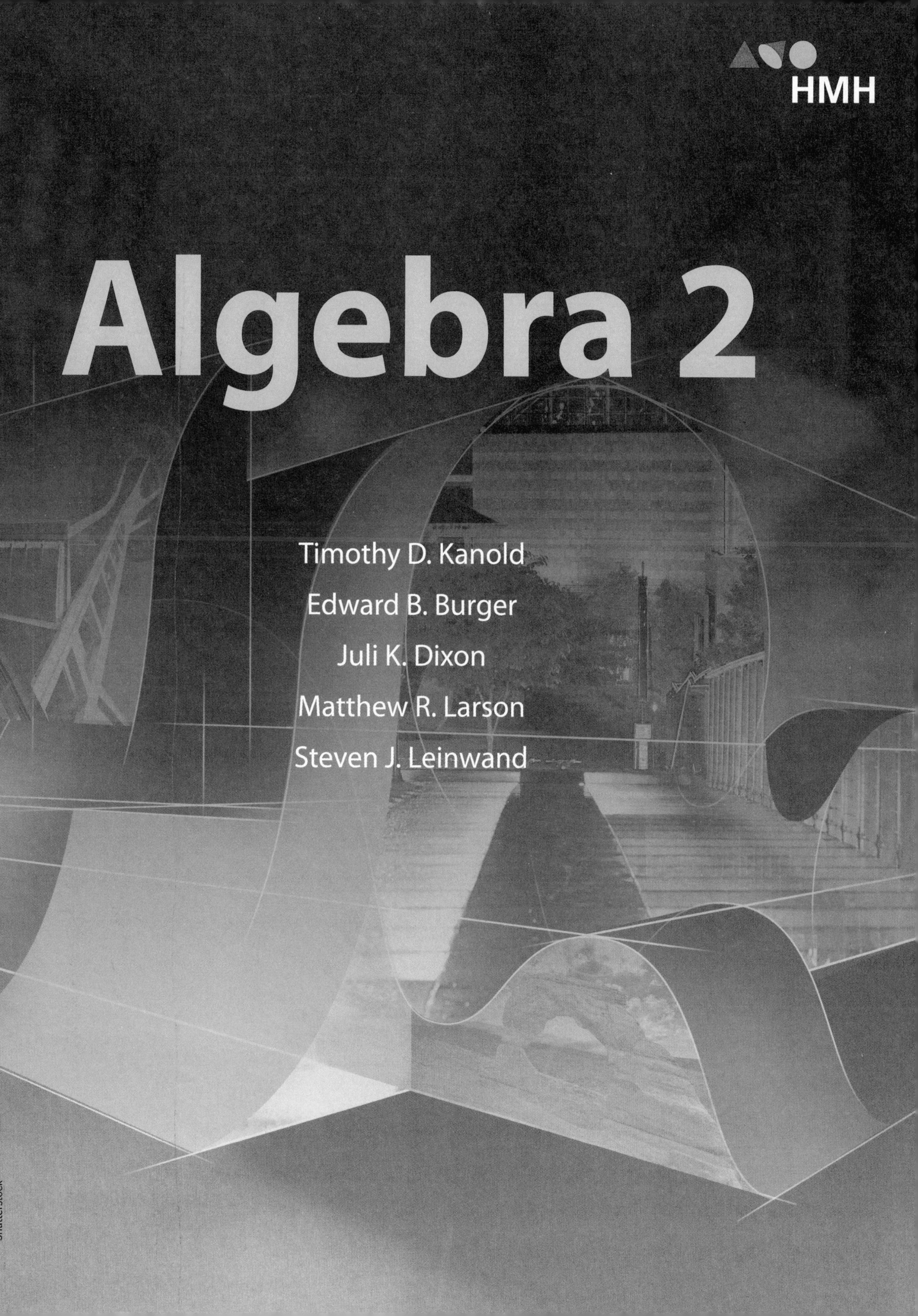

HMH

Algebra 2

Timothy D. Kanold

Edward B. Burger

Juli K. Dixon

Matthew R. Larson

Steven J. Leinwand

Printed in the U.S.A.

ISBN 978-1-328-90004-3

3 4 5 6 7 8 9 10 0868 26 25 24 23 22 21 20 19 18

4500712737 A B C D E F G H

Authors

Timothy D. Kanold, Ph.D., is an award-winning international educator, author, and consultant. He is a former superintendent and director of mathematics and science at Adlai E. Stevenson High School District 125 in Lincolnshire, Illinois. He is a past president of the National Council of Supervisors of Mathematics (NCSM) and the Council for the Presidential Awardees of Mathematics (CPAM). He has served on several writing and leadership commissions for NCTM during the past decade. He presents motivational professional development seminars with a focus on developing professional learning communities (PLC's) to improve the teaching, assessing, and learning of students. He has recently authored nationally recognized articles, books, and textbooks for mathematics education and school leadership, including *What Every Principal Needs to Know about the Teaching and Learning of Mathematics*.

Edward B. Burger, Ph.D., is the President of Southwestern University, a former Francis Christopher Oakley Third Century Professor of Mathematics at Williams College, and a former vice provost at Baylor University. He has authored or coauthored more than sixty-five articles, books, and video series; delivered over five hundred addresses and workshops throughout the world; and made more than fifty radio and television appearances. He is a Fellow of the American Mathematical Society as well as having earned many national honors, including the Robert Foster Cherry Award for Great Teaching in 2010. In 2012, Microsoft Education named him a "Global Hero in Education."

Juli K. Dixon, Ph.D., is a Professor of Mathematics Education at the University of Central Florida. She has taught mathematics in urban schools at the elementary, middle, secondary, and post-secondary levels. She is an active researcher and speaker with numerous publications and conference presentations. Key areas of focus are deepening teachers' content knowledge and communicating and justifying mathematical ideas. She is a past chair of the NCTM Student Explorations in Mathematics Editorial Panel and member of the Board of Directors for the Association of Mathematics Teacher Educators.

Matthew R. Larson, Ph.D., is the K-12 mathematics curriculum specialist for the Lincoln Public Schools and served on the Board of Directors for the National Council of Teachers of Mathematics from 2010 to 2013. He is a past chair of NCTM's Research Committee and was a member of NCTM's Task Force on Linking Research and Practice. He is the author of several books on implementing the Common Core Standards for Mathematics. He has taught mathematics at the secondary and college levels and held an appointment as an honorary visiting associate professor at Teachers College, Columbia University.

Steven J. Leinwand is a Principal Research Analyst at the American Institutes for Research (AIR) in Washington, D.C., and has over 30 years in leadership positions in mathematics education. He is past president of the National Council of Supervisors of Mathematics and served on the NCTM Board of Directors. He is the author of numerous articles, books, and textbooks and has made countless presentations with topics including student achievement, reasoning, effective assessment, and successful implementation of standards.

Performance Task Consultant

Robert Kaplinsky
Teacher Specialist, Mathematics
Downey Unified School District
Downey, California

STEM Consultants

Science, Technology, Engineering, and Mathematics

Michael A. DiSpezio
Global Educator
North Falmouth, Massachusetts

Michael R. Heithaus
Executive Director, School of Environment, Arts, and Society
Professor, Department of Biological Sciences
Florida International University
North Miami, Florida

Reviewers

Mindy Eden
Richwoods High School
Peoria School District
Peoria, IL

Dustin Johnson
Badger High School Math Teacher
Department Chair
Lake Geneva-Genoa City Union High School District
Lake Geneva, WI

Ashley D. McSwain
Murray High School
Murray City School District
Salt Lake City, UT

Rebecca Quinn
Doherty Memorial High School
Worcester Public Schools District
Worcester, MA

Ted Ryan
Madison LaFollette High School
Madison Metropolitan School District
Madison, WI

Tony Scoles
Fort Zumwalt School District
O'Fallon, MO

Cynthia L. Smith
Higley Unified School District
Gilbert, AZ

Phillip E. Spellane
Doherty Memorial High School
Worcester Public Schools District
Worcester, MA

Mona Toncheff
Math Content Specialist
Phoenix Union High School District
Phoenix, AZ

Functions

UNIT 1

MODULE 1

Analyzing Functions

MODULE 2

Absolute Value Functions, Equations, and Inequalities

UNIT 2

Quadratic Functions, Equations, and Relations

MODULE 3

Quadratic Equations

MODULE 4

Quadratic Relations and Systems of Equations

Polynomial Functions, Expressions, and Equations

UNIT 3

MODULE 5

Polynomial Functions

MODULE 6

Polynomials

MODULE 7

Polynomial Equations

Rational Functions, Expressions, and Equations

UNIT 4

MODULE 8

Rational Functions

MODULE 9

Rational Expressions and Equations

UNIT 5

Radical Functions, Expressions, and Equations

MODULE 10

Radical Functions

MODULE 11

Radical Expressions and Equations

Exponential and Logarithmic Functions and Equations

UNIT 6

MODULE 12

Sequences and Series

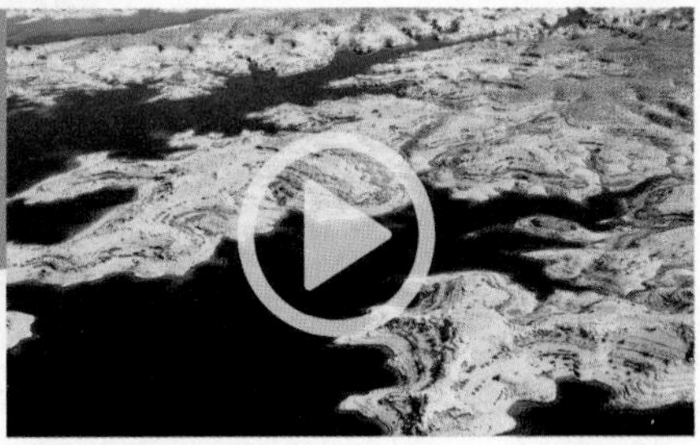

MODULE 13

Exponential Functions

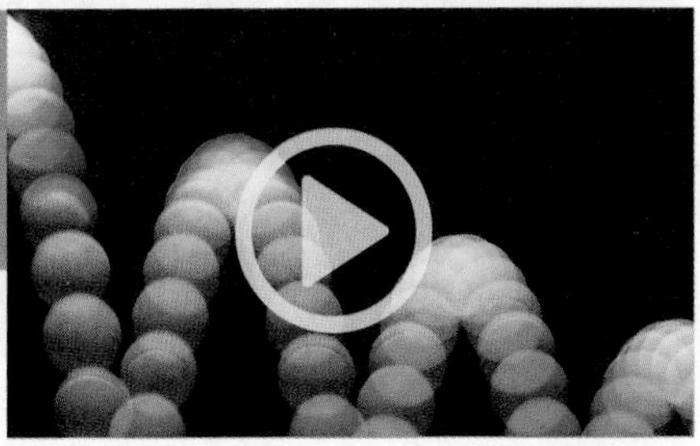

MODULE 14 Modeling with Exponential and Other Functions

MODULE 15 Logarithmic Functions

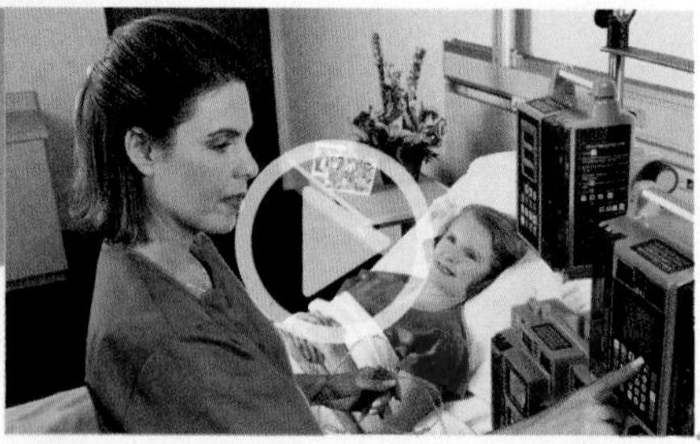

MODULE 16

Logarithmic Properties and Exponential Equations

UNIT 7

Trigonometric Functions

MODULE 17

Unit-Circle Definition of Trigonometric Functions

MODULE 18

Graphing Trigonometric Functions

Probability

UNIT 8

MODULE 19 Introduction to Probability

MODULE 20 Conditional Probability and Independence of Events

MODULE 21

Probability and Decision Making

Statistics

UNIT 9

MODULE 22

Gathering and Displaying Data

MODULE 23

Data Distributions

MODULE 24

Making Inferences from Data

Contents of Student Edition Resources

UNIT 1

Functions

MATH IN CAREERS

Community Theater Owner
A community theater owner uses math to determine revenue, profit, and expenses related to operating the theater. Probability and statistical methods are useful for determining the types of performances that will appeal to the public and attract patrons. Community theater owners should also understand the geometry of stage sets, and algebraic formulas for stage lighting, including those used to calculate light beam spread, throw distance, angle, and overall length.

If you are interested in a career as a community theater owner, you should study these mathematical subjects:

- Algebra
- Geometry
- Trigonometry
- Business Math
- Probability
- Statistics

Research other careers that require determining revenue, profit, and expenses. Check out the career activity at the end of the unit to find out how **Community Theater Owners** use math.

Visualize Vocabulary

Use the ✔ words to complete the graphic. You can put more than one word on each spoke of the information wheel.

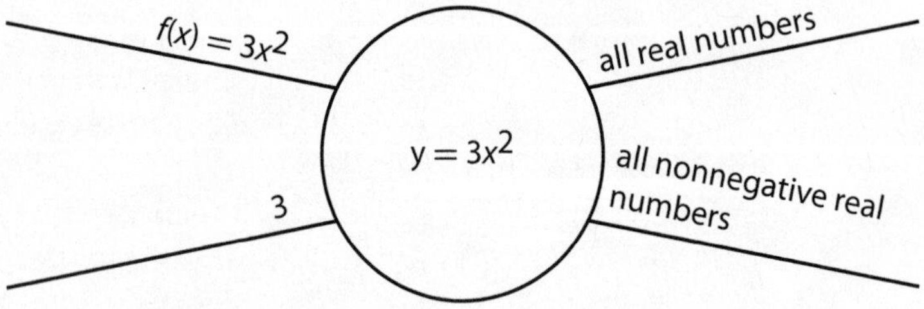

Vocabulary

Review Words

✔ coefficient *(coeficiente)*
✔ domain *(dominio)*
✔ function *(función)*
✔ inequality *(desigualdad)*
✔ interval *(intervalo)*
✔ quadratic function *(función cuadrática)*
✔ range *(rango)*
✔ transformation *(transformación)*

Preview Words

conjunction *(conjunción)*
disjunction *(disyunción)*
even function *(función par)*
inverse function *(función inversa)*
odd function *(función impar)*
parameter *(parámetro)*

Understand Vocabulary

To become familiar with some of the vocabulary terms in the module, consider the following. You may refer to the module, the glossary, or a dictionary.

1. A __?__ is a constant in the equation of a curve that yields a family of similar curves as it changes.
2. A function $f(x)$ such that $f(x) = f(-x)$ is an __?__ .
3. A compound statement that uses the word *or* is a __?__ .

Active Reading

Three-Panel Flip Chart Before beginning each lesson, create a three-panel flip chart to help you summarize important aspects of the lesson. As you study each lesson, record algebraic examples of functions on the first flap, their graphs on the second flap, and analyses of the functions on the third flap. Add to flip charts from previous lessons by extending the analyses of the functions when possible. For equations and inequalities, record an example on the first flap, a worked out solution on the second flap, and a graph on the third flap.

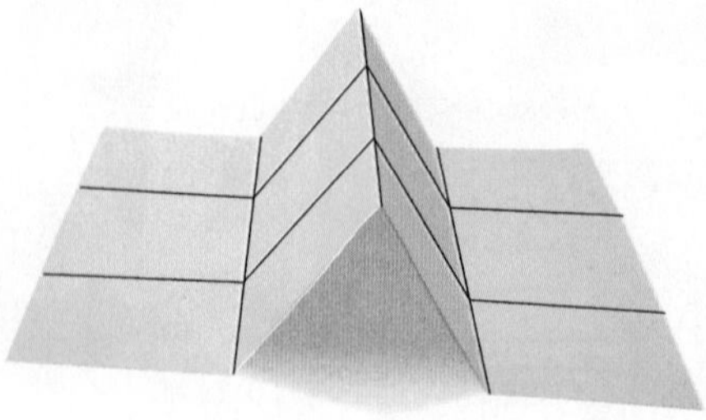

Analyzing Functions

MODULE 1

Essential Question: How can you analyze functions to solve real-world problems?

REAL WORLD VIDEO
Pole vaulting is just one of many track-and-field events that feature a person or object flying through the air. The path of a pole vaulter or of a shot put can be modeled using a quadratic function.

MODULE PERFORMANCE TASK PREVIEW

How High Does a Pole Vaulter Go?

In pole vaulting, a person jumps over a horizontal bar with the assistance of a long fiberglass or carbon-fiber pole. The flexible pole makes it possible for vaulters to achieve much greater heights than jumping without a pole. The goal is to clear the bar without knocking it down. How can mathematics be used to compare the heights of a pole vaulter for two different vaults? Let's jump in and find out!

Are YOU Ready?

Complete these exercises to review skills you will need for this module.

Personal Math Trainer

- Online Homework
- Hints and Help
- Extra Practice

Algebraic Representations of Transformations

Example 1

Rotate $A(-6,3)$ 90° clockwise.
$(-6(-1), 3) = (6, 3)$ Multiply.
$A(-6, 3) \rightarrow A'(3, 6)$ Switch.

Translate $B(4,7)$ 5 units down.
$(4, 7 - 5) = (4, 2)$ Subtract.
$B(4, 7) \rightarrow B'(4,2)$

Find the location of A' given that A is (1, 5).

1. Rotate 90° clockwise.

2. Translate 1 unit left.

3. Reflect across the x-axis.

Linear Functions

Example 2

Name the x- and y-intercepts for $y = -2x + 1$.

x-intercept: $0 = -2x + 1$, so $x = 0.5$.

y-intercept: $y = -2(0) + 1 = 1$

Find the x- and y-intercepts for each equation.

4. $y = 8x - 4$

5. $y = -x + 12$

6. $y = 1.2x + 4.8$

Properties of Translations, Reflections, and Rotations

Example 3

The point $P(1, -8)$ is reflected across the y-axis.
Name the quadrant that contains the image, P'.
$P(1, -8) \rightarrow P'(-1, -8)$, so P' is in Quadrant III.

Name the quadrant that contains the image of $R(7, 3)$ under the given transformation.

7. reflection across the x-axis

8. translation 8 units down

9. rotation 270° clockwise

Rate of Change and Slope

Example 4

Two points on a line are $(-3, 3)$ and $(4, 1)$. Find the slope.

$\frac{y_1 - y_2}{x_1 - x_2} = \frac{3 - 1}{-3 - 4} = -\frac{2}{7}$ The slope is $-\frac{2}{7}$.

Find the slope of the line that passes through the two points.

10. (0, 5) and (−9, −4)

11. (6, −2) and (1, −1)

12. (−7, 3) and (−4, −12)

1.1 Domain, Range, and End Behavior

Essential Question: How can you determine the domain, range, and end behavior of a function?

Resource Locker

Explore Representing an Interval on a Number Line

An **interval** is a part of a number line without any breaks. A *finite interval* has two endpoints, which may or may not be included in the interval. An *infinite interval* is unbounded at one or both ends.

Suppose an interval consists of all real numbers greater than or equal to 1. You can use the inequality $x \geq 1$ to represent the interval. You can also use *set notation* and *interval notation*, as shown in the table.

Description of Interval	Type of Interval	Inequality	Set Notation	Interval notation
All real numbers from a to b, including a and b	Finite	$a \leq x \leq b$	$\{x \mid a \leq x \leq b\}$	$[a, b]$
All real numbers greater than a	Infinite	$x > a$	$\{x \mid x > a\}$	$(a, +\infty)$
All real numbers less than or equal to a	Infinite	$x \leq a$	$\{x \mid x \leq a\}$	$(-\infty, a]$

For set notation, the vertical bar means "such that," so you read $\{x \mid x \geq 1\}$ as "the set of real numbers x such that x is greater than or equal to 1."

For interval notation, do the following:

- Use a square bracket to indicate that an interval includes an endpoint and a parenthesis to indicate that an interval doesn't include an endpoint.
- For an interval that is unbounded at its positive end, use the symbol for positive infinity, $+\infty$. For an interval that unbounded at its negative end, use the symbol for negative infinity, $-\infty$. Always use a parenthesis with positive or negative infinity.

So, you can write the interval $x \geq 1$ as $[1, +\infty)$.

Ⓐ Complete the table by writing the finite interval shown on each number line as an inequality, using set notation, and using interval notation.

Finite Interval	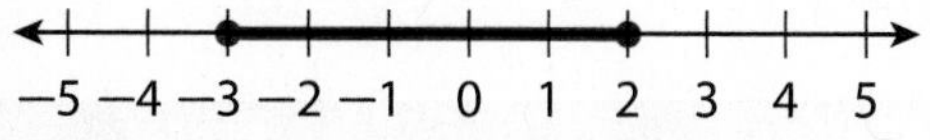	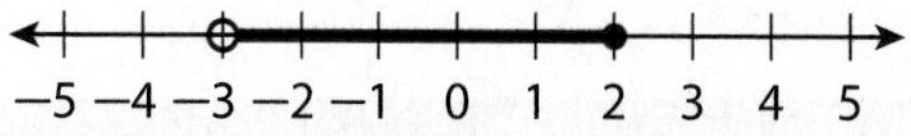
Inequality	?	?
Set Notation	?	?
Interval Notation	?	?

Ⓑ Complete the table by writing the infinite interval shown on each number line as an inequality, using set notation, and using interval notation.

Infinite Interval	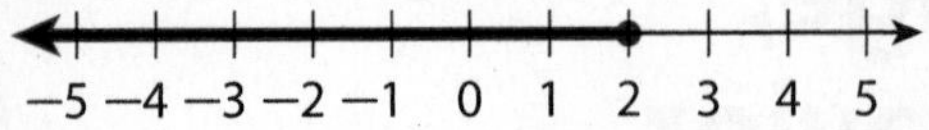	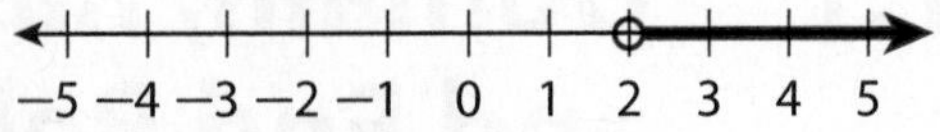
Inequality	?	?
Set Notation	?	?
Interval Notation	?	?

Reflect

1. Consider the interval shown on the number line.

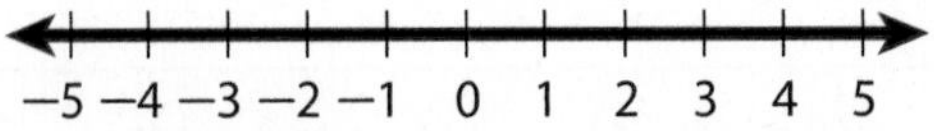

a. Represent the interval using interval notation.

b. What numbers are in this interval?

2. What do the intervals [0, 5], [0, 5), and (0, 5) have in common? What makes them different?

3. **Discussion** The symbol ∪ represents the *union* of two sets. What do you think the notation $(-\infty, 0) \cup (0, +\infty)$ represents?

Explain 1 Identifying a Function's Domain, Range and End Behavior from its Graph

Recall that the *domain* of a function *f* is the set of input values *x*, and the *range* is the set of output values $f(x)$. The **end behavior** of a function describes what happens to the $f(x)$-values as the *x*-values either increase without bound (approach positive infinity) or decrease without bound (approach negative infinity). For instance, consider the graph of a linear function shown. From the graph, you can make the following observations.

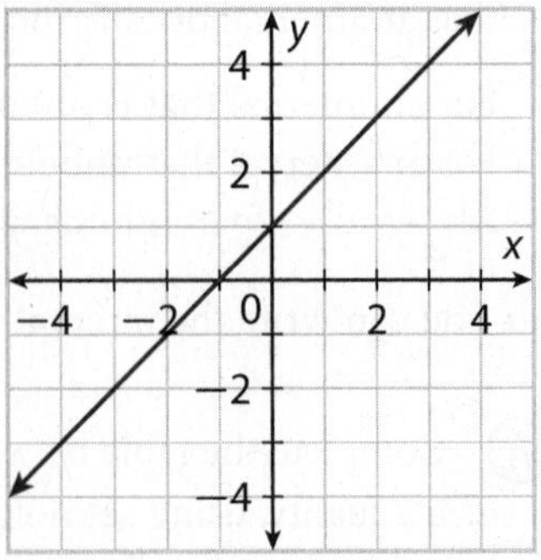

Statement of End Behavior	Symbolic Form of Statement
As the *x*-values increase without bound, the *f*(*x*)-values also increase without bound.	As $x \to +\infty$, $f(x) \to +\infty$.
As the *x*-values decrease without bound, the *f*(*x*)-values also decrease without bound.	As $x \to -\infty$, $f(x) \to -\infty$.

Example 1 **Write the domain and the range of the function as an inequality, using set notation, and using interval notation. Also describe the end behavior of the function.**

(A) The graph of the quadratic function $f(x) = x^2$ is shown.

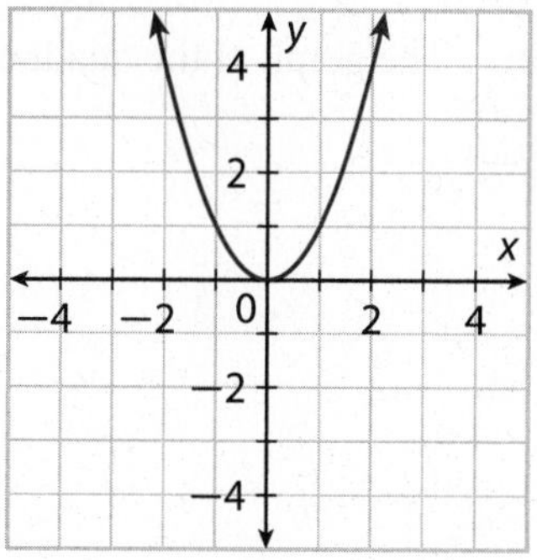

Domain:

Inequality: $-\infty < x < +\infty$

Set notation: $\{x \mid -\infty < x < +\infty\}$

Interval notation: $(-\infty, +\infty)$

Range:

Inequality: $y \geq 0$

Set notation: $\{y \mid y \geq 0\}$

Interval notation: $[0, +\infty)$

End behavior:

As $x \to +\infty$, $f(x) \to +\infty$.

As $x \to -\infty$, $f(x) \to +\infty$.

(B) The graph of the exponential function $f(x) = 2^x$ is shown.

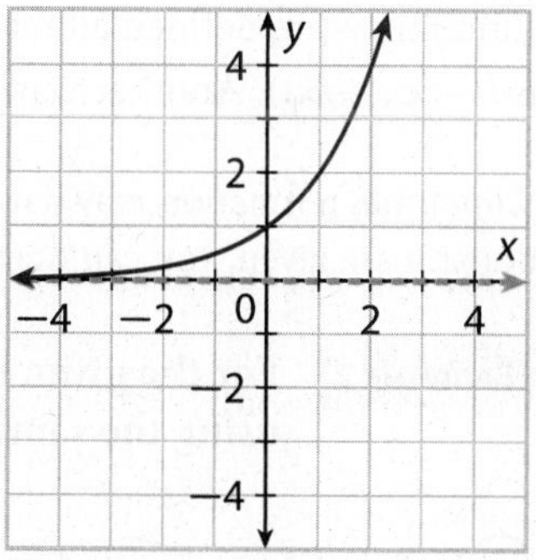

Domain:

Inequality: $-\infty < x < +\infty$

Set notation: $\{x \mid -\infty < x < +\infty\}$

Interval notation: $(-\infty, +\infty)$

Range:

Inequality: $y > 0$

Set notation: $\{y \mid y > 0\}$

Interval notation: $(0, +\infty)$

End behavior:

As $x \to +\infty$, $f(x) \to +\infty$.

As $x \to -\infty$, $f(x) \to 0$.

Reflect

4. Why is the end behavior of a quadratic function different from the end behavior of a linear function?

5. In Part B, the $f(x)$-values decrease as the x-values decrease. So, why can't you say that $f(x) \to -\infty$ as $x \to -\infty$?

Your Turn

Write the domain and the range of the function as an inequality, using set notation, and using interval notation. Also describe the end behavior of the function.

6. The graph of the quadratic function $f(x) = -x^2$ is shown.

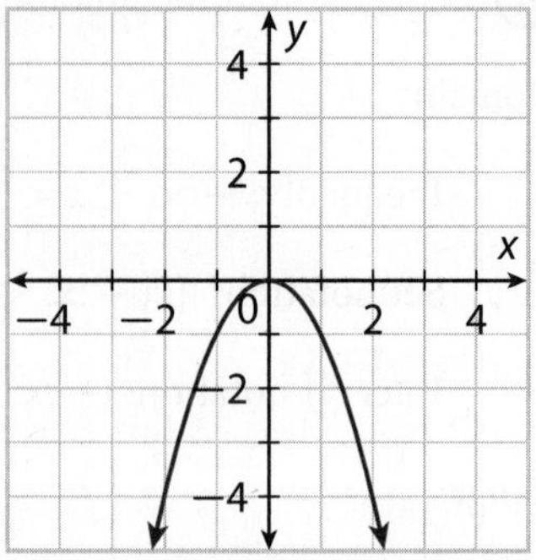

Explain 2 Graphing a Linear Function on a Restricted Domain

Unless otherwise stated, a function is assumed to have a domain consisting of all real numbers for which the function is defined. Many functions—such as linear, quadratic, and exponential functions—are defined all real numbers, so their domain, when written in interval notation, is $(-\infty, +\infty)$. Another way to write the set of real numbers is $\mathbb{R}$.

Sometimes a function may have a restricted domain. If the rule for a function and its restricted domain are given, you can draw its graph and then identify its range.

Example 2 **For the given function and domain, draw the graph and identify the range using the same notation as the given domain.**

(A) $f(x) = \frac{3}{4}x + 2$ with domain $[-4, 4]$

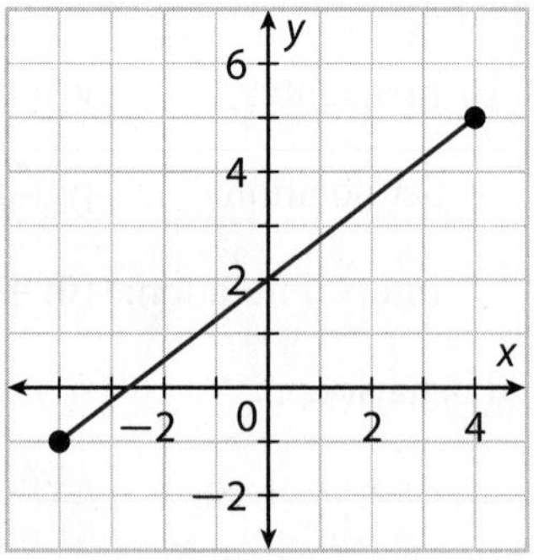

Since $f(x) = \frac{3}{4}x + 2$ is a linear function, the graph is a line segment with endpoints at $(-4, f(-4))$, or $(-4, -1)$, and $(4, f(4))$, or $(4, 5)$. The endpoints are included in the graph.

The range is $[-1, 5]$.

(B) $f(x) = -x - 2$ with domain $\{x | x > -3\}$

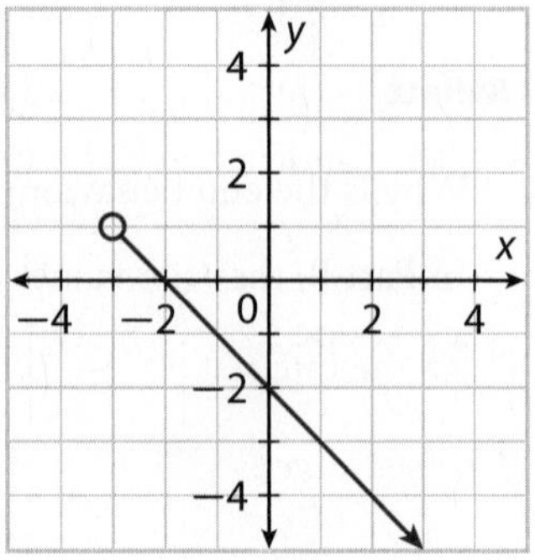

Since $f(x) = -x - 2$ is a linear function, the graph is a ray with its endpoint at $(-3, f(-3))$, or $(-3, 1)$. The endpoint is not included in the graph. The range is $\{y | y < 1\}$.

Reflect

7. In Part A, how does the graph change if the domain is $(-4, 4)$ instead of $[-4, 4]$?

8. In Part B, what is the end behavior as x increases without bound? Why can't you talk about the end behavior as x decreases without bound?

Your Turn

For the given function and domain, draw the graph and identify the range using the same notation as the given domain.

9. $f(x) = -\frac{1}{2}x + 2$ with domain $-6 \le x < 2$

10. $f(x) = \frac{2}{3}x - 1$ with domain $(-\infty, 3]$

Explain 3 Modeling with a Linear Function

Recall that when a real-world situation involves a constant rate of change, a linear function is a reasonable model for the situation. The situation may require restricting the function's domain.

Example 3 **Write a function that models the given situation. Determine a domain from the situation, graph the function using that domain, and identify the range.**

(A) Joyce jogs at a rate of 1 mile every 10 minutes for a total of 40 minutes. (Use inequalities for the domain and range of the function that models this situation.)

Joyce's jogging rate is 0.1 mi/min. Her jogging distance d (in miles) at any time t (in minutes) is modeled by $d(t) = 0.1t$. Since she jogs for 40 minutes, the domain is restricted to the interval $0 \le t \le 40$.

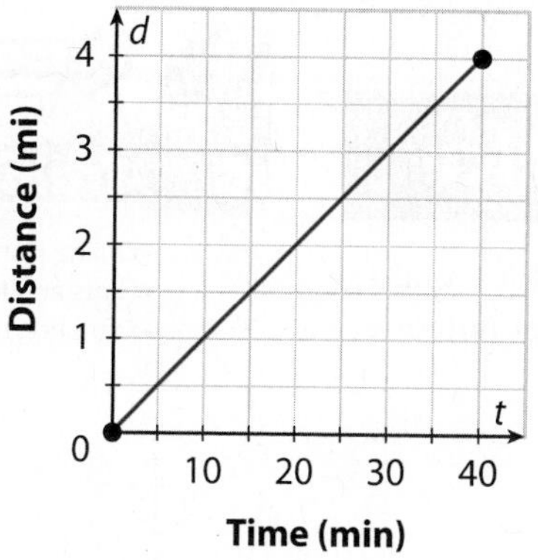

The range is $0 \le d \le 4$.

(B) A candle 6 inches high burns at a rate of 1 inch every 2 hours for 5 hours. (Use interval notation for the domain and range of the function that models this situation.)

The candle's burning rate is -0.5 in./h.
The candle's height h (in inches) at any time t (in hours) is modeled by $h(t) = 6 - 0.5t$. Since the candle burns for 5 hours, the domain is restricted

to the interval $[0, \boxed{5}]$.

The range is [3.5, 6].

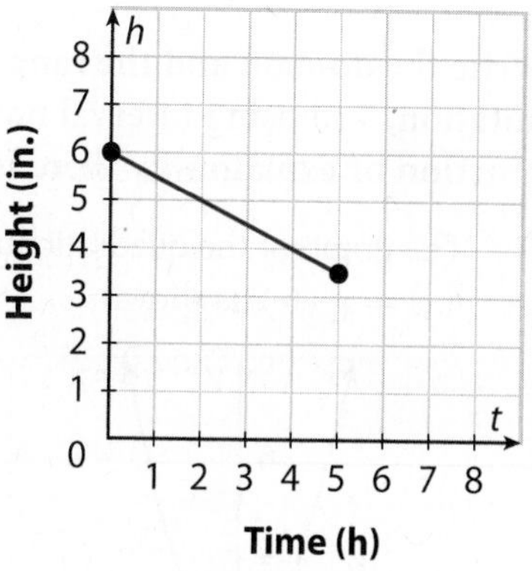

Reflect

11. In Part A, suppose Joyce jogs for only 30 minutes.

A. How does the domain change?

B. How does the graph change?

C. How does the range change?

Your Turn

12. While standing on a moving walkway at an airport, you are carried forward 25 feet every 15 seconds for 1 minute. Write a function that models this situation. Determine the domain from the situation, graph the function, and identify the range. Use set notation for the domain and range.

Elaborate

13. If a and b are real numbers such that $a < b$, use interval notation to write four different intervals having a and b as endpoints. Describe what numbers each interval includes.

14. What impact does restricting the domain of a linear function have on the graph of the function?

15. **Essential Question Check-In** How does slope determine the end behavior of a linear function with an unrestricted domain?

Evaluate: Homework and Practice

Personal Math Trainer
- Online Homework
- Hints and Help
- Extra Practice

1. Write the interval shown on the number line as an inequality, using set notation, and using interval notation.

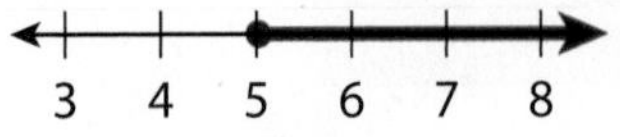

2. Write the interval (5, 100] as an inequality and using set notation.

3. Write the interval $-25 \leq x < 30$ using set notation and interval notation.

4. Write the interval $\{x \mid -3 < x < 5\}$ as an inequality and using interval notation.

Write the domain and the range of the function as an inequality, using set notation, and using interval notation. Also describe the end behavior of the function or explain why there is no end behavior.

5. The graph of the quadratic function $f(x) = x^2 + 2$ is shown.

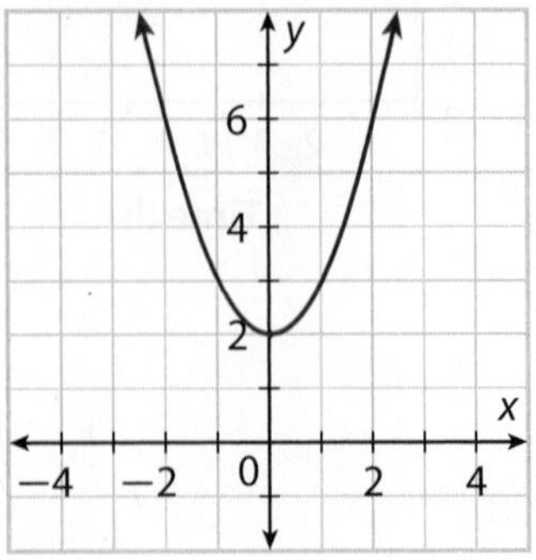

6. The graph of the exponential function $f(x) = 3^x$ is shown.

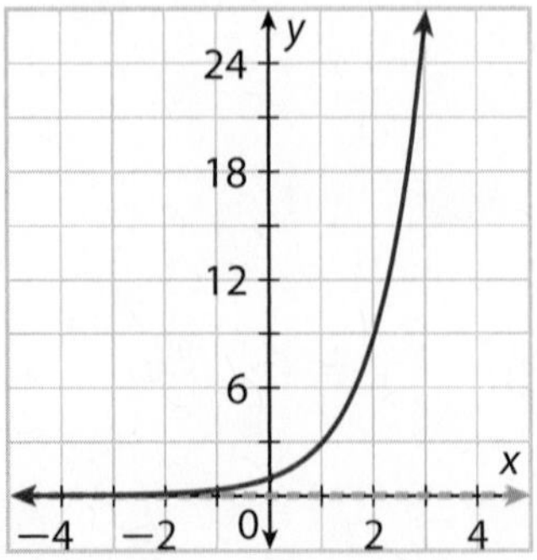

7. The graph of the linear function $g(x) = 2x - 2$ is shown.

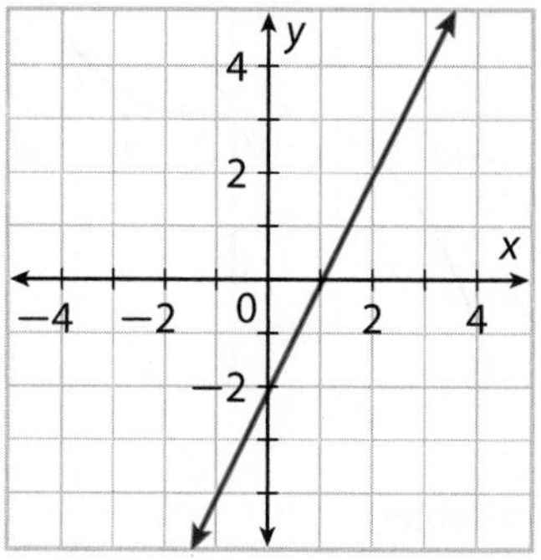

8. The graph of a function is shown.

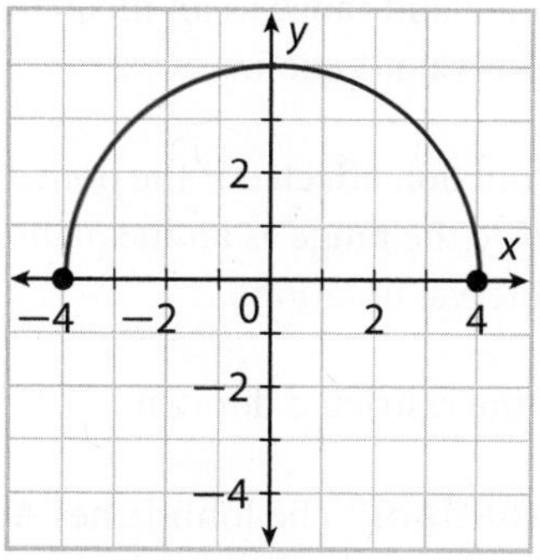

For the given function and domain, draw the graph and identify the range using the same notation as the given domain.

9. $f(x) = -x + 5$ with domain $[-3, 2]$

10. $f(x) = \frac{3}{2}x + 1$ with domain $\{x \mid x > -2\}$

Write a function that models the given situation. Determine the domain from the situation, graph the function using that domain, and identify the range.

11. A bicyclist travels at a constant speed of 12 miles per hour for a total of 45 minutes. (Use set notation for the domain and range of the function that models this situation.)

12. An elevator in a tall building starts at a floor of the building that is 90 meters above the ground. The elevator descends 2 meters every 0.5 second for 6 seconds. (Use an inequality for the domain and range of the function that models this situation.)

H.O.T. Focus on Higher Order Thinking

13. Explain the Error Cameron sells tickets at a movie theater. On Friday night, she worked from 4 p.m. to 10 p.m. and sold about 25 tickets every hour. Cameron says that the number of tickets, n, she has sold at any time t (in hours) can be modeled by the function $n(t) = 25t$, where the domain is $0 \le t \le 1$ and the range is $0 \le n \le 25$. Is Cameron's function, along with the domain and range, correct? Explain.

14. Multi-Step The graph of the cubic function $f(x) = x^3$ is shown.

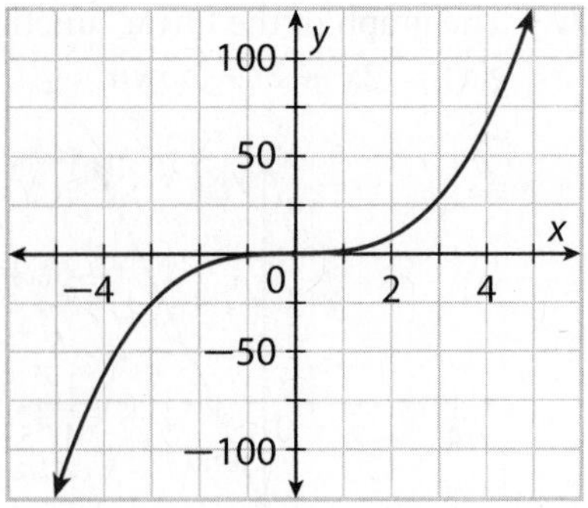

a. What are the domain, range, and end behavior of the function? (Write the domain and range as an inequality, using set notation, and using interval notation.)

b. How is the range of the function affected if the domain is restricted to $[-4, 4]$? (Write the range as an inequality, using set notation, and using interval notation.)

c. Graph the function with the restricted domain.

15. Represent Real-World Situations The John James Audubon Bridge is a cable-stayed bridge in Louisiana that opened in 2011. The height from the bridge deck to the top of the tower where a particular cable is anchored is about 500 feet, and the length of that cable is about 1200 feet. Draw the cable on a coordinate plane, letting the x-axis represent the bridge deck and the y-axis represent the tower. (Only use positive values of x and y.) Write a linear function whose graph models the cable. Identify the domain and range, writing each as an inequality, using set notation, and using interval notation.

Lesson Performance Task

The fuel efficiency for a 2007 passenger car was 31.2 mi/gal. For the same model of car, the fuel efficiency increased to 35.6 mi/gal in 2012. The gas tank for this car holds 16 gallons of gas.

a. Write and graph a linear function that models the distance that each car can travel for a given amount of gas (up to one tankful).

b. Write the domain and range of each function using interval notation.

c. Write and simplify a function $f(g)$ that represents the *difference* in the distance that the 2012 car can travel and the distance that the 2007 car can travel on the same amount of gas. Interpret this function using the graphs of the functions from part a. Also find and interpret $f(16)$.

d. Write the domain and range of the difference function using set notation.

1.2 Characteristics of Function Graphs

Essential Question: What are some of the attributes of a function, and how are they related to the function's graph?

Resource Locker

Explore Identifying Attributes of a Function from Its Graph

You can identify several attributes of a function by analyzing its graph. For instance, for the graph shown, you can see that the function's domain is $\{x|0 \leq x \leq 11\}$ and its range is $\{y| -1 \leq y \leq 1\}$. Use the graph to explore the function's other attributes.

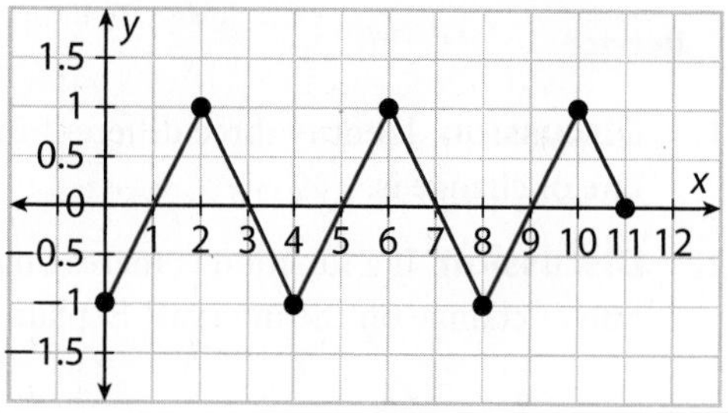

(A) Are the values of the function on the interval $\{x|1 < x < 3\}$ positive or negative?

(B) Are the values of the function on the interval $\{x|8 < x < 9\}$ positive or negative?

A function is **increasing** on an interval if $f(x_1) < f(x_2)$ when $x_1 < x_2$ for any x-values x_1 and x_2 from the interval. The graph of a function that is increasing on an interval rises from left to right on that interval. Similarly, a function is **decreasing** on an interval if $f(x_1) > f(x_2)$ when $x_1 < x_2$ for any x-values x_1 and x_2 from the interval. The graph of a function that is decreasing on an interval falls from left to right on that interval.

(C) Is the given function increasing or decreasing on the interval $\{x|2 \leq x \leq 4\}$?

(D) Is the given function increasing or decreasing on the interval $\{x|4 \leq x \leq 6\}$?

For the two points $(x_1, f(x_1))$ and $(x_2, f(x_2))$ on the graph of a function, the **average rate of change** of the function is the ratio of the change in the function values, $f(x_2) - f(x_1)$, to the change in the x-values, $x_2 - x_1$. For a linear function, the rate of change is constant and represents the slope of the function's graph.

(E) What is the given function's average rate of change on the interval $\{x|0 \leq x \leq 2\}$?

A function may change from increasing to decreasing or from decreasing to increasing at *turning points.* The value of $f(x)$ at a point where a function changes from increasing to decreasing is a **maximum value**. A maximum value occurs at a point that appears higher than all nearby points on the graph of the function. Similarly, the value of $f(x)$ at a point where a function changes from decreasing to increasing is a **minimum value**. A minimum value occurs at a point that appears lower than all nearby points on the graph of the function. If the graph of a function has an endpoint, the value of $f(x)$ at that point is considered a maximum or minimum value of the function if the point is higher or lower, respectively, than all nearby points.

(F) At how many points does the given function change from increasing to decreasing?

(G) What is the function's value at these points?

(H) At how many points does the given function change from decreasing to increasing?

(I) What is the function's value at these points?

A **zero** of a function is a value of x for which $f(x) = 0$. On a graph of the function, the zeros are the x-intercepts.

(J) How many x-intercepts does the given function's graph have?

(K) Identify the zeros of the function.

Reflect

1. **Discussion** Identify three different intervals that have the same average rate of change, and state what the rate of change is.

2. **Discussion** If a function is increasing on an interval $\{x | a \leq x \leq b\}$, what can you say about its average rate of change on the interval? Explain.

Explain 1 Sketching a Function's Graph from a Verbal Description

By understanding the attributes of a function, you can sketch a graph from a verbal description.

Example 1 **Sketch a graph of the following verbal descriptions.**

(A) Lyme disease is a bacterial infection transmitted to humans by ticks. When an infected tick bites a human, the probability of transmission is a function of the time since the tick attached itself to the skin. During the first 24 hours, the probability is 0%. During the next three 24-hour periods, the rate of change in the probability is always positive, but it is much greater for the middle period than the other two periods. After 96 hours, the probability is almost 100%. Sketch a graph of the function for the probability of transmission.

Probability of Transmission from Infected Tick

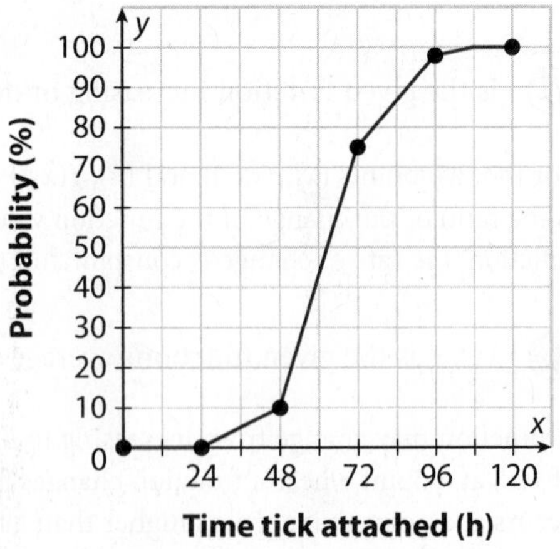

Identify the axes and scales.

The x-axis will be time (in hours) and will run from 0 to at least 96. The y-axis will be the probability of infection (as a percent) from 0 to 100.

Identify key intervals.

The intervals are in increments of 24 hours: 0 to 24, 24 to 48, 48 to 72, 72 to 96, and 96 to 120.

Sketch the graph of the function.

Draw a horizontal segment at $y = 0$ for the first 24-hour interval. The function increases over the next three 24-hour intervals with the middle interval having the greatest increase (the steepest slope). After 96 hours, the graph is nearly horizontal at 100%.

(B) The incidence of a disease is the rate at which a disease occurs in a population. It is calculated by dividing the number of new cases of a disease in a given time period (typically a year) by the size of the population. **To avoid small decimal numbers, the rate is often expressed in terms of a large number of people rather than a single person.** For instance, the incidence of measles in the United States in 1974 was about 10 cases per 100,000 people.

From 1974 to 1980, there were drastic fluctuations in the incidence of measles in the United States. In 1975, there was a slight increase in incidence from 1974. The next two years saw a substantial increase in the incidence, which reached a maximum in 1977 of about 26 cases per 100,000 people. From 1977 to 1979, the incidence fell to about 5 cases per 100,000 people. The incidence fell much faster from 1977 to 1978 than from 1978 to 1979. Finally, from 1979 to 1980, the incidence stayed about the same. **Sketch a graph of the function for the incidence of measles.**

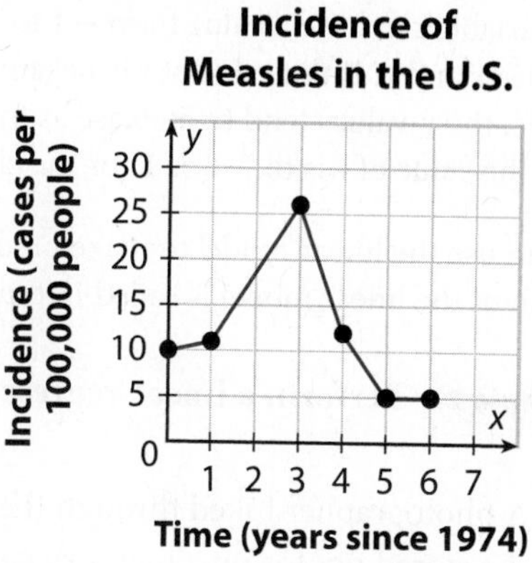

Identify the axes and scales.

The x-axis will represent time given by years and will run from 0 to 6. The y-axis will represent incidence of measles, measured in cases per 100,000 people, and will run from 0 to 30.

Identify key intervals.

The intervals are one-year increments from 0 to 6.

Sketch the graph of the function.

The first point on the graph is (0, 10). The graph slightly rises from $x = 0$ to $x = 1$.

From $x = 1$ to $x = 3$, the graph rises to a maximum y-value of 26.

The graph falls steeply from $x = 3$ to $x = 4$ and then falls less steeply from $x = 4$ to $x = 5$.

The graph is horizontal from $x = 5$ to $x = 6$.

Reflect

3. In Part B, the graph is horizontal from 1979 to 1980. What can you say about the rate of change for the function on this interval?

Your Turn

4. A grocery store stocks shelves with 100 cartons of strawberries before the store opens. For the first 3 hours the store is open, the store sells 20 cartons per hour. Over the next 2 hours, no cartons of strawberries are sold. The store then restocks 10 cartons each hour for the next 2 hours. In the final hour that the store is open, 30 cartons are sold. Sketch a graph of the function.

Explain 2 Modeling with a Linear Function

When given a set of paired data, you can use a scatter plot to see whether the data show a linear trend. If so, you can use a graphing calculator to perform linear regression and obtain a linear function that models the data. You should treat the least and greatest x-values of the data as the boundaries of the domain of the linear model.

When you perform linear regression, a graphing calculator will report the value of the *correlation coefficient r*. This variable can have a value from -1 to 1. It measures the direction and strength of the relationship between the variables x and y. If the value of r is negative, the y-values tend to decrease as the x-values increase. If the value of r is positive, the y-values tend to increase as the x-values increase. The more linear the relationship between x and y is, the closer the value of r is to -1 or 1 (or the closer the value of r^2 is to 1).

You can use the linear model to make predictions and decisions based on the data. Making a prediction within the domain of the linear model is called *interpolation*. Making a prediction outside the domain is called *extrapolation*.

Example 2 **Perform a linear regression for the given situation and make predictions.**

Ⓐ A photographer hiked through the Grand Canyon. Each day she stored photos on a memory card for her digital camera. When she returned from the trip, she deleted some photos from each memory card, saving only the best. The table shows the number of photos she kept from all those stored on each memory card. Use a graphing calculator to create a scatter plot of the data, find a linear regression model, and graph the model. Then use the model to predict the number of photos the photographer will keep if she takes 150 photos.

Grand Canyon Photos

Photos Taken	Photos Kept
117	25
128	31
140	39
157	52
110	21
188	45
170	42

Step 1: Create a scatter plot of the data.

Let x represent the number of photos taken, and let y represent the number of photos kept. Use a viewing window that shows x-values from 100 to 200 and y-values from 0 to 60.

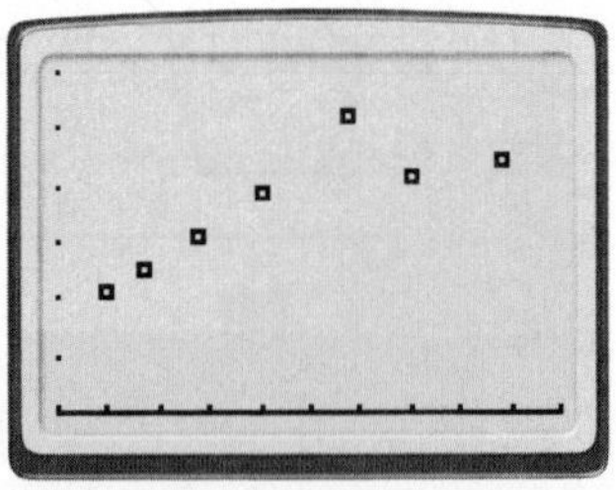

Notice that the trend in the data appears to be roughly linear, with y-values generally increasing as x-values increase.

Step 2: Perform linear regression. Write the linear model and its domain.

The linear regression model is $y = 0.33x - 11.33$. Its domain is $\{x|110 \leq x \leq 188\}$.

Step 3: Graph the model along with the data to obtain a visual check on the goodness of fit.

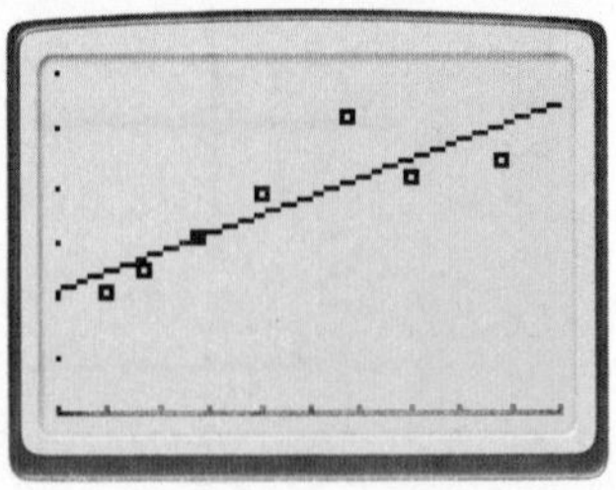

Notice that one of the data points is much farther from the line than the other data points are. The value of the correlation coefficient r would be closer to 1 without this data point.

Step 4: Predict the number of photos this photographer will keep if she takes 150 photos.

Evaluate the linear function when $x = 150$: $y = 0.33(150) - 11.33 \approx 38$. So, she will keep about 38 photos if she takes 150 photos.

(B) As a science project, Shelley is studying the relationship of car mileage (in miles per gallon) and speed (in miles per hour). The table shows the data Shelley gathered using her family's vehicle. Use a graphing calculator to create a scatter plot of the data, find a linear regression model, and graph the model. Then use the model to predict the gas mileage of the car at a speed of 20 miles per hour.

Speed (mi/h)	30	40	50	60	70
Mileage (mi/gal)	34.0	33.5	31.5	29.0	27.5

Step 1: Create a scatter plot of the data.

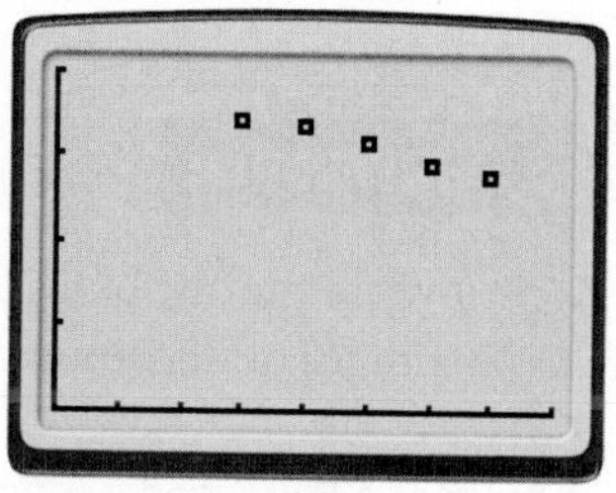

What do x and y represent?
Let x represent the car's speed, and let y represent the car's gas mileage.

What viewing window will you use?
Use a window that shows x-values from 0 to 80 and y-values from 0 to 40.

What trend do you observe?
The trend in the data appears to be quite linear, with y-values generally decreasing as x-values increase.

Step 2: Perform linear regression. Write the linear model and its domain.

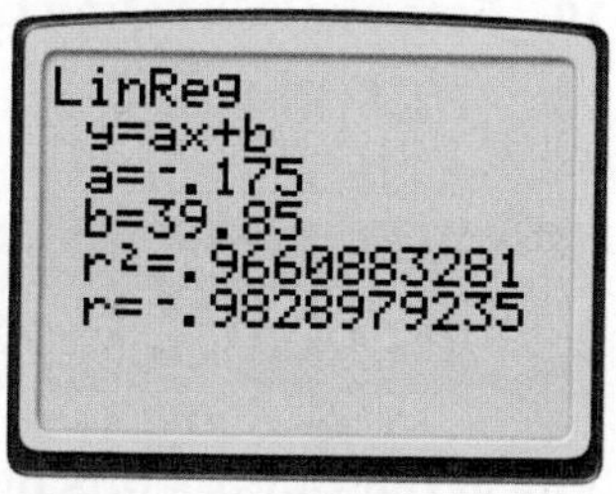

The linear regression model is $y = -0.175x + 39.85$. Its domain is $\{x | 30 \le x \le 70\}$.

Step 3: Graph the model along with the data to obtain a visual check on the goodness of fit.

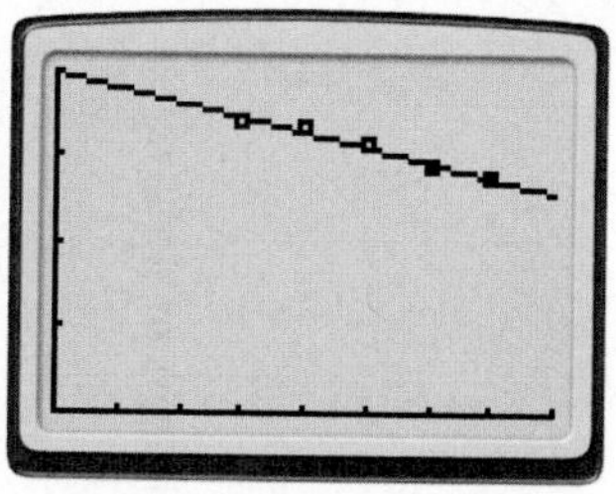

What can you say about the goodness of fit? As expected from the fact that the value of r from Step 2 is very close to -1, the line passes through or comes close to passing through all the data points.

Step 4: Predict the gas mileage of the car at a speed of 20 miles per hour.

Evaluate the linear function when x = 20: $y = -0.175(20) + 39.85 \approx 36.4$. So, the car's gas mileage should be about 36.4 mi/gal at a speed of 20 mi/h.

Reflect

5. Identify whether each prediction in Parts A and B is an interpolation or an extrapolation.

Your Turn

6. Vern created a website for his school's sports teams. He has a hit counter on his site that lets him know how many people have visited the site. The table shows the number of hits the site received each day for the first two weeks. Use a graphing calculator to find the linear regression model. Then predict how many hits there will be on day 15.

Day	1	2	3	4	5	6	7	8	9	10	11	12	13	14
Hits	5	10	21	24	28	36	33	21	27	40	46	50	31	38

Elaborate

7. How are the attributes of increasing and decreasing related to average rate of change? How are the attributes of maximum and minimum values related to the attributes of increasing and decreasing?

8. How can line segments be used to sketch graphs of functions that model real-world situations?

9. When making predictions based on a linear model, would you expect interpolated or extrapolated values to be more accurate? Justify your answer.

10. **Essential Question Check-In** What are some of the attributes of a function?

Evaluate: Homework and Practice

Personal Math Trainer

- Online Homework
- Hints and Help
- Extra Practice

The graph shows a function that models the value *V* (in millions of dollars) of a stock portfolio as a function of time *t* (in months) over an 18-month period.

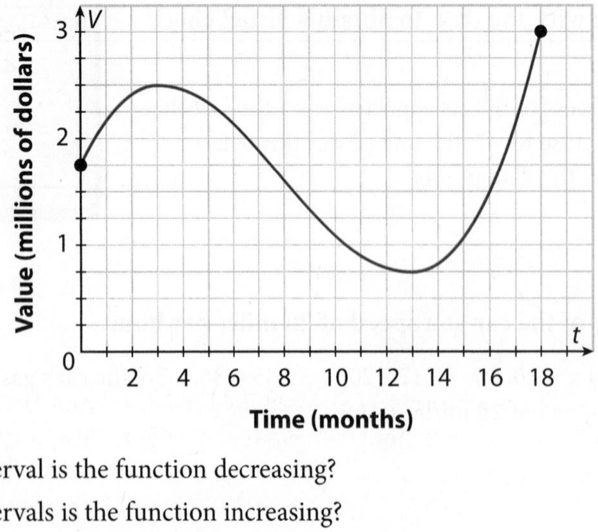

1. On what interval is the function decreasing?

On what intervals is the function increasing?

2. Identify any maximum values and minimum values.

3. What are the function's domain and range?

The table of values gives the probability $P(n)$ for getting all 5's when rolling a number cube n times.

n	1	2	3	4	5
$P(n)$	$\frac{1}{6}$	$\frac{1}{36}$	$\frac{1}{216}$	$\frac{1}{1296}$	$\frac{1}{7776}$

4. Is $P(n)$ increasing or decreasing? Explain the significance of this.

5. What is the end behavior of $P(n)$? Explain the significance of this.

6. The table shows some values of a function. On which intervals is the function's average rate of change positive? Select all that apply.

x	0	1	2	3
$f(x)$	50	75	40	65

a. From $x = 0$ to $x = 1$

b. From $x = 0$ to $x = 2$

c. From $x = 0$ to $x = 3$

d. From $x = 1$ to $x = 2$

e. From $x = 1$ to $x = 3$

f. From $x = 2$ to $x = 3$

Use the graph of the function $f(x)$ to identify the function's specified attributes.

7. Find the function's average rate of change over each interval.

a. From $x = -3$ to $x = -2$

b. From $x = -2$ to $x = 1$

c. From $x = 0$ to $x = 1$

d. From $x = 1$ to $x = 2$

e. From $x = -1$ to $x = 0$

f. From $x = -1$ to $x = 2$

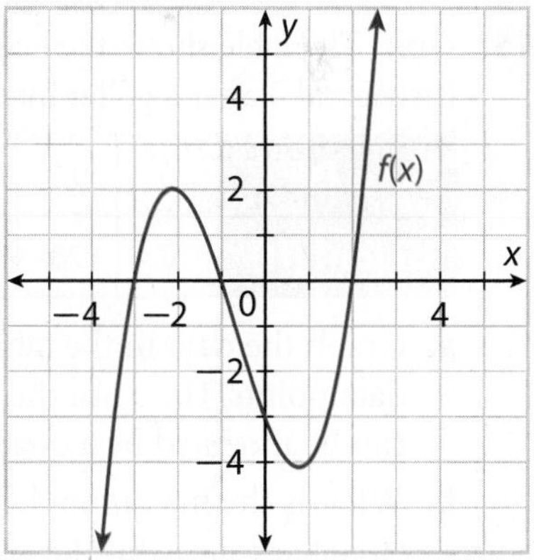

8. On what intervals are the function's values positive?

9. On what intervals are the function's values negative?

10. What are the zeros of the function?

11. The following describes the United States nuclear stockpile from 1944 to 1974. From 1944 to 1958, there was a gradual increase in the number of warheads from 0 to about 5000. From 1958 to 1966, there was a rapid increase in the number of warheads to a maximum of about 32,000. From 1966 to 1970, there was a decrease in the number of warheads to about 26,000. Finally, from 1970 to 1974, there was a small increase to about 28,000 warheads. Sketch a graph of the function.

12. The following describes the unemployment rate in the United States from 2003 to 2013. In 2003, the unemployment rate was at 6.3%. The unemployment rate began to fall over the years and reached a minimum of about 4.4% in 2007. A recession that began in 2007 caused the unemployment rate to increase over a two-year period and reach a maximum of about 10% in 2009. The unemployment rate then decreased over the next four years to about 7.0% in 2013. Sketch a graph of the function.

13. The following describes the incidence of mumps in the United States from 1984 to 2004. From 1984 to 1985, there was no change in the incidence of mumps, staying at about 1 case per 100,000 people. Then there was a spike in the incidence of mumps, which reached a peak of about 5.5 cases per 100,000 in 1987. Over the next year, there was a sharp decline in the incidence of mumps, to about 2 cases per 100,000 people in 1988. Then, from 1988 to 1989, there was a small increase to about 2.5 cases per 100,000 people. This was followed by a gradual decline, which reached a minimum of about 0.1 case per 100,000 in 1999. For the next five years, there was no change in the incidence of mumps. Sketch a graph of the function.

14. Aviation The table gives the lengths and wingspans of airplanes in an airline's fleet.

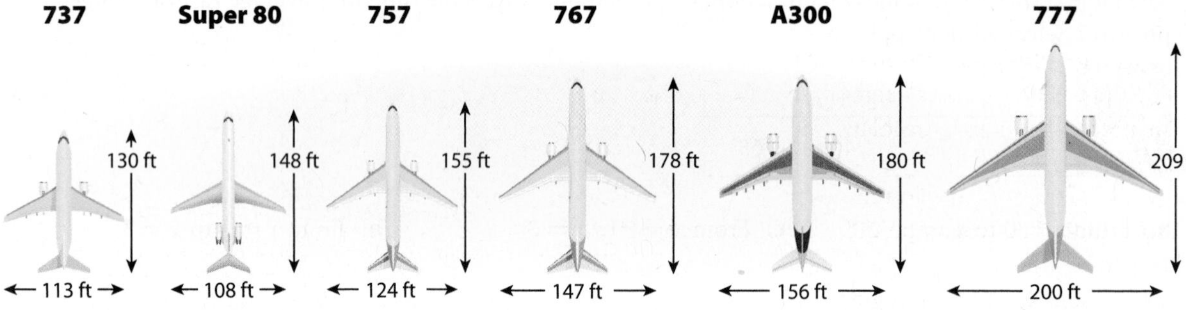

a. Make a scatter plot of the data with x representing length and y representing wingspan.

b. Sketch a line of fit.

c. Use the line of fit to predict the wingspan of an airplane with a length of 220 feet.

15. Golf The table shows the height (in feet) of a golf ball at various times (in seconds) after a golfer hits the ball into the air.

Time (s)	0	0.5	1	1.5	2	2.5	3	3.5	4
Height (ft)	0	28	48	60	64	60	48	28	0

a. Graph the data in the table. Then draw a smooth curve through the data points. (Because the golf ball is a projectile, its height h at time t can be modeled by a quadratic function whose graph is a parabola.)

b. What is the maximum height that the golf ball reaches?

c. On what interval is the golf ball's height increasing?

d. On what interval is the golf ball's height decreasing?

16. The model $a = 0.25t + 29$ represents the median age a of females in the United States as a function of time t (in years since 1970).

a. Predict the median age of females in 1995.

b. Predict the median age of females in 2015 to the nearest tenth.

H.O.T. Focus on Higher Order Thinking

17. Make a Prediction Anthropologists who study skeletal remains can predict a woman's height just from the length of her humerus, the bone between the elbow and the shoulder. The table gives data for humerus length and overall height for various women.

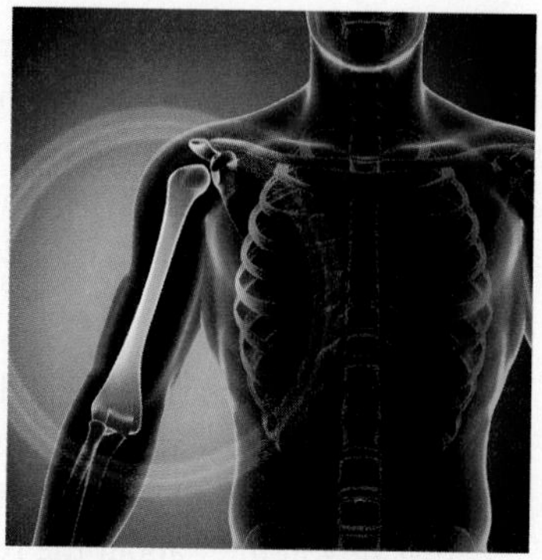

Humerus Length (cm)	35	27	30	33	25	39	27	31
Height (cm)	167	146	154	165	140	180	149	155

Using a graphing calculator, find the linear regression model and state its domain. Then predict a woman's height from a humerus that is 32 cm long, and tell whether the prediction is an interpolation or an extrapolation.

18. Make a Prediction Hummingbird wing beat rates are much higher than those in other birds. The table gives data about the mass and the frequency of wing beats for various species of hummingbirds.

Mass (g)	3.1	2.0	3.2	4.0	3.7	1.9	4.5
Frequency of Wing Beats (beats per second)	60	85	50	45	55	90	40

a. Using a graphing calculator, find the linear regression model and state its domain.

b. Predict the frequency of wing beats for a Giant Hummingbird with a mass of 19 grams.

c. Comment on the reasonableness of the prediction and what, if anything, is wrong with the model.

19. Explain the Error A student calculates a function's average rate of change on an interval and finds that it is 0. The student concludes that the function is constant on the interval. Explain the student's error, and give an example to support your explanation.

20. Communicate Mathematical Ideas Describe a way to obtain a linear model for a set of data without using a graphing calculator.

Lesson Performance Task

Since 1980 scientists have used data from satellite sensors to calculate a daily measure of Arctic sea ice extent. Sea ice extent is calculated as the sum of the areas of sea ice covering the ocean where the ice concentration is greater than 15%. The graph here shows seasonal variations in sea ice extent for 2012, 2013, and the average values for the 1980s.

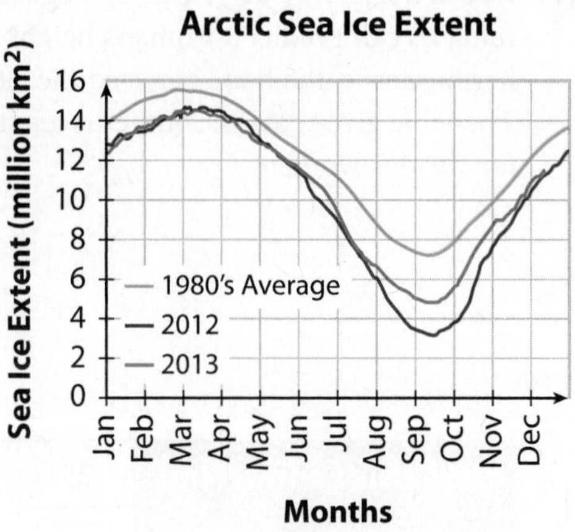

a. According to the graph, during which month does sea ice extent usually reach its maximum? During which month does the minimum extent generally occur? What can you infer about the reason for this pattern?

b. Sea ice extent reached its lowest level to date in 2012. About how much less was the minimum extent in 2012 compared with the average minimum for the 1980s? About what percentage of the 1980s average minimum was the 2012 minimum?

c. How does the maximum extent in 2012 compare with the average maximum for the 1980s? About what percentage of the 1980s average maximum was the 2012 maximum?

d. What do the patterns in the maximum and minimum values suggest about how climate change may be affecting sea ice extent?

e. How do the 2013 maximum and minimum values compare with those for 2012? What possible explanation can you suggest for the differences?

1.3 Transformations of Function Graphs

Resource Locker

Essential Question: What are the ways you can transform the graph of the function f(x)?

Explore 1 Investigating Translations of Function Graphs

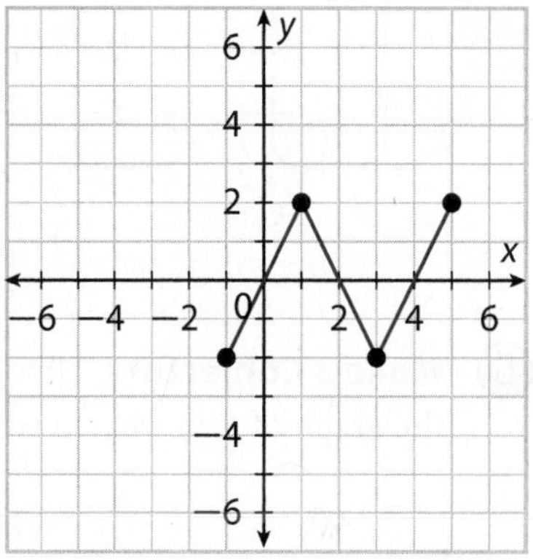

You can transform the graph of a function in various ways. You can translate the graph horizontally or vertically, you can stretch or compress the graph horizontally or vertically, and you can reflect the graph across the x-axis or the y-axis. How the graph of a given function is transformed is determined by the way certain numbers, called **parameters**, are introduced in the function.

The graph of $f(x)$ is shown. Copy this graph and use the same grid for the exploration.

(A) First graph $g(x) = f(x) + k$ where k is the parameter. Let $k = 4$ so that $g(x) = f(x) + 4$. Complete the input-output table and then graph $g(x)$. In general, how is the graph of $g(x) = f(x) + k$ related to the graph of $f(x)$ when k is a positive number?

x	f(x)	f(x) + 4
−1	−2	2
1	2	6
3	−2	?
5	2	?

(B) Now try a negative value of k in $g(x) = f(x) + k$. Let $k = -3$ so that $g(x) = f(x) - 3$. Complete the input-output table and then graph $g(x)$ on the same grid. In general, how is the graph of $g(x) = f(x) + k$ related to the graph of $f(x)$ when k is a negative number?

x	f(x)	f(x) − 3
−1	−2	−5
1	2	−1
3	−2	?
5	2	?

(C) Now graph $g(x) = f(x - h)$ where h is the parameter. Let $h = 2$ so that $g(x) = f(x - 2)$. Complete the mapping diagram and then graph $g(x)$ with $f(x)$. (To complete the mapping diagram, you need to find the inputs for g that produce the inputs for f after you subtract 2. Work backward from the inputs for f to the missing inputs for g by adding 2.) In general, how is the graph of $g(x) = f(x - h)$ related to the graph of $f(x)$ when h is a positive number?

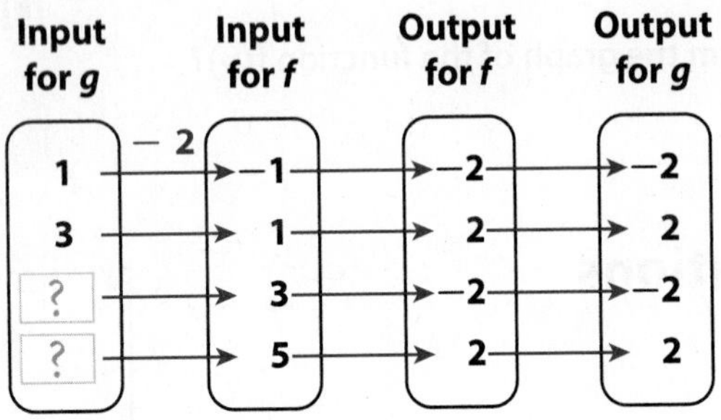

(D) **Make a Conjecture** How would you expect the graph of $g(x) = f(x - h)$ to be related to the graph of $f(x)$ when h is a negative number?

Reflect

1. Suppose a function $f(x)$ has a domain of $[x_1, x_2]$ and a range of $[y_1, y_2]$. When the graph of $f(x)$ is translated vertically k units where k is either positive or negative, how do the domain and range change?

2. Suppose a function $f(x)$ has a domain of $[x_1, x_2]$ and a range of $[y_1, y_2]$. When the graph of $f(x)$ is translated horizontally h units where h is either positive or negative, how do the domain and range change?

3. You can transform the graph of $f(x)$ to obtain the graph of $g(x) = f(x - h) + k$ by combining transformations. Predict what will happen by completing the table.

Sign of h	Sign of k	Transformations of the Graph of $f(x)$
+	+	Translate right h units and up k units.
+	−	?
−	+	?
−	−	?

Explore 2 Investigating Stretches and Compressions of Function Graphs

In this activity, you will consider what happens when you multiply by a positive parameter inside or outside a function. Throughout, you will use the same function $f(x)$ that you used in the previous activity.

Ⓐ First graph $g(x) = a \cdot f(x)$ where a is the parameter. Let $a = 2$ so that $g(x) = 2f(x)$. Complete the input-output table and then graph $g(x)$ with $f(x)$. In general, how is the graph of $g(x) = a \cdot f(x)$ related to the graph of $f(x)$ when a is greater than 1?

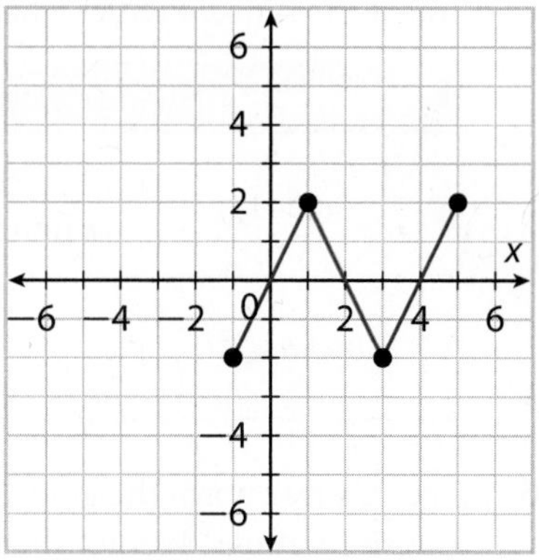

x	f(x)	2f(x)
−1	−2	−4
1	2	4
3	−2	?
5	2	?

Ⓑ Now try a value of a between 0 and 1 in $g(x) = a \cdot f(x)$. Let $a = \frac{1}{2}$ so that $g(x) = \frac{1}{2}f(x)$. Complete the input-output table and then graph $g(x)$ with $f(x)$. In general, how is the graph of $g(x) = a \cdot f(x)$ related to the graph of $f(x)$ when a is a number between 0 and 1?

x	f(x)	$\frac{1}{2}f(x)$
−1	−2	−1
1	2	1
3	−2	?
5	2	?

Ⓒ Now graph $g(x) = f\left(\frac{1}{b} \cdot x\right)$ where b is the parameter. Let $b = 2$ so that $g(x) = f\left(\frac{1}{2}x\right)$. Complete the mapping diagram and then graph $g(x)$ with $f(x)$. (To complete the mapping diagram, you need to find the inputs for g that produce the inputs for f after you multiply by $\frac{1}{2}$. Work backward from the inputs for f to the missing inputs for g by multiplying by 2.) In general, how is the graph of $g(x) = f\left(\frac{1}{b}x\right)$ related to the graph of $f(x)$ when b is a number greater than 1?

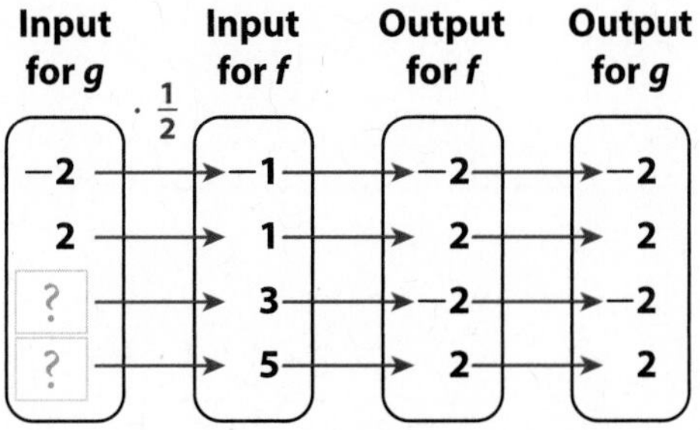

Ⓓ **Make a Conjecture** How would you expect the graph of $g(x) = f\left(\frac{1}{b} \cdot x\right)$ to be related to the graph of $f(x)$ when b is a number between 0 and 1?

Reflect

4. Suppose a function $f(x)$ has a domain of $[x_1, x_2]$ and a range of $[y_1, y_2]$. When the graph of $f(x)$ is stretched or compressed vertically by a factor of a, how do the domain and range change?

5. You can transform the graph of $f(x)$ to obtain the graph of $g(x) = a \cdot f(x-h) + k$ by combining transformations. Predict what will happen by completing the table.

Value of a	Transformations of the Graph of $f(x)$
$a > 1$	Stretch vertically by a factor of a, and translate h units horizontally and k units vertically.
$0 < a < 1$	?

6. You can transform the graph of $f(x)$ to obtain the graph of $g(x) = f\left(\frac{1}{b}(x - h)\right) + k$ by combining transformations. Predict what will happen by completing the table.

Value of b	Transformations of the Graph of $f(x)$
$b > 1$	Stretch horizontally by a factor of b, and translate h units horizontally and k units vertically.
$0 < b < 1$	?

Explore 3 Investigating Reflections of Function Graphs

When the parameter in a stretch or compression is negative, another transformation called a *reflection* is introduced. Examining reflections will also tell you whether a function is an *even function* or an *odd function*. An **even function** is one for which $f(-x) = f(x)$ for all x in the domain of the function, while an **odd function** is one for which $f(-x) = -f(x)$ for all x in the domain of the function. A function is not necessarily even or odd; it can be neither.

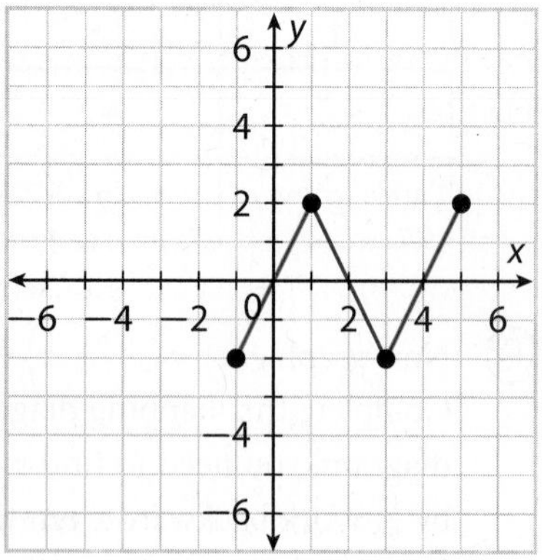

Ⓐ First graph $g(x) = a \cdot f(x)$ where $a = -1$. Complete the input-output table and then graph $g(x) = -f(x)$ with $f(x)$. In general, how is the graph of $g(x) = -f(x)$ related to the graph of $f(x)$?

x	$f(x)$	$-f(x)$
−1	−2	2
1	2	−2
3	−2	?
5	2	?

Ⓑ Now graph $g(x) = f\left(\frac{1}{b} \cdot x\right)$ where $b = -1$. Complete the input-output table and then graph $g(x) = f(-x)$ with $f(x)$. In general, how is the graph of $g(x) = f(-x)$ related to the graph of $f(x)$?

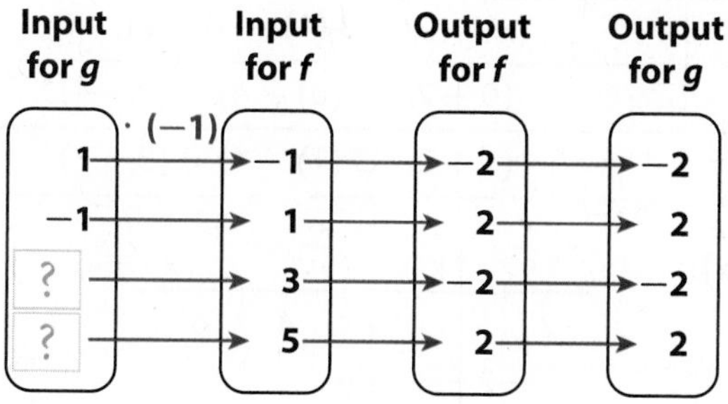

Reflect

7. **Discussion** Suppose a function $f(x)$ has a domain of $[x_1, x_2]$ and a range of $[y_1, y_2]$. When the graph of $f(x)$ is reflected across the x-axis, how do the domain and range change?

8. For a function $f(x)$, suppose the graph of $f(-x)$, the reflection of the graph of $f(x)$ across the y-axis, is identical to the graph of $f(x)$. What does this tell you about $f(x)$? Explain.

9. Is the function whose graph you reflected across the axes in Steps A and B an even function, an odd function, or neither? Explain.

Explain 1 Transforming the Graph of the Parent Quadratic Function

You can use transformations of the graph of a basic function, called a *parent function*, to obtain the graph of a related function. To do so, focus on how the transformations affect reference points on the graph of the parent function.

For instance, the parent quadratic function is $f(x) = x^2$. The graph of this function is a U-shaped curve called a *parabola* with a turning point, called a *vertex*, at (0, 0). The vertex is a useful reference point, as are the points (−1, 1) and (1, 1).

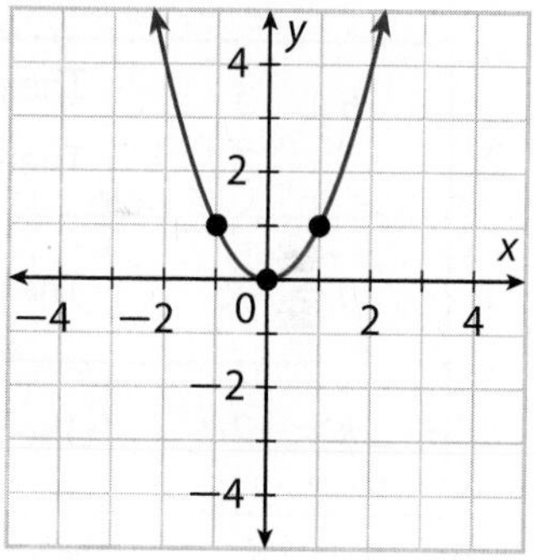

Example 1 **Describe how to transform the graph of $f(x) = x^2$ to obtain the graph of the related function $g(x)$. Then draw the graph of $g(x)$.**

Ⓐ $g(x) = -3f(x - 2) - 4$

Parameter and Its Value	Effect on the Parent Graph
$a = -3$	vertical stretch of the graph of $f(x)$ by a factor of 3 and a reflection across the x-axis
$b = 1$	Since $b = 1$, there is no horizontal stretch or compression.
$h = 2$	horizontal translation of the graph of $f(x)$ to the right 2 units
$k = -4$	vertical translation of the graph of $f(x)$ down 4 units

Applying these transformations to a point (x, y) on the parent graph results in the point $(x + 2, -3y - 4)$. The table shows what happens to the three reference points on the graph of $f(x)$.

Point on the Graph of $f(x)$	Corresponding Point on $g(x)$
$(-1, 1)$	$(-1 + 2, -3(1) - 4) = (1, -7)$
$(0, 0)$	$(0 + 2, -3(0) - 4) = (2, -4)$
$(1, 1)$	$(1 + 2, -3(1) - 4) = (3, -7)$

Use the transformed reference points to graph $g(x)$.

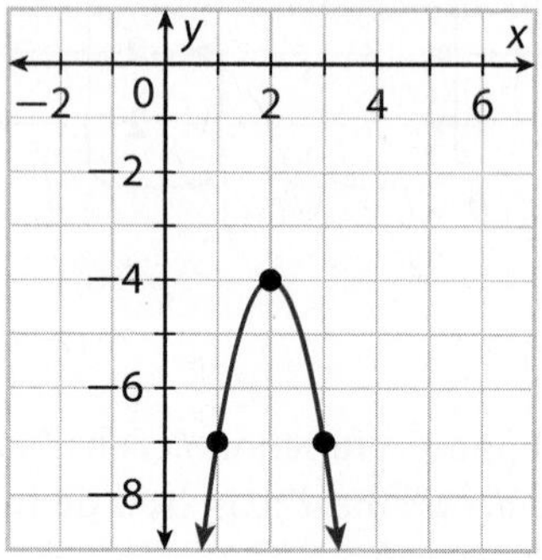

Ⓑ $g(x) = f\left(\frac{1}{2}(x + 5)\right) + 2$

Parameter and Its Value	Effect on the Parent Graph
$a =$ 1	Since $a = 1$, there is no vertical stretch, no vertical compression, and no reflection across the x-axis.
$b =$ 2	The parent graph is stretched horizontally by a factor of 2. There is no reflection across the y-axis.
$h =$ −5	The parent graph is translated −5 units horizontally.
$k =$ 2	The parent graph is translated 2 units vertically.

Applying these transformations to a point on the parent graph results in the point $(2x - 5, y + 2)$. The table shows what happens to the three reference points on the graph of $f(x)$.

Point on the Graph of $f(x)$	Corresponding Point on the Graph of $g(x)$
$(-1, 1)$	$(2(-1) - 5, 1 + 2) = (-7, 3)$
$(0, 0)$	$(2(0) - 5, 0 + 2) = (-5, 2)$
$(1, 1)$	$(2(1) - 5, 1 + 2) = (-3, 3)$

Use the transformed reference points to graph $g(x)$.

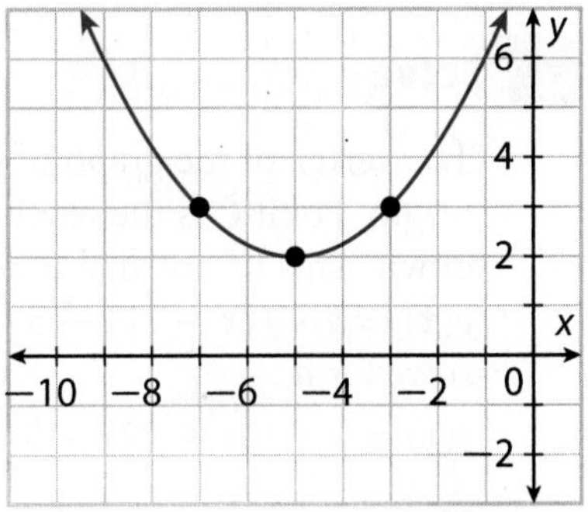

Reflect

10. Is the function $f(x) = x^2$ an even function, an odd function, or neither? Explain.

11. The graph of the parent quadratic function $f(x) = x^2$ has the vertical line $x = 0$ as its axis of symmetry. Identify the axis of symmetry for each of the graphs of $g(x)$ in Parts A and B. Which transformation(s) affect the location of the axis of symmetry?

Your Turn

12. Describe how to transform the graph of $f(x) = x^2$ to obtain the graph of the related function $g(x) = f\left(-4(x - 3)\right) + 1$. Then draw the graph of $g(x)$.

Explain 2 Modeling with a Quadratic Function

You can model real-world objects that have a parabolic shape using a quadratic function. In order to fit the function's graph to the shape of the object, you will need to determine the values of the parameters in the function $g(x) = a \cdot f\left(\frac{1}{b}(x - h)\right) + k$ where $f(x) = x^2$. Note that because $f(x)$ is simply a squaring function, it's possible to pull the parameter b outside the function and combine it with the parameter a. Doing so allows you to model real-objects using $g(x) = a \cdot f(x - h) + k$, which has only three parameters.

When modeling real-world objects, remember to restrict the domain of $g(x) = a \cdot f(x - h) + k$ to values of x that are based on the object's dimensions.

Example 2

An old stone bridge over a river uses a parabolic arch for support. In the illustration shown, the unit of measurement for both axes is feet, and the vertex of the arch is point C. Find a quadratic function that models the arch, and state the function's domain.

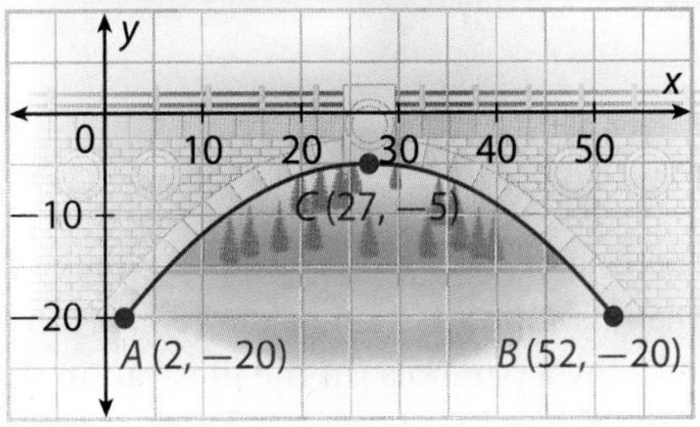

Analyze Information

Identify the important information.

- The shape of the arch is a parabola.
- The vertex of the parabola is $C(27, -5)$.
- Two other points on the parabola are $A(2, -20)$ and $B(52, -20)$.

Formulate a Plan

You want to find the values of the parameters a, h, and k in $g(x) = a \cdot f(x - h) + k$ where $f(x) = x^2$. You can use the coordinates of point C to find the values of h and k. Then you can use the coordinates of one of the other points to find the value of a.

Solve

The vertex of the graph of $g(x)$ is point C, and the vertex of the graph of $f(x)$ is the origin. Point C is the result of translating the origin 27 units to the right and 5 units down. This means that $h = 27$ and $k = -5$. Substituting these values into $g(x)$ gives $g(x) = a \cdot f(x - 27) - 5$. Now substitute the coordinates of point B into $g(x)$ and solve for a.

$g(x) = a \cdot f(x - 27) - 5$	Write the general function.
$g(\boxed{52}) = a \cdot f(52 - 27) - 5$	Substitute 52 for x.
$-20 = a \cdot f(52 - 27) - 5$	Replace $g(52)$ with -20, the y-value of B.
$-20 = a \cdot f(\boxed{25}) - 5$	Simplify.
$-20 = a(625) - 5$	Evaluate $f(25)$ for $f(x) = x^2$.
$a = \boxed{-\frac{3}{125}}$	Solve for a.

Substitute the value of a into $g(x)$.

$$g(x) = -\frac{3}{125} f(x - 27) - 5$$

The arch exists only between points A and B, so the domain of $g(x)$ is $\{x \mid 2 \le x \le 52\}$.

Justify and Evaluate

To justify the answer, verify that $g(2) = -20$.

$g(x) = -\frac{3}{125} f(x - 27) - 5$	Write the function.
$g(\boxed{2}) = -\frac{3}{125} f(\boxed{2} - 27) - 5$	Substitute 2 for x.
$= -\frac{3}{125} f(\boxed{-25}) - 5$	Subtract.
$= -\frac{3}{125} \cdot (\boxed{625}) - 5$	Evaluate $f(-25)$.
$= -20$ ✓	Simplify.

Your Turn

13. The netting of an empty hammock hangs between its supports along a curve that can be modeled by a parabola. In the illustration shown, the unit of measurement for both axes is feet, and the vertex of the curve is point C. Find a quadratic function that models the hammock's netting, and state the function's domain.

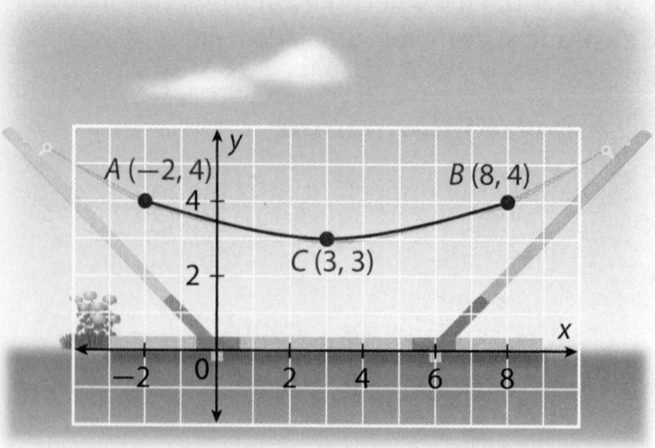

Elaborate

14. What is the general procedure to follow when graphing a function of the form $g(x) = a \cdot f(x - h) + k$ given the graph of $f(x)$?

15. What are the general steps to follow when determining the values of the parameters a, h, and k in $f(x) = a(x - h)^2 + k$ when modeling a parabolic real-world object?

16. **Essential Question Check-In** How can the graph of a function $f(x)$ be transformed?

Evaluate: Homework and Practice

Personal Math Trainer
- Online Homework
- Hints and Help
- Extra Practice

Write $g(x)$ in terms of $f(x)$ after performing the given transformation of the graph of $f(x)$.

1. Translate the graph of $f(x)$ to the left 3 units.

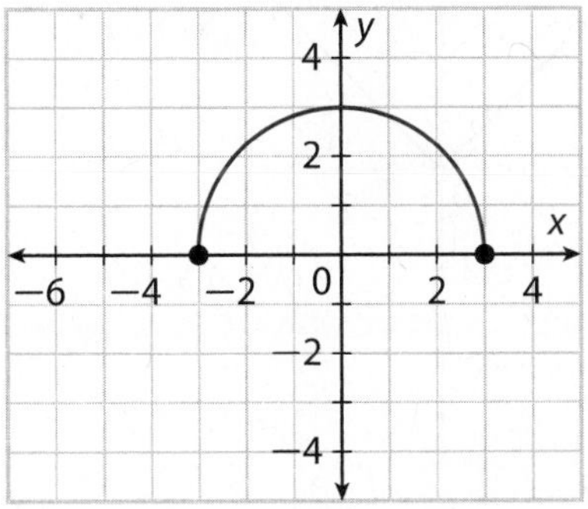

2. Translate the graph of $f(x)$ up 2 units.

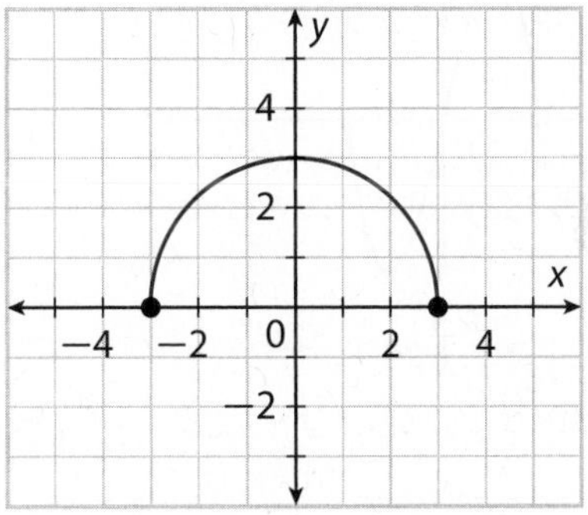

3. Translate the graph of $f(x)$ to the right 4 units.

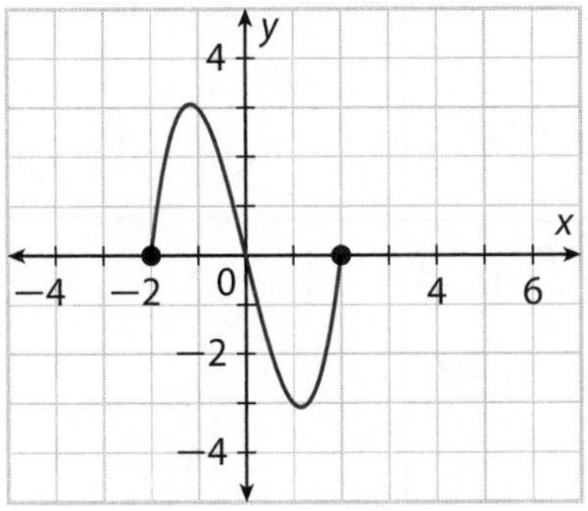

4. Translate the graph of $f(x)$ down 3 units.

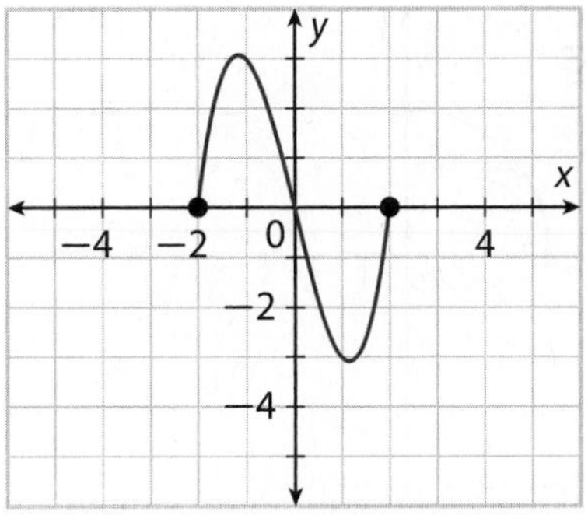

5. Stretch the graph of $f(x)$ horizontally by a factor of 3.

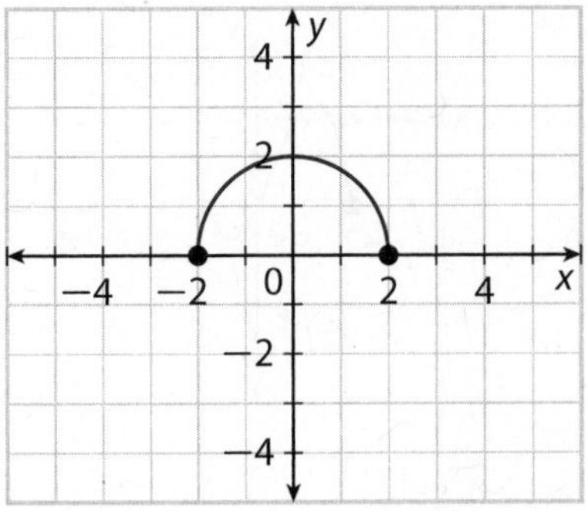

6. Stretch the graph of $f(x)$ vertically by a factor of 2.

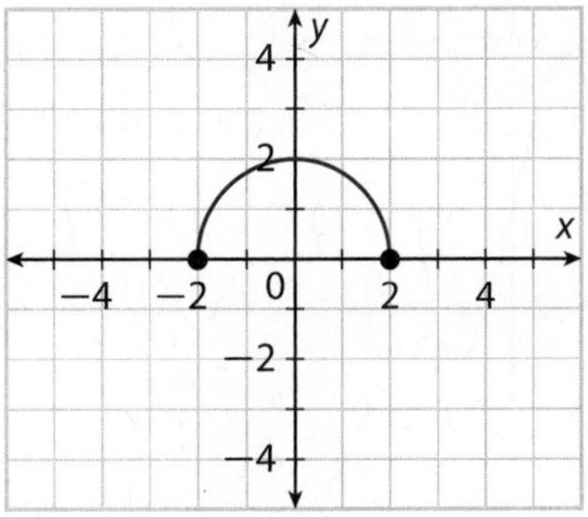

7. Compress the graph of $f(x)$ horizontally by a factor of $\frac{1}{3}$.

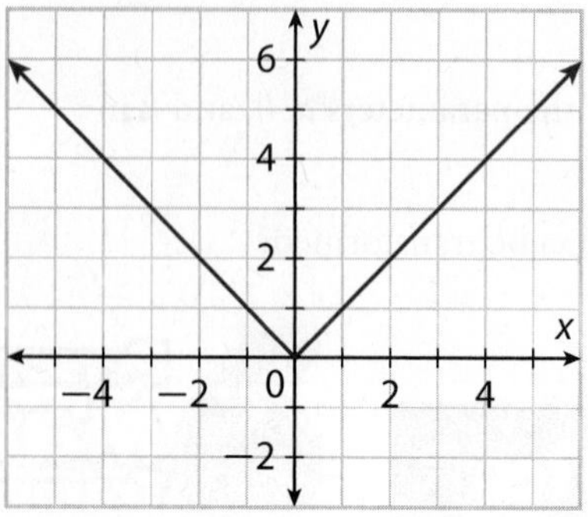

8. Compress the graph of $f(x)$ vertically by a factor of $\frac{1}{2}$.

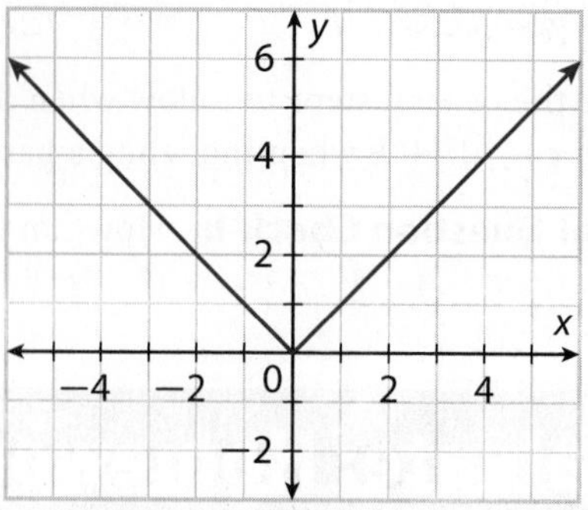

9. Reflect the graph of $f(x)$ across the y-axis.

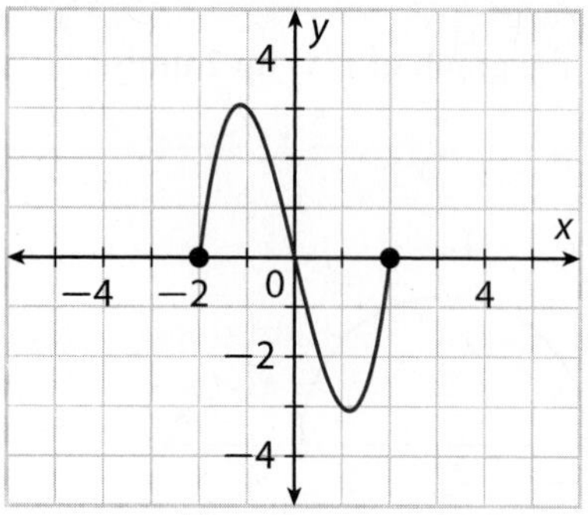

10. Reflect the graph of $f(x)$ across the x-axis.

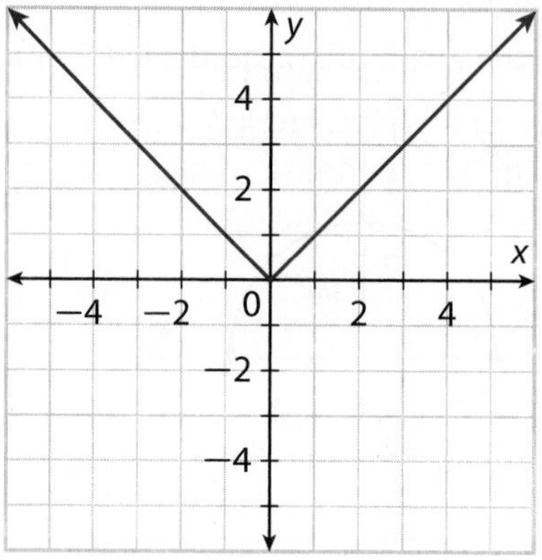

11. Reflect the graph of $f(x)$ across the y-axis.

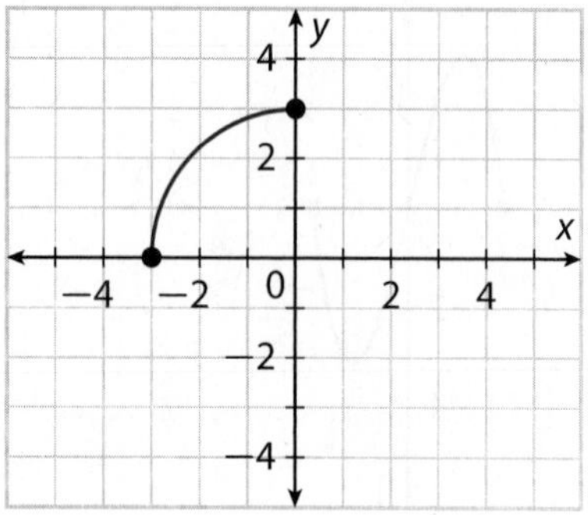

12. Reflect the graph of $f(x)$ across the x-axis.

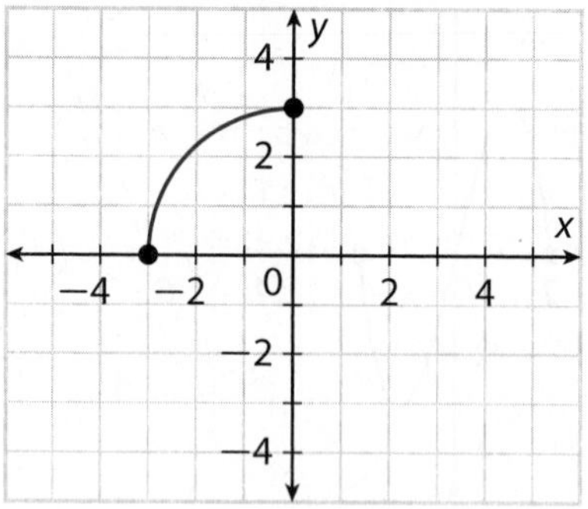

13. Determine if each function is an even function, an odd function, or neither.

a.

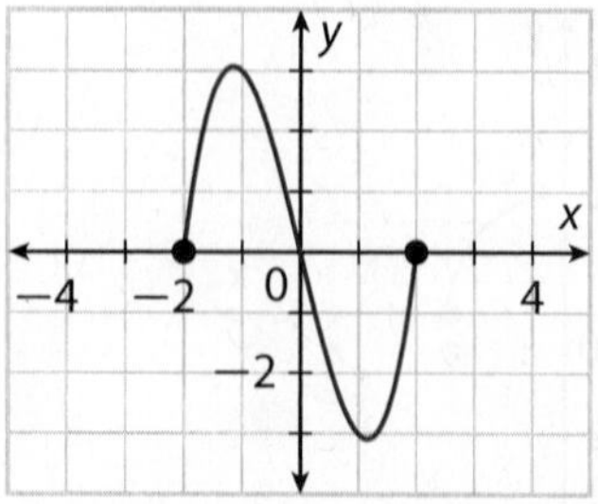

b.

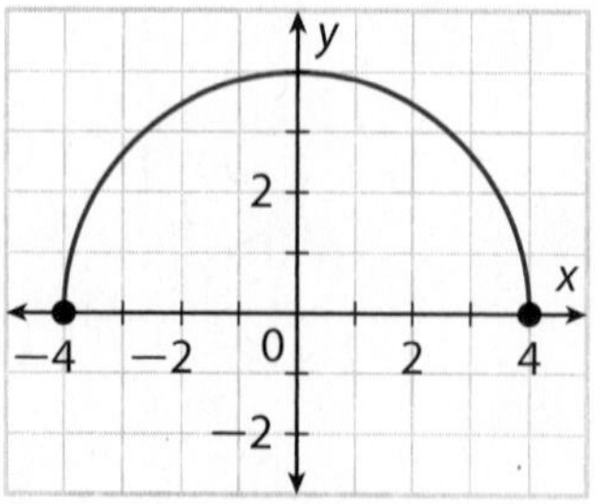

c.

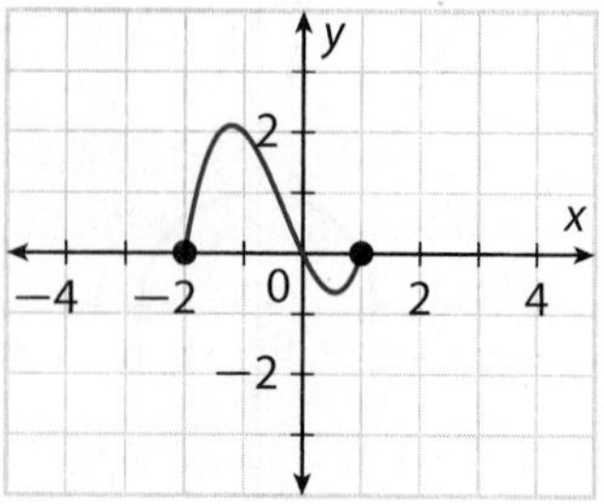

14. Determine whether each quadratic function is an even function. Answer *yes* or *no*.

a. $f(x) = 5x^2$

b. $f(x) = (x - 2)^2$

c. $f(x) = \left(\frac{x}{3}\right)^2$

d. $f(x) = x^2 + 6$

Describe how to transform the graph of $f(x) = x^2$ to obtain the graph of the related function $g(x)$. Then draw the graph of $g(x)$.

15. $g(x) = -\dfrac{f(x+4)}{3}$

16. $g(x) = f(2x) + 2$

17. Architecture Flying buttresses were used in the construction of cathedrals and other large stone buildings before the advent of more modern construction materials to prevent the walls of large, high-ceilinged rooms from collapsing.

The design of a flying buttress includes an arch. In the illustration shown, the unit of measurement for both axes is feet, and the vertex of the arch is point C. Find a quadratic function that models the arch, and state the function's domain.

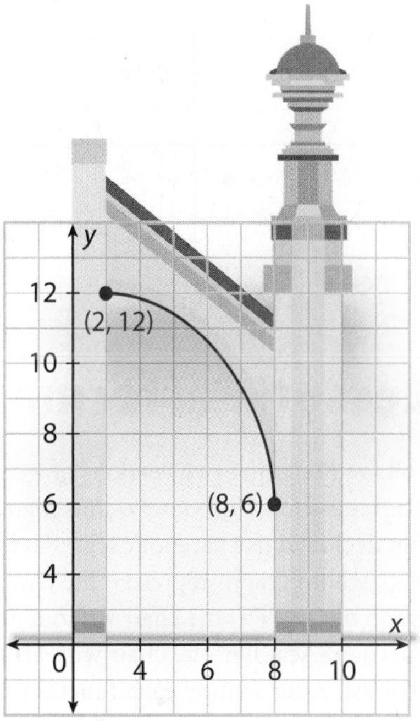

18. A red velvet rope hangs between two stanchions and forms a curve that can be modeled by a parabola. In the illustration shown, the unit of measurement for both axes is feet, and the vertex of the curve is point C. Find a quadratic function that models the rope, and state the function's domain.

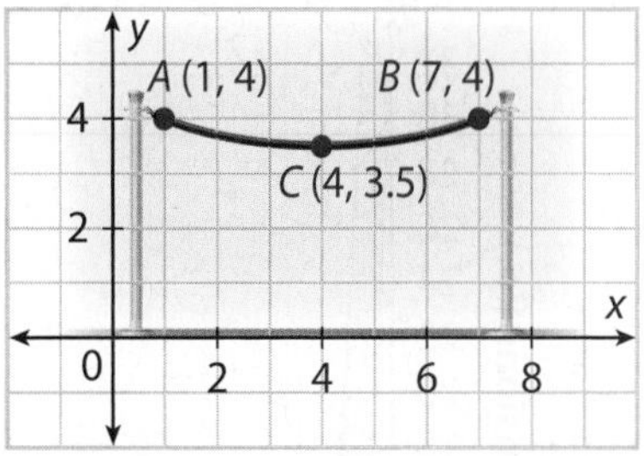

H.O.T. Focus on Higher Order Thinking

19. Multiple Representations The graph of the function $g(x) = \left(\frac{1}{2}x + 2\right)^2$ is shown.

Use the graph to identify the transformations of the graph of $f(x) = x^2$ needed to produce the graph of $g(x)$. (If a stretch or compression is involved, give it in terms of a horizontal stretch or compression rather than a vertical one.) Use your list of transformations to write $g(x)$ in the form $g(x) = f\left(\frac{1}{b}(x - h)\right) + k$. Then show why the new form of $g(x)$ is algebraically equivalent to the given form.

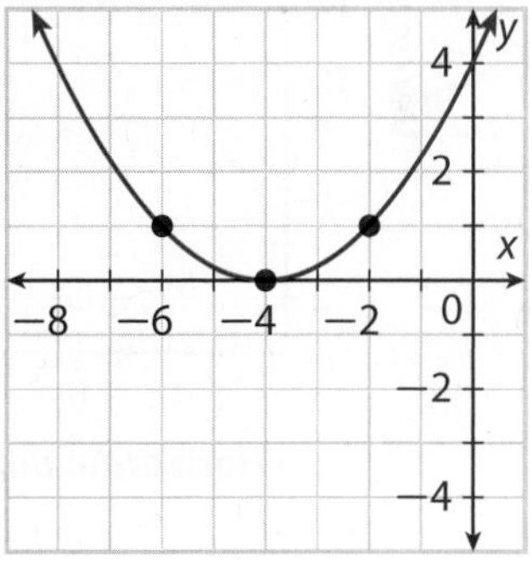

20. **Represent Real-World Situations** The graph of the ceiling function, $f(x) = \lceil x \rceil$, is shown. This function accepts any real number x as input and delivers the least integer greater than or equal to x as output. For instance, $f(1.3) = 2$ because 2 is the least integer greater than or equal to 1.3. The ceiling function is a type of *step function*, so named because its graph looks like a set of steps.

Write a function $g(x)$ whose graph is a transformation of the graph of $f(x)$ based on this situation: A parking garage charges \$4 for the first hour or less and \$2 for every additional hour or fraction of an hour. Then graph $g(x)$.

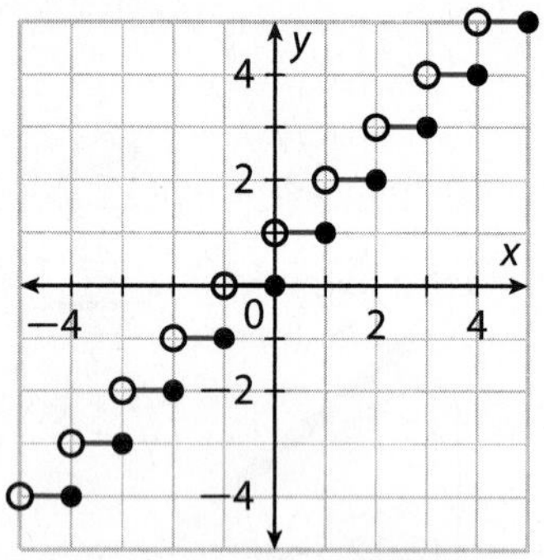

Lesson Performance Task

You are designing two versions of a chair, one without armrests and one with armrests. The diagrams show side views of the chair. Rather than use traditional straight legs for your chair, you decide to use parabolic legs. Given the function $f(x) = x^2$, write two functions, $g(x)$ and $h(x)$, whose graphs represent the legs of the two chairs and involve transformations of the graph of $f(x)$. For the chair without armrests, the graph of $g(x)$ must touch the bottom of the chair's seat. For the chair with armrests, the graph of $h(x)$ must touch the bottom of the armrest. After writing each function, graph it.

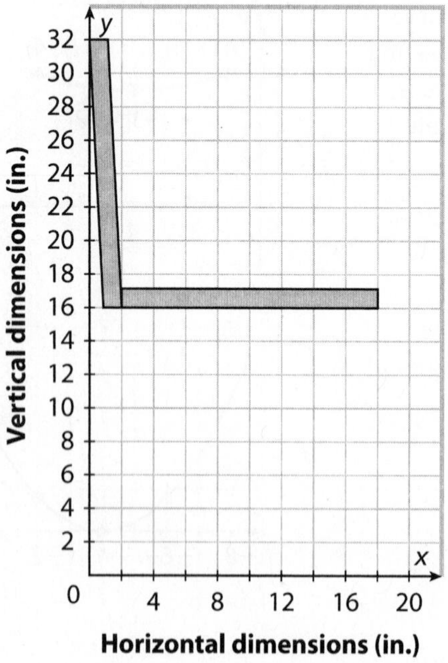

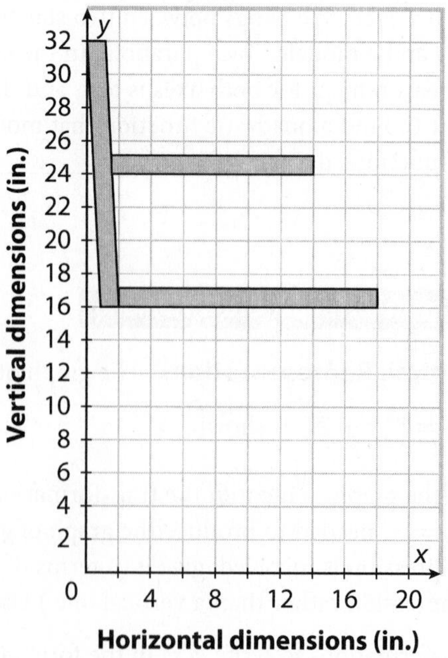

1.4 Inverses of Functions

Essential Question: What is an inverse function, and how do you know it's an inverse function?

Resource Locker

Explore Understanding Inverses of Functions

Recall that a *relation* is any pairing of the elements of one set (the domain) with the elements of a second set (the range). The elements of the domain are called inputs, while the elements of the range are called outputs. A function is a special type of relation that pairs every input with exactly one output. In a *one-to-one function*, no output is ever used more than once in the function's pairings. In a *many-to-one function*, at least one output is used more than once.

An **inverse relation** reverses the pairings of a relation. If a relation pairs an input x with an output y, then the inverse relation pairs an input y with an output x. The inverse of a function may or may not be another function. If the inverse of a function $f(x)$ is also a function, it is called the **inverse function** and is written $f^{-1}(x)$. If the inverse of a function is not a function, then it is simply an inverse relation.

Ⓐ The mapping diagrams show a function and its inverse. Complete the diagram for the inverse of the function.

Is the function one-to-one or many-to-one? Explain.

Is the inverse of the function also a function? Explain.

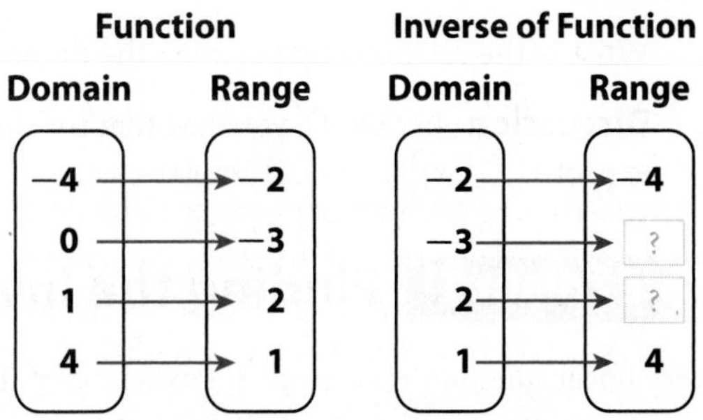

Ⓑ The mapping diagrams show a function and its inverse. Complete the diagram for the inverse of the function.

Is the function one-to-one or many-to-one? Explain.

Is the inverse of the function also a function? Explain.

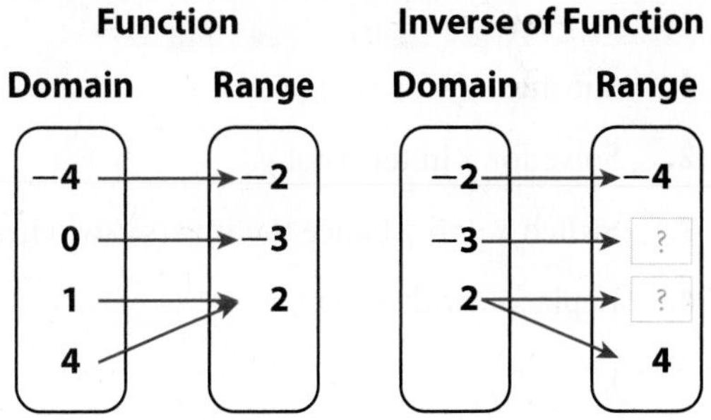

Ⓒ The graph of the original function in Step A is shown. Note that the graph also shows the dashed line $y = x$. Write the inverse of the function as a set of ordered pairs and graph them along with the original function.

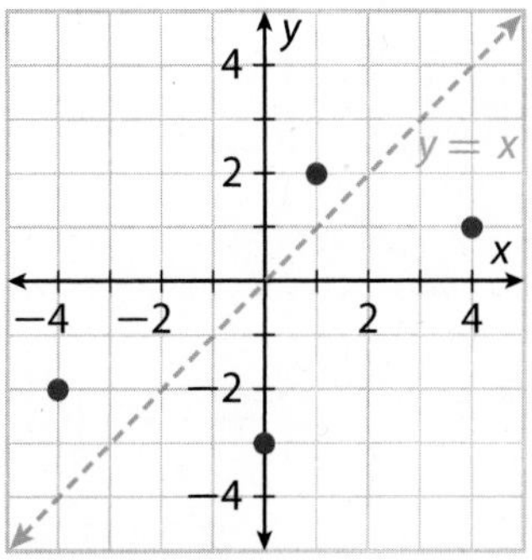

Function: $\{(-4, -2), (0, -3), (1, 2), (4, 1)\}$

Inverse of function:

$\{(?, ?), (?, ?), (?, ?), (?, ?)\}$

What do you observe about the graphs of the function and its inverse in relationship to the line $y = x$? Why does this make sense?

(D) The **composition of two functions** $f(x)$ and $g(x)$, written $f(g(x))$ and read as "f of g of x," is a new function that uses the output of $g(x)$ as the input of $f(x)$. For example, consider the functions f and g with the following rules.

f: Add 1 to an input. g: Double an input.

Notice that $g(1) = 2(1) = 2$. So, $f(g(1)) = f(2) = 2 + 1 = 3$.

You can also find $g(f(x))$. Notice that $f(1) = 1 + 1 = 2$. So, $g(f(1)) = g(2) = 2(2) = 4$.

For these two functions, you can see that $f(g(1)) \neq g(f(1))$.

You can compose a function and its inverse. For instance, the mapping diagram shown illustrates $f^{-1}(f(x))$ where $f(x)$ is the original function from Step A and $f^{-1}(x)$ is its inverse. Notice that the range of $f(x)$ serves as the domain of $f^{-1}(x)$. Complete the diagram. What do you notice about the outputs of $f^{-1}(f(x))$? Explain why this makes sense.

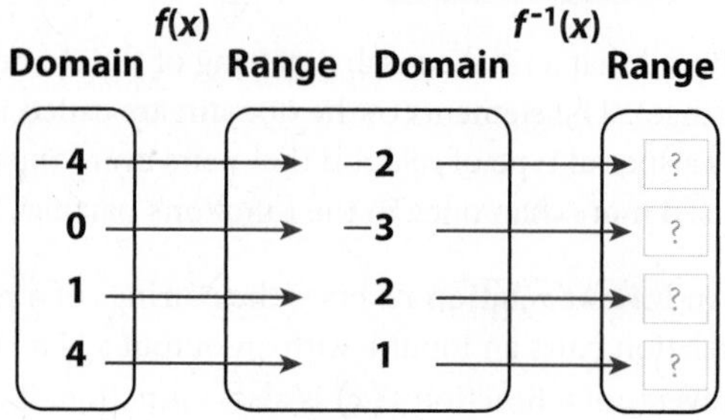

Reflect

1. What is the relationship between the domain and range of a relation and its inverse?

2. **Discussion** In Step D, you saw that for inverse functions, $f^{-1}(f(x)) = x$. What do you expect $f(f^{-1}(x))$ to equal? Explain.

Explain 1 Finding the Inverse of a Linear Function

Every linear function $f(x) = mx + b$ where $m \neq 0$ is a one-to-one function. So, its inverse is also a function. To find the inverse function, use the fact that inverse functions undo each other's pairings.

To find the inverse of a function $f(x)$:

1. Substitute y for $f(x)$.

2. Solve for x in terms of y.

3. Switch x and y (since the inverse switches inputs and outputs).

4. Replace y with $f^{-1}(x)$.

To check your work and verify that the functions are inverses, show that $f(f^{-1}(x)) = x$ and that $f^{-1}(f(x)) = x$.

Example 1 **Find the inverse function $f^{-1}(x)$ for the given function $f(x)$. Use composition to verify that the functions are inverses. Then graph the function and its inverse.**

(A) $f(x) = 3x + 4$

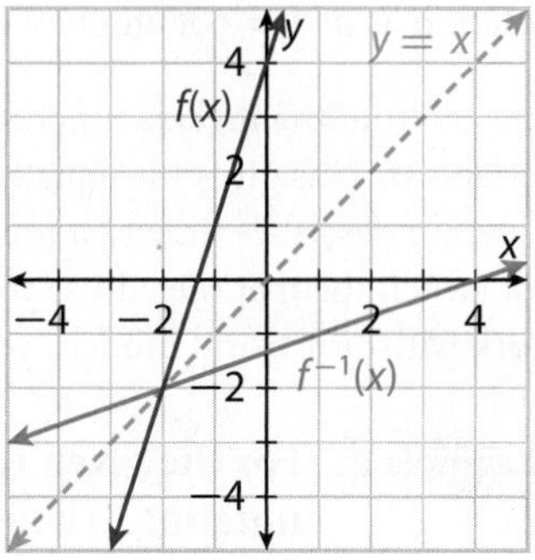

Replace $f(x)$ with y. $\quad y = 3x + 4$

Solve for x. $\quad y - 4 = 3x$

$$\frac{y-4}{3} = x$$

Interchange x and y. $\quad y = \frac{x-4}{3}$

Replace y with $f^{-1}(x)$. $\quad f^{-1}(x) = \frac{x-4}{3}$

Check: Verify that $f^{-1}\big(f(x)\big) = x$ and $f\big(f^{-1}(x)\big) = x$.

$$f^{-1}\big(f(x)\big) = f^{-1}(3x+4) = \frac{(3x+4)-4}{3} = \frac{3x}{3} = x$$

$$f\big(f^{-1}(x)\big) = f\left(\frac{x-4}{3}\right) = 3\left(\frac{x-4}{3}\right) + 4 = (x-4) + 4 = x$$

(B) $f(x) = 2x - 2$

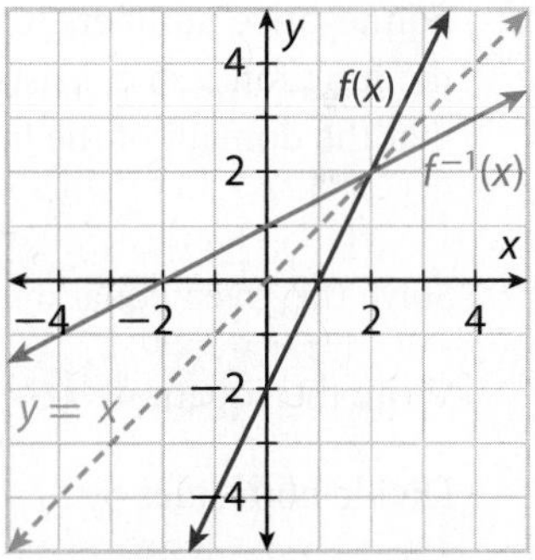

Replace $f(x)$ with y. $\quad y = \boxed{2x - 2}$

Solve for x. $\quad y \boxed{+2} = 2x$

$$\frac{y+2}{2} = x$$

Interchange x and y. $\quad y = \boxed{\frac{x+2}{2}}$

Replace y with $f^{-1}(x)$. $\quad \boxed{f^{-1}(x)} = \frac{x+2}{2}$

Check: Verify that $f^{-1}\big(f(x)\big) = x$ and $f\big(f^{-1}(x)\big) = x$.

$$f^{-1}\big(f(x)\big) = f^{-1}\left(\boxed{2x-2}\right) = \frac{(2x-2) + \boxed{2}}{\boxed{2}} = \frac{2x}{2} = \boxed{x}$$

$$f\big(f^{-1}(x)\big) = f\left(\boxed{\frac{x+2}{2}}\right) = \boxed{2}\left(\frac{x+2}{2}\right) - \boxed{2} = \left(\boxed{x+2}\right) - 2 = \boxed{x}$$

Reflect

3. What is the significance of the point where the graph of a linear function and its inverse intersect?

4. The graph of a constant function $f(x) = c$ for any constant c is a horizontal line through the point $(0, c)$. Does a constant function have an inverse? Does it have an inverse function? Explain.

Your Turn

Find the inverse function $f^{-1}(x)$ for the given function $f(x)$. Use composition to verify that the functions are inverses. Then graph the function and its inverse.

5. $f(x) = -2x + 3$

Explain 2 Modeling with the Inverse of a Linear Function

In a model for a real-world situation, the variables have specific real-world meanings. For example, the distance d (in miles) traveled in time t (in hours) at a constant speed of 60 miles per hour is $d = 60t$. Writing this in function notation as $d(t) = 60t$ emphasizes that this equation describes distance as a function of time.

You can find the inverse function for $d = 60t$ by solving for the independent variable t in terms of the dependent variable d. This gives the equation $t = \frac{d}{60}$. Writing this in function notation as $t(d) = \frac{d}{60}$ emphasizes that this equation describes time as a function of distance. Because the meanings of the variables can't be interchanged, you do not switch them at the end as you would switch x and y when working with purely mathematical functions. As you work with real-world models, you may have to restrict the domain and range.

Example 2 **For the given function, state the domain of the inverse function using set notation. Then find an equation for the inverse function, and graph it. Interpret the meaning of the inverse function.**

Ⓐ The equation $C = 3.5g$ gives the cost C (in dollars) as a function of the number of gallons of gasoline g when the price is \$3.50 per gallon.

The domain of the function $C = 3.5g$ is restricted to nonnegative numbers to make real-world sense, so the range of the function also consists of nonnegative numbers. This means that the domain of the inverse function is $\{C \mid C \geq 0\}$.

Solve the given equation for g to find the inverse function.

Write the equation. $C = 3.5g$

Divide both sides by 3.5. $\frac{C}{3.5} = g$

So, the inverse function is $g = \frac{C}{3.5}$.

Graph the inverse function.

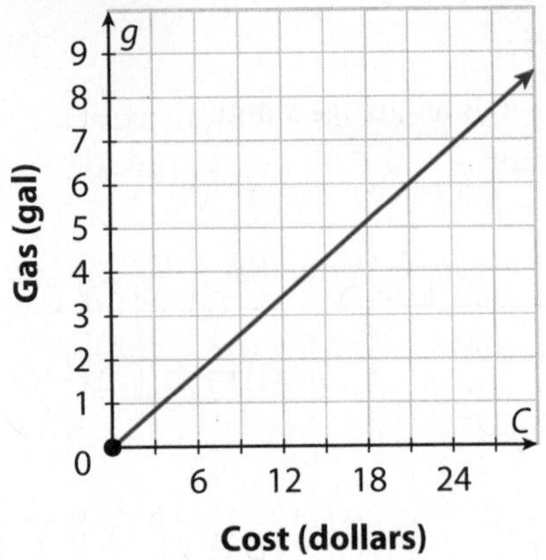

The inverse function gives the number of gallons of gasoline as a function of the cost (in dollars) when the price of gas is \$3.50 per gallon.

Ⓑ A car's gas tank, which can hold 14 gallons of gas, contains 4 gallons of gas when the driver stops at a gas station to fill the tank. The gas pump dispenses gas at a rate of 5 gallons per minute. The equation $g = 5t + 4$ gives the number of gallons of gasoline g in the tank as a function of the pumping time t(in minutes).

The range of the function $g = 5t + 4$ is the number of gallons of gas in the tank, which varies from 4 gallons to 14 gallons. So, the domain of the inverse function is $\left\{g \mid \boxed{4} \leq g \leq \boxed{14}\right\}$.

Solve the given equation for g to find the inverse function.

Write the equation. $g = \boxed{5}\,t + \boxed{4}$

Solve for t. $\dfrac{\boxed{g-4}}{5} = t$

So, the inverse function is $t = \boxed{\dfrac{g-4}{5}}$.

Graph the inverse function.

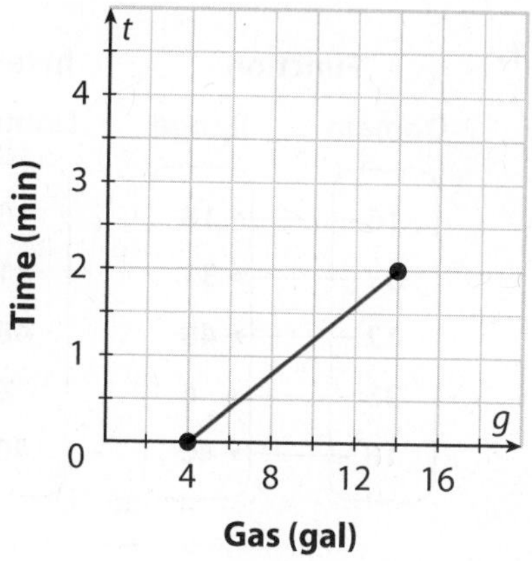

The inverse function gives the pumping time (in minutes) as a function of the amount of gas in the tank (in gallons) .

Your Turn

For the given function, determine the domain of the inverse function. Then find an equation for the inverse function, and graph it. Interpret the meaning of the inverse function.

6. A municipal swimming pool containing 600,000 gallons of water is drained. The amount of water w (in thousands of gallons) remaining in the pool at time t (in hours) after the draining begins is $w = 600 - 20t$.

Elaborate

7. What must be true about a function for its inverse to be a function?

8. A function rule indicates the operations to perform on an input to produce an output. What is the relationship between these operations and the operations indicated by the inverse function?

9. How can you use composition to verify that two functions $f(x)$ and $g(x)$ are inverse functions?

10. Describe a real-world situation modeled by a linear function for which it makes sense to find an inverse function. Give an example of how the inverse function might also be useful.

11. **Essential Question Check-In** What is an inverse relation?

Evaluate: Homework and Practice

Personal Math Trainer

- Online Homework
- Hints and Help
- Extra Practice

The mapping diagrams show a function and its inverse. Complete the diagram for the inverse of the function. Then tell whether the inverse is a function, and explain your reasoning.

1.

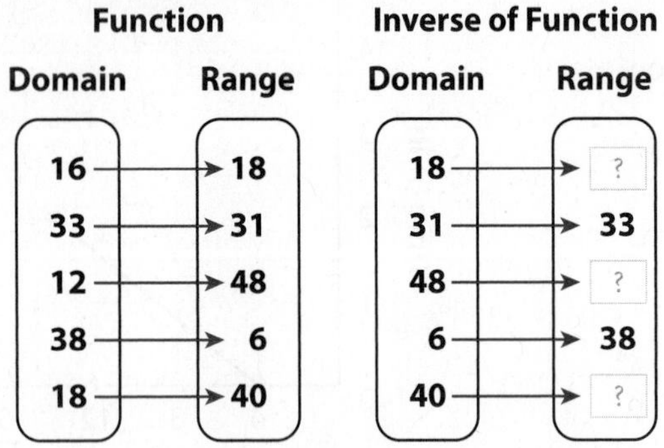

2.

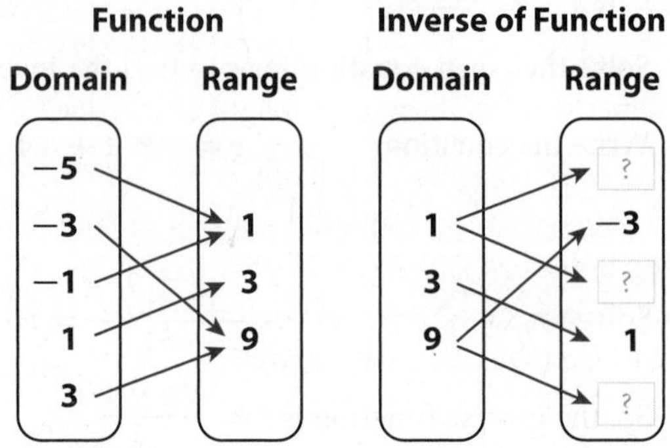

Write the inverse of the given function as a set of ordered pairs and then graph the function and its inverse on a coordinate plane.

3. Function:

$\{(-4, -3), (-2, -4), (0, -2), (1, 0), (2, 3)\}$

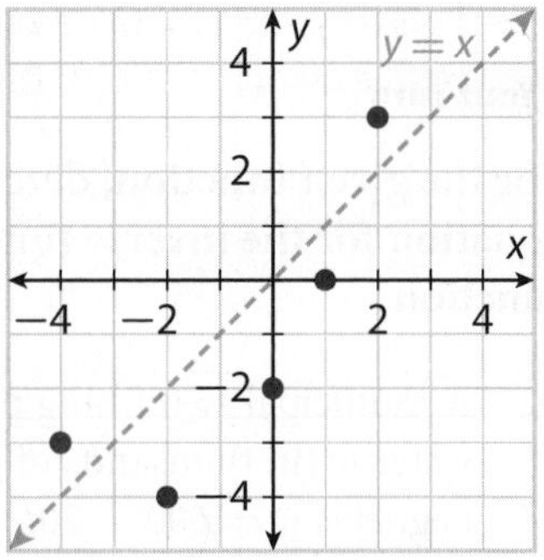

4. Function:

$\{(-3, -4), (-2, -3), (-1, 2), (1, 2), (2, 4), (3, 4)\}$

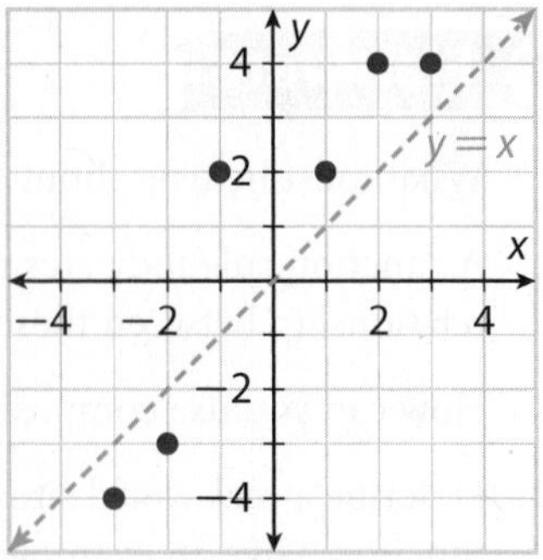

Find the inverse function $f^{-1}(x)$ for the given function $f(x)$.

5. $f(x) = 4x - 8$

6. $f(x) = \frac{x}{3}$

7. $f(x) = \frac{x + 1}{6}$

8. $f(x) = -0.75x$

Find the inverse function $f^{-1}(x)$ for the given function $f(x)$. Use composition to verify that the functions are inverses. Then graph the function and its inverse.

9. $f(x) = -3x + 3$

10. $f(x) = \frac{2}{5}x - 2$

For the given function, determine the domain of the inverse function. Then find an equation for the inverse function, and graph it. Interpret the meaning of the inverse function.

11. **Geometry** The equation $A = \frac{1}{2}(20)h$ gives the area A (in square inches) of a triangle with a base of 20 inches as a function of its height h (in inches).

12. The label on a gallon of paint says that it will cover from 250 square feet to 450 square feet depending on the surface that is being painted. A painter has 12 gallons of paint on hand. The equation $A = 12c$ gives the area A (in square feet) that the 12 gallons of paint will cover if applied at a coverage rate c (in square feet per gallon).

The graph of a function is given. Tell whether the function's inverse is a function, and explain your reasoning. If the inverse is not a function, tell how can you restrict the domain of the function so that its inverse is a function.

13.

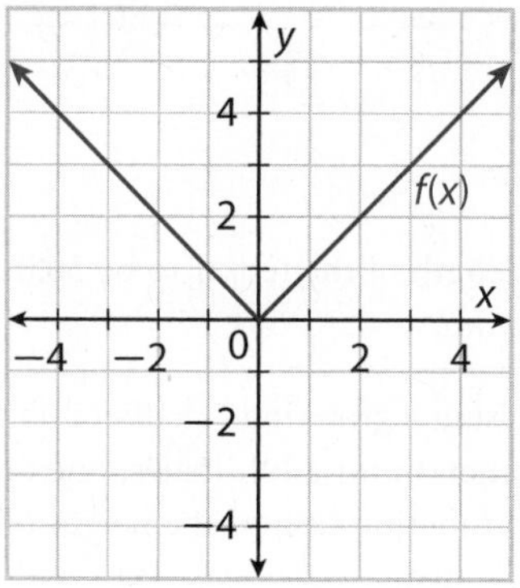

14.

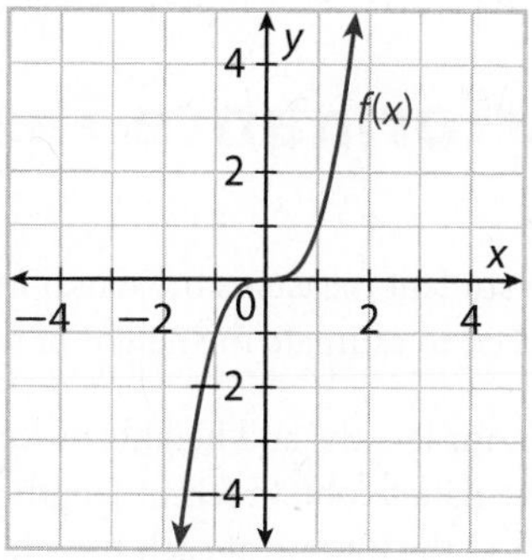

15. Multiple Response Identify the domain intervals over which the inverse of the graphed function is also a function. Select all that apply.

A. $[4, +\infty)$ D. $(-\infty, +\infty)$ G. $(4, 8)$

B. $(0, +\infty)$ E. $(-\infty, 4]$ H. $(8, +\infty)$

C. $[-4, +\infty)$ F. $(-\infty, 4)$ I. $(0, 8]$

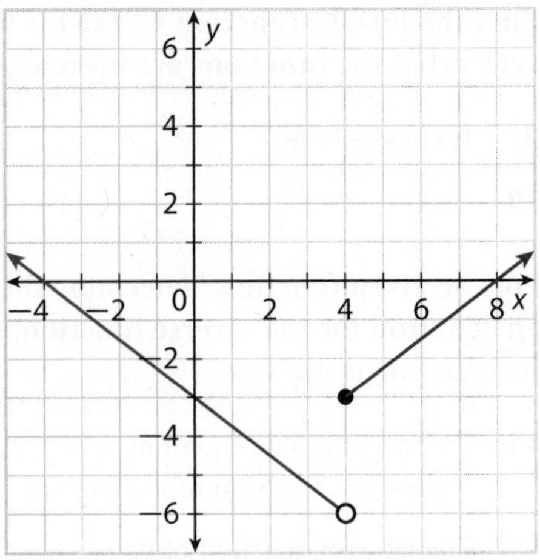

H.O.T. Focus on Higher Order Thinking

16. Draw Conclusions Identify all linear functions that are their own inverse.

17. Make a Conjecture Among linear functions (excluding constant functions), quadratic functions, absolute value functions, and exponential functions, which types of function do you have to restrict the domain for the inverse to be a function? Explain.

18. Find the Error A student was asked to find the inverse of $f(x) = 2x + 1$. The student's work is shown. Explain why the student is incorrect and what the student should have done to get the correct answer.

> The function $f(x) = 2x + 1$ involves two operations: multiplying by 2 and adding 1. The inverse operations are dividing by 2 and subtracting 1. So, the inverse function is $f^{-1}(x) = \frac{x}{2} - 1$.

Lesson Performance Task

In an anatomy class, a student measures the femur of an adult male and finds the length of the femur to be 50.0 cm. The student is then asked to estimate the height of the male that the femur came from.

The table shows the femur lengths and heights of some adult males and females. Using a graphing calculator, perform linear regression on the data to obtain femur length as a function of height (one function for adult males, one for adult females). Then find the inverse of each function. Use the appropriate inverse function to find the height of the adult male and explain how the inverse functions would be helpful to a forensic scientist.

Femur Length (cm)	30	38	46	54	62
Male Height (cm)	138	153	168	183	198
Female Height (cm)	132	147	163	179	194

STUDY GUIDE REVIEW

Analyzing Functions

MODULE 1

Essential Question: How can you analyze functions to solve real-world problems?

Key Vocabulary

finite interval *(intervalo finito)*
infinite interval *(intervalo infinito)*
domain *(dominio)*
range *(rango)*
end behavior *(comportamiento final)*

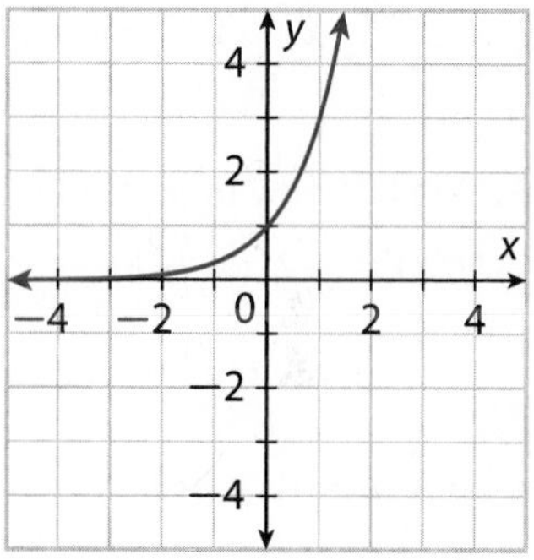

KEY EXAMPLE *(Lesson 1.1)*

Write the domain and range of $f(x) = 3^x$ as an inequality, using set notation, and using interval notation. Then describe the end behavior of the function.

	Domain	Range
Inequality	$-\infty < x < +\infty$	$y > 0$
Set notation	$\{x \mid -\infty < x < +\infty\}$	$\{y \mid y > 0\}$
Interval notation	$(-\infty, +\infty)$	$(0, +\infty)$

End behavior: As $x \to +\infty$, $f(x) \to +\infty$, and as $x \to -\infty$, $f(x) \to 0$.

KEY EXAMPLE *(Lesson 1.3)*

Describe how to transform the graph of $f(x) = x^2$ to obtain the graph of the related function $g(x) = 2f(x - 1) + 3$.

Parameter	Effect on the Parent Graph
$a = 2$	vertical stretch of the graph of $f(x)$ by a factor of 2
$h = 1$	translation of the graph of $f(x)$ to the right 1 unit
$k = 3$	translation of the graph of $f(x)$ up 3 units

A point (x, y) on the graph of $f(x) = x^2$ becomes the point $(x + 1, 2y + 3)$.

KEY EXAMPLE *(Lesson 1.4)*

Find the inverse function $f^{-1}(x)$ for $f(x) = -2x + 3$.

$y = -2x + 3$ — Replace $f(x)$ with y.

$\frac{y - 3}{-2} = x$ — Solve for x.

$y = \frac{x - 3}{-2}$ — Switch x and y.

$f^{-1}(x) = \frac{x - 3}{-2}$ — Replace y with $f^{-1}(x)$.

EXERCISES

Write the domain and range of the function as an inequality, using set notation, and using interval notation. *(Lesson 1.1)*

1.

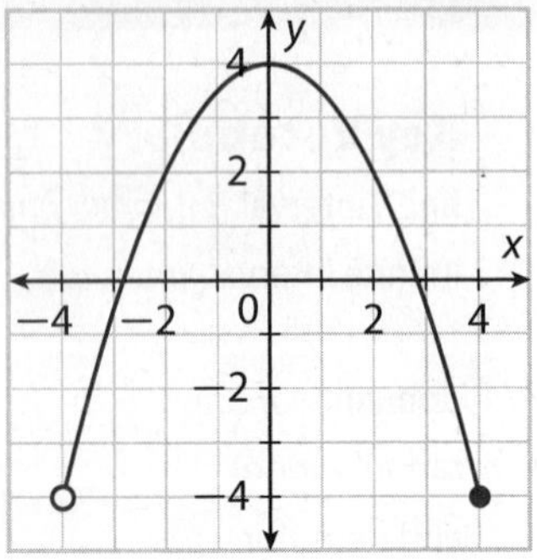

2.

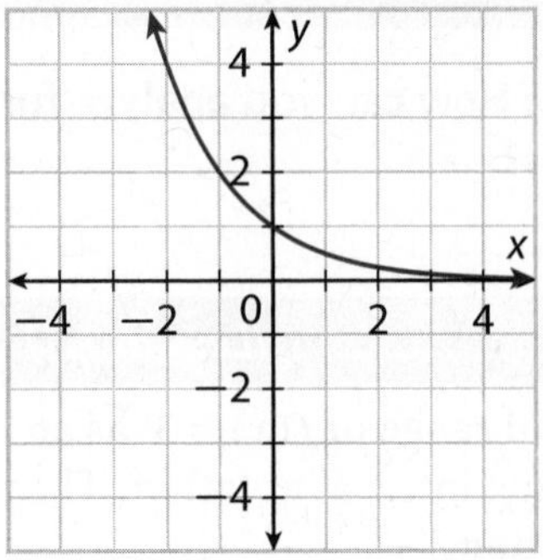

Find the inverse function $f^{-1}(x)$ for the given function $f(x)$. *(Lesson 1.4)*

3. $f(x) = \dfrac{x+3}{5}$

4. $f(x) = 2x + 6$

5. Explain how to transform the graph of the function $f(x) = x^2$ to obtain the graph of the related function $g(x) = -2f(x+1) - 3$. *(Lesson 1.3)*

MODULE PERFORMANCE TASK

How High Does a Pole-Vaulter Go?

A pole-vaulter performs two vaults, which can be modeled using the functions $h_1(t) = 9.8t - 4.9t^2$ and $h_2(t) = 8.82t - 4.9t^2$ where h is the height in meters at time t in seconds. How do the two jumps compare graphically in terms of the vertices and intercepts, and what do these represent? Which was the higher jump? How do you know?

As you complete the task, be sure to write down all your data and assumptions. Then use graphs, numbers, words, or algebra to explain how you reached your conclusions.

Ready to Go On?

1.1–1.4 Analyzing Functions

Personal Math Trainer
- Online Homework
- Hints and Help
- Extra Practice

Write the domain and range of the function $g(x) = 3x^2 - 4$ as an inequality, using set notation, and using interval notation. Then, compare the function to $f(x) = x^2$ and describe the transformations. *(Lessons 1.1, 1.3)*

1.	Domain	Range	Transformations
Inequality	?	?	?
Set notation	?	?	
Interval notation	?	?	

Find the inverse for each linear function. *(Lesson 1.4)*

2. $f(x) = -2x + 4$

3. $g(x) = \frac{x}{4} - 3$

4. $h(x) = \frac{3}{4}x + 1$

5. $j(x) = 5x - 6$

ESSENTIAL QUESTION

6. What are two ways the graphed function could be used to solve real-world problems? *(Lesson 1.2)*

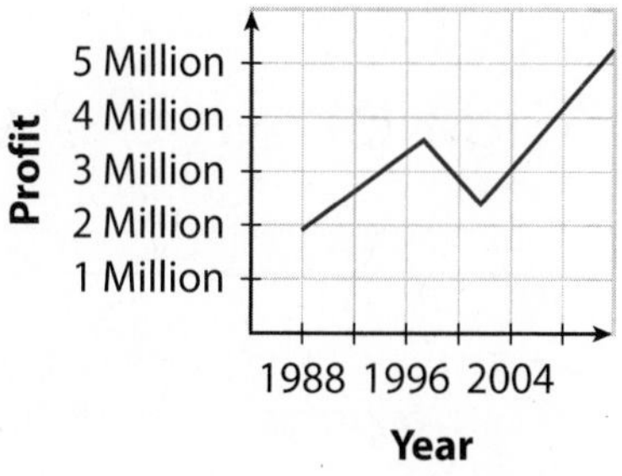

MODULE 1
MIXED REVIEW

Assessment Readiness

1. Look at each equation. Tell whether the graph of the equation has an end behavior that approaches infinity (∞) as $x \to -\infty$.

A. $y = -2x - 5$

B. $y = 5(x + 2)^2 - 3$

C. $y = -3^x$

2. Consider the function $g(x) = -f(x + 3) - 2$. Determine if each statement is True or False.

A. When compared to $f(x) = x^2$, $g(x)$ will have a vertical stretch of 3.

B. When compared to $f(x) = x^2$, $g(x)$ will be reflected over the x-axis.

C. When compared to $f(x) = x^2$, $g(x)$ will be translated left 3 units.

3. A bike rider starts at a fast pace and rides 40 miles in 2 hours. He gets tired, and slows down, traveling only 20 miles in the next 3 hours. He takes a rest for an hour, then rides back to where he started at a steady pace without stopping for 4 hours. Draw a graph to match the real world situation. Explain your choices.

4. The function to convert Fahrenheit to Celsius is $°C = f(°F) = \frac{5(°F - 32)}{9}$. The inverse function will convert Celsius to Fahrenheit. What is the inverse function? Explain how determining this inverse is different than determining the previous inverses.

Absolute Value Functions, Equations, and Inequalities

MODULE 2

Essential Question: How can you use absolute value functions to solve real-world problems?

REAL WORLD VIDEO
Gold jewelry is sold with a rating for purity. For instance, 18-karat gold is 75% pure by weight. The purity level has to meet tolerances that can be expressed using absolute value inequalities.

MODULE PERFORMANCE TASK PREVIEW
What Is the Purity of Gold?

Because gold is such a soft metal, it is usually mixed with another metal such as copper or silver. Pure gold is 24 karat, and 18 karat indicates a mixture of 18 parts gold and 6 parts of another metal or metals. Imagine someone wants to sell you a ring and claims it is 18 karat. How can you use math to be sure the gold is indeed 18 karat? Let's find out!

Are YOU Ready?

Complete these exercises to review skills you will need for this module.

Personal Math Trainer
- Online Homework
- Hints and Help
- Extra Practice

One-Step Equations

Example 1 Solve $x - 6.8 = 2$ for x.

$x - 6.8 + 6.8 = 2 + 6.8$ Add.

$x = 8.8$ Combine like terms.

Solve each equation.

1. $r + 9 = 7$ **2.** $\frac{w}{4} = -3$ **3.** $10b = 14$

Slope and Slope-Intercept Form

Example 2 Find the slope and y-intercept of $3x - y = 6$.

$-3x + 3x - y = -3x + 6$ Write the equation in $y = mx + b$ form.

$-y(-1) = (-3x + 6)(-1)$

$y = 3x - 6$ The slope is 3 and the y-intercept is -6.

Find the slope and y-intercept for each equation.

4. $y - 8 = 2x + 9$ **5.** $3y = 2(x - 3)$ **6.** $2y + 8x = 1$

Linear Inequalities in Two Variables

Example 3 Graph $y < 2x - 3$.

Graph the y-intercept of $(0, -3)$.

Use the slope of 2 to plot a second point, and draw a dashed line connecting the points. Shade below the line.

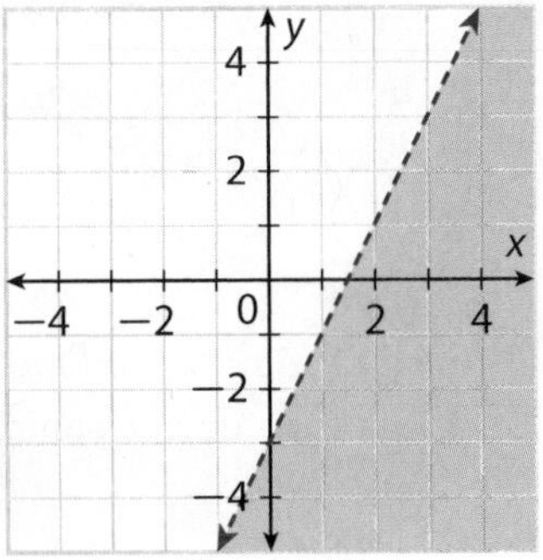

Graph and label each inequality on a coordinate plane.

7. $y \geq -x + 2$ **8.** $y < x - 1$

2.1 Graphing Absolute Value Functions

Essential Question: How can you identify the features of the graph of an absolute value function?

Resource Locker

Explore 1 Graphing and Analyzing the Parent Absolute Value Function

Absolute value, written as $|x|$, represents the distance between x and 0 on a number line. As a distance, absolute value is always nonnegative. For every point on a number line (except at 0), there is another point on the opposite side of 0 that is the same distance from 0. For example, both 5 and –5 are five units away from 0. Thus, $|-5| = 5$ and $|5| = 5$.

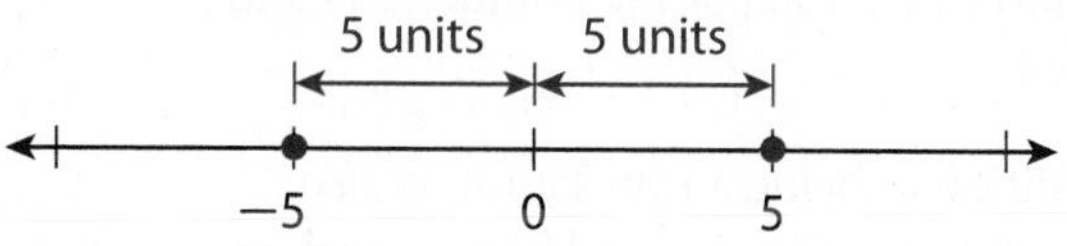

The absolute value function $|x|$, can be defined piecewise as $|x| = \begin{cases} x & x \geq 0 \\ -x & x < 0 \end{cases}$. When x is nonnegative, the function simply returns the number. When x is negative, the function returns the opposite of x.

(A) Complete the input-output table for $f(x)$.

$$f(x) = |x| = \begin{cases} x & x \geq 0 \\ -x & x < 0 \end{cases}$$

x	f(x)
-8	?
-4	?
0	?
4	?
8	?

(B) Plot the points you found on a coordinate grid. Use the points to complete the graph of the function.

(C) Now, examine your graph of $f(x) = |x|$ and complete the following statements about the function.

$f(x) = |x|$ is symmetric about the ? and therefore is a(n) ? function.

The domain of $f(x) = |x|$ is ? .

The range of $f(x) = |x|$ is ? .

Reflect

1. Use the definition of the absolute value function to show that $f(x) = |x|$ is an even function.

Explain 1 Graphing Absolute Value Functions

You can apply general transformations to absolute value functions by changing parameters in the equation $g(x) = a\left|\frac{1}{b}(x - h)\right| + k$.

Example 1 **Given the function $g(x) = a\left|\frac{1}{b}(x - h)\right| + k$, find the vertex of the function. Use the vertex and two other points to help you graph $g(x)$.**

(A) $g(x) = 4|x - 5| - 2$

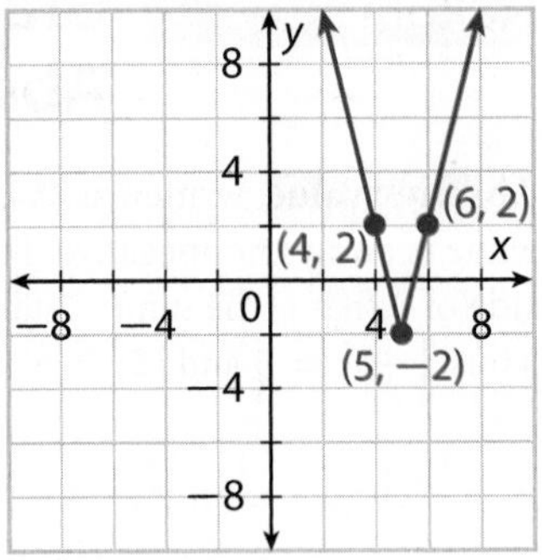

The vertex of the parent absolute value function is at (0, 0).

The vertex of $g(x)$ will be the point to which (0, 0) is mapped by $g(x)$.

$g(x)$ involves a translation of $f(x)$ 5 units to the right and 2 units down.

The vertex of $g(x)$ will therefore be at (5, –2).

Next, determine the location to which each of the points (1, 1) and (–1, 1) on $f(x)$ will be mapped.

Since $a > 1$, then $g(x)$, in addition to being a translation, is also a vertical stretch of $f(x)$ by a factor of 4. The x-coordinate of each point will be shifted 5 units to the right while the y-coordinate will be stretched by a factor of 4 and then moved down 2 units. So, (1, 1) moves to $(1 + 5, 4 \cdot |1| - 2) = (6, 2)$, and (–1, 1) moves to $(-1 + 5, 4 \cdot |1| - 2) = (4, 2)$. Now plot the three points and graph $g(x)$.

(B) $g(x) = \left|-\frac{1}{2}(x + 3)\right| + 1$

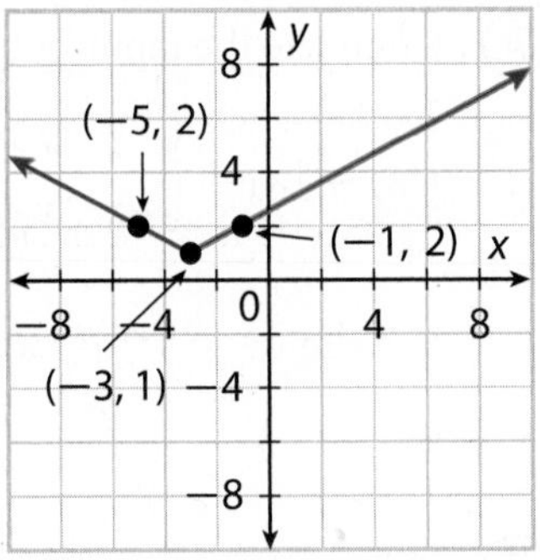

The vertex of the parent absolute value function is at (0, 0).

$g(x)$ is a translation of $f(x)$ 3 units to the left and 1 unit up.

The vertex of $g(x)$ will therefore be at $\left(\boxed{-3}, \boxed{1}\right)$.

Next, determine to where the points $(2, 2)$ and $(-2, 2)$ on $f(x)$ will be mapped.

Since $|b| = 2$, $g(x)$ is also a horizontal stretch of $f(x)$ and since b is negative, a reflection across the y-axis.

The x-coordinate will be reflected in the y-axis and stretched by a factor of 2, then moved 3 units to the left.

The y-coordinate will move up 1 unit.

So, (2, 2) becomes $\left(\boxed{-2(2) - 3}, \boxed{2 + 1}\right) = \left(\boxed{-7}, \boxed{3}\right)$, and $(-2, 2)$ becomes $\left(\boxed{1}, \boxed{3}\right)$. Now plot the three points and use them to sketch $g(x)$.

Your Turn

2. Given $g(x) = -\frac{1}{5}\left|(x + 6)\right| + 4$, find the vertex and two other points and use them to help you graph $g(x)$.

Explain 2 Writing Absolute Value Functions from a Graph

If an absolute value function in the form $g(x) = a\left|\frac{1}{b}(x - h)\right| + k$ has values other than 1 for both a and b, you can rewrite that function so that the value of at least one of a or b is 1.

When a and b are positive: $a\left|\frac{1}{b}(x - h)\right| = \left|\frac{a}{b}(x - h)\right| = \left|\frac{a}{b}\right|(x - h)\Big|$.

When a is negative and b is positive, you can move the opposite of a inside the absolute value expression. This leaves -1 outside the absolute value symbol: $-2\left|\frac{1}{b}\right| = -1(2)\left|\frac{1}{b}\right| = -1\left|\frac{2}{b}\right|$.

When b is negative, you can rewrite the equation without a negative sign, because of the properties of absolute value: $a\left|\frac{1}{b}(x - h)\right| = a\left|\frac{1}{-b}(x - h)\right|$. This case has now been reduced to one of the other two cases.

Example 2 **Given the graph of an absolute value function, write the function in the form $g(x) = a\left|\frac{1}{b}(x - h)\right| + k$.**

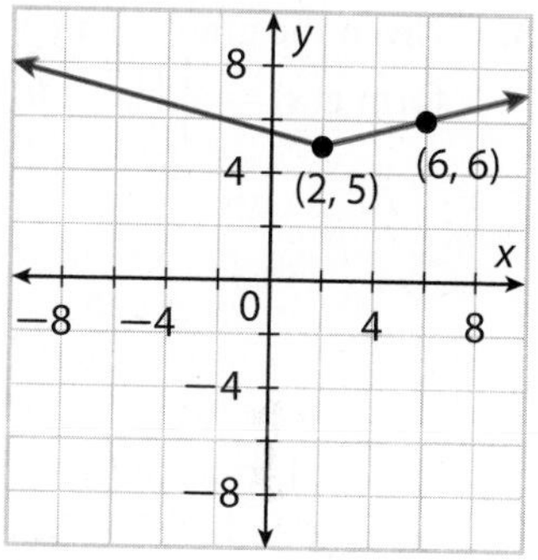

(A) Let $a = 1$.

The vertex of $g(x)$ is at (2, 5). This means that $h = 2$ and $k = 5$.
The value of a is given: $a = 1$.

Substitute these values into $g(x)$, giving $g(x) = \left|\frac{1}{b}(x - 2)\right| + 5$.

Choose a point on $g(x)$ like (6, 6), Substitute these values into $g(x)$, and solve for b.

Substitute. $6 = \left|\frac{1}{b}(6 - 2)\right| + 5$

Simplify. $6 = \left|\frac{1}{b}(4)\right| + 5$

Subtract 5 from each side. $1 = \left|\frac{4}{b}\right|$

Rewrite the absolute value as two equations. $1 = \frac{4}{b}$ or $1 = -\frac{4}{b}$

Solve for b. $b = 4$ or $b = -4$

Based on the problem conditions, only consider $b = 4$. Substitute into $g(x)$ to find the equation for the graph.

$g(x) = \left|\frac{1}{4}(x - 2)\right| + 5$

(B) Let $b = 1$.

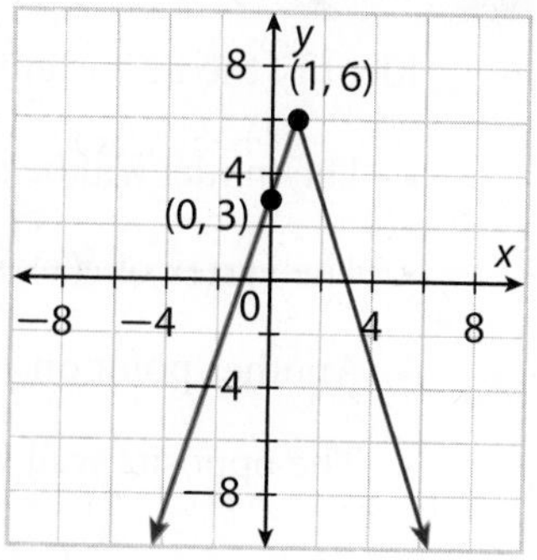

The vertex of $g(x)$ is at (1, 6). This means that $h =$ 1 and $k =$ 6 The value of b is given: $b = 1$.

Substitute these values into $g(x)$, giving $g(x) = a\left|x - 1\right| + 6$.

Now, choose a point on $g(x)$ with integer coordinates, (0, 3).

Substitute these values into $g(x)$ and solve for a.

$$g(x) = a\left|x - \boxed{1}\right| + \boxed{6}$$

Substitute. $\boxed{3} = a|0 - 1| + 6$

Simplify. $\boxed{3} = a|-1| + 6$

Solve for a. $\boxed{-3} = a$

Therefore $g(x) = \boxed{-3|x-1| + 6}$.

Your Turn

3. Given the graph of an absolute value function, write the function in the form $g(x) = a\left|\frac{1}{b}(x - h)\right| + k$.

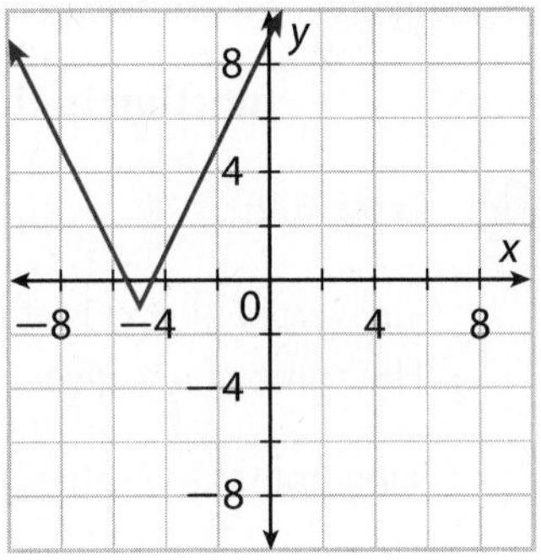

Explain 3 Modeling with Absolute Value Functions

Light travels in a straight line and can be modeled by a linear function. When light is reflected off a mirror, it travels in a straight line in a different direction. From physics, the angle at which the light ray comes in is equal to the angle at which it is reflected away: the angle of incidence is equal to the angle of reflection. You can use an absolute value function to model this situation.

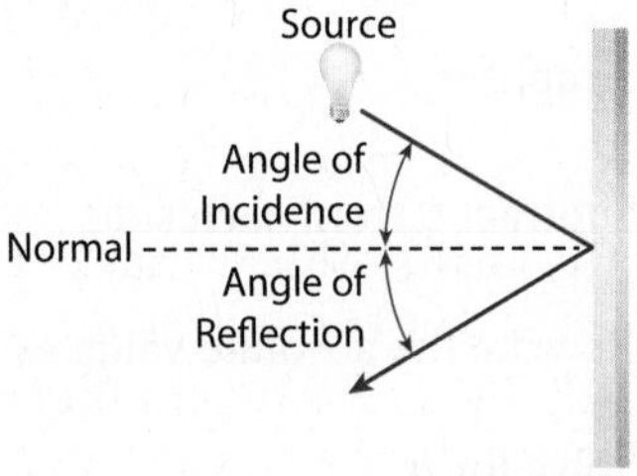

Law of Reflection

Example 3 **Solve the problem by modeling the situation with an absolute value function.**

At a science museum exhibit, a beam of light originates at a point 10 feet off the floor. It is reflected off a mirror on the floor that is 15 feet from the wall the light originates from. How high off the floor on the opposite wall does the light hit if the other wall is 8.5 feet from the mirror?

Analyze Information

Identify the important information.

- The model will be of the form $g(x) = a\left|\frac{1}{b}(x - h)\right| + k$.
- The vertex of $g(x)$ is (15, 0).
- Another point on $g(x)$ is (0, 10).
- The opposite wall is 23.5 feet from the first wall.

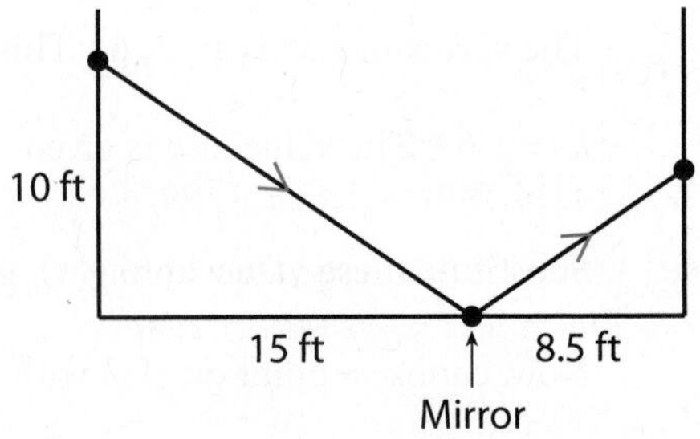

Formulate a Plan

Let the base of the first wall be the origin. You want to find the value of $g(x)$ at $x =$ 23.5 , which will give the height of the beam on the opposite wall. To do so, find the value of the parameters in the transformation of the parent function. In this situation, let $b = 1$. The vertex of $g(x)$ will give you the values of h and k. Use a second point to solve for a. Evaluate $g(23.5)$.

Solve

The vertex of $g(x)$ is at $(15, 0)$. Substitute, giving $g(x) = a|x - 15| + 0$.

Evaluate $g(x)$ at (0,10) and solve for a.

Substitute. $10 = a|0 - 15| + 0$

Simplify. $10 = a|-15|$

Simplify. $10 = 15a$

Solve for a. $a = \frac{2}{3}$

Therefore $g(x) = \frac{2}{3}|(x - 15)|$. Find $g(23.5)$. $g(23.5) = \frac{17}{3} \approx 5.67$

Justify and Evaluate

The answer of 5.67 makes sense because the function is symmetric with respect to the line x = 15. The distance from this line to the second wall is a little more than half the distance from the line to the beam's origin. Since the beam originates at a height of 10 feet, it should hit the second wall at a height of a little over 5 feet.

Your Turn

4. Two students are passing a ball back and forth, allowing it to bounce once between them. If one student bounce-passes the ball from a height of 1.4 m and it bounces 3 m away from the student, where should the second student stand to catch the ball at a height of 1.2 m? Assume the path of the ball is linear over this short distance.

Elaborate

5. In the general form of the absolute value function, what does each parameter represent?

6. **Discussion** Explain why the vertex of $f(x) = |x|$ remains the same when $f(x)$ is stretched or compressed but not when it is translated.

7. **Essential Question Check-In** What are the features of the graph of an absolute value function?

Personal Math Trainer
- Online Homework
- Hints and Help
- Extra Practice

Evaluate: Homework and Practice

Predict what the graph of each given function will look like. Verify your prediction using a graphing calculator. Then sketch the graph of the function.

1. $g(x) = 5|x - 3|$

2. $g(x) = -4|x + 2| + 5$

3. $g(x) = \left|\frac{7}{5}(x - 6)\right| + 4$

4. $g(x) = \left|\frac{3}{7}(x - 4)\right| + 2$

5. $g(x) = \frac{7}{4}|(x - 2)| - 3$

Graph the given function and identify the domain and range.

6. $g(x) = |x|$

7. $g(x) = \frac{4}{3}|(x - 5)| + 7$

8. $g(x) = -\frac{7}{6}|(x - 2)|$

9. $g(x) = \left|\frac{3}{4}(x - 2)\right| - 7$

10. $g(x) = \left|\frac{5}{7}(x - 4)\right|$

11. $g(x) = \left|-\frac{7}{3}(x + 5)\right| - 4$

Write the absolute value function in standard form for the given graph. Use *a* or *b* as directed, $b > 0$.

12. Let $a = 1$.

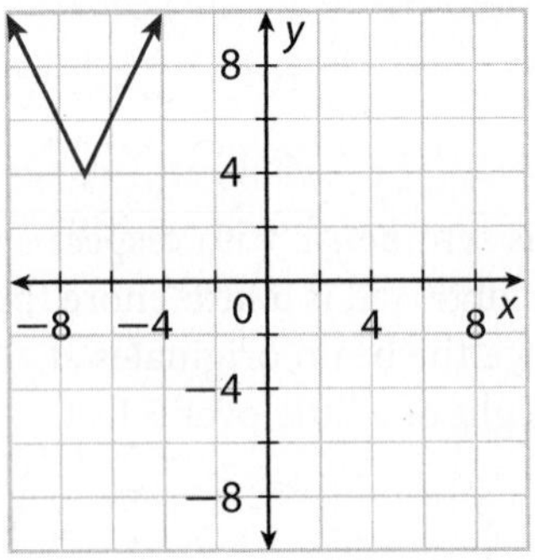

13. Let $b = 1$.

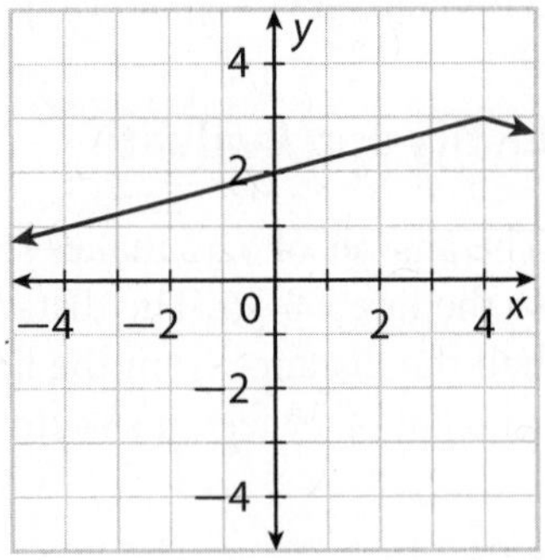

14. A rainstorm begins as a drizzle, builds up to a heavy rain, and then drops back to a drizzle. The rate r (in inches per hour) at which it rains is given by the function $r = -0.5|t - 1| + 0.5$, where t is the time (in hours). Graph the function. Determine for how long it rains and when it rains the hardest.

15. While playing pool, a player tries to shoot the eight ball into the corner pocket as shown. Imagine that a coordinate plane is placed over the pool table. The eight ball is at $\left(5, \frac{5}{4}\right)$ and the pocket they are aiming for is at $(10, 5)$. The player is going to bank the ball off the side at $(6, 0)$.

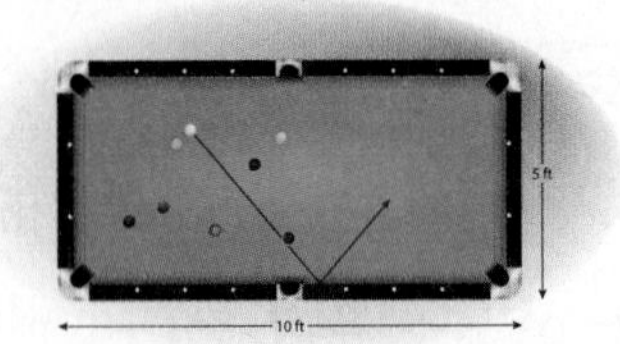

a. Write an equation for the path of the ball.

b. Did the player make the shot? How do you know?

16. Sam is sitting in a boat on a lake. She can get burned by the sunlight that hits her directly and by sunlight that reflects off the water. Sunlight reflects off the water at the point (2, 0) and hits Sam at the point (3.5, 3). Write and graph the function that shows the path of the sunlight.

17. The Transamerica Pyramid is an office building in San Francisco. It stands 853 feet tall and is 145 feet wide at its base. Imagine that a coordinate plane is placed over a side of the building. In the coordinate plane, each unit represents one foot. Write an absolute value function whose graph is the V-shaped outline of the sides of the building, ignoring the "shoulders" of the building.

18. Match each graph with its function.

a. ___?___ $y = |x + 6| - 4$ **b.** ___?___ $y = |x - 6| - 4$ **c.** ___?___ $y = |x - 6| + 4$

A
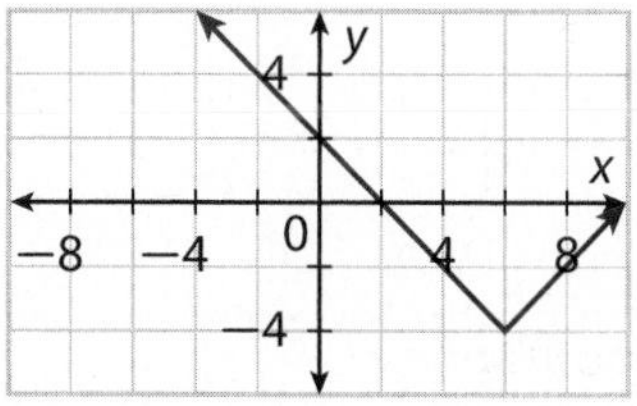

B
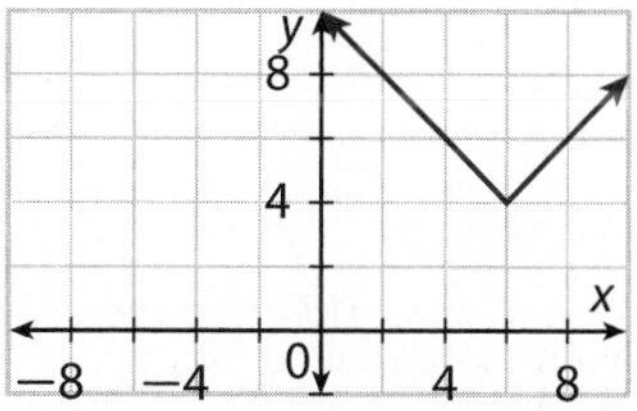

C
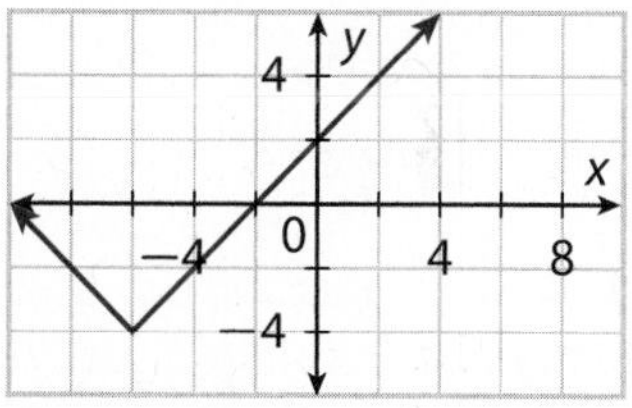

H.O.T. Focus on Higher Order Thinking

19. Explain the Error Explain why the graph shown is not the graph of $y = |x + 3| + 2$. What is the correct equation shown in the graph?

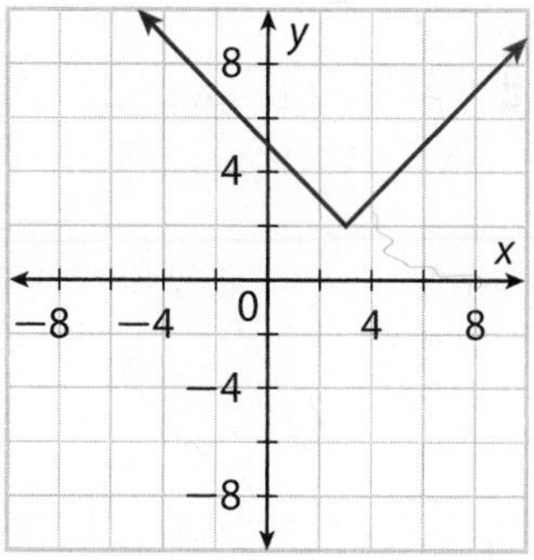

20. Multi-Step A golf player is trying to make a hole-in-one on the miniature golf green shown. Imagine that a coordinate plane is placed over the golf green. The golf ball is at (2.5, 2) and the hole is at (9.5, 2). The player is going to bank the ball off the side wall of the green at (6, 8).

a. Write an equation for the path of the ball.

b. Use the equation in part a to determine if the player makes the shot.

Lesson Performance Task

Suppose a musical piece calls for an orchestra to start at *fortissimo* (about 90 decibels), decrease steadily in loudness to *pianissimo* (about 50 decibels) in four measures, and then increase steadily back to *fortissimo* in another four measures.

a. Write a function to represent the sound level s in decibels as a function of the number of measures m.

b. After how many measures should the orchestra be at the loudness of *mezzo forte* (about 70 decibels)?

c. Describe what the graph of this function would look like.

2.2 Solving Absolute Value Equations

Essential Question: How can you solve an absolute value equation?

Resource Locker

Explore Solving Absolute Value Equations Graphically

Absolute value equations differ from linear equations in that they may have two solutions. This is indicated with a **disjunction**, a mathematical statement created by a connecting two other statements with the word "or." To see why there can be two solutions, you can solve an absolute value equation using graphs.

(A) Solve the equation $2|x - 5| - 4 = 2$.

Plot the function $f(x) = 2|x - 5| - 4$ on a grid. Then plot the function $g(x) = 2$ as a horizontal line on the same grid, and mark the points where the graphs intersect.

(B) Write the solution to this equation as a disjunction:

$x =$? or $x =$?

Reflect

1. Why might you expect most absolute value equations to have two solutions? Why not three or four?

2. Is it possible for an absolute value equation to have no solutions? one solution? If so, what would each look like graphically?

Explain 1 Solving Absolute Value Equations Algebraically

To solve absolute value equations algebraically, first isolate the absolute value expression on one side of the equation the same way you would isolate a variable. Then use the rule:

If $|x| = a$ (where a is a positive number), then $x = a$ OR $x = -a$.

Notice the use of a **disjunction** here in the rule for values of x. You cannot know from the original equation whether the expression inside the absolute value bars is positive or negative, so you must work through both possibilities to finish isolating x.

Example 1 **Solve each absolute value equation algebraically. Graph the solutions on a number line.**

Ⓐ $|3x| + 2 = 8$

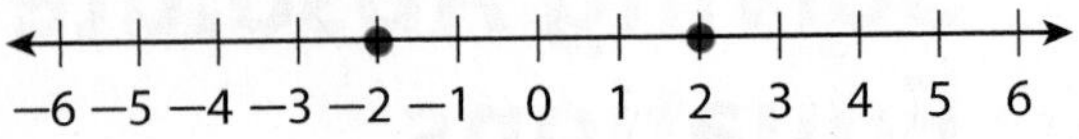

Subtract 2 from both sides. $|3x| = 6$

Rewrite as two equations. $3x = 6$ or $3x = -6$

Solve for x. $x = 2$ or $x = -2$

Ⓑ $3|4x - 5| - 2 = 19$

Add 2 to both sides. $3|4x - 5| = 21$

Divide both sides by 3. $|4x - 5| = 7$

Rewrite as two equations. $4x - 5 = 7$ or $4x - 5 = -7$

Add 5 to all four sides. $4x = 12$ or $4x = -2$

Solve for x. $x = 3$ or $x = -\frac{1}{2}$

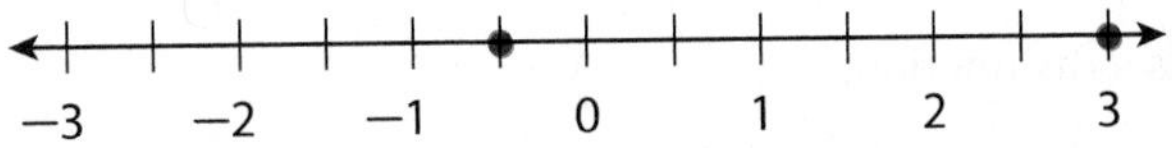

Your Turn

Solve each absolute value equation algebraically. Graph the solutions on a number line.

3. $\frac{1}{2}|x + 2| = 10$

4. $-2|3x - 6| + 5 = 1$

Explain 2 Absolute Value Equations with Fewer than Two Solutions

You have seen that absolute value equations have two solutions when the isolated absolute value expression is equal to a positive number. When the absolute value is equal to zero, there is a single solution because zero is its own opposite. When the absolute value expression is equal to a negative number, there is no solution because absolute value is never negative.

Example 2 **Isolate the absolute value expression in each equation to determine if the equation can be solved. If so, finish the solution. If not, write "no solution."**

(A) $-5|x+1|+2=12$

Subtract 2 from both sides.	$-5|x+1|=10$
Divide both sides by -5.	$|x+1|=-2$
Absolute values are never negative.	No Solution

(B) $\frac{3}{5}|2x-4|-3=-3$

Add 3 to both sides.	$\frac{3}{5}|2x-4|=$ 0
Multiply both sides by $\frac{5}{3}$.	$|2x-4|=$ 0
Rewrite as one equation.	$2x-4=$ 0
Add 4 to both sides.	$2x=$ 4
Divide both sides by 2.	$x=$ 2

Your Turn

Isolate the absolute value expression in each equation to determine if the equation can be solved. If so, finish the solution. If not, write "no solution."

5. $3\left|\frac{1}{2}x+5\right|+7=5$

6. $9\left|\frac{4}{3}x-2\right|+7=7$

Elaborate

7. Why is important to solve both equations in the disjunction arising from an absolute value equation? Why not just pick one and solve it, knowing the solution for the variable will work when plugged backed into the equation?

8. **Discussion** Discuss how the range of the absolute value function differs from the range of a linear function. Graphically, how does this explain why a linear equation always has exactly one solution while an absolute value equation can have one, two, or no solutions?

9. **Essential Question Check-In** Describe, in your own words, the basic steps to solving absolute value equations and how many solutions to expect.

Evaluate: Homework and Practice

Personal Math Trainer

- Online Homework
- Hints and Help
- Extra Practice

Solve the following absolute value equations by graphing.

1. $|x - 3| + 2 = 5$

2. $2|x + 1| + 5 = 9$

3. $-2|x + 5| + 4 = 2$

4. $\left|\frac{3}{2}(x - 2)\right| + 3 = 2$

Solve each absolute value equation algebraically. Graph the solutions on a number line.

5. $|2x| = 3$

6. $\left|\frac{1}{3}x + 4\right| = 3$

7. $3|2x - 3| + 2 = 3$

8. $-8|-x - 6| + 10 = 2$

Isolate the absolute value expressions in the following equations to determine if they can be solved. If so, find and graph the solution(s). If not, write "no solution".

9. $\frac{1}{4}|x + 2| + 7 = 5$

10. $-3|x - 3| + 3 = 6$

11. $2(|x + 4| + 3) = 6$

12. $5|2x + 4| - 3 = -3$

Solve the absolute value equations.

13. $|3x - 4| + 2 = 1$

14. $7\left|\frac{1}{2}x + 3\frac{1}{2}\right| - 2 = 5$

15. $|2(x + 5) - 3| + 2 = 6$

16. $-5|-3x + 2| - 2 = -2$

17. The bottom of a river makes a V-shape that can be modeled with the absolute value function, $d(h) = \frac{1}{5}|h - 240| - 48$, where d is the depth of the river bottom (in feet) and h is the horizontal distance to the left-hand shore (in feet).

A ship risks running aground if the bottom of its keel (its lowest point under the water) reaches down to the river bottom. Suppose you are the harbormaster and you want to place buoys where the river bottom is 30 feet below the surface. How far from the left-hand shore should you place the buoys?

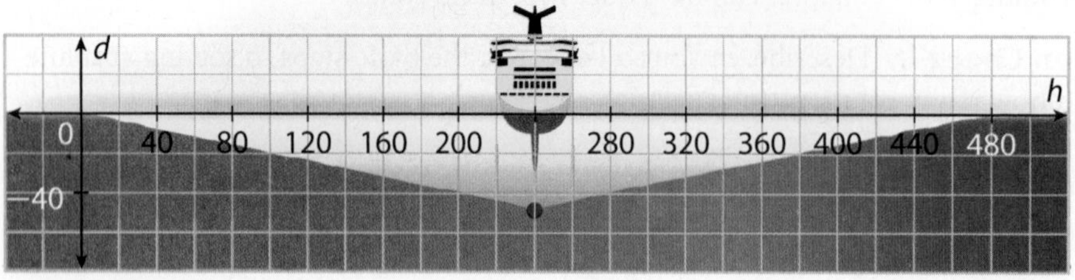

18. A flock of geese is approaching a photographer, flying in formation. The photographer starts taking photographs when the lead goose is 300 feet horizontally from her, and continues taking photographs until it is 100 feet past. The flock is flying at a steady 30 feet per second. Write and solve an equation to find the times after the photographing begins that the lead goose is at a horizontal distance of 75 feet from the photographer.

19. **Geometry** Find the points where a circle centered at (3, 0) with a radius of 5 crosses the x-axis. Use an absolute value equation and the fact that all points on a circle are the same distance (the radius) from the center.

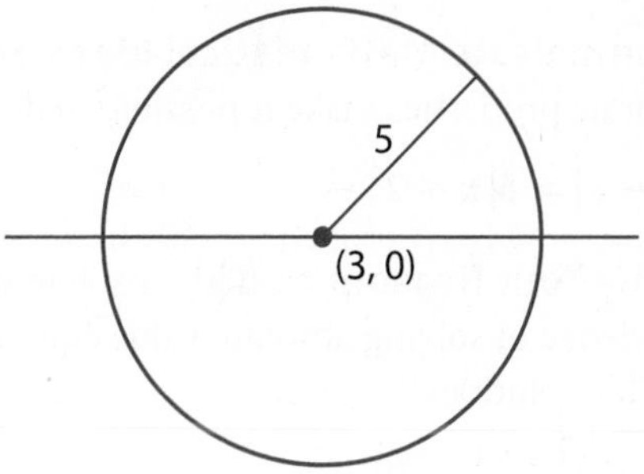

20. Select the value or values of x that satisfy the equation $-\frac{1}{2}|3x - 3| + 2 = 1$.

A. $x = \frac{5}{3}$

B. $x = -\frac{5}{3}$

C. $x = \frac{1}{3}$

D. $x = -\frac{1}{3}$

E. $x = 3$

F. $x = -3$

G. $x = 1$

H. $x = -1$

21. Terry is trying to place a satellite dish on the roof of his house at the recommended height of 30 feet. His house is 32 feet wide, and the height of the roof can be described by the function $h(x) = -\frac{3}{2}|x - 16| + 24$, where x is the distance along the width of the house. Where should Terry place the dish?

H.O.T. Focus on Higher Order Thinking

22. Explain the Error While attempting to solve the equation $-3|x-4|-4=3$, a student came up with the following results. Explain the error and find the correct solution:

$$-3|x-4|-4=3$$
$$-3|x-4|=7$$
$$|x-4|=-\frac{7}{3}$$
$$x-4=-\frac{7}{3} \quad \text{or} \quad x-4=\frac{7}{3}$$
$$x=\frac{5}{3} \quad \text{or} \quad x=\frac{19}{3}$$

23. Communicate Mathematical Ideas Solve this absolute value equation and explain what algebraic properties make it possible to do so.

$3|x-2|=5|x-2|-7$

24. Justify Your Reasoning This absolute value equation has nested absolute values. Use your knowledge of solving absolute value equations to solve this equation. Justify the number of possible solutions.

$\big||2x+5|-3\big|=10$

25. Check for Reasonableness For what type of real-world quantities would the negative answer for an absolute value equation not make sense?

Lesson Performance Task

A snowball comes apart as a child throws it north, resulting in two halves traveling away from the child. The child is standing 12 feet south and 6 feet east of the school door, along an east-west wall. One fragment flies off to the northeast, moving 2 feet east for every 5 feet north of travel, and the other moves 2 feet west for every 5 feet north of travel. Write an absolute value function that describes the northward position, $n(e)$, of both fragments as a function of how far east of the school door they are. How far apart are the fragments when they strike the wall?

2.3 Solving Absolute Value Inequalities

Resource Locker

Essential Question: What are two ways to solve an absolute value inequality?

Explore — Visualizing the Solution Set of an Absolute Value Inequality

You know that when solving an absolute value equation, it's possible to get two solutions. Here, you will explore what happens when you solve absolute value inequalities.

(A) Determine whether each of the integers from -5 to 5 is a solution of the inequality $|x| + 2 < 5$. If a number is a solution, plot it on a number line.

(B) Determine whether each of the integers from -5 to 5 is a solution of the inequality $|x| + 2 > 5$. If a number is a solution, plot it on a number line.

(C) State the solutions of the equation $|x| + 2 = 5$ and relate them to the solutions you found for the inequalities in Steps A and B.

(D) If x is any real number and not just an integer, graph the solutions of $|x| + 2 < 5$ and $|x| + 2 > 5$.

Reflect

1. It's possible to describe the solutions of $|x| + 2 < 5$ and $|x| + 2 > 5$ using inequalities that don't involve absolute value. For instance, you can write the solutions of $|x| + 2 < 5$ as $x > -3$ and $x < 3$. Notice that the word *and* is used because x must be both greater than -3 and less than 3. How would you write the solutions of $|x| + 2 > 5$? Explain.

2. Describe the solutions of $|x| + 2 \leq 5$ and $|x| + 2 \geq 5$ using inequalities that don't involve absolute value.

Explain 1 Solving Absolute Value Inequalities Graphically

You can use a graph to solve an absolute value inequality of the form $f(x) > g(x)$ or $f(x) < g(x)$, where $f(x)$ is an absolute value function and $g(x)$ is a constant function. Graph each function separately on the same coordinate plane and determine the intervals on the x-axis where one graph lies above or below the other. For $f(x) > g(x)$, you want to find the x-values for which the graph $f(x)$ is above the graph of $g(x)$. For $f(x) < g(x)$, you want to find the x-values for which the graph of $f(x)$ is below the graph of $g(x)$.

Example 1 **Solve the inequality graphically.**

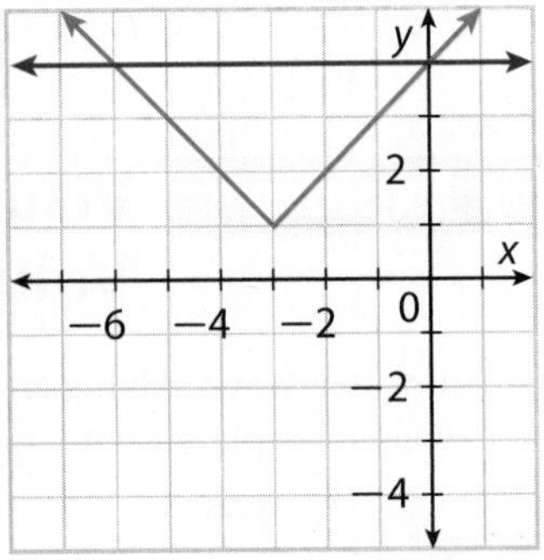

(A) $|x+3|+1>4$

The inequality is of the form $f(x) > g(x)$, so determine the intervals on the x-axis where the graph of $f(x) = |x+3|+1$ lies above the graph of $g(x) = 4$.

The graph of $f(x) = |x+3|+1$ lies above the graph of $g(x) = 4$ to the left of $x = -6$ and to the right of $x = 0$, so the solution of $|x+3|+1>4$ is $x < -6$ or $x > 0$.

(B) $|x-2|-3<1$

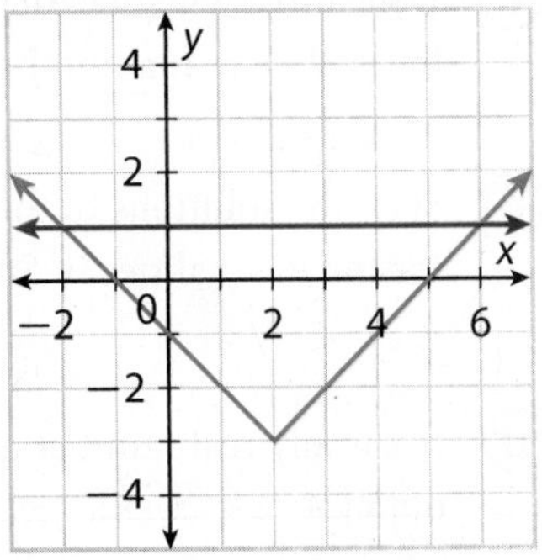

The inequality is of the form $f(x) < g(x)$, so determine the intervals on the x-axis where the graph of $f(x) = |x-2|-3$ lies below the graph of $g(x) = 1$.

The graph of $f(x) = |x-2|-3$ lies below the graph of $g(x) = 1$

between $x =$ [−2] and $x =$ [6], so the solution of

$|x-2|-3<1$ is $x >$ [−2] *and* $x <$ [6].

Reflect

3. Suppose the inequality in Part A is $|x+3|+1 \geq 4$ instead of $|x+3|+1>4$. How does the solution change?

4. In Part B, what is another way to write the solution $x > -2$ and $x < 6$?

5. **Discussion** Suppose the graph of an absolute value function $f(x)$ lies entirely above the graph of the constant function $g(x)$. What is the solution of the inequality $f(x) > g(x)$? What is the solution of the inequality $f(x) < g(x)$?

Your Turn

6. Solve $|x+1|-4 \leq -2$ graphically.

Explain 2 Solving Absolute Value Inequalities Algebraically

To solve an absolute value inequality algebraically, start by isolating the absolute value expression. When the absolute value expression is by itself on one side of the inequality, apply one of the following rules to finish solving the inequality for the variable.

Solving Absolute Value Inequalities Algebraically

1. If $|x| > a$ where a is a positive number, then $x < -a$ or $x > a$.
2. If $|x| < a$ where a is a positive number, then $-a < x < a$.

Example 2 **Solve the inequality algebraically. Graph the solution on a number line.**

(A) $|4 - x| + 15 > 21$

$|4 - x| > 6$

$4 - x < -6$ or $4 - x > 6$

$-x < -10$ or $-x > 2$

$x > 10$ or $x < -2$

The solution is $x > 10$ or $x < -2$.

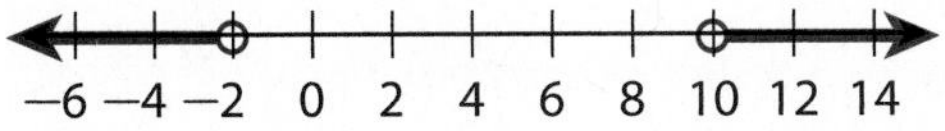

(B) $|x + 4| - 10 \leq -2$

$|x + 4| \leq$ 8

$x + 4 \geq$ −8 and $x + 4 \leq$ 8

$x \geq$ −12 and $x \leq$ 4

The solution is $x \geq$ −12 and $x \leq$ 4,

or −12 $\leq x \leq$ 4.

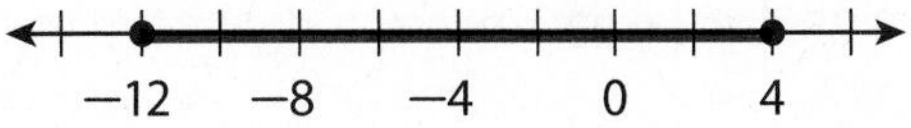

Reflect

7. In Part A, suppose the inequality were $|4 - x| + 15 > 14$ instead of $|4 - x| + 15 > 21$. How would the solution change? Explain.

8. In Part B, suppose the inequality were $|x + 4| - 10 \leq -11$ instead of $|x + 4| - 10 \leq -2$. How would the solution change? Explain.

Your Turn

Solve the inequality algebraically. Graph the solution on a number line.

9. $3|x - 7| \geq 9$

10. $|2x + 3| < 5$

Explain 3 Solving a Real-World Problem with Absolute Value Inequalities

Absolute value inequalities are often used to model real-world situations involving a margin of error or *tolerance*. Tolerance is the allowable amount of variation in a quantity.

Example 3

A machine at a lumber mill cuts boards that are 3.25 meters long. It is acceptable for the length to differ from this value by at most 0.02 meters. Write and solve an absolute value inequality to find the range of acceptable lengths.

Analyze Information

Identify the important information.

- The boards being cut are 3.25 meters long.
- The length can differ by at most 0.02 meters.

Formulate a Plan

Let the length of a board be ℓ. Since the sign of the difference between ℓ and 3.25 doesn't matter, take the absolute value of the difference. Since the absolute value of the difference can be at most 0.02, the inequality that models the situation is

$|\ell - 3.25| \leq 0.02$.

Solve

$|\ell - 3.25| \leq 0.02$

$\ell - 3.25 \geq -0.02$ and $\ell - 3.25 \leq 0.02$

$\ell \geq 3.23$ and $\ell \leq 3.27$

So, the range of acceptable lengths is $3.23 \leq \ell \leq 3.27$.

Justify and Evaluate

The bounds of the range are positive and close to 3.25, so this is a reasonable answer.

The answer is correct since $3.23 + 0.02 = 3.25$ and $3.27 - 0.02 = 3.25$.

Your Turn

11. A box of cereal is supposed to weigh 13.8 oz, but it's acceptable for the weight to vary as much as 0.1 oz. Write and solve an absolute value inequality to find the range of acceptable weights.

Elaborate

12. Describe the values of x that satisfy the inequalities $|x| < a$ and $|x| > a$ where a is a positive constant.

13. How do you algebraically solve an absolute value inequality?

14. Explain why the solution of $|x| > a$ is all real numbers if a is a negative number.

15. **Essential Question Check-In** How do you solve an absolute value inequality graphically?

Evaluate: Homework and Practice

Personal Math Trainer

- Online Homework
- Hints and Help
- Extra Practice

1. Determine whether each of the integers from -5 to 5 is a solution of the inequality $|x - 1| + 3 \geq 5$. If a number is a solution, plot it on a number line.

2. Determine whether each of the integers from -5 to 5 is a solution of the inequality $|x + 1| - 2 \leq 1$. If a number is a solution, plot it on a number line.

Solve each inequality graphically.

3. $2|x| \leq 6$

4. $|x - 3| - 2 > -1$

5. $\frac{1}{2}|x| + 2 < 3$

6. $|x + 2| - 4 \geq -2$

Match each graph with the corresponding absolute value inequality. Then give the solution of the inequality.

A. $2|x| + 1 > 3$ **B.** $2|x + 1| < 3$ **C.** $2|x| - 1 > 3$ **D.** $2|x - 1| < 3$

7.

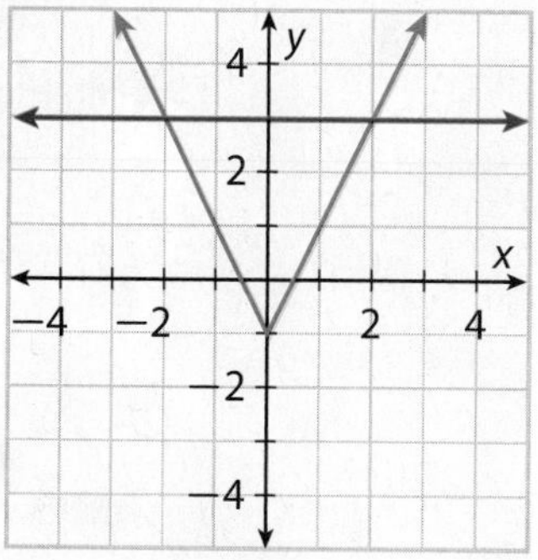

8.

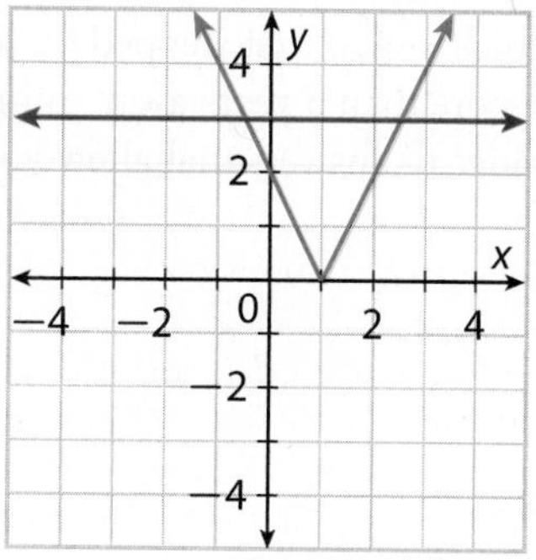

9.

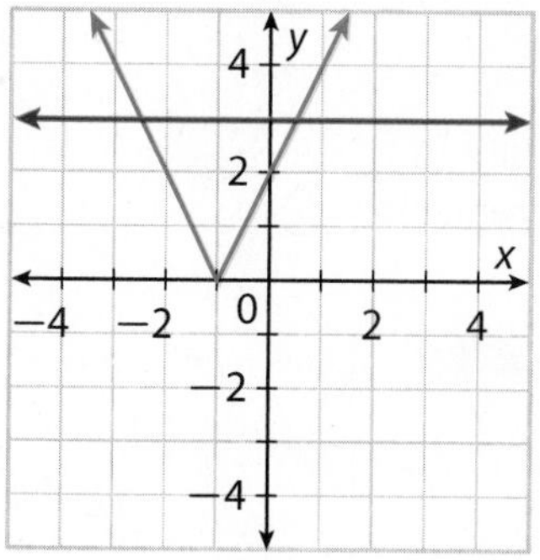

10.

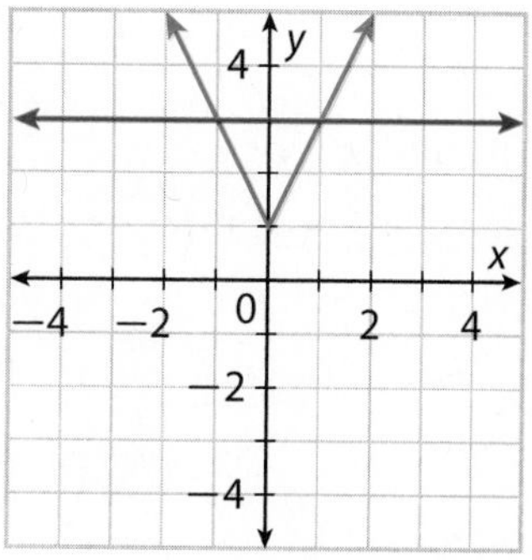

Solve each absolute value inequality algebraically. Graph the solution on a number line.

11. $2\left|x - \frac{7}{2}\right| + 3 > 4$

12. $|2x + 1| - 4 < 5$

13. $3|x + 4| + 2 \geq 5$

14. $|x + 11| - 8 \leq -3$

15. $-5|x - 3| - 5 < 15$

16. $8|x + 4| + 10 < 2$

Solve each problem using an absolute value inequality.

17. The thermostat for a house is set to 68 °F, but the actual temperature may vary by as much as 2 °F. What is the range of possible temperatures?

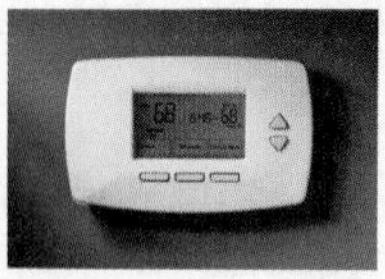

18. The balance of Jason's checking account is \$320. The balance varies by as much as \$80 each week. What are the possible balances of Jason's account?

19. On average, a squirrel lives to be 6.5 years old. The lifespan of a squirrel may vary by as much as 1.5 years. What is the range of ages that a squirrel lives?

20. You are playing a history quiz game where you must give the years of historical events. In order to score any points at all for a question about the year in which a man first stepped on the moon, your answer must be no more than 3 years away from the correct answer, 1969. What is the range of answers that allow you to score points?

21. The speed limit on a road is 30 miles per hour. Drivers on this road typically vary their speed around the limit by as much as 5 miles per hour. What is the range of typical speeds on this road?

H.O.T. Focus on Higher Order Thinking

22. **Represent Real-World Problems** A poll of likely voters shows that the incumbent will get 51% of the vote in an upcoming election. Based on the number of voters polled, the results of the poll could be off by as much as 3 percentage points. What does this mean for the incumbent?

23. **Explain the Error** A student solved the inequality $|x-1|-3>1$ graphically. Identify and correct the student's error.

I graphed the functions $f(x)=|x-1|-3$ and $g(x)=1$. Because the graph of $g(x)$ lies above the graph of $f(x)$ between $x=-3$ and $x=5$, the solution of the inequality is $-3<x<5$.

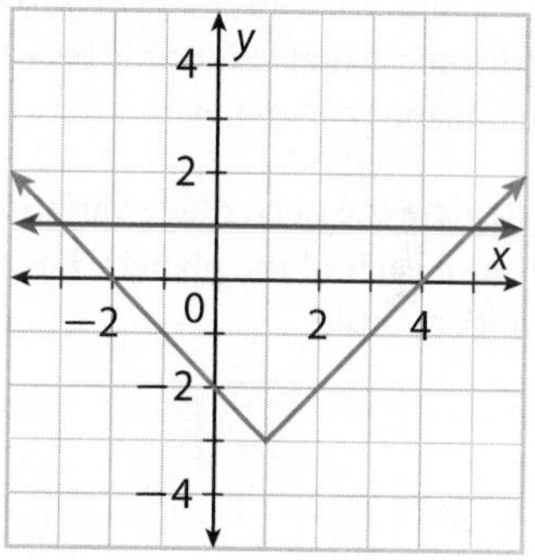

24. **Multi-Step** Recall that a literal equation or inequality is one in which the constants have been replaced by letters.

a. Solve $|ax+b|>c$ for x. Write the solution in terms of a, b, and c. Assume that $a>0$ and $c\geq 0$.

b. Use the solution of the literal inequality to find the solution of $|10x+21|>14$.

c. In Part a, explain how the restrictions $a>0$ and $c\geq 0$ affect finding the solutions of the inequality.

Lesson Performance Task

The distance between the Sun and each planet in our solar system varies because the planets travel in elliptical orbits around the Sun. Here is a table of the average distance and the variation in the distance for the five innermost planets in our solar system.

	Average Distance	Variation
Mercury	36.0 million miles	7.39 million miles
Venus	67.2 million miles	0.43 million miles
Earth	93.0 million miles	1.55 million miles
Mars	142 million miles	13.2 million miles
Jupiter	484 million miles	23.2 million miles

a. Write and solve an inequality to represent the range of distances that can occur between the Sun and each planet.

b. Calculate the percentage variation (variation divided by average distance) in the orbit of each of the planets. Based on these percentages, which planet has the most elliptical orbit?

STUDY GUIDE REVIEW

Absolute Value Functions, Equations, and Inequalities

MODULE 2

Essential Question: How can you use absolute value functions to solve real-world problems?

Key Vocabulary

absolute value *(valor absoluto)*
absolute-value equation *(ecuación de valor absoluto)*
coefficient *(coeficiente)*
disjunction *(disyunción)*
domain *(dominio)*
function *(función)*
inequality *(desigualdad)*
parameter *(parámetro)*
range *(rango)*
symmetry *(simetría)*
vertex *(vértice)*

KEY EXAMPLE *(Lesson 2.1)*

Given the function $g(x) = \left|\frac{1}{3}(x+6)\right| - 1$, predict what the graph will look like compared to the parent function, $f(x) = |x|$.

The graph of $g(x)$ will be the graph of $f(x)$ translated down 1 unit and left 6 units. There will also be a horizontal stretch of $f(x)$ by a factor of 3.

KEY EXAMPLE *(Lesson 2.2)*

Solve $6|2x+3| + 1 = 25$ algebraically.

$6|2x+3| = 24$	Subtract 1 from both sides.
$|2x+3| = 4$	Divide both sides by 6.
$2x+3 = 4$ or $2x+3 = -4$	Rewrite as two equations.
$2x = 1$ or $2x = -7$	Subtract 3 from both sides.
$x = \frac{1}{2}$ or $x = -\frac{7}{2}$	Solve for x.

So, $x = \frac{1}{2}$ or $-\frac{7}{2}$.

KEY EXAMPLE *(Lesson 2.3)*

Solve $|x+2| - 4 < 4$ algebraically, then graph the solution on a number line.

$$|x+2| - 4 < 4$$

$|x+2| < 8$	Add 4 to both sides.
$x+2 < 8$ and $x+2 > -8$	Rewrite as two inequalities.
$x < 6$ and $x > -10$	Subtract 2 from both sides.

The solution is $x < 6$ and $x > -10$.

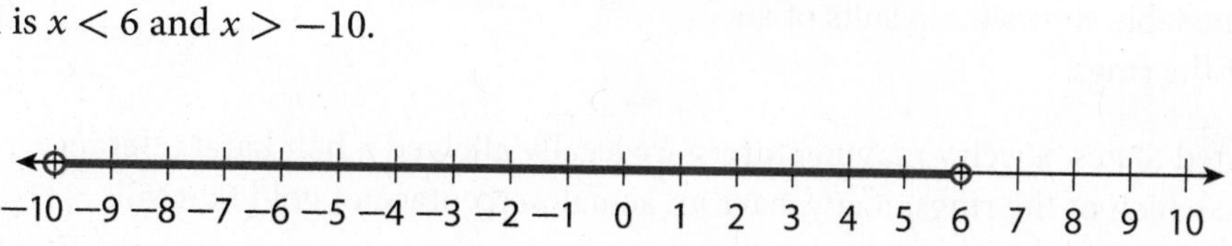

EXERCISES

Solve. *(Lessons 2.2, 2.3)*

1. $-10|x+2| = -70$

2. $|3x+7| = 27$

3. $\frac{1}{7}|8+x| \le 5$

4. $|x-2| - 5 > 10$

5. Explain how the graph of $g(x) = \left|\frac{3}{7}(x-4)\right| + 2$ compares to the graph of $h(x) = \frac{3}{7}(x-4) + 2$. *(Lesson 2.1)*

6. Leroy wants to place a chimney on his roof. It is recommended that the chimney be set at a height of at least 25 feet. The height of the roof is described by the function $r(x) = -\frac{4}{3}|x-10| + 35$, where x is the width of the roof. Where should Leroy place the chimney if the house is 40 feet wide? *(Lesson 2.3)*

MODULE PERFORMANCE TASK

What Is the Purity of Gold?

The purity of gold in jewelry is measured in "karats," with 24-karat gold the highest purity (100% pure gold). You have three gold rings labeled 10 karat, 14 karat, and 18 karat, and would like to know if the rings are correctly labeled. The table shows the results of an analysis of the rings.

Ring Label	Actual Percentage of Gold
10-karat	40.6%
14-karat	59.5%
18-karat	71.2%

In the United States, jewelry manufacturers are legally allowed a half karat tolerance. Determine which of the rings, if any, have an actual percentage of gold that falls outside this tolerance.

List any additional information you will need and then complete the task. Be sure to write down all your data and assumptions. Then use graphs, numbers, words, or algebra to explain how you reached your conclusion.

Ready to Go On?

2.1–2.3 Absolute Value Functions, Equations, and Inequalities

Personal Math Trainer

- Online Homework
- Hints and Help
- Extra Practice

Solve. *(Lesson 2.2)*

1. $|-2x - 3| = 6$

2. $\frac{1}{4}|-4 - 3x| = 2$

3. $|3x + 8| = 2$

4. $4|x + 7| + 3 = 59$

Solve each inequality using the method indicated. *(Lesson 2.3)*

5. $|5x + 2| \leq 13$ (algebraically)

6. $|x - 2| + 1 \leq 5$ (graphically)

ESSENTIAL QUESTION

7. Write a real world situation that could be modeled by $|x - 14| = 3$.

MODULE 2
MIXED REVIEW

Assessment Readiness

1. Look at each equation. Tell whether the graph of the equation be will reflected over the x-axis when compared to $f(x) = |x|$.

A. $g(x) = 3|x - 4|$

B. $h(x) = -\frac{1}{2}|x|$

C. $j(x) = |x + 3| - 2$

2. Consider the absolute value equation $\frac{2}{3}|x - 4| + 2 = 5$. Determine if each statement is True or False.

A. Solving $\frac{2}{3}|x - 4| + 2 = 5$ gives the same x-values as solving $\left|\frac{2}{3}(x - 4)\right| + 2 = 5$.

B. To solve the equation for x, the first step is to add 4 to both sides.

C. Before the step to rewrite as two equations, the equation looks like: $|x - 4| = 3$.

3. Describe the domain, range, and vertex of the function $f(x) = 3|x - 4| + 2$. Explain your answers.

4. Laurie wants to put a portable cellular phone mini-tower on her roof. The tower cannot be placed higher than 30 feet. The slant of her roof can be represented by the equation $r(x) = -\frac{1}{4}|x| + 60$. If her house is 40 feet wide, where could she place the tower? Explain.

Assessment Readiness

Personal Math Trainer
- Online Homework
- Hints and Help
- Extra Practice

1. Consider the function $f(x) = 2(x - 1)^2 + 5$. Determine if each statement is True or False.

A. The range is $y \geq 5$.

B. The range is $y \geq 7$.

C. The domain is $-\infty < x < \infty$.

2. Consider the function $g(x) = -3f(x + 1) - 1$. Determine if each statement is True or False.

A. When compared to $f(x) = 2x$, $g(x)$ will be reflected over the x-axis.

B. When compared to $f(x) = 2x$, $g(x)$ will have a vertical stretch of 3.

C. When compared to $f(x) = 2x$, $g(x)$ will be translated right 1 unit and up 1 unit.

3. Consider the equation $f(x) = \frac{1}{2}x - 5$. Tell whether each equation below is the inverse of $f(x)$.

A. $f^{-1}(x) = 2x - 10$

B. $f^{-1}(x) = -\frac{1}{2}x + 5$

C. $f^{-1}(x) = 2x + 10$

4. Consider the equation $3|x - 2| + 6 = 12$. Determine if each statement is True or False.

A. The equation can be solved using the Pythagorean Theorem.

B. The solutions of the equation are $x = 4$ and $x = 0$.

C. The first step to solving the equation could be subtracting 6 from both sides of the equation.

5. Look at each function. Will the graph of the function be stretched or compressed in the horizontal direction when compared to $f(x) = |x|$? Write Yes or No for A–C.

A. $g(x) = 2|x + 1| - 4$

B. $h(x) = |x - 2| - 1$

C. $j(x) = \left|\frac{1}{2}x - 7\right| + 2$

6. A triathlete is training for her next race and starts by swimming 2 miles in 1 hour. She rests for 1 hour and then rides her bike 100 miles in 5 hours. She rests another hour and runs 20 miles in 5 hours. Draw a graph showing the distance she travels over time. Explain your choice.

7. The maximum number of oranges in a box of volume one cubic foot can be modeled by the inequality $|x - 17| \leq 5$, depending on the size of the oranges. Solve the inequality to find the greatest and least numbers of oranges that could be in a box. Explain your answer.

8. How does the end behavior of $f(x) = (x - 2)^2 + 3$ differ from that of $g(x) = -(3x + 7)^2 - 8$ as $x \to -\infty$? Explain your answer.

Performance Tasks

★ 9. The revenue from an amusement park ride is given by the admission price of $3 times the number of riders. As part of a promotion, the first 10 riders ride for free.

A. What kind of transformation describes the change in the revenue based on the promotion?

B. Write a function rule for this transformation.

★★**10.** An automotive mechanic charges $50 to diagnose the problem in a vehicle and $65 per hour for labor to fix it.

A. If the mechanic increases his diagnostic fee to $60, what kind of transformation is this to the graph of the total repair bill?

B. If the mechanic increases his labor rate to $75 per hour, what kind of transformation is this to the graph of the total repair bill?

C. If it took 3 hours to repair your car, which of the two rate increases would have a greater effect on your total bill?

★★★**11. Diving** Scuba divers must know that the deeper the dive, the greater the water pressure in pounds per square inch (psi) for fresh water diving, as shown in the table.

Depth (feet)	Pressure (psi)
34	29.4
68	44.1
102	58.8

A. Write the pressure as a function of depth, and identify a reasonable domain and range for this function.

B. Find the inverse of the function from part **A**. What does the inverse function represent?

C. The point (25.9, 25.9) is an approximate solution to both the function from part **A** and its inverse. What does this point mean in the context of the problem?

Community Theater Owner A community theater currently sells 200 season tickets at $50 each. In order to increase its season-ticket revenue, the theater surveys its season-ticket holders to see if they would be willing to pay more. The survey finds that for every $5 increase in the price of a season ticket, the theater would lose 10 season-ticket holders. What action, if any, should the theater owner take to increase revenue?

a. Let n be the number of $5 price increases in the cost of a season ticket. Write an expression for the cost of a season ticket after n price increases, and an expression for the number of season-ticket holders after n price increases.

b. Use the expressions from part **a** to create a revenue function, $R(n)$, from the survey information.

c. Determine a constraint on the value of n. That is, write and solve an inequality that represents an upper bound on the value of n, then state a reasonable domain for the revenue function.

d. Graph the revenue function. Be sure to label the axes with the quantities they represent and indicate the axis scales by showing numbers for some grid lines.

e. Write a brief paragraph describing what actions the theater owner should take to maximize revenue. Include what happens to the number of season-ticket holders as well as the season-ticket prices.

UNIT 2

Quadratic Functions, Equations, and Relations

MATH IN CAREERS

Toy Manufacturer A toy manufacturer uses math to calculate the cost of manufacturing, including labor and materials, as well as to predict sales, determine profits, and keep track of orders and inventory. Toy manufacturers study market trends and use statistics to understand the economics of supply and demand for their products. They may also apply three-dimensional modeling to determine the amount of materials needed for toy construction.

If you are interested in a career as a toy manufacturer, you should study these mathematical subjects:

- Algebra
- Geometry
- Trigonometry
- Business Math
- Technical Math

Research other careers that require understanding how to predict sales of goods. Check out the career activity at the end of the unit to find out how **Toy Manufacturers** use math.

Reading Start-Up

Visualize Vocabulary

Use the ✔ words to complete the graphic. Place one word in each of the four sections of the frame.

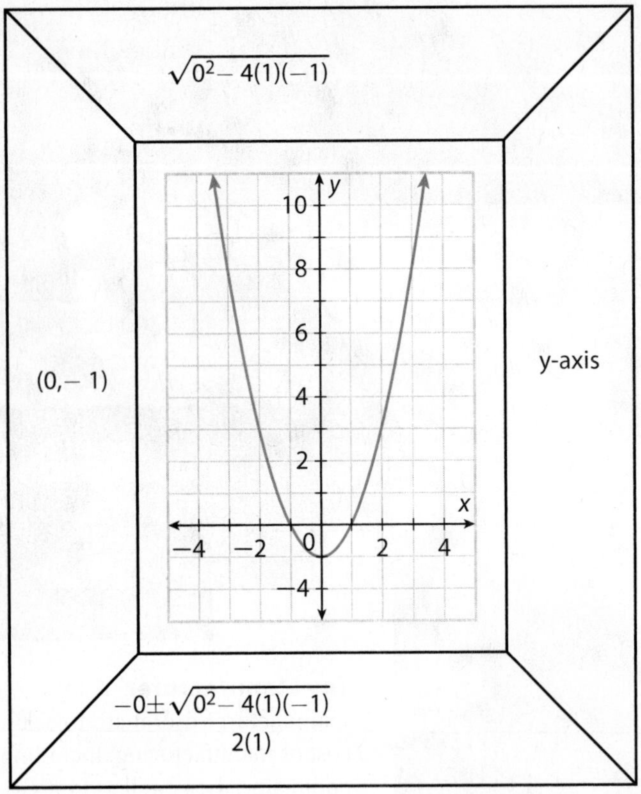

Vocabulary

Review Words

✔ axis of symmetry *(eje de simetría)*
✔ discriminant *(discriminante)*
✔ elimination *(eliminación)*
✔ parabola *(parábola)*
✔ quadratic formula *(fórmula cuadrática)*
✔ quadratic formula *(fórmula cuadrática)*
✔ quadratic function *(función cuadrática)*
✔ substitution *(sustitución)*
✔ vertex *(vértice)*

Preview Words

complex number *(número complejo)*
directrix *(directriz)*
focus *(foco)*
imaginary number *(número imaginario)*
matrix *(matriz)*

Understand Vocabulary

To become familiar with some of the vocabulary terms in the module, consider the following. You may refer to the module, the glossary, or a dictionary.

1. Every point on a parabola is equidistant from a fixed line, called the __?__, and a fixed point, called the __?__.

2. A __?__ is any number that can be written as $a + bi$, where a and b are real numbers and $i = \sqrt{-1}$.

3. A __?__ is a rectangular array of numbers.

Active Reading

Four-Corner Fold Before beginning each lesson, create a four-corner fold to help you organize the characteristics of key concepts. As you study each lesson, define new terms, including an example and a graph or diagram where applicable.

Quadratic Equations

MODULE 3

Essential Question: How can you use quadratic equations to solve real-world problems?

REAL WORLD VIDEO
Safe drivers are aware of stopping distances and carefully judge how fast they can travel based on road conditions. Stopping distance is one of many everyday functions that can be modeled with quadratic equations.

MODULE PERFORMANCE TASK PREVIEW

Can You Stop in Time?

When a driver applies the brakes, the car continues to travel for a certain distance until coming to a stop. The stopping distance for a vehicle depends on many factors, including the initial speed of the car and road conditions. How far will a car travel after the brakes are applied? Let's hit the road and find out!

Are YOU Ready?

Complete these exercises to review skills you will need for this module.

Personal Math Trainer

- Online Homework
- Hints and Help
- Extra Practice

One-Step Inequalities

Example 1 Solve $-2x \leq 9$ for x.
$x \geq -4.5$

Divide both sides by −2. Because you are dividing by a negative number, flip the inequality symbol.

Solve each inequality.

1. $n - 12 > 9$ **2.** $-3p < -27$ **3.** $\frac{k}{4} \geq -1$

Exponents

Example 2 Simplify $\frac{3a^5b^2}{9a^2b}$.

$$\frac{3a^5b^2}{9a^2b} = \frac{3^1a^5b^2}{3^2a^2b^1} = \frac{a^{5-2}b^{2-1}}{3^{2-1}} = \frac{a^3b}{3}$$

Subtract exponents when dividing.

Simplify each expression.

4. $\frac{16p^2}{2p^4}$ **5.** $5vw^5 \cdot 2v^4$ **6.** $\frac{3x^7y}{6x^4y^2}$

Solving Quadratic Equations by Factoring

Example 3 Factor to solve $x^2 + 2x - 15 = 0$ for x.

Pairs of factors of −15 are:
1 and −15
3 and −5
5 and −3
15 and −1

The pair with the sum of the middle term, 2, is 5 and −3.

$(x + 5)(x - 3) = 0$

Either $x + 5 = 0$ or $x - 3 = 0$, so the solutions are −5 and 3.

Factor to solve each equation.

7. $x^2 - 7x + 6 = 0$ **8.** $x^2 - 18x + 81 = 0$ **9.** $x^2 - 16 = 0$

3.1 Solving Quadratic Equations by Taking Square Roots

Resource Locker

Essential Question: What is an imaginary number, and how is it useful in solving quadratic equations?

Explore Investigating Ways of Solving Simple Quadratic Equations

There are many ways to solve a quadratic equation. Here, you will use three methods to solve the equation $x^2 = 16$: by graphing, by factoring, and by taking square roots.

(A) Solve $x^2 = 16$ by graphing.

First treat each side of the equation as a function, and graph the two functions, which in this case are $f(x) = x^2$ and $g(x) = 16$, on the same coordinate plane.

Then identify the x-coordinates of the points where the two graphs intersect.

$x =$? or $x =$?

(B) Solve $x^2 = 16$ by factoring.

This method involves rewriting the equation so that 0 is on one side in order to use the *zero-product property*, which says that the product of two numbers is 0 if and only if at least one of the numbers is 0.

Write the equation. $x^2 = 16$

Subtract 16 from both sides. $x^2 -$? $= 0$

Factor the difference of two squares. $(x +$? $)(x - 4) = 0$

Apply the zero-product property. $x +$? $= 0$ or $x - 4 = 0$

Solve for x. $x =$? or $x = 4$

(C) Solve $x^2 = 16$ by taking square roots.

A real number x is a *square root* of a nonnegative real number a provided $x^2 = a$. A square root is written using the radical symbol $\sqrt{}$. Every positive real number a has both a positive square root, written $\sqrt{a}$, and a negative square root, written $-\sqrt{a}$. For instance, the square roots of 9 are $\pm\sqrt{9}$ (read "plus or minus the square root of 9"), or ± 3. The number 0 has only itself as its square root: $\pm\sqrt{0} = 0$.

Write the equation. $x^2 = 16$

Use the definition of square root. $x = \pm\sqrt{16}$

Simplify the square roots. $x =$?

Reflect

1. Which of the three methods would you use to solve $x^2 = 5$? Explain, and then use the method to find the solutions.
2. Can the equation $x^2 = -9$ be solved by any of the three methods? Explain.

Explain 1 Finding Real Solutions of Simple Quadratic Equations

When solving a quadratic equation of the form $ax^2 + c = 0$ by taking square roots, you may need to use the following properties of square roots to simplify the solutions. (In a later lesson, these properties are stated in a more general form and then proved.)

Property Name	Words	Symbols	Numbers
Product property of square roots	The square root of a product equals the product of the square roots of the factors.	$\sqrt{ab} = \sqrt{a} \cdot \sqrt{b}$ where $a \geq 0$ and $b \geq 0$	$\sqrt{12} = \sqrt{4 \cdot 3}$ $= \sqrt{4} \cdot \sqrt{3}$ $= 2\sqrt{3}$
Quotient property of square roots	The square root of a fraction equals the quotient of the square roots of the numerator and the denominator.	$\sqrt{\frac{a}{b}} = \frac{\sqrt{a}}{\sqrt{b}}$ where $a \geq 0$ and $b > 0$	$\sqrt{\frac{5}{9}} = \frac{\sqrt{5}}{\sqrt{9}}$ $= \frac{\sqrt{5}}{3}$

Using the quotient property of square roots may require an additional step of *rationalizing the denominator* if the denominator is not a rational number. For instance, the quotient property allows you to write $\sqrt{\frac{2}{7}}$ as $\frac{\sqrt{2}}{\sqrt{7}}$, but $\sqrt{7}$ is not a rational number. To rationalize the denominator, multiply $\frac{\sqrt{2}}{\sqrt{7}}$ by $\frac{\sqrt{7}}{\sqrt{7}}$ (a form of 1) and get this result: $\frac{\sqrt{2}}{\sqrt{7}} \cdot \frac{\sqrt{7}}{\sqrt{7}} = \frac{\sqrt{14}}{\sqrt{49}} = \frac{\sqrt{14}}{7}$.

Example 1 **Solve the quadratic equation by taking square roots.**

(A) $2x^2 - 16 = 0$

Add 16 to both sides.	$2x^2 = 16$
Divide both sides by 2.	$x^2 = 8$
Use the definition of square root.	$x = \pm\sqrt{8}$
Use the product property.	$x = \pm\sqrt{4} \cdot \sqrt{2}$
Simplify.	$x = \pm 2\sqrt{2}$

(B) $-5x^2 + 9 = 0$

Subtract 9 from both sides. $-5x^2 = \boxed{-9}$

Divide both sides by $\boxed{-5}$. $x^2 = \boxed{\frac{9}{5}}$

Use the definition of square root. $x = \pm\sqrt{\boxed{\frac{9}{5}}}$

Use the quotient property. $x = \pm\boxed{\frac{\sqrt{9}}{\sqrt{5}}}$

Simplify the numerator. $x = \pm\boxed{\frac{3}{\sqrt{5}}}$

Rationalize the denominator. $x = \pm\boxed{\frac{3\sqrt{5}}{5}}$

Your Turn

Solve the quadratic equation by taking square roots.

3. $x^2 - 24 = 0$

4. $-4x^2 + 13 = 0$

Explain 2 Solving a Real-World Problem Using a Simple Quadratic Equation

Two commonly used quadratic models for falling objects near Earth's surface are the following:

- Distance fallen (in feet) at time t (in seconds): $d(t) = 16t^2$
- Height (in feet) at time t (in seconds): $h(t) = h_0 - 16t^2$ where h_0 is the object's initial height (in feet)

For both models, time is measured from the instant that the object begins to fall. A negative value of t would represent a time before the object began falling, so negative values of t are excluded from the domains of these functions. This means that for any equation of the form $d(t) = c$ or $h(t) = c$ where c is a constant, a negative solution should be rejected.

Example 2 **Write and solve an equation to answer the question. Give the exact answer and, if it's irrational, a decimal approximation (to the nearest tenth of a second).**

(A) If you drop a water balloon, how long does it take to fall 4 feet?

Using the model $d(t) = 16t^2$, solve the equation $d(t) = 4$.

Write the equation. $16t^2 = 4$

Divide both sides by 16. $t^2 = \frac{1}{4}$

Use the definition of square root. $t = \pm\sqrt{\frac{1}{4}}$

Use the quotient property. $t = \pm\frac{1}{2}$

Reject the negative value of t. The water balloon falls 4 feet in $\frac{1}{2}$ second.

Ⓑ The rooftop of a 5-story building is 50 feet above the ground. How long does it take the water balloon dropped from the rooftop to pass by a third-story window at 24 feet?

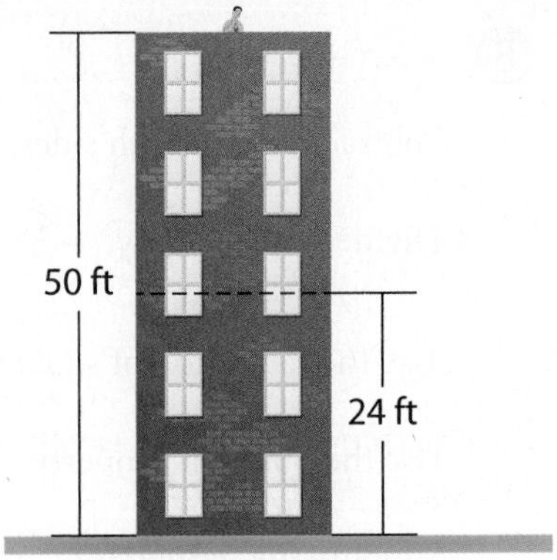

Using the model $h(t) = h_0 - 16t^2$, solve the equation $h(t) = 24$. (When you reach the step at which you divide both sides by -16, leave 16 in the denominator rather than simplifying the fraction because you'll get a rational denominator when you later use the quotient property.)

Write the equation. $\boxed{50} - 16t^2 = \boxed{24}$

Subtract 50 from both sides. $-16t^2 = \boxed{-26}$

Divide both sides by -16. $t^2 = \boxed{\frac{26}{16}}$

Use the definition of square root. $t = \pm\sqrt{\boxed{\frac{26}{16}}}$

Use the quotient property to simplify. $t = \pm\boxed{\frac{\sqrt{26}}{4}}$

Reject the negative value of t. The water balloon passes by the third-story window in $\boxed{\frac{\sqrt{26}}{4}} \approx \boxed{1.3}$ seconds.

Reflect

5. Discussion Explain how the model $h(t) = h_0 - 16t^2$ is built from the model $d(t) = 16t^2$.

Your Turn

Write and solve an equation to answer the question. Give the exact answer and, if it's irrational, a decimal approximation (to the nearest tenth of a second).

6. How long does it take the water balloon described in Part B to hit the ground?

7. On the moon, the distance d (in feet) that an object falls in time t (in seconds) is modeled by the function $d(t) = \frac{8}{3}t^2$. Suppose an astronaut on the moon drops a tool. How long does it take the tool to fall 4 feet?

Explain 3 Defining Imaginary Numbers

You know that the quadratic equation $x^2 = 1$ has two real solutions, the equation $x^2 = 0$ has one real solution, and the equation $x^2 = -1$ has no real solutions. By creating a new type of number called *imaginary numbers*, mathematicians allowed for solutions of equations like $x^2 = -1$.

Imaginary numbers are the square roots of negative numbers. These numbers can all be written in the form bi where b is a nonzero real number and i, called the **imaginary unit**, represents $\sqrt{-1}$. Some examples of imaginary numbers are the following:

- $2i$
- $-5i$
- $-\frac{i}{3}$ or $-\frac{1}{3}i$
- $i\sqrt{2}$ (Write the i in front of the radical symbol for clarity.)
- $\frac{i\sqrt{3}}{2}$ or $\frac{\sqrt{3}}{2}i$

Given that $i = \sqrt{-1}$, you can conclude that $i^2 = -1$. This means that the square of any imaginary number is a negative real number. When squaring an imaginary number, use the power of a product property of exponents: $(ab)^m = a^m \cdot b^m$.

Example 3 **Find the square of the imaginary number.**

(A) $5i$

$$(5i)^2 = 5^2 \cdot i^2$$
$$= 25(-1)$$
$$= -25$$

(B) $-i\sqrt{2}$

$$(-i\sqrt{2})^2 = \left(\boxed{-\sqrt{2}}\right)^2 \cdot i^2$$
$$= \boxed{2}(-1) = \boxed{-2}$$

Reflect

8. By definition, i is a square root of -1. Does -1 have another square root? Explain.

Your Turn

Find the square of the imaginary number.

9. $-2i$

10. $\frac{\sqrt{3}}{3}i$

Explain 4 Finding Imaginary Solutions of Simple Quadratic Equations

Using imaginary numbers and the fact that for a positive real number r, $\sqrt{-r} = i\sqrt{r}$, you can solve simple quadratic equations that do not have real solutions.

Example 4 **Solve the quadratic equation by taking square roots. Allow for imaginary solutions.**

(A) $x^2 + 12 = 0$

Write the equation.	$x^2 + 12 = 0$
Subtract 12 from both sides.	$x^2 = -12$
Use the definition of square root.	$x = \pm\sqrt{-12}$
Use the fact that for $r > 0$, $\sqrt{-r} = i\sqrt{r}$.	$x = \pm i\sqrt{12}$
Use the product property of square roots.	$x = \pm i\sqrt{(4)(3)} = \pm 2i\sqrt{3}$

(B) $4x^2 + 11 = 6$

Write the equation.	$4x^2 + 11 = 6$
Use subtraction and division to solve for x^2.	$x^2 = \boxed{-\frac{5}{4}}$
Use the definition of square root.	$x = \pm\sqrt{\boxed{-\frac{5}{4}}}$
Use the fact that for $r > 0$, $\sqrt{-r} = i\sqrt{r}$.	$x = \pm i\sqrt{\frac{5}{4}}$
Use the qoutient property of square roots.	$x = \pm \boxed{\frac{\sqrt{5}}{2}i}$

Your Turn

Solve the quadratic equation by taking square roots. Allow for imaginary solutions.

11. $\frac{1}{4}x^2 + 9 = 0$

12. $-5x^2 + 3 = 10$

Elaborate

13. The quadratic equations $4x^2 + 32 = 0$ and $4x^2 - 32 = 0$ differ only by the sign of the constant term. Without actually solving the equations, what can you say about the relationship between their solutions?

14. What kind of a number is the square of an imaginary number?

15. Why do you reject negative values of t when solving equations based on the models for a falling object near Earth's surface, $d(t) = 16t^2$ for distance fallen and $h(t) = h_0 - 16t^2$ for height during a fall?

16. **Essential Question Check-In** Describe how to find the square roots of a negative number.

Evaluate: Homework and Practice

Personal Math Trainer
- Online Homework
- Hints and Help
- Extra Practice

1. Solve the equation $x^2 - 2 = 7$ using the indicated method.

a. Solve by graphing. **b.** Solve by factoring. **c.** Solve by taking square roots.

2. Solve the equation $2x^2 + 3 = 5$ using the indicated method.

a. Solve by graphing. **b.** Solve by factoring. **c.** Solve by taking square roots.

Solve the quadratic equation by taking square roots.

3. $4x^2 = 24$

4. $-\frac{x^2}{5} + 15 = 0$

5. $2(5 - 5x^2) = 5$

6. $3x^2 - 8 = 12$

Write and solve an equation to answer the question. Give the exact answer and, if it's irrational, a decimal approximation (to the nearest tenth of a second).

7. A squirrel in a tree drops an acorn. How long does it take the acorn to fall 20 feet?

8. A person washing the windows of an office building drops a squeegee from a height of 60 feet. How long does it take the squeegee to pass by another window washer working at a height of 20 feet?

Geometry **Determine the lengths of the sides of the rectangle using the given area. Give answers both exactly and approximately (to the nearest tenth).**

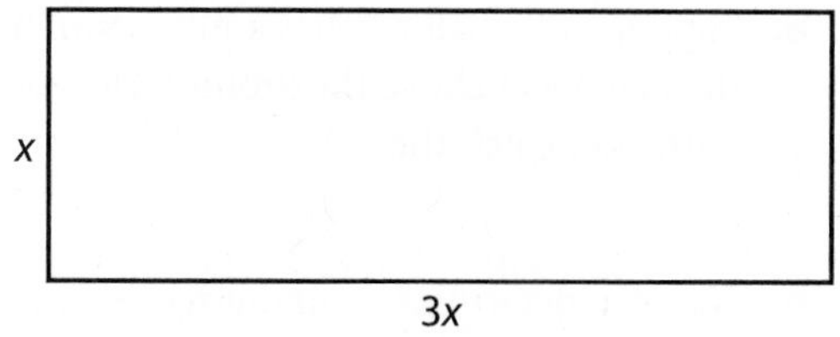

9. The area of the rectangle is 45 cm^2.

10. The area of the rectangle is 54 cm^2.

Find the square of the imaginary number.

11. $3i$

12. $i\sqrt{5}$

13. $-i\frac{\sqrt{2}}{2}$

Determine whether the quadratic equation has real solutions or imaginary solutions by solving the equation.

14. $15x^2 - 10 = 0$

15. $\frac{1}{2}x^2 + 12 = 4$

16. $5(2x^2 - 3) = 4(x^2 - 10)$

Solve the quadratic equation by taking square roots. Allow for imaginary solutions.

17. $x^2 = -81$

18. $x^2 + 64 = 0$

19. $5x^2 - 4 = -8$

20. $7x^2 + 10 = 0$

Geometry **Determine the length of the sides of each square using the given information. Give answers both exactly and approximately (to the nearest tenth).**

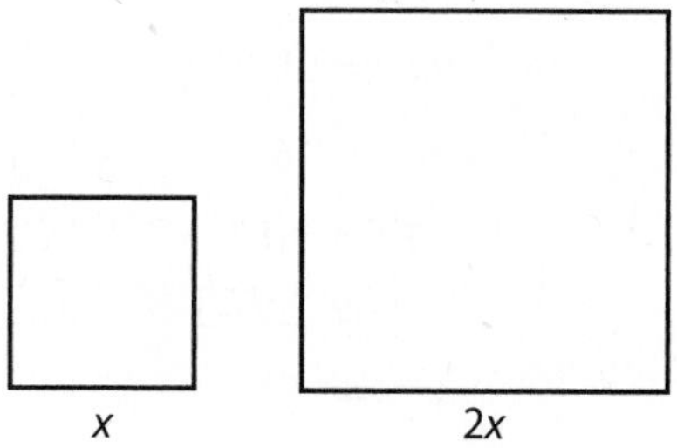

21. The area of the larger square is 42 cm^2 more than the area of the smaller square.

22. If the area of the larger square is decreased by 28 cm^2, the result is half of the area of the smaller square.

23. Determine whether each of the following numbers is real or imaginary.

a. i

b. A square root of 5

c. $(2i)^2$

d. $(-5)^2$

e. $\sqrt{-3}$

f. $-\sqrt{10}$

H.O.T. Focus on Higher Order Thinking

24. **Critical Thinking** When a batter hits a baseball, you can model the ball's height using a quadratic function that accounts for the ball's initial vertical velocity. However, once the ball reaches its maximum height, its vertical velocity is momentarily 0 feet per second, and you can use the model $h(t) = h_0 - 16t^2$ to find the ball's height h (in feet) at time t (in seconds) as it falls to the ground.

a. Suppose a fly ball reaches a maximum height of 67 feet and an outfielder catches the ball 3 feet above the ground. How long after the ball begins to descend does the outfielder catch the ball?

b. Can you determine (without writing or solving any equations) the total time the ball was in the air? Explain your reasoning and state any assumptions you make.

25. **Represent Real-World Situations** The aspect ratio of an image on a screen is the ratio of image width to image height. An HDTV screen shows images with an aspect ratio of 16:9. If the area of an HDTV screen is 864 in^2, what are the dimensions of the screen?

26. **Explain the Error** Russell wants to calculate the amount of time it takes for a load of dirt to fall from a crane's clamshell bucket at a height of 16 feet to the bottom of a hole that is 32 feet deep. He sets up the following equation and tries to solve it.

$$16 - 16t^2 = 32$$
$$-16t^2 = 16$$
$$t^2 = -1$$
$$t = \pm\sqrt{-1}$$
$$t = \pm \boldsymbol{i}$$

Does Russell's answer make sense? If not, find and correct Russell's error.

Lesson Performance Task

A suspension bridge uses two thick cables, one on each side of the road, to hold up the road. The cables are suspended between two towers and have a parabolic shape. Smaller vertical cables connect the parabolic cables to the road. The table gives the lengths of the first few vertical cables starting with the shortest one.

Displacement from the Shortest Vertical Cable (m)	Height of Vertical Cable (m)
0	3
1	3.05
2	3.2
3	3.45

Find a quadratic function that describes the height (in meters) of a parabolic cable above the road as a function of the horizontal displacement (in meters) from the cable's lowest point. Use the function to predict the distance between the towers if the parabolic cable reaches a maximum height of 48 m above the road at each tower.

3.2 Complex Numbers

Essential Question: What is a complex number, and how can you add, subtract, and multiply complex numbers?

Resource Locker

Explore Exploring Operations Involving Complex Numbers

In this lesson, you'll learn to perform operations with *complex numbers*, which have a form similar to linear binomials such as $3 + 4x$ and $2 - x$.

(A) Add the binomials $3 + 4x$ and $2 - x$.

Group like terms. $(3 + 4x) + (2 - x) = (3 + \boxed{?}) + (4x + \boxed{?})$

Combine like terms. $= (\boxed{?} + \boxed{?})$

(B) Subtract $2 - x$ from $3 + 4x$.

Rewrite as addition. $(3 + 4x) - (2 - x) = (3 + 4x) + (-2 + \boxed{?})$

Group like terms. $= (3 + \boxed{?}) + (4x + \boxed{?})$

Combine like terms. $= (\boxed{?} + \boxed{?})$

(C) Multiply the binomials $3 + 4x$ and $2 - x$.

Use FOIL. $(3 + 4x)(2 - x) = 6 + (-3x) + \boxed{?} + \boxed{?}$

Combine like terms. $= 6 + \boxed{?} + \boxed{?}$

Reflect

1. In Step A, you found that $(3 + 4x) + (2 - x) = 5 + 3x$. Suppose $x = i$ (the imaginary unit). What equation do you get?
2. In Step B, you found that $(3 + 4x) + (2 - x) = 1 + 5x$. Suppose $x = i$ (the imaginary unit). What equation do you get?
3. In Step C, you found that $(3 + 4x)(2 - x) = 6 + 5x - 4x^2$. Suppose $x = i$ (the imaginary unit). What equation do you get? How can you further simplify the right side of this equation?

Explain 1 Defining Complex Numbers

A **complex number** is any number that can be written in the form $a + bi$, where a and b are real numbers and $i = \sqrt{-1}$. For a complex number $a + bi$ a is called the *real part* of the number, and b is called the *imaginary part*. (Note that "imaginary part" refers to the real multiplier of i; it does not refer to the imaginary number bi.) The Venn diagram shows some examples of complex numbers.

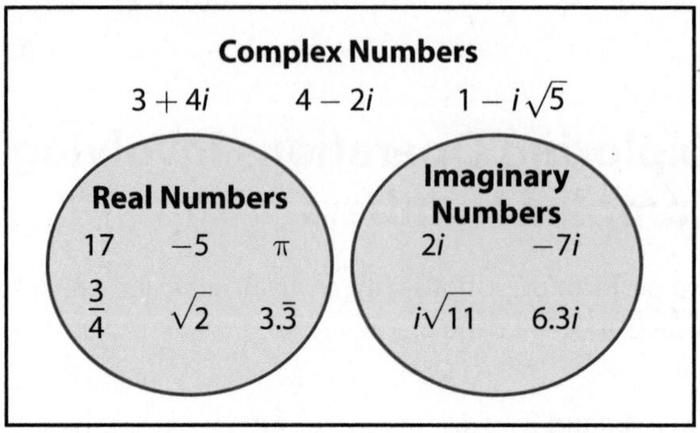

Notice that the set of real numbers is a subset of the set of complex numbers. That's because a real number a can be written in the form $a + 0i$ (whose imaginary part is 0). Likewise, the set of imaginary numbers is also a subset of the set of complex numbers, because an imaginary number bi (where $b \neq 0$) can be written in the form $0 + bi$ (whose real part is 0).

Example 1 **Identify the real and imaginary parts of the given number. Then tell which of the following sets the number belongs to: real numbers, imaginary numbers, and complex numbers.**

(A) $9 + 5i$

The real part of $9 + 5i$ is 9, and the imaginary part is 5. Because both the real and imaginary parts of $9 + 5i$ are nonzero, the number belongs only to the set of complex numbers.

(B) $-7i$

The real part of $-7i$ is 0, and the imaginary part is -7. Because the real part is 0, the number belongs to these sets: imaginary numbers and complex numbers.

Your Turn

Identify the real and imaginary parts of the given number. Then tell which of the following sets the number belongs to: real numbers, imaginary numbers, and complex numbers.

4. 11

5. $-1 + i$

Explain 2 Adding and Subtracting Complex Numbers

To add or subtract complex numbers, add or subtract the real parts and the imaginary parts separately.

Example 2 **Add or subtract the complex numbers.**

(A) $(-7 + 2i) + (5 - 11i)$

Group like terms. $(-7 + 2i) + (5 - 11i) = (-7 + 5) + (2i + (-11i))$

Combine like terms. $= -2 + (-9i)$

Write addition as subtraction. $= -2 - 9i$

(B) $(18 + 27i) - (2 + 3i)$

Group like terms. $(18 + 27i) - (2 + 3i) = \left(18 - \boxed{2}\right) + \left(\boxed{27i} - 3i\right)$

Combine like terms. $= \boxed{16} + \boxed{24}\,i$

Reflect

6. Is the sum $(a + bi) + (a - bi)$ where a and b are real numbers, a real number or an imaginary number? Explain.

Your Turn

Add or subtract the complex numbers.

7. $(17 - 6i) - (9 + 10i)$

8. $(16 + 17i) + (-8 - 12i)$

Explain 3 Multiplying Complex Numbers

To multiply two complex numbers, use the distributive property to multiply each part of one number by each part of the other. Use the fact that $i^2 = -1$ to simplify the result.

Example 3 **Multiply the complex numbers.**

(A) $(4 + 9i)(6 - 2i)$

Use the distributive property. $(4 + 9i)(6 - 2i) = 24 - 8i + 54i - 18i^2$

Substitute -1 for i^2. $= 24 - 8i + 54i - 18(-1)$

Combine like terms. $= 42 + 46i$

(B) $(-3 + 12i)(7 + 4i)$

Use the distributive property. $(-3 + 12i)(7 + 4i) = \boxed{-21} - 12i + \boxed{84i} + 48i^2$

Substitute -1 for i^2. $= \boxed{-21} - 12i + \boxed{84i} + 48(-1)$

Combine like terms. $= \boxed{-69} + \boxed{72}\, i$

Reflect

9. Is the product of $(a + bi)(a - bi)$, where a and b are real numbers, a real number or an imaginary number? Explain.

Your Turn

Multiply the complex numbers.

10. $(6 - 5i)(3 - 10i)$

11. $(8 + 15i)(11 + i)$

Explain 4 Solving a Real-World Problem Using Complex Numbers

Electrical engineers use complex numbers when analyzing electric circuits. An electric circuit can contain three types of components: resistors, inductors, and capacitors. As shown in the table, each type of component has a different symbol in a circuit diagram, and each is represented by a different type of complex number based on the phase angle of the current passing through it.

Circuit Component	Symbol in Circuit Diagram	Phase Angle	Representation as a Complex Number
Resistor		0°	A real number a
Inductor		90°	An imaginary number bi where $b > 0$
Capacitor	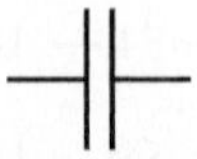	−90°	An imaginary number bi where $b < 0$

A diagram of an alternating current (AC) electric circuit is shown along with the *impedance* (measured in ohms, Ω) of each component in the circuit. An AC power source, which is shown on the left in the diagram and labeled 120 V (for volts), causes electrons to flow through the circuit. Impedance is a measure of each component's opposition to the electron flow.

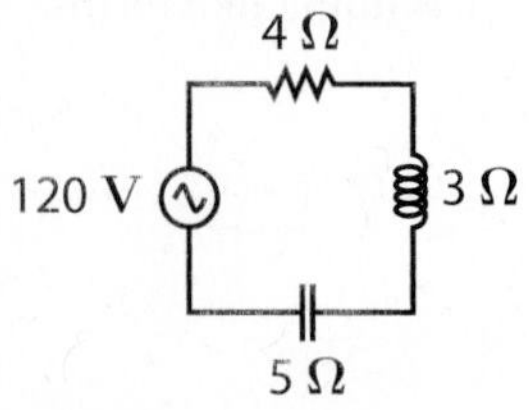

Example 4 **Use the diagram of the electric circuit to answer the following questions.**

Ⓐ The total impedance in the circuit is the sum of the impedances for the individual components. What is the total impedance for the given circuit?

Write the impedance for each component as a complex number.

- Impedance for the resistor: 4
- Impedance for the inductor: $3i$
- Impedance for the capacitor: $-5i$

Then find the sum of the impedances.

Total impedance $= 4 + 3i + (-5i) = 4 - 2i$

Ⓑ Ohm's law for AC electric circuits says that the voltage V (measured in volts) is the product of the current I (measured in amps) and the impedance Z (measured in ohms): $V = I \cdot Z$. For the given circuit, the current I is $24 + 12i$ amps. What is the voltage V for each component in the circuit?

Use Ohm's law, $V = I \cdot Z$, to find the voltage for each component. Remember that Z is the impedance from Part A.

Voltage for the resistor $= I \cdot Z = (24 + 12i)\left(\boxed{4} \right) = 96 + \boxed{48}\, i$

Voltage for the inductor $= I \cdot Z = (24 + 12i)\left(\boxed{3i} \right) = -36 + \boxed{72}\, i$

Voltage for the capacitor $= I \cdot Z = (24 + 12i)\left(\boxed{-5i} \right) = \boxed{60} - 120i$

Reflect

12. Find the sum of the voltages for the three components in Part B. What do you notice?

Your Turn

13. Suppose the circuit analyzed in Example 4 has a second resistor with an impedance of 2 Ω added to it. Find the total impedance. Given that the circuit now has a current of $18 + 6i$ amps, also find the voltage for each component in the circuit.

Elaborate

14. What kind of number is the sum, difference, or product of two complex numbers?

15. When is the sum of two complex numbers a real number? When is the sum of two complex numbers an imaginary number?

16. **Discussion** What are the similarities and differences between multiplying two complex numbers and multiplying two binomial linear expressions in the same variable?

17. **Essential Question Check-In** How do you add and subtract complex numbers?

Evaluate: Homework and Practice

Personal Math Trainer
- Online Homework
- Hints and Help
- Extra Practice

1. Find the sum of the binomials $3 + 2x$ and $4 - 5x$. Explain how you can use the result to find the sum of the complex numbers $3 + 2i$ and $4 - 5i$.

2. Find the product of the binomials $1 - 3x$ and $2 + x$. Explain how you can use the result to find the product of the complex numbers $1 - 3i$ and $2 + i$.

Identify the real and imaginary parts of the given number. Then tell which of the following sets the number belongs to: real numbers, imaginary numbers, and complex numbers.

3. $5 + i$

4. $7 - 6i$

5. 25

6. $i\sqrt{21}$

Add.

7. $(3 + 4i) + (7 + 11i)$

8. $(2 + 3i) + (6 - 5i)$

9. $(-1 - i) + (-10 + 3i)$

10. $(-9 - 7i) + (6 + 5i)$

Subtract.

11. $(2 + 3i) - (7 + 6i)$

12. $(4 + 5i) - (14 - i)$

13. $(-8 - 3i) - (-9 - 5i)$

14. $(5 + 2i) - (5 - 2i)$

Multiply.

15. $(2 + 3i)(3 + 5i)$

16. $(7 + i)(6 - 9i)$

17. $(-4 + 11i)(-5 - 8i)$

18. $(4 - i)(4 + i)$

Use the diagram of the electric circuit and the given current to find the total impedance for the circuit and the voltage for each component.

19.

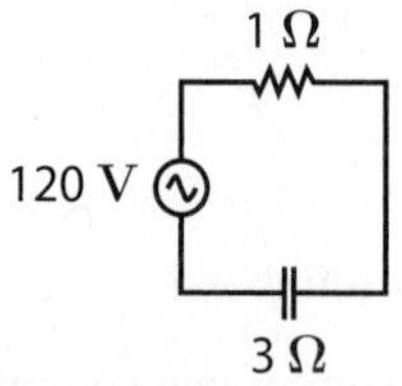

The circuit has a current of $12 + 36i$ amps.

20.

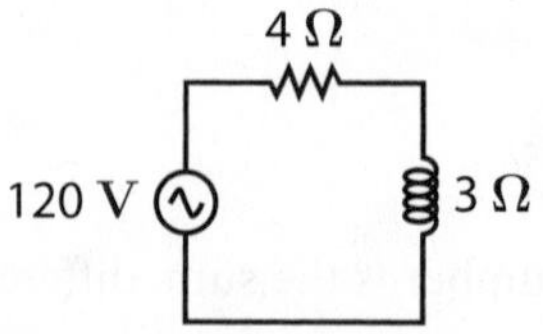

The circuit has a current of $19.2 - 14.4i$ amps.

21.

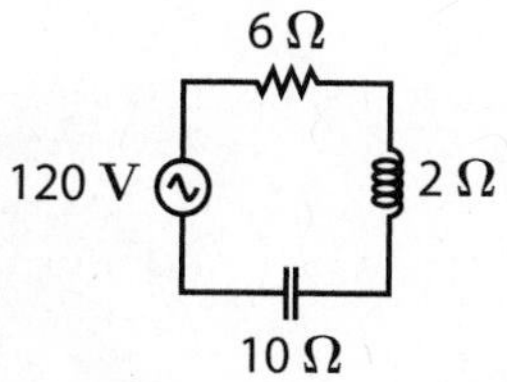

The circuit has a current of $7.2 + 9.6i$ amps.

22.

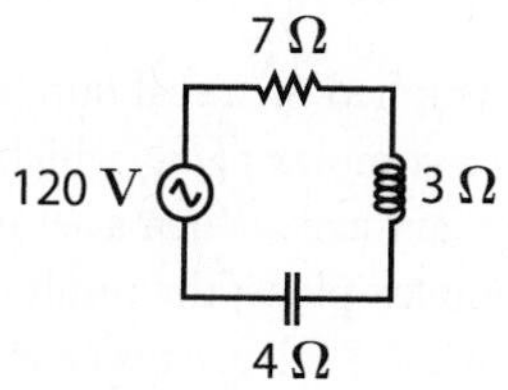

The circuit has a current of $16.8 + 2.4i$ amps.

23. Match each product on the right with the corresponding expression on the left.

A. $(3 - 5i)(3 + 5i)$ **a.** ___?___ $-16 + 30i$

B. $(3 + 5i)(3 + 5i)$ **b.** ___?___ -34

C. $(-3 - 5i)(3 + 5i)$ **c.** ___?___ 34

D. $(3 - 5i)(-3 - 5i)$ **d.** ___?___ $16 - 30i$

H.O.T. Focus on Higher Order Thinking

24. Explain the Error While attempting to multiply the expression $(2 - 3i)(3 + 2i)$, a student made a mistake. Explain and correct the error.

$$\begin{aligned}(2 - 3i)(3 + 2i) &= 6 - 9i + 4i - 6i^2 \\ &= 6 - 9(-1) + 4(-1) - 6(1) \\ &= 6 + 9 - 4 - 6 \\ &= 5\end{aligned}$$

25. Critical Thinking Show that $\sqrt{3} + i\sqrt{3}$ and $-\sqrt{3} - i\sqrt{3}$ are the square roots of $6i$.

26. Justify Reasoning What type of number is the product of two complex numbers that differ only in the sign of their imaginary parts? Prove your conjecture.

Lesson Performance Task

Just as real numbers can be graphed on a real number line, complex numbers can be graphed on a complex *plane*, which has a horizontal real axis and a vertical imaginary axis. When a set that involves complex numbers is graphed on a complex plane, the result can be an elaborate self-similar figure called a *fractal*. Such a set is called a Julia set.

Consider Julia sets having the quadratic recursive rule $f(n+1) = \left(f(n)\right)^2 + c$ for some complex number $f(0)$ and some complex constant c. For a given value of c, a complex number $f(0)$ either belongs or doesn't belong to the "'filled-in" Julia set corresponding to c depending on what happens with the sequence of numbers generated by the recursive rule.

a. Letting $c = i$, generate the first few numbers in the sequence defined by $f(0) = 1$ and $f(n+1) = \left(f(n)\right)^2 + i$. Copy the table to record your results.

n	$f(n)$	$f(n+1) = \left(f(n)\right)^2 + i$
0	$f(0) = 1$	$f(1) = \left(f(0)\right)^2 + i = (1)^2 + i = 1 + i$
1	$f(1) = 1 + i$	$f(2) = \left(f(1)\right)^2 + i = (1+i)^2 + i =$?
2	$f(2) =$?	$f(3) = \left(f(2)\right)^2 + i = \left(\ ?\ \right)^2 + i =$?
3	$f(3) =$?	$f(4) = \left(f(3)\right)^2 + i = \left(\ ?\ \right)^2 + i =$?

b. The *magnitude* of a complex number $a + bi$ is the real number $\sqrt{a^2 + b^2}$. In the complex plane, the magnitude of a complex number is the number's distance from the origin. If the magnitudes of the numbers in the sequence generated by a Julia set's recursive rule, where $f(0)$ is the starting value, remain bounded, then $f(0)$ belongs to the "filled-in" Julia set. If the magnitudes increase without bound, then $f(0)$ doesn't belong to the "filled-in" Julia set. Based on your completed table for $f(0) = 1$, would you say that the number belongs to the "filled-in" Julia set corresponding to $c = i$? Explain.

c. Would you say that $f(0) = i$ belongs to the "filled-in" Julia set corresponding to $c = i$? Explain.

3.3 Finding Complex Solutions of Quadratic Equations

Resource Locker

Essential Question: How can you find the complex solutions of any quadratic equation?

Explore Investigating Real Solutions of Quadratic Equations

(A) Complete the table.

$ax^2 + bx + c = 0$	$ax^2 + bx = -c$	$f(x) = ax^2 + bx$	$g(x) = -c$
$2x^2 + 4x + 1 = 0$	?	?	?
$2x^2 + 4x + 2 = 0$	?	?	?
$2x^2 + 4x + 3 = 0$	?	?	?

(B) The graph of $f(x) = 2x^2 + 4x$ is shown. Copy it, then graph each $g(x)$ on the same grid. Complete the table.

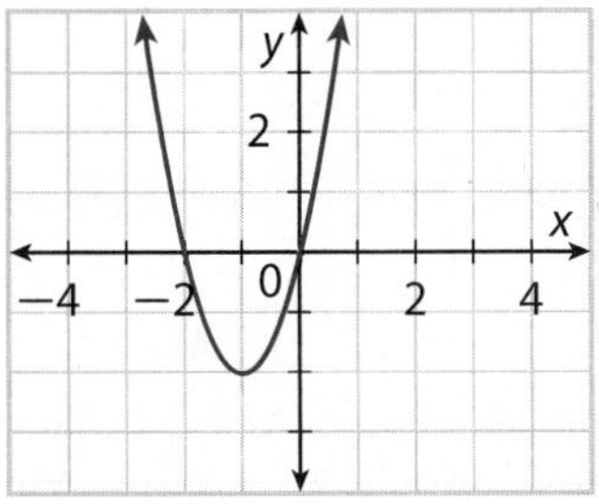

Equation	Number of Real Solutions
$2x^2 + 4x + 1 = 0$	?
$2x^2 + 4x + 2 = 0$	?
$2x^2 + 4x + 3 = 0$	?

(C) Repeat Steps A and B when $f(x) = -2x^2 + 4x$.

$ax^2 + bx + c = 0$	$ax^2 + bx = -c$	$f(x) = ax^2 + bx$	$g(x) = -c$
$-2x^2 + 4x - 1 = 0$	?	?	?
$-2x^2 + 4x - 2 = 0$	?	?	?
$-2x^2 + 4x - 3 = 0$	?	?	?

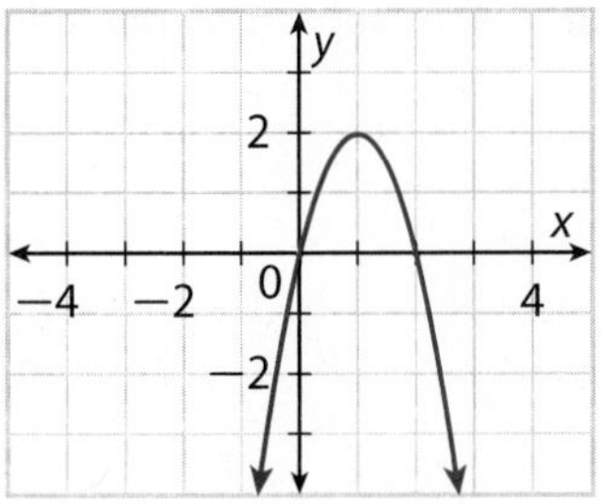

Equation	Number of Real Solutions
$-2x^2 + 4x - 1 = 0$	?
$-2x^2 + 4x - 2 = 0$	?
$-2x^2 + 4x - 3 = 0$	?

Reflect

1. Look back at Steps A and B. Notice that the minimum value of $f(x)$ in Steps A and B is -2. Complete the table by identifying how many real solutions the equation $f(x) = g(x)$ has for the given values of $g(x)$.

Value of $g(x)$	Number of Real Solutions of $f(x) = g(x)$
$g(x) = -2$	?
$g(x) > -2$	?
$g(x) < -2$	?

2. Look back at Step C. Notice that the maximum value of $f(x)$ in Step C is 2. Complete the table by identifying how many real solutions the equation $f(x) = g(x)$ has for the given values of $g(x)$.

Value of $g(x)$	Number of Real Solutions of $f(x) = g(x)$
$g(x) = 2$	?
$g(x) > 2$	?
$g(x) < 2$	?

3. You can generalize Reflect 1: For $f(x) = ax^2 + bx$ where $a > 0$, $f(x) = g(x)$ where $g(x) = -c$ has real solutions when $g(x)$ is greater than or equal to the minimum value of $f(x)$. The minimum value of $f(x)$ is

$$f\left(-\frac{b}{2a}\right) = a\left(-\frac{b}{2a}\right)^2 + b\left(-\frac{b}{2a}\right) = a\left(\frac{b^2}{4a^2}\right) - \frac{b^2}{2a} = \frac{b^2}{4a} - \frac{b^2}{2a} = \frac{b^2}{4a} - \frac{2b^2}{4a} = -\frac{b^2}{4a}.$$

So, $f(x) = g(x)$ has real solutions when $g(x) \geq -\frac{b^2}{4a}$.

Substitute $-c$ for $g(x)$. $\quad -c \geq -\frac{b^2}{4a}$

Add $\frac{b^2}{4a}$ to both sides. $\quad \frac{b^2}{4a} - c \geq 0$

Multiply both sides by $4a$, which is positive. $\quad b^2 - 4ac \geq 0$

In other words, the equation $ax^2 + bx + c = 0$ where $a > 0$ has real solutions when $b^2 - 4ac \geq 0$.

Generalize the results of Reflect 2 in a similar way. What do you notice?

Explain 1 Finding Complex Solutions by Completing the Square

Recall that completing the square for the expression $x^2 + bx$ requires adding $\left(\frac{b}{2}\right)^2$ to it, resulting in the perfect square trinomial $x^2 + bx + \left(\frac{b}{2}\right)^2$, which you can factor as $\left(x + \frac{b}{2}\right)^2$. Don't forget that when $x^2 + bx$ appears on one side of an equation, adding $\left(\frac{b}{2}\right)^2$ to it requires adding $\left(\frac{b}{2}\right)^2$ to the other side as well.

Example 1 **Solve the equation by completing the square. State whether the solutions are real or non-real.**

(A) $3x^2 + 9x - 6 = 0$

1. Write the equation in the form $x^2 + bx = c$.

$$3x^2 + 9x - 6 = 0$$
$$3x^2 + 9x = 6$$
$$x^2 + 3x = 2$$

2. Identify b and $\left(\frac{b}{2}\right)^2$.

$$b = 3$$
$$\left(\frac{b}{2}\right)^2 = \left(\frac{3}{2}\right)^2 = \frac{9}{4}$$

3. Add $\left(\frac{b}{2}\right)^2$ to both sides of the equation.

$$x^2 + 3x + \frac{9}{4} = 2 + \frac{9}{4}$$

4. Solve for x.

$$\left(x + \frac{3}{2}\right)^2 = 2 + \frac{9}{4}$$
$$\left(x + \frac{3}{2}\right)^2 = \frac{17}{4}$$
$$x + \frac{3}{2} = \pm\sqrt{\frac{17}{4}}$$
$$x + \frac{3}{2} = \pm\frac{\sqrt{17}}{2}$$
$$x = -\frac{3}{2} \pm \frac{\sqrt{17}}{2}$$
$$x = \frac{-3 \pm \sqrt{17}}{2}$$

There are two real solutions: $\frac{-3 + \sqrt{17}}{2}$ and $\frac{-3 - \sqrt{17}}{2}$.

(B) $x^2 - 2x + 7 = 0$

1. Write the equation in the form $x^2 + bx = c$.

$$x^2 - 2x = -7$$

2. Identify b and $\left(\frac{b}{2}\right)^2$.

$$b = \boxed{-2}$$
$$\left(\frac{b}{2}\right)^2 = \left(\frac{\boxed{-2}}{2}\right)^2 = \boxed{1}$$

3. Add $\left(\frac{b}{2}\right)^2$ to both sides.

$$x^2 - 2x + \boxed{1} = -7 + \boxed{1}$$

4. Solve for x.

$$x^2 - 2x + \boxed{1} = -7 + \boxed{1}$$
$$\left(x - \boxed{1}\right)^2 = \boxed{-6}$$
$$x - \boxed{1} = \pm\sqrt{\boxed{-6}}$$
$$x = 1 \pm \sqrt{\boxed{-6}}$$

There are two non-real solutions: $1 + i\sqrt{6}$ and $1 - i\sqrt{6}$.

Reflect

4. How many complex solutions do the equations in Parts A and B have? Explain.

Your Turn

Solve the equation by completing the square. State whether the solutions are real or non-real.

5. $x^2 + 8x + 17 = 0$

6. $x^2 + 10x - 7 = 0$

Explain 2 Identifying Whether Solutions Are Real or Non-real

By completing the square for the general quadratic equation $ax^2 + bx + c = 0$, you can obtain the *quadratic formula*, $x = \frac{-b \pm \sqrt{b^2 - 4ac}}{2a}$, which gives the solutions of the general quadratic equation. In the quadratic formula, the expression under the radical sign, $b^2 - 4ac$, is called the *discriminant*, and its value determines whether the solutions of the quadratic equation are real or non-real.

Value of Discriminant	Number and Type of Solutions
$b^2 - 4ac > 0$	Two real solutions
$b^2 - 4ac = 0$	One real solution
$b^2 - 4ac < 0$	Two non-real solutions

Example 2 **Answer the question by writing an equation and determining whether the solutions of the equation are real or non-real.**

(A) A ball is thrown in the air with an initial vertical velocity of 14 m/s from an initial height of 2 m. The ball's height h (in meters) at time t (in seconds) can be modeled by the quadratic function $h(t) = -4.9t^2 + 14t + 2$. Does the ball reach a height of 12 m?

Set $h(t)$ equal to 12. $-4.9t^2 + 14t + 2 = 12$

Subtract 12 from both sides. $-4.9t^2 + 14t - 10 = 0$

Find the value of the discriminant. $14^2 - 4(-4.9)(-10) = 196 - 196 = 0$

Because the discriminant is zero, the equation has one real solution, so the ball does reach a height of 12 m.

(B) A person wants to create a vegetable garden and keep the rabbits out by enclosing it with 100 feet of fencing. The area of the garden is given by the function $A(w) = w(50 - w)$ where w is the width (in feet) of the garden. Can the garden have an area of 700 ft^2?

Set $A(w)$ equal to 700. $w(50 - w) = \boxed{700}$

Multiply on the left side. $50w - w^2 = \boxed{700}$

Subtract 700 from both sides. $-w^2 + 50w - \boxed{700} = 0$

Find the value of the discriminant. $50^2 - 4(-1)(-700) = 2500 - 2800 = -300$

Because the discriminant is negative, the equation has two non-real solutions, so the garden cannot have an area of 700 ft^2.

Your Turn

Answer the question by writing an equation and determining if the solutions are real or non-real.

7. A hobbyist is making a toy sailboat. For the triangular sail, she wants the height h (in inches) to be twice the length of the base b (in inches). Can the area of the sail be 10 in^2?

Explain 3 Finding Complex Solutions Using the Quadratic Formula

When using the quadratic formula to solve a quadratic equation, be sure the equation is in the form $ax^2 + bx + c = 0$.

Example 3 **Solve the equation using the quadratic formula. Check a solution by substitution.**

(A) $-5x^2 - 2x - 8 = 0$

Write the quadratic formula. $x = \dfrac{-b \pm \sqrt{b^2 - 4ac}}{2a}$

Substitute values. $= \dfrac{-(-2) \pm \sqrt{(-2)^2 - 4(-5)(-8)}}{2(-5)}$

Simplify. $= \dfrac{2 \pm \sqrt{-156}}{-10} = \dfrac{1 \pm i\sqrt{39}}{-5}$

So, the two solutions are $-\dfrac{1}{5} - \dfrac{i\sqrt{39}}{5}$ and $-\dfrac{1}{5} + \dfrac{i\sqrt{39}}{5}$.

Check by substituting one of the values.

Substitute. $-5\left(-\dfrac{1}{5} - \dfrac{i\sqrt{39}}{5}\right)^2 - 2\left(-\dfrac{1}{5} - \dfrac{i\sqrt{39}}{5}\right) - 8 \stackrel{?}{=} 0$

Square. $-5\left(\dfrac{1}{25} + \dfrac{2i\sqrt{39}}{25} - \dfrac{39}{25}\right) - 2\left(-\dfrac{1}{5} - \dfrac{i\sqrt{39}}{5}\right) - 8 \stackrel{?}{=} 0$

Distribute. $-\dfrac{1}{5} - \dfrac{2i\sqrt{39}}{5} + \dfrac{39}{5} + \dfrac{2}{5} + \dfrac{2i\sqrt{39}}{5} - 8 \stackrel{?}{=} 0$

Simplify. $\dfrac{40}{5} - 8 \stackrel{?}{=} 0$

$0 = 0$

(B) $7x^2 + 2x + 3 = -1$

Write the equation with 0 on one side. $7x^2 + 2x + \boxed{4} = 0$

Write the quadratic formula. $x = \dfrac{-b \pm \sqrt{b^2 - 4ac}}{2a}$

Substitute values. $= \dfrac{-\boxed{2} \pm \sqrt{\left(\boxed{2}\right)^2 - 4\left(\boxed{7}\right)\left(\boxed{4}\right)}}{2\left(\boxed{7}\right)}$

Simplify. $= \dfrac{-\boxed{2} \pm \sqrt{-\boxed{108}}}{14}$

$= \dfrac{-\boxed{2} \pm \boxed{6}\, i\sqrt{\boxed{3}}}{14} = \dfrac{-\boxed{1} \pm \boxed{3}\, i\sqrt{\boxed{3}}}{7}$

So, the two solutions are $-\dfrac{1}{7} + \dfrac{3i\sqrt{3}}{7}$ and $-\dfrac{1}{7} - \dfrac{3i\sqrt{3}}{7}$.

Check by substituting one of the values.

Substitute. $7\left(-\dfrac{1}{7} + \dfrac{3i\sqrt{3}}{7}\right)^2 + 2\left(-\dfrac{1}{7} + \dfrac{3i\sqrt{3}}{7}\right) + 4 \stackrel{?}{=} 0$

Square. $7\left(\dfrac{1}{49} - \dfrac{6i\sqrt{3}}{49} - \dfrac{27}{49}\right)^2 + 2\left(-\dfrac{1}{7} + \dfrac{3i\sqrt{3}}{7}\right)^2 + 4 \stackrel{?}{=} 0$

Distribute. $\dfrac{1}{7} - \dfrac{6i\sqrt{3}}{7} - \dfrac{27}{7} - \dfrac{2}{7} + \dfrac{6i\sqrt{3}}{7} + 4 \stackrel{?}{=} 0$

$-\dfrac{28}{7} + 4 \stackrel{?}{=} 0$

Simplify. $0 = 0$

Your Turn

Solve the equation using the quadratic formula. Check a solution by substitution.

8. $6x^2 - 5x - 4 = 0$

9. $x^2 + 8x + 12 = 2x$

Elaborate

10. Discussion Suppose that the quadratic equation $ax^2 + bx + c = 0$ has $p + qi$ where $q \neq 0$ as one of its solutions. What must the other solution be? How do you know?

11. Discussion You know that the graph of the quadratic function $f(x) = ax^2 + bx + c$ has the vertical line $x = -\frac{b}{2a}$ as its axis of symmetry. If the graph of $f(x)$ crosses the x-axis, where do the x-intercepts occur relative to the axis of symmetry? Explain.

12. Essential Question Check-In Why is using the quadratic formula to solve a quadratic equation easier than completing the square?

Evaluate: Homework and Practice

Personal Math Trainer

- Online Homework
- Hints and Help
- Extra Practice

1. The graph of $f(x) = x^2 + 6x$ is shown. Use the graph to determine how many real solutions the following equations have: $x^2 + 6x + 6 = 0$, $x^2 + 6x + 9 = 0$, and $x^2 + 6x + 12 = 0$. Explain.

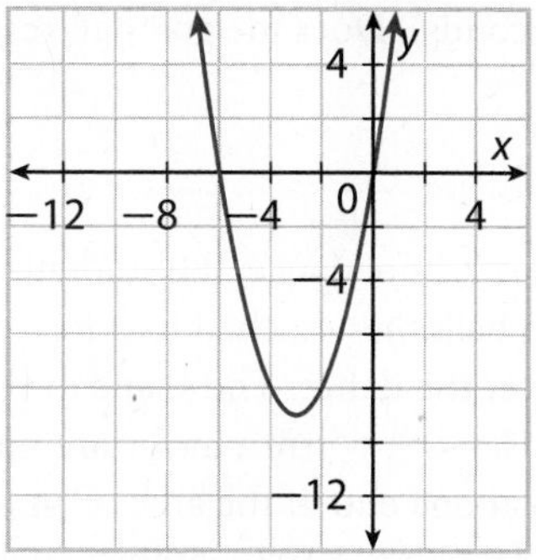

2. The graph of $f(x) = -\frac{1}{2}x^2 + 3x$ is shown. Use the graph to determine how many real solutions the following equations have: $-\frac{1}{2}x^2 + 3x - 3 = 0$, $-\frac{1}{2}x^2 + 3x - \frac{9}{2} = 0$, and $-\frac{1}{2}x^2 + 3x - 6 = 0$. Explain.

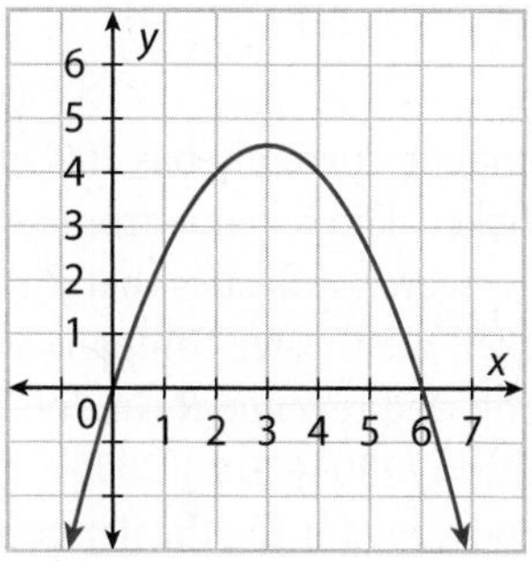

Solve the equation by completing the square. State whether the solutions are real or non-real.

3. $x^2 + 4x + 1 = 0$

4. $x^2 + 2x + 8 = 0$

5. $x^2 - 5x = -20$

6. $5x^2 - 6x = 8$

7. $7x^2 + 13x = 5$

8. $-x^2 - 6x - 11 = 0$

Without solving the equation, state the number of solutions and whether they are real or non-real.

9. $-16x^2 + 4x + 13 = 0$

10. $7x^2 - 11x + 10 = 0$

11. $-x^2 - \frac{2}{5}x = 1$

12. $4x^2 + 9 = 12x$

Answer the question by writing an equation and determining whether the solutions of the equation are real or non-real.

13. A gardener has 140 feet of fencing to put around a rectangular vegetable garden. The function $A(w) = 70w - w^2$ gives the garden's area A (in square feet) for any width w (in feet). Does the gardener have enough fencing for the area of the garden to be 1300 ft^2?

14. A golf ball is hit with an initial vertical velocity of 64 ft/s. The function $h(t) = -16t^2 + 64t$ models the height h (in feet) of the golf ball at time t (in seconds). Does the golf ball reach a height of 60 ft?

15. As a decoration for a school dance, the student council creates a parabolic arch with balloons attached to it for students to walk through as they enter the dance. The shape of the arch is modeled by the equation $y = x(5 - x)$, where x and y are measured in feet and where the origin is at one end of the arch. Can a student who is 6 feet 6 inches tall walk through the arch without ducking?

16. A small theater company currently has 200 subscribers who each pay \$120 for a season ticket. The revenue from season-ticket subscriptions is \$24,000. Market research indicates that for each \$10 increase in the cost of a season ticket, the theater company will lose 10 subscribers. A model for the projected revenue R (in dollars) from season-ticket subscriptions is $R(p) = (120 + 10p)(200 - 10p)$, where p is the number of \$10 price increases. According to this model, is it possible for the theater company to generate \$25,600 in revenue by increasing the price of a season ticket?

Solve the equation using the quadratic formula. Check a solution by substitution.

17. $x^2 - 8x + 27 = 0$

18. $x^2 - 30x + 50 = 0$

19. $x + 3 = x^2$

20. $2x^2 + 7 = 4x$

21. Identify whether each equation has two real solutions, one real solution, or two non-real solutions.

a. $x^2 - 3x + 1 = 0$

b. $x^2 - 2x + 1 = 0$

c. $x^2 - x + 1 = 0$

d. $x^2 + 1 = 0$

e. $x^2 + x + 1 = 0$

f. $x^2 + 2x + 1 = 0$

g. $x^2 + 3x + 1 = 0$

H.O.T. Focus on Higher Order Thinking

22. **Explain the Error** A student used the method of completing the square to solve the equation $-x^2 + 2x - 3 = 0$. Describe and correct the error.

$-x^2 + 2x - 3 = 0$

$-x^2 + 2x = 3$

$-x^2 + 2x + 1 = 3 + 1$

$(x + 1)^2 = 4$

$x + 1 = \pm\sqrt{4}$

$x + 1 = \pm 2$

$x = -1 \pm 2$

So, the two solutions are $-1 + 2 = 1$ and $-1 - 2 = -3$.

23. **Make a Conjecture** Describe the values of c for which the equation $x^2 + 8x + c = 0$ has two real solutions, one real solution, and two non-real solutions.

24. **Analyze Relationships** When you rewrite $y = ax^2 + bx + c$ in vertex form by completing the square, you obtain these coordinates for the vertex: $\left(-\frac{b}{2a}, c - \frac{b^2}{4a}\right)$. Suppose the vertex of the graph of $y = ax^2 + bx + c$ is located on the x-axis. Explain how the coordinates of the vertex and the quadratic formula are in agreement in this situation.

Lesson Performance Task

Matt and his friends are enjoying an afternoon at a baseball game. A batter hits a towering home run, and Matt shouts, "Wow, that must have been 110 feet high!" The ball was 4 feet off the ground when the batter hit it, and the ball came off the bat traveling vertically at 80 feet per second.

a. Model the ball's height h (in feet) at time t (in seconds) using the projectile motion model $h(t) = -16t^2 + v_0t + h_0$ where v_0 is the projectile's initial vertical velocity (in feet per second) and h_0 is the projectile's initial height (in feet). Use the model to write an equation based on Matt's claim, and then determine whether Matt's claim is correct.

b. Did the ball reach a height of 100 feet? Explain.

c. Let h_{max} be the ball's maximum height. By setting the projectile motion model equal to h_{max}, show how you can find h_{max} using the discriminant of the quadratic formula.

d. Find the time at which the ball reached its maximum height.

Quadratic Equations

Essential Question: How can you use quadratic equations to solve real-world problems?

Key Vocabulary
complex number
(número complejo)
imaginary number
(número imaginario)
imaginary unit
(unidad imaginaria)
pure imaginary number
(número imaginario puro)

KEY EXAMPLE *(Lessons 3.1, 3.2)*

Take square roots to solve the quadratic equations.

$3x^2 - 27 = 9$	
$3x^2 = 36$	Add 27 to both sides.
$x^2 = 12$	Divide both sides by 3.
$x = \pm\sqrt{12}$	Square root
$x = \pm\sqrt{4} \cdot \sqrt{3}$	Product Property
$x = \pm 2\sqrt{3}$	Simplify.

$x^2 + 20 = 0$	
$x^2 = -20$	Subtract 20 on both sides.
$x = \pm\sqrt{-20}$	Square root
$x = \pm\sqrt{(-1)(5)(4)}$	Product Property
$x = \pm 2i\sqrt{5}$	Simplify.

KEY EXAMPLE *(Lesson 3.3)*

Solve $2x^2 + 4x - 8 = 0$ by completing the square.

$2x^2 + 4x = 8$	Write the equation in the form $x^2 + bx = c$.
$x^2 + 2x = 4$	Divide both sides by 2.
$x^2 + 2x + 1 = 4 + 1$	Add $\left(\frac{b}{2}\right)^2$ to both sides of the equation.
$(x + 1)^2 = 5$	Solve for x.
$x + 1 = \pm\sqrt{5}$	
$x = -1 \pm \sqrt{5}$	

EXERCISES

Solve using the method stated. *(Lessons 3.1, 3.3)*

1. $x^2 - 16 = 0$ (square root)

2. $2x^2 - 10 = 0$ (square root)

3. $3x^2 - 6x - 12 = 0$ (completing the square)

4. $x^2 + 6x + 10 = 0$ (completing the square)

5. $x^2 - 4x + 4 = 0$ (factoring)

6. $x^2 - x - 30 = 0$ (factoring)

7. Explain when a quadratic equation can be solved using factoring. *(Lessons 3.1, 3.3)*

8. Can any quadratic equation be solved by completing the square? Explain. *(Lessons 3.1, 3.3)*

MODULE PERFORMANCE TASK

Can You Stop in Time?

A driver sees a tree fall across the road 125 feet in front of the car. The driver is barely able to stop the car before hitting the tree. Below what speed in miles per hour must the car have been traveling when the driver saw the tree fall?

The equation for braking distance is $d = \frac{s^2}{2\mu g} + 1.5s$, where d is braking distance, s is the speed of the car, μ is the coefficient of friction between the tires and the road, and g is the acceleration due to gravity, 32.2 ft/s^2.

Start by listing the information you will need and the steps you will take to solve the problem. Then complete the task, using numbers, words, or algebra to explain how you reached your conclusion.

Ready to Go On?

3.1–3.3 Quadratic Equations

Personal Math Trainer

- Online Homework
- Hints and Help
- Extra Practice

Solve the equations by taking square roots, completing the square, factoring, or using the quadratic formula. *(Lessons 3.1, 3.2, 3.3)*

1. $2x^2 - 16 = 0$

2. $2x^2 - 6x - 20 = 0$

3. $2x^2 + 2x - 2 = 0$

4. $x^2 + x = 30$

5. $x^2 - 5x = 24$

6. $-4x^2 + 8 = 24$

7. $x^2 + 30 = 24$

8. $x^2 + 4x + 3 = 0$

ESSENTIAL QUESTION

9. Write a real world situation that could be modeled by the equation $7m \cdot 5m = 875$. *(Lesson 3.1)*

MODULE 3
MIXED REVIEW

Assessment Readiness

1. Which of the following equations, when graphed, has two *x*-intercepts?

A. $x^2 + 16 = 0$

B. $2x^2 - 20 = 10$

C. $-3x^2 - 6 = 0$

2. Consider the equation $4x^2 + 4x - 16 = 0$. Determine if each statement is True or False.

A. To solve this equation using complete the square, $\left(\frac{b}{2}\right)^2 = \left(\frac{4}{2}\right)^2 = 4$.

B. If solving this equation using factoring, then $(x + 4)(x - 4) = 0$

C. After completing the square, $x = -\frac{1}{2} \pm \frac{\sqrt{17}}{2}$.

3. Consider the equation $ax^2 + bx = 25$. For what values of *a* and *b* would you solve this equation by taking a square root? For what values of *a* would the square root result in an imaginary number? Explain your answers.

4. Consider the equation $f(x) = ax^2 + bx + c$. For what values of *a* would the quadratic function open upward? For what values of *a* would the quadratic function open downward? What would happen to the function if the value of *a* were 0? Explain.

Quadratic Relations and Systems of Equations

MODULE 4

Essential Question: How can you use systems of equations to solve real-world problems?

REAL WORLD VIDEO
Video game designers need a solid understanding of algebra, including systems of quadratic equations, in order to program realistic interactions within the game environment.

MODULE PERFORMANCE TASK PREVIEW

How Can You Hit a Moving Target with a Laser Beam?

Video games can be a lot of fun. They can also help players to develop and hone skills such as following instructions, using logic in problem solving, hand-eye coordination, and fine motor and spatial abilities. Video game designers often use mathematics to program realistic interactions in the video world. How can math be used to aim a laser beam to hit a virtual clay disk flying through the air? Set your sights on the target and let's get started!

Are YOU Ready?

Complete these exercises to review skills you will need for this module.

Personal Math Trainer

- Online Homework
- Hints and Help
- Extra Practice

Graphing Linear Nonproportional Relationships

Example 1 Graph $y = -2x - 3$.

x	0	-2	-3
y	-3	1	3

Make a table of values. Plot the points and draw a line through them.

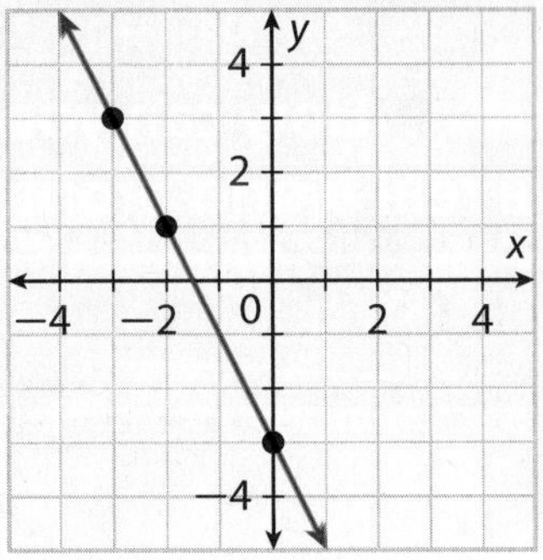

Graph each equation.

1. $y = -x + 5$

2. $y = 3x - 2$

Multi-Step Equations

Example 2 Solve $4(x - 2) = 12$ for x.

$4x - 8 = 12$ Distribute.

$4x = 20$ Add 8 to both sides.

$x = 5$ Divide by 4.

Solve each equation.

3. $5 - 3x = 7(x - 1)$

4. $3x + 2(x - 1) = 28$

5. $2(6 - 5x) = 5x + 9$

Solving Systems of Two Linear Equations

Example 3 Solve the system $\begin{cases} y = 2x + 8 \\ 3x + 2y = 2 \end{cases}$.

$3x + 2(2x + 8) = 2$ Substitute.

$x = -2$ Solve for x.

$y = 2(-2) + 8 = 4$ Solve for y.

The solution is $(-2, 4)$.

Solve each system.

6. $\begin{cases} y = 10 - 3x \\ 5x - y = 6 \end{cases}$

7. $\begin{cases} 2x - 3y = 4 \\ -x + 2y = 3 \end{cases}$

8. $\begin{cases} 5x - 2y = 4 \\ 3x + 2y = -12 \end{cases}$

4.1 Circles

Essential Question: What is the standard form for the equation of a circle, and what does the standard form tell you about the circle?

Resource Locker

Explore Deriving the Standard-Form Equation of a Circle

Recall that a circle is the set of points in a plane that are a fixed distance, called the radius, from a given point, called the center.

(A) The coordinate plane shows a circle with center $C(h, k)$ and radius r. $P(x, y)$ is an arbitrary point on the circle but is not directly above or below or to the left or right of C. $A(x, k)$ is a point with the same x-coordinate as P and the same y-coordinate as C. Explain why $\triangle CAP$ is a right triangle.

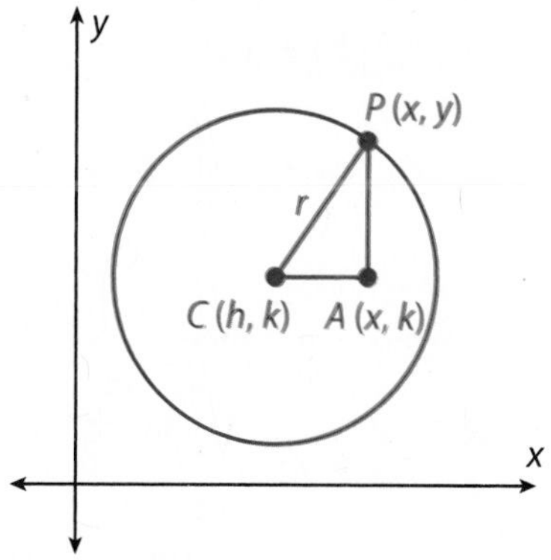

(B) Identify the lengths of the sides of $\triangle CAP$. Remember that point P is arbitrary, so you cannot rely upon the diagram to know whether the x-coordinate of P is greater than or less than h or whether the y-coordinate of P is greater than or less than k, so you must use absolute value for the lengths of the legs of $\triangle CAP$. Also, remember that the length of the hypotenuse of $\triangle CAP$ is just the radius of the circle.

The length of segment AC is $|\ ?\ |$.

The length of segment AP is $|\ ?\ |$.

The length of segment CP is ? .

(C) Apply the Pythagorean Theorem to $\triangle CAP$ to obtain an equation of the circle.

$$(x - ?)^2 + (y - ?)^2 = ?^2$$

Reflect

1. **Discussion** Why isn't absolute value used in the equation of the circle?
2. **Discussion** Why does the equation of the circle also apply to the cases in which P has the same x-coordinate as C or the same y-coordinate as C so that $\triangle CAP$ doesn't exist?

Explain 1 Writing the Equation of a Circle

The standard-form equation of a circle with center $C(h, k)$ and radius r is $(x - h)^2 + (y - k)^2 = r^2$. If you solve this equation for r, you obtain the equation $r = \sqrt{(x - h)^2 + (y - k)^2}$, which gives you a means for finding the radius of a circle when the center and a point $P(x, y)$ on the circle are known.

Example 1 **Write the equation of the circle.**

(A) The circle with center $C(-3, 2)$ and radius $r = 4$

Substitute -3 for h, 2 for k, and 4 for r into the general equation and simplify.

$$(x - (-3))^2 + (y - 2)^2 = 4^2$$

$$(x + 3)^2 + (y - 2)^2 = 16$$

(B) The circle with center $C(-4, -3)$ and containing the point $P(2, 5)$

Step 1 Find the radius.

$$r = CP$$

$$= \sqrt{\left(\boxed{2} - (-4)\right)^2 + \left(\boxed{5} - (-3)\right)^2}$$

$$= \sqrt{\left(\boxed{6}\right)^2 + \left(\boxed{8}\right)^2}$$

$$= \sqrt{\boxed{36} + \boxed{64}}$$

$$= \sqrt{\boxed{100}} = \boxed{10}$$

Step 2 Write the equation of the circle.

$$(x - (-4))^2 + (y - (-3))^2 = \boxed{10}^2$$

$$(x + 4)^2 + (y + 3)^2 = \boxed{100}$$

Your Turn

Write the equation of the circle.

3. The circle with center $C(1, -4)$ and radius $r = 2$

4. The circle with center $C(-2, 5)$ and containing the point $P(-2, -1)$

Explain 2 Rewriting an Equation of a Circle to Graph the Circle

Expanding the standard-form equation $(x - h)^2 + (y - k)^2 = r^2$ results in a general second-degree equation in two variables having the form $x^2 + y^2 + cx + dy + e = 0$. In order to graph such an equation or an even more general equation of the form $ax^2 + ay^2 + cx + dy + e = 0$. you must complete the square on both x and y to put the equation in standard form and identify the circle's center and radius.

Example 2 **Graph the circle after writing the equation in standard form.**

Ⓐ $x^2 + y^2 - 10x + 6y + 30 = 0$

Write the equation. $x^2 + y^2 - 10x + 6y + 30 = 0$

Prepare to complete the square on x and y. $\left(x^2 - 10x + \boxed{?}\right) + \left(y^2 + 6y + \boxed{?}\right) = -30 + \boxed{?} + \boxed{?}$

Complete both squares. $\left(x^2 - 10x + 25\right) + \left(y^2 + 6y + 9\right) = -30 + 25 + 9$

Factor and simplify. $(x - 5)^2 + (y + 3)^2 = 4$

The center of the circle is $C(5, -3)$, and the radius is $r = \sqrt{4} = 2$.

Graph the circle.

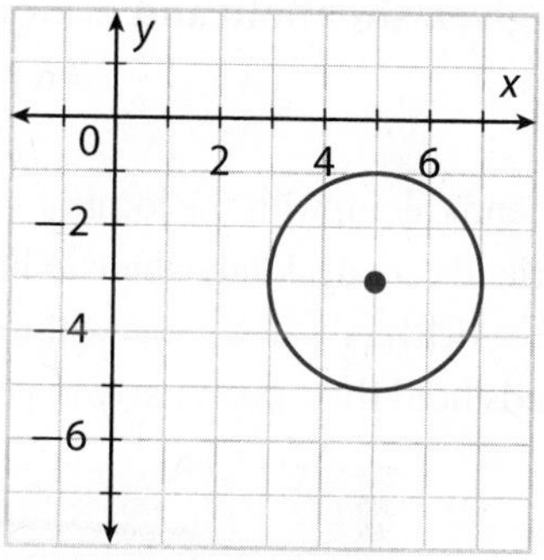

Ⓑ $4x^2 + 4y^2 + 8x - 16y + 11 = 0$

Write the equation. $4x^2 + 4y^2 + 8x - 16y + 11 = 0$

Factor 4 from the x terms and the y terms. $4\left(x^2 + 2x\right) + 4\left(y^2 - 4y\right) + 11 = 0$

Prepare to complete the square on x and y. $4\left(x^2 + 2x + \boxed{?}\right) + 4\left(y^2 - 4y + \boxed{?}\right) = -11 + 4\left(\boxed{?}\right) + 4\left(\boxed{?}\right)$

Complete both squares. $4\left(x^2 + 2x + \boxed{1}\right) + 4\left(y^2 - 4y + \boxed{4}\right) = -11 + 4\left(\boxed{1}\right) + 4\left(\boxed{4}\right)$

Factor and simplify. $4\left(x + \boxed{1}\right)^2 + 4\left(y - \boxed{2}\right)^2 = \boxed{9}$

Divide both sides by 4. $\left(x + \boxed{1}\right)^2 + \left(y - \boxed{2}\right)^2 = \boxed{\frac{9}{4}}$

The center is $C\left(\boxed{-1}, \boxed{2}\right)$, and the radius is $r = \sqrt{\boxed{\frac{9}{4}}} = \boxed{\frac{3}{2}}$.

Graph the circle.

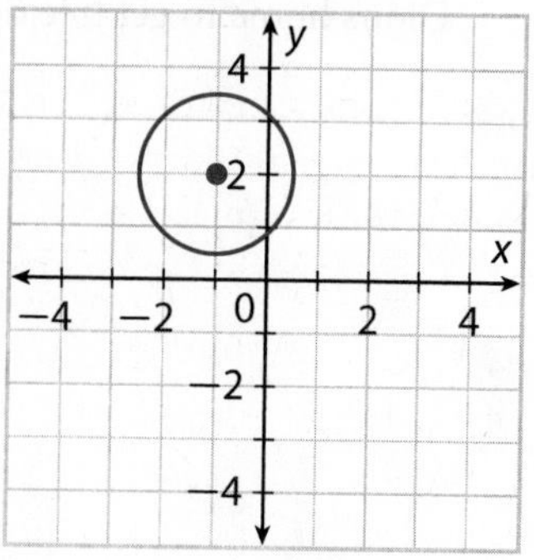

Your Turn

Graph the circle after writing the equation in standard form.

5. $x^2 + y^2 + 4x + 6y + 4 = 0$

6. $9x^2 + 9y^2 - 54x - 72y + 209 = 0$

Explain 3 Solving a Real-World Problem Involving a Circle

A circle in a coordinate plane divides the plane into two regions: points inside the circle and points outside the circle. Points inside the circle satisfy the inequality $(x - h)^2 + (y - k)^2 < r^2$, while points outside the circle satisfy the inequality $(x - h)^2 + (y - k)^2 > r^2$.

Example 3 **Write an inequality representing the given situation, and draw a circle to solve the problem.**

(A) The table lists the locations of the homes of five friends along with the locations of their favorite pizza restaurant and the school they attend. The friends are deciding where to have a pizza party based on the fact that the restaurant offers free delivery to locations within a 3-mile radius of the restaurant. At which homes should the friends hold their pizza party to get free delivery?

Place	Location
Alonzo's home	$A(3, 2)$
Barbara's home	$B(2, 4)$
Constance's home	$C(-2, 3)$
Dion's home	$D(0, -1)$
Eli's home	$E(1, -4)$
Pizza restaurant	$(-1, 1)$
School	$(1, -2)$

Write the equation of the circle with center $(-1, 1)$ and radius 3.

$(x - (-1))^2 + (y - 1)^2 = 3^2$, or $(x + 1)^2 + (y - 1)^2 = 9$

The inequality $(x + 1)^2 + (y - 1)^2 < 9$ represents the situation. Plot the points from the table and graph the circle.

The points inside the circle satisfy the inequality. So, the friends should hold their pizza party at either Constance's home or Dion's home to get free delivery.

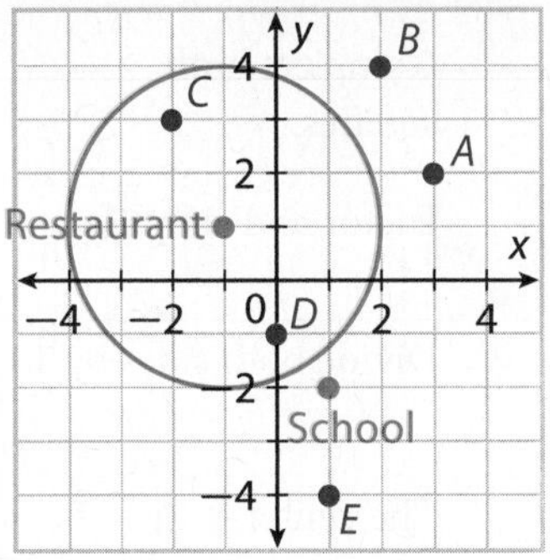

(B) In order for a student to ride the bus to school, the student must live more than 2 miles from the school. Which of the five friends are eligible to ride the bus?

Write the equation of the circle with center $(1, -2)$ and radius 2.

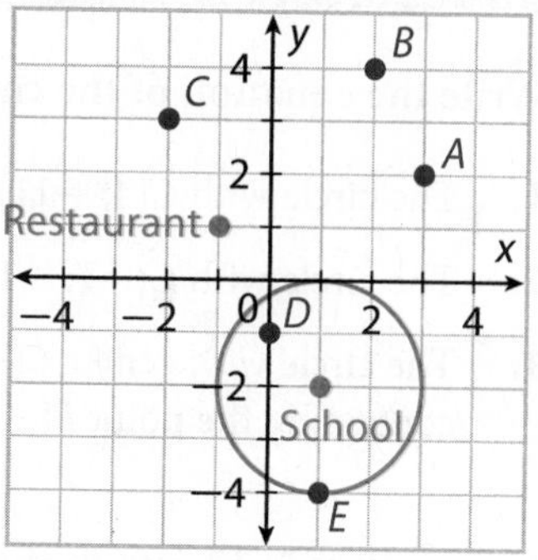

$$(x - 1)^2 + (y - (-2))^2 = 2^2$$

$$(x - 1)^2 + (y + 2)^2 = 4$$

The inequality $(x - 1)^2 + (y + 2)^2 > 4$ represents the situation.

Use the coordinate grid in Part A to graph the circle.

The points outside the circle satisfy the inequality. So, Alonzo, Barbara, and Constance are eligible to ride the bus.

Reflect

7. For Part B, how do you know that point E isn't outside the circle?

Your Turn

Write an inequality representing the given situation, and draw a circle to solve the problem.

8. Sasha delivers newspapers to subscribers that live within a 4-block radius of her house. Sasha's house is located at point $(0, -1)$. Points A, B, C, D, and E represent the houses of some of the subscribers to the newspaper. To which houses does Sasha deliver newspapers?

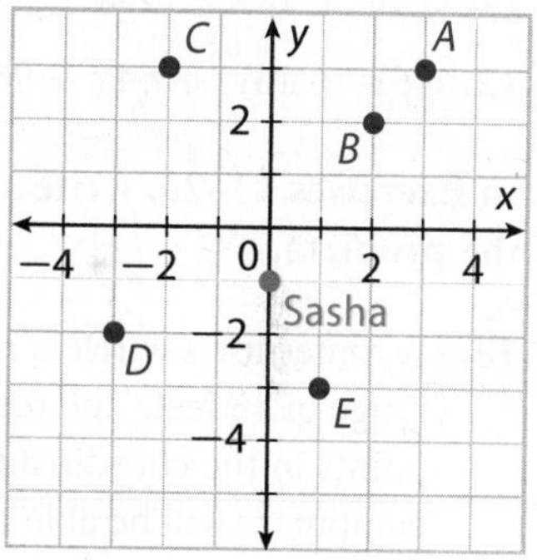

Elaborate

9. Describe the process for deriving the equation of a circle given the coordinates of its center and its radius.

10. What must you do with the equation $ax^2 + ay^2 + cx + dy + e = 0$ in order to graph it?

11. What do the inequalities $(x - h)^2 + (y - k)^2 < r^2$ and $(x - h)^2 + (y - k)^2 > r^2$ represent?

12. **Essential Question Check-In** What information must you know or determine in order to write an equation of a circle in standard form?

Evaluate: Homework and Practice

Personal Math Trainer
- Online Homework
- Hints and Help
- Extra Practice

Write the equation of the circle.

1. The circle with $C(4, -11)$ and radius $r = 16$

2. The circle with $C(-7, -1)$ and radius $r = 13$

3. The circle with center $C(-8, 2)$ and containing the point $P(-1, 6)$

4. The circle with center $C(5, 9)$ and containing the point $P(4, 8)$

In Exercises 5–12, graph the circle after writing the equation in standard form.

5. $x^2 + y^2 - 2x - 8y + 13 = 0$

Graph the circle after writing the equation in standard form.

6. $x^2 + y^2 + 6x - 10y + 25 = 0$

7. $x^2 + y^2 + 4x + 12y + 39 = 0$

8. $x^2 + y^2 - 8x + 4y + 16 = 0$

9. $8x^2 + 8y^2 - 16x - 32y - 88 = 0$

10. $2x^2 + 2y^2 + 20x + 12y + 50 = 0$

11. $12x^2 + 12y^2 - 96x - 24y + 201 = 0$

12. $16x^2 + 16y^2 + 64x - 96y + 199 = 0$

In Exercises 13–20, write an inequality representing the problem, and draw a circle to solve the problem.

13. A router for a wireless network on a floor of an office building has a range of 35 feet. The router is located at the point (30, 30). The lettered points in the coordinate diagram represent computers in the office. Which computers will be able to connect to the network through the router?

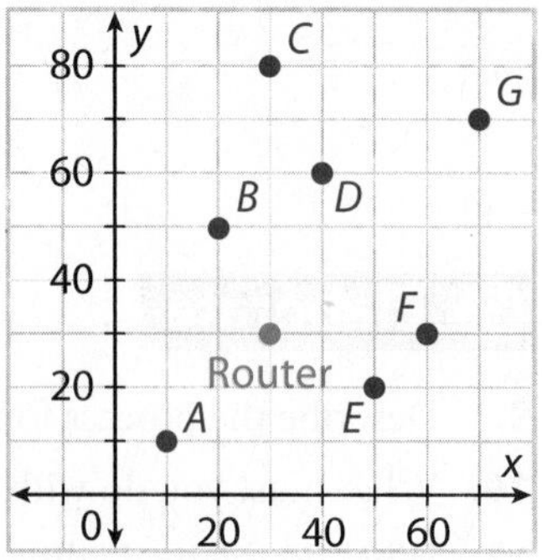

Write an inequality representing the problem, and draw a circle to solve the problem.

14. The epicenter of an earthquake is located at the point $(20, -30)$. The earthquake is felt up to 40 miles away. The labeled points in the coordinate diagram represent towns near the epicenter. In which towns is the earthquake felt?

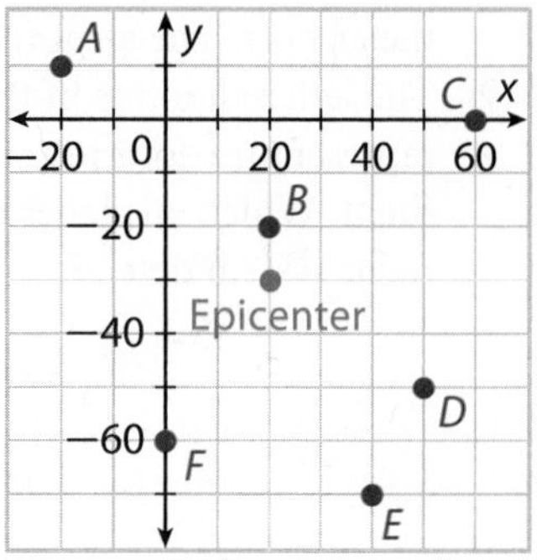

15. Aida's cat has disappeared somewhere in her apartment. The last time she saw the cat, it was located at the point $(30, 40)$. Aida knows all of the cat's hiding places, which are indicated by the lettered points in the coordinate diagram. If she searches for the cat no farther than 25 feet from where she last saw it, which hiding places will she check?

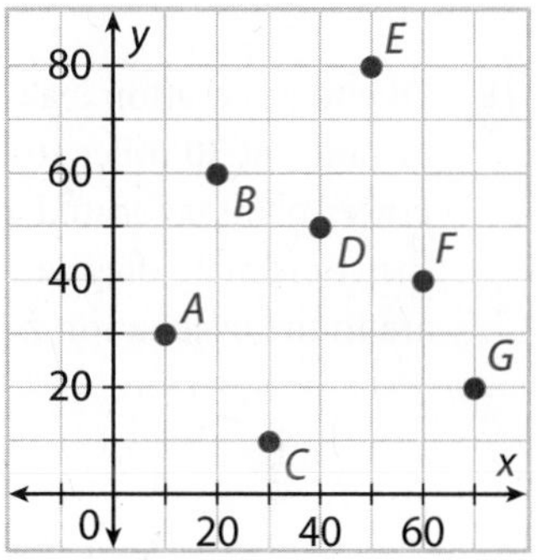

16. A rock concert is held in a large state park. The concert stage is located at the point $(-2, 2)$, and the music can be heard as far as 4 miles away. The lettered points in the coordinate diagram represent campsites within the park. At which campsites can the music be heard?

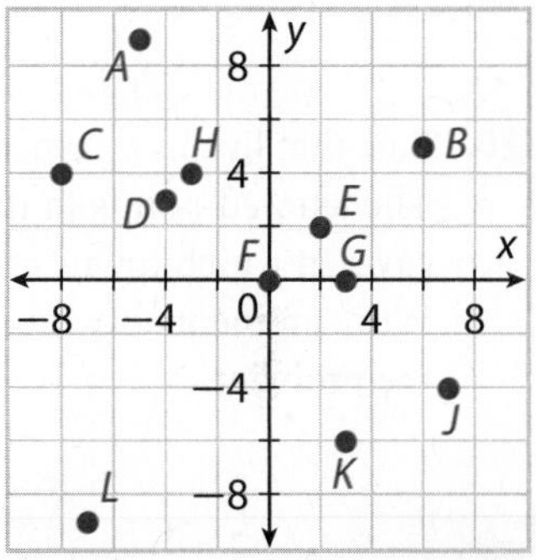

17. **Business** When Claire started her in-home computer service and support business, she decided not to accept clients located more than 10 miles from her home. Claire's home is located at the point (5, 0), and the lettered points in the coordinate diagram represent the homes of her prospective clients. Which prospective clients will Claire not accept?

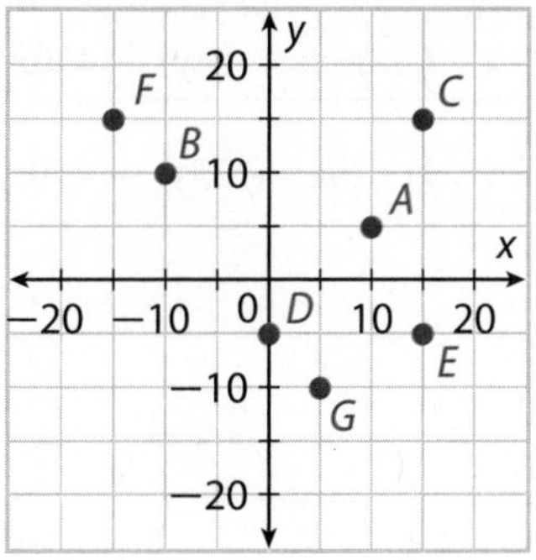

18. **Aviation** An airport's radar system detects airplanes that are in flight as far as 60 miles from the airport. The airport is located at $(-20, 40)$. The lettered points in the coordinate diagram represent the locations of airplanes currently in flight. Which airplanes does the airport's radar system detect?

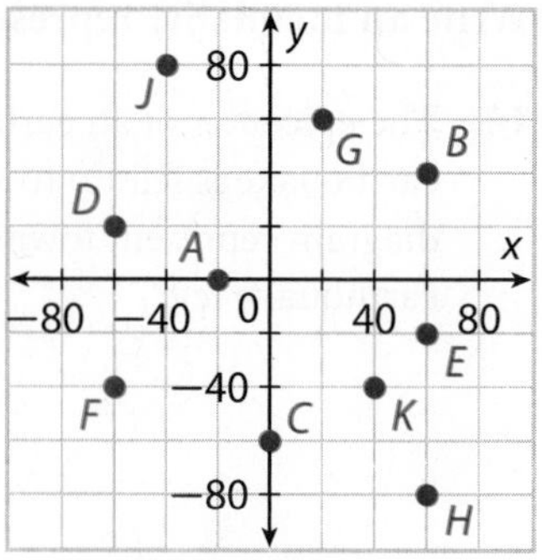

19. Due to a radiation leak at a nuclear power plant, the towns up to a distance of 30 miles from the plant are to be evacuated. The nuclear power plant is located at the point $(-10, -10)$. The lettered points in the coordinate diagram represent the towns in the area. Which towns are in the evacuation zone?

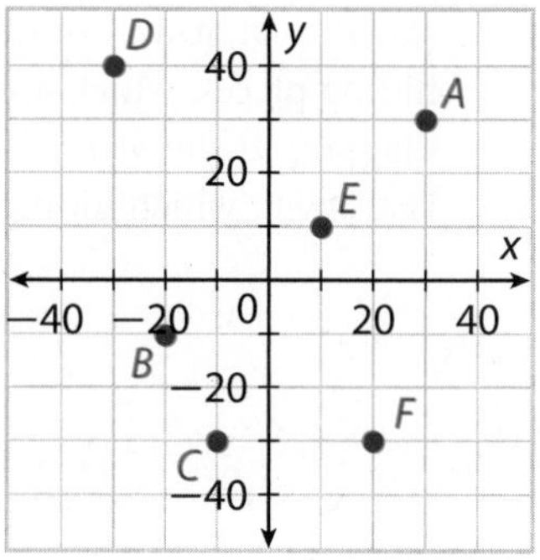

20. Bats that live in a cave at point $(-10, 0)$ have a feeding range of 40 miles. The lettered points in the coordinate diagram represent towns near the cave. In which towns are bats from the cave not likely to be observed? Write an inequality representing the problem, and draw a circle to solve the problem.

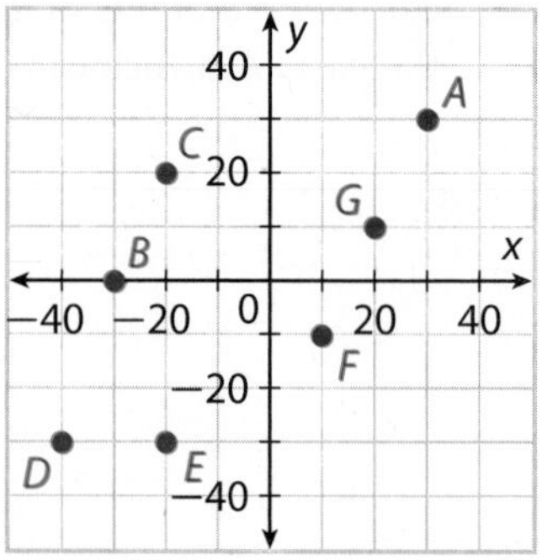

21. Match the equations to the center and radius of the circle each represents. Show your work.

A. $x^2 + y^2 + 18x + 22y - 23 = 0$ **a.** ___?___ $C(9, -11); r = 13$

B. $x^2 + y^2 - 18x + 22y + 33 = 0$ **b.** ___?___ $C(9, 11); r = 15$

C. $25x^2 + 25y^2 - 450x - 550y - 575 = 0$ **c.** ___?___ $C(-9, -11); r = 15$

D. $25x^2 + 25y^2 + 450x - 550y + 825 = 0$ **d.** ___?___ $C(-9, 11); r = 13$

H.O.T. Focus on Higher Order Thinking

22. Multi-Step A garden sprinkler waters the plants in a garden within a 12-foot spray radius. The sprinkler is located at the point $(5, -10)$. The lettered points in the coordinate diagram represent the plants. Use the diagram for parts a–c.

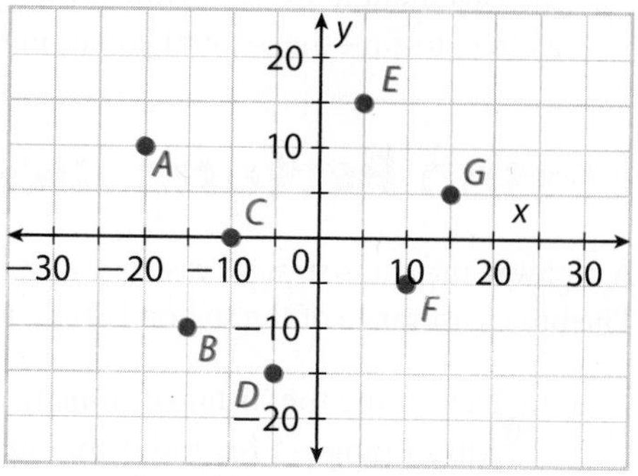

a. Write an inequality that represents the region that does not get water from the sprinkler. Then draw a circle and use it to identify the plants that do not get water from the sprinkler.

b. Suppose a second sprinkler with the same spray radius is placed at the point $(10, 10)$. Write a system of inequalities that represents the region that does not get water from either sprinkler. Then draw a second circle and use it to identify the plants that do not get water from either sprinkler.

c. Where would you place a third sprinkler with the same spray radius so all the plants get water from a sprinkler? Write a system of inequalities that represents the region that does not get water from any of the sprinklers. Then draw a third circle to show that every plant receives water from a sprinkler.

23. Represent Real-World Situations The orbit of the planet Venus is nearly circular. An astronomer develops a model for the orbit in which the Sun has coordinates $S(0, 0)$, the circular orbit of Venus passes through $V(41, 53)$, and each unit of the coordinate plane represents 1 million miles. Write an equation for the orbit of Venus. How far is Venus from the sun?

24. Draw Conclusions The *unit circle* is defined as the circle with radius 1 centered at the origin. A *Pythagorean triple* is an ordered triple of three positive integers, (a, b, c), that satisfy the relationship $a^2 + b^2 = c^2$. An example of a Pythagorean triple is (3, 4, 5). In parts a–d, you will draw conclusions about Pythagorean triples.

a. Write the equation of the unit circle.

b. Use the Pythagorean triple $(3, 4, 5)$ and the symmetry of a circle to identify the coordinates of two points on the part of the unit circle that lies in Quadrant I. Explain your reasoning.

c. Use your answer from part b and the symmetry of a circle to identify the coordinates of six other points on the unit circle. This time, the points should be in Quadrants II, III, and IV.

d. Find a different Pythagorean triple and use it to identify the coordinates of eight points on the unit circle.

25. Make a Conjecture In a two-dimensional plane, coordinates are given by ordered pairs of the form (x, y). You can generalize coordinates to three-dimensional space by using ordered triples of the form (x, y, z) where the coordinate z is used to indicate displacement above or below the xy-plane. Generalize the standard-form equation of a circle to find the general equation of a sphere. Explain your reasoning.

Lesson Performance Task

A highway that runs straight east and west passes 6 miles south of a radio tower. The broadcast range of the station is 10 miles.

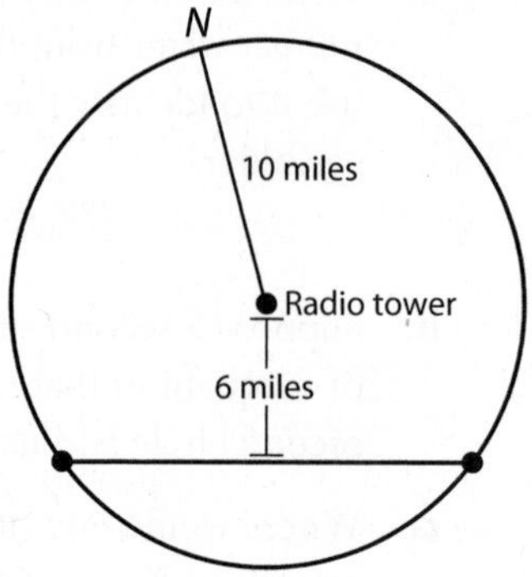

a. Determine the distance along the highway that a car will be within range of the radio station's signal.

b. Given that the car is traveling at a constant speed of 60 miles per hour, determine the amount of time the car is within range of the signal.

4.2 Parabolas

Essential Question: How is the distance formula connected with deriving equations for both vertical and horizontal parabolas?

Resource Locker

Explore Deriving the Standard-Form Equation of a Parabola

A **parabola** is defined as a set of points equidistant from a line (called the **directrix**) and a point (called the **focus**). The focus will always lie on the axis of symmetry, and the directrix will always be perpendicular to the axis of symmetry. This definition can be used to derive the equation for a horizontal parabola opening to the right with its vertex at the origin using the distance formula. (The derivations of parabolas opening in other directions will be covered later.)

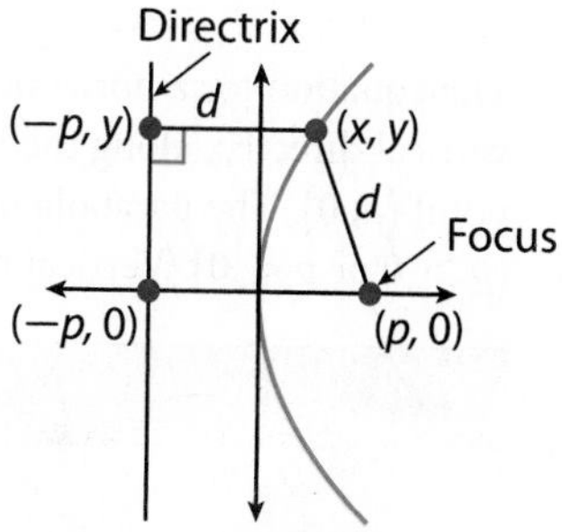

Ⓐ The coordinates for the focus are given by ? .

Ⓑ Write down the expression for the distance from a point (x, y) to the coordinates of the focus:

$$d = \sqrt{(? - ?)^2 + (? - ?)^2}$$

Ⓒ The distance from a point to a line is measured by drawing a perpendicular line segment from the point to the line. Find the point where a horizontal line from (x, y) intersects the directrix (defined by the line $x = -p$ for a parabola with its vertex on the origin).

?

Ⓓ Write down the expression for the distance from a point, (x, y) to the point from Step C:

$$d = \sqrt{(? - ?)^2 + (? - ?)^2}$$

Ⓔ Setting the two distances the same and simplifying gives

$$\sqrt{(x - p)^2 + y^2} = \sqrt{(x + p)^2}$$

To continue solving the problem, square both sides of the equation and expand the squared binomials.

$$? \, x^2 + ? \, xp + ? \, p^2 + y^2 = ? \, x^2 + ? \, xp + ? \, p^2$$

Ⓕ Collect terms.

$$? \, x^2 + ? \, px + ? \, p^2 + y^2 = 0$$

Ⓖ Finally, simplify and arrange the equation into the **standard form for a horizontal parabola** (with vertex at (0, 0)):

$$y^2 = ?$$

Reflect

1. Why was the directrix placed on the line $x = -p$?

2. **Discussion** How can the result be generalized to arrive at the standard form for a horizontal parabola with a vertex at (h, k):
$(y - k)^2 = 4p(x - h)$?

Explain 1 Writing the Equation of a Parabola with Vertex at (0, 0)

The equation for a horizontal parabola with vertex at $(0, 0)$ is written in the standard form as $y^2 = 4px$. It has a vertical directrix along the line $x = -p$, a horizontal axis of symmetry along the line $y = 0$, and a focus at the point $(p, 0)$. The parabola opens toward the focus, whether it is on the right or left of the origin $(p > 0$ or $p < 0)$. Vertical parabolas are similar, but with horizontal directrices and vertical axes of symmetry:

Parabolas with Vertices at the Origin

	Vertical	**Horizontal**
Equation in standard form	$x^2 = 4py$	$y^2 = 4px$
$p > 0$	Opens upward	Opens rightward
$p < 0$	Opens downward	Opens leftward
Focus	$(0, p)$	$(p, 0)$
Directrix	$y = -p$	$x = -p$
Axis of Symmetry	$x = 0$	$y = 0$

Example 1 **Find the equation of the parabola from the description of the focus and directrix. Then make a sketch showing the parabola, the focus, and the directrix.**

(A) Focus $(-8, 0)$, directrix $x = 8$

A vertical directrix means a horizontal parabola.

Confirm that the vertex is at $(0, 0)$:

a. The y-coordinate of the vertex is the same as the focus: 0.

b. The x-coordinate is halfway between the focus (-8) and the directrix $(+8)$: 0.

c. The vertex is at $(0, 0)$.

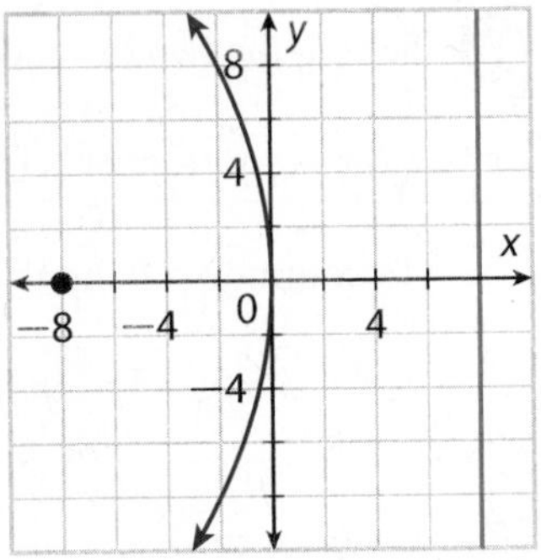

Use the equation for a horizontal parabola, $y^2 = 4px$, and replace p with the x coordinate of the focus: $y^2 = 4(-8)x$

Simplify: $y^2 = -32x$

Plot the focus and directrix and sketch the parabola.

Ⓑ Focus $(0, -2)$, directrix $y = 2$

A horizontal directrix means a vertical parabola.

Confirm that the vertex is at $(0, 0)$:

a. The x-coordinate of the vertex is the same as the focus: 0.

b. The y-coordinate is halfway between the focus, -2 and the directrix, 2 : 0

c. The vertex is at $(0, 0)$.

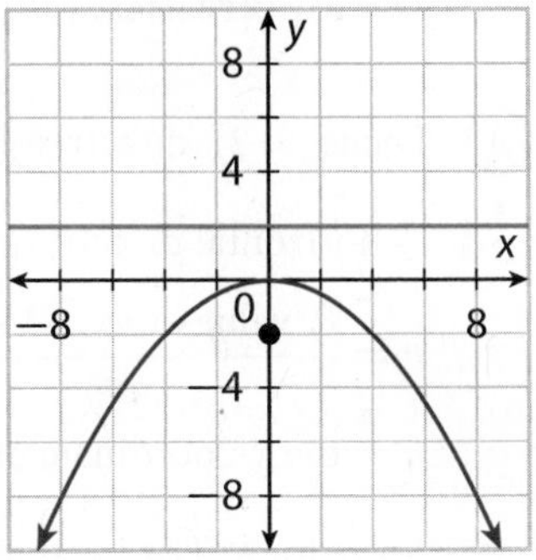

Use the equation for a vertical parabola, $x^2 = 4py$, and replace p with the y-coordinate of the focus: $x^2 = 4 \cdot -2 \cdot y$

Simplify: $x^2 = -8y$

Plot the focus, the directrix, and the parabola.

Your Turn

Find the equation of the parabola from the description of the focus and directrix. Then make a sketch showing the parabola, the focus, and the directrix.

3. Focus $(2, 0)$, directrix $x = -2$

4. Focus $\left(0, -\frac{1}{2}\right)$, directrix $y = \frac{1}{2}$

Explain 2 Writing the Equation of a Parabola with Vertex at (h, k)

The standard equation for a parabola with a vertex (h, k) can be found by translating from $(0, 0)$ to (h, k): substitute $(x - h)$ for x and $(y - k)$ for y. This also translates the focus and directrix each by the same amount.

Parabolas with Vertex (h, k)		
	Vertical	**Horizontal**
Equation in standard form	$(x-h)^2 = 4p(y-k)$	$(y-k)^2 = 4p(x-h)$
$p > 0$	Opens upward	Opens rightward
$p < 0$	Opens downward	Opens leftward
Focus	$(h, k+p)$	$(h+p, k)$
Directrix	$y = k - p$	$x = h - p$
Axis of Symmetry	$x = h$	$y = k$

p is found halfway from the directrix to the focus:

- For vertical parabolas: $p = \dfrac{(y \text{ value of focus}) - (y \text{ value of directrix})}{2}$
- For horizontal parabolas: $p = \dfrac{(x \text{ value of focus}) - (x \text{ value of directrix})}{2}$

The vertex can be found from the focus by relating the coordinates of the focus to h, k, and p.

Example 2 **Find the equation of the parabola from the description of the focus and directrix. Then make a sketch showing the parabola, the focus, and the directrix.**

(A) Focus $(3, 2)$, directrix $y = 0$

A horizontal directrix means a vertical parabola.

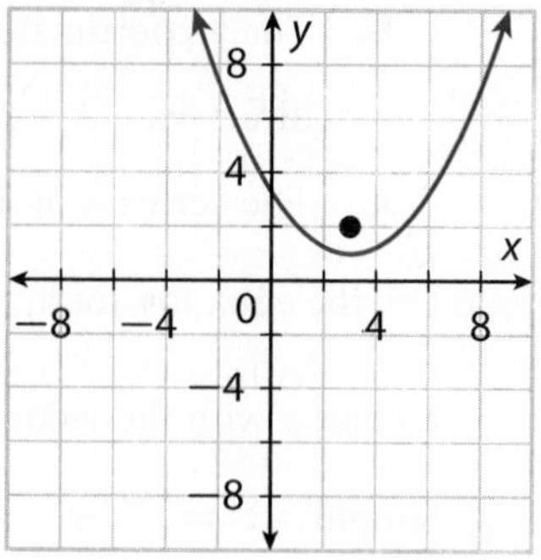

$$p = \frac{(y \text{ value of focus}) - (y \text{ value of directrix})}{2} = \frac{2 - 0}{2} = 1$$

$h =$ the x-coordinate of the focus $= 3$

Solve for k: The y-value of the focus is $k + p$, so

$k + p = 2$

$k + 1 = 2$

$k = 1$

Write the equation: $(x - 3)^2 = 4(y - 1)$

Plot the focus, the directrix, and the parabola.

(B) Focus $(-1, -1)$, directrix $x = 5$

A vertical directrix means a horizontal parabola.

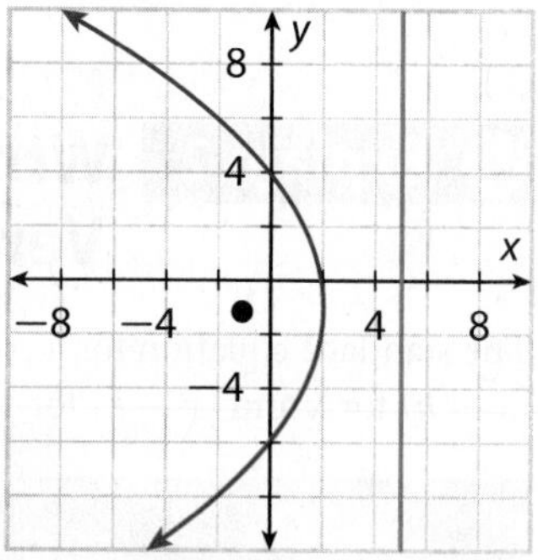

$$p = \frac{(x \text{ value of focus}) - (x \text{ value of directrix})}{2} = \frac{\boxed{-1} - \boxed{5}}{2} = \boxed{-3}$$

$k =$ the y-coordinate of the focus $= \boxed{-1}$

Solve for h: The x-value of the focus is $h + p$, so

$h + p = \boxed{-1}$

$h + (-3) = \boxed{-1}$

$h = \boxed{2}$

Write the equation: $(y + 1)^2 = \boxed{-12}\left(x - \boxed{2}\right)$

Your Turn

Find the equation of the parabola from the description of the focus and directrix. Then make a sketch showing the parabola, the focus, and the directrix.

5. Focus $(5, -1)$, directrix $x = -3$

6. Focus $(-2, 0)$, directrix $y = 4$

Explain 3 Rewriting the Equation of a Parabola to Graph the Parabola

A **second-degree equation in two variables** is an equation constructed by adding terms in two variables with powers no higher than 2. The general form looks like this:

$ax^2 + by^2 + cx + dy + e = 0$

Expanding the standard form of a parabola and grouping like terms results in a second-degree equation with either $a = 0$ or $b = 0$, depending on whether the parabola is vertical or horizontal. To graph an equation in this form requires the opposite conversion, accomplished by completing the square of the squared variable.

Example 3 **Convert the equation to the standard form of a parabola and graph the parabola, the focus, and the directrix.**

(A) $x^2 - 4x - 4y + 12 = 0$

Isolate the x terms and complete the square on x.

Isolate the x terms. $x^2 - 4x = 4y - 12$

Add $\left(\frac{-4}{2}\right)^2$ to both sides. $x^2 - 4x + 4 = 4y - 8$

Factor the perfect square trinomial on the left side. $(x - 2)^2 = 4y - 8$

Factor out 4 from the right side. $(x - 2)^2 = 4(y - 2)$

This is the standard form for a vertical parabola. Now find p, h, and k from the standard form $(x - h)^2 = 4p(y - k)$ in order to graph the parabola, focus, and directrix.

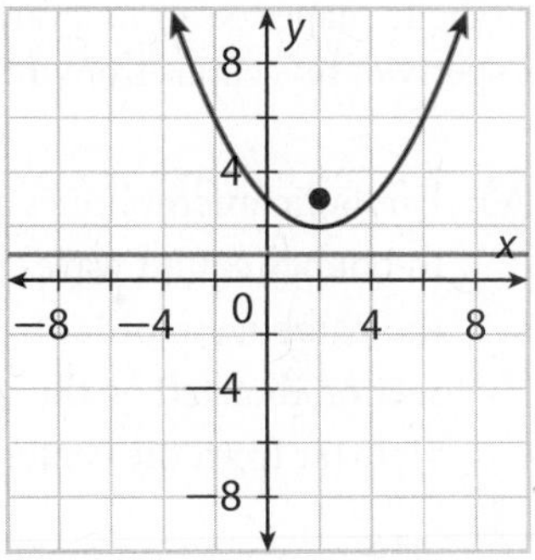

$4p = 4$, so $p = 1$. Vertex $= (h, k) = (2, 2)$.

$h = 2, k = 2$. Focus $= (h, k + p) = (2, 2 + 1) = (2, 3)$.

Directrix: $y = k - p = 2 - 1$, or $y = 1$.

(B) $y^2 + 2x + 8y + 18 = 0$

Isolate the y terms. $y^2 + 8y = -2x - 18$

Add $\left(\frac{8}{2}\right)^2$ to both sides. $y^2 + 8y + 16 = -2x - 2$

Factor the perfect square trinomial. $(y + 4)^2 = -2x - 2$

Factor out -2 on the right. $(y + 4)^2 = -2(x + 1)$

Identify the features of the graph using the standard form of a horizontal parabola, $(y - k)^2 = 4p(x - h)$:

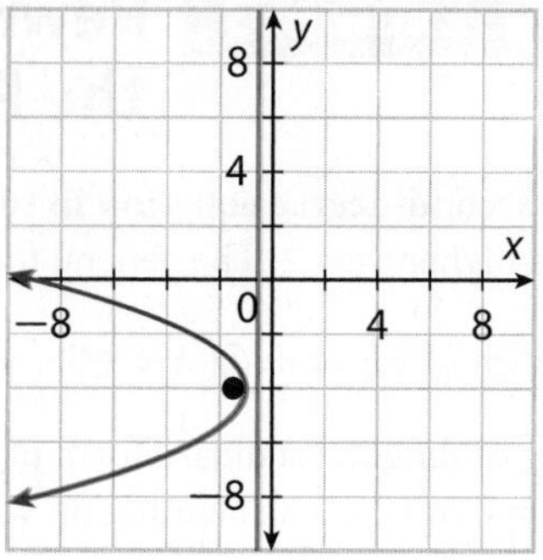

$4p = \boxed{-2}$, so $p = \boxed{-\frac{1}{2}}$.

$h = \boxed{-1}$, $k = \boxed{-4}$

Vertex $= (h, k) = \left(\boxed{-1}, \boxed{-4}\right)$

Focus $= (h + p, k) = \left(\boxed{-\frac{3}{2}}, \boxed{-4}\right)$

Directrix: $x = h - p$ or $x = \boxed{-\frac{1}{2}}$

Your Turn

Convert the equation to the standard form of a parabola and graph the parabola, the focus, and the directrix.

7. $y^2 - 12x - 4y + 64 = 0$

8. $x^2 + 8x - 16y - 48 = 0$

Explain 4 Solving a Real-World Problem

Parabolic shapes occur in a variety of applications in science and engineering that take advantage of the concentrating property of reflections from the parabolic surface at the focus.

(A) Parabolic microphones are so-named because they use a parabolic dish to bounce sound waves toward a microphone placed at the focus of the parabola in order to increase sensitivity. The dish shown has a cross section dictated by the equation $y^2 = 32x$ where x and y are in inches. How far from the center of the dish should the microphone be placed?

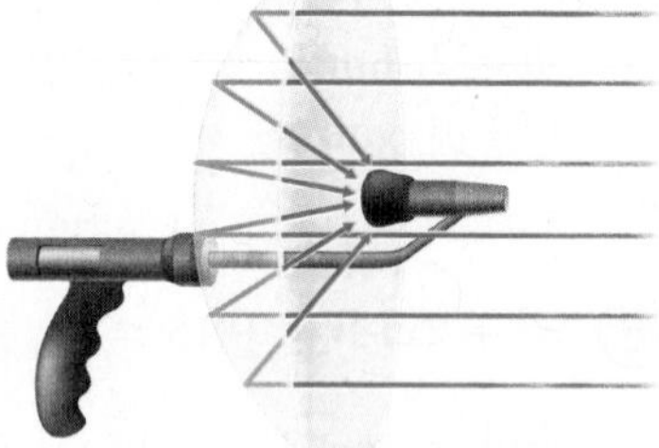

The cross section matches the standard form of a horizontal parabola with $h = 0$, $k = 0$, $p = 8$.

Therefore the vertex, which is the center of the dish, is at $(0, 0)$ and the focus is at $(8, 0)$, 8 inches away.

(B) A reflective telescope uses a parabolic mirror to focus light rays before creating an image with the eyepiece. If the focal length (the distance from the bottom of the mirror's bowl to the focus) is 140 mm and the mirror has a 70 mm diameter (width), what is the depth of the bowl of the mirror?

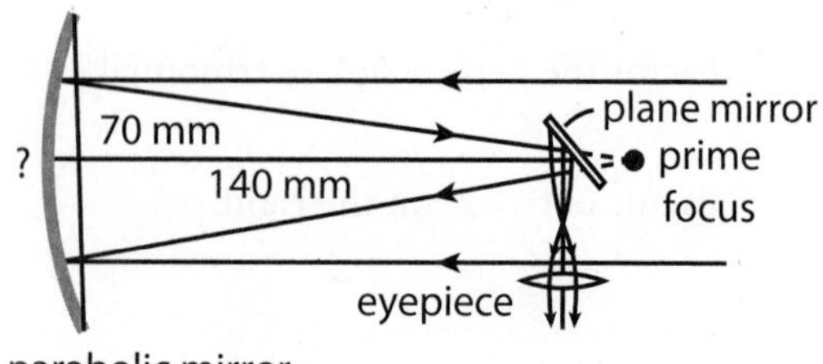

The distance from the bottom of the mirror's bowl to the focus is p. The vertex location is not specified (or needed), so use $(0, 0)$ for simplicity. The equation for the mirror is a horizontal parabola (with x the distance along the telescope and y the position out from the center).

$$\left(y - \boxed{0}\right)^2 = 4p\left(x - \boxed{0}\right)$$

$$y^2 = \boxed{560}\,x$$

Since the diameter of the bowl of the mirror is 70 mm, the points at the rim of the mirror have y-values of 35 mm and -35 mm. The x-value of either point will be the same as the x-value of the point directly above the bottom of the bowl, which equals the depth of the bowl. Since the points on the rim lie on the parabola, use the equation of the parabola to solve for the x-value of either edge of the mirror.

$$\boxed{35}^2 = \boxed{560}\,x$$

$$x \approx \boxed{2.19}\text{ mm}$$

The bowl is approximately 2.19 mm deep.

Your Turn

9. A football team needs one more field goal to win the game. The goalpost that the ball must clear is 10 feet (~3.3 yd) off the ground. The path of the football after it is kicked for a 35-yard field goal is given by the equation $y - 11 = -0.0125\left(x - 20\right)^2$, in yards. Does the team win?

Elaborate

10. Examine the graphs in this lesson and determine a relationship between the separation of the focus and the vertex, and the shape of the parabola. Demonstrate this by finding the relationship between p for a vertical parabola with vertex of $(0, 0)$ and a, the coefficient of the quadratic parent function $y = ax^2$.

11. Essential Question Check-In How can you use the distance formula to derive an equation relating x and y from the definition of a parabola based on focus and directrix?

Evaluate: Homework and Practice

Personal Math Trainer

- Online Homework
- Hints and Help
- Extra Practice

Find the equation of the parabola with vertex at $(0, 0)$ from the description of the focus and directrix and plot the parabola, the focus, and the directrix.

1. Focus at $(3, 0)$, directrix: $x = -3$

2. Focus at $(0, -5)$, directrix: $y = 5$

3. Focus at $(-1, 0)$, directrix: $x = 1$

4. Focus at $(0, 2)$, directrix: $y = -2$

Find the equation of the parabola with the given information.

5. Vertex: $(-3, 6)$; Directrix: $x = -1.75$

6. Vertex: $(6, 20)$; Focus: $(6, 11)$

Find the equation of the parabola with vertex at (h, k) from the description of the focus and directrix and plot the parabola, the focus, and the directrix.

7. Focus at $(5, 3)$, directrix: $y = 7$

8. Focus at $(-3, 3)$, directrix: $x = 3$

Convert the equation to the standard form of a parabola and graph the parabola, the focus, and the directrix.

9. $y^2 - 20x - 6y - 51 = 0$

10. $x^2 - 14x - 12y + 73 = 0$

11. **Communications** The equation for the cross section of a parabolic satellite television dish is $y = \frac{1}{50}x^2$, measured in inches. How far is the focus from the vertex of the cross section?

12. **Engineering** The equation for the cross section of a spotlight is $y + 5 = \frac{1}{12}x^2$, measured in inches. The bulb is located at the focus. How far is the bulb from the vertex of the cross section?

13. When a ball is thrown into the air, the path that the ball travels is modeled by the parabola $y - 7 = -0.0175(x - 20)^2$, measured in feet. What is the maximum height the ball reaches? How far does the ball travel before it hits the ground?

14. A cable for a suspension bridge is modeled by $y - 55 = 0.0025x^2$, where x is the horizontal distance, in feet, from the support tower and y is the height, in feet, above the bridge. How far is the lowest point of the cable above the bridge?

15. Match each equation to its graph.

a. ___?___ $y + 1 = \frac{1}{16}(x - 2)^2$ b. ___?___ $y - 1 = \frac{1}{16}(x + 2)^2$ c. ___?___ $x + 1 = -\frac{1}{16}(y - 2)^2$

A. 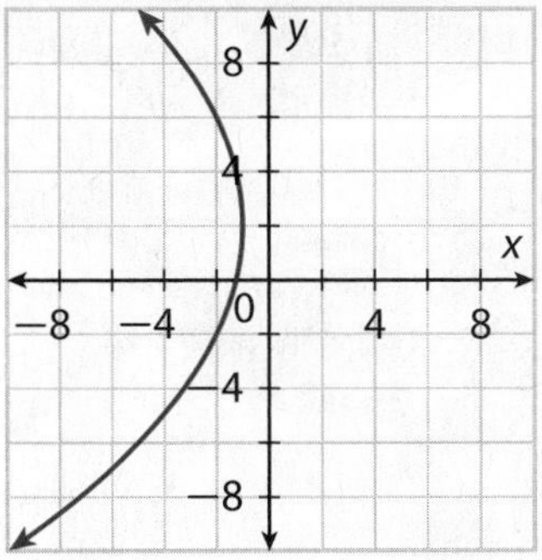

B. 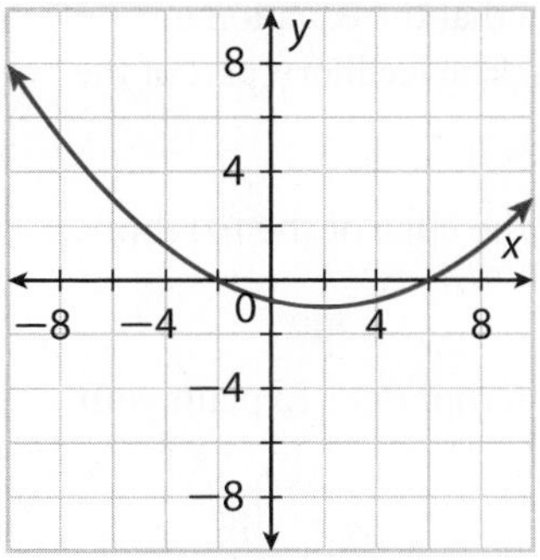

C. 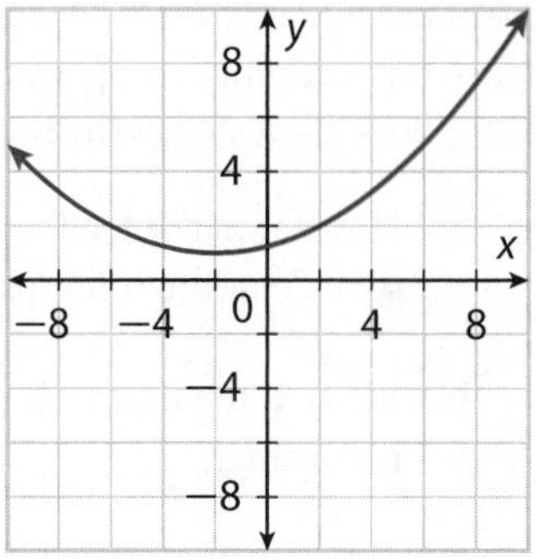

Derive the equation of the parabolas with the given information.

16. An upward-opening parabola with a focus at $(0, p)$ and a directrix $y = -p$.

17. A leftward-opening parabola with a focus at $(-p, 0)$ and directrix $x = p$.

H.O.T. Focus on Higher Order Thinking

18. Multi-Step A tennis player hits a tennis ball just as it hits one end line of the court. The path of the ball is modeled by the equation $y - 4 = -\frac{4}{1521}(x - 39)^2$ where $x = 0$ is at the end line. The tennis net is 3 feet high, and the total length of the court is 78 feet.

a. How far is the net located from the player?

b. Explain why the ball will go over the net.

c. Will the ball land "in," that is, inside the court or on the opposite endline?

19. Critical Thinking The latus rectum of a parabola is the line segment perpendicular to the axis of symmetry through the focus, with endpoints on the parabola. Find the length of the latus rectum of a parabola. Justify your answer. Hint: Set the coordinate system such that the vertex is at the origin and the parabola opens rightward with the focus at $(p, 0)$.

20. Explain the Error Lois is finding the focus and directrix of the parabola $y - 8 = -\frac{1}{2}(x + 2)^2$. Her work is shown. Explain what Lois did wrong, and then find the correct answer.

$h = -2, k = 8$

$4p = -\frac{1}{2}$, so $p = -\frac{1}{8}$, or $p = -0.125$

Focus $= (h, k + p) = (-2, 7.875)$

Directrix: $y = k - p$, or $y = 8.125$

Lesson Performance Task

Parabolic microphones are used for field audio during sports events. The microphones are manufactured such that the equation of their cross section is $x = \frac{1}{34}y^2$, in inches. The feedhorn part of the microphone is located at the focus.

a. How far is the feedhorn from the edge of the parabolic surface of the microphone?

b. What is the diameter of the microphone? Explain your reasoning.

c. If the diameter is increased by 5 inches, what is the new equation of the cross section of the microphone?

4.3 Solving Linear-Quadratic Systems

Resource Locker

Essential Question: How can you solve a system composed of a linear equation in two variables and a quadratic equation in two variables?

Explore Investigating Intersections of Lines and Graphs of Quadratic Equations

There are many real-world situations that can be modeled by linear or quadratic functions. What happens when the two situations overlap? Examine graphs of linear functions and quadratic functions and determine the ways they can intersect.

(A) Examine the two graphs below to consider the ways a line could intersect the parabola.

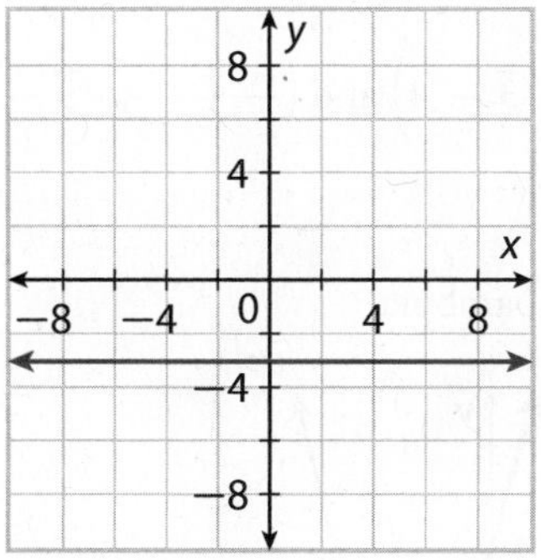

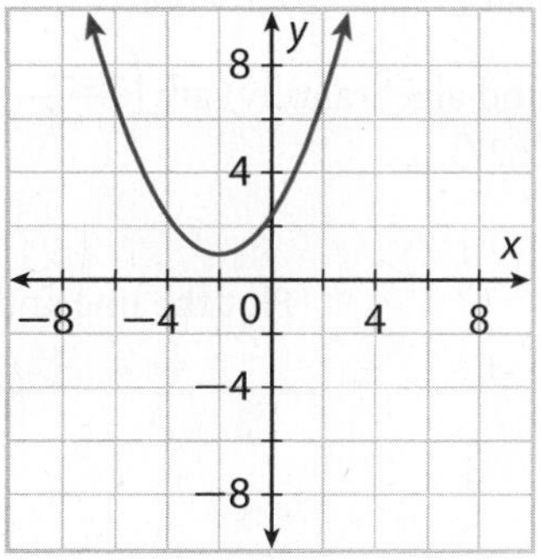

(B) Sketch three graphs of a line and a parabola: one showing intersection in one point, one showing intersection in two points, and one not showing intersection.

(C) So a constant linear function and a quadratic function can intersect at ? points.

Reflect

1. If a line intersects a circle at one point, what is the relationship between the line and the radius of the circle at that point?

2. **Discussion** Does a line have to be horizontal to intersect a parabola at exactly one point?

Explain 1 Solving Linear-Quadratic Systems Graphically

Graph each equation by hand and find the set of points where the two graphs intersect.

Example 1 **Solve the given linear-quadratic system graphically.**

(A) $\begin{cases} 2x - y = 3 \\ y + 6 = 2(x+1)^2 \end{cases}$

Plot the line and the parabola.

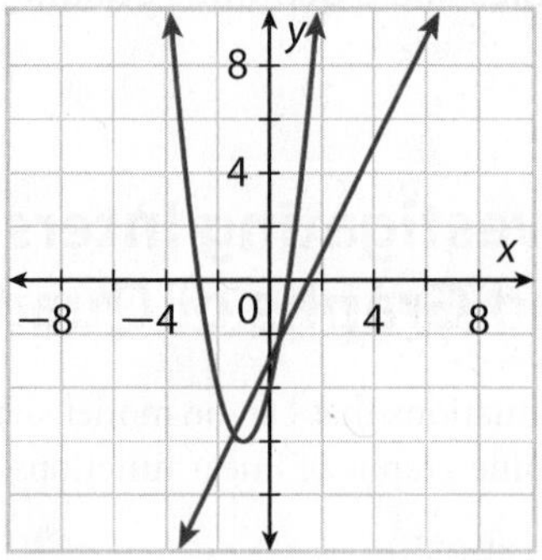

Solve each equation for y.

$$2x - y = 3$$
$$y = 2x - 3$$
$$y + 6 = 2(x+1)^2$$
$$y = 2(x+1)^2 - 6$$

Find the approximate points of intersection: Estimating from the graph, the intersection points appear to be near $(-1.5, -5.5)$ and $(0.5, -2.5)$.

The exact solutions (which can be found algebraically) are $\left(\frac{-1-\sqrt{3}}{2}, -\sqrt{3} - 4\right)$ and $\left(\frac{-1+\sqrt{3}}{2}, \sqrt{3} - 4\right)$, or about $(-1.37, -5.73)$ and $(0.37, -2.27)$.

(B) $\begin{cases} 3x + y = 4.5 \\ y = \frac{1}{2}(x-3)^2 \end{cases}$

Plot the line and the parabola.

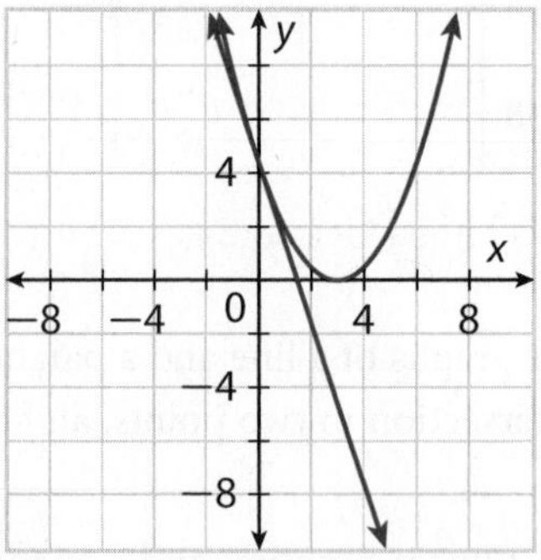

Solve each equation for y.

$$3x + y = 4.5$$

$y =$ **$-3x + 4.5$**

$y =$ **$\frac{1}{2}(x-3)^2$**

Find the approximate point(s) of intersection: (0, 4.5).

Note that checking these coordinates in the original system shows that this is an exact solution.

Your Turn

Solve the given linear-quadratic system graphically.

3. $\begin{cases} y + 3x = 0 \\ y - 6 = -3x^2 \end{cases}$

4. $\begin{cases} y + 1 = \frac{1}{2}(x-3)^2 \\ x - y = 6 \end{cases}$

Explain 2 Solving Linear-Quadratic Systems Algebraically

Use algebra to find the solution. Use substitution or elimination.

Example 2 **Solve the given linear-quadratic system algebraically.**

(A) $\begin{cases} 3x - y = 7 \\ y + 4 = 2(x+5)^2 \end{cases}$

Solve this system using elimination. First line up the terms.

$$7 + y = 3x$$
$$4 + y = 2(x+5)^2$$

Subtract the second equation from the first to eliminate the y variable.

$$7 + y = 3x$$
$$-\left(4 + y = 2(x + 5^2)\right)$$
$$3 = 3x - 2(x+5)^2$$

Solve the resulting equation for x using the quadratic formula.

$$3 = 3x - 2(x+5)^2$$
$$3 = 3x - 2(x^2 + 10x + 25)$$
$$3 = 3x - 2x^2 - 20x - 50$$
$$0 = -2x^2 - 17x - 53$$
$$2x^2 + 17x + 53 = 0$$
$$x = \frac{-17 \pm \sqrt{17^2 - 4 \cdot 2 \cdot 53}}{2 \cdot 2}$$
$$= \frac{-17 \pm \sqrt{289 - 424}}{4}$$
$$= \frac{-17 \pm \sqrt{-135}}{4}$$

There is no real number equivalent to $\sqrt{-135}$, so the system has no solution.

Ⓑ $\begin{cases} y = \frac{1}{4}(x-3)^2 \\ 3x - 2y = 13 \end{cases}$

Solve the system by substitution. The first equation is already solved for y. Substitute the expression $\frac{1}{4}(x-3)^2$ for y in the second equation.

$$3x - 2\left(\frac{1}{4}(x-3)^2\right) = 13$$

Now, solve for x.

$$13 = 3x - 2\left(\frac{1}{4}(x-3)^2\right)$$

$$13 = 3x - \boxed{\frac{1}{2}}(x-3)^2$$

$$13 = 3x - \frac{1}{2}\left(\boxed{x^2 - 6x + 9}\right)$$

$$13 = 3x - \frac{1}{2}x^2 + 3x - \frac{9}{2}$$

$$13 = -\frac{1}{2}x^2 + \boxed{6x} - \frac{9}{2}$$

$$0 = -\frac{1}{2}x^2 + 6x - \frac{35}{2}$$

$$0 = x^2 \boxed{-12x + 35}$$

$$0 = \left(x \boxed{-5}\right)\left(x \boxed{-7}\right)$$

$$x = \left(\boxed{5}\right) \text{ or } x = \left(\boxed{7}\right)$$

So the line and the parabola intersect at two points. Use the x-coordinates of the intersections to find the points.

Solve $3x - 2y = 13$ for y.

$$3x - 2y = 13$$

$$-2y = 13 - 3x$$

$$y = \boxed{-\left(\frac{13 - 3x}{2}\right)}$$

Find y when $x = 5$ and when $x = 7$.

$$y = -\frac{13 - 3 \cdot 5}{2} = -\frac{13 - 15}{2} = -\frac{-2}{2} = 1$$

$$y = -\frac{13 - 3 \cdot 7}{2} = -\frac{13 - 21}{2} = -\frac{-8}{2} = 4$$

So the solutions to the system are $(5, 1)$ and $(7, 4)$.

Reflect

5. How can you check algebraic solutions for reasonableness?

Your Turn

Solve the given linear-quadratic system algebraically.

6. $\begin{cases} x - 6 = -\frac{1}{6}y^2 \\ 2x + y = 6 \end{cases}$

7. $\begin{cases} x - y = 7 \\ x^2 - y = 7 \end{cases}$

Explain 3 Solving Real-World Problems

You can use the techniques from the previous examples to solve real-world problems.

Example 3 Solve each problem.

(A) A tour boat travels around an island in a pattern that can be modeled by the equation $36x^2 + 25y^2 = 900$. A fishing boat approaches the island on a path that can be modeled by the equation $3x - 2y = -8$. Is there a danger of collision? If so, where?

Write the system of equations.

$$\begin{cases} 36x^2 + 25y^2 = 900 \\ 3x - 2y = -8 \end{cases}$$

Solve the second equation for x.

$$3x - 2y = -8$$

$$3x = 2y - 8$$

$$x = \frac{2y - 8}{3}$$

Substitute for x in the first equation.

$$36x^2 + 25y^2 = 900$$

$$36\left(\frac{2y - 8}{3}\right)^2 + 25y^2 = 900$$

$$36\left(\frac{4y^2 - 32y + 64}{9}\right) + 25y^2 = 900$$

$$4(4y^2 - 32y + 64) + 25y^2 = 900$$

$$16y^2 - 128y + 256 + 25y^2 = 900$$

$$41y^2 - 128y - 644 = 0$$

Solve using the quadratic equation.

$$y = \frac{128 \pm \sqrt{128^2 - 4(41)(-644)}}{2(41)}$$

$$= \frac{128 \pm \sqrt{122{,}000}}{82}$$

$$\approx -2.70 \text{ or } 5.82$$

Collisions can occur when $y \approx -2.70$ or $y \approx 5.82$.

To find the x-values, substitute the y-values into $x = \frac{2y - 8}{3}$.

$$x = \frac{2(-2.70) - 8}{3} \qquad x = \frac{2(5.82) - 8}{3}$$

$$= \frac{-5.40 - 8}{3} \qquad = \frac{11.64 - 8}{3}$$

$$= \frac{-13.40}{3} \qquad = \frac{3.64}{3}$$

$$\approx -4.47 \qquad \approx 1.21$$

So the boats could collide at approximately $(-4.47, -2.70)$ or $(1.21, 5.82)$.

(B) The range of the signal from a radio station is bounded by a circle described by the equation $x^2 + y^2 = 2025$. A stretch of highway near the station is modeled by the equation $y - 15 = \frac{1}{20}x$. At which points, if any, does a car on the highway enter and exit the broadcast range of the station?

Write the system of equations.

$$\begin{cases} x^2 + y^2 = 2025 \\ y - 15 = \frac{1}{20}x \end{cases}$$

Solve the second equation for y.

$$y - 15 = \frac{1}{20}x$$

$$y = \boxed{\frac{1}{20}x + 15}$$

Substitute for x in the first equation.

$$x^2 + y^2 = 2025$$

$$x^2 + \left(\boxed{\frac{1}{20}x + 15}\right)^2 = 2025$$

$$x^2 + \boxed{\frac{1}{400}x^2 + \frac{3}{2}x + 225} = 2025$$

$$\boxed{\frac{401}{400}}x^2 + \frac{3}{2}x + 225 = 2025$$

$$\frac{401}{400}x^2 + \frac{3}{2}x - \boxed{1800} = 0$$

$$401x^2 + 600x - 720000 = 0$$

Solve using the quadratic formula.

$$y = \frac{-600 \pm \sqrt{600^2 - 4(401)(-720000)}}{2(401)}$$

$$= \frac{600 \pm \sqrt{1,155,240,000}}{802}$$

$$\approx \boxed{-41.63} \text{ or } \boxed{43.13} \text{ (rounded to the nearest hundredth)}$$

To find the y-values, substitute the x-values into $y = \frac{1}{20}x + 15$.

The car will be within the radio station's broadcast area between $(-41.63, 12.92)$ and $(43.13, 17.16)$.

Your Turn

8. An asteroid is traveling toward Earth on a path that can be modeled by the equation $y = \frac{1}{28}x - 7$. It approaches a satellite in orbit on a path that can be modeled by the equation $\frac{x^2}{49} + \frac{y^2}{51} = 1$. What are the approximate coordinates of the points where the satellite and asteroid might collide?

9. The owners of a circus are planning a new act. They want to have a trapeze artist catch another acrobat in mid-air as the second performer comes into the main tent on a zip-line. If the path of the trapeze can be modeled by the parabola $y = \frac{1}{4}x^2 + 16$ and the path of the zip-line can be modeled by $y = 2x + 12$, at what point can the trapeze artist grab the second acrobat?

Elaborate

10. A parabola opens to the left. Identify an infinite set of parallel lines that will intersect the parabola only once.

11. If a parabola can intersect a line from the set of lines $\{x = a \mid a \in R\}$ in 0, 1, or 2 points, what do you know about the parabola?

12. Essential Question Check-In How can you solve a system composed of a linear equation in two variables and a quadratic equation in two variables?

Evaluate: Homework and Practice

Personal Math Trainer

- Online Homework
- Hints and Help
- Extra Practice

1. How many points of intersection are on the graph?

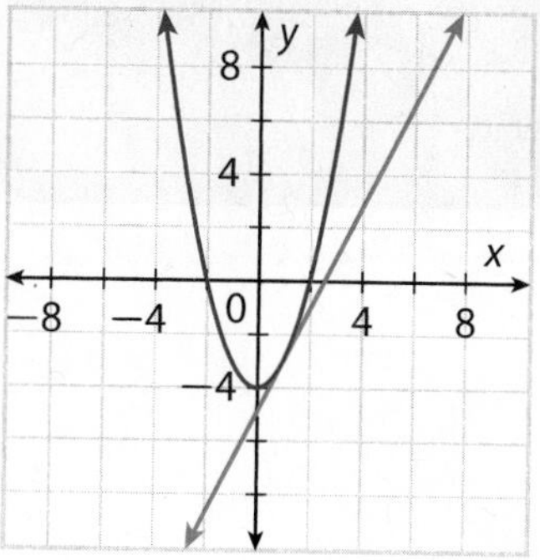

2. How many points of intersection are there on the graph of $\begin{cases} y = x^2 + 3x - 2 \\ y - x = 4 \end{cases}$?

Solve each given linear-quadratic system graphically. If necessary, round to the nearest integer.

3. $\begin{cases} y = -(x-2)^2 + 4 \\ y = -5 \end{cases}$

4. $\begin{cases} y - 3 = (x-1)^2 \\ 2x + y = 5 \end{cases}$

5. $\begin{cases} x = y^2 - 5 \\ -x + 2y = 12 \end{cases}$

6. $\begin{cases} x - 4 = (y+1)^2 \\ 3x - y = 17 \end{cases}$

7. $\begin{cases} (y-4)^2 + x^2 = -12x - 20 \\ x = y \end{cases}$

8. $\begin{cases} 5 - y = x^2 + x \\ y + 1 = \frac{3}{4}x \end{cases}$

Solve each linear-quadratic system algebraically.

9. $\begin{cases} 6x + y = -16 \\ y + 7 = x^2 \end{cases}$

10. $\begin{cases} y - 5 = (x-2)^2 \\ x + 2y = 6 \end{cases}$

11. $\begin{cases} y^2 - 26 = -x^2 \\ x - y = 6 \end{cases}$

12. $\begin{cases} y - 3 = x^2 - 2x \\ 2x + y = 1 \end{cases}$

13. $\begin{cases} y = x^2 + 1 \\ y - 1 = x \end{cases}$

14. $\begin{cases} y = x^2 + 2x + 7 \\ y - 7 = x \end{cases}$

15. Jason is driving his car on a highway at a constant rate of 60 miles per hour when he passes his friend Alan whose car is parked on the side of the road. Alan has been waiting for Jason to pass so that he can follow him to a nearby campground. To catch up to Jason's passing car, Alan accelerates at a constant rate. The distance d, in miles, that Alan's car travels as a function of time t, in hours, since Jason's car has passed is given by $d = 3600t^2$. Find how long it takes Alan's car to catch up with Jason's car.

16. The flight of a cannonball toward a hill is described by the parabola $y = 2 + 0.12x - 0.002x^2$.

The hill slopes upward along a path given by $y = 0.15x$.

Where on the hill does the cannonball land?

17. Amy throws a quarter from the top of a building at the same time that a balloon is released from the ground. The equation describing the height y above ground of the quarter in feet is $y = 64 - 2x^2$, where x is the time in seconds. The equation describing the elevation of the balloon in feet is $y = 6x + 8$, where x is the time in seconds. After how many seconds will the balloon and quarter pass each other? Check your solution for reasonableness.

18. The range of an ambulance service is a circular region bounded by the equation $x^2 + y^2 = 400$. A straight road within the service area is represented by $y = 3x + 20$. Find the length of the road, in miles, that lies within the range of the ambulance service (round your answer to the nearest hundredth).

Recall that the distance formula is $d = \sqrt{(x_2 - x_1)^2 + (y_2 - y_1)^2}$.

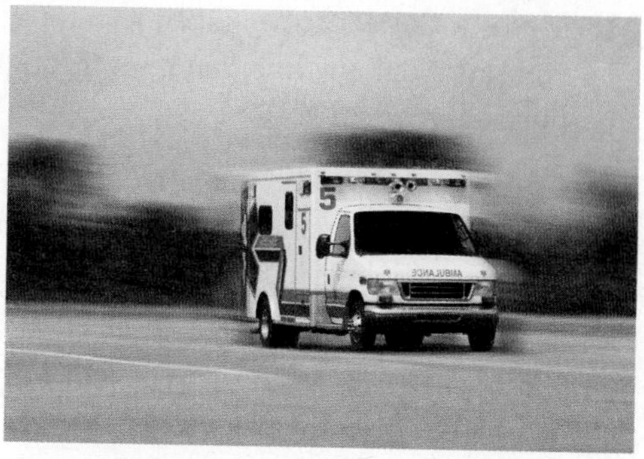

19. Match the equations with their solutions.

a. ___?___ $\begin{cases} y = x - 2 \\ -x^2 + y = 4x - 2 \end{cases}$ **A.** (4, 3) (−4, −3)

b. ___?___ $\begin{cases} y = (x - 2)^2 \\ y = -5x - 8 \end{cases}$ **B.** (0, −2) (5, 3)

c. ___?___ $\begin{cases} 4y = 3x \\ x^2 + y^2 = 25 \end{cases}$ **C.** (2, 0)

d. ___?___ $\begin{cases} y = (x - 2)^2 \\ y = 0 \end{cases}$ **D.** No solution

20. A student solved the system $\begin{cases} y - 7 = x^2 - 5x \\ y - 2x = 1 \end{cases}$ graphically and determined the only solution to be (1, 3). Was this a reasonable answer? How do you know?

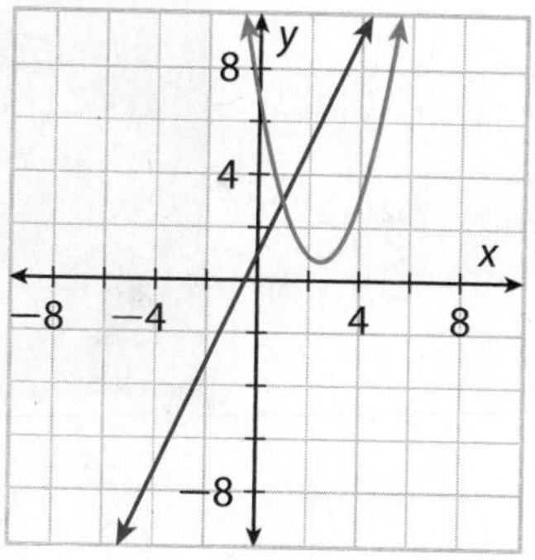

H.O.T. Focus on Higher Order Thinking

21. **Explain the Error** A student was asked to come up with a system of equations, one linear and one quadratic, that has two solutions. The student gave $\begin{cases} y^2 = -(x + 1)^2 + 9 \\ y = x^2 - 4x + 3 \end{cases}$ as the answer. What did the student do wrong?

22. Analyze Relationships The graph shows a quadratic function and a linear function $y = d$. If the linear function were changed to $y = d + 3$, how many solutions would the new system have? If the linear function were changed to $y = d - 5$, how many solutions would the new system have? Give reasons for your answers.

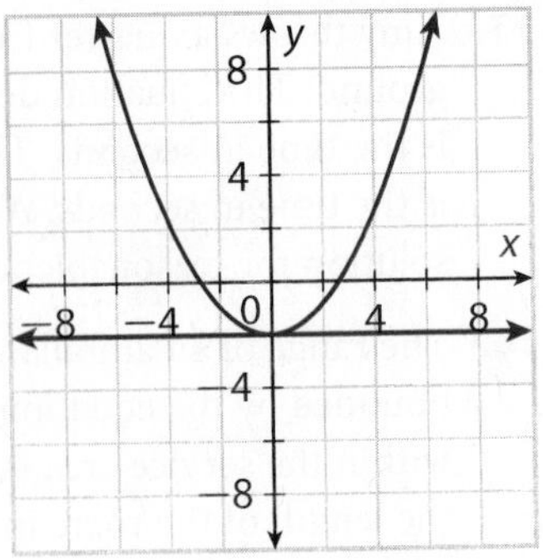

23. Make a Conjecture Given $y = 100x^2$ and $y = 0.0001x^2$, what can you say about any line that goes through the vertex of each but is not horizontal or vertical?

24. Communicate Mathematical Ideas Explain why a system of a linear equation and a quadratic equation cannot have an infinite number of solutions.

Lesson Performance Task

Suppose an aerial freestyle skier goes off a ramp with her path represented by the equation $y = -0.024(x - 25)^2 + 40$ where $x = 0$ represents the end of the ramp. If the surface of the mountain is represented by the linear equation $y = -0.5x + 25$, find the horizontal distance in feet the skier lands from the end of the ramp.

4.4 Solving Linear Systems in Three Variables

Resource Locker

Essential Question: How can you find the solution(s) of a system of three linear equations in three variables?

Explore Recognizing Ways that Planes Can Intersect

Recall that a linear equation in two variables defines a line. Consider a *linear equation in three variables.* An example is shown.

$$5 = 3x + 2y + 6z$$

A **linear equation in three variables** has three distinct variables, each of which is either first degree or has a coefficient of zero.

Just as the two numbers that satisfy a linear equation in two variables are called an ordered pair, the three numbers that satisfy a linear equation in three variables are called an **ordered triple** and are written (x, y, z).

The set of all ordered pairs satisfying a linear equation in two variables forms a line. Likewise the set of all ordered triples satisfying a linear equation in three variables forms a plane.

Three linear equations in three variables, considered together, form a system of three linear equations in three variables. The solutions of a system like this depend on the ways three planes can intersect.

(A) The diagrams show some ways three planes can intersect. How many points lie on all 3 planes?

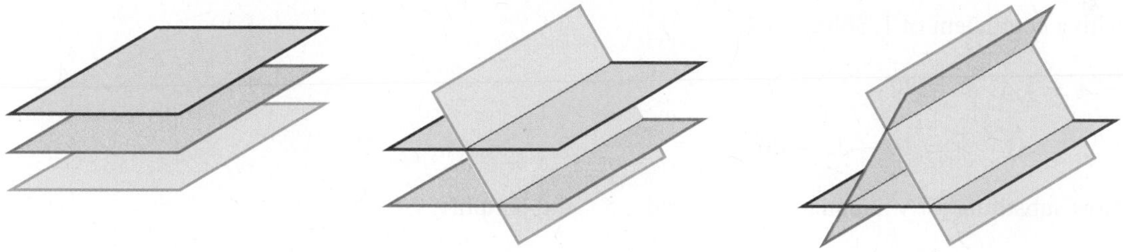

(B) The diagram shows three intersecting planes.

How many points lie on all 3 planes?

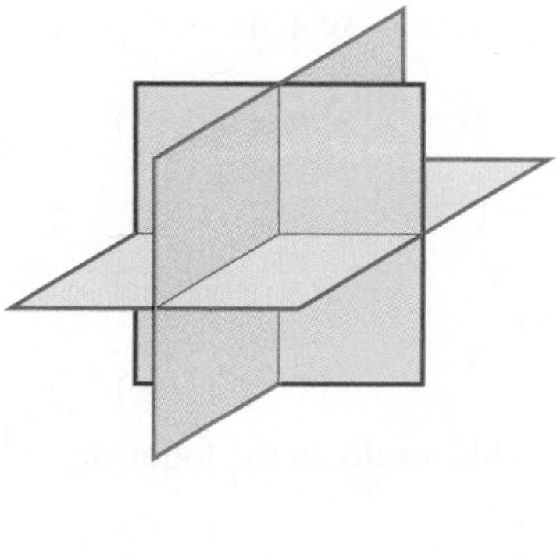

(C) The diagram shows planes intersecting in a different way.

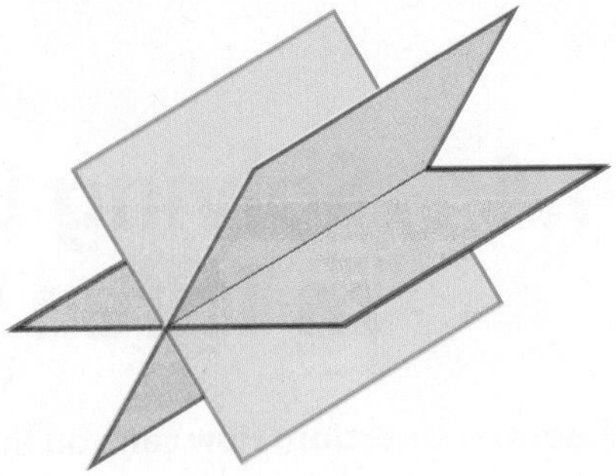

Describe the intersection.

How many points lie in all 3 planes?

Reflect

1. **Discussion** Give an example of three planes that intersect at exactly one point.

Explain 1 Solving a System of Three Linear Equations Using Substitution

A system of three linear equations is solved in the same manner as a system of two linear equations. It just has more steps.

Example 1 **Solve the system using substitution.**

(A)
$$\begin{cases} -2x + y + 3z = 20 & \boxed{1} \\ -3x + 2y + z = 21 & \boxed{2} \\ 3x - 2y + 3z = -9 & \boxed{3} \end{cases}$$

Choose an equation and variable to start with. The easiest equations to solve are those that have a variable with a coefficient of 1. Solve for y.

$-2x + y + 3z = 20$

$y = 2x - 3z + 20$

Now substitute for y in equations $\boxed{2}$ and $\boxed{3}$ and simplify.

$21 = -3x + 2(2x - 3z + 20) + z$

$21 = -3x + 4x - 6z + 40 + z$

$21 = x - 5z + 40$

$-19 = x - 5z$ $\boxed{4}$

$-9 = 3x - 2(2x - 3z + 20) + 3z$

$-9 = 3x - 4x + 6z - 40 + 3z$

$-9 = -x + 9z - 40$

$31 = -x + 9z$ $\boxed{5}$

This results in the following linear system in two variables:

$$\begin{cases} -19 = x - 5z & \boxed{4} \\ 31 = -x + 9z & \boxed{5} \end{cases}$$

Solve equation [4] for x.

$x = 5z - 19$

Substitute into equation [5] and solve for z. Then use the value for z to find the value of x.

$31 = -(5z - 19) + 9z$ $\qquad$ $31 = -x + 9(3)$

$31 = 4z + 19$ $\qquad$ $31 = -x + 27$

$3 = z$ $\qquad$ $-4 = x$

Finally, solve the equation for y when $x = -4$ and $z = 3$.

$y = 2x - 3z + 20$

$y = 2(-4) - 3(3) + 20$

$y = 3$

Therefore, the solution to the system of three linear equations is the ordered triple $(-4, 3, 3)$.

B There is a unique vertical parabola passing through any three noncollinear points in the coordinate plane provided that no two of the points have the same x-coordinate. Find the vertical parabola that passes through the points $(2, 1)$, $(-1, 4)$, and $(-2, 3)$.

The general form of a vertical parabola is the quadratic equation $y = ax^2 + bx + c$. In order to find the equation of the parabola, we must identify the values of a, b, and c. Since each point lies on the parabola, substituting the coordinates of each point into the general equation produces a different equation.

$$\begin{cases} 1 = a(2)^2 + b(2) + c \\ 4 = a(-1)^2 + b(-1) + c \\ 3 = a(-2)^2 + b(-2) + c \end{cases} \Rightarrow \begin{cases} 1 = 4a + 2b + c & [1] \\ 4 = a - b + c & [2] \\ 3 = 4a - 2b + c & [3] \end{cases}$$

Choose an equation in which it is relatively easy to isolate a variable. Solve equation [2] for c.

$c = 4 - a + b$ [2]

Now substitute for c in equations [1] and [3].

$1 = 4a + 2b + (4 - a + b)$ $\qquad$ $3 = 4a - 2b + (4 - a + b)$

$1 = 3a + 3b + 4$ $\qquad$ $3 = 3a - b + 4$

$-3 = 3a + 3b$ [4] $\qquad$ $-1 = 3a - b$ [5]

This results in the following linear system in two variables:

$$\begin{cases} 3a + 3b = -3 & [4] \\ 3a - b = -1 & [5] \end{cases}$$

Solve equation [5] for b.

$b = 3a + \boxed{1}$

Substitute into equation [4] and solve for a. Then use the value for a to find the values of b.

$3a + 3\left(\boxed{3a + 1}\right) = -3$

$3a + 9a + \boxed{3} = -3$

$12a = \boxed{-6}$

$a = \boxed{-\frac{1}{2}}$

$3\left(-\frac{1}{2}\right) + 3b = -3$

$\boxed{-\frac{3}{2}} + 3b = -3$

$3b = \boxed{-\frac{3}{2}}$

$b = \boxed{-\frac{1}{2}}$

Then use the values a and b to solve for c.

$c = 4 - a + b = 4 - \left(-\frac{1}{2}\right) + \left(-\frac{1}{2}\right) = 4$

So the equation of the parabola connecting (2, 1), (−1, 4), and (−2, 3) is

$y = \boxed{-\frac{1}{2}}x^2 - \boxed{\frac{1}{2}}x + \boxed{4}$.

Your Turn

Solve the system using substitution.

2. $\begin{cases} x + 2y + z = 8 \\ 2x + y - z = 4 \\ x + y + 3z = 7 \end{cases}$

3. $\begin{cases} 2x - y - 3z = 1 \\ 4x + 3y + 2z = -4 \\ -3x + 2y + 5z = -3 \end{cases}$

Explain 2 Solving a System of Three Linear Equations Using Elimination

You can also solve systems of three linear equations using elimination.

Example 2

(A) $\begin{cases} -2x + y + 3z = 20 & \boxed{1} \\ -3x + 2y + z = 21 & \boxed{2} \\ 3x - 2y + 3z = -9 & \boxed{3} \end{cases}$

Begin by looking for variables with coefficients that are either the same or additive inverses of each other. When subtracted or added, these pairs will eliminate that variable. Subtract equation [3] from equation [1] to eliminate the z variable.

$$\begin{array}{ll} [1] & -2x + y + 3z = 20 \\ [3] & \underline{3x - 2y + 3z = -9} \\ & -5x + 3y + 0 = 29 \quad [4] \end{array}$$

Next multiply [2] by -3 and add it to [1] to eliminate the same variable.

$$\begin{array}{llcl} [1] & -2x + y + 3z = 20 & & -2x + y + 3z = 20 \\ [2] & \underline{-3(-3x + 2y + z = 21)} & \Rightarrow & \underline{9x - 6y - 3z = -63} \\ & & & 7x - 5y + 0 = -43 \quad [5] \end{array}$$

This results in the system of two linear equations below.

$$\begin{cases} -5x + 3y = 29 & [4] \\ 7x - 5y = -43 & [5] \end{cases}$$

To solve this system, multiply [4] by 5 and add the result to the product of [5] and 3.

$$\begin{array}{llcl} [4] & 5(-5x + 3y = 29) & & -25x + 15y = 145 \\ [5] & \underline{3(7x - 5y = -43)} & \Rightarrow & \underline{21x - 15y = -129} \\ & & & -4x + 0 = 16 \\ & & & -4x = 16 \\ & & & x = -4 \end{array}$$

Substitute to solve for y and z.

$$\begin{array}{ll} -5x + 3y = 29 \quad [4] & -3x + 2y + z = 21 \quad [2] \\ -5(-4) + 3y = 29 & -3(-4) + 2(3) + z = 21 \\ y = 3 & z = 3 \end{array}$$

The solution to the system is the ordered triple $(-4, 3, 3)$.

(B) $\begin{cases} x + 2y + 3z = 9 & [1] \\ x + 3y + 2z = 5 & [2] \\ x + 4y - z = -5 & [3] \end{cases}$

Begin by subtracting equation [2] from equation [1] to eliminate x.

$$\begin{array}{lr} \boxed{1} & x + 2y + 3z = 9 \\ \boxed{2} & x + 3y + 2z = 5 \\ \hline & 0x - y + z = 4 \quad \boxed{4} \end{array}$$

Now subtract equation [3] from equation [1] to eliminate x.

$$\begin{array}{lr} \boxed{1} & x + 2y + 3z = 9 \\ \boxed{3} & x + 4y - z = -5 \\ \hline & 0x - 2y + 4z = 14 \quad \boxed{5} \end{array}$$

This results in a system of two linear equations:

$$\begin{cases} -y + z = 4 & \boxed{4} \\ -2y + 4z = 14 & \boxed{5} \end{cases}$$

To solve this system, multiply equation [5] by $-\frac{1}{2}$ and add it to equation [4].

$$\begin{array}{llcl} \boxed{4} & -y + z = 4 & & -y + z = 4 \\ \boxed{5} & -\frac{1}{2}(-2y + 4z = 14) & \Rightarrow & y - 2z = -7 \\ & & & 0y - z = -3 \\ & & & z = 3 \end{array}$$

Substitute to solve for y and x.

$$\begin{array}{lclc} -y + z = 4 & [4] & x + 2y + 3z = 9 & [1] \\ -y + 3 = 4 & & x + 2(-1) + 3(3) = 9 & \\ y = -1 & & x = 2 & \end{array}$$

The solution to the system is the ordered triple $(2, -1, 3)$.

Your Turn

Solve the system using elimination.

4. $\begin{cases} x + 2y + z = 8 & \boxed{1} \\ 2x + y - z = 4 & \boxed{2} \\ x + y + 3z = 7 & \boxed{3} \end{cases}$

5. $\begin{cases} 2x - y - 3z = 1 & \boxed{1} \\ 4x + 3y + 2z = -4 & \boxed{2} \\ -3x + 2y + 5z = -3 & \boxed{3} \end{cases}$

Explain 3 Solving a System of Three Linear Equations Using Matrices

You can represent systems of three linear equations in a *matrix.* A **matrix** is a rectangular array of numbers enclosed in brackets. Matrices are referred to by size: an m-by-n matrix has m rows and n columns.

A system of three linear equations can be written in a 3-by-4 matrix by first rearranging the equations so all of the variables are to the left of the equals sign and the constant term is to the right. Each row now corresponds to an equation. Enter the coefficients of the variables in the equation as the first three numbers in the row. Enter the constant that was on the right side of the equation as the fourth number.

The system $\begin{cases} 2x + y + 3z = 20 \\ 5x + 2y + z = 21 \\ 3x - 2y + 7z = -9 \end{cases}$ is expressed as $\begin{bmatrix} 2 & 1 & 3 & 20 \\ 5 & 2 & 1 & 21 \\ 3 & -2 & 7 & -9 \end{bmatrix}$ in matrix form.

Gaussian Elimination is a formalized process of using matrices to eliminate two of the variables in each equation in the system. This results in an easy way to find the solution set. The process involves using *elementary row operations* to generate equivalent matrices that lead to a solution.

The **elementary row operations** are

(1) Multiplying a row by a constant – When performing row multiplication, the product of the original value and the constant replaces each value in the row.

(2) Adding two rows – In row addition, each value in the second row mentioned in the addition is replaced by the sum of the values in the equivalent column of the two rows being added. These operations can also be performed together.

The elimination can be continued past this point to a matrix in which the solutions can be simply read directly out of the matrix. You can use a graphing calculator to perform these operations. The commands are shown in the table.

Command	Meaning	Syntax
*row(	replace each value in the row indicated with the product of the current value and the given number	*row(value,matrix,row)
row+(	replace rowB with the sum of rowA and the current rowB	row+(matrix,rowA,rowB)
*row+(	replace rowB with the product of the given value and rowA added to the current value of rowB	*row+(value,matrix,rowA,rowB)

Example 3 **Solve the system of three linear equations using matrices.**

(A) $\begin{cases} -2x + y + 3z = 20 \\ -3x + 2y + z = 21 \\ 3x - 2y + 3z = -9 \end{cases}$

Input the system as a 3-by-4 matrix. Multiply the first row by –0.5. Enter the command into your calculator. Press enter to view the result.

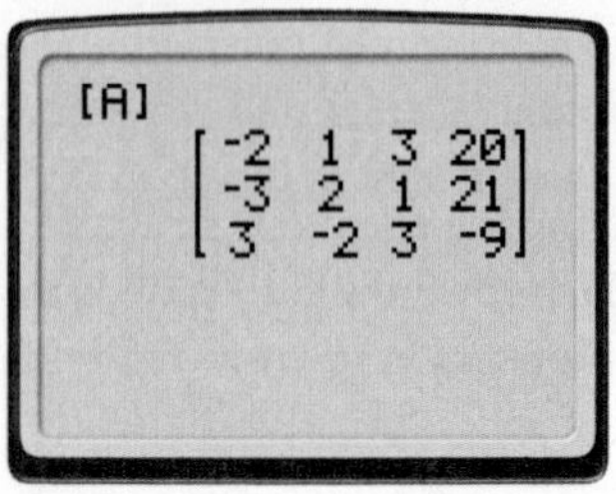

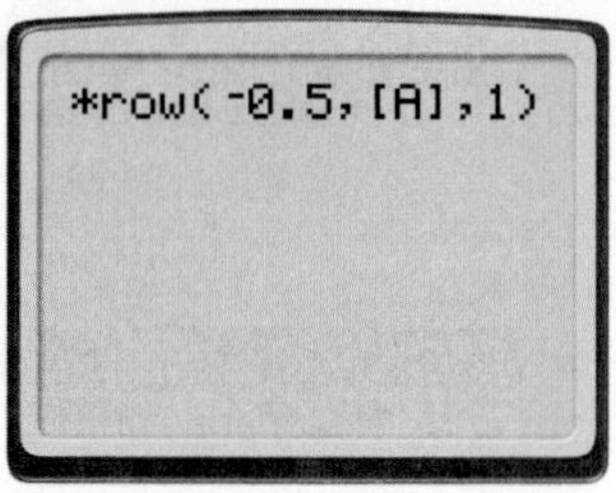

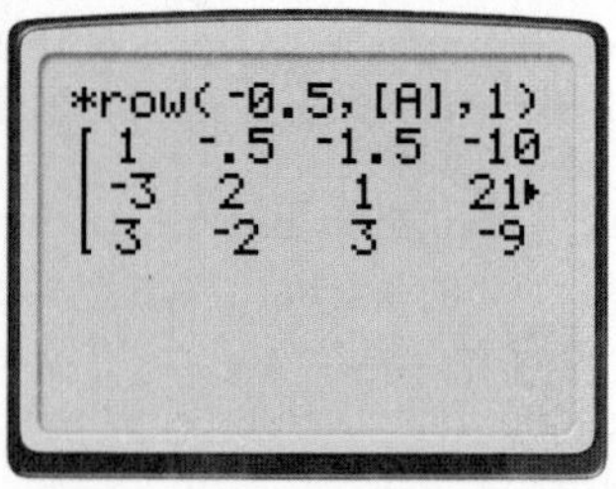

To reuse the resulting matrix, store it into Matrix B. Add 3 times row 1 to row 2. Press enter to view the result. Remember to store the result into a new matrix.

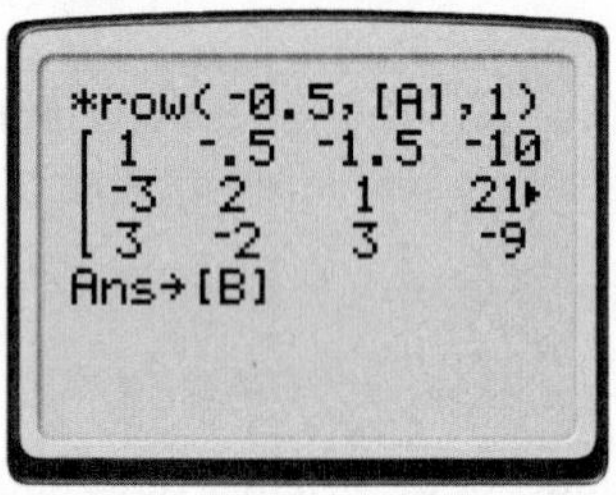

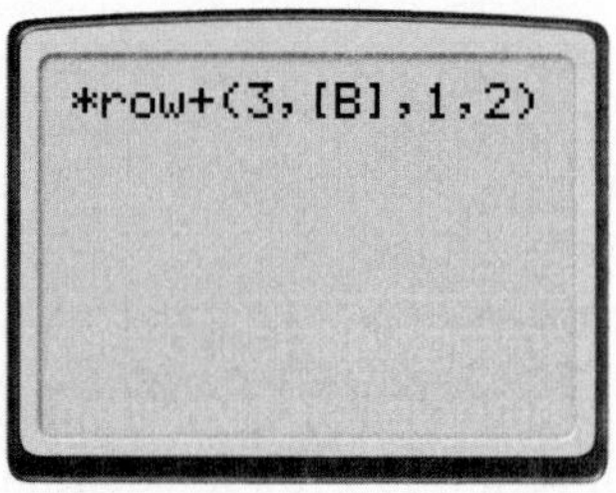

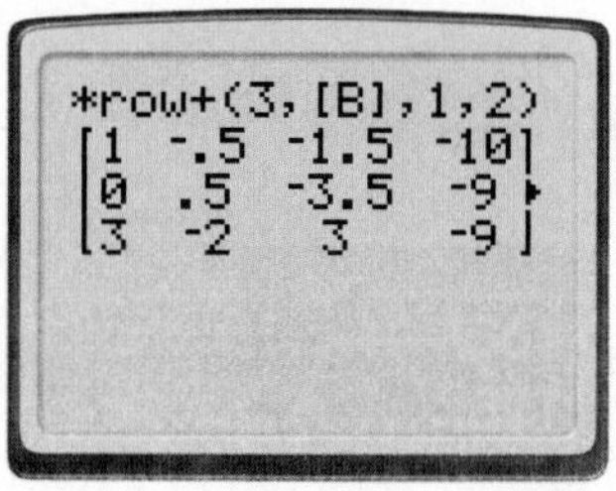

Multiply row 2 by 2.

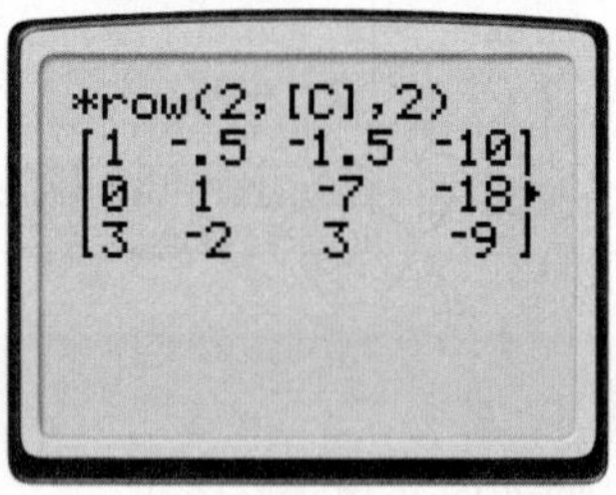

Add —3 times row 1 to row 3.

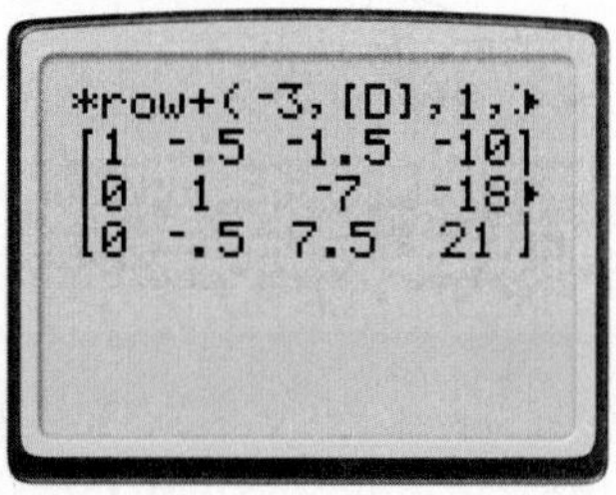

Add 0.5 times row 2 to row 3.

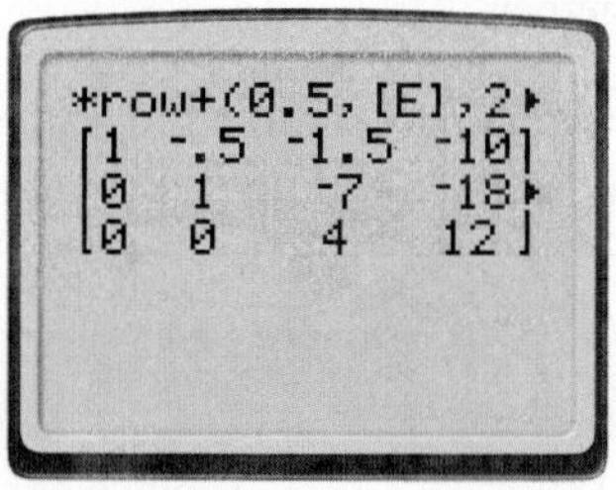

Multiply row 3 by 0.25.

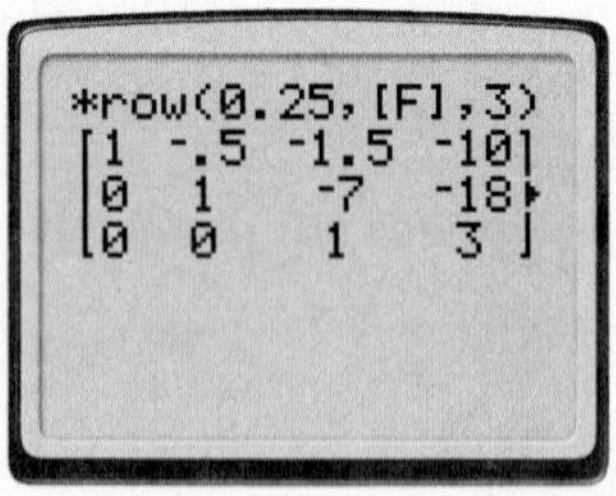

Add 7 times row 3 to row 2.

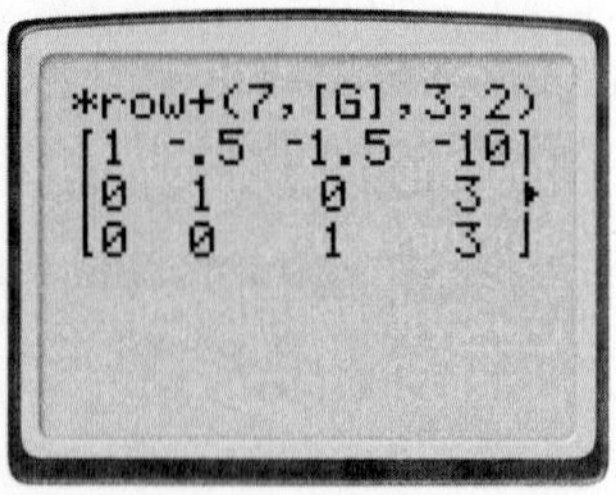

Add 1.5 times row 3 to row 1.

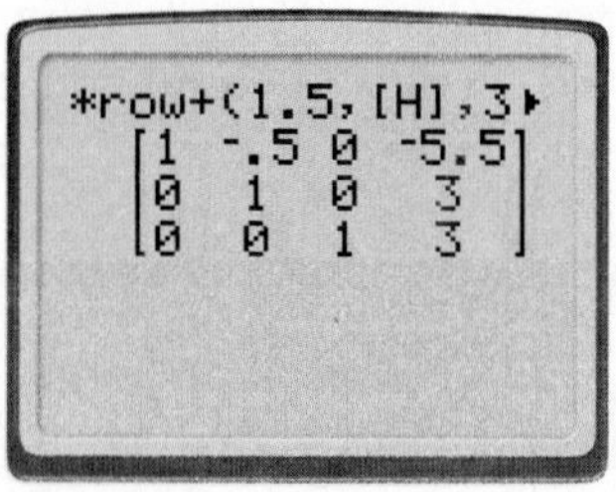

Add 0.5 times row 2 to row 1.

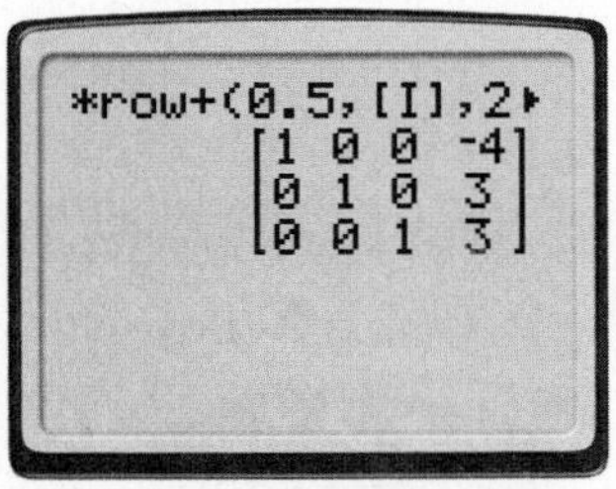

The first row tells us that $x = -4$, the second row tells us that $y = 3$, and the third row tells us that $z = 3$. So the solution is the ordered triple $(-4, 3, 3)$.

(B) $\begin{cases} x + 2y + 3z = 9 \\ x + 3y + 2z = 5 \\ x + 4y - z = -5 \end{cases}$

Write as a matrix. $\begin{bmatrix} 1 & 2 & 3 & 9 \\ 1 & 3 & 2 & 5 \\ 1 & 4 & -1 & -5 \end{bmatrix}$

Perform row operations.

$-r1 + r2$

$\begin{bmatrix} 1 & 2 & 3 & 9 \\ 0 & 1 & -1 & -4 \\ 1 & 4 & -1 & -5 \end{bmatrix}$

$-r1 + r3$

$\begin{bmatrix} 1 & 2 & 3 & 9 \\ 0 & 1 & -1 & -4 \\ 0 & 2 & -4 & -14 \end{bmatrix}$

$-2r2 + r3$

$\begin{bmatrix} 1 & 2 & 3 & 9 \\ 0 & 1 & -1 & -4 \\ 0 & 0 & -2 & -6 \end{bmatrix}$

$-0.5r3$

$\begin{bmatrix} 1 & 2 & 3 & 9 \\ 0 & 1 & -1 & -4 \\ 0 & 0 & 1 & 3 \end{bmatrix}$

$r3 + r2$

$\begin{bmatrix} 1 & 2 & 3 & 9 \\ 0 & 1 & 0 & -1 \\ 0 & 0 & 1 & 3 \end{bmatrix}$

$-3r3 + r1$

$\begin{bmatrix} 1 & 2 & 0 & 0 \\ 0 & 1 & 0 & -1 \\ 0 & 0 & 1 & 3 \end{bmatrix}$

$-2r2 + r1$

$\begin{bmatrix} 1 & 0 & 0 & 2 \\ 0 & 1 & 0 & -1 \\ 0 & 0 & 1 & 3 \end{bmatrix}$ The solution is the ordered triple $(2, -1, 3)$.

Your Turn

Solve the system of three linear equations using matrices.

6. $\begin{cases} x + 2y + z = 8 \\ 2x + y - z = 4 \\ x + y + 3z = 7 \end{cases}$

Explain 4 Solving a Real-World Problem

Example 4

(A) A child has \$6.17 in change in her piggy bank. The change consists of 113 coins in a mix of pennies, nickels, and quarters. If there are 8 times as many nickels as pennies, how many of each coin does the child have? Solve using substitution.

Begin by setting up a system of equations, and use p for the number of pennies, n for the number of nickels, and q for the number of quarters. Use the relationships in the problem statement to write the equations.

The total number of coins is the sum of the number of each coin. So, the first equation is $p + n + q = 113$.

The total value of the coins is \$6.17 or 617 cents (converting the value to cents will allow all coefficients to be integers). The second equation will be $p + 5n + 25q = 617$.

The third relationship given is that there are eight times as many nickels as pennies or, $n = 8p$. This gives the following system of equations:

$$\begin{cases} p + n + q = 113 & \boxed{1} \\ p + 5n + 25q = 617 & \boxed{2} \\ n = 8p & \boxed{3} \end{cases}$$

Equation $\boxed{3}$ is already solved for n. Substitute for n in equations $\boxed{1}$ and $\boxed{2}$ and simplify.

$$p + (8p) + q = 113$$
$$9p + q = 113 \quad \boxed{4}$$

$$p + 5(8p) + 25q = 617$$
$$p + 40p + 25q = 617$$
$$41p + 25q = 617 \quad \boxed{5}$$

This results in the following linear system in two variables:

$$\begin{cases} 9p + q = 113 & \boxed{4} \\ 41p + 25q = 617 & \boxed{5} \end{cases}$$

Solve equation $\boxed{4}$ for q.

$$9p + q = 113$$
$$q = 113 - 9p$$

Substitute for q in equation $\boxed{5}$ and solve for p.

$$41p + 25(113 - 9p) = 617$$
$$41p + 2825 - 225p = 617$$
$$12 = p$$

Use $p = 12$ to find q and n.

$$q = 113 - 9p \qquad n = 8p$$
$$q = 113 - 9(12) \qquad n = 8(12)$$
$$q = 5 \qquad n = 96$$

The child's piggy bank contains 12 pennies, 96 nickels, and 5 quarters.

(B) A student is shopping for clothes. The student needs to buy an equal number of shirts and ties. He also needs to buy four times as many shirts as pants. Shirts cost \$35, ties cost \$25, and pants cost \$40. If the student spends \$560, how many shirts, pants, and ties did he get?

Begin by setting up a system of equations, using s for the number of shirts, t for the number of ties, and p for the number pairs of pants. Use the relationships in the problem statement to write the equations.

The number of shirts is equal to the number of ties. So, the first equation is $s = t$.

The number of shirts is equal to 4 times the number of pairs of pants, so a second equation is $s =$ $4p$.

The total the student spent is the sum of the cost of the shirts, the ties, and the pairs of pants.

$35s + 25t + 40p =$ 560

The system of equations is below.

$$\begin{cases} s = t & \boxed{1} \\ s = 4p & \boxed{2} \\ 35s + 25t + 40p = 560 & \boxed{3} \end{cases}$$

Equation 1 is already solved for t. Solve equation 2 for p.

$4p = s$

$p = \frac{1}{4}s$

Substitute for p and t in equation 3 and solve for s.

$35s + 25(s) + 40\left(\frac{1}{4}s\right) = 560$

$35s + 25s + 10s = 560$

$70s = 560$

$s = 8$

Evaluate the equation solved for p above at $s = 8$ to find p.

$p = \frac{1}{4}s$

$p = \frac{1}{4}(8) = 2$

Recall that $s = t$, so $t = 8$.

The student bought 8 shirts, 8 ties, and 2 pairs of pants.

Your Turn

7. Louie Dampier is the leading scorer in the history of the American Basketball Association (ABA). His 13,726 points were scored on two-point baskets, three-point baskets, and one-point free throws. In his ABA career, Dampier made 2144 more two-point baskets than free throws and 1558 more free throws than three-point baskets. How many three-point baskets, two-point baskets, and free throws did Dampier make?

Elaborate

8. If you are given a system of linear equations in three variables, but the system only has two equations, what happens when you try to solve it?

9. **Discussion** Why does a system need to have at least as many equations as unknowns to have a unique solution?

10. **Essential Question Check-In** How can you find the solution to a system of three linear equations in three variables?

Evaluate: Homework and Practice

Solve the system using substitution.

1. $\begin{cases} 4x + y - 2z = -6 & \boxed{1} \\ 2x - 3y + 3z = 9 & \boxed{2} \\ x - 2y = 0 & \boxed{3} \end{cases}$

2. $\begin{cases} x + 5y + 3z = 4 & \boxed{1} \\ 4y - z = 3 & \boxed{2} \\ 6x - 2y + 4z = 0 & \boxed{3} \end{cases}$

Solve the system using elimination.

3. $\begin{cases} 4x + y - 2z = -6 & \boxed{1} \\ 2x - 3y + 3z = 9 & \boxed{2} \\ x - 2y = 0 & \boxed{3} \end{cases}$

4. $\begin{cases} x + 5y + 3z = 4 & \boxed{1} \\ 4y - z = 3 & \boxed{2} \\ 6x - 2y + 4z = 0 & \boxed{3} \end{cases}$

5. $\begin{cases} 2x - y + 3z = -12 & \boxed{1} \\ -x + 2y - 3z = 15 & \boxed{2} \\ y + 5z = -6 & \boxed{3} \end{cases}$

Solve the system of three linear equations using matrices.

6. $\begin{cases} 4x + y - 2z = -6 & \boxed{1} \\ 2x - 3y + 3z = 9 & \boxed{2} \\ x - 2y = 0 & \boxed{3} \end{cases}$

7. $\begin{cases} x + 5y + 3z = 4 & \boxed{1} \\ 4y - z = 3 & \boxed{2} \\ 6x - 2y + 4z = 0 & \boxed{3} \end{cases}$

Solve the system of linear equations using your method of choice.

8. $\begin{cases} 2x - y + 3z = 5 & \boxed{1} \\ -6x + 3y - 9z = -15 & \boxed{2} \\ 4x - 2y + 6z = 10 & \boxed{3} \end{cases}$

9. $\begin{cases} 3x + 4y - z = -7 & \boxed{1} \\ x - 5y + 2z = 19 & \boxed{2} \\ 5x + y - 2z = 5 & \boxed{3} \end{cases}$

10. Find the equation of the vertical parabola passing through the points $(3, 7)$, $(30, -11)$, and $(0, -1)$.

11. **Geometry** In triangle XYZ, the measure of angle X is eight times the sum of the measures of angles Y and Z. The measure of angle Y is three times the measure of angle Z. What are the measures of the angles?

12. The combined age of three relatives is 120 years. James is three times the age of Dan, and Paul is two times the sum of the ages of James and Dan. How old is each person?

13. **Economics** At a stock exchange there were a total of 10,000 shares sold in one day. Stock A had four times as many shares sold as Stock B. The number of shares sold for Stock C was equal to the sum of the numbers of shares sold for Stock A and Stock B. How many shares of each stock were sold?

H.O.T. Focus on Higher Order Thinking

14. **Communicate Mathematical Ideas** Explain how you know when a system has infinitely many solutions or when it has no solutions.

15. **Explain the Error** When given this system of equations, a student was asked to solve using matrices. Find and correct the student's error.

$$\begin{cases} 5x + 7y + 9z = 0 \\ x - y + z = -3 \\ 8x + y = 12 \end{cases}$$

$$\begin{bmatrix} 5 & 7 & 9 \\ 1 & -1 & 1 \\ 8 & 1 & 0 \end{bmatrix}$$

16. **Critical Thinking** Explain why the following system of equations cannot be solved.

$$\begin{cases} 7x + y + 6z = 1 \\ -x - 4y + 8z = 9 \end{cases}$$

Lesson Performance Task

A company that manufactures inline skates needs to order three parts—part *A*, part *B*, and part *C*. For one shipping order the company needs to buy a total of 6000 parts. There are four times as many *B* parts as *C* parts. The total number of *A* parts is one-fifth the sum of the *B* and *C* parts. On previous orders, the costs had been \$0.25 for part *A*, \$0.50 for part *B*, and \$0.75 for part *C*, resulting in a cost of \$3000 for all the parts in one order. When filling out an order for new parts, the company sees that it now costs \$0.60 for part *A*, \$0.40 for part *B*, and \$0.60 for part *C*. Will the company be able to buy the same quantity of parts at the same price as before with the new prices?

STUDY GUIDE REVIEW

Quadratic Relations and Systems of Equations

MODULE 4

Essential Question: How can you use systems of equations to solve real-world problems?

Key Vocabulary

directrix *(directriz)*

focus of a parabola *(foco de una parábola)*

linear equation in three variables *(ecuación lineal en tres variables)*

matrix *(matriz)*

ordered triple *(tripleta ordenada)*

KEY EXAMPLE *(Lesson 4.1)*

Write the equation of a circle that has a center at (–3, 5) and a radius of 9.

$(x-h)^2+(y-k)^2=r^2$	The standard form of the equation of a circle
$h=-3$	x-coordinate of center
$k=5$	y-coordinate of center
$r=9$	radius
$(x-(-3))^2+(y-5)^2=9^2$	Substitute.
$(x+3)^2+(y-5)^2=81$	Simplify.

KEY EXAMPLE *(Lesson 4.3)*

Solve the system using elimination.

$$\begin{cases} 5x+y=10 \\ y+2=3(x+4)^2 \end{cases}$$

$y-10=-5x$ First, line up the terms.

$y+2=3(x+4)^2$

$y-10=-5x$ Subtract the second equation from the first.

$$\begin{array}{r} y-10=-5x \\ \underline{\cancel{-y}+(-2)=-3(x+4)^2} \\ -12=5x-3(x+4)^2 \end{array}$$

$-12=5x-3(x+4)^2$

$-12=5x-3x^2-24x-48$

$0=-3x^2-19x-36$ Solve the resulting equation for x.

$$x=\frac{19\pm\sqrt{(-19)^2-4(-3)(-36)}}{2(-3)}$$

$$x=\frac{19\pm i\sqrt{71}}{-6}$$

There is no real number equivalent, so the system has no solution.

EXERCISES

Find the equation of the circle with the given characteristics. *(Lessons 4.1)*

1. Center: (3, 4)

Radius: 6

2. Center: (−7.5, 15)

Radius: 1.5

Find the center and radius of the given circle. *(Lessons 4.1)*

3. $(x-5)^2+(y-8)^2=144$

4. $x^2+(y+6)^2=50$

Find the solution to the system of equations using graphing or elimination. *(Lessons 4.2, 4.3, 4.4)*

5. $\begin{cases} 4x+3y=1 \\ y=x^2-x-1 \end{cases}$

6. $\begin{cases} x-3y=2 \\ y=x^2+2x-34 \end{cases}$

7. $\begin{cases} 3x+5y-2z=-7 \\ -2x+7y+6z=-3 \\ 8x+3y-10z=-11 \end{cases}$

8. $\begin{cases} 3x+24y+9z=9 \\ x-8y-3z=37 \\ 2x-16y-6z=75 \end{cases}$

MODULE PERFORMANCE TASK

How Can You Hit a Moving Target with a Laser Beam?

A video game designer is creating a game similar to skeet shooting, where a player will use a laser beam to hit a virtual clay disk launched into the air. The disk is launched from the ground and, if nothing blows it up, it reaches a maximum height of 30 meters and returns to the ground 60 meters away. The laser is fired from a height of 5 meters above the ground. Where should the designer point the laser to hit the disk at its maximum height?

As you complete the task, be sure to write down all your data and assumptions. Then use graphs, numbers, words, or algebra to explain how you reached your conclusion.

Ready to Go On?

4.1–4.4 Quadratic Relations and Systems of Equations

Personal Math Trainer

- Online Homework
- Hints and Help
- Extra Practice

Find the equation of the circle with the given characteristics. *(Lessons 4.1)*

1. Center: (0, –2)

Radius: 1

2. Center: (–4, 4.5)

Radius: 16

Find the center and radius of the given circle. *(Lesson 4.1)*

3. $x^2 + y^2 = 25$

4. $(x - 18)^2 + (y + 18)^2 = 70$

Solve the system of equations using any method. *(Lessons 4.3, 4.4)*

5. $\begin{cases} y + 12 = 4x \\ y - 20 = x^2 - 8x \end{cases}$

6 $\begin{cases} y = x + 2 \\ 2y - 12 = 2x^2 - 8x \end{cases}$

7. $\begin{cases} x + y + z = 9 \\ x - 8y - z = -27 \\ 2x - y + z = 6 \end{cases}$

8. $\begin{cases} -3x - 12y - 3z = 0 \\ x + 4y + z = 10 \\ -2x - 8y - 2z = -34 \end{cases}$

ESSENTIAL QUESTION

9. Describe a real world situation that might involve three linear equations in three variables. *(Lesson 4.4)*

MODULE 4
MIXED REVIEW

Assessment Readiness

1. Look at each focus and directrix. Is the resulting parabola horizontal? Write Yes or No for A–C.

A. Focus $(-5, 0)$, Directrix $x = 5$

B. Focus $(4, 0)$, Directrix $x = -4$

C. Focus $(0, -3)$, Directrix $y = 3$

2. Consider the system of equations $\begin{cases} y = x^2 + 6x + 10 \\ y + 6 = 2x \end{cases}$. Tell whether each statement is correct.

A. Another way to write this system is $\begin{cases} y = x^2 + 6x + 10 \\ y = 2x - 6 \end{cases}$.

B. The only way to solve this system is by graphing.

C. There is only one solution to the system, $(-4, 2)$.

3. Explain how a system of three equations in three variables can have infinitely many solutions.

4. Robin solved a quadratic equation using the process shown. Describe and correct her mistake.

$$0 = \frac{x^2}{4} - 2x + 7$$

$$x = \frac{-(-2) \pm \sqrt{(-2)^2 - 4\left(\frac{1}{4}\right)(7)}}{2(1/4)}$$

$$= \frac{2 \pm \sqrt{-4 - 7}}{\frac{1}{2}}$$

$$= 4 \pm 2\sqrt{-11}$$

$$= 4 \pm 2i\sqrt{11}$$

UNIT 2 MIXED REVIEW

Assessment Readiness

Personal Math Trainer

- Online Homework
- Hints and Help
- Extra Practice

1. Consider the function $f(x) = 3(x - 7)^2 + 2$. Determine if each statement is True or False.

A. The axis of symmetry for $f(x)$ is $x = 7$.

B. The range is $\left\{ y \mid y \in \Re \right\}$.

C. The vertex of $f(x)$ is $(7, -2)$.

2. Tell whether each quadratic equation has real roots.

A. $x^2 - 25 = 0$

B. $-\frac{1}{2}x^2 - 3 = 0$

C. $3x^2 - 4 = 2$

3. Consider the equation $3x^2 - 12x + 15 = 0$. Determine if each statement is True or False.

A. If solving this equation using factoring, then $(x - 5)(x + 1) = 0$.

B. After completing the square, $x = -2 \pm \sqrt{11}$.

C. To solve this equation using complete the square, $\left(\frac{b}{2}\right)^2 = \left(\frac{-4}{2}\right)^2 = 4$.

4. Consider the system of equations $\begin{cases} y = 2x^2 - 3x + 5 \\ y - 3 = x \end{cases}$. Determine if each statement is True or False.

A. The only way to solve this equation is by elimination.

B. Another way to write this system is $\begin{cases} y = 2x^2 - 3x + 5 \\ y = x + 3 \end{cases}$

C. There are three possible solutions to the system.

5. Look at each focus and directrix. Is the resulting parabola vertical? Write Yes or No for A–C.

A. Focus $(6, -3)$, Directrix $x = 2$

B. Focus $(-4, -2)$, Directrix $y = -3$

C. Focus $(0, 1)$, Directrix $y = 2$

6. Marcia shoots an arrow that hits a bull's–eye 80 feet away. The release point and bull's–eye are at the same height. Before hitting the bull's–eye, the arrow reaches a maximum height of 4 feet above its release point. If the bull's–eye is considered to be at (80, 0), what function (in standard form) could represent the path of the arrow if x is the horizontal distance from Marcia and y represents the height of the arrow in relation to its release point? How high is the arrow above its release point after traveling 20 feet horizontally? Explain.

7. Consider the equation $-4x^2 + x = 3$. What method should be used to most easily solve the equation if you have a choice between taking the square root, completing the square, using the quadratic formula, or factoring? Explain your reasoning, and then solve the equation.

8. Ronald says $f(x) = 0.5x + 1.5$ is the inverse of $g(x) = -1.5x + 4$. Is Ronald's answer correct? Explain why or why not.

Performance Tasks

★ 9. Keille is building a rectangular pen for a pet rabbit. She can buy wire fencing in a roll of 40 ft or a roll of 80 ft. The graph shows the area of pens she can build with each type of roll.

A. Describe the function for an 80 ft roll of fencing as a transformation of the function for a 40 ft roll of fencing.

B. Is the largest pen Keille can build with an 80 ft roll of fencing twice as large as the largest pen she can build with a 40 ft roll of fencing? Explain.

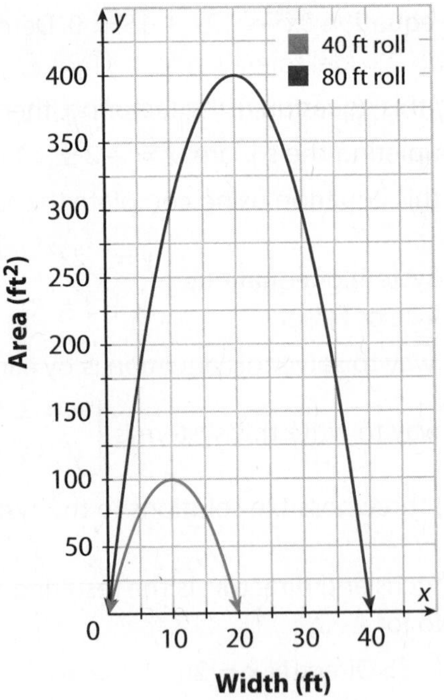

★★10. The spittlebug is the world's highest-jumping animal relative to its body length of about 6 millimeters. The height h of a spittlebug's jump in millimeters can be modeled by the function $h(t) = -4000t^2 + 3000t$, where t is the time in seconds.

A. What is the maximum height that the spittlebug will reach?

B. What is the ratio of a spittlebug's maximum jumping height to its body length? In the best human jumpers, this ratio is about 1.38 to 1. Compare the ratio for spittlebugs with the ratio for the best human jumpers.

★★★11. The light produced by high-pressure sodium vapor streetlamps for different energy usages is shown in the table.

High-Pressure Sodium Vapor Streetlamps					
Energy Use (watts)	35	50	70	100	150
Light Output (lumens)	2250	4000	5800	9500	16,000

A. Find a quadratic model for the light output with respect to energy use.

B. Find a linear model for the light output with respect to energy use.

C. Apply each model to estimate the light output in lumens of a 200-watt bulb.

D. Which model gives the better estimate? Explain.

MATH IN CAREERS

Toy Manufacturer A company is marketing a new toy. The function $s(p) = -50p^2 + 3000p$ models how the total sales s of the toy, in dollars, depends on the price p of the toy, in dollars.

a. Complete the square to write the function in vertex form.

b. Graph the function. Be sure to label the axes with the quantities they represent and indicate the axis scales by showing numbers for some grid lines.

c. What is the vertex of the graph? What does the vertex represent in this situation?

d. The model predicts that total sales will be \$40,000 when the toy price is \$20. At what other price does the model predict that the total sales will be \$40,000? Use the symmetry of the graph to support your answer.

e. According to the model, at what nonzero price should the manufacturer expect to sell no toys? How can you determine this price using the graph?

UNIT 3

Polynomial Functions, Expressions, and Equations

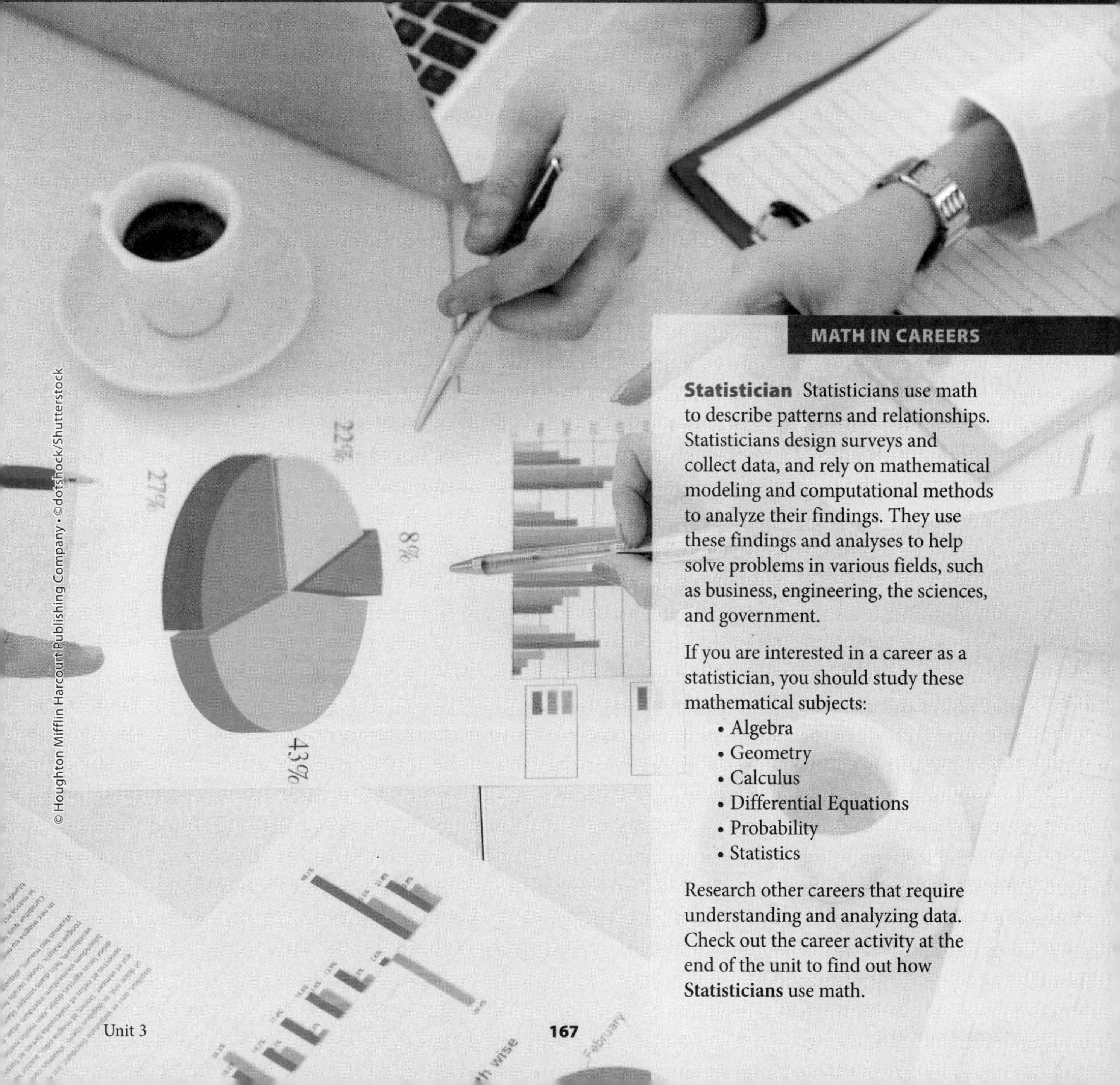

MATH IN CAREERS

Statistician Statisticians use math to describe patterns and relationships. Statisticians design surveys and collect data, and rely on mathematical modeling and computational methods to analyze their findings. They use these findings and analyses to help solve problems in various fields, such as business, engineering, the sciences, and government.

If you are interested in a career as a statistician, you should study these mathematical subjects:

- Algebra
- Geometry
- Calculus
- Differential Equations
- Probability
- Statistics

Research other careers that require understanding and analyzing data. Check out the career activity at the end of the unit to find out how **Statisticians** use math.

Reading Start-Up

Vocabulary

Review Words

- ✔ coefficient *(coeficiente)*
- ✔ factor *(factor)*
- ✔ parameter *(parámetro)*
- ✔ real number *(número real)*
- ✔ term *(término)*
- ✔ transformation *(transformación)*

Preview Words

binomial *(binomio)*
cubic function *(función cúbica)*
monomial *(monomio)*
polynomial *(polinomio)*
root *(raíz)*
trinomial *(trinomio)*

Visualize Vocabulary

Use the review words to complete the chart.

?	a number or expression that divides a product exactly.
?	a rational or irrational number
?	a number, variable, product, or quotient in an expression
?	one of the constants in a function or equation that may be changed
?	a change in the size, position, or shape of a figure or graph
?	a numerical factor in a term of an algebraic expression

Understand Vocabulary

To become familiar with some of the vocabulary terms in the module, consider the following. You may refer to the module, the glossary, or a dictionary.

1. A polynomial with two terms is a __?__.

2. A polynomial function of degree 3 is a __?__.

3. A __?__ of a polynomial is a zero of the function associated with that polynomial.

Active Reading

Key-Term Fold Before beginning the unit, create a key-term fold to help you organize what you learn. Write a vocabulary term on each tab of the key-term fold. Under each tab, write the definition of the term and an example.

Polynomial Functions

MODULE 5

Essential Question: How can polynomial functions help to solve real-world problems?

REAL WORLD VIDEO
Engineers who design roller coasters use mathematics, including polynomial functions, to model the shape of the track.

MODULE PERFORMANCE TASK PREVIEW

What's the Function of a Roller Coaster?

Nothing compares with riding a roller coaster. The thrill of a steep drop, the breathtaking speed, and the wind in your face make the ride unforgettable. How can a polynomial function model the path of a roller coaster? Hang on to your seat and let's find out!

Are YOU Ready?

Complete these exercises to review skills you will need for this module.

Personal Math Trainer

- Online Homework
- Hints and Help
- Extra Practice

Classifying Polynomials

Example 1 Classify the polynomial $2x^4 + x^3 - 1$ by its degree and number of terms.

Because the greatest exponent is 4, this is a quartic polynomial.

Because the polynomial has three terms, it is a trinomial.

The polynomial $2x^4 + x^3 - 1$ is a quartic trinomial.

Classify the polynomial by its degree and number of terms.

1. $3x^3$

2. $9x - 3y + 7$

3. $x^2 - 4$

4. $x^5 + x^4$

5. $5x^3 - 7y^2 + 2$

6. x

Transforming Cubic Functions

Example 2 The graph of $f(x) = 0.5(x - 3)^3 + 2$ is transformed 4 units right and 5 units down. Write the new function.

The inflection point is $(3, 2)$. Its location after the transformation is $(3 + 4, 2 - 5)$, or $(7, -3)$.

After the transformation, the function is $f'(x) = 0.5(x - 7)^3 - 3$.

Write the new function after the given transformation.

7. $g(x) = 0.25(x - 6)^3 - 1$
10 units left, 7 units down

8. $h(x) = (x + 9)^3 - 5$
6 units right, 4 units up

9. $f(x) = -0.5(x + 8)^3 + 12$
1 unit left, 3 units up

10. $f(x) = x^3$
3 units right, 2 units up

11. $g(x) = 5(x + 1)^3 - 4$
1 unit right, 4 units up

12. $h(x) = (x - 5)^3 + 5$
0.5 unit right, 1.5 units down

5.1 Graphing Cubic Functions

Essential Question: How are the graphs of $f(x) = a(x-h)^3 + k$ and $f(x) = \left(\frac{1}{b}(x-h)\right)^3 + k$ related to the graph of $f(x) = x^3$?

Resource Locker

Explore 1 Graphing and Analyzing $f(x) = x^3$

You know that a quadratic function has the standard form $f(x) = ax^2 + bx + c$ where a, b, and c are real numbers and $a \neq 0$. Similarly, a **cubic function** has the standard form $f(x) = ax^3 + bx^2 + cx + d$ where a, b, c and d are all real numbers and $a \neq 0$. You can use the basic cubic function, $f(x) = x^3$, as the parent function for a family of cubic functions related through transformations of the graph of $f(x) = x^3$.

(A) Complete the table, graph the ordered pairs, and then draw a smooth curve through the plotted points to obtain the graph of $f(x) = x^3$.

x	$y = x^3$
−2	?
−1	?
0	?
1	?
2	?

(B) Use the graph to analyze the function and complete the table.

Attributes of $f(x) = x^3$	
Domain	$\mathbb{R}$
Range	?
End behavior	As $x \to +\infty$, $f(x) \to$? . As $x \to -\infty$, $f(x) \to$? .
Zeros of the function	$x = 0$
Where the function has positive values	$x > 0$
Where the function has negative values	?
Where the function is increasing	?
Where the function is decreasing	The function never decreases.
Is the function even $(f(-x) = f(x))$, odd $(f(-x) = -f(x))$, or neither?	? , because $(x)^3 =$? .

Reflect

1. How would you characterize the rate of change of the function on the intervals $[-1, 0]$ and $[0, 1]$ compared with the rate of change on the intervals $[-2, -1]$ and $[1, 2]$? Explain.

2. A graph is said to be *symmetric about the origin* (and the origin is called the graph's *point of symmetry*) if for every point (x, y) on the graph, the point $(-x, -y)$ is also on the graph. Is the graph of $f(x) = x^3$ symmetric about the origin? Explain.

3. The graph of $g(x) = (-x)^3$ is a reflection of the graph of $f(x) = x^3$ across the y-axis, while the graph of $h(x) = -x^3$ is a reflection of the graph of $f(x) = x^3$ across the x-axis. If you graph $g(x)$ and $h(x)$ on a graphing calculator, what do you notice? Explain why this happens.

Explain 1 Graphing Combined Transformations of $f(x) = x^3$

When graphing transformations of $f(x) = x^3$, it helps to consider the effect of the transformations on the three reference points on the graph of $f(x)$: $(-1, -1)$, $(0, 0)$, and $(1,1)$. The table lists the three points and the corresponding points on the graph of $g(x) = a\left(\frac{1}{b}(x - h)\right)^3 + k$. Notice that the point $(0, 0)$, which is the point of symmetry for the graph of $f(x)$, is affected only by the parameters h and k. The other two reference points are affected by all four parameters.

$f(x) = x^3$		$g(x) = a\left(\frac{1}{b}(x-h)\right)^3 + k$	
x	y	x	y
-1	-1	$-b + h$	$-a + k$
0	0	h	k
1	1	$b + h$	$a + k$

Example 1 **Identify the transformations of the graph of $f(x) = x^3$ that produce the graph of the given function $g(x)$. Then graph $g(x)$ on the same coordinate plane as the graph of $f(x)$ by applying the transformations to the reference points $(-1, -1)$, $(0, 0)$, and $(1, 1)$.**

(A) $g(x) = 2(x - 1)^3 - 1$

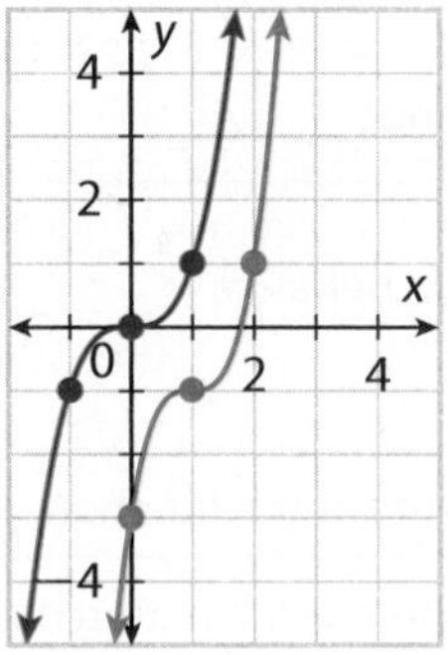

The transformations of the graph of $f(x)$ that produce the graph of $g(x)$ are:

- a vertical stretch by a factor of 2
- a translation of 1 unit to the right and 1 unit down

Note that the translation of 1 unit to the right affects only the x-coordinates of points on the graph of $f(x)$, while the vertical stretch by a factor of 2 and the translation of 1 unit down affect only the y-coordinates.

$f(x) = x^3$		$g(x) = 2(x-1)^3 - 1$	
x	y	x	y
-1	-1	$-1 + 1 = \mathbf{0}$	$2(-1) - 1 = -3$
0	0	$0 + 1 = 1$	$2(0) - 1 = -1$
1	1	$1 + 1 = 2$	$2(1) - 1 = 1$

Ⓑ $g(x) = \left(2(x+3)\right)^3 + 4$

The transformations of the graph of $f(x)$ that produce the graph of $g(x)$ are:

- a horizontal compression by a factor of $\frac{1}{2}$
- a translation of 3 units to the left and 4 units up

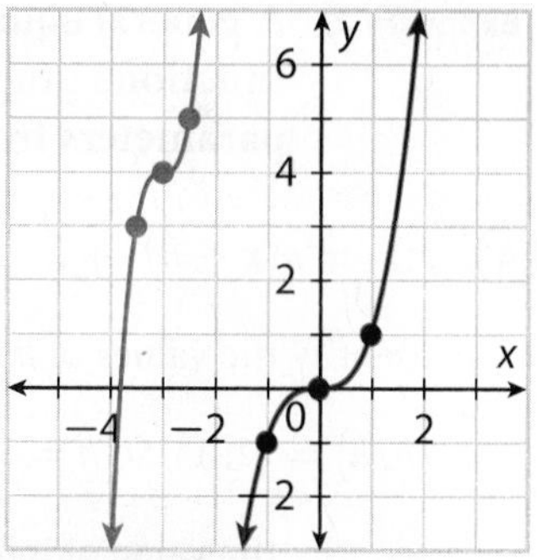

Note that the horizontal compression by a factor of $\frac{1}{2}$ and the translation of 3 units to the left affect only the x-coordinates of points on the graph of $f(x)$, while the translation of 4 units up affects only the y-coordinates.

$f(x) = x^3$		$g(x) = \left(2(x+3)\right)^3 + 4$	
x	y	x	y
−1	−1	$\frac{1}{2}(-1) + -3 = -3\frac{1}{2}$	$-1 + 4 = 3$
0	0	$\frac{1}{2}(0) + -3 = -3$	$0 + 4 = 4$
1	1	$\frac{1}{2}(1) + -3 = -2\frac{1}{2}$	$1 + 4 = 5$

Your Turn

Identify the transformations of the graph of $f(x) = x^3$ that produce the graph of the given function $g(x)$. Then graph $g(x)$ on the same coordinate plane as the graph of $f(x)$ by applying the transformations to the reference points $(-1, -1)$, $(0, 0)$, and $(1, 1)$.

4. $g(x) = -\frac{1}{2}(x-3)^3$

Explain 2 Writing Equations for Combined Transformations of $f(x) = x^3$

Given the graph of the transformed function $g(x) = a\left(\frac{1}{b}(x-h)\right)^3 + k$, you can determine the values of the parameters by using the same reference points that you used to graph $g(x)$ in the previous example.

Example 2 **A general equation for a cubic function $g(x)$ is given along with the function's graph. Write a specific equation by identifying the values of the parameters from the reference points shown on the graph.**

(A) $g(x) = a(x - h)^3 + k$

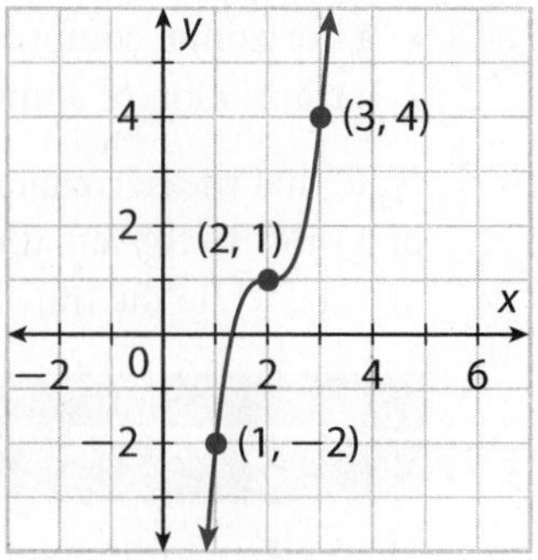

Identify the values of h and k from the point of symmetry.

$(h, k) = (2, 1)$, so $h = 2$ and $k = 1$.

Identify the value of a from either of the other two reference points.

The rightmost reference point has general coordinates $(h + 1, a + k)$. Substituting 2 for h and 1 for k and setting the general coordinates equal to the actual coordinates gives this result:

$(h + 1, a + k) = (3, a + 1) = (3, 4)$, so $a = 3$.

Write the function using the values of the parameters: $g(x) = 3(x - 2)^3 + 1$

(B) $g(x) = \left(\frac{1}{b}(x - h)\right)^3 + k$

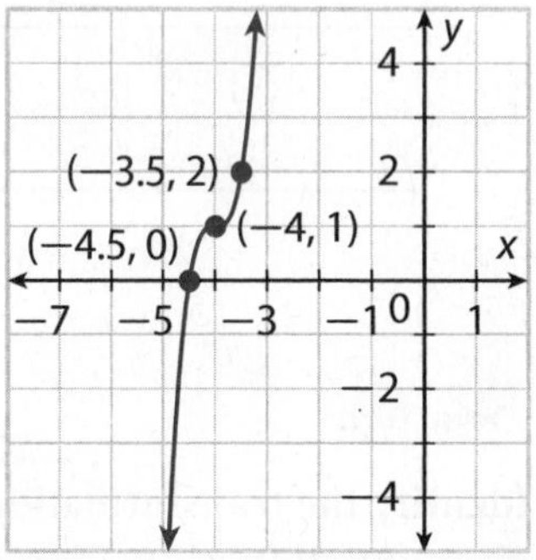

Identify the values of h and k from the point of symmetry.

$(h, k) = \left(-4, \boxed{1}\right)$, so $h = -4$ and $k = \boxed{1}$.

Identify the value of b from either of the other two reference points.

The rightmost reference point has general coordinates

$(b + h, 1 + k)$. Substituting -4 for h and 1 for k and setting the general coordinates equal to the actual coordinates gives this result:

$\left(b + h, 1 + \boxed{1}\right) = \left(b - 4, \boxed{2}\right) = (-3.5, 2)$, so $b = \boxed{0.5}$.

Write the function using the values of the parameters, and then simplify.

$$g(x) = \left(\frac{1}{\boxed{0.5}}\left(x - \boxed{-4}\right)\right)^3 + \boxed{1}$$

or

$$g(x) = \left(\boxed{2}\left(x + \boxed{4}\right)\right)^3 + \boxed{1}$$

Your Turn

A general equation for a cubic function $g(x)$ is given along with the function's graph. Write a specific equation by identifying the values of the parameters from the reference points shown on the graph.

5. $g(x) = a(x - h)^3 + k$

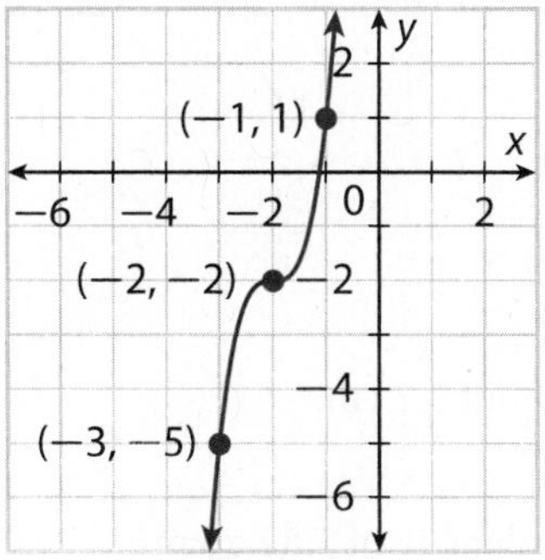

6. $g(x) = \left(\frac{1}{b}(x - h)\right)^3 + k$

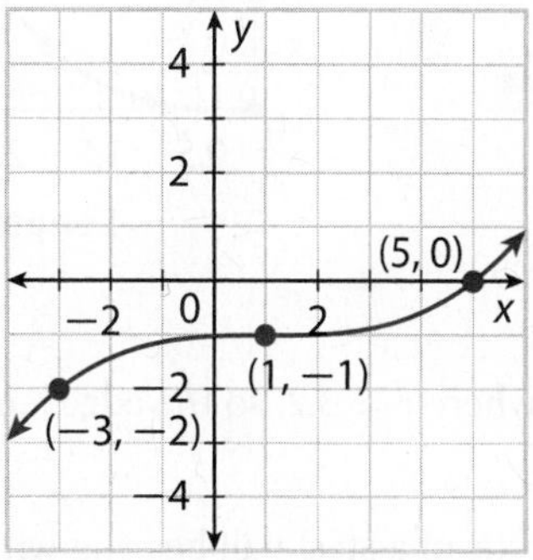

Explain 3 Modeling with a Transformation of $f(x) = x^3$

You may be able to model a real-world situation that involves volume with a cubic function. Sometimes mass may also be involved in the problem. Mass and volume are related through *density*, which is defined as an object's mass per unit volume. If an object has mass m and volume V, then its density d is $d = \frac{m}{V}$. You can rewrite the formula as $m = dV$ to express mass in terms of density and volume.

Example 3 **Use a cubic function to model the situation, and graph the function using calculated values of the function. Then use the graph to obtain the indicated estimate.**

(A) Estimate the length of an edge of a child's alphabet block (a cube) that has a mass of 23 g and is made from oak with a density of 0.72 g/cm³.

Let ℓ represent the length (in centimeters) of an edge of the block. Since the block is a cube, the volume V (in cubic centimeters) is $V(\ell) = \ell^3$. The mass m (in grams) of the block is $m(\ell) = 0.72 \cdot V(\ell) = 0.72\ell^3$. Make a table of values for this function.

Length (cm)	Mass (g)
0	0
1	0.72
2	5.76
3	19.44
4	46.08

Draw the graph of the mass function, recognizing that the graph is a vertical compression of the graph of the parent cubic function by a factor of 0.72. Then draw the horizontal line $m = 23$ and estimate the value of ℓ where the graphs intersect.

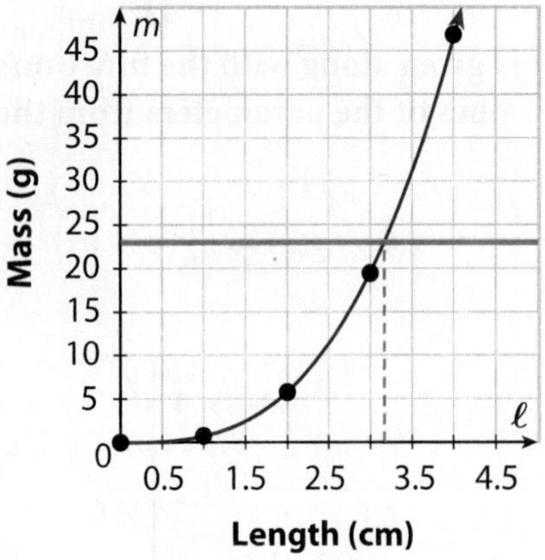

The graphs intersect where $\ell \approx 3.2$, so the edge length of the child's block is about 3.2 cm.

(B) Estimate the radius of a steel ball bearing with a mass of 75 grams and a density of 7.82 g/cm³.

Let r represent the radius (in centimeters) of the ball bearing.

The volume V (in cubic centimeters) of the ball bearing is $V(r) = \frac{4}{3}\pi\ r^3$. The mass m (in grams) of the ball bearing is $m(r) = 7.82 \cdot V(r) =$ 32.76 r^3.

Radius (cm)	Mass (g)
0	0
0.5	4.10
1	32.76
1.5	110.57
2	262.08

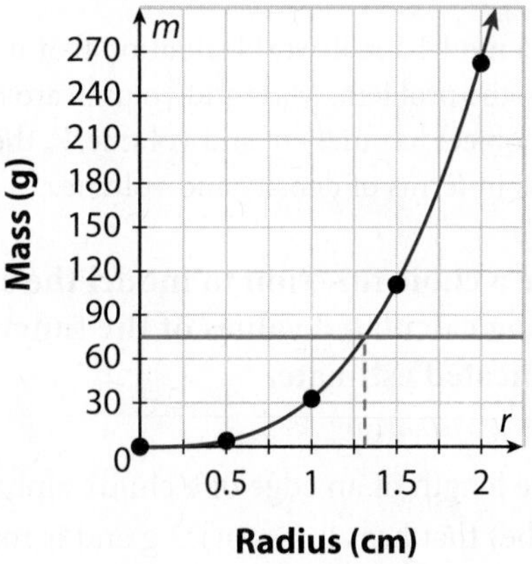

Draw the graph of the mass function, recognizing that the graph is a vertical stretch of the graph of the parent cubic function by a factor of 7.82. Then draw the horizontal line $m =$ 75 and estimate the value of r where the graphs intersect.

The graphs intersect where $r \approx$ 1.3, so the radius of the steel ball bearing is about 1.3 cm.

Reflect

7. Discussion Why is it important to plot multiple points on the graph of the volume function?

Your Turn

Use a cubic function to model the situation, and graph the function using calculated values of the function. Then use the graph to obtain the indicated estimate.

8. Polystyrene beads fill a cube-shaped box with an effective density of 0.00076 kg/cm³ (which accounts for the space between the beads). The filled box weighs 6 kilograms while the empty box had weighed 1.5 kilograms. Estimate the inner edge length of the box.

Elaborate

9. Identify which transformations (stretches or compressions, reflections, and translations) of $f(x) = x^3$ change the following attributes of the function.

a. End behavior

b. Location of the point of symmetry

c. Symmetry about a point

10. Essential Question Check-In Describe the transformations you must perform on the graph of $f(x) = x^3$ to obtain the graph of $g(x) = a(x - h)^3 + k$.

Evaluate: Homework and Practice

Personal Math Trainer
- Online Homework
- Hints and Help
- Extra Practice

1. Graph the parent cubic function $f(x) = x^3$ and use the graph to answer each question.

a. State the function's domain and range.

b. Identify the function's end behavior.

c. Identify the graph's x- and y-intercepts.

d. Identify the intervals where the function has positive values and where it has negative values.

e. Identify the intervals where the function is increasing and where it is decreasing.

f. Tell whether the function is even, odd, or neither. Explain.

g. Describe the graph's symmetry.

Describe how the graph of $g(x)$ is related to the graph of $f(x) = x^3$.

2. $g(x) = (x - 4)^3$

3. $g(x) = -5x^3$

4. $g(x) = x^3 + 2$

5. $g(x) = (3x)^3$

6. $g(x) = (x + 1)^3$

7. $g(x) = \frac{1}{4}x^3$

8. $g(x) = x^3 - 3$

9. $g(x) = \left(-\frac{2}{3}x\right)^3$

Identify the transformations of the graph of $f(x) = x^3$ that produce the graph of the given function $g(x)$. Then graph $g(x)$ on the same coordinate plane as the graph of $f(x)$ by applying the transformations to the reference points $(-1, -1)$, $(0, 0)$, and $(1, 1)$.

10. $g(x) = \left(\frac{1}{3}x\right)^3$

11. $g(x) = \frac{1}{3}x^3$

12. $g(x) = (x - 4)^3 - 3$

13. $g(x) = (x + 1)^3 + 2$

A general equation for a cubic function $g(x)$ is given along with the function's graph. Write a specific equation by identifying the values of the parameters from the reference points shown on the graph.

14. $g(x) = \left(\frac{1}{b}(x - h)\right)^3 + k$

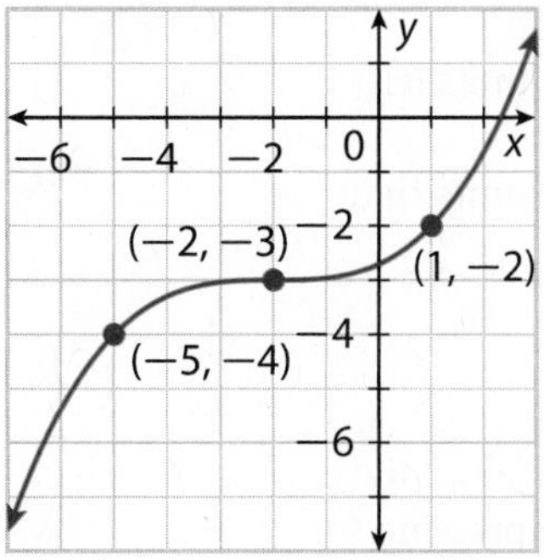

15. $g(x) = a(x - h)^3 + k$

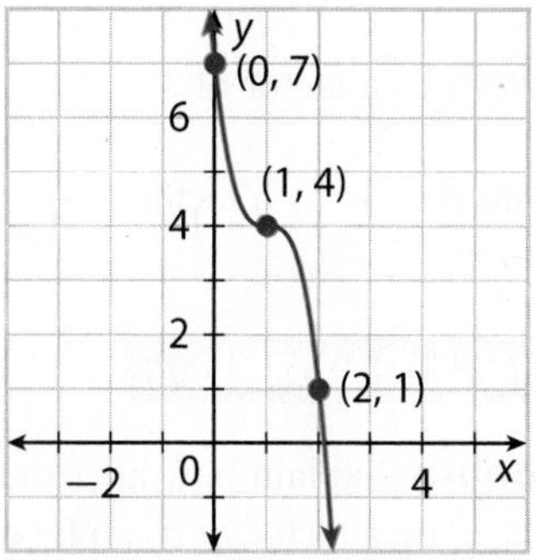

16. $g(x) = \left(\frac{1}{b}(x - h)\right)^3 + k$

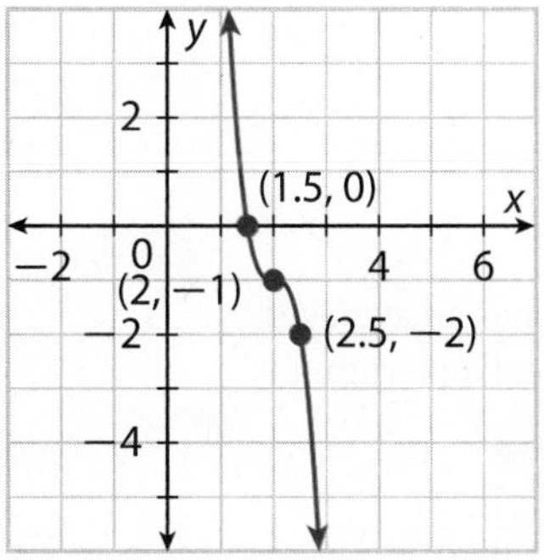

17. $g(x) = a(x - h)^3 + k$

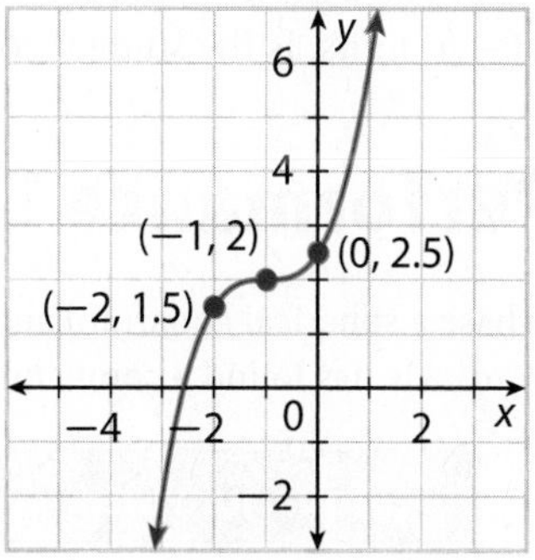

Use a cubic function to model the situation, and graph the function using calculated values of the function. Then use the graph to obtain the indicated estimate.

18. Estimate the edge length of a cube of gold with a mass of 1 kg. The density of gold is 0.019 kg/cm^3.

19. A proposed design for a habitable Mars colony is a hemispherical biodome used to maintain a breathable atmosphere for the colonists. Estimate the radius of the biodome if it is required to contain 5.5 billion cubic feet of air.

20. Multiple Response Select the transformations of the graph of the parent cubic function that result in the graph of $g(x) = \left(3(x-2)\right)^3 + 1$.

A. Horizontal stretch by a factor of 3

B. Horizontal compression by a factor of $\frac{1}{3}$

C. Vertical stretch by a factor of 3

D. Vertical compression by a factor of $\frac{1}{3}$

E. Translation 1 unit up

F. Translation 1 unit down

G. Translation 2 units left

H. Translation 2 units right

H.O.T. Focus on Higher Order Thinking

21. Justify Reasoning Explain how horizontally stretching (or compressing) the graph of $f(x) = x^3$ by a factor of b can be equivalent to vertically compressing (or stretching) the graph of $f(x) = x^3$ by a factor of a.

22. Critique Reasoning A student reasoned that $g(x) = (x - h)^3$ can be rewritten as $g(x) = x^3 - h^3$, so a horizontal translation of h units is equivalent to a vertical translation of $-h^3$ units. Is the student correct? Explain.

Lesson Performance Task

Julio wants to purchase a spherical aquarium and fill it with salt water, which has an average density of 1.027 g/cm^3. He has found a company that sells four sizes of spherical aquariums.

Aquarium Size	Diameter (cm)
Small	15
Medium	30
Large	45
Extra large	60

a. If the stand for Julio's aquarium will support a maximum of 50 kg, what is the largest size tank that he should buy? Explain your reasoning.

b. Julio's friend suggests that he could buy a larger tank if he uses fresh water, which has a density of 1.0 g/cm^3. Do you agree with the friend? Why or why not?

5.2 Graphing Polynomial Functions

Essential Question: How do you sketch the graph of a polynomial function in intercept form?

Resource Locker

Explore 1 Investigating the End Behavior of the Graphs of Simple Polynomial Functions

Linear, quadratic, and cubic functions belong to a more general class of functions called *polynomial functions*, which are categorized by their degree. Linear functions are polynomial functions of degree 1, quadratic functions are polynomial functions of degree 2, and cubic functions are polynomial functions of degree 3. In general, a **polynomial function of degree *n*** has the standard form $p(x) = a_n x^n + a_{n-1}x^{n-1} + ... + a_2 x^2 + a_1 x + a_0$, where $a_n, a_{n-1}, ..., a_2, a_1$, and a_0 are real numbers called the *coefficients* of the expressions $a_n x^n, a_{n-1}x^{n-1}, ..., a_2 x^2, a_1 x$, and a_0, which are the *terms* of the polynomial function. (Note that the constant term, a_0, appears to have no power of x associated with it, but since $x^0 = 1$, you can write a_0 as $a_0 x^0$ and treat a_0 as the coefficient of the term.)

A polynomial function of degree 4 is called a *quartic* function, while a polynomial function of degree 5 is called a *quintic* function. After degree 5, polynomial functions are generally referred to by their degree, as in "a sixth-degree polynomial function."

(A) Use a graphing calculator to graph the polynomial functions $f(x) = x$, $f(x) = x^2$, $f(x) = x^3$, $f(x) = x^4$, $f(x) = x^5$, and $f(x) = x^6$. Then use the graph of each function to determine the function's domain, range, and end behavior. (Use interval notation for the domain and range.)

Function	Domain	Range	End Behavior
$f(x) = x$	?	?	As $x \to +\infty$, $f(x) \to$? . As $x \to -\infty$, $f(x) \to$? .
$f(x) = x^2$	?	?	As $x \to +\infty$, $f(x) \to$? . As $x \to -\infty$, $f(x) \to$? .
$f(x) = x^3$	?	?	As $x \to +\infty$, $f(x) \to$? . As $x \to -\infty$, $f(x) \to$? .
$f(x) = x^4$	?	?	As $x \to +\infty$, $f(x) \to$? . As $x \to -\infty$, $f(x) \to$? .
$f(x) = x^5$	?	?	As $x \to +\infty$, $f(x) \to$? . As $x \to -\infty$, $f(x) \to$? .
$f(x) = x^6$	?	?	As $x \to +\infty$, $f(x) \to$? . As $x \to -\infty$, $f(x) \to$? .

Ⓑ Use a graphing calculator to graph the polynomial functions $f(x) = -x$, $f(x) = -x^2$, $f(x) = -x^3$, $f(x) = -x^4$, $f(x) = -x^5$, and $f(x) = -x^6$. Then use the graph of each function to determine the function's domain, range, and end behavior. (Use interval notation for the domain and range.)

Function	Domain	Range	End Behavior
$f(x) = -x$	?	?	As $x \to +\infty$, $f(x) \to$? . As $x \to -\infty$, $f(x) \to$? .
$f(x) = -x^2$	?	?	As $x \to +\infty$, $f(x) \to$? . As $x \to -\infty$, $f(x) \to$? .
$f(x) = -x^3$	?	?	As $x \to +\infty$, $f(x) \to$? . As $x \to -\infty$, $f(x) \to$? .
$f(x) = -x^4$	?	?	As $x \to +\infty$, $f(x) \to$? . As $x \to -\infty$, $f(x) \to$? .
$f(x) = -x^5$	?	?	As $x \to +\infty$, $f(x) \to$? . As $x \to -\infty$, $f(x) \to$? .
$f(x) = -x^6$	?	?	As $x \to +\infty$, $f(x) \to$? . As $x \to -\infty$, $f(x) \to$? .

Reflect

1. How can you generalize the results of this Explore for $f(x) = x^n$ and $f(x) = -x^n$ where n is positive whole number?

Explore 2 Investigating the x-intercepts and Turning Points of the Graphs of Polynomial Functions

The cubic function $f(x) = x^3$ has three factors, all of which happen to be x. One or more of the x's can be replaced with other linear factors in x, such as $x - 2$, without changing the fact that the function is cubic. In general, a polynomial function of the form $p(x) = a(x - x_1)(x - x_2)...(x - x_n)$ where $a, x_1, x_2,...,$ and x_n are real numbers (that are not necessarily distinct) has degree n where n is the number of variable factors.

The graph of $p(x) = a(x - x_1)(x - x_2)...(x - x_n)$ has $x_1, x_2,...,$ and x_n as its x-intercepts, which is why the polynomial is said to be in *intercept form.* Since the graph of $p(x)$ intersects the x-axis only at its x-intercepts, the graph must move away from and then move back toward the x-axis between each pair of successive x-intercepts, which means that the graph has a *turning point* between those x-intercepts. Also, instead of crossing the x-axis at an x-intercept, the graph can be *tangent* to the x-axis, and the point of tangency becomes a turning point because the graph must move toward the x-axis and then away from it near the point of tangency.

The y-coordinate of each turning point is a maximum or minimum value of the function at least near that turning point. A maximum or minimum value is called *global* or *absolute* if the function never takes on a value that is greater than the maximum or less than the minimum. A *local maximum* or *local minimum*, also called a *relative maximum* or *relative minimum*, is a maximum or minimum within some interval around the turning point that need not be (but may be) a global maximum or global minimum.

(A) Use a graphing calculator to graph the cubic functions $f(x) = x^3$, $f(x) = x^2(x - 2)$, and $f(x) = x(x - 2)(x + 2)$. Then use the graph of each function to answer the questions in the table.

Function	$f(x) = x^3$	$f(x) = x^2(x - 2)$	$f(x) = x(x - 2)(x + 2)$
How many distinct factors does $f(x)$ have?	?	?	?
What are the graph's x-intercepts?	?	?	?
Is the graph tangent to the x-axis or does it cross the x-axis at each x-intercept?	?	?	?
How many turning points does the graph have?	?	?	?
How many global maximum values? How many local maximum values that are not global?	?	?	?
How many global minimum values? How many local minimum values that are not global?	?	?	?

Ⓑ Use a graphing calculator to graph the quartic functions $f(x) = x^4$, $f(x) = x^3(x - 2)$, $f(x) = x^2(x - 2)(x + 2)$, and $f(x) = x(x - 2)(x + 2)(x + 3)$. Then use the graph of each function to answer the questions in the table.

Function	$f(x) = x^4$	$f(x) = x^3(x - 2)$	$f(x) = x^2(x - 2)(x + 2)$	$f(x) = x(x - 2)(x + 2)(x + 3)$
How many distinct factors?	?	?	?	?
What are the x-intercepts?	?	?	?	?
Tangent to or cross the x-axis at x-intercepts?	?	?	?	?
How many turning points?	?	?	?	?
How many global maximum values? How many local maximum values that are not global?	?	?	?	?
How many global minimum values? How many local minimum values that are not global?	?	?	?	?

Reflect

2. What determines how many x-intercepts the graph of a polynomial function in intercept form has?

3. What determines whether the graph of a polynomial function in intercept form crosses the x-axis or is tangent to it at an x-intercept?

4. Suppose you introduced a factor of -1 into each of the quartic functions in Step B. (For instance, $f(x) = x^4$ becomes $f(x) = -x^4$.) How would your answers to the questions about the functions and their graphs change?

Explain 1 Sketching the Graph of Polynomial Functions in Intercept Form

Given a polynomial function in intercept form, you can sketch the function's graph by using the end behavior, the x-intercepts, and the sign of the function values on intervals determined by the x-intercepts. The sign of the function values tells you whether the graph is above or below the x-axis on a particular interval. You can find the sign of the function values by determining the sign of each factor and recognizing what the sign of the product of those factors is.

Example 1 **Sketch the graph of the polynomial function.**

Ⓐ $f(x) = x(x + 2)(x - 3)$

Identify the end behavior. For the function $p(x) = a(x - x_1)(x - x_2)\ldots(x - x_n)$, the end behavior is determined by whether the degree n is even or odd and whether the constant factor a is positive or negative. For the given function $f(x)$, the degree is 3 and the constant factor a, which is 1, is positive, so $f(x)$ has the following end behavior:

As $x \to +\infty$, $f(x) \to +\infty$.

As $x \to -\infty$, $f(x) \to -\infty$.

Identify the graph's x-intercepts, and then use the sign of $f(x)$ on intervals determined by the x-intercepts to find where the graph is above the x-axis and where it's below the x-axis.

The x-intercepts are $x = 0$, $x = -2$, and $x = 3$. These three x-intercepts divide the x-axis into four intervals: $x < -2$, $-2 < x < 0$, $0 < x < 3$, and $x > 3$.

Interval	Sign of the Constant Factor	Sign of x	Sign of $x+2$	Sign of $x-3$	Sign of $f(x) = x(x+2)(x-3)$
$x < -2$	+	−	−	−	−
$-2 < x < 0$	+	−	+	−	+
$0 < x < 3$	+	+	+	−	−
$x > 3$	+	+	+	+	+

So, the graph of $f(x)$ is above the x-axis on the intervals $-2 < x < 0$ and $x > 3$, and it's below the x-axis on the intervals $x < -2$ and $0 < x < 3$.

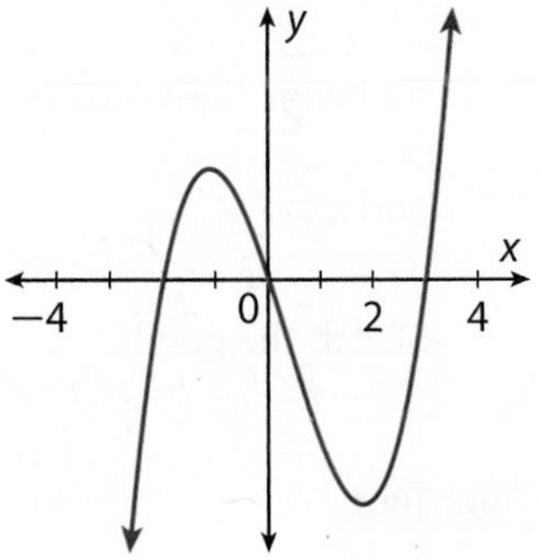

Sketch the graph.

While you should be precise about where the graph crosses the x-axis, you do not need to be precise about the y-coordinates of points on the graph that aren't on the x-axis. Your sketch should simply show where the graph lies above the x-axis and where it lies below the x-axis.

(B) $f(x) = -(x - 4)(x - 1)(x + 1)(x + 2)$

Identify the end behavior.

As $x \to +\infty$, $f(x) \to$ $-\infty$.

As $x \to -\infty$, $f(x) \to$ $-\infty$.

Identify the graph's x-intercepts, and then use the sign of $f(x)$ on intervals determined by the x-intercepts to find where the graph is above the x-axis and where it's below the x-axis.

The x-intercepts are $x =$ -2 , $x =$ -1 , $x =$ 1 , $x =$ 4 .

Interval	Sign of the Constant Factor	Sign of $x-4$	Sign of $x-1$	Sign of $x+1$	Sign of $x+2$	Sign of $f(x)=-(x-4)(x-1)(x+1)(x+2)$
$x< -2$	−	−	−	−	−	−
$-2<x< -1$	−	−	−	−	+	+
$-1<x< 1$	−	−	−	+	+	−
$1<x< 4$	−	−	+	+	+	+
$x> 4$	−	+	+	+	+	−

So, the graph of $f(x)$ is above the x-axis on the intervals

$-2 < x < -1$ and $1 < x < 4$, and

it's below the x-axis on the intervals $x < -2$, $-1 < x < 1$,

and $x > 4$.

Sketch the graph.

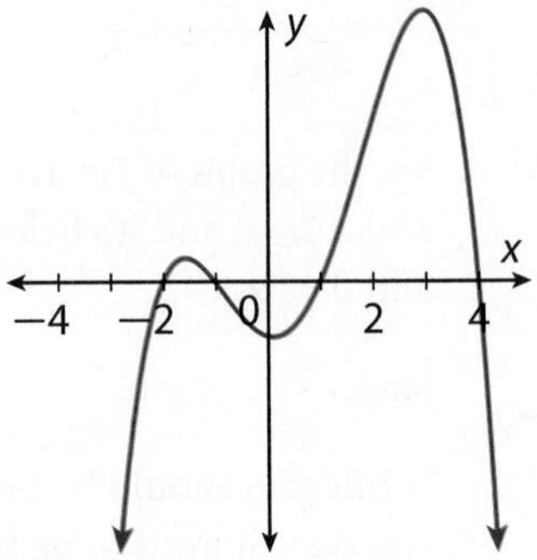

Your Turn

Sketch the graph of the polynomial function

5. $f(x) = -x^2(x-4)$

Explain 2 Modeling with a Polynomial Function

You can use cubic functions to model real-world situations. For example, you find the volume of a box (a rectangular prism) by multiplying the length, width, and height. If each dimension of the box is given in terms of x, then the volume is a cubic function of x.

Example 2

To create an open-top box out of a sheet of cardboard that is 9 inches long and 5 inches wide, you make a square flap of side length x inches in each corner by cutting along one of the flap's sides and folding along the other side. (In the first diagram, a solid line segment in the interior of the rectangle indicates a cut, while a dashed line segment indicates a fold.) After you fold up the four sides of the box (see the second diagram), you glue each flap to the side it overlaps. To the nearest tenth, find the value of x that maximizes the volume of the box.

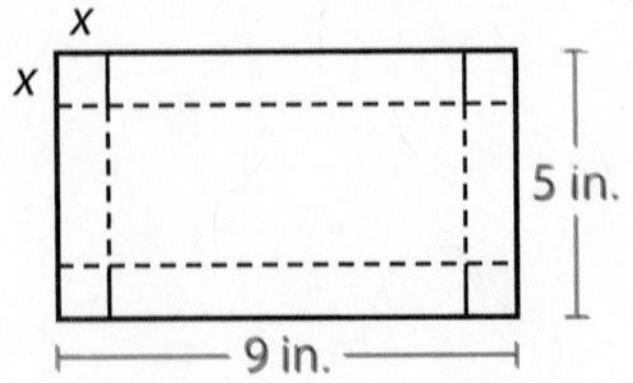

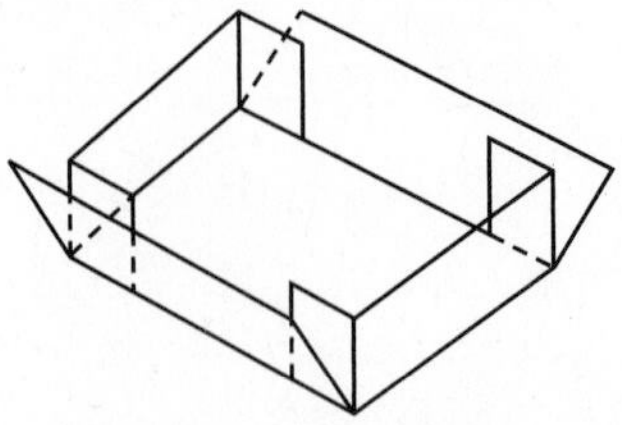

Analyze Information

Identify the important information.

A square flap of side length x inches is made in each corner of a rectangular sheet of cardboard.

The sheet of cardboard measures 9 inches by 5 inches.

Formulate a Plan

Find the dimensions of the box once the flaps have been made and the sides have been folded up. Create a volume function for the box, graph the function on a graphing calculator, and use the graph to find the value of x that maximizes the volume.

Solve

1. Write expressions for the dimensions of the box.

Length of box: $9 - 2x$

Width of box: $5 - 2x$

Height of box: x

2. Write the volume function and determine its domain.

$$V(x) = (9 - 2x)(5 - 2x)x$$

Because the length, width, and height of the box must all be positive, the volume function's domain is determined by the following three constraints:

$9 - 2x > 0$, or $x < 4.5$

$5 - 2x > 0$, or $x < 2.5$

$x > 0$

Taken together, these constraints give a domain of $0 < x < 2.5$.

3. Use a graphing calculator to graph the volume function on its domain.

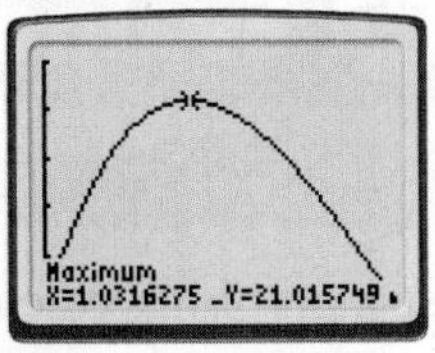

Adjust the viewing window so you can see the maximum. From the graphing calculator's **CALC** menu, select **4: maximum** to locate the point where the maximum value occurs.

So, $V(x) \approx 21.0$ when $x \approx 1.0$, which means that the box has a maximum volume of about 21 cubic inches when square flaps with a side length of 1 inch are made in the corners of the sheet of cardboard.

Justify and Evaluate

Making square flaps with a side length of 1 inch means that the box will be 7 inches long, 3 inches wide, and 1 inch high, so the volume is 21 cubic inches. As a check on this result, consider making square flaps with a side length of 0.9 inch and 1.1 inches:

$V(0.9) = (9 - 1.8)(5 - 1.8)(0.9) =$ 20.736

$V(1.1) = (9 - 2.2)(5 - 2.2)(1.1) =$ 20.944

Both volumes are slightly less than 21 cubic inches, which suggests that 21 cubic inches is the maximum volume.

Reflect

6. **Discussion** Although the volume function has three constraints on its domain, the domain involves only two of them. Why?

Your Turn

7. To create an open-top box out of a sheet of cardboard that is 25 inches long and 13 inches wide, you make a square flap of side length x inches in each corner by cutting along one of the flap's sides and folding along the other. (In the diagram, a solid line segment in the interior of the rectangle indicates a cut, while a dashed line segment indicates a fold.) Once you fold up the four sides of the box, you glue each flap to the side it overlaps. To the nearest tenth, find the value of x that maximizes the volume of the box.

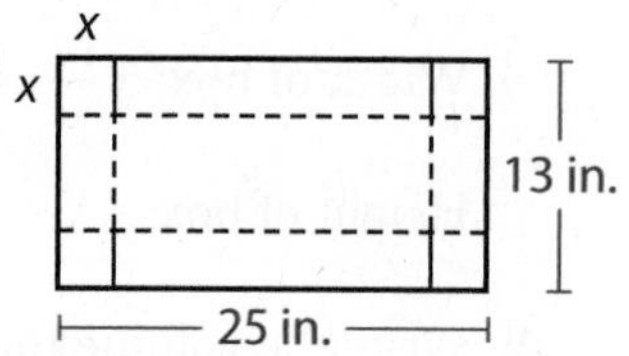

Elaborate

8. Compare and contrast the domain, range, and end behavior of $f(x) = x^n$ when n is even and when n is odd.

9. **Essential Question Check-In** For a polynomial function in intercept form, why is the constant factor important when graphing the function?

Evaluate: Homework and Practice

Personal Math Trainer

- Online Homework
- Hints and Help
- Extra Practice

Use a graphing calculator to graph the polynomial function. Then use the graph to determine the function's domain, range, and end behavior. (Use interval notation for the domain and range.)

1. $f(x) = x^7$

2. $f(x) = -x^9$

3. $f(x) = x^{10}$

4. $f(x) = -x^8$

Use a graphing calculator to graph the function. Then use the graph to determine the number of turning points and the number and type (global, or local but not global) of any maximum or minimum values.

5. $f(x) = x(x + 1)(x + 3)$

6. $f(x) = (x + 1)^2(x - 1)(x - 2)$

7. $f(x) = -x(x - 2)^2$

8. $f(x) = -(x - 1)(x + 2)^3$

Sketch the graph of the polynomial function.

9. $f(x) = x^2(x - 2)$

10. $f(x) = -(x + 1)(x - 2)(x - 3)$

11. $f(x) = x(x + 2)^2(x - 1)$

12. To create an open-top box out of a sheet of cardboard that is 6 inches long and 3 inches wide, you make a square flap of side length x inches in each corner by cutting along one of the flap's sides and folding along the other. Once you fold up the four sides of the box, you glue each flap to the side it overlaps. To the nearest tenth, find the value of x that maximizes the volume of the box.

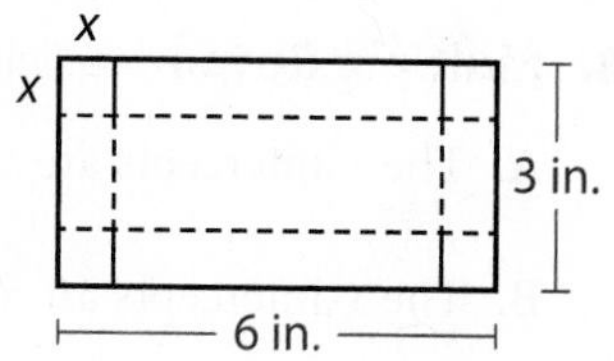

13. The template shows how to create a box from a square sheet of cardboard that has a side length of 36 inches. In the template, solid line segments indicate cuts, dashed line segments indicate folds, and grayed rectangles indicate pieces removed. The vertical strip that is 2 inches wide on the left side of the template is a flap that will be glued to the side of the box that it overlaps when the box is folded up. The horizontal strips that are $\frac{x}{2}$ inches wide at the top and bottom of the template are also flaps that will overlap to form the top and bottom of the box when the box is folded up. Write a volume function for the box in terms of x only. (You will need to determine a relationship between x and y first.) Then, to the nearest tenth, find the dimensions of the box with maximum volume.

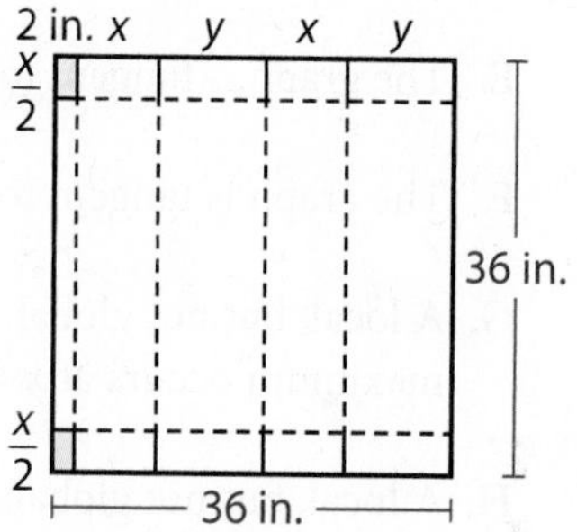

Write a cubic function in intercept form for the given graph, whose x-intercepts are integers. Assume that the constant factor a is either 1 or −1.

14.

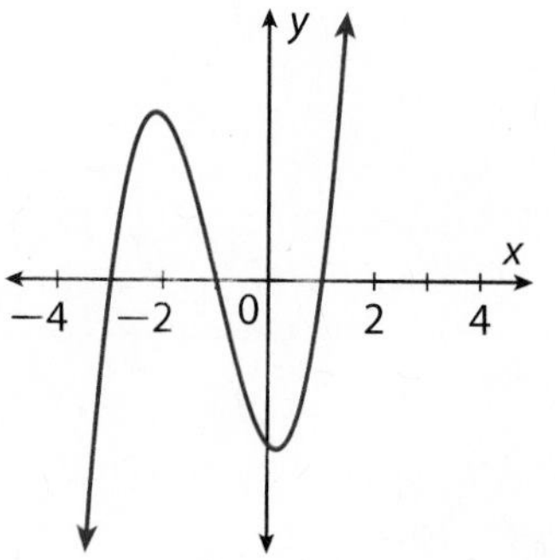

15.

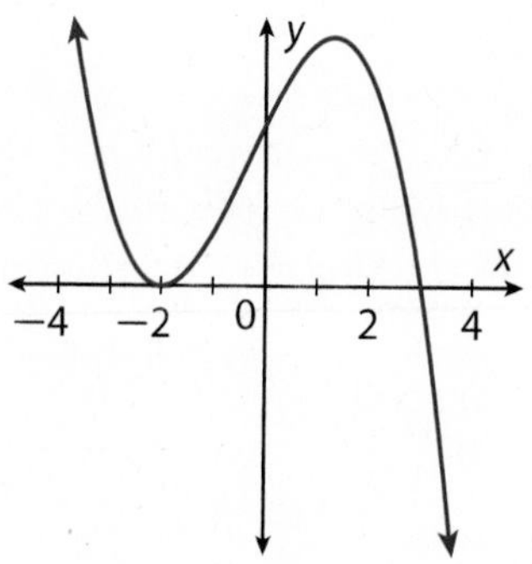

Write a quartic function in intercept form for the given graph, whose x-intercepts are integers. Assume that the constant factor a is either 1 or -1.

16.

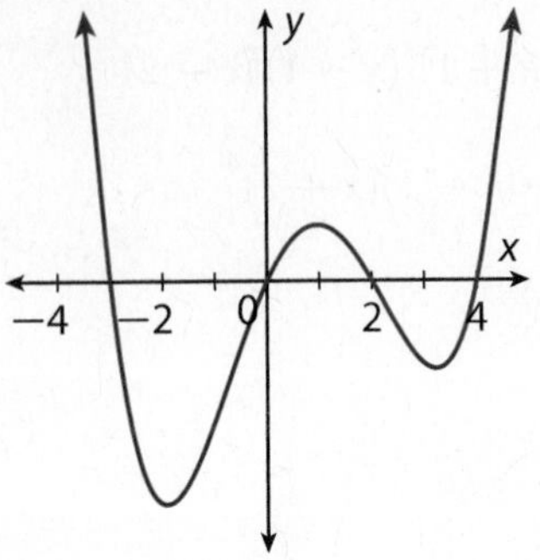

17.

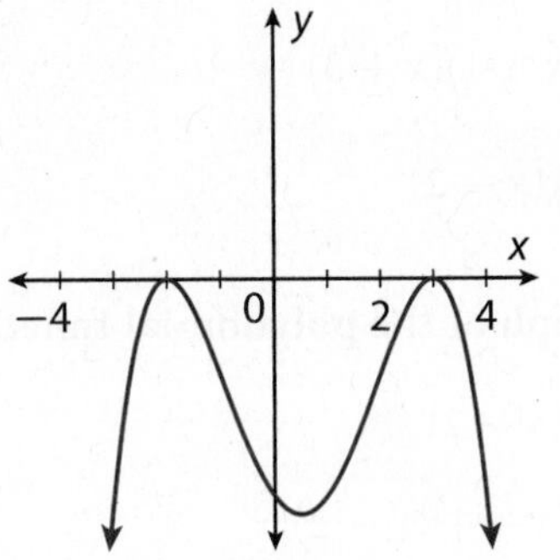

18. Multiple Response Select all statements that apply to the graph of $f(x) = (x - 1)^2(x + 2)$.

A. The x-intercepts are $x = 1$ and $x = -2$.

B. The x-intercepts are $x = -1$ and $x = 2$.

C. The graph crosses the x-axis at $x = 1$ and is tangent to the x-axis at $x = -2$.

D. The graph crosses the x-axis at $x = -1$ and is tangent to the x-axis at $x = 2$.

E. The graph is tangent to the x-axis at $x = 1$ and crosses the x-axis at $x = -2$.

F. The graph is tangent to the x-axis at $x = -1$ and crosses the x-axis at $x = 2$.

G. A local, but not global, minimum occurs on the interval $-2 < x < 1$, and a local, but not global, maximum occurs at $x = 1$.

H. A local, but not global, l maximum occurs on the interval $-2 < x < 1$, and a local, but not global, minimum occurs at $x = 1$.

I. A local, but not global, minimum occurs on the interval $-1 < x < 2$, and a local, but not global, maximum occurs at $x = 2$.

J. A local, but not global, maximum occurs on the interval $-1 < x < 2$, and a local, but not global, minimum occurs at $x = 2$.

H.O.T. Focus on Higher Order Thinking

19. Explain the Error A student was asked to sketch the graph of the function $f(x) = x^2(x - 3)$. Describe what the student did wrong. Then sketch the correct graph.

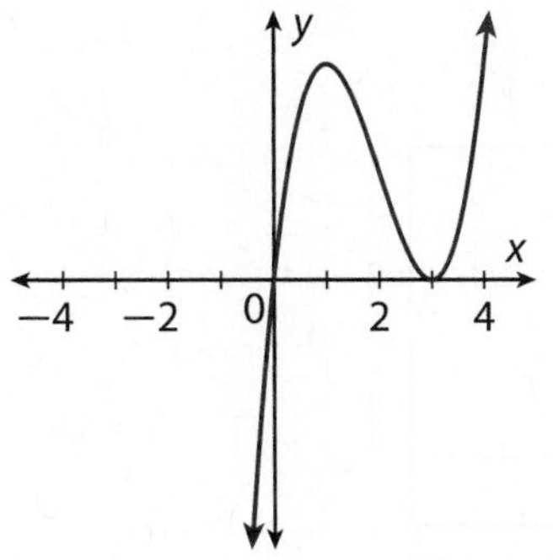

20. Make a Prediction Knowing the characteristics of the graphs of cubic and quartic functions in intercept form, sketch the graph of the quintic function $f(x) = x^2(x + 2)(x - 2)^2$.

21. Represent Real-World Situations A rectangular piece of sheet metal is rolled and riveted to form a circular tube that is open at both ends, as shown. The sheet metal has a perimeter of 36 inches. Each of the two sides of the rectangle that form the two ends of the tube has a length of x inches, but the tube has a circumference of $x - 1$ inches because an overlap of 1 inch is needed for the rivets. Write a volume function for the tube in terms of x. Then, to the nearest tenth, find the value of x that maximizes the volume of the tube.

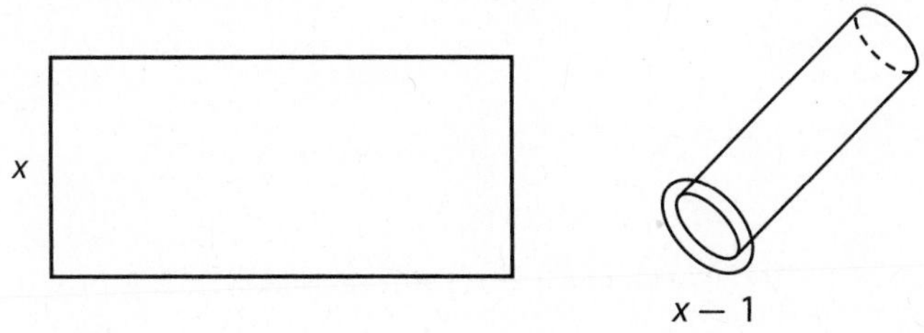

Lesson Performance Task

The template shows how to create a box with a lid from a sheet of card stock that is 10 inches wide and 24 inches long. In the template, solid line segments indicate cuts, and dashed line segments indicate folds. The square flaps, each with a side length of x inches, are glued to the sides they overlap when the box is folded up. The box has a bottom and four upright sides. The lid, which is attached to one of the upright sides, has three upright sides of its own. Assume that the three sides of the lid can be tucked inside the box when the lid is closed.

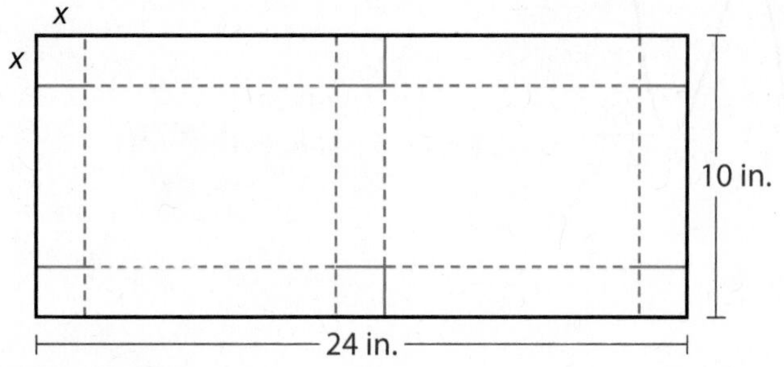

a. Write a polynomial function that represents the volume of the box, and state its domain.

b. Use a graphing calculator to find the value of x that will produce the box with maximum volume. What are the dimensions of that box?

Polynomial Functions

Essential Question: How can polynomial functions help to solve real-world problems?

Key Vocabulary
cubic function *(función cúbica)*
polynomial function *(función polinomial)*

KEY EXAMPLE *(Lesson 5.1)*

Identify the transformations of the graph $f(x) = x^3$ that produce the graph of the function $g(x) = \frac{1}{3}(x + 2)^3$. Then create a table with the corresponding input and output values.

- a vertical compression by a factor of $\frac{1}{3}$
- a translation of 2 units to the left

x	$f(x) = x^3$	$g(x) = \frac{1}{3}(x + 2)^3$
−2	−8	$\frac{1}{3}(-2 + 2)^3 = 0$
−1	−1	$\frac{1}{3}(-1 + 2)^3 = \frac{1}{3}$
0	0	$\frac{1}{3}(0 + 2)^3 = \frac{8}{3}$
1	1	$\frac{1}{3}(1 + 2)^3 = 9$
2	8	$\frac{1}{3}(2 + 2)^3 = \frac{64}{3}$

KEY EXAMPLE *(Lesson 5.2)*

Use a graphing calculator to graph $g(x) = x(x - 2)^2(x + 3)$. Then use the graph to determine the number of turning points, global maximums and minimums, and local maximums and minimums that are not global.

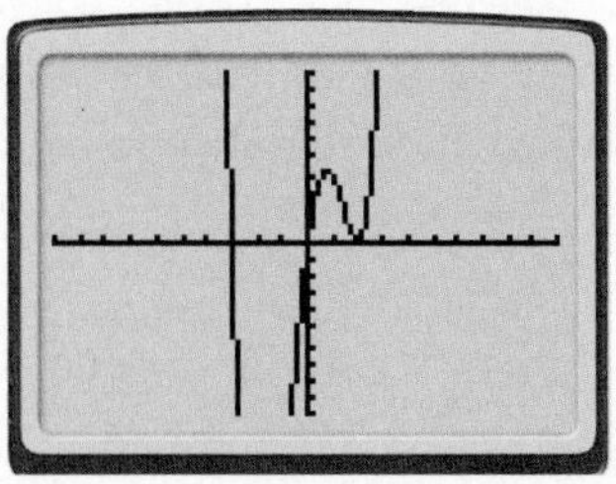

According to the graph, there are three turning points, one local maximum, one local minimum, and one global minimum.

EXERCISES

Identify the transformations of the graph $f(x) = x^3$ that produce the graph of the function. (Lesson 5.1)

1. $g(x) = \left(-\frac{1}{4}(x+2)\right)^3 + 3$

2. $h(x) = \frac{1}{3}(x-4)^3$

Use a graphing calculator to graph each function, then use the graph to determine the number of turning points, global maximums and minimums, and local maximums and minimums that are not global. (Lesson 5.2)

3. $s(x) = x(x+2)(x+1)^2$

4. $h(x) = x^2(x-3)(x+2)(x-2)$

5. Write a real world situation that could be modeled by the equation $V(w) = w(5w)(3w)$. (Lesson 5.2)

MODULE PERFORMANCE TASK

What's the Function of a Roller Coaster?

An engineer is designing part of a roller coaster track that can be modeled by the polynomial function

$$f(x) = 2.0 \times 10^{-6} x^4 - 0.0011x^3 + 0.195x^2 - 12.25x + 250$$

where $f(x)$ is the height in feet of a roller coaster car above ground level, and x is the horizontal distance in feet. For this section of track, the domain is $0 \leq x \leq 250$.

The factored form of this function is

$$f(x) = 2.0 \times 10^{-6}(x-200)(x-250)(x-50)^2.$$

Describe the experience of a rider who is riding a roller coaster on this track.

As you complete the task, be sure to write down all your data and assumptions. Then use graphs, numbers, words, or algebra to explain how you reached your conclusion.

Ready to Go On?

5.1–5.2 Polynomial Functions

Personal Math Trainer

- Online Homework
- Hints and Help
- Extra Practice

Identify the transformations of the graph of $f(x) = x^3$ that produce the graph of $g(x) = -\frac{1}{4}(x + 4)^3$. Apply the transformations to the reference points (−1, −1), (0, 0), and (1, 1) *(Lesson 5.1)*

1. Changes to x.

2. Changes to y.

3. Apply the transformations using the changes to x and y.

$f(x) = x^3$		$g(x) = -\frac{1}{4}(x + 4)^3$	
x	y	x	y
?	?	?	?
?	?	?	?
?	?	?	?

Graph the given function on your graphing calculator. Use the graph to state the number of turning points in the graph and the x-intercepts. *(Lesson 5.2)*

4. $g(x) = x^2(x - 3)$

5. $h(x) = (x - 4)(x - 3)(x + 2)^2$

ESSENTIAL QUESTION

6. Give a real world example of a cubic function. *(Lesson 5.1)*

MODULE 5
MIXED REVIEW

Assessment Readiness

1. Look at each equation. Is the vertex of the graph translated to the right and up when compared to $f(x) = x^3$?
Write Yes or No for A–C.

A. $y = (x + 6)^3 + 2$

B. $y = 5x^3 + 7$

C. $y = (x - 4)^3 + 2$

2. Consider the equation $h(x) = x(x - 1)(x + 3)^2$. Determine if each statement is True or False.

A. There are four turning points in the graph.

B. The graph crosses the x-axis at –3, –1, 0, and 1.

C. The graph has a global maximum.

3. Write a quartic function in intercept form for the given graph. Assume that the constant factor a is either 1 or –1. Explain your answer.

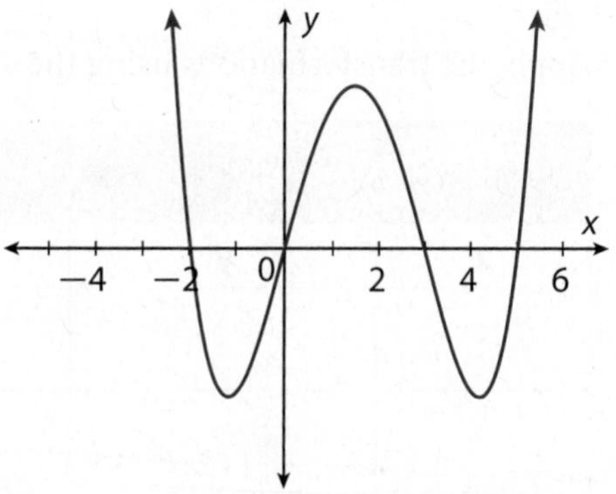

4. An ottoman shaped like a rectangular prism has a length of x, a width two inches shorter than the length, and a height two inches taller than the length. Write the function that represents the volume; then find the length, width, and height of the ottoman if the volume is 5760 in^3.

Polynomials

MODULE 6

Essential Question: How can you use polynomials to solve real-world problems?

REAL WORLD VIDEO
Meteorologists use mathematics and computer models to analyze climate patterns and forecast weather. For example, polynomial functions can be used to model temperature patterns.

MODULE PERFORMANCE TASK PREVIEW

What's the Temperature?

The weather is always a topic for conversation. Is it hot or cold outside? Is it T-shirt and shorts weather, or should you bundle up? What were the high and low temperatures for a particular day? You might suspect that the outdoor temperature follows a pattern. How can you use a polynomial to model the temperature? Let's find out!

Are YOU Ready?

Complete these exercises to review skills you will need for this module.

Personal Math Trainer

- Online Homework
- Hints and Help
- Extra Practice

Adding and Subtracting Polynomials

Example 1 Subtract.

$(7a^3 - 4a^2 + 11) - (3a^2 - 2a + 5)$

$7a^3 - 4a^2 + 11 - 3a^2 + 2a - 5$ Multiply by -1.

$7a^3 - 7a^2 + 2a + 6$ Combine like terms.

Add or subtract the polynomials.

1. $(m^5 + 4m^2 + 6) - (3m^5 - 8m^2)$

2. $(k^2 + 3k + 1) + (k^2 - 8)$

Algebraic Expressions

Example 2 Simplify the expression $5x^3 - 10x^2 + x^3 + 10$.

$6x^3 - 10x^2 + 10$ Combine like terms.

Simplify each expression.

3. $6x - 2x^2 - 2x$

4. $(5x)(2x^2) - x^2$

5. $4(2x - 3y) + 2(x + y)$

6. $4(a + b) - 7(a + 2b)$

Multiplying Polynomials

Example 3 Multiply. $(2a - b)(a + ab + b)$

$(2a - b)(a + ab + b) = 2a(a + ab + b) - b(a + ab + b)$

$= 2a \cdot a + 2a \cdot ab + 2a \cdot b - b \cdot a - b \cdot ab - b \cdot b$

$= 2a^2 + 2a^2b + 2ab - ab - ab^2 - b^2$

$= 2a^2 + 2a^2b + ab - ab^2 - b^2$

Multiply the polynomials.

7. $(x^2 - 4)(x + y)$

8. $(3m + 2)(3m^2 - 2m + 1)$

6.1 Adding and Subtracting Polynomials

Essential Question: How do you add or subtract two polynomials, and what type of expression is the result?

Resource Locker

Explore Identifying and Analyzing Monomials and Polynomials

A polynomial function of degree n has the *standard form* $p(x) = a_n x^n + a_{n-1} x^{n-1} + \dots + a_2 x^2 + a_1 x + a_0$, where $a_n, a_{n-1}, \dots, a_2, a_1$, and a_0 are real numbers and $a_n \neq 0$. The expression $a_n x^n + a_{n-1} x^{n-1} + \dots a_2 x^2 + a_1 x + a_0$ is called a **polynomial**, and each term of a polynomial is called a **monomial**. A monomial is the product of a number and one or more variables with whole-number exponents. A polynomial is a monomial or a sum of monomials. The *degree of a monomial* is the sum of the exponents of the variables, and the *degree of a polynomial* is the degree of the monomial term with the greatest degree. The *leading coefficient* of a polynomial is the coefficient of the term with the greatest degree.

(A) Which of the following are monomials?
$x^3, y + 3y^2 - 5y^3 + 10, a^2bc^{12}, 76$

(B) Identify the degree of each monomial.

Monomial	x^3	a^2bc^{12}	76
Degree	?	?	?

(C) Identify the terms of the polynomial $y + 3y^2 - 5y^3 + 10$.

(D) Identify the coefficient of each variable term.

Term	y	$3y^2$	$-5y^3$
Coefficient	?	?	?

(E) Identify the degree of each term.

Term	y	$3y^2$	$-5y^3$	10
Degree	?	?	?	?

(F) Write the polynomial in standard form.

(G) What is the leading coefficient of the polynomial?

Reflect

1. **Discussion** How can you find the degree of a polynomial with multiple variables in each term?

Explain 1 Adding Polynomials

To add polynomials, combine like terms.

Example 1 **Add the polynomials.**

Ⓐ $(4x^2 - x^3 + 2 + 5x^4) + (-x + 6x^2 + 3x^4)$

$$\begin{array}{rrrrr} 5x^4 & -x^3 & +4x^2 & & +2 \\ +3x^4 & & +6x^2 & -x & \\ \hline 8x^4 & -x^3 & +10x^2 & -x & +2 \end{array}$$

Write in standard form.
Align like terms.
Add.

Ⓑ $(10x - 18x^3 + 6x^4 - 2) + (-7x^4 + 5 + x + 2x^3)$

$(6x^4 - 18x^3 + 10x - 2) + (-7x^4 + 2x^3 + x + 5)$ Write in standard form.

$= (6x^4 - \boxed{7x^4}) + (\boxed{-18x^3} + 2x^3) + (\boxed{10x} + x) + (-2 + \boxed{5})$ Group like terms.

$= \boxed{-x^4} - 16x^3 + \boxed{11x} + 3$ Add.

Reflect

2. Is the sum of two polynomials always a polynomial? Explain.

Your Turn

Add the polynomials.

3. $(17x^4 + 8x^2 - 9x^7 + 4 - 2x^3) + (11x^3 - 8x^2 + 12)$

4. $(-8x + 3x^{11} + x^6) + (4x^4 - x + 17)$

Explain 2 Subtracting Polynomials

To subtract polynomials, combine like terms.

Example 2 **Subtract the polynomials.**

Ⓐ $(12x^3 + 5x - 8x^2 + 19) - (6x^2 - 9x + 3 - 18x^3)$

Write in standard form.
Align like terms and add the opposite.
Add.

$$\begin{array}{rrrr} 12x^3 & -8x^2 & +5x & +19 \\ +18x^3 & -6x^2 & +9x & -3 \\ \hline 30x^3 & -14x^2 & +14x & +16 \end{array}$$

(B) $\left(-4x^2 + 8x^3 + 19 - 5x^5\right) - \left(9 + 2x^2 + 10x^5\right)$

Write in standard form and add the opposite. $\left(-5x^5 + 8x^3 - 4x^2 + 19\right) + \left(-10x^5 - 2x^2 - 9\right)$

Group like terms $= \left(-5x^5 - \boxed{10x^5}\right) + \left(\boxed{8x^3}\right) + \left(\boxed{-4x^2} - 2x^2\right) + \left(\boxed{19} - 9\right)$

Add $= \boxed{-15x^5} + 8x^3 - \boxed{6x^2} + 10$

Reflect

5. Is the difference of two polynomials always a polynomial? Explain.

Your Turn

Subtract the polynomials.

6. $\left(23x^7 - 9x^4 + 1\right) - \left(-9x^4 + 6x^2 - 31\right)$

7. $\left(7x^3 + 13x - 8x^5 + 20x^2\right) - \left(-2x^5 + 9x^2\right)$

Explain 3 Modeling with Polynomial Addition and Subtraction

Polynomial functions can be used to model real-world quantities. If two polynomial functions model quantities that are two parts of a whole, the functions can be added to find a function that models the quantity as a whole. If the polynomial function for the whole and a polynomial function for a part are given, subtraction can be used to find the polynomial function that models the other part of the whole.

Example 3 **Find the polynomial that models the problem and use it to estimate the quantity.**

(A) The data from the U.S. Census Bureau for 2005–2009 shows that the number of male students enrolled in high school in the United States can be modeled by the function $M(x) = -10.4x^3 + 74.2x^2 - 3.4x + 8320.2$, where x is the number of years after 2005 and $M(x)$ is the number of male students in thousands. The number of female students enrolled in high school in the United States can be modeled by the function $F(x) = -13.8x^3 + 55.3x^2 + 141x + 7880$, where x is the number of years after 2005 and $F(x)$ is the number of female students in thousands. Estimate the total number of students enrolled in high school in the United States in 2009.

In the equation $T(x) = M(x) + F(x)$, $T(x)$ is the total number of students in thousands.

Add the polynomials.

$\left(-10.4x^3 + 74.2x^2 - 3.4x + 8320.2\right) + \left(-13.8x^3 + 55.3x^2 + 141x + 7880\right)$

$= \left(-10.4x^3 - 13.8x^3\right) + \left(74.2x^2 + 55.3x^2\right) + \left(-3.4x + 141x\right) + \left(8320.2 + 7880\right)$

$= -24.2x^3 + 129.5x^2 + 137.6x + 16{,}200.2$

The year 2009 is 4 years after 2005, so substitute 4 for x.

$-24.2(4)^3 + 129.5(4)^2 + 137.6(4) + 16{,}200.2 \approx 17{,}274$

About 17,274 thousand students were enrolled in high school in the United States in 2009.

(B) The data from the U.S. Census Bureau for 2000–2010 shows that the total number of overseas travelers visiting New York and Florida can be modeled by the function $T(x) = 41.5x^3 - 689.1x^2 + 4323.3x + 2796.6$, where x is the number of years after 2000 and $T(x)$ is the total number of travelers in thousands. The number of overseas travelers visiting New York can be modeled by the function $N(x) = -41.6x^3 + 560.9x^2 - 1632.7x + 6837.4$, where x is the number of years after 2000 and $N(x)$ is the number of travelers in thousands. Estimate the total number of overseas travelers to Florida in 2008.

In the equation $F(x) = T(x)$ [$-$] $N(x)$, $F(x)$ is the number of travelers to Florida in thousands.

Subtract the polynomials.

$(41.5x^3 - 689.1x^2 + 4323.3x + 2796.6)$ [$-$] $(-41.6x^3 + 560.9x^2 - 1632.7x + 6837.4)$

$= (41.5x^3 - 689.1x^2 + 4323.3x + 2796.6) + (41.6x^3 - 560.9x^2 + 1632.7x - 6837.4)$

$= (41.5x^3 +$ [$41.6x^3$] $) + ($ [$-689.1x^2$] $- 560.9x^2) + ($ [$4323.3x$] $+ 1632.7x) + (2796.6 -$ [6837.4] $)$

$=$ [83.1] $x^3 -$ [1250] $x^2 +$ [5956] $x -$ [4040.8]

The year 2008 is 8 years after 2000, so substitute [8] for x.

$83.1(8)^3 - 1250(8)^2 + 5956(8) - 4040.8 \approx$ [6154]

About [6154] thousand overseas travelers visited Florida in 2008.

Your Turn

8. According to the data from the U.S. Census Bureau for 1990–2009, the number of commercially owned automobiles in the United States can be modeled by the function $A(x) = 1.4x^3 - 130.6x^2 + 1831.3x + 128{,}141$, where x is the number of years after 1990 and $A(x)$ is the number of automobiles in thousands. The number of privately-owned automobiles in the United States can be modeled by the function $P(x) = -x^3 + 24.9x^2 - 177.9x + 1709.5$, where x is the number of years after 1990 and $P(x)$ is the number of automobiles in thousands. Estimate the total number of automobiles owned in 2005.

Elaborate

9. How is the degree of a polynomial related to the degrees of the monomials that comprise the polynomial?

10. How is polynomial subtraction based on polynomial addition?

11. How would you find the model for a whole if you have polynomial functions that are models for the two distinct parts that make up that whole?

12. **Essential Question Check-In** What is the result of adding or subtracting polynomials?

Evaluate: Homework and Practice

Personal Math Trainer

- Online Homework
- Hints and Help
- Extra Practice

1. Write the polynomial $-23x^7 + x^9 - 6x^3 + 10 + 2x^2$ in standard form, and then identify the degree and leading coefficient.

Add the polynomials.

2. $(82x^8 + 21x^2 - 6) + (18x + 7x^8 - 42x^2 + 3)$
3. $(15x - 121x^{12} + x^9 - x^7 + 3x^2) + (x^7 - 68x^2 - x^9)$
4. $(16 - x^2) + (-18x^2 + 7x^5 - 10x^4 + 5)$
5. $(x + 1 - 3x^2) + (8x + 21x^2 - 1)$
6. $(64 + x^3 - 8x^2) + (7x + 3 - x^2) + (19x^2 - 7x - 2)$
7. $(x^4 - 7x^3 + 2 - x) + (2x^3 - 3) + (1 - 5x^3 - x^4 + x)$

Subtract the polynomials.

8. $(-2x + 23x^5 + 11) - (5 - 9x^3 + x)$
9. $(7x^3 + 68x^4 - 14x + 1) - (-10x^3 + 8x + 23)$
10. $(57x^{18} - x^2) - (6x - 71x^3 + 5x^2 + 2)$
11. $(9x - 12x^3) - (5x^3 + 7x - 2)$
12. $(3x^5 - 9) - (11 + 13x^2 - x^4) - (10x^2 + x^4)$
13. $(10x^2 - x + 4) - (5x + 7) + (6x - 11)$

Find the polynomial that models the problem and use it to estimate the quantity.

14. A rectangle has a length of x and a width of $5x^3 + 4 - x^2$. Find the perimeter of the rectangle when the length is 5 feet.

15. A rectangle has a perimeter of $6x^3 + 9x^2 - 10x + 5$ and a length of x. Find the width of the rectangle when the length is 21 inches.

16. Cho is making a rectangular garden, where the length is x feet and the width is $4x - 1$ feet. He wants to add garden stones around the perimeter of the garden once he is done. If the garden is 4 feet long, how many feet will Cho need to cover with garden stones?

17. Employment The data from the U.S. Census Bureau for 1980–2010 shows that the median weekly earnings of full-time male employees who have at least a bachelor's degree can be modeled by the function $M(x) = 0.009x^3 - 0.29x^2 + 30.7x + 439.6$, where x is the number of years after 1980 and $M(x)$ is the median weekly earnings in dollars. The median weekly earnings of all full-time employees who have at least a bachelor's degree can be modeled by the function $T(x) = 0.012x^3 - 0.46x^2 + 56.1x + 732.3$, where x is the number of years after 1980 and $T(x)$ is the median weekly earnings in dollars. Estimate the median weekly earnings of a full-time female employee with at least a bachelor's degree in 2010.

18. Business From data gathered in the period 2008–2012, the yearly value of U.S. exports can be modeled by the function $E(x) = -228x^3 + 2552.8x^2 - 6098.5x + 11{,}425.8$, where x is the number of years after 2008 and $E(x)$ is the value of exports in billions of dollars. The yearly value of U.S. imports can be modeled by the function $I(x) = -400.4x^3 + 3954.4x^2 - 11{,}128.8x + 17{,}749.6$, where x is the number of years after 2008 and $I(x)$ is the value of imports in billions of dollars. Estimate the total value the United States imported and exported in 2012.

19. Education From data gathered in the period 1970–2010, the number of full-time students enrolled in a degree-granting institution can be modeled by the function $F(x) = 8.7x^3 - 213.3x^2 + 2015.5x + 3874.9$, where x is the number of years after 1970 and $F(x)$ is the number of students in thousands. The number of part-time students enrolled in a degree-granting institution can be modeled by the function $P(x) = 12x^3 - 285.3x^2 + 2217x + 1230$, where x is the number of years after 1970 and $P(x)$ is the number of students in thousands. Estimate the total number of students enrolled in a degree-granting institution in 2000.

20. Geography The data from the U.S. Census Bureau for 1982–2003 shows that the surface area of the United States that is covered by rural land can be modeled by the function $R(x) = 0.003x^3 - 0.086x^2 - 1.2x + 1417.4$, where x is the number of years after 1982 and $R(x)$ is the surface area in millions of acres. The total surface area of the United States can be modeled by the function $T(x) = 0.0023x^3 + 0.034x^2 - 5.9x + 1839.4$, where x is the number of years after 1982 and $T(x)$ is the surface area in millions of acres. Estimate the surface area of the United States that is not covered by rural land in 2001.

21. Determine which polynomials are monomials. Choose all that apply.

a. $4x^3y$

b. $12 - x^2 + 5x$

c. $152 + x$

d. 783

e. x

f. $19x^{-2}$

g. $4x^4x^2$

H.O.T. Focus on Higher Order Thinking

22. **Explain the Error** Colin simplified $(16x + 8x^2y - 7xy^2 + 9y - 2xy) - (-9xy + 8xy^2 + 10x^2y + x - 7y)$. His work is shown below. Find and correct Colin's mistake.

$$(16x + 8x^2y - 7xy^2 + 9y - 2xy) - (-9xy + 8xy^2 + 10x^2y + x - 7y)$$
$$= (16x + 8x^2y - 7xy^2 + 9y - 2xy) + (9xy - 8xy^2 - 10x^2y - x + 7y)$$
$$= (16x - x) + (8x^2y - 7xy^2 - 8xy^2 - 10x^2y) + (9y + 7y) + (-2xy + 9xy)$$
$$= 15x - 17x^2y^2 + 16y + 7xy$$

23. **Critical Reasoning** Janice is building a fence around a portion of her rectangular yard. The length of yard she will enclose is x, and the width is $2x^2 - 98x + 5$, where the measurements are in feet. If the length of the enclosed yard is 50 feet and the cost of fencing is \$13 per foot, how much will Janice need to spend on fencing?

24. **Multi-Step** Find a polynomial expression for the perimeter of a trapezoid with legs of length x and bases of lengths $0.1x^3 + 2x$ and $x^2 + 3x - 10$ where each is measured in inches.

   a. Find the perimeter of the trapezoid if the length of one leg is 6 inches.

   b. If the leg length is increased by 5 inches, will the perimeter also increase? By how much?

25. **Communicate Mathematical Ideas** Present a formal argument for why the set of polynomials is closed under addition and subtraction. Use the polynomials $ax^m + bx^m$ and $ax^m - bx^m$, for real numbers a and b and whole number m, to justify your reasoning.

Lesson Performance Task

The table shows the average monthly maximum and minimum temperatures for Death Valley throughout one year.

Month	Maximum Temperature	Minimum Temperature
January	67	40
February	73	46
March	82	55
April	91	62
May	101	73
June	110	81
July	116	88
August	115	86
September	107	76
October	93	62
November	77	48
December	65	38

Use a graphing calculator to find a good fourth-degree polynomial regression model for both the maximum and minimum temperatures. Then find a function that models the range in monthly temperatures and use the model to estimate the range during September. How does the range predicted by your model compare with the range shown in the table?

6.2 Multiplying Polynomials

Essential Question: How do you multiply polynomials, and what type of expression is the result?

Resource Locker

Explore — Analyzing a Visual Model for Polynomial Multiplication

The volume of a rectangular prism is the product of the length, width, and height of that prism. If the dimensions are all known, then the volume is a simple calculation. What if some of the dimensions are given as *binomials*? A **binomial** is a polynomial with two terms. How would you find the volume of a rectangular prism that is $x + 3$ units long, $x + 2$ units wide, and x units high? The images below show two methods for finding the solution.

$V = \text{length} \times \text{width} \times \text{height}$
$= (x + 3)(x + 2)x$

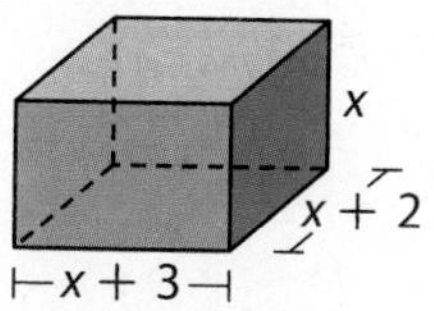

$V = V_1 + V_2 + V_3 + V_4$

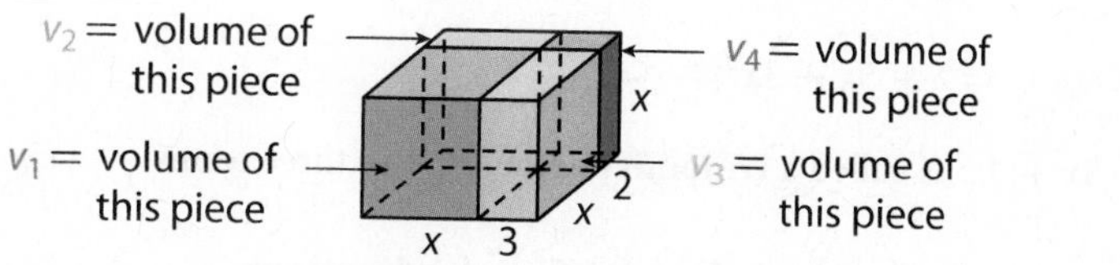

(A) The first model shows the rectangular prism, and its volume is calculated directly as the product of two binomials and a monomial.

(B) The second image divides the rectangular prism into ? smaller prisms, the dimensions of which are each ? .

(C) The volume of a cube (V_1) where all sides have a length of x, is ? .

(D) The volume of a rectangular prism (V_2) with dimensions x by x by 2 is ? .

(E) The volume of a rectangular prism (V_3) with dimensions x by x by 3 is ? .

(F) The volume of a rectangular prism (V_4) with dimensions x by 3 by 2 is ? .

(G) So the volume of the rectangular prism is the sum of the volumes of the four smaller regions.

$V_1 + V_2 + V_3 + V_4 =$? + ? + ? + ?

$=$?

Reflect

1. If all three dimensions were binomials, how many regions would the rectangular prism be divided into?
2. **Discussion** Can this method be applied to finding the volume of other simple solids? Are there solids that this process would be difficult to apply to? Are there any solids that this method cannot be applied to?

Explain 1 Multiplying Polynomials

Multiplying polynomials involves using the product rule for exponents and the distributive property. The product of two monomials is the product of the coefficients and the sum of the exponents of each variable.

$$5x \cdot 6x^3 = 30x^{1+3} \qquad -2x^2y^4z \cdot 5y^2z = -10x^2y^{4+2}z^{1+1}$$

$$= 30x^4 \qquad = -10x^2y^6z^2$$

When multiplying two binomials, the distributive property is used. Each term of one polynomial must be multiplied by each term of the other.

$$(2+3x)(1+x) = 2(1+x) + 3x(x+1)$$
$$= 2(1) + 2(x) + 3x(x) + 3x(1)$$
$$= 2 + 2x + 3x^{1+1} + 3x$$
$$= 2 + 5x + 3x^2$$

The polynomial $2 + 5x + 3x^2$ is called a **trinomial** because it has three terms.

Example 1 **Perform the following polynomial multiplications.**

Ⓐ $(x+2)(1-4x+2x^2)$

Find the product by multiplying horizontally.

$(x+2)(2x^2-4x+1)$	Write the polynomials in standard form.
$x(2x^2) + x(-4x) + x(1) + 2(2x^2) + 2(-4x) + 2(1)$	Distribute the x and the 2.
$2x^3 - 4x^2 + x + 4x^2 - 8x + 2$	Simplify.
$2x^3 - 7x + 2$	Combine like terms.

Therefore, $(x+2)(2x^2-4x+1) = 2x^3 - 7x + 2$.

Ⓑ $(3x-4)(2+x-7x^2)$

Find the product by multiplying vertically.

$-7x^2 + \boxed{x} + 2$ $3x - 4$	Write each polynomial in standard form.
$\boxed{28x^2} - 4x - 8$	Multipy −4 and $(-7x^2 + x + 2)$.
$\boxed{-21x^3} + 3x^2 + 6x$	Multipy $\boxed{3x}$ and $(-7x^2 + x + 2)$.
$-21x^3 + \boxed{31x^2} + 2x - 8$	Combine like terms.

Therefore, $(3x-4)(2+x-7x^2) = -21x^3 + 31x^2 + 2x - 8$.

Your Turn

Perform the following polynomial multiplications.

3. $(3 + 2x)(4 - 7x + 5x^2)$

4. $(x - 6)(3 - 8x - 4x^2)$

Explain 2 Modeling with Polynomial Multiplication

Many real-world situations can be modeled with polynomial functions. Sometimes, a situation will arise in which a model is needed that combines two quantities modeled by polynomial functions. In this case, the desired model would be the product of the two known models.

Example 2 **Find the polynomial function modeling the desired relationship.**

(A) Mr. Silva manages a manufacturing plant. From 1990 through 2005, the number of units produced (in thousands) can be modeled by $N(x) = 0.02x^2 + 0.2x + 3$, where x is the number of years since 1990. The average cost per unit (in dollars) can be modeled by $C(x) = -0.002x^2 - 0.1x + 2$, where x is the number of years since 1990. Write a polynomial $T(x)$ that can be used to model Mr. Silva's total manufacturing cost for those years.

The total manufacturing cost is the product of the number of units made and the cost per unit.

$T(x) = N(x) \cdot C(x)$

Multiply the two polynomials.

$$\begin{array}{rrr}
 & & 0.02x^2 + 0.2x + 3 \\
 & \times & -\ 0.002x^2 - 0.1x + 2 \\
\hline
 & & 0.04x^2 + 0.4x + 6 \\
 & -0.002x^3 & -\ 0.02x^2 - 0.3x \\
-0.00004x^4 - 0.0004x^3 & & -\ 0.006x^2 \\
\hline
-0.00004x^4 - 0.0024x^3 & & +\ 0.014x^2 + 0.1x + 6
\end{array}$$

Therefore, the total manufacturing cost can be modeled by the following polynomial, where x is the number of years since 1990.

$T(x) = -0.00004x^4 - 0.0024x^3 + 0.014x^2 + 0.1x + 6$

(B) Ms. Liao runs a small dress company. From 1995 through 2005, the number of dresses she made can be modeled by $N(x) = 0.3x^2 - 1.6x + 14$, and the average cost to make each dress can be modeled by $C(x) = -0.001x^2 - 0.06x + 8.3$, where x is the number of years since 1995. Write a polynomial that can be used to model Ms. Liao's total dressmaking costs, $T(x)$, for those years.

The total dressmaking cost is the product of the number of dresses made and the cost per dress.

$T(x) = N(x) \cdot C(x)$

Multiply the two polynomials.

$$\begin{array}{rrrrr} & & 0.3x^2 & -1.6x & +14 \\ & \times & -0.001x^2 & \boxed{-0.06x} & +8.3 \\ \hline & & 2.49x^2 & -13.28x & \boxed{+116.2} \\ & -0.018x^3 & \boxed{+0.096x^2} & -0.84x & \\ -0.0003x^{\boxed{4}} & +0.0016x^3 & -0.014x^2 & & \\ \hline -0.0003x^{\boxed{4}} & -0.0164x^3 & +2.572x^2 & \boxed{-14.12x} & +116.2 \end{array}$$

Therefore, the total dressmaking cost can be modeled by the following polynomial, where x is the number of years since 1995.

$T(x) = -0.0003x^4 - 0.0164x^3 + 2.572x^2 - 14.12x + 116.2$

Your Turn

5. Brent runs a small toy store specializing in wooden toys. From 2000 through 2012, the number of toys Brent made can be modeled by $N(x) = 0.7x^2 - 2x + 23$, and the average cost to make each toy can be modeled by $C(x) = -0.004x^2 - 0.08x + 25$, where x is the number of years since 2000. Write a polynomial that can be used to model Brent's total cost for making the toys, $T(x)$, for those years.

Explain 3 Verifying Polynomial Identities

You have already seen certain special polynomial relationships. For example, a difference of two squares can be easily factored: $x^2 - a^2 = (x + a)(x - a)$. This equation is an example of a **polynomial identity**, a mathematical relationship equating one polynomial quantity to another. Another example of a polynomial identity is

$$(x + a)^2 - (x - a)^2 = 4ax.$$

The identity can be verified by simplifying one side of the equation to match the other.

Example 3 **Verify the given polynomial identity.**

(A) $(x + a)^2 - (x - a)^2 = 4ax$

The right side of the identity is already fully simplified. Simplify the left-hand side.

$(x + a)^2 - (x - a)^2 = 4ax$	
$x^2 + 2ax + a^2 - (x^2 - 2ax + a^2) = 4ax$	Square each binomial.
$x^2 + 2ax + a^2 - x^2 + 2ax - a^2 = 4ax$	Distribute the negative.
$\cancel{x^2 - x^2} + 2ax + 2ax + \cancel{a^2 - a^2} = 4ax$	Rearrange terms.
$4ax = 4ax$	Simplify.

Therefore, $(x + a)^2 - (x - a)^2 = 4ax$ is a true statement.

(B) $(a+b)(a^2-ab+b^2)=a^3+b^3$

The right side of the identity is already fully simplified. Simplify the left-hand side.

$$(a+b)(a^2-ab+b^2)=a^3+b^3$$

$$a(a^2)+a(\boxed{-ab})+a(b^2)+b(a^2)+\boxed{b}(-ab)+b(b^2)=a^3+b^3 \quad \text{Distribute } a \text{ and } b.$$

$$a^3-a^2b+ab^2+\boxed{a^2b}-ab^2+\boxed{b^3}=a^3+b^3 \quad \text{Simplify.}$$

$$a^3-\boxed{a^2b}+a^2b+ab^2-\boxed{ab^2}+b^3=a^3+b^3 \quad \text{Rearrange terms.}$$

$$a^3\boxed{+}b^3=a^3+b^3 \quad \text{Combine like terms.}$$

Therefore, $(a+b)(a^2-ab+b^2)=a^3+b^3$ is a true statement.

Your Turn

6. Show that $a^5-b^5=(a-b)(a^4+a^3b+a^2b^2+ab^3+b^4)$.

7. Show that $(a-b)(a^2+ab+b^2)=a^3-b^3$.

Explain 4 Using Polynomial Identities

The most obvious use for polynomial identities is simplifying algebraic expressions, but polynomial identities often turn out to have nonintuitive uses as well.

Example 4 **For each situation, find the solution using the given polynomial identity.**

(A) The polynomial identity $(x^2+y^2)^2=(x^2-y^2)^2+(2xy)^2$ can be used to identify Pythagorean triples. Generate a Pythagorean triple using $x=4$ and $y=3$.

Substitute the given values into the identity.

$$(4^2+3^2)^2=(4^2-3^2)^2+(2\cdot 4\cdot 3)^2$$
$$(16+9)^2=(16-9)^2+(24)^2$$
$$(25)^2=(7)^2+(24)^2$$
$$625=49+576$$
$$625=625$$

Therefore, 7, 24, 25 is a Pythagorean triple.

(B) The identity $(x+y)^2=x^2+2xy+y^2$ can be used for mental-math calculations to quickly square numbers.

Find the square of 27.

Find two numbers whose sum is equal to 27.

Let $x=\boxed{20}$ and $y=7$

Evaluate

$$\left(20 + \boxed{7}\right)^2 = 20^2 + \boxed{2 \cdot 20 \cdot 7} + 7^2$$

$$27^2 = 400 + \boxed{280} + 49$$

$$27^2 = \boxed{729}$$

Verify by using a calculator to find 27^2.

$27^2 = \boxed{729}$

Your Turn

8. The identity $(x + y)(x - y) = x^2 - y^2$ can be used for mental-math calculations to quickly multiply two numbers in specific situations.

Find the product of 37 and 43. (Hint: What values should you choose for x and y so the equation calculates the product of 37 and 43?)

9. The identity $(x - y)^2 = x^2 - 2xy + y^2$ can also be used for mental-math calculations to quickly square numbers.

Find the square of 18. (Hint: What values should you choose for x and y so the equation calculates the square of 18?)

Elaborate

10. What property is employed in the process of polynomial multiplication?

11. How can you use unit analysis to justify multiplying two polynomial models of real-world quantities?

12. Give an example of a polynomial identity and how it's useful.

13. **Essential Question Check-In** When multiplying polynomials, what type of expression is the product?

Evaluate: Homework and Practice

Personal Math Trainer
- Online Homework
- Hints and Help
- Extra Practice

1. The dimensions for a rectangular prism are $x + 5$ for the length, $x + 1$ for the width, and x for the height. What is the volume of the prism?

Perform the following polynomial multiplications.

2. $(3x - 2)(2x^2 + 3x - 1)$

3. $(x^3 + 3x^2 + 1)(3x^2 + 6x - 2)$

4. $(x^2 + 9x + 7)(3x^2 + 9x + 5)$

5. $(2x + 5y)(3x^2 - 4xy + 2y^2)$

6. $(x^3 + x^2 + 1)(x^2 - x - 5)$

7. $(4x^2 + 3x + 2)(3x^2 + 2x - 1)$

Write a polynomial function to represent the new value.

8. The volume of a stock, or number of shares traded, is modeled over time during a given day by $S(x) = x^5 - 3x^4 + 10x^2 - 6x + 30$. The cost per share of that stock during that day is modeled by $C(x) = 0.004x^4 - 0.02x^2 + 0.3x + 4$. Write a polynomial function $V(x)$ to model the changing value during that day of the trades made of shares of that stock.

9. A businessman models the number of items (in thousands) that his company sold from 1998 through 2004 as $N(x) = -0.1x^3 + x^2 - 3x + 4$ and the average price per item (in dollars) as $P(x) = 0.2x + 5$, where x represents the number of years since 1998. Write a polynomial $R(x)$ that can be used to model the total revenue for this company.

10. Biology A biologist has found that the number of branches on a certain rare tree can be modeled by the polynomial $b(y) = 4y^2 + y$, where y is the number of years after the tree reaches a height of 6 feet. The number of leaves on each branch can be modeled by the polynomial $l(y) = 2y^3 + 3y^2 + y$. Write a polynomial describing the total number of leaves on the tree.

11. Physics An object thrown in the air has a velocity after t seconds that can be described by $v(t) = -9.8t + 24$ (in meters/second) and a height $h(t) = -4.9t^2 + 24t + 60$ (in meters). The object has mass $m = 2$ kilograms. The kinetic energy of the object is given by $K = \frac{1}{2}mv^2$, and the potential energy is given by $U = 9.8mh$. Find an expression for the total kinetic and potential energy $K + U$ as a function of time. What does this expression tell you about the energy of the falling object?

Verify the given polynomial identity.

12. $(x + y + z)^2 = x^2 + y^2 + z^2 + 2xy + 2xz + 2yz$

13. $a^5 + b^5 = (a + b)(a^4 - a^3b + a^2b^2 - ab^3 + b^4)$

14. $x^4 - y^4 = (x - y)(x + y)(x^2 + y^2)$

15. $(a^2 + b^2)(x^2 + y^2) = (ax - by)^2 + (bx + ay)^2$

Find the square of the number or the product of the numbers using one or more of these identities.

$(x + y)^2 = x^2 + 2xy + y^2$, $(x + y)(x - y) = x^2 - y^2$, or $(x - y)^2 = x^2 - 2xy + y^2$.

16. 43^2

17. 32^2

18. 89^2

19. 47^2

20. $54 \cdot 38$

21. $58 \cdot 68$

22. Explain the Error A polynomial identity for the difference of two cubes is $a^3 - b^3 = (a - b)(a^2 + ab + b^2)$. A student uses the identity to factor $64 - 27x^6$. Identify the error the student made, and then correct it.

Each term of $64 - 27x^6$ is a perfect cube. Let $a = 4$ and $b = 3x^2$. Then:

$$64 - 27x^6 = 4^3 - (3x^2)^3$$
$$= (4 - 3x^2)(4^2 + 4(-3x^2) + (-3x^2)^2)$$
$$= (4 - 3x^2)(16 - 12x^2 + 9x^4)$$

23. Determine whether there will be 1, 2, 3, or 4 terms after performing the polynomial multiplication.

a. $(5x)(3x)$

b. $(3x)(2x + 1)$

c. $(x + 1)(x - 1)$

d. $(x + 2)(3x^2 - 2x + 1)$

H.O.T. Focus on Higher Order Thinking

24. Multi-Step Given the polynomial identity: $x^6 + y^6 = (x^2 + y^2)(x^4 - x^2y^2 + y^4)$

a. Verify directly by expanding the right hand side.

b. Use another polynomial identity to verify this identity. $\left(\text{Note that } a^6 = (a^2)^3 = (a^3)^2\right)$

25. Communicate Mathematical Ideas Explain why the set of polynomials is closed under multiplication.

26. Critical Thinking Explain why every other term of the polynomial product $(x - y)^5$ written in standard form is subtracted when $(x - y)$ is raised to the fifth power.

Lesson Performance Task

The table presents data about oil wells in the state of Oklahoma from 1992 through 2008.

Year	Number of Wells	Average Daily Oil Production per Well (Barrels)
2008	83,443	2.178
2007	82,832	2.053
2006	82,284	2.108
2005	82,551	2.006
2004	83,222	2.10
2003	83,415	2.12
2002	83,730	2.16
2001	84,160	2.24
2000	84,432	2.24
1999	85,043	2.29
1998	85,691	2.49
1997	86,765	2.62
1996	88,144	2.66
1995	90,557	2.65
1994	91,289	2.73
1993	92,377	2.87
1992	93,192	2.99

a. Given the data in this table, use regression to find models for the number of producing wells (cubic regression) and average daily well output (quadratic regression) in terms of t years since 1992.

b. Find a function modeling the total daily oil output for the state of Oklahoma.

6.3 The Binomial Theorem

Essential Question: How is the Binomial Theorem useful?

Resource Locker

Explore 1 Generating Pascal's Triangle

Pascal's Triangle is a famous number pattern named after the French mathematician Blaise Pascal (1623–1662). You can use Pascal's Triangle to help you expand a power of a binomial of the form $(a + b)^n$.

Use the tree diagram shown to generate Pascal's Triangle. Notice that from each node in the diagram to the nodes immediately below it there are two paths, a left path (L) and a right path (R). You can describe a path from the single node in row 0 to any other node in the diagram using a string of Ls and Rs.

First, notice that there is only one possible path to each node in row 1, which is why a 1 appears in those nodes. In row 2, there is only one possible path, LL, to the first node and only one possible path, RR, to the last node, but there are two possible paths, LR and RL, to the center node.

(A) Copy the diagram, and complete only rows 3 and 4 of Pascal's Triangle. (You will complete rows 5 and 6 in Step C.) In each node, write the number of possible paths from the top down to that node.

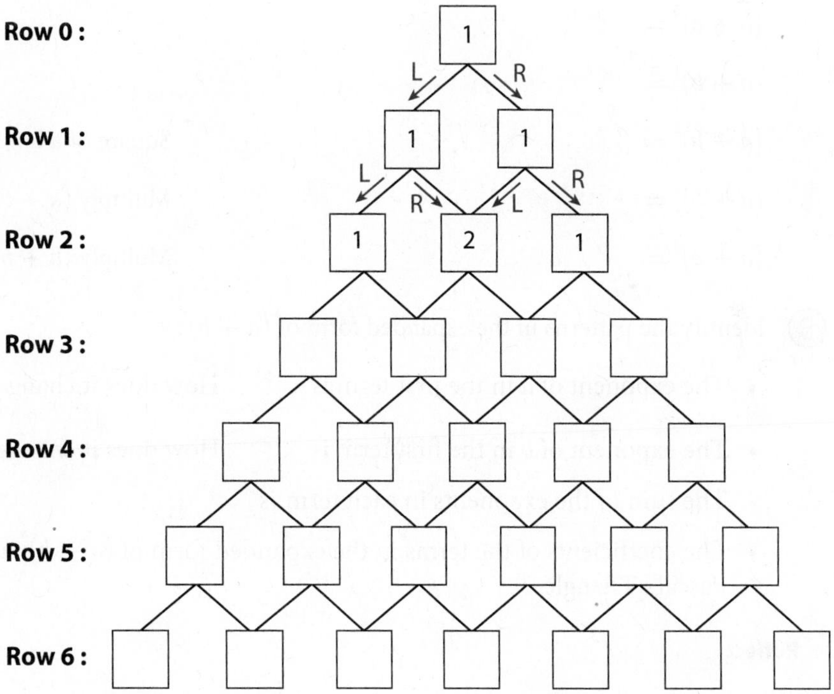

(B) Look for patterns in the tree diagram.

What is the value in the first and last node in each row? ?

For every other node, the value in the node is the ? of the two values above it.

(C) Using the patterns in Step B, go back to Pascal's Triangle in Step A and complete rows 5 and 6.

Reflect

1. Using strings of Ls and Rs, write the paths that lead to the second node in row 3 of Pascal's Triangle. How are the paths alike, and how are they different?

2. The path LLRLR leads to which node in which row of Pascal's Triangle? What is the value of that node?

Explore 2 Relating Pascal's Triangle to Powers of Binomials

As shown, the value in position r of row n of Pascal's Triangle is written as ${}_nC_r$, where the position numbers in each row start with 0. In this Explore, you will see how the values in Pascal's Triangle are related to powers of a binomial.

Row 0 : ⟶ ${}_0C_0$

Row 1 : ⟶ ${}_1C_0$ ${}_1C_1$

Row 2 : ⟶ ${}_2C_0$ ${}_2C_1$ ${}_2C_2$

Row 3 : ⟶ ${}_3C_0$ ${}_3C_1$ ${}_3C_2$ ${}_3C_3$

Ⓐ Expand each power.

$(a+b)^0 =$?

$(a+b)^1 =$?

$(a+b)^2 =$? Square of a binomial

$(a+b)^3 =$? Multiply $(a+b)^2$ by $(a+b)$.

$(a+b)^4 =$? Multiply $(a+b)^3$ by $(a+b)$.

Ⓑ Identify the patterns in the expanded form of $(a+b)^n$.

- The exponent of a in the first term is ? . How does it change in each successive term? ?
- The exponent of b in the first term is ? . How does it change in each successive term? ?
- The sum of the exponents in each term is ? .
- The coefficients of the terms in the expanded form of $(a+b)^n$ are the values in row ? of Pascal's Triangle.

Reflect

3. How many terms are in the expanded form of $(a+b)^n$?

4. Without expanding the power, determine the middle term of $(a+b)^6$. Explain how you found your answer.

5. Without expanding the power, determine the first term of $(a+b)^{15}$. Explain how you found your answer.

Explain 1 Expanding Powers of Binomials Using the Binomial Theorem

The **Binomial Theorem** states the connection between the terms of the expanded form of $(a + b)^n$ and Pascal's Triangle.

Binomial Theorem
For any whole number n, the binomial expansion of $(a + b)^n$ is given by
$(a+b)^n = {}_nC_0a^nb^0 + {}_nC_1a^{n-1}b^1 + {}_nC_2a^{n-2}b^2 + \ldots + {}_nC_{n-1}a^1b^{n-1} + {}_nC_na^0b^n$
where ${}_nC_r$ is the value in position r (where r starts at 0) of the nth row of Pascal's Triangle.

Since it can be cumbersome to look up numbers from Pascal's Triangle each time you want to expand a power of a binomial, you can use a calculator instead. To do so, enter the value of n, press **MATH**, go to the **PRB** menu, select **3:nCr**, and then enter the value of r. The calculator screen shows the values for ${}_6C_1$, ${}_6C_2$, and ${}_6C_3$.

Example 1 **Use the Binomial Theorem to expand each power of a binomial.**

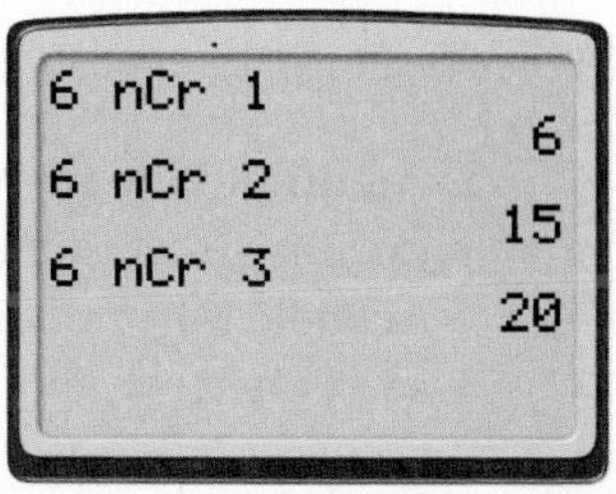

(A) $(x - 2)^3$

Step 1 Identify the values in row 3 of Pascal's Triangle.

1, 3, 3, and 1

Step 2 Expand the power as described by the Binomial Theorem, using the values from Pascal's Triangle as coefficients.

$$(x - 2)^3 = 1x^3(-2)^0 + 3x^2(-2)^1 + 3x^1(-2)^2 + 1x^0(-2)^3$$

Step 3 Simplify.

$$(x - 2)^3 = x^3 - 6x^2 + 12x - 8$$

(B) $(x + y)^7$

Step 1 Use a calculator to determine the values of ${}_7C_0$, ${}_7C_1$, ${}_7C_2$, ${}_7C_3$, ${}_7C_4$, ${}_7C_5$, ${}_7C_6$, and ${}_7C_7$.

1, 7, 21, 35, 35, 21, 7, and 1

Step 2 Expand the power as described by the Binomial Theorem, using the values of ${}_7C_0$, ${}_7C_1$, ${}_7C_2$, ${}_7C_3$, ${}_7C_4$, ${}_7C_5$, ${}_7C_6$, and ${}_7C_7$ as coefficients.

$$(x + y)^7 = 1x^7y^0 + 7x^6y^1 + 21x^5y^2 + 35x^4y^3 + 35x^3y^4 + 21x^2y^5 + 7x^1y^6 + 1x^0y^7$$

Step 3 Simplify.

$$(x + y)^7 = x^7 + 7x^6y + 21x^5y^2 + 35x^4y^3 + 35x^3y^4 + 21x^2y^5 + 7xy^6 + y^7$$

Reflect

6. What happens to the signs of the terms in the expanded form of $(x - 2)^3$? Why does this happen?
7. If the number 11 is written as the binomial $(10 + 1)$, how can you use the Binomial Theorem to find 11^2, 11^3, and 11^4? What is the pattern in the digits?

Your Turn

8. Use the Binomial Theorem to expand $(x - y)^4$.

Explain 2 Solving a Real-World Problem Using Binomial Probabilities

Recall that the probability of an event A is written as $P(A)$ and is expressed as a number between 0 and 1, where 0 represents impossibility and 1 represents certainty.

When dealing with probabilities, you will find these two rules helpful.

1. **Addition Rule for Mutually Exclusive Events:** If events A and B are *mutually exclusive* (that is, they cannot occur together), then $P(A \text{ or } B) = P(A) + P(B)$. For example, when rolling a die, getting a 1 and getting a 2 are mutually exclusive events, so $P(1 \text{ or } 2) = P(1) + P(2) = \frac{1}{6} + \frac{1}{6} = \frac{1}{3}$.
2. **Complement Rule:** The *complement* of event A consists of all of the possible outcomes that are not part of A, and the probability that A does not occur is $P(\text{not } A) = 1 - P(A)$. For example, when rolling a die, the probability of not getting a 2 is $P(\text{not } 2) = 1 - P(2) = 1 - \frac{1}{6} = \frac{5}{6}$.

A **binomial experiment** involves many trials where each trial has only two possible outcomes: success or failure. If the probability of success in each trial is p and the probability of failure in each trial is $q = 1 - p$, the **binomial probability** of exactly r successes in n trials is given by $P(r) = {}_nC_r p^r q^{n-r}$. Since ${}_nC_r = {}_nC_{n-r}$, you can rewrite $P(r)$ as $P(r) = {}_nC_{n-r} p^r q^{n-r}$, which represents the $(n - r)$th term in the expanded form of $(p + q)^n$.

Example 2 **One in 5 boats traveling down a river bypass a harbor at the mouth of the river and head out to sea. Currently, 4 boats are traveling down the river and approaching the mouth of the river.**

Ⓐ What is the probability that exactly 2 of the 4 boats head out to sea?

The probability that a boat will head out to sea is $\frac{1}{5}$, or 0.2.

Substitute 4 for n, 2 for r, 0.2 for p, and 0.8 for q.

$$P(2) = {}_4C_2(0.2)^2(0.8)^{4-2}$$
$$= 6(0.2)^2(0.8)^2$$
$$= 6(0.04)(0.64)$$
$$= 0.1536$$

So, the probability that exactly 2 of the 4 boats will head out to sea is 0.1536, or 15.36%.

(B) What is the probability that at least 2 of the 4 boats will head out to sea?

To find the probability that at least 2 of the 4 boats will head out to sea, find the probability that 2, 3, or 4 boats will head out to sea and add the probabilities.

From Part A, you know that $P(2) = 0.1536$.

$P(3) = {}_4C_{3}(0.2)^{3}(0.8)^{1}$

$= 4(0.008)(0.8)$

$= 0.0256$

$P(4) = {}_4C_{4}(0.2)^{4}(0.8)^{0}$

$= 1(0.0016)(1)$

$= 0.0016$

$P(\text{at least } 2) = P(2 \text{ or } 3 \text{ or } 4)$

$= P(2) + P(3) + P(4)$

$= 0.1536 + 0.0256 + 0.0016$

$= 0.1808$

So, the probability that at least 2 of the 4 boats will head out to sea is 0.1808, or 18.08%.

Reflect

9. In words, state the complement of the event that at least 2 of the 4 boats will head out to sea. Then find the probability of the complement.

Your Turn

10. Students are assigned randomly to 1 of 3 guidance counselors at a school. What is the probability that Ms. Banks, one of the school's guidance counselors, will get exactly 2 of the next 3 students assigned?

Elaborate

11. How do the numbers in one row of Pascal's Triangle relate to the numbers in the previous row?

12. How does Pascal's Triangle relate to the power of a binomial?

13. The expanded form of $(p + q)^3$ is $p^3 + 3p^2q + 3pq^2 + q^3$. In terms of a binomial experiment with a probability p of success and a probability q of failure on each trial, what do each of the terms p^3, $3p^2q$, $3pq^2$, and q^3 represent?

14. **Essential Question Check-In** The Binomial Theorem says that the expanded form of $(a + b)^n$ is a sum of terms of the form ${}_nC_r a^{n-r} b^r$ for what values of r?

Evaluate: Homework and Practice

Personal Math Trainer

- Online Homework
- Hints and Help
- Extra Practice

1. The path LLRRLLR leads to which node in which row of Pascal's Triangle? What is the value of that node?

2. Without expanding the power, determine the middle term of $(a + b)^8$. Explain how you found your answer.

Use the Binomial Theorem to expand each power of a binomial.

3. $(x + 6)^3$
4. $(x - 5)^4$
5. $(x + 3)^6$
6. $(2x - 1)^3$
7. $(3x + 4)^5$
8. $(2x - 3)^7$
9. $(x + 2y)^5$
10. $(3x - y)^4$
11. $(5x + y)^4$
12. $(x - 6y)^5$
13. $(5x - 4y)^3$
14. $(4x + 3y)^6$

Use the Binomial Theorem to find the specified term of the given power of a binomial. (Remember that *r* starts at 0 in the Binomial Theorem, so finding, say, the second term means that $r = 1$.)

15. Find the fourth term in the expanded form of $(x - 1)^6$.
16. Find the second term in the expanded form of $(2x + 1)^4$.
17. Find the third term in the expanded form of $(3x - 2y)^5$.
18. Find the fifth term in the expanded form of $(6x + 8y)^7$.

Ellen takes a multiple-choice quiz that has 5 questions, with 4 answer choices for each question.

19. What is the probability that she will get exactly 2 answers correct by guessing?
20. What is the probability that Ellen will get at least 3 answers correct by guessing?

Manufacturing **A machine that makes a part used in cars has a 98% probability of producing the part within acceptable tolerance levels. The machine makes 25 parts per hour.**

21. What is the probability that the machine will make exactly 20 acceptable parts in an hour?

22. What is the probability that the machine makes 23 or fewer acceptable parts?

23. Match each term of an expanded power of a binomial on the right with the corresponding description of the term on the left. (Remember that r starts at 0 in the Binomial Theorem, so finding, say, the second term means that $r = 1$.)

A. Fifth term in the expanded form of $(x + 2)^6$ — a. ___?___ $640x^2$

B. Fourth term in the expanded form of $(x + 4)^5$ — b. ___?___ $48x^2$

C. Third term in the expanded form of $(x + 8)^4$ — c. ___?___ $240x^2$

D. Second term in the expanded form of $(x + 16)^3$ — d. ___?___ $384x^2$

H.O.T. Focus on Higher Order Thinking

24. **Construct Arguments** Identify the symmetry in the rows of Pascal's Triangle and give an argument based on strings of Ls and Rs to explain why the symmetry exists.

25. **Communicate Mathematical Ideas** Explain why the numbers from Pascal's Triangle show up in the Binomial Theorem.

26. **Represent Real-World Situations** A small airline overbooks flights on the assumption that some passengers will not show up. The probability that a passenger shows up is 0.8. What number of tickets can the airline sell for a 20-seat flight and still have a probability of seating everyone that is at least 90%? Explain your reasoning.

Lesson Performance Task

Suppose that a basketball player has just been fouled while attempting a 3-point shot and is awarded three free throws. Given that the player is 85% successful at making free throws, calculate the probability that the player successfully makes zero, one, two, or all three of the free throws. Which situation is most likely to occur?

6.4 Factoring Polynomials

Essential Question: What are some ways to factor a polynomial, and how is factoring useful?

Resource Locker

Explore Analyzing a Visual Model for Polynomial Factorization

Factoring a polynomial of degree n involves finding factors of lesser a degree that can be multiplied together to produce the polynomial. When a polynomial has degree 3, for example, you can think of it as the volume of a rectangular prism whose dimensions you need to determine.

(A) The volumes of the parts of the rectangular prism are as follows:

Red(R): $V = x^3$

Green(G): $V = 2x^2$

Yellow(Y): $V = 8x$

Blue(B): $V = 4x^2$

Total volume: $V = x^3 + 6x^2 + 8x$

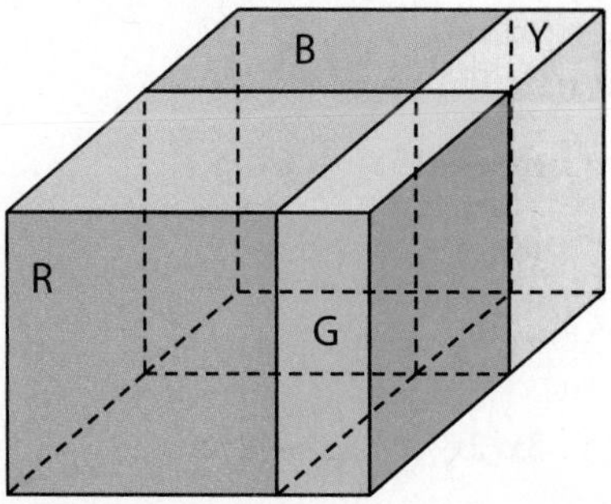

(B) The volume of the red piece is found by cubing the length of one edge. What is the height of this piece? ?

(C) The volume of a rectangular prism is $V = lwh$, where l is the length, w is the width, and h is the height of the prism. Notice that the green prism shares two dimensions with the cube. What are these dimensions? ?

(D) What is the length of the third edge of the green prism? ?

(E) You showed that the width of the cube is ? and the width of the green prism is ? . What is the width of the entire prism? ?

(F) You determined that the length of the green piece is x. Use the volume of the yellow piece and the information you have derived to find the length of the prism. ?

(G) Since the dimensions of the overall prism are x, $x+2$, and $x+4$, the volume of the overall prism can be rewritten in factored form as $V=(x)(x+2)(x+4)$. Multiply these polynomials together to verify that this is equal to the original given expression for the volume of the overall figure. ?

Reflect

1. **Discussion** What is one way to double the volume of the prism?

Explain 1 Factoring Out the Greatest Common Monomial First

Most polynomials cannot be *factored over the integers*, which means to find factors that use only integer coefficients. But when a polynomial can be factored, each factor has a degree less than the polynomial's degree. While the goal is to write the polynomial as a product of linear factors, this is not always possible. When a factor of degree 2 or greater cannot be factored further, it is called an **irreducible factor**.

Example 1 **Factor each polynomial over the integers.**

(A) $6x^3+15x^2+6x$

$6x^3+15x^2+6x$	Write out the polynomial.
$x(6x^2+15x+6)$	Factor out a common monomial, an x.
$3x(2x^2+5x+2)$	Factor out a common monomial, a 3.
$3x(2x+1)(x+2)$	Factor into simplest terms.

Note: The second and third steps can be combined into one step by factoring out the greatest common monomial.

(B) $2x^3-20x$

$2x^3-20x$	Write out the polynomial.
$2x(x^2-10)$	Factor out the greatest common monomial.

Reflect

2. Why wasn't the factor $x^2 - 10$ further factored?

3. Consider what happens when you factor $x^2 - 10$ over the real numbers and not merely the integers. Find a such that $x^2 - 10 = (x - a)(x + a)$.

Your Turn

Factor the polynomial over the integers.

4. $3x^3 + 7x^2 + 4x$

Explain 2 Recognizing Special Factoring Patterns

Remember the factoring patterns you already know:

Difference of two squares: $a^2 - b^2 = (a + b)(a - b)$

Perfect square trinomials: $a^2 + 2ab + b^2 = (a + b)^2$ and $a^2 - 2ab + b^2 = (a - b)^2$

There are two other factoring patterns that will prove useful:

Sum of two cubes: $a^3 + b^3 = (a + b)(a^2 - ab + b^2)$

Difference of two cubes: $a^3 - b^3 = (a - b)(a^2 + ab + b^2)$

Notice that in each of the new factoring patterns, the quadratic factor is irreducible over the integers.

Example 2 **Factor the polynomial using a factoring pattern.**

(A) $27x^3 + 64$

$27x^3 + 64$	Write out the polynomial.
$27x^3 = (3x)^3$	Check if $27x^3$ is a perfect cube.
$64 = (4)^3$	Check if 64 is a perfect cube.
$a^3 + b^3 = (a + b)(a^2 - ab + b^2)$	Use the sum of two cubes formula to factor.
$(3x)^3 + 4^3 = (3x + 4)((3x)^2 - (3x)(4) + 4^2)$	
$27x^3 + 64 = (3x + 4)(9x^2 - 12x + 16)$	

(B) $8x^3 - 27$

$8x^3 - 27$	Write out the polynomial.
$8x^3 = (2x)^3$	Check if $8x^3$ is a perfect cube.
$27 = (3)^3$	Check if 27 is a perfect cube.
$a^3 - b^3 = (a - b)(a^2 + ab + b^2)$	Use the difference of two cubes formula to factor.
$8x^3 - 27 = (2x - 3)(4x^2 + 6x + 9)$	

Reflect

5. The equation $8x^3 - 27 = 0$ has three roots. How many of them are real, what are they, and how many are nonreal?

Your Turn

Factor the polynomial using a factoring pattern.

6. $40x^4 + 5x$

Explain 3 Factoring by Grouping

Another technique for factoring a polynomial is grouping. If the polynomial has pairs of terms with common factors, factor by grouping terms with common factors and then factoring out the common factor from each group. Then look for a common factor of the groups in order to complete the factorization of the polynomial.

Example 3 **Factor the polynomial by grouping.**

(A) $x^3 - x^2 + x - 1$

Write out the polynomial.	$x^3 - x^2 + x - 1$
Group by common factor.	$(x^3 - x^2) + (x - 1)$
Factor.	$x^2(x - 1) + 1(x - 1)$
Regroup.	$(x^2 + 1)(x - 1)$

(B) $x^4 + x^3 + x + 1$

Write out the polynomial.	$x^4 + x^3 + x + 1$
Group by common factor.	$(x^4 + x^3) + (x + 1)$
Factor.	$x^3(x + 1) + 1(x + 1)$
Regroup.	$(x^3 + 1)(x + 1)$
Apply sum of two cubes to the first term.	$(x^2 - x + 1)(x + 1)(x + 1)$
Substitute this into the expression and simplify.	$(x + 1)^2(x^2 - x + 1)$

Your Turn

Factor the polynomial by grouping.

7. $x^3 + 3x^2 + 3x + 2$

Explain 4 Solving a Real-World Problem by Factoring a Polynomial

Remember that the zero-product property is used in solving factorable quadratic equations. It can also be used in solving factorable polynomial equations.

Example 4 **Write and solve a polynomial equation for the situation described.**

(A) A water park is designing a new pool in the shape of a rectangular prism. The sides and bottom of the pool are made of material 5 feet thick. The interior length must be twice the interior height (depth), and the interior width must be three times the interior height. The volume of water that the pool holds must be 6000 cubic feet. What are the exterior dimensions of the pool?

Let x represent the exterior height of the pool, that is, including its bottom. Let h, l, and w represent the interior dimensions. Then the dimensions of the interior of the pool are the following:

$h = x - 5$

$l = 2x - 10$

$w = 3x - 15$

The formula for the volume of a rectangular prism is $V = lwh$. Plug the values into the volume equation.

$V = (2x - 10)(3x - 15)(x - 5)$

$V = (6x^2 - 60x + 150)(x - 5)$

$V = 6x^3 - 90x^2 + 450x - 750$

Now solve for $V = 6000$.

$6000 = 6x^3 - 90x^2 + 450x - 750$

$0 = 6x^3 - 90x^2 + 450x - 6750$

Factor the resulting new polynomial.

$6x^3 - 90x^2 + 450x - 6750$

$= 6x^2(x - 15) + 450(x - 15)$

$= (6x^2 + 450)(x - 15)$

The only real root is $x = 15$. This is the exterior height of the pool.

The interior height of the pool will be 10 feet, the interior length 20 feet, and the interior width 30 feet. Because each side wall of the pool is 5 feet thick, the exterior height is 15 feet, the exterior length is 30 feet, and the exterior width is 40 feet.

(B) **Engineering** To build a hefty wooden feeding trough for a zoo, its sides and bottom should be 2 feet thick, and its outer length should be twice its outer width and height.

What should the outer dimensions of the trough be if it is to hold 288 cubic feet of water?

Volume = Interior Length(feet) · Interior Width(feet) · Interior Height(feet)

$$288 = (2x - 4)(x - 4)(x - 2)$$

$$288 = 2x^3 - 16x^2 + 40x - 32$$

$$0 = 2x^3 - 16x^2 + 40x - 320$$

$$0 = 2x^2(x - 8) + 40(x - 8)$$

$$0 = 2(x^2 + 20)(x - 8)$$

The only real solution is $x = 8$. The trough is 16 feet long, 8 feet wide, and 8 feet high.

Your Turn

8. **Engineering** A small bank vault is being designed in the shape of a rectangular prism. The vault's sides and top should all be 3 feet thick. The outer length of the vault should be twice the outer width. The outer height should be the same as the outer width. What should the outer dimensions of the vault be if it is to have 972 cubic feet of space?

Elaborate

9. Describe how the method of grouping incorporates the method of factoring out the greatest common monomial.

10. How do you decide if an equation fits in the sum of two cubes pattern?

11. How can factoring be used to solve a polynomial equation of the form $p(x) = a$, where a is a nonzero constant?

12. **Essential Question Check-In** What are two ways to factor a polynomial?

Evaluate: Homework and Practice

Personal Math Trainer

- Online Homework
- Hints and Help
- Extra Practice

Factor the polynomial, or identify it as irreducible.

1. $x^3 + x^2 - 12x$

2. $x^3 + 5$

3. $x^3 - 125$

4. $x^3 + 5x^2 + 6x$

5. $8x^3 + 125$

6. $2x^3 + 6x$

7. $216x^3 + 64$

8. $8x^3 - 64$

9. $10x^3 - 80$

10. $2x^4 + 7x^3 + 5x^2$

11. $x^3 + 10x^2 + 16x$

12. $x^3 + 9769$

Factor the polynomial by grouping.

13. $x^3 + 8x^2 + 6x + 48$

14. $x^3 + 4x^2 - x - 4$

15. $8x^4 + 8x^3 + 27x + 27$

16. $27x^4 + 54x^3 - 64x - 128$

17. $x^3 + 2x^2 + 3x + 6$

18. $4x^4 - 4x^3 - x + 1$

Write and solve a polynomial equation for the situation described.

19. Engineering A rectangular two-story horse barn is being designed for a farm. The upper floor will be used for storing hay, and the lower floor will have horse stalls that extend 5 feet from both of the longer walls. The barn's length is twice the barn's width, and the lower floor's ceiling height is 6 feet less than the barn's width. What should the dimensions of the lower floor be if the space not used for stalls is to have a volume of 1920 cubic feet?

20. Arts A piece of rectangular crafting supply is being cut for a new sculpture. You want its length to be 4 times its height and its width to be 2 times its height. If you want the wood to have a volume of 64 cubic centimeters, what will its length, width, and height be?

21. Engineering A new rectangular holding tank is being built. The tank's sides and bottom should be 1 foot thick. Its outer length should be twice its outer width and height.

What should the outer dimensions of the tank be if it is to have a volume of 36 cubic feet?

22. Construction A piece of granite is being cut for a building foundation. You want its length to be 8 times its height and its width to be 3 times its height. If you want the granite to have a volume of 648 cubic yards, what will its length, width, and height be?

23. State which, if any, special factoring pattern each of the following polynomial expressions follows:

a. $x^2 - 4$

b. $3x^3 + 5$

c. $4x^2 + 25$

d. $27x^3 + 1000$

e. $64x^3 - x^2 + 1$

H.O.T. Focus on Higher Order Thinking

24. Communicate Mathematical Ideas What is the relationship between the degree of a polynomial and the degree of its factors?

25. Critical Thinking Why is there no sum-of-two-squares factoring pattern?

26. Explain the Error Jim was trying to factor a polynomial and produced the following result:

$3x^3 + x^2 + 3x + 1$	Write out the polynomial.
$3x^2(x + 1) + 3(x + 1)$	Group by common factor.
$3(x^2 + 1)(x + 1)$	Regroup.

Explain Jim's error.

27. Factoring can also be done over the complex numbers. This allows you to find all the roots of an equation, not just the real ones.

Complete the steps showing how to use a special factor identity to factor $x^2 + 4$ over the complex numbers.

$x^2 + 4$	Write out the polynomial.
$x^2 - (-4)$	___?___
$(x +$ ___?___$)(x -$ ___?___$)$	Factor.
$(x + 2i)($ ___?___ $)$	Simplify.

28. Find all the imaginary roots of the equation $x^4 - 16 = 0$.

29. Factor $x^3 + x^2 + x + 1$ over the complex numbers.

Lesson Performance Task

Sabrina is building a rectangular raised flower bed. The boards on the two shorter sides are 6 inches thick, and the boards on the two longer sides are 4 inches thick. Sabrina wants the outer length of her bed to be 4 times its height and the outer width to be 2 times its height. She also wants the boards to rise 4 inches above the level of the soil in the bed. What should the outer dimensions of the bed be if she wants it to hold 3136 cubic inches of soil?

6.5 Dividing Polynomials

Essential Question: What are some ways to divide polynomials, and how do you know when the divisor is a factor of the dividend?

Resource Locker

Explore — Evaluating a Polynomial Function Using Synthetic Substitution

Polynomials can be written in something called nested form. A polynomial in nested form is written in such a way that evaluating it involves an alternating sequence of additions and multiplications. For instance, the nested form of $p(x) = 4x^3 + 3x^2 + 2x + 1$ is $p(x) = x\big(x(4x + 3) + 2\big) + 1$, which you evaluate by starting with 4, multiplying by the value of x, adding 3, multiplying by x, adding 2, multiplying by x, and adding 1.

(A) Given $p(x) = 4x^3 + 3x^2 + 2x + 1$, find $p(-2)$.

You can set up an array of numbers that captures the sequence of multiplications and additions needed to find $p(a)$. Using this array to find $p(a)$ is called **synthetic substitution**.

Given $p(x) = 4x^3 + 3x^2 + 2x + 1$, find $p(-2)$ by using synthetic substitution. The dashed arrow indicates bringing down, the diagonal arrows represent multiplication by -2, and the solid down arrows indicate adding.

The first two steps are to bring down the leading number, 4, then multiply by the value you are evaluating at, -2.

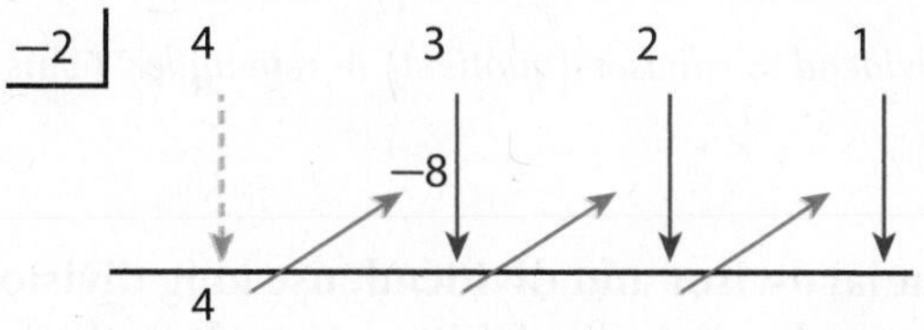

(B) Add 3 and -8.

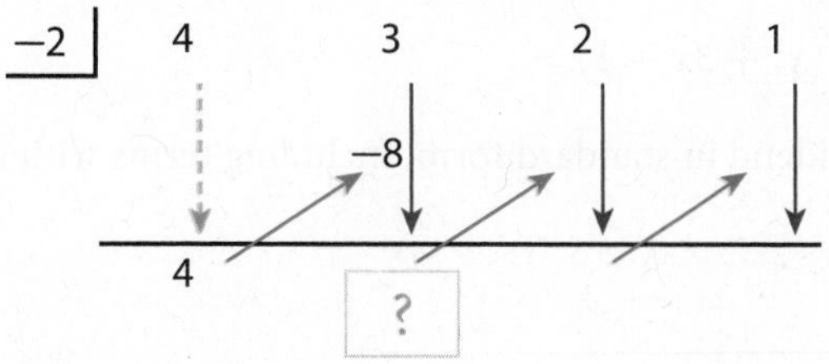

(C) Multiply the previous answer by −2.

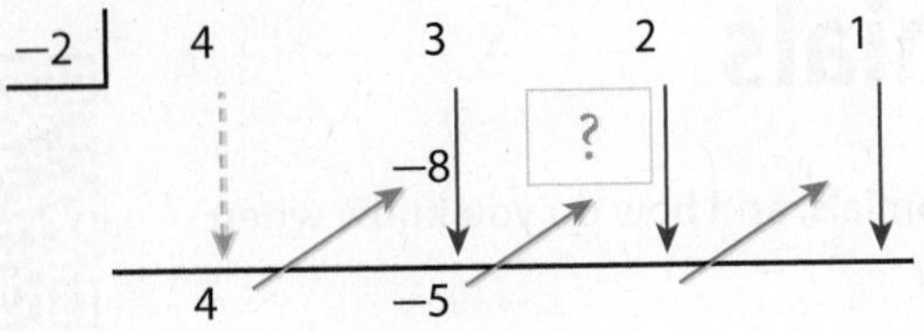

(D) Continue this sequence of steps until you reach the last addition.

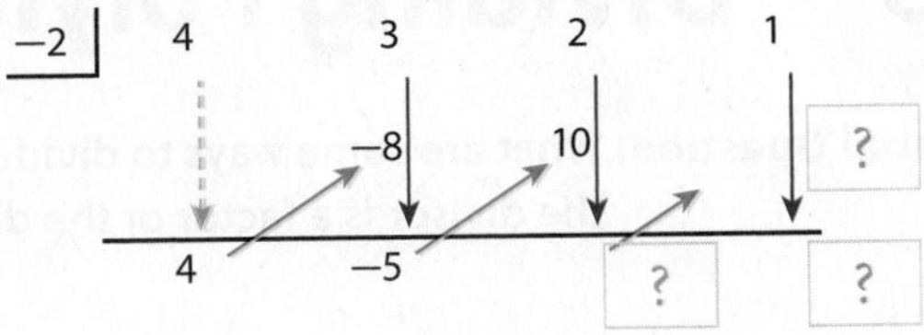

(E) $p(-2) =$?

Reflect

1. **Discussion** After the final addition, what does this sum correspond to?

Explain 1 Dividing Polynomials Using Long Division

Recall that arithmetic long division proceeds as follows.

$$\begin{array}{rl} & 23 \leftarrow \text{Quotient} \\ \text{Divisor} \rightarrow 12\overline{)\,277} & \leftarrow \text{Dividend} \\ 24 & \\ \hline 37 & \\ 36 & \\ \hline 1 & \leftarrow \text{Remainder} \end{array}$$

Notice that the long division leads to the result $\frac{\textit{dividend}}{\textit{divisor}} = \textit{quotient} + \frac{\textit{remainder}}{\textit{divisor}}$. Using the numbers from above, the arithmetic long division leads to $\frac{277}{12} = 23 + \frac{1}{12}$. Multiplying through by the divisor yields the result $\textit{dividend} = (\textit{divisor})(\textit{quotient}) + \textit{remainder}$. (This can be used as a means of checking your work.)

Example 1 **Given a polynomial divisor and dividend, use long division to find the quotient and remainder. Write the result in the form *dividend* = (*divisor*)(*quotient*) + *remainder* and then carry out the multiplication and addition as a check.**

(A) $(4x^3 + 2x^2 + 3x + 5) \div (x^2 + 3x + 1)$

Begin by writing the dividend in standard form, including terms with a coefficient of 0 (if any).

$4x^3 + 2x^2 + 3x + 5$

Write division in the same way as you would when dividing numbers.

$x^2 + 3x + 1\overline{)\,4x^3 + 2x^2 + 3x + 5}$

Find the value you need to multiply the divisor by so that the first term matches with the first term of the dividend. In this case, in order to get $4x^2$, we must multiply x^2 by $4x$. This will be the first term of the quotient.

$$\begin{array}{r} 4x \\ x^2+3x+1 \overline{\smash{)}\, 4x^3+2x^2+3x+5} \end{array}$$

Next, multiply the divisor through by the term of the quotient you just found and subtract that value from the dividend. $(x^2+3x+1)(4x) = 4x^3 + 12x^2 + 4x$, so subtract $4x^3 + 12x^2 + 4x$ from $4x^3 + 2x^2 + 3x + 5$.

$$\begin{array}{r} 4x \\ x^2+3x+1 \overline{\smash{)}\, 4x^3+2x^2+3x+5} \\ \underline{-(4x^3+12x^2+4x)} \\ -10x^2-x+5 \end{array}$$

Taking this difference as the new dividend, continue in this fashion until the largest term of the remaining dividend is of lower degree than the divisor.

$$\begin{array}{r} 4x-10 \\ x^2+3x+1 \overline{\smash{)}\, 4x^3+2x^2+3x+5} \\ \underline{-(4x^3+12x^2+4x)} \\ -10x^2-x+5 \\ \underline{-(-10x^2-30x-10)} \\ 29x+15 \end{array}$$

Since $29x + 5$ is of lower degree than $x^2 + 3x + 1$, stop. $29x + 15$ is the remainder.

Write the final answer.

$4x^3 + 2x^2 + 3x + 5 = (x^2 + 3x + 1)(4x - 10) + 29x + 15$

Check.

$$\begin{aligned} 4x^3 + 2x^2 + 3x + 5 &= (x^2 + 3x + 1)(4x - 10) + 29x + 15 \\ &= 4x^3 + 12x^2 + 4x - 10x^2 - 30x - 10 + 29x + 15 \\ &= 4x^3 + 2x^2 + 3x + 5 \end{aligned}$$

(B) $(6x^4 + 5x^3 + 2x + 8) \div (x^2 + 2x - 5)$

Write the dividend in standard form, including terms with a coefficient of 0.

$6x^4 + 5x^3 + 0x^2 + 2x + 8$

Write the division in the same way as you would when dividing numbers.

$$x^2+2x-5 \overline{\smash{)}\, 6x^4+5x^3+0x^2+2x+8}$$

Divide.

$$\begin{array}{r} 6x^2 - \boxed{7x} + \boxed{44} \\ x^2 + 2x - 5 \overline{) 6x^4 + 5x^3 + 0x^2 + 2x + 8} \\ -(6x^4 + 12x^3 - 30x^2) \\ \hline -7x^3 + 30x^2 + 2x \\ -(-7x^3 \boxed{-14x^2 + 35x}) \\ \hline \boxed{44x^2 - 33x} + 8 \\ -(\boxed{44x^2 + 88x - 220}) \\ \hline \boxed{-121x + 228} \end{array}$$

Write the final answer.

$6x^4 + 5x^3 + 2x + 8 =$ $\boxed{(x^2 + 2x - 5)(6x^2 - 7x + 44) - 121x + 228}$

Check.

$$6x^4 + 5x^3 + 2x + 8 = (x^2 + 2x - 5)(6x^2 - 7x + 44) - 121x + 228$$

$$= 6x^4 - 7x^3 + 44x^2 + 12x^3 - 14x^2 + 88x - 30x^2 + 35x - 220 - 121x + 228$$

$$= 6x^4 + 5x^3 + 2x + 8$$

Reflect

2. How do you include the terms with coefficients of 0?

Your Turn

Use long division to find the quotient and remainder. Write the result in the form *dividend* = (*divisor*)(*quotient*) + *remainder* and then carry out a check.

3. $(15x^3 + 8x - 12) \div (3x^2 + 6x + 1)$

4. $(9x^4 + x^3 + 11x^2 - 4) \div (x^2 + 16)$

Explain 2 Dividing $p(x)$ by $x - a$ Using Synthetic Division

Compare long division with synthetic substitution. There are two important things to notice. The first is that $p(a)$ is equal to the remainder when $p(x)$ is divided by $x - a$. The second is that the numbers to the left of $p(a)$ in the bottom row of the synthetic substitution array give the coefficients of the quotient. For this reason, synthetic substitution is also called **synthetic division**.

Long Division	Synthetic Substitution
$\begin{array}{r} 3x^2 + 10x + 20 \\ x - 2 \overline{) 3x^3 + 4x^2 + 0x + 10} \\ \underline{-(3x^3 - 6x^2)} \\ 10x^2 + 0x \\ \underline{-(10x^2 - 20x)} \\ 20x + 10 \\ \underline{-20x - 40} \\ 50 \end{array}$	$\begin{array}{r|rrrr} 2 & 3 & 4 & 0 & 10 \\ & & 6 & 20 & 40 \\ \hline & 3 & 10 & 20 & \boxed{50} \end{array}$

Example 2 **Given a polynomial $p(x)$, use synthetic division to divide by $x - a$ and obtain the quotient and the (nonzero) remainder. Write the result in the form $p(x) = (x - a)(quotient) + p(a)$, then carry out the multiplication and addition as a check.**

(A) $(7x^3 - 6x + 9) \div (x + 5)$

By inspection, $a = -5$. Write the coefficients and a in the synthetic division format.

$$\begin{array}{r|rrrr} -5 & 7 & 0 & -6 & 9 \\ & & & & \\ \hline & & & & \end{array}$$

Bring down the first coefficient. Then multiply and add for each column.

$$\begin{array}{r|rrrr} -5 & 7 & 0 & -6 & 9 \\ & & -35 & 175 & -845 \\ \hline & 7 & -35 & 169 & \boxed{-836} \end{array}$$

Write the result, using the non-remainder entries of the bottom row as the coefficients.

$$(7x^3 - 6x + 9) = (x + 5)(7x^2 - 35x + 169) - 836$$

Check.

$$\begin{aligned} (7x^3 - 6x + 9) &= (x + 5)(7x^2 - 35x + 169) - 836 \\ &= 7x^3 - 35x^2 - 35x^2 - 175x + 169x + 845 - 836 \\ &= 7x^3 - 6x + 9 \end{aligned}$$

(B) $(4x^4 - 3x^2 + 7x + 2) \div \left(x - \frac{1}{2}\right)$

Find a. Then write the coefficients and a in the synthetic division format.

Find a = $\boxed{\frac{1}{2}}$

$$\begin{array}{r|rrrrr} \frac{1}{2} & 4 & 0 & -3 & 7 & 2 \\ & & & & & \\ \hline & & & & & \end{array}$$

Bring down the first coefficient. Then multiply and add for each column.

$$\begin{array}{r|rrrrr} \frac{1}{2} & 4 & 0 & -3 & 7 & 2 \\ & & 2 & 1 & -1 & 3 \\ \hline & 4 & 2 & -2 & 6 & \boxed{5} \end{array}$$

Write the result.

$(4x^4 - 3x^2 + 7x + 2) = \left(x - \frac{1}{2}\right)\left(4x^3 + 2x^2 - 2x + 6\right) + 5$

Check.

$(4x^4 - 3x^2 + 7x + 2) = \left(x - \frac{1}{2}\right)\left(4x^3 + 2x^2 - 2x + 6\right) + 5$

$= 4x^4 + 2x^3 - 2x^2 + 6x - 2x^3 - x^2 + x - 3 + 5$

$= 4x^4 - 3x^2 + 7x + 2$

Reflect

5. Can you use synthetic division to divide a polynomial by $x^2 + 3$? Explain.

Your Turn

Given a polynomial $p(x)$, use synthetic division to divide by $x - a$ and obtain the quotient and the (nonzero) remainder. Write the result in the form $p(x) = (x - a)(quotient) + p(a)$. You may wish to perform a check.

6. $\left(2x^3 + 5x^2 - x + 7\right) \div (x - 2)$

7. $\left(6x^4 - 25x^3 - 3x + 5\right) \div \left(x + \frac{1}{3}\right)$

Explain 3 Using the Remainder Theorem and Factor Theorem

When $p(x)$ is divided by $x - a$, the result can be written in the form $p(x) = (x - a)q(x) + r$ where $q(x)$ is the quotient and r is a number. Substituting a for x in this equation gives $p(a) = (a - a)q(a) + r$. Since $a - a = 0$, this simplifies to $p(a) = r$. This is known as the **Remainder Theorem**.

If the remainder $p(a)$ in $p(x) = (x - a)q(x) + p(a)$ is 0, then $p(x) = (x - a)q(x)$, which tells you that $x - a$ is a factor of $p(x)$. Conversely, if $x - a$ is a factor of $p(x)$, then you can write $p(x)$ as $p(x) = (x - a)q(x)$, and when you divide $p(x)$ by $x - a$, you get the quotient $q(x)$ with a remainder of 0. These facts are known as the **Factor Theorem**.

Example 3 **Determine whether the given binomial is a factor of the polynomial $p(x)$. If so, find the remaining factors of $p(x)$.**

(A) $p(x) = x^3 + 3x^2 - 4x - 12;\ (x + 3)$

Use synthetic division.

−3	1	3	−4	−12
		−3	0	12
	1	0	−4	0

Since the remainder is 0, $x + 3$ is a factor.

Write $q(x)$ and then factor it.

$q(x) = x^2 - 4 = (x + 2)(x - 2)$

So, $p(x) = x^3 + 3x^2 - 4x - 12 = (x + 2)(x - 2)(x + 3)$.

B $p(x) = x^4 - 4x^3 - 6x^2 + 4x + 5;\ (x + 1)$

Use synthetic division.

$$\begin{array}{r|rrrrr} -1 & 1 & -4 & -6 & 4 & 5 \\ & & -1 & 5 & 1 & -5 \\ \hline & 1 & -5 & -1 & 5 & \boxed{0} \end{array}$$

Since the remainder is 0, $(x + 1)$ is a factor. Write $q(x)$.

$q(x) =$ $x^3 - 5x^2 - x + 5$

Now factor $q(x)$ by grouping.

$q(x) =$ $x^3 - 5x^2 - x + 5$

$=$ $x^2(x - 5) - (x - 5)$

$=$ $(x^2 - 1)(x - 5)$

$=$ $(x + 1(x - 1))(x - 5)$

So, $p(x) = x^4 - 4x^3 - 6x^2 + 4x + 5 =$ $(x + 1)(x + 1)(x - 1)(x - 5)$.

Your Turn

Determine whether the given binomial is a factor of the polynomial $p(x)$. If it is, find the remaining factors of $p(x)$.

8. $p(x) = 2x^4 + 8x^3 + 2x + 8;\ (x + 4)$

9. $p(x) = 3x^3 - 2x + 5;\ (x - 1)$

Elaborate

10. Compare long division and synthetic division of polynomials.

11. How does knowing one linear factor of a polynomial help find the other factors?

12. What conditions must be met in order to use synthetic division?

13. **Essential Question Check-In** How do you know when the divisor is a factor of the dividend?

Evaluate: Homework and Practice

Personal Math Trainer
- Online Homework
- Hints and Help
- Extra Practice

Given $p(x)$, find $p(-3)$ by using synthetic substitution.

1. $p(x) = 8x^3 + 7x^2 + 2x + 4$

2. $p(x) = x^3 + 6x^2 + 7x - 25$

3. $p(x) = 2x^3 + 5x^2 - 3x$

4. $p(x) = -x^4 + 5x^3 - 8x + 45$

Given a polynomial divisor and dividend, use long division to find the quotient and remainder. Write the result in the form *dividend* = (*divisor*)(*quotient*) + *remainder*. You may wish to carry out a check.

5. $(18x^3 - 3x^2 + x - 1) \div (x^2 - 4)$

6. $(6x^4 + x^3 - 9x + 13) \div (x^2 + 8)$

7. $(x^4 + 6x - 2.5) \div (x^2 + 3x + 0.5)$

8. $(x^3 + 250x^2 + 100x) \div \left(\frac{1}{2}x^2 + 25x + 9\right)$

Given a polynomial $p(x)$, use synthetic division to divide by $x - a$ and obtain the quotient and the (nonzero) remainder. Write the result in the form $p(x) = (x - a)(\text{quotient}) + p(a)$. You may wish to carry out a check.

9. $(7x^3 - 4x^2 - 400x - 100) \div (x - 8)$

10. $(8x^4 - 28.5x^2 - 9x + 10) \div (x + 0.25)$

11. $(2.5x^3 + 6x^2 - 5.5x - 10) \div (x + 1)$

Determine whether the given binomial is a factor of the polynomial $p(x)$. If so, find the remaining factors of $p(x)$.

12. $p(x) = x^3 + 2x^2 - x - 2$; $(x + 2)$

13. $p(x) = 2x^4 + 6x^3 - 5x - 10$; $(x + 2)$

14. $p(x) = x^3 - 22x^2 + 157x - 360$; $(x - 8)$

15. $p(x) = 4x^3 - 12x^2 + 2x - 5$; $(x - 3)$

16. The volume of a rectangular prism whose dimensions are binomials with integer coefficients is modeled by the function $V(x) = x^3 - 8x^2 + 19x - 12$. Given that $x - 1$ and $x - 3$ are two of the dimensions, find the missing dimension of the prism.

17. Given that the height of a rectangular prism is $x + 2$ and the volume is $x^3 - x^2 - 6x$, write an expression that represents the area of the base of the prism.

18. Physics A Van de Graaff generator is a machine that produces very high voltages by using small, safe levels of electric current. One machine has a current that can be modeled by $I(t) = t + 2$, where $t > 0$ represents time in seconds. The power of the system can be modeled by $P(t) = 0.5t^3 + 6t^2 + 10t$. Write an expression that represents the voltage of the system. Recall that $V = \frac{P}{I}$.

19. Geometry The volume of a hexagonal pyramid is modeled by the function $V(x) = \frac{1}{3}x^3 + \frac{4}{3}x^2 + \frac{2}{3}x - \frac{1}{3}$. Given the height $x + 1$, use polynomial division to find an expression for the area of the base.
(Hint: For a pyramid, $V = \frac{1}{3}Bh$.)

20. Explain the Error Two students used synthetic division to divide $3x^3 - 2x - 8$ by $x - 2$. Determine which solution is correct. Find the error in the other solution.

A.	B.
$\begin{array}{r|rrrr} 2 & 3 & 0 & -2 & -8 \\ & & 6 & 12 & 20 \\ \hline & 3 & 6 & 10 & 12 \end{array}$	$\begin{array}{r|rrrr} -2 & 3 & 0 & -2 & -8 \\ & & -6 & 12 & -20 \\ \hline & 3 & -6 & 10 & -28 \end{array}$

H.O.T. Focus on Higher Order Thinking

21. Multi-Step Use synthetic division to divide $p(x) = 3x^3 - 11x^2 - 56x - 50$ by $(3x + 4)$. Then check the solution.

22. Critical Thinking The polynomial $ax^3 + bx^2 + cx + d$ is factored as $3(x - 2)(x + 3)(x - 4)$. What are the values of a and d? Explain.

23. Analyze Relationships Investigate whether the set of whole numbers, the set of integers, and the set of rational numbers are closed under each of the four basic operations. Then consider whether the set of polynomials in one variable is closed under the four basic operations, and determine whether polynomials are like whole numbers, integers, or rational numbers with respect to closure. Use the table to organize.

	Whole Numbers	Integers	Rational Numbers	Polynomials
Addition	?	?	?	?
Subtraction	?	?	?	?
Multiplication	?	?	?	?
Division (by nonzero)	?	?	?	?

Lesson Performance Task

The table gives the attendance data for all divisions of NCAA Women's Basketball.

NCAA Women's Basketball Attendance			
Season	Years since 2006–2007	Number of teams in all 3 divisions	Attendance (in thousands) for all 3 divisions
2006–2007	0	1003	10,878.3
2007–2008	1	1013	11,120.8
2008–2009	2	1032	11,160.3
2009–2010	3	1037	11,134.7
2010–2011	4	1048	11,160.0
2011–2012	5	1055	11,201.8

Enter the data from the second, third, and fourth columns of the table and perform linear regression on the data pairs (t, T) and cubic regression on the data pairs (t, A) where $t =$ years since the 2006–2007 season, $T =$ number of teams, and $A =$ attendance (in thousands).

Then create a model for the average attendance per team: $A_{avg}(t) = \frac{A(t)}{T(t)}$. Carry out the division to write $A_{avg}(t)$ in the form $quadratic\ quotient + \frac{remainder}{T(t)}$.

Use an online computer algebra system to carry out the division of $A(t)$ by $T(t)$.

Polynomials

Essential Question: How can you use polynomials to solve real-world problems?

Key Vocabulary
binomial *(binomio)*
monomial *(monomio)*
polynomial *(polinomio)*
synthetic division *(división sintética)*
trinomial *(trinomio)*

KEY EXAMPLE *(Lesson 6.1)*

Subtract: $\left(5x^4 - x^3 + 2x + 1\right) - \left(2x^3 + 3x^2 - 4x - 7\right)$

$$\begin{array}{r} 5x^4 - x^3 + 0x^2 + 2x + 1 \\ + \quad -2x^3 - 3x^2 + 4x + 7 \\ \hline 5x^4 - 3x^3 - 3x^2 + 6x + 8 \end{array}$$

Write in standard form.
Align like terms and add the opposite.
Add.

Therefore, $\left(5x^4 - x^3 + 2x + 1\right) - \left(2x^3 + 3x^2 - 4x - 7\right) = 5x^4 - 3x^3 - 3x^2 + 6x + 8$.

KEY EXAMPLE *(Lesson 6.2)*

Multiply: $(3x - 2)\left(2x^2 - 5x + 1\right)$

$(3x - 2)\left(2x^2 - 5x + 1\right)$ — Write in standard form.

$3x\left(2x^2\right) + 3x(-5x) + 3x(1) + (-2)\left(2x^2\right) + (-2)(-5x) + (-2)(1)$ — Distribute the $3x$ and the -2.

$6x^3 - 15x^2 + 3x - 4x^2 + 10x - 2$ — Simplify.

$6x^3 - 19x^2 + 13x - 2$ — Combine like terms.

Therefore, $(3x - 2)\left(2x^2 - 5x + 1\right) = 6x^3 - 19x^2 + 13x - 2$.

KEY EXAMPLE *(Lesson 6.5)*

Divide: $\left(x^3 + 10x^2 + 13x + 36\right) \div (x + 9)$

$$\begin{array}{r} x^2 + x + 4 \\ x + 9 \,\big)\, x^3 + 10x^2 + 13x + 36 \\ -\left(x^3 + 9x^2\right) \qquad\qquad \\ \hline x^2 + 13x \qquad \\ -\left(x^2 + 9x\right) \qquad \\ \hline 4x + 36 \\ -(4x + 36) \\ \hline 0 \end{array}$$

In order to get x^3, multiply by x^2.
Multiply the divisor through by x^2, then subtract.
In order to get x^2, multiply by x.
Multiply the divisor through by x, then subtract.
In order to get $4x$, multiply by 4.
Multiply the divisor through by 4, then subtract.

Therefore, $\left(x^3 + 10x^2 + 13x + 36\right) \div (x + 9) = x^2 + x + 4$.

EXERCISES

Simplify. *(Lessons 6.1, 6.2, 6.5)*

1. $(9x^2 + 2x + 12) + (7x^2 + 10x - 13)$

2. $(6x^6 - 4x^5) - (10x^5 - 15x^4 + 8)$

3. $(x - 3)(4x^2 - 2x + 3)$

4. $(9x^4 + 27x^3 + 23x^2 + 10x) \div (x^2 + 2x)$

5. Mr. Alonzo runs a car repair garage. The average income from repairing a car can be modeled by $C(x) = 45x + 150$. If, for one year, the number of cars repaired can be modeled by $N(x) = 9x^2 + 7x + 6$, write a polynomial that can be used to model Mr. Alonzo's business income for that year. Explain. *(Lesson 6.2)*

MODULE PERFORMANCE TASK

What's the Temperature?

A meteorologist studying the temperature patterns for Redding, California, found the average of the daily minimum and maximum temperatures for each month, but the August temperatures are missing.

Month	Jan	Feb	Mar	Apr	May	June	July	Aug	Sep	Oct	Nov	Dec
Average Max Temperature (°F)	55.3	61.3	62.5	69.6	80.5	90.4	98.3	?	89.3	77.6	62.1	54.7
Average Min Temperature (°F)	35.7	40	41.7	46	52.3	61.8	64.7	?	58.8	49.2	41.4	35.2

How can she find the averages for August? She began by fitting the polynomial function shown below to the data for the average maximum temperature, where x is the month, with $x = 1$ corresponding to January, and the temperature is in degrees Fahrenheit.

$$T_{max}(x) = 0.0095x^5 - 0.2719x^4 + 2.5477x^3 - 9.1882x^2 + 17.272x + 45.468$$

She also thinks that a vertical compression of this function will create a function that fits the average minimum temperature data for Redding.

Use this information to find the average high and low temperature for August. Use graphs, numbers, words, or algebra to explain how you reached your conclusion.

Ready to Go On?

6.1–6.5 Polynomials

Personal Math Trainer
- Online Homework
- Hints and Help
- Extra Practice

Factor the polynomial. *(Lesson 6.4)*

1. $3x^2 + 4x - 4$

2. $2x^3 + 4x^2 - 30x$

3. $9x^2 - 25$

4. $4x^2 - 16x + 16$

Complete the polynomial operation. *(Lesson 6.1, 6.2, 6.3, 6.5)*

5. $(8x^3 - 2x^2 - 4x + 8) + (5x^2 + 6x - 4)$

6. $(-4x^2 - 2x + 8) - (x^2 + 8x - 5)$

7. $5x(x + 2)(3x - 7)$

8. $(3x^3 + 12x^2 + 11x - 2) \div (x + 2)$

9. $(x + y)^6$

ESSENTIAL QUESTION

10. Write a real-world situation that would require adding polynomials. *(Lesson 6.1)*

MODULE 6
MIXED REVIEW

Assessment Readiness

1. Look at each polynomial division problem. Can the polynomials be divided without a remainder?
Write Yes or No for A–C.

A. $(3x^3 - 5x^2 + 10x + 4) \div (3x + 1)$

B. $(2x^2 - 5x - 1) \div (x - 3)$

C. $(x^3 - 4x^2 + 2x - 3) \div (x + 2)$

2. Consider the polynomial $x^3 - x^2 - 6x$.
Determine if each statement is True or False.

A. $6x$ can be factored out of every term.

B. The completely factored polynomial is $x(x + 2)(x - 3)$.

C. $f(x) = x^3 - x^2 - 6x$ has a global minimum.

3. Alana completed a problem where she had to find the sum of the polynomials $(3x^2 + 8x - 4)$ and $(-8x^3 - 3x + 4)$. Her answer is 0. Describe and correct her mistake. When graphed, how many times does the sum change directions?

4. A rectangular plot of land has a length of $(2x^2 + 5x - 20)$ and a width of $(3x + 4)$. What polynomial represents the area of the plot of land? Explain how you got your answer.

Polynomial Equations

MODULE 7

Essential Question: How can you use polynomial equations to solve real-world problems?

REAL WORLD VIDEO
The population of the Texas horned lizard has decreased rapidly, and the species is now considered threatened. Biologists use polynomials and other mathematical models to study threatened and endangered species.

MODULE PERFORMANCE TASK PREVIEW

What Do Polynomials Have to Do with Endangered Species?

A species is considered to be endangered when the population is so low that the species is at risk of becoming extinct. Biologists use mathematics to model the population of species, and they use their models to help them predict the future population and to determine whether or not a species is at risk of extinction. How can a polynomial be used to model a species population? Let's find out!

Are YOU Ready?

Complete these exercises to review skills you will need for this module.

Personal Math Trainer

- Online Homework
- Hints and Help
- Extra Practice

Real Numbers

Example 1 Compare $2\sqrt{64}$ and $\sqrt{225}$.

$2\sqrt{64} = 2 \cdot 8$ and $\sqrt{225} = 15$ Evaluate the radicals.

$16 > 15$ Multiply and compare.

Since $16 > 15$, $2\sqrt{64} > \sqrt{225}$.

Compare. Use $>$ or $<$.

1. $4\sqrt{25}$ ___?___ $25\sqrt{4}$ **2.** $0.75\sqrt{144}$ ___?___ $8\sqrt{16}$ **3.** $2.2\sqrt{100}$ ___?___ $3\sqrt{36}$

Add and Subtract Rational Numbers

Example 2 Add $\frac{3}{4} + \frac{5}{6}$.

$\left(\frac{3}{3}\right) \cdot \frac{3}{4} + \left(\frac{2}{2}\right) \cdot \frac{5}{6}$ The LCM is 12. Multiply by 1.

$\frac{9}{12} + \frac{10}{12}$ Add.

$\frac{19}{12}$

Add or subtract.

4. $\frac{1}{3} + \frac{5}{8}$ **5.** $\frac{7}{12} - \frac{4}{9}$ **6.** $\frac{9}{8} - \frac{5}{6}$

Solving Quadratic Equations by Factoring

Example 3 Solve $x^2 + 3x - 10 = 0$ for x.

$(x - 2)(x + 5) = 0$ Factor.

Either $(x - 2) = 0$ or $(x + 5) = 0$

$x = 2$ or $x = -5$ Solve.

The solutions for x are 2 and -5.

Solve for x.

7. $x^2 - 5x + 4 = 0$ **8.** $x^2 + 11x + 30 = 0$ **9.** $x^2 + 6x = 16$

7.1 Finding Rational Solutions of Polynomial Equations

Essential Question: How do you find the rational roots of a polynomial equation?

Resource Locker

Explore — Relating Zeros and Coefficients of Polynomial Functions

The zeros of a polynomial function and the coefficients of the function are related. Consider the polynomial function $f(x) = (x + 2)(x - 1)(x + 3)$.

(A) Identify the zeros of the polynomial function.

(B) Multiply the factors to write the function in standard form.

(C) How are the zeros of $f(x)$ related to the standard form of the function?

(D) Now consider the polynomial function $g(x) = (2x + 3)(4x - 5)(6x - 1)$. Identify the zeros of this function.

(E) Multiply the factors to write the function in standard form.

(F) How are the zeros of $g(x)$ related to the standard form of the function?

Reflect

1. In general, how are the zeros of a polynomial function related to the function written in standard form?
2. **Discussion** Does the relationship from the first Reflect question hold if the zeros are all integers? Explain.
3. If you use the zeros, you can write the factored form of $g(x)$ as $g(x) = \left(x + \frac{3}{2}\right)\left(x - \frac{5}{4}\right)\left(x - \frac{1}{6}\right)$, rather than as $g(x) = (2x + 3)(4x - 5)(6x - 1)$. What is the relationship of the factors between the two forms? Give this relationship in a general form.

Explain 1 Finding Zeros Using the Rational Zero Theorem

If a polynomial function $p(x)$ is equal to $(a_1x + b_1)(a_2x + b_2)(a_3x + b_3)$, where a_1, a_2, a_3, b_1, b_2, and b_3 are integers, the leading coefficient of $p(x)$ will be the product $a_1a_2a_3$ and the constant term will be the product $b_1b_2b_3$. The zeros of $p(x)$ will be the rational numbers $-\frac{b_1}{a_1}$, $-\frac{b_2}{a_2}$, $-\frac{b_3}{a_3}$.

Comparing the zeros of $p(x)$ to its coefficient and constant term shows that the numerators of the polynomial's zeros are factors of the constant term and the denominators of the zeros are factors of the leading coefficient. This result can be generalized as the Rational Zero Theorem.

Rational Zero Theorem

If $p(x)$ is a polynomial function with integer coefficients, and if $\frac{m}{n}$ is a zero of $p(x)$ $\left(p\left(\frac{m}{n}\right) = 0\right)$, then m is a factor of the constant term of $p(x)$ and n is a factor of the leading coefficient of $p(x)$.

Example 1 **Find the rational zeros of the polynomial function; then write the function as a product of factors. Make sure to test the possible zeros to find the actual zeros of the function.**

(A) $f(x) = x^3 + 2x^2 - 19x - 20$

a. Use the Rational Zero Theorem to find all possible rational zeros.
Factors of -20: $\pm1, \pm2, \pm4, \pm5, \pm10, \pm20$

b. Test the possible zeros. Use a synthetic division table to organize the work. In this table, the first row (shaded) represents the coefficients of the polynomial, the first column represents the divisors, and the last column represents the remainders.

$\frac{m}{n}$	1	2	−19	−20
1	1	3	−16	−36
2	1	4	−11	−42
4	1	6	5	0
5	1	7	16	60

c. Factor the polynomial. The synthetic division by 4 results in a remainder of 0, so 4 is a zero and the polynomial in factored form is given as follows:

$$(x - 4)(x^2 + 6x + 5) = 0$$

$$(x - 4)(x + 5)(x + 1) = 0$$

$$x = 4, x = -5, \text{ or } x = -1$$

The zeros are $x = 4$, $x = -5$, and $x = -1$.

(B) $f(x) = x^4 - 4x^3 - 7x^2 + 22x + 24$

a. Use the Rational Zero Theorem to find all possible rational zeros.

Factors of 24: $\pm1, \pm2, \pm3, \pm4, \pm6, \pm8, \pm12, \pm24$

b. Test the possible zeros. Use a synthetic division table.

$\frac{m}{n}$	1	−4	−7	22	24
1	1	−3	−10	12	36
2	1	−2	−11	0	24
3	1	−1	−10	−8	0

c. Factor the polynomial. The synthetic division by 3 results in a remainder of 0, so 3 is a zero and the polynomial in factored form is given as follows:
$(x-3)(x^3-x^2-10x-8)=0$

d. Use the Rational Zero Theorem again to find all possible rational zeros of $g(x)=x^3-x^2-10x-8$.

Factors of −8: ±1, ±2, ±4, ±8

e. Test the possible zeros. Use a synthetic division table.

$\frac{m}{n}$	1	−1	−10	−8
1	1	0	−10	−18
2	1	1	−8	−24
4	1	3	2	0

f. Factor the polynomial. The synthetic division by 4 results in a remainder of 0, so 4 is a zero and the polynomial in factored form is:

$(x-3)(x-4)(1x^2+3x+2)=0$

$(x-3)(x-4)(x+2)(x+1)=0$

$x=3, x=4, x=-2$, or $x=-1$

The zeros are $x=3$, $x=4$, $x=-2$, and $x=-1$.

Reflect

4. How is using synthetic division on a 4th degree polynomial to find its zeros different than using synthetic division on a 3rd degree polynomial to find its zeros?

5. Suppose you are trying to find the zeros the function $f(x)=x^2+1$. Would it be possible to use synthetic division on this polynomial? Why or why not?

6. Using synthetic division, you find that $\frac{1}{2}$ is a zero of $f(x)=2x^3+x^2-13x+6$. The quotient from the synthetic division array for $f\left(\frac{1}{2}\right)$ is $2x^2+2x-12$. Show how to write the factored form of $f(x)=2x^3+x^2-13x+6$ using integer coefficients.

Your Turn

7. Find the zeros of $f(x) = x^3 + 3x^2 - 13x - 15$.

Explain 2 Solving a Real-World Problem Using the Rational Root Theorem

Since a zero of a function $f(x)$ is a value of x for which $f(x) = 0$, finding the zeros of a polynomial function $p(x)$ is the same thing as find the solutions of the polynomial equation $p(x) = 0$. Because a solution of a polynomial equation is known as a **root**, the Rational Zero Theorem can be also expressed as the Rational Root Theorem.

Rational Root Theorem

If the polynomial $p(x)$ has integer coefficients, then every rational root of the polynomial equation $p(x) = 0$ can be written in the form $\frac{m}{n}$, where m is a factor of the constant term of $p(x)$ and n is a factor of the leading coefficient of $p(x)$.

Engineering A pen company is designing a gift container for their new premium pen. The marketing department has designed a pyramidal box with a rectangular base. The base width is 1 inch shorter than its base length and the height is 3 inches taller than 3 times the base length. The volume of the box must be 6 cubic inches. What are the dimensions of the box? Graph the volume function and the line $y = 6$ on a graphing calculator to check your solution.

Analyze Information

The important information is that the base width must be 1 inch shorter than the base length, the height must be 3 inches taller than 3 times the base length, and the box must have a volume of 6 cubic inches.

Formulate a Plan

Write an equation to model the volume of the box.

Let x represent the base length in inches. The base width is $x - 1$ and the height is $3x + 3$, or $3(x + 1)$.

$$\frac{1}{3}\ell w h = V$$

$$\frac{1}{3}(x)(x-1)(3)(x+1) = 6$$

$$1x^3 - 1x - 6 = 0$$

Solve

Use the Rational Root Theorem to find all possible rational roots.

Factors of -6: $\pm1, \pm2, \pm3, \pm6$
Test the possible roots. Use a synthetic division table.

$\frac{m}{n}$	1	0	-1	-6
1	1	1	0	-6
2	1	2	3	0
3	1	3	8	18

Factor the polynomial. The synthetic division by 2 results in a remainder of 0, so 2 is a root and the polynomial in factored form is as follows: $(1x - 2)(1x^2 + 2x + 3) = 0$.
The quadratic polynomial produces only complex roots, so the only possible answer for the base length is 2 inches. The base width is 1 inch and the height is 9 inches.

Justify and Evaluate

The x-coordinates of the points where the graphs of two functions, f and g, intersect is the solution of the equation $f(x) = g(x)$. Using a graphing calculator to graph the volume function and $y = 6$ results in the graphs intersecting at the point (2, 6). Since the x-coordinate is 2, the answer is correct.

Your Turn

8. **Engineering** A box company is designing a new rectangular gift container. The marketing department has designed a box with a width 2 inches shorter than its length and a height 3 inches taller than its length. The volume of the box must be 56 cubic inches. What are the dimensions of the box?

Elaborate

9. For a polynomial function with integer coefficients, how are the function's coefficients and rational zeros related?

10. Describe the process for finding the rational zeros of a polynomial function with integer coefficients.

11. How is the Rational Root Theorem useful when solving a real-world problem about the volume of an object when the volume function is a polynomial and a specific value of the function is given?

12. **Essential Question Check-In** What does the Rational Root Theorem find?

Evaluate: Homework and Practice

Personal Math Trainer

- Online Homework
- Hints and Help
- Extra Practice

Find the rational zeros of each polynomial function. Then write each function in factored form.

1. $f(x) = x^3 - x^2 - 10x - 8$

2. $f(x) = x^3 + 2x^2 - 23x - 60$

3. $j(x) = 2x^3 - x^2 - 13x - 6$

4. $g(x) = x^3 - 9x^2 + 23x - 15$

5. $h(x) = x^3 - 5x^2 + 2x + 8$

6. $h(x) = 6x^3 - 7x^2 - 9x - 2$

7. $s(x) = x^3 - x^2 - x + 1$

8. $t(x) = x^3 + x^2 - 8x - 12$

9. $k(x) = x^4 + 5x^3 - x^2 - 17x + 12$

10. $g(x) = x^4 - 6x^3 + 11x^2 - 6x$

11. $h(x) = x^4 - 2x^3 - 3x^2 + 4x + 4$

12. $f(x) = x^4 - 5x^2 + 4$

13. **Manufacturing** A laboratory supply company is designing a new rectangular box in which to ship glass pipes. The company has created a box with a width 2 inches shorter than its length and a height 9 inches taller than twice its length. The volume of each box must be 45 cubic inches. What are the dimensions?

14. **Engineering** A natural history museum is building a pyramidal glass structure for its tree snake exhibit. Its research team has designed a pyramid with a square base and with a height that is 2 yards more than a side of its base. The volume of the pyramid must be 147 cubic yards. What are the dimensions?

15. **Engineering** A paper company is designing a new, pyramid-shaped paperweight. Its development team has decided that to make the length of the paperweight 4 inches less than the height and the width of the paperweight 3 inches less than the height. The paperweight must have a volume of 12 cubic inches. What are the dimensions of the paperweight?

16. Match each set of roots with its polynomial function.

A. $x = 2, x = 3, x = 4$

B. $x = -2, x = -4, x = \frac{3}{2}$

C. $x = \frac{1}{2}, x = \frac{5}{4}, x = -\frac{7}{3}$

D. $x = -\frac{4}{5}, x = \frac{6}{7}, x = 4$

a. ___?___ $f(x) = (x + 2)(x + 4)\left(x - \frac{3}{2}\right)$

b. ___?___ $f(x) = \left(x - \frac{1}{2}\right)\left(x - \frac{5}{4}\right)\left(x + \frac{7}{3}\right)$

c. ___?___ $f(x) = (x - 2)(x - 3)(x - 4)$

d. ___?___ $f(x) = \left(x + \frac{4}{5}\right)\left(x - \frac{6}{7}\right)(x - 4)$

17. Identify the zeros of $f(x) = (x + 3)(x - 4)(x - 3)$, write the function in standard form, and state how the zeros are related to the standard form.

H.O.T. Focus on Higher Order Thinking

18. **Critical Thinking** Consider the polynomial function $g(x) = 2x^3 - 6x^2 + \pi x + 5$. Is it possible to use the Rational Zero Theorem and synthetic division to factor this polynomial? Explain.

19. **Explain the Error** Sabrina was told to find the zeros of the polynomial function $h(x) = x(x - 4)(x + 2)$. She stated that the zeros of this polynomial are $x = 0$, $x = -4$, and $x = 2$. Explain her error.

20. **Justify Reasoning** If $\frac{c}{b}$ is a rational zero of a polynomial function $p(x)$, explain why $bx - c$ must be a factor of the polynomial.

21. **Justify Reasoning** A polynomial function $p(x)$ has degree 3, and its zeros are −3, 4, and 6. What do you think is the equation of $p(x)$? Do you think there could be more than one possibility? Explain.

Lesson Performance Task

For the years from 2001–2010, the number of Americans traveling to other countries by plane can be represented by the polynomial function $A(t) = 20t^4 - 428t^3 + 2760t^2 - 4320t + 33{,}600$, where A is the number of thousands of Americans traveling abroad by airplane and t is the number of years since 2001. In which year were there 40,000,000 Americans traveling abroad? Use the Rational Root Theorem to find your answer. [Hint: consider the function's domain and range before finding all possible rational roots.]

7.2 Finding Complex Solutions of Polynomial Equations

Resource Locker

Essential Question: What do the Fundamental Theorem of Algebra and its corollary tell you about the roots of the polynomial equation p(x) = 0 where p(x) has degree n?

Explore Investigating the Number of Complex Zeros of a Polynomial Function

You have used various algebraic and graphical methods to find the roots of a polynomial equation $p(x) = 0$ or the zeros of a polynomial function $p(x)$. Because a polynomial can have a factor that repeats, a zero or a root can occur multiple times.

The polynomial $p(x) = x^3 + 8x^2 + 21x + 18 = (x + 2)(x + 3)^2$ has -2 as a zero once and -3 as a zero twice, or *with multiplicity 2*. The **multiplicity** of a zero of $p(x)$ or a root of $p(x) = 0$ is the number of times that the related factor occurs in the factorization.

In this Explore, you will use algebraic methods to investigate the relationship between the degree of a polynomial function and the number of zeros that it has.

Ⓐ Find all zeros of $p(x) = x^3 + 7x^2$. Include any multiplicities greater than 1.

$$p(x) = x^3 + 7x^2$$

Factor out the GCF. $p(x) = \boxed{?}(x + 7)$

What are all the zeros of $p(x)$? $\boxed{?}$

Ⓑ Find all zeros of $p(x) = x^3 - 64$. Include any multiplicities greater than 1.

$$p(x) = x^3 - 64$$

Factor the difference of two cubes. $p(x) = \left(x \boxed{?} 4\right)\left(x^2 + \boxed{?} + \boxed{?}\right)$

What are the real zeros of $p(x)$? $\boxed{?}$

Solve $x^2 + 4x + 16 = 0$ using the quadratic formula.

$$x = \frac{-b \pm \sqrt{b^2 - 4ac}}{2a}$$

$$x = \frac{\boxed{?} \pm \sqrt{4^2 - 4 \cdot 1 \cdot \boxed{?}}}{2 \cdot \boxed{?}} \qquad x = \frac{-4 \pm \sqrt{\boxed{?}}}{2} \qquad x = \frac{-4 \pm \boxed{?}\sqrt{3}}{2}$$

$$x = -2 \pm 2i\sqrt{3}$$

What are the non-real zeros of $p(x)$? $\boxed{?}$

Ⓒ Find all zeros of $p(x) = x^4 + 3x^3 - 4x^2 - 12x$. Include any multiplicities greater than 1.

$$p(x) = x^4 + 3x^3 - 4x^2 - 12x$$

Factor out the GCF. $p(x) = x\left(\boxed{?}\right)$

Group terms to begin factoring by grouping. $p(x) = x\left((x^3 + 3x^2) - \left(\boxed{?}\right)\right)$

Factor out common monomials. $p(x) = x\left(\boxed{?}(x+3) - \boxed{?}(x+3)\right)$

Factor out the common binomial. $p(x) = x(x+3)(x^2 - 4)$

Factor the difference of squares. $p(x) = x(x+3)\left(\boxed{?}\right)\left(\boxed{?}\right)$

What are all the zeros of $p(x)$? $\boxed{?}$

Ⓓ Find all zeros of $p(x) = x^4 - 16$. Include any multiplicities greater than 1.

$$p(x) = x^4 - 16$$

Factor the difference of squares. $p(x) = \left(\boxed{?}\right)(x^2 + 4)$

Factor the difference of squares. $p(x) = \left(\boxed{?}\right)\left(\boxed{?}\right)(x^2 + 4)$

What are the real zeros of $p(x)$? $\boxed{?}$

Solve $x^2 + 4 = 0$ by taking square roots.

$x^2 + 4 = 0$

$x^2 = -4$

$x = \pm\sqrt{-4}$

$x = \pm \boxed{?}$

What are the non-real zeros of $p(x)$? $\boxed{?}$

Ⓔ Find all zeros of $p(x) = x^4 + 5x^3 + 6x^2 - 4x - 8$. Include multiplicities greater than 1.

By the Rational Zero Theorem, possible rational zeros are ±1, ±2, ±4, and ±8. Use a synthetic division table to test possible zeros.

$\frac{m}{n}$	1	5	6	−4	−8
1	1	6	12	8	0

The remainder is 0. Therefore, is 1 a zero? $\boxed{?}$

$p(x)$ factors as $(x - 1)\left(\boxed{?}\right)$.

Test for zeros in the cubic polynomial.

$\frac{m}{n}$	1	6	12	8
1	1	7	19	27
−1	1	5	7	1
2	1	8	28	64
−2	1	4	4	0

Which factor is a zero? ?

$p(x)$ factors as $(x-1)(x+2)($? $)$. The quadratic is a perfect square trinomial.

So, $p(x)$ factors completely as $p(x) = (x-1)$? .

What are all the zeros of $p(x)$? ?

(F) Complete the table to summarize your results from Steps A–E.

Polynomial Function in Standard Form	Polynomial Function Factored over the Integers	Real Zeros and Their Multiplicities	Non-real Zeros and Their Multiplicities
$p(x) = x^3 + 7x^2$	?	?	?
$p(x) = x^3 - 64$	?	?	?
$p(x) = x^4 + 3x^3 - 4x^2 - 12x$	?	?	?
$p(x) = x^4 - 16$	?	?	?
$p(x) = x^4 + 5x^3 + 6x^2 - 4x - 8$	?	?	?

Reflect

1. Examine the table. For each function, count the number of unique zeros, both real and non-real. How does the number of unique zeros compare with the degree?
2. Examine the table again. This time, count the total number of zeros for each function, where a zero of multiplicity m is counted as m zeros. How does the total number of zeros compare with the degree?
3. **Discussion** Describe the apparent relationship between the degree of a polynomial function and the number of zeros it has.

Explain 1 Applying the Fundamental Theorem of Algebra to Solving Polynomial Equations

The Fundamental Theorem of Algebra and its corollary summarize what you have observed earlier while finding rational zeros of polynomial functions and in completing the Explore.

The Fundamental Theorem of Algebra
Every polynomial function of degree $n \geq 1$ has at least one zero, where a zero may be a complex number.
Corollary: Every polynomial function of degree $n \geq 1$ has exactly n zeros, including multiplicities.

Because the zeros of a polynomial function $p(x)$ give the roots of the equation $p(x) = 0$, the theorem and its corollary also extend to finding all roots of a polynomial equation.

Example 1 **Solve the polynomial equation by finding all roots.**

(A) $2x^3 - 12x^2 - 34x + 204 = 0$

The polynomial has degree 3, so the equation has exactly 3 roots.

$$2x^3 - 12x^2 - 34x + 204 = 0$$

Divide both sides by 2. $\quad x^3 - 6x^2 - 17x + 102 = 0$

Group terms. $\quad (x^3 - 6x^2) - (17x - 102) = 0$

Factor out common monomials. $\quad x^2(x - 6) - 17(x - 6) = 0$

Factor out the common binomial. $\quad (x^2 - 17)(x - 6) = 0$

One root is $x = 6$. Solving $x^2 - 17 = 0$ gives $x^2 = 17$, or $x = \pm\sqrt{17}$.

The roots are $-\sqrt{17}$, $\sqrt{17}$, and 6.

(B) $x^4 - 6x^2 - 27 = 0$

The polynomial has degree 4, so the equation has exactly 4 roots.

Notice that $x^4 - 6x^2 - 27$ has the form $u^2 - 6u - 27$, where $u = x^2$. So, you can factor it like a quadratic trinomial.

$$x^4 - 6x^2 - 27 = 0$$

Factor the trinomial. $\quad \left(x^2 - \boxed{9}\right)\left(x^2 + \boxed{3}\right) = 0$

Factor the difference of squares. $\left(x + \boxed{3}\right)\left(x - \boxed{3}\right)\left(x^2 + 3\right) = 0$

The real roots are -3 and 3. Solving $x^2 + 3 = 0$ gives $x^2 = -3$, or

$x = \pm\sqrt{-3} = \pm \boxed{i}\sqrt{\boxed{3}}$.

The roots are $-3, 3, -i\sqrt{3}, i\sqrt{3}$.

Reflect

4. Restate the Fundamental Theorem of Algebra and its corollary in terms of the roots of equations.

Your Turn

Solve the polynomial equation by finding all roots.

5. $8x^3 - 27 = 0$

6. $p(x) = x^4 - 13x^3 + 55x^2 - 91x$

Explain 2 Writing a Polynomial Function From Its Zeros

You may have noticed in finding roots of quadratic and polynomial equations that any irrational or complex roots come in pairs. These pairs reflect the "±" in the quadratic formula. For example, for any of the following number pairs, you will never have a polynomial equation for which only one number in the pair is a root.

$$\sqrt{5} \text{ and } -\sqrt{5};\ 1 + \sqrt{7} \text{ and } 1 - \sqrt{7};\ i \text{ and } -i;\ 2 + 14i \text{ and } 2 - 14i;\ \frac{11}{6} + \frac{1}{6}i\sqrt{3} \text{ and } \frac{11}{6} - \frac{1}{6}i\sqrt{3}$$

The irrational root pairs $a + b\sqrt{c}$ and $a - b\sqrt{c}$ are called *irrational conjugates*. The complex root pairs $a + bi$ and $a - bi$ are called *complex conjugates*.

Irrational Root Theorem

If a polynomial $p(x)$ has rational coefficients and $a + b\sqrt{c}$ is a root of the equation $p(x) = 0$, where a and b are rational and $\sqrt{c}$ is irrational, then $a - b\sqrt{c}$ is also a root of $p(x) = 0$.

Complex Conjugate Root Theorem

If $a + bi$ is an imaginary root of a polynomial equation with real-number coefficients, then $a - bi$ is also a root.

Because the roots of the equation $p(x) = 0$ give the zeros of a polynomial function, corresponding theorems apply to the zeros of a polynomial function. You can use this fact to write a polynomial function from its zeros. Because irrational and complex conjugate pairs are a sum and difference of terms, the product of irrational conjugates is always a rational number and the product of complex conjugates is always a real number.

$\left(2 - \sqrt{10}\right)\left(2 + \sqrt{10}\right) = 2^2 - \left(\sqrt{10}\right)^2 = 4 - 10 = -6$

$\left(1 - i\sqrt{2}\right)\left(1 + i\sqrt{2}\right) = 1^2 - \left(i\sqrt{2}\right)^2 = 1 - (-1)(2) = 3$

Example 2 **Write the polynomial function with least degree and a leading coefficient of 1 that has the given zeros.**

(A) 5 and $3 + 2\sqrt{7}$

Because irrational zeros come in conjugate pairs, $3 - 2\sqrt{7}$ must also be a zero of the function. Use the 3 zeros to write a function in factored form, then multiply to write it in standard form.

$$p(x) = \left[x - \left(3 + 2\sqrt{7}\right)\right]\left[x - \left(3 - 2\sqrt{7}\right)\right](x - 5)$$

Multiply the first two factors using FOIL. $= \left[x^2 - \left(3 - 2\sqrt{7}\right)x - \left(3 + 2\sqrt{7}\right)x + \left(3 + 2\sqrt{7}\right)\left(3 - 2\sqrt{7}\right)\right](x - 5)$

Multipy the conjugates. $= \left[x^2 - \left(3 - 2\sqrt{7}\right)x - \left(3 + 2\sqrt{7}\right)x + (9 - 4 \cdot 7)\right](x - 5)$

Combine like terms. $= \left[x^2 + \left(-3 + 2\sqrt{7} - 3 - 2\sqrt{7}\right)x + (-19)\right](x - 5)$

Simplify. $= \left[x^2 - 6x - 19\right](x - 5)$

Distributive property $= x(x^2 - 6x - 19) - 5(x^2 - 6x - 19)$

Multiply. $= x^3 - 6x^2 - 19x - 5x^2 + 30x + 95$

Combine like terms. $= x^3 - 11x^2 + 11x + 95$

The polynomial function is $p(x) = x^3 - 11x^2 + 11x + 95$.

(B) 2, 3 and $1 - i$

Because complex zeros come in conjugate pairs, $1 + i$ must also be a zero of the function.

Use the 4 zeros to write a function in factored form, then multiply to write it in standard form.

$$p(x) = \left[x - (1 + i)\right]\left[x - \left(\boxed{1 - i}\right)\right](x - 2)(x - 3)$$

Multiply the first two factors using FOIL. $= \left[x^2 - (1 - i)x - \left(\boxed{1 + i}\right)x + (1 + i)(1 - i)\right](x - 2)(x - 3)$

Multipy the conjugates. $= \left[x^2 - (1 - i)x - (1 + i)x + \left(1 - \left(\boxed{-1}\right)\right)\right](x - 2)(x - 3)$

Combine like terms. $= \left[x^2 + (-1 + i - 1 - i)x + 2\right](x - 2)(x - 3)$

Simplify. $= \left(\boxed{x^2 - 2x + 2}\right)(x - 2)(x - 3)$

Multipy the binomials. $= (x^2 - 2x + 2)\ \boxed{(x^2 - 5x + 6)}$

Distributive property $= x^2(x^2 - 5x + 6)\boxed{- 2x}\ (x^2 - 5x + 6) + 2(x^2 - 5x + 6)$

Multipy. $= (x^4 - 5x^3 + 6x^2) + (-2x^3 + 10x^2 - 12x) + (2x^2 - 10x + 12)$

Combine like terms. $= \boxed{x^4 - 7x^3 + 18x^2 - 22x + 12}$

The polynomial function is $p(x) = x^4 - 7x^3 + 18x^2 - 22x + 12$.

Reflect

7. Restate the Irrational Root Theorem in terms of the zeros of polynomial functions.

8. Restate the Complex Conjugates Zero Theorem in terms of the roots of equations.

Your Turn

Write the polynomial function with the least degree and a leading coefficient of 1 that has the given zeros.

9. $2 + 3i$ and $4 - 7\sqrt{2}$

Explain 3 Solving a Real-World Problem by Graphing Polynomial Functions

You can use graphing to help you locate or approximate any real zeros of a polynomial function. Though a graph will not help you find non-real zeros, it can indicate that the function has non-real zeros. For example, look at the graph of $p(x) = x^4 - 2x^2 - 3$.

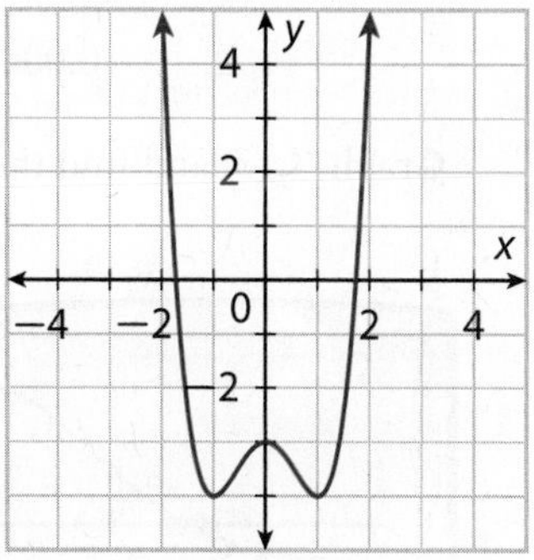

The graph intersects the x-axis twice, which shows that the function has two real zeros. By the corollary to the Fundamental Theorem of Algebra, however, a fourth degree polynomial has four zeros. So, the other two zeros of $p(x)$ must be non-real. The zeros are $-\sqrt{3}$, $\sqrt{3}$, i, and $-i$. (A polynomial whose graph has a turning point on the x-axis has a real zero of even multiplicity at that point. If the graph "bends" at the x-axis, there is a real zero of odd multiplicity greater than 1 at that point.)

Ⓐ The following polynomial models approximate the total oil consumption C (in millions of barrels per day) for North America (NA) and the Asia Pacific region (AP) over the period from 2001 to 2011, where t is in years and $t = 0$ represents 2001.

$$C_{NA}(t) = 0.00494t^4 - 0.0915t^3 + 0.442t^2 - 0.239t + 23.6$$

$$C_{AP}(t) = 0.00877t^3 - 0.139t^2 + 1.23t + 21.1$$

Use a graphing calculator to plot the functions and approximate the x-coordinate of the intersection in the region of interest. What does this represent in the context of this situation? Determine when oil consumption in the Asia Pacific region overtook oil consumption in North America using the requested method.

Graph $Y1 = 0.00494x^4 - 0.0915x^3 + 0.442x^2 - 0.239x + 23.6$ and $Y2 = 0.00877x^3 - 0.139x^2 + 1.23x + 21.1$. Use the "Calc" menu to find the point of intersection. Here are the results for Xmin = 0, Xmax = 10, Ymin = 20, Ymax = 30. (The graph for the Asia Pacific is the one that rises upward on all segments.)

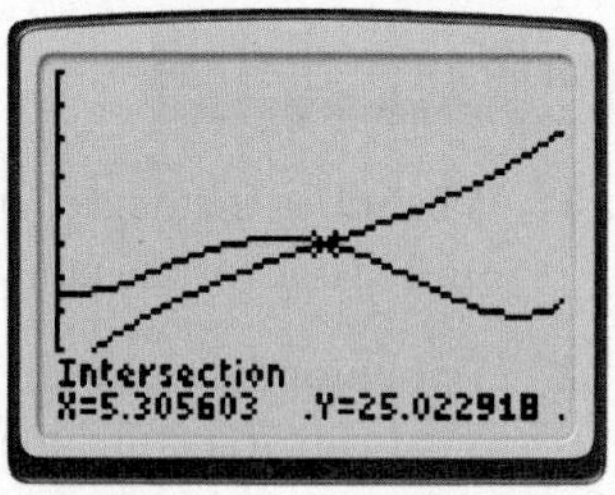

The functions intersect at about $x = 5$, which represents the year 2006. This means that the models show oil consumption in the Asia Pacific equaling and then overtaking oil consumption in North America about 2006.

(B) Find a single polynomial model for the situation in Example 3A whose zero represents the time that oil consumption for the Asia Pacific region overtakes consumption for North America. Plot the function on a graphing calculator and use it to find the x-intercept.

Let the function $C_D(t)$ represent the difference in oil consumption in the Asia Pacific and North America.

A difference of 0 indicates the time that consumption is equal.

$$C_D(t) = C_{AP}(t) - C_{NA}(t)$$

$$= 0.00877t^3 - 0.139t^2 + 1.23t + 21.1 - \left(0.00494t^4 - 0.0915t^3 + 0.442t^2 - 0.239t + 23.6\right)$$

Remove parentheses and rearrange terms.

$$= -0.00494t^4 + 0.00877t^3 + 0.0915t^3 - 0.139t^2 - 0.442t^2 + 1.23t + 0.239t + 21.1 - 23.6$$

Combine like terms. Round to three significant digits.

$$= -0.00494t^4 + 0.100t^3 - 0.581t^2 + 1.47t - 2.50$$

Graph $C_D(t)$ and find the x-intercept. (The graph with Ymin = −4, Ymax = 6 is shown.)

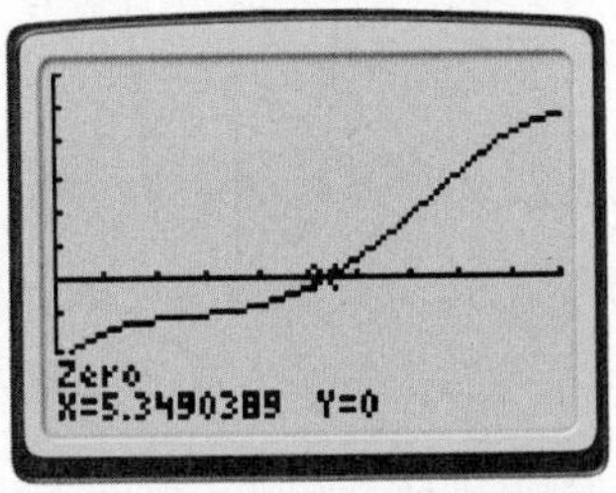

Within the rounding error, the results for the x-coordinate of the intersection of $C_{NA}(t)$ and $C_{AP}(t)$ and the x-intercept of $C_D(t)$ are the same.

Your Turn

10. An engineering class is designing model rockets for a competition. The body of the rocket must be cylindrical with a cone-shaped top. The cylinder part must be 60 cm tall, and the height of the cone must be twice the radius. The volume of the payload region must be 558π cm^3 in order to hold the cargo. Use a graphing calculator to graph the rocket's payload volume as a function of the radius x. On the same screen, graph the constant function for the desired payload. Find the intersection to find x.

Elaborate

11. What does the degree of a polynomial function $p(x)$ tell you about the zeros of the function or the roots of the equation $p(x) = 0$?

12. A polynomial equation of degree 5 has the roots 0.3, 2, 8, and 10.6 (each of multiplicity 1). What can you conclude about the remaining root? Explain your reasoning.

13. Discussion Describe two ways you can use graphing to determine when two polynomial functions that model a real-world situation have the same value.

14. Essential Question Check-In What are possible ways to find all the roots of a polynomial equation?

Evaluate: Homework and Practice

Personal Math Trainer

- Online Homework
- Hints and Help
- Extra Practice

Find all zeros of $p(x)$. Include any multiplicities greater than 1.

1. $p(x) = 3x^3 - 10x^2 + 10x - 4$

2. $p(x) = x^3 - 3x^2 + 4x - 12$

Solve the polynomial equation by finding all roots.

3. $2x^3 - 3x^2 + 8x - 12 = 0$

4. $x^4 - 5x^3 + 3x^2 + x = 0$

Write the polynomial function with least degree and a leading coefficient of 1 that has the given zeros.

5. 0, $\sqrt{5}$, and 2

6. $4i$, 2, and -2

7. 1, -1 (multiplicity 3), and $3i$

8. 3(multiplicity of 2) and $3i$

9. Forestry Height and trunk volume measurements from 10 giant sequoias between the heights of 220 and 275 feet in California give the following model, where h is the height in feet and V is the volume in cubic feet.

$$V(h) = 0.131h^3 - 90.9h^2 + 21{,}200h - 1{,}627{,}400$$

The "President" tree in the Giant Forest Grove in Sequoia National Park has a volume of about 45,100 cubic feet. Use a graphing calculator to plot the function $V(h)$ and the constant function representing the volume of the President tree together. (Use a window of 220 to 275 for X and 30,000 to 55,000 for Y.) Find the x-coordinate of the intersection of the graphs. What does this represent in the context of this situation?

10. Business Two competing stores, store A and store B, opened the same year in the same neighborhood. The annual revenue R (in millions of dollars) for each store t years after opening can be approximated by the polynomial models shown.

$$R_A(t) = 0.0001(-t^4 + 12t^3 - 77t^2 + 600t + 13{,}650)$$

$$R_B(t) = 0.0001(-t^4 + 36t^3 - 509t^2 + 3684t + 3390)$$

Using a graphing calculator, graph the models from $t = 0$ to $t = 10$, with a range of 0 to 2 for R. Find the x-coordinate of the intersection of the graphs, and interpret the graphs.

11. Personal Finance A retirement account contains cash and stock in a company. The cash amount is added to each week by the same amount until week 32, then that same amount is withdrawn each week. The functions shown model the balance B (in thousands of dollars) over the course of the past year, with the time t in weeks.

$$B_C(t) = -0.12|t - 32| + 13$$

$$B_S(t) = 0.00005t^4 - 0.00485t^3 + 0.1395t^2 - 1.135t + 15.75$$

Use a graphing calculator to graph both models (Use 0 to 50 for the domain and 0 to 20 for the range.). Find the x-coordinate of any points of intersection. Then interpret your results in the context of this situation.

12. Match the roots with their equation. Roots may be used more than once.

A. 1

B. -2

C. 2

D. -1

E. $2i$

F. $-2i$

a. ___?___ $x^4 + x^3 + 2x^2 + 4x - 8 = 0$

b. ___?___ $x^4 - 5x^2 + 4 = 0$

H.O.T. Focus on Higher Order Thinking

13. **Draw Conclusions** Find all of the roots of $x^6 - 5x^4 - 125x^2 + 15{,}625 = 0$. (Hint: Rearrange the terms with a sum of cubes followed by the two other terms.)

14. **Explain the Error** A student is asked to write the polynomial function with least degree and a leading coefficient of 1 that has the zeros $1 + i$, $1 - i$, $\sqrt{2}$, and -3. The student uses these zeros to find the corresponding factors, and multiplies them together to obtain $p(x) = x^4 + (1 - \sqrt{2})x^3 - (4 + \sqrt{2})x^2 + (6 + 4\sqrt{2})x - 6\sqrt{2}$. What error did the student make? What is the correct function?

15. **Critical Thinking** What is the least degree of a polynomial equation that has $3i$ as a root with a multiplicity of 3, and $2 - \sqrt{3}$ as a root with multiplicity 2? Explain.

Lesson Performance Task

In 1984 the MPAA introduced the PG-13 rating to their movie rating system. Recently, scientists measured the incidences of a specific type of violence depicted in movies. The researchers used specially trained coders to identify the specific type of violence in one half of the top grossing movies for each year since 1985. The trend in the average rate per hour of 5-minute segments of this type of violence in movies rated G/PG, PG-13, and R can be modeled as a function of time by the following equations:

$$V_{G/PG}(t) = -0.015t + 1.45$$

$$V_{PG\text{-}13}(t) = 0.000577t^3 - 0.0225t^2 + 0.26t + 0.8$$

$$V_R(t) = 2.15$$

V is the average rate per hour of 5-minute segments containing the specific type of violence in movies, and t is the number of years since 1985.

a. Interestingly, in 1985 or $t = 0$, $V_{G/PG}(0) > V_{PG\text{-}13}(0)$. Can you think of any reasons why this would be true?

b. What do the equations indicate about the relationship between $V_{G/PG}(t)$ and $V_{PG\text{-}13}(t)$ as t increases?

c. Graph the models for $V_{G/PG}(t)$ and $V_{PG\text{-}13}(t)$ and find the year in which $V_{PG\text{-}13}(t)$ will be greater than $V_{G/PG}(t)$.

STUDY GUIDE REVIEW

Polynomial Equations

MODULE 7

Essential Question: How can you use polynomial equations to solve real-world problems?

Key Vocabulary
root *(raíz)*
multiplicity *(multiplicidad)*

KEY EXAMPLE *(Lesson 7.1)*

Find the rational zeros of $f(x) = x^3 + 6x^2 + 11x + 6$; then write the function as a product of factors.

Factors of 6: $\pm1, \pm2, \pm3, \pm6$ — Use the Rational Zero Theorem.

Test the roots in a synthetic division table.

$\frac{m}{n}$	1	6	11	6
1	1	7	18	24
2	1	8	27	60
3	1	9	38	120
6	1	12	83	504
−1	1	5	6	0

$(x + 1)(x^2 + 5x + 6)$ — Factor the trinomial.

$(x + 1)(x + 2)(x + 3)$

$x = -1, x = -2, x = -3$

KEY EXAMPLE *(Lesson 7.2)*

Find all the zeros of $m(x) = 2x^4 - 4x^3 + 8x^2 - 16x$.

$2x^4 - 4x^3 - 8x^2 - 16x$

$2x(x^3 - 2x^2 - 4x + 8)$ — Factor out the GCF.

$2x((x^3 - 2x^2) - (4x - 8))$ — Group the terms.

$2x(x^2(x - 2) - 4(x - 2))$ — Factor out common monomials.

$2x(x^2 - 4)(x - 2)$ — Factor out the common binomial.

$2x(x + 2)(x - 2)(x - 2)$ — Difference of two squares

So, the zeros of $m(x)$ are 0, −2, 2 (mult. 2).

EXERCISES

Rewrite the function as a product of factors, and state all of the zeros. *(Lessons 7.1, 7.2)*

1. $r(x) = x^3 + 13x^2 + 48x + 36$

2. $m(x) = 3x^4 - 3x^2$

3. $n(x) = x^3 + 5x^2 - 8x - 12$

4. $p(x) = x^3 - 8$

5. $b(x) = x^4 - 81$

6. $t(x) = 15x^3 + 27x^2 - 6x$

7. Give an example of a fourth-degree polynomial function with all real zeros. Explain how you got your function. *(Lesson 7.1)*

MODULE PERFORMANCE TASK

What Do Polynomials Have to Do With Endangered Species?

A biologist has been studying a particular species of frog in an area for many years and has compiled population data. She used the data to create a model of the population, given here, where x is the years since 2000.

$$P(x) = -x^4 + 27x^3 - 198x^2 + 372x + 1768$$

Describe the trends for the population, and explain what the model predicts for the future population of this species of frog.

As you complete the task, be sure to write down all your data and assumptions. Then use graphs, numbers, words, or algebra to explain how you reached your conclusions.

Ready to Go On?

7.1–7.2 Polynomial Functions

Personal Math Trainer
- Online Homework
- Hints and Help
- Extra Practice

Write the function as a product of factors. *(Lesson 7.1)*

1. $f(x) = 7x^3 - 14x^2 - x + 2$

2. $g(x) = 3x^2 + 2x - 8$

3. $h(x) = 4x^2 - 25$

4. $t(x) = 8x^3 - 512$

List the zeros. *(Lessons 7.1, 7.2)*

5. $m(x) = x^4 + 3x^2 - 18$

6. $r(x) = x^3 + 3x^2 - x - 3$

7. $q(x) = x^3 - 1$

8. $p(x) = 9x^2 - 100$

ESSENTIAL QUESTION

9. Give an example of how factoring polynomials might be used in geometry. *(Lesson 7.1)*

MODULE 7
MIXED REVIEW

Assessment Readiness

1. Look at each equation. Does the polynomial function have all real zeros?

   A. $f(x) = x^4 - 2x^2 - 5$

   B. $g(x) = x^2 - 9$

   C. $h(x) = x^4 - 256$

2. Consider the polynomial function $m(x) = x^4 - 16x^2$. Determine if each statement is True or False.

   A. There will be both real and imaginary zeros of this function.

   B. Factoring the polynomial involves the difference of two squares.

   C. The zeros of the function are 0 (mult. 2), 4, −4.

3. Explain why some polynomial functions with real coefficients have non-real zeros.

4. By analyzing a quickly growing oil town, an analyst states that the predicted population P of the town t years from now can be modeled by the function $P(t) = 5t^3 - 2t^2 + 15{,}000$. If we assume the function is accurate, in approximately how many years will the town have a population of 225,000? How did you get your answer?

UNIT 3 MIXED REVIEW

Assessment Readiness

Personal Math Trainer

- Online Homework
- Hints and Help
- Extra Practice

1. Identify the transformations of the graph of $f(x) = x^3$ that produce the graph of the function $g(x) = -2(x - 5)^3$. Determine if each statement is True or False.

A. When compared with f(x), the graph of g(x) is vertically compressed by a factor of $\frac{1}{2}$.

B. When compared with f(x), the graph of g(x) is translated 5 units to the right.

C. When compared with f(x), the graph of g(x) is reflected across the x-axis.

2. Consider the polynomial $3x^3 + 9x^2 - 12x$. Determine if each statement is True or False.

A. $3x$ can be factored out of every term.

B. The polynomial cannot be factored as it is written.

C. The completely factored polynomial is $3x(x - 1)(x + 4)$.

3. Tell whether each expression is equivalent to the polynomial operation $3x(x - 2)(5x + 2)$.

A. $(3x^2 - 6x)(5x + 2)$

B. $3x(5x^2 - 8x - 4)$

C. $15x^3 - 24x^2 - 12x$

D. $3x(5x^2 - 5x - 2)$

4. Consider the polynomial function $g(x) = 3x^3 + 6x^2 - 9x$. Determine if each statement is True or False.

A. The polynomial has only real zeros.

B. Factoring the polynomial involves a common monomial.

C. The zeros of the polynomial are 0, –3, 1, 3.

5. Consider the function $m(x) = x^4 - 16$. Are these zeros of the function?

A. $-2i, 2i$

B. $2 \pm 2i$

C. $-2, 2$

6. Use a graphing calculator to graph the function $f(x) = -x(x + 1)(x - 4)^2$, and then use the graph to determine the number of turning points and global maximums and minimums, and local maximums and minimums that are not global.

7. Ms. Flores grows tomatoes on her farm. The price per pound of tomatoes can be modeled by $P(x) = 20x + 4$. If the total income that she wants to earn from tomatoes for one year can be modeled by $I(x) = 60x^3 - 8x^2 + 136x + 28$, write a polynomial that can be used to model the number of pounds of tomatoes Ms. Flores needs to grow in one year. Explain your answer.

8. During a discussion in class, Hannah stated that she liked the quadratic formula more than completing the square and factoring, because it works on every quadratic equation. The teacher then proposed the equation $-3x(x + 7) = 14$. Explain how Hannah can adjust this equation so she can use the quadratic formula to solve it.

Performance Tasks

★ 9. A bottom for a box can be made by cutting congruent squares from each of the four corners of a piece of cardboard. The volume of a box made from an 8.5-by-11-inch piece of cardboard would be represented by $V(x) = x(11 - 2x)(8.5 - 2x)$, where x is the side length of one square.

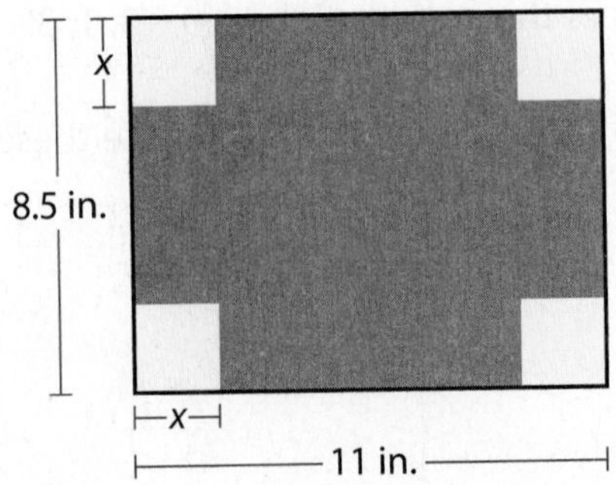

A. Express the volume as a sum of monomials.

B. Find the volume when $x = 1$ inch.

★★10. The volume of several planets in cubic kilometers can be modeled by $v(d) = \frac{1}{6}\pi d^3$, where d is the diameter of the planet in kilometers. The mass of each planet in kilograms in terms of diameter d can be modeled by $M(d) = (3.96 \times 10^{12})d^3 - (6.50 \times 10^{17})d^2 + (2.56 \times 10^{22})d - 5.56 \times 10^{25}$.

A. The density of a planet in kilograms per cubic kilometer can be found by dividing the planet's mass by its volume. Use polynomial division to find a model for the density of a planet in terms of its diameter.

B. Use the model to estimate the density of Jupiter, with diameter $d = 142{,}984$ km.

★★★11. The profit of a small business (in thousands of dollars) since it was founded can be modeled by the polynomial $f(t) = -t^4 + 44t^3 - 612t^2 + 2592t$, where t represents the number of years since 1980.

A. Factor $f(t)$ completely.

B. What was the company's profit in 1985?

C. Find and interpret $f(15)$.

D. What can you say about the company's long-term prospects?

MATH IN CAREERS

Statistician According to data from the U.S. Census Bureau, the total number of people in the United States labor force can be approximated by the function $T(x) = -0.011x^2 + 2x + 107$, where x is the number of years since 1980 and $T(x)$ is the number of workers in millions. The number of women in the United States labor force can be approximated by the function $W(x) = -0.012x^2 + 1.26x + 45.5$.

a. Use the function $T(x)$ to estimate the number of workers in millions in 2010.

b. Write a polynomial function $M(x)$ that models the number of men in the labor force, and explain how you found your function.

c. Use the function found in part *b* to estimate the number of male workers in millions in 2010.

d. Explain how you could have found the answer to part *c* without using the function $M(x)$.

UNIT 4

Rational Functions, Expressions, and Equations

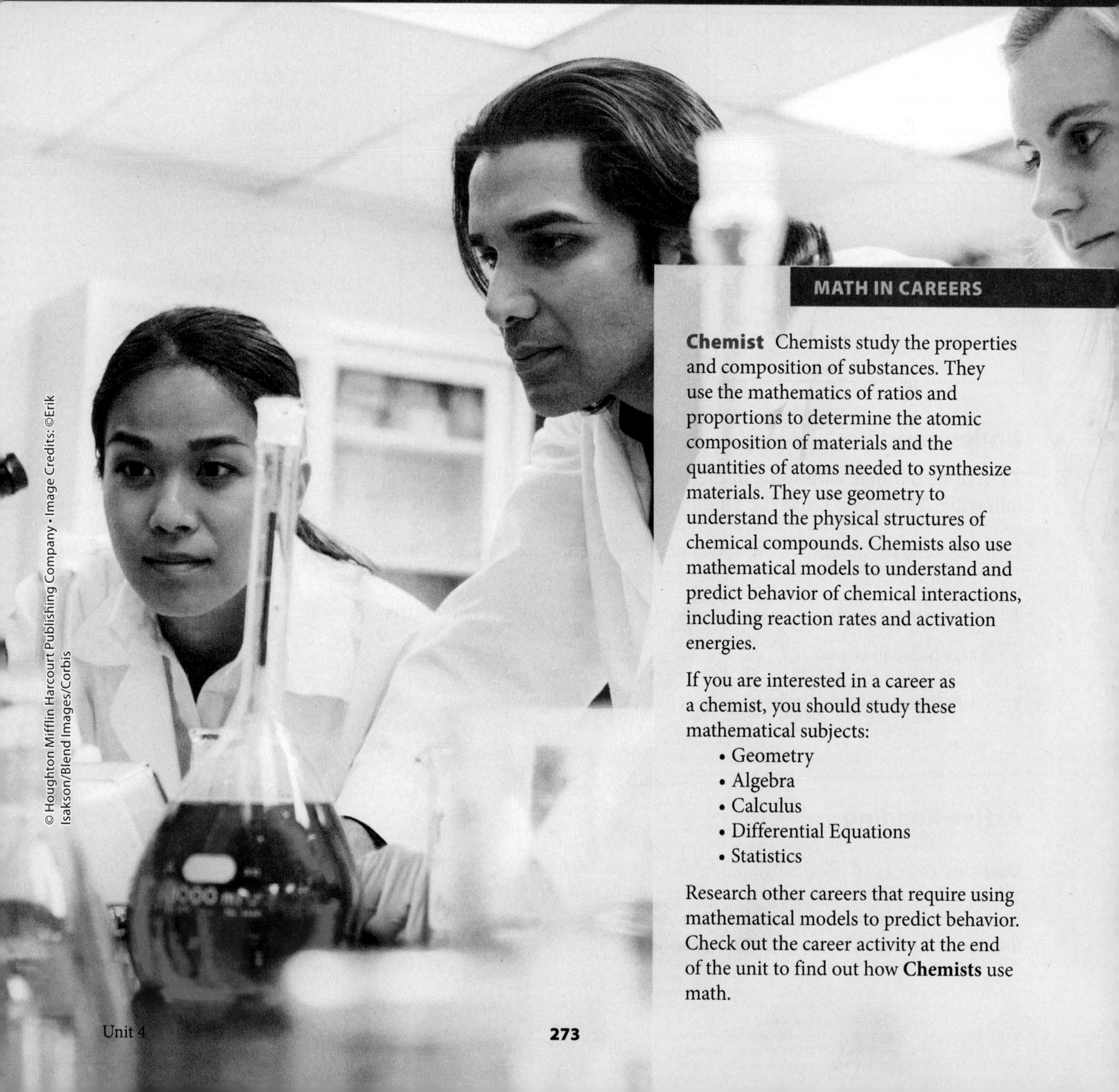

MATH IN CAREERS

Chemist Chemists study the properties and composition of substances. They use the mathematics of ratios and proportions to determine the atomic composition of materials and the quantities of atoms needed to synthesize materials. They use geometry to understand the physical structures of chemical compounds. Chemists also use mathematical models to understand and predict behavior of chemical interactions, including reaction rates and activation energies.

If you are interested in a career as a chemist, you should study these mathematical subjects:

- Geometry
- Algebra
- Calculus
- Differential Equations
- Statistics

Research other careers that require using mathematical models to predict behavior. Check out the career activity at the end of the unit to find out how **Chemists** use math.

Visualize Vocabulary

Use the ✓ words to complete the chart.

?	the set of output values of a function or relation
?	a linear relationship between two variables, x and y, that can be written in the form $y = kx$, where k is a nonzero constant
?	the multiplicative inverse of a number
?	the simplest function with the defining characteristics of the function family
?	the set of all possible input values of a relation or function
?	an algebraic expression whose numerator and denominator are polynomials

Review Words

✔ direct variation (*variación directa*)

✔ domain (*dominio*)

✔ parent function (*función madre*)

✔ range (*rango*)

✔ rational expression (*expresión racional*)

✔ reciprocal (*recíproco*)

Preview Words

asymptote (asíntota)

closure (cerradura)

inverse variation (variación inversa)

rational function (función racional)

Understand Vocabulary

To become familiar with some of the vocabulary terms in the module, consider the following. You may refer to the module, the glossary, or a dictionary.

1. __?__ is a relationship between two variables, x and y, that can be written in the form $y = \frac{k}{x}$, where k is a nonzero constant and $x \neq 0$.
2. A line that a graph approaches as the value of the variable becomes extremely large or small is a/an __?__.
3. A function whose rule can be written as a rational expression is a/an __?__.

Active Reading

Double-Door Fold Before beginning each lesson, create a double-door fold to compare the characteristics of two expressions, functions, or variations. This can help you identify the similarities and differences between the topics.

Rational Functions

MODULE 8

Essential Question: How can you use rational functions to solve real-world problems?

REAL WORLD VIDEO
As a consumer, you may shop around for the best deal on a new bike helmet. Check out the video to see how sporting goods manufacturers can use rational functions to help set pricing and sales goals.

MODULE PERFORMANCE TASK PREVIEW

What Is the Profit?

Like any business, a manufacturer of bike helmets must pay attention to ways to minimize costs and maximize profit. Businesses use mathematical functions to calculate and predict various quantities, including profits, costs, and revenue. What are some of the ways a business can use a profit function? Let's find out!

Are YOU Ready?

Complete these exercises to review skills you will need for this module.

Personal Math Trainer
- Online Homework
- Hints and Help
- Extra Practice

Graphing Linear Nonproportional Relationships

Example 1 Graph $y = -\frac{1}{2}x - 3$

Plot the y-intercept $(0, -3)$

The slope is $-\frac{1}{2}$, so from $(0, -3)$, plot the next point up 1 and left 2.

Draw a line through the two points.

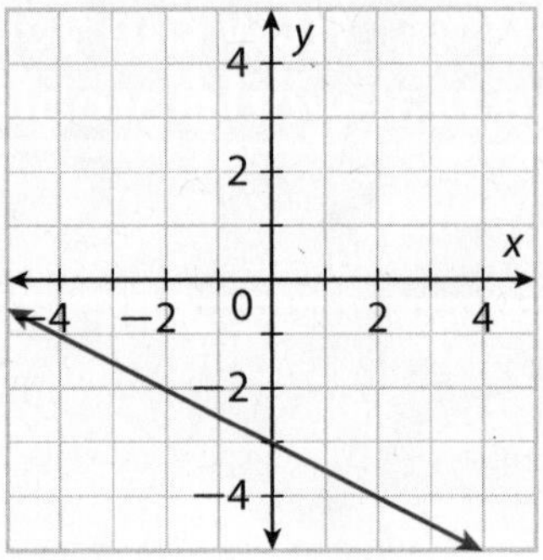

Graph each relationship.

1. $y = 3x - 4$

2. $y = -\frac{3}{4}x + 1$

Direct and Inverse Variation

Example 2 The graph of a direct variation function passes through $(1, 10)$. Write the equation for the function.

$k = \frac{y}{x} = \frac{10}{1} = 10$,
so the equation is $y = 10x$.

Example 3 The graph of an inverse variation function passes through $(4, 3)$. Write the equation for the function.

$k = xy = 4 \cdot 3 = 12$,
so the equation is $y = \frac{12}{x}$.

Write a direct variation equation for the graph that passes through the point.

3. $(2, 5)$ **4.** $(3, 6)$ **5.** $(4, 1)$

Write an inverse variation equation for the graph that passes through the point.

6. $(8, 1)$ **7.** $(5, 10)$ **8.** $(2, 6)$

8.1 Graphing Simple Rational Functions

Resource Locker

Essential Question: How are the graphs of $f(x) = a\left(\frac{1}{x-h}\right) + k$ and $f(x) = \frac{1}{\frac{1}{b}(x-h)} + k$ related to the graph of $f(x) = \frac{1}{x}$?

Explore 1 Graphing and Analyzing $f(x) = \frac{1}{x}$

A **rational function** is a function of the form $f(x) = \frac{p(x)}{q(x)}$ where $p(x)$ and $q(x)$ are polynomials, where $q(x) \neq 0$. The most basic rational function with a variable expression in the denominator is $f(x) = \frac{1}{x}$.

(A) State the domain of $f(x) = \frac{1}{x}$.

The function accepts all real numbers except ?, because division by ? is undefined. So, the function's domain is as follows:

- As an inequality: $x <$? or $x >$?
- In set notation: $\{x \mid x \neq$? $\}$
- In interval notation (where the symbol ∪ means *union*):

$(-\infty,$? $) \cup ($? $, +\infty)$

(B) Determine the end behavior of $f(x) = \frac{1}{x}$.

First, complete the tables.

x Increases without Bound	
x	$f(x) = \frac{1}{x}$
100	?
1000	?
10,000	?

x Decreases without Bound	
x	$f(x) = \frac{1}{x}$
−100	?
−1000	?
−10,000	?

Next, summarize the results.

- As $x \to +\infty$, $f(x) \to$? .
- As $x \to -\infty$, $f(x) \to$? .

Ⓒ Be more precise about the end behavior of $f(x) = \frac{1}{x}$, and determine what this means for the graph of the function.

You can be more precise about the end behavior by using the notation $f(x) \to 0^+$, which means that the value of $f(x)$ approaches 0 from the positive direction (that is, the value of $f(x)$ is positive as it approaches 0), and the notation $f(x) \to 0^-$, which means that the value of $f(x)$ approaches 0 from the negative direction. So, the end behavior of the function is more precisely summarized as follows:

- As $x \to +\infty$, $f(x) \to$? .
- As $x \to -\infty$, $f(x) \to$? .

The end behavior indicates that the graph of $f(x)$ approaches, but does not cross, the ? , so that axis is an asymptote for the graph.

Ⓓ Examine the behavior of $f(x) = \frac{1}{x}$ near $x = 0$, and determine what this means for the graph of the function.

First, complete the tables.

x Approaches 0 from the Positive Direction

x	$f(x) = \frac{1}{x}$
0.01	?
0.001	?
0.0001	?

x Approaches 0 from the Negative Direction

x	$f(x) = \frac{1}{x}$
−0.01	?
−0.001	?
−0.0001	?

Next, summarize the results.

- As $x \to 0^+$, $f(x) \to$? .
- As $x \to 0^-$, $f(x) \to$? .

The behavior of $f(x) = \frac{1}{x}$ near $x = 0$ indicates that the graph of $f(x)$ approaches, but does not cross, the ? , so that axis is also an asymptote for the graph.

Ⓔ Graph $f(x) = \frac{1}{x}$.

First, determine the sign of $f(x)$ on the two parts of its domain.

- When x is a negative number, $f(x)$ is a ? number.
- When x is a positive number, $f(x)$ is a ? number.

Next, complete the tables.

Negative Values of x	
x	$f(x)=\frac{1}{x}$
−2	?
−1	?
−0.5	?

Positive Values of x	
x	$f(x)=\frac{1}{x}$
0.5	?
1	?
2	?

Finally, use the information from this step and all previous steps to draw the graph. Draw asymptotes as dashed lines.

(F) State the range of $f(x)=\frac{1}{x}$.

The function takes on all real numbers except ?, so the function's range is as follows:

- As an inequality: $y <$? or $y >$?
- In set notation: $\{y \mid y \neq$? $\}$
- In interval notation (where the symbol ∪ means *union*): $(-\infty,$? $) \cup ($? $, +\infty)$

(G) Identify the intervals where the function is increasing and where it is decreasing. ?

(H) Determine whether $f(x)=\frac{1}{x}$ is an even function, an odd function, or neither. ?

Reflect

1. How does the graph of $f(x)=\frac{1}{x}$ show that the function has no zeros?

2. **Discussion** A graph is said to be *symmetric about the origin* (and the origin is called the graph's *point of symmetry*) if for every point (x, y) on the graph, the point $(-x, -y)$ is also on the graph. Is the graph of $f(x)=\frac{1}{x}$ symmetric about the origin? Explain.

3. Give any line(s) of symmetry for the graph of $f(x)=\frac{1}{x}$.

Explain 1 Graphing Simple Rational Functions

When graphing transformations of $f(x)=\frac{1}{x}$, it helps to consider the effect of the transformations on the following features of the graph of $f(x)$: the vertical asymptote, $x=0$; the horizontal asymptote, $y=0$; and two reference points, $(-1,-1)$ and $(1, 1)$. The table lists these features of the graph of $f(x)$ and the corresponding features of the graph of $g(x)=a\left(\frac{1}{\frac{1}{b}(x-h)}\right)+k$. Note that the asymptotes are affected only by the parameters h and k, while the reference points are affected by all four parameters.

Feature	$f(x)=\frac{1}{x}$	$g(x)=a\left(\frac{1}{\frac{1}{b}(x-h)}\right)+k$
Vertical asymptote	$x=0$	$x=h$
Horizontal asymptote	$y=0$	$y=k$
Reference point	$(-1,-1)$	$(-b+h,-a+k)$
Reference point	$(1, 1)$	$(b+h, a+k)$

Example 1 **Identify the transformations of the graph of $f(x) = \frac{1}{x}$ that produce the graph of the given function $g(x)$. Then graph $g(x)$ on the same coordinate plane as the graph of $f(x)$ by applying the transformations to the asymptotes $x = 0$ and $y = 0$ to the reference points $(-1, -1)$ and $(1, 1)$. Also state the domain and range of $g(x)$ using inequalities, set notation, and interval notation.**

Ⓐ $g(x) = 3\left(\frac{1}{x-1}\right) + 2$

The transformations of the graph of $f(x)$ that produce the graph of $g(x)$ are:

- a vertical stretch by a factor of 3
- a translation of 1 unit to the right and 2 units up

Note that the translation of 1 unit to the right affects only the x-coordinates, while the vertical stretch by a factor of 3 and the translation of 2 units up affect only the y-coordinates.

Feature	$f(x) = \frac{1}{x}$	$g(x) = 3\left(\frac{1}{x-1}\right) + 2$
Vertical asymptote	$x = 0$	$x = 1$
Horizontal asymptote	$y = 0$	$y = 2$
Reference point	$(-1, -1)$	$(-1 + 1, 3(-1) + 2) = (0, -1)$
Reference point	$(1, 1)$	$(1 + 1, 3(1) + 2) = (2, 5)$

Domain of $g(x)$:

Inequality: $x < 1$ or $x > 1$

Set notation: $\{x \mid x \neq 1\}$

Interval notation: $(-\infty, 1) \cup (1, +\infty)$

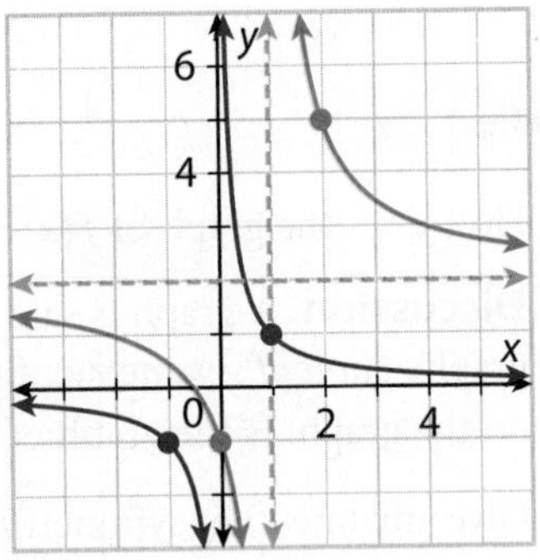

Range of $g(x)$:

Inequality: $y < 2$ or $y > 2$

Set notation: $\{y \mid y \neq 2\}$

Interval notation: $(-\infty, 2) \cup (2, +\infty)$

Ⓑ $g(x) = \frac{1}{2(x+3)} - 1$

The transformations of the graph of $f(x)$ that produce the graph of $g(x)$ are:

- a horizontal compression by a factor of $\frac{1}{2}$
- a translation of 3 units to the left and 1 unit down

Note that the horizontal compression by a factor of $\frac{1}{2}$ and the translation of 3 units to the left affect only the x-coordinates of points on the graph of $f(x)$, while the translation of 1 unit down affects only the y-coordinates.

Feature	$f(x) = \frac{1}{x}$	$g(x) = \frac{1}{2(x+3)} - 1$
Vertical asymptote	$x = 0$	$x = -3$
Horizontal asymptote	$y = 0$	$y = -1$
Reference point	$(-1, -1)$	$\left(\frac{1}{2}(-1) - 3, -1 - 1\right) = \left(-3\frac{1}{2}, -2\right)$
Reference point	$(1, 1)$	$\left(\frac{1}{2}(1) - 3, 1 - 1\right) = \left(-2\frac{1}{2}, 0\right)$

Domain of $g(x)$:

Inequality: $x < -3$ or $x > -3$

Set notation: $\{x \mid x \neq -3\}$

Interval notation: $(-\infty, -3) \cup (-3, +\infty)$

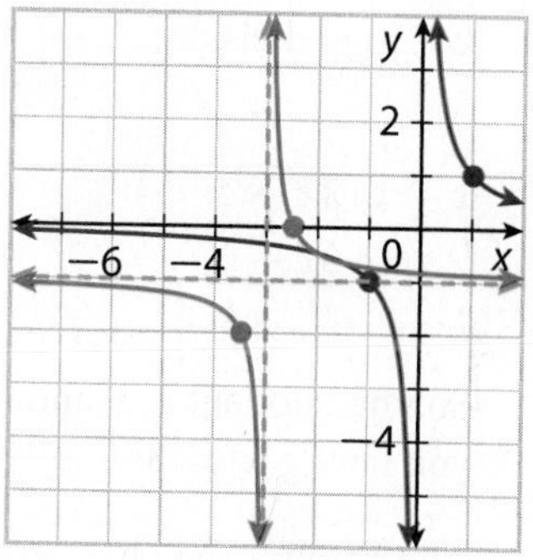

Range of $g(x)$:

Inequality: $y < -1$ or $y > -1$

Set notation: $\{y \mid y \neq -1\}$

Interval notation: $(-\infty, -1) \cup (-1, +\infty)$

Your Turn

Identify the transformations of the graph of $f(x) = \frac{1}{x}$ that produce the graph of the given function $g(x)$. Then graph $g(x)$ on the same coordinate plane as the graph of $f(x)$ by applying the transformations to the asymptotes $x = 0$ and $y = 0$ to the reference points $(-1, -1)$ and $(1, 1)$. Also state the domain and range of $g(x)$ using inequalities, set notation, and interval notation.

4. $g(x) = -0.5\left(\frac{1}{x+1}\right) - 3$

5. $g(x) = \frac{1}{-0.5(x-2)} + 1$

Explain 2 Rewriting Simple Rational Functions in Order to Graph Them

When given a rational function of the form $g(x) = \frac{mx + n}{px + q}$, where $m \neq 0$ and $p \neq 0$, you can carry out the division of the numerator by the denominator to write the function in the form $g(x) = a\left(\frac{1}{x - h}\right) + k$ or $g(x) = \frac{1}{\frac{1}{b}(x - h)} + k$ in order to graph it.

Example 2 **Rewrite the function in the form $g(x) = a\left(\frac{1}{x - h}\right) + k$ or $g(x) = \frac{1}{\frac{1}{b}(x - h)} + k$ and graph it. Also state the domain and range using inequalities, set notation, and interval notation.**

(A) $g(x) = \frac{3x - 4}{x - 1}$

Use long division.

$$\begin{array}{r} 3 \\ x - 1 \overline{\smash{)}\, 3x - 4} \\ \underline{3x - 3} \\ -1 \end{array}$$

So, the quotient is 3, and the remainder is -1. Using the fact that *dividend* = *quotient* + $\frac{\textit{remainder}}{\textit{divisor}}$, you have $g(x) = 3 + \frac{-1}{x - 1}$, or $g(x) = -\frac{1}{x - 1} + 3$.

The graph of $g(x)$ has vertical asymptote $x = 1$, horizontal asymptote $y = 3$, and reference points $\left(-1 + 1, -(-1) + 3\right) = (0, 4)$ and $(1 + 1, -(1) + 3) = (2, 2)$.

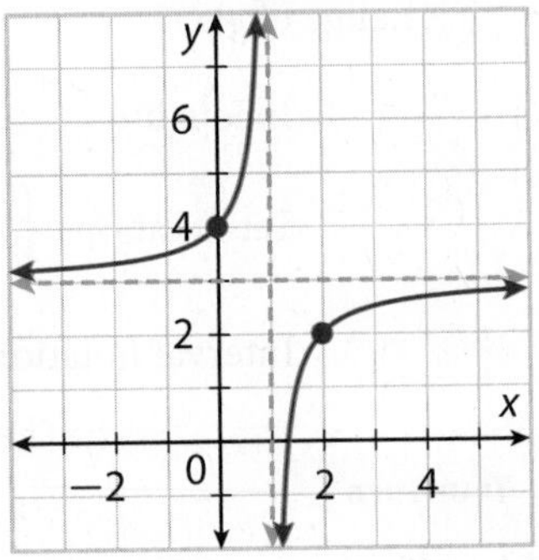

Domain of $g(x)$:

Inequality: $x < 1$ or $x > 1$

Set notation: $\{x | x \neq 1\}$

Interval notation: $(-\infty, 1) \cup (1, +\infty)$

Range of $g(x)$:

Inequality: $y < 3$ or $y > 3$

Set notation: $\{y | y \neq 3\}$

Interval notation: $(-\infty, 3) \cup (3, +\infty)$

(B) $g(x) = \frac{4x - 7}{-2x + 4}$

Use long division.

$$\begin{array}{r} -2 \\ -2x + 4 \overline{\smash{)}\, 4x - 7} \\ \underline{4x - 8} \\ \boxed{1} \end{array}$$

So, the quotient is -2, and the remainder is 1. Using the fact that *dividend* = *quotient* + $\frac{\textit{remainder}}{\textit{divisor}}$, you have

$g(x) = -2 + \frac{\boxed{1}}{-2x + 4}$, or $g(x) = \frac{\boxed{1}}{-2\left(x - \boxed{2}\right)} - 2$.

The graph of $g(x)$ has vertical asymptote $x = \boxed{2}$, horizontal asymptote $y = -2$, and reference points $\left(-\frac{1}{2}(-1) + \boxed{2}, -1 - 2\right) = \left(\boxed{2\frac{1}{2}}, -3\right)$ and $\left(-\frac{1}{2}(1) + \boxed{2}, 1 - 2\right) = \left(\boxed{1\frac{1}{2}}, -1\right)$.

Domain of $g(x)$:

Inequality: $x < \boxed{2}$ or $x > \boxed{2}$

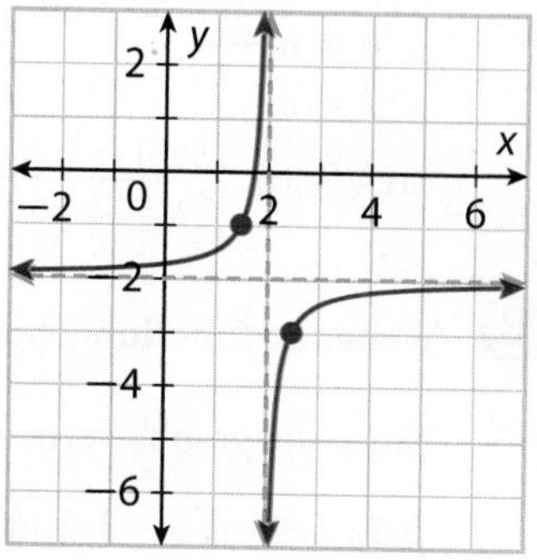

Set notation: $\{x \mid x \neq \boxed{2}\}$

Interval notation: $\left(-\infty, \boxed{2}\right) \cup \left(\boxed{2}, +\infty\right)$

Range of $g(x)$:

Inequality: $y < \boxed{-2}$ or $y > \boxed{-2}$

Set notation: $\{y \mid y \neq \boxed{-2}\}$

Interval notation: $\left(-\infty, \boxed{-2}\right) \cup \left(\boxed{-2}, +\infty\right)$

Reflect

6. In Part A, the graph of $g(x)$ is the result of what transformations of the graph of $f(x) = \frac{1}{x}$?

7. In Part B, the graph of $g(x)$ is the result of what transformations of the graph of $f(x) = \frac{1}{x}$?

Your Turn

Rewrite the function in the form $g(x) = a\left(\frac{1}{x-h}\right) + k$ or $g(x) = \frac{1}{\frac{1}{b}(x-h)} + k$ and graph it. Also state the domain and range using inequalities, set notation, and interval notation.

8. $g(x) = \dfrac{3x + 8}{x + 2}$

Explain 3 Writing Simple Rational Functions

When given the graph of a simple rational function, you can write its equation using one of the general forms $g(x) = a\left(\frac{1}{x-h}\right) + k$ and $g(x) = \frac{1}{\frac{1}{b}(x-h)} + k$ after identifying the values of the parameters using information obtained from the graph.

Example 3

Ⓐ **Write the function whose graph is shown. Use the form $g(x) = a\left(\frac{1}{x-h}\right) + k$.**

Since the graph's vertical asymptote is $x = 3$, the value of the parameter h is 3. Since the graph's horizontal asymptote is $y = 4$, the value of the parameter k is 4.

Substitute these values into the general form of the function.

$$g(x) = a\left(\frac{1}{x-3}\right) + 4$$

Now use one of the points, such as (4, 6), to find the value of the parameter a.

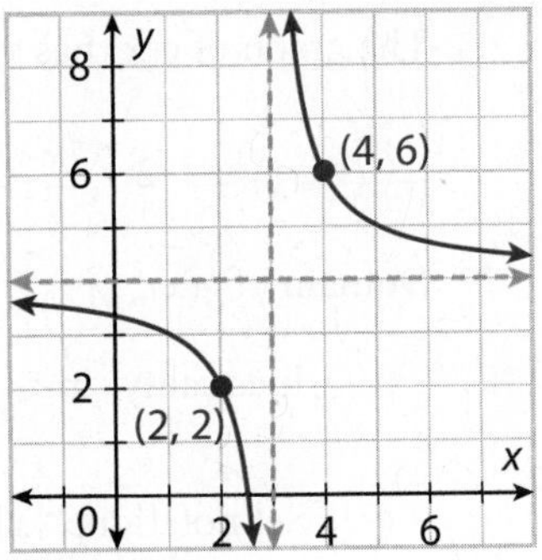

$$g(x) = a\left(\frac{1}{x-3}\right) + 4$$
$$6 = a\left(\frac{1}{4-3}\right) + 4$$
$$6 = a + 4$$
$$2 = a$$

So, $g(x) = 2\left(\frac{1}{x-3}\right) + 4$.

B **Write the function whose graph is shown. Use the form $g(x) = \frac{1}{\frac{1}{b}(x-h)} + k$.**

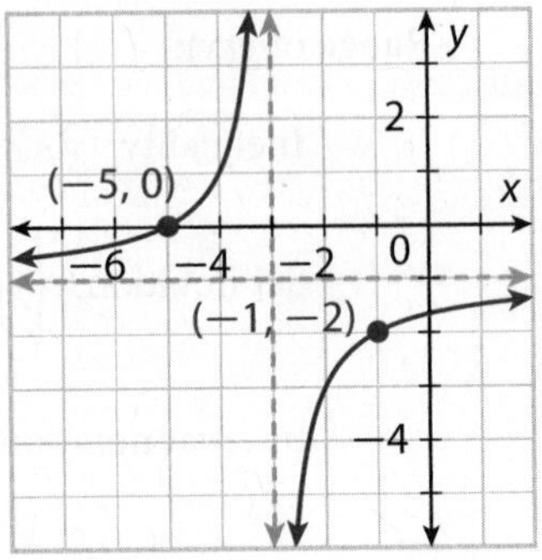

Since the graph's vertical asymptote is $x = -3$, the value of the parameter h is -3. Since the graph's horizontal asymptote is $y = -1$,

the value of the parameter k is -1.

Substitute these values into the general form of the function.

$$g(x) = \frac{1}{\frac{1}{b}(x+3)} + -1$$

Now use one of the points, such as (−5, 0), to find the value of the parameter a.

$$g(x) = \frac{1}{\frac{1}{b}(x+3)} + -1$$
$$0 = \frac{1}{\frac{1}{b}(-5+3)} + -1$$
$$1 = \frac{1}{\frac{1}{b}(-2)}$$
$$\frac{1}{b}(-2) \cdot 1 = 1$$
$$\frac{1}{b} = \frac{-1}{2}$$
$$b = -2$$

So, $g(x) = \frac{1}{\frac{1}{-2}(x+3)} + -1$, or $g(x) = \frac{1}{-0.5(x+3)} - 1$.

Reflect

9. **Discussion** In Parts A and B, the coordinates of a second point on the graph of $g(x)$ are given. In what way can those coordinates be useful?

Your Turn

10. Write the function whose graph is shown.
Use the form $g(x) = a\left(\frac{1}{x-h}\right) + k$.

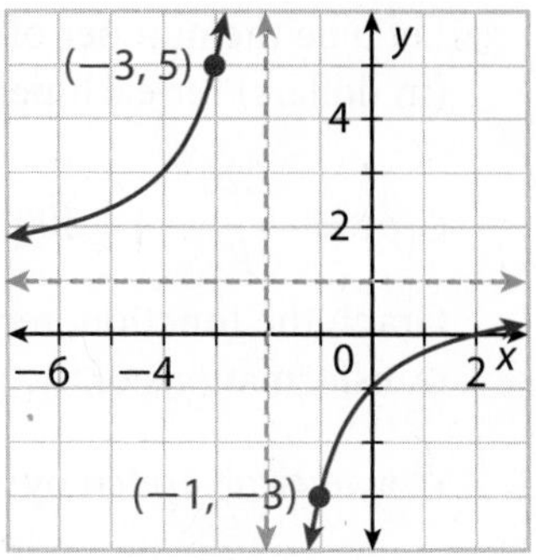

11. Write the function whose graph is shown. Use the form $g(x) = \frac{1}{\frac{1}{b}(x-h)} + k$.

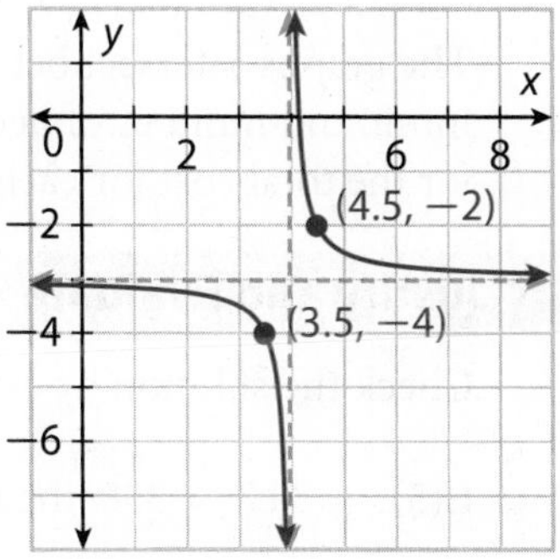

Explain 4 Modeling with Simple Rational Functions

In a real-world situation where there is a shared cost and a per-person or per-item cost, you can model the situation using a rational function that has the general form $f(x) = \frac{a}{x-h} + k$ where $f(x)$ is the total cost for each person or item.

Example 4

(A) **Mary and some of her friends are thinking about renting a car while staying at a beach resort for a vacation. The cost per person for staying at the beach resort is \$300, and the cost of the car rental is \$220. If the friends agree to share the cost of the car rental, what is the minimum number of people who must go on the trip so that the total cost for each person is no more than \$350?**

Analyze Information

Identify the important information.

- The cost per person for the resort is \$300.
- The cost of the car rental is \$220.
- The most that each person will spend is \$350.

Formulate a Plan

Create a rational function that gives the total cost for each person. Graph the function, and use the graph to answer the question.

Solve

Let p be the number of people who agree to go on the trip. Let $C(p)$ be the cost (in dollars) for each person.

$$C(p) = \frac{220}{p} + 300$$

Graph the function, recognizing that the graph involves two transformations of the graph of the parent rational function:

- a vertical stretch by a factor of 220
- a vertical translation of 300 units up

Also draw the line $C(p) = 350$.

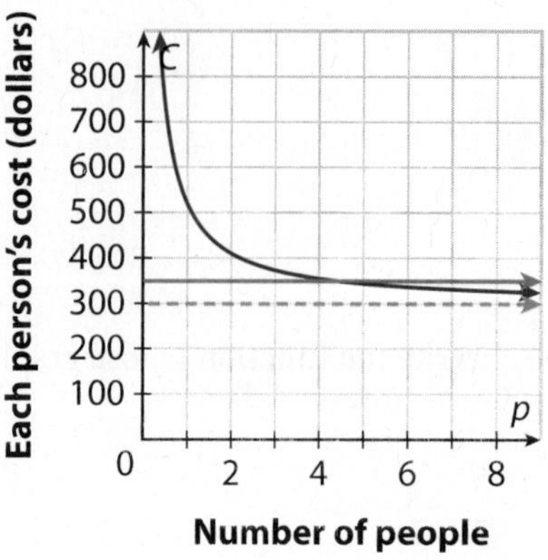

The graphs intersect between $p = $ 4 and $p = $ 5, so the minimum number of people who must go on the trip in order for the total cost for each person to be no more than \$350 is 5.

Justify and Evaluate

Check the solution by evaluating the function $C(p)$. Since $C(4) = $ 355 > 350 and

$C(5) = $ 344 < 350, the minimum number of people who must go on the trip is 5.

Your Turn

12. Justin has purchased a basic silk screening kit for applying designs to fabric. The kit costs \$200. He plans to buy T-shirts for \$10 each, apply a design that he creates to them, and then sell them. Model this situation with a rational function that gives the average cost of a silk-screened T-shirt when the cost of the kit is included in the calculation. Use the graph of the function to determine the minimum number of T-shirts that brings the average cost below \$17.50.

Elaborate

13. Compare and contrast the attributes of $f(x) = \frac{1}{x}$ and the attributes of $g(x) = -\frac{1}{x}$.

14. State the domain and range of $f(x) = a\left(\frac{1}{x-h}\right) + k$ using inequalities, set notation, and interval notation.

15. Given that the model $C(p) = \frac{100}{p} + 50$ represents the total cost C (in dollars) for each person in a group of p people when there is a shared expense and an individual expense, describe what the expressions $\frac{100}{p}$ and 50 represent.

16. **Essential Question Check-In** Describe the transformations you must perform on the graph of $f(x) = \frac{1}{x}$ to obtain the graph of $f(x) = a\left(\frac{1}{x-h}\right) + k$.

Evaluate: Homework and Practice

Personal Math Trainer

- Online Homework
- Hints and Help
- Extra Practice

Describe how the graph of $g(x)$ is related to the graph of $f(x) = \frac{1}{x}$.

1. $g(x) = \frac{1}{x} + 4$

2. $g(x) = 5\left(\frac{1}{x}\right)$

3. $g(x) = \frac{1}{x + 3}$

4. $g(x) = \frac{1}{0.1x}$

5. $g(x) = \frac{1}{x} - 7$

6. $g(x) = \frac{1}{x - 8}$

7. $g(x) = -0.1\left(\frac{1}{x}\right)$

8. $g(x) = \frac{1}{-3x}$

Identify the transformations of the graph of $f(x)$ that produce the graph of the given function $g(x)$. Then graph $g(x)$ on the same coordinate plane as the graph of $f(x)$ by applying the transformations to the asymptotes $x = 0$ and $y = 0$ and to the reference points $(-1, -1)$ and $(1, 1)$. Also state the domain and range of $g(x)$ using inequalities, set notation, and interval notation.

9. $g(x) = 3\left(\frac{1}{x + 1}\right) - 2$

10. $g(x) = \frac{1}{-0.5(x - 3)} + 1$

11. $g(x) = -0.5\left(\frac{1}{x - 1}\right) - 2$

12. $g(x) = \frac{1}{2(x + 2)} + 3$

Rewrite the function in the form $g(x) = a\frac{1}{(x-h)} + k$ or $g(x) = \frac{1}{\frac{1}{b}(x-h)} + k$ and graph it. Also state the domain and range using inequalities, set notation, and interval notation.

13. $g(x) = \frac{3x-5}{x-1}$

14. $g(x) = \frac{x+5}{0.5x+2}$

15. $g(x) = \frac{-4x+11}{x-2}$

16. $g(x) = \frac{4x+13}{-2x-6}$

17. Write the function whose graph is shown. Use the form $g(x) = a\left(\frac{1}{x-h}\right) + k$.

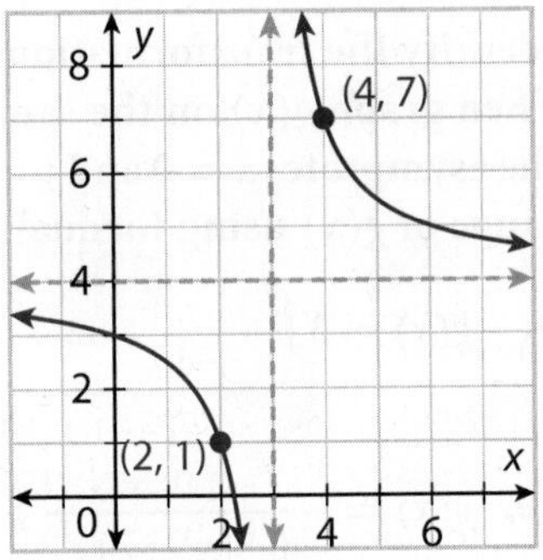

18. Write the function whose graph is shown. Use the form $g(x) = \frac{1}{\frac{1}{b}(x-h)} + k$

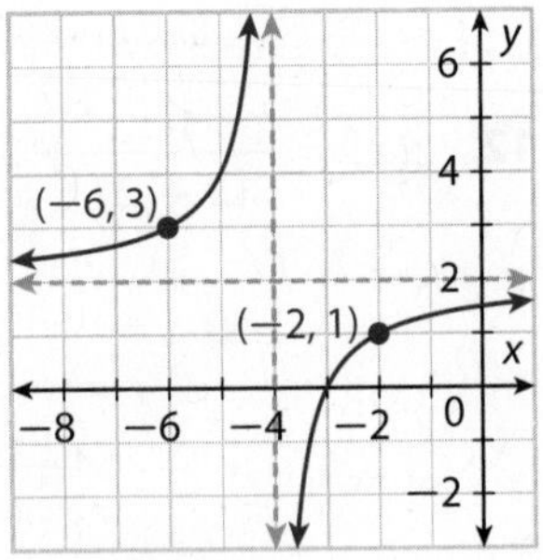

19. Write the function whose graph is shown. Use the form $g(x) = \frac{1}{\frac{1}{b}(x-h)} + k$.

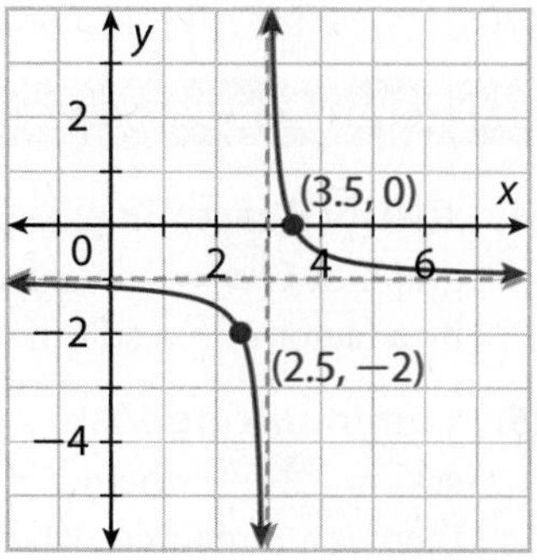

20. Write the function whose graph is shown. Use the form $g(x) = a\left(\frac{1}{x-h}\right) + k$

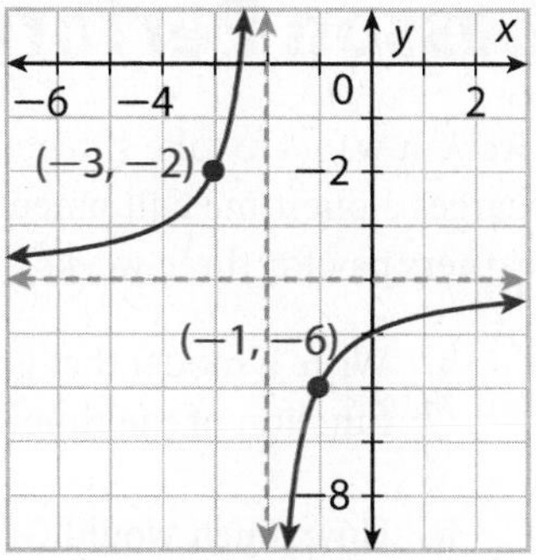

21. Maria has purchased a basic stained glass kit for \$100. She plans to make stained glass suncatchers and sell them. She estimates that the materials for making each suncatcher will cost \$15. Model this situation with a rational function that gives the average cost of a stained glass suncatcher when the cost of the kit is included in the calculation. Use the graph of the function to determine the minimum number of suncatchers that brings the average cost below \$22.50.

22. Amy has purchased a basic letterpress kit for \$140. She plans to make wedding invitations. She estimates that the cost of the paper and envelope for each invitation is \$2. Model this situation with a rational function that gives the average cost of a wedding invitation when the cost of the kit is included in the calculation. Use the graph of the function to determine the minimum number of invitations that brings the average cost below \$5.

23. Multiple Response Select the transformations of the graph of the parent rational function that result in the graph of $g(x) = \frac{1}{2(x-3)} + 1$

A. Horizontal stretch by a factor of 2

B. Horizontal compression by a factor of $\frac{1}{2}$

C. Vertical stretch by a factor of 2

D. Vertical compression by a factor of $\frac{1}{2}$

E. Translation 1 unit up

F. Translation 1 unit down

G. Translation 3 units right

H. Translation 3 units left

H.O.T. Focus on Higher Order Thinking

24. Justify Reasoning Explain why, for positive numbers a and b, a vertical stretch or compression of the graph of $f(x) = \frac{1}{x}$ by a factor of a and, separately, a horizontal stretch or compression of the graph of $f(x)$ by a factor of b result in the same graph when a and b are equal.

25. Communicate Mathematical Ideas Determine the domain and range of the rational function $g(x) = \frac{mx + n}{px + q}$ where $p \neq 0$. Give your answer in set notation, and explain your reasoning. Assume that there is a remainder when dividing $mx + n$ by $px + q$.

Lesson Performance Task

Graham wants to take snowboarding lessons at a nearby ski resort that charges $40 per week. The resort also charges a one-time equipment-rental fee of $99 for uninterrupted enrollment in classes. The resort requires that learners pay for three weeks of classes at a time.

a. Write a model that gives Graham's average weekly enrollment cost (in dollars) as a function of the time (in weeks) that Graham takes classes.

b. How much would Graham's average weekly enrollment cost be if he took classes only for the minimum of three weeks?

c. For how many weeks would Graham need to take classes for his average weekly enrollment cost to be at most $60? Describe how you can use a graphing calculator to graph the function from part a in order to answer this question, and then state the answer.

8.2 Graphing More Complicated Rational Functions

Resource Locker

Essential Question: What features of the graph of a rational function should you identify in order to sketch the graph? How do you identify those features?

Explore 1 Investigating Domains and Vertical Asympotes of More Complicated Rational Functions

You know that the rational function $f(x) = \frac{1}{x-2} + 3$ has the domain $\{x | x \neq 2\}$ because the function is undefined at $x = 2$. Its graph has the vertical asymptote $x = 2$ because as $x \to 2^+$ (x approaches 2 from the right), $f(x) \to +\infty$, and as $x \to 2^-$ (x approaches 2 from the left), $f(x) \to -\infty$. In this Explore, you will investigate the domains and vertical asymptotes of other rational functions.

(A) Complete the table by identifying each function's domain based on the x-values for which the function is undefined. Write the domain using an inequality, set notation, and interval notation. Then state the equations of what you think the vertical asymptotes of the function's graph are.

Function	Domain	Possible Vertical Asymptotes
$f(x) = \frac{x+3}{x-1}$	?	?
$f(x) = \frac{(x+5)(x-1)}{x+1}$	?	?
$f(x) = \frac{x-4}{(x+1)(x-1)}$	?	?
$f(x) = \frac{2x^2-3x-9}{x^2-x-6}$	?	?

(B) Using a graphing calculator, graph each of the functions from Step A, and check to see if vertical asymptotes occur where you expect. Are there any unexpected results? ?

(C) Examine the behavior of $f(x) = \frac{x+3}{x-1}$ near $x = 1$.

First, complete the tables.

x approaches 1 from the right	
x	$f(x) = \frac{x+3}{x-1}$
1.1	?
1.01	?
1.001	?

x approaches 1 from the left	
x	$f(x) = \frac{x+3}{x-1}$
0.9	?
0.99	?
0.999	?

Next, summarize the results.

- As $x \to 1^+$, $f(x) \to$? .
- As $x \to 1^-$, $f(x) \to$? .

Based on the behavior of $f(x) = \frac{x+3}{x-1}$ near $x = 1$, does the graph of $f(x)$ have a vertical asymptote at $x = 1$? ?

(D) Examine the behavior of $f(x) = \frac{(x+5)(x-1)}{(x+1)}$ near $x = -1$.

First, complete the tables.

x approaches −1 from the right	
x	$f(x) = \frac{(x+5)(x-1)}{x+1}$
−0.9	?
−0.99	?
−0.999	?

x approaches −1 from the left	
x	$f(x) = \frac{(x+5)(x-1)}{x+1}$
−1.1	?
−1.01	?
−1.001	?

Next, summarize the results.

- As $x \to -1^+$, $f(x) \to$? .
- As $x \to -1^-$, $f(x) \to$? .

Based on the behavior of $f(x) = \frac{(x+5)(x-1)}{(x+1)}$ near $x = -1$, does the graph of $f(x)$ have a vertical asymptote at $x = -1$? ?

(E) Examine the behavior of $f(x) = \dfrac{x - 4}{(x + 1)(x - 1)}$ near $x = -1$ and $x = 1$.

First, complete the tables. Round results to the nearest tenth.

x approaches -1 from the right	
x	$f(x) = \dfrac{x - 4}{(x + 1)(x - 1)}$
-0.9	?
-0.99	?
-0.999	?

x approaches -1 from the left	
x	$f(x) = \dfrac{x - 4}{(x + 1)(x - 1)}$
-1.1	?
-1.01	?
-1.001	?

x approaches 1 from the right	
x	$f(x) = \dfrac{x - 4}{(x + 1)(x - 1)}$
1.1	?
1.01	?
1.001	?

x approaches 1 from the left	
x	$f(x) = \dfrac{x - 4}{(x + 1)(x - 1)}$
0.9	?
0.99	?
0.999	?

Next, summarize the results.

- As $x \to -1^+$, $f(x) \to$? .
- As $x \to -1^-$, $f(x) \to$? .
- As $x \to 1^+$, $f(x) \to$? .
- As $x \to 1^-$, $f(x) \to$? .

Based on the behavior of $f(x) = \frac{x - 4}{(x + 1)(x - 1)}$ near $x = -1$, does the graph of $f(x)$ have a vertical asymptote at $x = -1$? ? Based on the behavior of $f(x) = \frac{x - 4}{(x + 1)(x - 1)}$ near $x = 1$, does the graph of $f(x)$ have a vertical asymptote at $x = 1$? ?

(F) Examine the behavior of $f(x) = \dfrac{2x^2 - 3x - 9}{x^2 - x - 6}$ near $x = -2$ and $x = 3$.

First, complete the tables. Round results to the nearest ten thousandth if necessary.

x approaches -2 from the right	
x	$f(x) = \dfrac{2x^2 - 3x - 9}{x^2 - x - 6}$
-1.9	?
-1.99	?
-1.999	?

x approaches -2 from the left	
x	$f(x) = \dfrac{2x^2 - 3x - 9}{x^2 - x - 6}$
-2.1	?
-2.01	?
-2.001	?

x approaches 3 from the right	
x	$f(x) = \dfrac{2x^2 - 3x - 9}{x^2 - x - 6}$
3.1	?
3.01	?
3.001	?

x approaches 3 from the left	
x	$f(x) = \dfrac{2x^2 - 3x - 9}{x^2 - x - 6}$
2.9	?
2.99	?
2.999	?

Next, summarize the results.

- As $x \to -2^+$, $f(x) \to$?.
- As $x \to -2^-$, $f(x) \to$?.
- As $x \to 3^+$, $f(x) \to$?.
- As $x \to 3^-$, $f(x) \to$?.

Based on the behavior of $f(x) = \frac{2x^2 - 3x - 9}{x^2 - x - 6}$ near $x = -2$, does the graph of $f(x)$ have a vertical asymptote at $x = -2$? ? Based on the behavior of $f(x) = \frac{2x^2 - 3x - 9}{x^2 - x - 6}$ near $x = 3$, does the graph of $f(x)$ have a vertical asymptote at $x = 3$? ?

Reflect

1. Rewrite $f(x) = \dfrac{2x^2 - 3x - 9}{x^2 - x - 6}$ so that its numerator and denominator are factored. How does this form of the function explain the behavior of the function near $x = 3$?

2. **Discussion** When you graph $f(x) = \dfrac{2x^2 - 3x - 9}{x^2 - x - 6}$ on a graphing calculator, you can't tell that the function is undefined for $x = 3$. How does using the calculator's table feature help? What do you think the graph should look like to make it clear that the function is undefined at $x = 3$?

Explain 1 Sketching the Graphs of More Complicated Rational Functions

As you have seen, there can be breaks in the graph of a rational function. These breaks are called *discontinuities*, and there are two kinds:

1. When a rational function has a factor in the denominator that is not also in the numerator, an *infinite discontinuity* occurs at the value of x for which the factor equals 0. On the graph of the function, an infinite discontinuity appears as a vertical asymptote.

2. When a rational function has a factor in the denominator that is also in the numerator, a *point discontinuity* occurs at the value of x for which the factor equals 0. On the graph of the function, a point discontinuity appears as a "hole."

The graph of a rational function can also have a horizontal asymptote, or even an asymptote that is a line that is neither horizontal nor vertical. This is determined by the degrees and leading coefficients of the function's numerator and denominator. Examine the following rational expressions, which include polynomial quotients rewritten using long division as a quotient plus a remainder that approaches 0 as x increases or decreases without bound.

$$\frac{1}{x-1} \to 0 \text{ as } x \to \pm\infty$$

$$\frac{x+1}{x^2-1} = \frac{x+1}{(x+1)(x-1)} = \frac{1}{x-1} \ (x \neq -1), \text{ so } \frac{x+1}{x^2-1} \to 0 \text{ as } x \to \pm\infty$$

$$\frac{x+3}{x-1} = 1 + \frac{4}{x-1} \to 1 \text{ as } x \to \pm\infty$$

$$\frac{4x+3}{x-1} = 4 + \frac{7}{x-1} \to 4 \text{ as } x \to \pm\infty$$

$$\frac{3x^2+x-1}{x-1} = 3x + 4 + \frac{3}{x-1} \to 3x + 4 \text{ as } x \to \pm\infty$$

In general, if the numerator is a polynomial $p(x)$ in standard form with leading coefficient a and the denominator is a polynomial $q(x)$ in standard form with leading coefficient b, then an examination of the function's end behavior gives the following results.

Relationship between Degree of $p(x)$ and Degree of $q(x)$	Equation of Horizontal Asymptote (if one exists)
Degree of $p(x) <$ degree of $q(x)$	$y = 0$
Degree of $p(x) =$ degree of $q(x)$	$y = \frac{a}{b}$
Degree of $p(x) >$ degree of $q(x)$	There is no horizontal asymptote. The function instead increases or decreases without bound as x increases or decreases without bound. In particular, when the degree of the numerator is 1 more than the degree of the denominator, the function's graph approaches a slanted line, called a *slant asymptote*, as x increases or decreases without bound.

You can sketch the graph of a rational function by identifying where vertical asymptotes, "holes," horizontal asymptotes, and slant asymptotes occur. Using the factors of the numerator and denominator, you can also establish intervals on the x-axis where either an x-intercept or a discontinuity occurs and then check the signs of the factors on those intervals to determine whether the graph lies above or below the x-axis.

Example 1 **Sketch the graph of the given rational function. (If the degree of the numerator is 1 more than the degree of the denominator, find the graph's slant asymptote by dividing the numerator by the denominator.) Also state the function's domain and range using inequalities, set notation, and interval notation. (If your sketch indicates that the function has maximum or minimum values, use a graphing calculator to find those values to the nearest hundredth when determining the range.)**

Ⓐ $f(x) = \frac{x+1}{x-2}$

Identify vertical asymptotes and "holes."

The function is undefined when $x - 2 = 0$, or $x = 2$. Since $x - 2$ is not a factor of the numerator, there is a vertical asymptote rather than a "hole" at $x = 2$.

Identify horizontal asymptotes and slant asymptotes.

The numerator and denominator have the same degree and the leading coefficient of each is 1, so there is a horizontal asymptote at $y = \frac{1}{1} = 1$.

Identify x-intercepts.

An x-intercept occurs when $x + 1 = 0$, or $x = -1$.

Check the sign of the function on the intervals $x < -1$, $-1 < x < 2$, and $x > 2$.

Interval	Sign of $x+1$	Sign of $x-2$	Sign of $f(x) = \frac{x+1}{x-2}$
$x < -1$	−	−	+
$-1 < x < 2$	+	−	−
$x > 2$	+	+	+

Sketch the graph using all this information. Then state the domain and range.

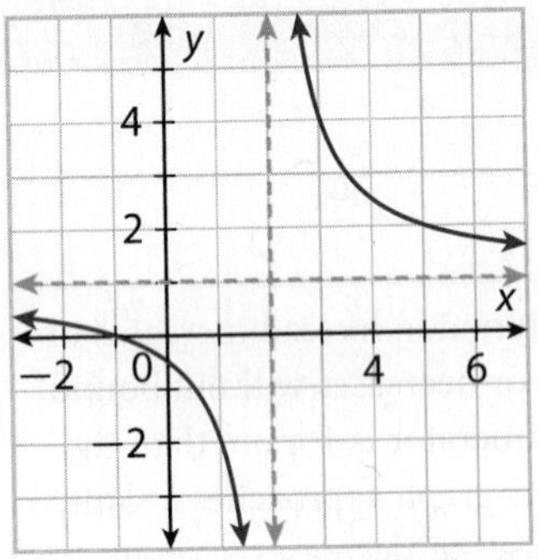

Domain:

Inequality: $x < 2$ or $x > 2$

Set notation: $\{x \mid x \neq 2\}$

Interval notation: $(-\infty, 2) \cup (2, +\infty)$

Range:

Inequality: $y < 1$ or $y > 1$

Set notation: $\{y \mid y \neq 1\}$

Interval notation: $(-\infty, 1) \cup (1, +\infty)$

B $f(x) = \dfrac{x^2 + x - 2}{x + 3}$

Factor the function's numerator.

$$f(x) = \frac{x^2 + x - 2}{x + 3} = \frac{(x-1)(x+2)}{x+3}$$

Identify vertical asymptotes and "holes."

The function is undefined when $x + 3 = 0$, or $x =$ -3. Since $x + 3$ is not a factor of the numerator, there is a vertical asymptote rather than a "hole" at $x =$ -3.

Identify horizontal asymptotes and slant asymptotes.

Because the degree of the numerator is 1 more than the degree of the denominator, there is no horizontal asymptote, but there is a slant asymptote. Divide the numerator by the denominator to identify the slant asymptote.

$$\begin{array}{r} x - 2 \\ x + 3 \overline{) x^2 + x - 2} \\ \underline{x^2 + 3x} \\ -2x - 2 \\ \underline{-2x - 6} \\ 4 \end{array}$$

So, the line $y = x - $ 2 is the slant asymptote.

Identify x-intercepts.

There are two x-intercepts: when $x - 1 = 0$, or $x =$ 1, and when $x + 2 = 0$, or $x =$ -2.

Check the sign of the function on the intervals $x < -3$, $-3 < x < -2$, $-2 < x < 1$, and $x > 1$.

Interval	Sign of $x+3$	Sign of $x+2$	Sign of $x-1$	Sign of $f(x) = \frac{(x-1)(x+2)}{x+3}$
$x < -3$	$-$	$-$	$-$	$-$
$-3 < x < -2$	$+$	$-$	$-$	$+$
$-2 < x < 1$	$+$	$+$	$-$	$-$
$x > 1$	$+$	$+$	$+$	$+$

Sketch the graph using all this information. Then state the domain and range.

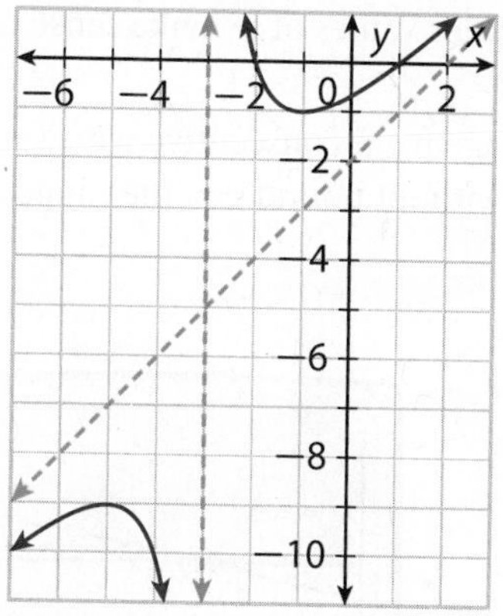

Domain:

Inequality: $x <$ -3 or $x >$ -3

Set notation: $\{x \mid x \neq -3\}$

Interval notation: $(-\infty, -3) \cup (-3, +\infty)$

The sketch indicates that the function has a maximum value and a minimum value. Using **3:minimum** from the **CALC** menu on a graphing calculator gives -1 as the minimum value. Using **4:maximum** from the **CALC** menu on a graphing calculator gives -5 as the maximum value.

Range: Inequality: $y <$ -5 or $y >$ -1

Set notation: $\{y \mid y < -5 \text{ or } y > -1\}$ Interval notation: $(-\infty, -5) \cup (-1, +\infty)$

Your Turn

Sketch the graph of the given rational function. (If the degree of the numerator is 1 more than the degree of the denominator, find the graph's slant asymptote by dividing the numerator by the denominator.) Also state the function's domain and range using inequalities, set notation, and interval notation. (If your sketch indicates that the function has maximum or minimum values, use a graphing calculator to find those values to the nearest hundredth when determining the range.)

3. $f(x) = \dfrac{x + 1}{x^2 + 3x - 4}$

Explain 2 Modeling with More Complicated Rational Functions

When two real-world variable quantities are compared using a ratio or rate, the comparison is a rational function. You can solve problems about the ratio or rate by graphing the rational function.

Example 2 **Write a rational function to model the situation, or use the given rational function. State a reasonable domain and range for the function using set notation. Then use a graphing calculator to graph the function and answer the question.**

(A) A baseball team has won 32 games out of 56 games played, for a winning percentage of $\frac{32}{56} \approx 0.571$. How many consecutive games must the team win to raise its winning percentage to 0.600?

Let w be the number of consecutive games to be won. Then the total number of games won is the function $T_{\text{won}}(w) = 32 + w$, and the total number of games played is the function $T_{\text{played}}(w) = 56 + w$.

The rational function that gives the team's winning percentage p (as a decimal) is

$$p(w) = \frac{T_{\text{won}}(w)}{T_{\text{played}}(w)} = \frac{32 + w}{56 + w}.$$

The domain of the rational function is $\{w \mid w \geq 0 \text{ and } w \text{ is a whole number}\}$. Note that you do not need to exclude -56 from the domain, because only nonnegative whole-number values of w make sense in this situation.

Since the function models what happens to the team's winning percentage from consecutive wins (no losses), the values of $p(w)$ start at 0.571 and approach 1 as w increases without bound. So, the range is

$\{p \mid 0.571 \leq p < 1\}$.

Graph $y = \frac{32 + x}{56 + x}$ on a graphing calculator using a viewing window that shows 0 to 10 on the x-axis and 0.5 to 0.7 on the y-axis. Also graph the line $y = 0.6$. To find where the graphs intersect, select **5: intersect** from the **CALC** menu.

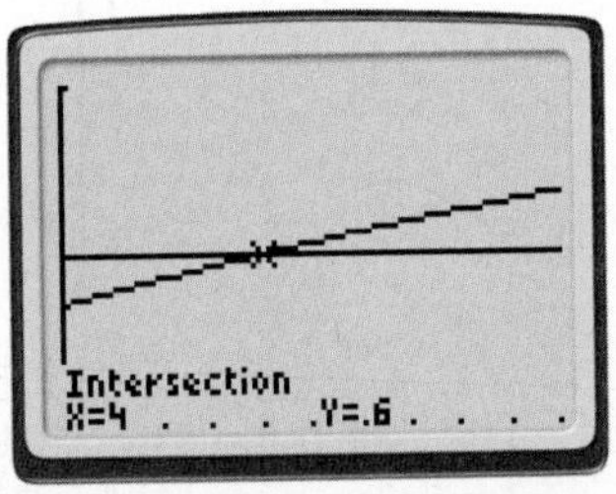

So, the team's winning percentage (as a decimal) will be 0.600 if the team wins 4 consecutive games.

(B) Two friends decide spend an afternoon canoeing on a river. They travel 4 miles upstream and 6 miles downstream. In still water, they know that their average paddling speed is 5 miles per hour. If their canoe trip takes 4 hours, what is the average speed of the river's current? To answer the question, use the rational function $t(c) = \frac{4}{5 - c} + \frac{6}{5 + c} = \frac{50 - 2c}{(5 - c)(5 + c)}$ where c is the average speed of the current (in miles per hour) and t is the time (in hours) spent canoeing 4 miles against the current at a rate of $5 - c$ miles per hour and 6 miles with the current at a rate of $5 + c$ miles per hour.

In order for the friends to travel upstream, the speed of the current must be less than their average paddling speed, so the domain of the function is $\{c \mid 0 \leq c < \boxed{5}\}$. If the friends canoed in still water $(c = 0)$, the trip would take a total of $\frac{4}{5} + \frac{6}{5} = \boxed{2}$ hours. As c approaches 5 from the left, the value of $\frac{6}{5+c}$ approaches $\frac{6}{10} = 0.6$ hour, but the value of $\frac{4}{5-c}$ increases without bound. So, the range of the function is $\{t \mid t \geq \boxed{2}\}$.

Graph $y = \dfrac{50 - 2x}{(5 - x)(5 + x)}$ on a graphing calculator using a viewing window that shows 0 to 5 on the x-axis and 2 to 5 on the y-axis. Also graph the line $y = \boxed{4}$. To find where the graphs intersect, select **5:intersect** from the **CALC** menu. The calculator shows that the average speed of the current is about 3.8 miles per hour.

Your Turn

Write a rational function to model the situation, or use the given rational function. State a reasonable domain and range for the function using set notation. Then use a graphing calculator to graph the function and answer the question.

4. A saline solution is a mixture of salt and water. A $p\%$ saline solution contains $p\%$ salt and $(100 - p)\%$ water by mass. A chemist has 300 grams of a 4% saline solution that needs to be strengthened to a 6% solution by adding salt. How much salt should the chemist add?

Elaborate

5. How can you show that the vertical line $x = c$, where c is a constant, is an asymptote for the graph of a rational function?

6. How can you determine the end behavior of a rational function?

7. **Essential Question Check-In** How do you identify any vertical asymptotes and "holes" that the graph of a rational function has?

Evaluate: Homework and Practice

State the domain using an inequality, set notation, and interval notation. For any x-value excluded from the domain, state whether the graph has a vertical asymptote or a "hole" at that x-value. Use a graphing calculator to check your answer.

1. $f(x) = \frac{x+5}{x+1}$

2. $f(x) = \frac{x^2+2x-3}{x^2-4x+3}$

Divide the numerator by the denominator to write the function in the form $f(x) = \text{quotient} + \frac{\text{remainder}}{\text{divisor}}$ and determine the function's end behavior. Then, using a graphing calculator to examine the function's graph, state the range using an inequality, set notation, and interval notation.

3. $f(x) = \frac{3x+1}{x-2}$

4. $f(x) = \frac{x}{(x-2)(x+3)}$

5. $f(x) = \frac{x^2-5x+6}{x-1}$

6. $f(x) = \frac{4x^2-1}{x^2+x-2}$

Sketch the graph of the given rational function. (If the degree of the numerator is 1 more than the degree of the denominator, find the graph's slant asymptote by dividing the numerator by the denominator.) Also state the function's domain and range using inequalities, set notation, and interval notation. (If your sketch indicates that the function has maximum or minimum values, use a graphing calculator to find those values to the nearest hundredth when determining the range.)

7. $f(x) = \frac{x-1}{x+1}$

8. $f(x) = \frac{x-1}{(x-2)(x+3)}$

9. $f(x) = \frac{(x+1)(x-1)}{x+2}$

10. $f(x) = \frac{-3x(x-2)}{(x-2)(x+2)}$

11. $f(x) = \frac{x^2+2x-8}{x-1}$

12. $f(x) = \frac{2x^2-4x}{x^2+4x+4}$

Write a rational function to model the situation, or use the given rational function. State a reasonable domain and range for the function using set notation. Then use a graphing calculator to graph the function and answer the question.

13. A basketball team has won 16 games out of 23 games played, for a winning percentage (expressed as a decimal) of $\frac{16}{23} \approx 0.696$. How many consecutive games must the team win to raise its winning percentage to 0.750?

14. So far this season, a baseball player has had 84 hits in 294 times at bat, for a batting average of $\frac{84}{294} \approx 0.286$. How many consecutive hits must the player get to raise his batting average to 0.300?

15. A kayaker traveled 5 miles upstream and then 8 miles downstream on a river. The average speed of the current was 3 miles per hour. If the kayaker was paddling for 5 hours, what was the kayaker's average paddling speed? To answer the question, use the rational function $t(s) = \frac{5}{s-3} + \frac{8}{s+3} = \frac{13s - 9}{(s-3)(s+3)}$ where s is the kayaker's average paddling speed (in miles per hour) and t is the time (in hours) spent kayaking 5 miles against the current at a rate of $s - 3$ miles per hour and 8 miles with the current at a rate of $s + 3$ miles per hour.

16. In aviation, *air speed* refers to a plane's speed in still air. A small plane maintains a certain air speed when flying to and from a city that is 400 miles away. On the trip out, the plane flies against a wind, which has an average speed of 40 miles per hour. On the return trip, the plane flies with the wind. If the total flight time for the round trip is 3.5 hours, what is the plane's average air speed? To answer this question, use the rational function $t(s) = \frac{400}{s-40} + \frac{400}{s+40} = \frac{800s}{(s-40)(s+40)}$, where s is the air speed (in miles per hour) and t is the total flight time (in hours) for the round trip.

17. Multiple Response Select the statements that apply to the rational function $f(x) = \frac{x-2}{x^2-x-6}$.

A. The function's domain is $\left\{x \mid x \neq -2 \text{ and } x \neq 3\right\}$.

B. The function's domain is $\left\{x \mid x \neq -2 \text{ and } x \neq -3\right\}$.

C. The function's range is $\left\{y \mid y \neq 0\right\}$.

D. The function's range is $\left\{y \mid -\infty < y < +\infty\right\}$.

E. The function's graph has vertical asymptotes at $x = -2$ and $x = 3$.

F. The function's graph has a vertical asymptote at $x = -3$ and a "hole" at $x = 2$.

G. The function's graph has a horizontal asymptote at $y = 0$.

H. The function's graph has a horizontal asymptote at $y = 1$.

H.O.T. Focus on Higher Order Thinking

18. Draw Conclusions For what value(s) of a does the graph of $f(x) = \frac{x+a}{x^2+4x+3}$ have a "hole"? Explain. Then, for each value of a, state the domain and the range of $f(x)$ using interval notation.

19. Critique Reasoning A student claims that the functions $f(x) = \frac{4x^2-1}{4x+2}$ and $g(x) = \frac{4x+2}{4x^2-1}$ have different domains but identical ranges. Which part of the student's claim is correct, and which is false? Explain.

Lesson Performance Task

In professional baseball, the smallest allowable volume of a baseball is 92.06% of the largest allowable volume, and the range of allowable radii is 0.04 inch.

a. Let r be the largest allowable radius (in inches) of a baseball. Write expressions, both in terms of r, for the largest allowable volume of the baseball and the smallest allowable volume of the baseball. (Use the formula for the volume of a sphere, $V = \frac{4}{3}\pi r^3$.)

b. Write and simplify a function that gives the ratio R of the smallest allowable volume of a baseball to the largest allowable volume.

c. Use a graphing calculator to graph the function from part b, and use the graph to find the smallest allowable radius and the largest allowable radius of a baseball. Round your answers to the nearest hundredth.

Rational Functions

Essential Question: How can you use rational functions to solve real-world problems?

Key Vocabulary

asymptote *(asíntota)*
constant of variation *(constante de variación)*
parent function *(función madre)*
rational function *(función racional)*

KEY EXAMPLE *(Lesson 8.1)*

Graph $y = -\frac{1}{x-2}$. State the domain, range, y-intercept, and identify any asymptotes.

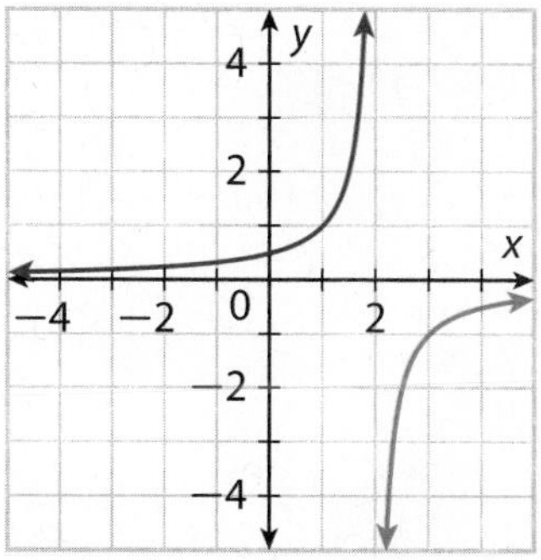

Domain: $x < 2$ or $x > 2$

Range: $y < 0$ or $y > 0$

y-intercept: $\left(0, \frac{1}{2}\right)$

The graph has a vertical asymptote at $x = 2$ and a horizontal asymptote at $y = 0$.

KEY EXAMPLE *(Lesson 8.2)*

Graph $y = \frac{2x^2}{x+2}$. State the domain, range, x-intercept, and identify any asymptotes.

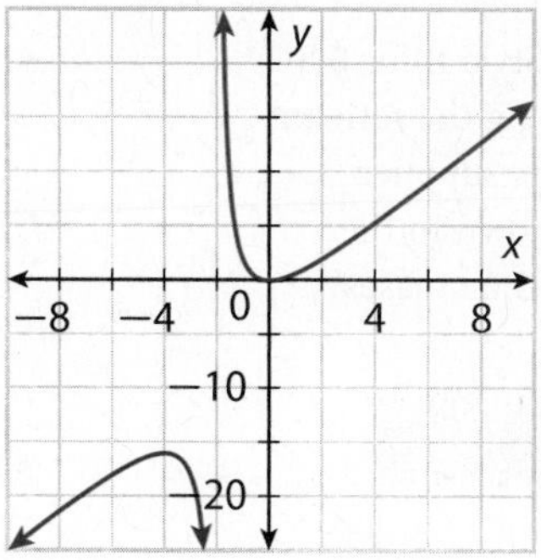

Domain: $x < -2$ or $x > -2$

Range: $y \leq -16$ or $y \geq 0$

The numerator has 0 as its only zero, so the x-intercept is $(0, 0)$.

The denominator has -2 as its only zero, so the graph has a vertical asymptote at $x = -2$.

EXERCISES

Describe how the graph of $g(x)$ is related to the graph of $f(x) = \frac{1}{x}$. *(Lesson 8.1)*

1. $g(x) = \dfrac{1}{x+4}$

2. $g(x) = \dfrac{1}{x-2} + 3$

3. $g(x) = \dfrac{-1}{x+3}$

Graph the function using a graphing calculator. State the domain, x-intercept(s), and identify asymptotes. *(Lesson 8.2)*

4. $f(x) = \dfrac{x^2 - 3x}{x+4}$

5. $f(x) = \dfrac{x-3}{x^2+6x+5}$

6. $f(x) = -\dfrac{(x^2-4)}{(x+1)}$

MODULE PERFORMANCE TASK

What Is the Profit?

A sporting goods store sells two styles of bike helmets: Style A for $30 each and Style B for $40 each. The store is trying to calculate its average profit on each style of helmet, using the rational function $A(x) = \frac{P(x)}{x}$, where $P(x)$ is the profit on the sale of x helmets. The helmet supplier offers a volume discount for orders up to 500 helmets, using the cost formulas shown in the table. For each style, how does per-helmet profit change as the number of helmets increases? What is the maximum per-helmet profit?

Number of Helmets (x)	100	200	300	400	500
Style A					
Revenue					
Cost: $100 + (20 - 0.01x)x$					
Profit					
Style B					
Revenue					
Cost: $250 + (30 - 0.03x)x$					
Profit					

Start by organizing your data in a table like the one shown. Then complete the task. Use graphs, numbers, words, or algebra to explain how you reached your conclusion.

Ready to Go On?

8.1–8.2 Rational Functions

Personal Math Trainer

- Online Homework
- Hints and Help
- Extra Practice

Describe how the graph of $g(x)$ is related to the graph of $f(x) = \frac{1}{x}$. *(Lesson 8.2)*

1. $g(x) = \frac{5}{x} - 3$

2. $g(x) = \frac{1}{-0.5(x - 2)} + 4$

3. $g(x) = \frac{-1}{x} + 5$

Graph the function using a graphing calculator. State the domain, x-intercept(s), and identify asymptotes. *(Lessons 8.2, 8.3)*

4. $f(x) = \frac{2x - 4}{x + 3}$

5. $f(x) = \frac{x^2 - 9}{x - 2}$

6. $f(x) = -\frac{(x + 2)}{(x^2 + 3x)}$

ESSENTIAL QUESTION

7. How do you identify any linear asymptotes of a rational function?

MODULE 8
MIXED REVIEW

Assessment Readiness

1. Consider the inequality $x^2 - 64 < 0$. Tell whether each of the following is a solution set of the inequality.
   A. $x < -8$ or $x > -8$
   B. $-8 < x < -8$
   C. $-64 < x < -64$

2. Consider the equation $y = \frac{2x + 5}{x - 1}$. Determine if each statement is True or False.
   A. The line $x = 1$ is an asymptote.
   B. The point $(0, -5)$ lies on the graph.
   C. The function is undefined for $x = -1$.

3. Consider the function $y = \frac{x^2 + 5x + 4}{x^2 - 9}$. State the domain, range, and x- and y-intercepts, and identify any asymptotes.

4. You have subscribed to a cable television service. The cable company charges a one-time installation fee of \$30 and a monthly fee of \$50. Write a model that gives the average cost per month as a function of months subscribed to the service. After how many months will the average cost be \$56? Explain your thinking and identify any asymptotes on the graph of the function.

Rational Expressions and Equations

MODULE 9

Essential Question: How can you use rational expressions and equations to solve real-world problems?

REAL WORLD VIDEO
Robotic arms and other prosthetic devices are among the wonders of robotics. Check out some of the other cutting-edge applications of modern robotics.

MODULE PERFORMANCE TASK PREVIEW

Robots and Resistors

Robotics engineers design robots and develop applications for them, such as executing high-precision tasks in factories, cleaning toxic waste, and locating and defusing bombs. People who work in robotics are skilled in areas such as electronics and computer programming. How can a rational expression be used to help design the circuitry for a robot? Let's find out!

Are YOU Ready?

Complete these exercises to review skills you will need for this module.

Personal Math Trainer

- Online Homework
- Hints and Help
- Extra Practice

Graphing Linear Proportional Relationships

Example 1

Graph $y = \frac{1}{2}x$.

When $x = 0$, $y = 0$, so plot $(0, 0)$ on the graph.

The slope is $\frac{1}{2}$, so from $(0, 0)$, plot the next point up 1 and over 2.

Draw a line through the two points.

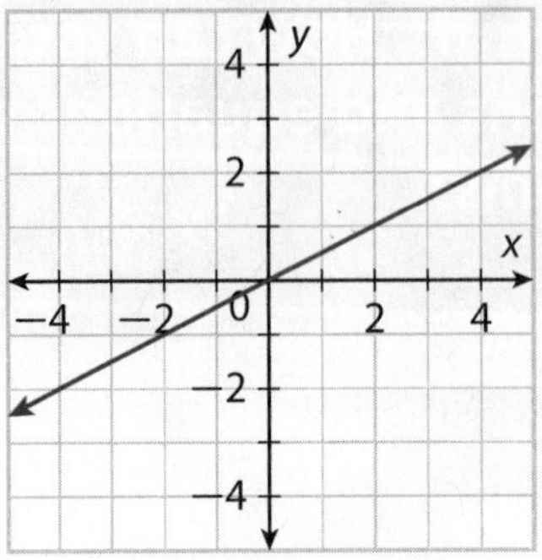

Graph each proportional relationship.

1. $y = 2x$

2. $y = \frac{2}{3}x$

Direct and Inverse Variation

Example 2

In a direct variation the constant is 4 and its graph passes through $(x, 10)$. Find x.

$y = kx \rightarrow 10 = 4x \rightarrow x = 2.5$

Example 3

In an inverse variation the constant is 2.4 and its graph passes through $(6, y)$. Find y.

$k = xy \rightarrow 2.4 = 6y \rightarrow y = 0.4$

Find the missing variable for each direct variation.

3. $k = -1$; $(x, -5)$

4. $k = 3$; $(9, y)$

5. $k = \frac{1}{3}$; $(x, -2)$

Find the missing variable for each inverse variation.

6. $k = 8$; $(x, -10)$

7. $k = -2$; $(5, y)$

8. $k = 6$; $(x, 1.5)$

9.1 Adding and Subtracting Rational Expressions

Essential Question: How can you add and subtract rational expressions?

Resource Locker

Explore Identifying Excluded Values

Given a rational expression, identify the excluded values by finding the zeroes of the denominator. If possible, simplify the expression.

(A) $\frac{(1 - x^2)}{x - 1}$

The denominator of the expression is ? .

(B) Since division by 0 is not defined, the excluded values for this expression are all the values that would make the denominator equal to 0.

$x - 1 = 0$

$x =$?

(C) Begin simplifying the expression by factoring the numerator.

$$\frac{(1 - x^2)}{x - 1} = \frac{(?)(?)}{x - 1}$$

(D) Divide out terms common to both the numerator and the denominator.

$$\frac{1 - x^2}{x - 1} = \frac{(?)(?)}{-1} - x = ? = ?$$

(E) The simplified expression is

$\frac{(1 - x^2)}{x - 1} =$? , whenever $x \neq$?

(F) What is the domain for this function? What is its range? ?

Reflect

1. What factors can be divided out of the numerator and denominator?

Explain 1 Writing Equivalent Rational Expressions

Given a rational expression, there are different ways to write an equivalent rational expression. When common terms are divided out, the result is an equivalent but simplified expression.

Example 1 **Rewrite the expression as indicated.**

(A) Write $\frac{3x}{(x+3)}$ as an equivalent rational expression that has a denominator of $(x+3)(x+5)$.

The expression $\frac{3x}{(x+3)}$ has a denominator of $(x+3)$.

The factor missing from the denominator is $(x+5)$.

Introduce a common factor, $(x+5)$.

$$\frac{3x}{(x+3)} = \frac{3x(x+5)}{(x+3)(x+5)}$$

$\frac{3x}{(x+3)}$ is equivalent to $\frac{3x(x+5)}{(x+3)(x+5)}$.

(B) Simplify the expression $\frac{(x^2+5x+6)}{(x^2+3x+2)(x+3)}$.

Write the expression. $\frac{(x^2+5x+6)}{(x^2+3x+2)(x+3)}$

Factor the numerator and denominator. $\frac{(x+2)(x+3)}{(x+1)(x+2)(x+3)}$

Divide out like terms. $\frac{1}{x+1}$

Your Turn

2. Write $\frac{5}{5x-25}$ as an equivalent expression with a denominator of $(x-5)(x+1)$.

3. Simplify the expression $\frac{(x+x^3)(1-x^2)}{(x^2-x^6)}$.

Explain 2 Identifying the LCD of Two Rational Expressions

Given two or more rational expressions, the least common denominator (LCD) is found by factoring each denominator and finding the least common multiple (LCM) of the factors. This technique is useful for the addition and subtraction of expressions with unlike denominators.

Least Common Denominator (LCD) of Rational Expressions

To find the LCD of rational expressions:

1. Factor each denominator completely. Write any repeated factors as powers.
2. List the different factors. If the denominators have common factors, use the highest power of each common factor.

Example 2 **Find the LCD for each set of rational expressions.**

Ⓐ $\frac{-2}{3x - 15}$ and $\frac{6x}{4x + 28}$

Factor each denominator completely.

$3x - 15 = 3(x - 5)$

$4x + 28 = 4(x + 7)$

List the different factors.

$3, 4, x - 5, x + 7$

The LCD is $3 \cdot 4(x - 5)(x + 7)$,

or $12(x - 5)(x + 7)$.

Ⓑ $\frac{-14}{x^2 - 11x + 24}$ and $\frac{9}{x^2 - 6x + 9}$

Factor each denominator completely.

$x^2 - 11x + 24 =$ $(x - 3)(x - 8)$

$x^2 - 6x + 9 =$ $(x - 3)(x - 3)$

List the different factors. $x - 3$ and $x - 8$

Taking the highest power of $(x - 3)$, the LCD is $(x - 3)^2(x - 8)$.

Reflect

4. **Discussion** When is the LCD of two rational expressions not equal to the product of their denominators?

Your Turn

Find the LCD for each set of rational expressions.

5. $\frac{x + 6}{8x - 24}$ and $\frac{14x}{10x - 30}$

6. $\frac{12x}{15x + 60}$ and $\frac{5}{x^2 + 9x + 20}$

Explain 3 Adding and Subtracting Rational Expressions

Adding and subtracting rational expressions is similar to adding and subtracting fractions.

Example 3 **Add or subtract. Identify any excluded values and simplify your answer.**

Ⓐ $\frac{x^2 + 4x + 2}{x^2} + \frac{x^2}{x^2 + x}$

Factor the denominators. $\frac{x^2 + 4x + 2}{x^2} + \frac{x^2}{x(x + 1)}$

Identify where the expression is not defined. The first expression is undefined when $x = 0$. The second expression is undefined when $x = 0$ and when $x = -1$.

Find a common denominator. The LCM for x^2 and $x(x + 1)$ is $x^2(x + 1)$.

Write the expressions with a common denominator by multiplying both by the appropriate form of 1.

$$\frac{(x + 1)}{(x + 1)} \cdot \frac{x^2 + 4x + 2}{x^2} + \frac{x^2}{x(x + 1)} \cdot \frac{x}{x}$$

Simplify each numerator.

$$= \frac{x^3 + 5x^2 + 6x + 2}{x^2(x + 1)} + \frac{x^3}{x^2(x + 1)}$$

Add.

$$= \frac{2x^3 + 5x^2 + 6x + 2}{x^2(x + 1)}$$

Since none of the factors of the denominator are factors of the numerator, the expression cannot be further simplified.

(B) $\dfrac{2x^2}{x^2-5x} - \dfrac{x^2+3x-4}{x^2}$

Factor the denominators. $\dfrac{2x^2}{\boxed{x(x-5)}} - \dfrac{x^2+3x-4}{x^2}$

Identify where the expression is not defined. The first expression is undefined when $x = 0$ and when $x = 5$. The second expression is undefined when $x = 0$.

Find a common denominator. The LCM for $x(x-5)$ and x^2 is $x^2(x-5)$.

Write the expressions with a common denominator by multiplying both by the appropriate form of 1. $\boxed{\dfrac{x}{x}} \cdot \dfrac{2x^2}{x(x-5)} - \dfrac{x^2+3x-4}{x^2} \cdot \dfrac{x-5}{x-5}$

Simplify each numerator. $= \dfrac{2x^3}{x^2(x-5)} - \dfrac{x^3-2x^2-19x+20}{x^2(x-5)}$

Subtract. $= \dfrac{\boxed{x^3} + 2x^2 + 19x - 20}{x^2(x-5)}$

Since none of the factors of the denominator are factors of the numerator, the expression cannot be further simplified.

Your Turn

Add each pair of expressions, simplifying the result and noting the combined excluded values. Then subtract the second expression from the first, again simplifying the result and noting the combined excluded values.

7. $-x^2$ and $\dfrac{1}{(1-x^2)}$

8. $\dfrac{x^2}{(4-x^2)}$ and $\dfrac{1}{(2-x)}$

Explain 4 Adding and Subtracting with Rational Models

Rational expressions can model real-world phenomena, and can be used to calculate measurements of those phenomena.

Example 4 Find the sum or difference of the models to solve the problem.

(A) Two groups have agreed that each will contribute \$2000 for an upcoming trip. Group A has 6 more people than group B. Let x represent the number of people in group A. Write and simplify an expression in terms of x that represents the difference between the number of dollars each person in group A must contribute and the number each person in group B must contribute.

$$\frac{2000}{x} - \frac{2000}{x-6} = \frac{2000(x-6)}{x(x-6)} - \frac{2000x}{(x-6)x}$$

$$= \frac{2000x - 12{,}000 - 2000x}{x(x-6)}$$

$$= -\frac{12{,}000}{x(x-6)}$$

Ⓑ A freight train averages 30 miles per hour traveling to its destination with full cars and 40 miles per hour on the return trip with empty cars. Find the total time in terms of d. Use the formula $t = \frac{d}{r}$.

Let d represent the one-way distance.

$$\text{Total time: } \frac{d}{30} + \frac{d}{40} = \frac{d \cdot \boxed{40}}{30 \cdot \boxed{40}} + \frac{d \cdot \boxed{30}}{40 \cdot \boxed{30}}$$

$$= \frac{d \cdot \boxed{40} + d \cdot \boxed{30}}{\boxed{1200}}$$

$$= \frac{\boxed{7}}{\boxed{120}}d$$

Your Turn

9. A hiker averages 1.4 miles per hour when walking downhill on a mountain trail and 0.8 miles per hour on the return trip when walking uphill. Find the total time in terms of d. Use the formula $t = \frac{d}{r}$.

10. Yvette ran at an average speed of 6.20 feet per second during the first two laps of a race and an average speed of 7.75 feet per second during the second two laps of a race. Find her total time in terms of d, the distance around the racecourse.

Elaborate

11. Why do rational expressions have excluded values?

12. How can you tell if your answer is written in simplest form?

13. **Essential Question Check-In** Why must the excluded values of each expression in a sum or difference of rational expressions also be excluded values for the simplified expression?

Evaluate: Homework and Practice

Personal Math Trainer

- Online Homework
- Hints and Help
- Extra Practice

Given a rational expression, identify the excluded values by finding the zeroes of the denominator.

1. $\dfrac{x-1}{x^2+3x-4}$

2. $\dfrac{4}{x(x+17)}$

Write the given expression as an equivalent rational expression that has the given denominator.

3. Expression: $\dfrac{x-7}{x+8}$
Denominator: x^3+8x^2

4. Expression: $\dfrac{3x^3}{3x-6}$
Denominator: $(2-x)(x^2+9)$

Simplify the given expression.

5. $\dfrac{(-4-4x)}{(x^2-x-2)}$

6. $\dfrac{-x-8}{x^2+9x+8}$

7. $\dfrac{6x^2+5x+1}{3x^2+4x+1}$

8. $\dfrac{x^4-1}{x^2+1}$

Find the LCD for each set of rational expressions.

9. $\dfrac{x}{2x+16}$ and $\dfrac{-4x}{3x-27}$

10. $\dfrac{x^2-4}{5x-30}$ and $\dfrac{5x+13}{7x-42}$

11. $\dfrac{4x+12}{x^2+5x+6}$ and $\dfrac{5x+15}{10x+20}$

12. $\dfrac{-11}{x^2-3x-28}$ and $\dfrac{2}{x^2-2x-24}$

13. $\dfrac{12}{3x^2-21x-54}$ and $\dfrac{-1}{21x^2-84}$

14. $\dfrac{3x}{5x^2-40x+60}$ and $\dfrac{17}{-7x^2+56x+84}$

Add or subtract the given expressions, simplifying each result and noting the combined excluded values.

15. $\dfrac{1}{1+x}+\dfrac{1-x}{x}$

16. $\dfrac{x+4}{x^2-4}+\dfrac{-2x-2}{x^2-4}$

17. $\dfrac{1}{2+x}-\dfrac{2-x}{x}$

18. $\dfrac{4x^4+4}{x^2+1}-\dfrac{8}{x^2+1}$

19. $\dfrac{x^4-2}{x^2-2}+\dfrac{2}{-x^2+2}$

20. $\dfrac{1}{x^2+3x-4}-\dfrac{1}{x^2-3x+2}$

21. $\dfrac{3}{x^2-4}-\dfrac{x+5}{x+2}$

22. $\dfrac{-3}{9x^2-4}+\dfrac{1}{3x^2+2x}$

23. $\dfrac{x-2}{x+2}+\dfrac{1}{x^2-4}-\dfrac{x+2}{2-x}$

24. $\dfrac{x-3}{x+3}-\dfrac{1}{x-3}+\dfrac{x+2}{3-x}$

25. A company has two factories, factory A and factory B. The cost per item to produce q items in factory A is $\frac{200+13q}{q}$. The cost per item to produce q items in factory B is $\frac{300+25q}{2q}$. Find an expression for the sum of these costs per item. Then divide this expression by 2 to find an expression for the average cost per item to produce q items in each factory.

26. An auto race consists of 8 laps. A driver completes the first 3 laps at an average speed of 185 miles per hour and the remaining laps at an average speed of 200 miles per hour. Let d represent the length of one lap. Find the time in terms of d that it takes the driver to complete the race.

27. The junior and senior classes of a high school are cleaning up a beach. Each class has pledged to clean 1600 meters of shoreline. The junior class has 12 more students than the senior class. Let s represent the number of students in the senior class. Write and simplify an expression in terms of s that represents the difference between the number of meters of shoreline each senior must clean and the number of meters each junior must clean.

28. **Architecture** The Renaissance architect Andrea Palladio believed that the height of a room with vaulted ceilings should be the harmonic mean of the length and width. The harmonic mean of two positive numbers a and b is equal to $\frac{2}{\frac{1}{a}+\frac{1}{b}}$. Simplify this expression. What are the excluded values? What do they mean in this problem?

29. Match each expression with the correct excluded value(s).

A. $\dfrac{3x+5}{x+2}$ — a. ___?___ no excluded values

B. $\dfrac{1+x}{x^2-1}$ — b. ___?___ $x \neq 0, -2$

C. $\dfrac{3x^4-12}{x^2+4}$ — c. ___?___ $x \neq 1, -1$

D. $\dfrac{3x+6}{x^2(x+2)}$ — d. ___?___ $x \neq -2$

H.O.T. Focus on Higher Order Thinking

30. **Explain the Error** George was asked to write the expression $2x - 3$ three times, once each with excluded values at $x = 1$, $x = 2$, and $x = -3$. He wrote the following expressions:

a. $\dfrac{2x-3}{x-1}$

b. $\dfrac{2x-3}{x-2}$

c. $\dfrac{2x-3}{x+3}$

What error did George make? Write the correct expressions, then write an expression that has all three excluded values.

31. **Communicate Mathematical Ideas** Write a rational expression with excluded values at $x = 0$ and $x = 17$.

32. Critical Thinking Sketch the graph of the rational equation $y = \frac{x^2 + 3x + 2}{x + 1}$. Think about how to show graphically that a graph exists over a domain except at one point.

Lesson Performance Task

A kayaker spends an afternoon paddling on a river. She travels 3 miles upstream and 3 miles downstream in a total of 4 hours. In still water, the kayaker can travel at an average speed of 2 miles per hour. Based on this information, can you estimate the average speed of the river's current? Is your answer reasonable?

Next, assume the average speed of the kayaker is an unknown, k, and not necessarily 2 miles per hour. What is the range of possible average kayaker speeds under the rest of the constraints?

9.2 Multiplying and Dividing Rational Expressions

Essential Question: How can you multiply and divide rational expressions?

Resource Locker

Explore Relating Multiplication Concepts

Use the facts you know about multiplying rational numbers to determine how to multiply rational expressions.

(A) How do you multiply $\frac{4}{5} \cdot \frac{5}{6}$?

Multiply 4 by ? to find the ? of the product, and multiply 5 by ? to find the ? .

(B) $\frac{4}{5} \cdot \frac{5}{6} = \frac{?}{?}$

(C) To simplify, factor the numerator and denominator.

$20 =$?

$30 =$?

(D) Cancel common factors in the numerator and denominator to simplify the product.

$\frac{4}{5} \cdot \frac{5}{6} = \frac{20}{30} = \frac{2 \cdot 2 \cdot 5}{2 \cdot 3 \cdot 5} = \frac{?}{?}$

(E) Based on the steps used for multiplying rational numbers, how can you multiply the rational expression $\frac{x+1}{x-1} \cdot \frac{3}{2(x+1)}$? ?

Reflect

1. **Discussion** Multiplying rational expressions is similar to multiplying rational numbers. Likewise, dividing rational expressions is similar to dividing rational numbers. How could you use the steps for dividing rational numbers to divide rational expressions?

Explain 1 Multiplying Rational Expressions

To multiply rational expressions, multiply the numerators to find the numerator of the product, and multiply the denominators to find the denominator. Then, simplify the product by cancelling common factors.

Note the excluded values of the product, which are any values of the variable for which the expression is undefined.

Example 1 **Find the products and any excluded values.**

(A) $\dfrac{3x^2}{x^2-2x-8} \cdot \dfrac{2x^2-6x-20}{x^2-3x-10}$

$\dfrac{3x^2}{x^2-2x-8} \cdot \dfrac{2x^2-6x-20}{x^2-3x-10} = \dfrac{3x^2}{(x+2)(x-4)} \cdot \dfrac{2(x+2)(x-5)}{(x+2)(x-5)}$ Factor the numerators and denominators.

$= \dfrac{6x^2(x+2)(x-5)}{(x+2)(x-4)(x+2)(x-5)}$ Multiply the numerators and multiply the denominators.

$= \dfrac{6x^2\cancel{(x+2)}\cancel{(x-5)}}{\cancel{(x+2)}(x-4)(x+2)\cancel{(x-5)}}$ Cancel the common factors in the numerator and denominator.

$= \dfrac{6x^2}{(x+2)(x-4)}$

Determine what values of x make each expression undefined.

$\dfrac{3x^2}{x^2-2x-8}$: The denominator is 0 when $x = -2$ and $x = 4$.

$\dfrac{2x^2-6x-20}{x^2-3x-10}$: The denominator is 0 when $x = -2$ and $x = 5$.

Excluded values: $x = -2$, $x = 4$, and $x = 5$

(B) $\dfrac{x^2-8x}{14(x^2+8x+15)} \cdot \dfrac{7x+35}{x+8}$

$\dfrac{x^2-8x}{14(x^2+8x+15)} \cdot \dfrac{7x+35}{x+8} = \dfrac{\boxed{x}\,(x-8)}{14\left(\boxed{x+3}\right)(x+5)} \cdot \dfrac{7\left(\boxed{x+5}\right)}{x+8}$ Factor the numerators and denominators.

$= \dfrac{7x(x-8)\left(\boxed{x+5}\right)}{14\left(\boxed{x+3}\right)(x+5)(x+8)}$ Multiply the numerators and multiply the denominators.

$= \dfrac{\boxed{x(x-8)}}{\boxed{2(x+3)(x+8)}}$ Cancel the common factors in the numerator and denominator.

Determine what values of x make each expression undefined.

$\dfrac{x^2-8x}{14(x^2+8x+15)}$: The denominator is 0 when $\boxed{x = -3 \text{ and } x = -5}$.

$\dfrac{7x+35}{x+8}$: The denominator is 0 when $\boxed{x = -8}$.

Excluded values: $\boxed{x = -3,\ x = -5, \text{ and } x = -8}$

Your Turn

Find the products and any excluded values.

2. $\dfrac{x^2 - 9}{x^2 - 5x - 24} \cdot \dfrac{x - 8}{2x^2 - 18x}$

3. $\dfrac{x}{x - 9} \cdot \dfrac{3x - 27}{x + 1}$

Explain 2 Dividing Rational Expressions

To divide rational expressions, change the division problem to a multiplication problem by multiplying by the reciprocal. Then, follow the steps for multiplying rational expressions.

Example 2 **Find the quotients and any excluded values.**

(A) $\dfrac{(x+7)^2}{x^2} \div \dfrac{x^2 + 9x + 14}{x^2 + x - 2}$

$\dfrac{(x+7)^2}{x^2} \div \dfrac{x^2 + 9x + 14}{x^2 + x - 2} = \dfrac{(x+7)^2}{x^2} \cdot \dfrac{x^2 + x - 2}{x^2 + 9x + 14}$ Multiply by the reciprocal.

$= \dfrac{(x+7)(x+7)}{x^2} \cdot \dfrac{(x+2)(x-1)}{(x+7)(x+2)}$ Factor the numerators and denominators.

$= \dfrac{(x+7)(x+7)(x+2)(x-1)}{x^2(x+7)(x+2)}$ Multiply the numerators and multiply the denominators.

$= \dfrac{\cancel{(x+7)}(x+7)\cancel{(x+2)}(x-1)}{x^2\cancel{(x+7)}\cancel{(x+2)}}$ Cancel the common factors in the numerator and denominator.

$= \dfrac{(x+7)(x-1)}{x^2}$

Determine what values of x make each expression undefined.

$\dfrac{(x+7)^2}{x}$: The denominator is 0 when $x = 0$.

$\dfrac{x^2 + 9x + 14}{x^2 + x - 2}$: The denominator is 0 when $x = -2$ and $x = 1$.

$\dfrac{x^2 + x - 2}{x^2 + 9x + 14}$: The denominator is 0 when $x = -7$ and $x = -2$.

Excluded values: $x = 0$, $x = -7$, $x = 1$, and $x = -2$

(B) $\dfrac{6x}{3x - 30} \div \dfrac{9x^2 - 27x - 36}{x^2 - 10x}$

$\dfrac{6x}{3x - 30} \div \dfrac{9x^2 - 27x - 36}{x^2 - 10x} = \dfrac{6x}{3x - 30} \cdot \dfrac{\boxed{x^2 - 10x}}{\boxed{9x^2 - 27x - 36}}$ Multiply by the reciprocal.

$= \dfrac{6x}{3\left(\boxed{x - 10}\right)} \cdot \dfrac{x\left(\boxed{x - 10}\right)}{9(x+1)\left(\boxed{x - 4}\right)}$ Factor the numerators and denominators.

$$= \frac{6x^2\left(\boxed{x-10}\right)}{27\left(\boxed{x-10}\right)(x+1)\left(\boxed{x-4}\right)}$$

Multiply the numerators and multiply the denominators.

$$= \frac{\boxed{2x^2}}{\boxed{9(x+1)(x-4)}}$$

Cancel the common factors in the numerator and denominator.

Determine what values of x make each expression undefined.

$\frac{6x}{3x-30}$: The denominator is 0 when $\boxed{x = 10}$.

$\frac{9x^2-27x-36}{x^2-10x}$: The denominator is 0 when $\boxed{x = 10 \text{ and } x = 0}$.

$\frac{x^2-10x}{9x^2-27x-36}$: The denominator is 0 when $\boxed{x = -1 \text{ and } x = 4}$.

Excluded values: $\boxed{x = 0, x = 10, x = -1, \text{ and } x = 4}$

Your Turn

Find the quotients and any excluded values.

4. $\frac{x+11}{4x} \div \frac{2x+6}{x^2+2x-3}$

5. $\frac{20}{x^2-7x} \div \frac{5x^2-40x}{x^2-15x+56}$

Explain 3 Activity: Investigating Closure

A set of numbers is said to be closed, or to have **closure**, under a given operation if the result of the operation on any two numbers in the set is also in the set.

(A) Recall whether the set of whole numbers, the set of integers, and the set of rational numbers are closed under each of the four basic operations.

	Addition	Subtraction	Multiplication	Division
Whole Numbers	?	?	?	?
Integers	?	?	?	?
Rational Numbers	?	?	?	?

(B) Look at the set of rational expressions. Use the rational expressions $\frac{p(x)}{q(x)}$ and $\frac{r(x)}{s(x)}$ where $p(x)$, $q(x)$, $r(x)$ and $s(x)$ are nonzero. Add the rational expressions.

$\frac{p(x)}{q(x)} + \frac{r(x)}{s(x)} =$?

(C) Is the set of rational expressions closed under addition? Explain. ?

Ⓓ Subtract the rational expressions.

$\frac{p(x)}{q(x)} - \frac{r(x)}{s(x)} =$?

Ⓔ Is the set of rational expressions closed under subtraction? Explain. ?

Ⓕ Multiply the rational expressions.

$\frac{p(x)}{q(x)} \cdot \frac{r(x)}{s(x)} =$?

Ⓖ Is the set of rational expressions closed under multiplication? Explain. ?

Ⓗ Divide the rational expressions.

$\frac{p(x)}{q(x)} \div \frac{r(x)}{s(x)} =$?

Ⓘ Is the set of rational expressions closed under division? Explain. ?

Reflect

6. Are rational expressions most like whole numbers, integers, or rational numbers? Explain.

Explain 4 Multiplying and Dividing with Rational Models

Models involving rational expressions can be solved using the same steps to multiply or divide rational expressions.

Example 3 **Solve the problems using rational expressions.**

Ⓐ Leonard drives 40 miles to work every day. One-fifth of his drive is on city roads, where he averages 30 miles per hour. The other part of his drive is on a highway, where he averages 55 miles per hour. The expression $\frac{d_c r_h + d_h r_c}{r_c r_h}$ represents the total time spent driving, in hours. In the expression, d_c represents the distance traveled on city roads, d_h represents the distance traveled on the highway, r_c is the average speed on city roads, and r_h is the average speed on the highway. Use the expression to find the average speed of Leonard's drive.

The total distance traveled is 40 miles. Find an expression for the average speed, r, of Leonard's drive.

$r =$ Total distance traveled $\div$ Total time

$= 40 \div \frac{d_c r_h + d_h r_c}{r_c r_h}$

$= 40 \cdot \frac{r_c r_h}{d_c r_h + d_h r_c}$

$= \frac{40 r_c r_h}{d_c r_h + d_h r_c}$

Find the values of d_c and d_h.

$d_c = \frac{1}{5}(40) = 8$ miles

$d_h = 40 - 8 = 32$ miles

Solve for r by substituting in the given values from the problem.

$$r = \frac{d r_c r_h}{d_c r_h + d_h r_c}$$

$$= \frac{40 \cdot 55 \cdot 30}{8 \cdot 55 + 32 \cdot 30}$$

$$\approx 47 \text{ miles per hour}$$

The average speed of Leonard's drive is about 47 miles per hour.

(B) The fuel efficiency of Tanika's car at highway speeds is 35 miles per gallon. The expression $\frac{48E - 216}{E(E-6)}$ represents the total gas consumed, in gallons, when Tanika drives 36 miles on a highway and 12 miles in a town to get to her relative's house. In the expression, E represents the fuel efficiency, in miles per gallon, of Tanika's car at highway speeds. Use the expression to find the average rate of gas consumed on her trip.

The total distance traveled is 48 miles. Find an expression for the average rate of gas consumed, g, on Tanika's trip.

$g =$ Total gas consumed $\div$ Total distance traveled

$$= \frac{48E - 216}{E(E-6)} \div 48$$

$$= \frac{48E - 216}{48\,E(E-6)}$$

The value of E is 35.

Solve for g by substituting in the value of E.

$$g = \frac{48(35) - 216}{48(35)(35 - 6)}$$

$$= \frac{1464}{48{,}720}$$

$$\approx 0.03$$

The average rate of gas consumed on Tanika's trip is about 0.03 gallon per mile.

Your Turn

7. The distance traveled by a car undergoing constant acceleration, a, for a time, t, is given by $d = v_0 t + \frac{1}{2}at^2$, where v_0 is the initial velocity of the car. Two cars are side by side with the same initial velocity. One car accelerates and the other car does not. Write an expression for the ratio of the distance traveled by the accelerating car to the distance traveled by the nonaccelerating car as a function of time.

Elaborate

8. Explain how finding excluded values when dividing one rational expression by another is different from multiplying two rational expressions.

9. **Essential Question Check-In** How is dividing rational expressions related to multiplying rational expressions?

Evaluate: Homework and Practice

Personal Math Trainer
- Online Homework
- Hints and Help
- Extra Practice

1. Explain how to multiply the rational expressions.

$$\frac{x-3}{2} \cdot \frac{x^2-3x+4}{x^2-2x}$$

Find the products and any excluded values.

2. $\frac{x}{3x-6} \cdot \frac{x-2}{x+9}$

3. $\frac{5x^2+25x}{2} \cdot \frac{4x}{x+5}$

4. $\frac{x^2-2x-15}{10x+30} \cdot \frac{3}{x^2-3x-10}$

5. $\frac{x^2-1}{x^2+5x+4} \cdot \frac{x^2}{x^2-x}$

6. $\frac{x^2+14x+33}{4x} \cdot \frac{x^2-3x}{x+3} \cdot \frac{8x-56}{x^2+4x-77}$

7. $\frac{9x^2}{x-6} \cdot \frac{x^2-36}{3x-6} \cdot \frac{3}{4x^2+24x}$

Find the quotients and any excluded values.

8. $\frac{5x^2+10x}{x^2+2x+1} \div \frac{20x+40}{x^2-1}$

9. $\frac{x^2-9x+18}{x^2+9x+18} \div \frac{x^2-36}{x^2-9}$

10. $\frac{-x^2+x+20}{5x^2-25x} \div \frac{x+4}{2x-14}$

11. $\frac{x+3}{x^2+8x+15} \div \frac{x^2-25}{x-5}$

12. $\frac{x^2-10x+9}{3x} \div \frac{x^2-7x-18}{x^2+2x}$

13. $\frac{8x+32}{x^2+8x+16} \div \frac{x^2-6x}{x^2-2x-24}$

Let $p(x) = \frac{1}{x+1}$ and $q(x) = \frac{1}{x-1}$. Perform the operation, and show that it results in another rational expression.

14. $p(x) + q(x)$

15. $p(x) - q(x)$

16. $p(x) \cdot q(x)$

17. $p(x) \div q(x)$

18. The distance a race car travels is given by the equation $d = v_0t + \frac{1}{2}at^2$, where v_0 is the initial speed of the race car, a is the acceleration, and t is the time travelled. Near the beginning of a race, the driver accelerates for 9 seconds at a rate of 4 m/s². The driver's initial speed was 75 m/s. Find the driver's average speed during the acceleration.

19. Julianna is designing a circular track that will consist of three concentric rings. The radius of the middle ring is 6 meters greater than that of the inner ring and 6 meters less than that of the outer ring. Find an expression for the ratio of the length of the outer ring to the length of the middle ring and another for the ratio of the length of the outer ring to length of the inner ring. If the radius of the inner ring is set at 90 meters, how many times longer is the outer ring than the middle ring and the inner ring?

20. Geometry Find a rational expression for the ratio of the surface area of a cylinder to the volume of a cylinder. Then find the ratio when the radius is 3 inches and the height is 10 inches.

H.O.T. Focus on Higher Order Thinking

21. Explain the Error Maria finds an expression equivalent to $\frac{x^2 - 4x - 45}{3x - 15} \div \frac{6x^2 - 150}{x^2 - 5x}$.

Her work is shown. Find and correct Maria's mistake.

$$\frac{x^2 - 4x - 45}{3x - 15} \div \frac{6x^2 - 150}{x^2 - 5x} = \frac{(x-9)(x+5)}{3(x-5)} \div \frac{6(x+5)(x-5)}{x(x-5)}$$

$$= \frac{6(x-9)(x+5)(x+5)(x-5)}{3x(x-5)(x-5)}$$

$$= \frac{2(x-9)(x+5)^2}{x(x-5)}$$

22. Critical Thinking Multiply the expressions. What do you notice about the resulting expression?

$$\left(\frac{3}{x-4} + \frac{x^3 - 4x}{8x^2 - 32}\right)\left(\frac{3x+18}{x^2 + 2x - 24} - \frac{x}{8}\right)$$

23. Multi-Step Jordan is making a garden with an area of $x^2 + 13x + 30$ square feet and a length of $x + 3$ feet.

a. Find an expression for the width of Jordan's garden.

b. If Karl makes a garden with an area of $3x^2 + 48x + 180$ square feet and a length of $x + 6$, how many times larger is the width of Jon's garden than Jordan's?

c. If x is equal to 4, what are the dimensions of both Jordan's and Karl's gardens?

Lesson Performance Task

Who has the advantage, taller or shorter runners? Almost all of the energy generated by a long-distance runner is released in the form of heat. For a runner with height H and speed V, the rate h_g of heat generated and the rate h_r of heat released can be modeled by $h_g = k_1H^3V^2$ and $h_r = k_2H^2$, k_1 and k_2 being constants. So, how does a runner's height affect the amount of heat she releases as she increases her speed?

9.3 Solving Rational Equations

Essential Question: What methods are there for solving rational equations?

Resource Locker

Explore Solving Rational Equations Graphically

A rational equation is an equation that contains one or more rational expressions. The time t in hours it takes to travel d miles can be determined by using the equation $t = \frac{d}{r}$, where r is the average rate of speed. This equation is an example of a rational equation. One method to solving rational equations is by graphing.

Solve the rational equation $\frac{x}{x-3} = 2$ by graphing.

(A) First, identify any excluded values. A number is an excluded value of a rational expression if substituting the number into the expression results in a division by 0, which is undefined. Solve $x - 3 = 0$ for x.

$x - 3 = 0$

$x =$?

(B) So, 3 is an excluded value of the rational equation. Rewrite the equation with 0 on one side.

$\frac{x}{x-3} = 2$

? $= 0$

(C) Graph the left side of the equation as a function. Substitute y for 0 and complete the table below.

x	y	(x, y)
0	?	?
1	?	?
2	?	?
4	?	?
5	?	?
9	?	?

(D) Use the table to graph the function.

(E) Identify any x-intercepts of the graph.

There is an x-intercept at ? .

(F) Is the value of x an excluded value? What is the solution of $\frac{x}{x-3} = 2$? ?

Reflect

1. **Discussion** Why does rewriting a rational equation with 0 on one side help with solving the equation?

Explain 1 Solving Rational Equations Algebraically

Rational equations can be solved algebraically by multiplying through by the LCD and solving the resulting polynomial equation. However, this eliminates the information about the excluded values of the original equation. Sometimes an excluded value of the original equation is a solution of the polynomial equation, and in this case the excluded value will be an **extraneous solution** of the polynomial equation. Extraneous solutions are not solutions of an equation.

Example 1 **Solve each rational equation algebraically.**

(A) $\frac{3x + 7}{x - 5} = \frac{5x + 17}{2x - 10}$

Identify any excluded values.

$x - 5 = 0$ $\quad$ $2x - 10 = 0$

$x = 5$ $\quad$ $x = 5$

The excluded value is 5.

Identify the LCD by finding all factors of the denominators.

$2x - 10 = 2(x - 5)$

The different factors are 2 and $x - 5$.

The LCD is $2(x - 5)$.

Multiply each term by the LCD. $\quad$ $\frac{3x + 7}{x - 5} \cdot 2(x - 5) = \frac{5x + 17}{2(x - 5)} \cdot 2(x - 5)$

Divide out common factors. $\quad$ $\frac{3x + 7}{\cancel{x - 5}} \cdot 2\cancel{(x - 5)} = \frac{5x + 17}{\cancel{2}\cancel{(x - 5)}} \cdot \cancel{2}\cancel{(x - 5)}$

Simplify. $\quad$ $(3x + 7)2 = 5x + 17$

Use the Distributive Property. $\quad$ $6x + 14 = 5x + 17$

Solve for x. $\quad$ $x + 14 = 17$

$x = 3$

The solution $x = 3$ is not an excluded value. So, $x = 3$ is the solution of the equation.

(B) $\frac{2x - 9}{x - 7} + \frac{x}{2} = \frac{5}{x - 7}$

Identify any excluded values.

$x - 7 = 0$

$x =$ 7

The excluded value is 7.

Identify the LCD.

The different factors are 2 and $x - 7$.

The LCD is $2(x-7)$.

Multiply each term by the LCD. $\frac{2x-9}{x-7} \cdot \boxed{2(x-7)} + \frac{x}{2} \cdot \boxed{2(x-7)} = \frac{5}{x-7} \cdot \boxed{2(x-7)}$

Divide out common factors. $\frac{2x-9}{\cancel{x-7}} \cdot \boxed{2\cancel{(x-7)}} + \frac{x}{\cancel{2}} \cdot \boxed{\cancel{2}(x-7)} = \frac{5}{\cancel{x-7}} \cdot \boxed{2\cancel{(x-7)}}$

Simplify. $\boxed{2}(2x-9) + x\left(\boxed{x-7}\right) = 5\left(\boxed{2}\right)$

Use the Distributive Property. $\boxed{4x-18} + x^2 - 7x = \boxed{10}$

Write in standard form. $\boxed{x^2 - 3x - 28} = 0$

Factor. $\left(\boxed{x-7}\right)\left(\boxed{x+4}\right) = 0$

Use the Zero Product Property. $x - 7 = 0$ or $\boxed{x+4} = 0$

Solve for x. $x = 7$ or $x = \boxed{-4}$

The solution $x = \boxed{7}$ is extraneous because it is an excluded value. The only solution is $x = \boxed{-4}$.

Your Turn

Solve each rational equation algebraically.

2. $\frac{8}{x+3} = \frac{x+1}{x+6}$

Explain 2 Solving a Real-world Problem with a Rational Equation

Rational equations are used to model real-world situations. These equations can be solved algebraically.

Example 2 **Use a rational equation to solve the problem.**

(A) Kelsey is kayaking on a river. She travels 5 miles upstream and 5 miles downstream in a total of 6 hours. In still water, Kelsey can travel at an average speed of 3 miles per hour. What is the average speed of the river's current?

Analyze Information

Identify the important information:

- The answer will be the average speed of the current.
- Kelsey spends 6 hours kayaking.
- She travels 5 miles upstream and 5 miles downstream.
- Her average speed in still water is 3 miles per hour.

Formulate a Plan

Let c represent the speed of the current in miles per hour. When Kelsey is going upstream, her speed is equal to her speed in still water minus c. When Kelsey is going downstream, her speed is equal to her speed in still water plus c.
The variable c is restricted to positive real numbers.
Complete the table.

	Distance (mi)	Average speed (mi/h)	Time (h)
Upstream	5	$3 - c$	$\frac{5}{3 - c}$
Downstream	5	$3 + c$	$\frac{5}{3 + c}$

Use the results from the table to write an equation.
total time = time upstream + time downstream

$$6 = \boxed{\frac{5}{3-c}} + \boxed{\frac{5}{3+c}}$$

Solve

$3 - c = 0 \qquad 3 + c = 0$

$\boxed{3} = c \qquad c = \boxed{-3}$

Excluded values: 3 and -3

LCD: $(3 - c)(3 + c)$

Multiply by the LCD. $\quad 6 \cdot \boxed{(3-c)(3+c)} = \frac{5}{3-c} \cdot \boxed{(3-c)(3+c)} + \frac{5}{3+c} \cdot \boxed{(3-c)(3+c)}$

Divide out common factors. $\quad 6 \cdot \boxed{(3-c)(3+c)} = \frac{5}{\cancel{3-c}} \cdot \boxed{\cancel{(3-c)}(3+c)} + \frac{5}{\cancel{3+c}} \cdot \boxed{(3-c)\cancel{(3+c)}}$

Simplify. $\quad 6 \cdot \boxed{(3-c)(3+c)} = 5 \cdot \boxed{3+c} + 5 \cdot \boxed{3-c}$

Use the Distributive Property. $\quad \boxed{54 - 6c^2} = 15 + 5c + \boxed{15 - 5c}$

Write in standard form. $\quad 0 = \boxed{6c^2 - 24}$

Factor. $\quad 0 = 6(c + 2)\left(\boxed{c - 2}\right)$

Use the Zero Product Property. $\quad c + 2 = 0$ or $\boxed{c - 2} = 0$

Solve for c. $\quad c = \boxed{-2}$ or $c = \boxed{2}$

There are no extraneous solutions. The solutions are $c = -2$ or $c = 2$.

Justify and Evaluate

The solution $c = \boxed{-2}$ is unreasonable because the speed of the current cannot be negative, but the solution $c = \boxed{2}$ is reasonable because the speed of the current can be positive. If the speed of the current is 2 miles per hour, it would take Kelsey 5 hour(s) to go upstream and 1 hour(s) to go downstream, which is a total of 6 hours.

Reflect

3. Why does the domain of the variable have to be restricted in real-world problems that can be modeled with a rational equation?

Your Turn

4. Kevin can clean a large aquarium tank in about 7 hours. When Kevin and Lara work together, they can clean the tank in 4 hours. Write and solve a rational equation to determine how long, to the nearest tenth of an hour, it would take Lara to clean the tank if she works by herself. Explain whether the answer is reasonable.

Elaborate

5. Why is it important to check solutions to rational equations?

6. Why can extraneous solutions to rational equations exist?

7. **Essential Question Check In** How can you solve a rational equation without graphing?

Evaluate: Homework and Practice

- Online Homework
- Hints and Help
- Extra Practice

Solve each rational equation by graphing using a table of values.

1. $\frac{x}{x+4} = -3$

x	y	(x, y)
−8	?	?
−6	?	?
−5	?	?
−3.5	?	?
−2	?	?
0	?	?

2. $\dfrac{x}{2x-10}=3$

x	y	(x, y)
0	?	?
3	?	?
4	?	?
5.5	?	?
7	?	?
10	?	?

Solve each rational equation algebraically.

3. $\dfrac{9}{4x}-\dfrac{5}{6}=-\dfrac{13}{12x}$

4. $\dfrac{3}{x+1}+\dfrac{2}{7}=2$

5. $\dfrac{56}{x^2-2x-15}-\dfrac{6}{x+3}=\dfrac{7}{x-5}$

6. $\dfrac{x^2-29}{x^2-10x+21}=\dfrac{6}{x-7}+\dfrac{5}{x-3}$

7. $\dfrac{5}{2x+6}-\dfrac{1}{6}=\dfrac{2}{x+4}$

8. $\dfrac{5}{x^2-3x+2}-\dfrac{1}{x-2}=\dfrac{x+6}{3x-3}$

For 9 and 10, write a rational equation for each real-world application. Do not solve.

9. A save percentage in lacrosse is found by dividing the number of saves by the number of shots faced. A lacrosse goalie saved 9 of 12 shots. How many additional consecutive saves *s* must the goalie make to raise his save percentage to 0.850?

10. Jake can mulch a garden in 30 minutes. Together, Jake and Ross can mulch the same garden in 16 minutes. How much time *t*, in minutes, will it take Ross to mulch the garden when working alone?

11. Geometry A new ice skating rink will be approximately rectangular in shape and will have an area of 18,000 square feet. Using an equation for the perimeter *P*, of the skating rink in terms of its width *W*, what are the dimensions of the skating rink if the perimeter is 580 feet?

12. Water flowing through both a small pipe and a large pipe can fill a water tank in 9 hours. Water flowing through the large pipe alone can fill the tank in 17 hours. Write an equation that can be used to find the amount of time t, in hours, it would take to fill the tank using only the small pipe.

13. A riverboat travels at an average of 14 km per hour in still water. The riverboat travels 110 km east up the Ohio River and 110 km west down the same river in a total of 17.5 hours. To the nearest tenth of a kilometer per hour, what was the speed of the current of the river?

14. A baseball player's batting average is equal to the number of hits divided by the number of at bats. A professional player had 139 hits in 515 at bats in 2012 and 167 hits in 584 at bats in 2013. Write and solve an equation to find how many additional consecutive hits h the batter would have needed to raise his batting average in 2012 to be at least equal to his average in 2013.

15. The time required to deliver and install a computer network at a customer's location is $t = 5 + \frac{2d}{r}$, where t is time in hours, d is the distance (in miles) from the warehouse to the customer's location, and r is the average speed of the delivery truck. If it takes 8.2 hours for an employee to deliver and install a network for a customer located 80 miles from the warehouse, what is the average speed of the delivery truck?

16. Art A glassblower can produce several sets of simple glasses in about 3 hours. When the glassblower works with an apprentice, the job takes about 2 hours. How long would it take the apprentice to make the same number of sets of glasses when working alone?

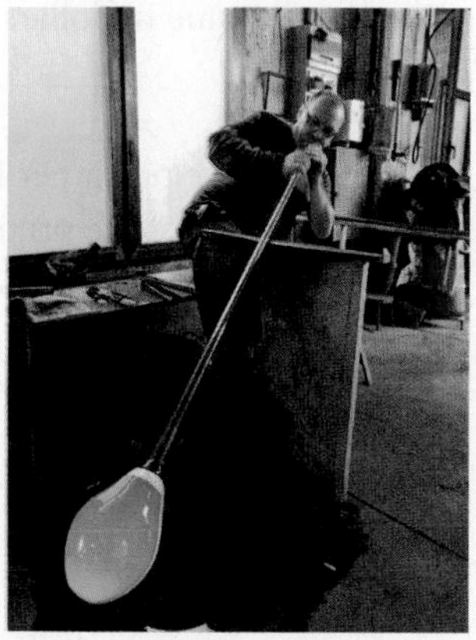

17. Which of the following equations have at least two excluded values? Select all that apply.

A. $\frac{3}{x} + \frac{1}{5x} = 1$

B. $\frac{x-4}{x-2} + \frac{3}{x} = \frac{5}{6}$

C. $\frac{x}{x-6} + 1 = \frac{5}{2x-12}$

D. $\frac{2x-3}{x^2-10x+25} + \frac{3}{7} = \frac{1}{x-5}$

E. $\frac{7}{x+2} + \frac{3x-4}{x^2+5x+6} = 9$

H.O.T. Focus on Higher Order Thinking

18. **Critical Thinking** An equation has the form $\frac{a}{x} + \frac{x}{b} = c$, where a, b, and c are constants and $b \neq 0$. How many solutions could this equation have? Explain.

19. **Multiple Representations** Write an equation whose graph is a straight line, but with an open circle at $x = 4$.

20. **Justify Reasoning** Explain why the excluded values do not change when multiplying by the LCD to add or subtract rational expressions.

21. **Critical Thinking** Describe how you would find the inverse of the rational function $f(x) = \frac{x-1}{x-2}$, $x \neq 2$. Then find the inverse.

Lesson Performance Task

Kasey creates comedy sketch videos and posts them on a popular video website and is selling an exclusive series of sketches on DVD. The total cost to make the series of sketches is $989. The materials cost $1.40 per DVD and the shipping costs $2.00 per DVD. Kasey plans to sell the DVDs for $12 each.

a. Let d be the number of DVDs Kasey sells. Create a profit-per-item model from the given information by writing a rule for $C(d)$, the total costs in dollars, $S(d)$, the total sales income in dollars, $P(d)$, the profit in dollars, and $P_{PI}(d)$, the profit per item sold in dollars.

b. What is the profit per DVD if Kasey sells 80 DVDs? Does this value make sense in the context of the problem?

c. Then use the function $P_{PI}(d)$ from part a to find how many DVDs Kasey would have to sell to break even. Identify all excluded values.

STUDY GUIDE REVIEW

Rational Expressions and Equations

MODULE 9

Essential Question: How can you use rational expressions and equations to solve real-world problems?

Key Vocabulary

closure *(cerradura)*
extraneous solution *(solución extraña)*
rational expression *(expresión racional)*
reciprocal *(recíproco)*

KEY EXAMPLE *(Lesson 9.1)*

Add $\frac{1}{3+x}$ and $\frac{3-x}{x}$, simplify the result, and note the excluded values.

$$\frac{1}{3+x}+\frac{3-x}{x}=\frac{1x}{(3+x)x}+\frac{(3-x)(3+x)}{x(3+x)}$$ Write with like denominators.

$$=\frac{x+(9-x^2)}{x(x+3)}$$ Add.

$$=\frac{-x^2+x+9}{x(x+3)},\ x\neq -3, 0$$ Simplify.

KEY EXAMPLE *(Lesson 9.2)*

Find the quotient $\frac{x+3}{x+2}\div\frac{x^2-9}{2x-4}$ and note any excluded values.

$$\frac{x+3}{x+2}\div\frac{x^2-9}{2x-4}=\frac{x+3}{x+2}\cdot\frac{2x-4}{x^2-9}$$ Multiply by the reciprocal.

$$=\frac{x+3}{x+2}\cdot\frac{2(x-2)}{(x+3)(x-3)}$$ Factor the numerators and denominators.

$$=\frac{2\cancel{(x+3)}(x-2)}{(x+2)\cancel{(x+3)}(x-3)}$$ Multiply and cancel the common factors.

$$=\frac{2(x-2)}{(x+2)(x-3)};\ x\neq \pm 2, \pm 3$$ Simplify.

KEY EXAMPLE *(Lesson 9.3)*

Solve the rational equation algebraically.

$$\frac{x}{x-3}+\frac{x}{2}=\frac{6x}{2x-6}$$

$$2\cancel{(x-3)}\frac{x}{\cancel{x-3}}+\cancel{2}(x-3)\frac{x}{\cancel{2}}=\cancel{2(x-3)}\frac{6x}{\cancel{2x-6}}$$ Multiply each term by the LCD and divide out common factors.

$$2x+x(x-3)=6x$$ Simplify.

$$x^2-7x=0$$ Write in standard form.

$$x(x-7)=0$$ Factor.

$$x=0 \text{ or } x=7$$ Solve for *x*.

EXERCISES

Add or subtract the given expressions, simplify the result, and note the excluded values. *(Lesson 9.1)*

1. $\frac{6x + 6}{x^2 - 9} + \frac{-3x + 3}{x^2 - 9}$

2. $\frac{4}{x^2 - 1} - \frac{x + 2}{x - 1}$

Multiply or divide the given expressions, simplify the result, and note the excluded values. *(Lesson 9.2)*

3. $\frac{x^2 - 4x - 5}{3x - 15} \cdot \frac{4}{x^2 - 2x - 3}$

4. $\frac{x + 2}{x - 4} \div \frac{x}{3x - 12}$

Solve each rational equation algebraically. *(Lesson 9.3)*

5. $x - \frac{10}{x} = 3$

6. $\frac{5}{x + 1} = \frac{2}{x + 4}$

MODULE PERFORMANCE TASK

Robots and Resistors

An engineer is designing part of a circuit that will control a robot. The circuit must have a certain total resistance to function properly. The engineer plans to use several resistors in *parallel*, which means each resistor is on its own branch of the circuit. The resistors available for this project are 20, 50, 80, and 200-ohm.

How can the engineer design a parallel circuit with a total resistance of 10 ohms using a maximum of 5 resistors, at least two of which must be different values? Find at least two possible circuit configurations that meet these criteria.

For another part of the circuit, the engineer wants to use resistors in parallel to create a total resistance of 6 ohms. Can she do it using the available resistor values? If so, how? If not, explain why not.

Begin by listing all of the information you will need to solve the problem. Then complete the task. Be sure to write down all your data and assumptions. Then use graphs, numbers, words, or algebra to explain how you reached your conclusion.

Ready to Go On?

9.1–9.3 Rational Expressions and Equations

Personal Math Trainer

- Online Homework
- Hints and Help
- Extra Practice

Perform the indicated operations, simplify the result, and note any excluded values. *(Lessons 9.1, 9.2)*

1. $\dfrac{4}{x+5} + \dfrac{2x}{x^2-25}$

2. $\dfrac{3x+2}{x-2} - \dfrac{x+5}{x-2}$

3. $\dfrac{x+3}{x+2} \cdot \dfrac{2x-4}{x^2-9}$

4. $\dfrac{x-3}{x-4} \div \dfrac{x-2}{x^2-16}$

Solve each rational equation. *(Lesson 9.3)*

5. $\dfrac{3}{x+2} + \dfrac{3}{2x+4} = \dfrac{x}{2x+4}$

6. $\dfrac{x}{x-8} = \dfrac{24-2x}{x-8}$

7. $\dfrac{8x}{x^2-4} - \dfrac{4}{x+2} = \dfrac{8}{x^2-4}$

8. $\dfrac{3x}{x+1} + \dfrac{6}{2x} = \dfrac{7}{x}$

ESSENTIAL QUESTION

9. How do you add or subtract rational expressions and identify any excluded values?

MODULE 9
MIXED REVIEW

Assessment Readiness

1. Tell whether each expression is equivalent to $x - 3$.

A. $\dfrac{(x-3)(x+5)}{x+3} + \dfrac{x+3}{x+5}$

B. $\dfrac{x+3}{x+5} + \dfrac{x-3}{x+5}$

C. $\dfrac{(x+3)(x+5)}{x-5} \div \dfrac{x+5}{x-5}$

2. Consider finding how many roots a quadratic equation has. Determine if each statement is True or False.

A. The quadratic equation $x^2 - 12 = 0$ has real roots.

B. The quadratic equation $x^2 + 25 = 0$ has imaginary roots.

C. The quadratic equation $-8x^2 + 20 = 0$ has one real root and one imaginary root.

3. A hiker averages 0.6 mile per hour walking up a mountain trail and 1.3 miles per hour walking down the trail. Find the total time in terms of *d*. Explain your answer.

4. A restaurant has two pastry ovens. When both ovens are used, it takes about 3 hours to bake the bread needed for one day. When only the large oven is used, it takes about 4 hours to bake the bread for one day. About how long would it take to bake the bread for one day if only the small oven were used? Explain how you got your answer.

UNIT 4 MIXED REVIEW

Assessment Readiness

Personal Math Trainer

- Online Homework
- Hints and Help
- Extra Practice

1. Consider each equation. Does the graph of the equation have an asymptote at $x = 5$? Write Yes or No for A–C.

A. $y = \dfrac{3x^3}{x-5}$

B. $y = \dfrac{x^2(x-4)}{x-4}$

C. $y = \dfrac{3x^2-6}{(x-2)(x-5)}$

2. Consider the equations $f(x) = \dfrac{1}{x}$ and $g(x) = 1 + \dfrac{1}{x+5}$. Determine if each statement is True or False.

A. $g(x)$ is translated 1 unit up and 5 units left from $f(x)$.

B. $g(x)$ is translated 1 unit up and 5 units right from $f(x)$.

C. $g(x)$ is reflected over the x-axis in comparison to $f(x)$.

3. Consider each equation. Does the equation have the solutions $x = -6, 4$? Write Yes or No for A–C.

A. $x + 2 = \dfrac{24}{x+6}$

B. $\dfrac{x+2}{x} = 24$

C. $x + 2 = \dfrac{24}{x}$

4. Consider each expression. Are both the values $x = 0$ and $x = 2$ excluded? Write Yes or No for A–C.

A. $\dfrac{1}{x+2} + \dfrac{4+x}{x}$

B. $\dfrac{1}{x-2} + \dfrac{4+x}{x}$

C. $\dfrac{1}{x^2-2} + \dfrac{4+x}{x^2+2}$

5. The time t it takes Sam to drive to his grandmother's house is inversely proportional to the speed v at which he drives. Write an equation for the one-way travel time. If it takes Sam 5 hours driving 50 miles per hour, how long would it take him if he drove at 65 miles per hour? Explain your answer.

6. A town has two trucks to collect garbage. When both trucks are in use, they take 6 hours to collect all the garbage. When only the small truck is in use, it takes 24 hours to collect the garbage. How long would it take to collect the garbage if only the large truck is in service? Explain your answer.

7. A farmer needs $3x^2 - 4x + 10$ seeds for each of $x^3 + 5x - 20$ fields. What expression would represent the seeds the farmer needs to plant all of the fields? Is $x = 1$ a reasonable value for this representation? Explain your answers.

Performance Tasks

★ 8. For a car moving with initial speed v_0 and acceleration a, the distance d that the car travels in time t is given by $d = v_0 t + \frac{1}{2}at^2$.

A. Write a rational expression in terms of t for the average speed of the car during a period of acceleration. Simplify the expression.

B. During a race, a driver accelerates for 3 s at a rate of 10 ft/s^2 in order to pass another car. The driver's initial speed was 264 ft/s. What was the driver's average speed during the acceleration?

★★ **9.** The average speed for the winner of the 2002 Indy 500 was 25 mi/h greater than the average speed for the 2001 winner. In addition, the 2002 winner completed the 500 mi race 32 min faster than the 2001 winner.

A. Let s represent the average speed of the 2001 winner in miles per hour. Write expressions in terms of s for the time in hours that it took the 2001 and 2002 winners to complete the race.

B. Write a rational equation that can be used to determine s. Solve your equation to find the average speed of the 2001 winner to the nearest mile per hour.

★★★ **10.** The Renaissance architect Andrea Palladio preferred that the length and width of rectangular rooms be limited to certain ratios. These ratios are listed in the table. Palladio also believed that the height of a room with vaulted ceilings should be the harmonic mean of the length and width.

Rooms with a Width of 30 ft

Length-to-Width Ratio	Length (ft)	Height (ft)
2:1	?	?
3:2	?	?
4:3	?	?
5:3	?	?
$\sqrt{2}$:1	?	?

A. The harmonic mean of two positive numbers a and b is equal to $\frac{2}{\frac{1}{a}+\frac{1}{b}}$. Simplify this expression.

B. Complete the table for a rectangular room with a width of 30 feet that meets Palladio's requirements for its length and height. If necessary, round to the nearest tenth.

C. A Palladian room has a length-to-width ratio of 4:3. If the length of this room is doubled, what effect should this change have on the room's width and height, according to Palladio's principles?

MATH IN CAREERS

Chemist A chemist mixes 5 mL of an acid with 15 mL of water. The concentration of acid in the acid-and-water mix is $\frac{5}{5+15} = \frac{5}{20} = 25\%$. If the chemist adds more acid to the mix, then the concentration C becomes a function of the additional amount a of acid added to the mix.

a. Write a rule for the function $C(a)$.

b. What is a reasonable domain for this function? Explain.

c. What concentration of acid does pure water have? What concentration of acid does pure acid have? So, what are the possible values of $C(a)$?

d. Graph the function. Be sure to label the axes with the quantities they represent and indicate the axis scales by showing numbers for some grid lines.

e. Analyze the function's rule to determine the vertical asymptote of the function's graph. Why is the asymptote irrelevant in this situation?

f. Analyze the function's rule to determine the horizontal asymptote of the function's graph. What is the relevance of the asymptote in this situation?

UNIT 5

Radical Functions, Expressions, and Equations

MATH IN CAREERS

Nutritionist Nutritionists provide services to individuals and institutions, such as schools and hospitals. Nutritionists must be able to calculate the amounts of different substances in a person's diet, including calories, fat, vitamins, and minerals. They must also calculate measures of fitness, such as body mass index. Nutritionists must use statistics when reviewing nutritional studies in scientific journals.

If you are interested in a career as a nutritionist, you should study these mathematical subjects:

- Algebra
- Statistics
- Business Math

Research other careers that require proficiency in understanding statistics in scientific articles. Check out the career activity at the end of the unit to find out how **Nutritionists** use math.

Reading Start-Up

Vocabulary

Review Words

✔ composition of functions (*composición de funciones*)
extraneous solution (*solución extraña*)
✔ inverse function (*función inversa*)
✔ many-to-one function (*función muchos a uno*)
✔ one-to-one function (*función uno a uno*)
radical expression (*expresión radical*)

Preview Words

cube root function (función de raíz cúbica)
index (índice)
square root function (función de raíz cuadrada)

Visualize Vocabulary

Use the ✓ words to complete the graphic. Put just one word in each section of the square.

The function that results from exchanging the input and output values of a function.	A function where each element of the range may correspond to more than one element of the domain.
A function where each element of the range corresponds to only one element of the domain.	A situation with two functions in which the output of one function is used as the input for the other.

Function Types

Understand Vocabulary

To become familiar with some of the vocabulary terms in the module, consider the following. You may refer to the module, the glossary, or a dictionary.

1. A function whose rule contains a variable under a square-root sign is a __?__.

2. A function whose rule contains a variable under a cube-root sign is a __?__.

3. In the radical expression $\sqrt[n]{x}$, n is the __?__.

Active Reading

Pyramid Fold Before beginning a module, create a pyramid fold to help you take notes from each lesson in the module. The three sides of the pyramid can summarize information about function families, their graphs, and their characteristics.

Radical Functions

MODULE 10

Essential Question: How can you use radical functions to solve real-world problems?

LESSON 10.1
Inverses of Simple Quadratic and Cubic Functions

LESSON 10.2
Graphing Square Root Functions

LESSON 10.3
Graphing Cube Root Functions

REAL WORLD VIDEO
A rocket must generate enough thrust to achieve escape velocity from Earth's gravitational field. Check out some of the calculations and preparations that go into a successful launch.

MODULE PERFORMANCE TASK PREVIEW
We Have Liftoff!

If you throw a ball straight up, it will eventually come back down. But if you could throw it with enough initial velocity, it would escape Earth's surface and go into orbit. If you could throw it even faster, it might even escape the solar system. What is the escape velocity for Earth, the minimum velocity for an object to leave Earth's surface and not return? What about the velocity necessary to escape other planets? Let's take off and find out!

Are YOU Ready?

Complete these exercises to review skills you will need for this module.

Personal Math Trainer

- Online Homework
- Hints and Help
- Extra Practice

Exponents

Example 1 Simplify .

$$x^2 \cdot x^3 - 2x^4 \cdot x = x^{2+3} - 2x^{4+1}$$
$$= x^5 - 2x^5$$
$$= -x^5$$

Simplify each expression.

1. $5x^3 \cdot 2x$

2. $-x^4 \cdot x^3$

3. $4x^2\left(2xy - x^2\right)$

Inverse Linear Functions

Example 2 Write the inverse function of $y = x + 9$.

$y - 9 = x + 9 - 9$ Subtract.

$y - 9 = x$ Simplify.

$x - 9 = y$

The inverse function of $y = x + 9$ is $y = x - 9$.

Example 3 Write the inverse function of $y = \frac{x}{-22}$.

$(-22)y = -\frac{x}{22}(-22)$ Multiply.

$-22y = x$ Simplify.

$-22x = y$

The inverse function of $y = \frac{x}{-22}$ is $y = -22x$.

Write the inverse of each function.

4. $y = x - 6$

5. $y = 7x$

6. $y = \frac{1}{2}x$

7. $y = x + 11$

8. $y = -18x$

9. $y = 21 + x$

10.1 Inverses of Simple Quadratic and Cubic Functions

Resource Locker

Essential Question: What functions are the inverses of quadratic functions and cubic functions, and how can you find them?

Explore Finding the Inverse of a Many-to-One Function

The function $f(x)$ is defined by the following ordered pairs: $(-2, 4)$, $(-1, 2)$, $(0, 0)$, $(1, 2)$, and $(2, 4)$.

(A) Find the inverse function of $f(x)$, $f^{-1}(x)$, by reversing the coordinates in the ordered pairs. ?

(B) Is the inverse also a function? Explain. ?

(C) If necessary, restrict the domain of $f(x)$ such that the inverse, $f^{-1}(x)$, is a function.

To restrict the domain of $f(x)$ so that its inverse is a function, you can restrict it to $\{x \mid x \geq$? $\}$.

(D) With the restricted domain of $f(x)$, what ordered pairs define the inverse function $f^{-1}(x)$? ?

Reflect

1. **Discussion** Look again at the ordered pairs that define $f(x)$. Without reversing the order of the coordinates, how could you have known that the inverse of $f(x)$ would not be a function?
2. How will restricting the domain of $f(x)$ affect the range of its inverse?

Explain 1 Finding and Graphing the Inverse of a Simple Quadratic Function

The function $f(x) = x^2$ is a many-to-one function, so its domain must be restricted in order to find its inverse function. If the domain is restricted to $x \geq 0$, then the inverse function is $f^{-1}(x) = \sqrt{x}$; if the domain is restricted to $x \leq 0$, then the inverse function is $f^{-1}(x) = -\sqrt{x}$.

The inverse of a quadratic function is a **square root function**, which is a function whose rule involves $\sqrt{x}$. **The parent square root function** is $g(x) = \sqrt{x}$. A square root function is defined only for values of x that make the expression under the radical sign nonnegative.

Example 1 **Restrict the domain of each quadratic function and find its inverse. Confirm the inverse relationship using composition. Graph the function and its inverse.**

(A) $f(x) = 0.5x^2$

Restrict the domain. $\{x | x \geq 0\}$

Find the inverse.

Replace $f(x)$ with y.	$y = 0.5x^2$
Multiply both sides by 2.	$2y = x^2$
Use the definition of positive square root.	$\sqrt{2y} = x$
Switch x and y to write the inverse.	$\sqrt{2x} = y$
Replace y with $f^{-1}(x)$.	$f^{-1}(x) = \sqrt{2x}$

Confirm the inverse relationship using composition.

$$f^{-1}(f(x)) = f^{-1}(0.5x^2) \qquad f(f^{-1}(x)) = 0.5(\sqrt{2x})^2$$
$$= \sqrt{2(0.5x^2)} \qquad = 0.5(2x)$$
$$= \sqrt{x^2} \qquad = x \text{ for } x \geq 0$$
$$= x \text{ for } x \geq 0$$

Since $f^{-1}(f(x)) = x$ for $x \geq 0$ and $f(f^{-1}(x)) = x$ for $x \geq 0$, it has been confirmed that $f^{-1}(x) = \sqrt{2x}$ for $x \geq 0$ is the inverse function of $f(x) = 0.5x^2$ for $x \geq 0$.

Graph $f^{-1}(x)$ by graphing $f(x)$ over the restricted domain and reflecting the graph over the line $y = x$.

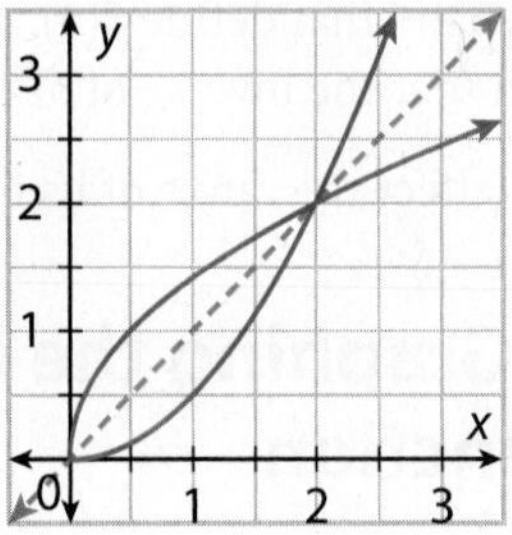

(B) $f(x) = x^2 - 7$

Find the inverse.

Restrict the domain. $\{x | x \geq 0\}$

Replace $f(x)$ with y.	$y = x^2 - 7$
Add 7 to both sides.	$y + 7 = x^2$
Use the definition of positive square root.	$\sqrt{x + 7} = x$

Switch x and y to write the inverse. $\sqrt{x+7} = y$

Replace y with $f^{-1}(x)$. $\sqrt{x+7} = f^{-1}(x)$

Confirm the inverse relationship using composition.

$$f^{-1}(f(x)) = f^{-1}\left(x^2 - 7 \right)$$
$$= \sqrt{(x^2 - 7) + 7}$$
$$= \sqrt{x^2}$$
$$= x \text{ for } x \geq 0$$

$$f(f^{-1}(x)) = f\left(\sqrt{x+7} \right)$$
$$\left(\sqrt{x+7} \right)^2 - 7$$
$$= x + 7 - 7$$
$$= x \geq -7$$

Since $f^{-1}(f(x)) = x$ for $x \geq 0$ it has been confirmed that $f^{-1}(x) = \sqrt{x+7}$ for $x \geq -7$ is the inverse function of $f(x) = x^2 - 7$ for $x \geq 0$.

Graph $f^{-1}(x)$ by graphing $f(x)$ over the restricted domain and reflecting the graph over the line $y = x$.

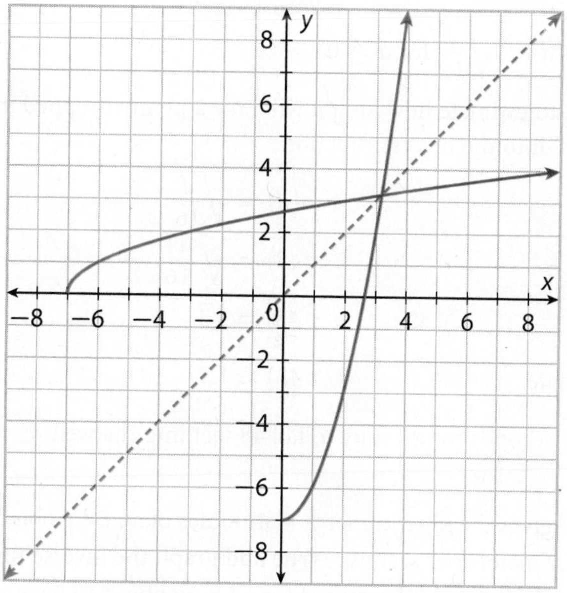

Your Turn

Restrict the domain of the quadratic function and find its inverse. Confirm the inverse relationship using composition. Graph the function and its inverse.

3. $f(x) = 3x^2$

Explain 2 Finding the Inverse of a Quadratic Model

In many instances, quadratic functions are used to model real-world applications. It is often useful to find and interpret the inverse of a quadratic model. Note that when working with real-world applications, it is more useful to use the notation $x(y)$ for the inverse of $y(x)$ instead of the notation $y^{-1}(x)$.

Example 2 **Find the inverse of each of the quadratic functions. Use the inverse to solve the application.**

Ⓐ The function $d(t) = 16t^2$ gives the distance d in feet that a dropped object falls in t seconds. Write the inverse function $t(d)$ to find the time t in seconds it takes for an object to fall a distance of d feet. Then estimate how long it will take a penny dropped into a well to fall 48 feet.

The original function $d(t) = 16t^2$ is a quadratic function with a domain restricted to $t \geq 0$.

Find the inverse function.

Write $d(t)$ as d. $\quad d = 16t^2$

Divide both sides by 16. $\quad \frac{d}{16} = t^2$

Use the definition of positive square root. $\quad \sqrt{\frac{d}{16}} = t$

Write t as $t(d)$. $\quad \sqrt{\frac{d}{16}} = t(d)$

The inverse function is $t(d) = \sqrt{\frac{d}{16}}$ for $d \geq 0$.

Use the inverse function to estimate how long it will take a penny dropped into a well to fall 48 feet. Substitute $d = 48$ into the inverse function.

Write the function. $\quad t(d) = \sqrt{\frac{d}{16}}$

Substitute 48 for d. $\quad t(48) = \sqrt{\frac{48}{16}}$

Simplify. $\quad t(48) = \sqrt{3}$

Use a calculator to estimate. $\quad t(48) \approx 1.7$

So, it will take about 1.7 seconds for a penny to fall 48 feet into the well.

Ⓑ The function $E(v) = 4v^2$ gives the kinetic energy E in Joules of an 8-kg object that is traveling at a velocity of v meters per second. Write and graph the inverse function $v(E)$ to find the velocity v in meters per second required for an 8-kg object to have a kinetic energy of E Joules. Then estimate the velocity required for an 8-kg object to have a kinetic energy of 60 Joules.

The original function $E(v) = 4v^2$ is a quadratic function with a domain restricted to $v \geq 0$.

Find the inverse function.

Write $E(v)$ as E. $\quad \boxed{E} = 4v^2$

Divide both sides by 4. $\quad \boxed{\frac{E}{4}} = v^2$

Use the definition of positive square root. $\quad \boxed{\sqrt{\frac{E}{4}}} = v$

Write v as $v(E)$. $v(E) = \sqrt{\frac{E}{4}}$

The inverse function is $v(E) = \sqrt{\frac{E}{4}}$ for $E \geq 0$.

Use the inverse function to estimate the velocity required for an 8-kg object to have a kinetic energy of 60 Joules.

Substitute $E = 60$ into the inverse function.

Write the function. $v(E) = \boxed{\sqrt{\frac{E}{4}}}$

Substitute 60 for E. $v\left(\boxed{60}\right) = \boxed{\sqrt{\frac{60}{4}}}$

Simplify. $v(60) = \sqrt{15}$

Use a calculator to estimate. $v(60) \approx 3.9$

So, an 8-kg object with kinetic energy of 60 Joules is traveling at a velocity of 3.9 meters per second.

Your Turn

Find the inverse of the quadratic function. Use the inverse to solve the application.

4. The function $A(r) = \pi r^2$ gives the area of a circular object with respect to its radius r. Write the inverse function $r(A)$ to find the radius r required for area of A. Then estimate the radius of a circular object that has an area of 40 cm^2.

Explain 3 Finding and Graphing the Inverse of a Simple Cubic Function

Note that the function $f(x) = x^3$ is a one-to-one function, so its domain does not need to be restricted in order to find its inverse function. The inverse of $f(x) = x^3$ is $f^{-1}(x) = \sqrt[3]{x}$.

The inverse of a cubic function is a **cube root function**, which is a function whose rule involves $\sqrt[3]{x}$. The **parent cube root function** is $g(x) = \sqrt[3]{x}$.

Example 3 **Find the inverse of each cubic function. Confirm the inverse relationship using composition. Graph the function and its inverse.**

(A) $f(x) = 0.5x^3$

Find each inverse. Graph the function and its inverse.

Replace $f(x)$ with y. $y = 0.5x^3$

Multiply both sides by 2. $2y = x^3$

Use the definition of cube root. $\sqrt[3]{2y} = x$

Switch x and y to write the inverse. $\sqrt[3]{2x} = y$

Replace y with $f^{-1}(x)$. $\sqrt[3]{2x} = f^{-1}(x)$

Confirm the inverse relationship using composition.

$$f^{-1}(f(x)) = f^{-1}(0.5x^3) = \sqrt[3]{2(0.5x^3)} = \sqrt[3]{x^3} = x$$

$$f(f^{-1}(x)) = f(\sqrt[3]{2x}) = 0.5(\sqrt[3]{2x})^3 = 0.5(2x) = x$$

Since $f^{-1}(f(x)) = x$ and $f(f^{-1}(x)) = x$, it has been confirmed that $f^{-1}(x) = \sqrt[3]{2x}$ is the inverse function of $f(x) = 0.5x^3$.

Graph $f^{-1}(x)$ by graphing $f(x)$ and reflecting $f(x)$ over the line $y = x$.

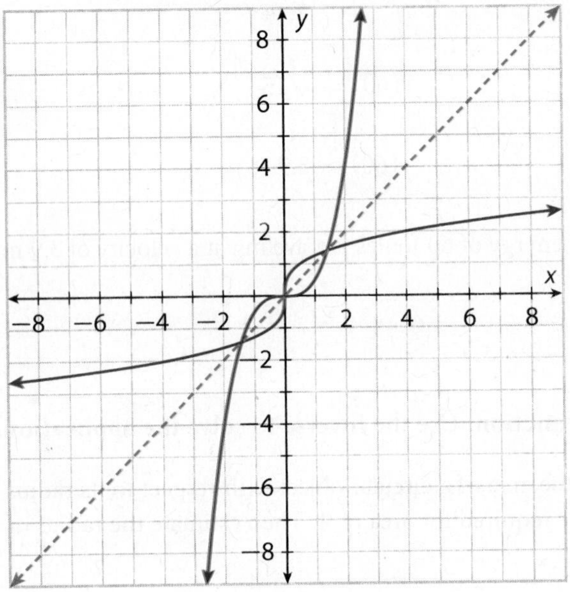

(B) $f(x) = x^3 - 9$

Find the inverse.

Replace $f(x)$ with y. $\quad y = x^3 - 9$

Add 9 to both sides. $\quad y + 9 = x^3$

Use the definition of cube root. $\quad \sqrt[3]{y + 9} = x$

Switch x and y to write the inverse. $\quad \sqrt[3]{x + 9} = y$

Replace y with $f^{-1}(x)$. $\quad \sqrt[3]{x + 9} = f^{-1}(x)$

Confirm the inverse relationship using composition.

$$f^{-1}(f(x)) = f^{-1}(x^3 - 9) = \sqrt[3]{(x^3 - 9) + 9} = \sqrt[3]{x^3} = x$$

$$f(f^{-1}(x)) = f(\sqrt[3]{y + 9}) = (\sqrt[3]{y + 9})^3 - 9 = x + 9 - 9 = x$$

Since $f^{-1}(f(x)) =$ x and $f(f^{-1}(x)) =$ x , it has been confirmed that $f^{-1}(x) = \sqrt[3]{x + 9}$ is the inverse function of $f(x) = x^3 - 9$.

Graph $f^{-1}(x)$ by graphing $f(x)$ and reflecting $f(x)$ over the line $y = x$.

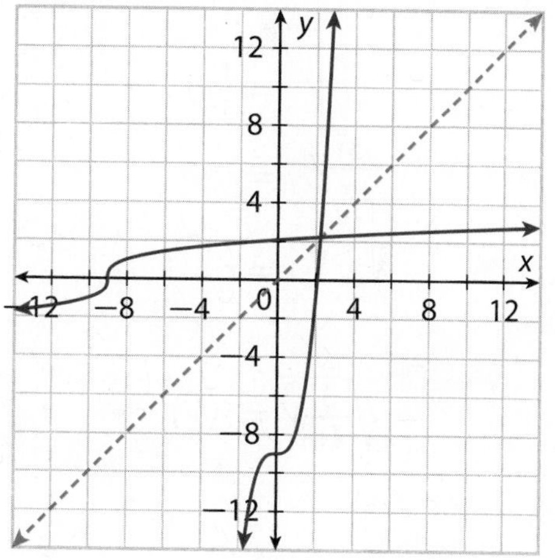

Your Turn

Find the inverse. Graph the function and its inverse.

5. $f(x) = 2x^3$

Explain 4 Finding the Inverse of a Cubic Model

In many instances, cubic functions are used to model real-world applications. It is often useful to find and interpret the inverse of cubic models. As with quadratic real-world applications, it is more useful to use the notation $x(y)$ for the inverse of $y(x)$ instead of the notation $y^{-1}(x)$.

Example 4 **Find the inverse of each of the following cubic functions.**

(A) The function $m(L) = 0.00001L^3$ gives the mass m in kilograms of a red snapper of length L centimeters. Find the inverse function $L(m)$ to find the length L in centimeters of a red snapper that has a mass of m kilograms.

The original function $m(L) = 0.00001L^3$ is a cubic function.

Find the inverse function.

Write $m(L)$ as m. $\quad m = 0.00001L^3$

Multiply both sides by 100,000. $\quad 100{,}000m = L^3$

Use the definition of cube root. $\quad \sqrt[3]{100{,}000m} = L$

Write L as $L(m)$. $\quad \sqrt[3]{100{,}000m} = L(m)$

The inverse function is $L(m) = \sqrt[3]{100{,}000m}$.

(B) The function $V(r) = \frac{4}{3}\pi r^3$ gives the volume V of a sphere with radius r. Find the inverse function $r(V)$ to find the radius r of a sphere with volume V.

The original function $V(r) = \frac{4}{3}\pi r^3$ is a cubic function.

Find the inverse function.

Write $V(r)$ as V. $$V = \frac{4}{3}\pi r^3$$

Divide both sides by $\frac{4}{3}\pi$. $$\frac{3}{4\pi}V = r^3$$

Use the definition of cube root. $$\sqrt[3]{\frac{3}{4\pi}V} = r$$

Write r as $r(V)$. $$\sqrt[3]{\frac{3}{4\pi}V} = r(V)$$

The inverse function is $r(V) = \sqrt[3]{\frac{3}{4\pi}V}$.

Your Turn

6. The function $m(r) = \frac{44}{3}\pi r^3$ gives the mass in grams of a spherical lead ball with a radius of r centimeters. Find the inverse function $r(m)$ to find the radius r of a lead sphere with mass m.

Elaborate

7. What is the general form of the inverse function for the function $f(x) = ax^2$? State any restrictions on the domains.

8. What is the general form of the inverse function for the function $f(x) = ax^3$? State any restrictions on the domains.

9. **Essential Question Check-In** Why must the domain be restricted when finding the inverse of a quadratic function, but not when finding the inverse of a cubic function?

Evaluate: Homework and Practice

Personal Math Trainer
- Online Homework
- Hints and Help
- Extra Practice

Restrict the domain of the quadratic function and find its inverse. Confirm the inverse relationship using composition. Graph the function and its inverse.

1. $f(x) = 0.2x^2$

2. $f(x) = 8x^2$

3. $f(x) = x^2 + 10$

Restrict the domain of the quadratic function and find its inverse. Confirm the inverse relationship using composition.

4. $f(x) = 15x^2$

5. $f(x) = x^2 - \frac{3}{4}$

6. $f(x) = 0.7x^2$

7. The function $d(s) = \frac{1}{14.9}s^2$ models the average depth d in feet of the water over which a tsunami travels, where s is the speed in miles per hour. Write the inverse function $s(d)$ to find the speed required for a depth of d feet. Then estimate the speed of a tsunami over water with an average depth of 1500 feet.

8. The function $x(T) = 9.8\left(\frac{T}{2\pi}\right)^2$ gives the length x in meters for a pendulum to swing for a period of T seconds. Write the inverse function to find the period of a pendulum in seconds. The period of a pendulum is the time it takes the pendulum to complete one back-and-forth swing. Find the period of a pendulum with length of 5 meters.

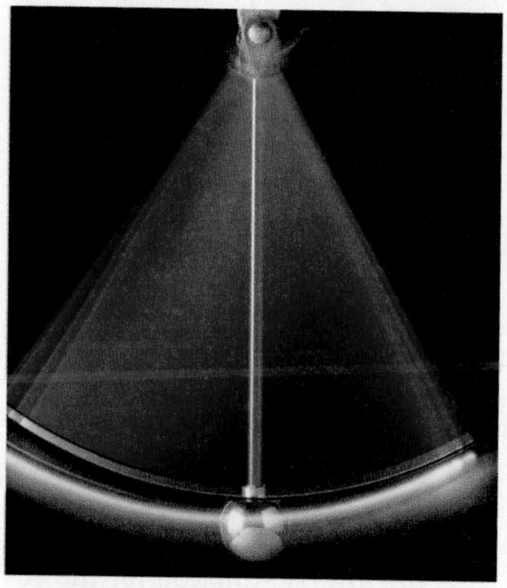

Find the inverse of each cubic function. Confirm the inverse relationship using composition. Graph the function and its inverse.

9. $f(x) = 0.25x^3$

10. $f(x) = -12x^3$

Find the inverse of the cubic function. Confirm the inverse relationship using composition.

11. $f(x) = x^3 - \frac{5}{6}$

12. $f(x) = x^3 + 9$

13. The function $m(r) = 31r^3$ models the mass in grams of a spherical zinc ball as a function of the ball's radius in centimeters. Write the inverse model to represent the radius r in cm of a spherical zinc ball as a function of the ball's mass m in g.

14. The function $m(r) = 21r^3$ models the mass in grams of a spherical titanium ball as a function of the ball's radius in centimeters. Write the inverse model to represent the radius r in centimeters of a spherical titanium ball as a function of the ball's mass m in grams.

15. After an initial deposit of $2000, a bank account pays interest at an annual rate $r\%$ compounded annually. The value V of the account after 3 years can be represented by the model $V(r) = 2000\,(1 + r)^3$. Write the inverse function $r(V)$ to find the interest rate needed for the account to have value V after the 3 years.

H.O.T. Focus on Higher Order Thinking

16. Explain the Error A student was asked to find the inverse of the function $f(x) = \left(\frac{x}{2}\right)^3 + 9$. What did the student do wrong? Find the correct inverse.

$$f(x) = \left(\frac{x}{2}\right)^3 + 9$$
$$y = \left(\frac{x}{2}\right)^3 + 9$$
$$y - 9 = \left(\frac{x}{2}\right)^3$$
$$2y - 18 = x^3$$
$$\sqrt[3]{2y - 18} = x$$
$$y = \sqrt[3]{2x - 18}$$
$$f^{-1}(x) = \sqrt[3]{2x - 18}$$

17. Multi-Step A framing store uses the function $\left(\frac{c - 0.2}{0.5}\right)^2 = a$ to determine the total area of a piece of glass with respect to the cost before installation of the glass. Write the inverse function for the cost c in dollars of glass for a picture with an area of a in square centimeters. Then write a new function to represent the total cost C the store charges if it costs \$6.00 for installation. Use the total cost function to estimate the cost if the area of the glass is 192 cm^2.

18. Make a Conjecture The function $f(x) = x^2$ must have its domain restricted to have its inverse be a function. The function $f(x) = x^3$ does not need to have its domain restricted to have its inverse be a function. Make a conjecture about which power functions need to have their domains restricted to have their inverses be functions and which do not.

Lesson Performance Task

One method used to irrigate crops is the center-pivot irrigation system. In this method, sprinklers rotate in a circle to water crops. The challenge for the farmer is to determine where to place the pivot in order to water the desired number of acres. The farmer knows the area but needs to find the radius of the circle necessary to define that area. How can the farmer determine this from the formula for the area of a circle $A = \pi r^2$? Find the formula the farmer could use to determine the radius necessary to irrigate a given number of acres, A. (Hint: One acre is 43,560 square feet.) What would be the radius necessary for the sprinklers to irrigate an area of 133 acres?

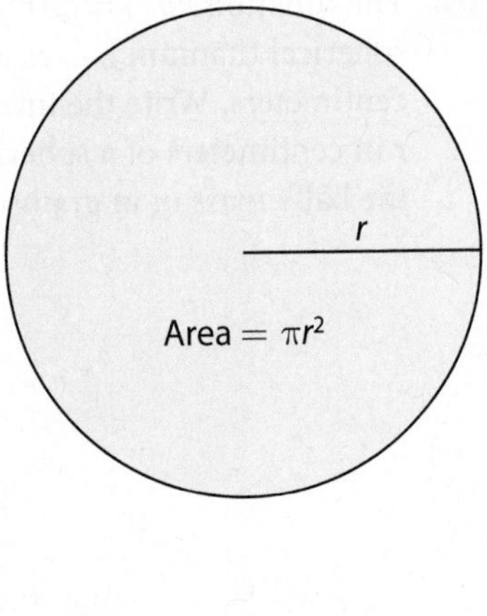

10.2 Graphing Square Root Functions

Essential Question: How can you use transformations of a parent square root function to graph functions of the form $g(x) = a\sqrt{(x-h)} + k$ or $g(x) = \sqrt{\frac{1}{b}(x-h)} + k$?

Resource Locker

Explore Graphing and Analyzing the Parent Square Root Function

Although you have seen how to use imaginary numbers to evaluate square roots of negative numbers, graphing complex numbers and complex valued functions is beyond the scope of this course. For purposes of graphing functions based on the square roots (and in most cases where a square root function is used in a real-world example), the domain and range should both be limited to real numbers.

The square root function is the inverse of a quadratic function with a domain limited to positive real numbers. The quadratic function must be a one-to-one function in order to have an inverse, so the domain is limited to one side of the vertex. The square root function is also a one-to-one function as all inverse functions are.

(A) The domain of the square root function (limited to real numbers) is given by $\{x \mid x \geq \boxed{?}\}$.

(B) Fill in the table.

x	$f(x) = \sqrt{x}$
0	?
1	?
4	?
9	?

(C) Plot the points on a coordinate grid, and connect them with a smooth curve.

(D) Recall that this function is the inverse of the parent quadratic $(f(x) = x^2)$ with a domain limited to the nonnegative real numbers. Write the range of this square root function:

$\{y \mid y \geq \boxed{?}\}$.

(E) The graph appears to be getting flatter as x increases, indicating that the rate of change ? as x increases.

(F) Describe the end behavior of the square root function, $f(x) = \sqrt{x}$. $f(x) \to$? as $x \to$?

Reflect

1. **Discussion** Why does the end behavior of the square root function only need to be described at one end?

2. The solution to the equation $x^2 = 4$ is sometimes written as $x = \pm 2$. Explain why the inverse of $f(x) = x^2$ cannot similarly be written as $g(x) = \pm\sqrt{x}$ in order to use all reals as the domain of $f(x)$.

Explore 2 Predicting the Effects of Parameters on the Graphs of Square Root Functions

You have learned how to transform the graph of a function using reflections across the x- and y-axes, vertical and horizontal stretches and compressions, and translations. Here, you will apply those transformations to the graph of the square root function $f(x) = \sqrt{x}$.

When transforming the parent function $f(x) = \sqrt{x}$, you can get functions of the form

$g(x) = a\sqrt{(x - h)} + k$ or $g(x) = \sqrt{\frac{1}{b}(x - h)} + k$.

For each parameter, predict the effect on the graph of the parent function, and then confirm your prediction with a graphing calculator.

(A) Predict the effect of the parameter, h, on the graph of $g(x) = \sqrt{x - h}$ for each function.

a. $g(x) = \sqrt{x - 2}$: The graph is a ? of the graph of $f(x)$? 2 units.

b. $g(x) = \sqrt{x + 2}$: The graph is a ? of the graph of $f(x)$? 2 units.

Check your answers using a graphing calculator.

(B) Predict the effect of the parameter k on the graph of $g(x) = \sqrt{x} + k$ for each function.

a. $g(x) = \sqrt{x} + 2$: The graph is a ? of the graph of $f(x)$? 2 units.

b. $g(x) = \sqrt{x} - 2$: The graph is a ? of the graph of $f(x)$? 2 units.

Check your answers using a graphing calculator.

(C) Predict the effect of the parameter a on the graph of $g(x) = a\sqrt{x}$ for each function.

a. $g(x) = 2\sqrt{x}$: The graph is a ? stretch of the graph of $f(x)$ by a factor of ? .

b. $g(x) = \frac{1}{2}\sqrt{x}$: The graph is a ? compression of the graph of $f(x)$ by a factor of ? .

c. $g(x) = -\frac{1}{2}\sqrt{x}$: The graph is a ? compression of the graph of $f(x)$ by a factor of ? as well as a ? across the ? .

d. $g(x) = -2\sqrt{x}$: The graph is a ? stretch of the graph of $f(x)$ by a factor of ? as well as a ? across the ? .

Check your answers using a graphing calculator.

(D) Predict the effect of the parameter, b, on the graph of $g(x) = \sqrt{\frac{1}{b}x}$ for each function.

a. $g(x) = \sqrt{\frac{1}{2}x}$: The graph is a ? stretch of the graph of $f(x)$ by a factor of ? .

b. $g(x) = \sqrt{2x}$: The graph is a ? compression of the graph of $f(x)$ by a factor of ? .

c. $g(x) = \sqrt{-\frac{1}{2}x}$: The graph is a ? stretch of the graph of $f(x)$ by a factor of ? as well as a ? across the ? .

d. $g(x) = \sqrt{-2x}$: The graph is a ? compression of the graph of $f(x)$ by a factor of ? as well as a ? across the ? .

Check your answers using a graphing calculator.

Reflect

3. **Discussion** Describe what the effect of each of the transformation parameters is on the domain and range of the transformed function.

Explain 1 Graphing Square Root Functions

When graphing transformations of the square root function, it is useful to consider the effect of the transformation on two reference points, $(0, 0)$ and $(1, 1)$, that lie on the parent function, and where they map to on the transformed function, $g(x)$.

$f(x) = \sqrt{x}$		$g(x) = a\sqrt{x-h}+k$		$g(x) = \sqrt{\frac{1}{b}(x-h)}+k$	
x	y	x	y	x	y
0	0	h	k	h	k
1	1	$h+1$	$k+a$	$h+b$	$k+1$

The transformed reference points can be found by recognizing that the initial point of the graph is translated from $(0, 0)$ to (h, k). When $g(x)$ involves the parameters a, h, and k, the second transformed reference point is 1 unit to the right of (h, k) and $|a|$ units up or down from (h, k), depending on the sign of a. When $g(x)$ involves the parameters b, h, and k, the second transformed reference point is $|b|$ units left or right from (h, k), depending on the sign of b, and 1 unit above (h, k).

Transformations of the square root function also affect the domain and range. In order to work with real valued inputs and outputs, the domain of the square root function cannot include values of x that result in a negative-valued expression. Negative values of x can be in the domain, as long as they result in nonnegative values of the expression that is inside the square root. Similarly, the value of the square root function is positive by definition, but multiplying the square root function by a negative number, or adding a constant to it changes the range and can result in negative values of the transformed function.

Example 1 **For each of the transformed square root functions, find the transformed reference points and use them to plot the transformed function on the same graph with the parent function. Describe the domain and range using set notation.**

(A) $g(x) = 2\sqrt{x-3} - 2$

To find the domain:

Square root input must be nonnegative. $x - 3 \geq 0$

Solve the inequality for x. $x \geq 3$

The domain is $\left\{x \mid x \geq 3\right\}$.

To find the range:

The square root function is nonnegative. $\sqrt{x-3} \geq 0$

Multiply by 2 $2\sqrt{x-3} \geq 0$

Subtract 2. $2\sqrt{x-3} - 2 \geq -2$

The expression on the left is $g(x)$. $g(x) \geq -2$

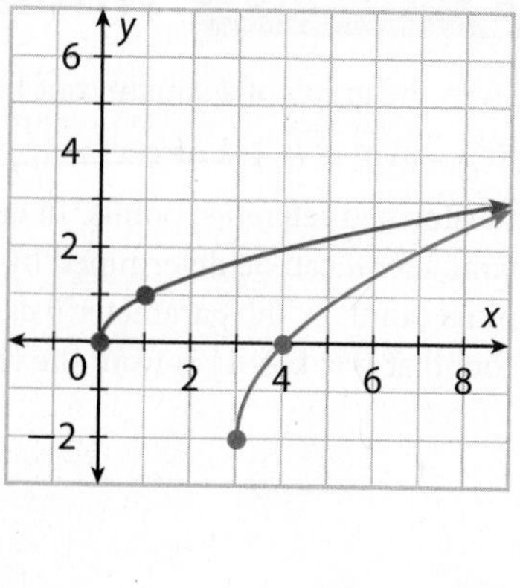

Since $g(x)$ is greater than or equal to -2 for all x in the domain, the range is $\{y \mid y \geq -2\}$.

$(0, 0) \rightarrow (3, -2)$

$(1, 1) \rightarrow (4, 0)$

(B) $g(x) = \sqrt{-\frac{1}{2}(x-2)} + 1$

To find the domain:

Square root input must be nonnegative. $-\frac{1}{2}(x-2) \geq$ 0

Multiply both sides by -2. $x - 2$ $\leq$ 0

Add 2 to both sides. x ≤ 2

Expressed in set notation, the domain is $\{x \mid$ $x \leq 2$ $\}$.

To find the range:

The square root function is nonnegative. $\sqrt{-\frac{1}{2}(x-2)}$ $\geq$ 0

Add 1 to both sides $\sqrt{-\frac{1}{2}(x-2)} + 1 \geq$ 1

Substitute in $g(x)$. $g(x) \geq 1$

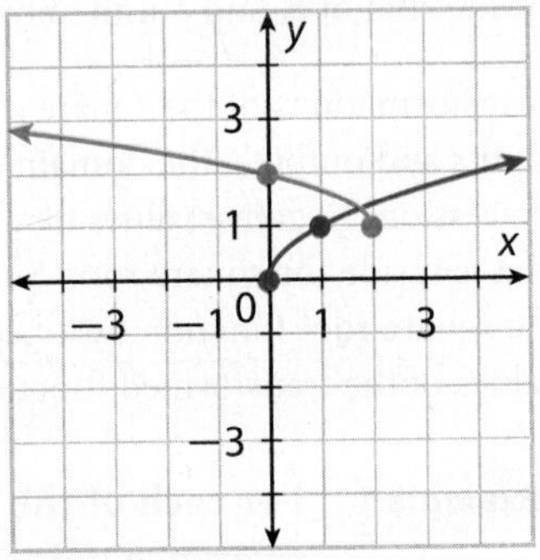

Since $g(x)$ is greater than 1 for all x in the domain,

the range (in set notation) is $\{y \mid$ $y \geq 1$ $\}$.

$(0, 0) \rightarrow$ $(2, 1)$

$(1, 1) \rightarrow$ $(0, 2)$

Your Turn

For each of the transformed square root functions, find the transformed reference points and use them to plot the transformed function on the same graph with the parent function. Describe the domain and range using set notation.

4. $g(x) = -3\sqrt{x-2} + 3$

5. $g(x) = \sqrt{\frac{1}{3}(x+2)} + 1$

Explain 2 Writing Square Root Functions

Given the graph of a square root function and the form of the transformed function, either $g(x) = a\sqrt{x-h} + k$ or $g(x) = \sqrt{\frac{1}{b}(x-h)} = k$, the transformation parameters can be determined from the transformed reference points. In either case, the initial point will be at (h, k) and readily apparent. The parameter a can be determined by how far up or down the second point (found at $x = h + 1$) is from the initial point, or the parameter b can be determined by how far to the left or right the second point (found at $y = k + 1$) is from the initial point.

Example 2 **Write the function that matches the graph using the indicated transformation format.**

Ⓐ $g(x) = \sqrt{\frac{1}{b}(x - h)} + k$

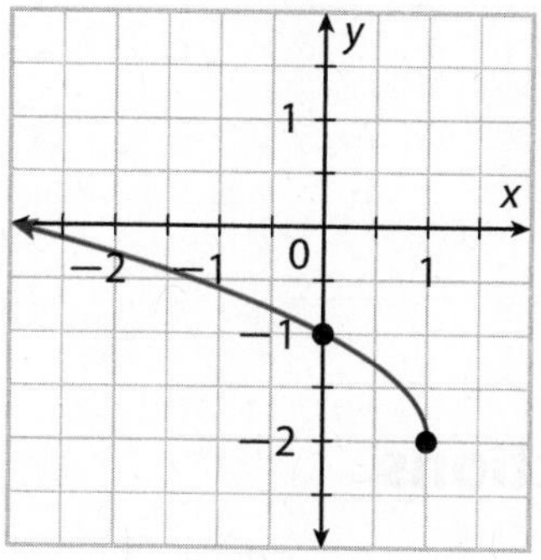

Initial point: $(h, k) = (1, -2)$

Second point:

$(h + b, k + 1) = (0, -1)$

$1 + b = 0$

$b = -1$

The function is $g(x) = \sqrt{-1(x - 1)} - 2$.

Ⓑ $g(x) = a\sqrt{x - h} + k$

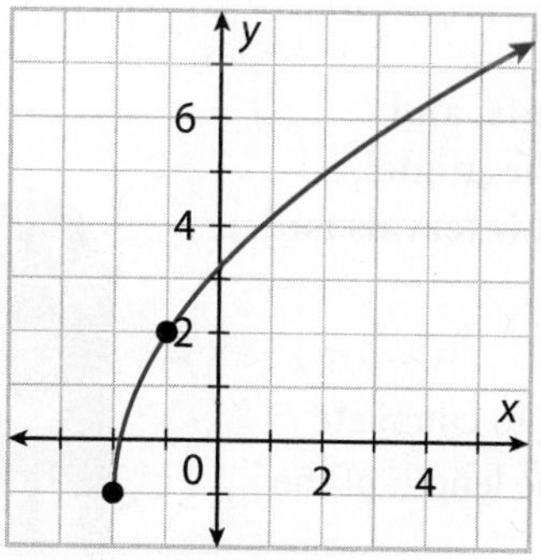

Initial point: $(h, k) = (-2, -1)$

Second point:

$(h + 1, k + a) = (-1, 2)$

$-1 + a = 2$

$a = 3$

The function is $g(x) = 3\sqrt{x + 2} - 1$.

Your Turn

Write the function that matches the graph using the indicated transformation format.

6. $g(x) = \sqrt{\frac{1}{b}(x - h)} + k$

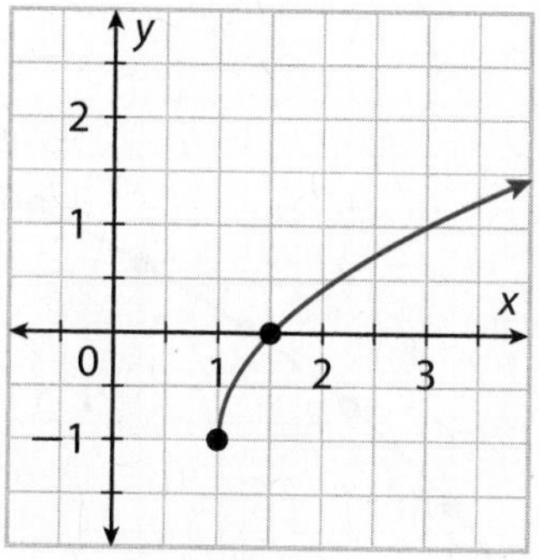

7. $g(x) = a\sqrt{(x - h)} + k$

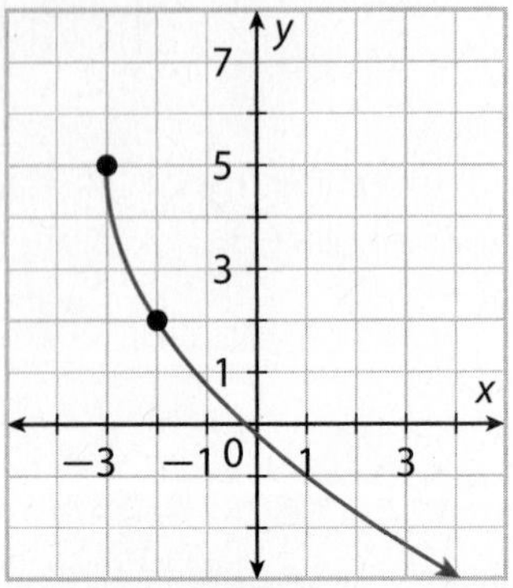

Explain 3 Modeling with Square Root Functions

Square root functions that model real-world situations can be used to investigate average rates of change.

Recall that the average rate of change of the function $f(x)$ over an interval from x_1 to x_2 is given by

$$\frac{f(x_2) - f(x_1)}{x_2 - x_1}.$$

Example 3 **Use a calculator to evaluate the model at the indicated points, and connect the points with a curve to complete the graph of the model. Calculate the average rates of change over the first and last intervals and explain what the rate of change represents.**

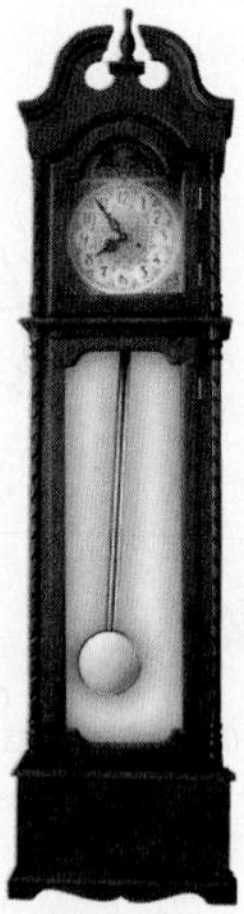

(A) The approximate period T of a pendulum (the time it takes a pendulum to complete one swing) is given in seconds by the formula $T = 0.32\sqrt{\ell}$, where ℓ is the length of the pendulum in inches. Use lengths of 2, 4, 6, 8, and 10 inches.

First find the points for the given x-values.

Length (inches)	Period (seconds)
2	0.45
4	0.64
6	0.78
8	0.91
10	1.01

Plot the points and draw a smooth curve through them.

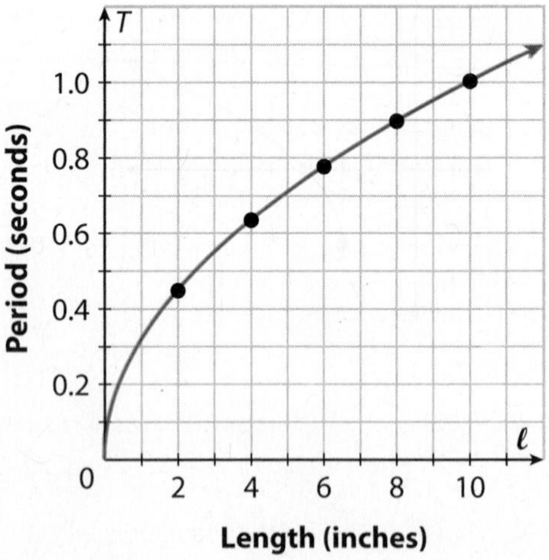

Find the average increase in period per inch increase in the pendulum length for the first interval and the last interval.

First interval:

$$\text{rate of change} = \frac{0.64 - 0.45}{4 - 2}$$

$$= 0.095$$

Last Interval:

$$\text{rate of change} = \frac{1.01 - 0.91}{10 - 8}$$
$$= 0.05$$

The average rate of change is less for the last interval. The average rate of change represents the increase in pendulum period with each additional inch of length. As the length of the pendulum increases, the increase in period time per inch of length becomes less.

(B) A car with good tires is on a dry road. The speed, in miles per hour, from which the car can stop in a given distance d, in feet, is given by $s(d) = \sqrt{96d}$. Use distances of 20, 40, 60, 80, and 100 feet.

First, find the points for the given x-values.

Distance	20	40	60	80	100
Speed	43.8	62.0	75.9	87.6	98.0

Plot the points and draw a smooth curve through them.

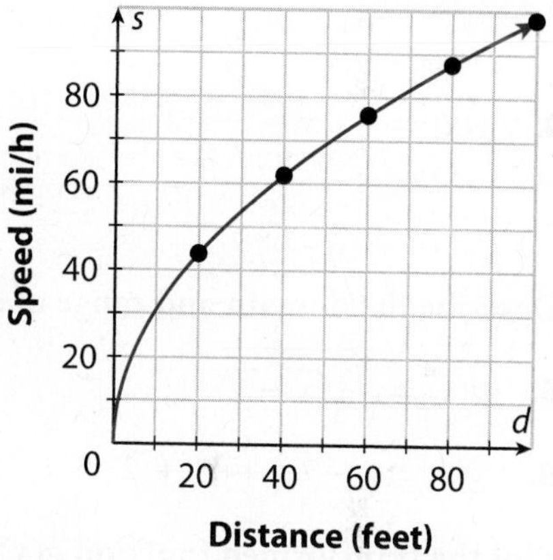

First interval:

$$\text{rate of change} = \frac{62.0 - 43.8}{40 - 20}$$
$$= 0.91$$

Last Interval:

$$\text{rate of change} = \frac{98.0 - 87.6}{100 - 80}$$
$$= 0.52$$

The average rate of change is less for the last interval. The average rate of change represents the increase in speed with each additional foot of distance. As the available stopping distance increases, the additional increase in speed per foot of stopping distance decreases.

Your Turn

Use a calculator to evaluate the model at the indicated points, and connect the points with a curve to complete the graph of the model. Calculate the average rates of change over the first and last intervals and explain what the rate of change represents.

8. The speed in miles per hour of a tsunami can be modeled by the function $s(d) = 3.86\sqrt{d}$, where d is the average depth in feet of the water over which the tsunami travels. Graph this function from depths of 1000 feet to 5000 feet and compare the change in speed with depth from the shallowest interval to the deepest. Use depths of 1000, 2000, 3000, 4000, and 5000 feet for the x-values.

Elaborate

9. What is the difference between the parameters inside the radical (b and h) and the parameters outside the radical (a and k)?

10. Which transformations change the square root function's end behavior?

11. Which transformations change the square root function's initial point location?

12. Which transformations change the square root function's domain?

13. Which transformations change the square root function's range?

14. **Essential Question Check-In** Describe in your own words the steps you would take to graph a function of the form $g(x) = a\sqrt{x-h} + k$ or $g(x) = \sqrt{\frac{1}{b}(x-h)} + k$ if you were given the values of h and k and using either a or b.

Evaluate: Homework and Practice

Personal Math Trainer

- Online Homework
- Hints and Help
- Extra Practice

1. Graph the functions $f(x) = \sqrt{x}$ and $g(x) = -\sqrt{x}$ on the same grid. Describe the domain, range and end behavior of each function. How are the functions related?

Describe the transformations of $g(x)$ from the parent function $f(x) = \sqrt{x}$.

2. $g(x) = \sqrt{\frac{1}{2}x} + 1$

3. $g(x) = -5\sqrt{x+1} - 3$

4. $g(x) = \frac{1}{4}\sqrt{x-5} - 2$

5. $g(x) = \sqrt{-7(x-7)}$

Describe the domain and range of each function using set notation.

6. $g(x) = \sqrt{\frac{1}{3}(x-1)}$

7. $g(x) = 3\sqrt{x+4} + 3$

8. $g(x) = \sqrt{-5(x+1)} + 2$

9. $g(x) = -7\sqrt{x-3} - 5$

Plot the transformed function $g(x)$ on a grid with the parent function, $f(x) = \sqrt{x}$. Describe the domain and range of each function using set notation.

10. $g(x) = -\sqrt{x} + 3$

11. $g(x) = \sqrt{\frac{1}{3}(x+4)} - 1$

12. $g(x) = \sqrt{-\frac{2}{3}\left(x - \frac{1}{2}\right)} - 2$

13. $g(x) = 4\sqrt{x+3} - 4$

Write the function that matches the graph using the indicated transformation format.

14. $g(x) = \sqrt{\frac{1}{b}(x-h)} + k$

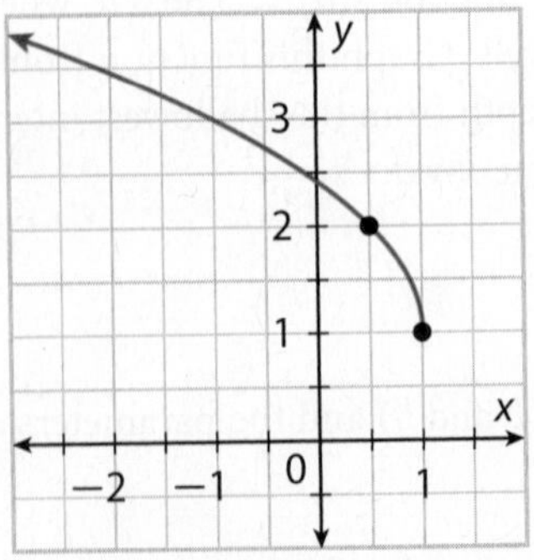

15. $g(x) = \sqrt{\frac{1}{b}(x-h)} + k$

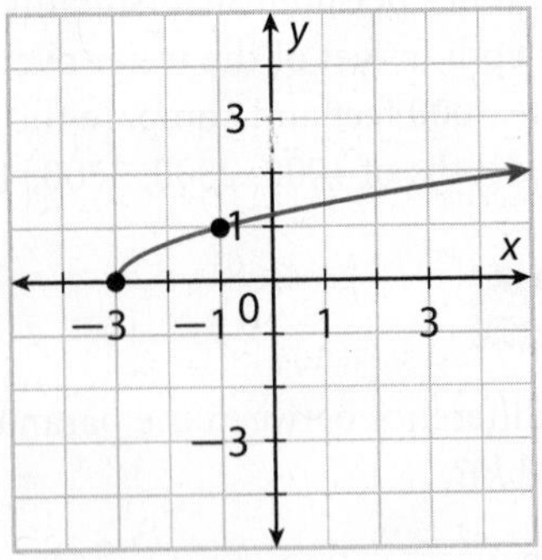

16. $g(x) = a\sqrt{x - h} + k$

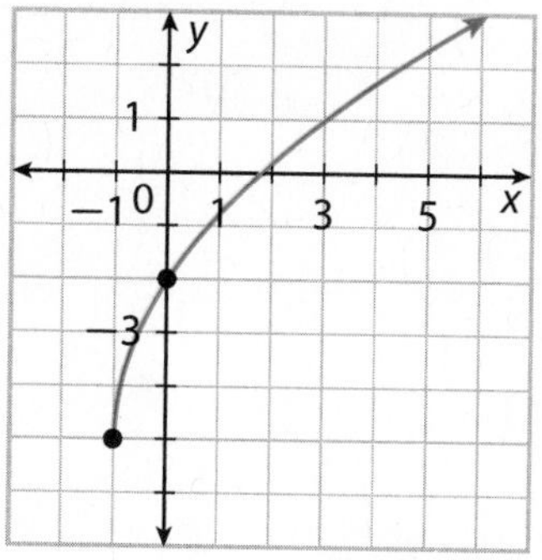

17. $g(x) = a\sqrt{x - h} + k$

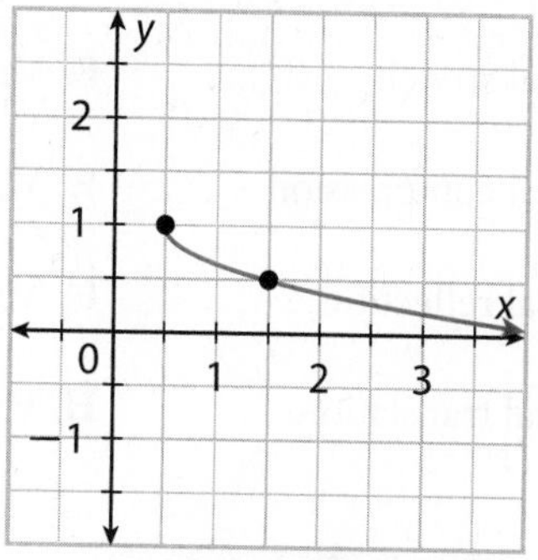

Use a calculator to evaluate the model at the indicated points, and connect the points with a curve to complete the graph of the model. Calculate the average rates of change over the first and last intervals and explain what the rate of change represents.

18. A farmer is trying to determine how much fencing to buy to make a square holding pen with a 6-foot gap for a gate. The length of fencing, f, in feet, required as a function of area, A, in square feet, is given by $f(A) = 4\sqrt{A} - 6$. Evaluate the function from 20 ft^2 to 100 ft^2 by calculating points every 20 ft^2.

19. The speed, s, in feet per second, of an object dropped from a height, h, in feet, is given by the formula $s(h) = \sqrt{64h}$. Evaluate the function for heights of 0 feet to 25 feet by calculating points every 5 feet.

20. Water is draining from a tank at an average speed, s, in feet per second, characterized by the function $s(d) = 8\sqrt{d - 2}$, where d is the depth of the water in the tank in feet. Evaluate the function for depths of 2, 3, 4, and 5 feet.

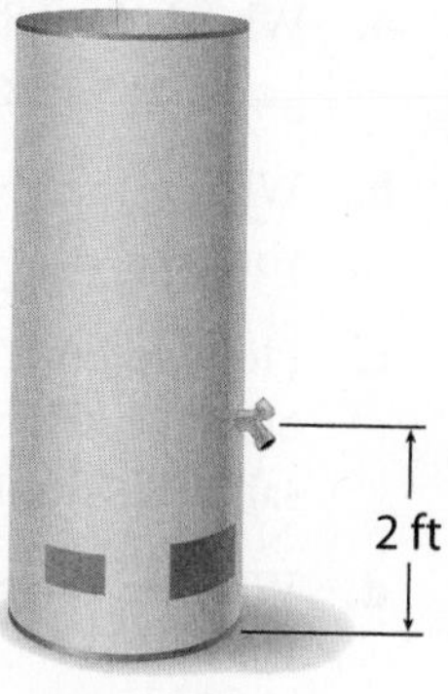

21. A research team studies the effects from an oil spill to develop new methods in oil clean-up. In the spill they are studying, the damaged oil tanker spilled oil into the ocean, forming a roughly circular spill pattern. The spill expanded out from the tanker, increasing the area at a rate of 100 square meters perhour. The radius of the circle is given by the function $r = \sqrt{\frac{100}{\pi}t}$, where t is the time (in hours) after the spill begins. Evaluate the function at hours 0, 1, 2, 3, and 4.

22. Give all of the transformations of the parent function $f(x) = \sqrt{x}$ that result in the function $g(x) = \sqrt{-2(x-3)} + 2$.

A. Horizontal stretch

B. Horizontal compression

C. Horizontal reflection

D. Horizontal translation

E. Vertical stretch

F. Vertical compression

G. Vertical reflection

H. Vertical translation

H.O.T. Focus on Higher Order Thinking

23. Draw Conclusions Describe the transformations to $f(x) = \sqrt{x}$ that result in the function $g(x) = \sqrt{-8x + 16} + 3$.

24. Analyze Relationships Show how a horizontally stretched square root function can sometimes be replaced by a vertical compression by equating the two forms of the transformed square root function.

$$g(x) = a\sqrt{x} = \sqrt{\frac{1}{b}x}$$

What must you assume about a and b for this replacement to result in the same function?

25. Multi-Step On a clear day, the view across the ocean is limited by the curvature of Earth. Objects appear to disappear below the horizon as they get farther from an observer. For an observer at height h above the water looking at an object with a height of H (both in feet), the approximate distance (d) in miles at which the object drops below the horizon is given by $d(h) = 1.21\sqrt{h + H}$.

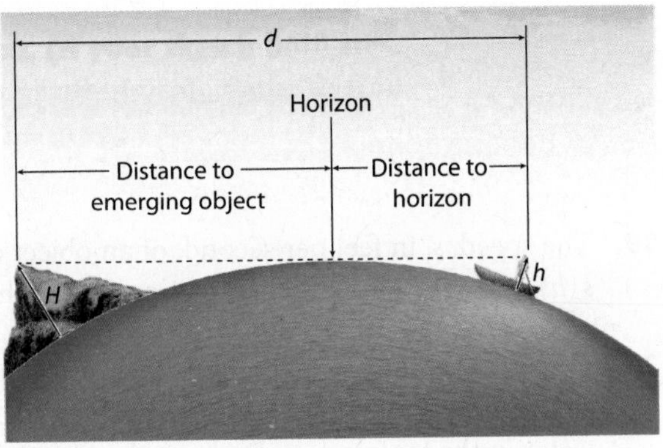

a. What is the effect of the object height, H, on the graph of $d(h)$?

b. What is the domain of the function $d(h)$? Explain your answer.

c. Plot two functions of distance required to see an object over the horizon versus observer height: one for seeing a 2-foot-tall buoy and one for seeing a 20-foot-tall sailboat. Calculate points every 10 feet from 0 to 40 feet.

d. Where is the greatest increase in viewing distance with observer height?

Lesson Performance Task

With all the coffee beans that come in for processing, a coffee manufacturer cannot sample all of them. Suppose one manufacturer uses the function $s(x) = \sqrt{x} + 1$ to determine how many samples that it must take from x containers in order to obtain a good representative sampling of beans. How does this function relate to the function $f(x) = \sqrt{x}$? Graph both functions. How many samples should be taken from a shipment of 45 containers of beans? Explain why this can only be a whole number answer.

10.3 Graphing Cube Root Functions

Essential Question: How can you use transformations of the parent cube root function to graph functions of the form $f(x) = a\sqrt[3]{(x - h)} + k$ or $g(x) = \sqrt[3]{\frac{1}{b}(x - h)} + k$?

Resource Locker

Explore Graphing and Analyzing the Parent Cube Root Function

The cube root parent function is $f(x) = \sqrt[3]{x}$. To graph $f(x)$, choose values of x and find corresponding values of y. Choose both negative and positive values of x.

Graph the function $f(x) = \sqrt[3]{x}$. Identify the domain and range of the function.

(A) Make a table of values.

x	y	x, y
−8	?	?
−1	?	?
0	?	?
1	?	?
8	?	?

(B) Use the table to graph the function.

(C) Identify the domain and range of the function.

The domain is ? .

The range is ? .

(D) Does the graph of $f(x) = \sqrt[3]{x}$ have any symmetry?

The graph has ? .

Reflect

1. Can the radicand in a cube root function be negative?

Explain 1 Graphing Cube Root Functions

Transformations of the Cube Root Parent Function $f(x) = \sqrt[3]{x}$		
Transformation	**f(x) Notation**	**Examples**
Vertical translation	$f(x) + k$	$y = \sqrt[3]{x} + 3$ 3 units up $y = \sqrt[3]{x} - 4$ 4 units down
Horizontal translation	$f(x - h)$	$y = \sqrt[3]{x - 2}$ 2 units right $y = \sqrt[3]{x + 1}$ 1 units left
Vertical stretch/compression	$af(x)$	$y = 6\sqrt[3]{x}$ vertical stretch by a factor of 6 $y = \frac{1}{2}\sqrt[3]{x}$ vertical compression by a factor of $\frac{1}{2}$
Horizontal stretch/ compression	$f\left(\frac{1}{b}x\right)$	$y = \sqrt[3]{\frac{1}{5}x}$ horizontal stretch by a factor of 5 $y = \sqrt[3]{3x}$ horizontal compression by a factor of $\frac{1}{3}$
Reflection	$-f(x)$ $f(-x)$	$y = -\sqrt[3]{x}$ across *x*-axis $y = \sqrt[3]{-x}$ across *y*-axis

For the function $f(x) = a\sqrt[3]{x - h} + k$, (h, k) is the graph's point of symmetry. Use the values of a, h, and k to draw each graph. Note that the point $(1, 1)$ on the graph of the parent function becomes the point $(1 + h, a + k)$ on the graph of the given function.

For the function $f(x) = \sqrt[3]{\frac{1}{b}(x - h)} + k$, (h, k) remains the graph's point of symmetry. Note that the point $(1, 1)$ on the graph of the parent function becomes the point $(b + h, 1 + k)$ on the graph of the given function.

Example 1 Graph the cube root functions.

Ⓐ Graph $g(x) = 2\sqrt[3]{x - 3} + 5$.

The transformations of the graph of $f(x) = \sqrt[3]{x}$ that produce the graph of $g(x)$ are:

- a vertical stretch by a factor of 2
- a translation of 3 units to the right and 5 units up

Choose points on $f(x) = \sqrt[3]{x}$ and find the transformed corresponding points on $g(x) = 2\sqrt[3]{x - 3} + 5$.

Graph $g(x) = 2\sqrt[3]{x - 3} + 5$ using the transformed points.

(See the table and graph on the next page.)

$f(x) = \sqrt[3]{x}$	$g(x) = 2\sqrt[3]{x-3} + 5$
(−8, −2)	(−5, 1)
(−1, −1)	(2, 3)
(0, 0)	(3, 5)
(1, 1)	(4, 7)
(8, 2)	(11, 9)

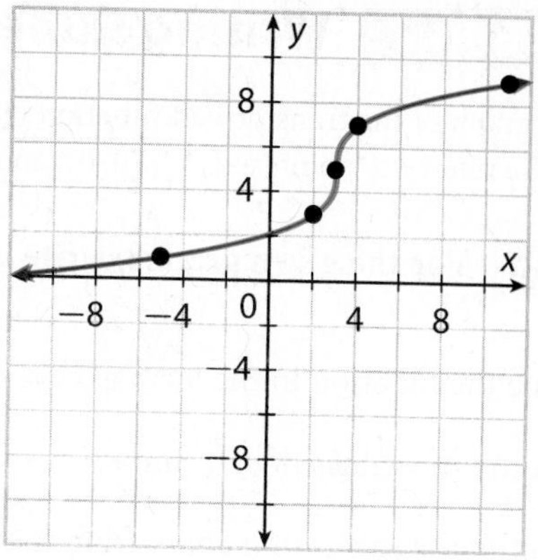

(B) Graph $g(x) = \sqrt[3]{\frac{1}{2}(x - 10)} + 4$.

The transformations of the graph of $f(x) = \sqrt[3]{x}$ that produce the graph of $g(x)$ are:

- a horizontal stretch by a factor of 2
- a translation of 10 units to the right and 4 units up

Choose points on $f(x) = \sqrt[3]{x}$ and find the transformed corresponding points on $g(x) = \sqrt[3]{\frac{1}{2}(x - 10)} + 4$.

Graph $g(x) = \sqrt[3]{\frac{1}{2}(x - 10)} + 4$ using the transformed points.

$f(x) = \sqrt[3]{x}$	$g(x) = \sqrt[3]{\frac{1}{2}(x - 10)} + 4$
(−8, −2)	(−6, 2)
(−1, −1)	(8, 3)
(0, 0)	(10, 4)
(1, 1)	(12, 5)
(8, 2)	(26, 6)

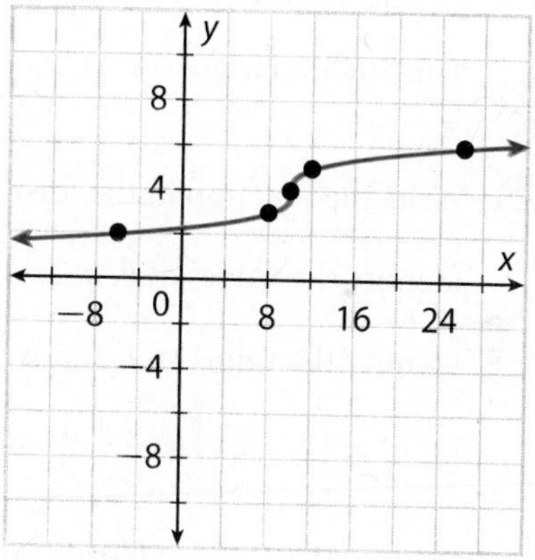

Your Turn

Graph the cube root function.

2. Graph $g(x) = \sqrt[3]{x - 3} + 6$.

$f(x) = \sqrt[3]{x}$	$g(x) = \sqrt[3]{x - 3} + 6$
(−8, −2)	?
(−1, −1)	?
(0, 0)	?
(1, 1)	?
(8, 2)	?

Explain 2 Writing Cube Root Functions

Given the graph of the transformed function $g(x) = a\sqrt[3]{\frac{1}{b}(x - h)} + k$, you can determine the values of the parameters by using the reference points $(-1, 1)$, $(0, 0)$, and $(1, 1)$ that you used to graph $g(x)$ in the previous example.

Example 2 **For the given graphs, write a cube root function.**

Ⓐ Write the function in the form $g(x) = a\sqrt[3]{x - h} + k$.

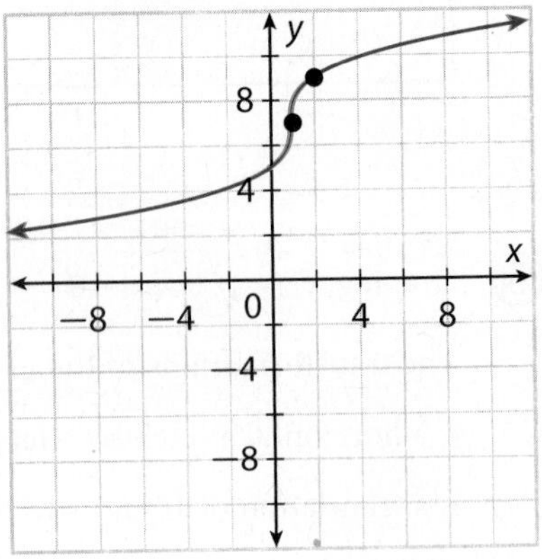

Identify the values of a, h, and k.

Identify the values of h and k from the point of symmetry.

$(h, k) = (1, 7)$, so $h = 1$ and $k = 7$.

Identify the value of a from either of the other two reference points $(-1, 1)$ or $(1, 1)$.

The reference point $(1, 1)$ has general coordinates $(h + 1, a + k)$. Substituting 1 for h and 7 for k and setting the general coordinates equal to the actual coordinates gives this result:

$(h + 1, a + k) = (2, a + 7) = (2, 9)$, so $a = 2$.

$a = 2$ $\quad\quad$ $h = 1$ $\quad\quad$ $k = 7$

The function is $g(x) = 2\sqrt[3]{x - 1} + 7$.

Ⓑ Write the function in the form $g(x) = \sqrt[3]{\frac{1}{b}(x - h)} + k$.

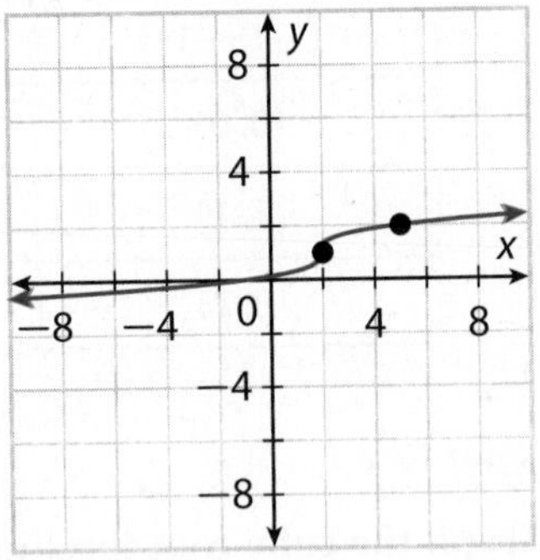

Identify the values of b, h, and k.

Identify the values of h and k from the point of symmetry.

$(h, k) = (2, \boxed{1})$ so $h = 2$ and $k = \boxed{1}$.

Identify the value of b from either of the other two reference points.

The rightmost reference point has general coordinates $(b + h, 1 + k)$. Substituting 2 for h and 1 for k and setting the general coordinates equal to the actual coordinates gives this result:

$(b + h, 1 + \boxed{1}) = (b + 2, \boxed{2}) = (5, 2)$, so $b = \boxed{3}$.

$b = \boxed{3}$ $\quad\quad$ $h = \boxed{2}$ $\quad\quad$ $k = \boxed{1}$

The function is $g(x) = \sqrt[3]{\frac{1}{3}(x - 2)} + 1$.

Your Turn

For the given graphs, write a cube root function.

3. Write the function in the form $g(x) = a\sqrt[3]{x - h} + k$.

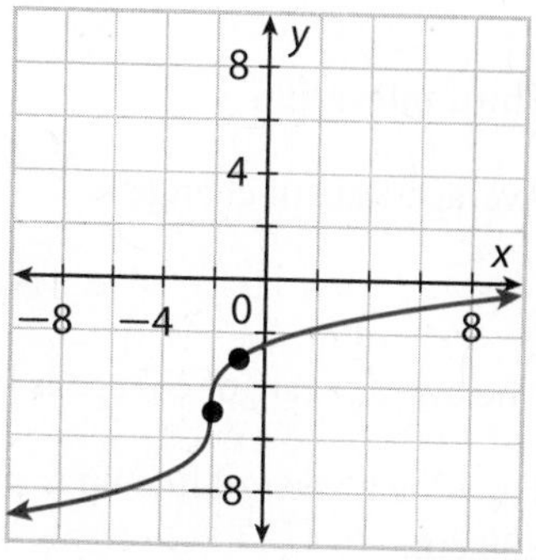

4. Write the function in the form $g(x) = \sqrt[3]{\frac{1}{b}(x - h)} + k$.

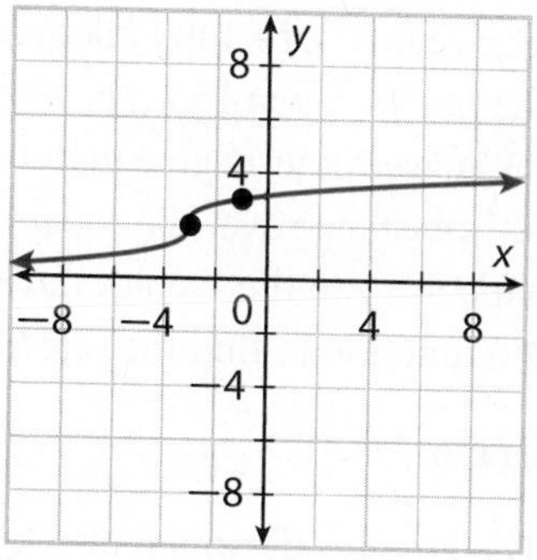

Explain 3 Modeling with Cube Root Functions

You can use cube root functions to model real-world situations.

Example 3

Ⓐ The shoulder height h (in centimeters) of a particular elephant is modeled by the function $h(t) = 62.1\sqrt[3]{t} + 76$, where t is the age (in years) of the elephant. Graph the function and examine its average rate of change over the equal t-intervals $(0, 20)$, $(20, 40)$, and $(40, 60)$. What is happening to the average rate of change as the t-values of the intervals increase? Use the graph to find the height when $t = 35$.

Graph $h(t) = 62.1\sqrt[3]{t} + 76$.

The graph is the graph of $f(x) = \sqrt[3]{x}$ translated up 76 and stretched vertically by a factor of 62.1. Graph the transformed points $(0, 76)$, $(8, 200.2)$, $(27, 262.3)$, and $(64, 324.4)$. Connect the points with a smooth curve.

First interval:

$$\text{Average Rate of change} \approx \frac{244.6 - 76}{20 - 0}$$

$$= 8.43$$

Second interval:

Average Rate of change $\approx \dfrac{288.4 - 244.6}{40 - 20}$

$= 2.19$

Third interval:

Average Rate of change $\approx \dfrac{319.1 - 288.4}{60 - 40}$

$= 1.54$

The average rate of change is becoming less.

Drawing a vertical line up from 35 gives a value of about 280 cm.

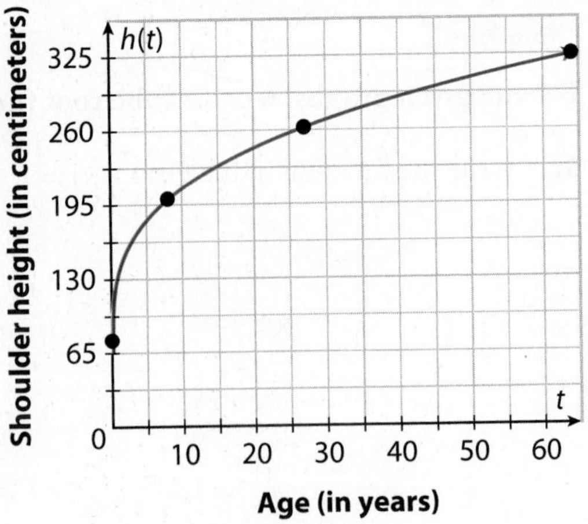

(B) The velocity of a 1400-kilogram car at the end of a 400-meter run is modeled by the function $v = 15.2\sqrt[3]{p}$, where v is the velocity in kilometers per hour and p is the power of its engine in horsepower. Graph the function and examine its average rate of change over the equal p-intervals $(0, 60)$, $(60, 120)$, and $(120, 180)$. What is happening to the average rate of change as the p-values of the intervals increase? Use the function to find the velocity when p is 100 horsepower.

Graph $v = 15.2\sqrt[3]{p}$.

The graph is the graph of $f(x) = \sqrt[3]{x}$ stretched vertically by a factor of 15.2. Graph the transformed points $(0, 0)$, $(8, 30.4)$, $(27, 45.6)$, $(64, 60.8)$, $(125, 76)$, and $(216, 91.2)$.

Connect the points with a smooth curve.

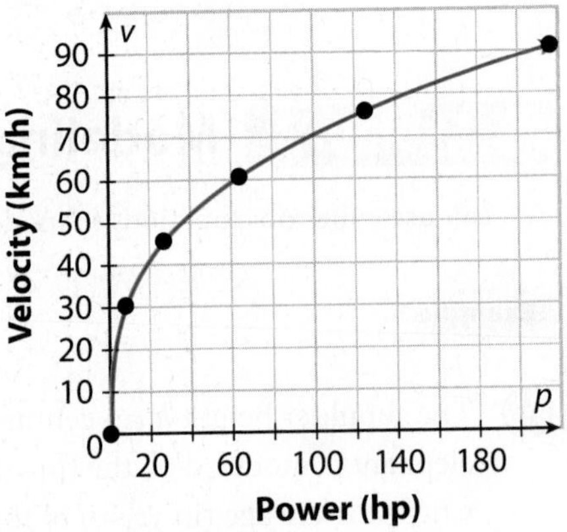

The average rate of change over the interval $(0, 60)$

is $\dfrac{59.5 - 0}{60 - 0}$ which is about 0.99.

The average rate of change over the interval $(60, 120)$

is $\dfrac{75.0 - 59.5}{120 - 60}$ which is about 0.26.

The average rate of change over the interval $(120, 180)$

is $\dfrac{85.8 - 75.0}{180 - 120}$ which is about 0.18.

The average rate of change is becoming less.

Substitute $p = 100$ in the function.

$v = 15.2\sqrt[3]{p}$

$v = 15.2\sqrt[3]{\boxed{100}}$

$v \approx 15.2\left(\boxed{4.64}\right)$

$v \approx \boxed{70.5}$

The velocity is about 70.5 km/h.

Your Turn

5. The fetch is the length of water over which the wind is blowing in a certain direction. The function $s(f) = 7.1\sqrt[3]{f}$, relates the speed of the wind s in kilometers per hour to the fetch f in kilometers. Graph the function and examine its average rate of change over the intervals $(20, 80)$, $(80, 140)$, and $(140, 200)$. What is happening to the average rate of change as the f-values of the intervals increase? Use the function to find the speed of the wind when $f = 64$.

Elaborate

6. **Discussion** Why is the domain of $f(x) = \sqrt[3]{x}$ all real numbers?

7. Identify which transformations (stretches or compressions, reflections, and translations) of $f(x) = \sqrt[3]{x}$ change the following attributes of the function.

   a. Location of the point of symmetry

   b. Symmetry about a point

8. **Essential Question Check-In** How do parameters a, b, h, and k effect the graphs of $f(x) = a\sqrt[3]{(x - h)} + k$ and $g(x) = \sqrt[3]{\frac{1}{b}(x - h)} + k$?

Evaluate: Homework and Practice

Personal Math Trainer

- Online Homework
- Hints and Help
- Extra Practice

1. Graph the function $g(x) = \sqrt[3]{x} + 3$. Identify the domain and range of the function.

2. Graph the function $g(x) = \sqrt[3]{x} - 5$. Identify the domain and range of the function.

Describe how the graph of the function compares to the graph of $f(x) = \sqrt[3]{x}$.

3. $g(x) = \sqrt[3]{x} + 6$

4. $g(x) = \sqrt[3]{x - 5}$

5. $g(x) = \frac{1}{3}\sqrt[3]{-x}$

6. $g(x) = \sqrt[3]{5x}$

7. $g(x) = -2\sqrt[3]{x} + 3$

8. $g(x) = \sqrt[3]{x + 4} - 3$

Graph the cube root functions.

9. $g(x) = 3\sqrt[3]{x+4}$

10. $g(x) = 2\sqrt[3]{x} + 3$

11. $g(x) = \sqrt[3]{x-3} + 2$

For the given graphs, write a cube root function.

12. Write the function in the form $g(x) = a\sqrt[3]{x-h} + k$.

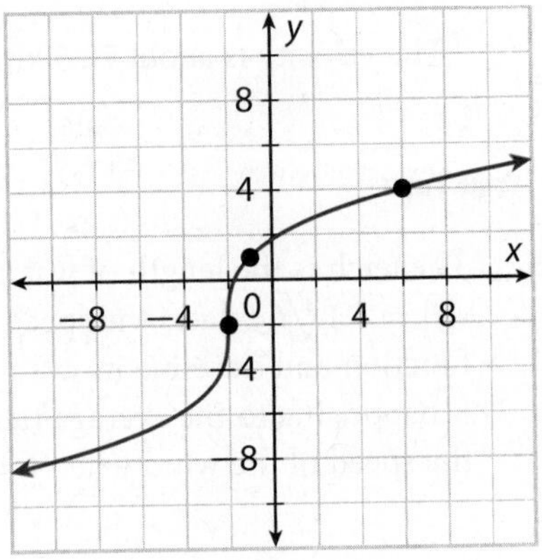

13. Write the function in the form $g(x) = a\sqrt[3]{x-h} + k$.

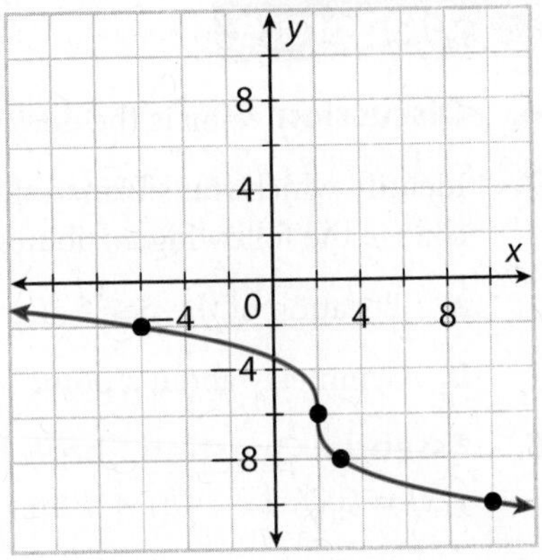

14. Write the function in the form $g(x) = \sqrt[3]{\frac{1}{b}(x-h)} + k$.

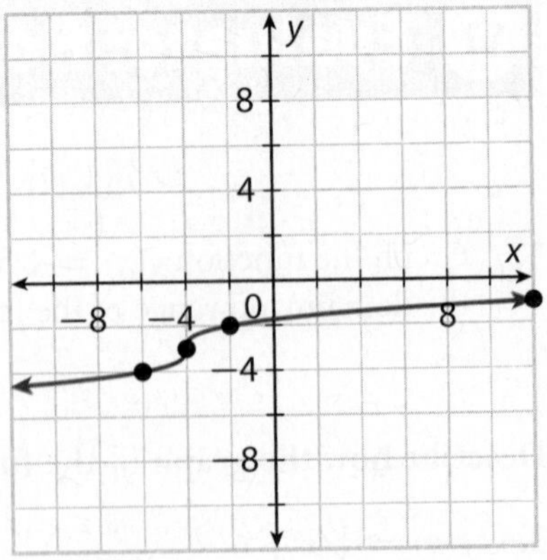

15. The length of the side of a cube is modeled by $s = \sqrt[3]{V}$. Graph the function. Use the graph to find s when $V = 48$.

16. The radius of a stainless steel ball, in centimeters, can be modeled by $r(m) = 0.31\sqrt[3]{m}$, where m is the mass of the ball in grams. Use the function to find r when $m = 125$.

17. Describe the steps for graphing $g(x) = \sqrt[3]{x+8} - 11$.

18. **Modeling** Write a situation that can be modeled by a cube root function. Give the function.

19. Find the y-intercept for the function $y = a\sqrt[3]{x-h} + k$.

20. Find the x-intercept for the function $y = a\sqrt[3]{x-h} + k$.

21. Describe the translation(s) used to get $g(x) = \sqrt[3]{x-9} + 12$ from $f(x) = \sqrt[3]{x}$. Select all that apply.

A. translated 9 units right

B. translated 9 units left

C. translated 9 units up

D. translated 9 units down

E. translated 12 units right

F. translated 12 units left

G. translated 12 units up

H. translated 12 units down

H.O.T. Focus on Higher Order Thinking

22. **Explain the Error** Tim says that to graph $g(x) = \sqrt[3]{x-6} + 3$, you need to translate the graph of $f(x) = \sqrt[3]{x}$ 6 units to the left and then 3 units up. What mistake did he make?

23. **Communicate Mathematical Ideas** Why does the square root function have a restricted domain but the cube root function does not?

24. **Justify Reasoning** Does a horizontal translation and a vertical translation of the function $f(x) = \sqrt[3]{x}$ affect the function's domain or range? Explain.

Lesson Performance Task

The side length of a 243-gram copper cube is 3 centimeters. Use this information to write a model for the radius of a copper sphere as a function of its mass. Then, find the radius of a copper sphere with a mass of 50 grams. How would changing the material affect the function?

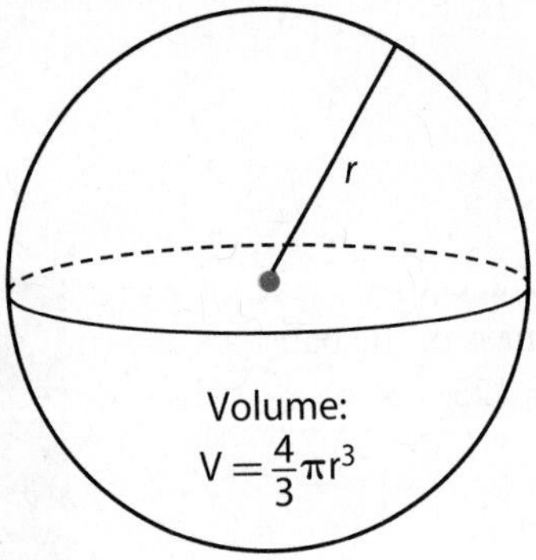

Radical Functions

Essential Question: How can you use radical functions to solve real-world problems?

Key Vocabulary
cube root function *(función de raíz cúbica)*
index *(índice)*
inverse function *(función inversa)*
square root function *(función de raíz cuadrada)*

KEY EXAMPLE *(Lesson 10.1)*

Find the inverse function $f^{-1}(x)$ for $f(x) = 2x^3 + 10$.

Replace $f(x)$ with y. $y = 2x^3 + 10$

Solve for x^3. $\frac{y - 10}{2} = x^3$

Take the cube root. $\sqrt[3]{\frac{y - 10}{2}} = x$

Switch x and y. $y = \sqrt[3]{\frac{x - 10}{2}}$

Replace y with $f^{-1}(x)$. $f^{-1}(x) = \sqrt[3]{\frac{x - 10}{2}}$

KEY EXAMPLE *(Lesson 10.2)*

Graph $y = -\sqrt{x - 3} + 2$. Describe the domain and range.

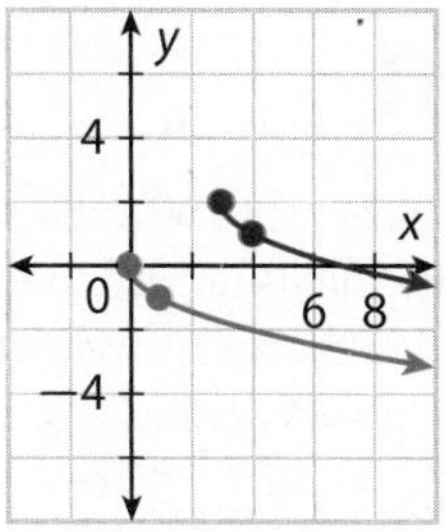

Sketch the graph of $y = -\sqrt{x}$.

It begins at the origin and passes through $(1, -1)$.

For $y = -\sqrt{x - 3} + 2$, $h = 3$ and $k = 2$.
Shift the graph of $y = -\sqrt{x}$ right 3 units and up 2 units. The graph begins at $(3, 2)$ and passes through $(4, 1)$.

Domain: $\{x \mid x \geq 3\}$ Range: $\{y \mid y \leq 2\}$

KEY EXAMPLE *(Lesson 10.3)*

Graph $y = \sqrt[3]{x + 2} - 4$.

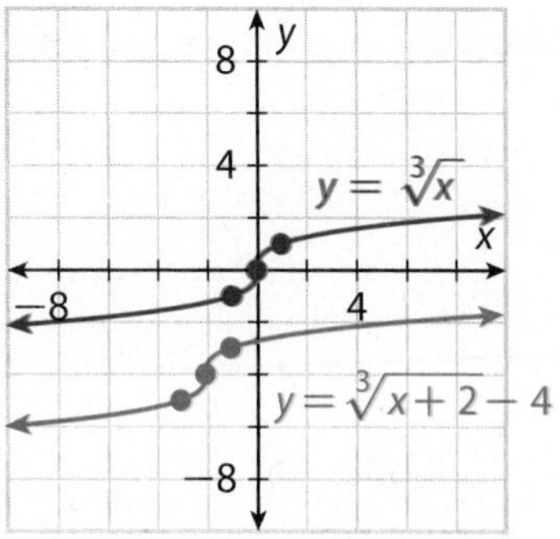

Sketch the graph of $y = \sqrt[3]{x}$.

It passes through $(-1, -1)$, $(0, 0)$, and $(1, 1)$.

For $y = \sqrt[3]{x + 2} - 4$, $h = -2$ and $k = -4$.
Shift the graph of $y = \sqrt[3]{x}$ left 2 units and down 4 units. The graph passes through $(-3, -5)$, $(-2, -4)$, and $(-1, -3)$.

EXERCISES

Find the inverse of each function. Restrict the domain where necessary. *(Lesson 10.1)*

1. $f(x) = 16x^2$

2. $f(x) = x^3 - 20$

Identify the transformations of the graph $f(x) = \sqrt{x}$ that produce the graph of the function. *(Lesson 10.2)*

3. $g(x) = -\sqrt{4x}$

4. $h(x) = \frac{1}{2}\sqrt{x} + 1$

Identify the transformations of the graph $f(x) = \sqrt[3]{x}$ that produce the graph of the function. *(Lesson 10.3)*

5. $g(x) = 4\sqrt[3]{x}$

6. $h(x) = \sqrt[3]{x - 5} + 3$

MODULE PERFORMANCE TASK

We Have Liftoff!

A rocket scientist is designing a rocket to visit the planets in the solar system. The velocity that is needed to escape a planet's gravitational pull is called the escape velocity. The escape velocity depends on the planet's radius and its mass, according to the equation $V_{escape} = \sqrt{2gR}$, where R is the radius and g is the gravitational constant for the particular planet. The rocket's maximum velocity is exactly double Earth's escape velocity. For which planets will the rocket have enough velocity to escape the planet's gravity?

Planet	Radius (m)	Mass (kg)	g (m/s^2)
Mercury	2.43×10^6	3.20×10^{23}	3.61
Venus	6.07×10^6	4.88×10^{24}	8.83
Mars	3.38×10^6	6.42×10^{23}	3.75
Jupiter	6.98×10^7	1.90×10^{27}	26.0
Saturn	5.82×10^7	5.68×10^{26}	11.2
Uranus	2.35×10^7	8.68×10^{25}	10.5
Neptune	2.27×10^7	1.03×10^{26}	13.3

Begin by listing any additional information you will need to solve the problem. Then complete the task. Be sure to write down all your data and assumptions. Then use graphs, numbers, words, or algebra to explain how you reached your conclusions.

Ready to Go On?

10.1–10.3 Radical Functions

Personal Math Trainer

- Online Homework
- Hints and Help
- Extra Practice

Find the inverse of each function. State any restrictions on the domain. *(Lesson 10.1)*

1. $f(x) = x^2 + 9$

2. $f(x) = -7x^3$

3. $f(x) = -2x^3 + 1$

4. $f(x) = 5x^2 + 3$

Identify the transformations of the graph $f(x) = \sqrt{x}$ or $h(x) = \sqrt[3]{x}$ that produce the graph of the function. *(Lessons 10.2, 10.3)*

5. $g(x) = \frac{1}{3}\sqrt{x - 5} - 4$

6. $g(x) = \sqrt[3]{4x} + 3$

7. $g(x) = \sqrt{x - 4} - 1$

8. $g(x) = \sqrt[3]{7x + 10}$

ESSENTIAL QUESTION

9. How do you use a parent square root or cube root function to graph a transformation of the function? *(Lessons 10.2, 10.3)*

MODULE 10
MIXED REVIEW

Assessment Readiness

1. Tell whether each equation is the inverse of $f(x) = x^3 - 16$.

A. $f^{-1}(x) = \sqrt[3]{x - 16}$

B. $f^{-1}(x) = \sqrt[3]{x + 16}$

C. $f^{-1}(x) = \sqrt[3]{x} + 16$

2. Consider the graphed function. Determine if each statement is True or False.

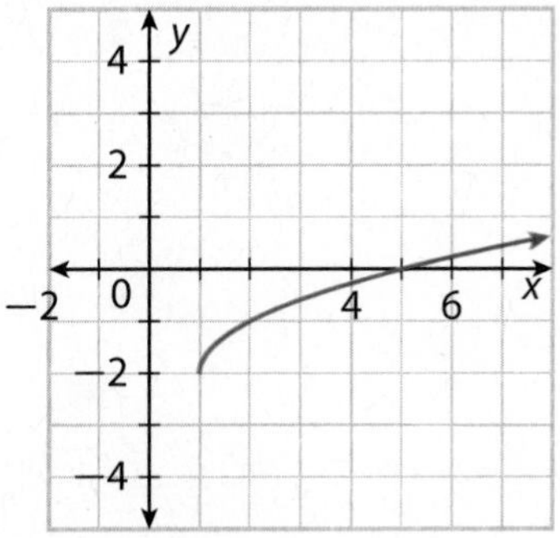

A. The equation for the function is $y = \sqrt{x - 1} - 2$.

B. The function has exactly one y-intercept.

C. The range of the function is $y \leq -2$.

3. A plane's average speed when flying from one city to another is 550 mi/h and is 430 mi/h on the return flight. To the nearest mile per hour, what is the plane's average speed for the entire trip? Explain your answer.

4. The kinetic energy E (in joules) of a 1250-kilogram compact car is given by the equation $E = 625s^2$, where s is the speed of the car (in meters per second). Write an inverse model that gives the speed of the car as a function of its kinetic energy. If the kinetic energy doubles, will the speed double? Explain why or why not.

Radical Expressions and Equations

MODULE 11

Essential Question: How can you use radical expressions and equations to solve real-world problems?

REAL WORLD VIDEO
A field biologist studying howler monkeys can use radical functions to calculate sound intensity, which decreases faster than linearly with distance.

MODULE PERFORMANCE TASK PREVIEW

Don't Disturb the Neighbors!

The loudness of a sound is subjective and depends on the listener's sensitivity to the frequencies of the sound waves. An objective measure, sound intensity, can be used to measure sounds. Sound intensity decreases the farther you get from the source of a sound. How far away do your neighbors have to be so that a loud band does not bother them? Let's find out!

Are YOU Ready?

Complete these exercises to review skills you will need for this module.

Personal Math Trainer

- Online Homework
- Hints and Help
- Extra Practice

Exponents

Example 1 Simplify $(x^3)^2 + x \cdot x^3 + 3x^4$.

$$(x^3)^2 + x \cdot x^3 + 3x^4 = (x^3)(x^3) + x \cdot x^3 + 3x^4 \quad \text{Start with the raised power.}$$

$$= x^{3+3} + x^{1+3} + 3x^4 \quad \text{Add exponents.}$$

$$= x^6 + x^4 + 3x^4 \quad \text{Simplify.}$$

$$= x^6 + 4x^4 \quad \text{Add like terms.}$$

Simplify each expression.

1. $(-x^5)^2$ **2.** $(3x^2)^5 - x^4 \cdot x^2$ **3.** $3x(2x)^2$

Inverse Linear Functions

Example 2 Write the inverse function of $y = 10x - 4$.

$$y + 4 = 10x \quad \text{Isolate the } x\text{-term.}$$

$$\frac{y+4}{10} = \frac{10x}{10} \quad \text{Divide.}$$

The inverse function of $y = 10x - 4$ is $y = \dfrac{x+4}{10}$.

Write the inverse function.

4. $y = 3x + 1$ **5.** $y = 2(x - 9)$ **6.** $y = \frac{1}{4}(3x + 4)$

Rational and Radical Exponents

Example 3 Write $\sqrt[9]{a^3}$ using a rational exponent.

$$\sqrt[9]{a^3} = a^{\frac{3}{9}} = a^{\frac{1}{3}}$$

Write each radical expression using a rational exponent.

7. $\sqrt[2]{x^5}$ **8.** $\sqrt[4]{a^2 b}$ **9.** $\sqrt[4]{p^8 q^2}$

11.1 Radical Expressions and Rational Exponents

Essential Question: How are rational exponents related to radicals and roots?

Resource Locker

Explore Defining Rational Exponents in Terms of Roots

Remember that a number a is an nth root of a number b if $a^n = b$. As you know, a square root is indicated by $\sqrt{}$ and a cube root by $\sqrt[3]{}$. In general, the nth root of a real number a is indicated by $\sqrt[n]{a}$, where n is the **index** of the radical and a is the radicand. (Note that when a number has more than one real root, the radical sign indicates only the principal, or positive, root.)

A *rational exponent* is an exponent that can be expressed as $\frac{m}{n}$, where m is an integer and n is a natural number. You can use the definition of a root and properties of equality and exponents to explore how to express roots using rational exponents.

(A) How can you express a square root using an exponent? That is, if $\sqrt{a} = a^m$, what is m?

Given $\quad \sqrt{a} = a^m$

Square both sides. $\quad (\sqrt{a})^2 = (a^m)^2$

Definition of square root $\quad ? = (a^m)^2$

Power of a power property $\quad a = a^{?}$

Definition of first power $\quad a^{?} = a^{2m}$

The bases are the same, so equate exponents. $\quad ? = ?$

Solve. $\quad m = ?$

So, $\quad \sqrt{a} = a^{?}$.

(B) How can you express a cube root using an exponent? That is, if $\sqrt[3]{a} = a^m$, what is m?

Given $\quad \sqrt[3]{a} = a^m$

Cube both sides. $\quad (\sqrt{a})^3 = (a^m)^3$

Definition of cube root $\quad ? = ?$

Power of a power property ? = ?

Definition of first power ? = ?

The bases are the same, so equate exponents. ? = ?

Solve. $m =$?

So, $\sqrt[3]{a} = a^{?}$.

Reflect

1. **Discussion** Examine the reasoning in Steps A and B. Can you apply the same reasoning for any *n*th root, $\sqrt[n]{a}$, where *n* is a natural number? Explain. What can you conclude?
2. For a positive number *a*, under what condition on *n* will there be only one real *n*th root? two real *n*th roots? Explain.
3. For a negative number *a*, under what condition on *n* will there be no real *n*th roots? one real *n*th root? Explain.

Explain 1 Translating Between Radical Expressions and Rational Exponents

In the Explore, you found that a rational exponent $\frac{m}{n}$ with $m = 1$ represents an *n*th root, or that $a^{\frac{1}{n}} = \sqrt[n]{a}$ for positive values of *a*. This is also true for negative values of *a* when the index is odd. When $m \neq 1$, you can think of the numerator *m* as the power and the denominator *n* as the root. The following ways of expressing the exponent $\frac{m}{n}$ are equivalent.

Rational Exponents

For any natural number *n*, integer *m*, and real number *a* when the *n*th root of *a* is real:

Words	Numbers	Algebra
The exponent $\frac{m}{n}$ indicates the *m*th power of the *n*th root of a quantity.	$27^{\frac{2}{3}} = (\sqrt[3]{27})^2 = 3^2 = 9$	$a^{\frac{m}{n}} = (\sqrt[n]{a})^m$
The exponent $\frac{m}{n}$ indicates the *n*th root of the *m*th power of a quantity.	$4^{\frac{3}{2}} = \sqrt{4^3} = \sqrt{64} = 8$	$a^{\frac{m}{n}} = \sqrt[n]{a^m}$

Notice that you can evaluate each example in the "Numbers" column using the equivalent definition.

$$27^{\frac{2}{3}} = \sqrt[3]{27^2} = \sqrt[3]{729} = 9 \qquad 4^{\frac{3}{2}} = (\sqrt{4})^3 = 2^3 = 8$$

Example 1 **Translate radical expressions into expressions with rational exponents, and vice versa. Simplify numerical expressions when possible. Assume all variables are positive.**

(A) **a.** $(-125)^{\frac{4}{3}}$ **b.** $x^{\frac{11}{8}}$ **c.** $\sqrt[5]{6^4}$ **d.** $\sqrt[4]{x^3}$

a. $(-125)^{\frac{4}{3}} = \left(\sqrt[3]{-125}\right)^4 = (-5)^4 = 625$

b. $x^{11/8} = \sqrt[8]{x^{11}}$ or $\left(\sqrt[8]{x}\right)^{11}$

c. $\sqrt[5]{6^4} = 6^{\frac{4}{5}}$

d. $\sqrt[4]{x^3} = x^{\frac{3}{4}}$

(B) **a.** $\left(\frac{81}{16}\right)^{\frac{3}{4}}$ **b.** $(xy)^{\frac{5}{3}}$ **c.** $\sqrt[3]{11^6}$ **d.** $\sqrt[3]{\left(\frac{2x}{y}\right)^5}$

a. $\left(\frac{81}{16}\right)^{\frac{3}{4}} = \left(\sqrt[4]{\frac{81}{16}}\right)^3 = \left(\boxed{\frac{3}{2}}\right)^3 = \boxed{\frac{27}{8}}$

b. $(xy)^{\frac{5}{3}} = \sqrt[3]{(xy)^5}$ or $\left(\sqrt[3]{xy}\right)^5$

c. $\sqrt[3]{11^6} = 11^{\boxed{\frac{6}{3}}} = 11^{\boxed{2}} = \boxed{121}$

d. $\sqrt[3]{\left(\frac{2x}{y}\right)^5} = \left(\frac{2x}{y}\right)^{\boxed{\frac{5}{3}}}$

Reflect

4. How can you use a calculator to show that evaluating $0.001728^{\frac{4}{3}}$ as a power of a root and as a root of a power are equivalent methods?

Your Turn

5. Translate radical expressions into expressions with rational exponents, and vice versa. Simplify numerical expressions when possible. Assume all variables are positive.

a. $\left(-\frac{32}{243}\right)^{\frac{2}{5}}$

b. $(3y)^{\frac{b}{c}}$

c. $\sqrt[3]{0.5^9}$

d. $\left(\sqrt[u]{st}\right)^v$

Explain 2 Modeling with Power Functions

The following functions all involve a given power of a variable.

$A = \pi r^2$ (area of a circle)

$V = \frac{4}{3}\pi r^3$ (volume of a sphere)

$T = 1.11 \cdot L^{\frac{1}{2}}$ (the time T in seconds for a pendulum of length L feet to complete one back-and-forth swing)

These are all examples of *power functions.* A power function has the form $y = ax^b$ where a is a real number and b is a rational number.

Example 2 **Solve each problem by modeling with power functions.**

(A) **Biology** The function $R = 73.3\sqrt[4]{M^3}$, known as Kleiber's law, relates the basal metabolic rate R in Calories per day burned and the body mass M of a mammal in kilograms. The table shows typical body masses for some members of the cat family.

Typical Body Mass

Animal	Mass (kg)
House cat	4.5
Cheetah	55
Lion	170

a. Rewrite the formula with a rational exponent.

b. What is the value of R for a cheetah to the nearest 50 Calories?

c. From the table, the mass of the lion is about 38 times that of the house cat. Is the lion's metabolic rate more or less than 38 times the cat's rate? Explain.

a. Because $\sqrt[n]{a^m} = a^{\frac{m}{n}}$, $\sqrt[4]{M^3} = M^{\frac{3}{4}}$, so the formula is $R = 73.3M^{\frac{3}{4}}$.

b. Substitute 55 for M in the formula and use a calculator.

The cheetah's metabolic rate is about 1500 Calories.

c. Less; find the ratio of R for the lion to R for the house cat.

$$\frac{73.3(170)^{\frac{3}{4}}}{73.3(4.5)^{\frac{3}{4}}} = \frac{170^{\frac{3}{4}}}{4.5^{\frac{3}{4}}} \approx \frac{47.1}{3.1} \approx 15$$

The metabolic rate for the lion is only about 15 times that of the house cat.

(B) The function $h(m) = 241m^{-\frac{1}{4}}$ models an animal's approximate resting heart rate h in beats per minute given its mass m in kilograms.

a. A common shrew has a mass of only about 0.01 kg. To the nearest 10, what is the model's estimate for this shrew's resting heart rate?

b. What is the model's estimate for the resting heart rate of an American elk with a mass of 300 kg?

c. Two animal species differ in mass by a multiple of 10. According to the model, about what percent of the smaller animal's resting heart rate would you expect the larger animal's resting heart rate to be?

a. Substitute 0.01 for m in the formula and use a calculator.

$$h(m) = 241\left(\boxed{0.01}\right)^{-\frac{1}{4}} \approx \boxed{760}$$

The model estimates the shrew's resting heart rate to be about 760 beats per minute.

b. Substitute 300 for m in the formula and use a calculator.

$$h(m) = 241\left(\boxed{300}\right)^{-\frac{1}{4}} \approx \boxed{60}$$

The model estimates the elk's resting heart rate to be about 60 beats per minute.

c. Find the ratio of $h(m)$ for the larger animal to the smaller animal. Let 1 represent the mass of the smaller animal.

$$\frac{241 \cdot \boxed{10}^{-\frac{1}{4}}}{241 \cdot 1^{-\frac{1}{4}}} = \boxed{10}^{-\frac{1}{4}} = \frac{1}{10^{\boxed{\frac{1}{4}}}} \approx \boxed{0.56}$$

You would expect the larger animal's resting heart rate to be about 56% of the smaller animal's resting heart rate.

Reflect

6. What is the difference between a power function and an exponential function?

7. In Part B, the exponent is negative. Are the results consistent with the meaning of a negative exponent that you learned for integers? Explain.

Your Turn

8. Use Kleiber's law from Part A.

a. Find the basal metabolic rate for a 170 kilogram lion to the nearest 50 Calories. Then find the formula's prediction for a 70 kilogram human.

b. Use your metabolic rate result for the lion to find what the basal metabolic rate for a 70 kilogram human *would* be *if* metabolic rate and mass were directly proportional. Compare the result to the result from Part a.

Elaborate

9. Explain how can you use a radical to write and evaluate the power $4^{2.5}$.

10. When $y = kx$ for some constant k, y varies directly as x. When $y = kx^2$, y varies directly as the square of x; and when $y = k\sqrt{x}$, y varies directly as the square root of x. How could you express the relationship $y = kx^{\frac{3}{5}}$ for a constant k?

11. Essential Question Check-In Which of the following are true? Explain.

- To evaluate an expression of the form $a^{\frac{m}{n}}$, first find the nth root of a. Then raise the result to the mth power.
- To evaluate an expression of the form $a^{\frac{m}{n}}$, first find the mth power of a. Then find the nth root of the result.

Evaluate: Homework and Practice

Personal Math Trainer

- Online Homework
- Hints and Help
- Extra Practice

Translate expressions with rational exponents into radical expressions. Simplify numerical expressions when possible. Assume all variables are positive.

1. $64^{\frac{5}{3}}$

2. $x^{\frac{p}{q}}$

3. $(-512)^{\frac{2}{3}}$

4. $3^{\frac{2}{7}}$

5. $-\left(\frac{729}{64}\right)^{\frac{5}{6}}$

6. $0.125^{\frac{4}{3}}$

7. $vw^{\frac{2}{3}}$

8. $(-32)^{0.6}$

Translate radical expressions into expressions with rational exponents. Simplify numerical expressions when possible. Assume all variables are positive.

9. $\sqrt[7]{y^5}$

10. $\sqrt[7]{(-6)^6}$

11. $\sqrt[3]{3^{15}}$

12. $\sqrt[4]{(\pi z)^3}$

13. $\sqrt[6]{(bcd)^4}$

14. $\sqrt{6^6}$

15. $\sqrt[5]{32^2}$

16. $\sqrt[3]{\left(\frac{4}{x}\right)^9}$

17. Music Frets are small metal bars positioned across the neck of a guitar so that the guitar can produce the notes of a specific scale. To find the distance a fret should be placed from the bridge, multiply the length of the string by $2^{-\frac{n}{12}}$, where n is the number of notes higher than the string's root note. Where should a fret be placed to produce a F note on a B string (6 notes higher) given that the length of the string is 64 cm?

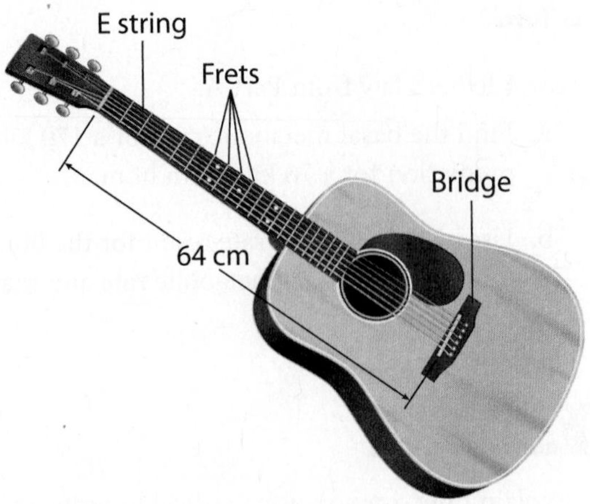

18. **Meteorology** The function $W = 35.74 + 0.6215T - 35.75V^{\frac{4}{25}} + 0.4275TV^{\frac{4}{25}}$ relates the windchill temperature W to the air temperature T in degrees Fahrenheit and the wind speed V in miles per hour. Use a calculator to find the wind chill temperature to the nearest degree when the air temperature is 28 °F and the wind speed is 35 miles per hour.

19. **Astronomy** New stars can form inside a cloud of interstellar gas when a cloud fragment, or *clump*, has a mass M greater than the *Jean's mass* M_J. The Jean's mass is $M_J = 100n^{-\frac{1}{2}}(T + 273)^{\frac{3}{2}}$ where n is the number of gas molecules per cubic centimeter and T is the gas temperature in degrees Celsius. A gas clump has $M = 137$, $n = 1000$, and $T = -263$. Will the clump form a star? Justify your answer.

20. **Urban geography** The total wages W in a metropolitan area compared to its total population p can be approximated by a power function of the form $W = a \cdot p^{\frac{9}{8}}$ where a is a constant. About how many times as great does the model predict the total earnings for a metropolitan area with 3,000,000 people will be as compared to a metropolitan area with a population of 750,000?

21. Which statement is true?

A. In the expression $8x^{\frac{3}{4}}$, $8x$ is the radicand.

B. In the expression $(-16)x^{\frac{4}{5}}$, 4 is the index.

C. The expression $1024^{\frac{n}{m}}$ represents the mth root of the nth power of 1024.

D. $50^{-\frac{2}{5}} = -50^{\frac{2}{5}}$

E. $\sqrt{(xy)^3} = xy^{\frac{3}{2}}$

H.O.T. Focus on Higher Order Thinking

22. **Explain the Error** A teacher asked students to evaluate $10^{-\frac{3}{5}}$ using their graphing calculators. The calculator entries of several students are shown below. Which entry will give the incorrect result? Explain.

$10^{(-3/5)}$ $\quad \sqrt[5]{10^{-3}}$ $\quad 10^{-6}$ $\quad 1/10^{5/3}$ $\quad \left(1/10^{1/5}\right)^3$

23. Critical Thinking The graphs of three functions of the form $y = ax^{\frac{m}{n}}$ are shown for a specific value of a, where m and n are natural numbers. What can you conclude about the relationship of m and n for each graph? Explain.

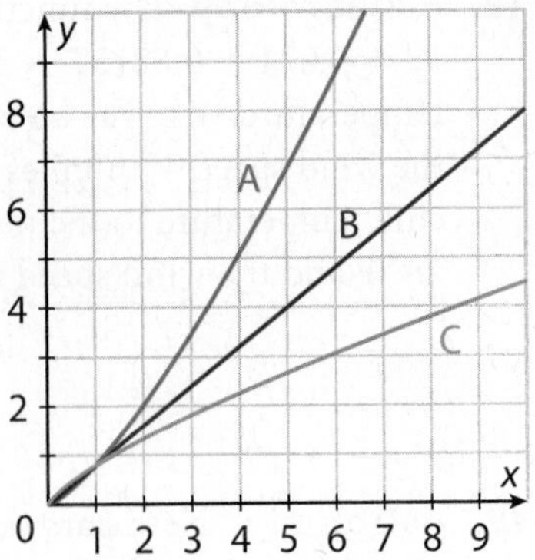

24. Critical Thinking For a negative real number a, under what condition(s) on m and n $(n \neq 0)$ is $a^{\frac{m}{n}}$ a real number? Explain. (Assume $\frac{m}{n}$ is written in simplest form.)

Lesson Performance Task

The formula $W = 35.74 + 0.6215T - 35.75V^{\frac{4}{25}} + 0.4275TV^{\frac{4}{25}}$ relates the wind chill temperature W to the air temperature T in degrees Fahrenheit and the wind speed V in miles per hour. Find the wind chill to the nearest degree when the air temperature is 40 °F and the wind speed is 35 miles per hour. If the wind chill is about 23 °F to the nearest degree when the air temperature is 40 °F, what is the wind speed to the nearest mile per hour?

11.2 Simplifying Radical Expressions

Essential Question: How can you simplify expressions containing rational exponents or radicals involving *n*th roots?

Resource Locker

Explore — Establishing the Properties of Rational Exponents

In previous courses, you have used properties of integer exponents to simplify and evaluate expressions, as shown here for a few simple examples:

$4^2 \cdot 4^3 = 4^{2+3} = 4^5 = 1024$

$(4 \cdot x)^2 = 4^2 \cdot x^2 = 16x^2$

$(4^2)^3 = 4^{2 \cdot 3} = 4^6 = 4096$

$\frac{4^2}{4^3} = 4^{2-3} = 4^{-1} = \frac{1}{4}$

$\left(\frac{4}{x}\right)^3 = \frac{4^3}{x^3} = \frac{64}{x^3}$

Now that you have been introduced to expressions involving rational exponents, you can explore the properties that apply to simplifying them.

(A) Let $a = 64$, $b = 4$, $m = \frac{1}{3}$, and $n = \frac{3}{2}$. Evaluate each expression by substituting and applying exponents individually, as shown.

Expression	Substitute	Simplify	Result
$a^m \cdot a^n$	$64^{\frac{1}{3}} \cdot 64^{\frac{3}{2}}$	$4 \cdot 512$	2048
$(a \cdot b)^n$	$(64 \cdot 4)^{\frac{3}{2}}$	$256^{\frac{3}{2}}$	?
$(a^m)^n$	?	?	?
$\frac{a^n}{a^m}$	?	?	?
$\left(\frac{a}{b}\right)^n$	?	?	?

(B) Complete the table again. This time, however, apply the rule of exponents that you would use for integer exponents.

Expression	Apply Rule and Substitute	Simplify	Result
$a^m \cdot a^n$	$64^{\frac{1}{3}+\frac{3}{2}}$	$64^{\frac{11}{6}}$	?
$(a \cdot b)^n$	?	?	?
$(a^m)^n$	?	?	?
$\frac{a^n}{a^m}$	?	?	?
$\left(\frac{a}{b}\right)^n$	?	?	?

Reflect

1. Compare your results in Steps A and B. What can you conclude?
2. In Steps A and B, you evaluated $\frac{a^n}{a^m}$ two ways. Now evaluate $\frac{a^m}{a^n}$ two ways, using the definition of negative exponents. Are your results consistent with your previous conclusions about integer and rational exponents?

Explain 1 Simplifying Rational-Exponent Expressions

Rational exponents have the same properties as integer exponents.

Properties of Rational Exponents

For all nonzero real numbers a and b and rational numbers m and n

Words	Numbers	Algebra
Product of Powers Property To multiply powers with the same base, add the exponents.	$12^{\frac{1}{2}} \cdot 12^{\frac{3}{2}} = 12^{\frac{1}{2}+\frac{3}{2}} = 12^2 = 144$	$a^m \cdot a^n = a^{m+n}$
Quotient of Powers Property To divide powers with the same base, subtract the exponents.	$\frac{125^{\frac{2}{3}}}{125^{\frac{1}{3}}} = 125^{\frac{2}{3}-\frac{1}{3}} = 125^{\frac{1}{3}} = 5$	$\frac{a^m}{a^n} = a^{m-n}$
Power of a Power Property To raise one power to another, multiply the exponents.	$\left(8^{\frac{2}{3}}\right)^3 = 8^{\frac{2}{3}\cdot 3} = 8^2 = 64$	$(a^m)^n = a^{m \cdot n}$
Power of a Product Property To find a power of a product, distribute the exponent.	$(16 \cdot 25)^{\frac{1}{2}} = 16^{\frac{1}{2}} \cdot 25^{\frac{1}{2}} = 4 \cdot 5 = 20$	$(ab)^m = a^m b^m$
Power of a Quotient Property To find the power of a qoutient, distribute the exponent.	$\left(\frac{16}{81}\right)^{\frac{1}{4}} = \frac{16^{\frac{1}{4}}}{81^{\frac{1}{4}}} = \frac{2}{3}$	$\left(\frac{a}{b}\right)^m = \frac{a^m}{b^m}$

Example 1 **Simplify the expression. Assume that all variables are positive. Exponents in simplified form should all be positive.**

Ⓐ **a.** $25^{\frac{3}{5}} \cdot 25^{\frac{7}{5}}$

$= 25^{\frac{3}{5}+\frac{7}{5}}$ Product of Powers Prop.

$= 25^2$ Simplify.

$= 625$

b. $\frac{8^{\frac{1}{3}}}{8^{\frac{2}{3}}}$

$= 8^{\frac{1}{3}-\frac{2}{3}}$ Quotient of Powes Prop.

$= 8^{-\frac{1}{3}}$ Simplify.

$= \frac{1}{8^{\frac{1}{3}}}$ Definition of neg. power

$= \frac{1}{2}$ Simplify.

Ⓑ a. $\left(\dfrac{y^{\frac{4}{3}}}{16y^{\frac{2}{3}}}\right)^{\frac{3}{2}}$

$= \left(\dfrac{y^{\frac{4}{3}-\frac{2}{3}}}{16}\right)^{\frac{3}{2}}$ Quotient of Powers Prop.

$= \left(\dfrac{y^{\boxed{\frac{2}{3}}}}{16}\right)^{\frac{3}{2}}$ Simplify.

$= \dfrac{\left(y^{\frac{2}{3}}\right)^{\frac{3}{2}}}{16^{\frac{3}{2}}}$ Power of a Quotient Prop.

$= \dfrac{y^{\frac{2}{3}\cdot\frac{3}{2}}}{16^{\frac{3}{2}}}$ Power of a Power Prop.

$= \boxed{\dfrac{y}{64}}$ Simplify.

b. $\left(27x^{\frac{3}{4}}\right)^{\frac{2}{3}}$

$= \boxed{27}^{\frac{2}{3}}\left(\boxed{x^{\frac{3}{4}}}\right)^{\frac{2}{3}}$ Power of a Product Prop.

$= 27^{\frac{2}{3}}\left(x^{\boxed{\frac{3}{4}\cdot\frac{2}{3}}}\right)$ Power of a Power Prop.

$= \boxed{9x^{\frac{1}{2}}}$ Simplify.

Your Turn

Simplify the expression. Assume that all variables are positive. Exponents in simplified form should all be positive.

3. $\left(12^{\frac{2}{3}} \cdot 12^{\frac{4}{3}}\right)^{\frac{3}{2}}$

4. $\dfrac{\left(6x^{\frac{1}{3}}\right)^{2}}{x^{\frac{5}{3}}y}$

Explain 2 Simplifying Radical Expressions Using the Properties of Exponents

When you are working with radical expressions involving *n*th roots, you can rewrite the expressions using rational exponents and then simplify them using the properties of exponents.

Example 2 **Simplify the expression by writing it using rational exponents and then using the properties of rational exponents. Assume that all variables are positive. Exponents in simplified form should all be positive.**

Ⓐ $x\left(\sqrt[3]{2y}\right)\left(\sqrt[3]{4x^2y^2}\right)$

$= x(2y)^{\frac{1}{3}}\left(4x^2y^2\right)^{\frac{1}{3}}$ Write using rational exponents.

$= x\left(2y \cdot 4x^2y^2\right)^{\frac{1}{3}}$ Power of a Product Property

$= x\left(8x^2y^3\right)^{\frac{1}{3}}$ Product of Powers Property

$= x\left(2x^{\frac{2}{3}}y\right)$ Power of a Product Property

$= 2x^{\frac{5}{3}}y$ Product of Powers Property

(B) $\dfrac{\sqrt{64y}}{\sqrt[3]{64y}}$

$= \dfrac{(64y)^{\frac{1}{2}}}{(64y)^{\frac{1}{3}}}$ Write using rational exponents.

$= (64y)^{\boxed{\frac{1}{2} - \frac{1}{3}}}$ Quotient of Powers Property

$= (64y)^{\boxed{\frac{1}{6}}}$ Simplify.

$= \boxed{64^{\frac{1}{6}}y^{\frac{1}{6}}}$ Power of a Product Property

$= \boxed{2y^{\frac{1}{6}}}$ Simplify.

Your Turn

Simplify the expression by writing it using rational exponents and then using the properties of rational exponents.

5. $\dfrac{\sqrt{x^3}}{\sqrt[3]{x^2}}$

6. $\sqrt[6]{16^3} \cdot \sqrt[4]{4^6} \cdot \sqrt[3]{8^2}$

Explain 3 Simplifying Radical Expressions Using the Properties of nth Roots

From working with square roots, you know, for example, that $\sqrt{8} \cdot \sqrt{2} = \sqrt{8 \cdot 2} = \sqrt{16} = 4$ and $\dfrac{\sqrt{8}}{\sqrt{2}} \cdot = \sqrt{\dfrac{8}{2}} = \sqrt{4} = 2$. The corresponding properties also apply to *n*th roots.

Properties of *n*th Roots

For a > 0 and b > 0

Words	Numbers	Algebra
Product Property of Roots The *n*th root of a product is equal to the product of the *n*th roots.	$\sqrt[3]{16} = \sqrt[3]{8} \cdot \sqrt[3]{2} = 2\sqrt[3]{2}$	$\sqrt[n]{ab} = \sqrt[n]{a} \cdot \sqrt[n]{b}$
Quotient Property of Roots The *n*th root of a Quotient is equal to the Quotient of the *n*th roots.	$\sqrt{\dfrac{25}{16}} = \dfrac{\sqrt{25}}{\sqrt{16}} = \dfrac{5}{4}$	$\sqrt[n]{\dfrac{a}{b}} = \dfrac{\sqrt[n]{a}}{\sqrt[n]{b}}$

Example 3 **Simplify the expression using the properties of *n*th roots. Assume that all variables are positive. Rationalize any irrational denominators.**

(A) $\sqrt[3]{256x^3y^7}$

$\sqrt[3]{256x^3y^7}$

$= \sqrt[3]{2^8 \cdot x^3y^7}$ Write 256 as a power.

$= \sqrt[3]{2^6 \cdot x^3y^6} \cdot \sqrt[3]{2^2 \cdot y}$ Product Property of Roots

$= \sqrt[3]{2^6} \cdot \sqrt[3]{x^3} \cdot \sqrt[3]{y^6} \cdot \sqrt[3]{4y}$ Factor out perfect cubes.

$= 4xy^2\sqrt[3]{4y}$ Simplify.

(B) $\sqrt[4]{\frac{81}{x}}$

$\sqrt[4]{\frac{81}{x}}$

$= \frac{\sqrt[4]{81}}{\sqrt[4]{x}}$ Quotient Property of Roots

$= \frac{3}{\sqrt[4]{x}}$ Simplify.

$= \frac{3}{\sqrt[4]{x}} \cdot \frac{\sqrt[4]{x^3}}{\sqrt[4]{x^3}}$ Rationalize the denominator.

$= \frac{3\sqrt[4]{x^3}}{\sqrt[4]{x^4}}$ Product Property of Roots

$= \frac{3\sqrt[4]{x^3}}{x}$ Simplify.

Reflect

7. In Part B, why was $\sqrt[4]{x^3}$ used when rationalizing the denominator? What factor would you use to rationalize a denominator of $\sqrt[5]{4y^3}$?

Your Turn

Simplify the expression using the properties of *n*th roots. Assume that all variables are positive.

8. $\sqrt[3]{216x^{12}y^{15}}$

9. $\sqrt[4]{\frac{16}{x^{14}}}$

Explain 4 Rewriting a Radical-Function Model

When you find or apply a function model involving rational powers or radicals, you can use the properties in this lesson to help you find a simpler expression for the model.

(A) **Manufacturing** A can that is twice as tall as its radius has the minimum surface area for the volume it contains. The formula $S = 6\pi\left(\frac{V}{2\pi}\right)^{\frac{2}{3}}$ expresses the surface area of a can with this shape in terms of its volume.

a. Use the properties of rational exponents to simplify the expression for the surface area. Then write the approximate model with the coefficient rounded to the nearest hundredth.

b. Graph the model using a graphing calculator. What is the surface area in square centimeters for a can with a volume of 440 cm^3?

a. $S = 6\pi\left(\frac{V}{2\pi}\right)^{\frac{2}{3}}$

Power of a Quotient Property $= 6\pi \cdot \frac{V^{\frac{2}{3}}}{(2\pi)^{\frac{2}{3}}}$

Group Powers of 2π. $= \frac{3(2\pi)}{(2\pi)^{\frac{2}{3}}} \cdot V^{\frac{2}{3}}$

Quotient of Powers Property $= 3(2\pi)^{1-\frac{2}{3}} \cdot V^{\frac{2}{3}}$

Simplify. $= 3(2\pi)^{\frac{1}{3}} \cdot V^{\frac{2}{3}}$

Use a calculator. $\approx 5.54V^{\frac{2}{3}}$

A simplified model is $S = 3(2\pi)^{\frac{1}{3}} \cdot V^{\frac{2}{3}}$, which gives $S \approx 5.54V^{\frac{2}{3}}$.

b.

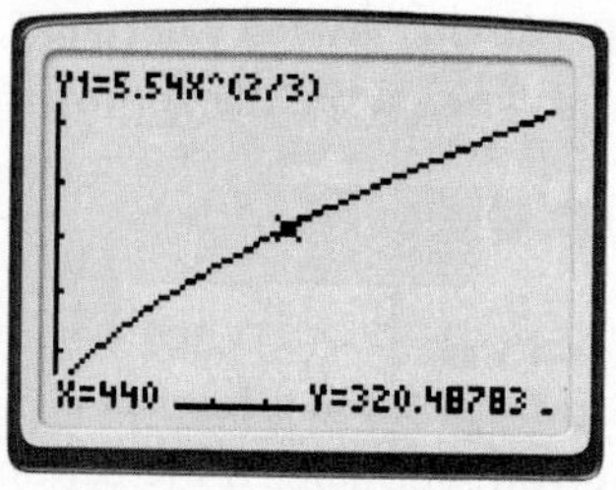

The surface area is about 320 cm^2.

(B) **Commercial fishing** The buoyancy of a fishing float in water depends on the volume of air it contains. The radius of a spherical float as a function of its volume is given by $r = \sqrt[3]{\frac{3V}{4\pi}}$.

a. Use the properties of roots to rewrite the expression for the radius as the product of a coefficient term and a variable term. Then write the approximate formula with the coefficient rounded to the nearest hundredth.

b. What should the radius be for a float that needs to contain 4.4 ft^3 of air to have the proper buoyancy?

a. $r = \sqrt[3]{\frac{3V}{4\pi}}$

Rewrite radicand. $= \sqrt[3]{\frac{3}{4\pi} \cdot \boxed{V}}$

Product Property of Roots $= \sqrt[3]{\frac{3}{4\pi}} \cdot \boxed{\sqrt[3]{V}}$

Use a calculator $\approx \boxed{0.62\sqrt[3]{V}}$

The rewritten formula is $r = \boxed{\sqrt[3]{\frac{3}{4\pi}} \cdot \sqrt[3]{V}}$, which gives $r \approx \boxed{0.62\sqrt[3]{V}}$.

b. Substitute 4.4 for V.

$r = 0.62\sqrt[3]{4.4} \approx \boxed{1.02}$

The radius is about 1.0 feet.

Reflect

10. Discussion What are some reasons you might want to rewrite an expression involving radicals into an expression involving rational exponents?

Your Turn

11. The surface area as a function of volume for a box with a square base and a height that is twice the side length of the base is $S = 10\left(\frac{V}{2}\right)^{\frac{2}{3}}$. Use the properties of rational exponents to simplify the expression for the surface area so that no fractions are involved. Then write the approximate model with the coefficient rounded to the nearest hundredth.

Elaborate

12. In problems with a radical in the denominator, you rationalized the denominator to remove the radical. What can you do to remove a rational exponent from the denominator? Explain by giving an example.

13. Show why $\sqrt[n]{a^n}$ is equal to a for all natural numbers a and n using the definition of nth roots and using rational exponents.

14. Show that the Product Property of Roots is true using rational exponents.

15. Essential Question Check-In Describe the difference between applying the Power of a Power Property and applying the Power of a Product Property for rational exponents using an example that involves both properties.

Evaluate: Homework and Practice

Personal Math Trainer

- Online Homework
- Hints and Help
- Extra Practice

Simplify the expression. Assume that all variables are positive. Exponents in simplified form should all be positive.

1. $\left(\left(\frac{1}{16}\right)^{-\frac{2}{3}}\right)^{\frac{3}{4}}$

2. $\dfrac{x^{\frac{1}{3}} \cdot x^{\frac{5}{6}}}{x^{\frac{1}{6}}}$

3. $\dfrac{9^{\frac{3}{2}} \cdot 9^{\frac{1}{2}}}{9^{-2}}$

4. $\left(\dfrac{16^{\frac{5}{3}}}{16^{\frac{5}{6}}}\right)^{\frac{9}{5}}$

5. $\dfrac{2xy}{\left(x^{\frac{1}{3}}y^{\frac{2}{3}}\right)^{\frac{3}{2}}}$

6. $\dfrac{3y^{\frac{3}{4}}}{2xy^{\frac{3}{2}}}$

Simplify the expression by writing it using rational exponents and then using the properties of rational exponents. Assume that all variables are positive. Exponents in simplified form should all be positive.

7. $\sqrt[4]{25} \cdot \sqrt[3]{5}$

8. $\dfrac{\sqrt[4]{2^{-2}}}{\sqrt[6]{2^{-9}}}$

9. $\dfrac{\sqrt[4]{3^3} \cdot \sqrt[3]{x^2}}{\sqrt{3x}}$

10. $\dfrac{\sqrt[4]{x^4y^6} \cdot \sqrt{x^6}}{y}$

11. $\dfrac{\sqrt[6]{s^4t^9}}{\sqrt[3]{st}}$

12. $\sqrt[4]{27} \cdot \sqrt{3} \cdot \sqrt[6]{81^3}$

Simplify the expression using the properties of *n*th roots. Assume that all variables are positive. Rationalize any irrational denominators.

13. $\dfrac{\sqrt[4]{36} \cdot \sqrt[4]{216}}{\sqrt[4]{6}}$

14. $\sqrt[4]{4096x^6y^8}$

15. $\dfrac{\sqrt[3]{x^8y^4}}{\sqrt[3]{x^2y}}$

16. $\sqrt[5]{\dfrac{125}{w^6}} \cdot \sqrt[5]{25v}$

17. Weather The volume of a sphere as a function of its surface area is given by $V = \frac{4\pi}{3}\left(\frac{S}{4\pi}\right)^{\frac{3}{2}}$.

a. Use the properties of roots to rewrite the expression for the volume as the product of a simplified coefficient term (with positive exponents) and a variable term. Then write the approximate formula with the coefficient rounded to the nearest thousandth.

b. A spherical weather balloon has a surface area of 500 ft^2. What is the approximate volume of the balloon?

18. Amusement parks An amusement park has a ride with a free fall of 128 feet. The formula $t = \sqrt{\frac{2d}{g}}$ gives the time t in seconds it takes the ride to fall a distance of d feet. The formula $v = \sqrt{2gd}$ gives the velocity v in feet per second after the ride has fallen d feet. The letter g represents the gravitational constant.

a. Rewrite each formula so that the variable d is isolated. Then simplify each formula using the fact that $g \approx 32$ ft/s^2.

b. Find the time it takes the ride to fall halfway and its velocity at that time. Then find the time and velocity for the full drop.

c. What is the ratio of the time it takes for the whole drop to the time it takes for the first half? What is the ratio of the velocity after the second half of the drop to the velocity after the first half? What do you notice?

19. Which choice(s) is/are equivalent to $\sqrt{2}$?

A. $\left(\sqrt[8]{2}\right)^4$

B. $\frac{2^3}{2^{-\frac{5}{2}}}$

C. $\left(4^{\frac{2}{3}} \cdot 2^{\frac{2}{3}}\right)^{\frac{1}{4}}$

D. $\frac{\sqrt[3]{2^2}}{\sqrt[6]{2}}$

E. $\frac{\sqrt{2^{-\frac{3}{4}}}}{\sqrt{2^{-\frac{7}{4}}}}$

20. Home Heating A propane storage tank for a home is shaped like a cylinder with hemispherical ends, and a cylindrical portion length that is 4 times the radius.

The formula $S = 12\pi \left(\frac{3V}{16\pi}\right)^{\frac{2}{3}}$ expresses the surface area of a tank with this shape in terms of its volume.

a. Use the properties of rational exponents to rewrite the expression for the surface area so that the variable V is isolated. Then write the approximate model with the coefficient rounded to the nearest hundredth.

b. Graph the model using a graphing calculator. What is the surface area in square feet for a tank with a volume of 150 ft^3 ?

H.O.T. Focus on Higher Order Thinking

21. Critique Reasoning Aaron's work in simplifying an expression is shown. What mistake(s) did Aaron make? Show the correct simplification.

$$625^{-\frac{1}{3}} \div 625^{-\frac{4}{3}}$$
$$= 625^{-\frac{1}{3} - \left(-\frac{4}{3}\right)}$$
$$= 625^{-\frac{1}{3}\left(-\frac{3}{4}\right)}$$
$$= 625^{\frac{1}{4}}$$
$$= 5$$

22. Critical Thinking Use the definition of nth root to show that the Product Property of Roots is true, that is, that $\sqrt[n]{ab} = \sqrt[n]{a} \cdot \sqrt[n]{b}$. (Hint: Begin by letting x be the nth root of a and letting y be the nth root of b.)

23. Critical Thinking For what real values of a is $\sqrt[4]{a}$ greater than a? For what real values of a is $\sqrt[5]{a}$ greater than a?

Lesson Performance Task

You've been asked to help decorate for a school dance, and the theme chosen is "The Solar System." The plan is to have a bunch of papier-mâché spheres serve as models of the planets, and your job is to paint them. All you're told are the volumes of the individual spheres, but you need to know their surface areas so you can get be sure to get enough paint. How can you write a simplified equation using rational exponents for the surface area of a sphere in terms of its volume?

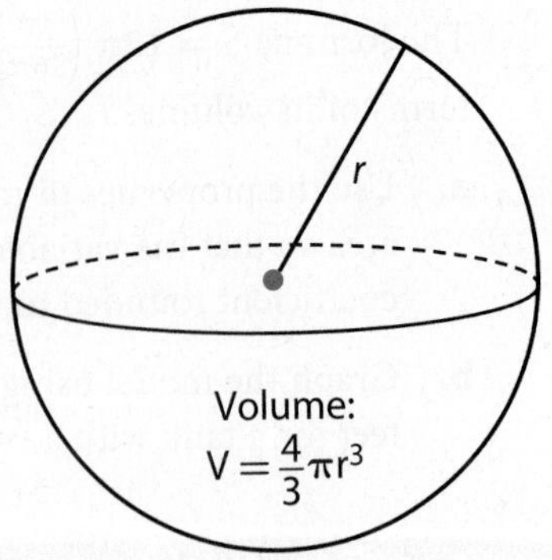

(The formula for the volume of a sphere is $V = \frac{4}{3}\pi r^3$ and the formula for the surface area of a sphere is $A = 4\pi r^2$.)

11.3 Solving Radical Equations

Essential Question: How can you solve equations involving square roots and cube roots?

Resource Locker

Explore Investigating Solutions of Square Root Equations

When solving quadratic equations, you have learned that the number of real solutions depends upon the values in the equation, with different equations having 0, 1, or 2 real solutions. How many real solutions does a square root equation have? In the Explore, you will investigate graphically the numbers of real solutions for different square root equations.

(A) Remember that you can graph the two sides of an equation as separate functions to find solutions of the equation: a solution is any x-value where the two graphs intersect.

The graph of $y = \sqrt{x-3}$ is shown on a calculator window of $-4 \leq x \leq 16$ and $-2 \leq y \leq 8$. Reproduce the graph on your calculator. Then add the graph of $y = 2$.

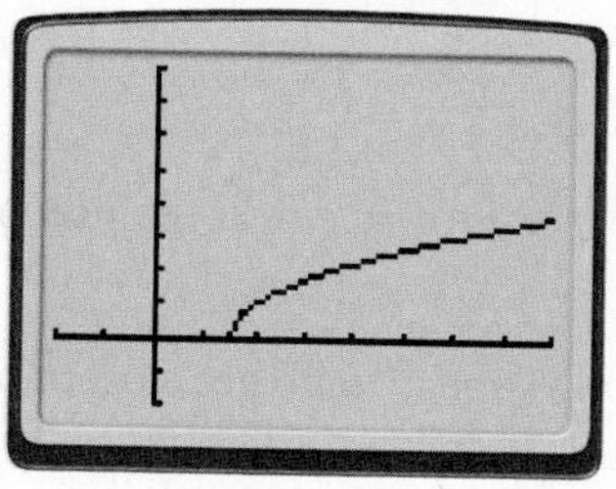

How many solutions does the equation $\sqrt{x-3} = 2$ have? ? How do you know? ?

On your calculator, replace the graph of $y = 2$ with the graph of $y = -1$.

How many solutions does the equation $\sqrt{x-3} = -1$ have? ? How do you know? ?

(B) Graph $y = \sqrt{x-3} + 2$ on your calculator (you can use the same viewing window as in Step A).

Add the graph of $y = 3$ to the graph of $y = \sqrt{x-3} + 2$.

How many solutions does $\sqrt{x-3} + 2 = 3$ have? ?

Replace the graph of $y = 3$ with the graph of $y = 1$.

How many solutions does $\sqrt{x-3} + 2 = 1$ have? ?

Ⓒ Graph both sides of $\sqrt{4x-4} = x + 1$ as separate functions on your calculator.

How many solutions does $\sqrt{4x-4} = x + 1$ have? ?

Replace the graph of $y = x + 1$ with the graph of $y = \frac{1}{2}x$.

How many solutions does $\sqrt{4x-4} = \frac{1}{2}x$ have? ?

Replace the graph of $y = \frac{1}{2}x$ with the graph of $y = 2x - 5$.

How many solutions does $\sqrt{4x-4} = 2x - 5$ have? ?

Ⓓ Graph both sides of $\sqrt{2x-3} = \sqrt{x}$ as separate functions on your calculator.

How many solutions does $\sqrt{2x-3} = \sqrt{x}$ have? ?

Replace the graph of $y = \sqrt{x}$ with the graph of $y = \sqrt{2x+3}$.

How many solutions does $\sqrt{2x-3} = \sqrt{2x+3}$ have? ?

Reflect

1. For a square root equation of the form $\sqrt{bx-h} = c$, what can you conclude about the number of solutions based on the sign of c?
2. For a square root equation of the form $\sqrt{bx-h} + k = c$, what can you conclude about the number of solutions based on the values of k and c?
3. For a cube root equation of the form $\sqrt[3]{bx-h} = c$, will the number of solutions depend on the sign of c? Explain.
4. The graphs in the second part of Step D appear to be get closer and closer as x increases. How can you be sure that they never meet, that is, that $\sqrt{2x-3} = \sqrt{2x+3}$ really has no solutions?

Explain 1 Solving Square Root and $\frac{1}{2}$-Power Equations

A *radical equation* contains a variable within a radical or a variable raised to a (non-integer) rational power. To solve a square root equation, or, equivalently, an equation involving the power $\frac{1}{2}$, you can square both sides of the equation and solve the resulting equation.

Because opposite numbers have the same square, squaring both sides of an equation may introduce an apparent solution that is not an actual solution (an extraneous solution). For example, while the only solution of $x = 2$ is 2, the equation that is the square of each side, $x^2 = 4$, has two solutions, −2 and 2. But −2 is not a solution of the original equation.

Example 1 **Solve the equation. Check for extraneous solutions.**

(A) $2 + \sqrt{x + 10} = x$

	$2 + \sqrt{x + 10} = x$
Isolate the radical.	$\sqrt{x + 10} = x - 2$
Square both sides.	$\left(\sqrt{x + 10}\right)^2 = (x - 2)^2$
Simplify.	$x + 10 = x^2 - 4x + 4$
Simplify.	$0 = x^2 - 5x - 6$
Factor.	$0 = (x - 6)(x + 1)$
Zero Product Property	$x = 6$ or $x = -1$

Check:

$2 + \sqrt{x + 10} = x$	$2 + \sqrt{x + 10} = x$
$2 + \sqrt{6 + 10} \stackrel{?}{=} 6$	$2 + \sqrt{-1 + 10} \stackrel{?}{=} -1$
$2 + \sqrt{16} \stackrel{?}{=} 6$	$2 + \sqrt{9} \stackrel{?}{=} -1$
$6 = 6$ ✓	$5 \neq -1$
$x = 6$ is a solution.	$x = -1$ is not a solution.

The solution is $x = 6$.

(B) $(x + 6)^{\frac{1}{2}} - (2x - 4)^{\frac{1}{2}} = 0$

Rewrite with radicals.	$\sqrt{x + 6} - \sqrt{2x - 4} = 0$
Isolate radicals on each side.	$\sqrt{x + 6} = \boxed{\sqrt{2x - 4}}$
Square both sides.	$\left(\sqrt{x + 6}\right)^2 = \left(\boxed{\sqrt{2x - 4}}\right)^2$
Simplify.	$\boxed{x + 6} = \boxed{2x - 4}$
Solve.	$\boxed{10} = x$

Check:

$$\sqrt{x + 6} - \sqrt{2x - 4} = 0$$

$$\sqrt{10 + 6} - \sqrt{2\left(\boxed{10}\right) - 4} \stackrel{?}{=} 0$$

$$\boxed{\sqrt{16}} - \boxed{\sqrt{16}} \stackrel{?}{=} 0$$

$$\boxed{0} = 0$$

The solution is $x = 10$.

Reflect

5. The graphs of each side of the equation from Part A are shown on the graphing calculator screen below. How can you tell from the graph that one of the two solutions you found algebraically is extraneous?

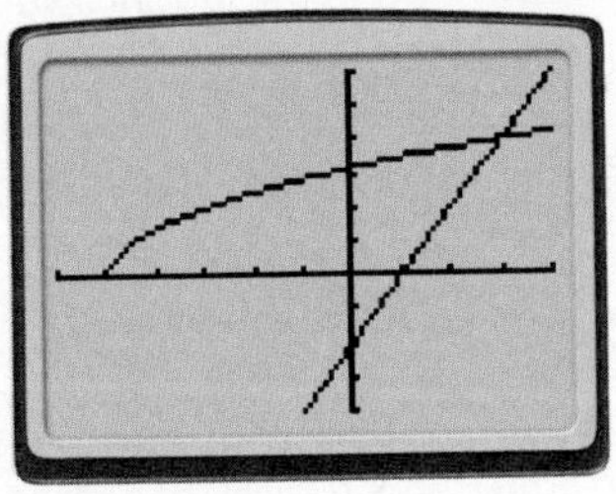

Your Turn

6. Solve $(x + 5)^{\frac{1}{2}} - 2 = 1$.

Explain 2 Solving Cube Root and $\frac{1}{3}$-Power Equations

You can solve radical equations that involve roots other than square roots by raising both sides to the index of the radical. So, to solve a cube root equation, or, equivalently, an equation involving the power $\frac{1}{3}$, you can cube both sides of the equation and solve the resulting equation.

Example 2 **Solve the equation.**

(A) $\sqrt[3]{x + 2} + 7 = 5$

$$\sqrt[3]{x + 2} + 7 = 5$$

Isolate the radical. $\sqrt[3]{x + 2} = -2$

Cube both sides. $\left(\sqrt[3]{x + 2}\right)^3 = (-2)^3$

Simplify. $x + 2 = -8$

Solve for x $x = -10$

The solution is $x = -10$.

(B) $\sqrt[3]{x - 5} = x + 1$

$$\sqrt[3]{x - 5} = x + 1$$

Cube both sides. $\left(\sqrt[3]{x - 5}\right)^3 = (x + 1)^3$

Simplify $x - 5 = x^3 + 3x^2 + 3x + 1$

Simplify. $0 = x^3 + 3x^2 + 2x + 6$

Begin to factor by grouping. $0 = x^2(x + 3) + 2(x + 3)$

Complete factoring $0 = (x^2 + 2)(x + 3)$

By the Zero Product Property, $x^2 + 2$ $= 0$ or $x + 3$ $= 0$.

Because there are no real values of x for which $x^2 =$ -2, the only solution is $x = -3$.

Reflect

7. **Discussion** Example 1 shows checking for extraneous solutions, while Example 2 does not. While it is always wise to check your answers, can a cubic equation have an extraneous solution? Explain your answer.

Your Turn

8. Solve $2(x - 50)^{\frac{1}{3}} = -10$.

Explain 3 Solving a Real-World Problem

(A) **Driving** The speed s in miles per hour that a car is traveling when it goes into a skid can be estimated by using the formula $s = \sqrt{30fd}$, where f is the coefficient of friction and d is the length of the skid marks in feet.

After an accident, a driver claims to have been traveling the speed limit of 55 mi/h. The coefficient of friction under the conditions at the time of the accident was 0.6, and the length of the skid marks is 190 feet. Is the driver telling the truth about the car's speed? Explain.

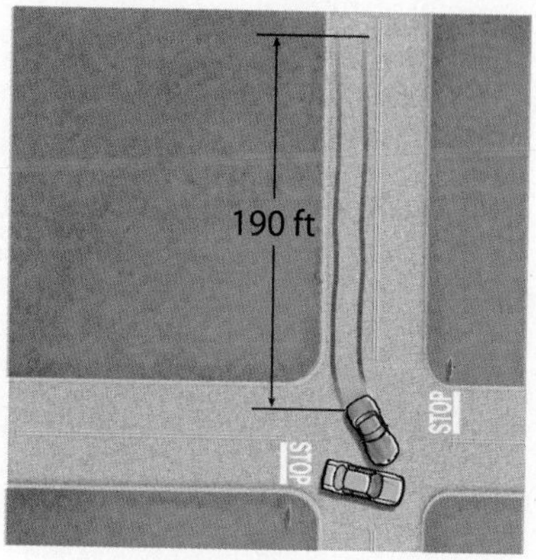

Use the formula to find the length of a skid at a speed of 55 mi/h. Compare this distance to the actual skid length of 190 feet.

$$s = \sqrt{30fd}$$

Substitute 55 for s and 0.6 for f $\quad 55 = \sqrt{30(0.6)d}$

Simplify. $\quad 55 = \sqrt{18d}$

Square both sides. $\quad 55^2 = \left(\sqrt{18d}\right)^2$

Simplify. $\quad 3025 = 18d$

Solve for d. $\quad 168 \approx d$

If the driver had been traveling at 55 mi/h, the skid marks would measure about 168 feet. Because the skid marks actually measure 190 feet, the driver must have been driving faster than 55 mi/h.

(B) **Construction** The diameter d in inches of a rope needed to lift a weight of w tons is given by the formula $d = \frac{\sqrt{15w}}{\pi}$. How much weight can be lifted with a rope with a diameter of 1.0 inch?

Use the formula for the diameter as a function of weight, and solve for the weight given the diameter.

$$d = \frac{\sqrt{15w}}{\pi}$$

Substitute. $\quad \boxed{1.0} = \frac{\sqrt{15w}}{\pi}$

Square both sides. $\quad \boxed{\pi} = \boxed{\sqrt{15w}}$

Isolate the radical. $\quad \left(\boxed{\pi}\right)^2 = \left(\sqrt{15w}\right)^2$

Simplify. $\quad \boxed{\pi^2} = 15w$

Solve for w. $\quad \boxed{0.66} \approx w$

A rope with a diameter of 1.0 can hold about 0.66 ton, or about 1320 pounds.

Your Turn

9. **Biology** The trunk length (in inches) of a male elephant can be modeled by $l = 23\sqrt[3]{t} + 17$, where t is the age of the elephant in years. If a male elephant has a trunk length of 100 inches, about what is his age?

Elaborate

10. A student asked to solve the equation $\sqrt{4x + 8} + 9 = 1$ isolated the radical, squared both sides, and solved for x to obtain $x = 14$, only to find out that the apparent solution was extraneous. Why could the student have stopped trying to solve the equation after isolating the radical?

11. When you see a cube root equation with the radical expression isolated on one side and a constant on the other, what should you expect for the number of solutions? Explain. What are some reasons you should check your answer anyway?

12. **Essential Question Check-In** Solving a quadratic equation of the form $x^2 = a$ involves taking the square root of both sides. Solving a square root equation of the form $\sqrt{x} = b$ involves squaring both sides of the equation. Which of these operations can create an equation that is not equivalent to the original equation? Explain how this affects the solution process.

Evaluate: Homework and Practice

Personal Math Trainer

- Online Homework
- Hints and Help
- Extra Practice

Solve the equation.

1. $\sqrt{x-9}=5$

2. $\sqrt{3x}=6$

3. $\sqrt{x+3}=x+1$

4. $\sqrt{(15x+10)}=2x+3$

5. $(x+4)^{\frac{1}{2}}=6$

6. $(45-9x)^{\frac{1}{2}}=x-5$

7. $(x-6)^{\frac{1}{2}}=x-2$

8. $4(x-2)^{\frac{1}{2}}=(x+13)^{\frac{1}{2}}$

9. $5-\sqrt[3]{x-4}=2$

10. $2\sqrt[3]{3x+2}=\sqrt[3]{4x-9}$

11. $\sqrt[3]{69x+35}=x+5$

12. $\sqrt[3]{x+5}=x-1$

13. $(x+7)^{\frac{1}{3}}=(4x)^{\frac{1}{3}}$

14. $(5x+1)^{\frac{1}{4}}=4$

15. $(-44x-18)^{\frac{1}{3}}=-2x+3$

16. $2(x-1)^{\frac{1}{5}}=(2x-17)^{\frac{1}{5}}$

17. **Driving** The formula for the speed versus skid length in Example 3A assumes that all 4 wheel brakes are working at top efficiency. If this is not true, another parameter is included in the equation so that the equation becomes $s=\sqrt{30fdn}$ where n is the percent braking efficiency as a decimal. Accident investigators know that the rear brakes failed on a car, reducing its braking efficiency to 60%. On a dry road with a coefficient of friction of 0.7, the car skidded 250 feet. Was the car going above the speed limit of 60 mi/h when the skid began?

18. **Anatomy** The surface area S of a human body in square meters can be approximated by $S=\sqrt{\frac{hm}{36}}$ where h is height in meters and m is mass in kilograms. A basketball player with a height of 2.1 meters has a surface area of about 2.7 m^2. What is the player's mass?

19. Biology The approximate antler length L (in inches) of a deer buck can be modeled by $L = 9\sqrt[3]{t} + 15$ where t is the age in years of the buck. If a buck has an antler length of 36 inches, what is its age?

20. Amusement Parks For a spinning amusement park ride, the velocity v in meters per second of a car moving around a curve with radius r meters is given by $v = \sqrt{ar}$ where a is the car's acceleration in m/s^2. If the ride has a maximum acceleration of 30 m/s^2 and the cars on the ride have a maximum velocity of 12 m/s, what is the smallest radius that any curve on the ride may have?

21. For each radical equation, state the number of solutions that exist.

A. $\sqrt{x - 4} = -5$

B. $\sqrt{x - 4} + 6 = 11$

C. $4 = -2\sqrt[3]{x + 2}$

D. $\sqrt{x + 40} = 0$

E. $\sqrt[3]{2x + 5} = -18$

H.O.T. Focus on Higher Order Thinking

22. Critical Thinking For an equation of the form $\sqrt{x+a}=b$ where b is a constant, does the sign of a affect whether or not there is a solution for a given value of b? If so, how? If not, why not?

23. Explain the Error Below is a student's work in solving the equation $2\sqrt{3x+3}=12$. What mistake did the student make? What is the correct solution?

$$2\sqrt{3x+3}=12$$

$$2\left(\sqrt{3x+3}\right)^2=12^2$$

$$2(3x+3)=144$$

$$6x+6=144$$

$$x=23$$

24. Communicate Mathematical Ideas Describe the key difference between solving radical equations for which you solve by raising both sides to an even power and those you solve by raising both sides to an odd power.

25. Critical Thinking How could you solve an equation for which one side is a rational power expression and the other side is a constant? Give an example. Under what condition would you have to be especially careful to check your solutions?

Lesson Performance Task

For many years scientists have used a scale known as the Fujita Scale to categorize different types of tornados in relation to the velocity of the winds produced. The formula used to generate the scale is given by $V = k(F + 2)^{\frac{3}{2}}$. The scale employs a constant, k, and the tornado's category number to determine wind speed. If you wanted to determine the different category numbers, how could you solve the radical equation for the variable F? (The value for k is about 14.1.) Solve the equation for F then verify the different categories using the minimum wind velocity. Do the values seem reasonable given the value for k?

Fujita Tornado Scale			
Damage Level	**Category**	**Minimum Wind Velocity (mi/h)**	**Calculations**
Moderate	F1	73	?
Significant	F2	113	?
Severe	F3	158	?
Devastating	F4	207	?
Incredible	F5	261	?

Radical Expressions and Equations

Essential Question: How can you use radical expressions and equations to solve real-world problems?

Key Vocabulary

extraneous solution *(solución extraña)*
radical expression *(expresión radical)*
rational exponent *(exponente racional)*

KEY EXAMPLE *(Lesson 11.1)*

Evaluate the expression.

$$\left(\sqrt[4]{16}\right)^5 = 2^5 = 32$$

$$27^{\frac{4}{3}} = \left(\sqrt[3]{27}\right)^4 = 3^4 = 81$$

KEY EXAMPLE *(Lesson 11.2)*

Write the expression in simplest form. Assume all variables are positive.

$\sqrt[3]{48} = \sqrt[3]{8 \cdot 6}$ Factor out a perfect cube.

$= \sqrt[3]{8} \cdot \sqrt[3]{6}$ Apply the Product Property of Radicals.

$= 2\sqrt[3]{6}$ Evaluate.

$\left(\frac{x^4}{y^8}\right)^{\frac{1}{2}} = \frac{\left(x^4\right)^{\frac{1}{2}}}{\left(y^8\right)^{\frac{1}{2}}}$ Apply the Power of a Quotient Property.

$= \frac{x^{4 \cdot \frac{1}{2}}}{y^{8 \cdot \frac{1}{2}}}$ Apply the Power of a Power Property.

$= \frac{x^2}{y^4}$ Simplify.

KEY EXAMPLE *(Lesson 11.3)*

Solve the equation. $\sqrt{x + 15} = x - 5$

$\left(\sqrt{x + 15}\right)^2 = (x - 5)^2$ Square both sides.

$x + 15 = x^2 - 10x + 25$

$x^2 - 11x + 10 = 0$ Write in standard form.

$(x - 10)(x - 1) = 0$ Factor.

$x = 10$ or $x = 1$ Solve for x.

$\sqrt{10 + 15} \stackrel{?}{=} 10 - 5$ $\quad \sqrt{1 + 15} \stackrel{?}{=} 1 - 5$ Check.

$5 = 5$ $\quad 4 \neq -4$

The solution $x = 1$ is extraneous. The only solution is $x = 10$.

EXERCISES

Evaluate the expression. *(Lesson 11.1)*

1. $\sqrt[3]{-64}$

2. $81^{\frac{1}{4}}$

3. $256^{\frac{3}{4}}$

Write the expression in simplest form. Assume that all variables are positive. *(Lesson 11.2)*

4. $\sqrt[3]{80}$

5. $(3^4 \cdot 5^4)^{-\frac{1}{4}}$

6. $(25a^{10}b^{16})^{\frac{1}{2}}$

7. $\sqrt[5]{\frac{c}{d^8}}$

Solve each equation. *(Lesson 11.3)*

8. $\sqrt[3]{5x-4} = 2$

9. $\sqrt{x+6} - 7 = -2$

MODULE PERFORMANCE TASK

Don't Disturb the Neighbors!

The faintest sound an average person can detect has an intensity of 1×10^{-12} watts per square meter, where watts are a unit of power. The intensity of a sound is given by $I = \frac{P}{4\pi d^2}$, where P is the power of the sound and d is the distance from the source. Yolanda wants to throw a party at her house and plans to invite a band to perform. The power of the sound from the band's speakers is typically 3.0 watts. Yolanda's neighborhood has a rule that between 7 p.m. and 11 p.m., a sound intensity up to $I = 5.0 \times 10^{-5}$ W/m^2 is acceptable; after 11 p.m., the acceptable intensity is $I = 5.0 \times 10^{-7}$ W/m^2. How far away would Yolanda's closest neighbors need to be for the band to play till 11 p.m.? How far would they need to be for the band to play all night?

Start by listing the information you will need to solve the problem. Then complete the task. Be sure to write down all your data and assumptions. Then use graphs, numbers, words, or algebra to explain how you reached your conclusion.

Ready to Go On?

11.1–11.3 Radical Expressions and Equations

Personal Math Trainer

- Online Homework
- Hints and Help
- Extra Practice

Simplify each expression. Assume that all variables are positive. *(Lessons 11.1, 11.2)*

1. $32^{\frac{1}{5}}$

2. $\left(\sqrt[3]{64}\right)^4$

3. $\sqrt[3]{27x^6}$

4. $\sqrt[4]{2x^6y^8}$

Solve each equation. *(Lesson 11.3)*

5. $\sqrt{10x} = 3\sqrt{x+1}$

6. $\sqrt[3]{2x-2} = 6$

7. $(4x+7)^{\frac{1}{2}} = 3$

8. $(x+3)^{\frac{1}{3}} = -6$

ESSENTIAL QUESTION

9. How do you solve a radical equation and identify any extraneous roots?

MODULE 11
MIXED REVIEW

Assessment Readiness

1. Tell whether each expression can be simplified to a rational number.

   A. $\sqrt{2} + \sqrt{2}$

   B. $\sqrt{4} \cdot \sqrt{20}$

   C. $\left(\sqrt{12}\right)^2$

2. Consider the function $f(x) = \frac{2x^2 - 5x - 3}{x - 3}$. Determine if each statement is True or False.

   A. This function looks like a straight line when graphed.

   B. There is a hole in this function at $(3, 7)$.

   C. There is a hole in this function at $(-0.5, 0)$.

3. Explain how to find the product of $(4 - 3i)(2 - i)$, then state the product.

4. The formula $s = \sqrt{\frac{A}{4.828}}$ can be used to approximate the side length s of a regular octagon with area A. A stop sign is shaped like a regular octagon with a side length of 12.4 in. To the nearest square inch, what is the area of the stop sign? Explain how you got your answer.

UNIT 5 MIXED REVIEW

Assessment Readiness

Personal Math Trainer

- Online Homework
- Hints and Help
- Extra Practice

1. Consider the graph of $g(x) = \frac{1}{3}\sqrt{x-1}$ as related to the graph of $f(x) = \sqrt{x}$. Determine if each statement is True or False.

A. $g(x)$ is a vertical stretching by a factor of $\frac{1}{3}$ and a translation of 1 unit up from $f(x)$.

B. $g(x)$ is a vertical compression by a factor of $\frac{1}{3}$ and a translation 1 unit right from $f(x)$.

C. $g(x)$ is a vertical compression by a factor of $\frac{1}{3}$ and a translation 1 unit left from $f(x)$.

2. Consider each transformation in relation to $f(x) = \sqrt[3]{x}$.
Determine if each statement is True or False.

A. $g(x) = 5\sqrt[3]{x+1} - 2$ is a transformation of $f(x)$ by a vertical stretch by a factor of 5 and a translation 1 unit left and 2 units down.

B. $g(x) = 5\sqrt[3]{x-1} + 2$ is a transformation of $f(x)$ by a horizontal stretch by a factor of 5 and a translation of 1 unit left and 2 units down.

C. $g(x) = \frac{1}{5}\sqrt[3]{x+1} - 2$ is a transformation of $f(x)$ by a horizontal stretch by a factor of $\frac{1}{5}$ and a translation of 1 unit left and 2 units down.

3. Tell whether each equation is the inverse of $f(x) = \frac{1}{2}x^3 + 5$.

A. $f^{-1}(x) = \sqrt[3]{2(x-5)}$

B. $f^{-1}(x) = \sqrt[3]{2(x+5)}$

C. $f^{-1}(x) = \sqrt[3]{\frac{1}{2}(x-5)}$

4. Tell whether each expression can be simplified to 25.

A. $\left(\sqrt[2]{125}\right)^3$

B. $\left(\sqrt[3]{125}\right)^2$

C. $\left(\sqrt{125}\right)^{\frac{1}{3}}$

5. A company produces canned tomatoes. They want the height h of each can to be twice the diameter d. Write an equation for the surface area A of the can in terms of the radius r. If the company wants to use no more than 90 square inches of metal for each can, what is the maximum radius of the can they will produce?

6. The period T of a pendulum in seconds is given by $T = 2\pi\sqrt{\frac{L}{9.81}}$, where L is the length of the pendulum in meters. If you want to use a pendulum as a clock, with a period of 2 seconds, how long should the pendulum be?

7. Tandra says that $\sqrt[3]{\frac{8x^6}{y}}$ can be simplified to $\frac{2x^2}{\sqrt[3]{y}}$. Elizabeth says that $\sqrt[3]{\frac{6x^6}{y}}$ can be simplified to $\frac{2x^2}{\sqrt[3]{y}}$. Who is correct, or are they both correct? Explain.

Performance Tasks

★ 8. The formula $P = 73.3\sqrt[4]{m^3}$, known as Kleiber's law, relates the metabolism rate P of an organism in Calories per day and the body mass m of the organism in kilograms. The table shows the typical body mass of several members of the cat family.

Typical Body Mass	
Animal	**Mass(kg)**
House cat	4.5
Cheetah	55.0
Lion	170.0

A. What is the metabolism rate of a cheetah to the nearest Calorie per day?

B. Approximately how many more Calories of food does a lion need to consume each day than a house cat does?

★★ **9.** On a clear day, the approximate distance d in miles that a person can see is given by $d = 1.2116\sqrt{h}$, where h is the person's height in feet above the ocean.

A. To the nearest tenth of a mile, how far can the captain on a clipper ship 15 feet above the ocean see?

B. How much farther, to the nearest tenth of a mile, will a sailor at the top of a mast 120 feet above the ocean be able to see than will the captain?

C. A pirate ship is approaching the clipper ship at a relative speed of 10 miles per hour. Approximately how many minutes sooner will the sailor be able to see the pirate ship than will the captain?

★★★**10.** The time it takes a pendulum to make one complete swing back and forth depends on its string length, as shown in the table.

String Length (m)	2	4	6	8	10
Time (s)	2.8	4.0	4.9	5.7	6.3

A. Graph the relationship between string length and time, and identify the parent function which best describes the data.

B. The function $T(x) = 2\pi\sqrt{\frac{x}{9.8}}$ gives the period in seconds of a pendulum of length x. The period of a pendulum is the time it takes the pendulum to complete one back-and-forth swing. Describe the graph of T as a transformation of $f(x) = \sqrt{x}$.

C. By what factor must the length of a pendulum be increased to double its period?

Nutritionist Body mass index (BMI) is a measure used to determine healthy body mass based on a person's height. BMI is calculated by dividing a person's mass in kilograms by the square of his or her height in meters. The median BMI measures for a group of boys, ages 2 to 10 years are given in the chart below.

Age of Boys	2	3	4	5	6	7	8	9	10
Median BMI	16.6	16.0	15.6	15.4	15.4	15.5	15.8	16.2	16.6

a. Create a scatter plot for the data in the table, treating age as the independent variable x and median BMI as the dependent variable y.

b. Use a calculator to find a quadratic regression model for the data. What is your model?

c. Give the domain of $f(x)$ based on the data set. Because $f(x)$ is quadratic, it is not one-to-one and its inverse is not a function. Restrict the domain of $f(x)$ to values of x for which $f(x)$ is increasing so that its inverse will be a function. What is the restricted domain of $f(x)$?

d. Find and graph the inverse of $f(x)$. What does $f^{-1}(x)$ model?

UNIT 6

Exponential and Logarithmic Functions and Equations

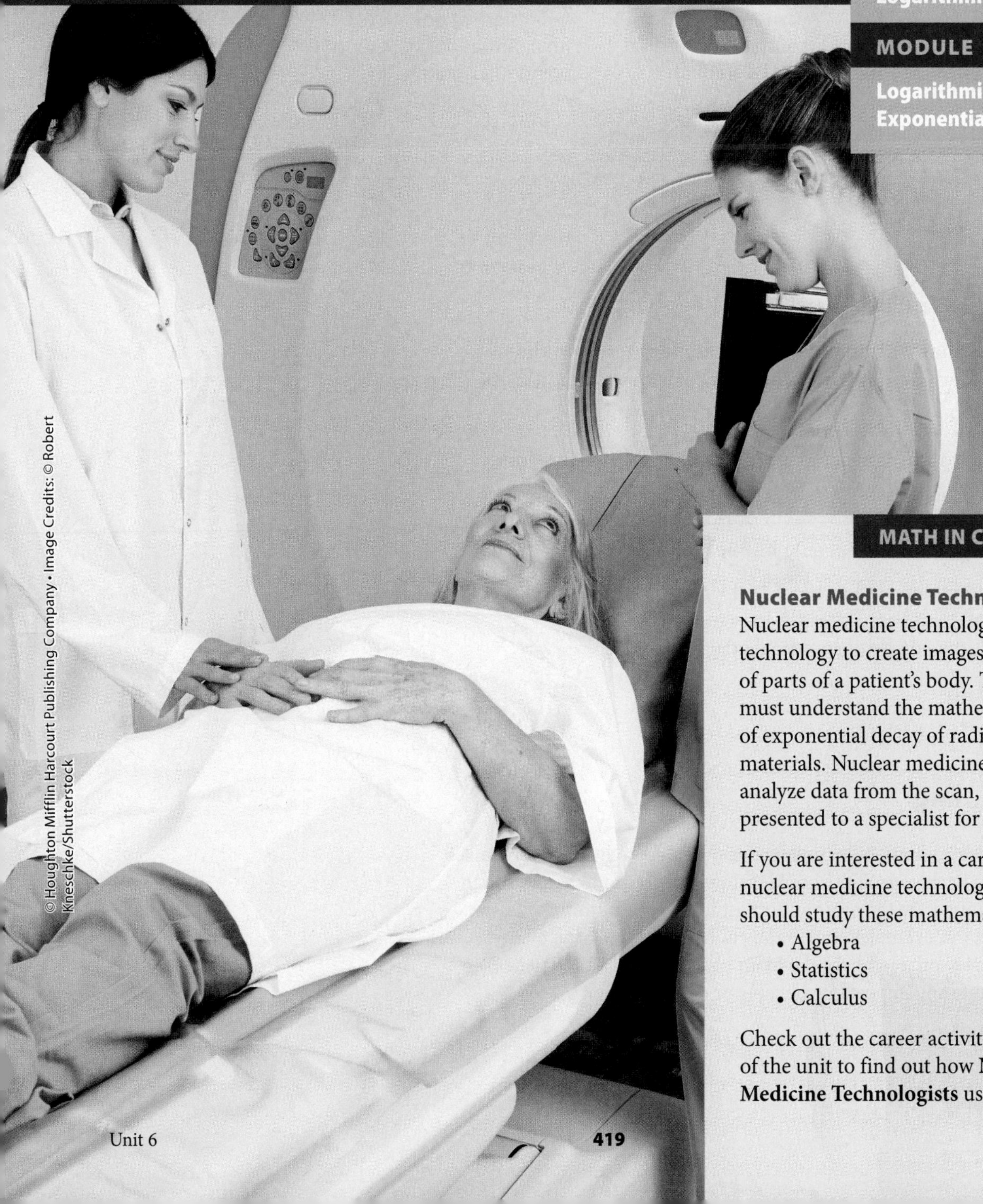

MATH IN CAREERS

Nuclear Medicine Technologist
Nuclear medicine technologists use technology to create images, or *scans*, of parts of a patient's body. They must understand the mathematics of exponential decay of radioactive materials. Nuclear medicine technologists analyze data from the scan, which are presented to a specialist for diagnosis.

If you are interested in a career as a nuclear medicine technologist, you should study these mathematical subjects:

- Algebra
- Statistics
- Calculus

Check out the career activity at the end of the unit to find out how **Nuclear Medicine Technologists** use math.

Reading Start-Up

Visualize Vocabulary

Use the ✓ words to complete the graphic.

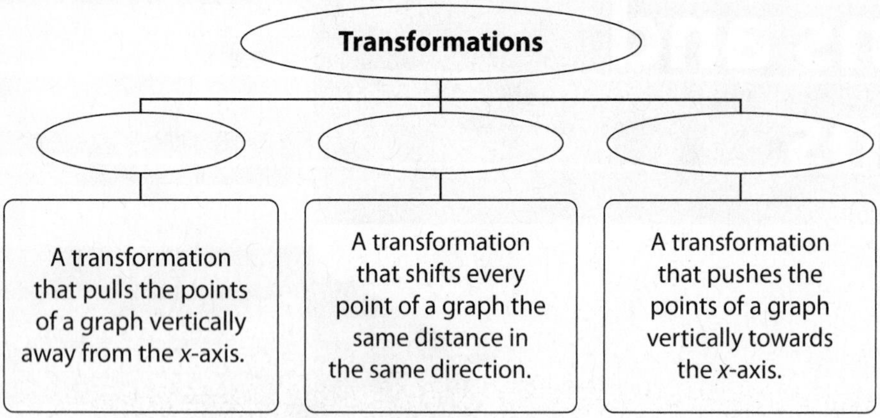

Vocabulary

Review Words

asymptote (*asíntota*)

inverse function (*función inversa*)

✔ translation (*traslación*)

✔ vertical compression (*compresión vertical*)

✔ vertical stretch (*estiramiento vertical*)

Preview Words

explicit formula (*fórmula explícita*)

geometric sequence (*sucesión geométrica*)

logarithmic function (*función logarítmica*)

recursive formula (*fórmula recurrente*)

Understand Vocabulary

To become familiar with some of the vocabulary terms in the module, consider the following. You may refer to the module, the glossary, or a dictionary.

1. A sequence in which the ratio of successive terms is a constant r, where $r \neq 0$ or 1 , is a __?__.

2. A __?__ is a rule for a sequence in which one or more previous terms are used to generate the next term.

3. A __?__ is the inverse of an exponential function.

Active Reading

Booklet Before beginning the unit, create a booklet to help you organize what you learn. Each page of the booklet should correspond to a lesson in the unit and summarize the most important information from the lesson. Include definitions, examples, and graphs to help you recall the main elements of the lesson. Highlight the main idea and use colored pencils to help you illustrate any important concepts or differences.

Sequences and Series

MODULE 12

Essential Question: How do sequences and series help to solve real-world problems?

REAL WORLD VIDEO
Fractal geography is the study of fractal patterns that occur in geographic features such as coastlines and watersheds. Check out how geometric series are involved in determining the area and perimeter of fractals.

MODULE PERFORMANCE TASK PREVIEW

How Big Is That Snowflake?

Did you ever make cutout snowflakes in school? If you did, you folded the paper a few times and snipped little triangles from the edges. The more you snipped, the more you decreased the overall area. In this module, you'll explore a fractal pattern called a Koch snowflake that starts with a triangle and adds smaller and smaller triangles to the edges. So, what is the total area of a Koch snowflake? The answer to this will crystalize later in the module.

Are YOU Ready?

Complete these exercises to review skills you will need for this module.

Personal Math Trainer

- Online Homework
- Hints and Help
- Extra Practice

Real Numbers

Example 1 Add: $\frac{5}{6} + \frac{5}{7} + \frac{5}{8}$

$\frac{5}{2 \cdot 3} + \frac{5}{7} + \frac{5}{2^3}$ Use prime factors in denominators.

$\frac{5(2^2 \cdot 7)}{2 \cdot 3(2^2 \cdot 7)} + \frac{5(2^3 \cdot 3)}{7(2^3 \cdot 3)} + \frac{5(3 \cdot 7)}{2^3(3 \cdot 7)}$ Use the LCD to rewrite fractions.

$\frac{365}{168}$ Simplify and add numerators.

Add.

1. $\frac{1}{2} + \frac{2}{3} + \frac{3}{4}$

2. $\frac{2}{3} + \frac{1}{2} + \frac{2}{5}$

3. $\frac{1}{8} + \frac{3}{10} + \frac{5}{12}$

Exponential Functions

Example 2 Write the values for $f(x)$ for $x = \{3, 4, 5\}$, if

$f(x) = \frac{1}{8}(4)^x$

$f(3) = \frac{1}{8}(4)^3 = \frac{1}{8}(64) = 8$

$f(4) = \frac{1}{8}(4)^4 = \frac{1}{8}(256) = 32$

$f(5) = \frac{1}{8}(4)^5 = \frac{1}{8}(1024) = 128$

The solution set is {8, 32, 128}.

Write the solution set for $f(x)$ for $x = \{3, 4, 5\}$.

4. $f(x) = 0.2(5)^x$

5. $f(x) = \frac{2}{3}(3)^x$

6. $f(x) = 0.75(2)^x$

12.1 Arithmetic Sequences

Essential Question: What are algebraic ways to define an arithmetic sequence?

Resource Locker

Explore Investigating Arithmetic Sequences

Consider a staircase where the vertical distance between steps is 7.5 inches and you must walk up 14 steps to get from the first floor to the second floor, a total vertical distance of 105 inches. Define two functions: $B(s)$, which models the distance from the bottom of the staircase (the first floor) to the bottom of your foot, and $T(s)$, which models the distance from the bottom of your foot to the top of the staircase (the second floor). For both functions, the independent variable s represents the number of steps that you have walked up.

(A) Complete the table. Show your calculations.

s	$B(s)$	$T(s)$
0	0	105
1	$0 + 7.5 = 7.5$	?
2	$0 + 2(7.5) = 15$	?
3	?	?
4	?	?

(B) Based on the patterns in the table, write rules for the two functions in terms of s.

$B(s) =$?

$T(s) =$?

(C) Identify the domain and range of $B(s)$.

- The domain of $B(s)$ is $\{0, 1, 2, 3, 4,$?, ?, ?, ?, ?, ?, ?, ?, ?, ?$\}$.
- The range of $B(s)$ is $\{0, 7.5, 15,$?, ?, ?, ?, ?, ?, ?, ?, ?, ?, ?, ?$\}$.

(D) Graph $B(s)$.

(E) Identify the domain and range of $T(s)$.

- The domain of $T(s)$ is

$\{0, 1, 2, 3, 4,$? , ? , ? , ? , ? , ? , ? , ? , ? , ? $\}$.

- The range of $T(s)$ is

$\{105,$? , ? , ? , ? , ? , ? , ? , ? , ? , ? , ? , ? ,

? , ? $\}$.

(F) Graph $T(s)$.

Reflect

1. Both $B(s)$ and $T(s)$ are linear functions, but their graphs consist of discrete points. Why?

2. How are $B(s)$ and $T(s)$ different? Why?

Explain 1 Writing Explicit and Recursive Rules for Arithmetic Sequences

A **sequence** is an ordered list of numbers. Each number in the list is called a *term* of the sequence. You can think of a sequence as a function with a subset of the set of integers as the domain and the set of terms of the sequence as the range. An **explicit rule** for a sequence defines the term in position n as a function of n. A **recursive rule** for a sequence defines the term in position n by relating it to one or more previous terms.

An **arithmetic sequence**, also known as a *discrete linear function*, is a sequence for which consecutive terms have a *common difference*. For instance, the terms of the sequence 0, 7.5, 15, 22.5, 30, 37.5, 45, 52.5, 60, 67.5, 75, 82.5, 90, 97.5, 105, which are the values of the function $B(s)$ from the Explore, have a common difference of 7.5. Likewise, the terms of the sequence 105, 97.5, 90, 82.5, 75, 67.5, 60, 52.5, 45, 37.5, 30, 22.5, 15, 7.5, 0, which are the values of the function $T(s)$ from the Explore, have a common difference of −7.5. Both sequences are arithmetic.

You can write different explicit and recursive rules for a sequence depending on what integer you use as the position number for the initial term of the sequence. The most commonly used starting position numbers are 0 and 1. The table shows rules for the sequences that you examined in the Explore.

	Sequence	
	0, 7.5, 15, 22.5, 30, 37.5, 45, 52.5, 60, 67.5, 75, 82.5, 90, 97.5, 105	105, 97.5, 90, 82.5, 75, 67.5, 60, 52.5, 45, 37.5, 30, 22.5, 15, 7.5, 0
Explicit rule when starting position is 0	$f(n) = 0 + 7.5n$ for $0 \leq n \leq 14$	$f(n) = 105 - 7.5n$ for $0 \leq n \leq 14$
Explicit rule when starting position is 1	$f(n) = 0 + 7.5(n - 1)$ for $1 \leq n \leq 15$	$f(n) = 105 - 7.5(n - 1)$ for $1 \leq n \leq 15$
Recursive rule when starting position is 0	$f(0) = 0$ and $f(n) = f(n - 1) + 7.5$ for $1 \leq n \leq 14$	$f(0) = 105$ and $f(n) = f(n - 1) - 7.5$ for $1 \leq n \leq 14$
Recursive rule when starting position is 1	$f(1) = 0$ and $f(n) = f(n - 1) + 7.5$ for $2 \leq n \leq 15$	$f(1) = 105$ and $f(n) = f(n - 1) - 7.5$ for $2 \leq n \leq 15$

In general, when 0 is the starting position for the initial term a of an arithmetic sequence with common difference d, the sequence has the explicit rule $f(n) = a + dn$ for $n \geq 0$ and the recursive rule $f(0) = a$ and $f(n) = f(n-1) + d$ for $n \geq 1$. When 1 is the starting position of the initial term, the sequence has the explicit rule $f(n) = a + d(n-1)$ for $n \geq 1$ and the recursive rule $f(1) = a$ and $f(n) = f(n-1) + d$ for $n \geq 2$.

Example 1 **Use the given table to write an explicit and a recursive rule for the sequence.**

(A)

n	0	1	2	3	4	5
$f(n)$	2	5	8	11	14	17

First, check the differences of consecutive values of $f(n)$:

$5 - 2 = 3$, $8 - 5 = 3$, $11 - 8 = 3$, $14 - 11 = 3$, and $17 - 14 = 3$

The differences are the same, so the sequence is arithmetic.

The initial term a of the sequence is 2, and its position number is 0. As already observed, the common difference d is 3.

So, the explicit rule for the sequence is $f(n) = 2 + 3n$ for $0 \leq n \leq 5$. The recursive rule is $f(0) = 2$ and $f(n) = f(n-1) + 3$ for $1 \leq n \leq 5$.

(B)

n	1	2	3	4	5	6
$f(n)$	29	25	21	17	13	9

First, check the differences of consecutive values of $f(n)$:

$25 - 29 = -4$, $21 - 25 = -4$, $17 - 21 = -4$, $13 - 17 = -4$, and $9 - 13 = -4$

The differences are the same, so the sequence is arithmetic.

The initial term a of the sequence is 29, and its position number is 1. As already observed, the common difference d is -4.

So, the explicit rule for the sequence is $f(n) = 29 - 4n$ for $1 \leq n \leq 6$. The recursive rule is $f(1) = 29$ and $f(n) = f(n-1) + -4$ for $2 \leq n \leq 6$.

Your Turn

Use the given table to write an explicit and a recursive rule for the sequence.

3.

n	0	1	2	3	4	5
$f(n)$	−7	−2	3	8	13	18

4.

n	1	2	3	4	5	6
$f(n)$	11	5	−1	−7	−13	−19

Explain 2 Graphing Arithmetic Sequences

As you saw in the Explore, the graph of an arithmetic sequence consists of points that lie on a line. The arithmetic sequence 3, 7, 11, 15, 19 has a final term, so it is called a *finite* sequence and its graph has a countable number of points. The arithmetic sequence 3, 7, 11, 15, 19, ... does not have a final term (indicated by the three dots), so it is called an *infinite* sequence and its graph has infinitely many points. Since you cannot show the complete graph of an infinite sequence, you should simply show as many points as the grid allows.

Example 2 **Write the terms of the given arithmetic sequence and then graph the sequence.**

(A) $f(n) = -1 + 2n$ for $0 \leq n \leq 4$

Make a table of values.

n	$f(n)$
0	$-1 + 2(0) = -1$
1	$-1 + 2(1) = 1$
2	$-1 + 2(2) = 3$
3	$-1 + 2(3) = 5$
4	$-1 + 2(4) = 7$

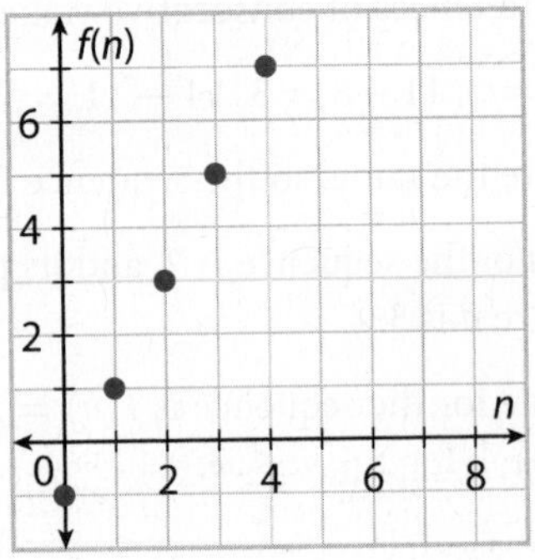

So, the sequence is −1, 1, 3, 5, 7.

Graph the sequence.

(B) $f(1) = 4$ and $f(n) = f(n-1) - 0.25$ for $n \geq 2$

Make a table of values, bearing in mind that the table could be extended because the sequence is infinite.

n	$f(n)$
1	4
2	$f(2) = f(1) - 0.25 = 4 - 0.25 =$ 3.75
3	$f(3) = f(2) - 0.25 =$ 3.75 $- 0.25 =$ 3.5
4	$f(4) = f(3) - 0.25 =$ 3.5 $- 0.25 =$ 3.25
5	$f(5) = f(4) - 0.25 =$ 3.25 $- 0.25 =$ 3

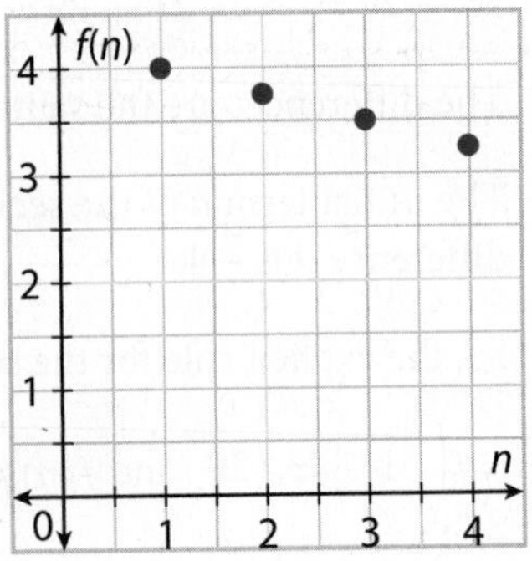

So, the sequence is 4, 3.75, 3.5, 3.25, 3, ...

Graph the sequence.

Your Turn

Write the terms of the given arithmetic sequence and then graph the sequence.

5. $f(n) = 8 - \frac{2}{3}(n-1)$ for $1 \leq n \leq 7$

6. $f(0) = -3$ and $f(n) = f(n-1) - 1$ for $n \geq 1$

Explain 3 Modeling with Arithmetic Sequences

Some real-world situations, like the situation in the Explore, can be modeled with an arithmetic sequence. You can then use a rule for the sequence to solve problems related to the situation.

Example 3 **Write a recursive rule and an explicit rule for an arithmetic sequence that models the situation. Then use the rule to answer the question.**

(A) There are 19 seats in the row nearest the stage of a theater. Each row after the first one has 2 more seats than the row before it. How many seats are in the 13th row?

Let n represent the row number, starting with 1 for the first row. The verbal description gives you a recursive rule: $f(1) = 19$ and $f(n) = f(n-1) + 2$ for $n \geq 2$. Since the initial term is 19 and the common difference is 2, an explicit rule is $f(n) = 19 + 2(n-1)$ for $n \geq 1$.

To find the number of seats in the 13th row, find using the explicit rule.

$f(13) = 19 + 2(13 - 1) = 43$

So, there are 43 seats in the 13th row.

(B) A student with a part-time job borrowed money from her parents to purchase a bicycle. The graph shows the amount the student owes her parents as she makes equal weekly payments. The amount owed is shown only for the first 5 weeks.

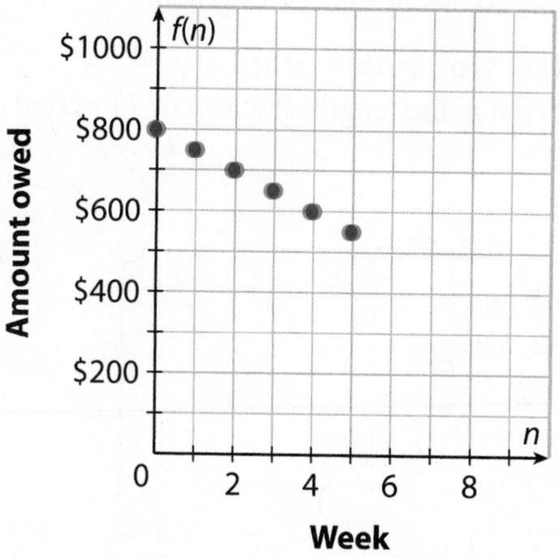

In how many weeks after purchasing the bicycle will the loan be paid off?

Let n represent the number of weeks since the loan was made, starting with 0 for the time at which the loan was made. The sequence of amounts owed is arithmetic because the weekly payments are equal. To determine the amount of the weekly payment, let $f(n)$ represent the amount owed

at week n, and observe from the graph that $f(0) =$ 800 and $f(2) =$ 700. The general explicit rule for the sequence is $f(n) = a + dn$. Substituting 2 for n, the value of $f(0)$ for a, and the value of $f(2)$ for $f(n)$ in $f(n) = a + dn$, you can solve for the common difference d:

$f(2) = f(0) + 2d$

$700 = 800 + 2d$

$-100 = 2d$

$-50 = d$

So, the amount of the weekly payment is \$50 , and an explicit rule for the sequence is $f(n) = \boxed{800} + \left(\boxed{-50}\right)n$. A recursive rule for the sequence is $f(0) = \boxed{800}$ and $f(n) = f(n-1) + \boxed{-50}$ for $n \geq 1$.

To determine when the loan will be paid off, you want to find the value of n for which $f(n) = 0$. Use the explicit rule.

$$f(n) = 0$$

$$\boxed{800} + \left(\boxed{-50}\right)n = 0$$

$$\boxed{-50}\, n = \boxed{-800}$$

$$n = \boxed{16}$$

So, the loan will be paid off in 16 weeks.

Your Turn

Write a recursive rule and an explicit rule for an arithmetic sequence that models the situation. Then use the rule to answer the question.

7. The starting salary for a summer camp counselor is \$395 per week. In each of the subsequent weeks, the salary increases by \$45 to encourage experienced counselors to work for the entire summer. If the salary is \$710 for the last week of the camp, for how many weeks does the camp run?

8. The graph shows the length, in inches, of a row of grocery carts when various numbers of carts are nested together. What is the length of a row of 25 nested carts?

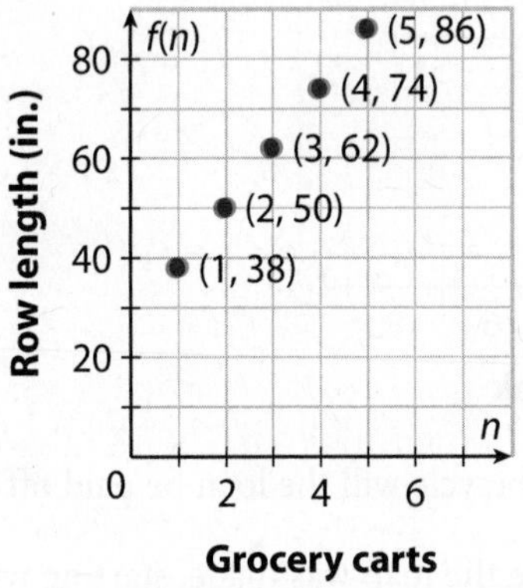

Elaborate

9. **Discussion** Is it easier to use an explicit rule or a recursive rule to find the 10th term in an arithmetic sequence? Explain.

10. What do you know about the terms in an arithmetic sequence with a common difference of 0?

11. Describe the difference between the graph of an arithmetic sequence with a positive common difference and the graph of an arithmetic sequence with a negative common difference.

12. **Essential Question Check-In** Does the rule $f(n) = -2 + 5n$ for $n \geq 0$ define an arithmetic sequence, and is the rule explicit or recursive? How do you know?

Evaluate: Homework and Practice

1. Consider the staircase in the Explore. How would the functions $B(s)$ and $T(s)$ change if the staircase were a spiral staircase going from the first floor to the third floor, with the same step height and distance between floors?

Personal Math Trainer
- Online Homework
- Hints and Help
- Extra Practice

Use the given table to write an explicit and a recursive rule for the sequence.

2.

n	0	1	2	3	4
$f(n)$	−6	1	8	15	22

3.

n	0	1	2	3	4
$f(n)$	8	5	2	−1	−4

Given the recursive rule for an arithmetic sequence, write the explicit rule.

4. $f(0) = 6$ and $f(n) = f(n-1) + 5$ for $n \geq 1$

5. $f(1) = 19$ and $f(n) = f(n-1) - 10$ for $n \geq 2$

Given the explicit rule for an arithmetic sequence, write the recursive rule.

6. $f(n) = 9.6 - 0.2(n-1)$ for $n \geq 1$

7. $f(n) = 14 + 8n$ for $n \geq 0$

Write the terms of the given arithmetic sequence and then graph the sequence.

8. $f(n) = 7 - \frac{1}{2}n$ for $n \geq 0$

9. $f(n) = 3 + 2(n-1)$ for $1 \leq n \leq 5$

10. $f(1) = -0.5$ and $f(n) = f(n-1) - 0.5$ for $n \geq 2$

11. $f(0) = -5$ and $f(n) = f(n-1) + 3$ for $1 \leq n \leq 4$

Write a recursive rule and an explicit rule for an arithmetic sequence that models the situation. Then use the rule to answer the question.

12. Thomas begins an exercise routine for 20 minutes each day. Each week he plans to add 5 minutes per day to the length of his exercise routine. For how many minutes will he exercise each day of the 6th week?

13. The Louvre pyramid in Paris, France, is built of glass panes. There are 4 panes in the top row, and each additional row has 4 more panes than the previous row. How many panes are in the 17th row?

14. Clarissa is buying a prom dress on layaway. The dress costs $185. She makes a down payment of $20 to put the dress on layaway and then makes weekly payments of $15. In how many weeks is the dress paid off?

15. The graph shows the height, in inches, of a stack of various numbers of identical plastic cups. The stack of cups will be placed on a shelf with 12 inches of vertical clearance with the shelf above. What number of cups can be in the stack without having a tight fit?

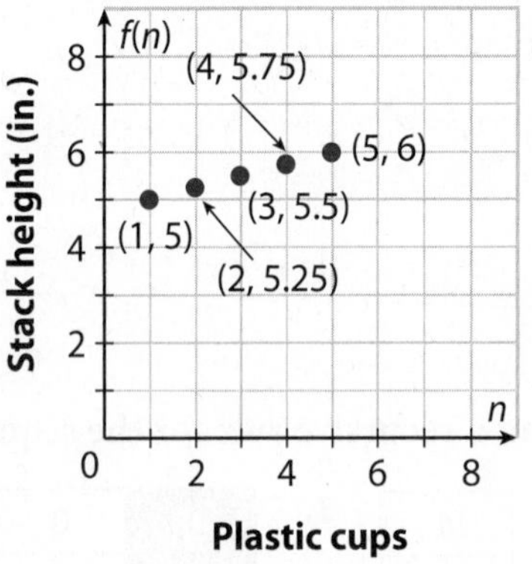

16. Determine whether each of the following sequences is arithmetic or is not arithmetic.

A. 1, 1, 2, 3, 5, 8, 13, 21, 34

B. 1, 4, 7, 10, 13, 16, 19

C. 1, 2, 4, 9, 16, 25

D. −4, 3, 10, 17, 24, 31

E. $\frac{1}{2}, \frac{2}{3}, \frac{3}{4}, \frac{4}{5}, \frac{5}{6}, \frac{6}{7}, \frac{7}{8}, \frac{8}{9}$

F. 18.5, 13, 7.5, 2, −3.5, −9

H.O.T. Focus on Higher Order Thinking

17. Multiple Representations The graphs of two arithmetic sequences are shown.

Graph of sequence A

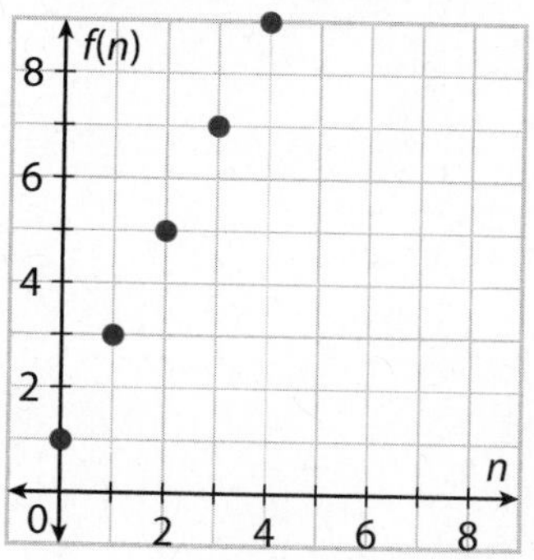

Graph of sequence B

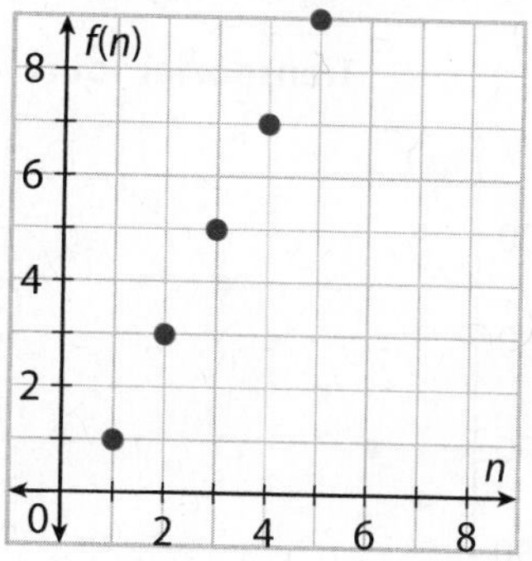

a. Are the sequences the same or different? Explain.

b. Write an explicit rule for each sequence.

c. How do the explicit rules indicate the geometric relationship between the two graphs?

18. Communicate Mathematical Ideas You know that if $(x_1, f(x_1))$ and $(x_2, f(x_2))$ are two points on the graph of a linear function, the slope of the function's graph is $m = \frac{f(x_2) - f(x_1)}{x_2 - x_1}$. Suppose $(n_1, f(n_1))$ and $(n_2, f(n_2))$ are two points on the graph of an arithmetic sequence with the explicit rule $f(n) = a + dn$. What does the expression $\frac{f(n_2) - f(n_1)}{n_2 - n_1}$ tell you about the arithmetic sequence? Justify your answer.

19. Construct Arguments Show how the recursive rule $f(0) = a$ and $f(n) = f(n-1) + d$ for $n \geq 1$ generates the explicit rule $f(n) = a + dn$ for $n \geq 0$.

Lesson Performance Task

The graph shows how the cost of a personal transporter tour depends on the number of participants. Write explicit and recursive rules for the cost of the tour. Then calculate the cost of the tour for 12 participants.

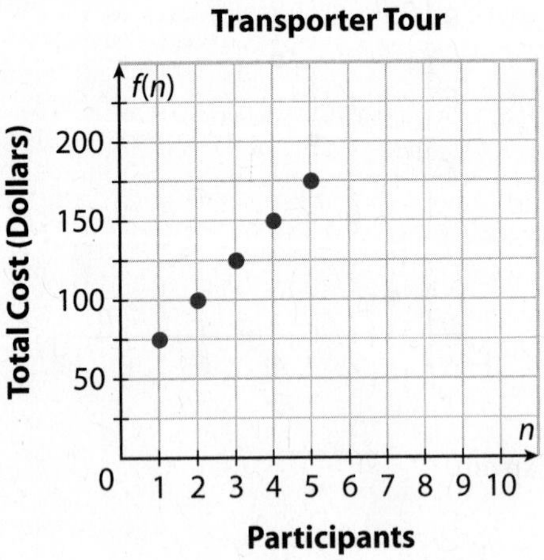

12.2 Geometric Sequences

Essential Question: How can you define a geometric sequence algebraically?

Resource Locker

Explore Investigating Geometric Sequences

As a tree grows, limbs branch off of the trunk, then smaller limbs branch off these limbs and each branch splits off into smaller and smaller copies of itself the same way throughout the entire tree. A mathematical object called a *fractal tree* resembles this growth.

Start by drawing a vertical line at the bottom of a piece of paper. This is Stage 0 of the fractal tree and is considered to be one 'branch'. The length of this branch defines 1 unit.

For Stage 1, draw 2 branches off of the top of the first branch. For this fractal tree, each smaller branch is $\frac{1}{2}$ the length of the previous branch and is at a 45-degree angle from the direction of the parent branch. The first four iterations, Stages 0-3, are shown.

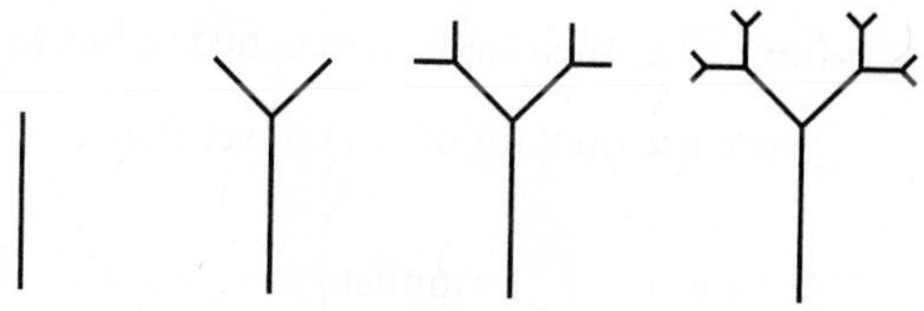

(A) In Stage 2, there are 2 branches drawn on the end of each of the 2 branches drawn in Stage 1. There are ? new branches in Stage 2. Each one of these branches will be $\frac{1}{2}$ the length of its predecessors or ? unit in length.

(B) For Stage 3, there are 8 new branches in total. To draw Stage 4, a total of ? branches must be drawn and to draw Stage 5, a total of ? branches must be drawn. Thus, each stage adds ? times as many branches as the previous stage did.

(C) Complete the table.

Stage	New Branches	Pattern	New Branches as a Power
Stage 0	1	1	2^0
Stage 1	2	$2 \cdot 1$	2^1
Stage 2	4	$2 \cdot 2$	2^2
Stage 3	8	$2 \cdot$?	?
Stage 4	16	$2 \cdot$?	?
Stage 5	32	$2 \cdot$?	?
Stage 6	64	$2 \cdot$?	?

Ⓓ The procedure for each stage after Stage 0 is to draw [?] branches on [?] branch added in the previous step.

Ⓔ Using the description above, write an equation for the number of new branches in a stage given the previous stage. Represent stage s as N_s; Stage 3 will be N_3.

$N_4 =$ [?] · [?]

$N_6 =$ [?] · [?]

$N_5 =$ [?] · [?]

$N_s =$ [?] · [?]

Ⓕ Rewrite the rule for Stage s as a function $N(s)$ that has a stage number as an input and the number of new branches in the stage as an output.

$N(s) =$ [?]

Ⓖ Recall that the domain of a function is the set of all numbers for which the function is defined. $N(s)$ is a function of s and s is the stage number. Since the stage number refers to the [?] the tree has branched, it has to be [?].

Write the domain of $N(s)$ in set notation.

$\{s \mid s$ is a [?] number$\}$

Ⓗ Similarly, the range of a function is the set of all possible values that the function can output over the domain. Let $N(s) = b$, the [?].

The range of $N(s)$ is $\{1, 2, 4$ [?], [?], [?], ...$\}$.

The range of $N(s)$ is $\{N \mid N = 2^s$, where s is [?]$\}$.

Ⓘ Graph the first five values of $N(s)$ on a grid with axes labeled as shown. The first value has been graphed for you.

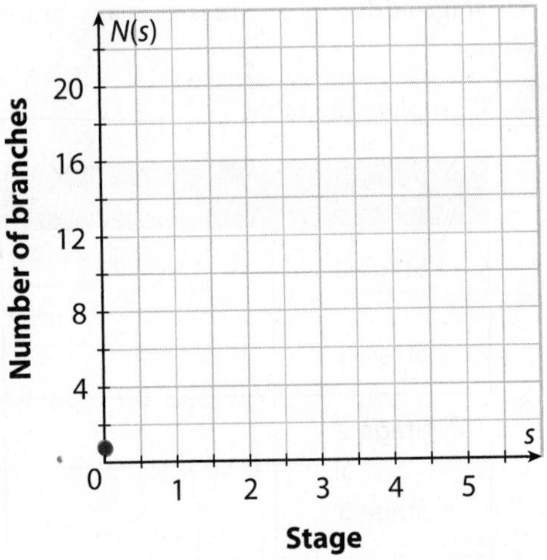

Ⓙ As s increases, $N(s)$ [?].

$N(s)$ is a(n) [?] function.

(K) Complete the table for branch length.

Stage Number	Number of Branches	Branch Length
0	1	1
1	2	$\frac{1}{2}$
2	4	$\frac{1}{4}$
3	8	$\frac{1}{?}$
4	16	$\frac{1}{?}$
5	32	$\frac{1}{?}$
⋮	⋮	⋮
n	2^n	$\frac{1}{?}$

(L) Write $L(s)$ expressing the branch length as a function of the Stage.

$$L(s) = \left(\frac{1}{?}\right)^{?}$$

(M) Write the domain and range of $L(s)$ in set notation.

The domain of $L(s)$ is $\{s \mid s \text{ is a } ? \text{ number}\}$.

The range of $L(s)$ is $\left\{1, \frac{1}{2}, \frac{1}{4}, ?, ?, ?, \ldots\right\}$.

The range of $L(s)$ is $\left\{L \mid L = \left(\frac{1}{2}\right)^s, \text{ where } s \text{ is } ?\right\}$.

(N) Graph the first five values of $L(s)$ on a grid with axes labeled as shown. The fifth point has been graphed for you.

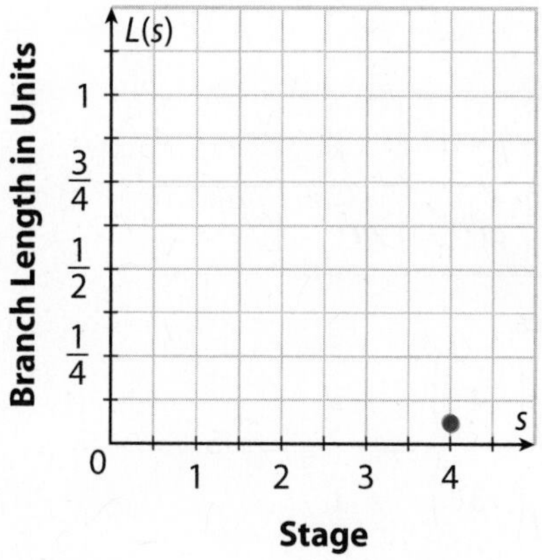

(O) As s increases, $L(s)$? . $L(s)$ is a(n) ? function.

Reflect

1. What is the total length added at each stage?
2. Is the total length of all the branches a sequence? If so, identify the sequence.

Explain 1 Writing Explicit and Recursive Rules for Geometric Sequences

A sequence is a set of numbers related by a common rule. All sequences start with an initial term. In a **geometric sequence**, the ratio of any term to the previous term is constant. This constant ratio is called the **common ratio** and is denoted by r $(r \neq 1)$. In the **explicit form** of the sequence, each term is found by evaluating the function $f(n) = ar^n$ or $f(n) = ar^{n-1}$ where a is the initial value and r is the common ratio, for some whole number n. Note that there are two forms of the explicit rule because it is permissible to call the initial value the first term or to call ar the first term.

A geometric sequence can also be defined recursively by $f(n) = r \cdot f(n-1)$ where either $f(0) = a$ or $f(1) = a$, again depending on the way the terms of the sequence are numbered. $f(n) = r \cdot f(n-1)$ is called the **recursive rule** for the sequence.

Example 1 **Write the explicit and recursive rules for a geometric sequence given a table of values.**

(A)

n	0	1	2	3	4	…	$j-1$	j	…
$f(n)$	3	6	12	24	48	…	$ar^{(j-1)}$	ar^j	…

Determine a and r, then write the explicit and recursive rules.

Find the common ratio: $\frac{f(n)}{f(n-1)} = r.$ $\frac{f(1)}{f(0)} = \frac{6}{3} = 2 = r$

Find the initial value, $a = f(0)$, from the table. $f(0) = 3 = a$

Find the explicit rule: $f(n) = ar^n$. $f(n) = 3 \cdot (2)^n$

Write the recursive rule. $f(n) = 2 \cdot f(n-1), n \geq 1$ and $f(0) = 3$

The explicit rule is $f(n) = 3 \cdot (2)^n$ and the recursive rule is $f(n) = 2 \cdot f(n-1), n \geq 1$ and $f(0) = 3$.

(B)

n	1	2	3	4	5	…	$j-1$	j	…
$f(n)$	$\frac{1}{25}$	$\frac{1}{5}$	1	5	25	…	$ar^{(j-1)}$	ar^j	…

Determine a and r, then write the explicit and recursive rules.

Find the common ratio: $\frac{f(n)}{f(n-1)} = r.$ $\frac{f(4)}{f(3)} = \frac{5}{1} = 5 = r$

Find the initial value, $a = f(1)$, from the table. $f(1) = \frac{1}{25} = a$

Find the explicit rule: $f(n) = ar^{n-1}$. $f(n) = \frac{1}{25} \cdot (5)^{n-1}$

Write the recursive rule. $f(n) = 5 \cdot f(n-1), n \geq 2$ and $f(1) = \frac{1}{25}$

The explicit rule is $f(n) = \frac{1}{25} \cdot (5)^{n-1}$ and the recursive rule is $f(n) = 5 \cdot f(n-1), n \geq 2$ where $f(1) = \frac{1}{25}$.

Reflect

3. **Discussion** If you were told that a geometric sequence had an initial value of $f(5) = 5$, could you write an explicit and a recursive rule for the function? What would the explicit rule be?

Your Turn

Write the explicit and recursive rules for a geometric sequence given a table of values.

4.

n	0	1	2	3	4	5	6	...
$f(n)$	$\frac{1}{27}$	$\frac{1}{9}$	$\frac{1}{3}$	1	3	9	27	...

5.

n	1	2	3	4	5	6	7	...
$f(n)$	0.001	0.01	0.1	1	10	100	1000	...

Explain 2 Graphing Geometric Sequences

To graph a geometric sequence given an explicit or a recursive rule you can use the rule to generate a table of values and then graph those points on a coordinate plane. Since the domain of a geometric sequence consists only of whole numbers, its graph consists of individual points, not a smooth curve.

Example 2 **Given either an explicit or recursive rule for a geometric sequence, use a table to generate values and draw the graph of the sequence.**

(A) Explicit rule: $f(n) = 2 \cdot 2^n, n \geq 0$

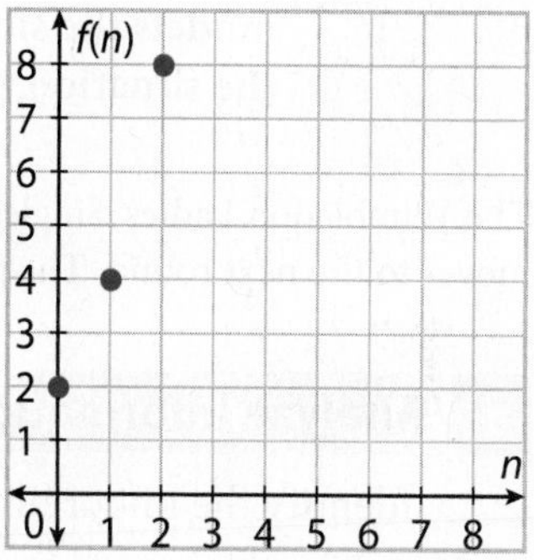

Use a table to generate points.

n	0	1	2	3	4	5	...
$f(n)$	2	4	8	16	32	64	...

Plot the first three points on the graph.

(B) Recursive rule: $f(n) = 0.5 \cdot f(n-1), n \geq 1$ and $f(0) = 16$

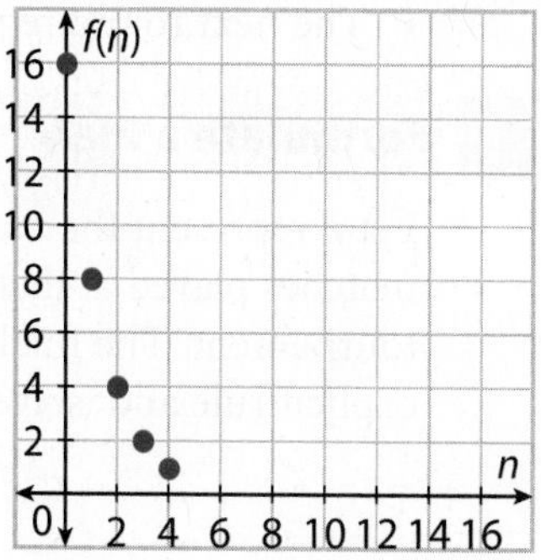

Use a table to generate points.

n	0	1	2	3	4	5	6	...
$f(n)$	16	8	4	2	1	0.5	0.25	...

Your Turn

Given either an explicit or recursive rule for a geometric sequence, use a table to generate values and draw the graph of the sequence.

6. $f(n) = 3 \cdot 2^{n-1}, n \geq 1$

n	1	2	3	4	5	...
f(n)						...

7. $f(n) = 3 \cdot f(n-1), n \geq 2$ and $f(1) = 2$

n	1	2	3	4	5	...
f(n)						...

Explain 3 Modeling With a Geometric Sequence

Given a real-world situation that can be modeled with a geometric sequence, you can use an explicit or a recursive rule to answer a question about the situation.

Example 3 **Write both an explicit and recursive rule for the geometric sequence that models the situation. Use the sequence to answer the question asked about the situation.**

The Wimbledon Ladies' Singles Championship begins with 128 players. Each match, two players play and only one moves to the next round. The players compete until there is one winner. How many rounds must the winner play?

Analyze Information

Identify the important information:

- The first round requires 64 matches, so $a =$ 64 .
- The next round requires half as many matches, so $r = \frac{1}{2}$.

Formulate a Plan

Let n represent the number of rounds played and let $f(n)$ represent the number of matches played at that round. Create the explicit rule and the recursive rule for the tournament. The final round will have 1 match(es), so substitute this value into the explicit rule and solve for n.

Solve

The explicit rule is $f(n) = \boxed{64 \cdot \left(\frac{1}{2}\right)^{n-1}}$, $n = \geq 1$.

The recursive rule is $f(n) = \boxed{\frac{1}{2}} \cdot f(n-1)$, $n \geq 2$ and $f(1) = \boxed{64}$.

The final round will have 1 match, so substitute 1 for $f(n)$ into the explicit rule and solve for n.

$$f(n) = 64 \cdot \left(\frac{1}{2}\right)^{n-1}$$

$$\boxed{1} = 64 \cdot \left(\frac{1}{2}\right)^{n-1}$$

$$\boxed{\frac{1}{64}} = \left(\frac{1}{2}\right)^{n-1}$$

$$\left(\frac{1}{2}\right)^{\boxed{6}} = \left(\frac{1}{2}\right)^{n-1}$$

Two powers with the same positive base other than 1 are equal if and only if the exponents are equal.

$$\left(\frac{1}{2}\right)^{\boxed{6}} = \left(\frac{1}{2}\right)^{n-1}$$

$$\boxed{6} = n - 1$$

$$\boxed{7} = n$$

The winner must play in 7 rounds.

Justify and Evaluate

The answer of 7 rounds makes sense because using the explicit rule gives $f(7) = \boxed{1}$ and the final round will have 1 match. This result can be checked using the recursive rule, which again results in $f(7) = \boxed{1}$.

Your Turn

Write both an explicit and recursive rule for the geometric sequence that models the situation. Use the sequence to answer the question asked about the situation.

8. A particular type of bacteria divides into two new bacteria every 20 minutes. A scientist growing the bacteria in a laboratory begins with 200 bacteria. How many bacteria are present 4 hours later?

Elaborate

9. Describe the difference between an explicit rule for a geometric sequence and a recursive rule.

10. How would you decide to use $n = 0$ or $n = 1$ as the starting value of n for a geometric sequence modeling a real-world situation?

11. **Essential Question Check-In** How can you define a geometric sequence in an algebraic way? What information do you need to write these rules?

Evaluate: Homework and Practice

Personal Math Trainer
- Online Homework
- Hints and Help
- Extra Practice

You are creating self-similar fractal trees. You start with a trunk of length 1 unit (at Stage 0). Then the trunk splits into two branches each one-third the length of the trunk. Then each one of these branches splits into two new branches, with each branch one-third the length of the previous one.

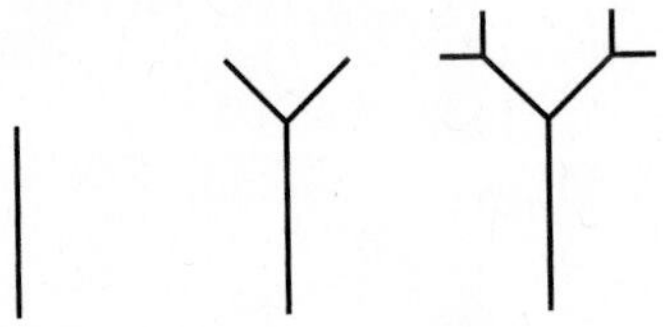

1. Can the length of the new branches at each stage be described with a geometric sequence? Explain. If so, find the explicit form for the length of each branch.
2. Can the number of new branches at each stage be described with a geometric sequence? Explain. If so, find the recursive rule for the number of new branches.
3. Can the total length of the new branches at each stage be modeled with a geometric sequence? Explain. (The total length of the new branches is the sum of the lengths of all the new branches.)

Write the explicit and recursive rules for a geometric sequence given a table of values.

4.

n	0	1	2	3	4	...
$f(n)$	0.1	0.3	0.9	2.7	8.1	...

5.

n	0	1	2	3	4	...
$f(n)$	100	10	1	0.1	0.01	...

6.

n	1	2	3	4	5	...
$f(n)$	1000	100	10	1	0.1	...

7.

n	1	2	3	4	5	...
$f(n)$	10^{50}	10^{47}	10^{44}	10^{41}	10^{38}	...

Given either an explicit or recursive rule for a geometric sequence, use a table to generate values and draw the graph of the sequence.

8. $f(n) = \left(\frac{1}{2}\right) \cdot 4^n,\ n \geq 0$

n	0	1	2	3	4	...
$f(n)$						...

9. $f(n) = 2 \cdot f(n-1), n \geq 1$ and $f(0) = 0.5$

n	0	1	2	3	4	...
f(n)						...

10. $f(n) = 0.5 \cdot f(n-1), n \geq 2$ and $f(1) = 8$

n	1	2	3	4	5	...
f(n)						...

11. $f(n) = \frac{2}{3} \cdot f(n-1), n \geq 2$ and $f(1) = 1$

n	1	2	3	4	5	...
f(n)						...

Write both an explicit and recursive rule for the geometric sequence that models the situation. Use the sequence to answer the question asked about the situation.

12. The Alphaville Youth Basketball committee is planning a single-elimination tournament (for all the games at each round, the winning team advances and the losing team is eliminated). The committee wants the winner to play 4 games. How many teams should the committee invite?

13. An online video game tournament begins with 1024 players. Four players play in each game. In each game there is only one winner, and only the winner advances to the next round. How many games will the winner play?

14. **Genealogy** You have 2 biological parents, 4 biological grandparents, and 8 biological great-grandparents.

a. How many direct ancestors do you have if you trace your ancestry back 6 generations? How many direct ancestors do you have if you go back 12 generations?

b. **What if...?** How does the explicit rule change if you are considered the first generation?

15. Fractals **Waclaw Sierpinski designed various fractals. He would take a geometric figure, shade it in, and then start removing the shading to create a fractal pattern.**

a. The Sierpinski triangle is a fractal based on a triangle. In each iteration, the center of each shaded triangle is removed.

Given that the area of the original triangle is 1 square unit, write a sequence for the area of the nth iteration of the Sierpinski triangle. (The first iteration is the original triangle.)

b. The Sierpinski carpet is a fractal based on a square. In each iteration, the center of each shaded square is removed.

Given that the area of the original square is 1 square unit, write a sequence for the area of the nth iteration of the Sierpinski carpet. (The first iteration is the original square.)

c. Find the shaded area of the fourth iteration of the Sierpinski carpet.

16. A piece of paper is 0.1 millimeter thick. When folded, the paper is twice as thick.

a. Find both the explicit and recursive rule for this geometric sequence.

b. Studies have shown that you can fold a piece of paper a maximum of 7 times. How thick will the paper be if it is folded on top of itself 7 times?

c. Assume that you could fold the paper as many times as you want. How many folds would be required for the paper to be taller than Mount Everest at 8850 meters? (*Hint:* Use a calculator to generate two large powers of 2 and check if the required number of millimeters is between those two powers. Continue to refine your guesses.)

H.O.T. Focus on Higher Order Thinking

17. Justify Reasoning Suppose you have the following table of points of a geometric sequence. The table is incomplete so you do not know the initial value. Determine whether each of the following can or cannot be the rule for the function in the table. If a function cannot be the rule for the sequence, explain why.

n	...	4	5	6	7	...
$f(n)$	...	6	12	24	48	...

A. $f(n) = 2^n$

B. $f(n) = \frac{3}{8} \cdot (2)^n$

C. $f(n) = 2 \cdot f(n-1),\ n \geq 1$ and $f(0) = 6$

D. $f(n) = \frac{3}{4} \cdot (2)^{n-1}$

E. $f(n) = 2 \cdot f(n-1),\ n \geq 1$ and $f(0) = \frac{3}{8}$

F. $f(n) = 2 \cdot f(n-1),\ n \geq 1$ and $f(1) = \frac{3}{4}$

G. $f(n) = (1.5) \cdot (2)^{n-2}$

H. $f(n) = 3 \cdot (2)^{n-3}$

18. Communicate Mathematical Ideas Show that the rules $f(n) = ar^n$ for $n \geq 0$ and $f(n) = ar^{n-1}$ for $n \geq 1$ for a geometric sequence are equivalent.

Lesson Performance Task

Have you ever heard of musical octaves? An octave is the interval between a musical note and the same musical note in the next higher or lower pitch. The frequencies of the sound waves of successive octaves of a note form a geometric sequence. For example, the table shows the frequencies in hertz (Hz), or cycles per second, produced by playing the note D in ascending octaves, D_0 being the lowest D note audible to the human ear.

Scale of D's	
Note	**Frequency (Hz)**
D_0	18.35
D_1	36.71
D_2	73.42
D_3	146.83

a. Explain how to write an explicit rule and a recursive rule for the frequency of D notes in hertz, where $n = 1$ represents D_1.

b. The note commonly called "middle D" is D_4. Use the explicit rule or the recursive rule from part **a** to predict the frequency for middle D.

c. Humans generally cannot hear sounds with frequencies greater than 20,000 Hz. What is the first D note that humans cannot hear? Explain.

12.3 Geometric Series

Essential Question: How do you find the sum of a finite geometric series?

Resource Locker

Explore 1 Investigating a Geometric Series

A **series** is the expression formed by adding the terms of a sequence. If the sequence is geometric and has a finite number of terms, it is called a **finite geometric series**. In this Explore, you will generate several related finite geometric series and find a formula for calculating the sum of each series.

Ⓐ Start with a rectangular sheet of paper and assume the sheet has an area of 1 square unit. Cut the sheet in half and lay down one of the half-pieces. Then cut the remaining piece in half, and lay down one of the quarter-pieces as if rebuilding the original sheet of paper. Continue the process: At each stage, cut the remaining piece in half, and lay down one of the two pieces as if rebuilding the original sheet of paper.

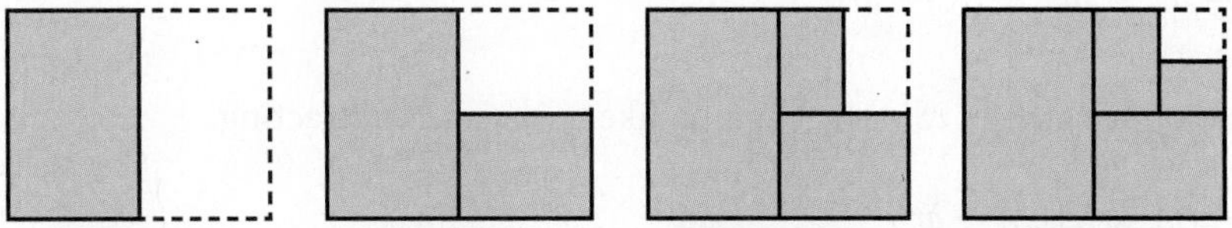

Ⓑ Complete the table by expressing the total area of the paper that has been laid down in two ways:

- as the sum of the areas of the pieces that have been laid down, and
- as the difference between 1 and the area of the remaining piece.

Stage	Sum of the areas of the pieces that have been laid down	Difference of 1 and the area of the remaining piece
1	$\frac{1}{2}$	$1 - \frac{1}{2} =$?
2	$\frac{1}{2} +$? $=$?	$1 -$? $=$?
3	$\frac{1}{2} +$? $+$? $=$?	$1 -$? $=$?
4	$\frac{1}{2} +$? $+$? $+$? $=$?	$1 -$? $=$?

Reflect

1. Write the sequence formed by the areas of the individual pieces that are laid down. What type of sequence is it?

2. In the table from Step B, you wrote four related finite geometric series: $\frac{1}{2}$, $\frac{1}{2} + \frac{1}{4}$, $\frac{1}{2} + \frac{1}{4} + \frac{1}{8}$, and $\frac{1}{2} + \frac{1}{4} + \frac{1}{8} + \frac{1}{16}$. One way you found the sum of each series was simply to add up the terms. Describe another way you found the sum of each series.

3. If the process of cutting the remaining piece of paper and laying down one of the two pieces is continued, you obtain the finite geometric series $\frac{1}{2} + \frac{1}{4} + \dots + \left(\frac{1}{2}\right)^n$ at the nth stage. Use your answer to the previous question to find the sum of this series.

Explore 2 Deriving a Formula for the Sum of a Finite Geometric Series

To find a general formula for the sum of a finite geometric series with n terms, begin by writing the series as $S(n) = a + ar + ar^2 + \dots + ar^{n-1}$.

(A) Find an expression for $rS(n)$.

$$rS(n) = ar + ar^2 + ar^{?} \dots + ar^{?}$$

(B) Find an expression for $S(n) - rS(n)$ by aligning like terms and subtracting.

$$S(n) = a + ar + ar^2 + \dots + ar^{n-1}$$

$$rS(n) = ar + ar^2 + \dots + ar^{n-1} + ar^n$$

$$S(n) - rS(n) = a + \boxed{?} + \boxed{?} + \dots + \boxed{?} - ar^n$$

(C) Simplify the expression for $S(n) - rS(n)$.

$$S(n) - rS(n) = \boxed{?}$$

(D) Factor the left and right sides of the equation in Step C.

$$S(n)\boxed{?} = \boxed{?}\,(1 - r^{?})$$

(E) Divide both sides of the equation in Step D by $1 - r$.

$$S(n) = a\left(\frac{\boxed{?} - \boxed{?}}{1 - r}\right)$$

Reflect

4. Check to see if the formula in Step E gives the same result as the answer you wrote for Reflect 3.

5. What restrictions are there on the values of r that can be used in the formula for the sum of a finite geometric series? Explain.

Explain 1 Finding the Sum of a Finite Geometric Series

The formula $S(n) = a\left(\frac{1 - r^n}{1 - r}\right)$ for the sum of a geometric series requires knowing the values of a, r, and n.

Recall that you learned how to find a and r for a geometric sequence, and the technique is no different for a series: a is the value of the first term, and r is the ratio of any two successive terms. To find n, you can simply count the terms if they are all listed. For instance, for the finite geometric series $3 + 6 + 12 + 24 + 48$, you can see that $a = 3$, $r = 2$, and $n = 5$.

If some of the terms of a finite geometric series have been replaced by an ellipsis, as in $2 + 6 + 18 + \ldots + 1458$, you obviously can't count the terms. One way to deal with this situation is to generate the missing terms by using the common ratio, which in this case is 3. The next term after 18 is $3(18) = 54$, and repeatedly multiplying by 3 to generate successive terms gives $2 + 6 + 18 + 54 + 162 + 486 + 1458$, so the series has 7 terms.

Another way to find the number of terms in $2 + 6 + 18 + \ldots + 1458$ is to recognize that the nth term in a geometric series is ar^{n-1}. For the series $2 + 6 + 18 + \ldots + 1458$ whose nth term is $2(3)^{n-1}$, find n as follows:

$2(3)^{n-1} = 1458$	Set the nth term equal to the last term.
$(3)^{n-1} = 729$	Divide both as power of 3
$(3)^{n-1} = 3^6$	Write 729 as a power of 3
$n - 1 = 6$	When the bases are the same, you can equate the exponents.
$n = 7$	Add 1 to both sides

Find the sum of the finite geometric series.

(A) $5 + 15 + 45 + 135 + 405 + 1215$

Step 1 Find the values of a, r, and n.

The first term in the series is a.	$a = 5$
Find the common ratio r by dividing two successive terms.	$r = \frac{15}{5} = 3$
Count the terms to find n.	$n = 6$

Step 2 Use the formula $S(n) = a\left(\frac{1 - r^n}{1 - r}\right)$.

Substitute the values of a, r, and n.	$S(6) = 5\left(\frac{1 - 3^6}{1 - 3}\right)$
Evaluate the power in the numerator.	$= 5\left(\frac{1 - 729}{1 - 3}\right)$
Simplify the numerator and denominator.	$= 5\left(\frac{-728}{-2}\right)$
Simplify the fraction.	$= 5(364)$
Multiply.	$= 1820$

Ⓑ $\frac{1}{4} + \frac{1}{8} + \frac{1}{16} + \dots + \frac{1}{512}$

Step 1 Find the values of a, r, and n.

The first term in the series is a. $a = \boxed{\frac{1}{4}}$

Find the common ratio by dividing two successive terms. $r = \frac{\boxed{\frac{1}{8}}}{\boxed{\frac{1}{4}}} = \boxed{\frac{1}{2}}$

Set the nth term, $\frac{1}{4}\left(\frac{1}{2}\right)^{n-1}$, equal to the last term to find n. $\frac{1}{4}\left(\frac{1}{2}\right)^{n-1} = \frac{1}{512}$

Multiply both sides by $\boxed{4}$. $\left(\frac{1}{2}\right)^{n-1} = \frac{1}{128}$

Write $\frac{1}{128}$ as a power of $\frac{1}{2}$. $\left(\frac{1}{2}\right)^{n-1} = \left(\frac{1}{2}\right)^{\boxed{7}}$

Equate the exponents. $n - 1 = \boxed{7}$

Add 1 to both sides. $n = \boxed{8}$

Step 2 Use the formula $S(n) = a\left(\frac{1-r^n}{1-r}\right)$.

Substitute the values of a, r, and n. $S(8) = \boxed{\frac{1}{4}}\left(\frac{1-\left(\boxed{\frac{1}{2}}\right)^{\boxed{8}}}{1-\boxed{\frac{1}{2}}}\right)$

Evaluate the power in the numerator. $= \frac{1}{4}\left(\frac{1-\boxed{\frac{1}{256}}}{1-\frac{1}{2}}\right)$

Simplify the numerator and denominator. $= \frac{1}{4}\left(\frac{\boxed{\frac{255}{256}}}{\frac{1}{2}}\right)$

Simplify the fraction. $= \frac{1}{4}\left(\boxed{\frac{255}{128}}\right)$

Multiply. $= \boxed{\frac{255}{512}}$

Your Turn

Find the sum of the finite geometric series.

6. $1 - 2 + 4 - 8 + 16 - 32$

7. $\frac{1}{2} - \frac{1}{4} + \frac{1}{8} \dots - \frac{1}{256}$

Explain 2 Solving a Real-World Problem Involving a Finite Geometric Series

Some financial problems can be modeled by a geometric series. For instance, an *annuity* involves equal payments made at regular intervals for a fixed amount of time. Because money can be invested and earn interest, comparing the value of money today to the value of money in the future requires accounting for the effect of interest. The *future value* of an annuity is how much the annuity payments will be worth at some point in the future. The *present value* of an annuity is how much the annuity payments are worth in the present.

Although an interest rate is typically expressed as an annual rate, it can be converted to a rate for other periods of time. For instance, an annual interest rate of $r\%$ results in a monthly interest rate of $\frac{r}{12}\%$. In general, if interest is earned n times per year, an annual interest rate of $r\%$ is divided by n.

Example 2

Ⓐ Niobe is saving for a down payment on a new car, which she intends to buy a year from now. At the end of each month, she deposits \$200 from her paycheck into a dedicated savings account, which earns 3% annual interest that is applied to the account balance each month. After making 12 deposits, how much money will Niobe have in her savings account?

Niobe is interested in the future value of her annuity (savings plan). A 3% annual interest rate corresponds to a $\frac{3}{12}\% = 0.25\%$ monthly interest rate.

First, calculate the sequence of end-of-month account balances. Recognize the recursive nature of the calculations:

- The end-of-month balance for month 1 is \$200 because the first deposit of \$200 is made at the end of the month, but the deposit doesn't earn any interest that month.
- The end-of-month balance for any other month is the sum of the previous month's end-of-month balance, the interest earned on the previous month's end-of-month balance, and the next deposit.

So, if $B(m)$ represents the account balance for month m, then a recursive rule for the account balances is $B(1) = 200$ and $B(m) = B(m-1) + B(m-1) \cdot 0.0025 + 200$. Notice that you can rewrite the equation $B(m) = B(m-1) + B(m-1) \cdot 0.0025 + 200$ as $B(m) = B(m-1) \cdot 1.0025 + 200$ by using the Distributive Property.

Month	End-of-month balance of account
1	200
2	$200 \cdot 1.0025 + 200$
3	$[200(1.0025) + 200] \cdot 1.0025 + 200 = 200(1.0025)^2 + 200(1.0025) + 200$
4	$[200(1.0025)^2 + 200(1.0025) + 200] \cdot 1.0025 + 200 = 200(1.0025)^3 + 200(1.0025)^2 + 200(1.0025) + 200$
⋮	⋮
12	$[200(1.0025)^{10} + \cdots + 200] \cdot 1.0025 + 200 = 200(1.0025)^{11} + \cdots + 200(1.0025) + 200$

Next, find the sum of the finite geometric series that represents the end-of-month balance after 12 deposits. You may find it helpful to use the commutative property to rewrite $200(1.0025)^{11} + \cdots + 200(1.0025) + 200$ as $200 + 200(1.0025) + \cdots + 200(1.0025)^{11}$ so that it's easier to see that the initial term a is 200 and the common ratio r is 1.0025. Also, you know from the recursive process that this series has 12 terms. Apply the formula for the sum of a finite geometric series in order to obtain the final balance of the account.

$$S(12) = 200\left(\frac{1 - 1.0025^{12}}{1 - 1.0025}\right)$$

To evaluate the expression for the sum, use a calculator. You may find it helpful to enter the expression in parts and rely upon the calculator's Answer feature to accumulate the results. (You should avoid rounding intermediate calculations, because the round-off errors will compound and give an inaccurate answer.)

So, Niobe will have \$2433.28 in her account after she makes 12 deposits.

(B) Niobe decides to postpone buying a new car because she wants to get a new smart phone instead. She can pay the phone's full price of \$580 up front, or she can agree to pay an extra \$25 per month on her phone bill over the course of a two-year contract for phone service.

What is the present cost to Niobe if she agrees to pay \$25 per month for two years, assuming that she could put the money for the payments in a savings account that earns 3% annual interest and make \$25 monthly withdrawals for two years?

As in Part A, a 3% annual interest rate becomes a 0.25% monthly interest rate. If Niobe puts an amount M_1 in the savings account and lets it earn interest for 1 month, then she will have $M_1 + 0.0025M_1$, or $1.0025M_1$, available to make her first phone payment. Since she wants $1.0025M_1$ to equal \$25, M_1 must equal $\frac{\$25}{1.0025} \approx \$24.94$. This means that the present cost of her first phone payment is \$24.94, because that amount of money will be worth \$25 in 1 month after earning \$0.06 in interest.

Similarly, if Niobe puts an additional amount M_2 in the savings account and lets it earn interest for 2 months, then she will have $1.0025M_2$ after 1 month and $1.0025(1.0025M_2)$, or $(1.0025)^{2} M_2$, after 2 months. Since she wants $(1.0025)^{2} M_2$ to equal \$25, M_2 must equal $\frac{\$25}{(1.0025)^{2}} \approx \$\ 24.88$.

This means that the present cost of her second phone payment is \$ 24.88 . It also means that she must deposit a total of $M_1 + M_2 = \$24.94 + \$\ 24.88 = \$\ 49.82$ in the savings account in order to have enough money for her first two phone payments.

Generalize these results to complete the following table.

Number of Payments	Present Cost of Payments
1	$\frac{25}{1.0025}$
2	$\frac{25}{1.0025} + \frac{25}{(1.0025)^2}$
3	$\frac{25}{1.0025} + \frac{25}{(1.0025)^2} + \frac{25}{(1.0025)^3}$
⋮	⋮
24	$\frac{25}{1.0025} + \frac{25}{(1.0025)^2} + \cdots + \frac{25}{(1.0025)^{24}}$

Find the sum of the finite geometric series that represents the present cost of 24 payments.

$$a = \frac{25}{1.0025}$$

$$r = \frac{1}{1.0025}$$

$$n = 24$$

$$S(24) = \frac{25}{1.0025}\left(\frac{1 - \left(\frac{1}{1.0025}\right)^{24}}{1 - \frac{1}{1.0025}}\right)$$

$$\approx 581.65$$

Although Niobe will end up making total payments of $\$25 \cdot 24 = \$\ 600$, the present cost of the payments is \$581.65, which is only slightly more than the up-front price of the phone.

Your Turn

8. A lottery winner is given the choice of collecting \$1,000,000 immediately or collecting payments of \$6000 per month for the next 20 years. Assuming the lottery money can be invested in an account with an annual interest rate of 6% that is applied monthly, find the present value of the lottery's delayed-payout plan in order to compare it with the lump-sum plan and decide which plan is better.

Elaborate

9. An alternative way of writing the formula for the sum of a finite geometric series is $S(n) = \dfrac{a - r \cdot ar^{n-1}}{1 - r}$. Describe in words how to find the sum of a finite geometric series using this formula.

10. Describe how to find the number of terms in a finite geometric series when some of the terms have been replaced by an ellipsis.

11. **Discussion** When analyzing an annuity, why is it important to determine the annuity's present value or future value?

12. **Essential Question Check-In** What is the formula for the sum of the finite geometric series $a + ar + ar^2 + \cdots + ar^{n-1}$?

Evaluate: Homework and Practice

Personal Math Trainer
- Online Homework
- Hints and Help
- Extra Practice

1. Suppose you start with a square piece of paper that you divide into four quarters, cutting out an L-shaped piece using three of the quarters and laying it down to create the first term of a geometric series. You then use the remaining quarter to repeat the process three more times, as shown.

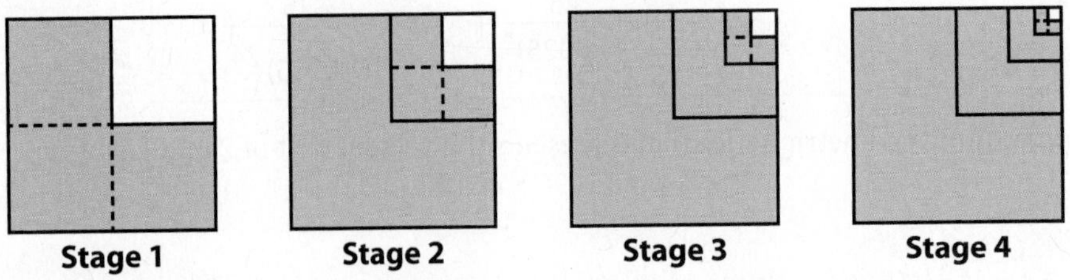

a. Complete the table.

Stage	Sum of the areas of the pieces that have been laid down	Difference of 1 and the area of the remaining piece
1	$\frac{3}{4}$	$1 - \frac{1}{4} = \frac{3}{4}$
2	?	?
3	?	?
4	?	?

b. Generalize the results in the table: At stage n, the second column gives you the finite geometric series $\frac{3}{4} + \frac{3}{16} + \cdots + 3\left(\frac{1}{4}\right)^n$. The third column gives you a way to find the sum of this series. What formula does the third column give you?

c. Show that the general formula for the sum of a finite geometric series agrees with the specific formula from part b.

2. In a later lesson you will learn how to use polynomial division to show that $\frac{x^n - 1}{x - 1} = x^{n-1} + x^{n-2} + \cdots + x^2 + x + 1$ for any integer n greater 0. Use this identity as an alternative method of deriving the formula for the sum of a finite geometric series with n terms. That is, given the series $a + ar + ar^2 + \cdots + ar^{n-1}$, show that its sum is $a\left(\frac{1 - r^n}{1 - r}\right)$.

Find the sum of the finite geometric series.

3. $-3 + 6 - 12 + 24 - 48 + 96 - 192 + 384$

4. $6 - 4 + \frac{8}{3} - \frac{16}{9} + \frac{32}{17}$

Determine how many terms the geometric series has, and then find the sum of the series.

5. $-12 - 4 - \frac{4}{3} - \cdots - \frac{4}{243}$

6. $0.3 + 0.03 + 0.003 + \cdots + 0.000003$

7. $6 + 30 + 150 + \cdots + 468{,}750$

8. $-3 + 9 - 27 + \cdots - 177{,}147$

Write the finite geometric series from its given description, and then find its sum.

9. A geometric series that starts with 2, ends with -6250, and has a common ratio of -5

10. A geometric series with 5 terms that begins with 1 and has a common ratio of $\frac{1}{3}$.

11. A geometric series with 7 terms that begins with 1000 and successively decreases by 20%

12. A geometric series where the first term is -12, the last term is -972, and each term after the first is triple the previous term

13. **Chess** The first international chess tournament was held in London in 1851. This single-elimination tournament (in which paired competitors played matches and only the winner of a match continued to the next round) began with 16 competitors. How many matches were played?

14. A ball is dropped from an initial height and allowed to bounce repeatedly. On the first bounce (one up-and-down motion), the ball reaches a height of 32 inches. On each successive bounce, the ball reaches 75% of its previous height. What is the total vertical distance that the ball travels in 10 bounces? (Do not include the initial height from which the ball is dropped.)

15. Medicine During a flu outbreak, health officials record 16 cases the first week, 56 new cases the second week, and 196 new cases the third week.

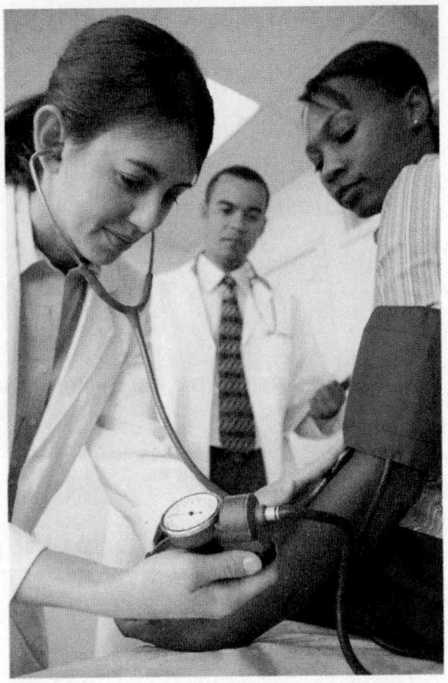

a. Assuming the pattern of new cases continues to follow a geometric sequence, what total number of new cases will have been recorded by the fifth week?

b. How many weeks will it take for the total number of recorded cases to exceed 40,000?

16. Finance A person deposits \$5000 into an investment account at the end of each year for 10 years. The account earns 4% interest annually. What is the future value of the annuity after the 10th deposit?

17. Business A business wants to buy a parcel of land in order to expand its operations. The owner of the land offers two purchase options: Buy the land today for \$100,000, or buy the land in five equal payments of \$22,000 where the payments are due a year apart and the first payment is due immediately. The chief financial officer for the business determines that money set aside for the purchase of the land can be invested and earn 5.4% interest annually. Which purchase option is the better deal for the business? Explain.

18. Match each finite geometric series on the left with its sum on the right.

A. $2 + 6 + 18 + \cdots + 1458$	**a.** ___?___	1094
B. $2 - 6 + 18 - \cdots + 1458$	**b.** ___?___	−2186
C. $-2 + 6 - 18 + \cdots - 1458$	**c.** ___?___	2186
D. $-2 - 6 - 8 - \cdots - 1458$	**d.** ___?___	−1094

H.O.T. Focus on Higher Order Thinking

19. Represent Real-World Problems The formula for the future value FV of an annuity consisting of n regular payments of p dollars at an interest rate of i (expressed as a decimal) is $FV = p\left(\frac{(1+i)^n - 1}{i}\right)$, which is valid for any payment rate (such as monthly or annually) as long as the interest rate has the same time unit. The formula assumes that the future value is calculated when the last payment is made. Show how to derive this formula.

20. Represent Real-World Problems The formula for the present value PV of an annuity consisting of n regular payments of p dollars at an interest rate of i (expressed as a decimal) is $PV = p\left(\frac{1 - (1+i)^{-n}}{i}\right)$, which is valid for any payment rate (such as monthly or annually) as long as the interest rate has the same time unit. The formula assumes that the present value is calculated one time unit before the first payment is made. Show how to derive this formula.

21. Draw Conclusions Consider whether it's possible for the infinite geometric series $a + ar + ar^2 + \cdots$ to have a finite sum. Since the formula $S(n) = a\left(\frac{1 - r^n}{1 - r}\right)$ gives the sum of the first n terms of the series, a reasonable approach to finding the sum of all terms in the series is to determine what happens to $S(n)$ as n increases without bound. Use this approach on each of the following series and draw a conclusion.

a. $1 + 2 + 4 + 8 + \cdots$

b. $1 + \frac{1}{2} + \frac{1}{4} + \frac{1}{8} + \cdots$

Lesson Performance Task

You've finally purchased your dream home after saving for a long time. You've made a nice down payment, and your mortgage loan is \$150,000. It is a 30-year loan with an annual interest rate of 4.5%, which is calculated monthly. Find a formula for calculating monthly mortgage payments. Then find the monthly payment needed to pay off your mortgage loan.

Let P be the principal, r be the monthly interest rate expressed as a decimal, and m be the monthly payment.

Sequences and Series

Essential Question: How can you use exponential functions to solve real-world problems?

Key Vocabulary

arithmetic sequence *(sucesión arithmética)*
explicit rule *(regla explícita)*
finite geometric series *(serie geométrica finito)*
geometric sequence *(sucesión geométrica)*
recursive rule *(regla recurrente)*
sequence *(sucesión)*
series *(regla recurrente)*

KEY EXAMPLE *(Lesson 12.2)*

Write the explicit rule for the sequence described by the points (0, 4), (1, −2), (2, −8), (3, −14), ...

$f(0) = 4 \rightarrow a = 4$ Use the fact that $f(0) = a$ to find a.

$f(1) = a + d$ Use $f(1) = a + d$ to find d.

$f(1) = 4 + d$

$-2 = 4 + d$

$d = -6$

$f(n) = 4 - 6n$ Substitute a and d into $f(n) = a + dn$

The explicit rule for the sequence is $f(n) = 4 - 6n$.

KEY EXAMPLE *(Lesson 12.2)*

Find the 12th term of the geometric sequence 5, 15, 45,...

$r = \frac{15}{5} = 3$ Find the common ratio of the sequence.

$a_n = a_1 r^{n-1}$ Write the formula for a geometric sequence

$a_{12} = 5(3)^{12-1}$ Substitute in $a, r,$ and n .

$a_{12} = 5(177{,}147)$ Use a calculator to solve for a_{12}.

$a_{12} = 885{,}735$ Simplify.

The 12th term of the geometric sequence is 885,735.

KEY EXAMPLE *(Lesson 12.3)*

Find the sum of the geometric series 2 − 4 + 8 − 16 + 32 − 64.

$a = 2,\ r = \frac{-4}{2} = -2,\ n = 6$ Find the values of a, r, and n.

$S(n) = 2\left(\frac{1 - r^n}{1 - r}\right)$

$S(6) = 2\left(\frac{1 - (-2)^6}{1 - (-2)}\right)$ Use the sum formula

$S(6) = -42$

The sum for the geometric series is −42.

EXERCISES

1. If the first three terms of a geometric sequence are 3, 12, and 48, what is the seventh term? *(Lesson 12.2)*

Write the explicit rule for the algebraic sequence. In every sequence, the first term is the $f(0)$ term. *(Lesson 12.1)*

2. 5, 7, 9, 11, 13 ...

3.

x	0	1	2	3	4
y	−3	1	5	9	13

Find the sum of the geometric series. *(Lesson 12.3)*

4. $4 + 16 + 64 + 256 + ... + 16{,}384$

5. $3 - 6 + 12 - 24 + ... - 1536$

6. $-2 - 6 - 18 - 54 - 162$

7. $-2 + 8 - 32 + ... +2048$

MODULE PERFORMANCE TASK

How Big Is That Snowflake?

The Koch snowflake is a special kind of shape called a fractal. It begins with an equilateral triangle. In the first iteration, each side of the triangle is divided into thirds. The middle third of each side becomes the base of a new equilateral triangle. In the second iteration, each of the sides is divided into thirds, forming the base of a new equilateral triangle. To make the full snowflake, this process continues infinitely. The first two iterations and the original triangle are shown.

What is the area of the Koch triangle after three iterations? By what factor is the area of the original triangle increased? Start by listing the information you will need to solve the problem. Be sure to write down all your data and assumptions. Then use graphs, numbers, tables, words, or algebra to explain how you reached your conclusion.

Ready to Go On?

12.1–12.3 Sequences and Series

Personal Math Trainer

- Online Homework
- Hints and Help
- Extra Practice

Write a recursive rule and an explicit rule for each sequence. *(Lessons 12.1, 12.2)*

1. 9, 27, 81, 243,...

2. 4, −3, −10, −17, ...

Find the stated term of the geometric sequence. *(Lesson 12.2)*

3. −3, −6, −12, −24, ...; 9th term

4. 4, −12, 36, −108, ...; 11th term

Find the sum of the geometric series. *(Lesson 12.3)*

5. $10 - 20 + 40 - 80 + 160 - ... + 2560$

6. $-1 + 3 - 9 + 27 - ... - 6561$

7. $2 + 12 + 72 + 432 + 2592 + 15{,}552$

8. $7 - 7 + 7 - 7 + 7 - ... + 7$

ESSENTIAL QUESTION

9. How can you tell whether a sequence is geometric or algebraic?

Assessment Readiness

1. Consider each sequence. Is the sequence geometric?

A. 10, 15, 20, 25,...

B. 5, 15, 45, 135,...

C. 1, 3, 5, 7,...

D. 2, 4, 8, 16,...

2. Consider the series 1, 5, 9, 13, 17, ... Determine if each statement is True or False.

A. If n represents the position in the sequence, the algebraic expression for the sequence is $4n - 3$.

B. If n represents the position in the sequence, the algebraic expression for the sequence is $n + 4$.

C. There is no algebraic expression for the sequence, because it is a geometric sequence.

3. Give the first five terms of the sequence $2n + 1$, and then create an example of a real world situation that could match the arithmetic sequence. If the sequence were plotted on a coordinate plane, what kind of function would it be?

4. Solve $\frac{3}{4}|x + 3| - 8 = 4$ for x. Explain your method.

5. Explain the difference between a geometric sequence and a geometric series.

Exponential Functions

MODULE 13

Essential Question: How can you use exponential functions to solve real-world problems?

REAL WORLD VIDEO
Check out how exponential functions can be used to model the path of a bouncing ball and other real-world patterns.

MODULE PERFORMANCE TASK PREVIEW

That's the Way the Ball Bounces

The height that a ball reaches after bouncing off a hard surface depends on several factors, including the height from which the ball was dropped and the material the ball is made of. The height of each successive bounce will be less than the previous bounce. How can mathematical modeling be used to represent a bouncing ball? Let's find out!

Are YOU Ready?

Complete these exercises to review skills you will need for this module.

Personal Math Trainer

- Online Homework
- Hints and Help
- Extra Practice

Real Numbers

Example 1 Write the multiplicative inverse of 0.3125.

$0.3125 = \frac{3125}{10{,}000}$ Write the decimal as a fraction.

$= \frac{5}{16} \rightarrow \frac{16}{5}$ Simplify, then take the reciprocal.

The multiplicative inverse of 0.3125 is $\frac{16}{5}$.

Write the multiplicative inverse.

1. 1.125 **2.** −0.6875 **3.** 0.444

Exponential Functions

Example 2 Evaluate $12(1.5)^{x-5}$ for $x = 8$.

$12(1.5)^{8-5}$ Substitute.

$12(1.5)^3$ Simplify.

$12(3.375) = 40.5$ Evaluate the exponent. Multiply.

Evaluate each expression.

4. $30(1.1)^{5x}$; $x = 0.4$ **5.** $8(2.5)^{\frac{x}{3}}$; $x = 12$ **6.** $2(x)^{2x+9}$; $x = -3$

Geometric Sequences

Example 3 List the first four terms of the sequence if $t_1 = 2$ and $t_n = -3t_{n-1}$.

$t_2 = -3t_{2-1} = -3t_1 = -3 \cdot 2 = -6$ Find the second term.

$t_3 = -3t_{3-1} = -3t_2 = -3 \cdot (-6) = 18$ Find the third term.

$t_4 = -3t_{4-1} = -3t_3 = -3 \cdot 18 = -54$ Find the fourth term.

The first four terms are 2, −6, 18, and −54.

List the first four terms of the sequence.

7. $t_1 = 0.02$

$t_n = 5t_{n-1}$

8. $t_1 = 3$

$t_n = 0.5t_{n-1}$

13.1 Exponential Growth Functions

Essential Question: How is the graph of $g(x) = ab^{x-h} + k$ where $b > 1$ related to the graph of $f(x) = b^x$?

Resource Locker

Explore 1 Graphing and Analyzing $f(x) = 2^x$ and $f(x) = 10^x$

An **exponential function** is a function of the form $f(x) = b^x$, where the base b is a positive constant other than 1 and the exponent x is a variable. Notice that there is no single parent exponential function because each choice of the base b determines a different function.

(A) Complete the input-output table for each of the parent exponential functions below.

x	$f(x) = 2^x$
−3	?
−2	?
−1	?
0	?
1	?
2	?
3	?

x	$p(x) = 10^x$
−3	?
−2	?
−1	?
0	?
1	?
2	?
3	?

(B) Graph the parent functions $f(x) = 2^x$ and $p(x) = 10^x$ by plotting points.

(C) What is the domain of each function?

Domain of $f(x) = 2^x$: $\{x \mid$? $\}$

Domain of $p(x) = 10^x$: $\{x \mid$? $\}$

(D) What is the range of each function?

Range of $f(x) = 2^x$: $\{y \mid$? $\}$

Range of $p(x) = 10^x$: $\{y \mid$? $\}$

(E) What is the y-intercept of each function?

y-intercept of $f(x) = 2^x$: ?

y-intercept of $p(x) = 10^x$: ?

(F) What is the trend of each function?

In both $f(x) = 2^x$ and $p(x) = 10^x$, as the value of x increases, does the value of y increase or decrease?

Reflect

1. Will the domain be the same for every exponential function? Why or why not?
2. Will the range be the same for every exponential function in the form $f(x) = b^x$, where b is a positive constant? Why or why not?
3. Will the value of the y-intercept be the same for every exponential function? Why or why not?

Explain 1 Graphing Combined Transformations of $f(x) = b^x$ Where $b > 1$

A given exponential function $g(x) = a(b^{x-h}) + k$ with base b can be graphed by recognizing the differences between the given function and its parent function, $f(x) = b^x$. These differences define the parameters of the transformation, where k represents the vertical translation, h is the horizontal translation, and a represents either the vertical stretch or compression of the exponential function and whether it is reflected across the x-axis.

You can use the parameters in $g(x) = a(b^x - h) + k$ to see what happens to two reference points during a transformation. Two points that are easily visualized on the parent exponential function are $(0, 1)$ and $(1, b)$.

In a transformation, the point $(0, 1)$ becomes $(h, a + k)$ and $(1, b)$ becomes $(1 + h, ab + k)$. The asymptote $y = 0$ for the parent function becomes $y = k$.

The graphs of $f(x) = 2^x$ and $p(x) = 10^x$ are shown below with the reference points and asymptotes labeled.

$f(x) = 2^x$	$p(x) = 10^x$
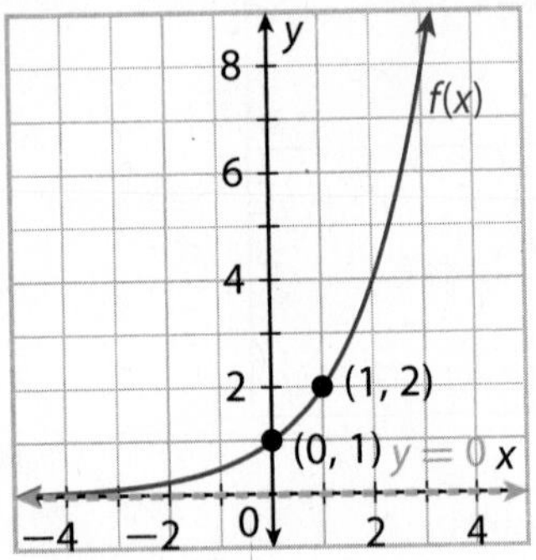	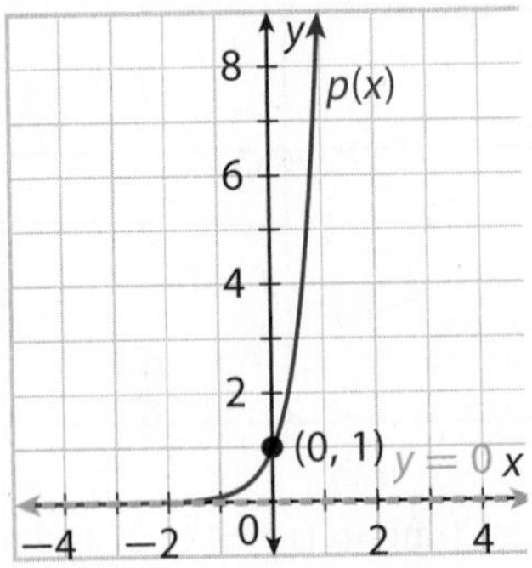

Example 1 **State the domain and range of the given function. Then identify the new values of the reference points and the asymptote. Use these values to graph the function.**

(A) $g(x) = -3\left(2^{x-2}\right) + 1$

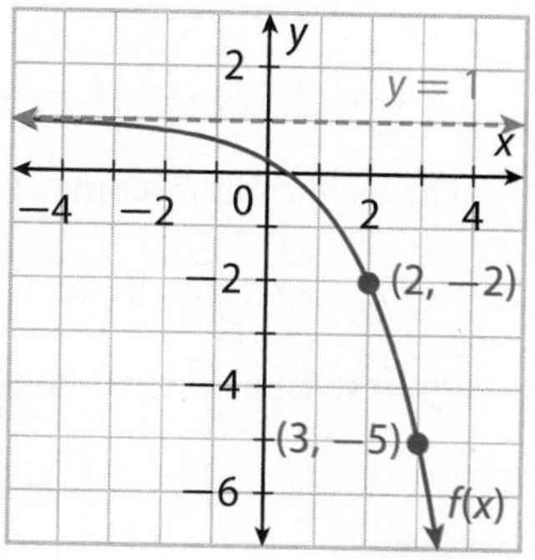

The domain of $g(x) = -3\left(2^{x-2}\right) + 1$ is $\left\{x \mid -\infty < x < \infty\right\}$.

The range of $g(x) = -3\left(2^{x-2}\right) + 1$ is $\left\{y \mid y < 1\right\}$.

Examine $g(x)$ and identify the parameters.

$a = -3$, which means that the function is reflected across the x-axis and vertically stretched by a factor of 3.

$h = 2$, so the function is translated 2 units to the right.

$k = 1$, so the function is translated 1 unit up.

The point $(0, 1)$ becomes $(h, a + k)$.

$$(h, a + k) = (2, -3 + 1)$$
$$= (2, -2)$$

$(1, b)$ becomes $(1 + h, ab + k)$.

$$(1 + h, ab + k) = (1 + 2, -3(2) + 1)$$
$$= (3, -6 + 1)$$
$$= (3, -5)$$

The asymptote becomes $y = k$.

$y = k \quad \rightarrow \quad y = 1$

Plot the transformed points and asymptote and draw the curve.

(B) $q(x) = 1.5\left(10^{x-3}\right) - 5$

The domain of $q(x) = 1.5\left(10^{x-3}\right) - 5$ is $\left\{x \mid -\infty < x < \infty\right\}$.

The range of $q(x) = 1.5\left(10^{x-3}\right) - 5$ is $\left\{y \mid y > -5\right\}$.

Examine $q(x)$ and identify the parameters.

$a =$ 1.5 so the function is stretched vertically by a factor of 1.5.

$h =$ 3 so the function is translated 3 units to the right.

$k =$ −5 so the function is translated 5 units down.

The point $(0,1)$ becomes $(h, a + k)$.

$(h, a + k) = (3, 1.5 - 5) = (3, -3.5)$

$(1, b)$ becomes $(1 + h, ab + k)$.

$(1 + h, ab + k) = (1 + 3, 1.5(10) - 5) = (4, 10)$

The asymptote becomes $y = k$.

$y = k \rightarrow y = -5$

Plot the transformed points and asymptote and draw the curve.

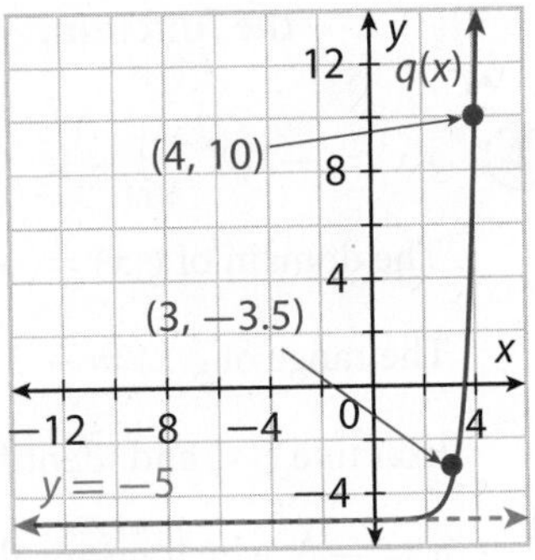

Your Turn

State the domain and range of the given function. Then identify the new values of the reference points and the asymptote. Use these values to graph the function.

4. $g(x) = 4(2^{x+2}) - 6$

5. $q(x) = -\frac{3}{5}(10^{x+2}) + 3$

Explain 2 Writing Equations for Combined Transformations of $f(x) = b^x$ Where $b > 1$

Given the graph of an exponential function, you can use your knowledge of the transformation parameters to write the function rule for the graph. Recall that the asymptote will give the value of k and the x-coordinate of the first reference point is h. Then let y_1 be the y-coordinate of the first point and solve the equation $y_1 = a + k$ for a.

Finally, use a, h, and k to write the function in the form $g(x) = a\left(b^{x-h}\right) + k$.

Example 2 **Write the exponential function that will produce the given graph, using the specified value of b. Verify that the second reference point is on the graph of the function. Then state the domain and range of the function in set notation.**

(A) Let $b = 2$.

The asymptote is $y = 1$, showing that $k = 1$.

The first reference point is $\left(-\frac{1}{3}, -\frac{1}{3}\right)$. This shows that $h = -\frac{1}{3}$ and that $a + k = -\frac{1}{3}$.

Substitute $k = 1$ and solve for a.

$a + k = -\frac{1}{3}$

$a + 1 = -\frac{1}{3}$

$a = -\frac{4}{3}$

$h = -\frac{1}{3}$

$k = 1$

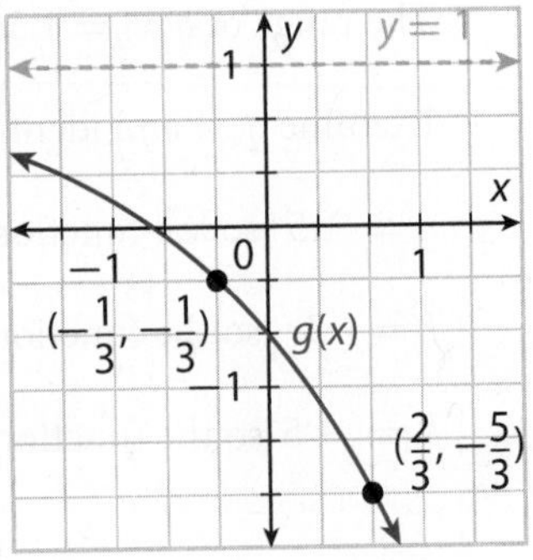

Substitute these values into $g(x) = a\left(b^{x-h}\right) + k$ to find $g(x)$.

$$g(x) = a\left(b^{x-h}\right) + k$$
$$= -\frac{4}{3}\left(2^{x+\frac{1}{3}}\right) + 1$$

Verify that $g\left(\frac{2}{3}\right) = -\frac{5}{3}$.

$$g\left(\frac{2}{3}\right) = -\frac{4}{3}\left(2^{\frac{2}{3}+\frac{1}{3}}\right) + 1$$
$$= -\frac{4}{3}\left(2^{1}\right) + 1$$
$$= -\frac{4}{3}(2) + 1$$
$$= \frac{3}{3} - \frac{8}{3}$$
$$= -\frac{5}{3}$$

The domain of $g(x)$ is $\left\{x \mid -\infty < x < +\infty\right\}$.

The range of $g(x)$ is $\left\{y \mid y < 1\right\}$.

(B) Let $b = 10$.

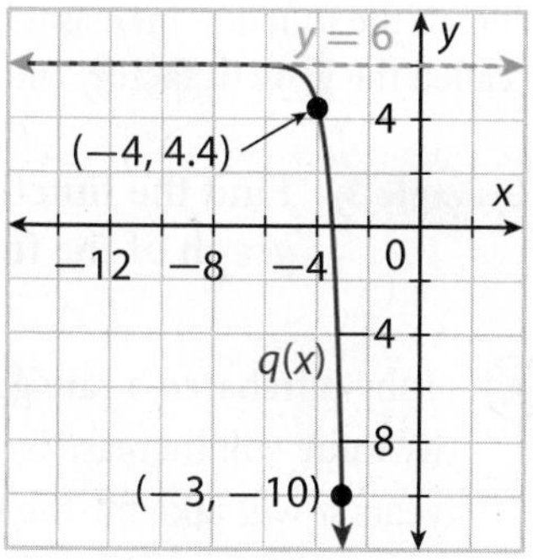

The asymptote is $y = $ 6 , showing that $k = $ 6 .

The first reference point is $(-4, 4.4)$. This shows that $h = $ −4 and that $a + k = $ 4.4 . Substitute for k and solve for a.

$a + k = $ 4.4

$a + $ 6 $=$ 4.4

$a = $ −1.6 $\quad h = $ −4 $\quad k = $ 6

Substitute these values into $q(x) = a\left(b^{x-h}\right) + k$ to find $q(x)$.

$q(x) = a\left(b^{x-h}\right) + k = $ −1.6 $\left(10^{x-(-4)}\right) + $ 6

Verify that $q(-3) = -10$.

$q(-3) = $ −1.6 $\left(10^{-3-(-4)}\right) + $ 6

$= $ −1.6 $\left(10^{1}\right) + $ 6

$= $ −16 $+$ 6

$= $ −10

The domain of $q(x)$ is $\left\{x \mid -\infty < x < +\infty\right\}$. The range of $q(x)$ is $\left\{y \mid y < 6\right\}$.

Your Turn

Write the exponential function that will produce the given graph, using the specified value of b. Verify that the second reference point is on the graph of the function. Then state the domain and range of the function in set notation.

6. $b = 2$

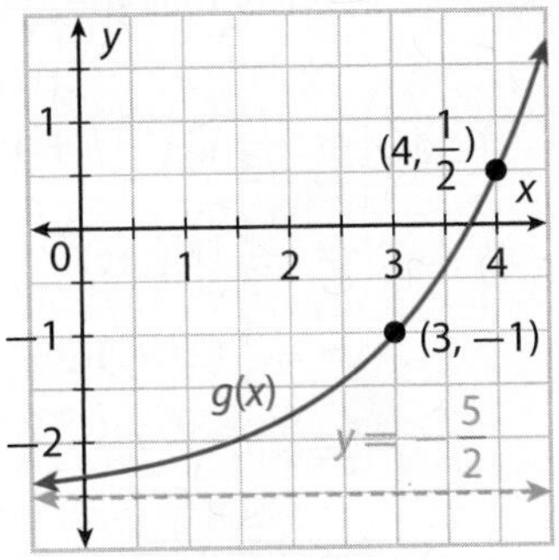

Explain 3 Modeling with Exponential Growth Functions

An **exponential growth function** has the form $f(t) = a(1 + r)^t$ where $a > 0$ and r is a constant percent increase (expressed as a decimal) for each unit increase in time t. That is, since $f(t + 1) = (1 + r) \cdot f(t) = f(t) + r \cdot f(t)$, the value of the function increases by $r \cdot f(t)$ on the interval $[t, t + 1]$. The base $1 + r$ of an exponential growth function is called the **growth factor**, and the constant percent increase r, in decimal form, is called the **growth rate**.

Example 3 **Find the function that corresponds with the given situation. Then use the graph of the function to make a prediction.**

(A) Tony purchased a rare guitar in 2000 for \$12,000. Experts estimate that its value will increase by 14% per year. Use a graph to find the number of years it will take for the value of the guitar to be \$60,000.

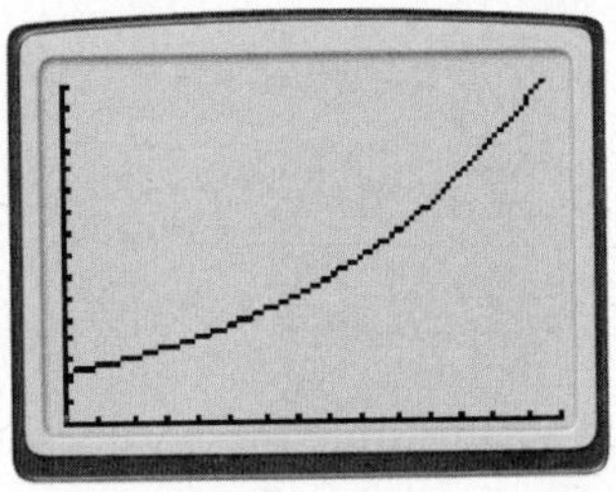

Write a function to model the growth in value for the guitar.

$$f(t) = a(1 + r)^t$$
$$= 12,000(1 + 0.14)^t$$
$$= 12,000(1.14)^t$$

Use a graphing calculator to graph the function.

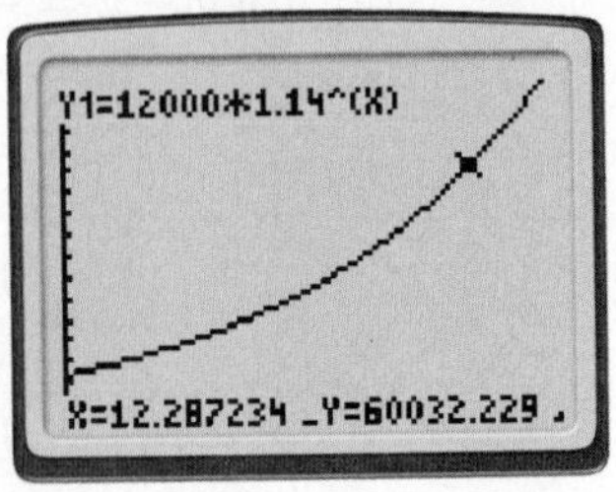

Use the graph to predict when the guitar will be worth \$60,000.

Use the TRACE feature to find the t-value where $f(t) \approx 60,000$.

So, the guitar will be worth \$60,000 approximately 12.29 years after it was purchased.

Ⓑ At the same time that Tony bought the $12,000 guitar, he also considered buying another rare guitar for $15,000. Experts estimated that this guitar would increase in value by 9% per year. Determine after how many years the two guitars will be worth the same amount.

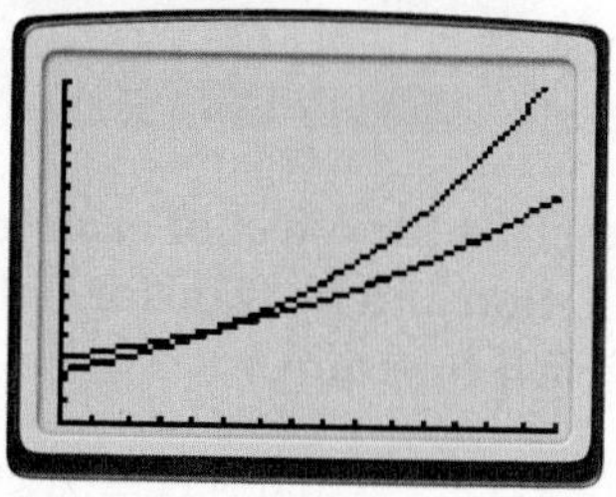

Write a function to model the growth in value for the second guitar.

$g(t) = a(1 + r)^t$

$= \boxed{15,000}\left(1 + \boxed{0.09}\right)^t$

$= \boxed{15,000}\left(\boxed{1.09}\right)^t$

Use a graphing calculator to graph the two functions.

Use the graph to predict when the two guitars will be worth the same amount.

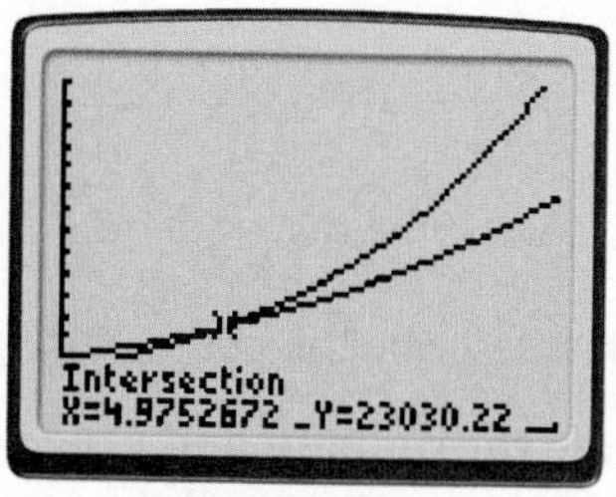

Use the intersection feature to find the t-value where $g(t) = \boxed{f(t)}$.

So, the two guitars will be worth the same amount 4.98 years after 2000.

Reflect

7. In part A, find the average rates of change over the intervals $(0, 4)$, $(4, 8)$, and $(8, 12)$. Do the rates increase, decrease, or stay the same?

Your Turn

Find the function that corresponds with the given situation. Then graph the function on a calculator and use the graph to make a prediction.

8. John researches a baseball card and finds that it is currently worth $3.25. However, it is supposed to increase in value 11% per year. In how many years will the card be worth $26?

Elaborate

9. How are reference points helpful when graphing transformations of $f(x) = b^x$ or when writing equations for transformed graphs?

10. Give the general form of an exponential growth function and describe its parameters.

11. **Essential Question Check-In** Which transformations of $f(x) = b^x$ change the function's end behavior? Which transformations change the function's y-intercept?

✪ Evaluate: Homework and Practice

Personal Math Trainer
- Online Homework
- Hints and Help
- Extra Practice

Describe the effect of each transformation on the parent function. Graph the parent function and its transformation. Then determine the domain, range, and *y*-intercept of each function.

1. $f(x) = 2^x$ and $g(x) = 2(2^x)$

2. $f(x) = 2^x$ and $g(x) = -5(2^x)$

3. $f(x) = 2^x$ and $g(x) = 2^{x+2}$

4. $f(x) = 2^x$ and $g(x) = 2^x + 5$

5. $f(x) = 10^x$ and $g(x) = 2(10^x)$

6. $f(x) = 10^x$ and $g(x) = -4(10^x)$

7. $f(x) = 10^x$ and $g(x) = 10^{x-2}$

8. $f(x) = 10^x$ and $g(x) = 10^x - 6$

9. Describe the graph of $g(x) = 2^{(x-3)} - 4$ in terms of $f(x) = 2^x$.

10. Describe the graph of $g(x) = 10^{(x+7)} + 6$ in terms of $f(x) = 10^x$.

State the domain and range of the given function. Then identify the new values of the reference points and the asymptote. Use these values to graph the function.

11. $h(x) = 2(3^{x+2}) - 1$

12. $k(x) = -0.5(4^{x-1}) + 2$

13. $f(x) = 3(6^{x-7}) - 8$

14. $f(x) = -3(2^{x+1}) + 3$

15. $h(x) = -\frac{1}{4}(5^{x+1}) - \frac{3}{4}$

16. $p(x) = 2(4^{x-3}) - 5$

Write the exponential function that will produce the given graph, using the specified value of *b*. Verify that the second reference point is on the graph of the function. Then state the domain and range of the function in set notation.

17. $b = 2$

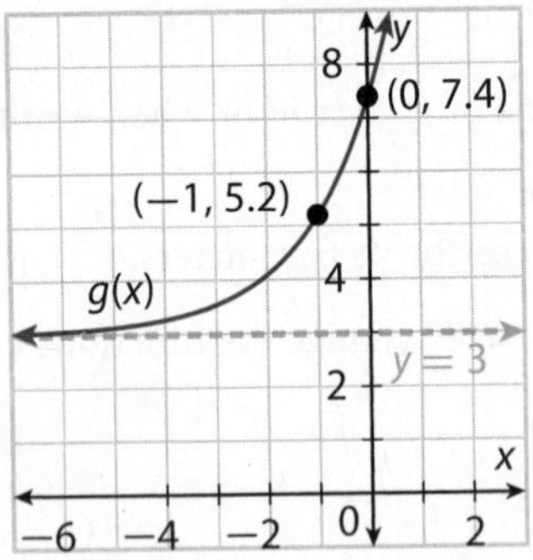

18. $b = 10$

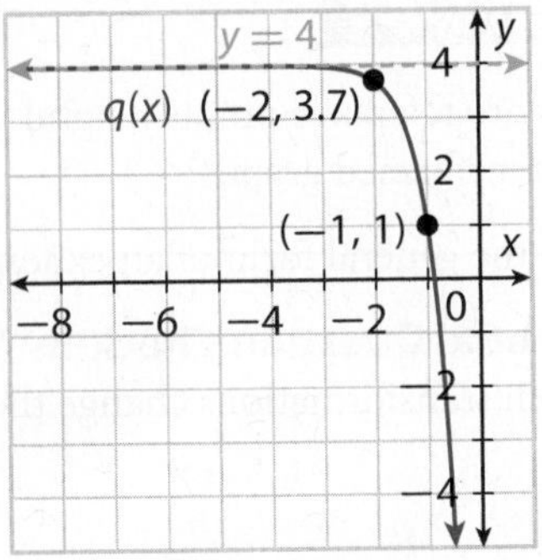

Find the function that corresponds with the given situation. Then graph the function on a calculator and use the graph to make a prediction.

19. A certain stock opens with a price of \$0.59. Over the first three days, the value of the stock increases on average by 50% per day. If this trend continues, how many days will it take for the stock to be worth \$6?

20. Sue has a lamp from her great-grandmother. She has it appraised and finds it is worth \$1000. She wants to sell it, but the appraiser tells her that the value is appreciating by 8% per year. In how many years will the value of the lamp be \$2000?

21. The population of a small town is 15,000. If the population is growing by 5% per year, how long will it take for the population to reach 25,000?

22. Bill invests \$3000 in a bond fund with an interest rate of 9% per year. If Bill does not withdraw any of the money, in how many years will his bond fund be worth \$5000?

H.O.T. Focus on Higher Order Thinking

23. Analyze Relationships Compare the end behavior of $g(x) = 2^x$ and $f(x) = x^2$. How are the graphs of the functions similar? How are they different?

24. Explain the Error A student has a baseball card that is worth \$6.35. He looks up the appreciation rate and finds it to be 2.5% per year. He wants to find how much it will be worth after 3 years. He writes the function $f(t) = 6.35(2.5)^t$ and uses the graph of that function to find the value of the card in 3 years.

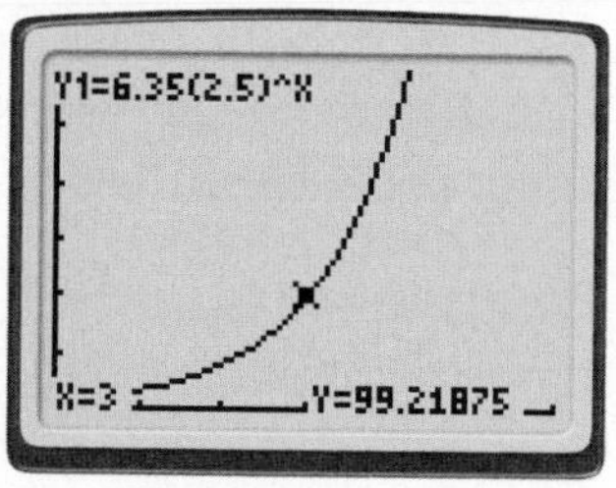

According to his graph, his card will be worth about \$99.22 in 3 years. What did the student do wrong? What is the correct answer?

Lesson Performance Task

Like all collectables, the price of an item is determined by what the buyer is willing to pay and the seller is willing to accept. The estimated value of a 1948 Tucker 48 automobile in excellent condition has risen at an approximately exponential rate from about $500,000 in December 2006 to about $1,400,000 in December 2013.

a. Find an equation in the form $V(t) = V_0\left(1 + r\right)^t$, where V_0 is the value of the car in dollars in December 2006, r is the average annual growth rate, t is the time in years since December 2006, and $V(t)$ is the value of the car in dollars at time t. (Hint: Substitute the known values and solve for r.)

b. What is the meaning of the value of r?

c. If this trend continues, what would be the value of the car in December 2017?

13.2 Exponential Decay Functions

Essential Question: How is the graph of $g(x) = ab^{x-h} + k$ where $0 < b < 1$ related to the graph of $f(x) = b^x$?

Resource Locker

Explore 1 Graphing and Analyzing $f(x) = \left(\frac{1}{2}\right)^x$ and $f(x) = \left(\frac{1}{10}\right)^x$

Exponential functions with bases between 0 and 1 can be transformed in a manner similar to exponential functions with bases greater than 1. Begin by plotting the parent functions of two of the more commonly used bases: $\frac{1}{2}$ and $\frac{1}{10}$.

(A) To begin, fill in the table in order to find points along the function $f(x) = \left(\frac{1}{2}\right)^x$. You may need to review the rules of the properties of exponents, including negative exponents.

x	$f(x) = \left(\frac{1}{2}\right)^x$
−3	8
−2	?
−1	?
0	?
1	?
2	?
3	?

(B) What does the end behavior of this function appear to be as x increases?

(C) Plot the points on a graph and draw a smooth curve through them.

(D) Complete the table for $f(x) = \left(\frac{1}{10}\right)^x$.

(E) Plot the points on a graph and draw a smooth curve through them.

x	$f(x) = \left(\frac{1}{10}\right)^x$
−3	1000
−2	?
−1	?
0	?
1	?
2	?
3	?

(F) Fill in the following table of properties:

	$f(x) = \left(\frac{1}{2}\right)^x$	$f(x) = \left(\frac{1}{10}\right)^x$
Domain	$\{x \mid -\infty < x < \infty\}$	$\{x \mid$? $\}$
Range	$\{y \mid$? $\}$	$\{y \mid$? $\}$
End behavior as $x \to \infty$	$f(x) \to$?	$f(x) \to$?
End behavior as $x \to -\infty$	$f(x) \to$?	$f(x) \to$?
y-intercept	(? , ?)	(? , ?)

(G) Do these functions both increase or both decrease throughout the domain?

(H) Of the two functions, $f(x) = \left(\frac{1}{?}\right)^x$ decreases faster.

Reflect

1. **Make a Conjecture** Look at the table of properties for the functions. What do you notice? Make a conjecture about these properties for exponential functions of the form $f(x) = \left(\frac{1}{n}\right)^x$, where n is a constant.

Explain 1 Graphing Combined Transformations of $f(x) = b^x$ Where $0 < b < 1$

When graphing transformations of $f(x) = b^x$ where $0 < b < 1$, it is helpful to consider the effect of the transformation on two reference points, $(0, 1)$ and $\left(-1, \frac{1}{b}\right)$, as well as the effect on the asymptote, $y = 0$. The table shows these reference points and the asymptote $y = 0$ for $f(x) = b^x$ and the corresponding points and asymptote for the transformed function, $g(x) = ab^{x-h} + k$.

	$f(x) = b^x$	$g(x) = ab^{x-h} + k$
First reference point	$(0, 1)$	$(h, a + k)$
Second reference point	$\left(-1, \frac{1}{b}\right)$	$\left(h - 1, \frac{a}{b} + k\right)$
Asymptote	$y = 0$	$y = k$

Example 1 **The graph of a parent exponential function is shown in blue. Use the reference points and the asymptote shown for the parent graph to graph the given transformed function. Then describe the domain and range of the transformed function using set notation.**

(A) $g(x) = 3\left(\frac{1}{2}\right)^{x-2} - 2$

Identify parameters: $a = 3$ $b = \frac{1}{2}$ $h = 2$ $k = -2$

Find reference points:

$$(h, a + k) = (2, 3 - 2) = (2, 1)$$

$$\left(h - 1, \frac{a}{b} + k\right) = \left(2 - 1, \frac{3}{\frac{1}{2}} - 2\right) = (1, 4)$$

Find the asymptote: $y = -2$

Plot the points and draw the asymptote. Then connect the points with a smooth curve that approaches the asymptote without crossing it.

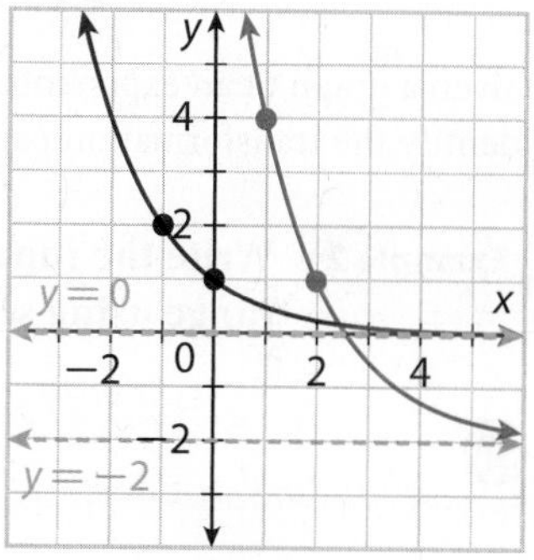

Domain: $\{x \mid -\infty < x < \infty\}$

Range: $\{y \mid y > -2\}$

(B) $g(x) = -\left(\frac{1}{10}\right)^{x+2} + 8$

Identify parameters:

$a = \boxed{-1}$ $b = \boxed{\frac{1}{10}}$ $h = \boxed{-2}$ $k = \boxed{8}$

Find reference points:

$$\left(h, \boxed{a + k}\right) = (-2, -1 + 8) = (-2, 7)$$

$$\left(h - 1, \frac{a}{b} + k\right) = \left(-2 - 1, \frac{\boxed{-1}}{\boxed{\frac{1}{10}}} + 8\right) = \left(\boxed{-3}, \boxed{-2}\right)$$

Find the asymptote:

$y = \boxed{8}$

Plot the points and draw the asymptote. Then connect the points with a smooth curve that approaches the asymptote without crossing it.

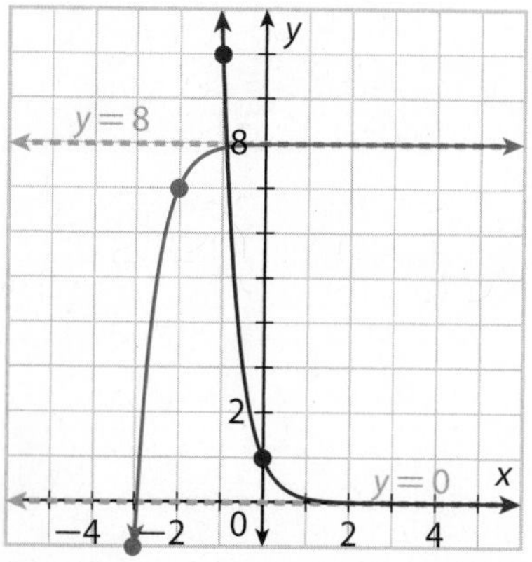

Domain: $\{x \mid \boxed{-\infty < x < \infty}\}$

Range: $\{y \mid \boxed{y < 8}\}$

Reflect

2. Which parameters make the domain and range of $g(x)$ differ from those of the parent function? Write the transformed domain and range for $g(x)$ in set notation.

Your Turn

Graph the given transformed function. Then describe the domain and range of the transformed function using set notation.

3. $g(x) = 3\left(\frac{1}{3}\right)^{x+2} - 4$

Explain 2 Writing Equations for Combined Transformations of $f(x) = b^x$ where $0 < b < 1$

Given a graph of an exponential function, $g(x) = ab^{x-h} + k$, the reference points and the asymptote can be used to identify the transformation parameters in order to write the function rule.

Example 2 **Write the function represented by this graph and state the domain and range using set notation.**

(A)

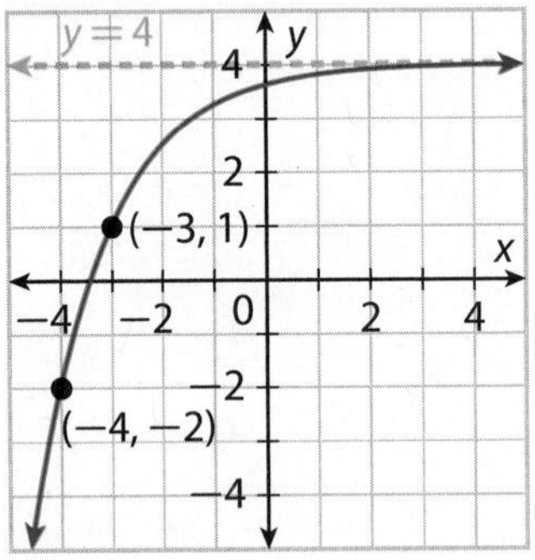

Find k from the asymptote: $k = 4$.

The first reference point is at $(-3,1)$.

Equate point value with parameters-based expression. $(-3, 1) = (h, a + k)$

Use the x-coordinate to solve for h. $h = -3$

Use the y-coordinate to solve for a. $a = 1 - k$

$= -3$

The second reference point is at $(-4, -2)$.

Equate point value with parameters-based expression. $(-4, -2) = \left(h - 1, \frac{a}{b} + k\right)$

Equate y-coordinate with parameters. $\frac{-3}{b} + 4 = -2$

Solve for b.

$$\frac{-3}{b} = -6$$

$$b = \frac{-3}{-6}$$

$$= \frac{1}{2}$$

$$g(x) = -3\left(\frac{1}{2}\right)^{x+3} + 4$$

Domain: $\{x \mid -\infty < x < \infty\}$

Range: $\{y \mid y < 4\}$

B

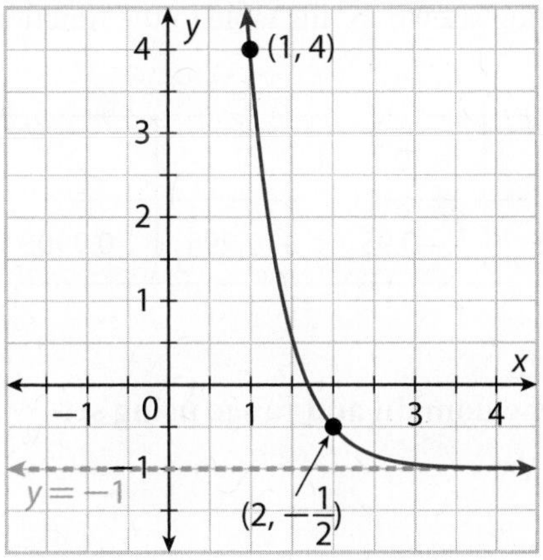

Find k from the asymptote: $k = \boxed{-1}$.

The first reference point is at $\left(\boxed{2}, \boxed{-\frac{1}{2}}\right)$, so $\left(\boxed{2}, -\frac{1}{2}\right) = \left(h, \boxed{a + k}\right)$

$h = \boxed{2}$ $\quad a = \boxed{-\frac{1}{2}} - k$

$$= \boxed{\frac{1}{2}}$$

The second reference point is at $\left(\boxed{1}, \boxed{4}\right)$, so $\left(\boxed{1}, 4\right) = \left(h - 1, \boxed{\frac{a}{b} + k}\right)$

$$\frac{\boxed{\frac{1}{2}}}{b} - 1 = \boxed{4}$$

$$\frac{\frac{1}{2}}{b} = \boxed{5}$$

$$b = \frac{\frac{1}{2}}{5}$$

$$= \boxed{\frac{1}{10}}$$

$g(x) = \boxed{\frac{1}{2}}\left(\frac{1}{10}\right)^{x-\boxed{2}} - \boxed{1}$

Domain: $\{x \mid -\infty < x < \infty\}$

Range: $\{y \mid y \boxed{>} -1\}$

Reflect

4. Compare the y-intercept and the asymptote of the function shown in this table to the function plotted in Example 2A.

x	−5	−4	−3	−2	−1	0	1	2
$g(x)$	−10	−4	−4	$\frac{1}{2}$	$1\frac{1}{4}$	$1\frac{5}{8}$	$1\frac{13}{16}$	$1\frac{29}{32}$

5. Compare the y-intercept and the asymptote of the function shown in this table to the function plotted in Example 2B.

x	−3	−2	−1	0	1	2
$g(x)$	49	4	−0.5	−0.95	−0.995	-0.9995

Your Turn

Write the function represented by this graph and state the domain and range using set notation.

6.

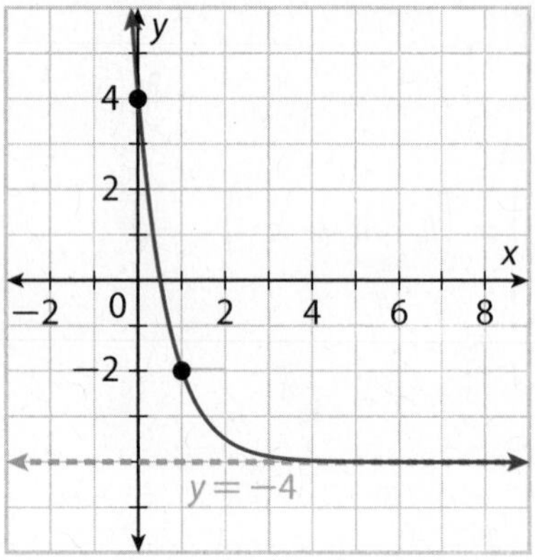

Explain 3 Modeling with Exponential Decay Functions

An **exponential decay function** has the form $f(t) = a(1 - r)^t$ where $a > 0$ and r is a constant percent decrease (expressed as a decimal) for each unit increase in time t. That is, since $f(t + 1) = (1 - r) \cdot f(t) = f(t) - r \cdot f(t)$, the value of the function decreases by $r \cdot f(t)$ on the interval $[t, t + 1]$. The base $1 - r$ of an exponential decay function is called the **decay factor**, and the constant percent decrease r, in decimal form, is called the **decay rate**.

Example 3 **Given the description of the decay terms, write the exponential decay function in the form $f(t) = a(1 - r)^t$ and graph it with a graphing calculator.**

Ⓐ The value of a truck purchased new for $28,000 decreases by 9.5% each year. Write an exponential function for this situation and graph it using a calculator. Use the graph to predict after how many years the value of the truck will be $5000.

"Purchased new for $28,000..." $a = 28{,}000$

"...decreases by 9.5% each year." $r = 0.095$

Substitute parameter values. $V_T(t) = 28{,}000(1 - 0.095)^t$

Simplify. $V_T(t) = 28{,}000(0.905)^t$

Graph the function with a graphing calculator. Use WINDOW to adjust the graph settings so that you can see the function and the function values that are important.

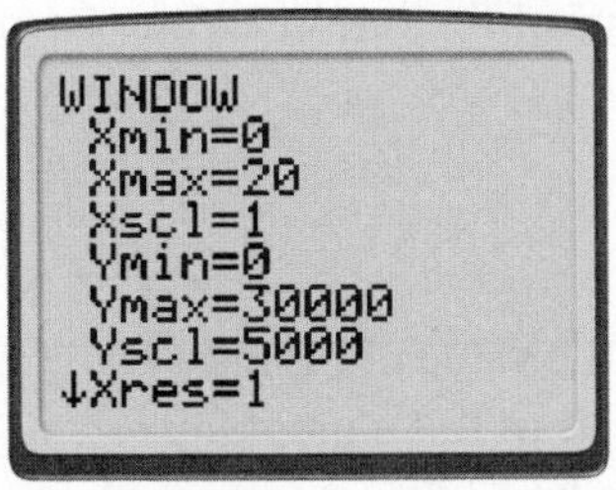

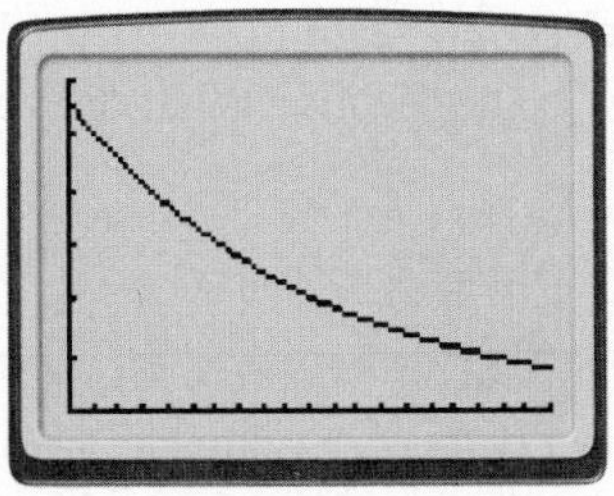

Find when the value reaches $5000 by finding the intersection between $V_T(t) = 28{,}000(0.905)^t$ and $V_T(t) = 5000$ on the calculator.

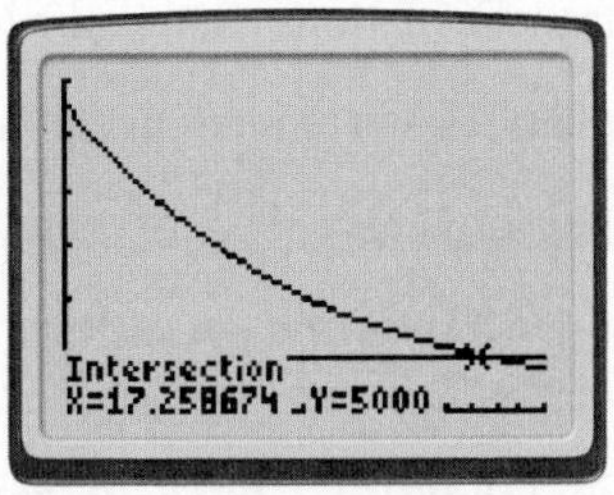

The intersection is at the point (17.26, 5000), which means after 17.26 years, the truck will have a value of $5000.

(B) The value of a sports car purchased new for \$45,000 decreases by 15% each year. Write an exponential function for the depreciation of the sports car, and plot it along with the previous example. After how many years will the two vehicles have the same value if they are purchased at the same time?

"Purchased new for \$45,000..." $a = 45{,}000$

"...decreases by 15% each year." $r = 0.15$

Substitute parameter values. $V_c(t) = 45{,}000\left(1 - 0.15\right)^t$

Simplify. $V_c(t) = 45{,}000\left(0.85\right)^t$

Add this plot to the graph for the truck value from Example A and find the intersection of the two functions to determine when the values are the same.

The intersection point is $(7.567, 13{,}155)$.

After 7.567 years, the values of both vehicles will be

\$ 13,155.

Reflect

7. What reference points could you use if you plotted the value function for the sports car on graph paper? Confirm that the graph passes through them using the calculate feature on a graphing calculator.

8. Using the sports car from example B, calculate the average rate of change over the course of the first year and the second year of ownership. What happens to the absolute value of the rate of change from the first interval to the second? What does this mean in this situation?

Your Turn

9. On federal income tax returns, self-employed people can depreciate the value of business equipment. Suppose a computer valued at \$2765 depreciates at a rate of 30% per year. Use a graphing calculator to determine the number of years it will take for the computer's value to be \$350.

Elaborate

10. Which transformations of $f(x) = \left(\frac{1}{2}\right)^x$ or $f(x) = \left(\frac{1}{10}\right)^x$ change the function's end behavior?

11. Which transformations change the location of the graph's y-intercept?

12. **Discussion** How are reference points and asymptotes helpful when graphing transformations of $f(x) = \left(\frac{1}{2}\right)^x$ or $f(x) = \left(\frac{1}{10}\right)^x$ or when writing equations for transformed graphs?

13. Give the general form of an exponential decay function based on a known decay rate and describe its parameters.

14. **Essential Question Check-In** How is the graph of $f(x) = b^x$ used to help graph the function $g(x) = ab^{x-h} + k$?

Evaluate: Homework and Practice

Personal Math Trainer
- Online Homework
- Hints and Help
- Extra Practice

Describe the transformation(s) from each parent function and give the domain and range of each function.

1. $g(x) = \left(\frac{1}{2}\right)^{x} + 3$

2. $g(x) = \left(\frac{1}{10}\right)^{x+4}$

3. $g(x) = -\left(\frac{1}{10}\right)^{x-1} + 2$

4. $g(x) = 3\left(\frac{1}{2}\right)^{x+3} - 6$

Graph the given transformed function. Then describe the domain and range of the transformed function using set notation.

5. $g(x) = -2\left(\frac{1}{2}\right)^{x-1} + 2$

6. $g(x) = \left(\frac{1}{4}\right)^{x+2} + 3$

7. $g(x) = \frac{1}{2}\left(\frac{1}{3}\right)^{x-\frac{1}{2}} + 2$

8. $g(x) = -3\left(\frac{1}{2}\right)^{x+2} + 7$

Write the function represented by each graph and state the domain and range using set notation.

9.

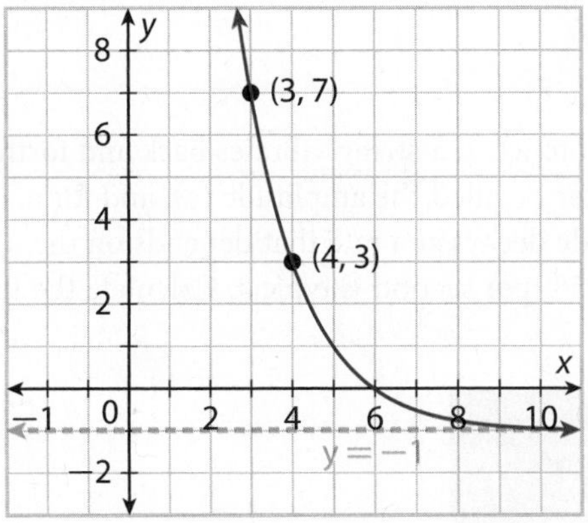

10.

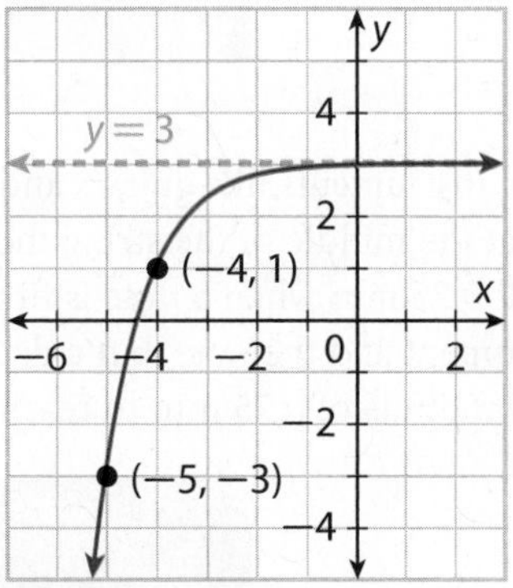

Write the exponential decay function described in the situation and use a graphing calculator to answer each question asked.

11. **Medicine** A quantity of insulin used to regulate sugar in the bloodstream breaks down by about 5% each minute after the injection. A bodyweight-adjusted dose is generally 10 units. How long does it take for the remaining insulin to be half of the original injection?

12. **Paleontology** Carbon-14 is a radioactive isotope of carbon that is used to date fossils. There are about 1.5 atoms of carbon-14 for every trillion atoms of carbon in the atmosphere, which known as 1.5 ppt (parts per trillion). Carbon in a living organism has the same concentration as carbon-14. When an organism dies, the carbon-14 content decays at a rate of 11.4% per millennium (1000 years). Write the equation for carbon-14 concentration (in ppt) as a function of time (in millennia) and determine how old a fossil must be that has a measured concentration of 0.2 ppt.

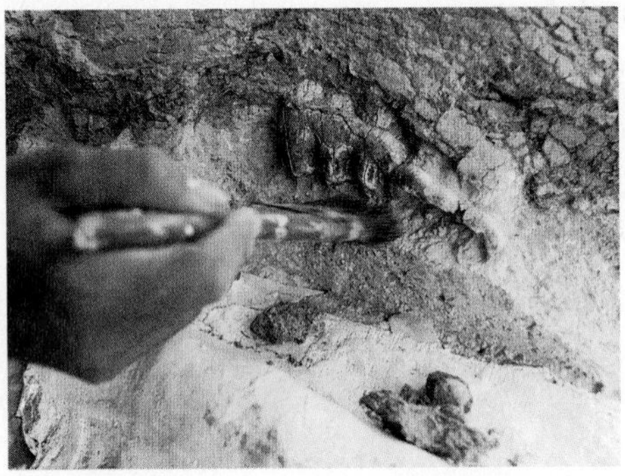

13. **Music** Stringed instruments like guitars and pianos create a note when a string vibrates back and forth. The distance that the middle of the string moves from the center is called the amplitude (a), and for a guitar, it starts at 0.75 mm when a note is first struck. Amplitude decays at a rate that depends on the individual instrument and the note, but a decay rate of about 25% per second is typical. Calculate the time it takes for an amplitude of 0.75 mm to reach 0.1 mm.

H.O.T. Focus on Higher Order Thinking

14. Analyze Relationships Compare the graphs of $f(x) = \left(\frac{1}{2}\right)^x$ and $g(x) = x^{\frac{1}{2}}$. Which of the following properties are the same? Explain.

a. Domain

b. Range

c. End behavior as x increases

d. End behavior as x decreases

15. Communicate Mathematical Ideas A quantity is reduced to half of its original amount during each given time period. Another quantity is reduced to one quarter of its original amount during the same given time period. Determine each decay rate, state which is greater, and explain your results.

16. Multiple Representations Exponential decay functions are written as transformations of the function $f(x) = b^x$, where $0 < b < 1$. However, it is also possible to use negative exponents as the basis of an exponential decay function. Use the properties of exponents to show why the function $f(x) = 2^{-x}$ is an exponential decay function.

17. Represent Real-World Problems You buy a video game console for \$500 and sell it 5 years later for \$100. The resale value decays exponentially over time. Write a function that represents the resale value, R, in dollars over the time, t, in years. Explain how you determined your function.

Lesson Performance Task

Sodium-24 is a radioactive isotope of sodium used as a diagnostic aid in medicine. It undergoes radioactive decay to form the stable isotope magnesium-24 and has a half-life of about 15 hours. This means that, in this time, half the amount of a sample mass of sodium-24 decays to magnesium-24. Suppose we start with an initial mass of 100 grams sodium-24.

a. Use the half-life of sodium-24 to write an exponential decay function of the form $m_{Na}(t) = m_0(1 - r)^t$, where m_0 is the initial mass of sodium-24, r is the decay rate, t is the time in hours, and $m_{Na}(t)$ is the mass of sodium-24 at time t. What is the meaning of r?

b. The combined amounts of sodium-24 and magnesium-24 must equal m_0, or 100, for all possible values of t. Show how to write a function for $m_{Mg}(t)$, the mass of magnesium-24 as a function of t.

c. Use a graphing calculator to graph $m_{Na}(t)$ and $m_{Mg}(t)$. Describe the graph of $m_{Mg}(t)$ as a series of transformations of $m_{Na}(t)$. What does the intersection of the graphs represent?

13.3 The Base e

Essential Question: How is the graph of $g(x) = ae^{x-h} + k$ related to the graph of $f(x) = e^x$?

Resource Locker

Explore 1 Graphing and Analyzing $f(x) = e^x$

The following table represents the function $f(x) = \left(1 + \frac{1}{x}\right)^x$ for several values of x.

x	1	10	100	1000	...
$f(x)$	2	2.5937...	2.7048...	2.7169...	...

As the value of x increases without bound, the value of $f(x)$ approaches a number whose decimal value is 2.718... This number is irrational and is called e. You can write this in symbols as $f(x) \to e$ as $x \to +\infty$.

If you graph $f(x)$ and the horizontal line $y = e$, you can see that $y = e$ is the horizontal asymptote of $f(x)$.

Even though e is an irrational number, it can be used as the base of an exponential function. The number e is sometimes called the natural base of an exponential function and is used extensively in scientific and other applications involving exponential growth and decay.

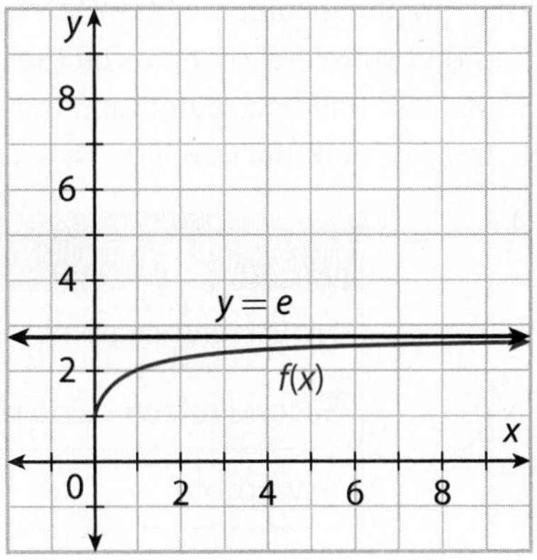

(A) Fill out the table of values below for the function $f(x) = e^x$. Use decimal approximations.

x	−10	−1	−0.5	0	0.5	1	1.5	2
$f(x) = e^x$	4.54×10^{-5}	$\frac{1}{e} = 0.367...$	0.606...	?	$\sqrt{e} =$?	?	?	?

(B) Plot the points on a graph.

(C) The domain of $f(x) = e^x$ is $\{x \mid ?\}$.

The range of $f(x) = e^x$ is $\{y \mid ?\}$.

(D) Is the function increasing or decreasing? For what values of x is it increasing/decreasing? ?

(E) The function's y-intercept is $(0, \boxed{?})$ because $f(0) = e^0 = \boxed{?}$ and $x = 0$ is in the domain of the function.

(F) Another point on the graph that can be used as a reference point is $(1, \boxed{?})$.

(G) Identify the end behavior.

$f(x) \to \boxed{?}$ as $x \to \infty$

$f(x) \to \boxed{?}$ as $x \to -\infty$

There is a horizontal asymptote at $y = \boxed{?}$.

Reflect

1. What is the relationship between the graphs of $f(x) = e^x$, $g(x) = 2^x$, and $h(x) = 3^x$? (Hint: Sketch the graphs on your own paper.)

Explain 1 Graphing Combined Transformations of $f(x) = e^x$

When graphing combined transformations of $f(x) = e^x$ that result in the function $g(x) = a \cdot e^{x-h} + k$, it helps to focus on two reference points on the graph of $f(x)$, $(0, 1)$ and $(1, e)$, as well as on the asymptote $y = 0$. The table shows these reference points and the asymptote $y = 0$ for $f(x) = e^x$ and the corresponding points and asymptote for the transformed function, $g(x) = a \cdot e^{x-h} + k$.

	$f(x) = e^x$	$g(x) = a \cdot e^{x-h} + k$
First reference point	$(0, 1)$	$(h, a + k)$
Second reference point	$(1, e)$	$(h + 1, ae + k)$
Asymptote	$y = 0$	$y = k$

Example 1 **Given a function of the form $g(x) = a \cdot e^{x-h} + k$, identify the reference points and use them to draw the graph. State the transformations that compose the combined transformation, the asymptote, the domain, and range. Write the domain and range using set notation.**

(A) $g(x) = 3 \cdot e^{x+1} + 4$

Compare $g(x) = 3 \cdot e^{x+1} + 4$ to the general form $g(x) = a \cdot e^{x-h} + k$ to find that $h = -1$, $k = 4$, and $a = 3$.

Find the reference points of $f(x) = 3 \cdot e^{x+1} + 4$.

$(0, 1) \to (h, a + k) = (-1, 3 + 4) = (-1, 7)$

$(1, e) \to (h + 1, ae + k) = (-1 + 1, 3e + 4) = (0, 3e + 4)$

State the transformations that compose the combined transformation.

$h = -1$, so the graph is translated 1 unit to the left.

$k = 4$, so the graph is translated 4 units up.

$a = 3$, so the graph is vertically stretched by a factor of 3.

a is positive, so the graph is not reflected across the x-axis.

The asymptote is vertically shifted to $y = k$, so $y = 4$.

The domain is $\left\{x \middle| -\infty < x < \infty\right\}$.

The range is $\left\{y \middle| y > 4\right\}$.

Use the information to graph the function $g(x) = 3 \cdot e^{x+1} + 4$.

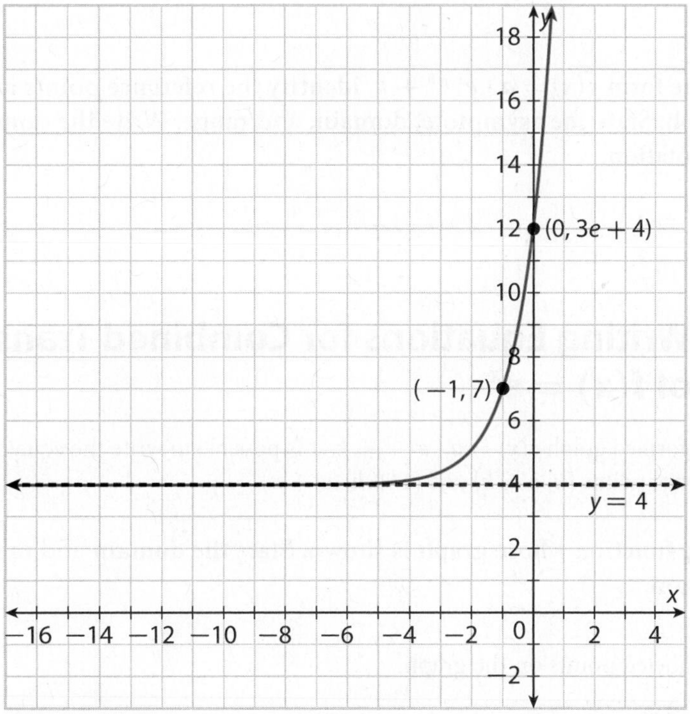

(B) $g(x) = -0.5 \cdot e^{x-2} - 1$

Compare $g(x) = -0.5 \cdot e^{x-2} - 1$ to the general form $g(x) = a \cdot e^{x-h} + k$ to find that $h =$ 2,

$k =$ −1, and $a =$ −0.5.

Find the reference points of $g(x) = -0.5 \cdot e^{x-2} - 1$.

$(0, 1) \rightarrow (h, a + k) = (2, -0.5 + -1) = (2, -1.5)$

$(1, e) \rightarrow (h + 1, ae + k) = (2 + 1, -0.5e + -1) = (3, -0.5e - 1)$

State the transformations that compose the combined transformation.

$h =$ 2, so the graph is translated 2 units to the right.

$k =$ −1, so the graph is translated 1 unit down.

$a =$ -0.5, so the graph is vertically compressed by a factor of 0.5.

a is negative, so the graph is reflected across the x-axis.

The asymptote is vertically shifted to $y = k$, so $y =$ -1.

The domain is $\left\{x \mid -\infty < x < \infty\right\}$.

The range is $\left\{y \mid y < -1\right\}$.

Use the information to graph the function $g(x) = -0.5 \cdot e^{x-2} - 1$.

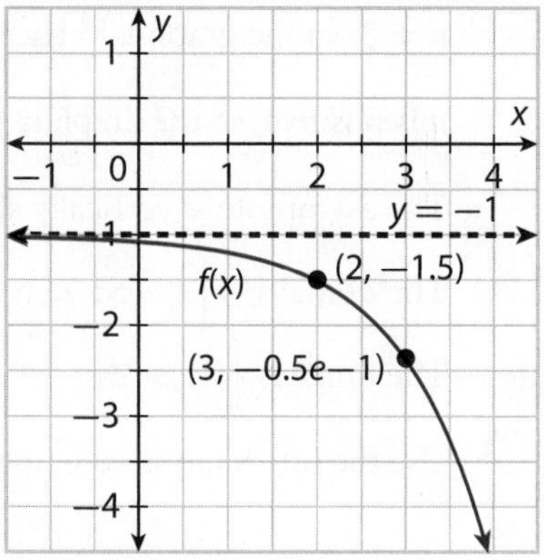

Your Turn

Given a function of the form $g(x) = a \cdot e^{x-h} + k$, identify the reference points and use them to draw the graph. State the asymptote, domain, and range. Write the domain and range using set notation.

2. $g(x) = (-1) \cdot e^{x+2} - 3$

Explain 2 Writing Equations for Combined Transformations of $f(x) = e^x$

If you are given the transformed graph $g(x) = a \cdot e^{x-h} + k$, it is possible to write the equation of the transformed graph by using the reference points $(h, a + k)$ and $(1 + h, ae + k)$.

Example 2 **Write the function whose graph is shown. State the domain and range in set notation.**

(A) First, look at the labeled points on the graph.

$(h, a + k) = (4, 6)$

$(1 + h, ae + k) = (5, 2e + 4)$

Find a, h, and k.

$(h, a + k) = (4, 6)$, so $h = 4$.

$(1 + h, ae + k) = (5, 2e + 4)$, so $ae + k = 2e + 4$.
Therefore, $a = 2$ and $k = 4$.

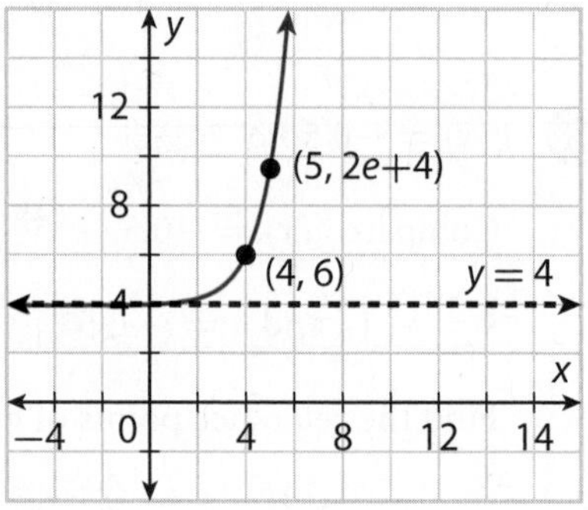

Write the equation by substituting the values of a, h, and k into the function $g(x) = a \cdot e^{x-h} + k$.

$g(x) = 2e^{x-4} + 4$

State the domain and range.

Domain: $\left\{x \mid -\infty < x < \infty\right\}$

Range: $\left\{y \mid y > 4\right\}$

(B) First, look at the labeled points on the graph.

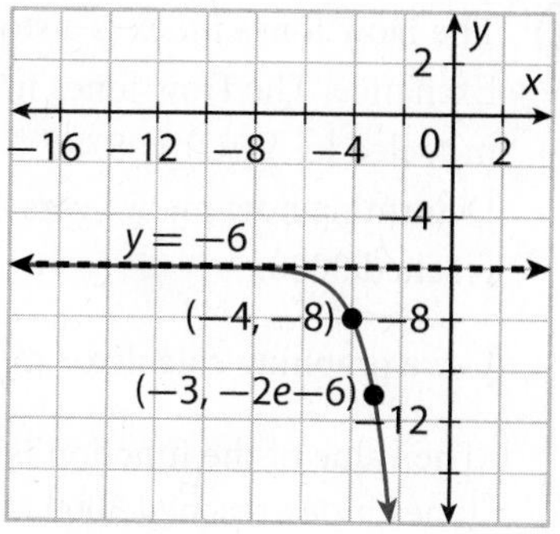

$(h, a + k) = (\boxed{-4}, \boxed{-8})$

$(1 + h, ae + k) = (\boxed{-3}, \boxed{-2e - 6})$

Find a, h, and k.

$(h, a + k) = (-4, -8)$, so $h = \boxed{-4}$.

$(1 + h, ae + k) = (-3, -2e - 6)$, so $ae + k = \boxed{-2e - 6}$.

Therefore, $a = \boxed{-2}$ and $k = \boxed{-6}$.

Write the equation by substituting the values of a, h, and k into the function $g(x) = a \cdot e^{x-h} + k$.

$g(x) = \boxed{-2e^{x+4} - 6}$

State the domain and range.

Domain: $\{x \mid \boxed{-\infty < x < \infty}\}$

Range: $\{y \mid \boxed{y < -6}\}$

Your Turn

Write the function whose graph is shown. State the domain and range in set notation.

3.

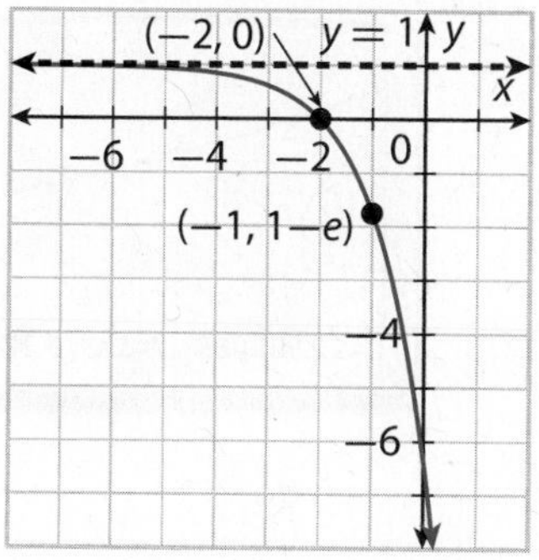

Explain 3 Modeling with Exponential Functions Having Base *e*

Although the function $f(x) = e^x$ has base $e \approx 2.718$, the function $g(x) = e^{cx}$ can have any positive base (other than 1) by choosing an appropriate positive or negative value of the constant c. This is because you can write $g(x)$ as $(e^c)^x$ by using the Power of a Power Property of Exponents.

Example 3 **Solve each problem using a graphing calculator. Then determine the growth rate or decay rate of the function.**

(A) The Dow Jones index is a stock market index for the New York Stock Exchange. The Dow Jones index for the period 1980-2000 can be modeled by $V_{DJ}(t) = 878e^{0.121t}$, where t is the number of years after 1980. Determine how many years after 1980 the Dow Jones index reached 3000.

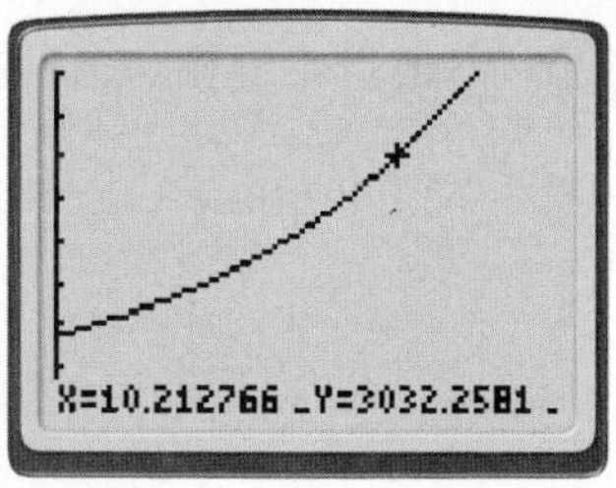

Use a graphing calculator to graph the function.

The value of the function is about 3000 when $x \approx 10.2$. So, the Dow Jones index reached 3000 after 10.2 years, or after the year 1990.

In an exponential growth model of the form $f(x) = ae^{cx}$, the growth factor $1 + r$ is equal to e^c.

To find r, first rewrite the function in the form $f(x) = a(e^c)^x$.

$$V_{DJ}(t) = 878e^{0.121t}$$

$$= 878\left(e^{0.121}\right)^t$$

Find r by using $1 + r = e^c$.

$$1 + r = e^c$$

$$1 + r = e^{0.121}$$

$$r = e^{0.121} - 1 \approx 0.13$$

So, the growth rate is about 13%.

(B) The Nikkei 225 index is a stock market index for the Tokyo Stock Exchange. The Nikkei 225 index for the period 1990-2010 can be modeled by $V_{N225}(t) = 23{,}500e^{-0.0381t}$, where t is the number of years after 1990. Determine how many years after 1990 the Nikkei 225 index reached 15,000.

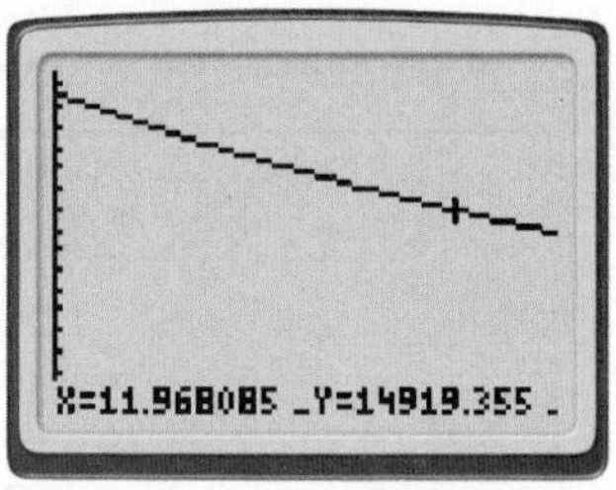

Use a graphing calculator to graph the function.

The value of the function is about 15,000 when $x \approx$ 12. So, the Nikkei 225 index reached 15,000 after 12 years, or after the year 2002.

In an exponential decay model of the form $f(x) = ae^{cx}$, the decay factor $1 - r$ is equal to e^c.

To find r, first rewrite the function in the form $f(x) = a(e^c)^x$.

$$V_{N225}(t) = 23{,}500e^{-0.0381t}$$

$$= 23{,}500\left(e^{-0.0381}\right)^t$$

Find r by using $1 - r = e^c$.

$$1 - r = e^c$$

$$1 - r = e^{-0.0381}$$

$$r = 1 - e^{-0.0381} \approx 0.037$$

So, the decay rate is 3.7 %.

Your Turn

4. A paleontologist uncovers a fossil of a saber-toothed cat in California. The paleontologist analyzes the fossil and concludes that the specimen contains 15% of its original carbon-14. The percent of original carbon-14 in a specimen after t years can be modeled by $N(t) = 100e^{-0.00012t}$, where t is the number of years after the specimen died. Use a graphing calculator to determine the age of the fossil. Then determine the decay rate of the function.

Elaborate

5. Which transformations of $f(x) = e^x$ change the function's end behavior?

6. Which transformations change the location of the graph's y-intercept?

7. Why can the function $f(x) = ae^{cx}$ be used as an exponential growth model and as an exponential decay model? How can you tell if the function represents growth or decay?

8. **Essential Question Check-In** How are reference points helpful when graphing transformations of $f(x) = e^x$ or when writing equations for transformed graphs?

Evaluate: Homework and Practice

Personal Math Trainer
- Online Homework
- Hints and Help
- Extra Practice

1. What does the value of $f(x) = \left(1 + \frac{1}{x}\right)^x$ approach as x increases without bound?

2. Identify the key attributes of $f(x) = e^x$, including the domain and range in set notation, the end behavior, and all intercepts.

Predict the effect of the parameters h, k, or a on the graph of the parent function $f(x) = e^x$. Identify any changes of domain, range, or end behavior.

3. $g(x) = f\left(x - \frac{1}{2}\right)$

4. $g(x) = f(x) - \frac{5}{2}$

5. $g(x) = -\frac{1}{4}f(x)$

6. $g(x) = \frac{27}{2}f(x)$

7. The graph of $f(x) = ce^x$ crosses the y-axis at $(0, c)$, where c is some constant. Where does the graph of $g(x) = f(x) - d$ cross the y-axis?

Given the function of the form $g(x) = a \cdot e^{x-h} + k$, identify the reference points and use them to draw the graph. State the domain and range in set notation.

8. $g(x) = e^{x-1} + 2$

9. $g(x) = -e^{x+1} - 1$

10. $g(x) = \frac{3}{2} e^{x-1} - 3$

11. $g(x) = -\frac{5}{3} e^{x-4} + 2$

Write the function whose graph is shown. State the domain and range in set notation.

12.

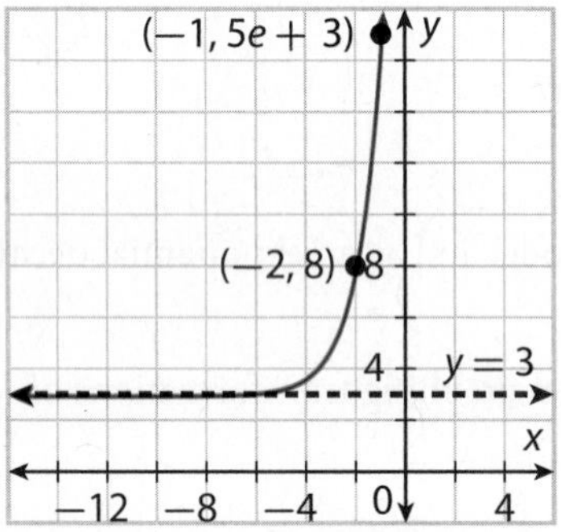

13.

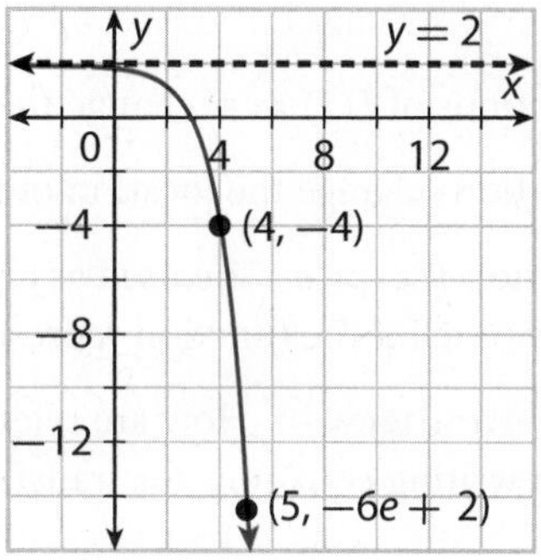

Solve each problem using a graphing calculator. Then determine the growth rate or decay rate of the function.

14. Medicine Technetium-99m, a radioisotope used to image the skeleton and the heart muscle, has a half-life of about 6 hours. Use the decay function $N(t) = N_0 e^{-0.1155t}$, where N_0 is the initial amount and t is the time in hours, to determine how many hours it takes for a 250 milligram dose to decay to 16 milligrams.

15. Ecology The George River herd of caribou in Canada was estimated to be about 4700 in 1954 and grew at an exponential rate to about 472,000 in 1984. Use the exponential growth function $P(t) = P_0 e^{0.154t}$, where P_0 is the initial population, t is the time in years after 1954, and $P(t)$ is the population at time t, to determine how many years after 1984 the herd reached 25 million.

H.O.T. Focus on Higher Order Thinking

16. **Explain the Error** A classmate claims that the function $g(x) = -4e^{x-5} + 6$ is the parent function $f(x) = e^x$ reflected across the y-axis, vertically compressed by a factor of 4, translated to the left 5 units, and translated up 6 units. Explain what the classmate described incorrectly and describe $g(x)$ as a series of transformations of $f(x)$.

17. **Multi-Step** Newton's law of cooling states that the temperature of an object decreases exponentially as a function of time, according to $T = T_s + (T_0 - T_s)e^{-kt}$, where T_0 is the initial temperature of the liquid, T_s is the surrounding temperature, and k is a constant. For a time in minutes, the constant for coffee is approximately 0.283. The corner coffee shop has an air temperature of 70°F and serves coffee at 206°F. Coffee experts say coffee tastes best at 140°F.

a. How long does it take for the coffee to reach its best temperature?

b. The air temperature on the patio outside the coffee shop is 86 °F. How long does it take for coffee to reach its best temperature there?

c. Find the time it takes for the coffee to cool to 71°F in both the coffee shop and the patio. Explain how you found your answer.

18. **Analyze Relationships** The graphing calculator screen shows the graphs of the functions $f(x) = 2^x$, $f(x) = 10^x$, and $f(x) = e^x$ on the same coordinate grid. Identify the common attributes and common point(s) of the three graphs. Explain why the point(s) is(are) common to all three graphs.

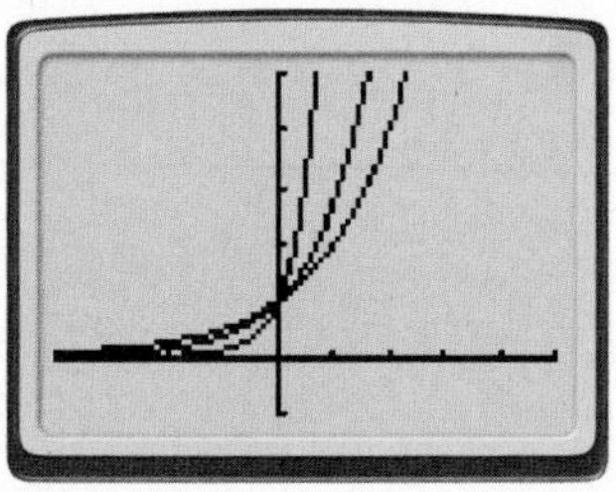

Lesson Performance Task

The ever-increasing amount of carbon dioxide in Earth's atmosphere is an area of concern for many scientists. In order to more accurately predict what the future consequences of this could be, scientists make mathematic models to extrapolate past increases into the future. A model developed to predict the annual mean carbon dioxide level L in Earth's atmosphere in parts per million t years after 1960 is $L(t) = 36.9 \cdot e^{0.0223t} + 280$.

a. Use the function $L(t)$ to describe the graph of $L(t)$ as a series of transformations of $f(t) = e^t$.

b. Find and interpret $L(80)$, the carbon dioxide level predicted for the year 2040. How does it compare to the carbon dioxide level in 2015?

c. Can $L(t)$ be used as a model for all positive values of t? Explain.

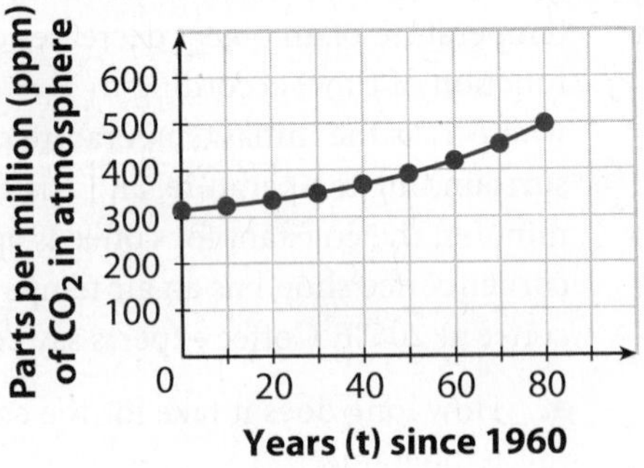

13.4 Compound Interest

Essential Question: How do you model the value of an investment that earns compound interest?

Resource Locker

Explore Comparing Simple and Compound Interest

A *bond* is a type of investment that you buy with cash and for which you receive interest either as the bond matures or when it matures. A *conventional bond* generates an interest payment, sometimes called a *coupon payment*, on a regular basis, typically twice a year. The interest payments end when the bond matures and the amount you paid up-front is returned to you.

A *zero-coupon bond*, on the other hand, requires you to invest less money up-front and pays you its maturity value, which includes all accumulated interest, when the bond matures. Over the life of the bond, the interest that is earned each period itself earns interest until the bond matures.

The basic difference between a conventional bond and a zero-coupon bond is the type of interest earned. A conventional bond pays simple interest, whereas a zero-coupon bond pays **compound interest**, which is interest that earns interest.

Ⓐ For $1000, you can buy a conventional bond that has a maturity value of $1000, has a maturity date of 4 years, and pays 5% annual interest. Calculate the interest that the investment earns annually by completing the table. (Bear in mind that interest earned is paid to you and not reinvested.)

Conventional Bond			
Year	**Value of Investment at Beginning of Year**	**Interest Earned for Year (Paid to the Investor)**	**Value of Investment at End of Year**
0	?	?	$1000
1	$1000	$1000(0.05) = $?	$?
2	$1000	$1000(0.05) = $?	$?
3	$1000	$1000(0.05) = $?	$?
4	$1000	$1000(0.05) = $?	$?

(B) For \$822.70, you can buy a zero-coupon bond that has a maturity value of \$1000, has a maturity date of 4 years, and pays 5% annual interest. Calculate the interest that the investment earns annually by completing the table. (Bear in mind that interest earned is reinvested and not paid to you until the bond matures.)

Zero-Coupon Bond

Year	Value of Investment at Beginning of Year	Interest Earned for Year (Reinvested)	Value of Investment at End of Year
0			\$822.70
1	\$822.70	\$822.70(0.05) = \$?	\$822.70 + \$? = \$?
2	\$?	\$? (0.05) = \$?	\$? + \$? = \$?
3	\$?	\$? (0.05) = \$?	\$? + \$? = \$?
4	\$?	\$? (0.05) = \$?	\$? + \$? = \$1000

Reflect

1. Describe the difference between how simple interest is calculated and how compound interest is calculated.

2. If $V(t)$ represents the value of an investment at time t, in whole numbers of years starting with $t = 0$ and ending with $t = 4$, write a constant function for the last column in the first table and an exponential function for the last column in the second table.

Explain 1 Modeling Interest Compounded Annually

Recall that the general exponential growth function is $f(t) = a(1 + r)^t$. When this function is applied to an investment where interest is compounded annually at a rate r, the function is written as $V(t) = P(1 + r)^t$ where $V(t)$ is the value V of the investment at time t and P is the *principal* (the amount invested).

(A) A person invests \$3500 in an account that earns 3% annual interest. Find when the value of the investment reaches \$10,000.

Let $P = 3500$ and $r = 0.03$. Then $V(t) = P(1 + r)^t = 3500(1.03)^t$.

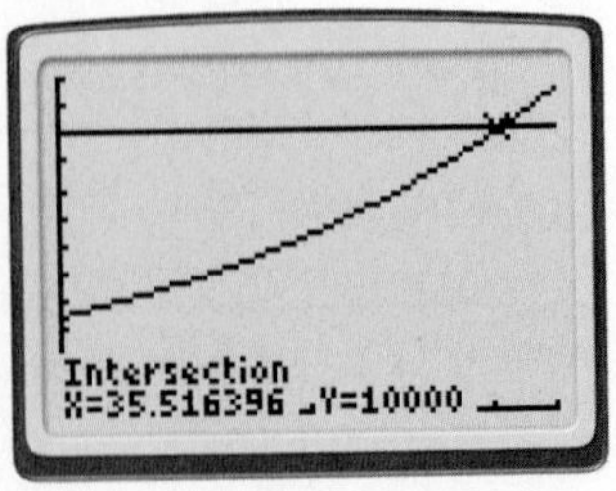

Graph $y = 3500(1.03)^x$ on a graphing calculator. Also graph the line $y = 10{,}000$ and find the point where the graphs intersect.

The value of the function is 10,000 at $x \approx 35.5$. So, the investment reaches a value of \$10,000 in approximately 35.5 years.

(B) A person invests \$200 in an account that earns 6.25% annual interest. Find when the value of the investment reaches \$5000.

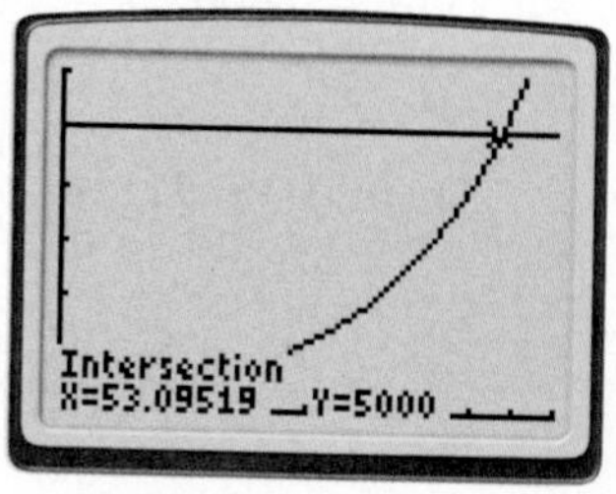

Let $P =$ 200 and $r =$ 0.0625.

Then $V(t) = P(1 + r)^t =$ 200 $\left(1.0625\right)^t$.

Graph the function on a graphing calculator. Also graph the line

$y =$ 5000 and find the point of intersection.

The value of the function is 5000 at $x \approx$ 53.1. So, the investment reaches a value of \$5000 in approximately 53.1 years.

Your Turn

3. A person invests \$1000 in an account that earns 5.5% annual interest. Find when the value of the investment has doubled.

Explain 2 Modeling Interest Compounded More than Once a Year

Interest may be earned more frequently than once a year, such as semiannually (every 6 months), quarterly (every 3 months), monthly, and even daily. If the number of times that interest is compounded in a year is n, then the interest rate per compounding period is $\frac{r}{n}$ (where r is the annual interest rate), and the number of times that interest is compounded in t years is nt. So, the exponential growth function becomes $V(t) = P\left(1 + \frac{r}{n}\right)^{nt}$.

(A) A person invests \$1200 in an account that earns 2% annual interest compounded quarterly. Find when the value of the investment reaches \$1500.

Let $P = 1200$, $r = 0.02$, and $n = 4$. Then $V(t) = P\left(1 + \frac{r}{n}\right)^{nt} = 1200\left(1 + \frac{0.02}{4}\right)^{4t} = 1200(1.005)^{4t}$.

Graph the function $y = 1200(1.005)^{4x}$ on a graphing calculator. Also graph the line $y = 1500$ and find the point where the graphs intersect.

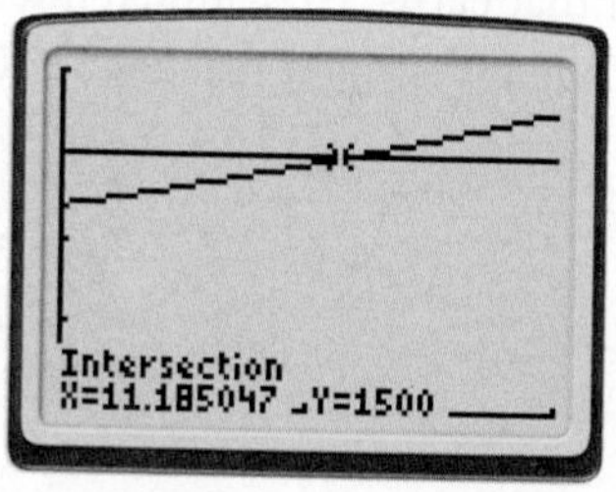

The value of the function is 1500 at $x \approx 11.2$. So, the investment reaches a value of \$1500 in approximately 11.2 years.

(B) A person invests \$600 in an account that earns 6.25% annual interest compounded semiannually. Find when the value of the investment reaches \$1700.

Let $P =$ 600, $r =$ 0.0625, and $n =$ 2.

Then $V(t) = P\left(1 + \frac{r}{n}\right)^{nt} = 600\left(1 + \frac{0.0625}{2}\right)^{2t} = 600(1.03125)^{2t}$.

Graph the function on a graphing calculator. Also graph the line $y =$ 1700 and find the point where the graphs intersect.

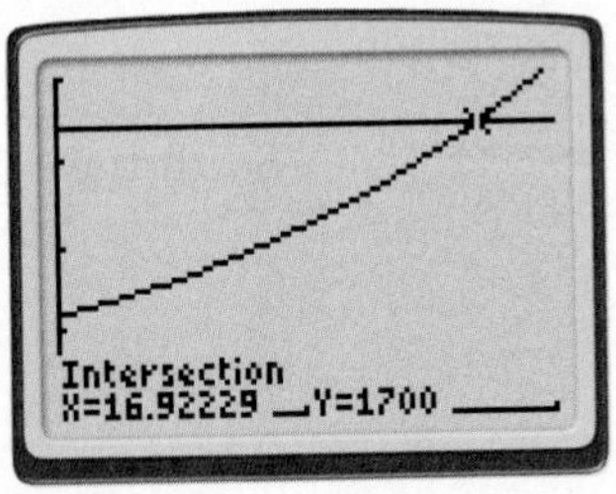

The value of the function is 1700 at $x \approx$ 16.9. So, the investment reaches a value of \$1700 in approximately 16.9 years.

Your Turn

4. A person invests \$8000 in an account that earns 6.5% annual interest compounded daily. Find when the value of the investment reaches \$20,000.

Explain 3 Modeling Interest Compounded Continuously

By letting $m = \frac{n}{r}$, you can rewrite the model $V(t) = P\left(1 + \frac{r}{n}\right)^{nt}$ as $V(t) = P\left(1 + \frac{1}{m}\right)^{mrt}$ because $\frac{r}{n} = \frac{1}{m}$ and $nt = mrt$. Then, rewriting $V(t) = P\left(1 + \frac{1}{m}\right)^{mrt}$ as $V(t) = P\left[\left(1 + \frac{1}{m}\right)^{m}\right]^{rt}$ and letting n increase without bound, which causes m to increase without bound, you see that $\left(1 + \frac{1}{m}\right)^{m}$ approaches e, and the model simply becomes $V(t) = Pe^{rt}$. This model gives the value of an investment with principal P and annual interest rate r when interest is compounded *continuously*.

(A) A person invests \$5000 in an account that earns 3.5% annual interest compounded continuously. Find when the value of the investment reaches \$12,000.

Let $P = 5000$ and $r = 0.035$. Then $V(t) = 5000e^{0.035t}$.

Graph $y = 5000e^{0.035x}$. on a graphing calculator. Also graph the line $y = 12{,}000$ and find the point where the graphs intersect.

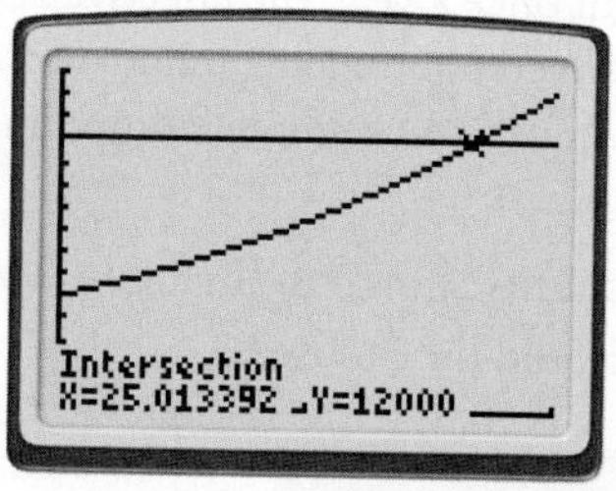

The value of the function is 12,000 at $x \approx 25$. So, the investment reaches a value of \$12,000 in approximately 25 years.

(B) The principal amount, \$350, earns 6% annual interest compounded continuously. Find when the value reaches \$1800.

Let $P =$ 350 and $r =$ 0.06. Then $V(t) =$ 350 $e^{0.06t}$.

Graph the function on a graphing calculator. Also graph the line $y =$ 1800 and find the point where the graphs intersect.

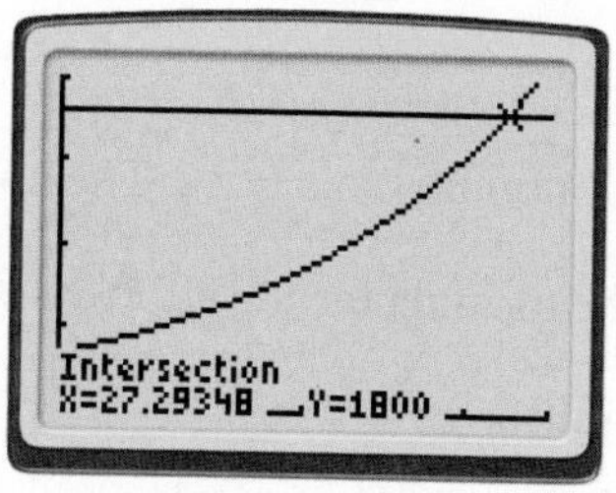

The value of the function is 1800 at $x \approx$ 27.3. So, the investment reaches a value of \$1800 in approximately 27.3 years.

Your Turn

5. A person invests \$1550 in an account that earns 4% annual interest compounded continuously. Find when the value of the investment reaches \$2000.

Explain 4 Finding and Comparing Effective Annual Interest Rates

The value-of-an-investment function $V(t) = P\left(1 + \frac{r}{n}\right)^{nt} = P\left[\left(1 + \frac{r}{n}\right)^{n}\right]^{t}$, where interest is compounded n times per year, is an exponential function of the form $f(t) = ab^t$ where $a = P$ and $b = \left(1 + \frac{r}{n}\right)^{n}$. When the base of an exponential function is greater than 1, the function is an exponential growth function where the base is the growth factor and 1 less than the base is the growth rate. So, the growth rate for $V(t) = P\left(1 + \frac{r}{n}\right)^{nt}$ is $b - 1 = \left(1 + \frac{r}{n}\right)^{n} - 1$. This growth rate is called the investment's *effective annual interest rate R*, whereas r is called the investment's *nominal annual interest rate.*

Similarly, for the value-of-an-investment function $V(t) = Pe^{rt} = P\left[e^r\right]^t$, where interest is compounded continuously, the growth factor is e^r, and the growth rate is $e^r - 1$. So, in this case, the effective annual interest rate is $R = e^r - 1$.

For an account that earns interest compounded more than once a year, the effective annual interest rate is the rate that would produce the same amount of interest if interest were compounded annually instead. The effective rate allows you to compare two accounts that have different nominal rates and different compounding periods.

(A) Arturo plans to make a deposit in one of the accounts shown in the table. To maximize the interest that the account earns, which account should he choose?

	Account X	Account Y
Nominal Annual Interest Rate	2.5%	2.48%
Compounding Period	Quarterly	Monthly

For Account X, interest is compounded quarterly, so $n = 4$. The nominal rate is 2.5%, so $r = 0.025$.

$R_X = \left(1 + \frac{r}{n}\right)^n - 1$ Use the formula for the effective rate.

$= \left(1 + \frac{0.025}{4}\right)^4 - 1$ Substitute.

≈ 0.02524 Simplify.

For Account Y, interest is compounded monthly, so $n = 12$. The nominal rate is 2.48%, so $r = 0.0248$.

$R_Y = \left(1 + \frac{r}{n}\right)^n - 1$ Use the formula for the effective rate.

$= \left(1 + \frac{0.0248}{12}\right)^{12} - 1$ Substitute.

≈ 0.02508 Simplify.

Account X has an effective rate of 2.524%, and Account Y has an effective rate of 2.508%, so Account X has a greater effective rate, and Arturo should choose Account X.

(B) Harriet plans to make a deposit in one of two accounts. Account A has a 3.24% nominal rate with interest compounded continuously, and Account B has a 3.25% nominal rate with interest compounded semiannually. To maximize the interest that the account earns, which account should she choose?

For Account A, interest is compounded continuously. The nominal rate is 3.24%, so $r =$ 0.0324.

$R_A = e^r - 1$ Use the formula for the effective rate.

$= e^{0.0324} - 1$ Substitute.

$\approx$ 0.03293 Simplify.

For Account B, interest is compounded semiannually, so so $n =$ 2. The nominal rate is 3.25%,

so $r =$ 0.0325

$$R_B = \left(1 + \frac{r}{n}\right)^n - 1 \qquad \text{Use the formula for the effective rate.}$$

$$= \left(1 + \frac{\boxed{0.0325}}{\boxed{2}}\right)^{\boxed{2}} - 1 \qquad \text{Substitute.}$$

$$\approx \boxed{0.03276} \qquad \text{Simplify.}$$

Account A has an effective rate of 3.293%, and Account B has an effective rate of 3.276%, so Account A has a greater effective rate, and Harriet should choose Account A.

Your Turn

6. Jaclyn plans to make a deposit in one of the accounts shown in the table. To maximize the interest that the account earns, which account should she choose?

	Account X	Account Y
Nominal Annual Interest Rate	4.24%	4.18%
Compounding Period	Annually	Daily

Elaborate

7. Explain the difference between an investment's nominal annual interest rate and its effective annual interest rate.

8. **Essential Question Check-In** List the three functions used to model an investment that earns compound interest at an annual rate r. Identify when each function is used.

Evaluate: Homework and Practice

Personal Math Trainer

- Online Homework
- Hints and Help
- Extra Practice

1. A person invests \$2560 in an account that earns 5.2% annual interest. Find when the value of the investment reaches \$6000.

2. A person invests \$1800 in an account that earns 2.46% annual interest. Find when the value of the investment reaches \$3500.

3. Emmanuel invests \$3600 and Kelsey invests \$2400. Both investments earn 3.8% annual interest. How much longer will it take Kelsey's investment to reach \$10,000 than Emmanuel's investment?

4. Jocelyn invests $1200 in an account that earns 2.4% annual interest. Marcus invests $400 in an account that earns 5.2% annual interest. Find when the value of Marcus's investment equals the value of Jocelyn's investment and find the common value of the investments at that time.

5. A person invests $350 in an account that earns 3.65% annual interest compounded semiannually. Find when the value of the investment reaches $5675.

6. Molly invests $8700 into her son's college fund, which earns 2% annual interest compounded daily. Find when the value of the fund reaches $12,000.

7. A person invests $200 in an account that earns 1.98% annual interest compounded quarterly. Find when the value of the investment reaches $500.

8. Hector invests $800 in an account that earns 6.98% annual interest compounded semiannually. Rebecca invests $1000 in an account that earns 5.43% annual interest compounded monthly. Find when the value of Hector's investment equals the value of Rebecca's investment and find the common value of the investments at that time.

9. A person invests $6750 in an account that earns 6.23% annual interest compounded continuously. Find when the value of the investment reaches $15,000.

10. A person invests $465 in an account that earns 3.1% annual interest compounded continuously. Find when the value of the investment reaches $2400.

11. Lucy invests $800 in an account that earns 6.12% annual interest compounded continuously. Juan invests $1600 in an account that earns 3.9% annual interest compounded continuously. Find when the value of Lucy's investment equals the value of Juan's investment and find the common value of the investments at that time.

12. Paula plans to make a deposit in one of the accounts shown in the table. To maximize the interest that the account earns, which account should she choose?

	Account X	Account Y
Nominal Annual Interest rate	2.83%	2.86%
Compounding Period	Continuously	Annually

13. Tanika plans to make a deposit to one of two accounts. Account A has a 3.78% nominal rate with interest compounded daily, and Account B has a 3.8% nominal rate with interest compounded monthly. To maximize the interest that the account earns, which account should she choose?

14. Kylie plans to deposit $650 in one of the accounts shown in the table. She chooses the account with the greater effective rate. How much money will she have in her account after 10 years?

	Account X	Account Y
Nominal Annual Interest Rate	4.13%	4.12%
Compounding Period	Semiannually	Quarterly

15. A person invests $2860 for 15 years in an account that earns 4.6% annual interest. Match each description of a difference in interest earned on the left with the actual difference listed on the right.

A. Difference between compounding interest semiannually and annually — **a.** ___?___ $14.89

B. Difference between compounding interest quarterly and semiannually — **b.** ___?___ $21.98

C. Difference between compounding interest monthly and quarterly — **c.** ___?___ $0.25

D. Difference between compounding interest daily and monthly — **d.** ___?___ $42.75

E. Difference between compounding interest continuously and daily — **e.** ___?___ $7.27

H.O.T. Focus on Higher Order Thinking

16. **Multi-Step** Ingrid and Harry are saving to buy a house. Ingrid invests $5000 in an account that earns 3.6% interest compounded quarterly. Harry invests $7500 in an account that earns 2.8% interest compounded semiannually.

a. Find a model for each investment.

b. Use a graphing calculator to find when the combined value of their investments reaches $15,000.

17. **Explain the Error** A student is asked to find when the value of an investment of $5200 in an account that earns 4.2% annual interest compounded quarterly reaches $16,500. The student uses the model $V(t) = 5200(1.014)^{3t}$ and finds that the investment reaches a value of $16,500 after approximately 27.7 years. Find and correct the student's error.

18. **Communicate Mathematical Ideas** For a certain price, you can buy a zero-coupon bond that has a maturity value of $1000, has a maturity date of 4 years, and pays 5% annual interest. How can the present value (the amount you pay for the bond) be determined from the future value (the amount you get when the bond matures)?

Lesson Performance Task

The grandparents of a newborn child decide to establish a college fund for her. They invest \$10,000 into a fund that pays 4.5% interest compounded continuously.

a. Write a model for the value of the investment over time and find the value of the investment when the child enters college at 18 years old.

b. In 2013, the average annual public in-state college tuition was \$8893, which was 2.9% above the 2012 cost. Use these figures to write a model to project the amount of money needed to pay for one year's college tuition 18 years into the future. What amount must be invested in the child's college fund to generate enough money in 18 years to pay for the first year's college tuition?

Exponential Functions

Essential Question: How can you use exponential functions to solve real-world problems?

Key Vocabulary
exponential decay *(decremento exponencial)*
exponential function *(función exponencial)*
exponential growth *(crecimiento exponencial)*

KEY EXAMPLE *(Lesson 13.2)*

$g(x) = 3^{x+1}$ is a transformation of the function $f(x) = 3^x$. Sketch a graph of $g(x) = 3^{x+1}$.

$g(x) = 3^{x+1} = f(x + 1)$

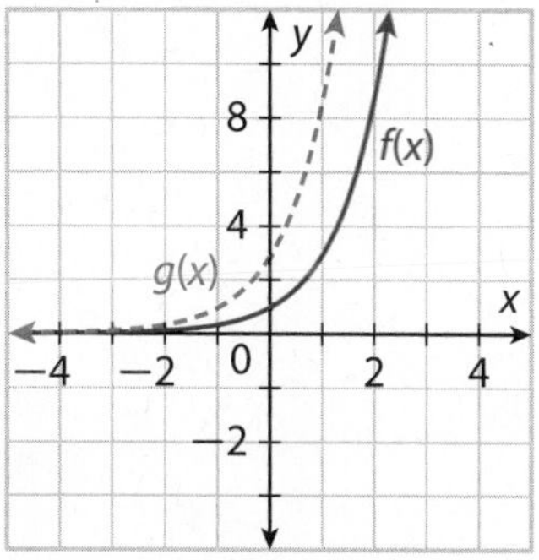

Because $g(x) = 3^{x+1} = f(x + 1)$, the graph of g can be obtained by shifting the graph of f one unit to the left, as shown.

The solid line represents $f(x) = 3^x$.
The dashed line represents $g(x) = 3^{x+1}$.

KEY EXAMPLE *(Lesson 13.4)*

Which of the following accounts has a greater effective rate?

	Account X	Account Y
Nominal Interest Rate	3.5%	3.49%
Compounding Period	Quarterly	Weekly

$$R_x = \left(1 + \frac{r}{n}\right)^n - 1$$ Use the formula for the effective rate.

$$= \left(1 + \frac{0.035}{4}\right)^4 - 1$$ Substitute.

$$\approx 0.03546$$ Simplify.

$$R_y = \left(1 + \frac{r}{n}\right)^n - 1$$ Use the formula for the effective rate.

$$= \left(1 + \frac{0.0349}{52}\right)^{52} - 1$$ Substitute.

$$\approx 0.0355$$ Simplify.

Account Y has the higher effective rate.

EXERCISES

Sketch the graphs of the following transformations. *(Lessons 13.1, 13.2, 13.3)*

1. $g(x) = -2(0.5)^x$

2. $f(x) = \left(\frac{1}{2}\right)^{-x}$

3. $f(x) = 2e^{x-2} + 1$

4. $g(x) = \left(\frac{3}{5}\right)^x$

MODULE PERFORMANCE TASK

That's The Way the Ball Bounces

Kingston is a chemical engineer who is testing the "bounciness" of two novel materials. He formed each material into two equal-sized spheres. Kingston then dropped each sphere on a hard surface and measured the heights the spheres reached after each bounce. The results are shown in the table.

	Heights (cm)					
	h_0	h_1	h_2	h_3	h_4	h_5
Material A	90	63.0	44.1	30.9	21.6	15.1
Material B	90	49.5	27.2	15.0	8.2	4.5

Use the data to create mathematical models for the heights of the spheres. Compare the two materials. One of the two materials will be used for the tip of a pogo stick. Which material should Kingston recommend and why?

As you complete the task, be sure to write down all your data and assumptions. Then use graphs, numbers, words, or algebra to explain how you reached your conclusion.

Ready to Go On?

13.1–13.4 Exponential Functions

Personal Math Trainer
- Online Homework
- Hints and Help
- Extra Practice

State the domain and range for the graphs of the following functions. *(Lessons 13.1, 13.2)*

1. $y = \left(\frac{1}{4}\right)^x$

2. $y = \left(\frac{1}{3}\right)^{(x-2)} + 2$

3. $y = -3 \cdot 2^{x+2}$

4. $y = 3^{x-2} - 1$

Identify the account that has the higher effective rate. *(Lessons 13.4)*

5.

	Account X	Account Y
Nominal Interest Rate	5%	5.2%
Compounding Period	Daily	Annually

6.

	Account A	Account B
Nominal Interest Rate	2.65%	2.6%
Compounding Period	Quarterly	Continuously

ESSENTIAL QUESTION

7. How can you tell whether an exponential function models exponential growth or exponential decay?

MODULE 13
MIXED REVIEW

Assessment Readiness

1. Consider the base of exponential functions. Tell whether the given base will cause exponential growth.
   A. A base between 0 and 1
   B. A base greater than 1
   C. A base equal to 1

2. Consider an investment of \$500 compounded annually with 3% interest. Determine if each statement is True or False.
   A. After 3 years, if no money is withdrawn, the account will have \$546.36
   B. The account will gain \$15.00 every year.
   C. After 5 years, if no money is withdrawn, the account will have \$562.75.

3. Jordan said that the asymptote of $y = \left(\frac{1}{2}\right)^{x-2} + 3$ is $y = 2$. Describe and correct his mistake.

4. Describe how $f(x) = |x|$ is changed to create $g(x) = \frac{3}{4}|x + 3| - 8$.

5. The graphs of $f(x) = 2^x$, $f(x) = 10^x$ and $f(x) = e^x$ all pass through a common point. Explain why the point $(0, 1)$ is common to all three functions.

Modeling with Exponential and Other Functions

MODULE 14

Essential Question: How can modeling with exponential and other functions help you to solve real-world problems?

REAL WORLD VIDEO
Most people have to save up money for a major purchase like a car or new home. Check out some of the factors to consider when investing for long-term goals.

MODULE PERFORMANCE TASK PREVIEW
Double Your Money!

If you had some money to invest, how would you pick the investment option that would let your money grow fastest? The return on an investment depends on factors such as the length of time of the investment and the return rate. How can you use an exponential model to find out when an investment will double in value? Let's find out!

Are YOU Ready?

Complete these exercises to review skills you will need for this module.

Personal Math Trainer

- Online Homework
- Hints and Help
- Extra Practice

Writing Linear Equations

Example 1 Write an equation for the line that passes through the points (2, 3) and (4, −1).

$\frac{-1-3}{4-2} = \frac{-4}{2} = -2$ Find the slope.

So $y = -2x + b$ Substitute slope for m in $y = mx + b$.

$3 = -2(2) + b$ Substitute (2, 3) for x- and y-values.

$b = 7$ Solve for b.

The equation is $y = -2x + 7$.

Write an equation for the line that passes through the given points.

1. $(2, -5), (6, -3)$

2. $(4, -3), (-2, 15)$

3. $(4, 7), (-2, -2)$

Transforming Linear Functions

Example 2 Write the equation of $y = 9x - 2$ after a reflection across the x-axis followed by a reflection across the y-axis.

$y = -1(9x - 2) \rightarrow y = -9x + 2$ Reflection across the x-axis

$y = -9(-x) + 2 \rightarrow y = 9x + 2$ Reflection across the y-axis

So $y = 9x + 2$ Reflected across both axes is $y = 9x + 2$.

Write the equation of each function after a reflection across both axes.

4. $y = 2x + 1$

5. $y = -3x - 4$

6. $y = -0.2x + 6$

Equations Involving Exponents

Example 3 Solve $x^{\frac{2}{3}} = 16$ for x.

$\left(x^{\frac{2}{3}}\right)^{\frac{3}{2}} = \pm (16)^{\frac{3}{2}}$ Raise both sides to the same power.

$x = \pm \left(16^{\frac{1}{2}}\right)^3 = \pm (4)^3 = \pm 64$ Evaluate the right side.

So, $x = \pm 64$.

Solve for x.

7. $x^6 = 4096$

8. $x^{\frac{3}{2}} = 27$

9. $\frac{1}{3}x^{\frac{2}{5}} = 3$

14.1 Fitting Exponential Functions to Data

Resource Locker

Essential Question: What are ways to model data using an exponential function of the form $f(x) = ab^x$?

Explore Identifying Exponential Functions from Tables of Values

Notice for an exponential function $f(x) = ab^x$ that $f(x+1) = ab^{x+1}$. By the product of powers property, $ab^{x+1} = a(b^x \cdot b^1) = ab^x \cdot b = f(x) \cdot b$. So, $f(x+1) = f(x) \cdot b$. This means that increasing the value of x by 1 multiplies the value of $f(x)$ by b. In other words, for successive integer values of x, each value of $f(x)$ is b times the value before it, or, equivalently, the ratio between successive values of $f(x)$ is b. This gives you a test to apply to a given set of data to see whether it represents exponential growth or decay.

Each table gives function values for successive integer values of x. Find the ratio of successive values of $f(x)$ to determine whether each set of data can be modeled by an exponential function.

(A)

x	0	1	2	3	4
f(x)	1	4	16	64	256

$\frac{f(1)}{f(0)} = \boxed{?}$; $\frac{f(2)}{f(1)} = \boxed{?}$; $\frac{f(3)}{f(2)} = \boxed{?}$; $\frac{f(4)}{f(3)} = \boxed{?}$

Are the data exponential?

(B)

x	0	1	2	3	4
f(x)	1	7	13	19	25

$\frac{f(1)}{f(0)} = \boxed{?}$; $\frac{f(2)}{f(1)} = \boxed{?}$; $\frac{f(3)}{f(2)} = \boxed{?}$; $\frac{f(4)}{f(3)} = \boxed{?}$

Are the data exponential?

(C)

x	0	1	2	3	4
f(x)	1	4	13	28	49

$\frac{f(1)}{f(0)} = \boxed{?}$; $\frac{f(2)}{f(1)} = \boxed{?}$; $\frac{f(3)}{f(2)} = \boxed{?}$; $\frac{f(4)}{f(3)} = \boxed{?}$

Are the data exponential?

(D)

x	0	1	2	3	4
$f(x)$	1	0.25	0.0625	0.015625	0.00390625

$\frac{f(1)}{f(0)} = $? ; $\frac{f(2)}{f(1)} = $? ; $\frac{f(3)}{f(2)} = $? ; $\frac{f(4)}{f(3)} = $?

Are the data exponential?

Reflect

1. In which step(s) does the table show exponential growth? Which show(s) exponential decay? What is the base of the growth or decay?
2. In which step are the data modeled by the exponential function $f(x) = 4^{-x}$?
3. What type of function model would be appropriate in each step not modeled by an exponential function? Explain your reasoning.
4. **Discussion** In the introduction to this Explore, you saw that the ratio between successive terms of $f(x) = ab^x$ is b. Find and simplify an expression for $f(x + c)$ where c is a constant. Then explain how this gives you a more general test to determine whether a set of data can be modeled by an exponential function.

Explain 1 Roughly Fitting an Exponential Function to Data

As the answer to the last Reflect question above indicates, if the ratios of successive values of the dependent variable in a data set for equally-spaced values of the independent variable are equal, an exponential function model fits. In the real world, sets of data rarely fit a model perfectly, but if the ratios are approximately equal, an exponential function can still be a good model.

Example 1

(A) **Population Statistics** The table gives the official population of the United States for the years 1790 to 1890.

Create an approximate exponential model for the data set. Then graph your function with a scatter plot of the data and assess its fit.

It appears that the ratio of the population in each decade to the population of the decade before it is pretty close to one and one third, so an exponential model should be reasonable.

For a model of the form $f(x) = ab^x$, $f(0) = a$. So, if x is the number of decades after 1790, the value when $x = 0$ is a, the initial population in 1790, or 3,929,214.

One way to estimate the growth factor, b, is to find the population ratios from decade to decade and average them:

Year	Total Population
1790	3,929,214
1800	5,308,483
1810	7,239,881
1820	9,638,453
1830	12,860,702
1840	17,063,353
1850	23,191,876
1860	31,443,321
1870	38,558,371
1880	50,189,209
1890	62,979,766

$$\frac{1.35 + 1.36 + 1.33 + 1.33 + 1.33 + 1.36 + 1.36 + 1.23 + 1.30 + 1.26}{10} \approx 1.32$$

An approximate model is $f(x) = 3.93(1.32)^x$, where $f(x)$ is in millions.

The graph is shown.

The graph looks like a good fit for the data. All of the points lie on, or close to, the curve.

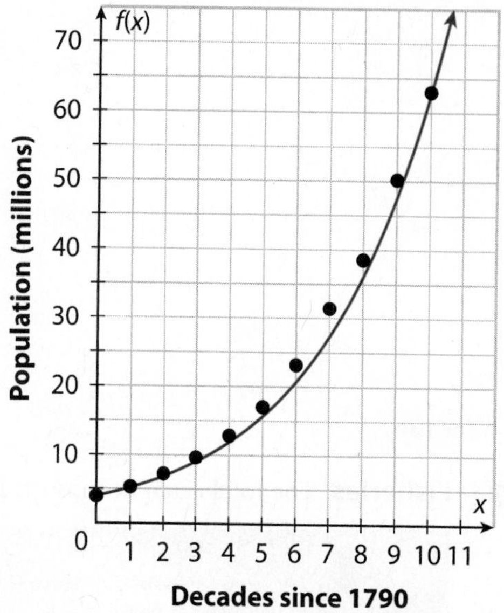

Another way to estimate b is to choose a point other than $(0, a)$ from the scatter plot that appears would lie on, or very close to, the best-fitting exponential curve. Substitute the coordinates in the general formula and solve for b. For the plot shown, the point (8, 38.56) looks like a good choice.

$$38.56 = 3.93 \cdot b^8$$

$$(9.81)^{\frac{1}{8}} \approx (b^8)^{\frac{1}{8}}$$

$$1.33 \approx b$$

This value of b results in a model very similar to the previous model.

(B) **Movies** The table shows the decline in weekly box office revenue from its peak for one of 2013's top-grossing summer movies.

Week	Revenue (in Millions of Dollars)
0	95.3
1	55.9
2	23.7
3	16.4
4	8.8
5	4.8
6	3.3
7	1.9
8	1.1
9	0.6

Create an approximate exponential model for the data set. Then graph your function with a scatter plot of the data and assess its fit.

Find the value of a in $f(x) = ab^x$.

When $x = 0$, $f(x) = 95.3$. So, $a = 95.3$.

Find an estimate for b.

Approximate the revenue ratios from week to week and average them:

$$\frac{0.59 + 0.42 + 0.69 + 0.54 + \boxed{0.55 + 0.69 + 0.58 + 0.58 + 0.55}}{\boxed{9}} \approx \boxed{0.58}$$

An approximate model is $f(x) = \boxed{95.3(0.58)^x}$.

The graph looks like a very good fit for the data. All of the points except one (2 weeks after peak revenue) lie on, or very close to, the curve.

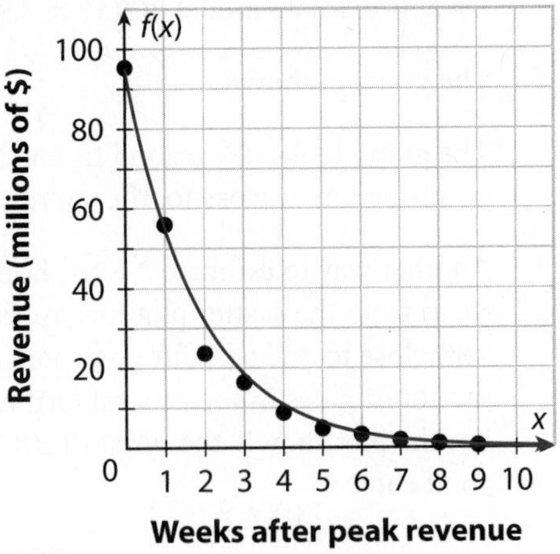

Your Turn

5. **Fisheries** The total catch in tons for Iceland's fisheries from 2002 to 2010 is shown in the table.

Year	Total Catch (Millions of Tons)
2002	2.145
2003	2.002
2004	1.750
2005	1.661
2006	1.345
2007	1.421
2008	1.307
2009	1.164
2010	1.063

Create an approximate exponential model for the data set. Then graph your function with a scatter plot of the data and assess its fit.

Explain 2 Fitting an Exponential Function to Data Using Technology

Previously you have used a graphing calculator to find a linear regression model of the form $y = ax + b$ to model data, and have also found quadratic regression models of the form $y = ax^2 + bx + c$. Similarly, you can use a graphing calculator to perform exponential regression to produce a model of the form $f(x) = ab^x$.

Example 2

Ⓐ **Population Statistics** Use the data from Example 1 Part A and a graphing calculator to find the exponential regression model for the data, and show the graph of the model with the scatter plot.

Using the STAT menu, enter the number of decades since 1790 in List1 and the population to the nearest tenth of a million in List2.

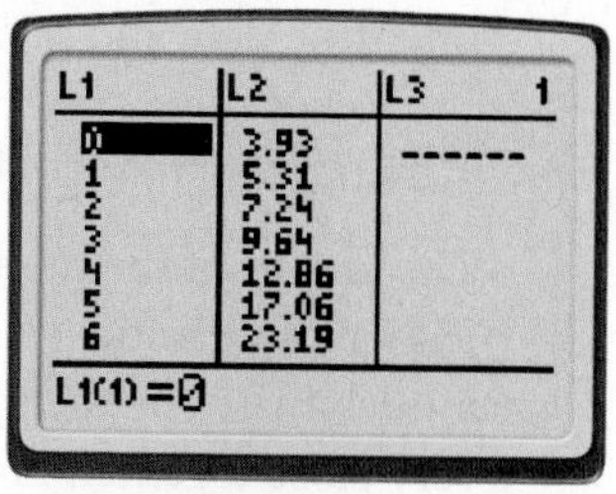

Using the STAT CALC menu, choose “ExpReg” and press ENTER until you see this screen:

An approximate model is $f(x) = 4.116(1.323)^x$.

Making sure that STATPLOT is turned “On,” enter the model into the Y = menu either directly or using the VARS menu and choosing “Statistics,” “EQ,” and “RegEQ.” The graphs are shown using the ZoomStat window:

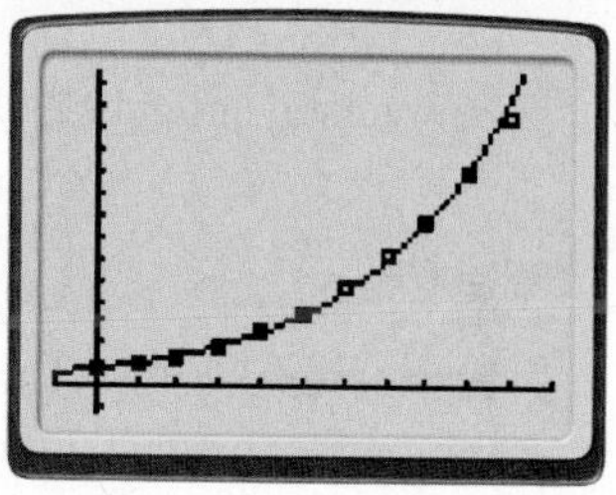

Plotted with the second graph from Example 1 (shown dotted), you can see that the graphs are nearly identical.

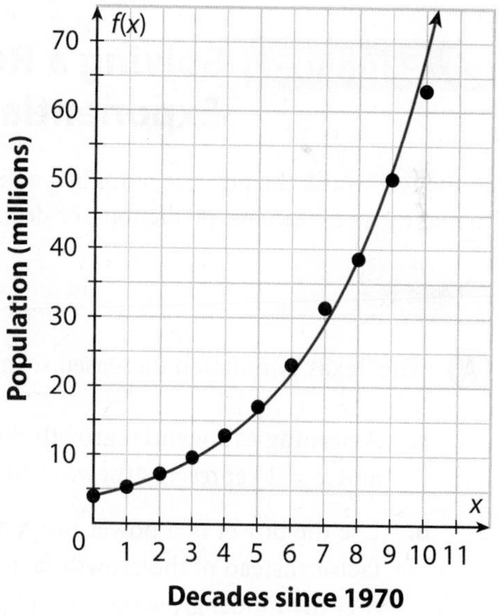

Ⓑ **Movies** Use the data from Example 1 Part B and a graphing calculator to find the exponential regression model for the data. Graph the regression model on the calculator, then graph the model from Example 1 on the same screen using a dashed curve. How do the graphs of the models compare? What can you say about the actual decline in revenue from one week after the peak to two weeks after the peak compared to what the regression model indicates?

Enter the data and perform exponential regression.

The model (using 3 digits of precision) is $f(x) =$ $86.2(0.576)^x$.

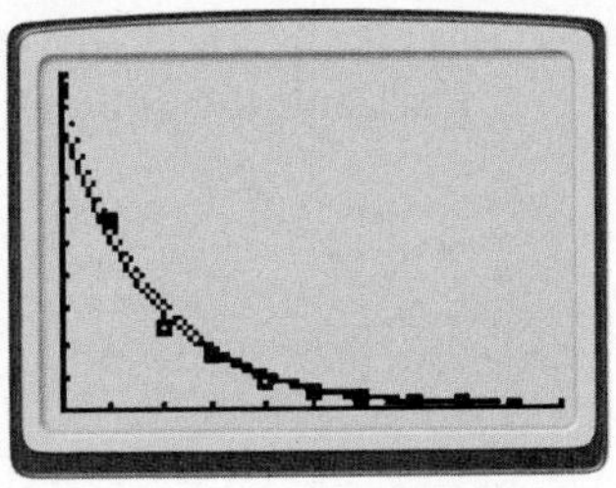

The graphs of the models are very close, but the regression equation starts with a lower initial value, and comes closer to the data point that the first model misses by the most. The last several weeks the models appear to be very close together. From the data, the decline from one week after the peak to two weeks after the peak was significantly larger than accounted for by the regression model.

Reflect

6. **Discussion** The U.S. population in 2014 was close to 320 million people. What does the regression model in Part A predict for the population in 2014? What does this tell you about extrapolating far into the future using an exponential model? How does the graph of the scatter plot with the regression model support this conclusion? (Note: The decade-to-decade U.S. growth dropped below 30% to stay after 1880, and below 20% to stay after 1910. From 2000 to 2010, the rate was below 10%.)

Your Turn

7. **Fisheries** Use the data from YourTurn5 and a graphing calculator to find the exponential regression model for the data. Graph the regression model on the calculator, then graph the model from your answer to YourTurn5 on the same screen. How do the graphs of the models compare?

Explain 3 Solving a Real-World Problem Using a Fitted Exponential Function

In the real world, the purpose of finding a mathematical model is to help identify trends or patterns, and to use them to make generalizations, predictions, or decisions based on the data.

Example 3

(A) The Texas population increased from 20.85 million to 25.15 million from 2000 to 2010.

a. Assuming exponential growth during the period, write a model where $x = 0$ represents the year 2000 and $x = 1$ represents the year 2010. What was the growth rate over the decade?

b. Use the power of a power property of exponents to rewrite the model so that b is the yearly growth factor instead of the growth factor for the decade. What is the yearly growth rate for this model? Verify that the model gives the correct population for 2010.

c. The Texas population was about 26.45 million in 2013. How does this compare with the prediction made by the model?

d. Find the model's prediction for the Texas population in 2035. Do you think it is reasonable to use this model to guide decisions about future needs for water, energy generation, and transportation needs. Explain your reasoning.

a. For a model of the form $f(x) = ab^x$, $a = f(0)$, so $a = 20.85$. To find an estimate for b, substitute $(x, f(x)) = (1, 25.5)$ and solve for b.

$$f(x) = a \cdot b^x$$

$$25.15 = 20.85 \cdot b^1$$

$$\frac{25.15}{20.85} = b$$

$$1.206 \approx b$$

An approximate model is $f(x) = 20.85(1.206)^x$. The growth rate was about 20.6%.

b. Because there are 10 years in a decade, the 10th power of the new b must give 1.206, the growth factor for the decade. So, $b^{10} = 1.206$, or $b = 1.206^{\frac{1}{10}}$. Use the power of a power property:

$$f(x) = 20.85(1.206)^x = 20.85\left(1.206^{\frac{1}{10}}\right)^{10x} \approx 20.85(1.019)^{10x}$$, where x is measured in decades.

If x is instead measured in years after 2000, the model is $f(x) = 20.85(1.019)^x$. The yearly growth rate is 1.9%.

The model gives a 2010 population of $f(x) = 20.85(1.019)^{10} \approx 25.17$. This agrees with the actual population within a rounding error.

c. Substitute $x = 13$ into the model $f(x) = 20.85(1.019)^x$:

$$f(13) = 20.85(1.019)^{13} \approx 26.63$$

The prediction is just a little bit higher than the actual population.

d. For 2035, $x = 35$: $f(35) = 20.85(1.019)^{35} \approx 40.3$. The model predicts a Texas population of about 40 million in 2035. Possible answer: Because it is very difficult to maintain a high growth rate with an already very large population, and with overall population growth slowing, it seems unreasonable that the population would increase from 25 to 40 million so quickly. But because using the model to project even to 2020 gives a population of over 30 million, it seems reasonable to make plans for the population to grow by several million people over a relatively short period.

(B) The average revenue per theater for the movie in Part B of the previous Examples is shown in the graph. (Note that for this graph, Week 0 corresponds to Week 2 of the graphs from the previous Examples.) The regression model is $y = 5.65(0.896)^x$.

a. From Week 3 to Week 4, there is a jump of over 60% in the average weekly revenue per theater, but the total revenue for the movie for the corresponding week fell by over 30%. What must have occurred for this to be true?

There must have been a sharp reduction in the number of theaters showing the movie.

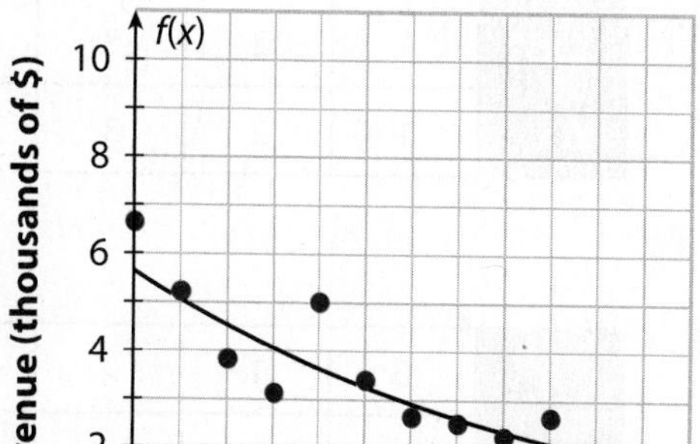

b. A new theater complex manager showing a similar summer movie in a single theater worries about quickly dropping revenue the first few weeks, and wants to stop showing the movie. Suppose you are advising the manager. Knowing that the model shown reflects the long-term trend well for such movies, what advice would you give the manager?

Be careful about removing the movie too quickly. Unless the amount of weekly revenue needed is very high, the model indicates that the longer-term trend may decline more slowly than the short-term trend.

Reflect

8. **Discussion** Consider the situation in Example 3B about deciding when to stop showing the movie. How does an understanding of what other theater managers might do affect your decision?

Your Turn

9. Graph the regression model for the catch in Icelandic fisheries, $f(x) = 2.119(0.9174^x)$, to find when the model predicts the total catches to drop below 0.5 million tons (remember that $x = 0$ corresponds to 2002). Should the model be used to project actual catch into the future? Why or why not? What are some considerations that the model raises about the fishery?

Elaborate

10. How can you tell whether a given set of data can reasonably be modeled using an exponential function?

11. What are some ways that an exponential growth or decay model can be used to guide decisions, preparations, or judgments about the future?

12. **Essential Question Check-In** What are some ways to find an approximate exponential model for a set of data without using a graphing calculator?

Evaluate: Homework and Practice

Personal Math Trainer
- Online Homework
- Hints and Help
- Extra Practice

Determine whether each set of data can be modeled by an exponential function. If it can, tell whether it represents exponential growth or exponential decay. If it can't, tell whether a linear or quadratic model is instead appropriate.

1.

x	0	1	2	3	4
$f(x)$	2	6	18	54	162

2.

x	1	2	3	4	5	6
$f(x)$	1	2	3	5	8	13

3.

x	0	1	2	3	4
$f(x)$	2	8	18	32	50

4.

x	5	10	15	20	25
$f(x)$	76.2	66.2	59.1	50.9	44.6

Three students, Anja, Ben, and Celia, are asked to find an approximate exponential model for the data shown. Use the data and scatter plot for Exercises 5–7.

x	0	1	2	3	4	5	6	7	8	9	10
$f(x)$	10	6.0	5.4	3.9	3.7	2.3	1.4	1.0	0.9	0.8	0.5

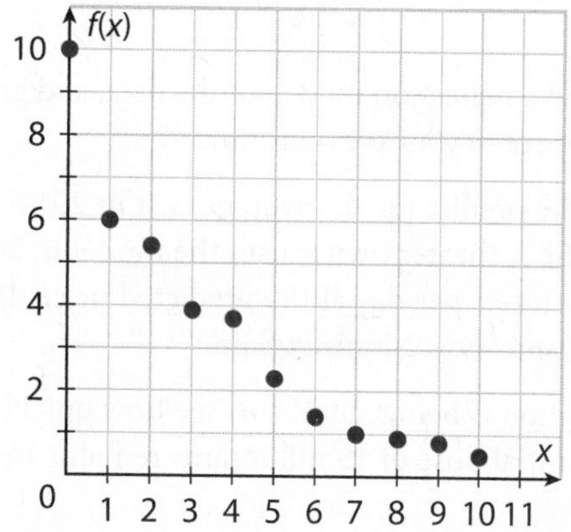

5. To find an approximate exponential model, Anja uses the first data point to find a, and then estimates b by finding the ratio of the first two function values. What is her model?

6. To find his model, Ben uses the first and last data points. What is his model?

7. Celia thinks that because the drop between the first two points is so large, the best model might actually have a y-intercept a little below 10. She uses $(0, 9.5)$ to estimate a in her model. To estimate b, she finds the average of the ratios of successive data values. What is her model? (Use two digits of precision for all quantities.)

8. Classic Cars The data give the estimated value in dollars of a model of classic car over several years.

15,300	16,100	17,300	18,400	19,600	20,700	22,000

a. Find an approximate exponential model for the car's value by averaging the successive ratios of the value. Then make a scatter plot of the data, graph your model with the scatter plot, and assess its fit to the data.

b. In the last year of the data, a car enthusiast spends \$15,100 on a car of the given model that is in need of some work. The owner then spends \$8300 restoring it. Use your model to create a table of values with a graphing calculator. How long does the function model predict the owner should keep the car before it can be sold for a profit of at least \$5000?

9. Movies The table shows the average price of a movie ticket in the United States from 2001 to 2010.

Year	2001	2002	2003	2004	2005	2006	2007	2008	2009	2010
Price ($)	5.66	5.81	6.03	6.21	6.41	6.55	6.88	7.18	7.50	7.89

a. Make a scatter plot of the data. Then use the first point and another point on the plot to find an approximate exponential model for the average ticket price. Then graph the model with your scatter plot and assess its fit to the data.

b. Use a graphing calculator to find a regression model for the data, and graph the model with the scatter plot. How does this model compare to your previous model?

c. What does the regression model predict for the average cost in 2014? How does this compare with the actual 2014 cost of about $8.35? A theater owner uses the model in 2010 to project income for 2014 assuming average sales of 490 tickets per day at the predicted price. If the actual price is instead $8.35, did the owner make a good business decision? Explain.

10. Pharmaceuticals A new medication is being studied to see how quickly it is metabolized in the body. The table shows how much of an initial dose of 15 milligrams remains in the bloodstream after different intervals of time.

Hours Since Administration	Amount Remaining (mg)
0	15
1	14.3
2	13.1
3	12.4
4	11.4
5	10.7
6	10.2
7	9.8

a. Use a graphing calculator to find a regression model. Use the calculator to graph the model with the scatter plot. How much of the drug is eliminated each hour?

b. The half-life of a drug is how long it takes for half of the drug to be broken down or eliminated from the bloodstream. Using the Table function, what is the half-life of the drug to the nearest hour?

c. Doctors want to maintain at least 7 mg of the medication in the bloodstream for maximum therapeutic effect, but do not want the amount much higher for a long period. This level is reached after 12 hours. A student suggests that this means that a 15 mg dose should be given every 12 hours. Explain whether you agree with the student. (*Hint*: Given the medicine's decay factor, how much will be in the bloodstream after the first few doses?)

11. Housing The average selling price of a unit in a high-rise condominium complex over 5 consecutive years was approximately \$184,300; \$195,600; \$204,500; \$215,300; \$228,200.

a. Find an exponential regression model where x represents years after the initial year and $f(x)$ is in thousands of dollars.

b. A couple wants to buy a unit in the complex. First, they want to save 20% of the selling price for a down payment. What is the model that represents 20% of the average selling price for a condominium?

c. At the time that the average selling price is \$228,200 (or when $x = 4$), the couple has \$20,000 saved toward a down payment. They are living with family, and saving \$1000 per month. Graph the model from Part b and a function that represents the couple's total savings on the same calculator screen. How much longer does the model predict it will take them to save enough money?

12. Business growth The growth in membership in thousands of a rapidly-growing Internet site over its first few years is modeled by $f(x) = 60(3.61)^x$ where x is in years and $x = 0$ represents the first anniversary of the site. Rewrite the model so that the growth factor represents weeks instead of years. What is the weekly growth factor? What does this model predict for the membership 20 weeks after the anniversary?

13. Which data set can be modeled by an exponential function $f(x) = ab^x$?

a. $(0, 0.1), (1, 0.5), (2, 2.5), (3, 12.5)$

b. $(0, 0.1), (1, 0.2), (2, 0.3), (3, 0.4)$

c. $(0, 1), (1, 2), (2, 4), (4, 8)$

d. $(0, 0.8), (1, 0.4), (2, 0.10), (3, 0.0125)$

H.O.T. Focus on Higher Order Thinking

14. Error analysis From the data $(2, 72.2), (3, 18.0), (4, 4.4), (5, 1.1), (6, 0.27)$, a student sees that the ratio of successive values of $f(x)$ is very close to 0.25, so that an exponential model is appropriate. From the first term, the student obtains $a = 72.2$, and writes the model $f(x) = 72.2(0.25)^x$. The student graphs the model with the data and observes that it does not fit the data well. What did the student do wrong? Correct the student's model.

15. Critical thinking For the data $(0, 5), (1, 4), (2, 3.5), (3, 3.25), (4, 3.125), (5, 3.0625)$, the ratio of consecutive y-values is not constant, so you cannot write an exponential model $f(x) = ab^x$. But the difference in the values from term to term, 1, 0.5, 0.25, 0.125, 0.0625, shows exponential decay with a decay factor of 0.5. How can you use this fact to write a model of the data that contains an exponential expression of the form ab^x?

16. Challenge Suppose that you have two data points (x_1, y_1) and (x_2, y_2) that you know are fitted by an exponential model $f(x) = ab^x$. Can you always find an equation for the model? Explain.

Lesson Performance Task

According to data from the U.S. Department of Agriculture, the number of farms in the United States has been decreasing over the past several decades. During this time, however, the average size of each farm has increased.

Year	Farms (Millions)
1940	6.35
1950	5.65
1960	3.96
1970	2.95
1980	2.44
1990	2.15
2000	2.17

Farms in the United States

a. The average size in acres of a U.S. farm from 1940 to 1980 can be modeled by the function $A(t) = 174e^{0.022t}$ where t is the number of years since 1940. What was the average farm size in 1940? In 1980?

b. The table shows the number of farms in the United States from 1940 to 2000. Find an exponential model for the data using a calculator.

c. If you were to determine the exponential model without a calculator, would the value for a be the same as the value from the calculator? Explain your answer.

d. Based on the data in the table, predict the number of farms in the United States in 2014.

e. Using a graphing calculator, determine how many years it takes for the number of farms to decrease by 50%.

f. Using a graphing calculator, determine when the number of farms in the United States will fall below 1 million.

g. Does an exponential model seem appropriate for all of the data listed in the table? Why or why not?

14.2 Choosing Among Linear, Quadratic, and Exponential Models

Resource Locker

Essential Question: How do you choose among, linear, quadratic, and exponential models for a given set of data?

Explore — Developing Rules of Thumb for Visually Choosing a Model

When you work with data, you may not know whether a linear, quadratic, or exponential model will be a good fit. If the data lie along a curve that rises and then falls or falls and then rises, the data may be well-fitted by a quadratic model. But sometimes it may not be as clear. Consider the following scatter plots.

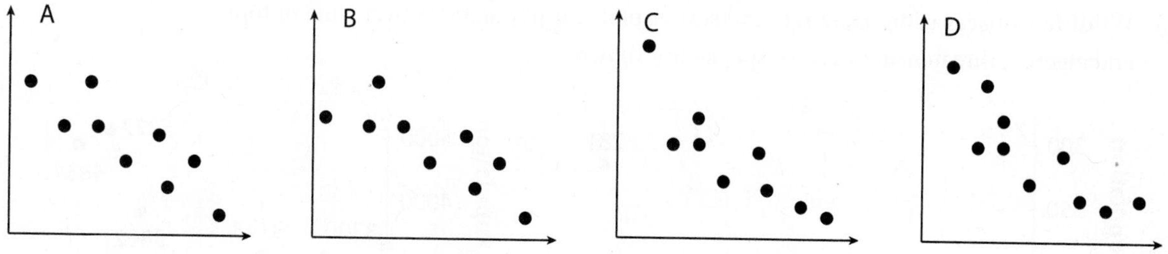

(A) Look at scatter plot A. Do you think a linear model will be appropriate? Explain your reasoning. If you think a linear model is appropriate, what do you know about the lead coefficient?

(B) Look at scatter plot B. What is different now that indicates that another kind of model might be appropriate? What characteristics would this model have?

(C) Look at scatter plot C. What about this plot indicates that yet another kind of model might be appropriate? What characteristics would this model have?

(D) Look at scatter plot D. This plot is very similar to plot C, but what indicates that a different model would be appropriate? What characteristics would this model have?

Reflect

1. When can it be difficult to distinguish whether a quadratic or an exponential model is most appropriate?
2. Under what circumstances might it be difficult to tell exponential or quadratic data from linear data?
3. For data that do not lie tightly along a curve or line, what is different about the last data point that can make it potentially more misleading than other points?

Explain 1 Modeling with a Linear Function

As noted in the Explore, it is not always immediately clear what kind of model best represents a data set. With experience, your ability to recognize signs and reasons for choosing one model over another will increase.

Example 1 **Examine each scatter plot. Then complete the steps below.**

Step 1: Choose the data set that appears to be best modeled by a linear function. Explain your choice, whether you think a linear model will be a close fit, and whether any other model might possibly be appropriate. What characteristics do you expect the linear model will have?

Step 2: Enter the data for your choice into your graphing calculator in two lists, and perform linear regression. Then give the model, defining your variables. What are the initial value and the rate of change of the model?

Step 3: Graph the model along with the scatter plot using your calculator, then assess how well the model appears to fit the data.

(A) **Wildlife Conservation** Data sets and scatter plots for populations over time of four endangered, threatened, or scarce species are shown.

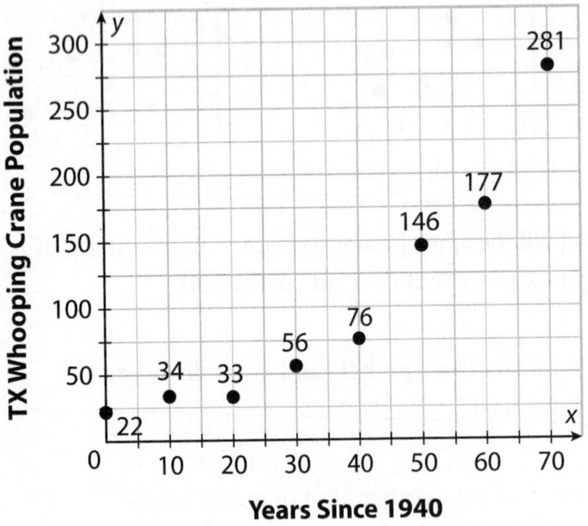

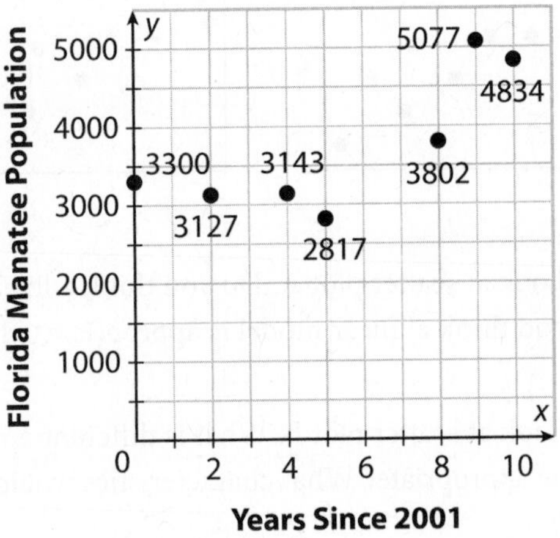

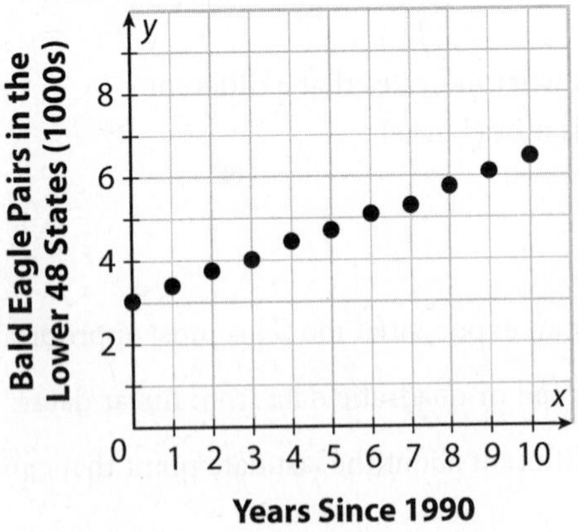

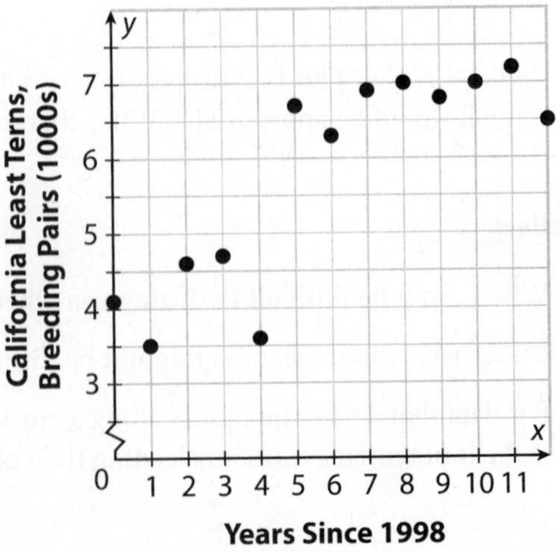

(1990, 3035)	(1994, 4449)	(1998, 5748)
(1991, 3399)	(1995, 4712)	(1999, 6104)
(1992, 3749)	(1996, 5094)	(2000, 6471)
(1993, 4015)	(1997, 5295)	

(1998, 4100)	(2003, 6700)	(2007, 6800)
(1999, 3500)	(2004, 6300)	(2008, 7000)
(2000, 4600)	(2005, 6900)	(2009, 7200)
(2001, 4700)	(2006, 7000)	(2010, 6500)
(2002, 3600)		

Step 1: The bald eagle population is clearly the one best modeled by a linear function, as the increase in the number of pairs is very steady, with no apparent curving or changes in the trend that might indicate a different model. The model will have a y-intercept of about 3 (in thousands) and will have a slope very close to 0.34, since the rate of change all along the graph remains close to the average rate of change from the first point to the last.

Step 2: A regression model is $y = 338.2x + 3042$ where x is the number of years after 1990 and y is the number of breeding pairs in thousands. The initial value is 3042, and the rate of change is about 338 pairs per year.

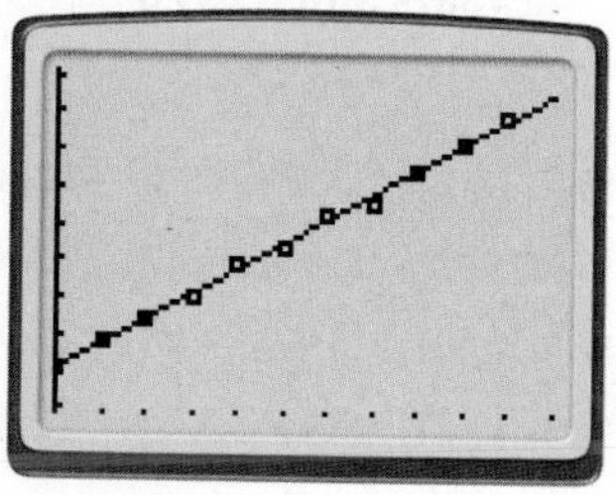

Step 3: The model is a very close fit to the data. It fits both the overall trend and the individual points very closely.

(B) **Automobiles** Data sets and scatter plots for various statistics about changes in automobiles of different model years are shown.

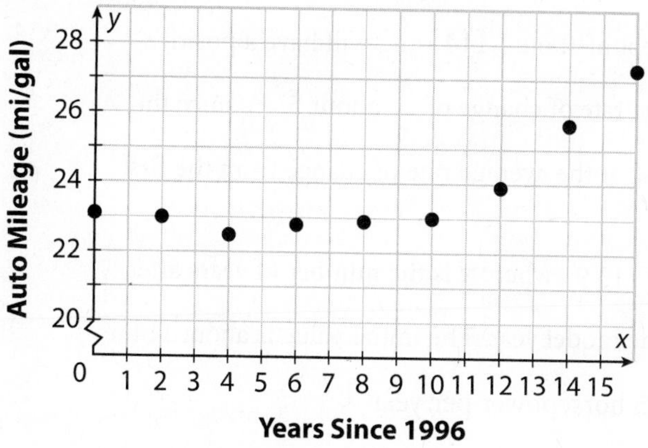

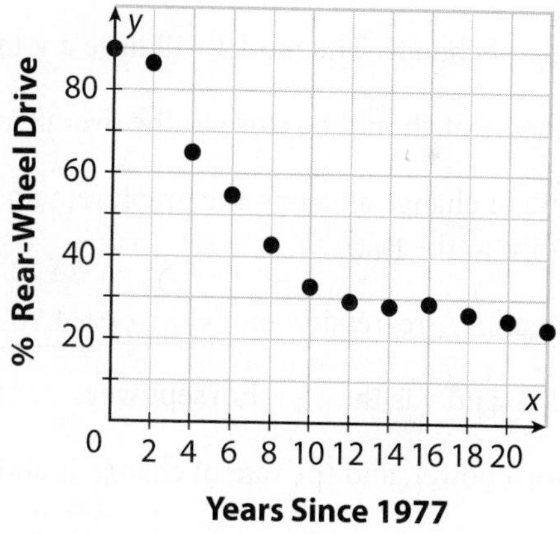

(1996, 23.1)	(2002, 22.8)	(2008, 23.9)
(1998, 23.0)	(2004, 22.9)	(2010, 25.7)
(2000, 22.5)	(2006, 23.0)	(2012, 27.3)

(1977, 89.8)	(1985, 42.9)	(1993, 28.8)
(1979, 86.5)	(1987, 32.8)	(1995, 26.3)
(1981, 65.0)	(1989, 29.3)	(1997, 24.9)
(1983, 54.8)	(1991, 28.1)	(1999, 22.9)

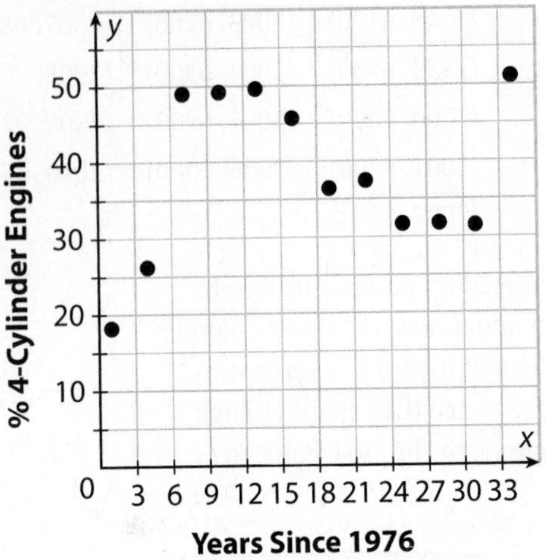

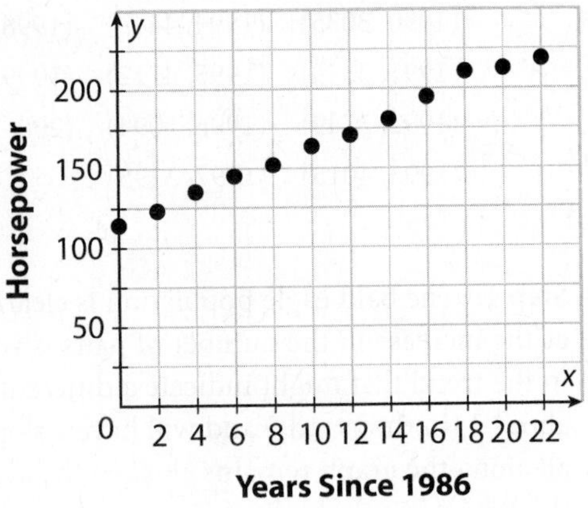

(1976, 18.2)	(1988, 49.6)	(2000, 31.7)
(1979, 26.2)	(1991, 45.7)	(2003, 31.8)
(1982, 49.0)	(1994, 36.4)	(2006, 31.5)
(1985, 49.2)	(1997, 37.4)	(2009, 51.1)

(1986, 114)	(1994, 152)	(2002, 195)
(1988, 123)	(1996, 164)	(2004, 211)
(1990, 135)	(1998, 171)	(2006, 213)
(1992, 145)	(2000, 181)	(2008, 219)

Step 1: The horsepower data are the data best modeled by a linear function, as the increase in horsepower over time is very steady, with the amount of increase never varying too much from the trend. All of the other data sets show clear variation in the rate of change. The model will have a *y*-intercept of about 114 and will have a positive slope that should be close to the overall average rate of change of about 5, since the rate of change all along the graph remains close to the average rate of change from the first point to the last.

Step 2: A regression model is $y = 4.967x + 113.9$ where x is the number of years after 1986 and y is the horsepower for the model year. The initial value is about 114 horsepower, and the rate of change is about 5 horsepower per year.

Step 3: The model fits both the overall trend and the individual points very closely.

Your Turn

4. Demographics Data sets and scatter plots for various changes in the United States population over time are shown. Using these data, complete the three steps described at the beginning of Example 1. Also, tell whether you would expect the trend indicated by your model to continue for a time after the data shown, or whether you expect that it would soon change, and explain your answer.

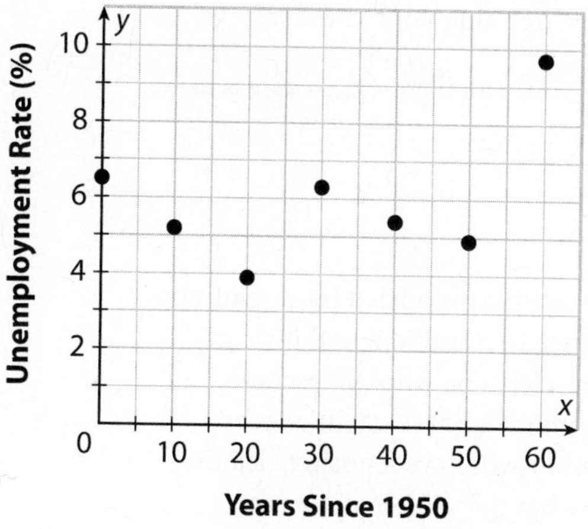

(1950, 6.5) (1980, 6.3) (2000, 4.9)
(1960, 5.2) (1990, 5.4) (2010, 9.7)
(1970, 3.9)

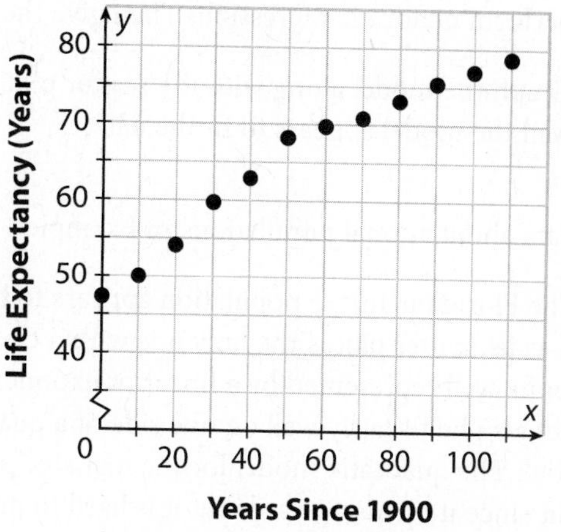

(1900, 47.3) (1930, 59.7) (1960, 69.7) (1990, 75.4)
(1910, 50.0) (1940, 62.9) (1970, 70.8) (2000, 77.0)
(1920, 54.1) (1950, 68.2) (1980, 73.1) (2010, 78.7)

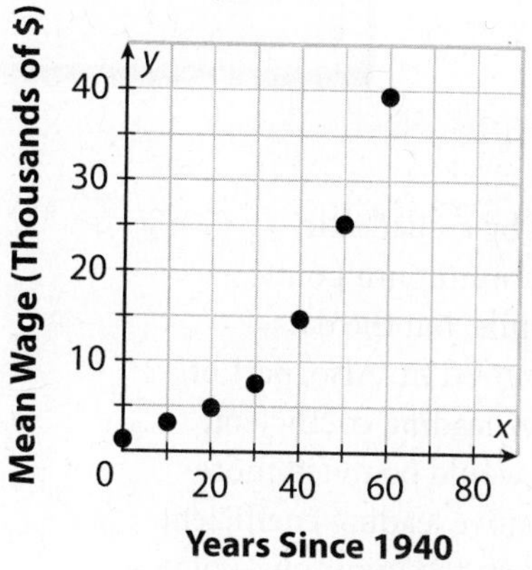

(1940, 1315) (1970, 7501) (1990, 25,236)
(1950, 3180) (1980, 14,610) (2000, 39,237)
(1960, 4816)

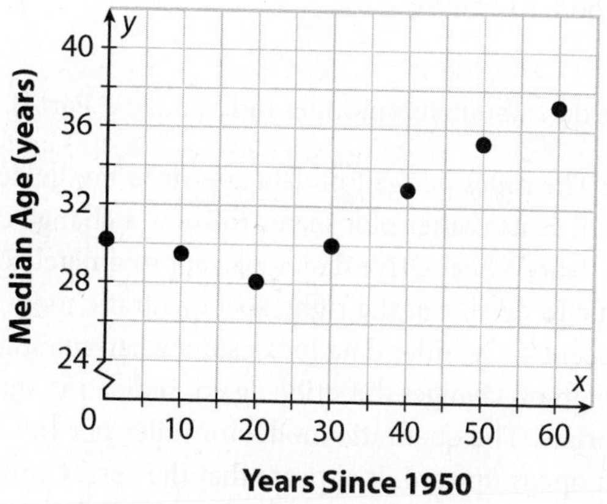

(1950, 30.2) (1980, 30.0) (2000, 35.3)
(1960, 29.5) (1990, 32.9) (2010, 37.2)
(1970, 28.1)

Explain 2 Modeling With a Quadratic Function

Example 2 **Using the groups of data sets and their scatter plots from Example 1:**

Step 1: Choose the data set that appears to be best modeled by a quadratic function. Explain your choice, whether you think a quadratic model will be a close fit, and whether any other model might possibly be appropriate. What characteristics do you expect the quadratic model will have?

Step 2: Enter the data for your choice into your graphing calculator in two lists, and perform quadratic regression. Then give the model, defining your variables.

Step 3: Graph the model along with the scatter plot using your calculator, then assess how well the model appears to fit the data.

(A) Use the data about animal populations in Example 1 Part A.

Step 1: The Florida manatee population appears to be the one best modeled by a quadratic function, as its scatter plot is the only one with a clear change in direction, and it clearly would not be well represented by a linear or exponential model. The whooping crane data might also be fit fairly well on one side of a quadratic model, but it might also be exponential. The quadratic model for the manatee population will have a positive leading coefficient since it opens upward, but it is hard to predict what the y-intercept or the vertex will be. Because the graph is not very symmetrical, the fit may not be very close.

Step 2: A regression model is $y = 48.50x^2 - 317.3x + 3411$ where x is the number of years after 2001 and y is the number of manatees

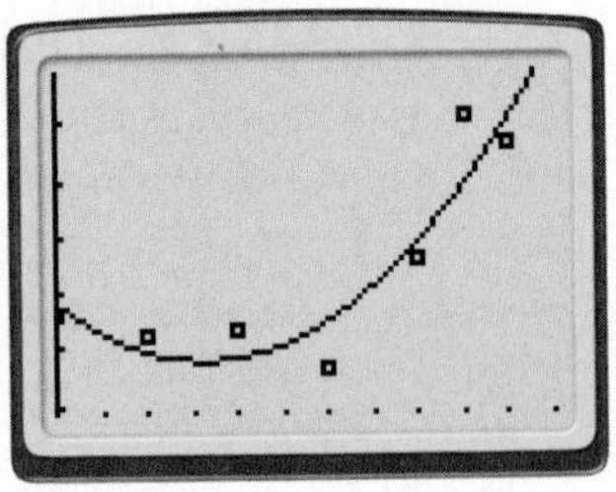

Step 3: The model is not a close fit, but it does look like an appropriate model for the overall trend during the time of the data. It misses the horizontal position for the vertex by a fairly wide margin, but otherwise is not too far from the data.

(B) Use the data about automobiles in Example 1 Part B.

Step 1: The miles per gallon data appear to be the data best modeled by a quadratic function, as its scatter plot seems to show a change of direction and a minimum point. The % Rear-Wheel Drive data looks approximately quadratic for a while, but the data continue to decline at the right, so a quadratic model would not be a good fit. Also, part of the percent 4-Cylinder data looks somewhat quadratic with a negative leading coefficient, but the graph changes direction again, indicating that a cubic model would be much more appropriate. The quadratic model for miles per gallon will have a positive leading coefficient since it opens upward. It appears that the vertex will not be too far from the minimum point on the plot, though it may be a little to the right.

Step 2: A regression model is $y = 0.0390x^2 - 0.3922x + 23.40$ where x is the number of years after 1996 and y is the average miles per gallon.

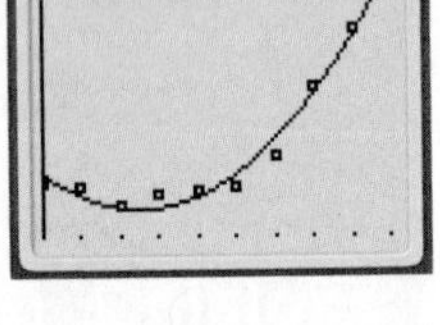

Step 3: The model is a fairly close fit to the data. Its minimum reflects the actual minimum miles per gallon closely, and the model reflects the trend at the right side of the data well.

Reflect

5. Discussion The Florida manatee has been under consideration for being downgraded from endangered to threatened. Do you believe the graph and model of the manatee population in Part A of this Example support this concept or argue against it? Explain your reasoning.

6. How might the model for miles per gallon affect a decision on when to purchase a car?

Your Turn

7. Using the data in Your Turn Exercise 4, complete the three steps described at the beginning of Example 2. Also, tell whether you would expect the trend indicated by your model to continue for a time after the data shown, or whether you expect that it would soon change, and explain your answer.

Explain 3 Modeling with an Exponential Function

Example 3 **Using the groups of data sets and their scatter plots from Example 1:**

Step 1: Choose the data set that appears to be best modeled by an exponential function. Explain your choice, whether you think an exponential model will be a close fit, and whether any other model might possibly be appropriate. What characteristics do you expect the exponential model will have?

Step 2: Enter the data for your choice into your graphing calculator in two lists, and perform exponential regression. Then give the model, defining your variables. What are the initial value, growth or decay factor, and growth or decay rate of the model?

Step 3: Graph the model along with the scatter plot using your calculator, then assess how well the model appears to fit the data.

(A) Use the data about animal populations in Example 1 Part A.

Step 1: The whooping crane population appears to be the one best modeled by an exponential function, as it rises increasingly quickly, but does not reflect a change in direction as a quadratic model can. Though the whooping crane plot is nearly linear in its midsection, the slow initial rise and fast later rise indicate that an exponential model is better. The California least tern data show a significant jump, but no clear pattern. An appropriate whooping crane model shows exponential growth, so the parameter b is greater than 1. Because the growth is not very large considering the time period of 70 years, however, the yearly growth factor will not be much above 1.

Step 2: A regression model is $y = 20.05(1.0374)^x$ where x is the number of years after 1940 and y is the population. The initial value for the model is 20 whooping cranes. The growth factor is 1.0374, and the growth rate is 0.0374, or about 3.74% per year.

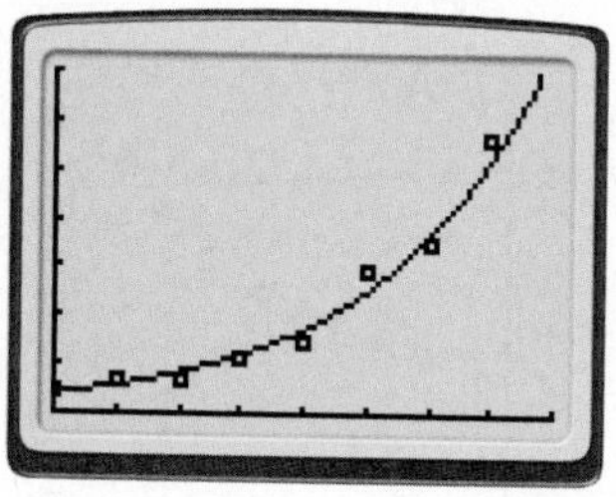

Step 3: The model is very good fit for the data. Some data points are a little above the curve and some a little below, but the fit is close and reflects the trend very well.

(B) Use the data about automobiles in Example 1 Part B.

Step 1: The percent of cars with rear-wheel drive data appears to be the data best modeled by an exponential function (exponential decay), as overall, the graph drops less and less steeply with time. None of the other plots has this characteristic. Because the data indicate exponential decay instead of growth, the parameter b is less than 1. The model will likely not be a really close fit, as it appears that the ratio of y-values from term to term varies a fair amount.

Step 2: A regression model is $y = 80.45(0.9371)^x$ where x is the number of years after 1977 and y is the percent of cars with rear-wheel drive. The initial value for the model is 80.45%. The decay factor is 0.9371, and the decay rate is $1 - 0.9371 = 0.0629$, or about 6.3%.

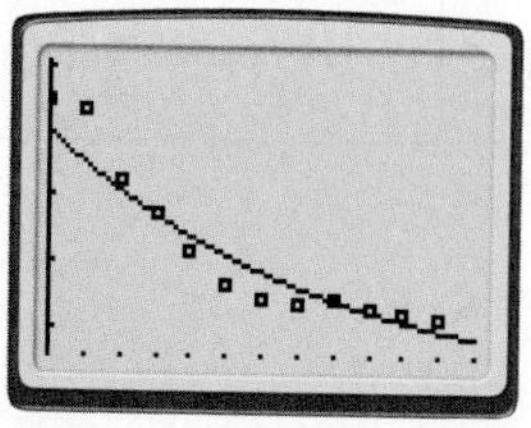

Step 3: The model is a fairly good fit, but not a close fit. The model falls well below the first two data points, and does not represent the middle of the data well. It does match the trend better toward the end of the data, though the model's decay rate is a little too high for the actual data.

Reflect

8. **Discussion** What does the model for the whooping crane population predict for the population in 2040? Do you think it is possible that the whooping crane will be removed from the endangered species list any time in the next few decades? Explain.

Your Turn

9. Using the data in YourTurn Exercise 4, complete the three steps described at the beginning of Example 3. Also, tell whether you would expect the trend indicated by your model to continue for a time after the data shown, or whether you expect that it would soon change, and explain your answer.

Elaborate

10. **Discussion** How does making a prediction from a model help make a decision or judgment based on a given set of data?

11. Describe the process for obtaining a regression model using a graphing calculator.

12. **Essential Question Check-In** How can a scatter plot of a data set help you determine the best type of model to choose for the data?

Evaluate: Homework and Practice

Personal Math Trainer

- Online Homework
- Hints and Help
- Extra Practice

1. Match each scatter plot with the most appropriate model from the following. Do not use any choice more than once.

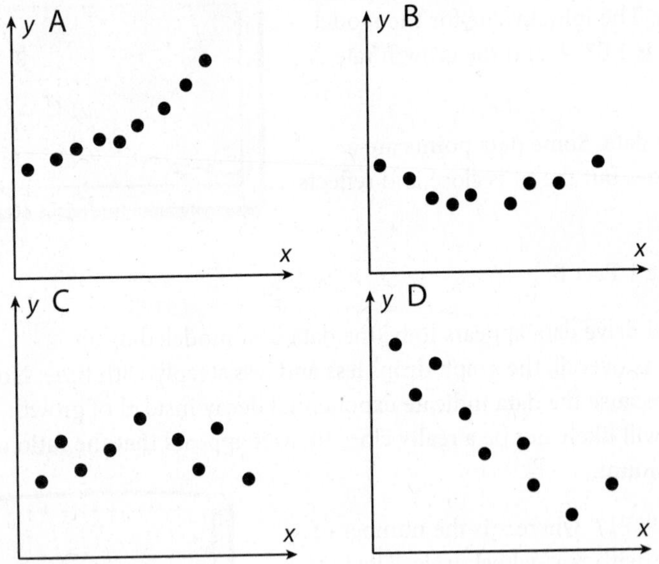

I. quadratic, $a > 0$
II. quadratic, $a < 0$
III. linear, $a < 0$
IV. exponential, $b > 1$
V. exponential, $b < 1$

In Exercises 2–5, for the data set given:

a. Create a scatter plot of the data. What kind of model do you think is most appropriate? Why? What characteristics do you expect that this model will have?

b. Use a graphing calculator to find an equation of the regression model. Then interpret the model, including the meaning of important parameters.

c. Graph the regression model with its scatter plot using a graphing calculator. How well does the model fit?

d. Answer the question following the data.

2. **Population Demographics** The data set shows the number of Americans living in multigenerational households.

Year	Number (in Millions)
1950	32
1960	27
1970	26
1980	28
1990	35
2000	42
2010	52

What does the model predict for the number in 2020? in 2040? Are these numbers reasonable? Explain.

3. **Cycling** The data set shows the inseam length for different frame sizes for road bicycles.

Frame Size (cm)	Inseam Length (cm)
46	69
48	71
49	74
51	76
53	79
54	81
58	86
60	89
61	91

Jarrell has an inseam of 84 cm, but the table does not give a frame size for him. He graphs the model on a graphing calculator and finds that a y-value of 84 is closest to an x-value of 56. He decides he needs a 56 cm frame. Do you think this is a reasonable conclusion. Explain.

4. **Population Geography** The data set shows the percent of the U.S. population living in central cities.

What does your model predict for the percent of the population living in central cities in 2010? How much confidence would you have in this prediction? Explain. Given that the actual number for 2010 was about 36.9%, does this support your judgment?

Year	% of Population
1910	21.2
1920	24.2
1930	30.8
1940	32.5
1950	32.8
1960	32.3
1970	31.4
1980	30.0

5. **Animal Migration** The data set shows the number of bald eagles counted passing a particular location on a migration route. Predict the number of bald eagles in 2033. How much confidence do you have in this prediction?

Year	Number of Eagles
1973	41
1978	79
1983	384
1988	261
1993	1725
1998	3289
2003	3356

6. **Smart Phones** For parts a–d, use the data in the table. The data set shows the percent of the world's population owning a smart phone.

a. Create a scatter plot of the data.

b. Use a graphing calculator to find equations for both exponential and quadratic regression models. Then interpret the models, including the meaning of important parameters.

c. Graph both regression models with the scatter plot using a graphing calculator. Do both models fit the data well? Does one seem significantly better than the other?

d. For how long after the data set do you think either model will be a good predictor? Explain your reasoning.

Year	% of Population
2006	1
2007	3
2008	4
2009	5
2010	7
2011	11
2012	16
2013	22

7. **Stock Market** The data set gives the U.S. stock market's average annual return rates for each of the last 11 decades.

Decade Ending	Annual Return Rate (%)
1910	9.96
1920	4.20
1930	14.95
1940	−0.63
1950	8.72
1960	19.28
1970	7.78
1980	5.82
1990	17.57
2000	18.17
2010	3.1

a. Make a scatter plot of the data.

b. What kind of model do you think is most appropriate for the data? Explain your reasoning.

c. Do the data give any kind of prediction about investing in the stock market for the future? Explain.

H.O.T. Focus on Higher Order Thinking

8. **Explain the Error** Out of curiosity, Julia enters the stock market data from Exercise 7 into her calculator and performs linear and quadratic regression. As she expected, there is almost no fit to the data at all. She then tries exponential regression, and get the message "ERR: DOMAIN." Why does she get this message?

9. **Critical Thinking** A student enters the road bicycle data from Exercise 3, accidentally performs quadratic regression instead of linear, and has the calculator graph the regression model with the scatter plot. The student sees this graph:

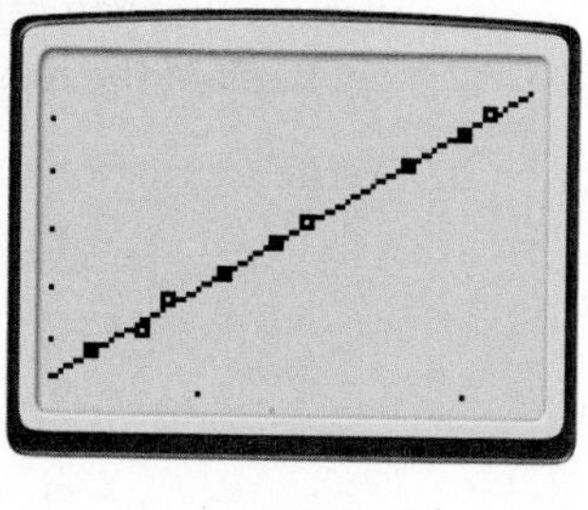

The model graphed by the calculator is $y = -0.001241x^2 + 1.587x - 1.549$. It is obviously a very close fit to the data, and looks almost identical to the linear model. Explain how this can be true. (*Hint*: What happens when you zoom out?)

10. Critical Thinking A graphing calculator returns a linear regression equation $y = ax + b$, a quadratic regression equation $y = ax^2 + bx + c$, and an exponential regression equation $y = a \cdot b^x$. For exponential regression, a is always positive, which is not true of the other models. How does an exponential model differ from the other two models regarding translations of a parent function?

11. Extension In past work, you have used the correlation coefficient r, which indicates how well a line fits the data. The closer $|r|$ is to 1, the better the fit, and the closer to 0, the worse the fit. When you perform quadratic or exponential regression with a calculator, the *coefficient of determination* r^2 or R^2 serves a similar purpose. Return to the smart phone data in Exercise 6, and perform the quadratic and exponential regression again. (Make sure that "Diagnostics" is turned on in the Catalog menu of your calculator first.) Which model is the closer fit to the data, that is, for which model is R^2 closest to 1?

Lesson Performance Task

A student is given $50 to invest. The student chooses the investment very well. The following data shows the amount that the investment is worth over several years.

x (Years)	*y* (Dollars)
0	50
1	147
2	462
3	1411
4	4220
5	4431
6	4642

a. Determine an appropriate model for the data. If it is reasonable to break up the data so that you can use different models over different parts of the time, then do so. Explain the reasoning for choosing your model(s).

b. Write a situation that may reflect the given data.

STUDY GUIDE REVIEW

Modeling with Exponential and Other Functions

MODULE 14

Essential Question: How can modeling with exponential and other functions help you to solve real-world problems?

Key Vocabulary
exponential regression
(regresión exponencial)

KEY EXAMPLE *(Lesson 14.1)*

What type of function is illustrated in the table?

x	−1	0	1	2	3
$f(x)$	9	3	1	$\frac{1}{3}$	$\frac{1}{9}$

Whenever x increases by 1, $f(x)$ is multiplied by the common ratio of $\frac{1}{3}$. Since this ratio is less than 1, the table represents an exponential decay function.

KEY EXAMPLE *(Lesson 14.2)*

Create a scatter plot for the data in the table. Treat age as the independent variable x and median BMI as the dependent variable y. Then, use a graphing calculator to find an appropriate regression model of the data. Explain why you chose that particular type of function.

Age	2	3	4	5	6	7	8	9	10
Median BMI	16.5	16.0	15.2	15.2	15.6	15.6	15.8	16.0	16.3

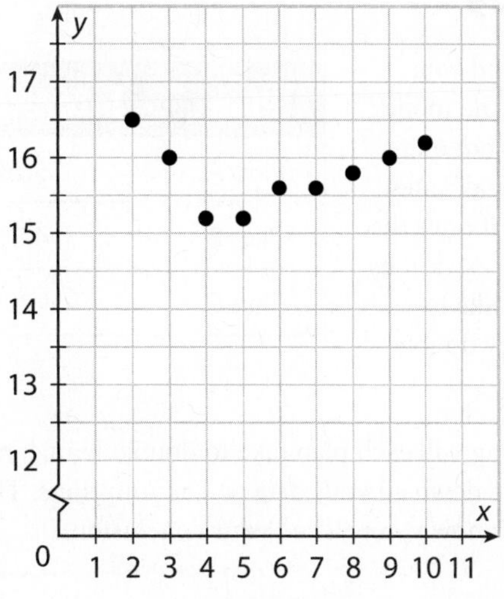

A quadratic regression of the data on a graphing calculator produces the equation $y = 0.0636x^2 - 0.7503x + 17.5867$. A quadratic function was chosen because the data points generally lie on a curve that approximates a parabola.

EXERCISES

Choose the type of function (linear, quadratic, or exponential) you would use to model the data. *(Lesson 14.2)*

1.

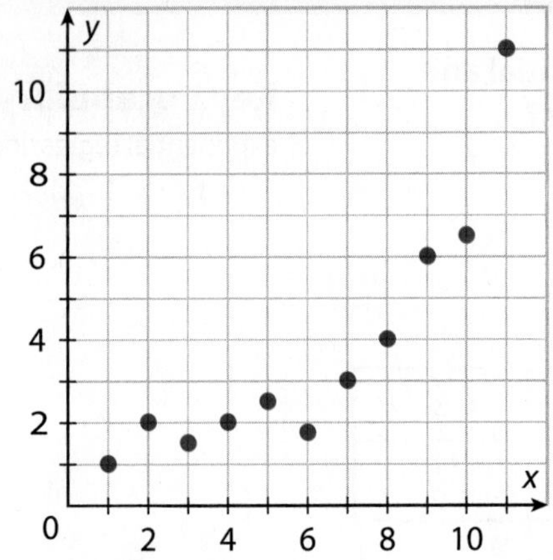

2.

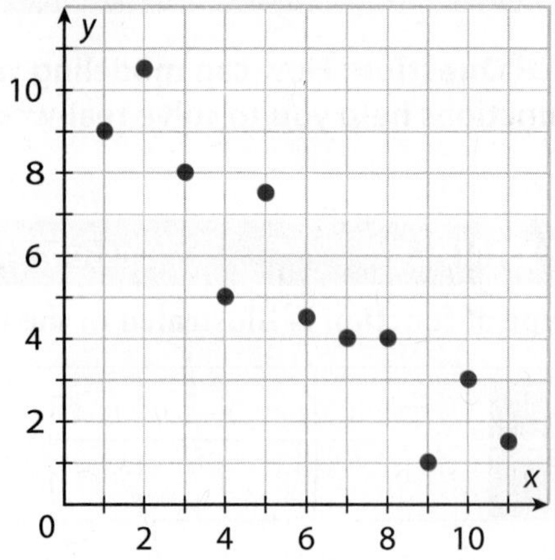

3. **How does the Product of Powers Property of Exponents help you in deciding whether a given set of data is exponential?** *(Lesson 14.1)*

MODULE PERFORMANCE TASK

Double Your Money

Jenna was a game show participant and won \$10,000! She eventually wants to use the money as a down payment on a home but is not quite ready for such a big commitment. She decides to invest the money and plans to use it once the amount reaches \$20,000. She researches various investment opportunities and would like to choose the one that will let her money double fastest.

Plan	Interest Rate	Compounding
Plan A	5.2%	Quarterly
Plan B	4.8%	Monthly
Plan C	4.25%	Continuously

To the nearest tenth of a year, how long will each plan take to double Jenna's money? Which should Jenna choose? Be sure to write down all your data and assumptions. Then use graphs, numbers, words, or algebra to explain how you reached your conclusion.

Ready to Go On?

14.1–14.2 Modeling with Exponential and Other Functions

Personal Math Trainer

- Online Homework
- Hints and Help
- Extra Practice

The isotope X has a half-life of 10 days. Complete the table showing the decay of a sample of X. *(Lessons 14.1, 14.2)*

1.

Number of Half-Lives	Number of Days (t)	Percent of Isotope Remaining (p)
0	0	100
1	10	50
2	20	?
3	?	?
4	?	?

2. Write the decay rate per half-life, r, as a fraction.

3. Write an expression for the number of half-lives in t days.

4. Write a function that models this situation. The function $p(t)$ should give the percent of the isotope remaining after t days.

ESSENTIAL QUESTION

5. What are two ways you can find an exponential function that models a given set of data?

MODULE 14
MIXED REVIEW

Assessment Readiness

1. Look at each exponential function. Does the function pass through (1, 2) and (3, 50)?

A. $y = \frac{3}{5} \cdot 5^x$

B. $y = \frac{2}{5} \cdot 5^x$

C. $y = \frac{1}{2} \cdot 5^x$

2. Consider the function $y = -2\left(\frac{1}{4}\right)^{x+1} + 7$. Determine if each statement is True or False.

A. The asymptote of the function is $y = 7$.

B. The asymptote of the function is $x = 7$.

C. The function has no asymptote.

3. Are there real solutions to the equation $x^3 - 5x^2 = 0$? Explain, then state the roots.

4. Describe the type of function illustrated in the table. Explain.

x	4	5	6	7	8
y	−4	−3	−4	−7	−12

5. How can you use the pattern formed by the points on a scatterplot to determine whether to fit the data to a linear, quadratic, or exponential function?

Logarithmic Functions

MODULE 15

Essential Question: How can you use logarithmic functions to solve real-world problems?

LESSON 15.1
Defining and Evaluating a Logarithmic Function

LESSON 15.2
Graphing Logarithmic Functions

REAL WORLD VIDEO
Check out some of the considerations that go into determining the proper dosage of a medication and learn about the role of logarithmic functions in this process.

MODULE PERFORMANCE TASK PREVIEW
What's the Dosage?

Scientists working in the pharmaceutical industry discover, develop, and test drugs for everything from relieving a headache to controlling high blood pressure. One important question regarding a specific drug is how long the drug stays in a person's system. How can logarithmic functions be used to answer this question? Let's find out!

Are YOU Ready?

Complete these exercises to review skills you will need for this module.

Personal Math Trainer

- Online Homework
- Hints and Help
- Extra Practice

Exponents

Example 1 Rewrite $x^{-3}y^2$ using only positive exponents.

$$x^{-3}y^2 = \frac{y^2}{x^3}$$

Rewrite each expression using only positive exponents.

1. $x^{-4}y^{-2}$ **2.** x^8y^{-5} **3.** $\frac{x^{-1}}{y^{-2}}$

Rational and Radical Exponents

Example 2 Write $\sqrt[4]{a^6b^4}$ using rational exponents.

$\sqrt[4]{a^6b^4} = (a^6b^4)^{\frac{1}{4}}$ Remove the radical symbol.

$= a^{\frac{3}{2}}b$ Simplify.

Write the expression using rational exponents.

4. $\sqrt[6]{a^3b^{12}}$ **5.** $\sqrt[3]{ab^2}$ **6.** $\sqrt[4]{81a^{12}b^8}$

Graphing Linear Nonproportional Relationships

Example 3 Graph $y = -3x + 1$.

Graph the y-intercept of $(0, 1)$.

Use the slope $\frac{-3}{1}$ to plot a second point.

Draw a line through the two points.

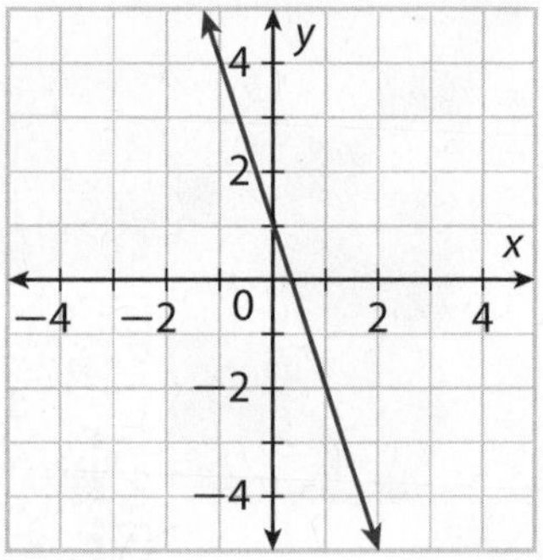

Graph each equation.

7. $y = \frac{2}{3}x - 4$ **8.** $y = 2x + 3$

15.1 Defining and Evaluating a Logarithmic Function

Essential Question: What is the inverse of the exponential function $f(x) = b^x$ where $b > 0$ and $b \neq 1$, and what is the value of $f^{-1}(b^m)$ for any real number m?

Resource Locker

Explore Understanding Logarithmic Functions as Inverses of Exponential Functions

An exponential function such as $f(x) = 2^x$ accepts values of the exponent as inputs and delivers the corresponding power of 2 as the outputs. The inverse of an exponential function is called a **logarithmic function**. For $f(x) = 2^x$, the inverse function is written $f^{-1}(x) = \log_2 x$, which is read either as "the logarithm with base 2 of x" or simply as "log base 2 of x." It accepts powers of 2 as inputs and delivers the corresponding exponents as outputs.

Ⓐ Graph $f^{-1}(x) = \log_2 x$ using the graph of $f(x) = 2^x$ shown for reference. Begin by reflecting the labeled points on the graph of $f(x) = 2^x$ across the line $y = x$ and labeling the reflected points with their coordinates. Then draw a smooth curve through the reflected points.

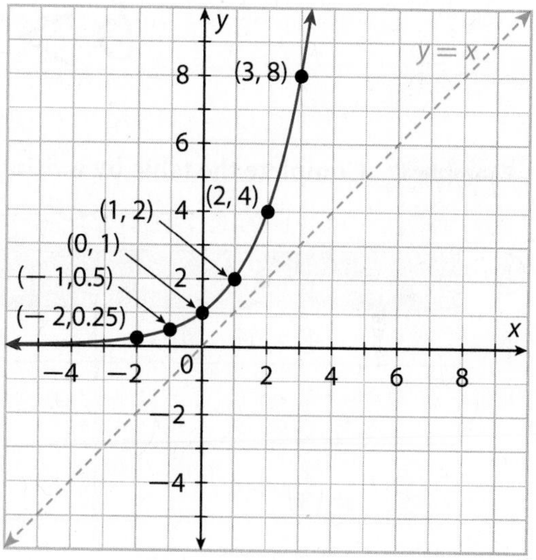

Ⓑ Using the labeled points on the graph of $f^{-1}(x)$, complete the following statements.

$f^{-1}(0.25) = \log_2$? = ?

$f^{-1}(0.5) = \log_2$? = ?

$f^{-1}(1) = \log_2$? = ?

$f^{-1}(2) = \log_2$? = ?

$f^{-1}(4) = \log_2$? = ?

$f^{-1}(8) = \log_2$? = ?

Reflect

1. Explain why the domain of $f(x) = 2^x$ doesn't need to be restricted in order for its inverse to be a function.
2. State the domain and range of $f^{-1}(x) = \log_2 x$ using set notation.
3. Identify any intercepts and asymptotes for the graph of $f^{-1}(x) = \log_2 x$.
4. Is $f^{-1}(x) = \log_2 x$ an increasing function or a decreasing function?

5. How does $f^{-1}(x) = \log_2 x$ behave as x increases without bound? As x decreases toward 0?

6. Based on the inverse relationship between $f(x) = 2^x$ and $f^{-1}(x) = \log_2 x$, complete this statement:

$f^{-1}(16) = \log_2$? $=$? because $f($? $) =$? .

Explain 1 Converting Between Exponential and Logarithmic Forms of Equations

In general, the exponential function $f(x) = b^x$, where $b > 0$ and $b \neq 1$, has the logarithmic function $f^{-1}(x) = \log_b x$ as its inverse. For instance, if $f(x) = 3^x$, then $f^{-1}(x) = \log_3 x$, and if $f(x) = \left(\frac{1}{4}\right)^x$, then $f^{-1}(x) = \log_{\frac{1}{4}} x$. The inverse relationship between exponential functions and logarithmic functions also means that you can write any exponential equation as a logarithmic equation and any logarithmic equation as an exponential equation.

Exponential Equation	**Logarithmic Equation**
$b^x = a$	$\log_b a = x$

$$b > 0, b \neq 1$$

Example 1 **Complete the table by writing each given equation in its alternate form.**

(A)

Exponential Equation	Logarithmic Equation
$4^3 = 64$	?
?	$\log_5 \frac{1}{25} = -2$
$\left(\frac{2}{3}\right)^p = q$	?
?	$\log_{\frac{1}{2}} m = n$

Think of each equation as involving an exponential function or a logarithmic function. Identify the function's base, input, and output. For the inverse function, use the same base but switch the input and output.

Think of the equation $4^3 = 64$ as involving an exponential function with base 4. The input is 3, and the output is 64. So, the inverse function (a logarithmic function) also has base 4, but its input is 64, and its output is 3.

Think of the equation $\log_5 \frac{1}{25} = -2$ as involving a logarithmic function with base 5. The input is $\frac{1}{25}$, and the output is -2. So, the inverse function (an exponential function) also has base 5, but its input is -2, and its output is $\frac{1}{25}$.

Think of the equation $\left(\frac{2}{3}\right)^p = q$ as involving an exponential function with base $\frac{2}{3}$. The input is p, and the output is q. So, the inverse function (a logarithmic function) also has base $\frac{2}{3}$, but its input is q, and its output is p.

Think of the equation $\log_{\frac{1}{2}} m = n$ as involving a logarithmic function with base $\frac{1}{2}$. The input is m, and the output is n. So, the inverse function (an exponential function) also has base $\frac{1}{2}$, but its input is n, and its output is m.

Exponential Equation	Logarithmic Equation
$4^3 = 64$	$\log_4 64 = 3$
$5^{-2} = \frac{1}{25}$	$\log_5 \frac{1}{25} = -2$
$\left(\frac{2}{3}\right)^p = q$	$\log_{\frac{2}{3}} q = p$
$\left(\frac{1}{2}\right)^n = m$	$\log_{\frac{1}{2}} m = n$

(B)

Exponential Equation	Logarithmic Equation
$3^5 = 243$	?
?	$\log_4 \frac{1}{64} = -3$
$\left(\frac{3}{4}\right)^r = s$	?
?	$\log_{\frac{1}{5}} v = w$

Think of the equation $3^5 = 243$ as involving an exponential function with base 3. The input is 5, and the output is 243. So, the inverse function (a logarithmic function) also has base 3, but its input is 243, and its output is 5. The logarithmic equation is $\boxed{\log_3 243 = 5}$.

Think of the equation $\log_4 \frac{1}{64} = -3$ as involving a logarithmic function with base 4. The input is $\frac{1}{64}$, and the output is -3. So, the inverse function (an exponential function) also has base 4, but its input is -3, and its output is $\frac{1}{64}$. The exponential equation is $\boxed{4^{-3} = \frac{1}{64}}$.

Think of the equation $\left(\frac{3}{4}\right)^r = s$ as involving an exponential function with base $\frac{3}{4}$. The input is r, and the output is s. So, the inverse function (a logarithmic function) also has base $\frac{3}{4}$, but its input is s, and its output is r. The logarithmic equation is $\boxed{\log_{\frac{3}{4}} s = r}$.

Think of the equation $\log_{\frac{1}{5}} v = w$ as involving a logarithmic function with base $\frac{1}{5}$. The input is v, and the output is w. So, the inverse function (an exponential function) also has base $\frac{1}{5}$, but its input is w, and its output is v. The exponential equation is $\boxed{\left(\frac{1}{5}\right)^w = v}$.

Reflect

7. A student wrote the logarithmic form of the exponential equation $5^0 = 1$ as $\log_5 0 = 1$. What did the student do wrong? What is the correct logarithmic equation?

Your Turn

8. Complete the table by writing each given equation in its alternate form.

Exponential Equation	Logarithmic Equation
$10^4 = 10{,}000$	?
?	$\log_2 \frac{1}{16} = -4$
$\left(\frac{2}{5}\right)^c = d$	?
?	$\log_{\frac{1}{3}} x = y$

Explain 2 Evaluating Logarithmic Functions by Thinking in Terms of Exponents

The logarithmic function $f(x) = \log_b x$ accepts a power of b as an input and delivers an exponent as an output. In cases where the input of a logarithmic function is a recognizable power of b, you should be able to determine the function's output. You may find it helpful first to write a logarithmic equation by letting the output equal y and then to rewrite the equation in exponential form. Once the bases on each side of the exponential equation are equal, you can equate their exponents to find y.

Example 2

(A) If $f(x) = \log_{10} x$, find $f(1000)$, $f(0.01)$, and $f(\sqrt{10})$.

$f(1000) = y$

$\log_{10} 1000 = y$

$10^y = 1000$

$10^y = 10^3$

$y = 3$

So, $f(1000) = 3$.

$f(0.01) = y$

$\log_{10} 0.01 = y$

$10^y = 0.01$

$10^y = 10^{-2}$

$y = -2$

So, $f(0.01) = -2$.

$f(\sqrt{10}) = y$

$\log_{10} \sqrt{10} = y$

$10^y = \sqrt{10}$

$10^y = 10^{\frac{1}{2}}$

$y = \frac{1}{2}$

So, $f(\sqrt{10}) = \frac{1}{2}$.

(B) If $f(x) = \log_{\frac{1}{2}} x$, find $f(4)$, $f\left(\frac{1}{32}\right)$ and $f(2\sqrt{2})$.

$f(4) = y$

$\log_{\frac{1}{2}} 4 = y$

$\left(\frac{1}{2}\right)^y = 4$

$\left(\frac{1}{2}\right)^y = 2^{\boxed{2}}$

$\left(\frac{1}{2}\right)^y = \left(\frac{1}{2}\right)^{\boxed{-2}}$

$y = \boxed{-2}$

So, $f(4) = \boxed{-2}$.

$f\left(\frac{1}{32}\right) = y$

$\log_{\frac{1}{2}} \frac{1}{32} = y$

$\left(\frac{1}{2}\right)^y = \frac{1}{32}$

$\left(\frac{1}{2}\right)^y = \frac{1}{2^{\boxed{5}}}$

$\left(\frac{1}{2}\right)^y = \left(\frac{1}{2}\right)^{\boxed{5}}$

$y = \boxed{5}$

So, $f\left(\frac{1}{32}\right) = \boxed{5}$.

$f(2\sqrt{2}) = y$

$\log_{\frac{1}{2}} 2\sqrt{2} = y$

$\left(\frac{1}{2}\right)^y = 2\sqrt{2}$

$\left(\frac{1}{2}\right)^y = \sqrt{2^2 \cdot 2}$

$\left(\frac{1}{2}\right)^y = \sqrt{2^{\boxed{3}}}$

$\left(\frac{1}{2}\right)^y = 2^{\boxed{\frac{3}{2}}}$

$\left(\frac{1}{2}\right)^y = \left(\frac{1}{2}\right)^{\boxed{-\frac{3}{2}}}$

$y = \boxed{-\frac{3}{2}}$

So $f(2\sqrt{2}) = \boxed{-\frac{3}{2}}$.

Your Turn

9. If $f(x) = \log_7 x$, find $f(343)$, $f\left(\frac{1}{49}\right)$, and $f(\sqrt{7})$.

Explain 3 Evaluating Logarithmic Functions Using a Scientific Calculator

You can use a scientific calculator to find the logarithm of any positive number x when the logarithm's base is either 10 or e. When the base is 10, you are finding what is called the *common logarithm* of x, and you use the calculator's LOG key because $\log_{10} x$ is also written as $\log x$ (where the base is understood to be 10). When the base is e, you are finding what is called the *natural logarithm* of x, and you use the calculator's LN key because $\log_e x$ is also written as $\ln x$.

Example 3 **Use a scientific calculator to find the common logarithm and the natural logarithm of the given number. Verify each result by evaluating the appropriate exponential expression.**

(A) 13

First, find the common logarithm of 13. Round the result to the thousandths place and raise 10 to that number to confirm that the power is close to 13.

So, log 13 ≈ 1.114.

Next, find the natural logarithm of 13. Round the result to the thousandths place and raise *e* to that number to confirm that the power is close to 13.

So, ln 13 ≈ 2.565.

(B) 0.42

First, find the common logarithm of 0.42. Round the result to the thousandths place and raise 10 to that number to confirm that the power is close to 0.42.

log 0.42 ≈ -0.377

$10^{-0.377} \approx 0.42$

Next, find the natural logarithm of 0.42. Round the result to the thousandths place and raise *e* to that number to confirm that the power is close to 0.42.

ln 0.42 ≈ -0.868

$e^{-0.868} \approx 0.42$

Reflect

10. For any $x > 1$, why is $\log x < \ln x$?

Your Turn

Use a scientific calculator to find the common logarithm and the natural logarithm of the given number. Verify each result by evaluating the appropriate exponential expression.

11. 0.25

12. 4

Explain 4 Evaluating a Logarithmic Model

There are standard scientific formulas that involve logarithms, such as the formulas for the acidity level (pH) of a liquid and the intensity level of a sound. It's also possible to develop your own models involving logarithms by finding the inverses of exponential growth and decay models.

Example 4

(A) The acidity level, or pH, of a liquid is given by the formula $\text{pH} = \log \frac{1}{[H^+]}$ where $[H^+]$ is the concentration (in moles per liter) of hydrogen ions in the liquid. In a typical chlorinated swimming pool, the concentration of hydrogen ions ranges from 1.58×10^{-8} moles per liter to 6.31×10^{-8} moles per liter. What is the range of the pH for a typical swimming pool?

Using the pH formula, substitute the given values of $[H^+]$.

$$\text{pH} = \log\left(\frac{1}{6.31 \times 10^{-8}}\right)$$

$$\approx \log 15{,}800{,}000$$

$$\approx 7.2$$

$$\text{pH} = \log\left(\frac{1}{1.58 \times 10^{-8}}\right)$$

$$\approx \log 63{,}300{,}000$$

$$\approx 7.8$$

So, the pH of a swimming pool ranges from 7.2 to 7.8.

(B) *Lactobacillus acidophilus* is one of the bacteria used to turn milk into yogurt. The population P of a colony of 3500 bacteria at time t (in minutes) can be modeled by the function $P(t) = 3500(2)^{\frac{t}{73}}$. How long does it take the population to reach 1,792,000?

Step 1 Solve $P = 3500(2)^{\frac{t}{73}}$ for t.

Write the model. $P = 3500(2)^{\frac{t}{73}}$

Divide both sides by 3500. $\frac{P}{3500} = (2)^{\frac{t}{73}}$

Rewrite in logarithmic form. $\log_2 \frac{P}{3500} = \frac{t}{73}$

Multiply both sides by 73. $73 \log_2 \frac{P}{3500} = t$

Step 2 Use the logarithmic model to find t when $P = 1{,}792{,}000$.

$$t = 73 \log_2 \frac{P}{3500} = 73 \log_2 \frac{1{,}792{,}000}{3500}$$

$$= 73 \log_2 512 = 73(9) = 657$$

So, the bacteria population will reach 1,792,000 in 657 minutes, or about 11 hours.

Your Turn

13. The intensity level L (in decibels, dB) of a sound is given by the formula $L = 10 \log \frac{I}{I_0}$ where I is the intensity (in watts per square meter, W/m^2) of the sound and I_0 is the intensity of the softest audible sound, about 10^{-12} W/m^2. What is the intensity level of a rock concert if the sound has an intensity of 3.2 W/m^2?

14. The mass (in milligrams) of beryllium-11, a radioactive isotope, in a 500-milligram sample at time t (in seconds) is given by the function $m(t) = 500e^{-0.05t}$. When will there be 90 milligrams of beryllium-11 remaining?

Elaborate

15. What is a logarithmic function? Give an example.

16. How can you turn an exponential model that gives y as a function of x into a logarithmic model that gives x as a function of y?

17. **Essential Question Check-In** Write the inverse of the exponential function $f(x) = b^x$ where $b > 0$ and $b \neq 1$.

Evaluate: Homework and Practice

Personal Math Trainer

- Online Homework
- Hints and Help
- Extra Practice

1. Complete the input-output table for $f(x) = \log_2 x$. Plot and label the ordered pairs from the table. Then draw the complete graph of $f(x)$.

x	f(x)
0.25	?
0.5	?
1	?
2	?
4	?
8	?

2. Use the graph of $f(x) = \log_2 x$ to do the following.

a. State the function's domain and range using set notation.

b. Identify the function's end behavior.

c. Identify the graph's x- and y-intercepts.

d. Identify the graph's asymptotes.

e. Identify the intervals where the function has positive values and where it has negative values.

f. Identify the intervals where the function is increasing and where it is decreasing

3. Consider the exponential function $f(x) = 3^x$.

a. State the function's domain and range using set notation.

b. Describe any restriction you must place on the domain of the function so that its inverse is also a function.

c. Write the rule for the inverse function.

d. State the inverse function's domain and range using set notation.

4. Consider the logarithmic function $f(x) = \log_4 x$.

a. State the function's domain and range using set notation.

b. Describe any restriction you must place on the domain of the function so that its inverse is also a function.

c. Write the rule for the inverse function.

d. State the inverse function's domain and range using set notation.

Write the given exponential equation in logarithmic form.

5. $5^3 = 125$

6. $\left(\frac{1}{10}\right)^{-2} = 100$

7. $3^m = n$

8. $\left(\frac{1}{2}\right)^p = q$

Write the given logarithmic equation in exponential form.

9. $\log_6 1296 = 4$

10. $\log_{\frac{1}{4}} \frac{1}{64} = 3$

11. $\log_8 x = y$

12. $\log_{\frac{2}{3}} c = d$

13. If $f(x) = \log_3 x$, find $f(243)$, $f\left(\frac{1}{27}\right)$, and $f\left(\sqrt{27}\right)$.

14. If $f(x) = \log_6 x$, find $f(36)$, $f\left(\frac{1}{6}\right)$ and $f\left(6\sqrt[3]{6}\right)$.

15. If $f(x) = \log_{\frac{1}{4}} x$, find $f\left(\frac{1}{64}\right)$, $f(256)$, and $f\left(\sqrt[3]{16}\right)$.

Use a scientific calculator to find the common logarithm and the natural logarithm of the given number. Verify each result by evaluating the appropriate exponential expression.

16. 19

17. 9

18. 0.6

19. 0.31

20. The acidity level, or pH, of a liquid is given by the formula $\text{pH} = \log \frac{1}{[\text{H}^+]}$ where $[\text{H}^+]$ is the concentration (in moles per liter) of hydrogen ions in the liquid. What is the pH of iced tea with a hydrogen ion concentration of 0.000158 mole per liter?

21. The intensity level L (in decibels, dB) of a sound is given by the formula $L = 10 \log \frac{I}{I_0}$ where I is the intensity (in watts per square meter, W/m^2) of the sound and I_0 is the intensity of the softest audible sound, about $10^{-12}\ \text{W/m}^2$. What is the intensity level of a lawn mower if the sound has an intensity of $0.00063\ \text{W/m}^2$?

22. Match each liquid with its pH given the concentration of hydrogen ions in the liquid.

Liquid	Hydrogen Ion Concentration	pH
A. Cocoa	5.2×10^{-7}	**a.** ___?___ 3.5
B. Cider	7.9×10^{-4}	**b.** ___?___ 3.3
C. Ginger Ale	4.9×10^{-4}	**c.** ___?___ 2.4
D. Honey	1.3×10^{-4}	**d.** ___?___ 4.5
E. Buttermilk	3.2×10^{-5}	**e.** ___?___ 6.3
F. Cranberry juice	4.0×10^{-3}	**f.** ___?___ 6.4
G. Pinneapple juice	3.1×10^{-4}	**g.** ___?___ 3.1
H. Tomato juice	6.3×10^{-2}	**h.** ___?___ 1.2
I. Carrot juice	4.0×10^{-7}	**i.** ___?___ 3.9

H.O.T. Focus on Higher Order Thinking

23. Explain the Error Jade is taking a chemistry test and has to find the pH of a liquid given that its hydrogen ion concentration is 7.53×10^{-9} moles per liter. She writes the following.

$$\begin{aligned} pH &= \ln \frac{1}{[H^+]} \\ &= \ln \frac{1}{7.53 \times 10^{-9}} \\ &\approx 18.7 \end{aligned}$$

She knows that the pH scale ranges from 1 to 14, so her answer of 18.7 must be incorrect, but she runs out of time on the test. Explain her error and find the correct pH.

24. Multi-step Exponential functions have the general form $f(x) = ab^{x-h} + k$ where a, b, h, and k are constants, $a \neq 0$, $b > 0$, and $b \neq 1$.

a. State the domain and range of $f(x)$ using set notation.

b. Show how to find $f^{-1}(x)$. Give a description of each step you take.

c. State the domain and range of $f^{-1}(x)$ using set notation.

25. Justify Reasoning Evaluate each expression without using a calculator. Explain your reasoning.

a. $\ln e^2$

b. $10^{\log 7}$

c. $4^{\log_2 5}$

Lesson Performance Task

Skydivers use an instrument called an altimeter to determine their height above Earth's surface. An altimeter measures atmospheric pressure and converts it to altitude based on the relationship between pressure and altitude. One model for atmospheric pressure P (in kilopascals, kPa) as a function of altitude a (in kilometers) is $P = 100e^{-a/8}$.

a. Since an altimeter measures pressure directly, pressure is the independent variable for an altimeter. Rewrite the model $P = 100e^{-a/8}$ so that it gives altitude as a function of pressure.

b. To check the function in part a, use the fact that atmospheric pressure at Earth's surface is about 100 kPa.

c. Suppose a skydiver deploys the parachute when the altimeter measures 87 kPa. Use the function in part a to determine the skydiver's altitude. Give your answer in both kilometers and feet. (1 kilometer ≈ 3281 feet)

15.2 Graphing Logarithmic Functions

Resource Locker

Essential Question: How is the graph of $g(x) = a \log_b (x - h) + k$ where $b > 0$ and $b \neq 1$ related to the graph of $f(x) = \log_b x$?

Explore 1 Graphing and Analyzing Parent Logarithmic Functions

The graph of the logarithmic function $f(x) = \log_2 x$, which you analyzed in the previous lesson, is shown. In this Explore, you'll graph and analyze other basic logarithmic functions.

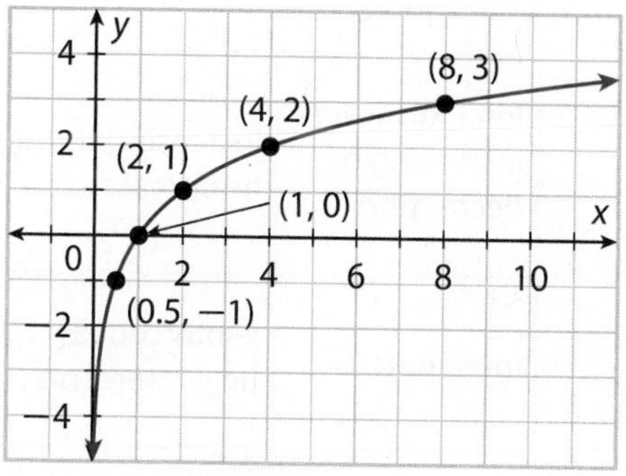

Ⓐ Complete the table for the function $f(x) = \log x$. (Remember that when the base of a logarithmic function is not specified, it is understood to be 10.) Then plot and label the ordered pairs from the table and draw a smooth curve through the points to obtain the graph of the function.

x	$f(x) = \log x$
0.1	?
1	?
10	?

Ⓑ Complete the table for the function $f(x) = \ln x$. (Remember that the base of this function is e.) Then plot and label the ordered pairs from the table and draw a smooth curve through the points to obtain the graph of the function.

x	$f(x) = \ln x$
$\frac{1}{e} \approx 0.368$	?
1	?
$e \approx 2.72$	?
$e^2 \approx 7.39$	?

Ⓒ Analyze the two graphs from Steps A and B, and then complete the table.

Function	$f(x) = \log_2(x)$	$f(x) = \log x$	$f(x) = \ln x$
Domain	$\{x \mid x > 0\}$	?	?
Range	$\{y \mid 0 < y < \infty\}$	?	?
End behavior	As $x \to +\infty$, $f(x) \to +\infty$. As $x \to 0^+$, $f(x) \to -\infty$.	?	?
Vertical and horizontal asymptotes	Vertical asymptote at $x = 0$; no horizontal asymptote	?	?
Intervals where increasing or decreasing	Increasing throughout its domain	?	?
Intercepts	x-intercept at $(1, 0)$; no y-intercepts	?	?
Intervals where positive or negative	Positive on $(1, +\infty)$; negative on $(0, 1)$	?	?

Reflect

1. What similarities do you notice about all logarithmic functions of the form $f(x) = \log_b x$ where $b > 1$? What differences do you notice?

Explain 1 Graphing Combined Transformations of $f(x) = \log_b x$ Where $b > 1$

When graphing transformations of $f(x) = \log_b x$ where $b > 1$, it helps to consider the effect of the transformations on the following features of the graph of $f(x)$: the vertical asymptote, $x = 0$, and two reference points, $(1, 0)$ and $(b, 1)$. The table lists these features as well as the corresponding features of the graph of $g(x) = a \log_b (x - h) + k$.

Function	$f(x) = \log_b x$	$g(x) = a \log_b (x - h) + k$
Asymptote	$x = 0$	$x = h$
Reference point	$(1, 0)$	$(1 + h, k)$
Reference point	$(b, 1)$	$(b + h, a + k)$

Example 1 **Identify the transformations of the graph of $f(x) = \log_b x$ that produce the graph of the given function $g(x)$. Then graph $g(x)$ on the same coordinate plane as the graph of $f(x)$ by applying the transformations to the asymptote $x = 0$ and to the reference points $(1, 0)$ and $(b, 1)$. Also state the domain and range of $g(x)$ using set notation.**

(A) $g(x) = -2 \log_2 (x - 1) - 2$

The transformations of the graph of $f(x) = \log_2 x$ that produce the graph of $g(x)$ are as follows:

- a vertical stretch by a factor of 2
- a reflection across the x-axis
- a translation of 1 unit to the right and 2 units down

Note that the translation of 1 unit to the right affects only the x-coordinates of points on the graph of $f(x)$, while the vertical stretch by a factor of 2, the reflection across the x-axis, and the translation of 2 units down affect only the y-coordinates.

Function	$f(x) = \log_2 x$	$g(x) = -2 \log_2 (x - 1) - 2$
Asymptote	$x = 0$	$x = 1$
Reference point	$(1, 0)$	$(1 + 1, -2(0) - 2) = (2, -2)$
Reference point	$(2, 1)$	$(2 + 1, -2(1) - 2) = (3, -4)$

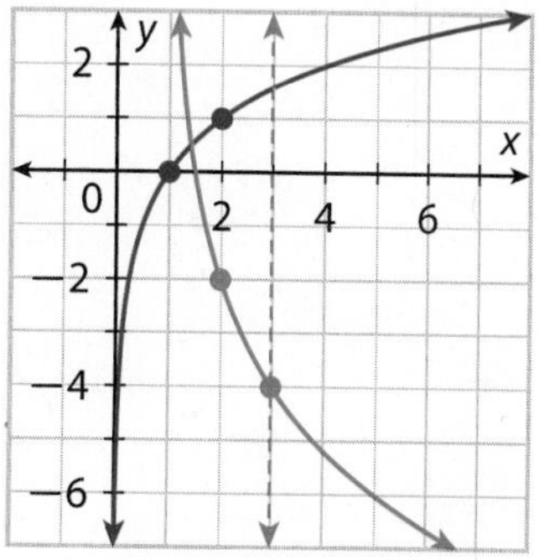

Domain: $\{x \mid x > 1\}$

Range: $\{y \mid \infty < y < +\infty\}$

(B) $g(x) = 2\log(x + 2) + 4$

The transformations of the graph of $f(x) = \log x$ that produce the graph of $g(x)$ are as follows:

- a vertical stretch by a factor of 2
- a translation of 2 units to the left and 4 units up

Note that the translation of 2 units to the left affects only the x-coordinates of points on the graph of $f(x)$, while the vertical stretch by a factor of 2 and the translation of 4 units up affect only the y-coordinates.

Function	$f(x) = \log x$	$g(x) = 2\log(x + 2) + 4$
Asymptote	$x = 0$	$x = -2$
Reference point	$(1, 0)$	$(1 - 2, 2(0) + 4) = (-1, 4)$
Reference point	$(10, 1)$	$(10 - 2, 2(1) + 4) = (8, 6)$

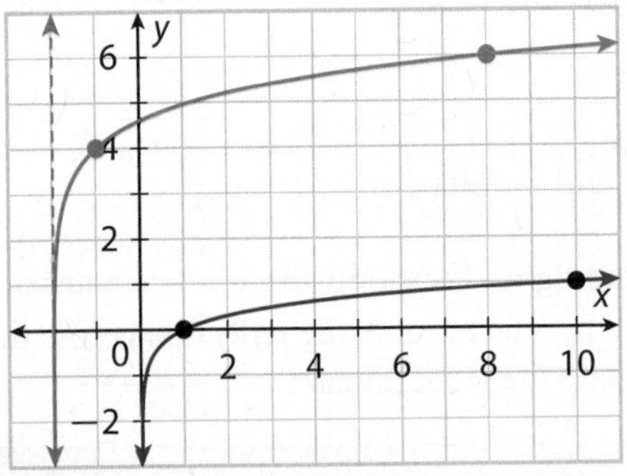

Domain: $\{x \mid x > -2\}$

Range: $\{y \mid -\infty < y < +\infty\}$

Your Turn

Identify the transformations of the graph of $f(x) = \log_b x$ that produce the graph of the given function $g(x)$. Then graph $g(x)$ on the same coordinate plane as a graph of $f(x)$ by applying the transformations to the asymptote $x = 0$ and to the reference points $(1, 0)$ and $(b, 1)$. Also state the domain and range of $g(x)$ using set notation.

2. $g(x) = \frac{1}{2}\log_2 (x + 1) + 2$

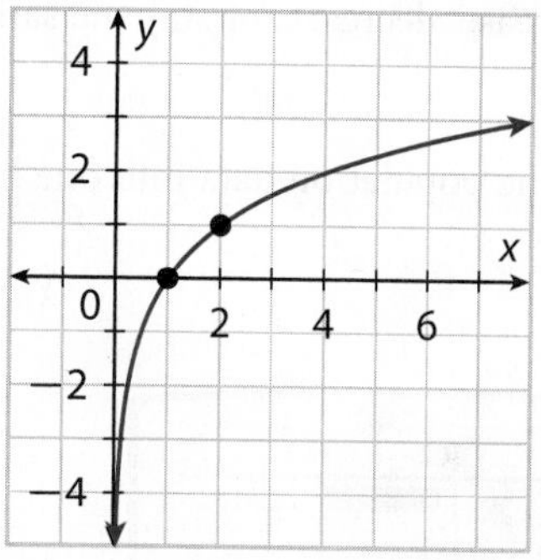

Explain 2 Writing, Graphing, and Analyzing a Logarithmic Model

You can obtain a logarithmic model for real-world data either by performing logarithmic regression on the data or by finding the inverse of an exponential model if one is available.

Example 2 **A biologist studied a population of foxes in a forest preserve over a period of time. The table gives the data that the biologist collected.**

Years Since Study Began	Fox Population
0	55
2	72
3	99
5	123
8	151
12	234
15	336
18	475

From the data, the biologist obtained the exponential model $P = 62(1.12)^t$ where P is the fox population at time t (in years since the study began). The biologist is interested in having a model that gives the time it takes the fox population to reach a certain level.

Ⓐ One way to obtain the model that the biologist wants is to perform logarithmic regression on a graphing calculator using the data set but with the variables switched (that is, the fox population is the independent variable and time is the dependent variable). After obtaining the logarithmic regression model, graph it on a scatter plot of the data. Analyze the model in terms of whether it is increasing or decreasing as well as its average rate of change from $P = 100$ to $P = 200$, from $P = 200$ to $P = 300$, and from $P = 300$ to $P = 400$. Do the model's average rates of change increase, decrease, or stay the same? What does this mean for the fox population?

Using a graphing calculator, enter the population data into one list (L1) and the time data into another list (L2).

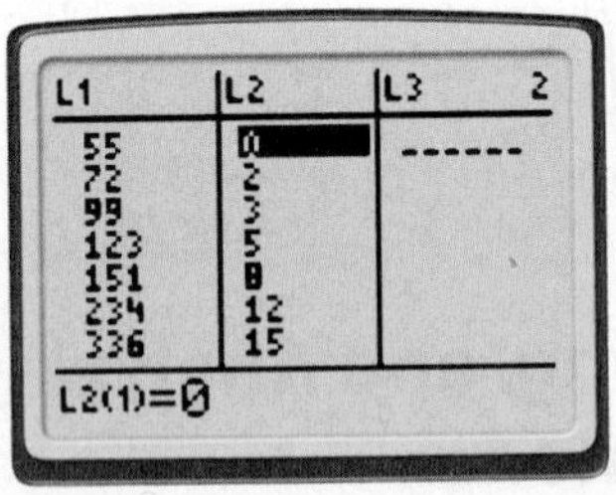

Perform logarithmic regression by pressing the STAT key, choosing the **CALC** menu, and selecting **9:LnReg**. Note that the calculator's regression model is a natural logarithmic function.

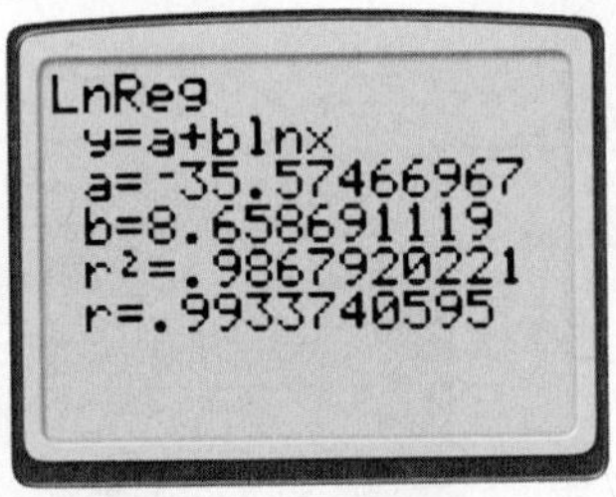

So, the model is $t = -35.6 + 8.66 \ln P$. Graphing this model on a scatter plot of the data visually confirms that the model is a good fit for the data.

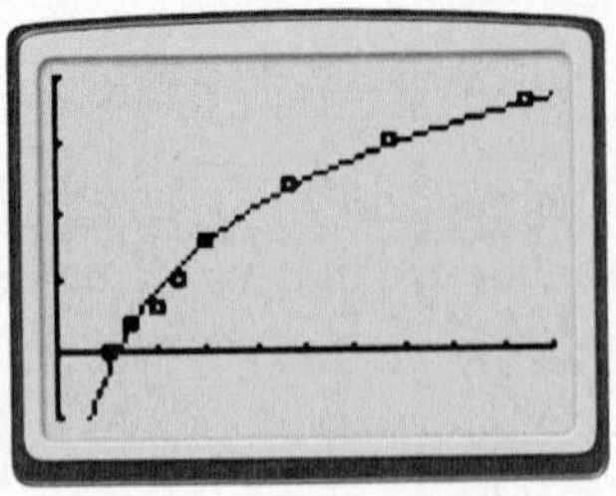

From the graph, you can see that the function is increasing. To find the model's average rates of change, divide the change in t (the dependent variable) by the change in P (the independent variable):

Average rate of change $= \frac{t_2 - t_1}{P_2 - P_1}$

Population	Number of Years to Reach That Population	Average Rate of Change
100	$t = -35.6 + 8.66 \ln 100 \approx 4.3$	
200	$t = -35.6 + 8.66 \ln 200 \approx 10.3$	$\frac{10.3 - 4.3}{200 - 100} = \frac{6.0}{100} = 0.060$
300	$t = -35.6 + 8.66 \ln 300 \approx 13.8$	$\frac{13.8 - 10.3}{300 - 200} = \frac{3.5}{100} = 0.035$
400	$t = -35.6 + 8.66 \ln 400 \approx 16.3$	$\frac{16.3 - 13.8}{400 - 300} = \frac{2.5}{100} = 0.025$

The model's average rates of change are decreasing. This means that as the fox population grows, it takes less time for the population to increase by another 100 foxes.

(B) Another way to obtain the model that the biologist wants is to find the inverse of the exponential model. Find the inverse model and compare it with the logarithmic regression model.

In order to compare the inverse of the biologist's model, $P = 62(1.12)^t$, with the logarithmic regression model, you must rewrite the biologist's model with base e so that the inverse will involve a natural logarithm. This means that you want to find a constant c such that $e^c = 1.12$. Writing the exponential equation $e^c = 1.12$ in logarithmic form gives $c = \ln 1.12$, so $c =$ 0.113 to the nearest thousandth.

Replacing 1.12 with $e^{0.113}$ in the biologist's model gives $P = 62\left(e^{0.113}\right)^t$, or $P = 62\,e^{0.113t}$. Now find the inverse of this function.

Write the equation. $P = 62e^{0.113t}$

Divide both sides by 62. $\frac{P}{62} = e^{0.113t}$

Write in logarithmic form. $\ln \frac{P}{62} = 0.113t$

Divide both sides by 0.113. $8.85 \ln \frac{P}{62} = t$

So, the inverse of the exponential model is $t = 8.85 \ln \frac{P}{62}$. To compare this model with the logarithmic regression model, use a graphing calculator to graph both $y = 8.85 \ln \frac{x}{62}$ and $y = -35.6 + 8.66 \ln x$. You observe that the graphs roughly coincide, so the models are basically equivalent.

Reflect

3. **Discussion** In a later lesson, you will learn the quotient property of logarithms, which states that $\log_b \frac{m}{n} = \log_b m - \log_b n$ for any positive numbers m and n. Explain how you can use this property to compare the two models in Example 3.

Your Turn

4. Maria made a deposit in a bank account and left the money untouched for several years. The table lists her account balance at the end of each year.

Years Since the Deposit Was Made	Account Balance
0	\$1000.00
1	\$1020.00
2	\$1040.40
3	\$1061.21

a. Write an exponential model for the account balance as a function of time (in years since the deposit was made).

b. Find the inverse of the exponential model after rewriting it with a base of e. Describe what information the inverse gives.

c. Perform logarithmic regression on the data (using the account balance as the independent variable and time as the dependent variable). Compare this model with the inverse model from part b.

Elaborate

5. Which transformations of $f(x) = \log_b(x)$ change the function's end behavior (both as x increases without bound and as x decreases toward 0 from the right)? Which transformations change the location of the graph's x-intercept?

6. How are reference points helpful when graphing transformations of $f(x) = \log_b(x)$?

7. What are two ways to obtain a logarithmic model for a set of data?

8. **Essential Question Check-In** Describe the transformations you must perform on the graph of $f(x) = \log_b(x)$ to obtain the graph of $g(x) = a\log_b(x - h) + k$.

Evaluate: Homework and Practice

Personal Math Trainer
- Online Homework
- Hints and Help
- Extra Practice

1. Graph the logarithmic functions $f(x) = \log_2 x$, $f(x) = \log x$, and $f(x) = \ln x$ on the same coordinate plane. To distinguish the curves, label the point on each curve where the y-coordinate is 1.

2. Describe the attributes that the logarithmic functions $f(x) = \log_2 x$, $f(x) = \log x$, and $f(x) = \ln x$ have in common and the attributes that make them different. Attributes should include domain, range, end behavior, asymptotes, intercepts, intervals where the functions are positive and where they are negative, intervals where the functions are increasing and where they are decreasing, and the average rate of change on an interval.

3. For each of the six functions, describe how its graph is a transformation of the graph of $f(x) = \log_2 x$. Also identify what attributes of $f(x) = \log_2 x$ change as a result of the transformation. Attributes to consider are the domain, the range, the end behavior, the vertical asymptote, the x-intercept, the intervals where the function is positive and where it is negative, and whether the function increases or decreases throughout its domain.

   a. $g(x) = \log_2 x - 5$

   b. $g(x) = 4 \log_2 x$

   c. $g(x) = \log_2 (x + 6)$

   d. $g(x) = -\frac{3}{4} \log_2 x$

   e. $g(x) = \log_2 x + 7$

   f. $g(x) = \log_2 (x - 8)$

Identify the transformations of the graph of $f(x) = \log_b x$ that produce the graph of the given function $g(x)$. Then graph $g(x)$ on the same coordinate plane as a graph of $f(x)$ by applying the transformations to the asymptote $x = 0$ and to the reference points $(1, 0)$ and $(b, 1)$. Also state the domain and range of $g(x)$ using set notation.

4. $g(x) = -4 \log_2 (x + 2) + 1$

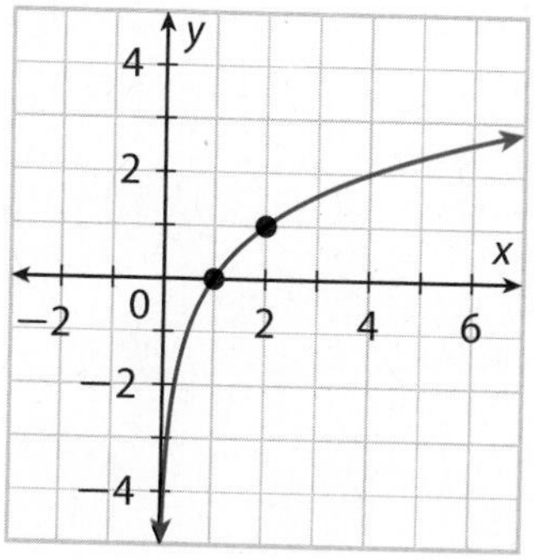

5. $g(x) = 3 \log (x - 1) - 1$

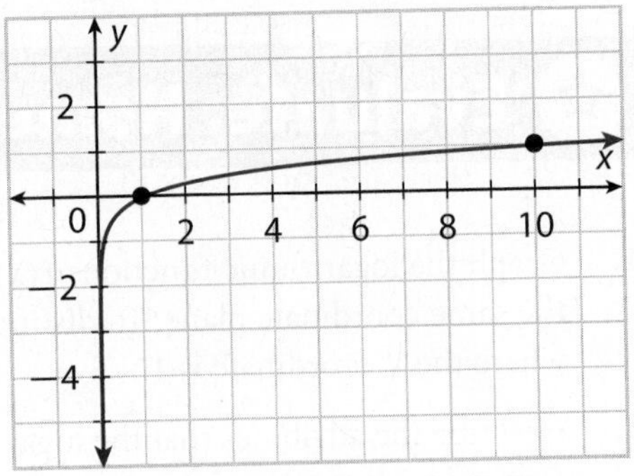

6. $f(x) = \frac{1}{2} \log_2 (x - 1) - 2$

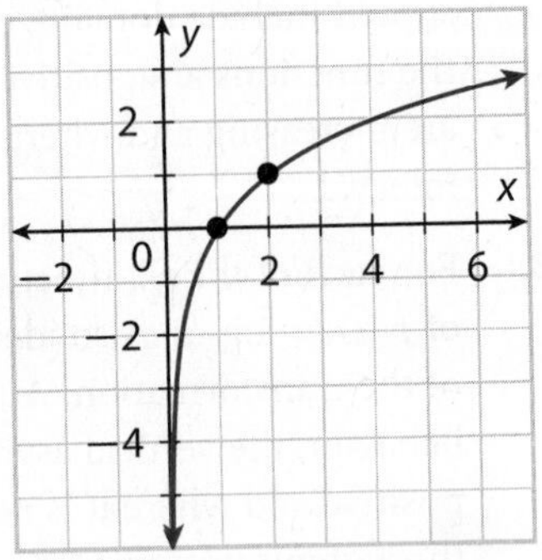

7. $g(x) = -4 \ln(x - 4) + 3$

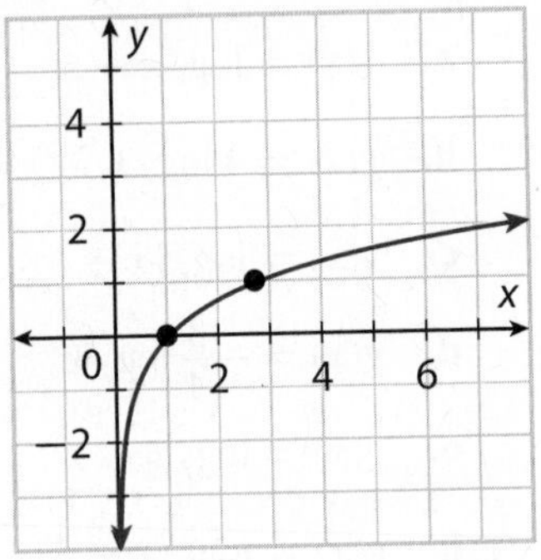

8. $g(x) = -2 \log(x + 2) + 5$

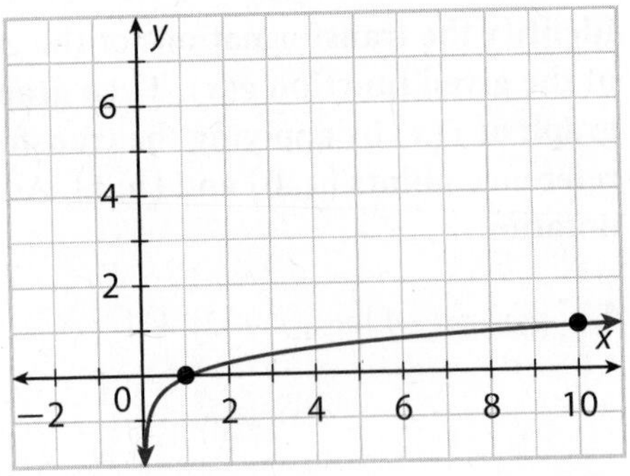

9. The radioactive isotope fluorine-18 is used in medicine to produce images of internal organs and detect cancer. It decays to the stable element oxygen-18. The table gives the percent of fluorine-18 that remains in a sample over a period of time.

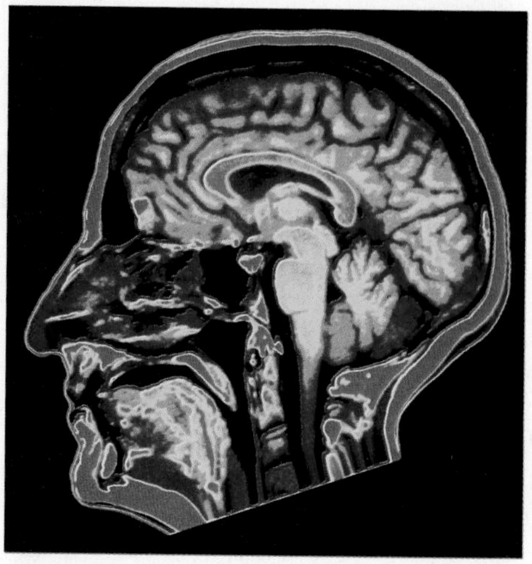

Time (hours)	Percent of Fluorine-18 Remaining
0	100
1	68.5
2	46.9
3	32.1

a. Write an exponential model for the percent of fluorine-18 remaining as a function of time (in hours).

b. Find the inverse of the exponential model after rewriting it with a base of e. Describe what information the inverse gives.

c. Perform logarithmic regression on the data (using the percent of fluorine-18 remaining as the independent variable and time as the dependent variable). Compare this model with the inverse model from part b.

10. During the period between 2001–2011, the average price of an ounce of gold doubled every 4 years. In 2001, the average price of gold was about $270 per ounce.

Year	Average Price of an Ounce of Gold
2001	$271.04
2002	$309.73
2003	$363.38
2004	$409.72
2005	$444.74
2006	$603.46
2007	$695.39
2008	$871.96
2009	$972.35
2010	$1224.53
2011	$1571.52

a. Use the fact that the average price of an ounce of gold doubled every 4 years to write an exponential model for the average price as a function of time (in years since 2001).

b. Find the inverse of the exponential model after rewriting it with a base of e. Describe what information the inverse gives.

c. Perform logarithmic regression on the data in the table (using the average price of an ounce of gold as the independent variable and time as the dependent variable). Compare this model with the inverse model from part b.

H.O.T. Focus on Higher Order Thinking

11. Multiple Representations For the function $g(x) = \log(x - h)$, what value of the parameter h will cause the function to pass through the point $(7, 1)$? Answer the question in two different ways: once by using the function's rule, and once by thinking in terms of the function's graph.

12. Explain the Error A student drew the graph of $g(x) = 2 \log_{\frac{1}{2}}(x - 2)$ as shown. Explain the error that the student made, and draw the correct graph.

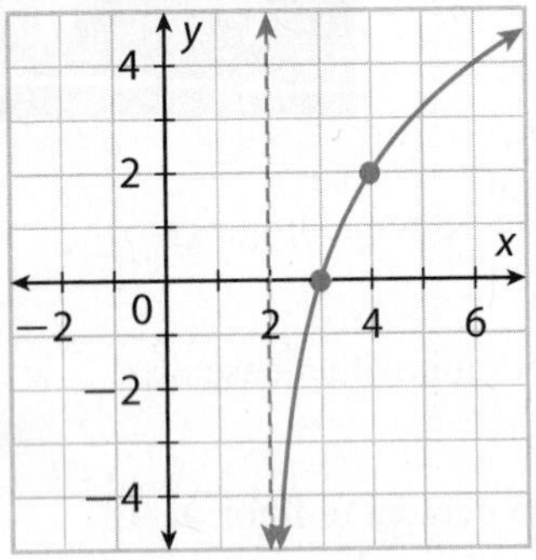

13. Construct Arguments Prove that $\log_{\frac{1}{b}} x = -\log_b x$ for any positive value of b not equal to 1. Begin the proof by setting $\log_{\frac{1}{b}} x$ equal to m and rewriting the equation in exponential form.

Lesson Performance Task

Given the following data about the heights of chair seats and table tops for children, make separate scatterplots of the ordered pairs (age of child, chair seat height) and the ordered pairs (age of child, table top height). Explain why a logarithmic model would be appropriate for each data set. Perform a logarithmic regression on each data set, and describe the transformations needed to obtain the graph of the model from the graph of the parent function $f(x) = \ln x$.

Age of Child (years)	Chair Seat Height (inches)	Table Top Height (inches)
1	5	12
1.5	6.5	14
2	8	16
3	10	18
5	12	20
7.5	14	22
11	16	25

Logarithmic Functions

Essential Question: How can you use logarithmic functions to solve real-world problems?

Key Vocabulary
asymptote
(asíntota)
common logarithm
(logaritmo común)
logarithm
(logaritmo)
logarithmic function
(función logarítmica)
natural logarithm
(logaritmo natural)

KEY EXAMPLE *(Lesson 15.1)*

Evaluate $f(x) = \log_4 x$ when $x = 1024$.

$f(1024) = \log_4 1024$

$4^{f(1024)} = 1024$ — by definition of logarithm

$4^{f(1024)} = 4^5$ — because $4^5 = 1024$

$f(1024) = 5$

KEY EXAMPLE *(Lesson 15.2)*

Graph $f(x) = 3 \log_2 (x + 1) - 4$.

The parameters for $f(x) = a \log_b (x - h) + k$ are $a = 3$, $b = 2$, $h = -1$, and $k = -4$.

Find reference points:

$(1 + h, k) = (0, -4)$

$(b + h, a + k) = (2 - 1, 3 - 4) = (1, -1)$

The two reference points are $(0, -4)$ and $(1, -1)$.

Find the asymptote:

$x = h = -1$

Plot the points and draw the asymptote. Connect the points with a curve that passes through the reference points and continually draws nearer the asymptote.

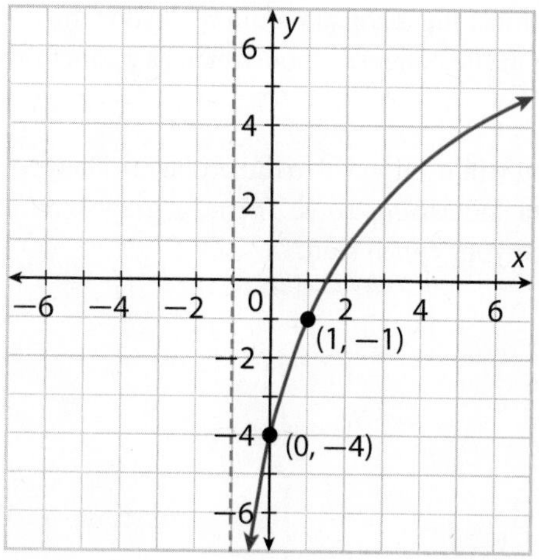

EXERCISES

Evaluate each logarithmic function for the given value. *(Lesson 15.1)*

1. $f(x) = \log_2 x$, for $f(256)$

2. $f(x) = \log_9 x$, for $f(6561)$

Graph each function. *(Lesson 15.2)*

3. $f(x) = 2\log_3(x - 2) + 1$

4. $f(x) = \log_5(x + 1) - 1$

MODULE PERFORMANCE TASK

What's the Dosage?

Kira is a scientist working for a pharmaceutical lab and has developed a new drug. According to her research, 30% of the drug is eliminated from the bloodstream every 6 hours. Her initial dosage plan is to have the patient take a 1200 mg pill of the drug every 12 hours.

The patient needs to have at least 500 mg of the drug in the bloodstream at all times, but the total amount should never exceed 2500 mg. The drug should be taken for no more than 4 days. Does Kira's proposed dosage plan meet the medical requirements for the drug? Find a function that describes the amount of drug in the patient's bloodstream as a function of the number of doses.

Start by listing the information you will need to solve the problem. Then complete the task. Be sure to write down all your data and assumptions. Then use graphs, numbers, words, or algebra to explain how you reached your conclusion.

Ready to Go On?

15.1–15.2 Logarithmic Functions

Personal Math Trainer
- Online Homework
- Hints and Help
- Extra Practice

Rewrite the given equation in exponential format. *(Lesson 15.1)*

1. $\log_6 x = r$

2. $\log_{\frac{3}{4}} 12x = 35y$

Evaluate each logarithmic function for the given value. *(Lesson 15.1)*

3. $f(x) = \log_5 x$ for $f(125)$

4. $f(x) = \log_3 x$ for $f(729)$

Graph each function. *(Lesson 15.2)*

5. $f(x) = -3 \log_e (x + 1) + 2$

6. $f(x) = 4 \log_{10} (x + 4) - 3$

ESSENTIAL QUESTION

7. How is the graph of the logarithmic function $f(x) = \log_4 x$ related to the graph of the exponential function $g(x) = 4^x$?

MODULE 15
MIXED REVIEW

Assessment Readiness

1. Tell whether each function shows exponential decay.

A. $f(x) = \left(\frac{1}{4}\right)^x$

B. $f(x) = 1.6\left(\frac{3}{4}\right)^x$

C. $f(x) = \frac{3}{5}(1.1)^x$

2. Consider the function $f(x) = \frac{1}{4}\log_5(x+3) - 2$. Determine if each statement is True or False.

A. The domain of this function is $\{x \mid x > -3\}$.

B. There is no range to this function.

C. The range of this function is $\{y \mid y > -2\}$

3. Shelby is canoeing in a river. She travels 4 miles upstream and 4 miles downstream in a total of 5 hours. In still water, Shelby can travel at an average speed of 2 miles per hour. To the nearest tenth, what is the average speed of the river's current? Explain.

4. Researchers have found that after 25 years of age, the average size of the pupil in a person's eye decreases. The relationship between pupil diameter d (in millimeters) and age a (in years) can be modeled by $d = -2.1158 \log_e a + 13.669$. What is the average diameter of a pupil for a person 25 years old? 50 years old? Explain how you got your answer.

Logarithmic Properties and Exponential Equations

MODULE 16

Essential Question: How do the properties of logarithms allow you to solve real-world problems?

REAL WORLD VIDEO
Scientists use radiocarbon dating and other techniques to study the fossils of mastodons and other extinct species found at the La Brea Tar Pits.

MODULE PERFORMANCE TASK PREVIEW

How Old Is That Bone?

All living organisms contain carbon. Carbon has two main isotopes, carbon-12 and carbon-14. C-14 is radioactive and decays at a steady rate. Living organisms continually replenish their stores of carbon, and the ratio between C-12 and C-14 stays relatively constant. When the organism dies, this ratio changes at a known rate as C-14 decays. How can we use a logarithmic equation and carbon dating to determine the age of a mastodon bone? Let's find out!

Are YOU Ready?

Complete these exercises to review skills you will need for this module.

Personal Math Trainer
- Online Homework
- Hints and Help
- Extra Practice

Exponents

Example 1 Simplify $\frac{40 \cdot x^6y}{5x^2y^5}$.

$\frac{40 \cdot x^6y}{5x^2y^5} = \frac{40}{5} \cdot x^{6-2}y^{1-5}$ Subtract exponents.

$= \frac{8x^4}{y^4}$ Simplify.

Simplify each expression.

1. $\frac{xy^2}{x^3y^2}$

2. $\frac{18x^3y^7}{2y^5}$

3. $\frac{12x^4}{8x^9y}$

Multi-Step Equations

Example 2 Solve $3(5 - 2x) = -x$ for x.

$15 - 6x = -x$ Distribute the 3.

$15 = 5x$ Add $6x$ to both sides.

$3 = x$ Divide both sides by 5.

The solution is $x = 3$.

Solve.

4. $5(4x + 9) = 2x$

5. $3(x + 12) = 2(4 - 2x)$

6. $(x - 2)^2 = 4(x + 1)$

Equations Involving Exponents

Example 3 Solve $2x^{\frac{1}{3}} - 1 = 3$ for x.

$2x^{\frac{1}{3}} = 4$ Add 1 to both sides.

$x^{\frac{1}{3}} = 2$ Divide both sides by 2.

$\left(x^{\frac{1}{3}}\right)^3 = (2)^3$ Raise both sides to the power of 3.

$x = 8$ Simplify.

Solve.

7. $3x^{\frac{1}{4}} + 2 = 11$

8. $8x^{\frac{1}{2}} + 20 = 100$

9. $4x^{\frac{1}{3}} + 15 = 35$

16.1 Properties of Logarithms

Essential Question: What are the properties of logarithms?

Resource Locker

Explore 1 Investigating the Properties of Logarithms

You can use a scientific calculator to evaluate a logarithmic expression.

(A) Evaluate the expressions in each set using a scientific calculator.

Set A	Set B
$\log \frac{10}{e} \approx$?	$\frac{1}{\log e} \approx$?
$\ln 10 \approx$?	$1 + \log e \approx$?
$\log e^{10} \approx$?	$1 - \log e \approx$?
$\log 10e \approx$?	$10 \log e \approx$?

(B) Match the expressions in Set A to the equivalent expressions in Set B.

$\log \frac{10}{e} =$?

$\ln 10 =$?

$\log e^{10} =$?

$\log 10e =$?

Reflect

1. How can you check the results of evaluating the logarithmic expressions in Set A? Use this method to check each.

2. **Discussion** How do you know that $\log e$ and $\ln 10$ are reciprocals? Given that the expressions are reciprocals, show another way to represent each expression.

Explore 2 Proving the Properties of Logarithms

A logarithm is the exponent to which a base must be raised in order to obtain a given number. So $\log_b b^m = m$. It follows that $\log_b b^0 = 0$, so $\log_b 1 = 0$. Also, $\log_b b^1 = 1$, so $\log_b b = 1$. Additional properties of logarithms are the Product Property of Logarithms, the Quotient Property of Logarithms, the Power Property of Logarithms, and the Change of Base Property of Logarithms.

Properties of Logarithms			
For any positive numbers a, m, n, b $(b \neq 1)$, and c $(c \neq 1)$, the following properties hold.			
Definition-Based Properties	$\log_b b^m = m$	$\log_b 1 = 0$	$\log_b b = 1$
Product Property of Logarithms	$\log_b mn = \log_b m + \log_b n$		
Quotient Property of Logarithms	$\log_b \frac{m}{n} = \log_b m - \log_b n$		
Power Property of Logarithms	$\log_b m^n = n\log_b m$		
Change of Base Property of Logarithms	$\log_c a = \frac{\log_b a}{\log_b c}$		

Given positive numbers m, n, and b $(b \neq 1)$, prove the Product Property of Logarithms.

(A) Let $x = \log_b m$ and $y = \log_b n$. Rewrite the expressions in exponential form.

$m =$?

$n =$?

(B) Substitute for m and n.

$\log_b mn = \log_b (\;?\;)$

(C) Use the Product of Powers Property of Exponents to simplify.

$\log_b (b^x \cdot b^y) = \log_b b^{?}$

(D) Use the definition of a logarithm $\log_b b^m = m$ to simplify further.

$\log_b b^{x+y} =$?

(E) Substitute for x and y.

$x + y =$?

Reflect

3. Prove the Power Property of Logarithms. Justify each step of your proof.

Explain 1 Using the Properties of Logarithms

Logarithmic expressions can be rewritten using one or more of the properties of logarithms.

Example 1 **Express each expression as a single logarithm. Simplify if possible. Then check your results by converting to exponential form and evaluating.**

(A) $\log_3 27 - \log_3 81$

$\log_3 27 - \log_3 81 = \log_3\left(\frac{27}{81}\right)$ Quotient Property of Logarithms

$= \log_3\left(\frac{1}{3}\right)$ Simplify.

$= \log_3 3^{-1}$ Write using base 3.

$= -1\log_3 3$ Power Property of Logarithms.

$= -1$ Simplify.

Check:

$\log_3\left(\frac{1}{3}\right) = -1$

$\frac{1}{3} = 3^{-1}$

$\frac{1}{3} = \frac{1}{3}$

(B) $\log_5\left(\frac{1}{25}\right) + \log_5 625$

$\log_5\left(\frac{1}{25}\right) + \log_5 625 = \log_5\left(\frac{1}{25} \cdot 625\right)$ Product Property of Logarithms

$= \log_5 25$ Simplify.

$= \log_5 5^2$ Write using base 5.

$= 2\log_5 5$ Power Property of Logarithms

$= 2$ Simplify.

Check:

$\log_5 25 = 2$

$25 = 5^{2}$

$25 = 25$

Your Turn

Express each expression as a single logarithm. Simplify if possible.

4. $\log_4 64^3$

5. $\log_8 18 - \log_8 2$

Explain 2 Rewriting a Logarithmic Model

There are standard formulas that involve logarithms, such as the formula for measuring the loudness of sounds. The loudness of a sound $L(I)$, in decibels, is given by the function $L(I) = 10\log\left(\frac{I}{I_0}\right)$, where I is the sound's intensity in watts per square meter and I_0 is the intensity of a barely audible sound. It's also possible to develop logarithmic models from exponential growth or decay models of the form $f(t) = a(1 + r)^t$ or $f(t) = a(1 - r)^t$ by finding the inverse.

Example 2 **Solve the problems using logarithmic models.**

(A) During a concert, an orchestra plays a piece of music in which its volume increases from one measure to the next, tripling the sound's intensity. Find how many decibels the loudness of the sound increases between the two measures.

Let I be the intensity in the first measure. So $3I$ is the intensity in the second measure.

Increase in loudness $= L(3I) - L(I)$	Write the expression.
$= 10\log\left(\frac{3I}{I_0}\right) - 10\log\left(\frac{I}{I_0}\right)$	Substitute.
$= 10\left(\log\left(\frac{3I}{I_0}\right) - \log\left(\frac{I}{I_0}\right)\right)$	Distributive Property
$= 10\left(\log 3 + \log\left(\frac{I}{I_0}\right) - \log\left(\frac{I}{I_0}\right)\right)$	Product Property of Logarithms
$= 10\log 3$	Simplify.
≈ 4.77	Evaluate the logarithm.

So the loudness of sound increases by about 4.77 decibels.

(B) The population of the United States in 2012 was 313.9 million. If the population increases exponentially at an average rate of 1% each year, how long will it take for the population to double?

The exponential growth model is $P = P_0(1+r)^t$, where P is the population in millions after t years, P_0 is the population in 2012, and r is the average growth rate.

$P_0 = 313.9$

$P = 2P_0 = 627.8$

$r = 0.01$

Find the inverse model of $P = P_0(1+r)^t$.

$$P = P_0(1+r)^t$$ Exponential model

$$\frac{P}{P_0} = (1+r)^t$$ Divide both sides by P_0.

$$\log_{1+r}\left(\frac{P}{P_0}\right) = \log_{1+r}(1+r)^t$$ Take the log of both sides.

$$\log_{1+r}\left(\frac{P}{P_0}\right) = t$$ Definition of a logarithm

$$\frac{\log\left(\frac{P}{P_0}\right)}{\log(1+r)} = t$$ Change of Base Property of Logarithms

Substitute and solve for t.

$$t = \frac{\log\left(\frac{627.8}{313.9}\right)}{\log(1+0.01)}$$ Substitute.

$$= \frac{\log 2}{\log 1.01}$$ Simplify.

$$= \frac{0.301}{0.004}$$ Evaluate the logarithms.

$$= 75.25$$ Simplify.

The population of the United States will double in 75.25 years from 2012, or in the year 2087.

Your Turn

6. A bank account earns 6% annual interest compounded annually. The balance B of the account after t years is given by the equation $B = B_0(1.06)^t$, where B_0 is the starting balance. If the account starts with a balance of $250, how long will it take to triple the balance of the account?

Elaborate

7. On what other properties do the proofs of the properties of logarithms rely?

8. What properties of logarithms would you use to rewrite the expression $\log_7 x + \log_7 4x$ as a single logarithm?

9. Explain how the properties of logarithms are useful in finding the inverse of an exponential growth or decay model.

10. **Essential Question Check-In** State each of the Product, Quotient, and Power Properties of Logarithms in a simple sentence.

Evaluate: Homework and Practice

- Online Homework
- Hints and Help
- Extra Practice

Express each expression as a single logarithm. Simplify if possible.

1. $\log_9 12 + \log_9 546.75$

2. $\log_2 76.8 - \log_2 1.2$

3. $\log_{\frac{2}{5}} 0.0256^3$

4. $\log_{11} 11^{23}$

5. $\log_5 5^{x+1} + \log_4 256^2$

6. $\log(\log_7 98 - \log_7 2)^x$

7. $\log_{x+1}(x^2 + 2x + 1)^3$

8. $\log_4 5 + \log_4 12 - \log_4 3.75$

Solve the problems using logarithmic models.

9. **Geology** Seismologists use the Richter scale to express the energy, or magnitude, of an earthquake. The Richter magnitude of an earthquake M is related to the energy released in ergs E shown by the formula $M = \frac{2}{3}\log\left(\frac{E}{10^{11.8}}\right)$. In 1964, an earthquake centered at Prince William Sound, Alaska registered a magnitude of 9.2 on the Richter scale. Find the energy released by the earthquake.

10. **Astronomy** The difference between the apparent magnitude (brightness) m of a star and its absolute magnitude M is given by the formula $m - M = 5\log\frac{d}{10}$, where d is the distance of the star from the Earth, measured in parsecs. Find the distance d of the star Rho Oph from Earth, where Rho Oph has an apparent magnitude of 5.0 and an absolute magnitude −0.4.

11. The intensity of the sound of a conversation ranges from 10^{-10} watts per square meter to 10^{-6} watts per square meter. What is the range in the loudness of the conversation? Use $I_0 = 10^{-12}$ watts per square meter.

12. The intensity of sound from the stands of a football game is 25 times as great when the home team scores a touchdown as it is when the away team scores. Find the difference in the loudness of the sound when the two teams score.

13. **Finance** A stock priced at \$40 increases at a rate of 8% per year. Write and evaluate a logarithmic expression for the number of years that it will take for the value of the stock to reach \$50.

14. Suppose that the population of one endangered species decreases at a rate of 4% per year. In one habitat, the current population of the species is 143. After how long will the population drop below 30?

15. The population P of bacteria in a culture after t minutes is given by the equation $P = P_0\,(1.12)^t$, where P_0 is the initial population. If the number of bacteria starts at 200, how long will it take for the population to increase to 1000?

16. **Chemistry** Most swimming pool experts recommend a pH of between 7.0 and 7.6 for water in a swimming pool. Use $\text{pH} = -\log\left[\text{H}^+\right]$ and write an expression for the difference in hydrogen ion concentration over this pH range.

17. Match the logarithmic expressions to equivalent expressions.

A. $\log_2 4x$	**a.** ___?___ $2x$
B. $\log_2 \frac{x}{4}$	**b.** ___?___ $2 + \log_2 x$
C. $\log_2 4^x$	**c.** ___?___ $\frac{\log x}{\log 2}$
D. $\log_2 x^4$	**d.** ___?___ $4\log_2 x$
E. $\log_2 x$	**e.** ___?___ $\log_2 x - 2$

18. Prove the Quotient Property of Logarithms. Justify each step of your proof.

19. Prove the Change of Base Property of Logarithms. Justify each step of your proof.

H.O.T. Focus on Higher Order Thinking

20. Multi-Step The radioactive isotope Carbon-14 decays exponentially at a rate of 0.0121% each year.

a. How long will it take 250 g of Carbon-14 to decay to 100 g?

b. The half-life for a radioactive isotope is the amount of time it takes for the isotope to reach half its initial value. What is the half-life of Carbon-14?

21. Explain the Error A student simplified the expression $\log_2 8 + \log_3 27$ as shown. Explain and correct the student's error.

$$\log_2 8 + \log_3 27 = \log(8 \cdot 27)$$
$$= \log(216)$$
$$\approx 2.33$$

22. Communicate Mathematical Ideas Explain why it is not necessary for a scientific calculator to have both a key for common logs and a key for natural logs.

23. Analyze Relationships Explain how to find the relationship between $\log_b a$ and $\log_{\frac{1}{b}} a$.

Lesson Performance Task

Given the population data for the state of Texas from 1920–2010, perform exponential regression to obtain an exponential growth model for population as a function of time (represent 1920 as Year 0).

Obtain a logarithmic model for time as a function of population two ways: (1) by finding the inverse of the exponential model, and (2) by performing logarithmic regression on the same set of data but using population as the independent variable and time as the dependent variable. Then confirm that the two expressions are equivalent by applying the properties of logarithms.

Year	U.S. Census Count
1920	4,663,228
1930	5,824,715
1940	6,414,824
1950	7,711,194
1960	9,579,677
1970	11,196,730
1980	14,229,191
1990	16,986,335
2000	20,851,820
2010	25,145,561

16.2 Solving Exponential Equations

Essential Question: What are some ways you can solve an equation of the form $ab^x = c$, where a and c are nonzero real numbers and b is greater than 0 and not equal to 1?

Resource Locker

Explore Solving Exponential Equations Graphically

One way to solve exponential equations is graphically. First, graph each side of the equation separately. The point(s) at which the two graphs intersect are the solutions of the equation.

(A) First, look at the equation $275e^{0.06x} = 1000$. To solve the equation graphically, split it into two separate equations.

$y_1 =$?

$y_2 =$?

(B) What will the graphs of y_1 and y_2 look like? ?

(C) Graph y_1 and y_2 using a graphing calculator.

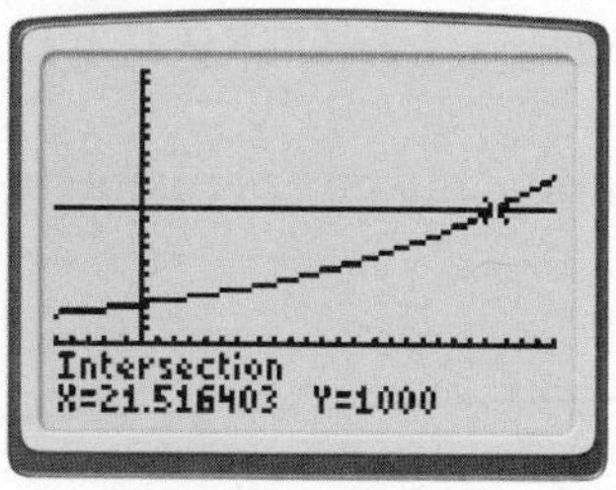

(D) The x-coordinate of the point of intersection is approximately ? .

(E) So, the solution of the equation is $x \approx$? .

(F) Now, look at the equation $10^{2x} = 10^4$. Split the equation into two separate equations.

$y_1 =$?

$y_2 =$?

Ⓖ What will the graphs of y_1 and y_2 look like? [?]

Ⓗ Graph y_1 and y_2 using a graphing calculator.

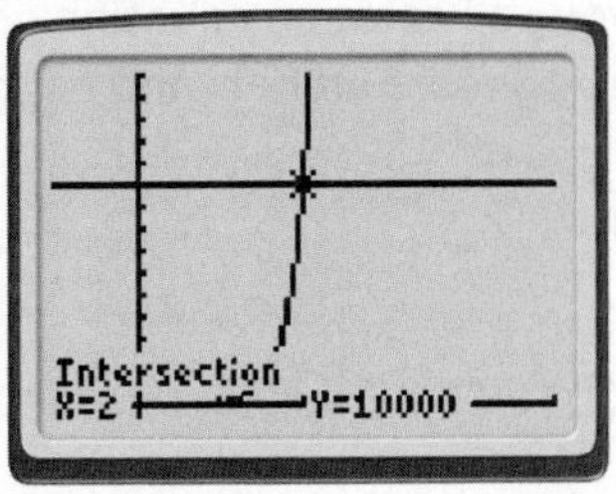

Ⓘ The x-coordinate of the point of intersection is [?].

Ⓙ So, the solution of the equation is $x \approx$ [?].

Reflect

1. How can you check the solution of an exponential equation after it is found graphically?

Explain 1 Solving Exponential Equations Algebraically

In addition to solving exponential equations graphically, exponential equations can be solved algebraically. One way to solve exponential equations is to rewrite them in logarithmic form. Another way is to use the Property of Equality for Logarithmic Equations which states that for any positive numbers x, y, and b $(b \neq 1)$, $\log_b x = \log_b y$ if and only if $x = y$.

Example 1 **Solve the equations. Give the exact solution and an approximate solution to three decimal places.**

Ⓐ $10 = 5e^{4x}$

$10 = 5e^{4x}$	Original equation
$2 = e^{4x}$	Divide both sides by 5.
$\ln 2 = 4x$	Rewrite in logarithmic form.
$\frac{\ln 2}{4} = \frac{4x}{4}$	Divide both sides by 4.
$\frac{\ln 2}{4} = x$	Simplify.
$0.173 \approx x$	Evaluate. Round to three decimal places.

(B) $5^x - 4 = 7$

$5^x - 4 = 7$	Original equation
$5^x - 4 + \boxed{4} = 7 + \boxed{4}$	Add $\boxed{4}$ to both sides.
$5^x = \boxed{11}$	Simplify.
$\log 5^x = \log \boxed{11}$	Take the common logarithm of both sides.
$\boxed{x \log 5} = \log 11$	Power Property of Logarithms
$x = \dfrac{\log \boxed{11}}{\log \boxed{5}}$	Divide both sides by $\log 5$.
$x \approx \boxed{1.490}$	Evaluate. Round to three decimal palces.

Reflect

2. Consider the equation $2^{x-3} = 85$. How can you solve this equation using logarithm base 2?

3. **Discussion** When solving an exponential equation with base e, what is the benefit of taking the natural logarithm of both sides of the equation?

Your Turn

Solve the equations. Give the exact solution and an approximate solution to three decimal places.

4. $2e^{x-1} + 5 = 80$

5. $6^{3x} = 12$

Explain 2 Solve a Real-World Problem by Solving an Exponential Equation

Suppose that \$250 is deposited into an account that pays 4.5% compounded quarterly. The equation $A = P\left(1 + \frac{r}{4}\right)^n$ gives the amount A in the account after n quarters for an initial investment P that earns interest at a rate r. Solve for n to find how long it will take for the account to contain at least \$500.

Analyze Information

Identify the important information.

- The initial investment P is \$ $\boxed{250}$.
- The interest rate is $\boxed{4.5}$ %, so r is $\boxed{0.045}$.
- The amount A in the account after n quarters is \$ $\boxed{500}$.

Formulate a Plan

Solve the equation for $A = P\left(1 + \frac{r}{4}\right)^n$ for $\boxed{n}$ by substituting in the known information and using logarithms.

Solve

$$\boxed{500} = \boxed{250}\left(1 + \frac{\boxed{0.045}}{4}\right)^n \quad \text{Substitute.}$$

$$\boxed{2} = \left(1 + \frac{0.045}{4}\right)^n \quad \text{Divide both sides by 250.}$$

$$2 = \boxed{1.01125}^n \quad \text{Evaluate the expression in parentheses.}$$

$$\log 2 = \log 1.01125^n \quad \text{Take the common logarithm of both sides.}$$

$$\log 2 = \boxed{n} \log \boxed{1.01125} \quad \text{Power Property of Logarithms}$$

$$\frac{\log \boxed{2}}{\log \boxed{1.01125}} = n \quad \text{Divide both sides by log 1.01125.}$$

$$\boxed{61.96} \approx n \quad \text{Evaluate.}$$

Justify and Evaluate

It will take about $\boxed{61.96}$ quarters, or about $\boxed{15.5}$ years, for the account to contain at least $500.

Check by substituting this value for n in the equation and solving for A.

$$A = 250\left(1 + \frac{0.045}{4}\right)^{\boxed{61.96}} \quad \text{Substitute.}$$

$$= 250\left(\boxed{1.01125}\right)^{61.96} \quad \text{Evaluate the expression in parentheses.}$$

$$\approx 250\left(\boxed{2}\right) \quad \text{Evaluate the exponent.}$$

$$\approx \boxed{500} \quad \text{Multiply.}$$

So, the answer is reasonable.

Your Turn

6. How long will it take to triple a $250 initial investment in an account that pays 4.5% compounded quarterly?

Elaborate

7. Describe how to solve an exponential equation graphically.

8. **Essential Question Check-In** Describe how to solve an exponential equation algebraically.

✩ Evaluate: Homework and Practice

Personal Math Trainer

- Online Homework
- Hints and Help
- Extra Practice

Solve the equations graphically.

1. $4e^{0.1x} = 60$

2. $120e^{2x} = 75e^{3x}$

3. $5 = 625e^{0.02x}$

Solve the equations graphically. Then check your solutions algebraically.

4. $10e^{6x} = 5e^{-3x}$

5. $450e^{0.4x} = 2000$

Solve the equations. Give the exact solution and an approximate solution to three decimal places.

6. $6^{3x-9} - 10 = -3$

7. $7e^{3x} = 42$

8. $11^{6x+2} = 12$

9. $e^{\frac{2x-1}{3}} = 250$

10. $(10^x)^2 + 90 = 105$

11. $5^{\frac{x}{4}} = 30$

Solve.

12. The price P of a gallon of gas after t years is given by the equation $P = P_0(1 + r)^t$, where P_0 is the initial price of gas and r is the rate of inflation. If the price of a gallon of gas is currently \$3.25, how long will it take for the price to rise to \$4.00 if the rate of inflation is 10.5%?

13. **Finance** The amount A in a bank account after t years is given by the equation $A = A_0\left(1 + \frac{r}{6}\right)^{6t}$, where A_0 is the initial amount and r is the interest rate. Suppose there is \$600 in the account. If the interest rate is 4%, after how many years will the amount triple?

14. A baseball player has a 25% chance of hitting a home run during a game. For how many games will the probability of hitting a home run in every game drop to 5%?

15. **Meteorology** In one part of the atmosphere where the temperature is a constant −70 °F, pressure can be expressed as a function of altitude by the equation $P(h) = 128(10)^{-0.682h}$, where P is the atmospheric pressure in kilopascals (kPa) and h is the altitude in kilometers above sea level. The pressure ranges from 2.55 kPa to 22.9 kPa in this region. What is the range of altitudes?

16. You can choose a prize of either a $20,000 car or one penny on the first day, double that (2 cents) on the second day, and so on for a month. On what day would you receive at least the value of the car?

17. **Population** The population of a small coastal resort town, currently 3400, grows at a rate of 3% per year. This growth can be expressed by the exponential equation $P = 3400(1 + 0.03)^t$, where P is the population after t years. Find the number of years it will take for the population to reach 10,000.

18. A veterinarian has instructed Harrison to give his 75-lb dog one 325-mg aspirin tablet for arthritis. The amount of aspirin A remaining in the dog's body after t minutes can be expressed by $A = 325\left(\frac{1}{2}\right)^{\frac{t}{15}}$. How long will it take for the amount of aspirin to drop to 50 mg?

19. **Agriculture** The number of farms in Iowa (in thousands) can be modeled by $N(t) = 119(0.987)^t$, where t is the number of years since 1980. According to the model, when will the number of farms in Iowa be about 80,000?

20. Match the equations with the solutions.

A. $9e^{3x} = 27$	**a.** __?__ $x \approx 1.099$
B. $9e^{x} = 27$	**b.** __?__ $x \approx 1.022$
C. $9e^{3x-4} = 27$	**c.** __?__ $x \approx 0.366$
D. $9e^{3x} + 2 = 27$	**d.** __?__ $x \approx 1.700$

H.O.T. Focus on Higher Order Thinking

21. Explain the Error A student solved the equation $e^{4x} - 6 = 10$ as shown. Find and correct the student's mistake. Is there an easier way to solve the problem? Verify that both methods result in the same answer.

$$e^{4x} - 6 = 10$$
$$e^{4x} = 16$$
$$\log e^{4x} = \log 16$$
$$4x \log e = \log 16$$
$$4x(1) = \log 16$$
$$x = \frac{\log 16}{4}$$
$$x \approx 0.301$$

22. Multi-Step The amount $\boldsymbol{A}$ in an account after $\boldsymbol{t}$ years is given by the equation $\boldsymbol{A = Pe^{rt}}$, where $\boldsymbol{P}$ is the initial amount and $\boldsymbol{r}$ is the interest rate.

a. Find an equation that models approximately how long it will take for the initial amount P in the account to double with the interest rate r. Write the equation in terms of the interest rate expressed as a percent.

b. The Rule of 72 states that you can find the approximate time it will take to double your money by dividing 72 by the interest rate. The rule uses 72 instead of 69 because 72 has more divisors, making it easier to calculate mentally. Use the Rule of 72 to find the approximate time it takes to double an initial investment of $300 with an interest rate of 3.75%. Determine that this result is reasonable by solving the equation $A = P_0(1.0375)^t$, where A is the amount after t years and P_0 is the initial investment.

23. Represent Real-World Problems Suppose you have an initial mass M_0 of a radioactive substance with a half-life of h. Then the mass of the parent isotopes at time t is $P(t) = M_0\left(\frac{1}{2}\right)^{\frac{t}{h}}$. Since the substance is decaying from the original parent isotopes into the new daughter isotopes while the mass of all the isotopes remains constant, the mass of the daughter isotopes at time t is $D(t) = M_0 - P(t)$. Find when the masses of the parent isotopes and daughter isotopes are equal. Explain the meaning of your answer and why it makes sense.

Lesson Performance Task

The frequency of a note on the piano, in Hz, is related to its position on the keyboard by the function $f(n) = 440 \cdot 2^{\frac{n}{12}}$, where n is the number of keys above or below the note concert A, concert A being the A key above middle C on the piano. Using this function, find the position n of the key that has a frequency of 110 Hz. Why is this number a negative value?

Logarithmic Properties and Exponential Equations

Essential Question: How do the properties of logarithms allow you to solve real-world problems?

Key Vocabulary
exponential equation
(ecuación exponencial)

KEY EXAMPLE *(Lesson 16.1)*

Simplify: $\log_5 5^{x+2} + \log_2 16^3$.

Apply properties of logarithms.

$$\begin{aligned}\log_5 5^{x+2} + \log_2 16^3 &= (x+2)\log_5 5 + 3\log_2 16 \\ &= (x+2) + 3\log_2 (2^4) \\ &= x + 2 + 3(4) \\ &= x + 14\end{aligned}$$

KEY EXAMPLE *(Lesson 16.2)*

Solve the equation: $4^{3x+1} = 6$.

$4^{3x+1} = 6$

$\log 4^{3x+1} = \log 6$ — Take the log of both sides.

$(3x+1)\log 4 = \log 6$ — Bring down the exponent.

$3x + 1 = \dfrac{\log 6}{\log 4}$ — Rearrange to isolate *x*.

$3x = \dfrac{\log 6}{\log 4} - 1$

$x = \dfrac{1}{3}\left(\dfrac{\log 6}{\log 4} - 1\right) \approx 0.0975$

EXERCISES

Use properties of logarithms to simplify. *(Lesson 16.1)*

1. $\log_{\frac{3}{5}} 0.216^4$

2. $\log_4 4^{x-2} + \log_3 243^2$

3. $\log_8 0.015625^x$

4. $\log 10^{2x+1} + \log_3 9$

Solve each equation. *(Lesson 16.2)*

5. $5^x = 50$

6. $6^{x+2} = 45$

7. $20^{2x+3} = 15$

8. $3^{5x+1} = 150$

MODULE PERFORMANCE TASK

How Old Is That Bone?

The La Brea Tar Pits in Los Angeles contain one of the best preserved collections of Pleistocene vertebrates, including over 660 species of organisms. An archeologist working at La Brea Tar Pits wants to assess the age of a mastodon bone fragment she discovered. She measures that the fragment has 22% as much carbon-14 as typical living tissue. Given that the half-life of carbon-14 is 5370 years, what is the bone fragment's age?

Start by listing the information you will need to solve the problem. Then complete the task. Be sure to write down all your data and assumptions. Then use graphs, numbers, words, or algebra to explain how you reached your conclusion.

Ready to Go On?

16.1–16.2 Logarithmic Properties and Exponential Equations

Personal Math Trainer

- Online Homework
- Hints and Help
- Extra Practice

Use properties of logarithms to simplify. *(Lesson 16.1)*

1. $\log_{\frac{6}{5}} 2.0736^5$

2. $\log_2 3.2 - \log_2 0.025$

3. $\log_7 7^{2x-1} + \log_3 81^2$

4. $\log_5 125 - \log 10^{5x}$

Solve each equation. Give the exact solution and an approximate solution to three decimal places. *(Lesson 16.2)*

5. $7^{2x} = 30$

6. $5^{2x-1} = 20$

7. $2^{0.5x+7} = 215$

8. $10^{3x-3} = 15$

ESSENTIAL QUESTION

9. How do you solve an exponential equation algebraically?

MODULE 16
MIXED REVIEW

Assessment Readiness

1. For each function below, determine if the function has an inverse defined for all real numbers.

A. $f(x) = 4x^3 - 1$

B. $f(x) = \sqrt{3x} + 2$

C. $f(x) = 4x^2 + 2$

2. Consider the equation $8^{x+1} = 12$. Determine if each statement is True or False.

A. After bringing down the exponent, the equation is $(x + 1)\log 8 = \log 12$.

B. The equation cannot be solved because the bases are not the same.

C. The approximate value of x is 0.195.

3. At a constant temperature, the pressure, P, of an enclosed gas is inversely proportional to the volume, V, of the gas. If $P = 50$ pounds per square inch when $V = 30$ cubic inches, how can you find the pressure when the volume is 125 cubic inches?

4. $A = P(1 + r)^n$ gives amount A in an account after n years after an initial investment P that earns interest at an annual rate r. How long will it take for \$250 to increase to \$500 at 4% annual interest? Explain how you got your answer.

Assessment Readiness

Personal Math Trainer

- Online Homework
- Hints and Help
- Extra Practice

1. Consider each sequence rule. Does the rule match the geometric sequence 5, 10, 20, 40, 80, ... ? Write Yes or No for A–C.

A. $a_n = 5(2)^n$

B. $a_n = 10(2n)$

C. $a_n = 5(2)^{n-1}$

2. Consider a situation where a population doubles every five years. Determine if each statement is True or False.

A. The situation could be modeled with an exponential equation.

B. The situation could not be modeled with a quadratic equation.

C. The situation could be modeled with a linear equation.

3. Consider the function $f(x) = \log_6 x$. Determine if each statement is True or False.

A. To evaluate $f(216)$, one way is to type it into the calculator as log 216 divided by log 6.

B. There is no way to evaluate $\log_6$ in the calculator, because the log function in the calculator has a base of 10.

C. When the function is evaluated for $x = 216$, $f(216) \approx 3$.

4. Tell whether each equation is the inverse function of $f(x) = 8x^3 + 2$.

A. $f^{-1}(x) = \dfrac{\sqrt[2]{x-2}}{2}$

B. $f^{-1}(x) = \dfrac{\sqrt[3]{x-2}}{2}$

C. $f^{-1}(x) = \dfrac{\sqrt[3]{x-2}}{8}$

D. $f^{-1}(x) = \dfrac{\sqrt[3]{x+2}}{2}$

5. In science class, Danny watched a video that talked about a type of spore that would have the following amount of spores in the petri dish each hour:

Hours	0	1	2	3	4
Spores	1	3	9	27	81

Danny wants to match the growth of the spores to a linear, quadratic, or exponential model. Using the information given, which model matches the spore growth? Explain.

6. A circular plot of land has a radius $3x - 1$. What is the polynomial representing the area of the land? Explain your answer.

7. The number of bacteria growing in a petri dish after *n* hours can be modeled by $b(t) = b_0 r^n$, where b_0 is the initial number of bacteria and *r* is the rate at which the bacteria grow. If the number of bacteria quadruples after 1 hour, how many hours will it take to produce 51,200 bacteria if there are initially 50 bacteria? Explain your answer.

Performance Tasks

★ 8. The amount of freight transported by rail in the United States was about 580 billion *ton-miles* in 1960 and has been increasing at a rate of 2.32% per year since then.

A. Write and graph a function representing the amount of freight, in billions of ton-miles, transported annually (1960 = year 0).

B. In what year would you predict that the number of ton-miles would have exceeded or would exceed 1 trillion (1000 billion)?

★★★ **9.** In one part of the atmosphere where the temperature is a constant −70°F, from about 11 km to 25 km above sea level, pressure can be expressed as a function of altitude by the equation $P(h) = 128(10)^{-0.0682h}$, where P is the atmospheric pressure in kilopascals (kPa) and h is the altitude in kilometers above sea level.

A. What is the altitude, to the nearest tenth of a kilometer, where the pressure is 5.54 kPa?

B. A kilopascal is 0.145 psi. Would the model predict a sea-level pressure less than or greater than the actual sea-level pressure, 14.7 psi? Explain.

★★★ **10.** The loudness of sound is measured on a logarithmic scale according to the formula $L = 10\log\left(\frac{I}{I_0}\right)$, where L is the loudness of sound in decibels (dB), I is the intensity of sound, and I_0 is the intensity of the softest audible sound.

Sound	Intensity
Jet takeoff	$10^{15}I_0$
Jackhammer	$10^{12}I_0$
Hair dryer	$10^{7}I_0$
Whisper	$10^{3}I_0$
Leaves rustling	$10^{2}I_0$
Softest audible sound	I_0

A. Find the loudness in decibels of each sound listed in the table.

B. The sound at a rock concert is found to have a loudness of 110 decibels. Find the intensity of this sound. Where should this sound be placed in the table in order to preserve the order from least to greatest intensity?

C. A decibel is $\frac{1}{10}$ of a bel. Is a jet plane louder than a sound that measures 20 bels? Explain.

MATH IN CAREERS

Nuclear Medicine Technologist The radioactive properties of the isotope technetium-99m can be used in combination with a tin compound to map circulatory system disorders. Technetium-99m has a half-life of 6 hours.

a. Write an exponential decay function that models this situation. The function $p(t)$ should give the percent of the isotope remaining after t hours.

b. Describe domain, range, and the end behavior of $p(t)$ as t increases without bound for the function found in part a.

c. Write the inverse of the decay function. Use a common logarithm for your final function.

d. How long does it take until 5% of the technetium-99m remains? Round to the nearest tenth of an hour.

UNIT 7

Trigonometric Functions

MODULE 17

Unit-Circle Definition of Trigonometric Functions

MODULE 18

Graphing Trigonometric Functions

MATH IN CAREERS

Boat Builder A boat builder builds and repairs all types of marine vessels, from sailboats to riverboats. Boat builders are responsible for drafting a boat's design; building the frame, hull, deck, and cabins; and fitting the engine. Boat builders often use computer technologies when designing a boat and must use geometry and trigonometry when interpreting blueprints and shaping and cutting materials to specified measurements. Boat builders need to be able to estimate and calculate costs of materials and labor and to understand mathematical models of different aspects of boats and boating.

If you are interested in a career as a boat builder, you should study these mathematical subjects:

- Geometry
- Algebra
- Trigonometry
- Business Math

Check out the career activity at the end of the unit to find out how **Boat Builders** use math.

Reading Start-Up

Visualize Vocabulary

Use the ✔ words to complete the graphic.

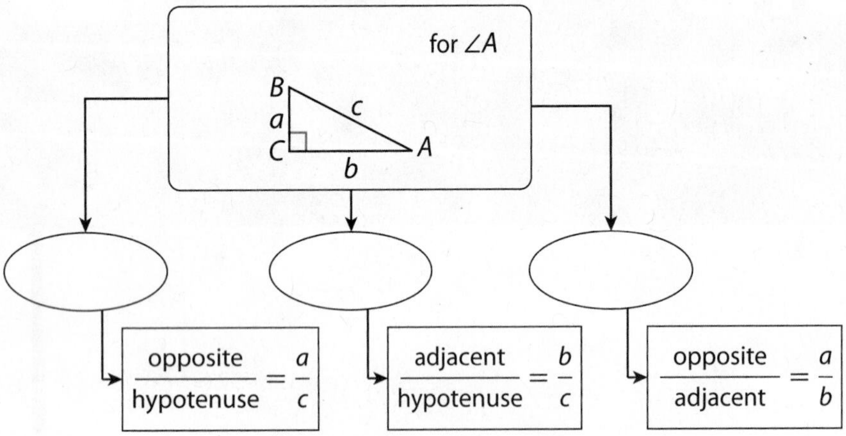

Vocabulary

Review Words

✔ cosine *(coseno)*
✔ sine *(seno)*
✔ tangent *(tangente)*
✔ trigonometric ratio *(razón trigonométrica)*

Preview Words

amplitude *(amplitud)*
angle of rotation *(ángulo de referencia)*
cosecant function *(función cosecante)*
cotangent function *(función cotangente)*
period *(periodo)*
periodic function *(function periódica)*
radian *(radián)*
reference angle *(ángulo de rotación)*
secant function *(función secante)*

Understand Vocabulary

To become familiar with some of the vocabulary terms in the module, consider the following. You may refer to the module, the glossary, or a dictionary.

1. An __?__ is formed by a rotating ray, called the terminal side, and a stationary ray, called the initial side.

2. A __?__ repeats exactly in regular intervals.

3. The __?__ of a periodic function is half the difference of the maximum and minimum values and is always positive.

Active Reading

Layered Book Before beginning each module in this unit, create a layered book to help you summarize the information in each lesson. Each flap of the layered book can correspond to definitions and examples of the trigonometric functions, their graphs, and transformations. Write details of each function on the appropriate flap to create a summary of the module.

Unit-Circle Definition of Trigonometric Functions

MODULE 17

Essential Question: How can the unit-circle definition of trigonometric functions help to solve real-world problems?

REAL WORLD VIDEO
How does a digital device like a smartphone display time on an analog clock? You may be surprised to learn that the answer involves trigonometry.

MODULE PERFORMANCE TASK PREVIEW

Telling Time with Trig

Imagine you are designing an analog clock widget that can be displayed on a variety of digital devices. You have to solve the problem of how to convert digital information about time into the corresponding positions of the hands of the clock. How can you use trigonometry to program your clock to display time accurately? It's time to find out!

Are YOU Ready?

Complete these exercises to review skills you will need for this module.

Personal Math Trainer

- Online Homework
- Hints and Help
- Extra Practice

Pythagorean Theorem

Example 1

Two sides of a right triangle measure 3 units and 1.5 units. Find the length of the third side. If possible, find the angle measures.

Use the Pythagorean Theorem $a^2 + b^2 = c^2$ to find the missing length.

The third side is either a leg or a hypotenuse.

If it's a hypotenuse, then it is c in the Pythagorean formula: $(1.5)^2 + 3^2 = c^2$, and $c = \sqrt{(1.5)^2 + 3^2} = \sqrt{2.25 + 9} = \sqrt{11.25} \approx 3.35$. The ratio of the side lengths is 1.5 : 3 : 3.35, so this triangle is not a special right triangle.

If it's a leg, then it is a in the Pythagorean formula: $a^2 + 1.5^2 = 3^2$, and $a = \sqrt{3^2 - 1.5^2} = \sqrt{9 - 2.25} = 1.5\sqrt{3}$. Since the ratio of the sides $1.5 : 1.5\sqrt{3} : 3$ are in the form $a : a\sqrt{3} : 2a$, the triangle is a 30°-60°-90° special right triangle.

Two side lengths of a right triangle are given. Find the possible lengths of the missing side. When the sides form a special right triangle, find the angle measures of the triangle.

1. $4\sqrt{3}, 2\sqrt{3}$

2. 8, 15

3. $3\sqrt{2}, 3$

Distance Formula

Example 2

Find the distance between the points $(7, -1)$ and $(16, 11)$.

$$d = \sqrt{(x_1 - x_2)^2 + (y_1 - y_2)^2} = \sqrt{(7 - 16)^2 + (-1 - 11)^2}$$
$$= \sqrt{81 + 144} = \sqrt{225} = 15$$

The distance is 15.

Find the distance between the given points.

4. $(-4, 20)$ and $(3, -4)$

5. $(8, 9)$ and $(0, -6)$

6. $(2.5, -2)$ and $(-5, 2)$

17.1 Angles of Rotation and Radian Measure

Essential Question: What is the relationship between the unit circle and radian measure?

Resource Locker

Explore 1 Drawing Angles of Rotation and Finding Coterminal Angles

In trigonometry, an **angle of rotation** is an angle formed by the starting and ending positions of a ray that rotates about its endpoint. The angle is in *standard position* in a coordinate plane when the starting position of the ray, or *initial side* of the angle, is on the positive *x*-axis and has its endpoint at the origin. To show the amount and direction of rotation, a curved arrow is drawn to the ending position of the ray, or *terminal side* of the angle.

In geometry, you were accustomed to working with angles having measures between 0° and 180°. In trigonometry, angles can have measures greater than 180° and even less than 0°. To see why, think in terms of revolutions, or complete circular motions. Let θ be an angle of rotation in standard position.

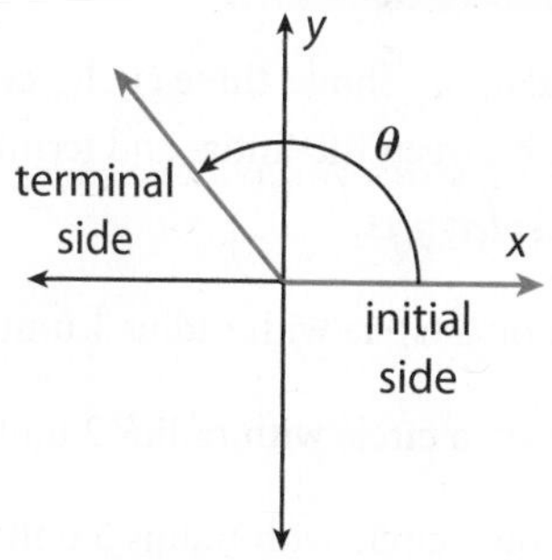

- If the rotation for an angle θ is less than 1 revolution in a counterclockwise direction, then the measure of θ is between 0° and 360°. An angle of rotation measured *clockwise* from standard position has a *negative* angle measure. **Coterminal angles** are angles that share the same terminal side. For example, the angles with measures of 257° and −103° are coterminal, as shown.

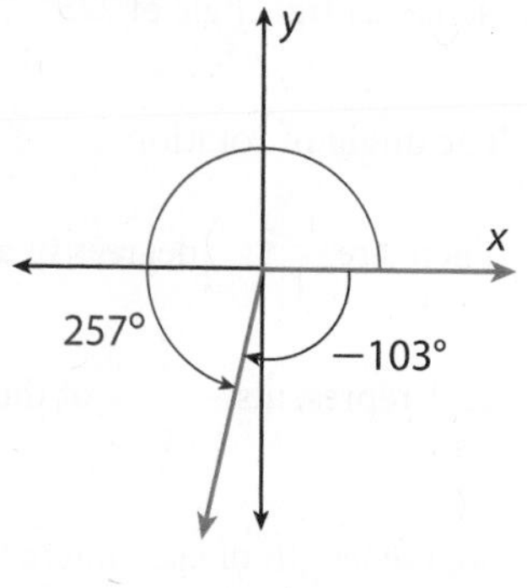

- If the rotation for θ is more than 1 revolution but less than 2 revolutions in a counterclockwise direction, then the measure of θ is between 360° and 720°, as shown. Because you can have any number of revolutions with an angle of rotation, there is a counterclockwise angle of rotation corresponding to any positive real number and a clockwise angle of rotation corresponding to any negative real number.

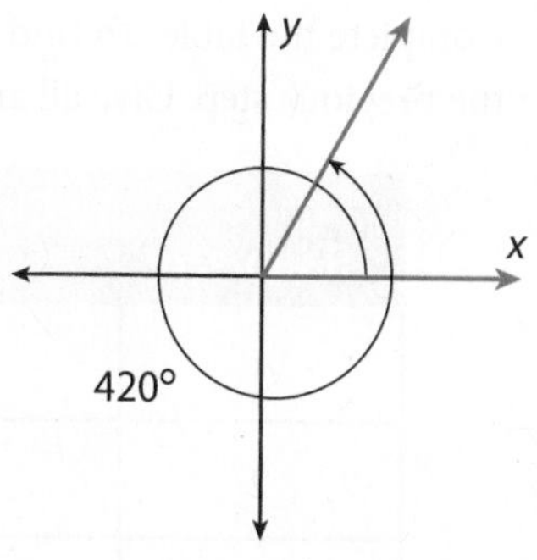

(A) On a pair of coordinate axes, draw an angle of rotation of 310°. In what quadrant is the terminal side of the angle?

(B) On the same graph from the previous step, draw a positive coterminal angle. What is the angle measure of your angle?

(C) On the same graph from the previous two steps, draw a negative coterminal angle. What is the angle measure of your angle?

Reflect

1. Is the measure of an angle of rotation in standard position completely determined by the position of its terminal side? Explain.

2. Find the measure between 720° and 1080° of an angle that is coterminal with an angle that has a measure of −30°. In addition, describe a general method for finding the measure of any angle that is coterminal with a given angle.

Explore 2 Understanding Radian Measure

The diagram shows three circles centered at the origin. The arcs that are on the circle between the initial and terminal sides of the 225° central angle are called *intercepted arcs*.

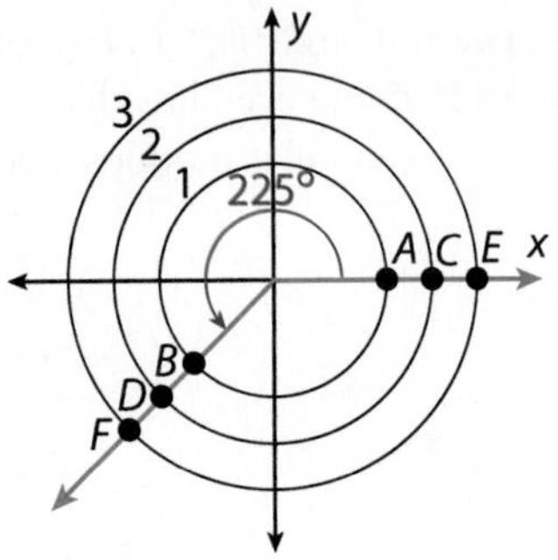

$\overset{\frown}{AB}$ is on a circle with radius 1 unit.

$\overset{\frown}{CD}$ is on a circle with radius 2 units.

$\overset{\frown}{EF}$ is on a circle with radius 3 units.

Notice that the intercepted arcs have different lengths, although they are intercepted by the same central angle of 225°. You will now explore how these arc lengths are related to the angle.

(A) The angle of rotation is ? degrees counterclockwise.

There are ? degrees in a circle.

225° represents $\frac{?}{?}$ of the total number of degrees in a circle.

So, the length of each intercepted arc is $\frac{?}{?}$ of the total circumference of the circle that it lies on.

(B) Complete the table. To find the length of the intercepted arc, use the fraction you found in the previous step. Give all answers in terms of π.

Radius, r	Circumference, C ($C = 2\pi r$)	Length of Intercepted Arc, s	Ratio of Arc Length to Radius, $\frac{s}{r}$
1	?	?	?
2	?	?	?
3	?	?	?

Reflect

3. What do you notice about the ratios $\frac{s}{r}$ in the fourth column of the table?

4. When the ratios of the values of a variable y to the corresponding values of another variable x all equal a constant k, y is said to be *proportional* to x, and the constant k is called the *constant of proportionality.* Because $\frac{y}{x} = k$, you can solve for y to get $y = kx$. In the case of the arcs that are intercepted by a 225° angle, is the arc length s proportional to the radius r? If so, what is the constant of proportionality, and what equation gives s in terms of r?

5. Suppose that the central angle is 270° instead of 225°. Would the arc length s still be proportional to the radius r? If so, would the constant of proportionality still be the same? Explain.

Explain 1 Converting Between Degree Measure and Radian Measure

For a central angle θ that intercepts an arc of length s on a circle with radius r, the **radian measure** of the angle is the ratio $\theta = \frac{s}{r}$. In particular, on a *unit circle*, a circle centered at the origin with a radius of 1 unit, $\theta = s$. So, 1 *radian* is the angle that intercepts an arc of length 1 on a unit circle, as shown.

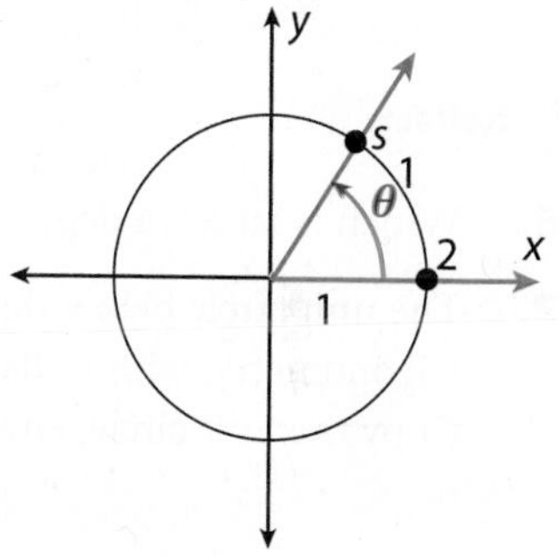

$\theta = 1$ radian

Recall that there are 360° in a full circle. Since the circumference of a circle of radius r is $s = 2\pi r$, the number of radians in a full circle is $\frac{2\pi r}{r} = 2\pi$. Therefore, $360° = 2\pi$ radians. So, $1° = \frac{2\pi}{360} = \frac{\pi}{180}$ radians and 1 radian $= \frac{360}{2\pi} = \frac{180}{\pi}$ degrees. This result is summed up in the following table.

CONVERTING DEGREES TO RADIANS	CONVERTING RADIANS TO DEGREES
Multiply the number of degrees by $\left(\frac{\pi \text{ radians}}{180°}\right)$.	Multiply the number of radians by $\left(\frac{180°}{\pi \text{ radians}}\right)$.

Example 1 **Convert each measure from degrees to radians or from radians to degrees.**

(A)

Degree measure	Radian measure
20°	$\frac{\pi}{180°} \cdot 20° = \frac{\pi}{9}$
315°	$\frac{\pi}{180°} \cdot 315° = \frac{7\pi}{4}$
600°	$\frac{\pi}{180°} \cdot 600° = \frac{10\pi}{3}$
−60°	$\frac{\pi}{180°} \cdot (-60°) = -\frac{\pi}{3}$
−540°	$\frac{\pi}{180°} \cdot (-540°) = -3\pi$

(B)

Radian measure	Degree measure
$\frac{\pi}{8}$	$\frac{180°}{\pi} \cdot \frac{\pi}{8} = 22.5°$
$\frac{4\pi}{3}$	$\frac{180}{\pi} \cdot \frac{4\pi}{3} = 240°$
$\frac{9\pi}{2}$	$\frac{180}{\pi} \cdot \frac{9\pi}{2} = 810°$
$-\frac{7\pi}{12}$	$\frac{180}{\pi} \cdot \left(-\frac{7\pi}{12}\right) = -105°$
$-\frac{13\pi}{6}$	$\frac{180}{\pi} \cdot \left(-\frac{13\pi}{6}\right) = -390°$

Reflect

6. Which is larger, a degree or a radian? Explain.

7. The unit circle below shows the measures of angles of rotation that are commonly used in trigonometry, with radian measures outside the circle and degree measures inside the circle. Copy the unit circle, and provide the missing measures.

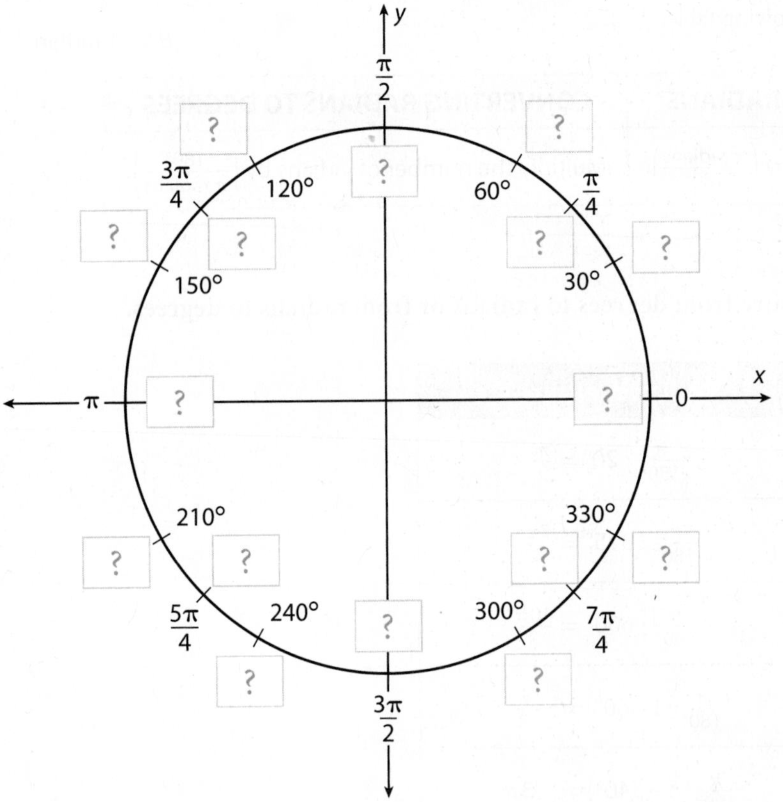

Your Turn

Convert each measure from degrees to radians or from radians to degrees.

8. $-495°$

9. $\frac{13\pi}{12}$

Explain 2 Solving a Real-World Problem Involving Arc Length

As you saw in the first Explain, for a central angle θ in radian measure, $\theta = \frac{s}{r}$ where s is the intercepted arc length. Multiplying both sides of the equation by r gives the arc length formula for a circle:

Arc Length Formula

For a circle of radius r, the arc length s intercepted by a central angle θ (measured in radians) is given by the following formula.

$$s = r\theta$$

Many problems involving arc length also involve *angular velocity*, which is the angle measure through which an object turns in a given time interval. For example, the second hand of a clock has an angular velocity of 360° per minute, or 6° per second. Angular velocity may also be expressed in radians per unit of time. This makes finding the arc length traversed in an amount of time especially easy by using the arc length formula.

(A) **The Sun** A point on the Sun's equator makes a full revolution once every 25.38 days. The Sun has a radius of about 432,200 miles at its equator. What is the angular velocity in radians per hour of a point on the Sun's equator? What distance around the Sun's axis does the point travel in one hour? How does this compare with the distance of about 1038 miles traveled by a point on Earth's equator in an hour?

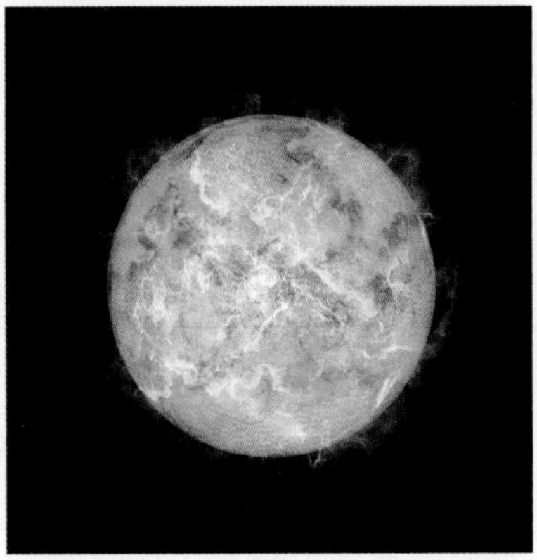

One revolution is 2π radians. The angular velocity in radians per day is $\frac{2\pi}{25.38}$. Convert this to radians per hour.

$$\frac{2\pi \text{ radians}}{25.38 \text{ days}} \cdot \frac{1 \text{ day}}{24 \text{ hours}} = \frac{2\pi \text{ radians}}{25.38(24) \text{ hours}}$$

$$\approx 0.01032 \text{ radians/h}$$

The distance the point travels in an hour is the arc length it traverses in an hour.

$$s = r\theta$$

$$= 432{,}200(0.01032)$$

$$\approx 4460$$

The point travels about 4460 miles around the Sun's axis in an hour. This is more than 4 times farther than a point on Earth's equator travels in the same time.

(B) **The Earth** Earth's equator is at a latitude of 0°. The Arctic circle is at a latitude of 66.52°N. The diameter of the equator is 7926 miles. The diameter of the Arctic circle is 3150 miles.

a. Find the angular velocity in degrees per minute of a point on the equator and of a point on the Arctic circle.

b. How far does a point on the Equator travel in 15 minutes?

c. How long will it take a point on the Arctic circle to travel this distance?

a. Every point on Earth completes 1 revolution of 360 degrees each 24 hours, so the angular velocities of the points will be the same. Convert the angular velocity to degrees per minute.

$$\frac{360^\circ}{24\text{ h}} \cdot \frac{1\text{ h}}{60\text{ min}} = \frac{360^\circ}{24(60)\text{ min}} = 0.25\ ^\circ/\text{min}$$

The angular velocity is 0.25 °/min.

b. Multiply the time by the angular velocity to find the angle through which a point rotates in 15 minutes.

$$15\text{ min} \cdot 0.25^\circ/\text{min} = 3.75^\circ$$

Write a proportion to find the distance to the nearest tenth that this represents at the equator, where Earth's circumference is $\pi \cdot 7926$ miles.

$$\frac{3.75^\circ}{360^\circ} = \frac{x\text{ mi}}{\pi \cdot 7926\text{ mi}}$$

$$x = \frac{3.75\pi(7926)}{360}$$

$$x \approx 259.4$$

A point at the equator travels about 259.4 miles in 15 minutes.

c. Write a proportion to find the angle of rotation to the nearest thousandth required to move a point 259.4 miles on the Arctic circle, where the circumference is $\pi \cdot 3150$ miles.

$$\frac{259.4\text{ mi}}{\pi \cdot 3150\text{ mi}} = \frac{x^\circ}{360^\circ}$$

$$x = \frac{259.4(360)}{3150\pi}$$

$$x \approx 9.437$$

Use the angular velocity to find the time t to the nearest hundredth required for a point on the Arctic circle to move through an angle of rotation of 9.437°.

$$\left(0.25^\circ/\text{min}\right)(t\text{ min}) = 9.437^\circ$$

$$t \approx 37.75$$

It takes about 37.75 minutes for a point on the Arctic circle to travel the same distance that a point on the equator travels in 15 minutes.

Reflect

10. How does using an angle of rotation to find the length of the arc on a circle intercepted by the angle differ when degrees are used from when radians are used?

Your Turn

11. **Astronomy** A neutron star (an incredibly dense collapsed star) in the Sagittarius Galaxy has a radius of 10 miles and completes a full revolution every 0.0014 seconds. Find the angular velocity of the star in radians per second, then use this velocity to determine how far a point on the equator of the star travels each second. How does this compare to the speed of light (about 186,000 mi/sec)?

12. **Geography** The northeastern corner of Maine is due north of the southern tip of South America in Chile. The difference in latitude between the locations is 103°. Using both degree measure and radian measure, and a north-south circumference of Earth of 24,860 miles, find the distance between the two locations.

Elaborate

13. Given the measure of two angles of rotation, how can you determine whether they are coterminal without actually drawing the angles?

14. What is the conversion factor to go from degrees to radians? What is the conversion factor to go from radians to degrees? How are the conversion factors related?

15. **Essential Question Check-In** An angle of rotation in standard position intercepts an arc of length 1 on the unit circle. What is the radian measure of the angle of rotation?

Evaluate: Homework and Practice

Personal Math Trainer

- Online Homework
- Hints and Help
- Extra Practice

Draw the indicated angle of rotation in standard position.

1. A positive angle coterminal to 130°

2. A negative angle coterminal to 130°

For each angle, find the nearest two positive coterminal angles and the nearest two negative coterminal angles.

3. 84°

4. 420°

5. $-\frac{\pi}{3}$

6. $\frac{5\pi}{2}$

Convert each measure from degrees to radians or from radians to degrees.

7. 70°

8. −270°

9. −945°

10. 2160°

11. $\frac{33\pi}{18}$

12. $\frac{11\pi}{4}$

13. $-\frac{5\pi}{3}$

14. $-\frac{7\pi}{2}$

15. **Geography** A student in the United States has an friend overseas with whom she corresponds by computer. The foreign student says, "If you write the latitude and longitude of my school in radians instead of degrees, you get the coordinates 0.6227 radians north latitude and 2.438 radians east longitude". Convert the coordinates back to degrees. Then use a globe, map, or app to identify the city.

16. **Geography** If a ship sailed due south from Iceland to Antarctica, it would sail through an angle of rotation of about 140° around Earth's center. Find this measure in radians. Then, using 3960 miles for Earth's radius, find how far the ship would travel.

17. **Geography** Acapulco, Mexico and Hyderabad, India both lie at 17° north latitude, and lie very nearly halfway around the world from each other in an east-west direction. The radius of Earth at a latitude of 17° is about 3790 miles. Suppose that you could fly from Acapulco directly west to Hyderabad or fly directly north to Hyderabad. Which way would be shorter, and by how much? Use 3960 miles for Earth's radius. (Hint: To fly directly north, you would go from 17° north latitude to 90° north latitude, and then back down to 17° north latitude.)

18. **Planetary Exploration** "Opportunity" and "Phoenix" are two of the robotic explorers on Mars. Opportunity landed at 2° south latitude, where Mars' radius is about 2110 miles. Phoenix landed at 68° north latitude, where Mars' radius is about 790 miles. Mars rotates on its axis once every 24.6 Earth-hours. How far does each explorer travel as Mars rotates by 1 radian? How many hours does it take Mars to rotate 1 radian? Using this answer, how fast is each explorer traveling around Mars' axis in miles per hour?

19. **Earth's Rotation** The 40th parallel of north latitude runs across the United States through Philadelphia, Indianapolis, and Denver. At this latitude, Earth's radius is about 3030 miles. The earth rotates with an angular velocity of $\frac{\pi}{12}$ radians (or 15°) per hour toward the east. If a jet flies due west with the same angular velocity relative to the ground at the equinox, the Sun as viewed from the jet will stop in the sky. How fast in miles per hour would the jet have to travel west at the 40th parallel for this to happen?

20. **Our Galaxy** It is about 30,000 light years from our solar system to the center of the Milky Way Galaxy. The solar system revolves around the center of the Milky Way with an angular velocity of about 2.6×10^{-8} radians per year.

a. What distance does the solar system travel in its orbit each year?

b. Given that a light year is about 5.88×10^{12} miles, how fast is the solar system circling the center of the galaxy in miles per hour?

21. **Driving** A windshield wiper blade turns through an angle of 135°. The bottom of the blade traces an arc with a 9-inch radius. The top of the blade traces an arc with a 23-inch radius. To the nearest inch, how much longer is the top arc than the bottom arc?

22. **Cycling** You are riding your bicycle, which has tires with a 30-inch diameter, at a steady 15 miles per hour. What is the angular velocity of a point on the outside of the tire in radians per second?

23. Select all angles that are coterminal with an angle of rotation of 300°.

A. $-420°$

B. $2100°$

C. $-900°$

D. $-\frac{\pi}{3}$ radians

E. $\frac{23\pi}{3}$ radians

F. $-\frac{7\pi}{3}$ radians

H.O.T. Focus on Higher Order Thinking

24. Explain the Error Lisa was told that a portion of the restaurant on the Space Needle in Seattle rotates at a rate of 8 radians per hour. When asked to find the distance through which she would travel if she sat at a table 40 feet from the center of rotation for a meal lasting 2 hours, she produced the following result:

$\theta = \frac{s}{r}$

$8 = \frac{s}{40}$

$320 = s$ The distance is 320 feet.

25. Represent Real-World Problems The minute hand on a clock has an angular velocity of 2π radians/hour, while the hour hand has an angular velocity of $\frac{\pi}{6}$ radians/hour. At 12:00, the hour and second hands both point straight up. The two hands will next come back together sometime after 1:00. At what exact time will this happen? (Hint: You want to find the next time when the angle of rotation made by the hour hand is coterminal with the angle made by the minute hand after it has first completed one full revolution.)

26. Critical Thinking Write a single rational expression that can be used to represent all angles that are coterminal with an angle of $\frac{5\pi}{8}$ radians.

27. Extension You know that the length s of the arc intercepted on a circle of radius r by an angle of rotation of θ radians is $s = r\theta$. Find an expression for the area of the sector of the circle with radius r that has a central angle of θ radians. Explain your reasoning.

Lesson Performance Task

At a space exploration center, astronauts are training on a human centrifuge that has a diameter of 70 feet.

a. The centrifuge makes 72 complete revolutions in 2 minutes. What is the angular velocity of the centrifuge in radians per second? What distance does an astronaut travel around the center each second?

b. Acceleration is the rate of change of velocity with time. An object moving at a constant velocity v in circular motion with a radius of r has an acceleration a of $a = \frac{v^2}{r}$. What is the astronaut's acceleration? (Note that the acceleration will have units of feet per second *squared*.)

c. One "g" is the acceleration caused on Earth's surface by gravity. This acceleration is what gives you your weight. Some roller coasters can produce an acceleration in a tight loop of 5 or even 6 g's. Earth's gravity produces an acceleration of 32 ft/s^2. How many g's is the astronaut experiencing in the centrifuge?

17.2 Defining and Evaluating the Basic Trigonometric Functions

Essential Question: How does the unit circle allow the trigonometric functions to be defined for all real numbers instead of just for acute angles?

Resource Locker

Explore Using Special Right Triangles in a Unit Circle

In geometry, you learned that sine, cosine, and tangent are ratios of the lengths of the sides of a right triangle. In particular, if θ is an acute angle in a right triangle, then:

$$\sin\theta = \frac{\text{length of the opposite leg}}{\text{length of the hypotenuse}}$$

$$\cos\theta = \frac{\text{length of the adjacent leg}}{\text{length of the hypotenuse}}$$

$$\tan\theta = \frac{\text{length of the opposite leg}}{\text{length of the adjacent leg}}$$

You also studied two sets of special right triangles: those with angles of 45°—45°—90° and those with angles of 30° —60° —90°, and found a general relationship for the lengths of the three sides in each type of triangle:

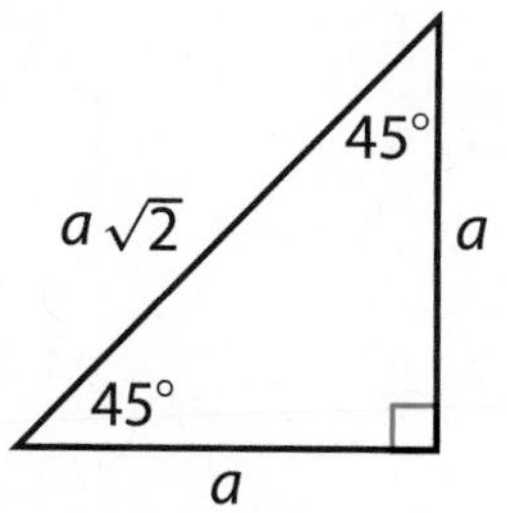

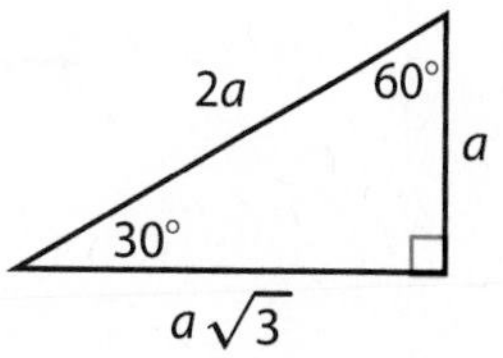

The variable, a, can take any positive value. To see how these triangles and the values of sine, cosine, and tangent for their angles relate to the unit circle, the hypotenuse must have a length of 1. This corresponds to leg lengths of $\frac{\sqrt{2}}{2}$ for the 45° —45° —90° triangle, and leg lengths of $\frac{\sqrt{3}}{2}$ and $\frac{1}{2}$ for the 30° —60° —90° triangle.

(A) A 45° —45° —90° triangle has been inscribed inside a unit circle. Copy the diagram, and use it to complete the following steps.

- Sketch the result of reflecting the triangle across the y-axis.
- Sketch the result of reflecting the triangle across the x-axis.
- Sketch the result of reflecting the triangle across both axes.

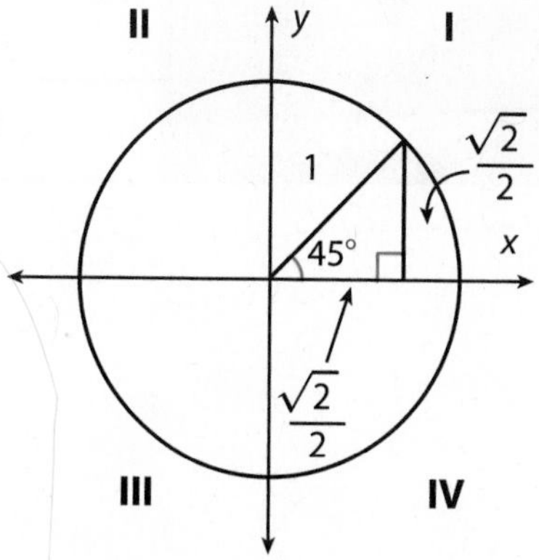

You should have a triangle in each of the four quadrants.

- For each triangle you drew, indicate the *signed* length of each leg. For example, a leg pointing left or down from the x- or y-axis should have a negative value.

Use the signed lengths of the legs and the ratios associated with the trigonometric functions to fill in the table.

	Quadrant I $0° < \theta < 90°$	Quadrant II $90° < \theta < 180°$	Quadrant III $180° < \theta < 270°$	Quadrant IV $270° < \theta < 360°$
Angle of rotation, θ	45°	?	?	?
$\sin \theta$	$\frac{\sqrt{2}}{2}$	?	?	?
$\cos \theta$	$\frac{\sqrt{2}}{2}$	?	?	?
$\tan \theta$	1	?	?	?

(B) Repeat the process from Step A for the 30° —60° —90° triangle that has been inscribed in the unit circle.

- Sketch the three reflected triangles and label the signed lengths of the legs.
- Use the signed lengths of the legs and the ratios associated with the trigonometric functions to fill in the table.

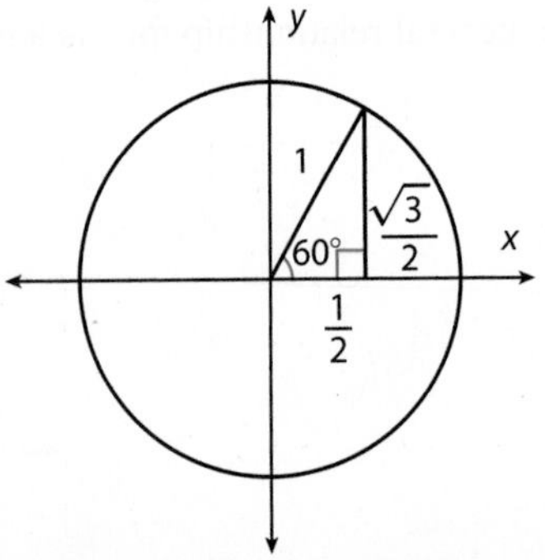

	Quadrant I $0° < \theta < 90°$	Quadrant II $90° < \theta < 180°$	Quadrant III $180° < \theta < 270°$	Quadrant IV $270° < \theta < 360°$
Angle of rotation, θ	60°	?	?	?
$\sin \theta$	$\frac{\sqrt{3}}{2}$	?	?	?
$\cos \theta$	$\frac{1}{2}$	?	?	?
$\tan \theta$	$\sqrt{3}$	?	?	?

(C) Repeat the process for this 30° —60° —90° triangle that has been inscribed in the unit circle.

- Sketch the three reflected triangles and label the signed lengths of the legs.
- Use the signed lengths of the legs and the ratios associated with the trigonometric functions to fill in the table.

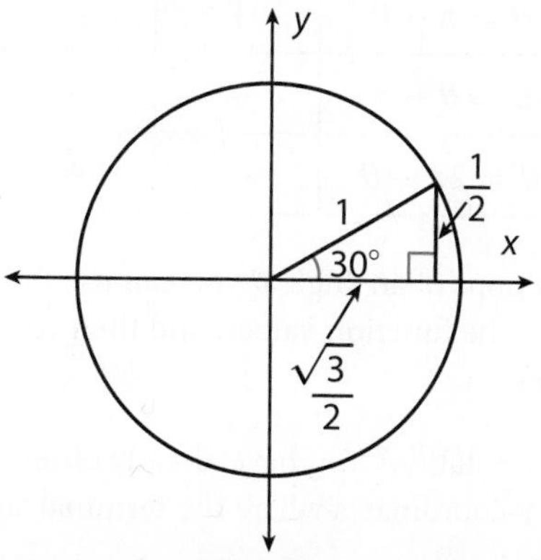

	Quadrant I $0° < \theta < 90°$	Quadrant II $90° < \theta < 180°$	Quadrant III $180° < \theta < 270°$	Quadrant IV $270° < \theta < 360°$
Angle of rotation, θ	30°	?	?	?
$\sin\theta$	$\frac{1}{2}$	?	?	?
$\cos\theta$	$\frac{\sqrt{3}}{2}$	?	?	?
$\tan\theta$	$\frac{\sqrt{3}}{3}$	?	?	?

Reflect

1. What do you observe about the absolute values of the trigonometric functions in any row of each table?

2. Identify which quadrants have positive values for sin θ and which quadrants have negative values. Do the same for cos θ and tan θ.

3. How do the signed lengths of the triangles' legs relate to the point where the triangle intersects the unit circle? Use this to relate the coordinates of the intersection points to the trigonometric functions of the angle θ.

Explain 1 Evaluating the Basic Trigonometric Functions for Special Angles

In the Explore, each of the reflected triangles has an interior angle with its vertex at the center of the circle whose measure is equal to the measure of the corresponding angle of the original triangle. These four angles serve as *reference angles* for the rotation angles listed in the table. This concept can be extended to any rotation angle.

The **reference angle** of a rotation angle is the acute angle from the terminal side of the rotation angle to the x-axis.

For rotation angles that represent less than one full revolution $\left(0° \leq \theta < 360° \text{ or } 0 \leq \theta < 2\pi\right)$ the measure of the reference angle can be found using a quadrant dependent formula. The quadrant also determines the signs of the trigonometric function. The formulas and signs are summarized in the table.

	Reference angle (θ')		Sign		
Quadrant	**Degrees**	**Radians**	**Sin**	**Cos**	**Tan**
I	$\theta' = \theta$	$\theta' = \theta$	+	+	+
II	$\theta' = 180° - \theta$	$\theta' = \pi - \theta$	+	−	−
III	$\theta' = \theta - 180°$	$\theta' = \theta - \pi$	−	−	+
IV	$\theta' = 360° - \theta$	$\theta' = 2\pi - \theta$	−	+	−

To find the values of the trigonometric functions of an angle θ you can use the ratios from the reference angle to find the absolute values of the function values, and then you can use the quadrant to determine the signs of the function values.

What about rotation angles larger than a full rotation? You have already observed that the values of $\cos\theta$ and $\sin\theta$ match the x- and y-coordinates where the terminal side of the angle intersects the circle.

Using this as the definition for sine and cosine, and including the definition of tangent as $\frac{y}{x}$, the trigonometric functions can be extended to any angle. Angles representing multiple revolutions, and negative angles give the same result for any trigonometric function as the coterminal angle between 0° and 360°.

Example 1 **Evaluate the trigonometric function by using the quadrant and the reference angle to determine the sign and absolute value of the function value.**

(A) $\cos\frac{16\pi}{3}$

Identify the coterminal angle between 0 and 2π. $\frac{16}{3}\pi = 4\pi + \frac{4}{3}\pi$

Find the reference angle for Quadrant III. $\theta' = \frac{4}{3}\pi - \pi$

$\theta' = \frac{\pi}{3}$

Identify the special right triangle angle. $\theta' = \frac{\pi}{3} \times \frac{180°}{\pi} = 60°$

Use the sides of a 30° —60° —90° triangle. $\cos\theta' = \frac{1}{2}$

Apply the sign of cosine in Quadrant III. $\cos\frac{16}{3}\pi = -\cos\frac{\pi}{3}$

$= -\frac{1}{2}$

(B) $\tan\frac{11\pi}{4}$

Identify the coterminal angle between 0 and 2π. $\frac{11}{4}\pi = 2\pi + \boxed{\frac{3}{4}\pi}$

Find the reference angle for Quadrant $\boxed{\text{II}}$. $\theta' = \boxed{\pi} - \frac{3}{4}\pi$

$\theta' = \boxed{\frac{\pi}{4}}$

Identify the special right triangle angle. $\theta' = \frac{\pi}{4} \times \boxed{\frac{180°}{\pi}} = 45°$

Use the ratios of the sides of a 45° — 45° — 90° triangle. $\tan\theta' = \boxed{1}$

Apply the sign of tangent in Quadrant II. $\tan\frac{11\pi}{4} = \boxed{-1}$

Reflect

4. Explain how defining sine, cosine, and tangent in terms of x- and y-coordinates instead of in terms of the sides of a right triangle also allows these functions to be evaluated at quadrantal angles.

Your Turn

Evaluate the trigonometric function by using the quadrant and the reference angle to determine the sign and absolute value of the function value.

5. $\sin \frac{5\pi}{6}$

6. $\cos 7\pi$

Explain 2 Evaluating the Basic Trigonometric Functions Using a Calculator

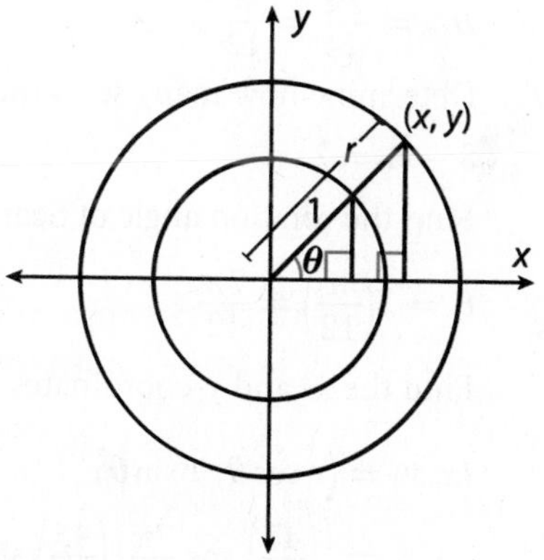

Using coordinates of points on the unit circle to define trigonometric functions, you can see that the sine and cosine functions can be defined for any angle measure. But because the ratio that describes the tangent function has the variable x as its denominator, the tangent function is not defined for any angle for which x is 0. This occurs at angles whose measures are $\cdots, -\frac{3\pi}{2}, -\frac{\pi}{2}, \frac{\pi}{2}, \frac{3\pi}{2}, \frac{5\pi}{2}, \cdots$, or $\left(\frac{2n+1}{2}\right)\pi$ for all integers n. These angle measures are not included in the domain of the tangent function.

Because the values of the sine and cosine functions are coordinates of points on the unit circle, the output of the sine and cosine functions will always range from -1 to 1. The output of the tangent function, however, can be arbitrarily large because the denominator can become arbitrarily small (as long as it does not equal 0).

	Sine	Cosine	Tangent
Domain	$\left\{\theta \mid \theta \in \mathbb{R}\right\}$	$\left\{\theta \mid \theta \in \mathbb{R}\right\}$	$\left\{\theta \mid \theta \neq \frac{(2n+1)\pi}{2}, n \in \mathbb{Z}\right\}$
Range	$\left\{\theta \mid -1 \leq \theta \leq 1\right\}$	$\left\{\theta \mid -1 \leq \theta \leq 1\right\}$	$\left\{\theta \mid \theta \in \mathbb{R}\right\}$

Using trigonometric functions to find coordinates of any point on a circle as a function of an angle is useful for solving real-world applications.

The diagram shows two concentric circles with a single angle inscribed in both. The inner circle is a unit circle, and the outer circle has a radius of r. The two inscribed right triangles are similar —we know this because they have two angles of the same size—, and the coordinates of the outer point can be determined by using the ratios of the sides of similar triangles. The base and height of the inside triangle are $\cos\theta$ and $\sin\theta$ respectively. The ratio of outer and inner widths and outer and inner heights are the same as the ratio of outer and inner hypotenuses, or $\frac{r}{1}$. Thus, the x- and y-coordinates of any point on a circular arc of radius r and angle θ are given by $(r\cos\theta,\ r\sin\theta)$.

The trigonometric ratios can be expanded to the coordinates (x, y) of any point on a circle with radius r centered at the origin:

$$\sin\theta = \frac{y}{r} \qquad \cos\theta = \frac{x}{r} \qquad \tan\theta = \frac{y}{x}, x \neq 0$$

Example 2 **Use trigonometric functions and a calculator to solve the problem.**

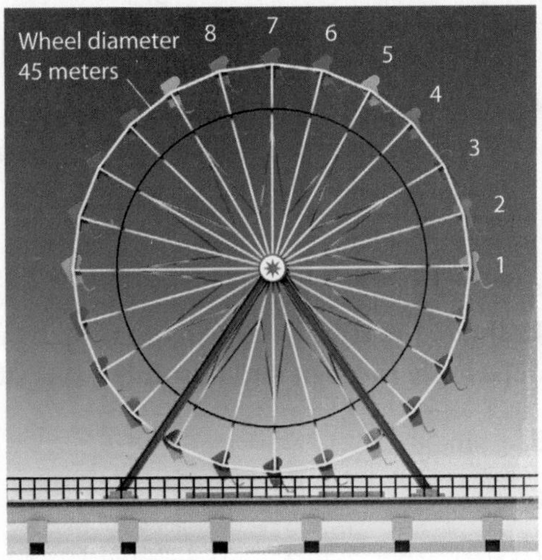

(A) A Ferris wheel with a diameter of 45 meters and 24 seats spread evenly around the outside wheel is stopped in the position shown in the diagram. Using the center of the Ferris wheel as the origin, what are the horizontal and vertical positions of Seat 8? How far above the bottom of the wheel is Seat 8? Solve the problem using radians. Give answers to the nearest tenth of a meter.

First check that your calculator is in radian mode. On a graphing calculator, the units for angle measure can be changed to radians by pressing MODE and selecting radians.

Determine the angle between two adjacent seats.

$\theta_{sep} = \frac{2\pi}{24} = \frac{\pi}{12}$

Determine how many seats there are from Seat 8 to Seat 1.

$8 - 1 = 7$

Find the rotation angle of Seat 8.

$\theta = 7\left(\frac{\pi}{12}\right) = \frac{7\pi}{12}$

Find the x- and y-coordinates.

$$\begin{aligned}(x, y) &= (r\cos\theta,\ r\sin\theta)\\ &= \left(\left(\frac{45}{2}\right)\cos\frac{7\pi}{12},\ \left(\frac{45}{2}\right)\sin\frac{7\pi}{12}\right)\\ &\approx (-5.8, 21.7)\end{aligned}$$

Seat 8 is about 5.8 meters to the left and 21.7 meters above the center of the wheel. The center is 22.5 meters above the bottom of the wheel, so Seat 8 is stopped 44.2 meters above the bottom of the wheel.

(B) An airplane begins to descend toward a runway 1 mile away at an angle of −5° to the horizontal. What is its change in elevation after it flies 5000 feet horizontally towards the runway?

First check that your calculator is in degree mode. On a graphing calculator, the units for angle measure can be changed to degrees by pressing MODE and selecting degrees.

Using the beginning of the descent as the origin, the horizontal distance traveled by the plane should be treated as the x-coordinate. The change in elevation is the y-coordinate.

$\tan \theta = \frac{y}{x}$

$\tan\left(-5°\right) = \frac{y}{5000}$

$5000 \tan(-5°) = y$

$y \approx -437.4$

The elevation drops by about 437.4 feet.

Reflect

7. How could you describe the position of Seat 8 in Example A with a negative angle measure?

Your Turn

8. How long a shadow does a 40-foot tall tree cast on the ground if the sun is at an angle of 0.5 radians relative to the horizon? Use a calculator to solve the problem.

Elaborate

9. Explain the meaning of the message "ERR:DOMAIN" if you try to evaluate $\tan\frac{\pi}{2}$ on a graphing calculator. Why do you get this error message?

10. Explain why it is helpful to find coterminal and reference angles when evaluating trigonometric functions of large positive and negative angles without a calculator.

11. **Essential Question Check-In** Explain how to define the sine and cosine of an angle in terms of a coordinate on the unit circle.

Evaluate: Homework and Practice

Personal Math Trainer

- Online Homework
- Hints and Help
- Extra Practice

1. A right triangle with an angle of approximately 53.1° is inscribed in the first quadrant of the unit circle, with a horizontal length of $\frac{3}{5}$ and a vertical length of $\frac{4}{5}$.

Complete the table for the following trigonometric functions.

Angle of rotation, θ	53.1	126.9	233.1	306.9
$\sin\theta$	?	?	?	?
$\cos\theta$	?	?	?	?
$\tan\theta$	?	?	?	?

Evaluate the trigonometric function without using a calculator. Angles are given in degrees.

2. $\cos 135°$

3. $\tan(-30°)$

4. $\sin 480°$

5. $\cos 720°$

Evaluate the trigonometric function without using a calculator. Angles are given in radians.

6. $\cos \frac{7\pi}{4}$

7. $\sin\left(-\frac{\pi}{2}\right)$

8. $\tan\left(-\frac{10\pi}{3}\right)$

9. $\tan \frac{16\pi}{3}$

Use a calculator to evaluate the trigonometric function of the angle given in degrees.

10. $\sin 132°$

11. $\cos(-203°)$

12. $\tan 43°$

13. $\cos 547°$

Use a calculator to evaluate the trigonometric function of the angle given in radians.

14. $\sin\left(\frac{5}{8}\pi\right)$

15. $\cos(1.2\pi)$

16. $\tan(10.5)$

17. $\sin(-3.7)$

Find a value or an expression for the coordinate on a circle centered at (0, 0) and at an angle θ from the *x*-axis.

18. radius $= 10$, $\theta = 135°$, *x*-coordinate

19. radius $= 5$, $\theta = 2.7$ radians, *y*-coordinate

20. radius $= r$, $\theta = \frac{17\pi}{4}$ radians , *x*-coordinate

21. radius $= 0.5$, $\theta = 2\phi$, *y*-coordinate

Use trigonometric functions to solve the real-world problems.

22. A swing hangs from a beam 10 feet high, with the seat hanging 2 feet above the ground. In motion, the swing moves back and forth from $-130°$ to $-50°$ to the horizontal. How far forward and back does the swing move along the ground at the extremes?

23. The Americans with Disabilities Act sets the maximum angle for a wheelchair ramp entering a business at 4.76°. Determine the horizontal distance needed to accommodate a ramp that goes up to a door 4 feet off the ground.

24. Jennifer is riding on a merry-go-round at a carnival that revolves at a speed of 3.3 revolutions per minute. She is sitting 7 feet from the center of the merry-go-round. If Jennifer's starting position is considered to be at 0 radians, what are her *x*- and *y*-coordinates after 57 seconds?

25. A car is traveling on a road that goes up a hill. The hill has an angle of 17° relative to horizontal. How high up the hill vertically will the car be after it has traveled 100 yards up the road?

26. Classify $f(\theta)$ of these trigonometric functions as less than, greater than, or equal to zero.

A. $f(\theta) = \sin\theta$, θ is in quadrant III

B. $f(\theta) = \tan\theta$, θ is in quadrant II

C. $f(\theta) = \cos\theta$, θ is in quadrant IV

D. $f(\theta) = \cos\theta$, $\theta = 180°$

E. $f(\theta) = \tan\theta$, $\theta = 540°$

F. $f(\theta) = \tan\theta$, θ in quadrant I

H.O.T. Focus on Higher Order Thinking

27. Explain the Error Sven used his calculator to find $\sin 10°$ and got an answer of approximately -0.5440, which seems wrong given that 10° is in the first quadrant. What did Sven do wrong? What is the correct answer?

28. Look for a Pattern Use the reference triangles and your calculator to make an observation about the rate of change of $\tan\theta$ over the interval 0 to 2π. Where does the rate of change increase? Where does it decrease? Are there any intervals where $\tan\theta$ is a decreasing function? Explain.

29. Analyze Relationships Use the unit circle and quadrant locations to prove that $\cos(-\theta) = \cos\theta$ for any angle, θ.

Lesson Performance Task

In Italy, there is a large circular test track that is used to test race cars and other high-speed automobiles.

a. Suppose a similar track has a radius of 6 kilometers. Find the circumference of the track.

b. While test-driving a new car on the similar track, a driver starts at the right-hand side of the circular track, travels in a counter-clockwise direction, and stops $\frac{3}{5}$ of the way around the track. Using the center of the track as the origin and the starting point as the intersection of the x-axis and the circle represented by the track, find the coordinates, to the nearest tenth, of the point where the driver stopped the car.

c. The driver continues in the same direction, but stops again approximately at the point $(5.2, 3.0)$. What is the car's position on the track relative to its starting point? Had the car made more or less than 1 revolution around the track when it stopped the second time? Explain.

d. If the car drove once around the track in 6 minutes and 48 seconds, what is its average velocity? Give your answer to the nearest tenth of a kilometer per hour.

17.3 Using a Pythagorean Identity

Essential Question: How can you use a given value of one of the trigonometric functions to calculate the values of the other functions?

Resource Locker

Explore Proving a Pythagorean Identity

In the previous lesson, you learned that the coordinates of any point (x, y) that lies on the unit circle where the terminal ray of an angle θ intersects the circle are $x = \cos\theta$ and $y = \sin\theta$, and that $\tan\theta = \frac{y}{x}$. Combining these facts gives the identity $\tan\theta = \frac{\sin\theta}{\cos\theta}$, which is true for all values of θ where $\cos\theta \neq 0$. In the following Explore, you will derive another identity based on the Pythagorean theorem, which is why the identity is known as a *Pythagorean identity.*

(A) The terminal side of an angle θ intersects the unit circle at the point (a, b) as shown. Write a and b in terms of trigonometric functions involving θ.

$a =$?

$b =$?

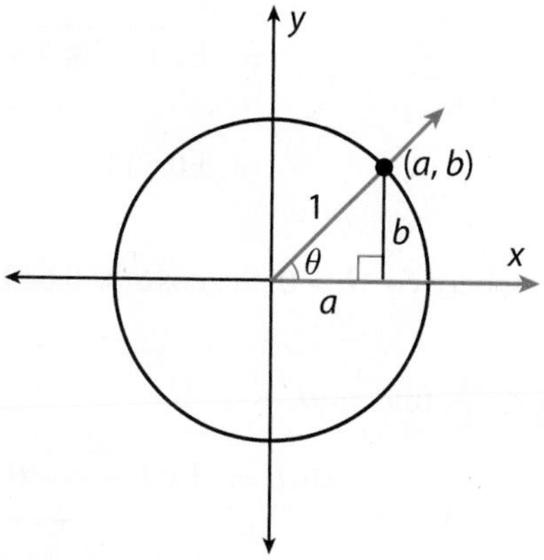

(B) Apply the Pythagorean theorem to the right triangle in the diagram. Note that when a trigonometric function is squared, the exponent is typically written immediately after the name of the function. For instance, $(\sin\theta)^2 = \sin^2\theta$.

Write the Pythagorean Theorem. $a^2 + b^2 = c^2$

Substitute for a, b, and c. $(?)^2 + (?)^2 = ?^2$

Square each expression. $? + ? = ?$

Reflect

1. The identity is typically written with the sine function first. Write the identity this way, and explain why it is equivalent to the one in Step B.

2. Confirm the Pythagorean identity for $\theta = \frac{\pi}{3}$.

3. Confirm the Pythagorean identity for $\theta = \frac{3\pi}{4}$.

Explain 1 Finding the Value of the Other Trigonometric Functions Given the Value of sin θ or cos θ

You can rewrite the identity $\sin^2\theta + \cos^2\theta = 1$ to express one trigonometric function in terms of the other. As shown, each alternate version of the identity involves both positive and negative square roots. You can determine which sign to use based on knowing the quadrant in which the terminal side of θ lies.

Solve for sin θ	Solve for cos θ
$\sin^2\theta + \cos^2\theta = 1$	$\sin^2\theta + \cos^2\theta = 1$
$\sin^2\theta = 1 - \cos^2\theta$	$\cos^2\theta = 1 - \cos^2\theta$
$\sin\theta = \pm\sqrt{1 - \cos^2\theta}$	$\cos\theta = \pm\sqrt{1 - \sin^2\theta}$

Example 1 **Find the approximate value of each trigonometric function.**

(A) Given that $\sin\theta = 0.766$ where $0 < \theta < \frac{\pi}{2}$, find $\cos\theta$.

Use the identity to solve for $\cos\theta$. $\cos\theta = \pm\sqrt{1 - \sin^2\theta}$

Substitute for $\sin\theta$. $= \pm\sqrt{1 - (0.766)^2}$

Use a calculator, then round. $\approx \pm 0.643$

The terminal side of θ lies in Quadrant I, where $\cos\theta > 0$. So, $\cos\theta \approx 0.643$.

(B) Given that $\cos\theta = -0.906$ where $\pi < \theta < \frac{3\pi}{2}$, find $\sin\theta$.

Use the identity to solve for $\sin\theta$. $\sin\theta = \pm\sqrt{1 - \cos^2\theta}$

Substitute for $\cos\theta$. $= \pm\sqrt{1 - \left(-0.906\right)^2}$

Use a calculator, then round. $\approx \pm$ 0.423

The terminal side of θ lies in Quadrant III, where $\sin\theta$ < 0. So, $\sin\theta \approx$ −0.423.

Reflect

4. Suppose that $\frac{\pi}{2} < \theta < \pi$ instead of $0 < \theta < \frac{\pi}{2}$ in part A of this Example. How does this affect the value of $\sin\theta$?

5. Suppose that $\frac{3\pi}{2} < \theta < 2\pi$ instead of $\pi < \theta < \frac{3\pi}{2}$ in part B of this Example. How does this affect the value of $\sin\theta$?

6. Explain how you would use the results of part A of this Example to determine the approximate value for $\tan\theta$. Then find it.

Your Turn

7. Given that $\sin\theta = -0.644$ where $\pi < \theta < \frac{3\pi}{2}$, find $\cos\theta$.

8. Given that $\cos\theta = -0.994$ where $\frac{\pi}{2} < \theta < \pi$, find $\sin\theta$. Then find $\tan\theta$.

Explain 2 Finding the Value of Other Trigonometric Functions Given the Value of tanθ

If you multiply both sides of the identity $\tan\theta = \frac{\sin\theta}{\cos\theta}$ by $\cos\theta$, you get the identity $\cos\theta\tan\theta = \sin\theta$, or $\sin\theta = \cos\theta\tan\theta$. Also, if you divide both sides of $\sin\theta = \cos\theta\tan\theta$ by $\tan\theta$, you get the identity $\cos\theta = \frac{\sin\theta}{\tan\theta}$. You can use the first of these identities to find the sine and cosine of an angle when you know the tangent.

Example 2 **Find the approximate value of each trigonometric function.**

(A) Given that $\tan\theta \approx -2.327$ where $\frac{\pi}{2} < \theta < \pi$, find the values of $\sin\theta$ and $\cos\theta$.

First, write $\sin\theta$ in terms of $\cos\theta$.

Use the identity $\sin\theta = \cos\theta\tan\theta$. $\quad \sin\theta = \cos\theta\tan\theta$

Substitute the value of $\tan\theta$. $\quad \approx -2.327\cos\theta$

Now use the Pythagorean Identity to find $\cos\theta$. Then find $\sin\theta$.

Use the Pythagorean Identity. $\quad \sin^2\theta + \cos^2\theta = 1$

Substitute for $\sin\theta$. $\quad (-2.327\cos\theta)^2 + \cos^2\theta \approx 1$

Square. $\quad 5.415\cos^2\theta + \cos^2\theta \approx 1$

Combine like terms. $\quad 6.415\cos^2\theta \approx 1$

Solve for $\cos^2\theta$. $\quad \cos^2\theta \approx 0.156$

Solve for $\cos\theta$. $\quad \cos\theta \approx \pm 0.395$

The terminal side of θ lies in Quadrant II, where $\cos\theta < 0$. Therefore, $\cos\theta \approx -0.395$ and $\sin\theta \approx -2.327\cos\theta \approx 0.919$.

(B) Given that $\tan\theta \approx -4.366$ where $\frac{3\pi}{2} < \theta < 2\pi$, find the values of $\sin\theta$ and $\cos\theta$.

First, write $\sin\theta$ in terms of $\cos\theta$.

Use the identity $\sin\theta = \cos\theta\tan\theta$. $\quad \sin\theta = \cos\theta\tan\theta$

Substitute the value of $\tan\theta$. $\quad \approx \boxed{-4.366}\cos\theta$

Now use the Pythagorean Identity to find $\cos\theta$. Then find $\sin\theta$.

Use the Pythagorean Identity. $\quad \sin^2\theta + \cos^2\theta = 1$

Substitute for $\sin\theta$. $\quad \left(\boxed{-4.366}\cos\theta\right)^2 + \cos^2\theta \approx 1$

Square. $\quad \boxed{19.062}\cos^2\theta + \cos^2\theta \approx 1$

Combine like terms. $\quad \boxed{20.062}\cos^2\theta \approx 1$

Solve for $\cos^2\theta$. $\quad \cos^2\theta \approx \boxed{0.050}$

Solve for $\cos\theta$. $\cos\theta \approx$ 0.223

The terminal side of θ lies in Quadrant IV, where $\cos\theta > 0$. Therefore, $\cos\theta \approx$ 0.223

and $\sin\theta \approx$ −4.366 $\cos\theta \approx$ −0.974.

Reflect

9. In part A of this Example, when you multiplied the given value of $\tan\theta$ by the calculated value of $\cos\theta$ in order to find the value of $\sin\theta$, was the product positive or negative? Explain why this is the result you would expect.

10. If $\tan\theta = 1$ where $0 < \theta < \frac{\pi}{2}$, show that you can solve for $\sin\theta$ and $\cos\theta$ exactly using the Pythagorean identity. Why is this so?

Your Turn

11. Given that $\tan\theta \approx 3.454$ where $\pi < \theta < \frac{3\pi}{2}$, find the values of $\sin\theta$ and $\cos\theta$.

Elaborate

12. What conclusions can you draw if you are given only the information that $\tan\theta = -1$?

13. **Discussion** Explain in what way the process of finding the sine and cosine of an angle from the tangent ratio is similar to the process of solving a linear equation in two variables by substitution.

14. **Essential Question Check-In** If you know only the sine or cosine of an angle and the quadrant in which the angle terminates, how can you find the other trigonometric ratios?

Evaluate: Homework and Practice

Personal Math Trainer

- Online Homework
- Hints and Help
- Extra Practice

Find the approximate value of each trigonometric function.

1. Given that $\sin\theta = 0.515$ where $0 < \theta < \frac{\pi}{2}$, find $\cos\theta$.

2. Given that $\cos\theta = 0.198$ where $\frac{3\pi}{2} < \theta < 2\pi$, find $\sin\theta$.

3. Given that $\sin\theta = -0.447$ where $\frac{3\pi}{2} < \theta < 2\pi$, find $\cos\theta$.

4. Given that $\cos\theta = -0.544$ where $\frac{\pi}{2} < \theta < 2\pi$, find $\sin\theta$.

5. Given that $\sin\theta = -0.908$ where $\pi < \theta < \frac{3\pi}{2}$, find $\cos\theta$.

6. Given that $\sin\theta = 0.313$ where $\frac{\pi}{2} < \theta < \pi$, find $\cos\theta$.

7. Given that $\cos\theta = 0.678$ where $0 < \theta < \frac{\pi}{2}$, find $\sin\theta$.

8. Given that $\cos\theta = -0.489$ where $\pi < \theta < \frac{3\pi}{2}$, find $\sin\theta$.

Find the approximate value of each trigonometric function.

9. Given that $\tan\theta \approx -3.966$ where $\frac{\pi}{2} < \theta < \pi$, find the values of $\sin\theta$ and $\cos\theta$.

10. Given that $\tan\theta \approx -4.580$ where $\frac{3\pi}{2} < \theta < 2\pi$, find the values of $\sin\theta$ and $\cos\theta$.

11. Given that $\tan\theta \approx 7.549$ where $0 < \theta < \frac{\pi}{2}$, find the values of $\sin\theta$ and $\cos\theta$.

12. Given that $\tan\theta \approx 4.575$ where $\pi < \theta < \frac{3\pi}{2}$, find the values of $\sin\theta$ and $\cos\theta$.

13. Given that $\tan\theta \approx -1.237$ where $\frac{3\pi}{2}, < \theta < 2\pi$ find the values of $\sin\theta$ and $\cos\theta$.

14. Given that $\tan\theta \approx 5.632$ where $\pi < \theta < \frac{3\pi}{2}$, find the values of $\sin\theta$ and $\cos\theta$.

15. Given that $\tan\theta \approx 6.653$ where $0 < \theta < \frac{\pi}{2}$, find the values of $\sin\theta$ and $\cos\theta$.

16. Given that $\tan\theta \approx -9.366$ where $\frac{\pi}{2}, < \theta < \pi$ find the values of $\sin\theta$ and $\cos\theta$.

17. Given the trigonometric function and the location of the terminal side of the angle, state whether the function value will be positive or negative.

A. $\cos\theta$, Quadrant I

B. $\sin\theta$, Quadrant IV

C. $\tan\theta$, Quadrant II

D. $\sin\theta$, Quadrant III

E. $\tan\theta$, Quadrant III

18. Confirm the Pythagorean identity $\sin^2\theta + \cos^2\theta = 1$ for $\theta = \frac{7\pi}{4}$.

19. Recall that the equation of a circle with radius r centered at the origin is $x^2 + y^2 = r^2$. Use this fact and the fact that the coordinates of a point on this circle are $(x, y) = (r\cos\theta, r\sin\theta)$ for a central angle θ to show that the Pythagorean identity derived above is true.

20. Sports A ski supply company is testing the friction of a new ski wax by placing a waxed block on an inclined plane covered with wet snow. The inclined plane is slowly raised until the block begins to slide. At the instant the block starts to slide, the component of the weight of the block parallel to the incline, $mg\sin\theta$, and the resistive force of friction, $\mu mg\cos\theta$, are equal, where μ is the coefficient of friction. Find the value of μ to the nearest hundredth if $\sin\theta = 0.139$ at the instant the block begins to slide.

21. Driving Tires and roads are designed so that the coefficient of friction between the rubber of the tires and the asphalt of the roads is very high, which gives plenty of traction for starting, stopping, and turning. For a particular road surface and tire, the steepest angle for which a car could rest on the slope without starting to slide has a sine of 0.643. This value satisfies the equation $mg\sin\theta = \mu mg\cos\theta$ where μ is the coefficient of friction. Find the value of μ to the nearest hundredth.

H.O.T. Focus on Higher Order Thinking

22. Explain the Error Julian was given that $\sin\theta = -0.555$ where $\frac{3\pi}{2} < \theta < 2\pi$ and told to find $\cos\theta$. He produced the following work:

$$\cos\theta = \pm\sqrt{1 - \sin^2\theta}$$
$$= \pm\sqrt{1 - (-0.555^2)}$$
$$\approx \pm 1.144$$

Since $\cos\theta > 0$ when $\frac{3\pi}{2} < \theta < 2\pi$, $\cos\theta \approx 1.144$.

Explain his error and state the correct answer.

Critical Thinking **Rewrite each trigonometric expression in terms of $\cos\theta$ and simplify.**

23. $\dfrac{\sin^2\theta}{1 - \cos\theta}$

24. $\cos\theta + \sin\theta\cos\theta - \tan\theta + \tan\theta\sin^2\theta$ (Hint: Begin by factoring $\tan\theta$ from the last two terms.)

25. Critical Thinking To what trigonometric function does the expression $\dfrac{\sqrt{1 - \cos^2\theta}}{\sqrt{1 - \sin^2\theta}}$ simplify? Explain your answer.

Lesson Performance Task

A tower casts a shadow that is 160 feet long at a particular time one morning. With the base of the tower as the origin, east as the positive x-axis, and north as the positive y-axis, the shadow at this time is in the northwest quadrant formed by the axes. Also at this time, the tangent of the angle of rotation measured so that the shadow lies on the terminal ray is $\tan\theta = -2.545$. What are the coordinates of the tip of the shadow to the nearest foot, and what do they indicate?

Unit-Circle Definition of Trigonometric Functions

Essential Question: How can the unit-circle definition of trigonometric functions help to solve real-world problems?

Key Vocabulary
angle of rotation
(ángulo de rotación)
coterminal angles
(ángulos coterminales)
radian measure
(medida del radián)
reference angle
(ángulo de referencia)

KEY EXAMPLE *(Lesson 17.1)*

A laboratory centrifuge with a diameter of 12 inches makes approximately 10,000 revolutions in 3 minutes. How long will it take for a test tube in the centrifuge to travel 360,000 degrees? How far will the test tube travel in inches?

$3 \text{ min} \cdot \dfrac{60 \text{ sec}}{1 \text{ min}} = 180 \text{ s}$ Convert minutes to seconds

$\dfrac{360°(10{,}000)}{180 \text{ sec}} = 20{,}000°/\text{s}$ Find the angular velocity in terms of degrees/s.

$\dfrac{360{,}000°}{\dfrac{20{,}000°}{1 \text{ sec}}} = 18 \text{ s}$ Divide the number of degrees by the velocity.

$360{,}000 \cdot \dfrac{\pi}{180} = 20{,}000\pi$ Convert degrees to radians.

$s = r\theta = 6 \cdot 2000\pi \approx 37{,}700$ Use the formula for the arc length to find the distance.

The test tube travels 360,000 degrees in 18 seconds, and travels approximately 37,700 inches.

KEY EXAMPLE *(Lesson 17.2)*

Evaluate the trigonometric function $\cos \frac{13\pi}{3}$ by using the quadrant and the reference angle to determine the sign and absolute value.

$\dfrac{13\pi}{3} = 4\pi + \dfrac{\pi}{3}$ Identify the coterminal angle between 0 and 2π.

$\theta' = \dfrac{\pi}{3}$ Find the reference angle for quadrant I.

$\theta' = \dfrac{\pi}{3} \times \dfrac{180°}{\pi} = 60°$ Identify the special right triangle angle.

$\cos\theta' = \dfrac{1}{2}$ Use the sides of a 30°-60°-90° triangle.

$\cos \dfrac{13\pi}{3} = +\cos \dfrac{\pi}{3}$ Apply the sign of cosine in quadrant I.

$\cos \dfrac{13\pi}{3} = \dfrac{1}{2}$

EXERCISES

A merry-go-round with the given radius turns through the given angle. How far, in feet, will a child on the edge of the merry-go-round travel? *(Lesson 17.1)*

1. 4 feet; 270°

2. 6 feet; 310°

3. 2 feet; 720°

4. 3 feet; 90°

A child is riding a carousel at an amusement park. How long will it take for the child to travel through the given angle at the given angular velocity? *(Lesson 17.1)*

5. 3 rev/min; 270°

6. 5 rev/min; 310°

Evaluate the trigonometric function by using the quadrant and the reference angle to determine the sign and absolute value. *(Lesson 17.2)*

7. $\sin \frac{13\pi}{4}$

8. $\tan \frac{4\pi}{3}$

MODULE PERFORMANCE TASK

Telling Time with Trig

An analog clock displays time on a computer screen. It is based on a unit circle, so the programmer can use cosine and sine to specify the positions of the ends of the hands. Draw a clock face and label each of the hour marks with its coordinates. What are the coordinates of each hand at 4:30?

Start by listing the information you will need to solve the problem. Then complete the task. Be sure to write down all your data and assumptions. Then use graphs, numbers, words, or algebra to explain how you reached your conclusion.

Ready to Go On?

17.1–17.3 Unit-Circle Definition of Trigonometric Functions

Personal Math Trainer

- Online Homework
- Hints and Help
- Extra Practice

A coin has a radius of 10 mm. How long will it take the coin to roll through the given angle measure at the given angular velocity? How far will it travel in that time?

1. 180°; 5 rev/s

2. 360°; 7 rev/s

3. 540°; 6 rev/s

4. 1800°; 4 rev/s

Evaluate the trigonometric function by using the quadrant and the reference angle to determine the sign and absolute value.

5. $\cos \frac{17\pi}{4}$

6. sin 410°

Find the approximate value of each trigonometric function.

7. Given $\sin \theta = 0.996$; find $\cos \theta$

8. Given $\cos \theta = 0.342$; find $\sin \theta$

ESSENTIAL QUESTION

9. How does using radian measure simplify finding distances around a circle compared to using degree measure?

MODULE 17
MIXED REVIEW

Assessment Readiness

1. Consider the radian measure $\frac{16\pi}{5}$. Tell whether each statement is correct.

   A. $\cos \frac{16\pi}{5} \approx -0.809$

   B. $\tan \frac{16\pi}{5} \approx 0.727$

   C. $\sin \frac{16\pi}{5} \approx 0.588$

2. Consider a situation where a colored ring is 10 inches in diameter. Determine if each statement is True or False.

   A. If the ring is rolling at a rate of 2 revolutions per second, it will take approximately 0.17 second to travel 120°.

   B. The angular velocity is needed to find the distance the ring will travel in rotating through 1080°.

   C. The radius is needed to find how long it will take the ring to rotate through 1080°.

3. Carlos wants to find the value of $\cos \theta$ given $\sin \theta = 0.707$, and he finds that $\cos \theta$ is the same value. Is this possible, or did he make a mistake? Explain.

4. Given the equation $y = x(x - 3)(2x + 7)$, find the rational roots. Explain how you determined your answer.

MODULE 18

Graphing Trigonometric Functions

Essential Question: How can graphing trigonometric functions help to solve real-world problems?

REAL WORLD VIDEO
Check out how data about periodic phenomena such as tides and phases of the moon can be represented by a sine function.

MODULE PERFORMANCE TASK PREVIEW

What's Your Sine?

The moon is visible only because we see the sun's light reflecting from the moon's surface. Depending on where the moon is in its orbit around Earth, we see no moon, a full moon, or any fraction of the moon's surface in between. How can we use a sine function to figure out what fraction of the moon's surface will be lit on any given night? Let's find out!

Are YOU Ready?

Complete these exercises to review skills you will need for this module.

Personal Math Trainer

- Online Homework
- Hints and Help
- Extra Practice

Stretching, Compressing, and Reflecting Quadratic Functions

Example 1 The graph of $g(x) = -2(x + 9)^2 - 4$ is vertically compressed by a factor of 0.5 and reflected over the y-axis. Write the new function.

Vertical compression:

$g'(x) = 0.5\left(-2(x + 9)^2 - 4\right) = -(x + 9)^2 - 2$

Reflection over the y—axis: $g''(x) = -(-x + 9)^2 - 2$

The new function is $g''(x) = -(-x + 9)^2 - 2$.

Write the new function for $f(x) = (x + 1)^2 - 2$ after the given transformation.

1. reflection over x—axis

2. horizontal compression, factor of 10

3. vertical stretch, factor of 2

Combining Transformations of Quadratic Functions

Example 2 The graph of $f(x) = -2(x + 5)^2 + 1$ is transformed 3 units right and 2 units down. Write the new function.

The vertex is $(-5, 1)$. Its location after the transformation is $(-5 + 3, 1 - 2)$, or $(-2, -1)$.

The new function is $f'(x) = -2(x + 2)^2 - 1$.

Write the new function after the given transformation.

4. $p(x) = 0.1(x - 8)^2 + 9$
5 units left, 6 units down

5. $q(x) = -0.5(x + 2)^2 - 12$
1 unit right, 9 units up

6. $h(x) = 0.8(x - 8)^2 - 10$
7 units left, 4 units up

18.1 Stretching, Compressing, and Reflecting Sine and Cosine Graphs

Resource Locker

Essential Question: What are the key features of the graphs of the sine and cosine functions?

Explore 1 Graphing the Basic Sine and Cosine Functions

Recall that the points around the unit circle have coordinates $(\cos \theta, \sin \theta)$ as shown.

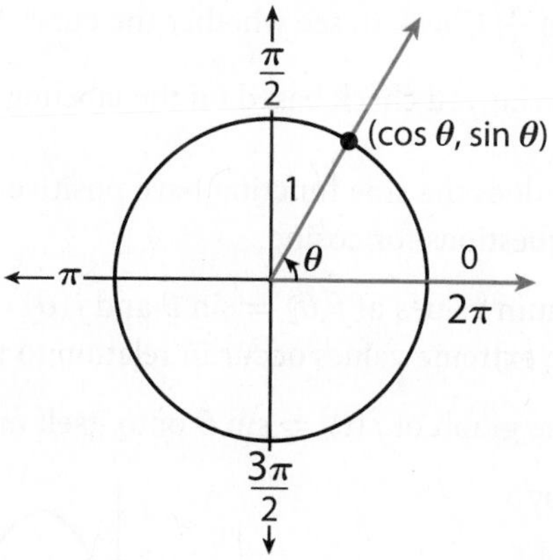

(A) Identify the following points on the graph of the sine function on the interval $[0, 2\pi]$.

A. the three points where x-intercepts occur

B. the point of maximum value

C. the point of minimum value

(B) Complete the table of values. On coordinate axes labeled as shown, plot the points from the table, and draw a smooth curve through them.

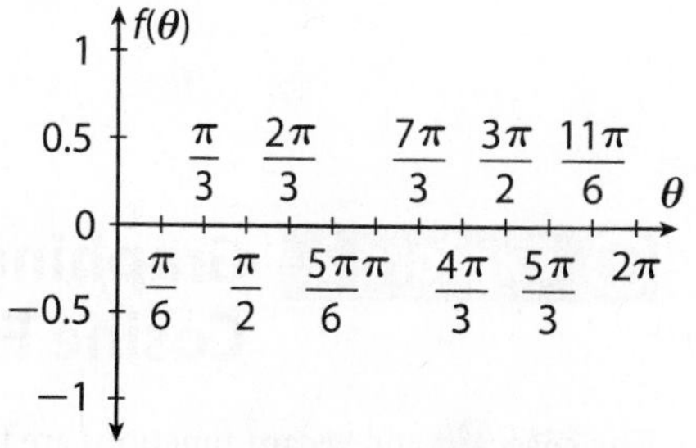

θ	0	$\frac{\pi}{6}$	$\frac{\pi}{2}$	$\frac{5\pi}{6}$	π	$\frac{7\pi}{6}$	$\frac{3\pi}{2}$	$\frac{11\pi}{6}$	2π
$f(\theta) = \sin \theta$	?	?	?	?	?	?	?	?	?

(C) Identify the following points on the graph of the cosine function on the interval $[0, 2\pi]$.

A. the two points where x-intercepts occur

B. the two points of maximum value

C. the point of minimum value

(D) Complete the table of values. On coordinate axes labeled as in part B, plot the points from the table, and draw a smooth curve through them.

θ	0	$\frac{\pi}{3}$	$\frac{\pi}{2}$	$\frac{2\pi}{3}$	π	$\frac{4\pi}{3}$	$\frac{3\pi}{2}$	$\frac{5\pi}{3}$	2π
$f(\theta) = \cos\theta$	?	?	?	?	?	?	?	?	?

Reflect

1. Give a decimal approximation of $\sin\frac{\pi}{3}$. Check to see whether the curve that you drew passes through the point $\left(\frac{\pi}{3}, \sin\frac{\pi}{3}\right)$. What other points can you check based on the labeling of the θ–axis?

2. On the interval $0 \leq \theta \leq 2\pi$, where does the sine function have positive values? Where does it have negative values? Answer the same questions for cosine.

3. What are the minimum and maximum values of $f(\theta) = \sin\theta$ and $f(\theta) = \cos\theta$ on the interval $0 \leq \theta \leq 2\pi$? Where do the extreme values occur in relation to the θ–intercepts?

4. Describe a rotation that will map the graph of $f(\theta) = \sin\theta$ onto itself on the interval $0 \leq \theta \leq 2\pi$.

5. Recall that coterminal angles differ by a multiple of 2π and have the same sine value and the same cosine value. This means that the graphs of sine and cosine on the interval $0 \leq \theta \leq 2\pi$ represent one *cycle* of the complete graphs and that the cycles repeat every 2π radians. Use this fact to sketch graphs of $f(\theta) = \sin\theta$ and $f(\theta) = \cos\theta$ that extend to the left and right by an additional 1 cycle.

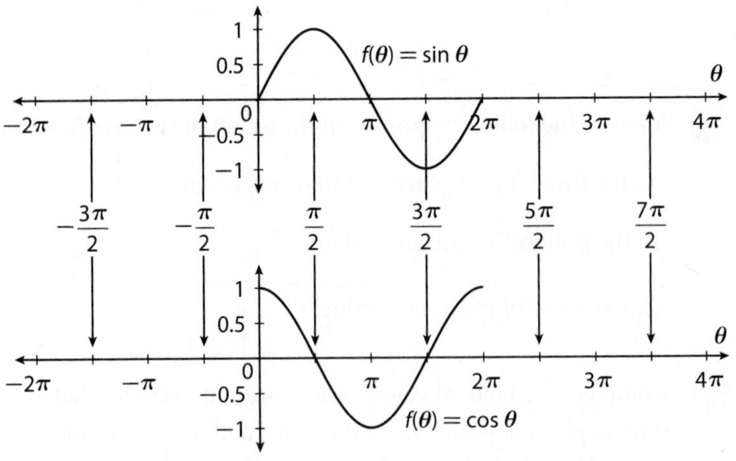

Explore 2 Graphing the Reciprocals of the Basic Sine and Cosine Functions

The **cosecant** and **secant** functions are the reciprocals of the sine and cosine functions, respectively.

$$\csc\theta = \frac{1}{\sin\theta} \qquad \sec\theta = \frac{1}{\cos\theta}$$

(A) Complete the table of values. Note that whenever $\sin \theta = 0$, $\csc \theta$ is undefined.

θ	0	$\frac{\pi}{6}$	$\frac{\pi}{2}$	$\frac{5\pi}{6}$	π	$\frac{7\pi}{6}$	$\frac{3\pi}{2}$	$\frac{11\pi}{6}$	2π
$f(\theta) = \sin \theta$	0	0.5	1	0.5	0	−0.5	−1	−0.5	0
$f(\theta) = \csc \theta$	?	?	?	?	?	?	?	?	?

(B) Complete each of the following statements.

A. As $\theta \to 0^+$, $\sin \theta \to$? and $\csc \theta \to$? .

B. As $\theta \to 0^-$, $\sin \theta \to$? and $\csc \theta \to$? .

What does this behavior tell you about the graph of the cosecant function? ?

(C) Copy the graph of the sine function. On the same axes, sketch the graph of $f(\theta) = \csc \theta$ over the interval $[0, 2\pi]$. Then, extend the graph to the left and right until the entire coordinate plane is filled.

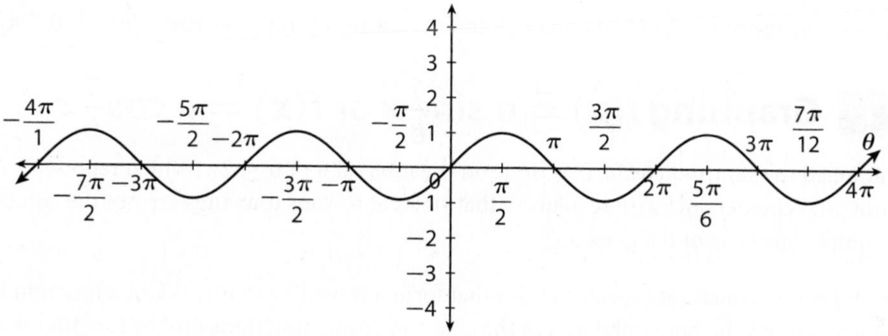

(D) Complete the table of values. Note that whenever $\cos \theta = 0$, $\sec \theta$ is undefined.

θ	0	$\frac{\pi}{3}$	$\frac{\pi}{2}$	$\frac{2\pi}{3}$	π	$\frac{4\pi}{3}$	$\frac{3\pi}{2}$	$\frac{5\pi}{3}$	2π
$f(\theta) = \cos \theta$	1	0.5	0	−0.5	−1	−0.5	0	0.5	1
$f(\theta) = \sec \theta$	?	?	?	?	?	?	?	?	?

(E) Complete each of the following statements.

A. As $\theta \to \frac{\pi}{2}^+$, $\cos \theta \to$? and $\sec \theta \to$? .

B. As $\theta \to \frac{\pi}{2}^-$, $\cos \theta \to$? and $\sec \theta \to$? .

What does this behavior tell you about the graph of the cosecant function? ?

Ⓕ Copy the graph of the cosine function. On the same axes, sketch the graph of $f(\theta) = \sec\theta$ over the interval $[0, 2\pi]$. Then, extend the graph to the left and right until the entire coordinate plane is filled.

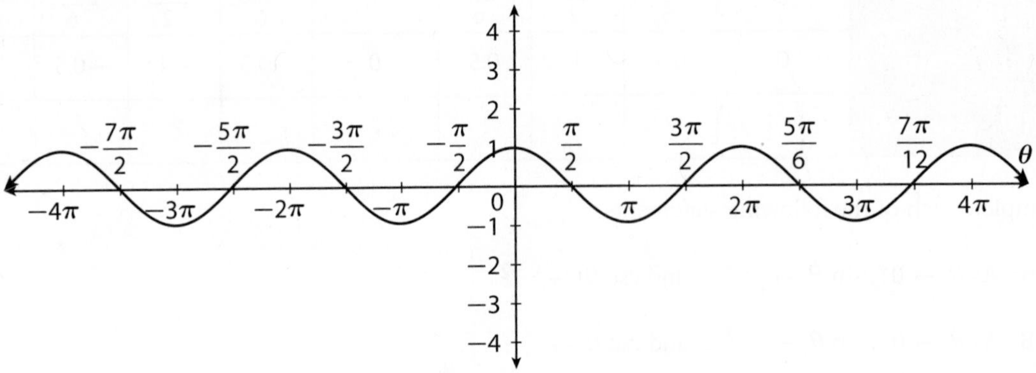

Reflect

6. How do the domain, range, maximum values, and minimum values compare between the sine and cosine functions and their reciprocals?

7. Describe the vertical asymptotes of the cosecant and secant functions over the interval $[0, 2\pi]$.

Explain 1 Graphing $f(x) = a \sin\frac{1}{b}x$ or $f(x) = a \cos\frac{1}{b}x$

In Explore 1, you graphed the sine and cosine functions on the interval $0 \leq \theta \leq 2\pi$, which represents all of the angles of rotation within the first counterclockwise revolution that starts at 0. Your drawings are not the complete graphs, however. They are simply one *cycle* of the graphs.

The graphs of sine and cosine consist of repeated cycles that form a wave-like shape. When a function repeats its values over regular intervals on the horizontal axis as the sine and cosine functions do, the function is called **periodic**, and the length of the interval is called the function's **period**. In Explore 1, you saw that the basic sine and cosine functions each have a period of 2π.

The wave-like shape of the sine and cosine functions has a "crest" (where the function's maximum value occurs) and a "trough" (where the function's minimum value occurs). Halfway between the "crest" and the "trough" is the graph's **midline**. The distance that the "crest" rises above the midline or the distance that the "trough" falls below the midline is called the graph's **amplitude**. In Explore 1, you saw that the basic sine and cosine functions each have an amplitude of 1.

Note that for trigonometric functions, the angle θ is the independent variable, and the output $f(\theta)$ is the dependent variable. You can graph these functions on the familiar xy-coordinate plane by letting x represent the angle and y represent the value of the function.

Example 1 **For each trigonometric function, identify the vertical stretch or compression and the horizontal stretch or compression. Then, graph the function and identify its period.**

Ⓐ $y = 3 \sin 2x$

The equation has the general form $y = a \sin\frac{1}{b}x$. The value of a is 3. Since $\frac{1}{b} = 2$, the value of b is $\frac{1}{2}$. So, the graph of the parent sine function must be vertically stretched by a factor of 3 and horizontally compressed by a factor of $\frac{1}{2}$.

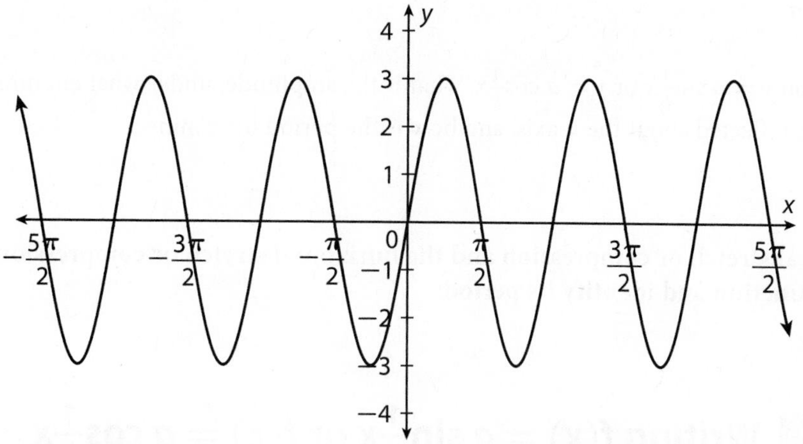

Horizontally stretching or compressing the parent function's graph by a factor of $|b|$ changes the period of the function. Since the parent function has a period of 2π, multiply 2π by $|b|$ to obtain the period of the transformed function.

Period: $2\pi \cdot |b| = 2\pi \cdot \frac{1}{2} = \pi$

(B) $y = -3 \cos \frac{x}{2}$

The equation has the general form $y = a \cos \frac{1}{b} x$. The value of a is -3. Since $\frac{1}{b} = \boxed{\frac{1}{2}}$, the value of b is 2.

So, the graph of the parent function must be vertically stretched by a factor of 3 and horizontally stretched by a factor of 2.

Graph the function. Note that since a is negative, the graph will be reflected across the x-axis.

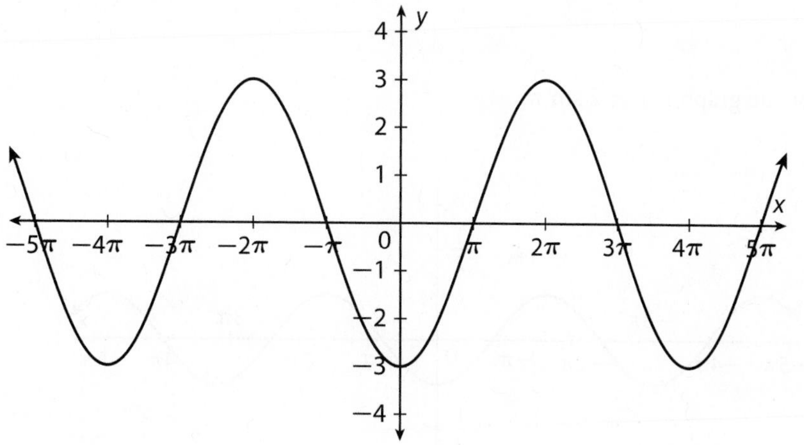

Find the function's period.

$2\pi \cdot |b| = 2\pi \cdot \boxed{2} = \boxed{4\pi}$

Reflect

8. For the function $y = a \sin\frac{1}{b}x$ or $y = a \cos\frac{1}{b}x$, what is the amplitude, under what circumstances is the graph of the function reflected about the x-axis, and how is the period determined?

Your Turn

Identify the vertical stretch or compression and the horizontal stretch or compression. Then, graph the function and identify its period.

9. $y = \frac{1}{2} \sin 4x$

Explain 2 Writing $f(x) = a \sin\frac{1}{b}x$ or $f(x) = a \cos\frac{1}{b}x$

You can write the equation of a trigonometric function if you are given its graph.

Example 2 **Write an equation for each graph.**

(A) Because the graph's y-intercept is 0, the graph is a sine function.

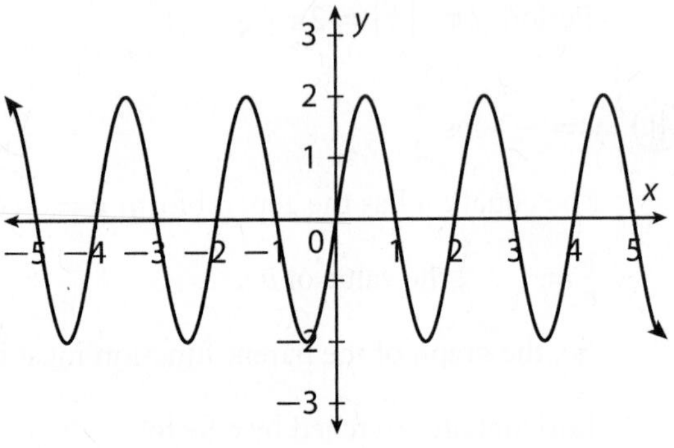

Since the maximum and minimum values are 2 and −2, respectively, the graph is a vertical stretch of the parent sine function by a factor of 2. So, $a = 2$.

The period of the function is 2.

Use the equation $2\pi b = 2$ to find a positive value for $\frac{1}{b}$.

.

$$2\pi b = 2$$

$$b = \frac{2}{2\pi} = \frac{1}{\pi}$$

$$\frac{1}{b} = \pi$$

An equation for the graph is $y = 2 \sin \pi x$.

(B)

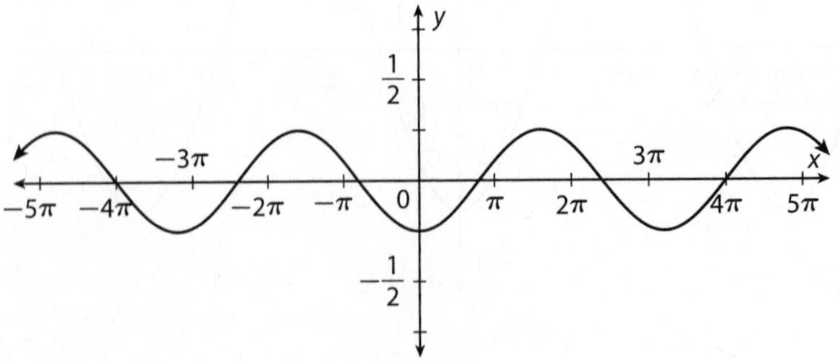

Because the graph's y-intercept is negative, the graph is a cosine function reflected across the x-axis.

Since the maximum and minimum in the graph are $\boxed{\frac{1}{4}}$ and $\boxed{-\frac{1}{4}}$, respectively, the graph will be a vertical compression of the graph of the parent cosine function by a factor of $\boxed{\frac{1}{4}}$.

The period of the function is $\boxed{10}$.

Use the equation $2\pi b = \boxed{10}$ to find a positive value for $\frac{1}{b}$.

$2\pi b = \boxed{10}$

$b = \frac{\boxed{10}}{2\pi} = \frac{\boxed{5}}{\pi}$

$\frac{1}{b} = \frac{\pi}{\boxed{5}}$

An equation for the graph is $y = \boxed{-\frac{1}{4}} \cos \boxed{\frac{\pi}{5}} x$.

Your Turn

Write an equation for the graph.

10.

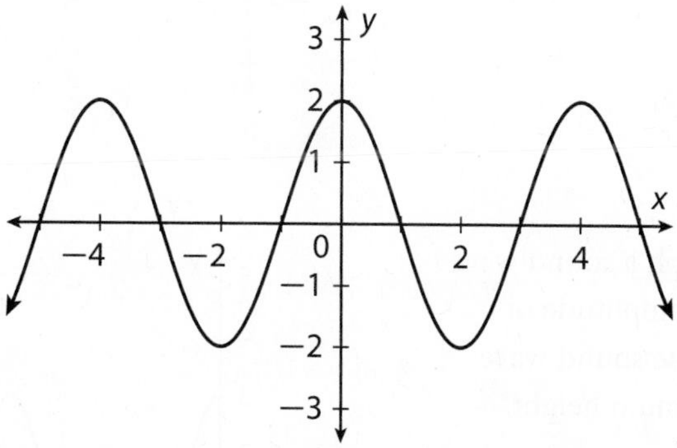

Explain 3 Modeling with Sine or Cosine Functions

Sine and cosine functions can be used to model real-world phenomena, such as sound waves. Different sounds create different waves. One way to distinguish sounds is to measure *frequency*. **Frequency** is the number of cycles in a given unit of time, so it is the reciprocal of the period of a function.

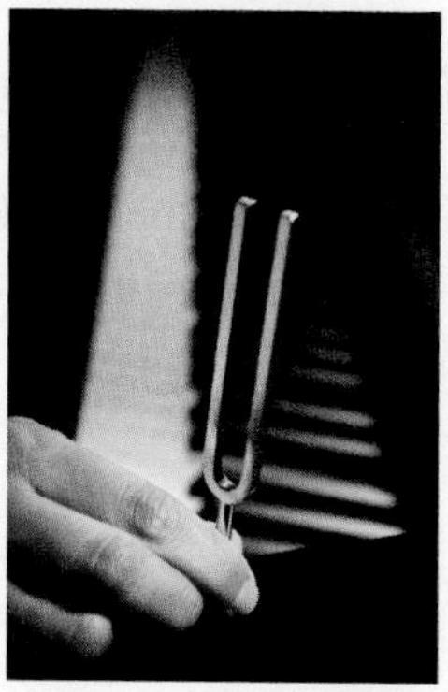

Hertz (Hz) is the standard measure of frequency and represents one cycle per second. For example, the sound wave made by a tuning fork for middle A has a frequency of 440 Hz. This means that the wave repeats 440 times in 1 second.

As a tuning fork vibrates, it creates fluctuations in air pressure. The maximum change in air pressure, typically measured in pascals, is the sound wave's amplitude.

Example 3 **Graph each function, and then find its frequency. What do the frequency, amplitude, and period represent in the context of the problem?**

Ⓐ **Physics** Use a sine function to graph a sound wave with a period of 0.004 second and an amplitude of 4 pascals.

Graph the function.

$$\text{frequency} = \frac{1}{\text{period}} = \frac{1}{0.004} = 250 \text{ Hz}$$

The frequency represents the number of cycles of the sound wave every second. The amplitude represents the maximum change in air pressure. The period represents the amount of time it takes for the sound wave to repeat.

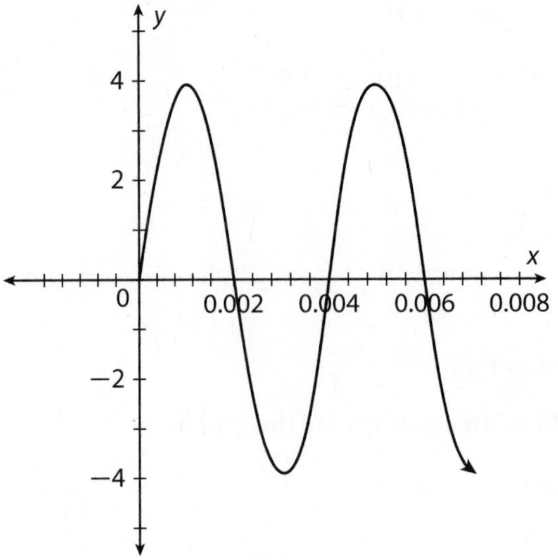

Ⓑ **Physics** Use a cosine function to graph a sound wave with a period of 0.010 second and an amplitude of 3 pascals. Note that the recording of the sound wave started when the wave was at its maximum height.

Graph the function.

$$\text{frequency} = \frac{1}{\text{period}} = \frac{1}{\boxed{0.010}} = \boxed{100} \text{ Hz}$$

The frequency represents the number cycles of the sound wave every second. The amplitude represents the maximum change in air pressure. The period represents the amount of time it takes for the sound wave to repeat.

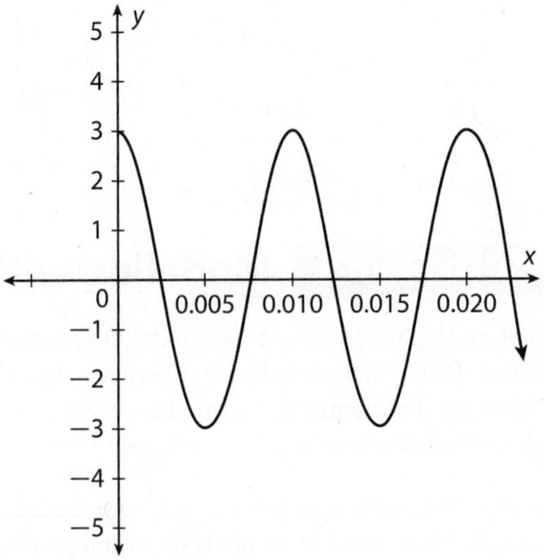

Your Turn

Graph the function, and then find its frequency. What do the frequency, amplitude, and period represent in the context of the problem?

11. A pendulum makes one back-and-forth swing every 1.5 seconds. Its horizontal displacement relative to its position at rest is measured in inches. Starting when the pendulum is 5 inches (its maximum displacement) to the right of its position at rest, use a cosine function to graph the pendulum's horizontal displacement over time.

Elaborate

12. The graphs of sine and cosine are periodic functions. Refer to angles of rotation and the unit circle to explain why this is so.

13. Referring to angles of rotation and the unit circle, explain why $\sin(-\theta) = -\sin \theta$, and why $\cos(-\theta) = \cos \theta$. Use the graphs of $\sin \theta$ and $\cos \theta$ for reference.

14. How does the unit circle explain why the 2 in $y = \sin 2x$ results in a horizontal compression of the graph of $y = \sin x$?

15. **Essential Question Check-In** What is one key difference between the graphs of the sine and cosine functions?

Evaluate: Homework and Practice

Personal Math Trainer
- Online Homework
- Hints and Help
- Extra Practice

For each trigonometric function, identify the vertical stretch or compression and the horizontal stretch or compression. Then, graph the function and identify its period.

1. $y = 4 \sin x$

2. $y = \frac{1}{2} \cos 2x$

3. $y = -3 \sin \frac{1}{6}x$

4. $y = -2 \cos \frac{1}{3}x$

5. $y = \frac{1}{3} \sin 2x$

6. $y = -\frac{1}{4} \cos 3x$

Write an equation for each graph.

7.

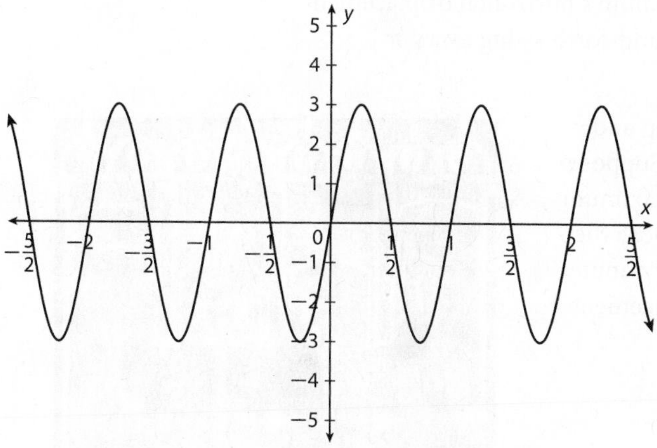

8.

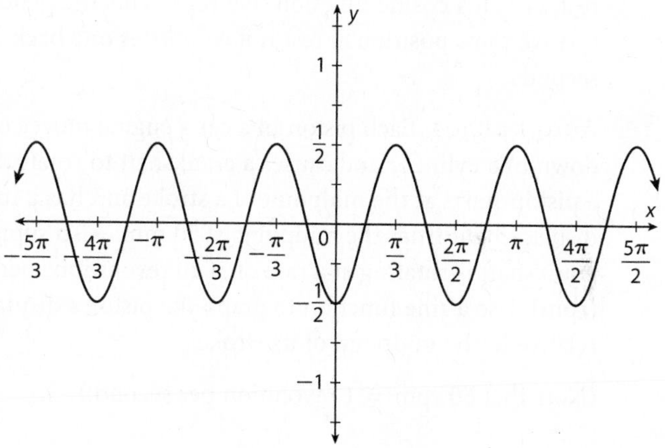

9.

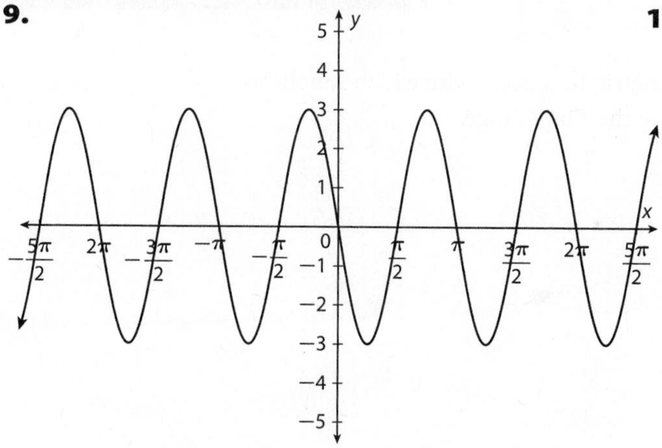

10.

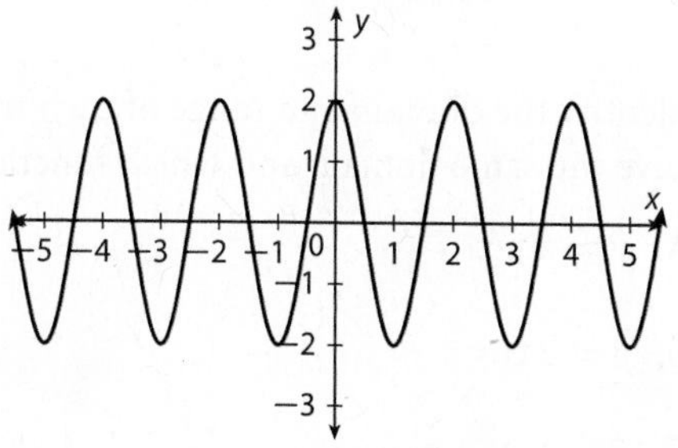

11.

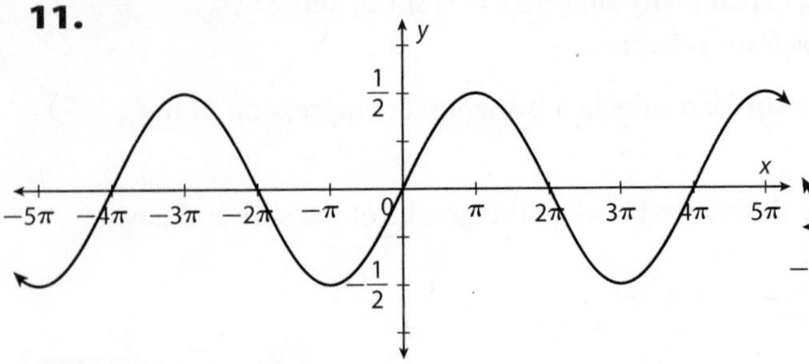

12.

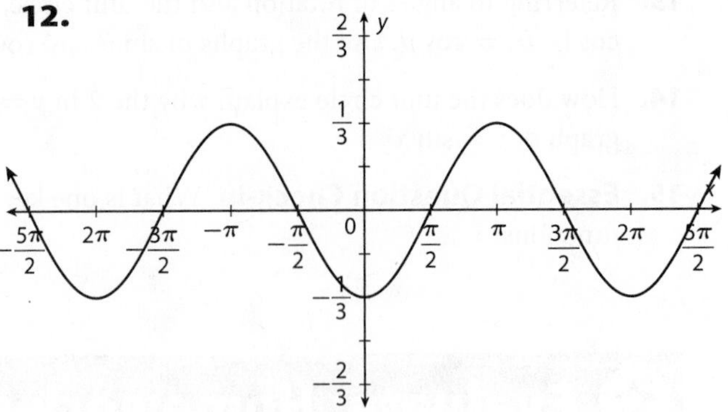

Graph each function, and then find its frequency. What do the frequency, amplitude, and period represent in the context of the problem?

13. **Physics** Use a sine function to graph a sound wave with a period of 0.003 second and an amplitude of 2 pascals.

14. **Physics** A mass attached to a spring oscillates up and down every 2 seconds. Draw a graph of the vertical displacement of the mass relative to its position at rest if the spring is stretched to a length of 15 cm before the mass is released.

15. **Physics** A pendulum is released at a point 5 meters to the right of its position at rest. Graph a cosine function that represents the pendulum's horizontal displacement relative to its position at rest if it completes one back-and-forth swing every π seconds.

16. **Automobiles** Each piston in a car's engine moves up and down in a cylinder and causes a crankshaft to rotate. Suppose a piston starts at the midpoint of a stroke and has a maximum displacement from the midpoint of 50 mm. Also suppose the crankshaft is rotating at a rate of 3000 revolutions per minute (rpm). Use a sine function to graph the piston's displacement relative to the midpoint of its stroke.

(Note that 60 rpm = 1 revolution per second.)

17. Identify the domain and range of each trigonometric function. State which functions have the same domain and which functions have the same range.

A. $y = \sin x$

B. $y = 2\cos x$

C. $y = -3\sin \frac{1}{2}x$

D. $y = -\frac{4}{5}\sin \pi x$

E. $y = 2\sin \frac{x}{4}$

18. Use Explore 1 for reference. State how the basic sine and cosine functions are similar and how they are different. How are the graphs of the functions geometrically related?

19. Describe the graphs of the cosecant and secant functions. Note any asymptotes, x-intercepts, and maximum or minimum values.

20. Compare the two sine functions in terms of their periods.

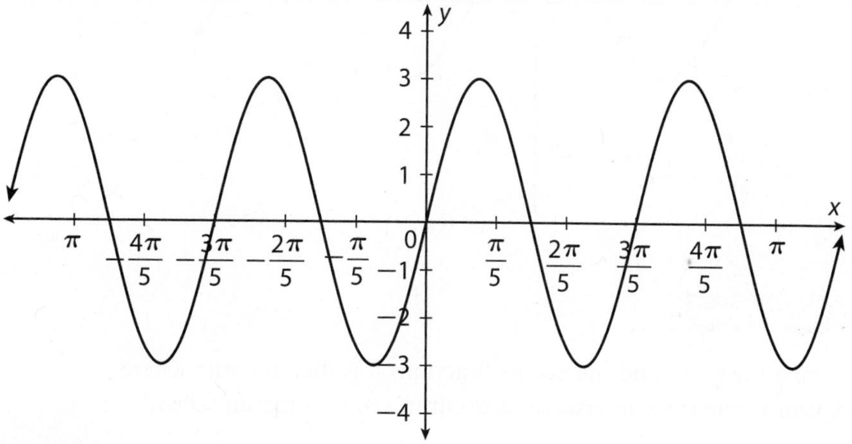

θ	0	$\frac{\pi}{6}$	$\frac{\pi}{2}$	$\frac{5\pi}{6}$	π	$\frac{7\pi}{6}$	$\frac{3\pi}{2}$	$\frac{11\pi}{6}$	2π
$f(\theta)$	0	1	2	1	0	−1	−2	−1	0

Sketch the graph of a cosecant or secant function, as appropriate, using the provided graph of a sine or cosine function as a reference. Be sure to include asymptotes.

21.

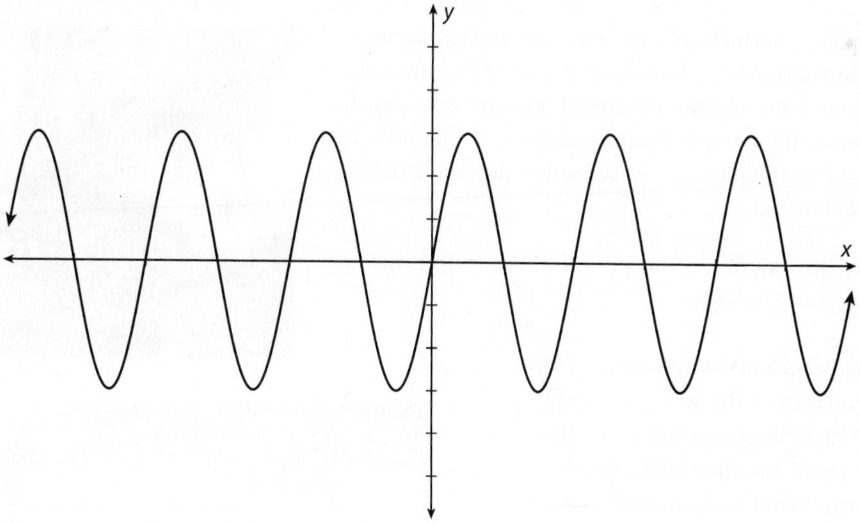

22.

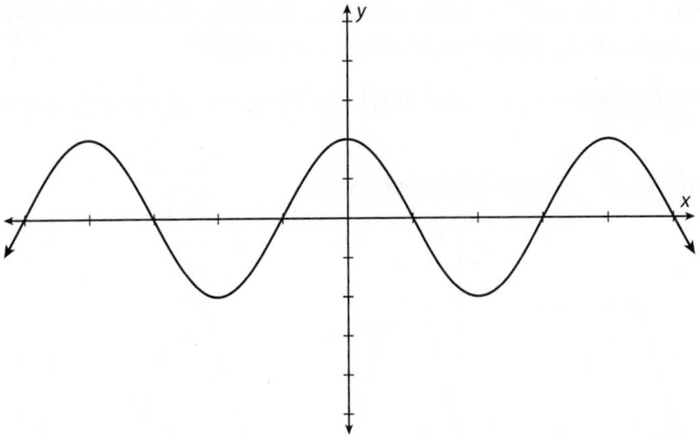

H.O.T. Focus on Higher Order Thinking

23. Critical Thinking Graph the basic sine and cosine functions together. Identify where $\sin\theta = \cos\theta$, and explain where these intersections occur in terms of the unit circle.

24. Explain the Error When instructed to write the equation of a sine function with a vertical stretch of 2 and a horizontal compression of $\frac{1}{2}$, Charles produced the answer $y = 2\sin\frac{1}{2}x$. Explain his error, and state the correct answer.

25. Critical Thinking State the domain and range of the secant function on the interval $[0, 2\pi]$. Explain how the domain and range indicate that the graph of the secant function has vertical asymptotes.

Lesson Performance Task

A vuvuzela is a plastic horn about 2 feet long and is used during soccer matches in South Africa. If the sound level of the vuvuzela is 120 decibels from 1 meter away, the sound pressure is 20 pascals. A function of the sound pressure P in pascals from the sound wave of a vuvuzela as a function of time t in seconds is approximately $P(t) = 20\sin(1464.612t)$.

a. Identify the amplitude and period of the sound wave. Explain your findings.

b. Use the period of the function to find the frequency of the sound in hertz (Hz). The table shows the notes and frequency of a section of a piano's keyboard. What is the note that the vuvuzela plays? Explain.

Note	Frequency (Hz)
Middle C	261.626
B	246.942
B-flat	233.082
A	220
A-flat	207.652
G	195.998
G-flat	184.997

c. A piano tuner strikes a tuning fork for middle A, which has a frequency 440 Hz, at 80 decibels from 1 meter away, or a sound pressure of 0.2 pascal. What is an equation that represents the sound pressure P in pascals as a function of time t in seconds? Show your work.

18.2 Stretching, Compressing, and Reflecting Tangent Graphs

Essential Question: What are the key features of the graph of the tangent function?

Resource Locker

Explore Graphing the Basic Tangent Function and Its Reciprocal

Recall that the tangent of an angle can be found from the relationship $\tan\theta = \frac{\sin\theta}{\cos\theta}$. Using the coordinates of the position on the unit circle, $(x, y) = (\cos\theta, \sin\theta)$, the value of the tangent function can also be found from the ratio of y to x.

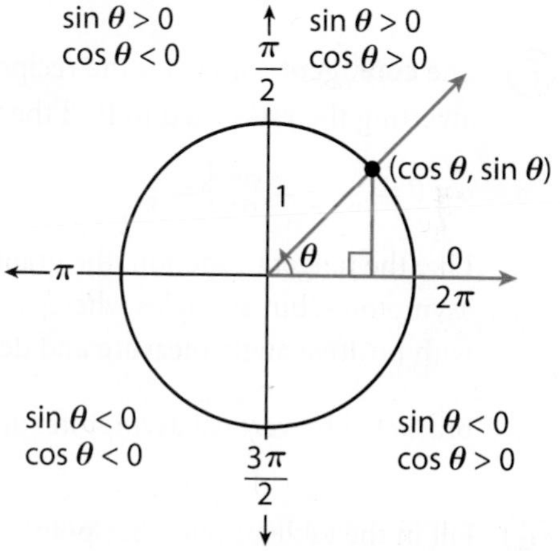

(A) The tangent of an angle is undefined when the denominator of the defining ratio is 0.

As θ increases from 0, the first angle (in radians) at which the tangent becomes undefined is ? .

As θ decreases from 0, the first angle (in radians) at which the tangent becomes undefined is ? .

The tangent is defined between these two angles. Use special triangles and the (x, y) coordinates of the unit circle to fill in the table of reference points (the x-intercept and the halfway points):

θ	$-\frac{\pi}{4}$	0	$\frac{\pi}{4}$
$\tan\theta$	?	?	?

(B) Use your calculator to evaluate tangent as it approaches $\frac{\pi}{2} \approx 1.5708$ and $-\frac{\pi}{2} \approx -1.5708$.

θ	1.492	1.555	1.569	...	$\frac{\pi}{2} \approx 1.5708$
$\tan\theta$	?	?	?	...	Undefined

θ	−1.492	−1.555	−1.569	...	$-\frac{\pi}{2} \approx -1.5708$
$\tan\theta$	?	?	?	...	Undefined

Does the tangent function increase or decrease without bound as the angle approaches $\frac{\pi}{2}$ from below? ?

Does it increase or decrease without bound as it approaches $-\frac{\pi}{2}$ from above? ? There are vertical ? at $\frac{\pi}{2}$ and $-\frac{\pi}{2}$.

(C) Use the reference points from Step A and the asymptotic behavior observed in Step B to graph $f(\theta) = \tan\theta$ from $-\frac{\pi}{2}$ to $\frac{\pi}{2}$. Draw the vertical asymptotes.

(D) Continue to graph $f(\theta) = \tan\theta$ from $\frac{\pi}{2}$ to $\frac{3\pi}{2}$ by finding the corresponding reference points and drawing in the next vertical asymptote at ? .

θ	$\frac{3\pi}{4}$	π	$\frac{5\pi}{4}$
$\tan\theta$	?	?	?

(E) Use the same technique to complete the graph from -2π to 4π.

(F) The **cotangent** (or cot) is the reciprocal of the tangent. It can be found by inverting the ratio used to find the tangent of an angle:

$$\cot\theta = \frac{1}{\tan\theta} = \frac{\cos\theta}{\sin\theta} = \frac{x}{y}$$

Like the tangent function, the graph of cotangent has regular vertical asymptotes, but at angles where $\sin\theta$ is equal to 0. The first interval with positive angle measure and defined values of cotangent is bracketed by vertical asymptotes at $\theta =$? and $\theta =$? .

(G) Fill in the table of reference points for $\cot\theta$.

θ	$\frac{\pi}{4}$	$\frac{\pi}{2}$	$\frac{3\pi}{4}$
$\cot\theta$	?	?	?

Cotangent is undefined everywhere tangent is equal to ? , and cotangent is equal to 1 or -1 when tangent is equal to ? or ? , respectively.

(H) Sketch the asymptotes at 0 and π and use the reference points to sketch the first cycle of $f(\theta) = \cot\theta$. Then continue the graph to the left and right using the same pattern of repeating asymptotes and reference points that you used to plot $f(\theta) = \tan\theta$.

Reflect

1. Describe the behavior of the graph of the tangent function. Include where the function equals 0, where it has asymptotes, what the period is, and over what regions it is increasing and/or decreasing.
2. Describe the behavior of the graph of the cotangent function. Include where the function equals 0, where it has asymptotes, what the period is, and over what regions it is increasing and/or decreasing.
3. Use reference angles to explain why the graph of $f(\theta) = \tan\theta$ appears to show $f(-\theta) = -\tan\theta$.

Explain 1 Graphing $f(x) = a\tan\left(\frac{1}{b}x\right)$

Tangent functions can be graphed on the xy–coordinate plane by letting x represent the angle in radians and y represent the value of the function.

The plot of a transformed tangent function can be found from the transformation parameters, as you have done for other families of functions. The parameter a causes the graph to stretch (for $|a| > 1$), compress (for $|a| < 1$), and/or reflect across the x-axis (for $a < 0$). The parameter b controls the horizontal stretches and compressions of the function and the locations of the vertical asymptotes, with the asymptotes $x = \frac{-\pi}{2}$ and $x = \frac{\pi}{2}$ moving in or out to $x = -\frac{b\pi}{2}$ and $x = \frac{b\pi}{2}$. Use the asymptotes to guide your sketch by keeping the curve (or curves if drawing more than one cycle) inside the asymptotes. The other guide to the shape comes from the halfway points at $\left(-\frac{\pi b}{4}, -a\right)$ and $\left(\frac{\pi b}{4}, a\right)$, which correspond to the points $\left(-\frac{\pi}{4}, -1\right)$ and $\left(\frac{\pi}{4}, 1\right)$ in the parent function.

Example 1 **Plot one cycle of the transformed tangent function $g(x)$ together with the parent function $f(x) = \tan x$.**

(A) $g(x) = \frac{1}{2}\tan\frac{x}{3}$

Assign values to a and b from the function rule.

$a = \frac{1}{2}, b = 3$

Draw the vertical asymptotes at $x = -\frac{3\pi}{2}$ and $x = \frac{3\pi}{2}$.

Draw the reference points at $\left(-\frac{3\pi}{4}, -\frac{1}{2}\right)$, $(0, 0)$, $\left(\frac{3\pi}{4}, \frac{1}{2}\right)$.

Sketch the function.

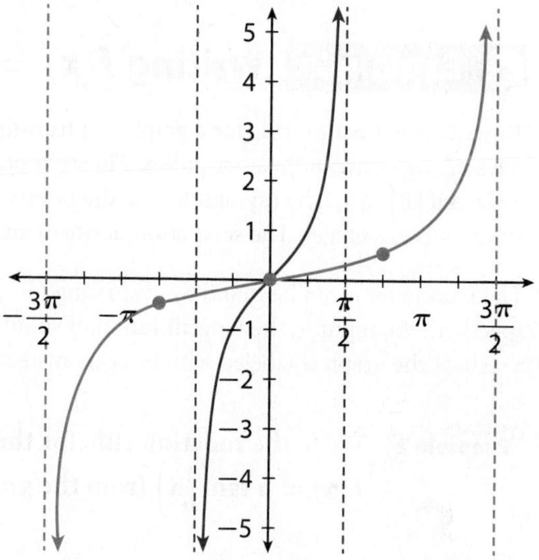

(B) $g(x) = -2\tan 2x$

Assign values to a and b from the function rule.

$a =$ -2 , $b =$ $\frac{1}{2}$

Draw the vertical asymptotes at $x =$ $-\frac{\pi}{4}$ and

$x =$ $\frac{\pi}{4}$.

Draw the reference points at $\left(-\frac{\pi}{8}, 2\right)$, $\left(0, 0\right)$,

$\left(\frac{\pi}{8}, -2\right)$.

Sketch the function.

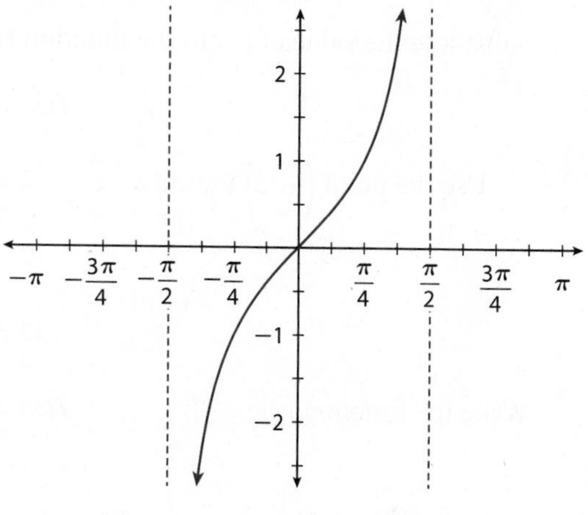

Reflect

4. Why is the vertical stretch parameter, a, referred to as the amplitude when transforming sine and cosine functions, but not tangent functions? If it is not the amplitude, how can it be used to help graph the function?

5. **Make a Conjecture** Do transformed functions of the form $f(x) = a \tan\left(\frac{1}{b}x\right)$ have the same behavior seen in the parent function, that is, $f(-x) = -f(x)$? Explain your answer and how it helps to graph transformed functions.

Your Turn

6. Graph $g(x) = -3 \tan\frac{x}{2}$.

Explain 2 Writing $f(x) = a\tan\left(\frac{1}{b}x\right)$

To write the function rule for a graph of a transformed tangent function, identify the value of b from the spacing between the asymptotes. The asymptotes spread apart by a factor of $|b|$ if $|b| > 1$ or move inward if $|b| < 1$. The asymptotes are the points where the function is undefined, or $\frac{x}{b} = \frac{\pi}{2} + n\pi$, where n is an integer. The separation between any two consecutive asymptotes is $b\pi$.

The parameter a can be found by evaluating $\tan\frac{x}{b}$ at a known point. Finally, unless degrees are specified, the input to the tangent function should be assumed to be in radians, even if the x-axis of the graph is labeled with integers instead of multiples of π.

Example 2 **Write the function rule for the transformed tangent function of the form $f(x) = a\tan\left(\frac{1}{b}x\right)$ from the graph.**

(A) Find b from the distance between the asymptotes.

$\pi b = 1 - (-1)$, so $b = \frac{2}{\pi}$

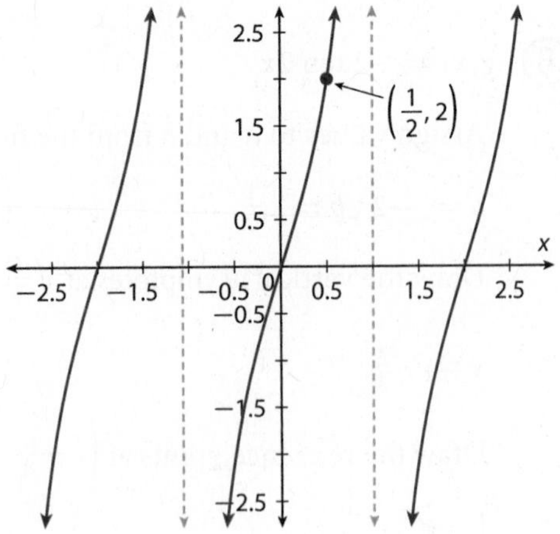

Substitute the value of b into the function rule.

$$f(x) = a\tan\frac{\pi}{2}x$$

Use the point $\left(\frac{1}{2}, 2\right)$ to find a. $\quad 2 = a\tan\left(\frac{\pi}{2} \cdot \frac{1}{2}\right)$

$$2 = a\tan\frac{\pi}{4}$$

$$2 = a$$

Write the function rule. $\quad f(x) = 2\tan\frac{\pi}{2}x$

(B) Find b from the distance between the asymptotes.

$$\pi b = \boxed{\frac{3\pi}{2}} - \left(\boxed{-\frac{3\pi}{2}}\right)$$

$$\pi b = \boxed{3\pi}$$

$$b = \boxed{3}$$

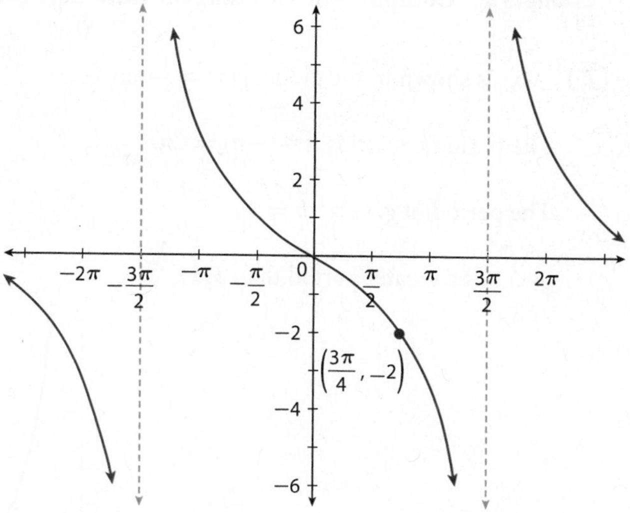

Substitute the value of b.

$$f(x) = a \tan \boxed{\frac{1}{3}} x$$

Use the point $\left(\frac{3\pi}{4}, -2\right)$ to find a.

$$\boxed{-2} = a \tan\left(\frac{1}{3} \cdot \boxed{\frac{3\pi}{4}}\right)$$

$$-2 = a \tan \boxed{\frac{\pi}{4}}$$

$$-2 = a$$

Write the function rule. $f(x) = \boxed{-2} \tan \boxed{\frac{x}{3}}$

Your Turn

7. Write the function rule for the transformed tangent function from its graph.

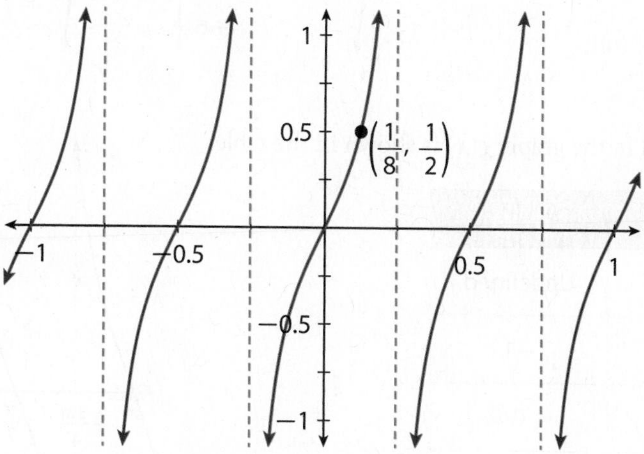

Explain 3 Comparing Tangent Functions

To compare tangent functions expressed in different forms such as graphs, tables, and equations, find the common elements that can be determined from each. Asymptotes are generally easy to recognize, and can be used to determine the period of the function.

Example 3 **Compare the two tangent functions indicated by comparing their periods.**

(A) $f(x)$ is shown in the graph; $g(x) = -\tan \frac{x}{3}$.

The period of $f(x)$ is $\pi - (-\pi) = 2\pi$.

The period of $g(x)$ is $\pi b = 3\pi$.

$g(x)$ has a greater period than $f(x)$.

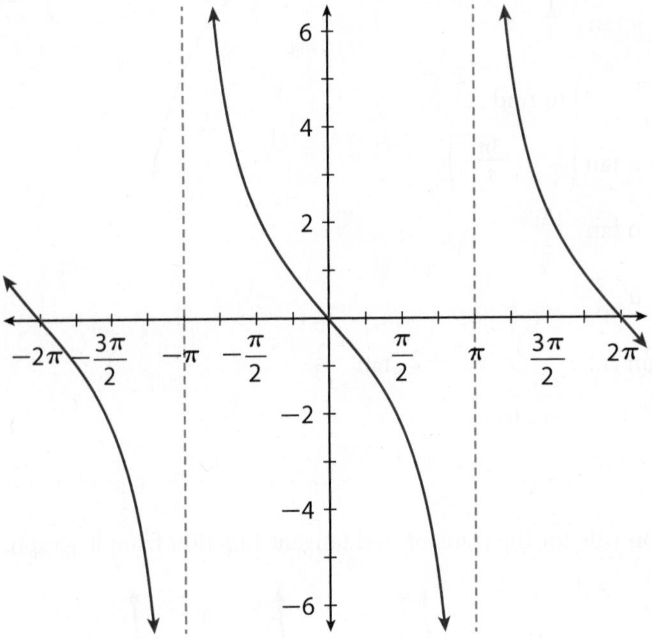

(B) $f(x)$ is shown in the graph; $g(x)$ is shown in the table.

x	$g(x)$
$-\frac{\pi}{4}$	Undefined
$-\frac{\pi}{8}$	−1
0	0
$\frac{\pi}{8}$	1
$\frac{\pi}{4}$	Undefined

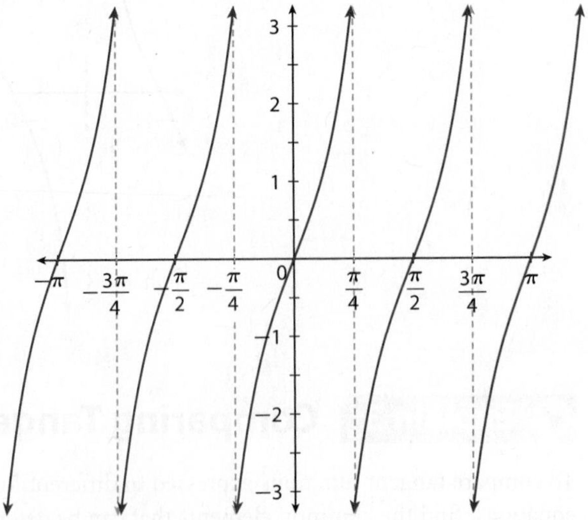

The period of $f(x)$ is $\boxed{\frac{\pi}{4}} - \left(\boxed{-\frac{\pi}{4}}\right) = \boxed{\frac{\pi}{2}}$.

The asymptotes of $g(x)$ can be found where the function is undefined.

The period of $g(x)$ is $\boxed{\frac{\pi}{4}} - \left(\boxed{-\frac{\pi}{4}}\right) = \boxed{\frac{\pi}{2}}$.

$g(x)$ has the same period as $f(x)$.

Your Turn

Compare the two tangent functions indicated by comparing their periods.

8. $f(x) = 3 \tan \frac{\pi}{3}x$

x	$g(x)$
$-\frac{1}{6}$	Undefined
$-\frac{1}{12}$	-1
0	0
$\frac{1}{12}$	1
$\frac{1}{6}$	Undefined

Explain 4 Modeling with Tangent Functions

Tangent functions can be used to model real-world situations that relate perpendicular measures (such as horizontal distance and height) to a changing angle.

Example 4 **Read the description and use a tangent function to model the quantities. Use a calculator to make a table of points and graph the model. Describe the significance of the asymptote(s) and determine the domain over which the model works.**

A climber is ascending the face of a 500-foot high vertical cliff at 5 feet per minute. Her climbing partner is observing from 150 feet away. Find the function that describes the amount of time climbing as a function of the angle of elevation of the observer's line-of-sight to the climber. Does the viewing angle ever reach 75 degrees?

Analyze Information

- The distance from the observer to the cliff base is 150 feet.
- The cliff is 500 feet high.
- The climber is climbing at 5 feet per minute.

Formulate a Plan

- A vertical line from the cliff base to the climber forms the second leg of a right triangle that can be used to find the appropriate trigonometric ratio.
- Use the right triangle to find a relationship between the height of the climber and the angle of elevation from which the observer is viewing.
- To find the time as a function of the angle, use the speed of the climber to rewrite the tangent expression.

Solve

The height as a function of viewing angle is $\tan \theta = \frac{h}{150}$.

The height of the climber is a function of time; $h = 5t$.

Substituting $5t$ for h in the second equation gives:

$$\tan \theta = \frac{5t}{150}$$

$$\tan \theta = \frac{t}{30}$$

$$t = 30 \tan \theta$$

θ	Time (minutes)
0	0.00
15	8.04
30	17.32
45	30.00
60	51.96

Justify and Evaluate

Using the function to calculate time, a viewing angle of 75 degrees should be reached in 111.96 minutes. However, the height at that time would be 559.8 feet, which is higher than the cliff top This means that a viewing angle of 75 degrees is impossible.

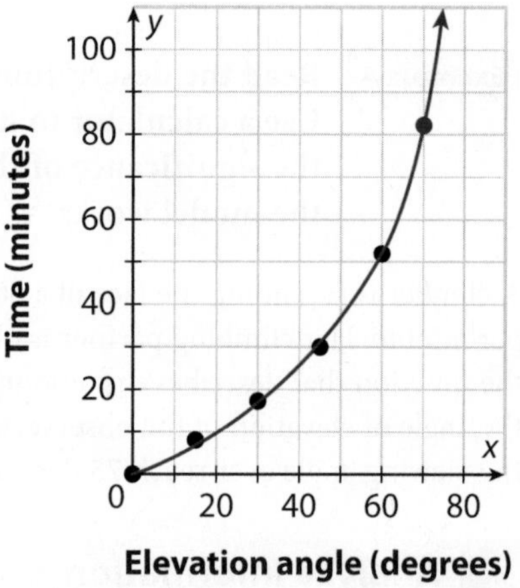

Your Turn

9. You observe a model rocket launch from 20 feet away. Find the rule for the rocket's elevation as a function of the elevation angle, and graph it.

Elaborate

10. If sine, cosine and tangent are all based on coordinates of the unit circle, why do sine and cosine have a domain of all real numbers while the tangent function does not?

11. Why does the tangent function have a different period than the sine and cosine functions if they are all defined using the unit circle?

12. **Essential Question Check-in** How do the asymptotes and x-intercepts help in graphing the tangent function and its transformations?

Evaluate: Homework and Practice

Personal Math Trainer

- Online Homework
- Hints and Help
- Extra Practice

1. Write the rules that describe all asymptotes of the functions $f(x) = \tan x$ and $f(x) = \cot x$.

Plot one cycle of the transformed tangent function $g(x)$ together with the parent function $f(x) = \tan x$.

2. $g(x) = \tan 3x$

3. $g(x) = 3 \tan \frac{2}{3}x$

4. $g(x) = -\tan \frac{x}{3}$

5. $g(x) = -\frac{1}{4} \tan 4x$

Write the function rule for the transformed tangent function of the form $g(x) = a \tan\left[\frac{1}{b}x\right]$ from the graph.

6.

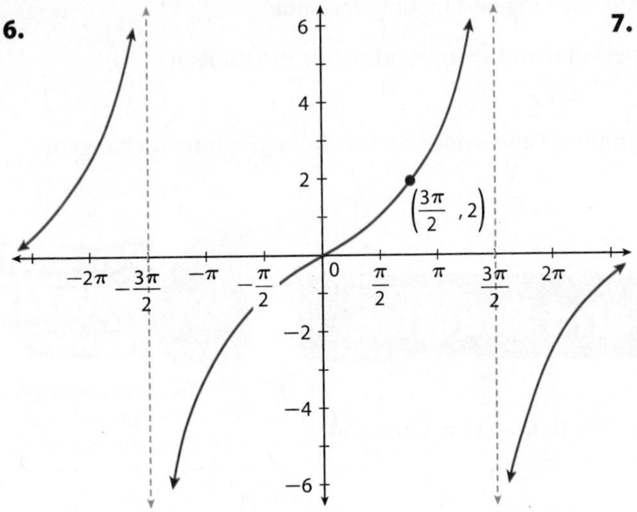

7.

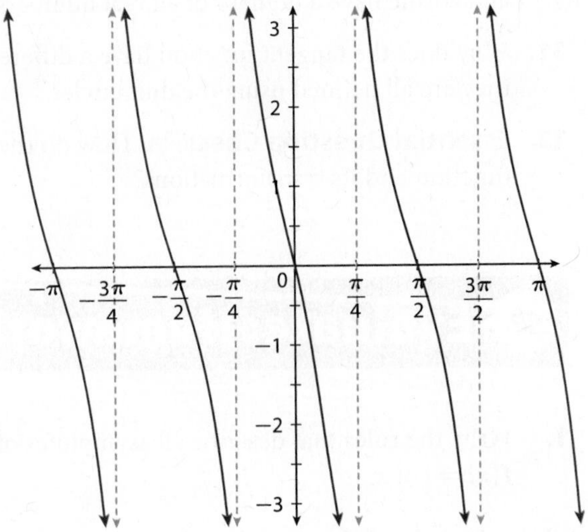

8.

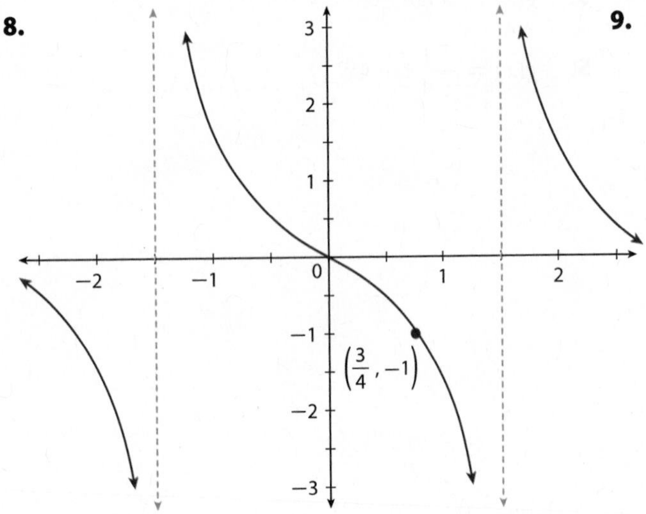

9.

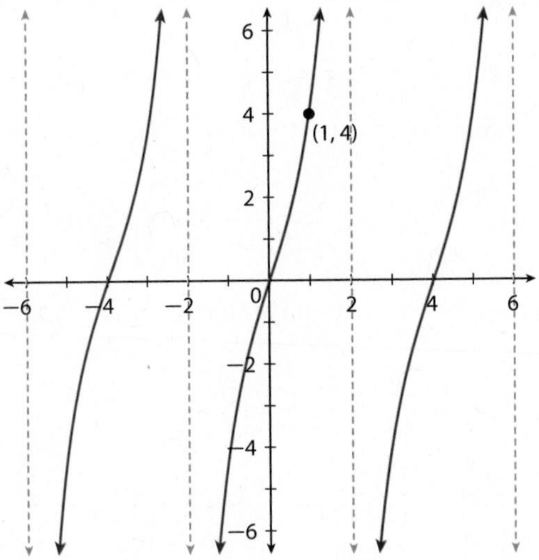

Compare the two tangent functions indicated by comparing their periods.

10.

x	$f(x)$
−12	undefined
−6	−3
0	0
6	3
12	undefined

$g(x)$ is a tangent function with asymptotes at -10 and 10.

11. $f(x) = 3 \tan 4x$; $g(x)$ is a tangent function whose graph passes through points with x-coordinates $-\frac{\pi}{4}$ and $\frac{\pi}{4}$ that are halfway between the x-intercept at 0 and the nearest vertical asymptotes.

12. $f(x)$ is shown in the graph.

$g(x)$ is a tangent function stretched horizontally by a factor of 2.

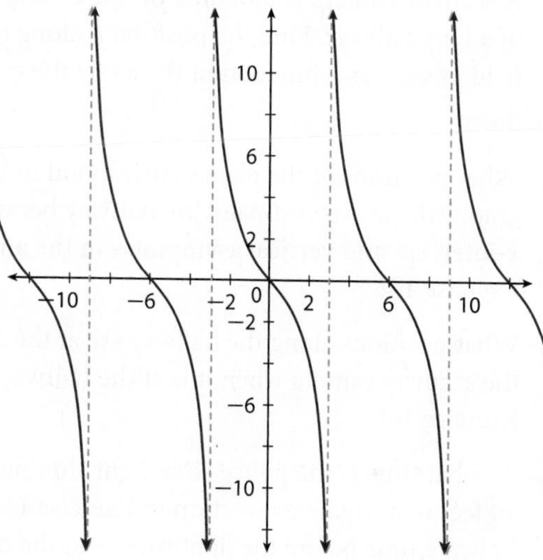

13. $f(x) = 3 \tan \pi x$

x	$g(x)$
−1	undefined
$-\frac{1}{2}$	2
0	0
$\frac{1}{2}$	−2
1	undefined

14. Sam is watching airplanes fly over his head at an airshow. The airplanes approach from the east at an altitude of 0.1 mile. Sam watches the airplanes approach and fly past. Measure angles from straight over Sam's head, with angles to the east being positive and angles to the west being negative. Find the horizontal position p of the planes from Sam as a function of the angle of Sam's view as the planes approach and fly over.

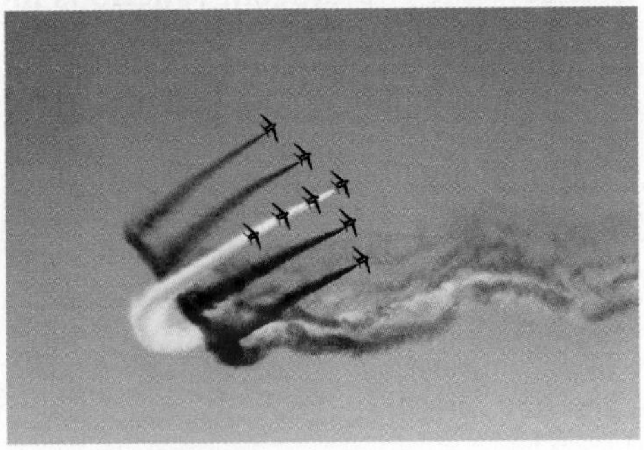

15. A police car stops in a long tunnel and parks 20 feet from the wall. The siren light makes a complete revolution once per second. Find the position p between the point where the center of the beam of light strikes the tunnel wall at time t and the point on the wall closest to the light's source. Graph the position as a function of time for $-0.25 < t < 0.25$ where at time $t = 0$ the beam is pointed directly at the wall.

16. A security camera is mounted on the ceiling 10 feet above the floor at the midpoint of a long hallway. Find the position p along the hallway of the center of the camera's field of view as a function of the angle the camera makes relative to pointing straight down.

17. What positions of the planes correspond to the points on the graph whose x-coordinates are halfway between the graph's x-intercept and vertical asymptotes in the airshow example in Exercise 14?

18. What positions along the hallway are at the center of the view of the security camera when it is at the halfway points of the graph in Exercise 16?

19. At what time is the police siren light shining on the wall at a distance of 20 feet in a negative direction in Exercise 15? (Note that negative values for time indicate time before the light rotates to the closest point on the wall.)

20. **Multiple Response** The function $g(x) = -3 \tan \pi x$ has which of the following transformations compared to the parent function $f(x) = \tan x$?

A. a vertical stretch by a factor of 3

B. a vertical compression by a factor of 3

C. a horizontal stretch by a factor of π

D. a horizontal compression by a factor of $\frac{1}{\pi}$

E. a reflection over the x-axis

F. a translation up by 3

G. a translation down by 3

H.O.T. Focus on Higher Order Thinking

21. Draw Conclusions In the security camera model of Exercise 16, imagine that the camera has a field of view that is 20° wide (i.e. if the center of the image is looking at 40°, the total image views from 30° to 50°). What center angle views the shortest stretch of the hallway? What center angle views the longest stretch?

22. Justify Reasoning In the police siren example of Exercise 15, if the graph were extended to longer times and encompassed more periods of the tangent function, explain whether it would make sense to include all other periods of the tangent function.

23. Communicate Mathematical Ideas How could you sketch a graph of a tangent function on a coordinate plane with no grid lines (except the *x*- and *y*-axes) that is already showing the sine and cosine functions?

Lesson Performance Task

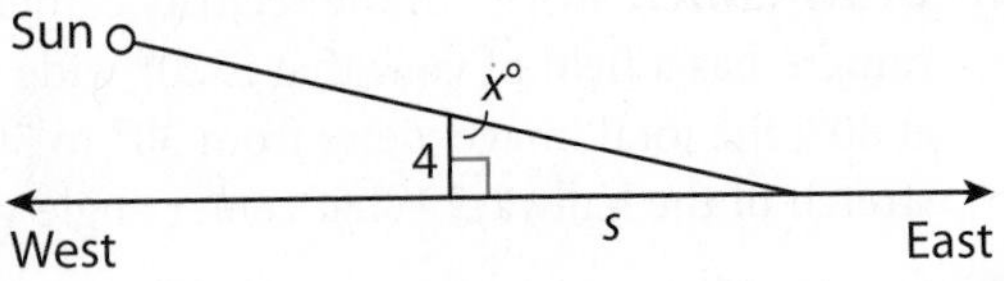

A community on the equator celebrates the equinox by having a festival at the town's sundial. Because the town is located at the equator, the sun rises directly in the east and sets directly in the west, passing directly overhead at solar noon, halfway through the 12 hours of daylight. The sundial rests on the ground, and its gnomon, the pointer that casts the shadow, is 4 feet above the ground. Let x be the angle of the sun from the sundial in degrees and let s be the length of the sundial's shadow in feet, as shown in the figure.

A. Write an equation that expresses the relationship between s and x, and then solve for s.

B. Let the angle off the sundial to the west be negative and the angle off the sundial to the east be positive. Write a function for the length of the sundial's shadow, s, in feet to the east as a function of time t hours after solar noon using the fact that the angle changes by $15°$ per hour.

C. Describe the graph of $s(t)$ from part B as a series of transformations from the parent function $f(t) = \tan t$. Also indicate the period of the function.

D. Since solar noon occurs at 12:15 p.m. local time, sunrise and sunset occur around 6:15 a.m. and 6:15 p.m., respectively. Complete the table to determine the values of t and $s(t)$, rounding to the nearest hundredth as needed. What is the meaning of the negative values for $s(t)$?

Local Time	t	$s(t)$
6:15 a.m.	?	?
8:15 a.m.	?	?
10:15 a.m.	?	?
12:15 p.m.	?	?
2:15 p.m.	?	?
4:15 p.m.	?	?
6:15 p.m.	?	?

E. Do the values of $s(t)$ make sense at sunrise and sunset? Explain your reasoning.

18.3 Translating Trigonometric Graphs

Resource Locker

Essential Question: How do the constants h and k in the functions $f(x) = a \sin\frac{1}{b}(x - h) + k$, $f(x) = a \cos\frac{1}{b}(x - h) + k$, and $f(x) = a \tan\frac{1}{b}(x - h) + k$ affect their graphs?

Explore Translating the Graph of a Trigonometric Function

In previous lessons, you saw in what ways the graphs of $f(x) = a \sin\left(\frac{1}{b}\right)x$, $f(x) = a \cos\left(\frac{1}{b}\right)x$, and $f(x) = a \tan\left(\frac{1}{b}\right)x$ were vertical and horizontal shrinks and stretches of the graphs of their parent functions. You saw that the vertical stretches and shrinks changed the amplitude of sine and cosine graphs, but did not change the midline on the x-axis, and the horizontal stretches and compressions changed the period of all of the graphs.

As with other types of functions, you can indicate horizontal and vertical translations in the equations for trigonometric functions. Trigonometric functions in the form $f(x) = a \sin\frac{1}{b}(x - h) + k$, $f(x) = a \cos\frac{1}{b}(x - h) + k$, or $f(x) = a \tan\frac{1}{b}(x - h) + k$ indicate a vertical translation by k and a horizontal translation by h.

(A) Answer the following questions about the graph of $f(x) = 0.5 \sin 3x$.

a. What is the period of the graph?

b. What are the first three x-intercepts for $x \geq 0$?

c. What are the maximum and minimum values of the first cycle for $x \geq 0$, and where do they occur?

d. What are the five key points of the graph that represent the values you found?

Use the key points to sketch one cycle of the graph.

(B) Identify h and k for $f(x) = 0.5 \sin 3\left(x - \frac{\pi}{3}\right) - 1.5$, and tell what translations they indicate. Find the images of the key points of the graph in Step A. Finally, sketch the graph from Step A again, along with the graph of its image, after the indicated translations.

(C) Answer the following questions about the graph of $f(x) = 2\tan\frac{1}{2}x$.

a. What is the period of the graph?

b. What is the x-intercept of the graph at or nearest the origin? What are the asymptotes?

c. What are the halfway points on either side of the x-intercept that you found?

d. What are the three key points of the graph that represent the values you found?

Use the key points to sketch one cycle of the graph. Also show the asymptotes.

(D) Identify h and k for $f(x) = 2\tan\frac{1}{2}(x + \pi) + 3$, and tell what translations they indicate. Find the images of the key points of the graph in Step A, and the new asymptotes. Finally, sketch the graph from Step A again, along with the graph of its image after the indicated translations. (Note: Show the asymptotes for the translated graph, but not for the original graph.)

Reflect

1. Suppose that you are told to extend the graph of the translated function you graphed in Step B to the left and to the right. Without actually drawing the graph, explain how you would do this.

2. What feature of the graphs of the trigonometric functions is represented by the value of the parameter k?

Explain 1 Graphing General Trigonometric Functions

Now you can combine all you have learned about the parameters a, b, h, and k in the equations for trigonometric functions to graph functions of the form $f(x) = a\sin\frac{1}{b}(x - h) + k$, $f(x) = a\cos\frac{1}{b}(x - h) + k$, or $f(x) = a\tan\frac{1}{b}(x - h) + k$ directly from their equations without first graphing parent functions.

Example 1 **For the function given, identify the period and the midline of the graph, and where the graph crosses the midline. For a sine or cosine function, identify the amplitude and the maximum and minimum values and where they occur. For a tangent function, identify the asymptotes and the values of the halfway points. Then graph one cycle of the function.**

(A) $f(x) = 3\sin(x - \pi) + 1$

Period: $\frac{1}{b} = 1$, so $b = 1$; period $= 2\pi \cdot 1 = 2\pi$

Midline: $y = k$, or $y = 1$

Amplitude: $a = 3$

The point $(0, 0)$ on the graph of the parent function $y = \sin x$ is translated $h = \pi$ units to the right and $k = 1$ unit up to $(\pi, 1)$. The graph also crosses the midline at the endpoint of the cycle , $(\pi + 2\pi, 1) = (3\pi, 1)$ and at the point halfway between $(\pi, 1)$ and $(3\pi, 1)$ or at $(2\pi, 1)$. So, the graph contains $(\pi, 1)$, $(2\pi, 1)$ and $(3\pi, 1)$.

Maximum: $a = 3$ units above the midline, or $k + a = 1 + 3 = 4$; occurs halfway between the first and second midline crossings, or at $x = \frac{\pi + 2\pi}{2} = \frac{3\pi}{2}$. So, the graph contains $\left(\frac{3\pi}{2}, 4\right)$.

Minimum: $a = 3$ units below the midline, or $k - a = 1 - 3 = -2$; occurs halfway between the second and third midline crossings, or at $x = \frac{2\pi + 3\pi}{2} = \frac{5\pi}{2}$. So, the graph contains $\left(\frac{5\pi}{2}, -2\right)$.

Plot the key points found and sketch the graph.

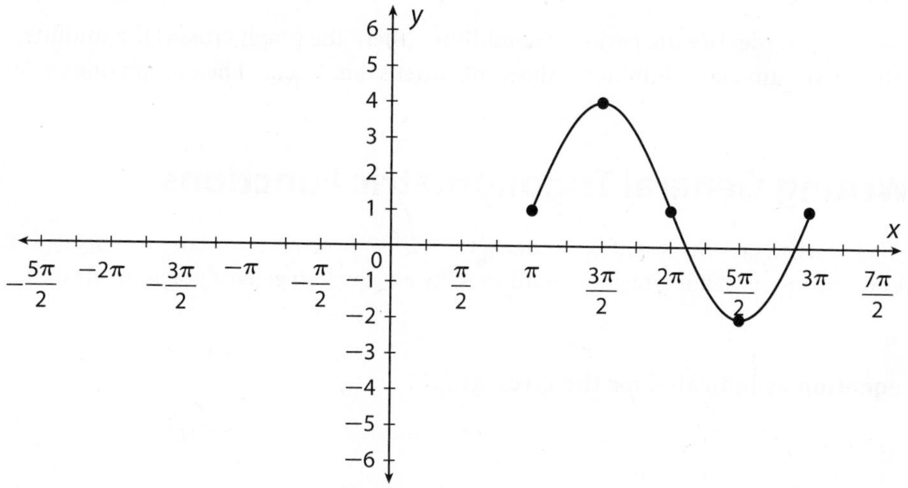

B $f(x) = -2\tan\frac{1}{2}(x - 2\pi) + 2$

Period: $\frac{1}{b} = \boxed{\frac{1}{2}}$, so $b = \boxed{2}$; period $= \boxed{\pi} \cdot 2 = \boxed{2\pi}$

Midline: $y = k$, or $y = \boxed{2}$

The point $(0, 0)$ on the graph of $y = \tan x$ is translated $h = \boxed{2\pi}$ units to the right and $k = \boxed{2}$ units up to $\left(\boxed{2\pi}, \boxed{2}\right)$. There are asymptotes half a cycle to the left and right of this point, or at $x = 2\pi - \boxed{\pi} = \boxed{\pi}$ and $x = 2\pi + \boxed{\pi} = \boxed{3\pi}$.

Halfway points occur halfway between the asymptotes and where the graph crosses its midline, or at

$$x = \frac{\boxed{\pi} + 2\pi}{2} = \frac{\boxed{3\pi}}{2}$$

and $x = \frac{2\pi + \boxed{3\pi}}{2} = \frac{\boxed{5\pi}}{2}$.

The halfway points of $y = \tan x$ have y–values of -1 and 1. Because $a = \boxed{-2}$ in $f(x) = -2\tan\frac{1}{2}(x - 2\pi) + 2$, the halfway points are reflected across the midline and stretched vertically from it by a factor of $\boxed{2}$. The halfway points are

$$\left(\frac{3\pi}{2}, a\left(\boxed{-1}\right) + k\right) = \left(\frac{3\pi}{2}, -2\left(\boxed{-1}\right) + 2\right) = \left(\frac{3\pi}{2}, \boxed{4}\right) \text{ and}$$

$$\left(\frac{5\pi}{2}, a\left(\boxed{1}\right) + k\right) = \left(\frac{5\pi}{2}, -2\left(\boxed{1}\right) + 2\right) = \left(\frac{5\pi}{2}, \boxed{0}\right).$$

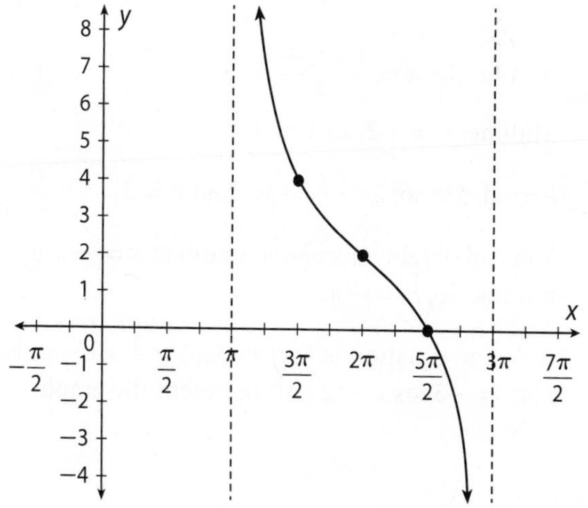

Plot the key points found and sketch the graph.

Your Turn

3. For $f(x) = 2\cos 2\left(x - \frac{\pi}{2}\right) + 1$, identify the period, the midline, where the graph crosses the midline, the amplitude, and the maximum and minimum values and where they occur. Then graph one cycle of the function.

Explain 2 Writing General Trigonometric Functions

Because the equations of $f(x) = a\sin\frac{1}{b}(x - h) + k$, $f(x) = a\cos\frac{1}{b}(x - h) + k$, or $f(x) = a\tan\frac{1}{b}(x - h) + k$ directly reflect the physical features of their graphs, it is straightforward to write an equation given a graph of one of these functions.

Example 2 **Write an equation as indicated for the given graph.**

(A) a cosine function

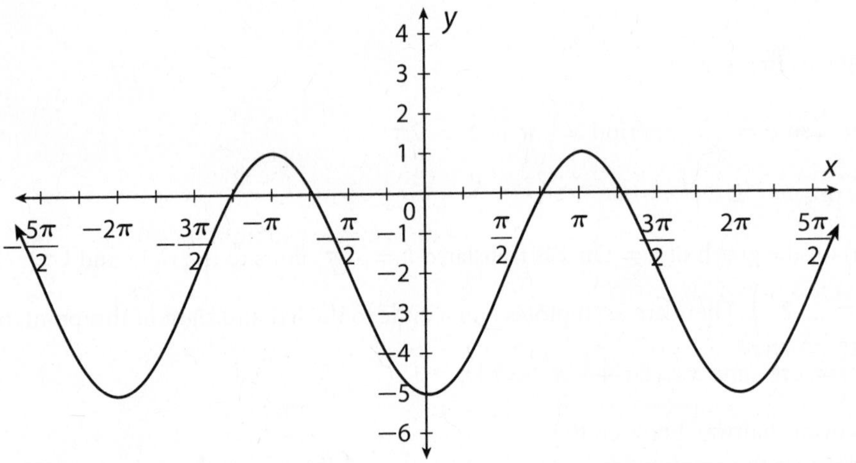

Amplitude: $a = \frac{1 - (-5)}{2} = 3$

Midline: $y = -2$, so $k = -2$.

Period: 2π; so, $2\pi \cdot b = 2\pi$, and $b = 1$.

You can obtain a local maximum at $x = -\pi$ by translating the graph of $y = \cos x$ to the left by π units. So, $h = -\pi$.

A cosine equation is $f(x) = 3\cos(x + \pi) - 2$. Notice that the equations $f(x) = 3\cos(x - \pi) - 2$ and $f(x) = -3\cos x - 2$ also represent the graph.

(B) a tangent function with midline and halfway points shown

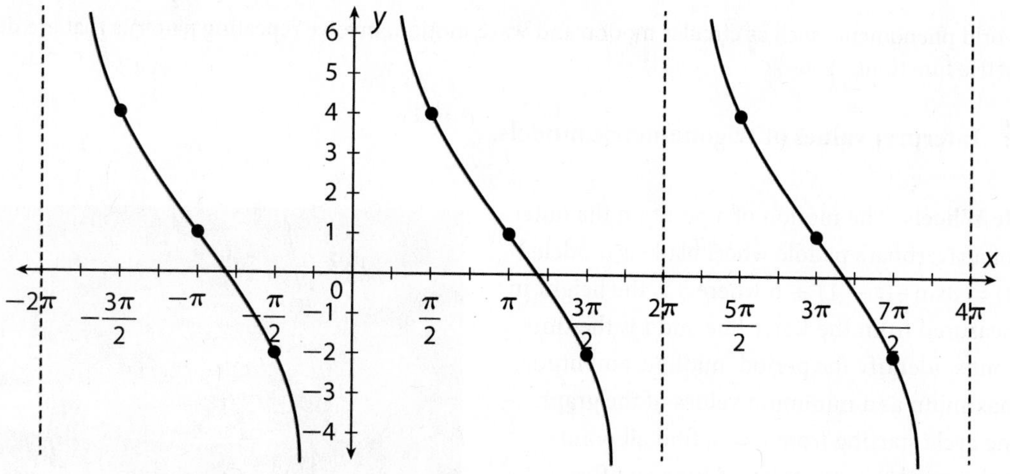

Midline: $y =$ [1], so $k =$ [1].

Period: 2π; so, [π] $\cdot\, b =$ [2π], and $b =$ [2].

The halfway points lie [3] units above and below the midline, so the graph is vertically stretched by a factor of [3]. Because the graph is falling from left to right for each cycle, the sign of a is negative. So, $a =$ [−3].

A cycle of the graph crosses the midline at $x = \pi$ instead of at $x = 0$ as for the graph of $y = \tan x$, so you can describe the graph by a translation to the right by [π] units. So, $h =$ [π].

A tangent equation is $f(x) =$ [−3] tan [$\frac{1}{2}$] $\left(x -\right.$ [π] $\left.\right) +$ [1]. Notice that the equation $f(x) = -3\tan\frac{1}{2}(x + \pi) + 1$ also represents the graph.

Reflect

4. How could you write a sine function from the cosine function first described by Example 2A?

5. What is true in general about the graph of a tangent function of the form $f(x) = a\tan\frac{1}{b}(x - h) + k$ when $a > 0$? when $a < 0$?

Your Turn

6. Write a sine function for the graph.

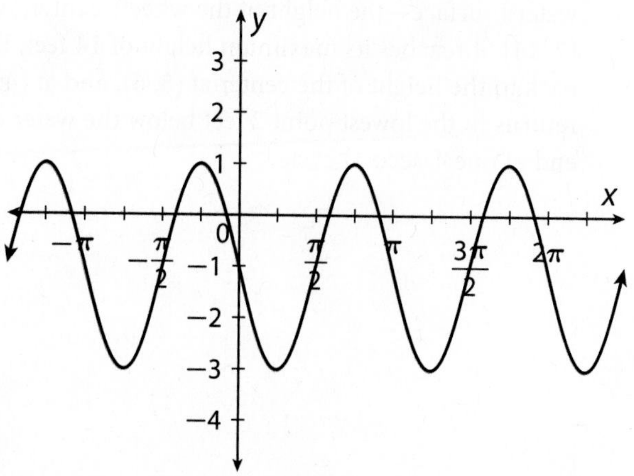

Explain 3 Modeling with General Trigonometric Functions

Many real-world phenomena, such as circular motion and wave motion, involve repeating patterns that are described by trigonometric functions.

Example 3 **Interpret values of trigonometric models.**

Ⓐ **Paddle Wheels** The motion of a point on the outer edge of a riverboat's paddle wheel blade is modeled by $h(t) = 8\sin\frac{\pi}{2}(t - 1) + 6$ where h is the height in feet measured from the water line and t is the time in seconds. Identify the period, midline, amplitude, and maximum and minimum values of the graph. For one cycle starting from $t = 0$, find all points where the graph intersects its midline and the coordinates of any local maxima and minima. Interpret these points in the context of the problem, and graph one cycle.

Period: $\frac{1}{b} = \frac{\pi}{2}$, so $b = \frac{2}{\pi}$, and $2\pi \cdot b = 4$;
Midline: $k = 6$, so the midline is $h(t) = 6$.

Amplitude: $a = 8$;
Maximum: $k + a = 6 + 8 = 14$;
Minimum: $k - a = 6 - 8 = -2$

When $t = 0$, $h(t) = 8\sin\frac{\pi}{2}(0 - 1) + 6 = 8\sin\left(-\frac{\pi}{2}\right) + 6$ $= 8(-1) + 6 = -2$. So, $(0, -2)$ is on the graph.

This is a minimum. There is a second minimum at the end of the cycle at $(0 + 4, -2) = (4, -2)$.

A maximum lies halfway between the x-values of the minima at $x = \frac{0 + 4}{2} = 2$. So, $(2, 14)$ is on the graph.

The graph crosses its midline halfway between each local maximum or minimum, or at $x = \frac{0 + 2}{2} = 1$ and $x = \frac{2 + 4}{2} = 3$. So, $(1, 6)$ and $(3, 6)$ are on the graph.

The point $(0, -2)$ means that the outer edge of the blade is 2 feet below the water's surface at time $t = 0$. One second later, it is at $(1, 6)$, or 6 feet above the water's surface—the height of the wheel's center. At $(2, 14)$, it reaches its maximum height of 14 feet, is back to the height of the center at $(3, 6)$, and at $(4, -2)$ returns to the lowest point 2 feet below the water at the end of one 4-second cycle.

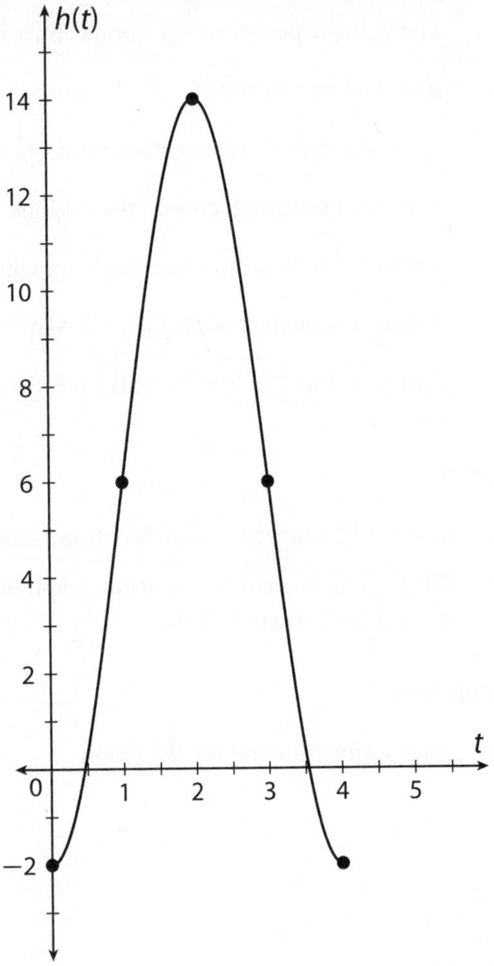

Ⓑ **Amusement Parks** The motion of a gondola car on the Ferris wheel at Navy Pier in Chicago can be modeled by $h(t) = 70\sin\frac{2\pi}{7}(t - 1.75) + 80$, where h is the height in feet and t is the time in minutes. Identify the period, midline, amplitude, and maximum and minimum values of the graph. For one cycle starting from $t = 0$, find all points where the graph intersects its midline and the coordinates of any local maxima and minima. Interpret these points in the context of the problem, and graph one cycle.

Period: $\frac{1}{b} = \boxed{\frac{2\pi}{7}}$, so $b = \boxed{\frac{7}{2\pi}}$, and $2\pi \cdot b = \boxed{7}$;

Midline: $k = \boxed{80}$, so the midline is $h(t) = \boxed{80}$.

Amplitude: $a = \boxed{70}$; Maximum: $k + a = \boxed{80} + \boxed{70} = \boxed{150}$;

Minimum: $k - a = \boxed{80} - \boxed{70} = \boxed{10}$

When $t = 0$, $h(t) = 70\sin\frac{2\pi}{7}\left(\boxed{0} - 1.75\right) + 80 = 70\sin\left(-\boxed{\frac{\pi}{2}}\right) + 80$

$= 70\left(\boxed{-1}\right) + 80 = \boxed{10}$. So, $\left(0, \boxed{10}\right)$ is on the graph. This is a minimum.

There is a second minimum at the end of the cycle at $\left(0 + \boxed{7}, 10\right)$

$= \left(\boxed{7}, 10.\right)$ A maximum lies halfway between the x-values of the minima

at $x = \frac{0 + \boxed{7}}{2} = \boxed{3.5}$. So, $\left(\boxed{3.5}, \boxed{150}\right)$ is on the graph.

The graph crosses its midline halfway between each local maximum or minimum, or at $x = \frac{0 + 3.5}{2} = 1.75$ and $x = \frac{3.5 + \boxed{7}}{2} = \boxed{5.25}$.

So, $\left(1.75, \boxed{80}\right)$ and $\left(\boxed{5.25}, \boxed{80}\right)$ are on the graph.

The point $(0, 10)$ means that the gondola is $\boxed{10}$ feet above the ground at time $t = 0$.

After 1.75 minutes, it is at $\left(1.75, \boxed{80}\right)$, or $\boxed{80}$ feet above the ground—the height of the wheel's center. At $\left(3.5, \boxed{150}\right)$ it reaches its maximum height of $\boxed{150}$ feet. It is back to the height of the center at $(5.25, 80)$, and at $(7, 10)$ it returns to the lowest point, 10 feet above the ground, at the end of one 7-minute cycle.

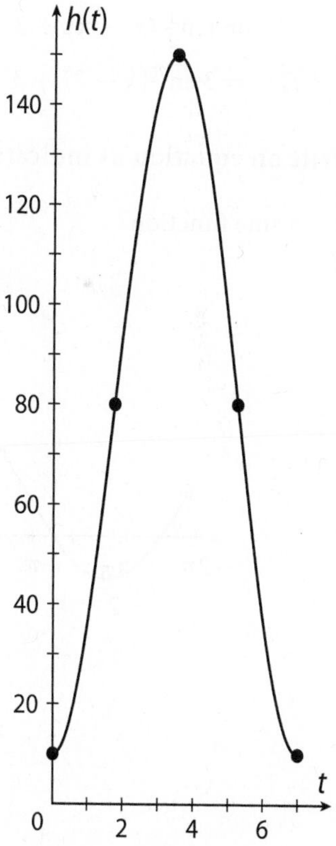

Your Turn

7. Amusement Parks The height h in feet of a car on a different Ferris wheel can be modeled by $h(t) = -16\cos\frac{\pi}{45}t + 24$, where t is the time in seconds. Identify the period, midline, amplitude, and maximum and minimum values of the graph. For one cycle starting from $t = 0$, find all points where the graph intersects its midline and the coordinates of any local maxima and minima. Interpret these points in the context of the problem, and graph one cycle.

Elaborate

8. How can being given the first local maximum and local minimum of a cosine function $(a > 0)$ help you write its equation?

9. **Essential Question Check-In** How do positive values of h affect the graph of a function in the form $f(x) = a \sin \frac{1}{b}(x - h) + k$? How do negative values of k affect the graph of this function?

Evaluate: Homework and Practice

Personal Math Trainer

- Online Homework
- Hints and Help
- Extra Practice

For each function, identify the period and the midline of the graph, and where the graph crosses the midline. For a sine or cosine function, identify the amplitude and the maximum and minimum values and where they occur. For a tangent function, identify the asymptotes and the values of the halfway points. Then graph one cycle.

1. $f(x) = -3 \sin(x + \pi) + 1$

2. $f(x) = 2 \cos 3x + 1$

3. $f(x) = \tan \frac{1}{2}(x - \pi) + 3$

4. $f(x) = 3 \sin \frac{\pi}{2}(x - 2) + 3$

Write an equation as indicated for the given graph.

5. a sine function

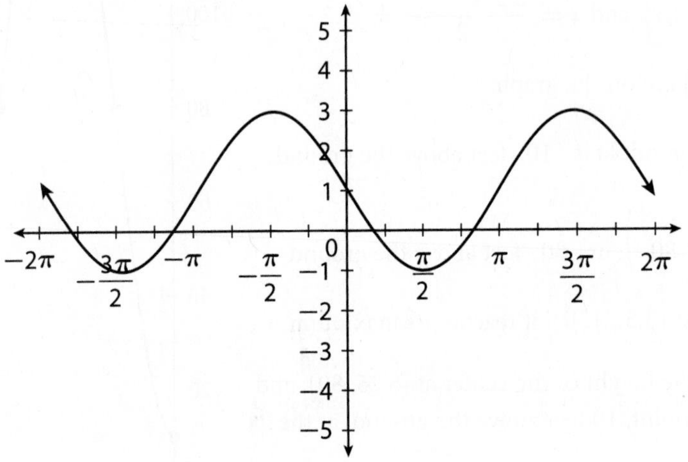

6. a cosine function

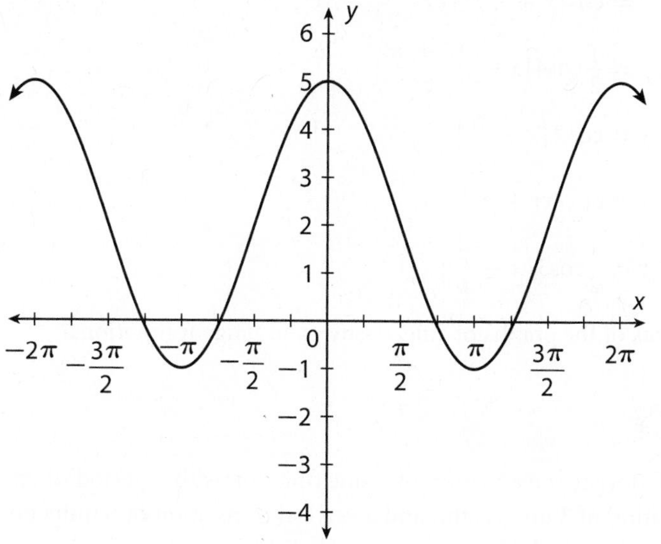

7. a tangent function

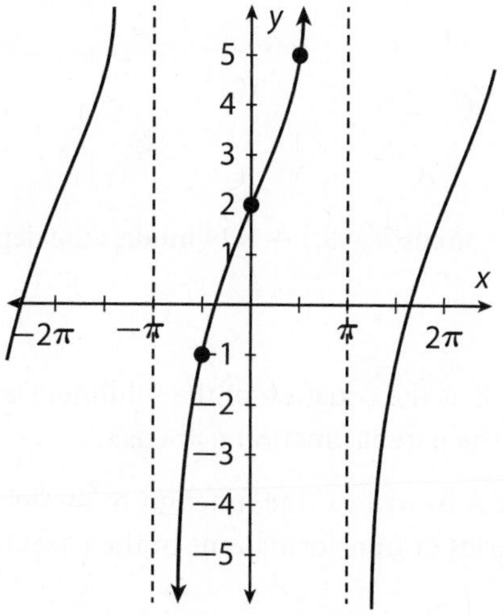

For the context described, identify the period, midline, amplitude, and maximum and minimum values of the graph. For one cycle starting from $t = 0$, find all points where the graph intersects its midline and the coordinates of any local maxima and minima. Interpret these points in the context of the problem, and graph one cycle.

8. **Historic Technology** Water turns a water wheel at an old mill. The water comes in at the top of the wheel through a wooden chute. The function $h(t) = 15\cos\frac{\pi}{5}t + 20$ models the height h in feet above the stream into which the water empties of a point on the wheel where t is the time in seconds.

9. **Games** A toy is suspended 36 inches above the floor on a spring. A child reaches up, pulls the toy, and releases it. The function $h(t) = 10\sin\pi(x - 0.5) + 36$ models the toy's height h in inches above the floor after t seconds.

10. Match each sine function with the cosine function that has the same graph.

a. ___?___ $y = \sin 2x$ 1. $y = \cos\left(x + \frac{\pi}{2}\right) + 1$

b. ___?___ $y = \frac{1}{2}\sin 3x$ 2. $y = \frac{1}{2}\cos 4\left(x - \frac{16 + \pi}{8}\right)$

c. ___?___ $y = \frac{1}{2}\sin 4(x - 2)$ 3. $y = \cos 2\left(x - \frac{\pi}{4}\right)$

d. ___?___ $y = \sin(x - \pi) + 1$ 4. $y = \cos(x) + 4$

e. ___?___ $y = \sin\left(x + \frac{\pi}{2}\right) + 4$ 5. $y = \frac{1}{2}\cos 3\left(x - \frac{\pi}{6}\right)$

11. How do h and k affect the key points of the graphs of sine, cosine, and tangent functions?

H.O.T. Focus on Higher Order Thinking

12. **Explain the Error** Sage was told to write the equation of a sine function with a period of 2π, an amplitude of 5, a horizontal translation of 3 units right, and a vertical translation of 6 units up. She wrote the equation $f(x) = 5\sin 2\pi(x - 3) + 6$. Explain Sage's error and give the correct equation.

13. **Critical Thinking** Can any sine or cosine function graph be represented by a sine equation with a positive coefficient a? Explain your answer.

14. **Make a Prediction** What will the graph of the function $f(x) = \cos^2 x + \sin^2 x$ look like? Explain your answer and check it on a graphing calculator.

Lesson Performance Task

At a location off a pier on the Maine coastline, the function $d(t) = 4.36\cos(0.499t) + 8.79$ models the depth d in feet of the water t hours after the first high tide during a first quarter moon.

a. Identify the amplitude and period of the function as well as the equation of the midline. Describe the graph of this function as a series of transformations of the parent function $y = \cos x$.

b. Explain how you can use the cosine function from part A to write a sine function to model the depth of the water. Describe the graph of this function as a series of transformations of the parent function $y = \sin x$.

c. The heights of astronomical tides are affected by the moon phase. A function that models the depth of the water at the same location after the first low tide during a new moon is $d(t) = 6.31\sin[0.503(t - 3.13)] + 8.75$. Identify the amplitude and period of the function as well as the equation of the midline. Describe the graph of this function as a series of transformations of the parent function $y = \sin x$.

d. Explain how you can use the sine function from part C on the previous page to write a cosine function to model the height of the water. Describe the graph of this function as a series of transformations of the parent function $y = \cos x$.

e. Compare the functions from parts A and B with the functions from parts C and D. How do the tides during a new moon compare to the tides during a first quarter moon?

18.4 Fitting Sine Functions to Data

Essential Question: How can you model data using a sine function?

Resource Locker

Explore Roughly Fitting a Sine Function to Data

When the graph of a set of data has a wave-like pattern, you can model the data with a sine function of the form $y = a \sin \frac{1}{b}(x - h) + k$. While it is also possible to use a cosine function as a model, it's not necessary because the basic sine and cosine curves are identical apart from a horizontal translation due to the fact that $\cos x = \sin\left(x + \frac{\pi}{2}\right)$.

Consider Chicago's monthly average temperatures in degrees Fahrenheit.

Month	1	2	3	4	5	6	7	8	9	10	11	12
Average temperature (°F)	23.8	27.7	37.9	48.9	59.1	68.9	74.0	72.4	64.6	52.5	40.3	27.7

(A) Graph the data.

(B) You want to write a model of the form $y = a \sin \frac{1}{b}(x - h) + k$ where x represents time (in months, starting with 1 for January), y represents average monthly temperature (in degrees Fahrenheit), and a, b, h, and k are constants. Begin by finding the value of b.

You know that the parameter b produces a horizontal stretch or compression of the graph of $y = \sin x$ by a factor of b. You also know that the period of $y = \sin x$ is 2π, so the period of $y = a \sin \frac{1}{b}(x-h) + k$ is $2\pi b$. Use this information to find the value of b for the temperature data. Explain your reasoning. Then substitute the value of b into the model.

(C) You know that the parameter k produces a vertical translation of the graph of $y = \sin x$. You also know that the graph of $y = \sin x$ has $y = 0$ as its midline, so the graph of $y = a \sin \frac{1}{b}(x - h) + k$ has $y = k$ as its midline. The midline, which is a horizontal line, occurs halfway between the highest and lowest data points. Use this information to find the value of k for the temperature data. Explain your reasoning. Then substitute the value of k into the model.

(D) You know that the parameter h produces a horizontal translation of the graph of $y = \sin x$. You also know that the graph of $y = \sin x$ crosses its midline at $x = 0$, so the graph of $y = a \sin \frac{1}{b}(x - h) + k$ crosses its midline at $x = h$. Use this information to find the value of h for the temperature data. Explain your reasoning. Then substitute the value of h into the model.

(E) You know that the parameter a produces a vertical stretch or compression of the graph of $y = \sin x$ as well as a reflection across the midline when a is negative. You also know that the graph of $y = \sin x$ has an amplitude of 1, so the graph of $y = a \sin \frac{1}{b}(x - h) + k$ has an amplitude of $|a|$. The amplitude is half the vertical distance between the highest and lowest data points. Use this information to find the value of a for the temperature data. Explain your reasoning. Then substitute the value of a into the model.

(F) Graph the model on the same coordinate grid on which you plotted the data from Step A.

Reflect

1. If the temperature data had been given in degrees Celsius rather than degrees Fahrenheit, how would the model change?
2. If you let t represent time and T represent temperature, what does the model become?
3. If you define January as month 0 instead of month 1, how does the graph of the data change, and what does the model become?

Explain 1 Fitting a Sine Function to Data Using Technology

You can obtain a sine model for a set of data by performing sine regression using a graphing calculator in the same way as you would perform linear regression, exponential regression, and so on.

(A) The table gives Chicago's monthly average temperatures as in the Explore. Use a graphing calculator to obtain a sine regression model for the data. Graph the regression model along with the model from the Explore, and compare the models visually.

Month	1	2	3	4	5	6	7	8	9	10	11	12
Average temperature (°F)	23.8	27.7	37.9	48.9	59.1	68.9	74.0	72.4	64.6	52.5	40.3	27.7

Step 1 Enter the data into lists L_1 and L_2. Then press the **STAT** key and select **C:SinReg** from the **CALC** menu.

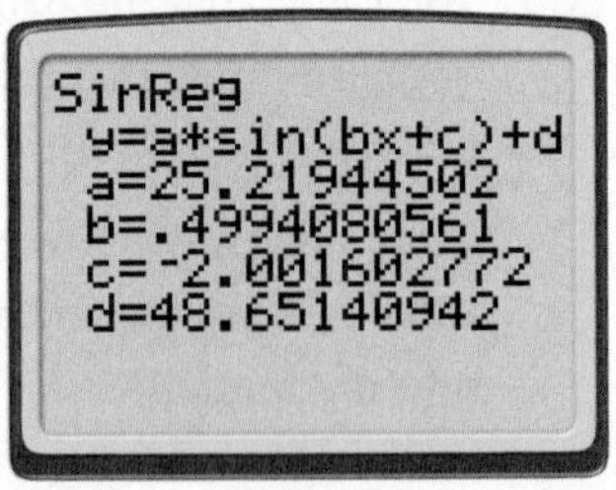

So, the regression model is $y = 25.2 \sin(0.5x - 2) + 48.7$.

Step 2 Graph the data, the regression model, and the model $y = 25.1 \sin\frac{\pi}{6}(x - 4) + 48.9$ from the Explore. Visually compare the models.

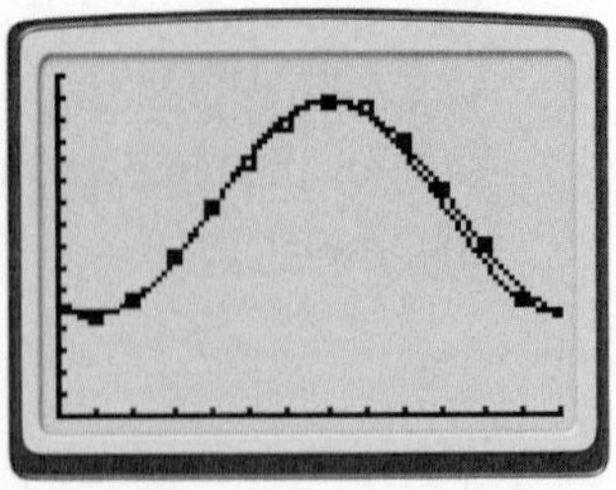

Both models appear to fit the data equally well from $x = 1$ to $x = 8$. For values of x greater than 8, the regression model fits the data better than the rough-fit model from the Explore does.

(B) The table gives the monthly mean minimum temperature, in degrees Celsius, for Canberra, Australia. Roughly fit a sine model of the form $y = a \sin\frac{1}{b}(x - h) + k$ to the data. Then obtain a sine regression model using a graphing calculator. Finally, visually compare the two models in relation to the data.

Month	1	2	3	4	5	6	7	8	9	10	11	12
Minimum temperature (°C)	13.2	13.1	10.7	6.7	3.2	1.0	−0.1	1.0	3.3	6.1	8.8	11.4

Step 1 Roughly fit a sine model of the form $y = a \sin\frac{1}{b}(x - h) + k$.

- The period $2\pi b$ must equal 12, so $b = \boxed{\frac{6}{\pi}}$ and $\frac{1}{b} = \boxed{\frac{\pi}{6}}$.
- The horizontal midline is halfway between the highest and lowest data points, so $k = \frac{13.2 + (-0.1)}{2} = \boxed{6.55}$.
- The first occurrence of a temperature close to 6.55 °C is in month 4, so $h = \boxed{4}$.
- The amplitude is half the vertical distance between the highest and lowest data points, so $|a| = \frac{13.2 - (-0.1)}{2} = \boxed{6.65}$. Because the temperatures are decreasing near $x = 4$, $a = \boxed{-6.65}$.

So, a sine model for the data is $y = \boxed{-6.65} \sin \boxed{\frac{\pi}{6}} \left(x - \boxed{4}\right) + \boxed{6.55}$.

Step 2 Enter the data into a graphing calculator and perform sine regression.

The sine regression model is $y = \boxed{6.65} \sin\left(\boxed{0.51}\, x + \boxed{1.07}\right) + \boxed{6.71}$.

Step 3 Visually compare the two models.

Both models appear to fit the data equally well from $x = 1$ to $x = 10$. For values of x greater than 10, the regression model fits the data better than the rough-fit model.

Reflect

4. Rewrite the regression model in Part A so that it has the form $y = a \sin\frac{1}{b}(x - h) + k$. Then compare this form of the regression model with the rough-fit model from the Explore.

5. **Discussion** Rewrite the regression model in Part B so that it has the form $y = a \sin\frac{1}{b}(x - h) + k$. Then compare this form of the regression model with the rough-fit model in Part B. How can you reconcile any differences you observe?

Your Turn

6. The table gives the monthly mean maximum temperature, in degrees Celsius, for Canberra, Australia. Roughly fit a sine model of the form $y = a\sin\frac{1}{b}(x - h) + k$ to the data. Then obtain a sine regression model using a graphing calculator. Finally, visually compare the two models in relation to the data.

Month	1	2	3	4	5	6	7	8	9	10	11	12
Maximum temperature (°C)	28.0	27.1	24.5	20.0	15.6	12.3	11.4	13.0	16.2	19.4	22.7	26.1

Explain 2 Solving a Real-World Problem Using a Sine Model

You can use the graph of a sine model to determine when the model takes on a value of interest.

Example 2 **The table gives the amount of daylight, in hours and minutes, in Chicago on the first day of every month. For what period of time during a year does Chicago get a minimum of 12 hours of daylight?**

Day	Jan. 1	Feb. 1	Mar. 1	Apr. 1	May 1	June 1	July 1	Aug. 1	Sept. 1	Oct. 1	Nov. 1	Dec. 1
Amount of daylight (h:min)	9:12	10:03	11:15	12:43	14:02	15:01	15:10	14:24	13:08	11:45	10:22	9:22

Analyze Information

The independent variable in this situation is time, given as calendar dates (the first day of every month).

The dependent variable is amount of daylight, measured in hours and minutes.

Formulate a Plan

You want a sine regression model for the data in order to find the period of time during a year that Chicago gets a minimum of 12 hours of daylight. To obtain the model, you need to convert each of the given calendar dates to the number of days since the start of the year. You also need to convert each corresponding amount of daylight from hours and minutes to decimal hours.

Solve

You can use an online day-of-year calendar to convert the calendar dates to days since the start of the year (assuming it's not a leap year). Converting hours and minutes to decimal hours simply involves dividing the minutes by 60 and adding the result to the hours. Complete the table, giving decimal hours to the nearest hundredth if necessary.

Day	1	32	60	91	121	152	182	213	244	274	305	335
Amount of daylight (hours)	9.2	10.05	11.25	12.72	14.03	15.02	15.17	14.4	13.13	11.75	10.37	9.37

Enter the data into a graphing calculator and perform sine regression. The sine regression model is $y = 3 \sin(0.0167x + -1.31) + 12.1$. Graph the model along with the line $y = 12$. Use **5:intersect** from the **CALC** menu to determine the coordinates of each of the points of intersection of the sine curve and the line.

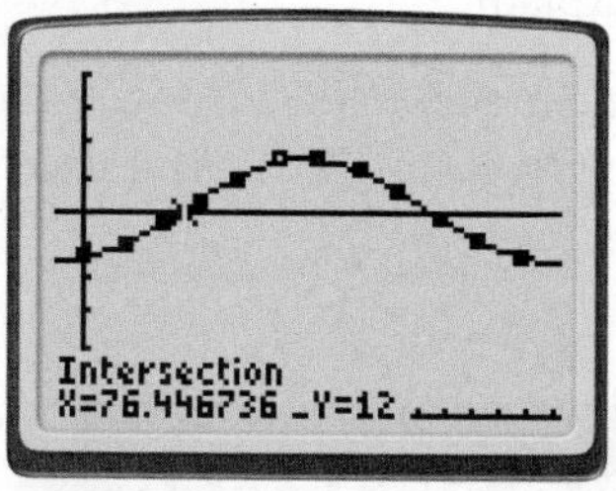

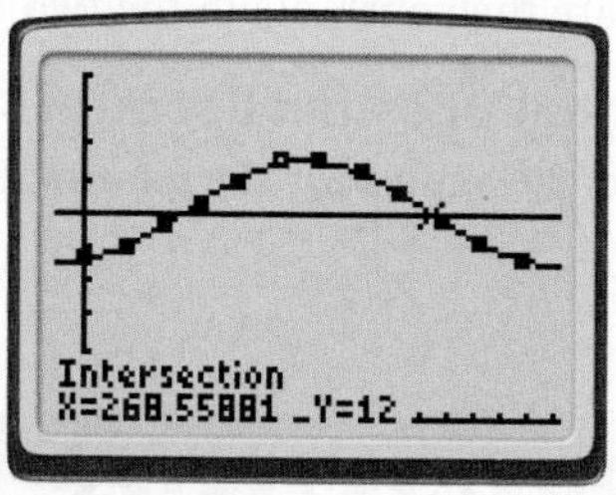

To the nearest whole number, the x-coordinate for the first point of intersection is 76, and the x-coordinate of the second point of intersection is 269. Using a day-of-year calendar, you find that 76 corresponds to March 17 and 269 corresponds to September 26. Since the graph of the sine model is above the line between those two dates, Chicago gets a minimum of 12 hours of daylight between March 17 and September 26.

Justify and Evaluate

Looking back at the table of data, you see that the first time the amount of daylight is 12 hours or greater is April 1 and the last time is September 1. These dates fall within the interval you found using the sine regression model, which confirms your answer.

Your Turn

7. The table gives the amount of daylight, in hours and minutes, in Sydney, Australia, on the first day of every month. For what period of time during a year does Sydney get a minimum of 12 hours of daylight?

Day	Jan. 1	Feb. 1	Mar. 1	Apr. 1	May 1	June 1	July 1	Aug. 1	Sept. 1	Oct. 1	Nov. 1	Dec. 1
Amount of daylight (h:min)	14:22	13:44	12:49	11:44	10:45	10:03	9:56	10:27	11:23	12:25	13:27	14:13

Data as ordered pairs with days of year and decimal hours: (1, 14.37), (32, 13.73), (60, 12.82), (91, 11.73), (121, 10.75), (152, 10.05), (182, 9.93), (213, 10.45), (244, 11.38), (274, 12.42), (305, 13.45), (335, 14.22)

Elaborate

8. What pattern must graphed data exhibit in order for a sine function to be an appropriate model for the data?

9. When modeling data with the function $y = a \sin \frac{1}{b}(x - h) + k$, how do you use the data to identify a reasonable value for the parameter a?

10. When you obtain both a rough-fit sine model and a sine regression model for a set of data, can you compare the constants in the two models directly? Explain.

11. **Essential Question Check-In** One way to fit a sine model to data is to use the data to identify reasonable values for the parameters a, b, h, and k in $y = a \sin \frac{1}{b}(x - h) + k$. What is another way?

Evaluate: Homework and Practice

Personal Math Trainer

- Online Homework
- Hints and Help
- Extra Practice

For the situation described:

(a) Graph the data, roughly fit a sine model of the form $y = a \sin \frac{1}{b}(x - h) + k$ to the data, and graph the model on the same grid as the data.

(b) Obtain a sine regression model using a graphing calculator, and then visually compare the two models in relation to the data.

1. The table gives the average monthly temperature in Nashville, Tennessee, in degrees Fahrenheit.

Month	1	2	3	4	5	6	7	8	9	10	11	12
Average temperature (°F)	37.7	41.7	50.0	59.0	67.5	75.7	79.4	78.7	71.5	60.3	49.8	40.4

2. The table shows the approximate US residential monthly electricity consumption in billions of kilowatt-hours (kWh) for one year where $x = 1$ represents January.

Month	1	2	3	4	5	6	7	8	9	10	11	12
Consumption (billions of kWh)	136	116	106	91	94	114	137	138	115	98	92	124

For the situation described:

(a) Graph the data, roughly fit a sine model of the form $y = a \sin \frac{1}{b}(x - h) + k$ to the data, and graph the model on the same grid as the data.

(b) Obtain a sine regression model using a graphing calculator, and then visually compare the two models in relation to the data.

(c) Use a graphing calculator and the regression model to answer the question.

3. The table shows the amount of daylight (in minutes) from sunrise to sunset on the 21st day of each month (given as the day of the year) in Green Bay, Wisconsin, where January 1 = day 1.

Day of year	21	52	80	111	141	172	202	233	264	294	325	355
Amount of daylight (minutes)	565	646	732	826	901	933	902	826	733	643	563	530

For about how long each year is the amount of daylight at most 10 hours?

4. The table shows the decimal portion of the moon's surface illuminated from Earth's view at midnight from Washington, D.C., in March, 2014, where x represents the day of the month.

Day	1	3	5	7	9	11	13	15	17	19	21	23	25	27	29	31
Portion of moon illuminated	0.00	0.05	0.19	0.37	0.56	0.74	0.89	0.98	1.00	0.94	0.80	0.60	0.37	0.17	0.03	0.00

A "gibbous moon" refers to the moon phases when more than half of the moon is illuminated, but it is not a full moon. About how long is the period that the moon is either a gibbous moon or a full moon?

H.O.T. Focus on Higher Order Thinking

5. **Make a Conjecture** Why does it make sense that a graphing calculator has a sine regression option but not a cosine regression option?

6. **Critical Thinking** In a science class lab, a mass is suspended from a spring above a tabletop. The mass is pulled down and released. By examining frames from a video as the mass bobs up and down, the class obtains the model $d(t) = 5 \sin 4(t - 0.39)$ for the displacement d of the mass relative to its resting position at time t in seconds. Cassandra notices that after several seconds the mass is not bobbing up and down as far, but it still seems to take about the same time for a cycle. Graph $y = e^{-0.05x}\left[5 \sin 4(x - 0.39)\right]$ on a graphing calculator with the original model for $0 \leq x \leq 10$. Explain how this model differs from the original model, and how it might account for Cassandra's observation.

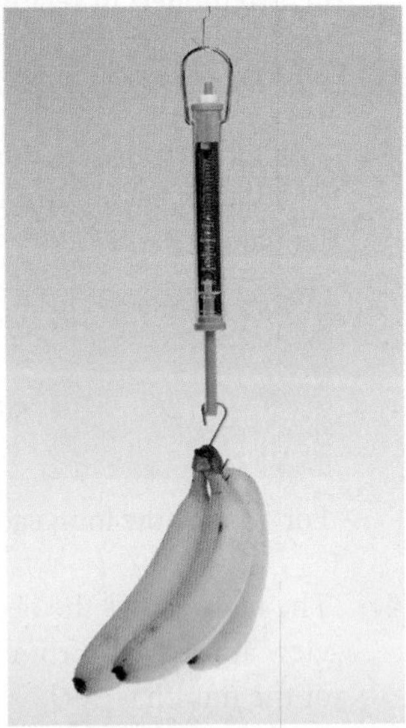

7. **Explain the Error** Given a set of data about the Sun's maximum angle θ (in degrees) above the horizon in Boston on any day of the year, Ryan uses his graphing calculator to obtain the regression model $\theta = 23.6 \sin(0.0168t - 1.32) + 47.4$ where t is the number of days since the start of a year. He concludes that the midline of the model's graph is $\theta = 47.4°$ and that the first time during the year that the Sun is reaches this maximum angle in Boston is $t = 1.32$, which corresponds to January 2. What is wrong with Ryan's conclusion? What is the correct conclusion?

Lesson Performance Task

For two years, a polling agency called a random sample of people every other month and asked them, "Do you think you have or are coming down with a cold or the flu today?" The percentage of those who responded "yes" to the pollsters is shown in the table.

Date	Percentage with cold or flu
January 15, 2012	9.3
March 15, 2012	6.4
May 15, 2012	4.2
July 15, 2012	3.1
September 15, 2012	5.2
November 15, 2012	7.9
January 15, 2013	10.8
March 15, 2013	7.1
May 15, 2013	4.7
July 15, 2013	3.0
September 15, 2013	5.3
November 15, 2013	7.7

a. Are the data periodic? If so, how many cycles do the data represent? Explain your reasoning.

b. When dealing with periodic phenomena, scientists often average corresponding data values from multiple cycles. For instance, for a given location, meteorologists often average the daily high temperatures and the daily low temperatures for corresponding days over a series of years. Why does it make sense to do so?

c. Complete the table by averaging the corresponding data values from the previous table. Also, replace the calendar dates in the cycle with the number of days since the start of a year (assuming it's not a leap year).

Days since start of year	Percentage with cold or flu
?	?
?	?
?	?
?	?
?	?
?	?

d. Roughly fit a sine model to the data in part c.

e. Use a graphing calculator to obtain a sine regression model for the data in part c. Visually compare this model with your rough-fit model.

f. Use the regression model to determine the period of time during the year when more than 6% of people have a cold or the flu.

Graphing Trigonometric Functions

Essential Question: How can graphing trigonometric functions help to solve real-world problems?

Key Vocabulary
amplitude *(amplitude)*
cosecant *(cosecante)*
cotangent *(cotangente)*
frequency *(frecuencia)*
midline *(línea media)*
period *(periodo)*
periodic function *(función periódica)*
secant function *(secante)*

KEY EXAMPLE (Lesson 18.1)

Find the amplitude and period of $f(x) = -\frac{1}{2}\cos 2x$.

$a = -\frac{1}{2}$

$\frac{1}{b} = 2$, so $b = \frac{1}{2}$

Identify a and b by comparing the function with the general equation $f(x) = a\cos\frac{1}{b}(x - h) + k$ or $f(x) = a\sin\frac{1}{b}(x - h) + k$.

amplitude $= |a| = \frac{1}{2}$ period $= 2\pi \cdot b = \frac{2\pi}{2} = \pi$

KEY EXAMPLE (Lesson 18.2)

Find the period, x-intercepts, and asymptotes of $f(x) = \cot\frac{\pi}{2}x$.

$\frac{1}{b} = \frac{\pi}{2}$, so $b = \frac{2}{\pi}$ — *Identify b by comparing the function with the general equation $f(x) = \tan\frac{1}{b}x$ or $f(x) = \cot\frac{1}{b}x$.*

period $= 2$ — *period $= \pi \cdot b = \pi \cdot \frac{2}{\pi} = 2$*

The first x-intercept is at 1. — *Identify the first x-intercept.*

The x-intercepts are at $1 + 2n$. — *Generalize the intercept locations (n = integer).*

The first asymptote is at $x = 0$. — *Identify the first asymptote.*

The asymptotes are at $x = 2n$. — *Generalize the asymptote locations.*

KEY EXAMPLE (Lesson 18.3)

Find the amplitude, period, horizontal and vertical shifts, maximum, minimum, and midline of $f(x) = 3\cos(x - \pi) - 1$.

$f(x) = 3$	$\cos 1(x$	$-\pi)$	-1
↑	↑	↑	↑
amplitude $= \|3\|$	period $2\pi \cdot 1$	horizontal shift	vertical shift
$= 3$	$= 2\pi$	$= \pi$	$= -1$

maximum = amplitude + vertical shift $= 3 + (-1) = 2 \rightarrow (\pi, 2); (3\pi, 2)$

minimum = −amplitude + vertical shift $= -3 + (-1) = -4 \rightarrow (2\pi, -4)$

midline: $y = \frac{\text{maximum} + \text{minimum}}{2} = \frac{2 + (-4)}{2} = -1$

KEY EXAMPLE (Lesson 18.4)

The table gives information on tides at Canada's Bay of Fundy. Assume that it takes 6.25 hours for the tide to come in and another 6.25 hours for the tide to retreat. Write a cosine function that models the height of the tide over time.

Tides at the Bay of Fundy		
	Time (*h*)	**Height (*m*)**
High Tide	$t = 0$	16.3
Low Tide	$t = 6.25$	0

amplitude: $(0.5)16.3 = 8.15 = a$

period: $12.5 = 2\pi \cdot |b| \rightarrow b = \frac{25}{4\pi}$ vertical shift: $(0.5)16.3 = 8.15$

function: $f(x) = 8.15\cos\frac{4\pi}{25}t + 8.15$

EXERCISES

1. Identify the amplitude and period of $f(x) = \frac{\pi}{2}\sin \pi x$ *(Lesson 18.1)*

2. Identify the period, x-intercepts, and asymptotes of $f(x) = \tan \pi x$. *(Lesson 18.2)*

3. Find the amplitude, period, horizontal shift, maximum, minimum, and midline of $f(x) = 2\sin\left(x - \frac{\pi}{2}\right) + 3$. *(Lesson 18.3)*

MODULE PERFORMANCE TASK

What's Your Sine?

During a new moon, 0% of the moon's surface visible from Earth is illuminated by the Sun. At the full moon, 100% of the moon is lit. The moon cycles back and forth between these extremes about every 29.5 days. The table gives the fraction of the moon that was lit on certain days in January 2014.

Day	1	5	10	13	16	20	25	28	31
Fraction Lit	0.00	0.20	0.70	0.92	1.00	0.86	0.40	0.11	0.00

Use this information to find a sine function that models this phenomenon. Then use your model to predict the fraction of the moon's visible surface that is lit on any given day in 2014.

Start by listing the information you will need to solve the problem. Then complete the task. Use graphs, numbers, words, or algebra to explain how you reached your conclusion.

Ready to Go On?

18.1–18.4 Graphing Trigonometric Functions

Personal Math Trainer

- Online Homework
- Hints and Help
- Extra Practice

1. Find the amplitude, period, horizontal shift, and x-intercepts of $f(x) = \sin\left(x - \frac{5\pi}{4}\right)$.

2. The displacement in inches of a mass attached to a spring is modeled by $y_1(t) = 3\sin\left(\frac{2\pi}{5}t + \frac{\pi}{2}\right)$, where t is the time in seconds.

a. What is the amplitude of the motion?

b. What is the period of the motion?

c. What is the initial displacement when $t = 0$?

3. The paddle wheel of a ship is 11 feet in diameter, revolves 15 times per minute when moving at top speed, and is 2 feet below the water's surface at its lowest point. Using this speed and starting from a point at the very top of the wheel, write a model for the height h (in feet) of the end of the paddle relative to the water's surface as a function of time t (in minutes).

ESSENTIAL QUESTION

4. What are the key features of the graphs of a trigonometric function, and how can you use a trigonometric function to model real-world data?

MODULE 18
MIXED REVIEW

Assessment Readiness

1. Consider the graph of the function $f(x) = \pi\cos\left(x + \frac{\pi}{2}\right) + 2$. Determine if each statement is True or False.

A. The period is π.

B. The amplitude is 1.

C. The horizontal shift is $-\frac{\pi}{2}$.

2. Tell whether each function has an amplitude of 4.

A. $f(x) = 4\csc x$

B. $f(x) = -4\sin \pi x$

C. $f(x) = \sin 4x + 4$

3. A basketball is dropped from a height of 15 feet. Can the height of the basketball be modeled by a trigonometric function? If so, write the function. If not, explain why not.

4. In photosynthesis, a plant converts carbon dioxide and water to sugar and oxygen. This process is studied by measuring a plant's carbon assimilation C (in micromoles of CO_2 per square meter per second). For a bean plant, $C(t) = 1.2 \sin \frac{\pi}{12}(t - 6) + 7$, where t is time in hours starting at midnight.

a. What is the period of the function?

b. What is the maximum and at what time does it occur?

Assessment Readiness

Personal Math Trainer

- Online Homework
- Hints and Help
- Extra Practice

1. Consider that $\sin\theta \approx 0.819$.

Tell whether each statement is possible.

A. $\cos\theta \approx 0.819$

B. $\cos\theta \approx -0.574$

C. $\cos\theta \approx 0.574$

2. Consider the graphs of the functions $f(x) = 0.25\cos 4\left(x - \frac{\pi}{2}\right) + 0.5$ and $g(x) = 0.25\cos 4\left(x + \frac{\pi}{2}\right) + 0.5$. Determine if each statement is True or False.

A. Both graphs look exactly the same.

B. $g(x)$ is translated up $\frac{\pi}{2}$, and $f(x)$ is translated down $\frac{\pi}{2}$.

C. $g(x)$ is translated left $\frac{\pi}{2}$, and $f(x)$ is translated right $\frac{\pi}{2}$.

3. Consider a ball that has a diameter of 10 inches rolling at a rate of 20 revolutions per second. Determine if each statement is True or False.

A. It will take 0.1 second to travel 7200 degrees.

B. It will take 5 minutes to travel 7200 degrees.

C. The ball will travel approximately 436 inches if it rolls through 5000 degrees.

4. Consider the radian measure $\frac{23\pi}{4}$. Tell whether each statement is correct.

A. $\cos\frac{23\pi}{4} \approx -0.707$

B. $\tan\frac{23\pi}{4} = -1$

C. $\sin\frac{23\pi}{4} \approx 0.707$

5. Hannah is graphing the functions $f(x) = 5\sin(x)$ and $g(x) = 5\csc(x)$ on the same coordinate plane. Explain what she should see if she graphs them correctly.

6. While completing an assignment in class, students were required to recognize the period and amplitude of a trigonometric function without graphing the function. Roland said that the function $f(x) = 4\sin\left(\frac{1}{2}x\right)$ has a period of 4 and an amplitude of $\frac{1}{2}$. Describe and correct his mistake.

7. Use two different methods to find the roots of the quadratic equation $h(x) = x^2 + 3x - 18$. Explain which methods you used, and why. Did you get the same roots?

Performance Tasks

★ 8. In women's fastpitch softball, the circular pitching motion occurs through about $1\frac{1}{2}$ arm revolutions. What radian measure does this represent? For a pitcher whose pitch radius is 2 feet, what circular distance does the ball travel during the pitching motion?

★★ **9.** A DVD's rotational speed varies from 1530 rpm (revolutions per minute) when the inner edge is being read to 630 rpm when the outer edge is being read.

A. What is the total rotation of the DVD in radians after 10 seconds, if the computer is reading data on the outer edge? Show how you got your answer.

B. In 10 seconds, what linear distance is covered by the part of the DVD that passes under the reader head from part A, which is about 6 cm from the center of the DVD?

C. If the computer is reading data on the inner edge (about 2.5 cm from the center of the DVD), what linear distance is covered by the part of the DVD that passes under the reader head in 10 seconds?

★★★**10.** Belinda recorded the dew point in her hometown in °F each day for a year (not a leap year) and entered the data into her graphing calculator, with $x = 0$ as January 1. She then performed a sinusoidal regression on her graphing calculator as shown.

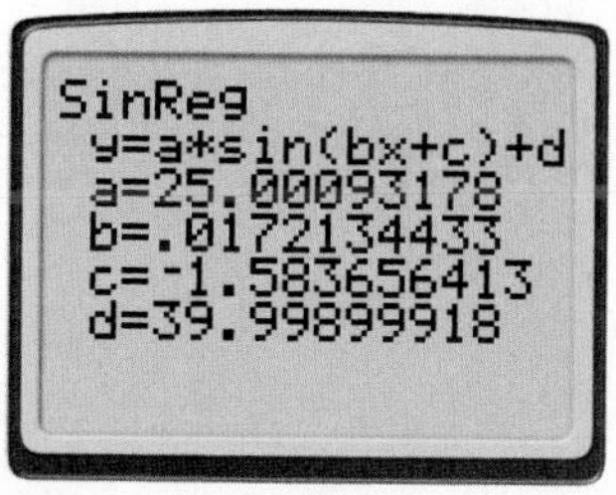

A. What is the model function? What are the function's period and amplitude? (Answers can be rounded to 2 decimal places, but don't round when calculating.)

B. Use the model function to find the approximate dew point on February 20. Also, determine on what day(s) the model says the dew point was 55 °F by using your graphing calculator.

C. What is the horizontal shift of the model function? What would the horizontal shift have been if the cosine function had been used instead of the sine function in the model? Support your answer.

MATH IN CAREERS

Boat Builder A side view of a riverboat's paddle wheel is shown. The paddle wheel has a diameter of 16 feet and rotates at a rate of 1 revolution every 4 seconds. Its lowest point is 2 feet below the water line. The function $h(t) = 8\sin\left[\frac{\pi}{2}(t-1)\right] + 6$ models the motion of the paddle point labeled P. The function gives the "height" (which is negative when the paddle is below the water line) at time t (in seconds).

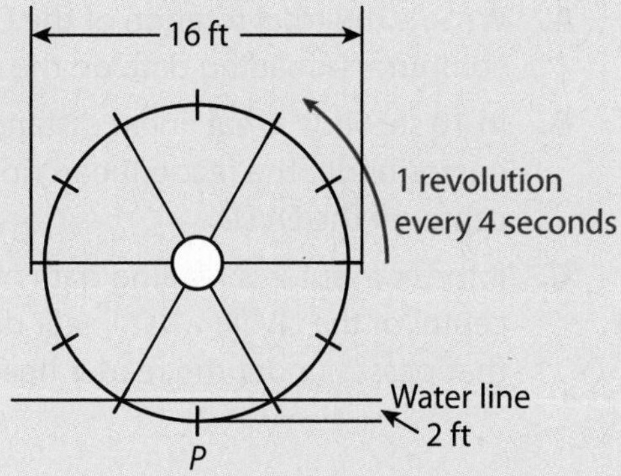

a. Graph the function on the interval $0 \leq t \leq 6$.

b. What is the significance of the graph's t-intercepts in the context of the situation?

c. What is the significance of the maximum and minimum values of h in the context of the situation?

d. If a point on the edge of the paddle travels a distance of 1 mile, through how many complete revolutions has the paddle wheel turned?

UNIT 8

Probability

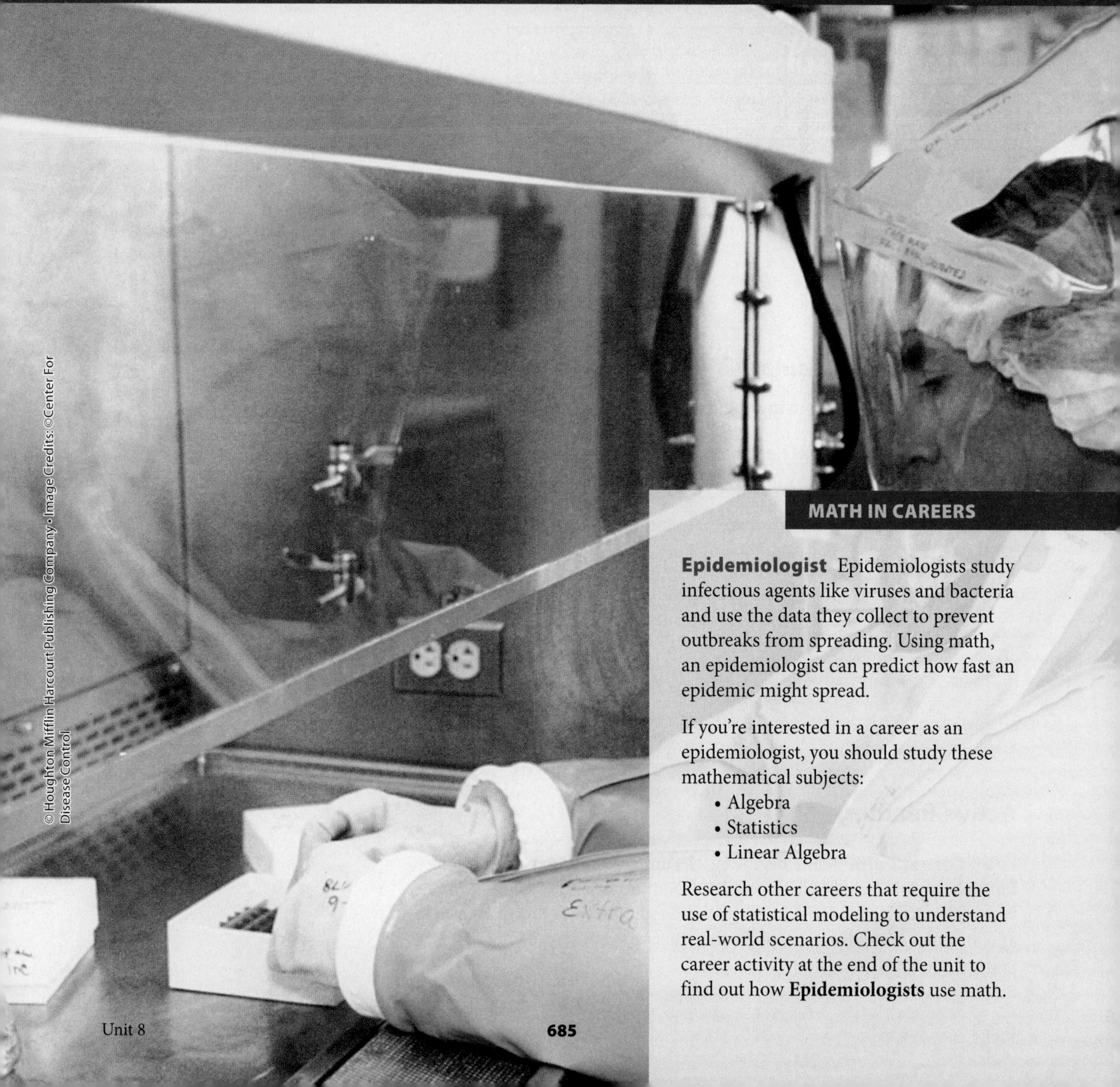

MATH IN CAREERS

Epidemiologist Epidemiologists study infectious agents like viruses and bacteria and use the data they collect to prevent outbreaks from spreading. Using math, an epidemiologist can predict how fast an epidemic might spread.

If you're interested in a career as an epidemiologist, you should study these mathematical subjects:

- Algebra
- Statistics
- Linear Algebra

Research other careers that require the use of statistical modeling to understand real-world scenarios. Check out the career activity at the end of the unit to find out how **Epidemiologists** use math.

Reading Start-Up

Vocabulary

Review Words

✔ event (*evento*)
✔ outcome (*resultado*)
✔ probability (*probabilidad*)
✔ sample space (*muestra de espacio*)
✔ trial (prueba)

Preview Words

combination (*combinación*)
complement (*complementar*)
conditional probability (*probabilidad condicional*)
dependent events (*eventos dependientes*)
element (*elemento*)
empty set (*conjunto vacío*)
factorial (*factorial*)
independent events (*eventos independientes*)
intersection (*intersección*)
permutation (*permutación*)
set (*conjunto*)
subset (*subconjunto*)
union (*unión*)

Visualize Vocabulary

Match the review words to their descriptions to complete the chart.

Word	Description
?	The measure of how likely an event is to occur
?	All possible outcomes of an experiment
?	Any set of outcomes
?	A single repetition or observation of an experiment
?	A result of an experiment

Understand Vocabulary

Complete the sentences using the preview words.

1. The __?__ contains no elements.

2. If the occurrence of one event does not affect the occurrence of another event, then the events are called __?__.

3. A(n) __?__ is a group of objects in a particular order.

4. To find the __?__ of a positive integer, find the product of the number and all of the positive integers less than the number.

Active Reading

Four-Corner Fold Before beginning the unit, create a four-corner fold for each module. Label each flap with lesson titles from the module. As you study each lesson, write important ideas such as vocabulary, diagrams, and formulas under the appropriate flap. Refer to your layered books as you complete exercises.

MODULE 19

Introduction to Probability

Essential Question: How can you use probability to solve real-world problems?

REAL WORLD VIDEO
Check out how principles of probability are used to derive and interpret baseball players' statistics.

MODULE PERFORMANCE TASK PREVIEW

Baseball Probability

In this module, you will use concepts of probability to determine the chances of various outcomes for a baseball player at bat. To successfully complete this task, you'll need to calculate a theoretical probability for a real-world situation. Batter up!

Are YOU Ready?

Complete these exercises to review skills you will need for this module.

Personal Math Trainer

- Online Homework
- Hints and Help
- Extra Practice

Probability of Simple Events

Example 1

Find the probability of rolling a 4 when using a normal six-sided die with each side having equal probability.

Each of the six faces has equal probability, so the probability of any face being rolled is $\frac{1}{6}$.

There is only one face with a four on it, so the probability of rolling a four is also $\frac{1}{6}$.

Find each probability.

1. The probability of flipping a coin and getting a heads, given that the probability of getting a tails is the same, and there is no chance that the coin lands on its side.

2. The probability of drawing a Jack of Hearts from a 52-card deck given the deck is properly shuffled.

3. The probability of any particular day being Sunday.

Probability of Compound Events

Example 2

Find the probability of drawing a red card or a black card when the probability of either is $\frac{1}{4}$ and you only draw one card.

Only one card is drawn and either card has a $\frac{1}{4}$ probability, so the probability of drawing one or the other is the sum of their probabilities.

Probability of drawing a red card or black card $\frac{1}{4} + \frac{1}{4} = \frac{1}{2}$.

Find each probability.

4. The probability of rolling a twelve-sided die and getting a 4 or a 6 given the probability of getting a 4 is $\frac{1}{12}$ and is equal to the probability of getting a 6.

5. The probability of pulling a red or a blue marble from a jar given the probability of drawing a red marble is $\frac{1}{4}$ and the probability of pulling a blue marble is $\frac{1}{2}$ and you only pull one marble.

19.1 Probability and Set Theory

Essential Question: How are sets and their relationships used to calculate probabilities?

Resource Locker

Explore Working with Sets

A **set** is a collection of distinct objects. Each object in a set is called an **element** of the set. A set is often denoted by writing the elements in braces.

The set with no elements is the **empty set**, denoted by ∅ or { }.

The set of all elements under consideration is the **universal set**, denoted by U.

Identifying the number of elements in a set is important for calculating probabilities.

(A) Use set notation to identify each set described in the table and identify the number of elements in each set.

Set	Set Notation	Number of Elements in the Set
Set A is the set of prime numbers less than 10.	$A = \{2, 3, ?, 7\}$	$n(A) = 4$
Set B is the set of even natural numbers less than 10.	$B = \{?, ?, ?, ?\}$	$n(B) = ?$
Set C is the set of natural numbers less than 10 that are multiples of 4.	$? = \{4, ?\}$	$n(C) = ?$
The universal set is all natural numbers less than 10.	$U = ?$	$?(?) = 9$

The following table identifies terms used to describe relationships among sets. Use sets A, B, C, and U from the previous table. You will supply the missing Venn diagrams for the Example column, including the referenced elements of the sets, as you complete steps B–I.

Term	Notation	Venn Diagram	Example
Set C is a **subset** of set B if every element of C is also an element of B.	$C \subset B$	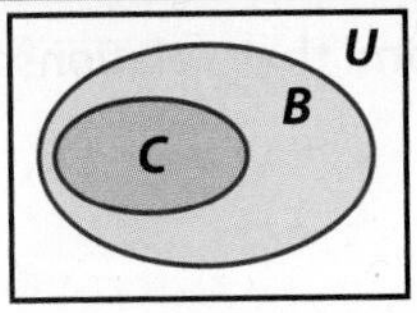	?
The **intersection** of sets A and B is the set of all elements that are in both A *and* B.	$A \cap B$	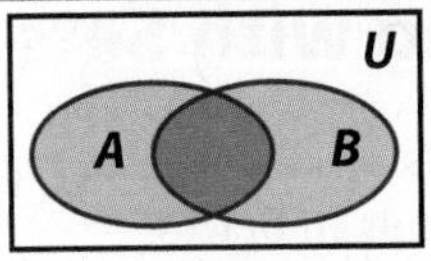 $A \cap B$ is the double-shaded region.	?
The **union** of sets A and B is the set of all elements that are in A *or* B.	$A \cup B$	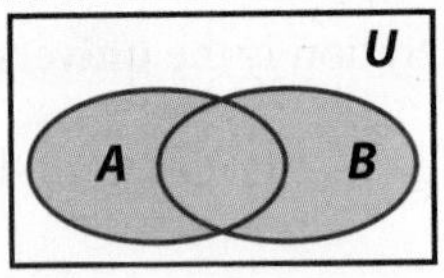 $A \cup B$ is the entire shaded region.	?
The **complement** of set A is the set of all elements in the universal set U that are *not* in A.	A^C or $\sim A$	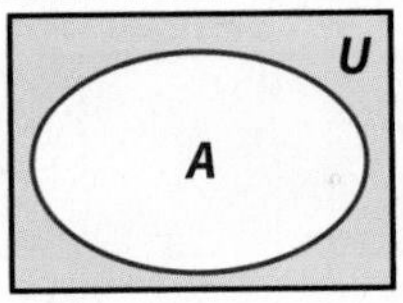 A^C is the shaded region.	?

(B) Since C is a subset of B, every element of set C, which consists of the numbers [?] and [?], is located not only in oval C, but also within oval B. Set B includes the elements of C as well as the additional elements [?] and [?], which are located in oval B outside of oval C. The universal set includes the elements of sets B and C as well as the additional elements [?], [?], [?], [?], and [?], which are located in region U outside of ovals B and C.

(C) For the first row of the table, draw the corresponding Venn diagram that includes the elements of B, C, and U.

(D) To determine the intersection of A and B, first define the elements of set A and set B separately, then identify all the elements found in both sets A *and* B.

$A = \{?, ?, ?, ?\}$

$B = \{?, ?, ?, ?\}$

$A \cap B = \{?\}$

(E) For the second row of the table, draw the Venn diagram for $A \cap B$ that includes the elements of A, B, and U and the double-shaded intersection region.

(F) To determine the union of sets A and B, identify all the elements found in either set A *or* set B by combining all the elements of the two sets into the union set.

$A \cup B = \{ ?, ?, ?, ?, ?, ?, ? \}$

(G) For the third row of the table, draw the Venn diagram for $A \cup B$ that includes the elements of A, B, and U and the shaded union region.

(H) To determine the complement of set A, first identify the elements of set A and universal set U separately, then identify all the elements in the universal set that are *not* in set A.

$A = \{ ?, ?, ?, ? \}$

$U = \{ ?, ?, ?, ?, ?, ?, ?, ?, ? \}$

$A^C = \{ ?, ?, ?, ?, ? \}$

(I) For the fourth row of the table, draw the Venn diagram for A^C that includes the elements of A and U and the shaded region that represents the complement of A.

Reflect

1. **Draw Conclusions** Do sets always have an intersection that is not the empty set? Provide an example to support your conclusion.

Explain 1 Calculating Theoretical Probabilities

A *probability experiment* is an activity involving chance. Each repetition of the experiment is called a *trial* and each possible result of the experiment is termed an *outcome*. A set of outcomes is known as an *event*, and the set of all possible outcomes is called the *sample space*.

Probability measures how likely an event is to occur. An event that is impossible has a probability of 0, while an event that is certain has a probability of 1. All other events have a probability between 0 and 1. When all the outcomes of a probability experiment are equally likely, the **theoretical probability** of an event A in the sample space S is given by

$$P(A) = \frac{\text{number of outcomes in the event}}{\text{number of outcomes in the sample space}} = \frac{n(A)}{n(S)}.$$

Example 1 **Calculate $P(A)$, $P(A \cup B)$, $P(A \cap B)$, and $P(A^C)$ for each situation.**

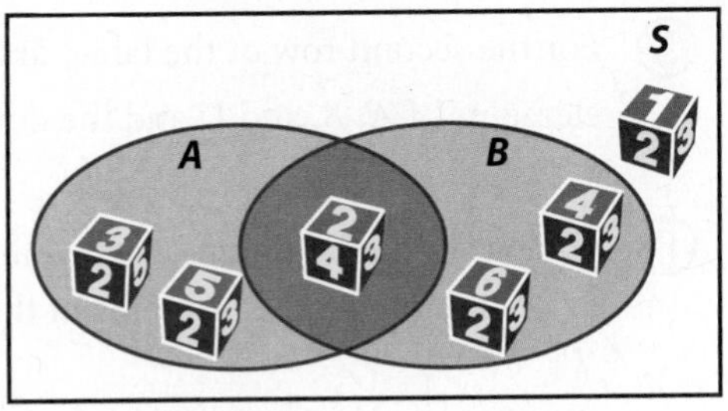

(A) You roll a number cube. Event A is rolling a prime number. Event B is rolling an even number.

$S = \{1, 2, 3, 4, 5, 6\}$, so $n(S) = 6$. $A = \{2, 3, 5\}$, so $n(A) = 3$.

So, $P(A) = \dfrac{n(A)}{n(S)} = \dfrac{3}{6} = \dfrac{1}{2}$.

$A \cup B = \{2, 3, 4, 5, 6\}$, so $n(A \cup B) = 5$. So, $P(A \cup B) = \dfrac{n(A \cup B)}{n(S)} = \dfrac{5}{6}$.

$A \cap B = \{2\}$, so $n(A \cap B) = 1$. So, $P(A \cap B) = \dfrac{n(A \cap B)}{n(S)} = \dfrac{1}{6}$.

$A^C = \{1, 4, 6\}$, so $n(A^C) = 3$. So, $P(A^C) = \dfrac{n(A^C)}{n(S)} = \dfrac{3}{6} = \dfrac{1}{2}$.

(B) Your grocery basket contains one bag of each of the following items: oranges, green apples, green grapes, green broccoli, white cauliflower, orange carrots, and green spinach. You are getting ready to transfer your items from your cart to the conveyer belt for check-out. Event A is picking a bag containing a vegetable first. Event B is picking a bag containing a green food first. All bags have an equal chance of being picked first.

Order of objects in sets may vary.

$S = \{\text{orange, apple, grape, broccoli, cauliflower, carrot, spinach}\}$, so $n(S) = 7$.

$A = \{\text{broccoli, cauliflower, carrot, spinach}\}$, so $n(A) = 4$. So $P(A) = \dfrac{n(A)}{n(S)} = \dfrac{4}{7}$.

$A \cup B = \{\text{broccoli, cauliflower, carrot, spinach, apple, grape}\}$, so $n(A \cup B) = 6$.

$P(A \cup B) = \dfrac{n(A \cup B)}{n(S)} = \dfrac{6}{7}$

$A \cap B = \{\text{broccoli, spinach}\}$, so $n(A \cap B) = 2$

$P(A \cap B) = \dfrac{n(A \cap B)}{n(S)} = \dfrac{2}{7}$

$$P(A^c) = \frac{n(A^c)}{n(S)} = \frac{3}{7}$$

Reflect

2. **Discussion** In Example 1B, which is greater, $P(A \cup B)$ or $P(A \cap B)$? Do you think this result is true in general? Explain.

Your Turn

The numbers 1 through 30 are written on slips of paper that are then placed in a hat. Students draw a slip to determine the order in which they will give an oral report. Event *A* is being one of the first 10 students to give their report. Event *B* is picking a multiple of 6. If you pick first, calculate each of the indicated probabilities.

3. $P(A)$

4. $P(A \cup B)$

5. $P(A \cap B)$

6. $P(A^c)$

Explain 2 Using the Complement of an Event

You may have noticed in the previous examples that the probability of an event occurring and the probability of the event not occurring (i.e., the probability of the complement of the event) have a sum of 1. This relationship can be useful when it is more convenient to calculate the probability of the complement of an event than it is to calculate the probability of the event.

Probabilities of an Event and Its Complement	
$P(A) + P(A^c) = 1$	The sum of the probability of an event and the probability of its complement is 1.
$P(A) = 1 - P(A^c)$	The probability of an event is 1 minus the probability of its complement.
$P(A^c) = 1 - P(A)$	The probability of the complement of an event is 1 minus the probability of the event.

Example 2 **Use the complement to calculate the indicated probabilities.**

(A) You roll a blue number cube and a white number cube at the same time. What is the probability that you do not roll doubles?

Step 1 **Define the events.** Let *A* be that you do not roll doubles and A^c that you do roll doubles.

Step 2 **Make a diagram.** A two-way table is one helpful way to identify all the possible outcomes in the sample space.

Blue Number Cube

White Number Cube	1	2	3	4	5	6
1	1, 1	1, 2	1, 3	1, 4	1, 5	1, 6
2	2, 1	2, 2	2, 3	2, 4	2, 5	2, 6
3	3, 1	3, 2	3, 3	3, 4	3, 5	3, 6
4	4, 1	4, 2	4, 3	4, 4	4, 5	4, 6
5	5, 1	5, 2	5, 3	5, 4	5, 5	5, 6
6	6, 1	6, 2	6, 3	6, 4	6, 5	6, 6

Step 3 Determine $P(A^c)$. Since there are fewer outcomes for rolling doubles, it is more convenient to determine the probability of rolling doubles, which is $P(A^c)$. To determine $n(A^c)$, draw a loop around the outcomes in the table that correspond to A^c and then calculate $P(A^c)$.

$$P(A^c) = \frac{n(A^c)}{n(S)} = \frac{6}{36} = \frac{1}{6}$$

Step 4 Determine $P(A)$. Use the relationship between the probability of an event and its complement to determine $P(A)$.

$$P(A) = 1 - P(A^c) = 1 - \frac{1}{6} = \frac{5}{6}$$

So, the probability of not rolling doubles is $\frac{5}{6}$.

(B) One pile of cards contains the numbers 2 through 6 in red hearts. A second pile of cards contains the numbers 4 through 8 in black spades. Each pile of cards has been randomly shuffled. If one card from each pile is chosen at the same time, what is the probability that the sum will be less than 12?

Step 1 Define the events. Let A be the event that the sum is less than 12 and A^c be the event that the sum is not less than 12.

Step 2 Make a diagram. Make a table to show all the outcomes in the sample space.

Step 3 Determine $P(A^c)$. Circle the outcomes in the table that correspond to A^c, then determine $P(A^c)$.

		Red Hearts ♥				
		2	3	4	5	6
Black Spades ♠	4	4+2	4+3	4+4	4+5	4+6
	5	5+2	5+3	5+4	5+5	5+6
	6	6+2	6+3	6+4	6+5	6+6
	7	7+2	7+3	7+4	7+5	7+6
	8	8+2	8+3	8+4	8+5	8+6

$$P(A^c) = \frac{n(A^c)}{n(S)} = \frac{6}{25}$$

Step 4 Determine $P(A)$. Use the relationship between the probability of an event and its complement to determine $P(A^c)$.

$$P(A) = 1 - P(A^c) = 1 - \frac{6}{25} = \frac{19}{25}$$

So, the probability that the sum of the two cards is less than 12 is $\frac{19}{25}$.

Reflect

7. Describe a different way to calculate the probability that the sum of the two cards will be less than 12.

Your Turn

One bag of marbles contains two red, one yellow, one green, and one blue marble. Another bag contains one marble of each of the same four colors. One marble from each bag is chosen at the same time. Use the complement to calculate the indicated probabilities.

8. Probability of selecting two different colors

9. Probability of not selecting a yellow marble

Elaborate

10. Can a subset of A contain elements of A^C? Why or why not?

11. For any set A, what does $A \cap \emptyset$ equal? What does $A \cup \emptyset$ equal? Explain.

12. **Essential Question Check-In** How do the terms *set*, *element*, and *universal set* correlate to the terms used to calculate theoretical probability?

Evaluate: Homework and Practice

Personal Math Trainer
- Online Homework
- Hints and Help
- Extra Practice

Set A is the set of factors of 12, set B is the set of even natural numbers less than 13, set C is the set of odd natural numbers less than 13, and set D is the set of even natural numbers less than 7. The universal set for these questions is the set of natural numbers less than 13.

So, $A = \{1, 2, 3, 4, 6, 12\}$, $B = \{2, 4, 6, 8, 10, 12\}$, $C = \{1, 3, 5, 7, 9, 11\}$, $D = \{2, 4, 6\}$, and $U = \{1, 2, 3, 4, 5, 6, 7, 8, 9, 10, 11, 12\}$. Answer each question.

1. Is $D \subset A$? Explain why or why not.

2. Is $B \subset A$? Explain why or why not.

3. What is $A \cap B$?

4. What is $A \cap C$?

5. What is $A \cup B$?

6. What is $A \cup C$?

7. What is A^C?

8. What is B^C?

You have a set of 10 cards numbered 1 to 10. You choose a card at random. Event A is choosing a number less than 7. Event B is choosing an odd number. Calculate the probability.

9. $P(A)$

10. $P(B)$

11. $P(A \cup B)$

12. $P(A \cap B)$

13. $P(A^C)$

14. $P(B^C)$

Use the complement of the event to find the probability.

15. You roll a 6-sided number cube. What is the probability that you do not roll a 2?

16. You choose a card at random from a standard deck of cards. What is the probability that you do not choose a red king?

17. You spin the spinner shown. The spinner is divided into 12 equal sectors. What is the probability of not spinning a 2?

18. A bag contains 2 red, 5 blue, and 3 green balls. A ball is chosen at random. What is the probability of not choosing a red ball?

19. Cards numbered 1–12 are placed in a bag. A card is chosen at random. What is the probability of not choosing a number less than 5?

20. Slips of paper numbered 1–20 are folded and placed into a hat, and then a slip of paper is drawn at random. What is the probability the slip drawn has a number which is not a multiple of 4 or 5?

21. You are going to roll two number cubes, a white number cube and a red number cube, and find the sum of the two numbers that come up.

a. What is the probability that the sum will be 6?

b. What is the probability that the sum will not be 6?

22. You have cards with the letters A, B, C, D, E, F, G, H, I, J, K, L, M, N, O, P. Event U is choosing the cards A, B, C or D. Event V is choosing a vowel. Event W is choosing a letter in the word "APPLE". Find $P(U \cap V \cap W)$.

A standard deck of cards has 13 cards (2, 3, 4, 5, 6, 7, 8, 9, 10, jack, queen, king, ace) in each of 4 suits (hearts, clubs, diamonds, spades). The hearts and diamonds cards are red. The clubs and spades cards are black. Answer each question.

23. You choose a card from a standard deck of cards at random. What is the probability that you do not choose an ace? Explain.

24. You choose a card from a standard deck of cards at random. What is the probability that you do not choose a club? Explain.

25. You choose a card from a standard deck of cards at random. Event A is choosing a red card. Event B is choosing an even number. Event C is choosing a black card. Find $P(A \cap B \cap C)$. Explain.

26. You are selecting a card at random from a standard deck of cards. Match each event with the correct probability.

A. Picking a card that is both red and a heart. **a.** ___?___ $\frac{1}{52}$

B. Picking a card that is both a heart and an ace. **b.** ___?___ $\frac{1}{4}$

C. Picking a card that is not both a heart and an ace. **c.** ___?___ $\frac{51}{52}$

H.O.T. Focus on Higher Order Thinking

27. Critique Reasoning A bag contains white tiles, black tiles, and gray tiles. Someone is going to choose a tile at random. $P(W)$, the probability of choosing a white tile, is $\frac{1}{4}$. A student claims that the probability of choosing a black tile, $P(B)$, is $\frac{3}{4}$ since $P(B) = 1 - P(W) = 1 - \frac{1}{4} = \frac{3}{4}$. Do you agree? Explain.

28. Communicate Mathematical Ideas A bag contains 5 red marbles and 10 blue marbles. You are going to choose a marble at random. Event A is choosing a red marble. Event B is choosing a blue marble. What is $P(A \cap B)$? Explain.

29. Critical Thinking Jeffery states that for a sample space S where all outcomes are equally likely, $0 \leq P(A) \leq 1$ for any subset A of S. Create an argument that will justify his statement or state a counterexample.

Lesson Performance Task

For the sets you've worked with in this lesson, membership in a set is binary: Either something belongs to the set or it doesn't. For instance, 5 is an element of the set of odd numbers, but 6 isn't

In 1965, Lofti Zadeh developed the idea of "fuzzy" sets to deal with sets for which membership is not binary. He defined a *degree* of membership that can vary from 0 to 1. For instance, a membership function $m_L(w)$ for the set L of large dogs where the degree of membership m is determined by the weight w of a dog might be defined as follows:

- A dog is a full member of the set L if it weighs 80 pounds or more. This can be written as $m_L(w) = 1$ for $w \geq 80$.
- A dog is not a member of the set L if it weighs 60 pounds or less. This can be written as $m_L(w) = 0$ for $w \leq 60$.
- A dog is a partial member of the set L if it weighs between 60 and 80 pounds. This can be written as $0 < m_L(w) < 1$ for $60 < w < 80$.

The "large dogs" portion of the graph shown displays the membership criteria listed above. Note that the graph shows only values of $m(w)$ that are positive.

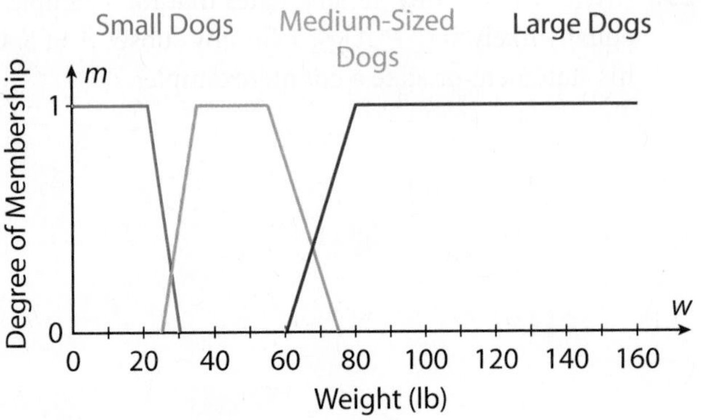

1. Using the graph, give the approximate weights for which a dog is considered a full member, a partial member, and not a member of the set S of small dogs.

2. The union of two "fuzzy" sets A and B is given by the membership rule $m_{A \cup B}(x) = \text{maximum}\big(m_A(x), m_B(x)\big)$. So, for a dog of a given size, the degree of its membership in the set of small or medium-sized dogs $(S \cup M)$ is the greater of its degree of membership in the set of small dogs and its degree of membership in the set of medium-sized dogs.

The intersection of A and B is given by the membership rule $m_{A \cap B}(x) = \text{minimum}\big(m_A(x), m_B(x)\big)$. So, for a dog of a given size, the degree of its membership in the set of dogs that are both small and medium-sized $(S \cap M)$ is the lesser of its degree of membership in the set of small dogs and its degree of membership in the set of medium-sized dogs.

Using the graph above and letting S be the set of small dogs, M be the set of medium-sized dogs, and L be the set of large dogs, draw the graph of each set.

a. $S \cup M$

b. $M \cap L$

19.2 Permutations and Probability

Essential Question: When are permutations useful in calculating probability?

Resource Locker

Explore Finding the Number of Permutations

A **permutation** is a selection of objects from a group in which order is important. For example, there are 6 permutations of the letters A, B, and C.

ABC	ACB	BAC	BCA	CAB	CBA

You can find the number of permutations with the **Fundamental Counting Principle**.

Fundamental Counting Principle

If there are n items and a_1 ways to choose the first item, a_2 ways to select the second item after the first item has been chosen, and so on, there are $a_1 \times a_2 \times \ldots \times a_n$ ways to choose n items.

There are 7 members in a club. Each year the club elects a president, a vice president, and a treasurer.

(A) What is the number of permutations of all 7 members of the club?

There are ? different ways to make the first selection.

Once the first person has been chosen, there are ? different ways to make the second selection.

Once the first two people have been chosen, there are ? different ways to make the third selection.

Continuing this pattern, there are ? permutations of all the members of the club.

(B) The club is holding elections for a president, a vice president, and a treasurer. How many different ways can these positions be filled?

There are ? different ways the position of president can be filled.

Once the president has been chosen, there are ? different ways the position of vice president can be filled. Once the president and vice president have been chosen, there are ? different ways the position of treasurer can be filled.

So, there are ? different ways that the positions can be filled.

(C) What is the number of permutations of the members of the club who were not elected as officers?

After the officers have been elected, there are ? members remaining. So there are ? different ways to make the first selection.

Once the first person has been chosen, there are ? different ways to make the second selection.

Continuing this pattern, there are ? permutations of the unelected members of the club.

(D) Divide the number of permutations of all the members by the number of permutations of the unelected members.

There are ? permutations of all the members of the club.

There are ? permutations of the unelected members of the club.

The quotient of these two values is ? .

Reflect

1. How does the answer to Step D compare to the answer to Step B?
2. **Discussion** Explain the effect of dividing the total number of permutations by the number of permutations of items not selected.

Explain 1 Finding a Probability Using Permutations

The results of the Explore can be generalized to give a formula for permutations. To do so, it is helpful to use *factorials*. For a positive integer n, n **factorial**, written $n!$, is defined as follows.

$$n! = n \times (n-1) \times (n-2) \times \ldots \times 3 \times 2 \times 1$$

That is, $n!$ is the product of n and all the positive integers less than n. Note that $0!$ is defined to be 1.

In the Explore, the number of permutations of the 7 objects taken 3 at a time is

$$7 \times 6 \times 5 = \frac{7 \times 6 \times 5 \times 4 \times 3 \times 2 \times 1}{4 \times 3 \times 2 \times 1} = \frac{7!}{4!} = \frac{7!}{(7-3)!}$$

This can be generalized as follows.

Permutations

The number of permutations of n objects taken r at a time is given by ${}_nP_r = \frac{n!}{(n-r)!}$.

Example 1 Use permutations to find the probabilities.

(A) A research laboratory requires a four-digit security code to gain access to the facility. A security code can contain any of the digits 0, 1, 2, 3, 4, 5, 6, 7, 8, and 9, but no digit is repeated. What is the probability that a scientist is randomly assigned a code with the digits 1, 2, 3, and 4 in any order?

The sample space S consists is the number of permutations of 4 digits selected from 10 digits.

$$n(S) = {}_{10}P_4 = \frac{10!}{(10-4)!} = \frac{10!}{6!} = 5040$$

Event A consists of permutations of a security code with the digits 1, 2, 3, and 4.

$$n(A) = {}_4P_4 = \frac{4!}{(4-4)!} = \frac{4!}{0!} = 24$$

The probability of getting a security code with the digits 1, 2, 3, and 4 is

$$P(A) = \frac{n(A)}{n(S)} = \frac{24}{5040} = \frac{1}{210}.$$

(B) A certain motorcycle license plate consists of 5 digits that are randomly selected. No digit is repeated. What is the probability of getting a license plate consisting of all even digits?

The sample space S consists of permutations of 5 digits selected from 10 digits.

$$n(S) = {}_{\boxed{10}}P_{\boxed{5}} = \frac{\boxed{10!}}{\boxed{5!}} = \boxed{30,240}$$

Event A consists of permutations of a license plate with all even digits.

$$n(A) = {}_{\boxed{5}}P_{\boxed{5}} \frac{\boxed{5!}}{\boxed{0!}} = \boxed{120}$$

The probability of getting a license plate with all even digits is

$$P(A) = \frac{n(A)}{n(S)} = \frac{\boxed{120}}{\boxed{30,240}} = \frac{\boxed{1}}{\boxed{252}}.$$

Your Turn

There are 8 finalists in the 100-meter dash at the Olympic Games. Suppose 3 of the finalists are from the United States, and that all finalists are equally likely to win.

3. What is the probability that the United States will win all 3 medals in this event?

4. What is the probability that the United States will win no medals in this event?

Explain 2 Finding the Number of Permutations with Repetition

Up to this point, the problems have focused on finding the permutations of distinct objects. If some of the objects are repeated, this will reduce the number of permutations that are distinguishable.

For example, here are the permutations of the letters A, B, and C.

ABC	ACB	BAC	BCA	CAB	CBA

Next, here are the permutations of the letters M, O, and M. Bold type is used to show the different positions of the repeated letter.

MOM	MO**M**	**M**MO	M**M**O	O**M**M	OM**M**

Shown without the bold type, here are the permutations of the letters M, O, and M.

MOM	MOM	MMO	MMO	OMM	OMM

Notice that since the letter M is repeated, there are only 3 distinguishable permutations of the letters. This can be generalized with a formula for permutations with repetition.

Permutations with Repetition

The number of different permutations of n objects where one object repeats a times, a second object repeats b times, and so on is

$$\frac{n!}{a! \times b! \times \ldots}$$

Example 2 **Find the number of permutations.**

(A) How many different permutations are there of the letters in the word ARKANSAS?

There are 8 letters in the word, and there are 3 A's and 2 S's, so the number of permutations of the letters in ARKANSAS is $\frac{8!}{3!2!} = 3360$.

(B) One of the zip codes for Anchorage, Alaska, is 99522. How many permutations are there of the numbers in this zip code?

There are 5 digits in the zip code, and there are 2 nines, and 2 twos in the zip code, so the number of permutations of the zip code is

$$\frac{5!}{2!2!} = 30.$$

Your Turn

5. How many different permutations can be formed using all the letters in MISSISSIPPI?

6. One of the standard telephone numbers for directory assistance is 555–1212. How many different permutations of this telephone number are possible?

Explain 3 Finding a Probability Using Permutations with Repetition

Permutations with repetition can be used to find probablilities.

Example 3 **The school jazz band has 4 boys and 4 girls, and they are randomly lined up for a yearbook photo.**

(A) Find the probability of getting an alternating boy-girl arrangement.

The sample space S consists of permutations of 8 objects, with 4 boys and 4 girls.

$n(S)\ \frac{8!}{4!4!} = 70$

Event A consists of permutations that alternate boy-girl or girl-boy. The possible permutations are BGBGBGBG and GBGBGBGB.

$n(A) = 2$

The probability of getting an alternating boy-girl arrangement is $P(A) = \frac{n(A)}{n(S)} = \frac{2}{70} = \frac{1}{35}$.

(B) Find the probability of getting all of the boys grouped together.

The sample space S consists of permutations of 8 students, with 4 boys and 4 girls.

$n(S) = \frac{8!}{4!4!} = 70$

Event A consists of permutations with all 4 boys in a row. The possible permutations are BBBBGGGG, GBBBBGGG, GGBBBBGG, GGGBBBBG, and GGGGBBBB.

$n(A) = 5$

The probability of getting all the boys grouped together is $P(A) = \frac{n(A)}{n(S)} = \frac{5}{70} = \frac{1}{14}$.

Your Turn

7. There are 2 mystery books, 2 romance books, and 2 poetry books to be randomly placed on a shelf. What is the probability that the mystery books are next to each other, the romance books are next to each other, and the poetry books are next to each other?

8. What is the probability that a random arrangement of the letters in the word APPLE will have the two P's next to each other?

Elaborate

9. If ${}_nP_a = {}_nP_b$, what is the relationship between a and b? Explain your answer.

10. It was observed that there are 6 permutations of the letters A, B, and C. They are ABC, ACB, BAC, BCA, CAB, and CBA. If the conditions are changed so that the order of selection does not matter, what happens to these 6 different groups?

11. **Essential Question Check-In** How do you determine whether choosing a group of objects involves permutations?

Evaluate: Homework and Practice

Personal Math Trainer

- Online Homework
- Hints and Help
- Extra Practice

1. An MP3 player has a playlist with 12 songs. You select the shuffle option, which plays each song in a random order without repetition, for the playlist. In how many different orders can the songs be played?

2. There are 10 runners in a race. Medals are awarded for 1st, 2nd, and 3rd place. In how many different ways can the medals be awarded?

3. There are 9 players on a baseball team. In how many different ways can the coach choose players for first base, second base, third base, and shortstop?

4. A bag contains 9 tiles, each with a different number from 1 to 9. You choose a tile without looking, put it aside, choose a second tile without looking, put it aside, then choose a third tile without looking. What is the probability that you choose tiles with the numbers 1, 2, and 3 in that order?

5. There are 11 students on a committee. To decide which 3 of these students will attend a conference, 3 names are chosen at random by pulling names one at a time from a hat. What is the probability that Sarah, Jamal, and Mai are chosen in any order?

6. A clerk has 4 different letters that need to go in 4 different envelopes. The clerk places one letter in each envelope at random. What is the probability that all 4 letters are placed in the correct envelopes?

7. A swim coach randomly selects 3 swimmers from a team of 8 to swim in a heat. What is the probability that she will choose the three strongest swimmers?

8. How many different sequences of letters can be formed using all the letters in ENVELOPE?

9. Yolanda has 3 each of red, blue, and green marbles. How many possible ways can the 9 marbles be arranged in a row?

10. Jane has 16 cards. Ten of the cards look exactly the same and have the number 1 on them. The other 6 cards look exactly the same and have the number 2 on them. Jane is going to make a row containing all 16 cards. How many different ways can she order the row?

11. Ramon has 10 cards, each with one number on it. The numbers are 1, 2, 3, 4, 4, 6, 6, 6, 6, 6. Ramon is going to make a row containing all 10 cards. How many different ways can he order the row?

12. A grocer has 5 apples and 5 oranges for a window display. The grocer makes a row of the 10 pieces of fruit by choosing one piece of fruit at random, making it the first piece in the row, choosing a second piece of fruit at random, making it the second piece in the row, and so on. What is the probability that the grocer arranges the fruits in alternating order? (Assume that the apples are not distinguishable and that the oranges are not distinguishable.)

13. The letters G, E, O, M, E, T, R, Y are on 8 tiles in a bag, one letter on each tile. If you select tiles randomly from the bag and place them in a row from left to right, what is the probability the tiles will spell out GEOMETRY?

14. There are 11 boys and 10 girls in a classroom. A teacher chooses a student at random and puts that student at the head of a line, chooses a second student at random and makes that student second in the line, and so on, until all 21 students are in the line. What is the probability that the teacher puts them in a line alternating boys and girls? where no two of the same gender stand together?

15. There are 4 female and 4 male kittens are sleeping together in a row. Assuming that the arrangement is a random arrangement, what is the probability that all the female kittens are together, and all the male kittens are together?

16. If a ski club with 12 members votes to choose 3 group leaders, what is the probability that Marsha, Kevin, and Nicola will be chosen in any order for President, Treasurer, and Secretary?

17. There are 7 books numbered 1–7 on the summer reading list. Peter randomly chooses 2 books. What is the probability that Peter chooses books numbered 1 and 2, in either order?

18. On an exam, students are asked to list 5 historical events in the order in which they occurred. A student randomly orders the events. What is the probability that the student chooses the correct order?

19. A fan makes 6 posters to hold up at a basketball game. Each poster has a letter of the word TIGERS. Six friends sit next to each other in a row. The posters are distributed at random. What is the probability that TIGERS is spelled correctly when the friends hold up the posters?

20. The 10 letter tiles S, A, C, D, E, E, M, I, I, and O are in a bag. What is the probability that the letters S-A-M-E will be drawn from the bag at random, in that order?

21. If three cards are drawn at random from a standard deck of 52 cards, what is the probability that they will all be 7s? (There are four 7s in a standard deck of 52 cards.)

22. A shop classroom has ten desks in a row. If there are 6 students in shop class and they choose their desks at random, what is the probability they will sit in the first six desks?

23. Match each event with its probability. All orders are chosen randomly.

A. There are 15 floats that will be in a town parade. Event *A*: The mascot float is chosen to be first and the football team float is chosen to be second. **a.** ___?___ $\frac{1}{1365}$

B. Beth is one of 10 students performing in a school talent show. Event *B*: Beth is chosen to be the fifth performer and her best friend is chosen to be fourth. **b.** ___?___ $\frac{1}{210}$

C. Sylvester is in a music competition with 14 other musicians. Event *C*: Sylvester is chosen to be last, and his two best friends are chosen to be first and second. **c.** ___?___ $\frac{1}{90}$

H.O.T. Focus on Higher Order Thinking

24. Explain the Error Describe and correct the error in evaluating the expression.

$$_5P_3 = \frac{5!}{3!} = \frac{5 \times 4 \times 3!}{3!} = 20$$

25. Make a Conjecture If you are going to draw four cards from a deck of cards, does drawing four aces from the deck have the same probability as drawing four 3s? Explain.

26. **Communicate Mathematical Ideas** Nolan has Algebra, Biology, and World History homework. Assume that he chooses the order that he does his homework at random. Explain how to find the probability of his doing his Algebra homework first.

27. **Explain the Error** A student solved the problem shown. The student's work is also shown. Explain the error and provide the correct answer.

A bag contains 6 tiles with the letters A, B, C, D, E, and F, one letter on each tile. You choose 4 tiles one at a time without looking and line them up from left to right as you choose them. What is the probability that your tiles spell BEAD?

Let S be the sample space and let A be the event that the tiles spell BEAD.

$$n(S) = {}_6P_4 = \frac{6!}{(6-4)!} = \frac{6!}{2!} = 360$$

$$n(A) = {}_4P_4 = \frac{4!}{(4-4)!} = \frac{4!}{0!} = 24$$

$$P(A) = \frac{n(A)}{n(S)} = \frac{24}{360} = \frac{1}{5}$$

Lesson Performance Task

How many different ways can a blue card, a red card, and a green card be arranged? The diagram shows that the answer is six.

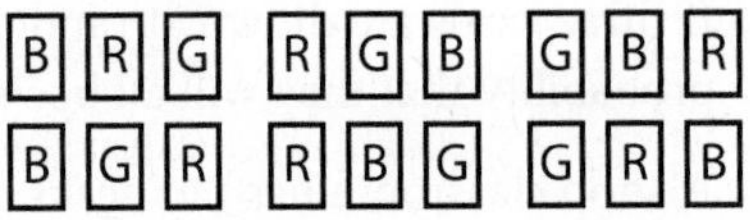

1. Now solve this problem: What is the least number of colors needed to color the pattern shown here, so that no two squares with a common boundary have the same color? Draw a sketch to show your answer.

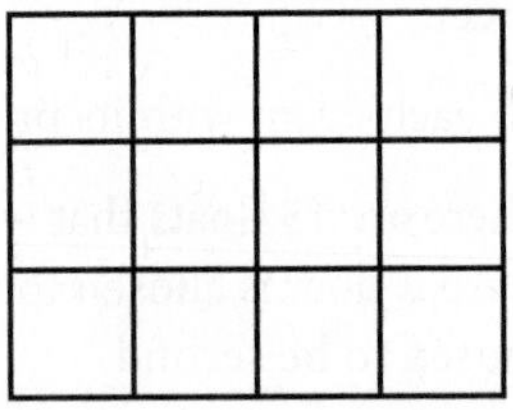

2. Now try this one. Again, find the least number of colors needed to color the pattern so that no two regions with a common boundary have the same color. Draw a sketch to show your answer.

3. In 1974, Kenneth Appel and Wolfgang Haken solved a problem that had confounded mathematicians for more than a century. They proved that no matter how complex a map is, it can be colored in a maximum of four colors, so that no two regions with a common boundary have the same color. Sketch the figure shown here. Can you color it in four colors? Can you color it in three colors?

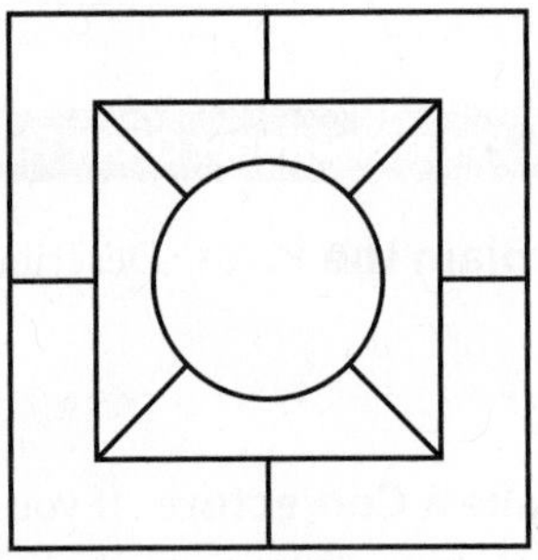

19.3 Combinations and Probability

Essential Question: What is the difference between a permutation and a combination?

Resource Locker

Explore Finding the Number of Combinations

A **combination** is a selection of objects from a group in which order is unimportant. For example, if 3 letters are chosen from the group of letters A, B, C, and D, there are 4 different combinations.

ABC	ABD	ACD	BCD

A restaurant has 8 different appetizers on the menu, as shown in the table. They also offer an appetizer sampler, which contains any 3 of the appetizers served on a single plate. How many different appetizer samplers can be created? The order in which the appetizers are selected does not matter.

Appetizers	
Nachos	Chicken Wings
Chicken Quesadilla	Vegetarian Egg Rolls
Potato Skins	Soft Pretzels
Beef Chili	Guacamole Dip

(A) Find the number appetizer samplers that are possible if the order of selection does matter. This is the number of permutations of 8 objects taken 3 at a time.

$${}_8P_3 = \frac{?}{(? - ?)!} = \frac{?}{?} = ?$$

(B) Find the number of different ways to select a particular group of appetizers. This is the number of permutations of 3 objects.

$${}_3P_3 = \frac{?}{(? - ?)!} = \frac{?}{?} = ?$$

(C) To find the number of possible appetizer samplers if the order of selection does not matter, divide the answer to part A by the answer to part B.

So the number of appetizer samplers that can be created is $\frac{?}{?} = ?$.

Reflect

1. Explain why the answer to Part A was divided by the answer to Part B.
2. On Mondays and Tuesdays, the restaurant offers an appetizer sampler that contains any 4 of the appetizers listed. How many different appetizer samplers can be created?
3. In general, are there more ways or fewer ways to select objects when the order does not matter? Why?

Explain 1 Finding a Probability Using Combinations

The results of the Explore can be generalized to give a formula for combinations. In the Explore, the number of combinations of the 8 objects taken 3 at a time is

$$_8P_3 \div {_3P_3} = \frac{8!}{(8-3)!} \div \frac{3!}{(3-3)!} = \frac{8!}{(8-3)!} \cdot \frac{0!}{3!} = \frac{8!}{(8-3)!} \cdot \frac{1}{3!} = \frac{8!}{3!(8-3)!}$$

This can be generalized as follows.

Combinations
The number of combinations of n objects taken r at a time is given by $_nC_r = \frac{n!}{r!(n-r)!}$

Example 1 **Find each probability.**

(A) There are 4 boys and 8 girls on the debate team. The coach randomly chooses 3 of the students to participate in a competition. What is the probability that the coach chooses all girls?

The sample space S consists of combinations of 3 students taken from the group of 12 students.

$$n(S) = {_{12}C_3} = \frac{12!}{3!9!} = 220$$

Event A consists of combinations of 3 girls taken from the set of 8 girls.

$$n(A) = {_8C_3} = \frac{8!}{3!5!} = 56$$

The probability that the coach chooses all girls is $P(A) = \frac{n(A)}{n(S)} = \frac{56}{220} = \frac{14}{55}$.

(B) There are 52 cards in a standard deck, 13 in each of 4 suits: clubs, diamonds, hearts, and spades. Five cards are randomly drawn from the deck. What is the probability that all five cards are diamonds?

The sample space S consists of combinations of 5 cards drawn from 52 cards.

$$n(S) = {_{52}C_5} = \frac{52!}{5!47!} = 2{,}598{,}960$$

Event A consists of combinations of 5 cards drawn from the 13 diamonds.

$$n(A) = {}_{13}C_{5} = \frac{13!}{5!8!} = 1287$$

The probability of randomly selecting 5 cards that are diamonds is

$$P(A) = \frac{n(A)}{n(S)} = \frac{1287}{2{,}598{,}960} = \frac{33}{66{,}640}.$$

Your Turn

4. A coin is tossed 4 times. What is the probability of getting exactly 3 heads?

5. A standard deck of cards is divided in half, with the red cards (diamonds and hearts) separated from the black cards (spades and clubs). Four cards are randomly drawn from the red half. What is the probability they are all diamonds?

Explain 2 Finding a Probability Using Combinations and Addition

Sometimes, counting problems involve the phrases "at least" or "at most." For these problems, combinations must be added.

For example, suppose a coin is flipped 3 times. The coin could show heads 0, 1, 2, or 3 times. To find the number of combinations with at least 2 heads, add the number of combinations with 2 heads and the number of combinations with 3 heads $({}_3C_2 + {}_3C_3)$.

Example 2 **Find each probability.**

(A) A coin is flipped 5 times. What is the probability that the result is heads at least 4 of the 5 times?

The number of outcomes in the sample space S can be found by using the Fundamental Counting Principle since each flip can result in heads or tails.

$n(S) = 2 \cdot 2 \cdot 2 \cdot 2 \cdot 2 = 2^5 = 32$

Let A be the event that the coin shows heads at least 4 times. This is the sum of 2 events, the coin showing heads 4 times and the coin showing heads 5 times. Find the sum of the combinations with 4 heads from 5 coins and with 5 heads from 5 coins.

$n(A) = {}_5C_4 + {}_5C_5 = \frac{5!}{4!1!} + \frac{5!}{5!0!} = 5 + 1 = 6$

The probability that the coin shows at least 4 heads is $P(A) = \frac{n(A)}{n(S)} = \frac{6}{32} = \frac{3}{16}$.

(B) Three number cubes are rolled and the result is recorded. What is the probability that at least 2 of the number cubes show 6?

The number of outcomes in the sample space S can be found by using the Fundamental Counting Principle since each roll can result in 1, 2, 3, 4, 5, or 6.

$$n(S) = 6^3 = 216$$

Let A be the event that at least 2 number cubes show 6. This is the sum of 2 events: 2 number cubes showing 6; and 3 number cubes showing 6. The event of getting 6 on 2 number cubes occurs 5 times since there are 5 possibilities for the other number cube.

$$n(A) = 5 \cdot {}_3C_2 + {}_3C_3 = 5 \cdot \frac{3!}{2!1!} + \frac{3!}{3!0!} = 15 + 1 = 16$$

The probability of getting a 6 at least twice in 3 rolls is $P(A) = \frac{n(A)}{n(S)} = \frac{16}{216} = \frac{2}{27}$.

Your Turn

6. A math department has a large database of true-false questions, half of which are true and half of which are false, that are used to create future exams. A new test is created by randomly selecting 6 questions from the database. What is the probability the new test contains at most 2 questions where the correct answer is "true"?

7. There are equally many boys and girls in the senior class. If 5 seniors are randomly selected to form the student council, what is the probability the council will contain at least 3 girls?

Elaborate

8. **Discussion** A coin is flipped 5 times, and the result of heads or tails is recorded. To find the probability of getting tails at least once, the events of 1, 2, 3, 4, or 5 tails can be added together. Is there a faster way to calculate this probability?

9. If ${}_nC_a = {}_nC_b$, what is the relationship between a and b? Explain your answer.

10. **Essential Question Check-In** How do you determine whether choosing a group of objects involves combinations?

Evaluate: Homework and Practice

Personal Math Trainer
- Online Homework
- Hints and Help
- Extra Practice

1. A cat has a litter of 6 kittens. You plan to adopt 2 of the kittens. In how many ways can you choose 2 of the kittens from the litter?

2. An amusement park has 11 roller coasters. In how many ways can you choose 4 of the roller coasters to ride during your visit to the park?

3. Four students from 30-member math club will be selected to organize a fundraiser. How many groups of 4 students are possible?

4. A school has 5 Spanish teachers and 4 French teachers. The school's principal randomly chooses 2 of the teachers to attend a conference. What is the probability that the principal chooses 2 Spanish teachers?

5. There are 6 fiction books and 8 nonfiction books on a reading list. Your teacher randomly assigns you 4 books to read over the summer. What is the probability that you are assigned all nonfiction books?

6. A bag contains 26 tiles, each with a different letter of the alphabet written on it. You choose 3 tiles from the bag without looking. What is the probability that you choose the tiles with the letters A, B, and C?

7. You are randomly assigned a password consisting of 6 different characters chosen from the digits 0 to 9 and the letters A to Z. As a percent, what is the probability that you are assigned a password consisting of only letters? Round your answer to the nearest tenth of a percent.

8. A bouquet of 6 flowers is made up by randomly choosing between roses and carnations. What is the probability the bouquet will have at most 2 roses?

9. A bag of fruit contains 10 pieces of fruit, chosen randomly from bins of apples and oranges. What is the probability the bag contains at least 6 oranges?

10. You flip a coin 10 times. What is the probability that you get at most 3 heads?

11. You flip a coin 8 times. What is the probability you will get at least 5 heads?

12. You flip a coin 5 times. What is the probability that every result will be tails?

13. There are 12 balloons in a bag: 3 each of blue, green, red, and yellow. Three balloons are chosen at random. Find the probability that all 3 balloons are green.

14. There are 6 female and 3 male kittens at an adoption center. Four kittens are chosen at random. What is the probability that all 4 kittens are female?

There are 21 students in your class. The teacher wants to send 4 students to the library each day. The teacher will choose the students to go to the library at random each day for the first four days from the list of students who have not already gone. Answer each question.

15. What is the probability you will be chosen to go on the first day?

16. If you have not yet been chosen to go on days 1–3, what is the probability you will be chosen to go on the fourth day?

17. Your teacher chooses 2 students at random to represent your homeroom. The homeroom has a total of 30 students, including your best friend. What is the probability that you and your best friend are chosen?

There are 12 peaches and 8 bananas in a fruit basket. You get a snack for yourself and three of your friends by choosing four of the pieces of fruit at random. Answer each question.

18. What is the probability that all 4 are peaches?

19. What is the probability that all 4 are bananas?

20. There are 30 students in your class. Your science teacher will choose 5 students at random to create a group to do a project. Find the probability that you and your 2 best friends in the science class will be chosen to be in the group.

21. On a television game show, 9 members of the studio audience are randomly selected to be eligible contestants.

a. Six of the 9 eligible contestants are randomly chosen to play a game on the stage. How many combinations of 6 players from the group of eligible contestants are possible?

b. You and your two friends are part of the group of 9 eligible contestants. What is the probability that all three of you are chosen to play the game on stage? Explain how you found your answer.

22. Determine whether you should use permutations or combinations to find the number of possibilities in each of the following situations.

a. Selecting a group of 5 people from a group of 8 people

b. Finding the number of combinations for a combination lock

c. Awarding first and second place ribbons in a contest

d. Choosing 3 books to read in any order from a list of 7 books

H.O.T. Focus on Higher Order Thinking

23. Communicate Mathematical Ideas Using the letters *A*, *B*, and *C*, explain the difference between a permutation and a combination.

24. a. Draw Conclusions Calculate ${}_{10}C_6$ and ${}_{10}C_4$.

b. What do you notice about these values? Explain why this makes sense.

c. Use your observations to help you state a generalization about combinations.

25. Justify Reasoning Use the formula for combinations to make a generalization about ${}_nC_n$. Explain why this makes sense.

26. Explain the Error Describe and correct the error in evaluating ${}_9C_4$.

$${}_9C_4 = \frac{9!}{(9-4)!} = \frac{9!}{5!} = 3024$$

Lesson Performance Task

1. In the 2012 elections, there were six candidates for the United States Senate in Vermont. In how many different orders, from first through sixth, could the candidates have finished?

2. The winner of the Vermont Senatorial election received 208,253 votes, 71.1% of the total votes cast. The candidate coming in second received 24.8% of the vote. How many votes did the second-place candidate receive? Round to the nearest ten.

3. Following the 2012 election there were 53 Democratic, 45 Republican, and 2 Independent senators in Congress.

   a. How many committees of 5 Democratic senators could be formed?

   b. How many committees of 48 Democratic senators could be formed?

   c. Explain how a clever person who knew nothing about combinations could guess the answer to (b) if the person knew the answer to (a).

4. Following the election, a newspaper printed a circle graph showing the make-up of the Senate. How many degrees were allotted to the sector representing Democrats, how many to Republicans, and how many to Independents?

19.4 Mutually Exclusive and Overlapping Events

Essential Question: How are probabilities affected when events are mutually exclusive or overlapping?

Resource Locker

Explore 1 Finding the Probability of Mutually Exclusive Events

Two events are **mutually exclusive events** if they cannot both occur in the same trial of an experiment. For example, if you flip a coin it cannot land heads up and tails up in the same trial. Therefore, the events are mutually exclusive.

A number dodecahedron has 12 sides numbered 1 through 12. What is the probability that you roll the cube and the result is an even number or a 7?

(A) Let A be the event that you roll an even number. Let B be the event that you roll a 7. Let S be the sample space.

Copy the Venn diagram and complete it by writing all outcomes in the sample space in the appropriate region.

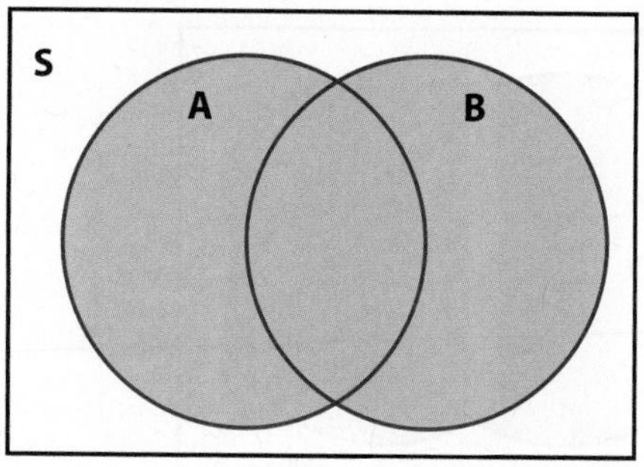

(B) Calculate $P(A)$.

$$P(A) = \frac{?}{?} = \frac{?}{?}$$

(C) Calculate $P(B)$.

$$P(B) = \frac{?}{?}$$

(D) Calculate $P(A \text{ or } B)$.

$n(S) = ?$

$n(A \text{ or } B) = n(A) + n(B)$

$= ? + ? = ?$

So, $P(A \text{ or } B) = \dfrac{n(A \text{ or } B)}{n(S)} = \dfrac{?}{?}$.

(E) Calculate $P(A) + P(B)$. Compare the answer to Step D.

$$P(A) + P(B) = \frac{?}{?} + \frac{?}{?} = \frac{?}{?}$$

$P(A) + P(B)$? $P(A \text{ or } B)$.

Reflect

1. **Discussion** How would you describe mutually exclusive events to another student in your own words? How could you use a Venn diagram to assist in your explanation?

2. Look back over the steps. What can you conjecture about the probability of the union of events that are mutually exclusive?

Explore 2 Finding the Probability of Overlapping Events

The process used in the previous Explore can be generalized to give the formula for the probability of mutually exclusive events.

Mutually Exclusive Events

If A and B are mutually exclusive events, then $P(A \text{ or } B) = P(A) + P(B)$.

Two events are **overlapping events** (or inclusive events) if they have one or more outcomes in common.

What is the probability that you roll a number dodecahedron and the result is an even number or a number greater than 7?

(A) Let A be the event that you roll an even number. Let B be the event that you roll a number greater than 7. Let S be the sample space.

Copy the Venn diagram and complete it by writing all outcomes in the sample space in the appropriate region.

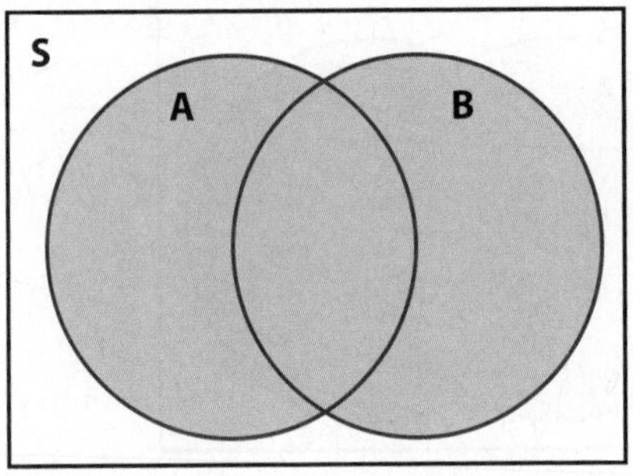

(B) Calculate $P(A)$.

$P(A) = \frac{?}{?} = \frac{?}{?}$

(C) Calculate $P(B)$.

$P(B) = \frac{?}{?}$

(D) Calculate $P(A \text{ and } B)$.

$P(A \text{ and } B) = \frac{?}{?} = \frac{?}{?}$

(E) Use the Venn diagram to find $P(A \text{ or } B)$.

$P(A \text{ or } B) = \frac{?}{?} = \frac{?}{?}$

(F) Now, use $P(A)$, $P(B)$, and $P(A \text{ and } B)$ to calculate $P(A \text{ or } B)$.

$P(A) =$? $P(B) =$? $P(A \text{ and } B) =$?

$P(A) + P(B) - P(A \text{ and } B) =$? + ? − ? = ?

Reflect

3. Why must you subtract $P(A \text{ and } B)$ from $P(A) + P(B)$ to determine $P(A \text{ or } B)$?

4. Look back over the steps. What can you conjecture about the probability of the union of two events that are overlapping?

Explain 1 Finding a Probability From a Two-Way Table of Data

The previous Explore leads to the following rule.

The Addition Rule

$P(A \text{ or } B) = P(A) + P(B) - P(A \text{ and } B)$

Example 1 **Use the given two-way tables to determine the probabilities.**

(A) $P(\text{senior or girl})$

	Freshman	Sophomore	Junior	Senior	TOTAL
Boy	98	104	100	94	396
Girl	102	106	96	108	412
Total	200	210	196	202	808

To determine $P(\text{senior or girl})$, first calculate $P(\text{senior})$, $P(\text{girl})$, and $P(\text{senior and girl})$.

$P(\text{senior}) = \frac{202}{808} = \frac{1}{4}$; $P(\text{girl}) = \frac{412}{808} = \frac{103}{202}$ $P(\text{senior and girl}) = \frac{108}{808} = \frac{27}{202}$

Use the addition rule to determine $P(\text{senior or girl})$.

$$P(\text{senior or girl}) = P(\text{senior}) + P(\text{girl}) - P(\text{senior and girl})$$
$$= \frac{1}{4} + \frac{103}{202} - \frac{27}{202}$$
$$= \frac{253}{404}$$

Therefore, the probability that a student is a senior or a girl is $\frac{253}{404}$.

(B) $P\left((\text{domestic or late})^c\right)$

	Late	On Time	Total
Domestic Flights	12	108	120
International Flights	6	54	60
Total	18	162	180

To determine $P\left((\text{domestic or late})^c\right)$, first calculate $P(\text{domestic or late})$.

$P(\text{domestic}) = \frac{120}{180} = \frac{2}{3}$; $P(\text{late}) = \frac{18}{180} = \frac{1}{10}$; $P(\text{domestic and late}) = \frac{12}{180} = \frac{1}{15}$

Use the addition rule to determine $P(\text{domestic or late})$.

$P(\text{domestic or late}) = P(\text{domestic}) + P(\text{late}) - P(\text{domestic and late})$

$$= \frac{2}{3} + \frac{1}{10} - \frac{1}{15} = \frac{7}{10}$$

Therefore, $P\left((\text{domestic or late})^c\right) = 1 - P(\text{domestic or late})$

$$= 1 - \frac{7}{10}$$

$$= \frac{3}{10}$$

Your Turn

5. Use the table to determine $P(\text{headache or no medicine})$.

	Took Medicine	No Medicine	TOTAL
Headache	12	15	27
No Headache	48	25	73
TOTAL	60	40	100

Elaborate

6. Give an example of mutually exclusive events and an example of overlapping events.

7. **Essential Question Check-In** How do you determine the probability of mutually exclusive events and overlapping events?

Evaluate: Homework and Practice

Personal Math Trainer
- Online Homework
- Hints and Help
- Extra Practice

1. A bag contains 3 blue marbles, 5 red marbles, and 4 green marbles. You choose one without looking. What is the probability that it is red or green?

2. A number icosahedron has 20 sides numbered 1 through 20. What is the probability that the result of a roll is a number less than 4 or greater than 11?

3. A bag contains 26 tiles, each with a different letter of the alphabet written on it. You choose a tile without looking. What is the probability that you choose a vowel (a, e, i, o, or u) or a letter in the word GEOMETRY?

4. **Persevere in Problem Solving** You roll two number cubes at the same time. Each cube has sides numbered 1 through 6. What is the probability that the sum of the numbers rolled is even or greater than 9? (*Hint:* Create and fill out a probability chart.)

The table shows the data for car insurance quotes for 125 drivers made by an insurance company in one week.

	Teen	Adult (20 or over)	Total
0 accidents	15	53	68
1 accident	4	32	36
2+ accidents	9	12	21
Total	28	97	125

You randomly choose one of the drivers. Find the probability of each event.

5. The driver is an adult.

6. The driver is a teen with 0 or 1 accident.

7. The driver is a teen.

8. The driver has 2+ accidents.

9. The driver is a teen and has 2+ accidents.

10. The driver is a teen or a driver with 2+ accidents.

Use the following information for Exercises 11–16. The table shown shows the results of a customer satisfaction survey for a cellular service provider, by location of the customer. In the survey, customers were asked whether they would recommend a plan with the provider to a friend.

	Arlington	Towson	Parkville	Total
Yes	40	35	41	116
No	18	10	6	34
Total	58	45	47	150

One of the customers that was surveyed was chosen at random. Find the probability of each event.

11. The customer was from Towson and said No.

12. The customer was from Parkville.

13. The customer said Yes.

14. The customer was from Parkville and said Yes.

15. The customer was from Parkville or said Yes.

16. Explain why you cannot use the rule $P(A \text{ or } B) = P(A) + P(B)$ in Exercise 15.

Use the following information for Exercises 17–21. Roberto is the owner of a car dealership. He is assessing the success rate of his top three salespeople in order to offer one of them a promotion. Over two months, for each attempted sale, he records whether the salesperson made a successful sale or not. The results are shown in the chart.

	Successful	Unsuccessful	Total
Becky	6	6	12
Raul	4	5	9
Darrell	6	9	15
Total	16	20	36

Roberto randomly chooses one of the attempted sales.

17. Find the probability that the sale was one of Becky's or Raul's successful sales.

18. Find the probability that the sale was one of the unsuccessful sales or one of Raul's successful sales.

19. Find the probability that the sale was one of Darrell's unsuccessful sales or one of Raul's unsuccessful sales.

20. Find the probability that the sale was an unsuccessful sale or one of Becky's attempted sales.

21. Find the probability that the sale was a successful sale or one of Raul's attempted sales.

22. You are going to draw one card at random from a standard deck of cards. A standard deck of cards has 13 cards (2, 3, 4, 5, 6, 7, 8, 9, 10, jack, queen, king, ace) in each of 4 suits (hearts, clubs, diamonds, spades). The hearts and diamonds cards are red. The clubs and spades cards are black. Which of the following have a probability of less than $\frac{1}{4}$? Choose all that apply.

a. Drawing a card that is a spade and an ace

b. Drawing a card that is a club or an ace

c. Drawing a card that is a face card or a club

d. Drawing a card that is black and a heart

e. Drawing a red card and a number card from 2–9

H.O.T. Focus on Higher Order Thinking

23. Draw Conclusions A survey of 1108 employees at a software company finds that 621 employees take a bus to work and 445 employees take a train to work. Some employees take both a bus and a train, and 321 employees take only a train. To the nearest percent, find the probability that a randomly chosen employee takes a bus or a train to work. Explain.

24. Communicate Mathematical Ideas Explain how to use a Venn diagram to find the probability of randomly choosing a multiple of 3 or a multiple of 4 from the set of numbers from 1 to 25. Then find the probability.

25. Explain the Error Sanderson attempted to find the probability of randomly choosing a 10 or a diamond from a standard deck of playing cards. He used the following logic:

Let S be the sample space, A be the event that the card is a 10, and B be the event that the card is a diamond.

There are 52 cards in the deck, so $n(S) = 52$.

There are four 10s in the deck, so $n(A) = 4$.

There are 13 diamonds in the deck, so $n(B) = 13$.

One 10 is a diamond, so $n(A \cap B) = 1$.

$$P(A \cup B) = \frac{n(A \cup B)}{n(S)} = \frac{n(A) \cdot n(B) - n(A \cap B)}{n(S)} = \frac{4 \cdot 13 - 1}{52} = \frac{51}{52}$$

Describe and correct Sanderson's mistake.

Lesson Performance Task

What is the smallest number of randomly chosen people that are needed in order for there to be a better than 50% probability that at least two of them will have the same birthday? The astonishing answer is 23. Follow these steps to find why.

1. Can a person have a birthday on two different days? Use the vocabulary of this lesson to explain your answer.

Looking for the probability that two or more people in a group of 23 have matching birthdays is a challenge. Maybe there is one match but maybe there are five matches or seven or fourteen. A much easier way is to look for the probability that there are *no* matches in a group of 23. In other words, all 23 have different birthdays. Then use that number to find the answer.

2. There are 365 days in a non-leap year.

   a. Write an expression for the number of ways you can assign different birthdays to 23 people. (Hint: Think of the people as standing in a line, and you are going to assign a different number from 1 to 365 to each person.)

   b. Write an expression for the number of ways you can assign any birthday to 23 people. (Hint: Now think about assigning any number from 1 to 365 to each of 23 people.)

   c. How can you use your answers to (a) and (b) to find the probability that no people in a group of 23 have the same birthday? Use a calculator to find the probability to the nearest ten-thousandth.

   d. What is the probability that at least two people in a group of 23 have the same birthday? Explain your reasoning.

STUDY GUIDE REVIEW

Introduction to Probability

MODULE 19

Essential Question: How can you use probability to solve real-world problems?

Key Vocabulary

set *(conjunto, juego)*
element *(elemento)*
empty set *(conjunto vacío)*
universal set *(conjunto universal)*
subset *(subconjunto)*
intersection *(intersección)*
union *(unión)*
complement *(complementar)*
theoretical probability *(probabilidad teórica)*
permutation *(permutación)*
Fundamental Counting Principle *(principio fundamental de conteo)*
factorial *(factorial)*
combination *(combinación)*

KEY EXAMPLE (Lesson 19.1)

When rolling two fair number cubes, what is the probability that the sum of the two cubes will not be even or prime?

The sum of two number cubes can be any integer from 2 through 12. Of these, the only possible sum that is not even or prime is 9. There are 36 possible outcomes for rolling two number cubes. Of these, the only ones that sum to 9 are (3, 6), (6, 3), (4, 5), and (5, 4). So, $P(\text{sum is not even or prime}) = \frac{4}{36} = \frac{1}{9}$.

KEY EXAMPLE (Lesson 19.2)

Ten marbles are placed in a jar. Of the 10 marbles, 3 are blue, 2 are red, 3 are green, 1 is orange, and 1 is yellow. The 10 marbles are randomly placed in a line. What is the probability that all marbles of the same color are next to each other?

Marbles of the same color are indistinguishable objects. The sample space S consists of permutations of 10 objects, with 3 of one type, 3 of another type, and 2 of a third type.

$$n(S) = \frac{10!}{3!3!2!} = 50{,}400$$

Event A consists of permutations that have all marbles of the same color next to each other, so it is the number of ways of ordering the 5 colors.

$$n(A) = 5! = 120$$

The probability that all marbles of the same color are next to each other is

$$P(A) = \frac{n(A)}{n(S)} = \frac{120}{50{,}400} = \frac{1}{420}.$$

KEY EXAMPLE (Lesson 19.3)

A class of 15 boys and 15 girls is putting together a random group of 3 students to do classroom chores. What is the probability that at least 2 of the students are boys?

The sample space S consists of combinations of three student groups.

$$n(S) = \frac{30!}{3!27!} = 4060$$

Event A consists of combinations that have 2 boys or 3 boys in the group. The event of getting 2 boys in the group occurs 15 times, once for each individual girl in the class.

$$n(A) = 15 \cdot {}_{15}C_2 + {}_{15}C_3 = 15 \cdot \frac{15!}{2!13!} + \frac{15!}{3!12!} = 2030$$

The probability that there will be at least 2 boys in the group is $P(A) = \frac{n(A)}{n(S)} = \frac{2030}{4060} = \frac{1}{2}$.

EXERCISES

Use the sets below to find the indicated set for problems 1–4. *(Lesson 19.1)*

$U = \{1, 2, 3, 4, 5, 6, 7, 8, 9\}$

$A = \{1, 3, 5, 7, 9\}$

$B = \{2, 4, 6, 8\}$

$C = \{1, 2, 4, 5, 7, 9\}$

1. $A \cup C$

2. $B \cap C$

3. A^C

4. $A \cap B$

5. A computer password can use all digits (0–9) and all letters (*a–z*) that are case sensitive (upper and lower). How many different permutations of 5-figure passwords are there if there is no repeated input? *(Lesson 19.2)*

6. Brandon is rolling a 10-sided number cube 5 times. What is the probability that he will roll at least two 7s? *(Lesson 19.3)*

Determine if the given events are mutually exclusive. If not, explain why. *(Lesson 19.4)*

7. Rolling a 3 or a 4 on a regular number cube

8. Drawing a queen or a red card from a standard deck of 52 cards

9. Flipping a coin and having it land on heads or tails

10. Rolling an even number or a prime number on a number cube

MODULE PERFORMANCE TASK

Baseball Probability

A baseball player will be batting three times during today's game. So far this season, the player has gotten an average of 1 hit in every 3 times at bat. Based on this data, what is the probability that the player will get exactly one hit in today's game? Is that outcome more or less likely than getting no hits?

Start by making notes about your plan for solving the problem. Then complete the task, using words, numbers, or diagrams to explain how your reached your conclusions.

Ready to Go On?

19.1–19.4 Introduction to Probability

Personal Math Trainer

- Online Homework
- Hints and Help
- Extra Practice

Find the probabilities.

1. Twenty-six tiles with the letters A through Z are placed face down on a table and mixed. (For the purpose of this exercise assume that the letter Y is a vowel.) Five tiles are drawn in order. Compute the probability that only consonants are selected.

2. The two-way table shows the results of a poll in a certain country that asked voters, sorted by political party, whether they supported or opposed a proposed government initiative. Find the given probabilities.

	Party A	Party B	Other Party	No Party	Total
Support	97	68	8	19	192
Oppose	32	81	16	11	140
Undecided	9	23	10	26	68
Total	138	172	34	56	400

a. $P(\text{no party or undecided})$

b. $P\left((\text{party A or support})^c\right)$

ESSENTIAL QUESTION

3. A teacher is assigning 32 presentation topics to 9 students at random. Each student will get 3 topics, and no topic will be repeated. Somil is very interested in 5 topics. What is the probability that Somil will be assigned at least one of his preferred topics? Explain how you arrived at your answer.

MODULE 19
MIXED REVIEW

Assessment Readiness

1. Jonah is arranging books on a shelf. The order of the books matters to him. There are 336 ways he can arrange the books. Determine if each statement is True or False.

A. He might be arranging 3 books from a selection of 8 different books.

B. He might be arranging 4 books from a selection of 8 different books.

C. He might be arranging 5 books from a selection of 8 different books.

2. Decide whether the probability of tossing the given sum with two dice is $\frac{5}{36}$.

A. A sum of 6.

B. A sum of 7.

C. A sum of 8.

3. Let H be the event that a coin flip lands with heads showing, and let T be the event that a flip lands with tails showing. (Note that $P(H) = P(T) = 0.5$.) What is the probability that you will get heads at least once if you flip the coin ten times? Explain your reasoning.

4. There are 8 girls and 6 boys on the student council. How many committees of 3 girls and 2 boys can be formed? Show your work.

Conditional Probability and Independence of Events

MODULE 20

Essential Question: How can you use conditional probability and independence of events to solve real-world problems?

REAL WORLD VIDEO
Check out how principles of conditional probability are used to understand the chances of events in playing cards.

MODULE PERFORMANCE TASK PREVIEW

Playing Cards

In this module, you will use concepts of conditional probability to determine the chance of drawing a hand of cards with a certain property. To successfully complete this task you'll need to master these skills:

- Distinguish between independent and dependent events.
- Apply the conditional probability formula to a real-world situation.
- Use the Multiplication Rule appropriately.

Are YOU Ready?

Complete these exercises to review skills you will need for this module.

Personal Math Trainer
- Online Homework
- Hints and Help
- Extra Practice

Probability of Compound Events

Example 1 Find the probability of rolling a pair of six-sided dice and the sum of their faces being even or equal to 3.

3 is not even, so the two probabilities are mutually exclusive. The probability is equal to the sums of the probabilities of rolling an even sum or rolling a sum of 3.

Probability of rolling an even sum $= \frac{18}{36}$ Count the number of outcomes for the first event.

Probability of rolling a sum of 3 $= \frac{2}{36}$ Count the number of outcomes for the second event.

Probability of rolling an even sum or a sum of 3 $= \frac{18}{36} + \frac{2}{36} = \frac{20}{36} = \frac{5}{9}$

Find each probability.

1. The probability of rolling two dice at the same time and getting a 4 with either die or the sum of the dice is 6.

2. The probability of rolling two dice at the same time and getting a 4 with either die and the sum of the dice is 6.

3. The probability of pulling red or blue marbles (or both) from a jar of only red and blue marbles when you pull out two marbles given that pulling red and pulling blue are equally likely events.

4. The probability of pulling a red marble and a blue marble from a jar of only red and blue marbles when you pull out two marbles given that pulling red and pulling blue are equally likely events.

5. The probability of flipping a coin three times and getting exactly two heads or at least one tails given the probability of getting a heads is $\frac{1}{2}$ and the probability of getting a tails is $\frac{1}{2}$.

6. The probability of flipping a coin three times and getting exactly two heads and at least one tails given the probability of getting a heads is $\frac{1}{2}$ and the probability of getting a tails is $\frac{1}{2}$.

7. The probability of flipping a coin three times and getting at least two heads or at least one tails given the probability of getting a heads is $\frac{1}{2}$ and the probability of getting a tails is $\frac{1}{2}$.

20.1 Conditional Probability

Essential Question: How do you calculate a conditional probability?

Resource Locker

Explore 1 Finding Conditional Probabilities from a Two-Way Frequency Table

The probability that event A occurs given that event B has already occurred is called the **conditional probability** of A given B and is written $P(A \mid B)$.

One hundred migraine headache sufferers participated in a study of a new medicine. Some were given the new medicine, and others were not. After one week, participants were asked if they had experienced a headache during the week. The two-way frequency table shows the results.

	Took medicine	No medicine	Total
Headache	11	13	24
No headache	54	22	76
Total	65	35	100

Let event A be the event that a participant did not get a headache. Let event B be the event that a participant took the medicine.

(A) To the nearest percent, what is the probability that a participant who took the medicine did not get a headache?

? participants took the medicine. So, $P(A \mid B) = \frac{?}{?} \approx$? %.

Of these, ? did not get a headache.

(B) To the nearest percent, what is the probability that a participant who did not get a headache took the medicine?

? participants did not get a headache. So, $P(B \mid A) = \frac{?}{?} \approx$? %.

Of these, ? took the medicine.

(C) Let $n(A)$ be the number of participants who did not get a headache, $n(B)$ be the number of participants who took the medicine, and $n(A \cap B)$ be the number of participants who took the medicine and did not get a headache.

$n(A) =$? $n(B) =$? $n(A \cap B) =$?

Express $P(A \mid B)$ and $P(B \mid A)$ in terms of $n(A)$, $n(B)$, and $n(A \cap B)$.

$P(A \mid B) = \frac{?}{?}$ $P(B \mid A) = \frac{?}{?}$

Reflect

1. For the question "What is the probability that a participant who did not get a headache took the medicine?", what event is assumed to have already occurred?

2. In general, does it appear that $P(A \mid B) = P(B \mid A)$? Why or why not?

Explore 2 Finding Conditional Probabilities from a Two-Way Relative Frequency Table

You can develop a formula for $P(A \mid B)$ that uses relative frequencies (which are probabilities) rather than frequencies (which are counts).

	Took medicine	No medicine	Total
Headache	11	13	24
No headache	54	22	76
Total	65	35	100

(A) To obtain relative frequencies, divide every number in the table by 100, the total number of participants in the study. Make a relative frequency table by replacing each number in the table with the corresponding relative frequency.

(B) Recall that event A is the event that a participant did not get a headache and that event B is the event that a participant took the medicine. Use the relative frequency table from Step A to find $P(A)$, $P(B)$, and $P(A \cap B)$.

(C) In the first Explore, you found the conditional probabilities $P(A \mid B) \approx 83\%$ and $P(B \mid A) \approx 71\%$ by using the frequencies in the two-way frequency table. Use the relative frequencies from the table in Step A to find the equivalent conditional probabilities.

$P(A \mid B) = \dfrac{P(A \cap B)}{P(B)} = \dfrac{?}{?} \approx ?\ \%$ $\qquad P(B \mid A) = \dfrac{P(A \cap B)}{P(A)} = \dfrac{?}{?} \approx ?\ \%$

(D) Generalize the results by using $n(S)$ as the number of elements in the sample space (in this case, the number of participants in the study). For instance, you can write $P(A) = \frac{n(A)}{n(S)}$. Write each of the following probabilities in a similar way.

$P(B) = \dfrac{?}{?}$ $\qquad P(A \cap B) = \dfrac{?}{?}$ $\qquad P(A \mid B) = \dfrac{\frac{n(A \cap B)}{?}}{\frac{n(B)}{?}} = \dfrac{P(A \cap B)}{?}$

Reflect

3. Why are the two forms of $P(A \cap B)$, $\frac{n(A \cap B)}{n(B)}$ and $\frac{P(A \cap B)}{P(B)}$, equivalent?

4. What is a formula for $P(B|A)$ that involves probabilities rather than counts? How do you obtain this formula from the fact that $P(B|A) = \frac{n(A \cap B)}{n(A)}$?

Explain 1 Using the Conditional Probability Formula

In the previous Explore, you discovered the following formula for conditional probability.

Conditional Probability

The conditional probability of A given B (that is, the probability that event A occurs given that event B occurs) is as follows:

$$P(A|B) = \frac{P(A \cap B)}{P(B)}$$

Example 1 **Find the specified probability.**

(A) For a standard deck of playing cards, find the probability that a red card randomly drawn from the deck is a jack.

Step 1 Find $P(R)$, the probability that a red card is drawn from the deck.

There are 26 red cards in the deck of 52 cards, so $P(R) = \frac{26}{52}$.

Step 2 Find $P(J \cap R)$, the probability that a red jack is drawn from the deck.

There are 2 red jacks in the deck, so $P(J \cap R) = \frac{2}{52}$.

Step 3 Substitute the probabilities from Steps 1 and 2 into the formula for conditional probability.

$$P(J|R) = \frac{P(J \cap R)}{P(R)} = \frac{\frac{2}{52}}{\frac{26}{52}}$$

Step 4 Simplify the result.

$$P(J|R) = \frac{\frac{2}{52} \cdot 52}{\frac{26}{52} \cdot 52} = \frac{2}{26} = \frac{1}{13}$$

(B) For a standard deck of playing cards, find the probability that a jack randomly drawn from the deck is a red card.

Step 1 Find $P(J)$, the probability that a jack is drawn from the deck.

There are 4 jacks in the deck of 52 cards, so $P(J) = \frac{\boxed{4}}{52}$.

Step 2 Find $P(J \cap R)$, the probability that a red jack is drawn from the deck.

There are 2 red jacks in the deck, so $P(J \cap R) = \frac{\boxed{2}}{52}$.

Step 3 Substitute the probabilities from Steps 1 and 2 into the formula for conditional probability.

$$P(R|J) = \frac{P(J \cap R)}{P(J)} = \frac{\frac{\boxed{2}}{52}}{\frac{\boxed{4}}{52}}$$

Step 4 Simplify the result.

$$P(R|J) = \frac{\frac{\boxed{2}}{52} \cdot 52}{\frac{\boxed{4}}{52} \cdot 52} = \frac{\boxed{2}}{\boxed{4}} = \frac{1}{\boxed{2}}$$

Your Turn

5. For a standard deck of playing cards, find the probability that a face card randomly drawn from the deck is a king. (The ace is *not* a face card.)

6. For a standard deck of playing cards, find the probability that a queen randomly drawn from the deck is a diamond.

Elaborate

7. When calculating a conditional probability from a two-way table, explain why it doesn't matter whether the table gives frequencies or relative frequencies.

8. **Discussion** Is it possible to have $P(B|A) = P(A|B)$ for some events A and B? What conditions would need to exist?

9. **Essential Question Check-In** In a two-way frequency table, suppose event A represents a row of the table and event B represents a column of the table. Describe how to find the conditional probability $P(A|B)$ using the frequencies in the table.

Evaluate: Homework and Practice

Personal Math Trainer
- Online Homework
- Hints and Help
- Extra Practice

In order to study the relationship between the amount of sleep a student gets and his or her school performance, a researcher collected data from 120 students. The two-way frequency table shows the number of students who passed and failed an exam and the number of students who got more or less than 6 hours of sleep the night before. Use the table to answer the questions in Exercises 1–3.

	Passed exam	Failed exam	Total
Less than 6 hours of sleep	12	10	22
More than 6 hours of sleep	90	8	98
Total	102	18	120

1. To the nearest percent, what is the probability that a student who failed the exam got less than 6 hours of sleep?

2. To the nearest percent, what is the probability that a student who got less than 6 hours of sleep failed the exam?

3. To the nearest percent, what is the probability that a student got less than 6 hours of sleep and failed the exam?

4. You have a standard deck of playing cards from which you randomly select a card. Event D is getting a diamond, and event F is getting a face card (a jack, queen, or king). Show that $P(D|F) = \frac{n(D \cap F)}{n(F)}$ and $P(D|F) = \frac{P(D \cap F)}{P(F)}$ are equal.

The table shows data in the previous table as relative frequencies (rounded to the nearest thousandth when necessary). Use the table for Exercises 5–7.

	Passed exam	Failed exam	Total
Less than 6 hours of sleep	0.100	0.083	0.183
More than 6 hours of sleep	0.750	0.067	0.817
Total	0.850	0.150	1.000

5. To the nearest percent, what is the probability that a student who passed the exam got more than 6 hours of sleep?

6. To the nearest percent, what is the probability that a student who got more than 6 hours of sleep passed the exam?

7. Which is greater, the probability that a student who got less than 6 hours of sleep passed the exam or the probability that a student who got more than 6 hours of sleep failed the exam? Explain.

You randomly draw a card from a standard deck of playing cards. Let A be the event that the card is an ace, let B be the event that the card is black, and let C be the event that the card is a club. Find the specified probability as a fraction.

8. $P(A|B)$

9. $P(B|A)$

10. $P(A|C)$

11. $P(C|A)$

12. $P(B|C)$

13. $P(C|B)$

14. A botanist studied the effect of a new fertilizer by choosing 100 orchids and giving 70% of these plants the fertilizer. Of the plants that got the fertilizer, 40% produced flowers within a month. Of the plants that did not get the fertilizer, 10% produced flowers within a month.

a. Use the given information to complete the two-way frequency table.

b. To the nearest percent, what is the probability that an orchid that produced flowers got fertilizer?

c. To the nearest percent, what is the probability that an orchid that got fertilizer produced flowers?

15. At a school fair, a box contains 24 yellow balls and 76 red balls. One-fourth of the balls of each color are labeled "Win a prize." Match each description of a probability with its value as a percent.

A. The probability that a randomly selected ball labeled "Win a prize" is yellow — **a.** ___?___ 76%

B. The probability that a randomly selected ball labeled "Win a prize" is red — **b.** ___?___ 25%

C. The probability that a randomly selected ball is labeled "Win a prize" and is red — **c.** ___?___ 24%

D. The probability that a randomly selected yellow ball is labeled "Win a prize" — **d.** ___?___ 19%

16. A teacher gave her students two tests. If 45% of the students passed both tests and 60% passed the first test, what is the probability that a student who passed the first test also passed the second?

17. You randomly select two marbles, one at a time, from a pouch containing blue and green marbles. The probability of selecting a blue marble on the first draw and a green marble on the second draw is 25%, and the probability of selecting a blue marble on the first draw is 56%. To the nearest percent, what is the probability of selecting a green marble on the second draw, given that the first marble was blue?

You roll two number cubes, one red and one blue. The table shows the probabilities for events based on whether or not a 1 is rolled on each number cube. Use the table to find the specified conditional probability, expressed as a fraction. Then show that the conditional probability is correct by listing the possible outcomes as ordered pairs of the form (number on red cube, number on blue cube) and identifying the successful outcomes.

	Rolling a 1 on the red cube	Not rolling a 1 on the red cube	Total
Rolling a 1 on the blue cube	$\frac{1}{36}$	$\frac{5}{36}$	$\frac{1}{6}$
Not rolling a 1 on the blue cube	$\frac{5}{36}$	$\frac{25}{36}$	$\frac{5}{6}$
Total	$\frac{1}{6}$	$\frac{5}{6}$	1

18. *P*(not rolling a 1 on the blue cube | rolling a 1 on the red cube)

19. *P*(not rolling a 1 on the blue cube | not rolling a 1 on the red cube)

20. The table shows the results of a quality-control study at a computer factory.

	Shipped	Not shipped	Total
Defective	3	7	10
Not defective	89	1	90
Total	92	8	100

a. To the nearest tenth of a percent, what is the probability that a shipped computer is not defective?

b. To the nearest tenth of a percent, what is the probability that a defective computer is shipped?

H.O.T. Focus on Higher Order Thinking

21. Analyze Relationships In the Venn diagram, the circles representing events *A* and *B* divide the sample space *S* into four regions: the overlap of the circles, the part of *A* not in the overlap, the part of *B* not in the overlap, and the part of *S* not in *A* or *B*. Suppose that the area of each region is proportional to the number of outcomes that fall within the region. Which conditional probability is greater: $P(A|B)$ or $P(B|A)$? Explain.

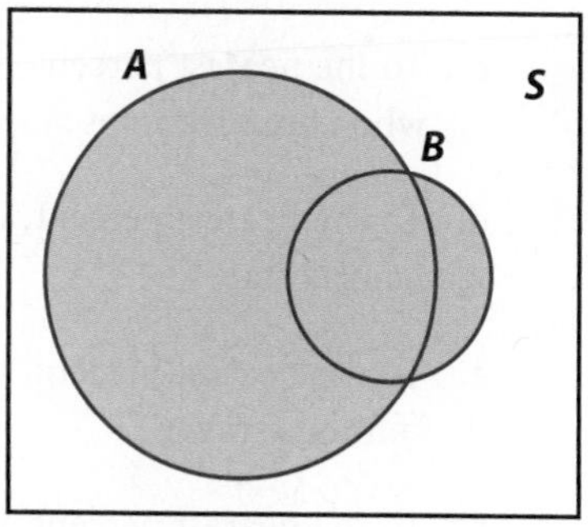

22. Explain the Error A student was asked to use the table shown to find the probability, to nearest percent, that a participant in a study of a new medicine for migraine headaches did not take the medicine, given that the participant reported no headaches.

	Took medicine	No medicine	Total
Headache	11	13	24
No headache	54	22	76
Total	65	35	100

The student made the following calculation.

$P(\text{no medicine} \mid \text{no headache}) = \frac{22}{35} \approx 0.63 = 63\%$

Explain the student's error, and find the correct probability.

23. Communicate Mathematical Ideas Explain how a conditional probability based on a two-way frequency table effectively reduces it to a one-way table. In your explanation, refer to the two-way table shown, which lists frequencies for events A, B, and their complements. Tell which part of the table supports your explanation.

	A	Not A	Total
B	$n(A \cap B)$	$n(\text{not } A \cap B)$	$n(B)$
Not B	$n(A \cap \text{not } B)$	$n(\text{not } A \cap \text{not } B)$	$n(\text{not } B)$
Total	$n(A)$	$n(\text{not } A)$	$n(S)$

Lesson Performance Task

The two-way frequency table gives the results of a survey that asked students this question: Which of these would you most like to meet: a famous singer, a movie star, or a sports star?

	Famous singer	Movie star	Sports star	Total
Boys	20	15	55	?
Girls	40	50	20	?
Total	?	?	?	?

a. Complete the table by finding the row totals, column totals, and grand total.

b. To the nearest percent, what is the probability that a student who chose “movie star” is a girl?

c. To the nearest percent, what is the probability that a student who chose “famous singer” is a boy?

d. To the nearest percent, what is the probability that a boy chose “sports star”?

e. To the nearest percent, what is the probability that a girl chose “famous singer”?

f. To the nearest percent, what is the probability that a student who chose either “famous singer” or “movie star” is a boy?

g. To the nearest percent, what is the probability that a girl did not choose “sports star”?

20.2 Independent Events

Essential Question: What does it mean for two events to be independent?

Resource Locker

Explore Understanding the Independence of Events

Suppose you flip a coin and roll a number cube. You would expect the probability of getting heads on the coin to be $\frac{1}{2}$ regardless of what number you get from rolling the number cube. Likewise, you would expect the probability of rolling a 3 on the number cube to be $\frac{1}{6}$ regardless of whether of the coin flip results in heads or tails.

When the occurrence of one event has no effect on the occurrence of another event, the two events are called **independent events**.

(A) A jar contains 15 red marbles and 17 yellow marbles. You randomly draw a marble from the jar. Let R be the event that you get a red marble, and let Y be the event that you get a yellow marble.

Since the jar has a total of ? marbles, $P(R) = \frac{?}{?}$ and $P(Y) = \frac{?}{?}$.

(B) Suppose the first marble you draw is a red marble, and you put that marble back in the jar before randomly drawing a second marble. Find $P(Y|R)$, the probability that you get a yellow marble on the second draw after getting a red marble on the first draw. Explain your reasoning.

Since the jar still has a total of ? marbles and ? of them are yellow,

$P(Y|R) = \frac{?}{?}$.

(C) Suppose you *don't* put the red marble back in the jar before randomly drawing a second marble. Find $P(Y|R)$, the probability that you get a yellow marble on the second draw after getting a red marble on the first draw. Explain your reasoning.

Since the jar now has a total of ? marbles and ? of them are yellow,

$P(Y|R) = \frac{?}{?}$.

Reflect

1. In one case you replaced the first marble before drawing the second, and in the other case you didn't. For which case was $P(Y|R)$ equal to $P(Y)$? Why?

2. In which of the two cases would you say the events of getting a red marble on the first draw and getting a yellow marble on the second draw are independent? What is true about $P(Y|R)$ and $P(Y)$ in this case?

Explain 1 Determining if Events are Independent

To determine the independence of two events A and B, you can check to see whether $P(A|B) = P(A)$ since the occurrence of event A is unaffected by the occurrence of event B if and only if the events are independent.

Example 1 **The two-way frequency table gives data about 180 randomly selected flights that arrive at an airport. Use the table to answer the question.**

	Late Arrival	On Time	Total
Domestic Flights	12	108	120
International Flights	6	54	60
Total	18	162	180

(A) Is the event that a flight is on time independent of the event that a flight is domestic?

Let O be the event that a flight is on time. Let D be the event that a flight is domestic. Find $P(O)$ and $P(O|D)$. To find $P(O)$, note that the total number of flights is 180, and of those flights, there are 162 on-time flights. So, $P(O) = \frac{162}{180} = 90\%$.

To find $P(O|D)$, note that there are 120 domestic flights, and of those flights, there are 108 on-time flights.

So, $P(O|D), = \frac{108}{120} = 90\%$.

Since $P(O|D) = P(O)$, the event that a flight is on time is independent of the event that a flight is domestic.

(B) Is the event that a flight is international independent of the event that a flight arrives late?

Let I be the event that a flight is international. Let L be the event that a flight arrives late. Find $P(I)$ and $P(I|L)$. To find $P(I)$, note that the total number of flights is 180, and of those flights, there are 60 international flights. So, $P(I) = \frac{60}{180} = 33\frac{1}{3}\%$.

To find $P(I|L)$, note that there are 18 flights that arrive late, and of those flights, there are 6 international flights. So, $P(I|L) = \frac{6}{18} = 33\frac{1}{3}\%$.

Since $P(I|L) = P(I)$, the event that a flight is international is independent of the event that a flight arrives late.

Your Turn

The two-way frequency table gives data about 200 randomly selected apartments in a city. Use the table to answer the question.

	1 Bedroom	2+ Bedrooms	Total
Single Occupant	64	12	76
Multiple Occupants	26	98	124
Total	90	110	200

3. Is the event that an apartment has a single occupant independent of the event that an apartment has 1 bedroom?

4. Is the event that an apartment has 2 or more bedrooms independent of the event that an apartment has multiple occupants?

Explain 2 Finding the Probability of Independent Events

From the definition of conditional probability you know that $P(A|B) = \frac{P(A \cap B)}{P(B)}$ for any events A and B. If those events happen to be independent, you can replace $P(A|B)$ with $P(A)$ and get $P(A) = \frac{P(A \cap B)}{P(B)}$. Solving the last equation for $P(A \cap B)$ gives the following result.

Probability of Independent Events

Events A and B are independent if and only if $P(A \cap B) = P(A) \cdot P(B)$.

Example 2 **Find the specified probability.**

(A) Recall the jar with 15 red marbles and 17 yellow marbles from the Explore. Suppose you randomly draw one marble from the jar. After you put that marble back in the jar, you randomly draw a second marble. What is the probability that you draw a yellow marble first and a red marble second?

Let Y be the event of drawing a yellow marble first. Let R be the event of drawing a red marble second. Then $P(Y) = \frac{17}{32}$ and, because the first marble drawn is replaced before the second marble is drawn, $P(R|Y) = P(R) = \frac{15}{32}$. Since the events are independent, you can multiply their probabilities: $P(Y \cap R) = P(Y) \cdot P(R) = \frac{17}{32} \cdot \frac{15}{32} = \frac{255}{1024} \approx 25\%$.

(B) You spin the spinner shown two times. What is the probability that the spinner stops on an even number on the first spin, followed by an odd number on the second spin?

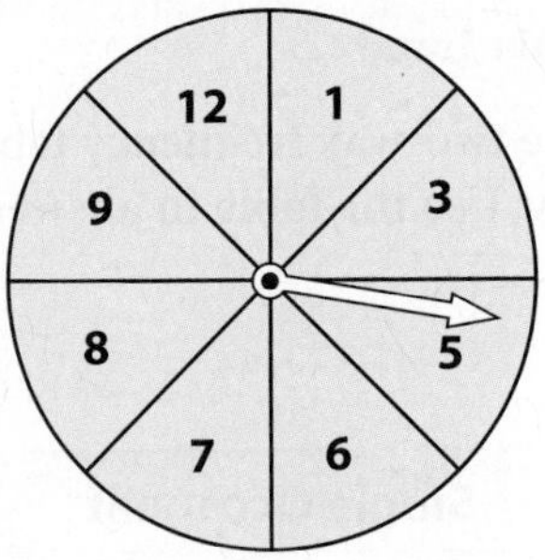

Let E be the event of getting an even number on the first spin. Let O be the event of getting an odd number on the second spin. Then $P(E) = \frac{3}{8}$ and, because the first spin has no effect on the second spin, $P(O|E) = P(O) = \frac{5}{8}$. Since the events are independent, you can multiply their probabilities: $P(E \cap O) = P(E) \cdot P(O) = \frac{3}{8} \cdot \frac{5}{8} = \frac{15}{64} \approx 23\%$.

Reflect

5. In Part B, what is the probability that the spinner stops on an odd number on the first spin, followed by an even number on the second spin? What do you observe? What does this tell you?

Your Turn

6. You spin a spinner with 4 red sections, 3 blue sections, 2 green sections, and 1 yellow section. If all the sections are of equal size, what is the probability that the spinner stops on green first and blue second?

7. A number cube has the numbers 3, 5, 6, 8, 10, and 12 on its faces. You roll the number cube twice. What is the probability that you roll an odd number on both rolls?

Explain 3 Showing That Events Are Independent

So far, you have used the formula $P(A \cap B) = P(A) \cdot P(B)$ when you knew that events A and B are independent. You can also use the formula to determine whether two events are independent.

Example 3 **Determine if the events are independent.**

(A) The two-way frequency table shows data for 120 randomly selected patients who have the same doctor. Determine whether a patient who takes vitamins and a patient who exercises regularly are independent events.

	Takes Vitamins	No Vitamins	Total
Regular Exercise	48	28	76
No regular Exercise	12	32	44
Total	60	60	120

Let V be the event that a patient takes vitamins. Let E be the event that a patient exercises regularly.

Step 1 Find $P(V)$, $P(E)$, and $P(V \cap E)$. The total number of patients is 120.

There are 60 patients who take vitamins, so $P(V) = \frac{60}{120} = \frac{1}{2}$.

There are 76 patients who exercise regularly, so $P(B) = \frac{76}{120} = \frac{19}{30}$.

There are 48 patients who take vitamins and exercise regularly, so $P(V \cap E) = \frac{48}{120} = 40\%$.

Step 2 Compare $P(V \cap E)$ and $P(V) \cdot P(E)$.

$P(V) \cdot P(E) = \frac{1}{2} \cdot \frac{19}{30} = \frac{19}{60} \approx 32\%$

Because $P(V \cap E) \neq P(V) \cdot P(E)$, the events are not independent.

(B) The two-way frequency table shows data for 60 randomly selected children at an elementary school. Determine whether a child who knows how to ride a bike and a child who knows how to swim are independent events.

	Knows how to Ride a Bike	Doesn't Know how to Ride a Bike	Total
Knows how to Swim	30	10	40
Doesn't Know how to Swim	15	5	20
Total	45	15	60

Let B be the event a child knows how to ride a bike. Let S be the event that a child knows how to swim.

Step 1 Find $P(B)$, $P(S)$, and $P(B \cap S)$. The total number of children is 60.

There are 45 children who know how to ride a bike, so $P(B) = \frac{45}{60} = \frac{3}{4}$.

There are 40 children who know how to swim, so $P(S) = \frac{40}{60} = \frac{2}{3}$.

There are 30 children who know how to ride a bike and swim, so $P(B \cap S) = \frac{30}{60} = \frac{1}{2}$.

Step 2 Compare $P(B \cap S)$ and $P(B) \cdot P(S)$.

$P(B) \cdot P(S) = \frac{3}{4} \cdot \frac{2}{3} = \frac{1}{2}$

Because $P(B \cap S)$ = $P(B) \cdot P(S)$, the events are independent.

Your Turn

8. A farmer wants to know if an insecticide is effective in preventing small insects called aphids from damaging tomato plants. The farmer experiments with 80 plants and records the results in the two-way frequency table. Determine whether a plant that was sprayed with insecticide and a plant that has aphids are independent events.

	Has Aphids	No Aphids	Total
Sprayed with Insecticide	12	40	52
Not Sprayed with Insecticide	14	14	28
Total	26	54	80

9. A student wants to know if right-handed people are more or less likely to play a musical instrument than left-handed people. The student collects data from 250 people, as shown in the two-way frequency table. Determine whether being right-handed and playing a musical instrument are independent events.

	Right-Handed	Left-Handed	Total
Plays a Musical Instrument	44	6	50
Does not Play a Musical Instrument	176	24	200
Total	220	30	250

Elaborate

10. What are the ways that you can show that two events A and B are independent?

11. How can you find the probability that two independent events A and B both occur?

12. **Essential Question Check-In** Give an example of two independent events and explain why they are independent.

Evaluate: Homework and Practice

Personal Math Trainer
- Online Homework
- Hints and Help
- Extra Practice

1. A bag contains 12 red and 8 blue chips. Two chips are separately drawn at random from the bag.

   a. Suppose that a single chip is drawn at random from the bag. Find the probability that the chip is red and the probability that the chip is blue.

   b. Suppose that two chips are separately drawn at random from the bag and that the first chip is returned to the bag before the second chip is drawn. Find the probability that the second chip drawn is blue given the first chip drawn was red.

   c. Suppose that two chips are separately drawn at random from the bag and that the first chip is not returned to the bag before the second chip is drawn. Find the probability that the second chip drawn is blue given the first chip drawn was red.

   d. In which situation—the first chip is returned to the bag or not returned to the bag—are the events that the first chip is red and the second chip is blue independent? Explain.

2. For each situation, identify whether the events are independent or not independent.

   a. Flip a coin twice and get tails both times.

   b. Roll a number cube and get 1 on the first roll and 6 on the second.

   c. Draw an ace from a shuffled deck, put the card back and reshuffle the deck, and then draw an 8.

   d. Rotate a bingo cage and draw the ball labeled B-4, set it aside, and then rotate the cage again and draw the ball labled N-38.

Answer the question using the fact that $P(A|B) = P(A)$ only when events A and B are independent.

3. The two-way frequency table shows data for 80 randomly selected people who live in a metropolitan area. Is the event that a person prefers public transportation independent of the event that a person lives in the city?

	Prefers to Drive	Prefers Public Transportation	Total
Lives in the City	12	24	36
Lives in the Suburbs	33	11	44
Total	45	35	80

4. The two-way frequency table shows data for 120 randomly selected people who take vacations. Is the event that a person prefers vacationing out of state independent of the event that a person is a woman?

	Prefers Vacationing Out of State	Prefers Vacationing in State	Total
Men	48	32	80
Women	24	16	40
Total	72	48	120

A jar contains marbles of various colors as listed in the table. Suppose you randomly draw one marble from the jar. After you put that marble back in the jar, you randomly draw a second marble. Use this information to answer the question, giving a probability as a percent and rounding to the nearest tenth of percent when necessary.

Color of Marble	Number of Marbles
Red	20
Yellow	18
Green	12
Blue	10

5. What is the probability that you draw a blue marble first and a red marble second?

6. What is the probability that you draw a yellow marble first and a green marble second?

7. What is the probability that you draw a yellow marble both times?

8. What color marble for the first draw and what color marble for the second draw have the greatest probability of occurring together? What is that probability?

You spin the spinner shown two times. Each section of the spinner is the same size. Use this information to answer the question, giving a probability as a percent and rounding to the nearest tenth of a percent when necessary.

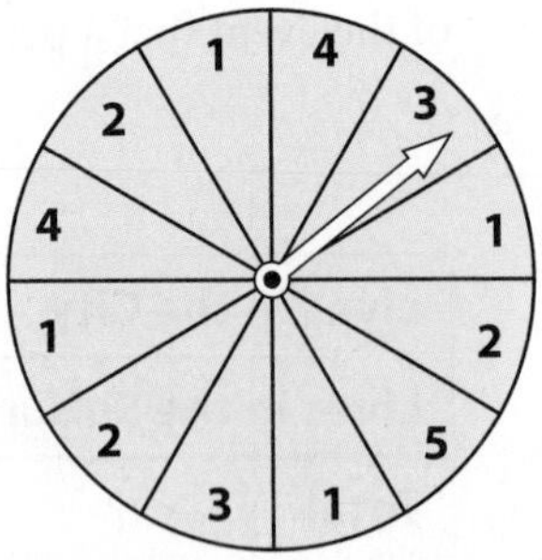

9. What is the probability that the spinner stops on 1 first and 2 second?

10. What is the probability that the spinner stops on 4 first and 3 second?

11. What is the probability that the spinner stops on an odd number first and an even number second?

12. What first number and what second number have the least probability of occurring together? What is that probability?

13. Find the probability of getting heads on every toss of a coin when the coin is tossed 3 times.

14. You are randomly choosing cards, one at a time and with replacement, from a standard deck of cards. Find the probability that you choose an ace, then a red card, and then a face card. (Remember that face cards are jacks, queens, and kings.)

Determine whether the given events are independent using the fact that $P(A \cap B) = P(A) \cdot P(B)$ only when events A and B are independent.

15. The manager of a produce stand wants to find out whether there is a connection between people who buy fresh vegetables and people who buy fresh fruit. The manager collects data on 200 randomly chosen shoppers, as shown in the two-way frequency table. Determine whether buying fresh vegetables and buying fresh fruit are independent events.

	Bought Vegetables	No Vegetables	Total
Bought Fruit	56	20	76
No Fruit	49	75	124
Total	105	95	200

16. The owner of a bookstore collects data about the reading preferences of 60 randomly chosen customers, as shown in the two-way frequency table. Determine whether being a female and preferring fiction are independent events.

	Prefers Fiction	Prefers Nonfiction	Total
Female	15	10	25
Male	21	14	35
Total	36	24	60

17. The psychology department at a college collects data about whether there is a relationship between a student's intended career and the student's like or dislike for solving puzzles. The two-way frequency table shows the collected data for 80 randomly chosen students. Determine whether planning for a career in a field involving math or science and a like for solving puzzles are independent events.

	Plans a Career in a Math/Science Field	Plans a Career in a Non-Math/Science Field	Total
Likes Solving Puzzles	35	15	50
Dislikes Solving Puzzles	9	21	30
Total	44	36	80

18. A local television station surveys some of its viewers to determine the primary reason they watch the station. The two-way frequency table gives the survey data. Determine whether a viewer is a man and a viewer primarily watches the station for entertainment are independent events.

	Primarily Watches for Information (News, Weather, Sports)	Primarily Watches for Entertainment (Comedies, Dramas)	Total
Men	28	12	40
Women	35	15	50
Total	63	27	90

19. Using what you know about independent events, complete the two-way frequency table in such a way that any event from a column will be independent of any event from a row. Give an example using the table to demonstrate the independence of two events.

	Women	Men	Total
Prefers Writing with a Pen	?	?	100
Prefers Writing with a Pencil	?	?	50
Total	60	90	150

H.O.T. Focus on Higher Order Thinking

20. Make a Prediction A box contains 100 balloons. The balloons come in two colors: 80 are yellow and 20 are green. The balloons are also either marked or unmarked: 50 are marked "Happy Birthday!" and 50 are not. A balloon is randomly chosen from the box. How many yellow "Happy Birthday!" balloons must be in the box if the event that a balloon is yellow and the event that a balloon is marked "Happy Birthday!" are independent? Explain.

21. Construct Arguments Given that events A and B are independent, prove that the complement of event A, A^c, is also independent of event B.

22. Multi-Step The two-way frequency table shows two events, A and B, and their complements, A^c and B^c. Let $P(A) = a$ and $P(B) = b$. Using a, b, and the grand total T, form the products listed in the table to find the number of elements in $A \cap B$, $A \cap B^c$, $A^c \cap B$, and $A^c \cap B^c$.

	A	**A^c**	**Total**
B	abT	$(1-a)bT$	?
B^c	$a(1-b)T$	$(1-a)(1-b)T$	?
Total	?	?	T

a. Find the table's missing row and column totals in simplest form.

b. Show that events A and B are independent using the fact that $P(A \mid B) = P(A)$ only when events A and B are independent.

c. Show that events A and B^c are independent.

d. Show that events A^c and B are independent.

e. Show that events A^c and B^c are independent.

Lesson Performance Task

Before the mid-1800s, little was known about the way that plants pass along characteristics such as color and height to their offspring. From painstaking observations of garden peas, the Austrian monk Gregor Mendel discovered the basic laws of heredity. The table shows the results of three of Mendel's experiments. In each experiment, he looked at a particular characteristic of garden peas by planting seeds exclusively of one type.

Characteristic	Type Planted	Results in Second Generation
Flower color	100% violet	705 violet, 224 white
Seed texture	100% round	5474 round, 1850 wrinkled
Seed color	100% yellow	6022 yellow, 2011 green

1. Suppose you plant garden peas with violet flowers and round, yellow seeds. Estimate the probability of obtaining second-generation plants with violet flowers, the probability of obtaining second-generation plants with round seeds, and the probability of obtaining second-generation plants with yellow seeds. Explain how you made your estimates.

Mendel saw that certain traits, such as violet flowers and round seeds, seemed stronger than others, such white flowers and wrinkled seeds. He called the stronger traits "dominant" and the weaker traits "recessive." Both traits can be carried in the genes of a plant, because a gene consists of two *alleles*, one received from the mother and one from the father. (For plants, the "father" is the plant from which the pollen comes, and the "mother" is the plant whose pistil receives the pollen.) When at least one of the alleles has the dominant trait, the plant exhibits the dominant trait. Only when both alleles have the recessive trait does the plant exhibit the recessive trait.

You can use a 2 × 2 Punnett square, like the one shown, to see the results of crossing the genes of two parent plants. In this Punnett square, *V* represents the dominant flower color violet and *v* represents the recessive flower color white. If each parent's genes contain both *V* and *v* alleles, the offspring may receive, independently and with equal probability, either a *V* allele or a *v* allele from each parent.

	V	**v**
V	VV	Vv
v	vV	vv

2. After planting a first generation of plants exhibiting only dominant traits, Mendel observed that the second generation consisted of plants with a ratio of about 3:1 dominant-to-recessive traits. Does the Punnett square support or refute Mendel's observation? Explain.

3. Draw a 4 × 4 Punnett square for finding the results of crossing two violet-flower-and-round-seed parent plants. Let *V* and *R* represent the dominant traits violet flowers and round seeds, respectively. Let *v* and *r* represent the recessive traits white flowers and wrinkled seeds, respectively. Each column heading and row heading of your Punnett square should contain a two-letter combination of *V* or *v* and *R* or *r*. Each cell of your Punnett square will then contain four letters. Use the Punnett square to find the probability that a second-generation plant will have white flowers and round seeds. Explain your reasoning.

20.3 Dependent Events

Essential Question: How do you find the probability of dependent events?

Resource Locker

Explore Finding a Way to Calculate the Probability of Dependent Events

You know two tests for the independence of events A and B:

1. If $P(A|B) = P(A)$, then A and B are independent.
2. If $P(A \cap B) = P(A) \cdot P(B)$, then A and B are independent.

Two events that fail either of these tests are **dependent events** because the occurrence of one event affects the occurrence of the other event.

(A) The two-way frequency table shows the results of a survey of 100 people who regularly walk for exercise. Let O be the event that a person prefers walking outdoors. Let M be the event that a person is male. Find $P(O)$, $P(M)$, and $P(O \cap M)$ as fractions. Then determine whether events O and M are independent or dependent.

	Prefers walking outdoors	Prefers walking on a treadmill	Total
Male	40	10	50
Female	20	30	50
Total	60	40	100

(B) Calculate the conditional probabilities $P(O|M)$ and $P(M|O)$.

$$P(O|M) = \frac{n(O \cap M)}{n(M)} = \frac{?}{?} = \frac{?}{5}$$

$$P(M|O) = \frac{n(O \cap M)}{n(O)} = \frac{?}{?} = \frac{?}{3}$$

Ⓒ Complete the multiplication table using the fractions for $P(O)$ and $P(M)$ from Step A and the fractions for $P(O|M)$ and $P(M|O)$ from Step B.

x	$P(O)$	$P(M)$
$P(O\|M)$	?	?
$P(M\|O)$	?	?

Ⓓ Do any of the four products in Step C equal $P(O \cap M)$, calculated in Step A? If so, which of the four products? ?

Reflect

1. In a previous lesson you learned the conditional probability formula $P(B|A) = \frac{P(A \cap B)}{P(A)}$. How does this formula explain the results you obtained in Step D?

2. Let F be the event that a person is female. Let T be the event that a person prefers walking on a treadmill. Write two formulas you can use to calculate $P(F \cap T)$. Use either one to find the value of $P(F \cap T)$, and then confirm the result by finding $P(F \cap T)$ directly from the two-way frequency table.

Explain 1 Finding the Probability of Two Dependent Events

You can use the Multiplication Rule to find the probability of dependent events.

Multiplication Rule

$P(A \cap B) = P(A) \cdot P(B|A)$ where $P(B|A)$ is the conditional probability of event B, given that event A has occurred.

Example 1 **There are 5 tiles with the letters A, B, C, D, and E in a bag. You choose a tile without looking, put it aside, and then choose another tile without looking. Use the Multiplication Rule to find the specified probability, writing it as a fraction.**

Ⓐ Find the probability that you choose a vowel followed by a consonant.

Let V be the event that the first tile is a vowel. Let C be the event that the second tile is a consonant. Of the 5 tiles, there are 2 vowels, so $P(V) = \frac{2}{5}$.

Of the 4 remaining tiles, there are 3 consonants, so $P(C|V) = \frac{3}{4}$.

By the Multiplication Rule, $P(V \cap C) = P(V) \cdot P(V|C) = \frac{2}{5} \cdot \frac{3}{4} = \frac{6}{20} = \frac{3}{10}$.

(B) Find the probability that you choose a vowel followed by another vowel.

Let $V1$ be the event that the first tile is a vowel. Let $V2$ be the event that the second tile is also a vowel. Of the 5 tiles, there are 2 vowels, so $P(V1) = \frac{2}{5}$.

Of the 4 remaining tiles, there is 1 vowel, so $P(V2|V1) = \frac{1}{4}$.

By the Multiplication Rule, $P(V1 \cap V2) = P(V1) \cdot P(V2|V1) = \frac{2}{5} \cdot \frac{1}{4} = \frac{2}{20} = \frac{1}{10}$.

Your Turn

A bag holds 4 white marbles and 2 blue marbles. You choose a marble without looking, put it aside, and choose another marble without looking. Use the Multiplication Rule to find the specified probability, writing it as a fraction.

3. Find the probability that you choose a white marble followed by a blue marble.

4. Find the probability that you choose a white marble followed by another white marble.

Explain 2 Finding the Probability of Three or More Dependent Events

You can extend the Multiplication Rule to three or more events. For instance, for three events A, B, and C, the rule becomes $P(A \cap B \cap C) = P(A) \cdot P(B|A) \cdot P(C|A \cap B)$.

Example 2 **You have a key ring with 7 different keys. You're attempting to unlock a door in the dark, so you try keys one at a time and keep track of which ones you try.**

(A) Find the probability that the third key you try is the right one.

Let $W1$ be the event that the first key you try is wrong. Let $W2$ be the event that the second key you try is also wrong. Let R be the event that the third key you try is right.

On the first try, there are 6 wrong keys among the 7 keys, so $P(W1) = \frac{6}{7}$.

On the second try, there are 5 wrong keys among the 6 remaining keys, so $P(W2|W1) = \frac{5}{6}$.

On the third try, there is 1 right key among the 5 remaining keys, so $P(R|W2 \cap W1) = \frac{1}{5}$.

By the Multiplication Rule, $P(W1 \cap W2 \cap R) = P(W1) \cdot P(W2|W1) \cdot P(R|W1 \cap W2) = \frac{6}{7} \cdot \frac{5}{6} \cdot \frac{1}{5} = \frac{1}{7}$.

(B) Find the probability that one of the first three keys you try is right.

There are two ways to approach this problem:

1. You can break the problem into three cases: (1) the first key you try is right; (2) the first key is wrong, but the second key is right; and (3) the first two keys are wrong, but the third key is right.

2. You can use the complement: The complement of the event that one of the first three keys is right is the event that *none* of the first three keys is right.

Use the second approach.

Let $W1$, $W2$, and $W3$ be the events that the first, second, and third keys, respectively, are wrong.

From Part A, you already know that $P(W1) = \frac{6}{7}$ and $P(W2|W1) = \frac{5}{6}$.

On the third try, there are 4 wrong keys among the 5 remaining keys, so $P(W3|W2 \cap W1) = \frac{4}{5}$.

By the Multiplication Rule,

$$P(W1 \cap W2 \cap W3) = P(W1) \cdot P(W2|W1) \cdot P(W3|W1 \cap W2) = \frac{6}{7} \cdot \frac{5}{6} \cdot \frac{4}{5} = \frac{4}{7}.$$

The event $W1 \cap W2 \cap W3$ is the complement of the one you want. So, the probability that one of the first three keys you try is right is $1 - P(W1 \cap W2 \cap W3) = 1 - \frac{4}{7} = \frac{3}{7}$.

Reflect

5. In Part B, show that the first approach to solving the problem gives the same result.

6. In Part A, suppose you don't keep track of the keys as you try them. How does the probability change? Explain.

Your Turn

Three people are standing in line at a car rental agency at an airport. Each person is willing to take whatever rental car is offered. The agency has 4 white cars and 2 silver ones available and offers them to customers on a random basis.

7. Find the probability that all three customers get white cars.

8. Find the probability that two of the customers get the silver cars and one gets a white car.

Elaborate

9. When are two events dependent?

10. Suppose you are given a bag with 3 blue marbles and 2 red marbles, and you are asked to find the probability of drawing 2 blue marbles by drawing one marble at a time and not replacing the first marble drawn. Why does not replacing the first marble make these events dependent? What would make these events independent? Explain.

11. **Essential Question Check-In** According to the Multiplication Rule, when finding $P(A \cap B)$ for dependent events A and B, you multiply $P(A)$ by what?

Evaluate: Homework and Practice

Personal Math Trainer

- Online Homework
- Hints and Help
- Extra Practice

1. Town officials are considering a property tax increase to finance the building of a new school. The two-way frequency table shows the results of a survey of 110 town residents.

	Supports a property tax increase	Does not support a property tax increase	Total
Lives in a household with children	50	20	70
Lives in a household without children	10	30	40
Total	60	50	110

a. Let C be the event that a person lives in a household with children. Let S be the event that a person supports a property tax increase. Are the events C and S independent or dependent? Explain.

b. Find $P(C|S)$ and $P(S|C)$. Which of these two conditional probabilities can you multiply with $P(C)$ to get $P(C \cap S)$? Which of the two can you multiply with $P(S)$ to get $P(C \cap S)$?

2. A mall surveyed 120 shoppers to find out whether they typically wait for a sale to get a better price or make purchases on the spur of the moment regardless of price. The two-way frequency table shows the results of the survey.

	Waits for a Sale	Buys on Impulse	Total
Woman	40	10	50
Man	50	20	70
Total	90	30	120

a. Let W be the event that a shopper is a woman. Let S be the event that a shopper typically waits for a sale. Are the events W and S independent or dependent? Explain.

b. Find $P(W|S)$ and $P(S|W)$. Which of these two conditional probabilities can you multiply with $P(W)$ to get $P(W \cap S)$? Which of the two can you multiply with $P(S)$ to get $P(W \cap S)$?

There are 4 green, 10 red, and 6 yellow marbles in a bag. Each time you randomly choose a marble, you put it aside before choosing another marble at random. Use the Multiplication Rule to find the specified probability, writing it as a fraction.

3. Find the probability that you choose a red marble followed by a yellow marble.

4. Find the probabilty that you choose one yellow marble followed by another yellow marble.

5. Find the probability that you choose a red marble, followed by a yellow marble, followed by a green marble.

6. Find the probability that you choose three red marbles.

The table shows the sums that are possible when you roll two number cubes and add the numbers. Use this information to answer the questions.

+	1	2	3	4	5	6
1	2	3	4	5	6	7
2	3	4	5	6	7	8
3	4	5	6	7	8	9
4	5	6	7	8	9	10
5	6	7	8	9	10	11
6	7	8	9	10	11	12

7. Let A be the event that you roll a 2 on the number cube represented by the row labeled 2. Let B be the event that the sum of the numbers on the cubes is 7.

a. Are these events independent or dependent? Explain.

b. What is $P(A \cap B)$?

8. Let A be the event that you roll a 3 on the number cube represented by the row labeled 3. Let B be the event that the sum of the numbers on the cubes is 5.

a. Are these events independent or dependent? Explain.

b. What is $P(A \cap B)$?

9. A cooler contains 6 bottles of apple juice and 8 bottles of grape juice. You choose a bottle without looking, put it aside, and then choose another bottle without looking. Match each situation with its probability. More than one situation can have the same probability.

A. Choose apple juice and then grape juice. **a.** ___?___ $\frac{4}{13}$

B. Choose apple juice and then apple juice. **b.** ___?___ $\frac{24}{91}$

C. Choose grape juice and then apple juice. **c.** ___?___ $\frac{15}{91}$

D. Choose grape juice and then grape juice.

10. Jorge plays all tracks on a playlist with no repeats. The playlist he's listening to has 12 songs, 4 of which are his favorites.

a. What is the probability that the first song played is one of his favorites, but the next two songs are not?

b. What is the probability that the first three songs played are all his favorites?

c. Jorge can also play the tracks on his playlist in a random order with repeats possible. If he does this, how does your answer to part b change? Explain why.

11. You are playing a game of bingo with friends. In this game, balls are labeled with one of the letters of the word BINGO and a number. Some of these letter-number combinations are written on a bingo card in a 5 × 5 array, and as balls are randomly drawn and announced, players mark their cards if the ball's letter-number combination appears on the cards. The first player to complete a row, column, or diagonal on a card says "Bingo!" and wins the game. In the game you're playing, there are 20 balls left. To complete a row on your card, you need N-32 called. To complete a column, you need G-51 called. To complete a diagonal, you need B-6 called.

a. What is the probability that the next two balls drawn do not have a letter-number combination you need, but the third ball does?

b. What is the probability that none of the letter-number combinations you need is called from the next three balls?

H.O.T. Focus on Higher Order Thinking

12. You are talking with 3 friends, and the conversation turns to birthdays.

a. What is the probability that no two people in your group were born in the same month?

b. Is the probability that at least two people in your group were born in the same month greater or less than $\frac{1}{2}$? Explain.

c. How many people in a group would it take for the probability that at least two people were born in the same month to be greater than $\frac{1}{2}$? Explain.

13. Construct Arguments Show how to extend the Multiplication Rule to three events A, B, and C.

14. Make a Prediction A bag contains the same number of red marbles and blue marbles. You choose a marble without looking, put it aside, and then choose another marble. Is there a greater-than-50% chance or a less-than-50% chance that you choose two marbles with different colors? Explain.

Lesson Performance Task

To prepare for an accuracy landing competition, a team of skydivers has laid out targets in a large open field. During practice sessions, team members attempt to land inside a target.

Two rectangular targets are shown on each field. Assuming a skydiver lands at random in the field, find the probabilities that the skydiver lands inside the specified target(s).

1. Calculate the probabilities using the targets shown here.

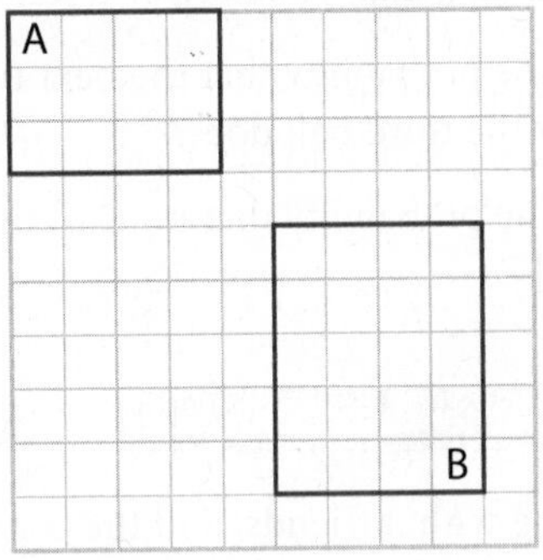

a. $P(A)$

b. $P(B)$

c. $P(A \cap B)$

d. $P(A \cup B)$

e. $P(A|B)$

f. $P(B|A)$

2. Calculate the probabilities using the targets shown here.

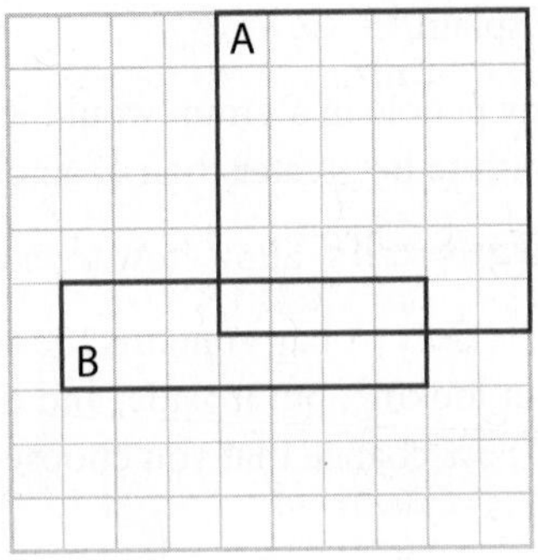

a. $P(A)$

b. $P(B)$

c. $P(A \cap B)$

d. $P(A \cup B)$

e. $P(A|B)$

f. $P(B|A)$

3. Calculate the probabilities using the targets shown here.

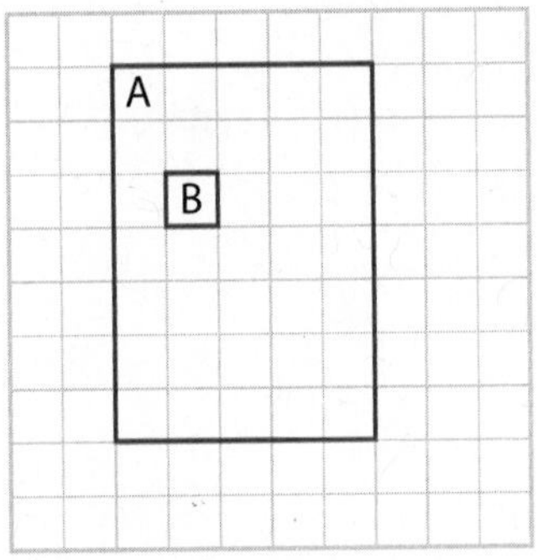

a. $P(A)$

b. $P(B)$

c. $P(A \cap B)$

d. $P(A \cup B)$

e. $P(A|B)$

f. $P(B|A)$

STUDY GUIDE REVIEW

Conditional Probability and Independence of Events

MODULE 20

Essential Question: How can you use conditional probability and independence of events to solve real-world problems?

Key Vocabulary
conditional probability
(probabilidad condicional)
independent events
(eventos independientes)
dependent events
(eventos dependientes)

KEY EXAMPLE *(Lesson 20.1)*

Find the probability that a black card drawn from the deck is a queen. (The deck is a standard one of 52 cards.)

The deck has 52 cards and 26 of them are black, so the probability of drawing a black card is $P(B) = \frac{26}{52}$. There are 2 black queens in the deck, so the probability of drawing one of them from the deck is $P(Q \cap B) = \frac{2}{52} = \frac{1}{26}$. Using the formula for conditional probability, $P(Q \mid B) = \frac{P(Q \cap B)}{P(B)} = \frac{\frac{2}{52}}{\frac{26}{52}} = \frac{1}{13}$.

KEY EXAMPLE *(Lesson 20.2)*

Jim rolled a set of two number cubes. If these are standard 6-sided number cubes, what is the probability of obtaining 12? (That means the values of the top faces add up to 12.)

The only way to get 12 is for both of the top sides of the number cubes to be 6. The events of obtaining 6s are independent. Each of these events has the probability of $\frac{1}{6}$ (1 out of 6 options), so the probability of getting 12 is $\frac{1}{6} \cdot \frac{1}{6} = \frac{1}{36}$ by the multiplication rule.

KEY EXAMPLE *(Lesson 20.3)*

What is the probability of selecting 2 blue marbles out of a jar of 20, half of them blue? How did you obtain it?

Let event A be selecting a blue marble on the first pick. Let event B be selecting a blue marble on the second one. The first marble is not replaced, so these are dependent events. Of the 20 marbles, half of them are blue, so $P(A) = \frac{1}{2}$. Of the remaining 19 marbles, 9 of them are blue, so the probability of selecting one is $P(B) = \frac{9}{19}$. Thus, the probability of selecting 2 blue marbles is $P(A \text{ and } B) = \frac{1}{2} \cdot \frac{9}{19} = \frac{9}{38}$, using the multiplication rule.

Exercises

Determine the conditional probability. *(Lesson 20.1)*

1. What is the probability that a diamond that is drawn from the deck is a queen?

2. What is the probability that a queen drawn is a diamond?

Show that the following situation refers to independent events. *(Lesson 20.2)*

3. Isabelle believes that right- and left-footed soccer players are equally likely to score goals. She collected data from 260 players from a local soccer league. Using the following two-way frequency table, show that being right-footed and scoring goals are independent events.

	Right-Footed	Left-Footed	Total
Has scored a goal	39	13	52
Has not scored a goal	156	52	208
TOTAL	195	65	260

Identify whether a situation involves independent or dependent events. *(Lesson 20.3)*

4. Jim has 2 blue, 2 green, and 2 black socks in his drawer. He picks out 2 socks, one after the other. Determine the probability of him getting a matching pair of blue socks.

MODULE PERFORMANCE TASK

Drawing Aces

You have a standard deck of 52 playing cards. You pick three cards in a row without replacement. What is the probability that all three are aces?

Now you replace the three cards, shuffle, and pick four cards in a row without replacement. What is the probability that none are aces?

Begin by making notes about your plan for approaching this problem. Then complete the task, using words, numbers, or diagrams to explain how you reached your conclusions.

Ready to Go On?

20.1–20.3 Conditional Probability and Independence of Events

Personal Math Trainer

- Online Homework
- Hints and Help
- Extra Practice

Compute the requested probability and explain how you obtained it.

1. A farmer wants to know if a particular fertilizer can cause blackberry shrubs to produce fruit early. Using the following two-way table, compute the probability of a plant producing fruit early without receiving fertilizer.

	Early Fruit	No Fruit	Total
Received Fertilizer	37	3	40
Did not receive fertilizer	19	21	40
TOTAL	56	24	80

2. Lisa flipped the same coin twice. Determine the probability of the coin landing on tails on the second try.

3. Lisa flipped the same coin three times. What is the probability she obtained all tails?

ESSENTIAL QUESTION

4. A jar contains 12 pennies, 5 nickels, and 18 quarters. You select 2 coins at random, one after the other.

Does selecting a nickel affect the probability of selecting another nickel? Does not selecting a dime affect the probability of selecting a nickel? Describe how you would find the probability of selecting 2 nickels.

MODULE 20
MIXED REVIEW

Assessment Readiness

1. Are the events independent? Write Yes or No for each situation.
   A. Picking a penny and a marble out of a jar of pennies and a jar of marbles.
   B. Drawing cards from a deck to form a 4-card hand.
   C. Choosing a color for a new shirt from a choice of red, yellow, or purple.

2. Of the boys running for School President, 2 are juniors and 3 are seniors. Of the girls who are running, 4 are juniors and 1 is a senior. Tell whether each situation has a probability of $\frac{2}{5}$.
   A. A girl wins.
   B. A candidate who is a boy is a junior.
   C. A candidate who is a junior is a boy.

3. You shuffle a standard deck of playing cards and deal one card. What is the probability that you deal an ace or a club? Explain your reasoning.

4. Claude has 2 jars of marbles. Each jar has 10 blue marbles and 10 green marbles. He selects 2 marbles from each jar. What is the probability they are all blue? Explain your reasoning.

Probability and Decision Making

MODULE 21

Essential Question: How can you use probability to solve real-world problems?

REAL WORLD VIDEO
Physicians today use many sophisticated tests and technologies to help diagnose illnesses, but they must still consider probability in their diagnoses and decisions about treatment.

MODULE PERFORMANCE TASK PREVIEW

What's the Diagnosis?

The science of medicine has come a long way since surgeries were performed by the neighborhood barber, and leeches were used to treat just about every ailment. Nevertheless, modern medicine isn't perfect, and widely used tests for diagnosing illnesses aren't always 100 percent accurate. In this module you'll learn how probability can be used to measure the reliability of tests, and then use what you learned to evaluate decisions about a diagnosis.

Are YOU Ready?

Complete these exercises to review skills you will need for this module.

Personal Math Trainer
- Online Homework
- Hints and Help
- Extra Practice

Probability of Simple Events

Example 1 Two 6-sided conventional number cubes are tossed. What is the probability that their sum is greater than 8?

+	1	2	3	4	5	6
1	2	3	4	5	6	7
2	3	4	5	6	7	8
3	4	5	6	7	8	9
4	5	6	7	8	9	10
5	6	7	8	9	10	11
6	7	8	9	10	11	12

There are 10 values greater than 8 and a total number of 36 values.

$$\frac{\text{number of favorable outcomes}}{\text{total number of outcomes}} = \frac{10}{36} = \frac{5}{18}$$

The probability that the sum of the two number cubes is greater than 8 is $\frac{5}{18}$.

Two number cubes are tossed. Find each probability.

1. The sum is prime. **2.** The product is prime. **3.** The product is a perfect square.

Making Predictions with Probability

Example 2 A fly lands on the target shown. What is the probability that the fly landed on red?

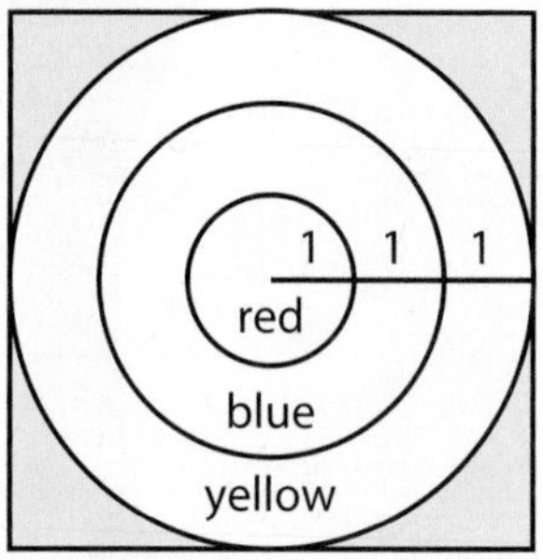

The area of the entire target is 6^2, or 36 units^2.

Red area is: $A = \pi r^2 = \pi(1)^2 = \pi$.

$$\frac{\text{number of favorable outcomes}}{\text{total number of outcomes}} = \frac{\pi}{36} \approx 8.7\%$$

Use the target to find the percent probability, to the nearest tenth.

4. Blue **5.** Yellow or red **6.** Not within a circle

21.1 Using Probability to Make Fair Decisions

Resource Locker

Essential Question: How can you use probability to help you make fair decisions?

Explore Using Probabilities When Drawing at Random

You are sharing a veggie supreme pizza with friends. There is one slice left and you and a friend both want it. Both of you have already had two slices. What is a fair way to solve this problem?

(A) Suppose you both decide to have the same amount of pizza. This means that the last slice will be cut into two pieces. Describe a fair way to split this last piece. ?

(B) Suppose instead you decide that one of you will get the whole slice. Complete the table so that the result of each option gives a fair chance for each of you to get the last slice. Why do each of these possibilities give a fair chance? ?

Option	Result (you get last slice)	Result (friend gets last slice)
Flip a coin	Heads	?
Roll a standard die	?	1, 3, 5
Play Rock, Paper, Scissors	You win.	You ? .
Draw lots using two straws of different lengths	?	Short straw

Reflect

1. Suppose, when down to the last piece, you tell your friend, "I will cut the last piece, and I will choose which piece you get." Why is this method unfair?

2. Your friend suggests that you shoot free throws to decide who gets the last piece. Use probability to explain why this might not be a fair way to decide.

Explain 1 Awarding a Prize to a Random Winner

Suppose you have to decide how to award a prize to a person at an event. You might want every person attending to have the same chance of winning, or you might want people to do something to improve their chance of winning. How can you award the prize fairly?

Example 1 **Explain whether each method of awarding a prize is fair.**

(A) The sponsor of an event wants to award a door prize to one attendee. Each person in attendance is given a ticket with a unique number on it. All of the numbers are placed in a bowl, and one is drawn at random. The person with the matching number wins the prize.

The method of awarding a door prize is fair. Each number has the same chance of being chosen, so each attendee has an equal probability of winning the prize. If n attendees are at the event, then the probability of winning the prize is $\frac{1}{n}$ for each attendee.

(B) A fundraiser includes a raffle in which half of the money collected goes to a charity, and the other half goes to one winner. Tickets are sold for $5 each. Copies of all the tickets are placed in a box, and one ticket is drawn at random. The person with the matching ticket wins the raffle.

The method of choosing a raffle winner is fair because each ticket has an equal probability of being drawn.

Reflect

3. In Example 1B, the probability may not be the same for each person to win the raffle. Explain why the method is still fair.

Your Turn

4. Each month, a company wants to award a special parking space to an employee at random. Describe a fair way to do this. Include a way to ensure that a person doesn't win a second time before each employee has won once.

Explain 2 Solving Real-World Problems Fairly

You can use a random number generator to choose a winner of a prize.

Example 2 **Use a problem solving plan.**

A class of 24 students sold 65 magazine subscriptions to raise money for a trip. The table shows three of the students and the number of subscriptions each sold. As an incentive to participate, you will award a prize to one student in the class. Describe a method of awarding the prize fairly. Use probabilities to explain why your method is fair for the students listed.

Student	Subscriptions Sold
Miri	5
Liam	2
Madison	0

Analyze Information

Identify the important information.

- There are 24 students.
- They sold 65 magazine subscriptions.
- There is one prize, so there will be one winner.

Formulate a Plan

To be fair, students who sold more subscriptions should have a better chance of winning the prize than the students who sold fewer.

Find a method of assigning outcomes so that the chance of winning is proportional to the number of subscriptions sold.

Solve

The class sold 65 subscriptions, so assign the numbers 1–65 to the students. Each student gets as many numbers as the number of subscriptions he or she sold.

Student	Subscriptions Sold	Numbers Assigned	Probability of Winning
Miri	5	1–5	$\frac{5}{65} \approx 7.7\%$
Liam	2	6, 7	$\frac{2}{65} \approx 3.1\%$
Madison	0	none	$\frac{0}{65} = 0\%$

Then use a calculator to find a random integer from 1 to 65 (randInt(1, 65)). Then, for instance, if the result is 7, Liam wins the prize.

Justify and Evaluate

This method seems fair because it gives everyone who sold subscriptions a chance of winning. You could award a prize to the student who sold the most subscriptions, but this might not be possible if multiple students all sold the same number, and it might not seem fair if some students have better access to buyers than others.

Reflect

5. A student suggests that it would be better to assign the numbers to students randomly rather than in numerical order. Would doing this affect the probability of winning?

6. A charity is giving a movie ticket for every 10 coats donated. Jacob collected 8 coats, Ben collected 6, and Ryan and Zak each collected 3. They decide to donate the coats together so that they will get 2 movie tickets. Describe how to use a random number generator to decide which 2 boys get a ticket.

Explain 3 Solving the Problem of Points

The decision-making process that you will apply in this example is based on the "Problem of Points" that was studied by the French mathematicians Blaise Pascal and Pierre de Fermat in the 17th century. Their work on the problem launched the branch of mathematics now known as probability.

Example 3 **Two students, Lee and Rory, find a box containing 100 baseball cards. To determine who should get the cards, they decide to play a game with the rules shown.**

Game Rules
• One of the students repeatedly tosses a coin.
• When the coin lands heads up, Lee gets a point.
• When the coin lands tails up, Rory gets a point.
• The first student to reach 20 points wins the game and gets the baseball cards.

As Lee and Rory are playing the game, they are interrupted and unable to continue. How should the 100 baseball cards be divided between the students given that the game was interrupted at the described moment?

(A) When they are interrupted, Lee has 19 points and Rory has 17 points.

At most, 3 coin tosses would have been needed for someone to win the game.

Make a list of all possible results using H for heads and T for tails. Draw boxes around the outcomes in which Lee wins the game.

0T, 3H	1T, 2H	2T, 1H	3T, 0H
HHH	THH	TTH	TTT
	HTH	THT	
	HHT	HTT	

There are 8 possible results. Lee wins in 7 of them and Rory wins in 1 of them.

The probability of Lee winning is $\frac{7}{8}$, so he should get $\frac{7}{8}$ of the cards which is 87.5 cards. The probability of Rory winning is $\frac{1}{8}$, so he should get $\frac{1}{8}$ of the cards which is 12.5 cards. Rather than split a card into two, they might decide to flip a coin for that card or let Lee have it because he was more likely to win it.

(B) When they are interrupted, Lee has 18 points and Rory has 17 points.

At most, four more coin tosses would have been needed.

List all possible results. Draw boxes around the outcomes in which Lee wins.

0T, 4H	1T, 3H	2T, 2H	3T, 1H	4T, 0H
HHHH	THHH	TTHH	TTTH	TTTT
	HTHH	THTH	TTHT	
	HHTH	THHT	THTT	
	HHHT	HTTH	HTTT	
		HTHT		
		HHTT		

There are 16 possible results. Lee wins in 11 of them and Rory wins in 5 of them.

The probability of Lee winning is $\frac{11}{16}$, so he should get 69 cards.

The probability of Rory winning is $\frac{5}{16}$, so he should get 31 cards.

Reflect

7. **Discussion** A student suggests that a better way to divide the cards in Example 3B would be to split the cards based on the number of points earned so far. Which method do you think is better?

Your Turn

8. Describe a situation where the game is interrupted, resulting in the cards needing to be divided evenly between the two players.

Elaborate

9. **Discussion** In the situation described in the Explore, suppose you like the crust and your friend does not. Is there a fair way to cut the slice of pizza that might not result in two pieces with the same area?

10. How would the solution to Example 2 need to change if there were two prizes to award? Assume that you do not want one student to win both prizes.

11. **Essential Question Check-In** Describe a way to use probability to make a fair choice of a raffle winner.

Evaluate: Homework and Practice

Personal Math Trainer

- Online Homework
- Hints and Help
- Extra Practice

1. You and a friend split the cost of a package of five passes to a climbing gym. Describe a way that you could fairly decide who gets to use the fifth pass.

2. In addition to prizes for first, second, and third place, the organizers of a race have a prize that they want each participant to have an equal chance of winning. Describe a fair method of choosing a winner for this prize.

Decide whether each method is a fair way to choose a winner based on whether each person has an equal chance of winning. Explain your answer by calculating each person's probability of winning.

3. Roll a standard die. Meri wins if the result is less than 3. Riley wins if the result is greater than 3.
4. Draw a card from a standard deck of cards. Meri wins if the card is red. Riley wins if the card is black.
5. Flip a coin. Meri wins if it lands heads. Riley wins if it lands tails.
6. Meri and Riley both jump as high as they can. Whoever jumps higher wins.
7. Roll a standard die. Meri wins if the result is even. Riley wins if the result is odd.
8. Randomly draw a stone from a box that contains 5 black stones and 4 white stones. Meri wins if the stone is black. Riley wins if the stone is white.

9. A chess club has received a chess set to give to one of its members. The club decides that everyone should have a chance of winning the set based on how many games they have won this season. Describe a fair method to decide who wins the set. Find the probability that each member will win it.

Member	Games Won	Probability of Winning	Member	Games Won	Probability of Winning
Kayla	30	?	Hailey	12	?
Noah	23	?	Gabe	12	?
Ava	18	?	Concour	5	?

10. Owen, Diego, and Cody often play a game of chance during lunch. When they can't finish, they calculate the probability that each will win given the current state of the game and assign partial wins. Today, when they had to stop, they calculated that there were 56 possibilities for how the game could be completed. Owen was the winner in 23 of the possibilities, Diego was the winner in 18 of them, and Cody was the winner in 15. To two decimal places, how should they assign partial wins?

Represent Real-World Problems **Twenty students, including Paige, volunteer to work at the school banquet. Each volunteer worked a nonzero whole number of hours. Paige worked 4 hours. The students worked a total of 45 hours. The organizers would like to award a prize to one of the volunteers.**

11. Describe a process for awarding the prize so that each volunteer has an equal chance of winning. Find the probability that Paige wins.

12. Describe a process for awarding the prize so that each volunteer's chance of winning is proportional to how many hours the volunteer worked. Find the probability that Paige wins.

There are 10,000 seats available in a sports stadium. Each seat has a package beneath it, and 20 of the seats have an additional prize-winning package with a family pass for the entire season.

13. Under what circumstances is this method of choosing winners of the family passes fair?

14. Assuming that the method of choosing winners is fair, what is the probability of winning a family pass if you attend the game?

15. What is the probability of not winning a family pass if you attend the game?

A teacher tells students, "For each puzzle problem you complete, I will assign you an entry number for a prize giveaway." In all, 10 students complete 53 puzzle problems. Leon completed 7. To award the prize, the teacher uses a calculator to generate a random integer from 1 to 53. Leon is assigned the numbers 18 to 24.

16. What is the probability that a particular number is chosen?

17. What is the probability that one of Leon's numbers will be chosen?

18. What is the probability that one of Leon's numbers will not be chosen?

19. Is this fair to Leon according to the original instructions? Explain.

H.O.T. Focus on Higher Order Thinking

20. **Make a Conjecture** Two teams are playing a game against one another in class to earn 10 extra points on an assignment. The teacher said that the points will be split fairly between the two teams, depending on the results of the game. If Team A earned 1300 points and Team B earned 2200 points, describe one way the teacher could split up the 10 extra points. Explain.

21. Persevere in Problem Solving Alexa and Sofia are at a yard sale, and they find a box of 20 collectible toys that they both want. They can't agree about who saw it first, so they flip a coin until Alexa gets 10 heads or Sofia gets 10 tails. When Alexa has 3 heads and Sofia has 6 tails, they decide to stop and divide the toys proportionally based on the probability each has of winning under the original rules. How should they divide the toys?

Lesson Performance Task

Three games are described below. For each game, tell whether it is fair (all players are equally likely to win) or unfair (one player has an advantage). Explain how you reached your decision, being sure to discuss how probability entered into your decision.

1. You and your friend each toss a quarter. If two heads turn up, you win. If a head and a tail turn up, your friend wins. If two tails turn up, you play again.
2. You and your friend each roll a number cube. If the sum of the numbers is odd, you get 1 point. If the sum is even, your friend gets 1 point.
3. You and your friend each roll a number cube. If the product of the numbers is odd, you get 1 point. If the product is even, your friend gets 1 point.

21.2 Analyzing Decisions

Essential Question: How can conditional probability help you make real-world decisions?

Resource Locker

Explore 1 Analyzing a Decision Using Probability

Suppose scientists have developed a test that can be used at birth to determine whether a baby is right-handed or left-handed. The test uses a drop of the baby's saliva and instantly gives the result. The test has been in development long enough for the scientists to track the babies as they grow into toddlers and to see whether their test is accurate. About 10% of babies turn out to be left-handed.

The scientists have learned that when children are left-handed, the test correctly identifies them as left-handed 92% of the time. Also, when children are right-handed, the test correctly identifies them as right-handed 95% of the time.

(A) In the first year on the market, the test is used on 1,000,000 babies. Complete the table. Begin with the grand total (lower-right table cell) and the row totals, and use those to help you fill in the four "Actually" versus "Tests" cells and then the two column totals.

	Tests Left-handed	Tests Right-handed	Total
Actually Left-handed	?	?	?
Actually Right-handed	?	?	?
Total	?	?	?

(B) What is the probability that a baby who tests left-handed actually is left-handed?

(C) What is the probability that a baby who tests right-handed actually is right-handed?

Reflect

1. Is the test a good test of right-handedness?

2. A baby is tested, and the test shows the baby will be left-handed. The parents decide to buy a left-handed baseball glove for when the baby is old enough to play baseball. Is this a reasonable decision?

3. **Discussion** Describe two ways in which the test can become a more reliable indicator of left-handedness.

Explore 2 Deriving Bayes' Theorem

Bayes' Theorem gives a formula for calculating an unknown conditional probability from other known probabilities. You can use Bayes' Theorem to calculate conditional probabilities like those in Steps B and C in Explore 1.

A Complete the steps to derive Bayes' Theorem.

(1) Write the formula for $P(B|A)$. ?

(2) Solve for $P(A \cap B)$. ?

(3) Write the formula for $P(A|B)$. ?

(4) Substitute the expression for $P(A \cap B)$ in step (2) into the formula for $P(A|B)$ in step (3). ?

B Complete the equations at the bottom of the tree diagram. Use the fact that the probability shown along each branch is the probability of the single event to which that branch leads. Each product of probabilities listed at the bottom of the tree diagram is the probability that two events occur together.

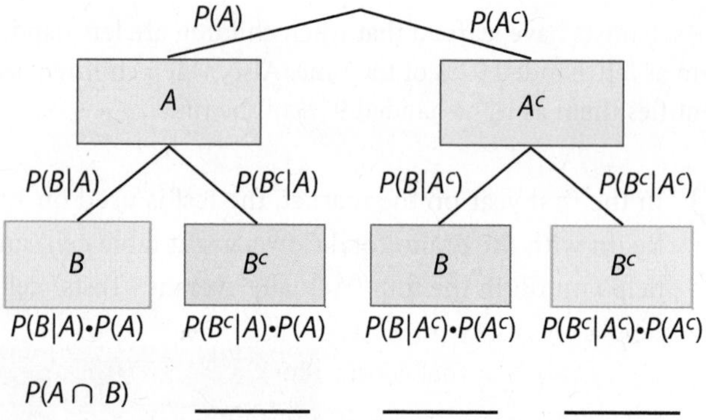

C Complete the explanation for finding $P(B)$ using the tree diagram in Step B.

Because events A and A^c are mutually exclusive, the events $A \cap B$ and ? are mutually exclusive. Since the union of $A \cap B$ and ? is ? ,

$P(B) = P(A \cap B) +$? $= P(A) \cdot P(B|A) +$? .

D Use your result from Step C to rewrite your final expression from Step A to get another form of Bayes' Theorem. ?

Reflect

4. Explain in words what each expression means in the context of Explore 1.

$P(A)$ is the probability of actually being left-handed.

$P(B)$ is the probability of testing left-handed.

$P(A|B)$ is ? .

$P(B|A)$ is ? .

5. Use Bayes' Theorem to calculate the probability that a baby actually is left-handed, given that the baby tests left-handed. Explain what this probability means.

Explain 1 Using Bayes' Theorem

Bayes' Theorem is a useful tool when you need to make or analyze decisions.

Bayes' Theorem

Given two events A and B with $P(B) \neq 0$, $P(A|B) = \frac{P(A) \cdot P(B|A)}{P(B)}$.

Another form is $P(A|B) = \frac{P(A) \cdot P(B|A)}{P(A) \cdot P(B|A) + P(A^c) \cdot P(B|A^c)}$.

Example 1 **Suppose Walter operates an order-filling machine that has an error rate of 0.5%. He installs a new order-filling machine that has an error rate of only 0.1%. The new machine takes over 80% of the order-filling tasks.**

(A) One day, Walter gets a call from a customer complaining that her order wasn't filled properly. Walter blames the problem on the old machine. Was he correct in doing so?

First, find the probability that the order was filled by the old machine given that there was an error in filling the order, P(old | error).

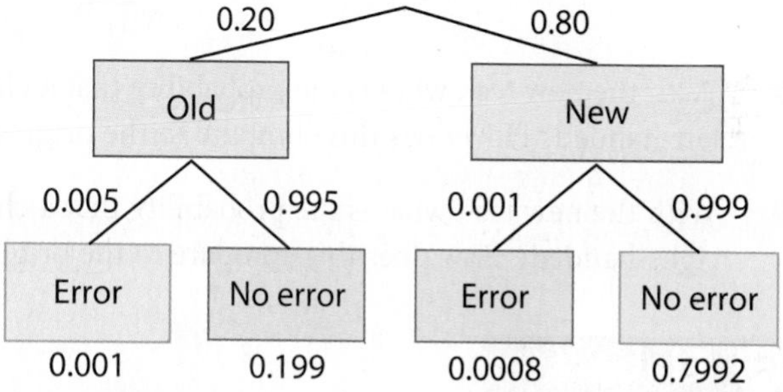

$$P(\text{old}|\text{error}) = \frac{P(\text{old}) \cdot P(\text{error}|\text{old})}{P(\text{error})}$$

$$= \frac{(0.20) \cdot 0.005}{0.001 + 0.0008} = \frac{0.001}{0.0018} = \frac{5}{9} \approx 0.56$$

Given that there is a mistake, the probability is about 56% that the old machine filled the order. The probability that the new machine filled the order is $1 - 0.56 = 44\%$. The old machine is only slightly more likely than the new machine to have filled the order. Walter shouldn't blame the old machine.

(B) Walter needs to increase capacity for filling orders so he increases the number of orders being filled by the old machine to 30% of the total orders. What percent of errors in filled orders are made by the old machine? Is Walter unreasonably increasing the risk of shipping incorrectly filled orders?

Find the probability that the order was filled by the old machine given that there is an error in filling, $P(\text{old}|\text{error})$.

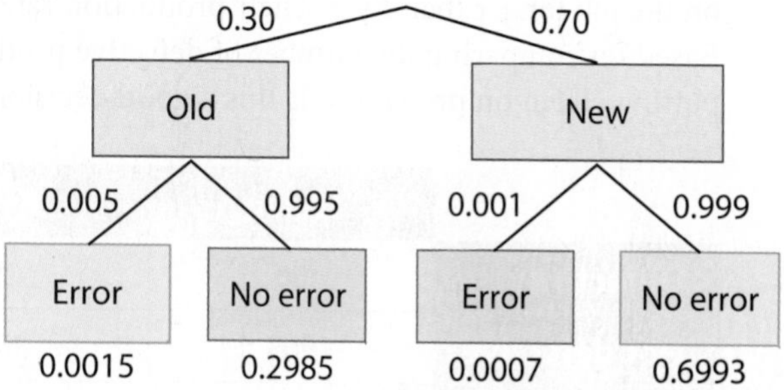

Use Bayes' Theorem.

$$P(\text{old}|\text{error}) = \frac{P(\text{old}) \cdot P(\text{error}|\text{old})}{P(\text{error})}$$

$$= \frac{0.30 \cdot 0.005}{0.0015 + 0.007} = \frac{0.0015}{0.0022} = \frac{15}{22} = 68\%$$

Describe the result of making this change.

Given that there is an error, the probability is about 68% that the old machine filled the package. Making this change increases the probability of an error from $0.001 + 0.0008 = 0.0018$ to $0.0015 + 0.0007 = 0.0022$, a difference of 0.0004, which means that there are 4 additional errors for every 10,000 orders. This seems like a worthwhile risk.

Reflect

6. Given that the old machine fills so few orders, how can it be responsible for more than half of the errors?

Your Turn

In the situation described in Explore 1, suppose the scientists have changed the test so that now it correctly identifies left-handed babies 100% of the time, and still correctly identifies right-handed babies 95% of the time.

7. Complete the tree diagram.

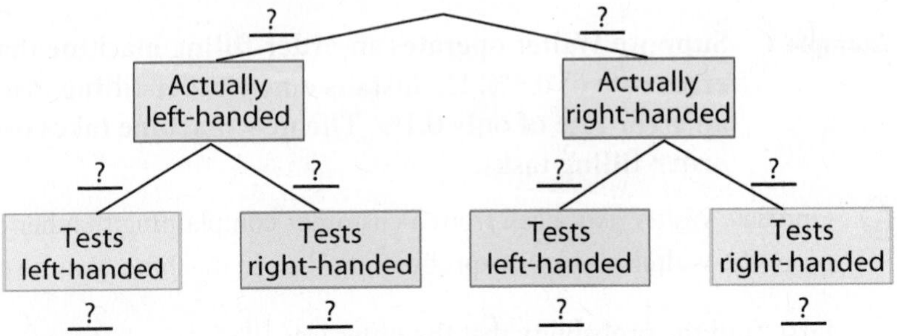

8. With the new test, what is the probability that a child who tests left-handed will be left-handed? How does this compare to the original test?

9. With the new test, what is the probability that a child who tests right-handed will be right-handed? How does this compare to the original test?

Elaborate

10. **Discussion** Compare the probabilities you found in Explore 1 and Your Turn 8 and 9. Why did the probability that a baby who tests right-handed actually is right-handed become 100%?

11. **Essential Question Check-In** How can you use probability to help you analyze decisions?

Evaluate: Homework and Practice

Personal Math Trainer
- Online Homework
- Hints and Help
- Extra Practice

1. A factory manager is assessing the work of two assembly-line workers. Helen has been on the job longer than Kyle. Their production rates for the last month are in the table. Based on comparing the number of defective products, the manager is considering putting Helen on probation. Is this a good decision? Why or why not?

	Helen	Kyle	Total
Defective	50	20	70
Not defective	965	350	1,315
Total	1,015	370	1,385

2. **Multiple Step** A reporter asked 150 voters if they plan to vote in favor of a new library and a new arena. The table shows the results. If you are given that a voter plans to vote no for the new arena, what is the probability that the voter also plans to vote no for the new library?

	Yes for Library	No for Library	Total
Yes for Arena	21	30	51
No for Arena	57	42	99
Total	78	72	150

3. You want to hand out coupons for a local restaurant to students who live off campus at a rural college with a population of 10,000 students. You know that 10% of the students live off campus and that 98% of those students ride a bike. Also, 62% of the students who live on campus do not have a bike. You decide to give a coupon to any student you see who is riding a bike. Complete the table. Then explain whether this a good decision.

	Bike	No bike	Total
On campus	?	?	?
Off campus	?	?	?
Total	?	?	?

4. A test for a virus correctly identifies someone who has the virus (by returning a positive result) 99% of the time. The test correctly identifies someone who does not have the virus (by returning a negative result) 99% of the time. It is known that 0.5% of the population has the virus. A doctor decides to treat anyone who tests positive for the virus. Complete the two-way table assuming a total population of 1,000,000 people have been tested. Is this a good decision?

	Tests Positive	Tests Negative	Total
Virus	?	?	?
No virus	?	?	?
Total	?	?	?

5. It is known that 2% of the population has a certain allergy. A test correctly identifies people who have the allergy 98% of the time. The test correctly identifies people who do not have the allergy 95% of the time. A website recommends that anyone who tests positive for the allergy should begin taking anti-allergy medication. Complete the two-way table. Do you think this is a good recommendation? Why or why not?

	Test Positive	Test Negative	Total
?	?	?	?
?	?	?	?
Total	?	?	10,000

6. Use the tree diagram shown.

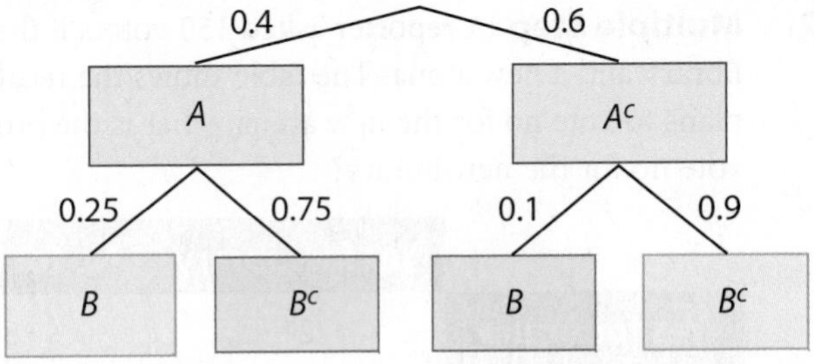

a. Find $P(A^c) \cdot P(B|A^c)$.

b. Find $P(B)$.

c. Use Bayes's Theorem to find $P(A^c|B)$.

7. The probabilities of drawing lemons and limes from a bag are shown in the tree diagram. Find the probability of drawing the two pieces of fruit randomly from the bag.

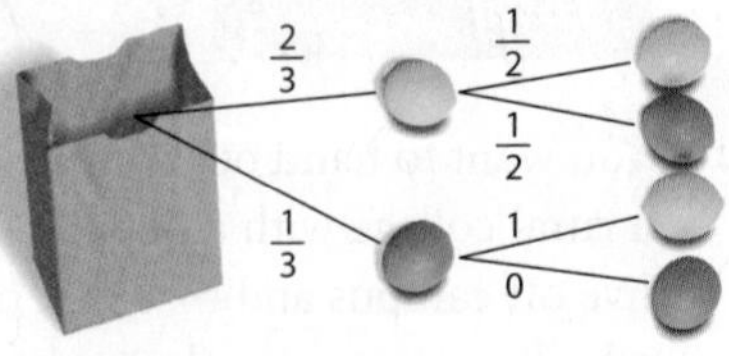

a. two lemons

b. two limes

c. lime then lemon

d. lemon then lime OR lime then lemon

8. **Multiple Step** A school principal plans a school picnic for June 2. A few days before the event, the weather forecast predicts rain for June 2, so the principal decides to cancel the picnic. Consider the following information.

- In the school's town, the probability that it rains on any day in June is 3%.
- When it rains, the forecast correctly predicts rain 90% of the time.
- When it does not rain, the forecast incorrectly predicts rain 5% of the time.

a. Find $P(\text{prediction of rain} \mid \text{rains})$ and $P(\text{rains})$.

b. Complete the tree diagram, and find $P(\text{prediction of rain})$.

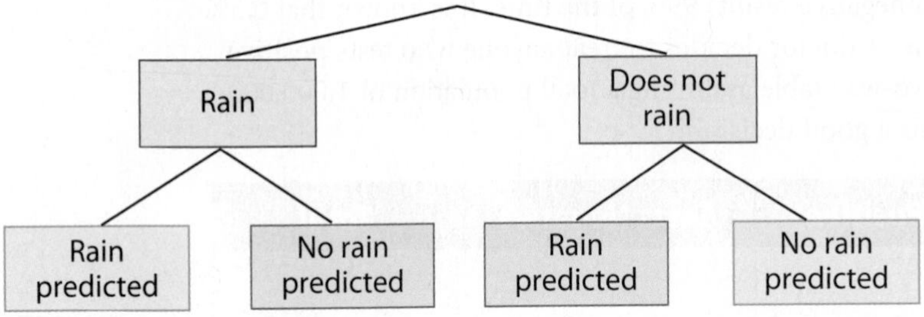

c. Find $P(\text{rains} \mid \text{prediction of rain})$.

d. Is the decision to cancel the picnic reasonable?

9. Pamela has collected data on the number of students in the sophomore class who play a sport or play a musical instrument. She has learned the following.

- 42.5% of all students in her school play a musical instrument.
- 20% of those who play a musical instrument also play a sport.
- 40% of those who play no instrument also play no sport.

Complete the tree diagram. Would it be reasonable to conclude that a student who doesn't play a sport plays a musical instrument?

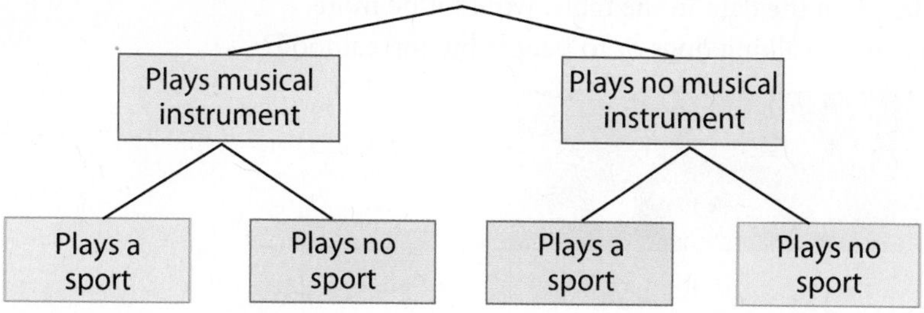

10. Interpret the Answer Company X supplies 35% of the phones to an electronics store and Company Y supplies the remainder. The manager of the store knows that 25% of the phones in the last shipment from Company X were defective, while only 5% of the phones from Company Y were defective. The manager chooses a phone at random and finds that it is defective. The manager decides that the phone must have come from Company X. Do you think this is a reasonable conclusion? Why or why not?

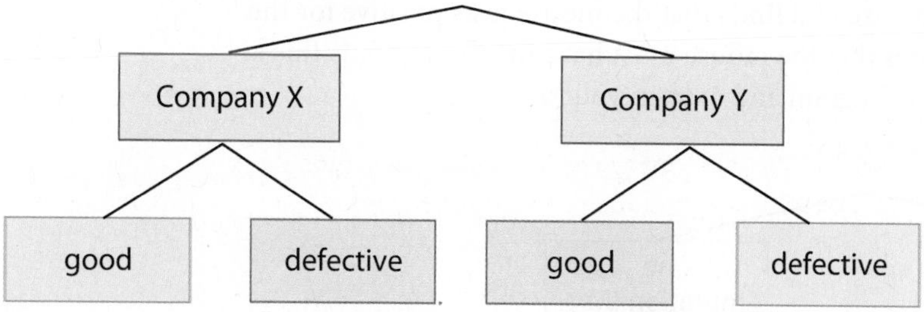

11. Suppose that strep throat affects 2% of the population and a test to detect it produces an accurate result 99% of the time. Create a tree diagram and use Bayes' Theorem to find the probability that someone who tests positive actually has strep throat.

12. Fundraising A hand-made quilt is first prize in a fund-raiser raffle. The table shows information about all the ticket buyers. Given that the winner of the quilt is a man, what is the probability that he resides in Sharonville?

	Men	Women	Total
Forestview	35	45	80
Sharonville	15	25	40
?	?	?	?

13. Recall that the Multiplication Rule says that $P(A \cap B) = P(A) \cdot P(B|A)$. If you switch the order of events A and B, then the rule becomes $P(B \cap A) = P(B) \cdot P(A|B)$. Use the Multiplication Rule and the fact that $P(B \cap A) = P(A \cap B)$ to prove Bayes' Theorem. (*Hint*: Divide each side by $P(B)$.)

14. Sociology A sociologist collected data on the types of pets in 100 randomly selected households. Suppose you want to offer a service to households that own both a cat and a dog. Complete the table. Based on the data in the table, would it be more effective to hand information to people walking dogs or to people buying cat food?

		Owns a Cat		
		Yes	No	?
Owns a Dog	Yes	15	24	?
	No	18	43	?
	?	?	?	?

15. Interpret the Answer It is known that 1% of all mice in a laboratory have a genetic mutation. A test for the mutation correctly identifies mice that have the mutation 98% of the time. The test correctly identifies mice that do not have the mutation 96% of the time. A lab assistant tests a mouse and finds that the mouse tests positive for the mutation. The lab assistant decides that the mouse must have the mutation. Is this a good decision? Complete the tree diagram and explain your answer.

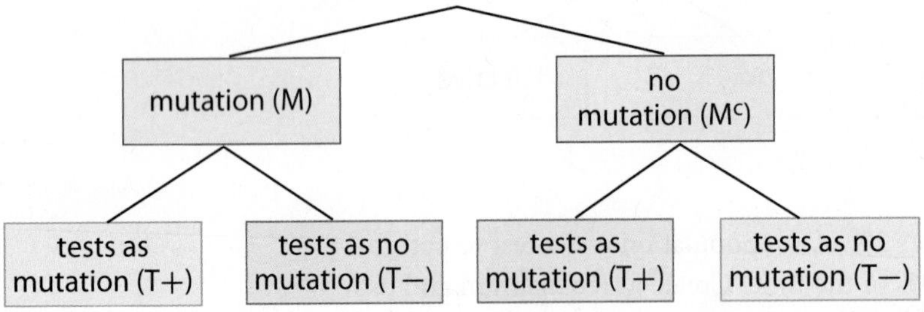

16. Interpret the Answer It is known that 96% of all dogs do not get trained. One professional trainer claims that 54% of trained dogs will sit on one of the first four commands to sit and that no other dogs will sit on command. A condominium community wants to impose a restriction on dogs that are not trained. They want each dog owner to show that his or her dog will sit on one of the first four commands. Assuming that the professional trainer's claim is correct, is this a fair way to identify dogs that have not been trained? Explain.

17. Multiple Steps Tomas has a choice of three possible routes to work. On each day, he randomly selects a route and keeps track of whether he is late. Based on this 40-day trial, which route makes Tomas least likely to be late for work?

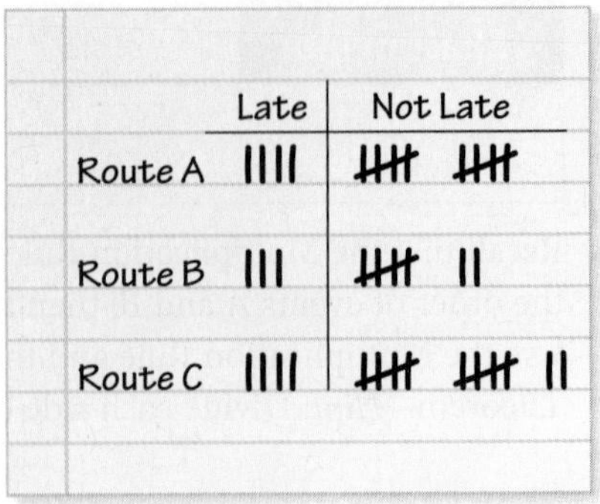

H.O.T. Focus on Higher Order Thinking

18. Critique Reasoning When Elisabeth saw this tree diagram, she said that the calculations must be incorrect. Do you agree? Justify your answer.

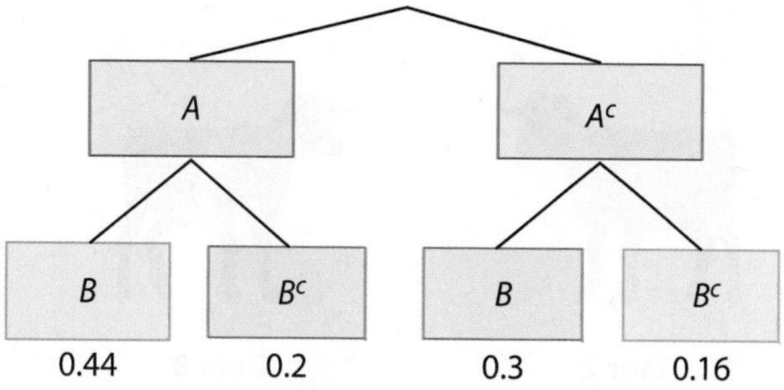

19. Multiple Representations The Venn diagram shows how many of the first 100 customers of a new bakery bought either bread or cookies, both, or neither. Taryn claims that the data indicate that a customer who bought cookies is more likely to have bought bread than a customer who bought bread is likely to have bought cookies. Is she correct?

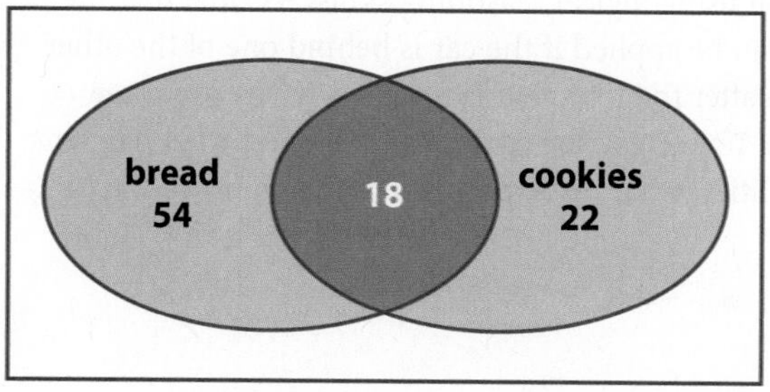

20. Persevere in Problem Solving At one high school, the probability that a student is absent today, given that the student was absent yesterday, is 0.12. The probability that a student is absent today, given that the student was present yesterday, is 0.05. The probability that a student was absent yesterday is 0.1. A teacher forgot to take attendance in several classes yesterday, so he assumed that attendance in his class today is the same as yesterday. If there were 40 students in these classes, how many errors would you expect by doing this?

Lesson Performance Task

You're a contestant on a TV quiz show. Before you are three doors. Behind two of the doors, there's a goat. Behind one of the doors, there's a new car. You are asked to pick a door. After you make your choice, the quizmaster opens one of the doors you *didn't* choose, revealing a goat.

Door 1

Door 2

Door 3

Now there are only two doors. You can stick with your original choice or you can switch to the one remaining door. Should you switch?

Intuition tells most people that, with two doors left, there's a 50% probability that they're right and a 50% probability that they're wrong. They conclude that it doesn't matter whether they switch or not.

Does it? Using Bayes' Theorem, it can be shown mathematically that you're much better off switching! You can reach the same conclusion using logical reasoning skills. Assume that the car is behind Door 1. (The same reasoning can be applied if the car is behind one of the other doors.) You've decided to switch your choice after the first goat is revealed. There are three possibilities based on which door you choose first. Describe each possibility and what happens when you switch. Based on the three possibilities, what is the probability that you win the car? Explain how you obtain the probability..

Probability and Decision Making

Essential Question: How can you use probability to solve real-world problems?

KEY EXAMPLE *(Lesson 21.1)*

Determine whether the method of awarding a prize is fair. Explain.

A festival has a baked goods fundraising raffle in which tickets are drawn for winners. The tickets are sold for \$2 each, and the purchaser of the ticket places his or her name on the ticket before placing the ticket into a fishbowl on a table. There are 20 cakes for prizes. A ticket is drawn at random from the fishbowl for each cake.

The method of awarding the prize is fair. This is because each ticket has an equal probability of being drawn. For each of n tickets bought, that ticket has a $\frac{1}{n}$ chance of being drawn. The more tickets someone buys, the better chance they have of winning a cake.

KEY EXAMPLE *(Lesson 21.2)*

Suppose Rhonda's Block Warehouse operates a block-making machine that has an error rate of 0.7%. Then Rhonda installs a new block-making machine that has an error rate of only 0.3%. The new machine takes over 75% of the block-making tasks. One day, Rhonda gets a call from a customer complaining that his block is not made properly. Rhonda blames the problem on the old machine. Was she correct in doing so?

Find the probability that the block was made by the old machine given that the block is bad, $P(\text{old}|\text{bad})$.

$$P(\text{old}|\text{bad}) = \frac{P(\text{old}) \cdot P(\text{bad}|\text{old})}{P(\text{old}) \cdot P(\text{bad}|\text{old}) + P(\text{new}) \cdot P(\text{bad}|\text{new})} \quad \text{Bayes' Theorem}$$

$$= \frac{0.25 \cdot 0.7}{0.25 \cdot 0.7 + 0.75 \cdot 0.3} \quad \text{Substitute known probabilities}$$

$$= 0.4375, \text{ or } 43.75\%$$

Given that the probability that a bad block is made by the old machine is less than 50%, Rhonda should not blame the old machine for the bad block.

EXERCISES

Determine whether the method of awarding a prize is fair. Explain. If it is not fair, describe a way that would be fair. *(Lesson 21.1)*

1. A teacher gives a ticket to each student who earns a 90 or above on any homework assignment. At the end of each week, the teacher draws from the ticket jar and gives the winning student a free homework pass for the next week.

Suppose that a card dealing machine has a probability of 23% of dealing a face card. An older machine has a 14% chance of dealing a face card. Use Bayes's Theorem to find the probability. *(Lesson 21.2)*

2. If each machine is used 50% of the time, and a face card is the next card dealt, what is the probability the new machine dealt the card?

MODULE PERFORMANCE TASK

What's the Diagnosis?

Lenny works in a factory that makes cleaning products. Lately he has been suffering from headaches. He asks his doctor if the chemicals used in the factory might be responsible for his headaches. The doctor performs a blood test that is routinely used to diagnose the kind of illness Lenny is concerned about.

Use the following facts to gauge the probability that Lenny has the illness if he tests positive:

1. The test has a reliability rate of 85 percent.
2. The test has a false positive rate of 8 percent.
3. The illness affects 3 percent of people who are Lenny's age and who work in conditions similar to those he works in.

Start by listing the information you will need to solve the problem. Then complete the task. Use numbers, words, or algebra to explain how you reached your conclusion.

Ready to Go On?

22.1–22.2 Probability and Decision Making

Personal Math Trainer
- Online Homework
- Hints and Help
- Extra Practice

Determine whether the method of awarding a prize is fair. Explain briefly.

1. Prize to every 500th customer

2. Ticket to every customer; drawing

3. Choose number 1–10; draw number

4. Ticket to all cars; two to red cars

Rodney's Repair Service has a lug nut tightening machine that works well 89% of the time. They got a new machine that works well 98% of the time. Each machine is used 50% of the time. Use Bayes's Theorem to find each probability.

5. new machine given malfunctioned

6. old machine given malfunctioned

7. old machine given worked well

8. new machine given worked well

ESSENTIAL QUESTION

9. How can probability and decision making help the organizer of a raffle?

MODULE 21
MIXED REVIEW

Assessment Readiness

1. Consider each situation. Is the method of awarding the prize fair?

A. Ticket for every $10 spent, random drawing

B. Prize to the person who can press a buzzer the quickest

C. Pair of number cubes is tossed; finalist A wins if the sum is 2–7 and finalist B wins if the sum is 8–12

2. Consider the situation of having four tiles in a bag spelling M-A-T-H drawn randomly without replacement. Determine if each statement is True or False.

A. There is one way to draw all 4 tiles from the bag, if order doesn't matter.

B. There are six ways to draw 2 tiles from the bag, if order matters.

C. There are twenty four ways to draw 3 tiles from the bag if order matters.

3. The band class has two trumpet players. Of the two, the first trumpet player plays a wrong note 4% of the time, and the second trumpet player plays a wrong note 9% of the time. If one song has the first trumpet player playing 75% of the song, and the second trumpet player playing the rest, use Bayes' Theorem to find the probability that a particular wrong note was played by the second trumpet player. Explain why your answer makes sense.

4. Gerald says that the sequence 4, 16, 64, 256,... can be described by the rule $2 \cdot 2^n = 4^n$. Describe and correct his mistake.

Assessment Readiness

Personal Math Trainer

- Online Homework
- Hints and Help
- Extra Practice

1. Figure *ABCDE* is similar to figure *LMNOP*. Determine if each statement is True or False.

A. $\frac{BC}{AE} = \frac{MN}{OP}$

B. $\frac{AB}{DE} = \frac{LM}{OP}$

C. $\frac{BD}{AE} = \frac{MN}{LP}$

2. The transformation $(x, y) \rightarrow (x - 2, y + 1)$ is applied to $\triangle XYZ$. Determine if each statement is True or False.

A. The area of $\triangle X'Y'Z'$ is the same as the area of $\triangle XYZ$.

B. The distance from X to X' is equal to the distance from Z to Z'.

C. The transformation is a rotation.

3. Tell whether each scenario describes independent events.

A. Drawing one card and then another from a standard deck of cards and having both be aces

B. Rolling a fair number cube twice and getting 6 on both rolls

C. Rolling a 3 on a fair number cube and flipping tails on a fair coin

4. Each student in a class has been assigned at random to draw a parallelogram, a rectangle, a rhombus, or a square. Consider the likelihood that the quadrilateral that the student draws will be a parallelogram. Determine if each statement is True or False.

A. It is unlikely, but not certain, because the probability is less than 0.5.

B. It is likely, but not certain, because the probability is more than 0.5.

C. It is impossible for it not to happen because the probability is 1.

5. The events *A* and *B* are independent. Determine if each statement is True or False.

A. $P(A \mid B) = P(B \mid A)$

B. $P(A \text{ and } B) = P(B) \cdot P(A)$

C. $P(A) = P(B)$

6. Vera needs to place 15 student volunteers at a local fire station. Five students will wash fire trucks, 7 will be assigned to paint, and 3 will be assigned to wash windows. What is the number of possible job assignments expressed using factorials and as a simplified number?

7. The table below shows the number of days that a meteorologist predicted it would be sunny and the number of days it was sunny. Based on the data in the table, what is the conditional probability that it will be sunny on a day when the meteorologist predicts it will be sunny? Show your work.

	Sunny	Not Sunny	Total
Predicts Sunny	570	20	590
Does Not Predict Sunny	63	347	410
Total	633	367	1000

8. Complete the two-way table below. Then find the fraction of red cards in a standard 52-card deck that have a number on them and find the fraction of numbered cards that are red.

	Red	Black	Total
Number	?	?	?
No Number	?	?	?
Total	?	?	?

Performance Tasks

★ **9.** Sixteen cards numbered 1 through 16 are placed face down, and Stephanie chooses one at random. What is the probability that the number on Stephanie's card is less than 5 or greater than 10? Show your work.

★★10. Students in 4 different classes are surveyed about their favorite movie type. What is the probability that a randomly selected student in class B prefers comedies? What is the probability that a randomly selected student who prefers comedies is in class B? Explain why the two probabilities are not the same. Show your work.

	A	B	C	D
Action	12	9	8	11
Comedy	13	11	15	4
Drama	6	11	7	18

★★★11. A Chinese restaurant has a buffet that includes ice cream for dessert. The table shows the selections made last week.

	Chocolate	Vanilla	Strawberry
Cone	24	18	12
Dish	12	21	15

A. Which flavor is the most popular? Which serving method? Is the combination of the most popular flavor and serving method the most popular dessert choice overall? Explain.

B. Which of the following is more likely? Explain.

- A customer chooses vanilla, given that the customer chose a cone.
- A customer chooses a cone, given that the customer chose vanilla?

C. A class of 24 students gets the buffet for lunch. If they all get ice cream, about how many will get a cone or vanilla? Explain.

MATH IN CAREERS

Epidemiologist An epidemiologist is aiding in the treatment of a community plagued by two different infectious agents, X and Z. Each infectious agent must be treated differently with a new treatment if the patient has been infected by both agents. The community has a total population of 15,000 people, where 5% are healthy and 60% are afflicted by the X infection. The same incident happened to 10 other communities with similar results as the first. What is the probability that people will be healthy? have the X affliction? have the Z affliction? have both afflictions?

UNIT 9

Statistics

MATH IN CAREERS

Pharmaceutical Scientist
Pharmaceutical scientists work in a variety of capacities, such as inventing and synthesizing new drugs, creating dosage delivery systems, and studying how a particular drug interacts in a living organism. They also design and conduct clinical trials to test the efficacy of novel medications. Pharmaceutical scientists make use of algebra, calculus, and differential equations to model and interpret the effects of a drug and the drug's rate of decay in the body. They also use statistics to help make informed decisions about a medication's usefulness.

If you are interested in a career as a pharmaceutical scientist, you should study these mathematical subjects:

- Algebra
- Statistics
- Calculus
- Differential Equations

Check out the career activity at the end of the unit to find out how **Pharmaceutical Scientists** use math.

Reading Start-Up

Visualize Vocabulary

Match the review words to their descriptions to complete the chart.

Word	Description
?	A probability experiment with a fixed number of independent trials in which each outcome falls into exactly one of two categories
?	A bell shaped probability distribution
?	In a binomial experiment, the probability of r successes $(0 \leq r \leq n)$ is $p(r) = {}_nC_r \cdot p^r q^{n-r}$, with probability of success p and probability of failure q and $p + q = 1$

Vocabulary

Review Words

✔ binomial experiment *(experimento binomial)*

✔ binomial probability *(probabilidad binomial)*

✔ normal distribution *(distribución normal)*

Preview Words

biased sample *(muestra no representativa)*

margin of error *(margen de error)*

null hypothesis *(hipótesis nula)*

observational study *(estudio de observación)*

population *(población)*

probability distribution *(distribución de probabilidad)*

sample *(muestra)*

standard normal value *(valor normal estándar)*

statistic *(estadística)*

Understand Vocabulary

To become familiar with some of the vocabulary terms in the module, consider the following. You may refer to the module, the glossary, or a dictionary.

1. A number that describes a sample is a __?__ .

2. A __?__ does not fairly represent the population.

3. A __?__ is a part of the population.

4. The __?__ is an assumption in statistics that there is no difference between the two groups being tested.

Active Reading

Key-Term Fold Before beginning each module in this unit, create a key-term fold to help you learn the definitions in each lesson. Each tab can contain a key term on one side and its definition on the other. When possible, include an example with the definition. Use the key-term fold to quiz yourself on the definitions of the key terms in the unit.

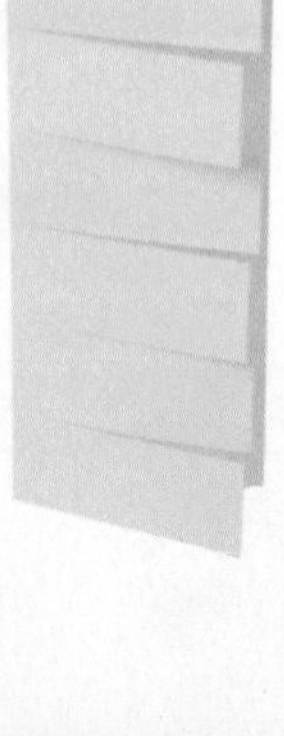

Gathering and Displaying Data

MODULE 22

Essential Question: How can gathering and displaying data help to solve real-world problems?

REAL WORLD VIDEO
Unlike packaged foods, fresh fruit and vegetables do not have nutrition labels. Check out some ways we can gather and analyze nutrition data for fresh produce.

MODULE PERFORMANCE TASK PREVIEW

Fruit Nutrition Data

Good nutrition is especially important while you are still growing. You can achieve good nutrition by monitoring the nutrients that you eat. You already know to eat plenty of fruits and vegetables, but how do the nutrients in, say, a pear compare with those of a peach? You've heard that you can't compare apples and oranges, but later on, that's exactly what we'll be doing!

Are YOU Ready?

Complete these exercises to review skills you will need for this module.

Personal Math Trainer

- Online Homework
- Hints and Help
- Extra Practice

Two-Way Tables

Example 1

The table shows the number of tickets sold for seats in the four areas of the local playhouse for showings in a three-day period. What percent of the tickets sold for the Saturday showing were for orchestra level seating?

	Friday	Saturday	Sunday
Box	12	4	2
Orchestra	856	891	773
Loge	492	540	411
Balcony	712	695	359

Saturday is the second to last column. The total tickets sold for the Saturday performance were $4 + 891 + 540 + 695$, which is a total of 2130 tickets. The percent of those tickets that were orchestra level is $\frac{891}{2130} \cdot 100$, or about 42%.

Use the table shown to find each percent.

1. What percent of all the loge tickets sold were for the Friday showing?

2. What percent of all tickets sold were for the Sunday showing?

3. What percent of all tickets sold were for seats at either the loge or balcony level?

Box Plots

Example 2

A box plot shows the least and greatest data items, the upper and lower quartiles, and the median of all the data. Find the lower quartile of these data:

20, 25, 8, 1, 17, 2, 9, 23, 21, 2, 16, 12

Order the data:

1, 2, 2, 8, 9, 12, 16, 17, 20, 21, 23, 25

The lower quartile is the median of the first half of the data:1, 2, 2, 8, 9, 12. The median is halfway between 2 and 8, which is 5.

Use the data in the example to find each measure.

4. Median

5. Upper quartile

6. Range

22.1 Data-Gathering Techniques

Essential Question: Under what circumstances should a sample statistic be used as an estimator of a population parameter?

Resource Locker

Explore Finding the Mean of Samples Obtained from Various Sampling Methods

You collect data about a **population** by surveying or studying some or all of the individuals in the population. When *all* the individuals in a population are surveyed or studied, the data-gathering technique is called a **census**. A **parameter** is a number that summarizes a characteristic of the population. When only some of the individuals in a population are surveyed or studied, the data-gathering technique is called **sampling**. A **statistic** is a number that summarizes a characteristic of a sample. Statistics can be used to estimate parameters.

Consider the following table, which lists the salaries (in thousands of dollars) of all 30 employees at a small company. In this Explore, you will take samples from this population and compute the mean (the sum of the data divided by the sample size).

Salaries at a Small Company									
21	24	26	28	30	32	33	35	37	41
44	46	47	49	50	51	52	54	55	57
58	62	62	64	64	65	70	71	73	80

(A) Suppose the employees whose salaries are 51, 57, 58, 65, 70, and 73 volunteer to be in the sample. This is called a *self-selected sample*. Compute the sample's mean, rounding to the nearest whole number.

(B) Suppose the six salaries in the first two columns of the table are chosen. This is called a *convenience sample* because the data are easy to obtain. Record the salaries, and then compute the sample's mean, rounding to the nearest whole number.

(C) Suppose every fifth salary in the list, reading from left to right in each row, is chosen. This is called a *systematic sample*. Record the salaries, and then compute the sample's mean, rounding to the nearest whole number.

(D) Label the data in the table with the identifiers 1–10 for the first row, 11–20 for the second row, and 21–30 for the third row. Then use a graphing calculator's random integer generator to generate six identifiers between 1 and 30, as shown. (If any identifiers are repeated, simply generate replacements for them until you have six unique identifiers.) This is called a *simple random sample*. Record the corresponding salaries, and then compute the sample's mean, rounding to the nearest whole number.

Reflect

1. Compute the mean of the population. Then list the four samples from best to worst in terms of how well each sample mean estimates the population mean.

2. With the way the table is organized, both the convenience sample and the systematic sample have means that are not too far from the population mean. Why?

Explain 1 Distinguishing Among Sampling Methods

The goal of sampling is to obtain a **representative sample**, because the statistic obtained from the sample is a good estimator of the corresponding population parameter. Some sampling methods can result in **biased samples** that may not be representative of the population and can produce statistics that lead to inaccurate conclusions about the corresponding population parameters.

Sampling Method	Description
Simple random sample	Each individual in the population has an equal chance of being selected.
Self-selected sample	Individuals volunteer to be part of the sample.
Convenience sample	Individuals are selected based on how accessible they are.
Systematic sample	Members of the sample are chosen according to a rule, such as every *n*th individual in the population.
Stratified sample	The population is divided into groups, and individuals from each group are selected (typically through a random sample within each group).
Cluster sample	The population is divided into groups, some of the groups are randomly selected, and either all the individuals in the selected groups are selected or just some of the individuals from the selected groups are selected (typically through a random sample within each selected group).

The Explore showed that simple random samples are likely to be representative of a population (as are other sampling methods that involve randomness) and are therefore preferred over sampling methods that don't involve randomness.

Example 1 **Identify the population, classify the sampling methods, and decide whether the sampling methods could result in a biased sample. Explain your reasoning.**

Ⓐ The officials of the National Football League (NFL) want to know how the players feel about some proposed changes to the NFL rules. They decide to ask a sample of 100 players.

a. The officials choose the first 100 players who volunteer their opinions.

b. The officials randomly choose 3 or 4 players from each of the 32 teams in the NFL.

c. The officials have a computer randomly generate a list of 100 players from a database of all NFL players.

The population consists of the players in the NFL.

a. This is a self-selected sample because the players volunteer their opinions. This could result in a biased sample because the players who feel strongly about the rules would be the first ones to volunteer and get their opinions counted.

b. This is a stratified sample because the players are separated by team and randomly chosen from each team. This is not likely to be biased since the players are chosen randomly and are taken from each team.

c. This is a simple random sample because each player has an equally likely chance of being chosen. This is not likely to be biased since the players are chosen randomly.

(B) Administrators at your school want to know if students think that more vegetarian items should be added to the lunch menu.

a. The administrators survey every 25th student who enters the cafeteria during the lunch period.

b. The administrators survey the first 50 students who get in the lunch line to buy lunch.

c. The administrators use a randomly generated list of 50 students from a master list of all students.

The population consists of the students at the school.

a. This is a systematic sample because the rule of every 25th student is used. This method isn't likely to result in a biased sample because a wide range of students will be surveyed.

b. This is a convenience sample because the students are easily accessible. This method is likely to result in a biased sample because it does not include students who bring their lunch.

c. This is a simple random sample because each student has an equally likely chance of being chosen. This method isn't likely to result in a biased sample because the students are chosen randomly.

Your Turn

Identify the population, classify the sampling methods, and decide whether the sampling methods could result in a biased sample. Explain your reasoning.

3. A local newspaper conducts a survey to find out if adult residents of the city think the use of hand-held cell phones while driving in the city should be banned.

a. The newspaper sends a text message to a random selection of 1000 subscribers whose cell phones are listed in the paper's subscription database.

b. Using the 10 neighborhoods into which the city is divided, the newspaper randomly contacts 100 adults living in each of the neighborhoods.

Explain 2 Making Predictions from a Random Sample

In statistics, you work with data. Data can be **numerical**, such as heights or salaries, or **categorical**, such as eye color or political affiliation. While a statistic like the mean is appropriate for numerical data, an appropriate statistic for categorical data is a **proportion**, which is the relative frequency of a category.

Example 2 **A community health center surveyed a small random sample of adults in the community about their exercise habits. The survey asked whether the person engages in regular cardio exercise (running, walking, swimming, or other) and, if so, what the duration and frequency of exercise are. Of the 25 people surveyed, 10 said that they do engage in regular cardio exercise. The table lists the data for those 10 people. Calculate statistics from the sample, and use the statistics to make predictions about the exercise habits of the approximately 5000 adults living in the community.**

Type of exercise	Duration (minutes spent exercising)	Frequency (times per week)
Running	30	4
Walking	20	5
Running	40	3
Running	60	6
Swimming	40	4
Other	90	2
Running	30	3
Walking	20	5
Running	30	4
Other	120	1

(A) Calculate the proportion of adults who get regular cardio exercise and the proportion of runners among those who get regular cardio exercise. Use the proportions to predict the number of runners among all adults living in the community.

Proportion of adults who get regular cardio exercise: $\frac{10}{25} = 0.4$ or 40%

Proportion of runners among those who get regular cardio exercise: $\frac{5}{10} = 0.5$ or 50%

To predict the number of runners in the community, multiply the number of adults in the community by the proportion of adults who get regular cardio exercise and then by the proportion of runners among those who get regular cardio exercise.

Predicted number of runners in the community: $5000 \cdot 0.4 \cdot 0.5 = 1000$

(B) Calculate the mean duration of exercise for those who get regular cardio exercise and the mean frequency of exercise for those who get regular cardio exercise. Use the means to predict, for those who get regular cardio exercise, the number of hours spent exercising each week. Show your calculations and include units.

Mean duration of exercise for those who get regular cardio exercise: 48 minutes

Mean frequency of exercise for those who get regular cardio exercise: 3.7 times per week

To predict the number of hours spent exercising, multiply the mean duration of exercise (in minutes) for those who get regular cardio exercise by the mean frequency of exercise (in times per week) for those who get regular cardio exercise. This product will be in minutes per week. To convert to hours per week, also multiply by the conversion factor $\frac{1 \text{ hour}}{60 \text{ minutes}}$.

Predicted time spent exercising: $\boxed{48}$ minutes $\cdot$ $\boxed{3.7}$ /week $\cdot$ $\frac{1 \text{ hour}}{60 \text{ minutes}} \approx \boxed{3}$ hours/week

Reflect

4. **Discussion** How much confidence do you have in the predictions made from the results of the survey? Explain your reasoning.

Your Turn

5. A ski resort uses the information gained from scanning season ski passes in lift lines to determine how many days out of each season the pass holders ski and how many lift rides they take each day. The table lists the data for a random sample of 16 pass holders. Calculate the mean number of days skied and the mean number of lift rides taken per day. Use the means to predict the number of lift rides taken per season by a pass holder.

Number of days	10	5	2	14	27	3	18	5
Number of lift rides	12	15	6	18	10	6	15	9

Number of days	4	16	7	12	19	14	25	13
Number of lift rides	11	13	14	10	8	6	15	18

Elaborate

6. Name a sampling method that is more likely to produce a representative sample and a sampling method that is more likely to produce a biased sample.

7. Why are there different statistics for numerical and categorical data?

8. **Essential Question Check-In** Explain the difference between a parameter and a statistic.

Evaluate: Homework and Practice

Personal Math Trainer

- Online Homework
- Hints and Help
- Extra Practice

1. A student council wants to know whether students would like the council to sponsor a mid-winter dance or a mid-winter carnival this year. Classify each sampling method.

   a. Survey every tenth student on the school's roster.

   b. Survey all students in three randomly selected homerooms.

   c. Survey 20 randomly selected freshmen, 20 randomly selected sophomores, 20 randomly selected juniors, and 20 randomly selected seniors.

   d. Survey those who ask the council president for a questionnaire.

   e. Survey a random selection of those who happen to be in the cafeteria at noon.

2. The officers of a neighborhood association want to know whether residents are interested in beautifying the neighborhood and, if so, how much money they are willing to contribute toward the costs involved. The officers are considering two methods for gathering data:

Method A: Call and survey every tenth resident on the association's roster.

Method B: Randomly select and survey 10 residents from among those who come to the neighborhood block party.

a. Identify the population.

b. Which sampling method is most likely to result in a representative sample of the population? Explain.

c. Describe another sampling method that is likely to result in a representative sample of the population.

d. Describe the categorical and numerical data that the officers of the neighborhood association want to gather.

Decide whether the sampling method could result in a biased sample. Explain your reasoning.

3. On the first day of school, all of the incoming freshmen attend an orientation program. Afterward, the principal wants to learn the opinions of the freshmen regarding the orientation. She decides to ask 25 freshmen as they leave the auditorium to complete a questionnaire.

4. The members of the school drama club want to know how much students are willing to pay for a ticket to one of their productions. They decide that each member of the drama club should ask 5 of his or her friends what they are each willing to pay.

5. A medical conference has 500 participating doctors. The table lists the doctors' specialties. A researcher wants to survey a sample of 25 of the doctors to get their opinions on proposed new rules for health care providers. Explain why it may be better for the researcher to use a stratified sample rather than a simple random sample.

Specialty	Number of Doctors
Dermatology	40
Geriatrics	120
Oncology	140
Pediatrics	100
Surgery	100

6. A researcher wants to conduct a face-to-face survey of 100 farmers in a large agricultural state to get their opinions about the risks and rewards of farming. The researcher has limited time and budget. Explain why it may be better for the researcher to use a cluster sample based on counties in the state rather than a simple random sample.

Identify the population and the sampling method.

7. A quality control inspector at a computer assembly plant needs to estimate the number of defective computers in a group of 250 computers. He tests 25 randomly chosen computers.

8. The manager of a movie theater wants to know how the movie viewers feel about the new stadium seating at the theater. She asks every 30th person who exits the theater each Saturday night for a month.

9. Eric is interested in purchasing a used sports car. He selects the make and model of the car at a website that locates all used cars of that make and model for sale within a certain distance of his home. The website delivers a list of 120 cars that meet his criteria. Eric randomly selects 10 of those cars and records what type of engine and transmission they have, as shown in the table.

Engine (L = liter)	Transmission
3.6 L V6	Manual
3.6 L V6	Automatic
6.2 L V8	Manual
3.6 L V6	Manual
6.2 L Supercharged V8	Manual
3.6 L V6	Automatic
6.2 L V8	Manual
3.6 L V6	Automatic
3.6 L V6	Manual
6.2 L V8	Automatic

a. If Eric can only drive cars with automatic transmissions, predict the number of such cars on the website's list. Show your calculations.

b. Eric knows that the 3.6 L V6 engine takes regular gasoline, but the 6.2 L V8 engine requires premium gasoline. To minimize his fuel costs, he wants a car with the 3.6 L V6 engine. Predict the number of such cars on the website's list. Show your calculations.

c. Predict the number of cars that have a 3.6 L V6 engine and an automatic transmission. Show your calculations.

10. A community theater association plans to produce three plays for the upcoming season. The association surveys a random sample of the approximately 7000 households in the community to see if an adult member of the household is interested in attending plays and, if so, what type of plays the person prefers (comedy, drama, or musical), how many members of the household (including the person surveyed) might attend plays, and how many of the three plays those household members might attend. Of the 50 adults surveyed, 12 indicated an interest in attending plays. The table lists the data for those 12 people.

Preferred Type of Play	Number of People Attending	Number of Plays Attending
Comedy	2	1
Musical	3	2
Musical	1	2
Drama	2	3
Comedy	3	2
Comedy	2	3
Musical	4	1
Drama	2	3
Comedy	2	2
Musical	2	3
Comedy	5	1
Drama	1	2

a. Describe the categorical and numerical data gathered in the survey.

b. Calculate the proportion of adults who indicated an interest in attending plays and calculate the proportion of adults who prefer dramas among those who are interested in attending plays. If approximately 15,000 adults live in the community, predict the number of adults who are interested in attending plays that are dramas. Show your calculations.

c. For an adult with an interest in attending plays, calculate the mean number of household members who might attend plays and the mean number of plays that those household members might attend. Round each mean to the nearest tenth. If the theater association plans to sells tickets to the plays for $40 each, predict the amount of revenue from ticket sales. Show your calculations and include units.

11. Match each description of a sample on the left with a sampling technique on the right.

A. A television reporter asks people walking by on the street to answer a question about an upcoming election.

B. A television reporter randomly selects voting precincts and then contacts voters randomly chosen from a list of registered voters residing in those precincts to ask about an upcoming election.

C. A television reporter contacts voters randomly chosen from a complete list of registered voters to ask about an upcoming election.

D. A television reporter contacts every 100th voter from a complete list of registered voters to ask about an upcoming election.

E. A television reporter contacts registered voters randomly chosen from every voting precinct to ask about an upcoming election.

F. A television reporter asks viewers to call in their response to a question about an upcoming election.

a. ___?___ Simple random sample

b. ___?___ Self-selected sample

c. ___?___ Convenience sample

d. ___?___ Systematic sample

e. ___?___ Stratified sample

f. ___?___ Cluster sample

H.O.T. Focus on Higher Order Thinking

12. Critical Thinking A reporter for a high school newspaper asked all members of the school's track team how many miles they run each week.

a. What type of data did the reporter gather?

b. Was the reporter's data-gathering technique a census or a sample? Explain.

c. Are the data representative of the entire student body? Why or why not?

13. Communicate Mathematical Ideas Categorical data can be nominal or ordinal. *Nominal data* refer to categories that do not have any "natural" ordering, while *ordinal data* refer to categories that do have an order. Similarly, numerical data can be discrete or continuous. *Discrete data* are typically counts or scores (which cannot be made more precise), while *continuous data* are typically measurements (which can be made more precise). For each description of a set of data, identify whether the data are nominal, ordinal, discrete, or continuous. Explain your reasoning. Also give another example of the same type of data.

a. A researcher records how many people live in a subject's household.

b. A researcher records the gender of each subject.

c. A researcher records the amount of time each subject spends using an electronic device during a day.

d. A researcher records whether each subject is a young adult, a middle-aged adult, or a senior.

14. Analyze Relationships The grid represents the entire population of 100 trees in an apple orchard. The values in the grid show the number of kilograms of apples produced by each tree during one year. Given the data, obtain three random samples of size 20 from the population and find the mean of each sample. Discuss how the means of those samples compare with the population mean, which is 68.9.

109	52	62	72	110	61	51	50	100	50
54	104	54	111	74	73	77	68	65	66
108	53	27	75	52	117	76	60	64	67
73	36	103	71	67	60	59	26	80	61
38	63	35	112	75	68	51	72	79	62
58	105	55	53	118	57	101	66	116	31
29	57	74	33	102	69	28	71	30	58
39	55	34	120	64	114	70	113	78	63
107	37	56	25	76	70	69	77	30	115
56	40	106	32	119	65	80	78	79	59

Lesson Performance Task

Think about your school's cafeteria and the food it serves. Suppose you are given the opportunity to conduct a survey about the cafeteria.

a. Identify the population to be surveyed.

b. Write one or more survey questions. For each question, state whether it will generate numerical data or categorical data.

c. Assuming that you aren't able to conduct a census of the population, describe how you could obtain a representative sample of the population.

d. Suppose you asked a random sample of 25 students in your school whether they were satisfied with cafeteria lunches and how often in a typical week they brought their own lunches. The tables give the results of the survey. If the school has 600 students, use the results to predict the number of students who are satisfied with cafeteria lunches and the number of lunches brought to school in a typical week.

Satisfied with cafeteria lunches?	
Response	**Number**
Yes	18
No	7

Bring own lunches how often in a week?	
Response	**Number**
5 times	2
4 times	1
3 times	4
2 times	2
1 time	4
0 times	12

22.2 Shape, Center, and Spread

Essential Question: Which measures of center and spread are appropriate for a normal distribution, and which are appropriate for a skewed distribution?

Resource Locker

Explore 1 Seeing the Shape of a Distribution

"Raw" data values are simply presented in an unorganized list. Organizing the data values by using the frequency with which they occur results in a **distribution** of the data. A distribution may be presented as a frequency table or as a data display. Data displays for numerical data, such as line plots, histograms, and box plots, involve a number line, while data displays for categorical data, such as bar graphs and circle graphs, do not. Data displays reveal the shape of a distribution.

The table gives data about a random sample of 20 babies born at a hospital.

Baby	Birth Month	Birth Weight (kg)	Mother's Age
1	5	3.3	28
2	7	3.6	31
3	11	3.5	33
4	2	3.4	35
5	10	3.7	39
6	3	3.4	30
7	1	3.5	29
8	4	3.2	30
9	7	3.6	31
10	6	3.4	32

Baby	Birth Month	Birth Weight (kg)	Mother's Age
11	9	3.6	33
12	10	3.5	29
13	11	3.4	31
14	1	3.7	29
15	6	3.5	34
16	5	3.8	30
17	8	3.5	32
18	9	3.6	30
19	12	3.3	29
20	2	3.5	28

(A) Make a line plot for the distribution of birth months.

(B) Make a line plot for the distribution of birth weights.

(C) Make a line plot for the distribution of mothers' ages.

Reflect

1. Describe the shape of the distribution of birth months.
2. Describe the shape of the distribution of birth weights.
3. Describe the shape of the distribution of mothers' ages.

Explore 2 Relating Measures of Center and Spread to the Shape of a Distribution

As you saw in the previous Explore, data distributions can have various shapes. Some of these shapes are given names in statistics.

- A distribution whose shape is basically level (that is, it looks like a rectangle) is called a **uniform distribution**.
- A distribution that is mounded in the middle with symmetric "tails" at each end (that is, it looks bell-shaped) is called a **normal distribution**.
- A distribution that is mounded but not symmetric because one "tail" is much longer than the other is called a **skewed distribution**. When the longer "tail" is on the left, the distribution is said to be *skewed left*. When the longer "tail" is on the right, the distribution is said to be *skewed right*.

The figures show the general shapes of normal and skewed distributions.

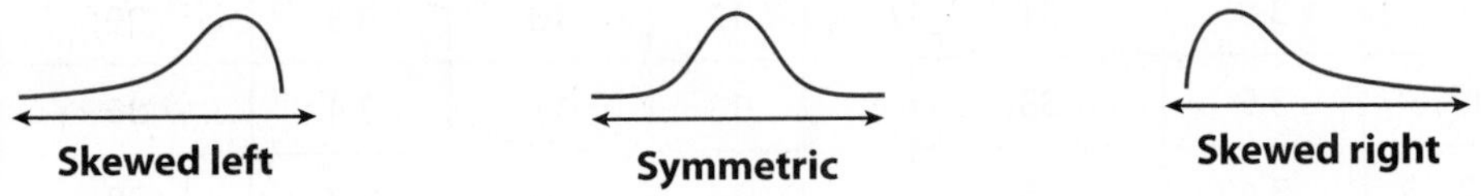

Shape is one way of characterizing a data distribution. Another way is by identifying the distribution's center and spread. You should already be familiar with the following measures of center and spread:

- The *mean* of n data values is the sum of the data values divided by n. If $x_1, x_2, ..., x_n$ are data values from a sample, then the mean $\bar{x}$ is given by:

$$\bar{x} = \frac{x_1 + x_2 + \cdots + x_n}{n}$$

- The *median* of n data values written in ascending order is the middle value if n is odd, and is the mean of the two middle values if n is even.
- The *standard deviation* of n data values is the square root of the mean of the squared deviations from the distribution's mean. If $x_1, x_2, ..., x_n$ are data values from a sample, then the standard deviation s is given by:

$$s = \sqrt{\frac{(x_1 - \bar{x})^2 + (x_2 - \bar{x})^2 + \cdots + (x_n - \bar{x})^2}{n}}$$

- The *interquartile range*, or IQR, of data values written in ascending order is the difference between the median of the upper half of the data, called the *third quartile* or Q_3, and the median of the lower half of the data, called the *first quartile* or Q_1. So, $IQR = Q_3 - Q_1$.

To distinguish a population mean from a sample mean, statisticians use the Greek letter mu, written μ, instead of $\bar{x}$. Similarly, they use the Greek letter sigma, written σ, instead of s to distinguish a population standard deviation from a sample standard deviation.

(A) Use a graphing calculator to compute the measures of center and the measures of spread for the distribution of baby weights and the distribution of mothers' ages from the previous Explore. Begin by entering the two sets of data into two lists on a graphing calculator as shown.

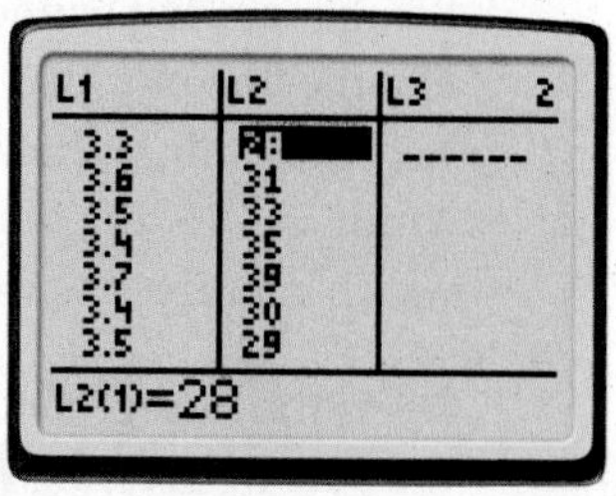

(B) Calculate the "1-Variable Statistics" for the distribution of baby weights. Record the statistics listed. (Note: Your calculator may report the standard deviation with a denominator of $n - 1$ as "s_x" and the standard deviation with a denominator of n as "σ_x." In statistics, when you want to use a sample's standard deviation as an estimate of the population's standard deviation, you use s_x, which is sometimes called the "corrected" sample standard deviation. Otherwise, you can just use σ_x, which you should do in this lesson.)

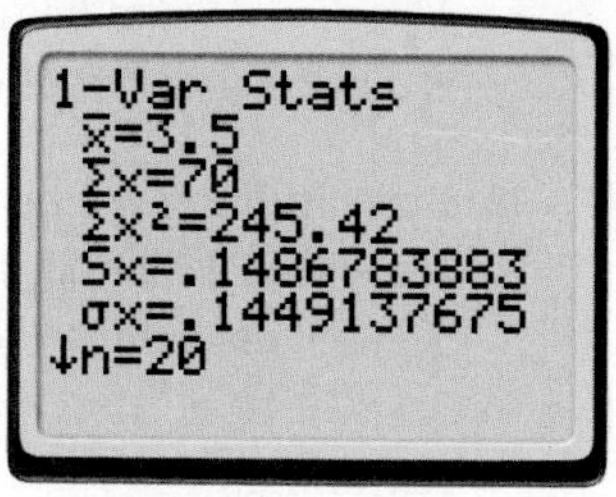

$\bar{x} =$?   Median = ?

$s \approx$? $\text{IQR} = Q_3 - Q_1 =$?

(C) Calculate the "1-Variable Statistics" for the distribution of mothers' ages. Record the statistics listed.

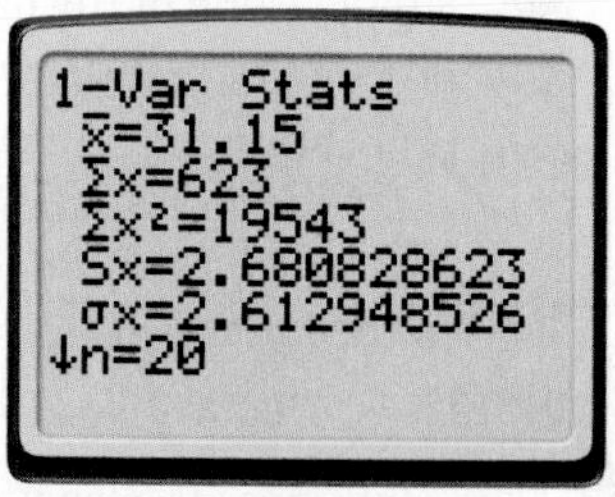

$\bar{x} =$?   Median = ?

$s \approx$? $\text{IQR} = Q_3 - Q_1 =$?

Reflect

4. What do you notice about the mean and median for the symmetric distribution (baby weights) as compared with the mean and median for the skewed distribution (mothers' ages)? Explain why this happens.

5. The standard deviation and IQR for the skewed distribution are significantly greater than the corresponding statistics for the symmetric distribution. Explain why this makes sense.

6. Which measures of center and spread would you report for the symmetric distribution? For the skewed distribution? Explain your reasoning.

Explain 1 Making and Analyzing a Histogram

You can use a graphing calculator to create a histogram of numerical data using the viewing window settings Xmin (the least x-value), Xmax (the greatest x-value), and Xscl (the width of an interval on the x-axis, which becomes the width of the histogram).

Example 1 **Use a graphing calculator to make a histogram of the given data and then analyze the graph.**

(A) **a.** Make a histogram of the baby weights from Explore 1. Based on the shape of the distribution, identify what type of distribution it is.

Begin by turning on a statistics plot, selecting the histogram option, and entering the list where the data are stored.

Set the viewing window. To obtain a histogram that looks very much like the line plot that you drew for this data set, use the values shown. Xscl determines the width of each bar, so when Xscl = 0.1 and Xmin = 3.15, the first bar covers the interval $3.15 \leq x < 3.25$, which captures the weight 3.2 kg.

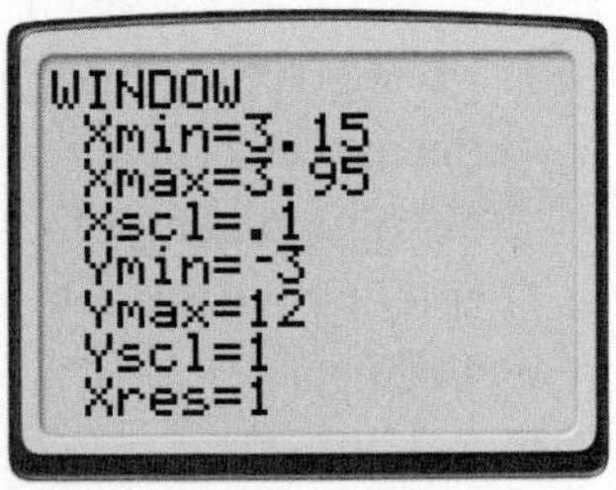

Draw the histogram by pressing GRAPH. You can obtain the heights of the bars by pressing TRACE and using the arrow keys.

The distribution has a central mound and symmetric tails, so it is a normal distribution.

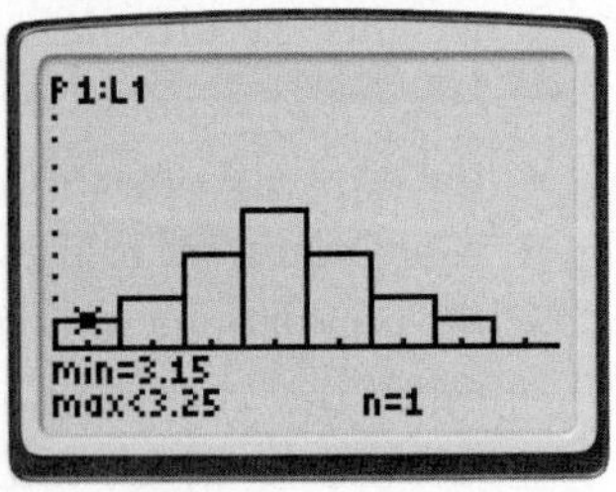

b. By examining the histogram, determine the percent of the data that are within 1 standard deviation ($s \approx 0.14$) of the mean ($\bar{x} = 3.5$). That is, determine the percent of the data in the interval $3.5 - 0.14 < x < 3.5 + 0.14$, or $3.36 < x < 3.64$. Explain your reasoning.

The bars for x-values that satisfy $3.36 < x < 3.64$ have heights of 4, 6, and 4, so 14 data values out of 20, or 70% of the data, are in the interval.

c. Suppose one of the baby weights is chosen at random. By examining the histogram, determine the probability that the weight is more than 1 standard deviation above the mean. That is, determine the probability that the weight is in the interval $x > 3.5 + 0.14$, or $x > 3.64$. Explain your reasoning.

The bars for x-values that satisfy $x > 3.64$ have heights of 2 and 1, so the probability that the weight is in the interval is $\frac{3}{20} = 0.15$ or 15%.

(B) The table gives the lengths (in inches) of the random sample of 20 babies from Explore 1.

Baby	Baby Length (in.)
1	17
2	21
3	20
4	19
5	22
6	19
7	20

Baby	Baby Length (in.)
8	18
9	21
10	19
11	21
12	20
13	19
14	22

Baby	Baby Length (in.)
15	20
16	23
17	20
18	21
19	18
20	20

a. Make a histogram of the baby lengths. Based on the shape of the distribution, identify what type of distribution it is.

The distribution has a central mound and symmetric tails, so it is a normal distribution.

b. By examining the histogram, determine the percent of the data that are within 2 standard deviations ($s \approx 1.4$) of the mean ($\bar{x} = 20$). Explain your reasoning.

The interval for data that are within 2 standard deviations of the mean is

$17.2 < x < 22.8$. The bars for x-values that satisfy $17.2 < x < 22.8$ have heights

of 2, 4, 6, 4, and 2, so 18 data values out of 20, or 90% of the data, are in the interval.

c. Suppose one of the baby lengths is chosen at random. By examining the histogram, determine the probability that the length is less than 2 standard deviations below the mean. Explain your reasoning.

The interval for data that are less than 2 standard deviations below the mean is

$x < 17.2$. The only bar for x-values that satisfy $x < 17.2$ has a height of 1, so the

probability that the length is in the interval is $\frac{1}{20} = 0.05$ or 5%.

Your Turn

7. The table lists the test scores of a random sample of 22 students who are taking the same math class.

Student	Math test scores
1	86
2	78
3	95
4	83
5	83
6	81
7	87
8	81

Student	Math test scores
9	90
10	85
11	83
12	99
13	81
14	75
15	85

Student	Math test scores
16	83
17	83
18	70
19	73
20	79
21	85
22	83

a. Use a graphing calculator to make a histogram of the math test scores. Based on the shape of the distribution, identify what type of distribution it is.

b. By examining the histogram, determine the percent of the data that are within 2 standard deviations ($s \approx 6.3$) of the mean ($\bar{x} \approx 83$). Explain your reasoning.

c. Suppose one of the math test scores is chosen at random. By examining the histogram, determine the probability that the test score is less than 2 standard deviations below the mean. Explain your reasoning.

Explain 2 Making and Analyzing a Box Plot

A box plot, also known as a box-and-whisker plot, is based on five key numbers: the minimum data value, the first quartile of the data values, the median (second quartile) of the data values, the third quartile of the data values, and the maximum data value. A graphing calculator will automatically compute these values when drawing a box plot. A graphing calculator also gives you two options for drawing box plots: one that shows outliers and one that does not. For this lesson, choose the second option.

Example 2 **Use a graphing calculator to make a box plot of the given data and then analyze the graph.**

(A) **a.** Make a box plot of the mothers' ages from Explore 1. How does the box plot show that this skewed distribution is skewed right?

Begin by turning on a statistics plot, selecting the second box plot option, and entering the list where the data are stored.

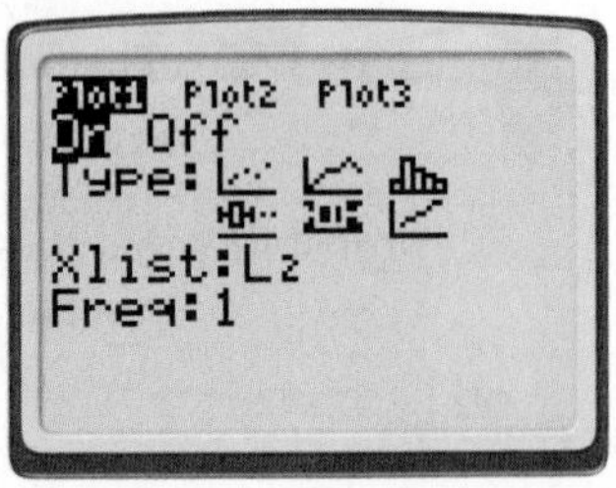

Set the viewing window. Use the values shown.

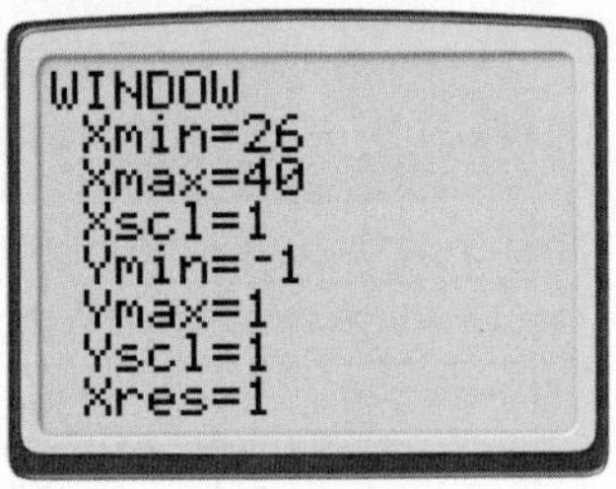

Draw the box plot by pressing GRAPH. You can obtain the box plot's five key values by pressing TRACE and using the arrow keys.

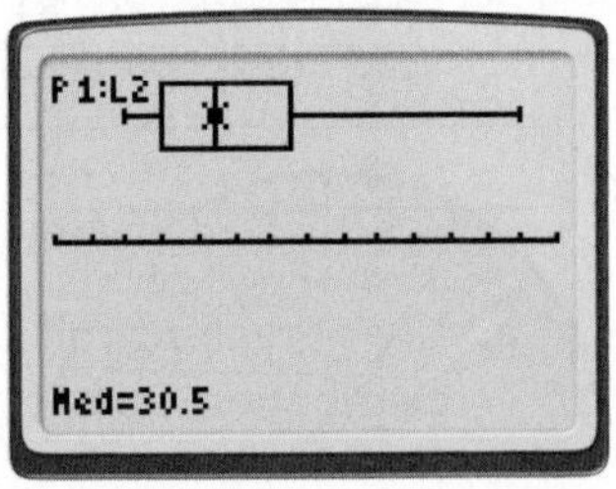

The part of the box to the right of the median is slightly wider than the part to the left, and the "whisker" on the right is much longer than the one on the left, so the distribution is skewed right.

b. Suppose one of the mothers' ages is chosen at random. Based on the box plot and not the original set of data, what can you say is the approximate probability that the age falls between the median, 30.5, and the third quartile, 32.5? Explain your reasoning.

The probability is about 25%, or 0.25, because Q_1, the median, and Q_3 divide the data into four almost-equal parts.

(B) The list gives the ages of a random sample of 16 people who visited a doctor's office one day.

80, 52, 78, 64, 70, 80, 78, 35, 78, 74, 82, 73, 80, 75, 62, 80

a. Make a box plot of the ages. How does the box plot show that this skewed distribution is skewed left?

The part of the box to the left of the median is slightly wider than the part to the right and the "whisker" on the left is much longer than the one on the right, so the distribution is skewed left.

b. Suppose one of the ages is chosen at random. Based on the box plot and not the original set of data, what can you say is the approximate probability that the age falls between the first quartile, 67, and the third quartile, 80? Explain your reasoning.

The probability is about 50%, or 0.5, because Q_1, the median, and Q_3 divide the data into four almost-equal parts and there are two parts that each represent about 25% of the data between the first and third quartiles.

Your Turn

8. The list gives the starting salaries (in thousands of dollars) of a random sample of 18 positions at a large company. Use a graphing calculator to make a box plot and then analyze the graph.

40, 32, 27, 40, 34, 25, 37, 39, 40, 37, 28, 39, 35, 39, 40, 43, 30, 35

a. Make a box plot of the starting salaries. How does the box plot show that this skewed distribution is skewed left?

b. Suppose one of the starting salaries is chosen at random. Based on the box plot and not the original set of data, what can you say is the approximate probability that the salary is less than the third quartile, 40? Explain your reasoning.

Elaborate

9. Explain the difference between a normal distribution and a skewed distribution.

10. Discussion Describe how you can use a line plot, a histogram, and a box plot of a set of data to answer questions about the percent of the data that fall within a specified interval.

11. Essential Question Check-In Why are the mean and standard deviation not appropriate statistics to use with a skewed distribution?

Evaluate: Homework and Practice

Personal Math Trainer

- Online Homework
- Hints and Help
- Extra Practice

1. Make a line plot of the data. Based on the shape of the distribution, identify what type of distribution it is.
   a. Ages of children: 4, 9, 12, 8, 7, 8, 7, 10, 8, 9, 6, 8
   b. Scores on a test: 80, 78, 70, 77, 75, 77, 76, 66, 77, 76, 75, 77
   c. Salaries (in thousands of dollars) of employees: 35, 35, 36, 40, 37, 36, 37, 35, 35, 38, 36, 34

In Exercises 2–3, use the data in the table. The table gives the heights and weights of a random sample of 14 college baseball players.

Height (in.)	Weight (lb)
70	160
69	165
72	170
70	170
68	150
71	175
70	160
69	165
71	165
70	170
67	155
69	165
71	165
73	185

2. a. Find the mean, median, standard deviation, and IQR of the height data.
   b. Use a graphing calculator to make a histogram of the height data. Based on the shape of the distribution, identify what type of distribution it is.
   c. By examining the histogram of the height distribution, determine the percent of the data that fall within 1 standard deviation of the mean. Explain your reasoning.
   d. Suppose one of the heights is chosen at random. By examining the histogram, determine the probability that the height is more than 1 standard deviation above the mean. Explain your reasoning.

3. **a.** Find the mean, median, standard deviation, and IQR of the weight data.

b. Use a graphing calculator to make a histogram of the weight data. Based on the shape of the distribution, identify what type of distribution it is.

c. By examining the histogram, determine the percent of the weight data that are within 2 standard deviations of the mean. Explain your reasoning.

d. Suppose one of the weights is chosen at random. By examining the histogram, determine the probability that the weight is less than 1 standard deviation above the mean. Explain your reasoning.

4. The line plot shows a random sample of resting heart rates (in beats per minute) for 24 adults.

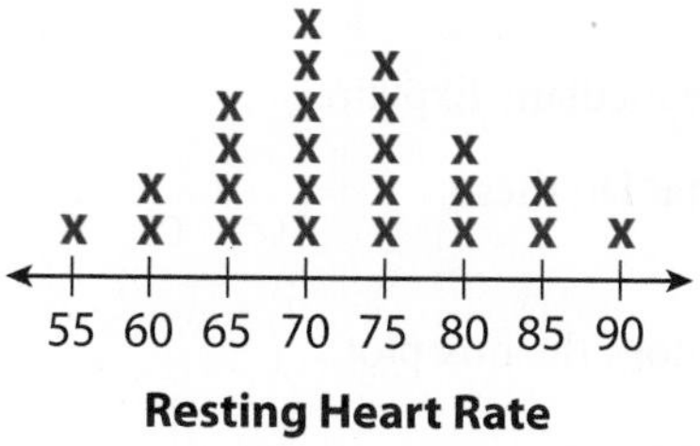

a. Find the mean, median, standard deviation, and IQR of the heart rates.

b. By examining the line plot, determine the percent of the data that are within 1 standard deviation of the mean. Explain your reasoning.

c. Suppose one of the heart rates is chosen at random. By examining the line plot, determine the probability that the heart rate is more than 1 standard deviation below the mean. Explain your reasoning.

5. The list gives the prices (in thousands of dollars) of a random sample of houses for sale in a large town.

175, 400, 325, 350, 500, 375, 350, 375, 400, 375, 250, 400, 200, 375, 400, 400, 375, 325, 400, 350

a. Find the mean, median, standard deviation, and IQR of the house prices. How do these statistics tell you that the distribution is not symmetric?

b. Use a graphing calculator to make a box plot of the house prices. How does the box plot show that this skewed distribution is skewed left?

c. Suppose one of the house prices is chosen at random. Based on the box plot and not the original set of data, what can you say is the approximate probability that the price falls between the first and the third quartiles? Explain your reasoning.

6. The line plot shows a random sample of the amounts of time (in minutes) that an employee at a call center spent on the phone with customers.

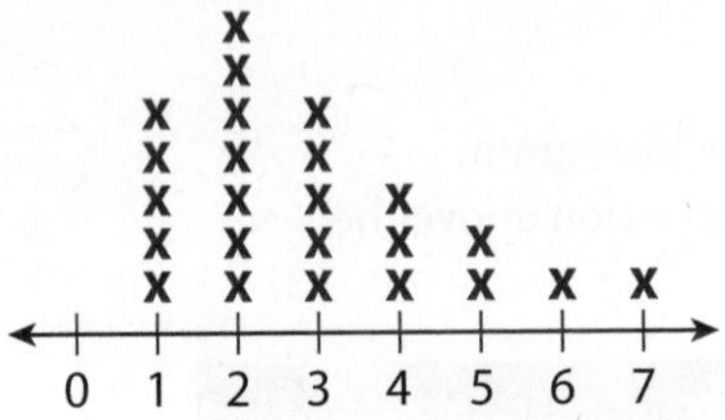

Time Spent With Customer

a. Do you expect the mean to be equal to, less than, or greater than the median? Explain.

b. Find the mean, median, standard deviation, and IQR of the time data. Do these statistics agree with your answer for part a?

c. Use a graphing calculator to make a box plot of the time data. How does the box plot show that the distribution is skewed right?

d. Suppose one of the times spent with a customer is chosen at random. Based on the box plot and not the original set of data, what can you say is the approximate probability that the time is greater than the third quartile? Explain your reasoning.

7. Classify each description as applying to a normal distribution or a skewed distribution.

A. Histogram is mound-shaped with two symmetric tails.

B. Mean and median are equal or almost equal.

C. Box plot has one "whisker" longer than the other.

D. Histogram is mounded with one tail longer than the other.

E. Box plot is symmetric with respect to the median.

F. Mean and median are significantly different.

H.O.T. Focus on Higher Order Thinking

8. **Explain the Error** A student was given the following data and asked to determine the percent of the data that fall within 1 standard deviation of the mean.

20, 21, 21, 22, 22, 22, 22, 23, 23, 23, 23, 24, 24, 24, 24, 24, 25, 25, 25, 26, 26, 26, 27, 27, 28

The student gave this answer: "The interval for data that are within 1 standard deviation of the mean is $24 - 3.5 < x < 24 + 3.5$, or $21.5 < x < 27.5$. The bars for x-values that satisfy $21.5 < x < 27.5$ have heights of 4, 4, 5, 3, 3, and 2, so 21 data values out of 25, or about 84% of the data, are in the interval." Find and correct the student's error.

9. **Analyze Relationships** The list gives the number of siblings that a child has from a random sample of 10 children at a daycare center.

5, 2, 3, 1, 0, 2, 3, 1, 2, 1

a. Use a graphing calculator to create a box plot of the data. Does the box plot indicate that the distribution is normal or skewed? Explain.

b. Find the mean, median, standard deviation, and IQR of the sibling data. What is the relationship between the mean and median?

c. Suppose that an 11th child at the daycare is included in the random sample, and that child has 1 sibling. How does the box plot change? How does the relationship between the mean and median change?

d. Suppose that a 12th child at the daycare is included in the random sample, and that child also has 1 sibling. How does the box plot change? How does the relationship between the mean and median change?

e. What is the general rule about the relationship between the mean and median when a distribution is skewed right? What has your investigation of the sibling data demonstrated about this rule?

10. **Draw Conclusions** Recall that a graphing calculator may give two versions of the standard deviation. The population standard deviation, which you can also use for the "uncorrected" sample standard deviation, is $\sigma_x = \sqrt{\frac{(x_1 - \bar{x})^2 + (x_2 - \bar{x})^2 + \cdots + (x_n - \bar{x})^2}{n}}$.

The "corrected" sample standard deviation is $s_x = \sqrt{\frac{(x_1 - \bar{x})^2 + (x_2 - \bar{x})^2 + \cdots + (x_n - \bar{x})^2}{n - 1}}$.

Write and simplify the ratio $\frac{\sigma_x}{s_x}$. Then determine what this ratio approaches as n increases without bound. What does this result mean in terms of finding standard deviations of samples?

Lesson Performance Task

The table gives data about a random sample of 16 cats brought to a veterinarian's office during one week.

Sex	Weight (pounds)	Age (years)
Male	12	11
Female	9	2
Female	8	12
Male	10	15
Female	10	10
Male	11	10
Male	10	11
Male	11	7

Sex	Weight (pounds)	Age (years)
Female	9	5
Male	12	8
Female	7	13
Male	11	11
Female	10	13
Male	13	9
Female	8	12
Female	9	16

a. Find the mean, median, standard deviation, and IQR of the weight data. Do the same for the age data.

b. Use a graphing calculator to make a histogram of the weight data and a separate histogram of the age data. Based on the shape of each distribution, identify what type of distribution it is. Explain your reasoning.

c. By examining the histogram of the weight distribution, determine the percent of the data that fall within 1 standard deviation of the mean. Explain your reasoning.

d. For the age data, $Q_1 = 8.5$ and $Q_3 = 12.5$. By examining the histogram of the age distribution, find the probability that the age of a randomly chosen cat falls between Q_1 and Q_3. Why does this make sense?

e. Investigate whether being male or female has an impact on a cat's weight and age. Do so by calculating the mean weight and age of female cats and the mean weight and age of male cats. For which variable, weight or age, does being male or female have a greater impact? How much of an impact is there?

Gathering and Displaying Data

Essential Question: How can gathering and displaying data help solve real-world problems?

Key Vocabulary

population *(población)*
census *(censo)*
parameter *(parámetro)*
sample *(muestra)*
sampling statistic *(estadística)*
representative sample *(muestra representantiva)*
biased sample *(muestra no representantiva)*
numerical data *(datos numéricos)*
categorical data *(datos categóricos)*
proportion *(proporción)*
distribution *(distribución)*
uniform distribution *(distribución uniforme)*
normal distribution *(distribución normal)*
skewed distribution *(distribución asimétrica)*

KEY EXAMPLE *(Lesson 22.1)*

A local community center surveyed a small random sample of people in the community about their time spent volunteering. The survey asked whether the person engaged in regular volunteer work (food kitchen, hospital, community center, or other) and, if so, the duration and frequency of the volunteer work.

Of the 20 people surveyed, 8 said they do engage in regular volunteer work. The table lists the data for those 8 people.

Type of Work	Duration (hours)	Days per Week
Food Kitchen	2	5
Hospital	3	3
Hospital	2	4
Food Kitchen	5	3
Comm. Center	4	5
Hospital	2	4
Other	3	5
Comm. Center	2	4

Calculate statistics from the sample, and use the statistics to make predictions about the volunteering habits of the approximately 10,000 people living in the community.

Proportion of adults who volunteer $= \frac{8}{20} = 0.4 = 40\%$

Proportion of hospital volunteers $= \frac{3}{8} = 0.375 = 37.5\%$

Use proportion and a verbal model to predict the number of hospital volunteers among all people living in the community.

Total hospital volunteers = Community × Prop. of Volunteers × Prop. of Hospital Volunteers
$= 10{,}000 \times 0.4 \times 0.375 = 1500$

KEY EXAMPLE *(Lesson 22.2)*

Using the volunteer table, make a line plot for the distribution of hours, and a line plot for the distribution of frequency (days per week).

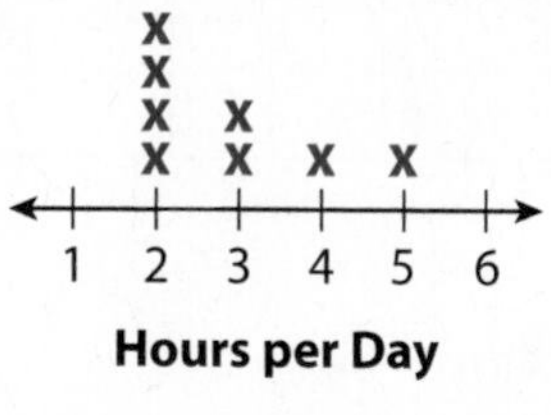

This line plot is skewed right.

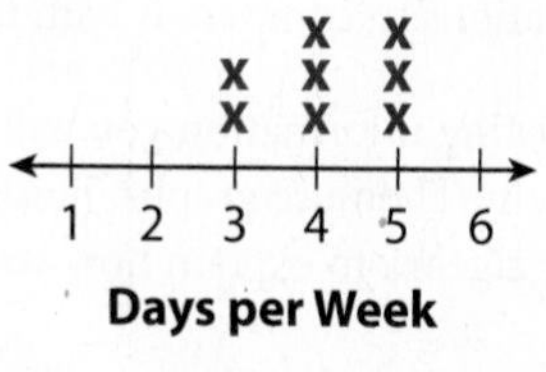

This line plot has a nearly uniform distribution.

EXERCISES

A local high school surveys a random sample of students out of a total of approximately 2500 students to see if a student is interested in attending sporting events and, if so, what type of sporting events the person prefers (football, baseball, volleyball, or track), how many friends they would bring along, and how many events they would be willing to attend a year.

Of the 25 students surveyed, 10 indicated an interest in attending sporting events. The table lists the data for those 10 people.

Sporting Event	Number of Friends	Number of Events
Football	3	5
Football	0	6
Baseball	2	4
Volleyball	2	8
Football	5	7
Track	1	3
Football	3	4
Volleyball	2	5
Baseball	4	2
Track	3	3

1. Using the statistics from the sample, create a verbal model to predict the number of students likely to attend a track meet, then predict the total attendance when they bring their friends. *(Lesson 22.1)*

MODULE PERFORMANCE TASK

Fruit Nutrition Data

The table compares the nutritional values of ten fruits. Specifically, the table shows how much of the recommended daily allowance of three different nutrients is met by a serving of each fruit.

You want to display the data so you can pick up a piece of fruit and know how it compares nutritionally to the other nine fruits. Make appropriate data representations and use them to describe the distributions for each of these data sets. Then, pick one fruit and use your data representations to compare it with the other fruits.

Start by listing information you will need to solve the problem. Then use graphs, numbers, tables, words, or algebra to explain how you reached your conclusion.

	Percentage of Daily Value		
Fruit	Potassium	Fiber	Vitamin C
Apple	7	20	8
Banana	13	12	15
Cantaloupe	7	4	80
Cherries	10	4	15
Orange	7	12	130
Peach	7	8	15
Pear	5	24	10
Pineapple	3	4	50
Strawberries	5	8	160
Watermelon	8	4	25

Ready to Go On?

23.1–23.2 Gathering and Displaying Data

Personal Math Trainer

- Online Homework
- Hints and Help
- Extra Practice

Use the table for exercises 1–4.

A local business surveys a random sample of about 500 employees to see if they are working overtime and, if so, how many hours per week and how many weeks per month. The company has four types of employees: sales, engineer, manager, and clerical.

The 40 employees surveyed were evenly split between the four employment categories. Ten worked overtime last month. The table lists the data for those 10 people.

Employee	Avg. Overtime/Week	Weeks/Month
Manager	8	3
Manager	10	2
Sales	3	1
Engineer	2	1
Manager	8	2
Clerical	8	2
Sales	4	3
Engineer	3	1
Manager	7	3
Sales	2	2

1. Predict the number of managers working overtime out of the employees of the company.

2. Predict the number of sales people working overtime out of the employees of the company.

3. Create the line plot for the number of weeks per month the sample of employees works overtime.

ESSENTIAL QUESTION

4. How can gathering and displaying data help a business owner?

MODULE 22
MIXED REVIEW

Assessment Readiness

1. Consider the equation $y = \frac{3x-2}{x+2}$. Is the function defined for the value of x? Answer Yes or No for A–C.

A. $x = 2$

B. $x = -2$

C. $x = 0$

2. Consider the distribution of data on line plots. Determine if each statement is True or False.

A. A distribution that is "skewed" has most of the data in the middle with two tails on each side.

B. A "uniform" distribution has a data distribution that is basically level, though it doesn't have to be exactly level.

C. A distribution that is "normal" looks bell-shaped.

3. The junior class at a local school would like to survey students to pick a theme for the junior-senior prom. They are considering the following survey methods:

- Survey every tenth student in the junior and senior classes on the school roster.
- Survey every fifteenth student on the school roster for freshman through seniors.
- Survey those who happen to be standing around outside in the morning before the first bell rings.

Which sampling method would most likely result in a theme that would please those attending the prom? Explain.

4. Solve the equation $2x^2 + 6x + 10 = 0$ for all values of x. Explain the method you used, and why.

MODULE 23

Data Distributions

Essential Question: How can you use data distributions to solve real-world problems?

REAL WORLD VIDEO
Regular, vigorous exercise is an important part of maintaining a healthy body weight. Check out some ways we can display and analyze data distributions for body weight in a population.

MODULE PERFORMANCE TASK PREVIEW

BMI and Obesity

Health experts use a variety of statistics to measure the overall health of a population. One of these is body mass index (BMI), which uses a person's weight and height to produce a number that describes whether he or she is overweight, underweight, or normal. How many people are within the normal range? How many are obese? These are weighty questions! An ounce of curiosity is all we will need to figure them out at the end of the module.

Are YOU Ready?

Complete these exercises to review skills you will need for this module.

Personal Math Trainer

- Online Homework
- Hints and Help
- Extra Practice

Measures of Center and Spread

Example 1 Find the median, mean, and range of these ordered data.

8, 15, 15, 26, 33, 49, 50, 54

Median: $\frac{26 + 33}{2} = 29.5$

Mean: $\frac{8 + 15 + 15 + 26 + 33 + 49 + 50 + 54}{8} = 31.25$

Range: $54 - 8 = 46$

Find the median, mean, and range.

1. 16, 38, 12, 19, 40

2. 14, 4, 10, 6, 16, 9, 1, 2, 5, 3

3. 15, 8, 12, 1, 10, 2

Normal Distributions

Example 2 The graph shows a normal distribution of Intelligence Quotient (IQ) scores. What percent of the population has an IQ score greater than the mean?

The curve is symmetrical about an IQ score of 100, which is the mean. So 50% of the population has an IQ score greater than the mean.

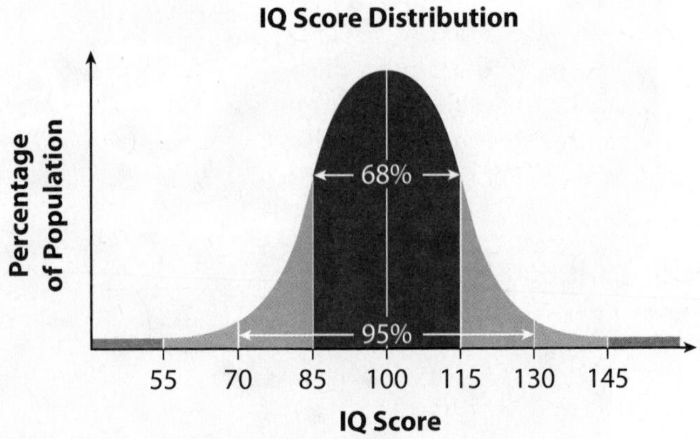

Use the graph to answer the questions.

4. What percent of the population has an IQ score above 130?

5. What percent of the population has an IQ score above 115?

6. What percent of the population has an IQ score between 70 and 85?

23.1 Probability Distributions

Essential Question: What is a probability distribution for a discrete random variable, and how can it be displayed?

Resource Locker

Explore Using Simulation to Obtain an Empirical Probability Distribution

A **random variable** is a variable whose value is determined by the outcome of a probability experiment. For example, when you roll a number cube, you can use the random variable X to represent the number you roll. The possible values of X are 1, 2, 3, 4, 5, and 6.

A **probability distribution** is a data distribution that gives the probabilities of the values of a random variable. A probability distribution can be represented by a histogram in which the values of the random variable—that is, the possible outcomes—are on the horizontal axis, and probabilities are on the vertical axis. The probability distribution for rolling a number cube is shown. Notice that it is a uniform distribution.

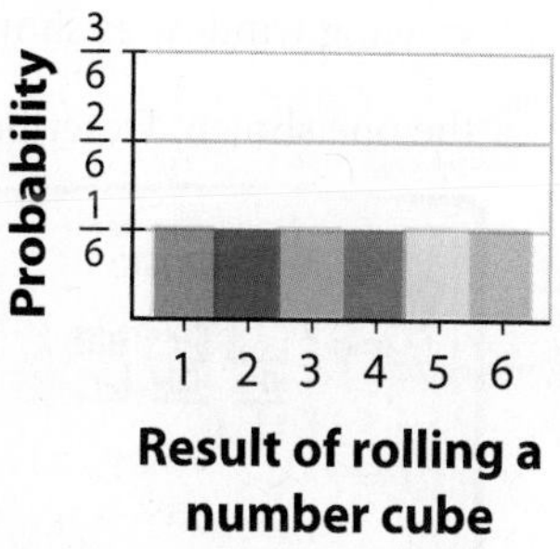

When the values of a random variable are discrete, as is the case for rolling a number cube, a histogram for the probability distribution typically shows bars that each have a width of 1 and are centered on a value of the variable. The area of each bar therefore equals the probability of the corresponding outcome, and the combined areas of the bars are the sum of the probabilities, which is 1.

A **cumulative probability** is the probability that a random variable is less than or equal to a given value. You can find cumulative probabilities from a histogram by adding the areas of the bars for all outcomes less than or equal to the given value.

Suppose you flip a coin 5 times in a row. Use a simulation to determine the probability distribution for the number of times the coin lands heads up.

(A) When you flip a coin, the possible outcomes are heads and tails. Use a graphing calculator to generate the integers 0 and 1 randomly, associating each 0 with tails and each 1 with heads.

To do the simulation, press MATH and then select the probability (**PRB**) menu. Choose **5:randInt** and enter a 0, a comma, a 1, and a closing parenthesis. Now press ENTER 5 times to generate a group of 0s and 1s. This simulates one trial (that is, one set of 5 coin flips).

Carry out 4 trials and record your results in a table.

Trial	1	2	3	4
Number of heads	?	?	?	?

(B) Report your results to your teacher in order to combine everyone's results. Use the combined class data to complete the table. To find the relative frequency for an outcome, divide the frequency of the outcome by the total number of trials in the class and round to the nearest hundredth. Record the results in a table.

Number of heads	0	1	2	3	4	5
Frequency	?	?	?	?	?	?
Relative frequency	?	?	?	?	?	?

(C) Enter the outcomes (0 through 5) into your calculator as list L_1. Enter the relative frequencies as list L_2. Make a histogram by turning on a statistics plot, selecting the histogram option, and using L_1 for Xlist and L_2 for Freq as shown. Then set the viewing window as shown. Finally, press GRAPH to obtain a histogram like the one shown. Describe the shape of the probability distribution.

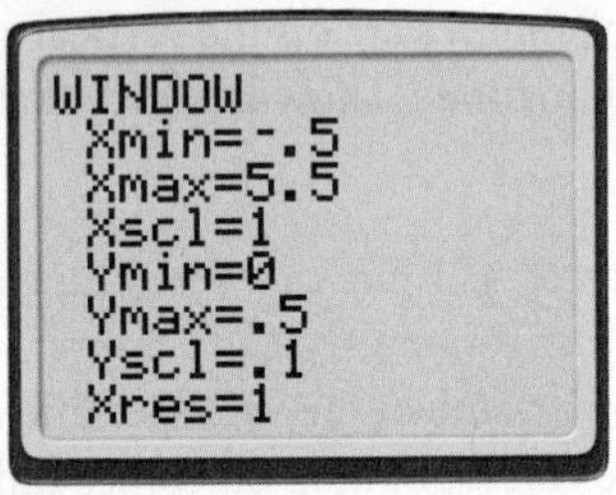

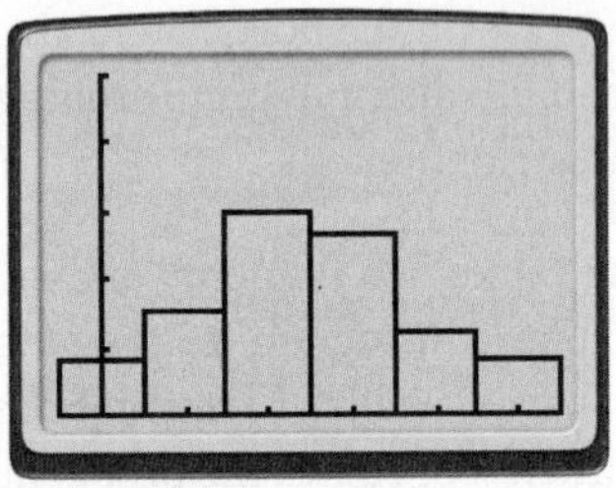

Reflect

1. **Discussion** If you flipped a coin 5 times and got 5 heads, would this cause you to question whether the coin is fair? Why or why not?

Explain 1 Displaying and Analyzing a Theoretical Probability Distribution

Recall that a binomial experiment involves repeated trials where each trial has only two outcomes: success or failure. The probability of success on each trial is p, and the probability of failure on each trial is $q = 1 - p$. The binomial probability of r successes in n trials is given by $P(X = r) = {}_nC_r p^r q^{n-r}$.

Example 1 **Calculate all the theoretical probabilities for the given binomial experiment. Then draw a histogram of the probability distribution, observe its shape, and use it to find the specified probabilities.**

(A) A binomial experiment consists of flipping a fair coin for 5 trials where getting heads is considered a success. Find the probability of getting 3 or more heads and the probability of getting at least 1 head.

To calculate the probabilities, set n equal to 5 and let r range from 0 to 5 in ${}_nC_r p^r q^{n-r}$. Since the coin is fair, $p = \frac{1}{2}$ and $q = \frac{1}{2}$.

Number of heads	0	1	2	3	4	5
Theoretical probability	$\frac{1}{32}$	$\frac{5}{32}$	$\frac{10}{32}$	$\frac{10}{32}$	$\frac{5}{32}$	$\frac{1}{32}$

Create a histogram.

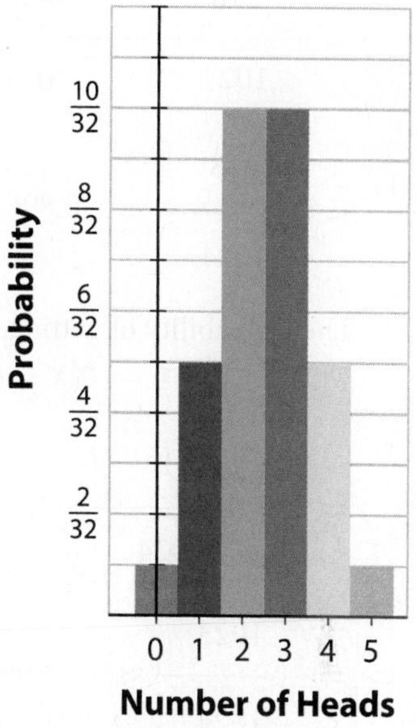

The distribution is mounded and has symmetric tails, so it is a normal distribution.

The probability of getting 3 or more heads is:

$$P(X \geq 3) = P(X = 3) + P(X = 4) + P(X = 5)$$
$$= \frac{10}{32} + \frac{5}{32} + \frac{1}{32}$$
$$= \frac{16}{32} = 0.5$$

The probability of getting at least 1 head is:

$$P(X \geq 1) = 1 - P(X = 0)$$
$$= 1 - \frac{1}{32}$$
$$= \frac{31}{32} \approx 0.969$$

(B) A binomial experiment consists of flipping a biased coin for 5 trials where getting heads is considered a success. The coin lands heads up 75% of the time. Find the probability of getting 3 or more heads and the probability of getting at least 1 head.

To calculate the probabilities, set n equal to 5 and let r range from 0 to 5 in ${}_nC_r\,p^r q^{n-r}$.

Since the coin is biased such that it lands heads up 75% of the time, $p = \frac{3}{4}$ and $q = \boxed{\frac{1}{4}}$.

Number of heads	0	1	2	3	4	5
Theoretical probability	$\frac{1}{1024}$	$\frac{15}{1024}$	$\frac{90}{1024}$	$\frac{270}{1024}$	$\frac{405}{1024}$	$\frac{243}{1024}$

Create a histogram.

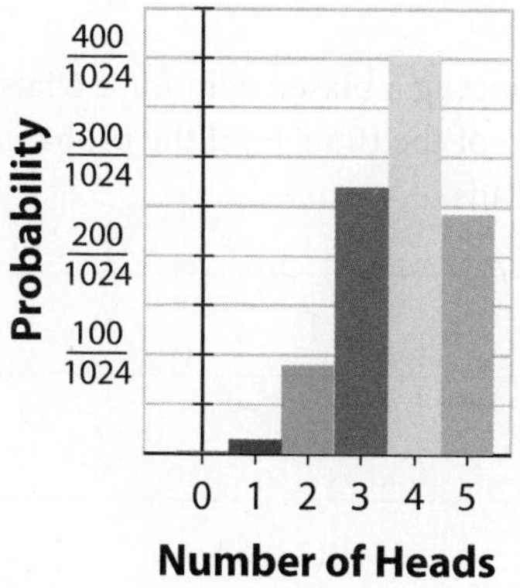

The distribution is mounded and has a tail to the left, so the distribution is skewed left.

The probability of getting 3 or more heads is:

$$P(X \geq 3) = P(X = 3) + P(X = 4) + P(X = 5)$$

$$= \frac{270}{1024} + \frac{405}{1024} + \frac{243}{1024}$$

$$= \frac{918}{1024} \approx 0.896$$

The probability of getting at least 1 head is:

$$P(X \geq 1) = 1 - P(X = 0)$$

$$= 1 - \frac{1}{1024}$$

$$= \frac{1023}{1024} \approx 0.999$$

Reflect

2. Why are the probabilities in the histogram you made in the Explore different from the probabilities given in the histogram from Part A?

3. For which coin, the fair coin in Part A or the biased coin in Part B, is flipping a coin 5 times and getting 5 heads more likely to occur? Explain.

4. **Discussion** Can you definitively conclude whether a coin that results in repeated heads when flipped is fair or biased? What might make you favor one conclusion over the other?

Your Turn

Calculate all the theoretical probabilities for the given binomial experiment. Then draw a histogram of the probability distribution, observe its shape, and use it to find the specified probabilities.

5. A binomial experiment consists of flipping a biased coin for 4 trials where getting heads is considered a success. The coin lands heads up 40% of the time. Find the probability of getting 2 or more heads and the probability of getting fewer than 4 heads.

Number of heads	0	1	2	3	4
Theoretical probability	?	?	?	?	?

Your Turn

6. A binomial experiment consists of flipping a biased coin for 4 trials where getting tails is considered a success. The coin lands heads up 40% of the time. Find the probability of getting 2 or more tails and the probability of getting fewer than 4 tails.

Number of heads	0	1	2	3	4
Theoretical probability	?	?	?	?	?

Elaborate

7. What is a random variable, and what makes a random variable discrete?

8. How can a histogram for a probability distribution be used to calculate a cumulative probability?

9. **Essential Question Check-In** What is a probability distribution for a discrete random variable?

Evaluate: Homework and Practice

Personal Math Trainer
- Online Homework
- Hints and Help
- Extra Practice

1. A spinner has three equal sections, labeled 1, 2, and 3. You spin the spinner twice and find the sum of the two numbers the spinner lands on.

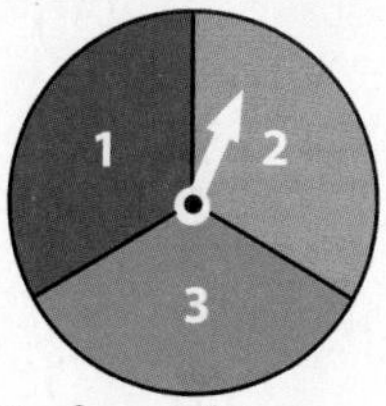

   a. Let X be a random variable that represents the sum of the two numbers. What are the possible values of X?

   b. Make a table that shows all possible sums and the probability for each sum.

   c. Make a histogram of the probability distribution.

   d. What is the probability that the sum is not 2? How is this probability represented in the histogram?

2. You roll two number cubes at the same time. Let X be a random variable that represents the absolute value of the difference of the numbers rolled.

a. What are the possible values of X?

b. Make a table that shows all possible absolute differences and the probability for each absolute difference.

c. Is this probability distribution symmetric? Why or why not?

d. Find the probability of getting a difference greater than 3.

3. A trick coin is designed to land heads up with a probability of 80%. You flip the coin 7 times.

a. Make a table that shows all possible numbers of heads and the probability for each number of heads.

b. Make a histogram of the probability distribution.

c. What is the probability of getting 6 or 7 heads?

d. What is the probability of getting 4 or more heads?

e. Which is greater, the probability of getting an even number of heads or the probability of getting an odd number of heads?

f. Suppose you flip a coin 7 times and get 7 heads. Based on what you know now, would you question whether the coin is fair? Why or why not?

4. You flip a coin 4 times in a row. The histogram shows the theoretical probability distribution for this situation.

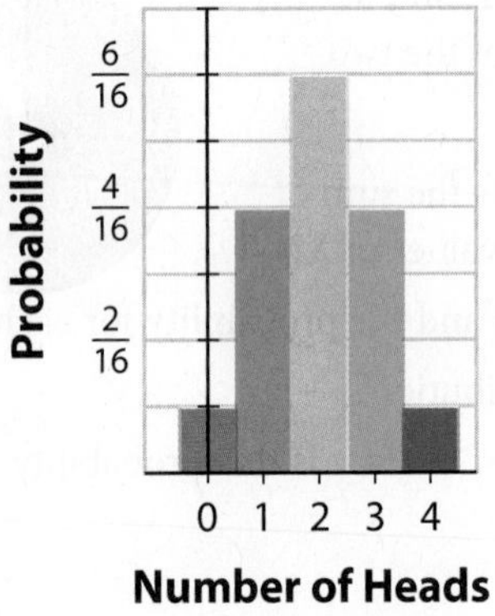

a. What is the probability of getting 3 or more heads?

b. What is the probability of getting at most 2 heads?

c. How do you know that the coin is fair?

5. A spinner has 4 equal sections that are labeled 1, 2, 3, and 4. You spin the spinner twice and find the sum of the 2 numbers it lands on. Let X be a random variable that represents the sum of the 2 numbers.

a. Complete the table.

Sum	2	3	4	5	6	7	8
Frequency	1	2	3	4	3	2	1
Probability	?	?	?	?	?	?	?

b. Make a histogram of the probability distribution.

c. What is the probability of getting a sum of 6 or more?

d. Without actually calculating any probabilities, determine the relationship between $P(X > 5)$ and $P(X < 5)$. Explain your reasoning.

6. You roll 2 number cubes at the same time. Let X be a random variable that represents the sum of the numbers rolled.

a. Create a table to show the sums that are possible. In the table, make the row heads the numbers that are possible on one number cube, and the column heads the numbers that are possible on the other number cube.

b. Create a table with row heads "sum", "frequency", and "probability", as in Exercise 5. In the "frequency" row of the table, show the number of ways that you can get each sum. Then find the probability of each sum to complete the third row.

c. Make a histogram of the probability distribution.

d. What is the probability that you roll a sum of 5 or less?

e. What is the probability that you roll a sum of 12 four times in a row? If this happened, would you question whether the number cubes are fair?

7. A fair coin is flipped 6 times. Match each specified probability on the left with its value on the right. (A value on the right may apply to more than one specified probability on the left.)

A. The probability of getting at least 4 heads — **a.** ___?___ $\frac{7}{64}$

B. The probability of getting no more than 1 head — **b.** ___?___ $\frac{21}{64}$

C. The probability of getting 1 or 2 heads — **c.** ___?___ $\frac{11}{32}$

D. The probability of getting no more than 2 heads — **d.** ___?___ $\frac{1}{2}$

E. The probability of getting an even number of heads

F. The probability of getting an odd number of heads

H.O.T. Focus on Higher Order Thinking

8. Represent Real-World Situations About 19.4% of the U.S. population that is 25 years old and over have a bachelor's degree only, and 10.5% have an advanced degree.

a. Find the probability that of 6 randomly selected people who are 25 years old or over, 4 have at least a bachelor's degree.

b. Find the probability that of 6 randomly selected people who are 25 years old or over, 4 do not have even a bachelor's degree.

c. Suppose all 6 of 6 randomly selected people have advanced degrees. Would you question the probability model? Explain.

9. Justify Reasoning Describe a way to get fair results from a coin that you suspect is biased. Explain how you know that the process is fair.

10. Construct Arguments Use the formula $P(X = r) = {}_nC_r\, p^r q^{n-r}$ for a binomial experiment to explain why the probability distribution for the number of heads obtained when a fair coin is flipped n times is symmetric.

Lesson Performance Task

According to the U.S. Census, in 2010 the number of people 18 years old or over in the U.S. was 229.1 million, and of those people, 129.5 million were married.

a. Find the probability that of 10 randomly selected people 18 years old or over, 6 are married.

b. Consider a survey where all 10 of the people surveyed are married. What conclusion might you draw about that survey?

23.2 Normal Distributions

Essential Question: How do you find percents of data and probabilities of events associated with normal distributions?

Resource Locker

Explore 1 Substituting a Normal Curve for a Symmetric Histogram

The table below gives the mass (in kilograms) of 20 babies at birth. You know that there are 20 babies, because that is the sum of the frequencies. You also know that the masses are normally distributed because the mass with the greatest frequency occurs at the center of the distribution and the other frequencies taper off symmetrically from that center. The mean of the data is 3.5 kg, and the standard deviation is 0.14 kg.

You can use a graphing calculator to draw a smooth bell-shaped curve, called a *normal curve*, that captures the shape of the histogram. A normal curve has the property that the area under the curve (and above the x-axis) is 1. This means that you must adjust the heights of the bars in the histogram so that the sum of the areas of the bars is 1.

(A) Find the relative frequency of each mass.

Mass (kg)	3.2	3.3	3.4	3.5	3.6	3.7	3.8
Frequency	1	2	4	6	4	2	1
Relative frequency	$\frac{1}{20} = 0.05$	?	?	?	?	?	?
Adjusted bar height	$\frac{0.05}{0.1} = 0.5$	?	?	?	?	?	?

(B) What is the sum of the relative frequencies?

(C) For a given mass, the relative frequency is the area that you want the bar to have. Since you used a bar width of 0.1 when you created the histogram, the area of the bar is $0.1h$ where h is the height of the bar. You want $0.1h$ to equal the relative frequency f, so solve $0.1h = f$ for h to find the adjusted bar height. Complete this row in the table.

(D) Enter each mass from the table into L_1 on your graphing calculator. Then enter each adjusted bar height into L_2.

(E) Turn on a statistics plot and select the histogram option. For Xlist, enter L_1. For Freq, enter L_2. Set the graphing window as shown. Then press GRAPH.

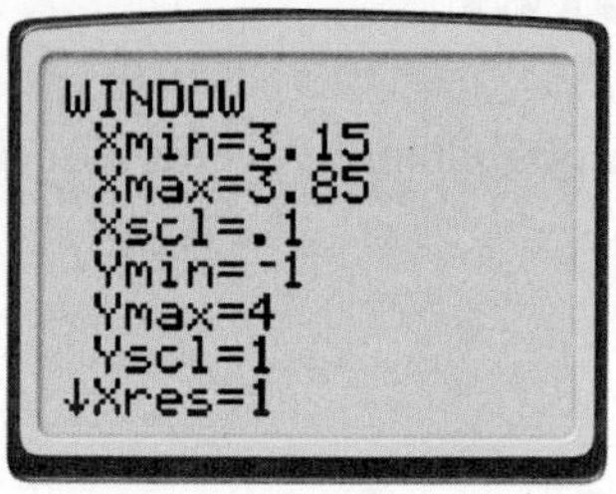

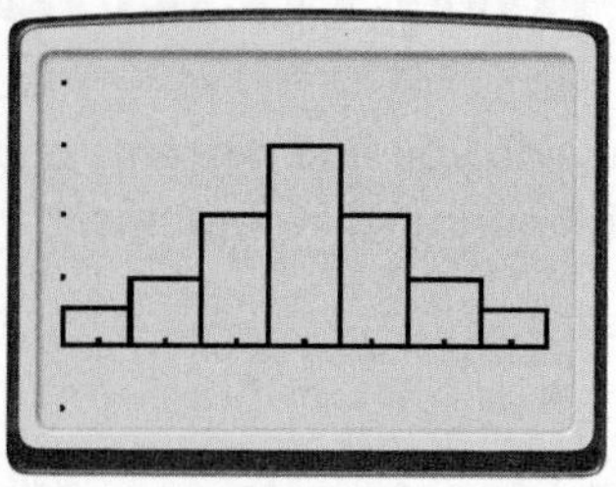

(F) Your calculator has a built-in function called a *normal probability density function*, which you can access by pressing 2nd VARS and selecting the first choice from the DISTR (distribution) menu. When entering this function to be graphed, you must include the mean and standard deviation of the distribution by entering **normalpdf(X, 3.5, 0.14)**. When you press GRAPH, the calculator will draw a normal curve that fits the histogram.

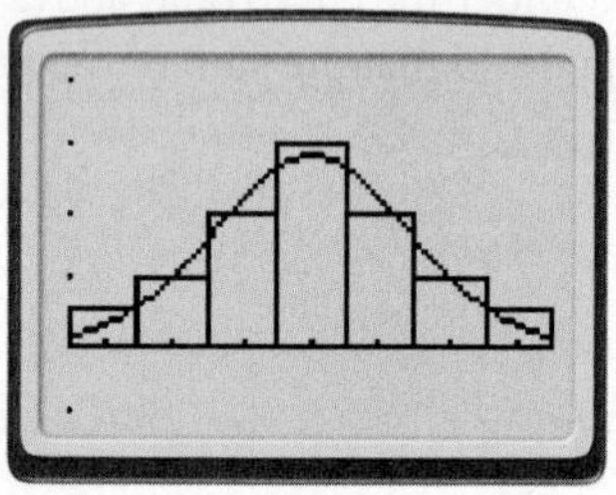

Reflect

1. Describe the end behavior of the normal probability density function.

2. **Discussion** If the area under the normal curve is 1, then what is the area under the curve to the left of the mean, 3.5? Describe how to obtain this area using the bars in the histogram. Show that your method gives the correct result.

3. Explain how you can use the bars in the histogram to estimate the area under the curve within 1 standard deviation of the mean, which is the interval from $3.5 - 0.14 = 3.36$ to $3.5 + 0.14 = 3.64$ on the x-axis. Then find the estimate.

4. Explain how you can use the bars in the histogram to estimate the area under the curve within 2 standard deviations of the mean, which is the interval from $3.5 - 2(0.14) = 3.22$ to $3.5 + 2(0.14) = 3.78$ on the x-axis. Then find the estimate.

Explain 1 Finding Areas Under a Normal Curve

All normal curves have the following properties, sometimes collectively called the 68–95–99.7 rule:

- 68% of the data fall within 1 standard deviation of the mean.
- 95% of the data fall within 2 standard deviations of the mean.
- 99.7% of the data fall within 3 standard deviations of the mean.

A normal curve's symmetry allows you to separate the area under the curve into eight parts and know the percent of the data in each part.

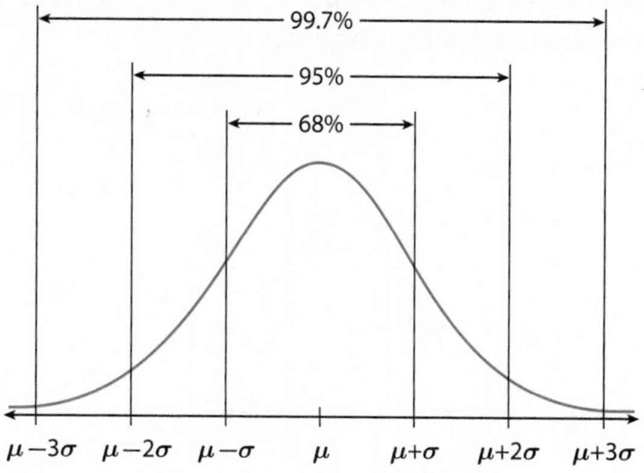

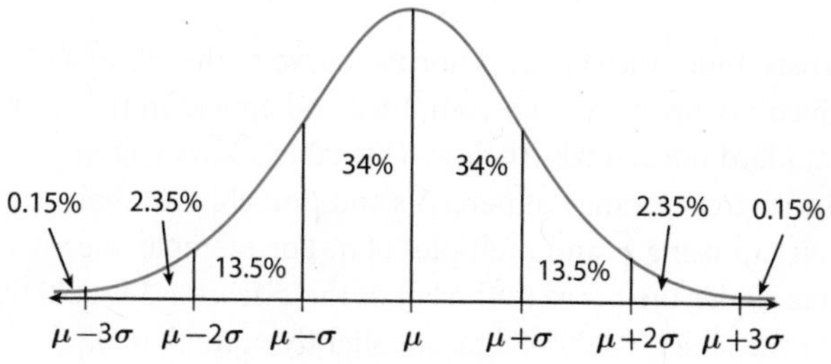

Example 1 **Suppose the heights (in inches) of men (ages 20–29) years old in the United States are normally distributed with a mean of 69.3 inches and a standard deviation of 2.92 inches. Find each of the following.**

Ⓐ The percent of men who are between 63.46 inches and 75.14 inches tall.

63.46 inches is 5.84 inches, or 2 standard deviations, below the mean.

75.14 inches is 5.84 inches, or 2 standard deviations, above the mean.

95% of the data in a normal distribution fall within 2 standard deviations of the mean.

So, 95% of males are between 63.46 inches and 75.14 inches tall.

Ⓑ The percent of men who are taller than 72.22 inches.

72.22 inches is 2.92 inches, or 1 standard deviation, above the mean.

When the area under a normal curve is separated into eight parts, the parts that satisfy the condition that the height will be greater than 72.22 inches have percents of 13.5%, 2.35%, and 0.15%.

The sum of these percents is 16%.

So, 16 % of males are taller than 72.22 inches.

Your Turn

Suppose the heights (in inches) of men (ages 20–29) in the United States are normally distributed with a mean of 69.3 inches and a standard deviation of 2.92 inches. Find each of the following.

5. The percent of men who are between 60.54 inches and 78.06 inches tall.

6. The percent of men who are shorter than 60.54 inches.

Explain 2 Using the Standard Normal Distribution

The **standard normal distribution** has a mean of 0 and a standard deviation of 1. A data value x from a normal distribution with mean μ and standard deviation σ can be standardized by finding its **z-score** using the formula $z = \frac{x - \mu}{\sigma}$.

Areas under the standard normal curve to the left of a given z-score have been computed and appear in the standard normal table below. This table allows you to find a greater range of percents and probabilities than you can using μ and multiples of σ. For example, the area under the curve to the left of the z-score 1.3 is 0.9032. (In the table, "0.0000+" means slightly more than 0, and "1.0000—" means slightly less than 1.)

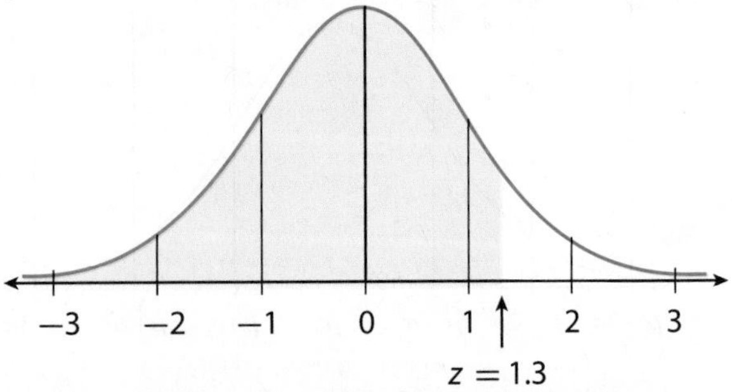

Standard Normal Table

z	.0	.1	.2	.3	.4	.5	.6	.7	.8	.9
−3	0.0013	0.0010	0.0007	0.0005	0.0003	0.0002	0.0002	0.0001	0.0001	0.0000+
−2	0.0228	0.0179	0.0139	0.0107	0.0082	0.0062	0.0047	0.0035	0.0026	0.0019
−1	0.1587	0.1357	0.1151	0.0968	0.0808	0.0668	0.0548	0.0446	0.0359	0.0287
−0	0.5000	0.4602	0.4207	0.3821	0.3446	0.3085	0.2743	0.2420	0.2119	0.1841
0	0.5000	0.5398	0.5793	0.6179	0.6554	0.6915	0.7257	0.7580	0.7881	0.8159
1	0.8413	0.8643	0.8849	0.9032	0.9192	0.9332	0.9452	0.9554	0.9641	0.9713
2	0.9772	0.9821	0.9861	0.9893	0.9918	0.9938	0.9953	0.9965	0.9974	0.9981
3	0.9987	0.9990	0.9993	0.9995	0.9997	0.9998	0.9998	0.9999	0.9999	1.000—

Example 2 **Suppose the heights (in inches) of women (ages 20–29) in the United States are normally distributed with a mean of 64.1 inches and a standard deviation of 2.75 inches. Find the percent of women who are no more than 65 inches tall and the probability that a randomly chosen woman is between 60 inches and 63 inches tall.**

Analyze Information

The mean of the heights is 64.1 inches.

The standard deviation of the heights is 2.75 inches.

Formulate a Plan

Convert the heights to z-scores and use the standard normal table to find the probabilities needed.

Solve

First, find the percent of women who are no more than 65 inches tall.

Convert 65 to a z-score (to the nearest tenth): $z_{65} = \frac{65 - \mu}{\sigma} = \frac{65 - \boxed{64.1}}{\boxed{2.75}} \approx \boxed{0.3}$

Recognize that the phrase "no more than 65 inches" means that $z \leq z_{65}$. Read the decimal from the appropriate row and column of the standard normal table: 0.6179

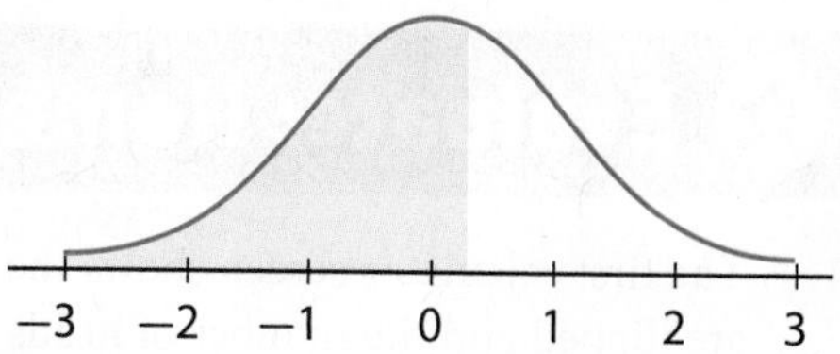

Write the decimal as a percent: 61.79%

Next, find the probability that a randomly chosen woman is between 60 inches and 63 inches tall.

Convert 60 to a z-score: $z_{60} = \frac{60 - \mu}{\sigma} = \frac{60 - 64.1}{2.75} \approx -1.5$

Convert 63 to a z-score: $z_{63} = \frac{63 - \mu}{\sigma} = \frac{63 - 64.1}{2.75} = -0.4$

Because the standard normal table gives areas under the standard normal curve to the left of a given z-score, you find $P(z_{60} \leq z \leq z_{63})$ by subtracting $P(z \leq z_{60})$ from $P(z \leq z_{63})$. Complete the following calculation using the appropriate values from the table:

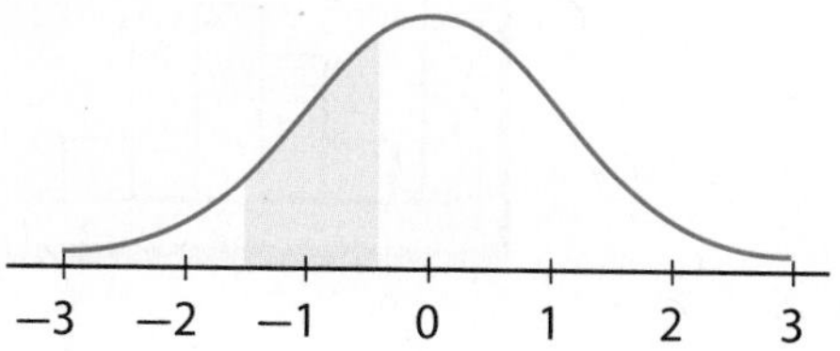

$P(z_{60} \leq z \leq z_{63}) = P(z \leq z_{63}) - P(z \leq z_{60}) = 0.3446 - 0.0668 = 0.2778$

Write the decimal as a percent: 27.78%

Justify and Evaluate

65 inches is slightly greater than the mean height. Since all the heights up to the mean represent 50% of the data, it makes sense that all the heights up to 65 inches are slightly more than 50%. Heights from 60–63 inches are within the area for heights less than 65 inches but there are fewer, so it makes sense that the probability is less than 50%.

Your Turn

Suppose the heights (in inches) of adult females (ages 20–29) in the United States are normally distributed with a mean of 64.1 inches and a standard deviation of 2.75 inches.

7. Find the percent of women who are at least 66 inches tall.

8. Find the percent of women who are less than or equal to 61.6 inches tall.

Elaborate

9. Explain how you know that the area under a normal curve between $\mu + \sigma$ and $\mu + 2\sigma$ represents 13.5% of the data if you know that the percent of the data within 1 standard deviation of the mean is 68% and the percent of the data within 2 standard deviations of the mean is 95%.

10. How can you use the 68-95-99.7 rule and the symmetry of a normal curve to find the percent of normally distributed data that are less than 1 standard deviation above the mean?

11. **Essential Question Check-In** Explain what a z-score is and how it's used.

Evaluate: Homework and Practice

Personal Math Trainer
- Online Homework
- Hints and Help
- Extra Practice

1. The first calculator screen shows the probability distribution when 6 coins are flipped and the number of heads is counted. The second screen shows the probability distribution of the number of correct answers given by a group of people on a 6-question quiz. For which distribution is it reasonable to use a normal curve as an approximation? Why?

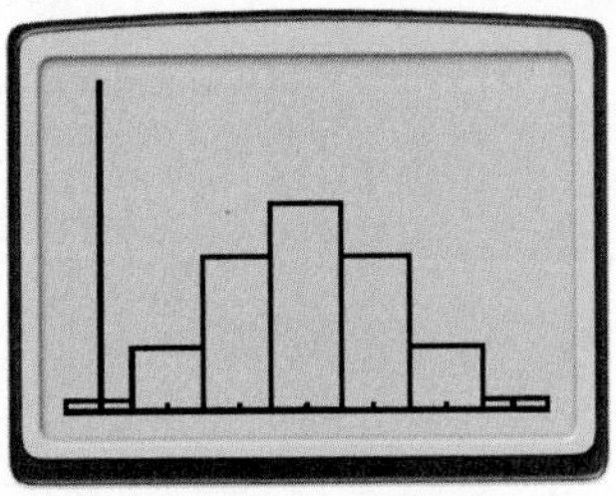

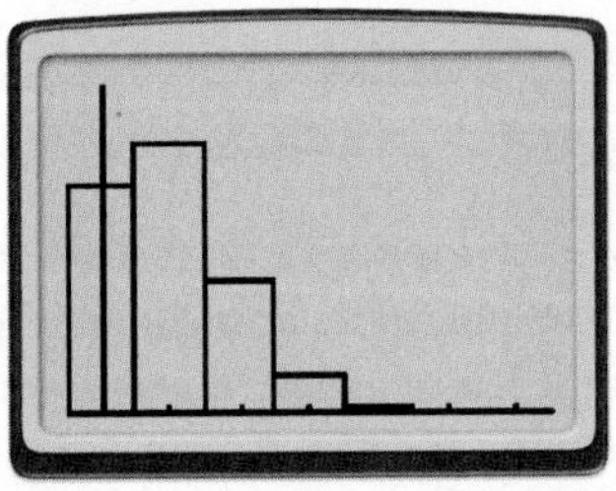

A college-entrance exam is designed so that scores are normally distributed with a mean of 500 and a standard deviation of 100.

2. What percent of exam scores are between 400 and 600?
3. What is the probability that a randomly chosen exam score is above 600?
4. What is the probability that a randomly chosen exam score is less than 300 or greater than 700?
5. What is the probability that a randomly chosen exam score is above 300?

Flight 202's arrival time is normally distributed with a mean arrival time of 4:30 p.m. and a standard deviation of 15 minutes. Find the probability that a randomly chosen arrival time is within the given time period.

6. After 4:45 p.m.
7. Between 4:15 p.m. and 5:00 p.m.
8. Between 3:45 p.m. and 4:30 p.m.
9. By 4:45 p.m.

Suppose the scores on a test given to all juniors in a school district are normally distributed with a mean of 74 and a standard deviation of 8. Find each of the following using the standard normal table.

10. Find the percent of juniors whose score is no more than 90.
11. Find the percent of juniors whose score is between 58 and 74.
12. Find the percent of juniors whose score is at least 74.
13. Find the probability that a randomly chosen junior has a score above 82.
14. Find the probability that a randomly chosen junior has a score between 66 and 90.
15. Find the probability that a randomly chosen junior has a score below 74.

Graphing Calculator On a graphing calculator, you can use the function normalcdf(lower bound, upper bound, μ, σ) on the DISTR menu to find the area under a normal curve for values of x between a specified lower bound and a specified upper bound. You can use −1E99 as the lower bound to represent negative infinity and 1E99 as the upper bound to represent positive infinity. Suppose that cans of lemonade mix have amounts of lemonade mix that are normally distributed with a mean of 350 grams and a standard deviation of 4 grams. Use this information and a graphing calculator to answer each question.

16. What percent of cans have less than 338 grams of lemonade mix?

17. What is the probability that a randomly chosen can has between 342 grams and 350 grams of lemonade mix?

18. What is the probability that a randomly chosen can has less than 342 grams or more than 346 grams of lemonade mix?

Spreadsheet In a spreadsheet, you can use the function NORM DIST(upper bound, μ, σ, TRUE) to find the area under a normal curve for values of x less than or equal to a specified upper bound. Suppose the heights of all the children in a state are normally distributed with a mean of 45 inches and a standard deviation of 6 inches. Use this information and a spreadsheet to answer each question.

19. What is the probability that a randomly chosen child is less than 40 inches tall?

20. What is the probability that a randomly chosen child is greater than 47 inches tall?

21. What percent of children are between 50 and 53 inches tall?

22. What is the probability that a randomly chosen child is less than 38 inches tall or more than 51 inches tall?

H.O.T. Focus on Higher Order Thinking

23. Explain the Error A student was asked to describe the relationship between the area under a normal curve for all x-values less than a and the area under the normal curve for all x-values greater than a. The student's response was "Both areas are 0.5 because the curve is symmetric." Explain the student's error.

24. Make a Conjecture A local orchard packages apples in bags. When full, the bags weigh 5 pounds each and contain a whole number of apples. The weights are normally distributed with a mean of 5 pounds and a standard deviation of 0.25 pound. An inspector weighs each bag and rejects all bags that weigh less than 5 pounds. Describe the shape of the distribution of the weights of the bags that are not rejected.

25. Analyze Relationships A biologist is measuring the lengths of frogs in a certain location. The lengths of 20 frogs are shown. If the mean is 7.4 centimeters and the standard deviation is 0.8 centimeter, do the data appear to be normally distributed? Complete the table and explain.

Length (cm)				
7.5	5.8	7.9	7.6	8.1
7.9	7.1	5.9	8.4	7.3
7.1	6.4	8.3	8.4	6.7
8.1	7.8	5.9	6.8	8.1

			Values $\leq x$	
z	Area $\leq z$	x	Projected	Actual
−2	0.02	5.8	$0.02 \cdot 20 = 0.4 \approx 0$	1
−1	0.16	6.6	?	?
0	0.5	?	?	?
1	0.84	8.2	?	?
2	0.98	?	?	?

Lesson Performance Task

Suppose a nurse records the temperatures of healthy men and women. The table represents the means and standard deviations of the data.

	Women	Men
°F	98.4 ± 0.7 °F	98.1 ± 0.7 °F
°C	36.9 ± 0.4 °C	36.7 ± 0.4 °C

A. What is the range of temperatures for 1, 2, and 3 standard deviations for both women and men? (Give temperatures in both degrees Fahrenheit and degrees Celsius.)

B. Assuming a normal distribution, find the probability that a randomly selected man's temperature is between 96.7 °F and 97.4 °F.

C. A fever is considered medically significant if body temperature reaches 100.4 °F (38 °C). What can you observe about this temperature?

23.3 Sampling Distributions

Essential Question: How is the mean of a sampling distribution related to the corresponding population mean or population proportion?

Resource Locker

Explore 1 Developing a Distribution of Sample Means

The tables provide the following data about the first 50 people to join a new gym: member ID number, age, and sex.

ID	Age	Sex	ID	Age	Sex	ID	Age	Sex	ID	Age	Sex	ID	Age	Sex
1	30	M	11	38	F	21	74	F	31	32	M	41	46	M
2	48	M	12	24	M	22	21	M	32	28	F	42	34	F
3	52	M	13	48	F	23	29	F	33	35	M	43	44	F
4	25	F	14	45	M	24	48	M	34	49	M	44	68	M
5	63	F	15	28	F	25	37	M	35	18	M	45	24	F
6	50	F	16	39	M	26	52	F	36	56	F	46	34	F
7	18	F	17	37	F	27	25	F	37	48	F	47	55	F
8	28	F	18	63	F	28	44	M	38	38	F	48	39	M
9	72	M	19	20	M	29	29	F	39	52	F	49	40	F
10	25	F	20	81	F	30	66	M	40	33	F	50	30	F

(A) Enter the age data into a graphing calculator and find the mean age μ and standard deviation σ for the population of the gym's first 50 members. Round each statistic to the nearest tenth.

(B) Use a graphing calculator's random number generator to choose a sample of 5 gym members. Find the mean age $\overline{x}$ for your sample. Round to the nearest tenth.

(C) Report your sample mean to your teacher. As other students report their sample means, create a class histogram. To do so, shade a square above the appropriate interval as each sample mean is reported. For sample means that lie on an interval boundary, shade a square on the interval to the *right*. For instance, if the sample mean is 39.5, shade a square on the interval from 39.5 to 40.5.

Make your own copy of the class histogram.

(D) Calculate the mean of the sample means, $\mu_{\bar{x}}$, and the standard deviation of the sample means, $\sigma_{\bar{x}}$.

(E) Now use a graphing calculator's random number generator to choose a sample of 15 gym members. Find the mean for your sample. Round to the nearest tenth.

(F) Report your sample mean to your teacher. As other students report their sample means, create a class histogram and make your own copy of it.

(G) Calculate the mean of the sample means, $\mu_{\bar{x}}$, and the standard deviation of the sample means, $\sigma_{\bar{x}}$.

Reflect

1. In the class histograms, how does the mean of the sample means compare with the population mean?
2. What happens to the standard deviation of the sample means as the sample size increases?
3. What happens to the shape of the histogram as the sample size increases?

Explore 2 Developing a Distribution of Sample Proportions

Use the tables of gym membership data from Explore 1. This time you will develop a sampling distribution based on a sample proportion rather than a sample mean.

(A) Find the proportion p of female gym members in the population.

(B) Use a graphing calculator's random number generator to choose a sample of 5 gym members. Find the proportion $\hat{p}$ of female gym members for your sample.

(C) Report your sample proportion to your teacher. As other students report their sample proportions, create a class histogram and make your own copy of it.

(D) Calculate the mean of the sample proportions, $\mu_{\hat{p}}$, and the standard deviation of the sample proportions, $\sigma_{\hat{p}}$. Round to the nearest hundredth.

(E) Now use your calculator's random number generator to choose a sample of 10 gym members. Find the proportion of female members $\hat{p}$ for your sample.

(F) Report your sample proportion to your teacher. As other students report their sample proportions, create a class histogram and make your own copy of it.

(G) Calculate the mean of the sample proportions, $\mu_{\hat{p}}$, and the standard deviation of the sample proportions, $\sigma_{\hat{p}}$. Round to the nearest hundredth.

Reflect

4. In the class histograms, how does the mean of the sample proportions compare with the population proportion?

5. What happens to the standard deviation of the sample proportions as the sample size increases?

Explain 1 Using the Sampling Distribution of the Sample Mean

The histograms that you made in the two Explores are *sampling distributions*. A **sampling distribution** shows how a particular statistic varies across all samples of n individuals from the same population. In Explore 1, you approximated sampling distributions of the sample mean, $\bar{x}$, for samples of size 5 and 15. (The reason your sampling distributions are approximations is that you did not find *all* samples of a given size.)

The mean of the sampling distribution of the sample mean is denoted $\mu_{\bar{x}}$. The standard deviation of the sampling distribution of the sample mean is denoted $\sigma_{\bar{x}}$ and is also called the **standard error of the mean.**

In Explore 1, you may have discovered that $\mu_{\bar{x}}$ is close to $\bar{x}$ regardless of the sample size and that $\sigma_{\bar{x}}$ decreases as the sample size n increases. You based these observations on simulations. When you consider all possible samples of n individuals, you arrive at one of the major theorems of statistics.

Properties of the Sampling Distribution of the Sample Mean

If a random sample of size n is selected from a population with mean μ and standard deviation σ, then

1. $\mu_{\bar{x}} = \mu$,

2. $\sigma_{\bar{x}} = \frac{\sigma}{\sqrt{n}}$, and

3. The sampling distribution of the sample mean is normal if the population is normal; for all other populations, the sampling distribution of the mean approaches a normal distribution as n increases.

The third property stated above is known as the Central Limit Theorem.

Example 1 **Boxes of Cruncho cereal have a mean mass of 323 grams with a standard deviation of 20 grams.**

(A) For random samples of 36 boxes, what interval centered on the mean of the sampling distribution captures 95% of the sample means?

Write the given information about the population and a sample.

$\mu = 323$ $\sigma = 20$ $n = 36$

Find the mean of the sampling distribution of the sample mean and the standard error of the mean.

$\mu_{\bar{x}} = \mu = 323$ $\sigma_{\bar{x}} = \frac{\sigma}{\sqrt{n}} = \frac{20}{\sqrt{36}} = \frac{20}{6} \approx 3.3$

The sampling distribution of the sample mean is approximately normal. In a normal distribution, 95% of the data fall within 2 standard deviations of the mean.

$\mu_{\bar{x}} - 2\sigma_{\bar{x}} = 323 - 2(3.3) = 316.4$ $\qquad \mu_{\bar{x}} + 2\sigma_{\bar{x}} = 323 + 2(3.3) = 329.6$

So, for random samples of 36 boxes, 95% of the sample means fall between 316.4 grams and 329.6 grams.

(B) What is the probability that a random sample of 25 boxes has a mean mass of at most 325 grams?

Write the given information about the population and the sample.

$\mu = \boxed{323} \qquad \sigma = \boxed{20} \qquad n = \boxed{25}$

Find the mean of the sampling distribution of the sample mean and the standard error of the mean.

$\mu_{\bar{x}} = \mu = \boxed{323}$ $\qquad \sigma_{\bar{x}} = \dfrac{\sigma}{\sqrt{n}} = \dfrac{\boxed{20}}{\sqrt{\boxed{25}}} = \dfrac{\boxed{20}}{\boxed{5}} = \boxed{4}$

The sampling distribution of the sample mean is approximately normal. Use a graphing calculator to find $P(\bar{x} \le 325)$.

$P(\bar{x} \le 325) = \text{normalcdf}\left(-1\text{E}99, \boxed{325}, \boxed{323}, \boxed{4}\right) \approx \boxed{0.69}$

So, the probability that the random sample has a mean mass of at most 325 grams is about 0.69.

Your Turn

Boxes of Cruncho cereal have a mean mass of 323 grams with a standard deviation of 20 grams.

6. For random samples of 50 boxes, what interval centered on the mean of the sampling distribution captures 99.7% of the sample means?

7. What is the probability that a random sample of 100 boxes has a mean mass of at least 320 grams?

Explain 2 Using the Sampling Distribution of the Sample Proportion

When you work with the sampling distribution of a sample proportion, p represents the proportion of individuals in the population that have a particular characteristic (that is, the proportion of "successes") and $\hat{p}$ is the proportion of successes in a sample. The mean of the sampling distribution of the sample proportion is denoted $\mu_{\hat{p}}$. The standard deviation of the sampling distribution of the sample proportion is denoted $\sigma_{\hat{p}}$ and is also called the **standard error of the proportion**.

Properties of the Sampling Distribution of the Sample Proportion

If a random sample of size n is selected from a population with proportion p of successes, then

1. $\mu_{\hat{p}} = p$,
2. $\sigma_{\hat{p}} = \sqrt{\dfrac{p(1-p)}{n}}$, and
3. if both np and $n(1-p)$ are at least 10, then the sampling distribution of the sample proportion is approximately normal.

Example 2 **40% of the students at a university live off campus. When sampling from this population, consider "successes" to be students who live off campus.**

(A) For random samples of 50 students, what interval centered on the mean of the sampling distribution captures 95% of the sample proportions?

Write the given information about the population and a sample.

$p = 0.4 \quad n = 50$

Find the mean of the sampling distribution of the sample proportion and the standard error of the proportion.

$\mu_{\hat{p}} = p = 0.4 \qquad \sigma_{\hat{p}} = \sqrt{\frac{p(1-p)}{n}} = \sqrt{\frac{0.4(1-0.4)}{50}} \approx 0.069$

Check that np and $n(1-p)$ are both at least 10.

$np = 50 \cdot 0.4 = 20 \qquad n(1-p) = 50 \cdot 0.6 = 30$

Since np and $n(1-p)$ are both greater than 10, the sampling distribution of the sample proportion is approximately normal. In a normal distribution, 95% of the data fall within 2 standard deviations of the mean.

$\mu_{\hat{p}} - 2\sigma_{\hat{p}} = 0.4 - 2(0.069) = 0.262 \qquad \mu_{\hat{p}} + 2\sigma_{\hat{p}} = 0.4 + 2(0.069) = 0.538$

So, for random samples of 50 students, 95% of the sample proportions fall between 26.2% and 53.8%.

(B) What is the probability that a random sample of 25 students has a sample proportion of at most 37%?

Write the given information about the population and the sample, where a success is a student who lives off campus.

$p = \boxed{0.4} \quad n = \boxed{25}$

Find the mean of the sampling distribution of the sample proportion and the standard error of the proportion.

$\mu_{\hat{p}} = p = \boxed{0.4} \qquad \sigma_{\hat{p}} = \sqrt{\frac{p(1-p)}{n}} = \sqrt{\frac{\boxed{0.4}\left(1 - \boxed{0.4}\right)}{\boxed{25}}} = \boxed{0.098}$

Check that np and $n(1-p)$ are both at least 10.

$np = \boxed{25} \cdot \boxed{0.4} = \boxed{10} \qquad n(1-p) = \boxed{25} \cdot \boxed{0.6} = \boxed{15}$

Since np and $n(1-p)$ are greater than or equal to 10, the sampling distribution of the sample proportion is approximately normal. Use a graphing calculator to find $P(\hat{p} \leq 0.37)$.

$P(\hat{p} \leq 0.37) = \text{normalcdf}\left(-1\text{E}99, \boxed{0.37}, \boxed{0.4}, \boxed{0.098}\right) \approx \boxed{0.38}$

So, the probability that the random sample has a sample proportion of at most 37% is about 0.38.

Your Turn

40% of the students at a university live off campus. When sampling from this population, consider "successes" to be students who live off campus.

8. For random samples of 80 students, what interval centered on the mean of the sampling distribution captures 68% of the sample proportions?

9. What is the probability that a random sample of 60 students includes more than 18 students who live off campus?

Elaborate

10. What is a sampling distribution?

11. What allows you to conclude that 95% of the sample means in a sampling distribution are within 2 standard deviations of the population mean?

12. When finding a sample mean or a sample proportion, why is using the greatest sample size possible (given constraints on the cost and time of sampling) a desirable thing to do?

13. **Essential Question Check-In** When you repeatedly take random samples of the same size from a population, what does the mean of the samples approximate?

Evaluate: Homework and Practice

Personal Math Trainer

- Online Homework
- Hints and Help
- Extra Practice

1. The general manager of a multiplex theater took random samples of size 10 from the audiences attending the opening weekend of a new movie. From each sample, the manager obtained the mean age and the proportion of those who said they liked the movie. The sample means and sample proportions are listed in the tables.

Sample number	Sample mean (age)	Sample proportion (liked the movie)
1	22.1	0.6
2	25.7	0.9
3	24.8	0.7
4	24.3	0.7
5	23.9	0.8
6	23.3	0.6
7	22.8	0.5
8	24.0	0.8
9	25.1	0.7
10	23.6	0.7

Sample number	Sample mean (age)	Sample proportion (liked the movie)
11	24.2	0.5
12	26.4	0.6
13	25.9	0.7
14	23.8	0.8
15	21.1	0.7
16	24.4	0.7
17	23.9	0.6
18	25.1	0.7
19	24.7	0.9
20	22.9	0.6

a. Based on the 20 samples, what is the best estimate for the mean age of all the people who saw the movie? Explain.

b. Based on this sample, what is the best estimate for the proportion of all the people who saw the movie and liked it? Explain.

c. What could the manager have done to improve the accuracy of both estimates?

On a standardized science test, the seniors at Fillmore High School have a mean score of 425 with a standard deviation of 80.

2. For random samples of 30 seniors, what interval centered on the mean of the sampling distribution captures 95% of the mean scores?

3. For random samples of 100 seniors, what interval centered on the mean of the sampling distribution captures 68% of the mean scores?

4. What is the probability that a random sample of 50 seniors has a mean score of at most 415?

5. What is the probability that a random sample of 25 seniors has a mean score of at least 430?

For Exercises 6–9, use the following information: The safety placard on an elevator states that up to 8 people (1200 kilograms) can ride the elevator at one time. Suppose the people who work in the office building where the elevator is located have a mean mass of 80 kilograms with a standard deviation of 25 kilograms.

6. For random samples of 8 people who work in the office building, what interval centered on the mean of the sampling distribution captures 95% of the mean masses?

7. For random samples of 8 people who work in the office building, what interval centered on the mean of the sampling distribution captures 99.7% of the mean masses?

8. What is the probability that a random sample of 8 people who work in the office building has a mean mass of at most 90 kilograms?

9. Based on the elevator's safety placard, what is the maximum mean mass of 8 people who can ride the elevator at one time? What is the probability that a random sample of 8 people who work in the office building exceeds this maximum mean mass?

A popcorn manufacturer puts a prize in 25% of its bags of popcorn. When sampling from this population, consider "successes" to be bags of popcorn containing a prize.

10. For random samples of 100 bags of popcorn, what interval centered on the mean of the sampling distribution captures 95% of the sample proportions?

11. For random samples of 80 bags of popcorn, what interval centered on the mean of the sampling distribution captures 68% of the sample proportions?

12. What is the probability that a random sample of 120 bags of popcorn has prizes in at most 30% of the bags?

13. What is the probability that a random sample of 60 bags has prizes in more than 12 bags?

About 28% of students at a large school play varsity sports. When sampling from this population, consider "successes" to be students who play varsity sports.

14. For random samples of 75 students, what interval centered on the mean of the sampling distribution captures 95% of the sample proportions?

15. For random samples of 100 students, what interval centered on the mean of the sampling distribution captures 99.7% of the sample proportions?

16. What is the probability that a random sample of 45 students includes more than 18 students who play varsity sports?

17. What is the probability that a random sample of 60 students includes from 12 to 24 students who play varsity sports?

18. Among the 450 seniors in a large high school, 306 plan to be in college in the fall following high school graduation. Suppose random samples of 100 seniors are taken from this population in order to obtain sample proportions of seniors who plan to be college in the fall. Which of the following are true statements?

a. Every sample proportion is 0.68.

b. The mean of the sampling distribution of the sample proportion is 0.68.

c. The standard error of the proportion is about 0.047.

d. The standard error of the proportion is about 0.0047.

e. The sampling distribution of the sample proportion is skewed.

f. The sampling distribution of the sample proportion is approximately normal.

H.O.T. Focus on Higher Order Thinking

19. Explain the Error A student was told that a population has a mean of 400 and a standard deviation of 25. The student was asked to find the probability that a random sample of size 45 taken from the population has a mean of at most 401. The student entered normalcdf $(-1\text{E}99, 401, 400, 25)$ on a graphing calculator and got a probability of about 0.516. What did the student do wrong? Show how to find the correct answer.

20. Draw Conclusions Amanda plans to use random sampling to estimate the percent of people who are truly ambidextrous (that is, they do not have a dominant right or left hand). She suspects that the percent is quite low, perhaps as low as 1%. If she wants the sampling distribution of the sample proportion to be approximately normal, what minimum sample size should she use? Explain.

21. Check for Reasonableness Given that about 90% of people are right-handed, you are interested in knowing what percent of people put their right thumb on top when they clasp their hands. Having no other information to go on, you assume that people who put their right thumb on top when they clasp their hands are those who are also right-handed. You then take a random sample of 100 people and find that 60 put their right thumb on top when they clasp their hands. Does this result lead you to question your assumption? Explain why or why not.

Lesson Performance Task

Among the data that the U.S. Census Bureau collects are the sizes of households, as shown in the table.

Number of people in household	Number of households	Number of people
1	31,886,794	?
2	38,635,170	?
3	18,044,529	?
4	15,030,350	?
5	6,940,508	?
6	2,704,873	?
7 or more	1,749,501	?

a. In the table above, assume that you can simply use 7 as the number of people in households with 7 or more people. Complete the third column of the table. Then use that column to approximate the population mean μ (that is, the mean number of people in a household). Explain your reasoning.

b. Is the actual population mean greater than or less than the mean that you calculated? Explain.

c. Given that $\mu \approx 2.49$ and $\sigma \approx 1.42$, find the probability that a random sample of 100 households in the United States has a mean size of 2.3 people or less.

d. Given that $\mu \approx 2.49$ and $\sigma \approx 1.42$, find the probability that a random sample of 100 households in the United States has a mean size of 2.6 people or more.

Data Distributions

Essential Question: How can data distributions help solve real-world problems?

Key Vocabulary
random variable
(variable aleatoria)
probability distribution
(distribución de probabilidad)
cumulative probability
(probabilidad acumulativa)
sampling distribution
(distribución muestral)
standard error of the mean
(error típico de la media)

KEY EXAMPLE (Lesson 23.1)

A spinner has four equal sections that are labeled 1, 2, 3, and 4. A number cube has six sides labeled 1, 2, 3, 4, 5, and 6. You spin the spinner and roll the number cube, then find the sum of the two numbers. Let x be a random variable that represents the sum of the two numbers. Make a histogram of the probability distribution of x.

First, complete the table. Then, make a histogram of the probability distribution.

Sum	2	3	4	5	6	7	8	9	10
Frequency	1	2	3	4	4	4	3	2	1
Probability	$\frac{1}{24}$	$\frac{2}{24}$	$\frac{3}{24}$	$\frac{4}{24}$	$\frac{4}{24}$	$\frac{4}{24}$	$\frac{3}{24}$	$\frac{2}{24}$	$\frac{1}{24}$

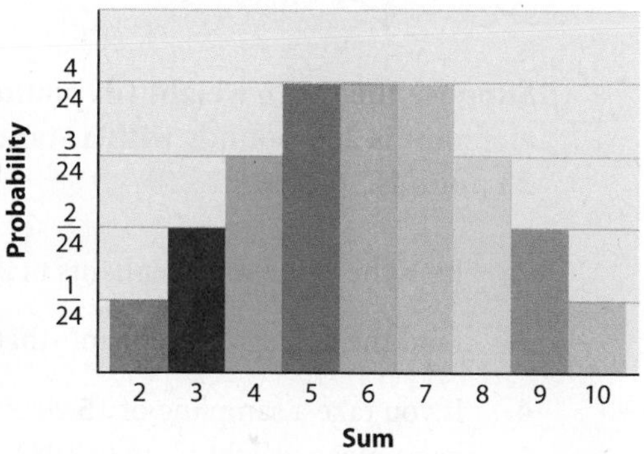

KEY EXAMPLE (Lesson 23.2)

Suppose the heights (in feet) of oak trees in the United States are normally distributed with a mean of 68.5 feet and a standard deviation of 12 feet. Find the percent of trees that are no more than 72 feet tall.

$z_{72} = \frac{72 - \mu}{\sigma} = \frac{72 - 68.5}{12} \approx 0.3$ Convert 72 to a z-score

$P(z \leq z_{72}) = 0.6179$ Read from standard normal table.

62% Write decimal as percent.

KEY EXAMPLE (Lesson 23.2)

Suppose the average birth weight of a full-term newborn is approximately 7.5 pounds with a standard deviation of 2 pounds. You choose a random sample at the hospital of 20 newborn weights. What is the probability that your sample has a mean weight of up to 7.75 pounds?

$\mu = 7.5, \sigma = 2, n = 20$ Write the given information.

$\mu_x = \mu = 7.5, \sigma_{\bar{x}} = \frac{\sigma}{\sqrt{20}} = \frac{2}{\sqrt{20}} \approx 0.447$ Find the mean of the sampling distribution and the standard error.

$z_{7.25} = \frac{7.75 - 7.5}{0.447} \approx 0.6$ Convert 7.75 to a z-score.

$P(z \leq z_{7.25}) = 0.7257 = 73\%$ Use the standard normal table.

EXERCISES

Create a frequency table, then create the histogram of the probability distribution.

1. **A spinner has five equal sections labeled 1, 2, 3, 4, and 5. You spin the spinner twice, then find the sum of the two numbers.** *(Lesson 23.1)*

Sum									
Frequency									
Probability									

Suppose the mean weight (in pounds) of a newborn elephant is 200 pounds with a standard deviation of 23 pounds. *(Lesson 23.2)*

2. Find the percent of elephants that are no more than 212 pounds.
3. Find the percent of elephants that are no more than 205 pounds.
4. If you take a sampling of 15 elephants, what is the probability that your sample has a mean weight of up to 198?

MODULE PERFORMANCE TASK

BMI and Obesity

You can calculate your BMI (body mass index) by dividing your weight in kilograms by the square of your height in meters. A person with a BMI from 18.5 to 24.9 is considered to have a healthy weight. An overweight adult has a BMI from 25.0 to 29.9. An obese person has a BMI greater than 29.9.

The BMI of 18-year-old males is approximately normally distributed with a mean of 24.2 and a standard deviation of 5.1. What percent of 18-year-old males are overweight? What percentage are obese?

Start by listing information you will need to solve the problem. Then use graphs, numbers, tables, words, or algebra to explain how you reached your conclusion.

Ready to Go On?

23.1–23.3 Data Distributions

Personal Math Trainer
- Online Homework
- Hints and Help
- Extra Practice

At a local company, the ages of all new employees hired during the last 10 years are normally distributed. The mean age is 35 years old, with a standard deviation of 10 years.

1. Find the percent of new employees that are no more than 27 years old.

2. Find the percent of new employees that are no more than 39 years old.

3. Find the percent of new employees that are at least 27 years old.

4. If you were to take a sampling of 10 employees, what is the probability that the mean age of the sample will be at least 32?

5. If you were to take a sampling of 10 employees, what is the probability that the mean age of the sample will be at least 38?

ESSENTIAL QUESTION

6. How could data distributions help a doctor do his or her job? Give an example.

MODULE 23
MIXED REVIEW

Assessment Readiness

1. Consider the histogram. Tell whether each statement is correct.

A. There are 16 data values.

B. Data is spread among 5 sums.

C. Each sum is equally likely.

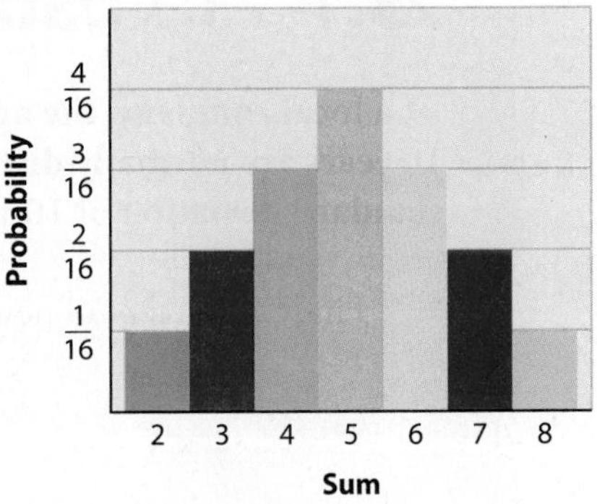

2. Consider the shape of a histogram with a normal distribution. Determine if each statement is True or False.

A. A histogram with normal distribution increases, but never decreases.

B. A histogram with normal distribution makes a bell curve. The bell could be wide or tall.

C. A histogram with normal distribution has the same shape as a line plot with normal distribution.

3. A local zoo plans to add a new animal display according to the desires of the community members who spend the most time at the zoo. They are considering the following survey methods:

- Put a survey up on their website and solicit responses from those visiting the site.
- Survey every 12th customer buying a ticket for the zoo.
- Survey every annual zoo pass purchaser.

Which sampling method would most likely result in a theme that would please those who spend the most time at the zoo? Explain.

4. Suppose the average time a student spends on homework at a certain school is 3.75 hours a night, with a standard deviation of 1.5 hours. You choose a random sample of 20 students. What is the probability that your sample has a mean time of up to 4.25 hours? Explain.

Making Inferences from Data

MODULE 24

Essential Question: How can making inferences from data help to solve real-world problems?

LESSON 24.1
Confidence Intervals and Margins of Error

LESSON 24.2
Surveys, Experiments, and Observational Studies

LESSON 24.3
Determining the Significance of Experimental Results

REAL WORLD VIDEO
Competitive athletes train hard and are always looking for training techniques that might give them an advantage over their competitors. How can we use data to make judgments about the effectiveness of various training strategies?

MODULE PERFORMANCE TASK PREVIEW

Sports Nutrition

The greatest sports players have to be in their best health in order to play at a high level. They exercise regularly and avoid unhealthy habits. Coaches tell them what to eat and what not to eat to play a good game. But really, how necessary is good nutrition for great athletic performance? By the end of this module, you'll have the means to answer this question.

Are YOU Ready?

Complete these exercises to review skills you will need for this module.

Personal Math Trainer

- Online Homework
- Hints and Help
- Extra Practice

Trend Lines and Predictions

Example 1 A pet store asked loyal customers the weight of their dog and monthly budgeted expenses for owning it. The scatter plot shows the results of this survey with a line of best fit. Approximate the monthly cost of a dog weighing 40 pounds.

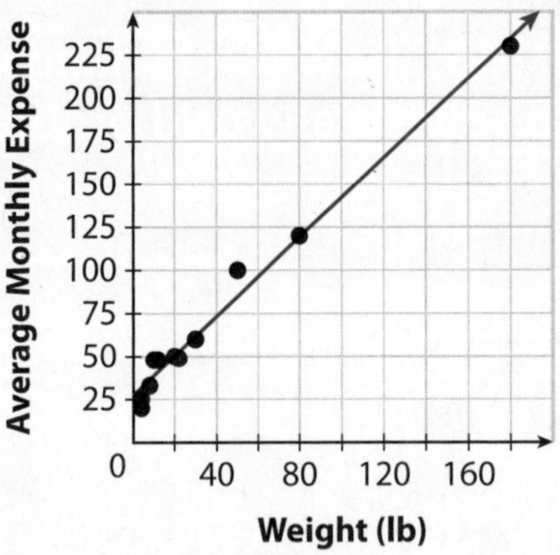

According to the graph, when $x = 40$ lbs, the expected monthly cost is about \$75.

Find the expected monthly cost of owning a dog at the given weight.

1. 60 lb

2. 100 lb

3. 150 lb

Making Inferences From a Random Sample

Example 2 A product quality engineer takes a random sample of 200 widgets and finds that 15 of them are defective. At this factory, the rule is if the defect rate is greater than 8.5%, the assembly line needs to be shut down for retooling. Should the engineer shut down the assembly line?

No. In the sample, only $\frac{15}{200} = 7.5\%$ of the widgets were defective.

For each sample size and number of defective widgets, should the engineer close down the assembly line or not? Explain.

4. Sample size = 5; defective widgets = 1

5. Sample size = 150; defective widgets = 27

24.1 Confidence Intervals and Margins of Error

Essential Question: How do you calculate a confidence interval and a margin of error for a population proportion or population mean?

Resource Locker

Explore Identifying Likely Population Proportions

In a previous lesson, you took samples from a population whose parameter of interest is known in order to see how well a sample statistic estimated that parameter. In this lesson, you will estimate a population parameter using a statistic obtained from a random sample, and you will quantify the accuracy of that estimate.

Suppose you survey a random sample of 50 students at your high school and find that 40% of those surveyed attended the football game last Saturday. Although you cannot survey the entire population of students, you would still like to know what population proportions are reasonably likely in this situation.

(A) Suppose the proportion p of the population that attended last Saturday's game is 30%. Find the reasonably likely values of the sample proportion $\hat{p}$.

In this case, $p =$? and $n =$? .

$\mu_{\hat{p}} = p =$? and $\sigma_{\hat{p}} = \sqrt{\frac{p(1-p)}{n}} = \sqrt{\frac{?(1-?)}{?}} \approx$?

(B) The reasonably likely values of $\hat{p}$ fall within 2 standard deviations of $\mu_{\hat{p}}$.

$\mu_{\hat{p}} - 2\sigma_{\hat{p}} =$? $- 2($? $) =$?

$\mu_{\hat{p}} + 2\sigma_{\hat{p}} =$? $+ 2($? $) =$?

Ⓒ Draw the graph on grid paper, then draw a horizontal line segment at the level of 0.3 on the vertical axis to represent the interval of likely values of $\hat{p}$ you found in Step B.

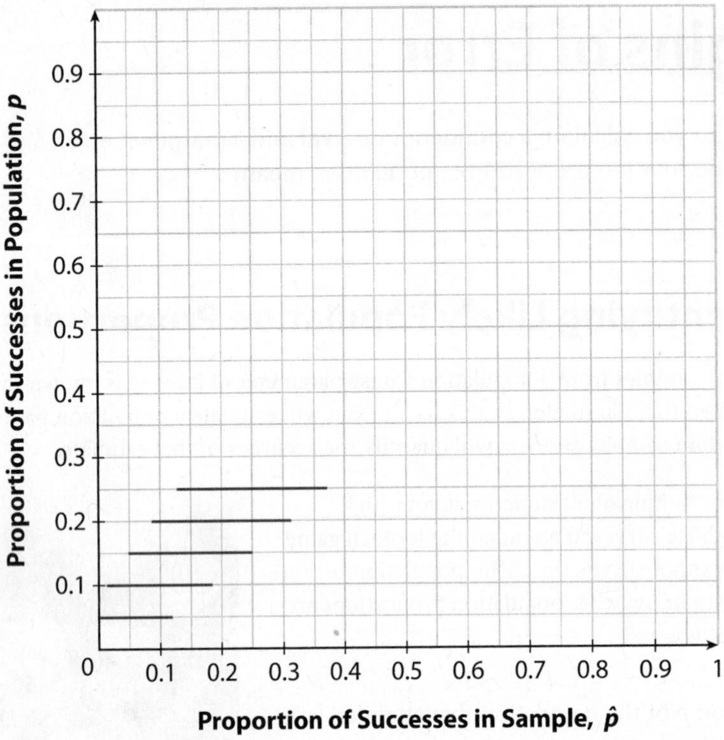

Ⓓ Now repeat the process for $p = 0.35, 0.4, 0.45$, and so on to complete the graph in Step C. You may wish to divide up the work with other students and pool your findings.

Ⓔ Draw a vertical line at 0.4 on the horizontal axis. This represents $\hat{p} = 0.4$. The line segments that this vertical line intersects are the population proportions for which a sample proportion of 0.4 is reasonably likely.

Reflect

1. **Discussion** Is it possible that 30% of all students at your school attended last Saturday's football game? Is it likely? Explain.
2. **Discussion** Is it possible that 60% of all students at your school attended last Saturday's football game? Is it likely? Explain.
3. **Discussion** Based on your graph, which population proportions do you think are reasonably likely? Why?

Explain 1 Finding a Confidence Interval for a Population Proportion

A **confidence interval** is an approximate range of values that is likely to include an unknown population parameter. The *level* of a confidence interval, such as 95%, gives the probability that the interval includes the true value of the parameter.

Recall that when data are normally distributed, 95% of the values fall within 2 standard deviations of the mean. Using this idea in the Explore, you found a 95% confidence interval for the proportion of all students who attended the football game last Saturday.

The graph that you completed in the Explore is shown. You can see from the graph that when the horizontal line segment at $p = 0.4$ is rotated 90° about the point $(0.4, 0.4)$, it becomes a vertical line segment that captures all of the likely population proportions. Since you already know the interval on the horizontal axis that defines the horizontal segment, you can find the interval on the vertical axis that defines the vertical segment by using the fact that $\mu_{\hat{p}} = p$ and interchanging the variables $\hat{p}$ on the horizontal axis) and p (on the vertical axis). So, the horizontal axis interval $\mu_{\hat{p}} - 2\sigma_{\hat{p}} \leq \hat{p} \leq \mu_{\hat{p}} + 2\sigma_{\hat{p}}$ becomes the vertical axis interval as follows:

Replace $\mu_{\hat{p}}$ with p.	$p - 2\sigma_{\hat{p}} \leq \hat{p} \leq p + 2\sigma_{\hat{p}}$
Interchange $\hat{p}$ and p.	$\hat{p} - 2\sigma_{\hat{p}} \leq p \leq \hat{p} + 2\sigma_{\hat{p}}$

In this case, the vertical axis interval is the 95% confidence interval for p. This result can be generalized to a c% confidence interval for p.

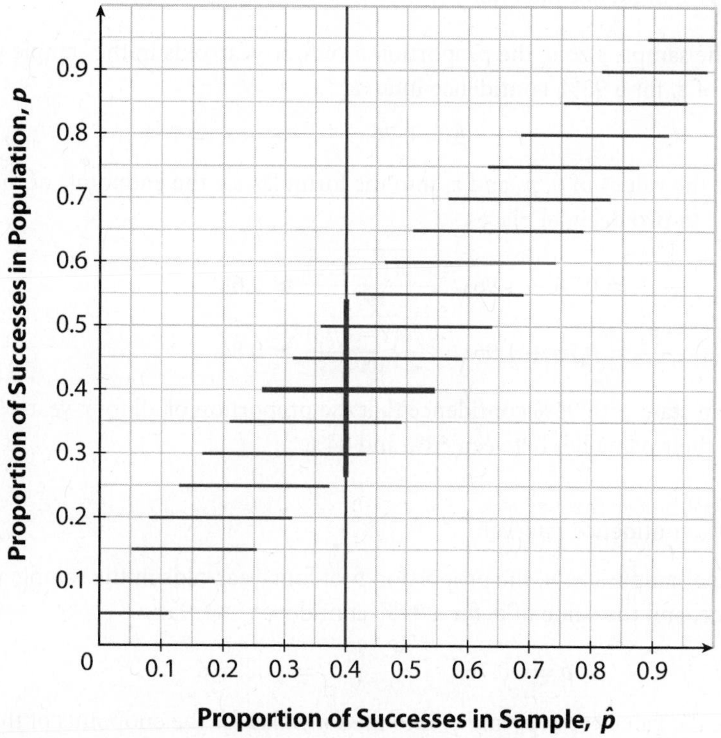

A Confidence Interval for a Population Proportion

A c% confidence interval for the proportion p of successes in a population is given by $\hat{p} - z_c\sqrt{\frac{\hat{p}(1-\hat{p})}{n}} \leq p \leq \hat{p} + z_c\sqrt{\frac{\hat{p}(1-\hat{p})}{n}}$, where $\hat{p}$ is the sample proportion, n is the sample size, and z_c depends upon the desired degree of confidence.

In order for this interval to describe the value of p reasonably accurately, three conditions must be met:

1. There are only two possible outcomes associated with the parameter of interest. The population proportion for one outcome is p, and the proportion for the other outcome is $1 - p$.
2. $n\hat{p}$ and $n(1 - \hat{p})$ must both be at least 10.
3. The size of the population must be at least 10 times the size of the sample, and the sample must be random.

Use the values in the table for z_c. Note that you should use 1.96 rather than 2 for $z_{95\%}$ for greater accuracy.

Desired degree of confidence	90%	95%	99%
Value of z_c	1.645	1.96	2.576

Example 1 **In a random sample of 100 four-year-old children in the United States, 76 were able to write their name. Find the specified confidence interval for the proportion p of four-year-olds in the United States who can write their name.**

(A) Find a 95% confidence interval.

Identify the sample size n, the proportion $\hat{p}$ of four-year-olds in the sample who can write their name, and the value of z_c for a 95% confidence interval.

$n = 100$ $\hat{p} = 0.76$ $z_c = 1.96$

Substitute the values of n, $\hat{p}$, and z_c into the formulas for the endpoints of the confidence interval. Simplify and round to two decimal places.

$$\hat{p} - z_c\sqrt{\frac{\hat{p}(1-\hat{p})}{n}} = 0.76 - 1.96\sqrt{\frac{0.76(1-0.76)}{100}} \approx 0.68$$

$$\hat{p} + z_c\sqrt{\frac{\hat{p}(1-\hat{p})}{n}} = 0.76 + 1.96\sqrt{\frac{0.76(1-0.76)}{100}} \approx 0.84$$

So, you can state with 95% confidence that the proportion of all four-year-olds in the United States who can write their name lies between 68% and 84%.

(B) Find a 99% confidence interval.

Identify the sample size n, the proportion $\hat{p}$ of four-year-olds in the sample who can write their name, and the value of z_c for a 99% confidence interval.

$n = $ 100 $\hat{p} = $ 0.76 $z_c = $ 2.576

Substitute the values of n, $\hat{p}$, and z_c into the formulas for the endpoints of the confidence interval. Simplify and round to two decimal places.

$$\hat{p} - z_c\sqrt{\frac{\hat{p}(1-\hat{p})}{n}} = 0.76 - 2.576\sqrt{\frac{0.76\left(1-0.76\right)}{100}} \approx 0.65$$

$$\hat{p} + z_c\sqrt{\frac{\hat{p}(1-\hat{p})}{n}} = 0.76 + 2.576\sqrt{\frac{0.76\left(1-0.76\right)}{100}} \approx 0.87$$

So, you can state with 99% confidence that the proportion of all four-year-olds in the United States who can write their name lies between 65% and 87%.

Reflect

4. **Discussion** Do the data from the sample of four-year-old children satisfy the three conditions for using the confidence interval formula? Explain.

5. **Discussion** Does increasing the value of c increase or decrease the range of values for a confidence interval of a population proportion? Explain why it happens mathematically and why it makes sense.

Your Turn

6. Isabelle surveys a random sample of 80 voters in her large town and finds that 46 support raising property taxes in order to build a new library. Find a 95% confidence interval for the proportion p of all voters in Isabelle's town who support raising property taxes in order to build a new library.

Explain 2 Finding a Confidence Interval for a Population Mean

You can use reasoning similar to the argument in the Explore to develop a formula for a confidence interval for a population mean.

A Confidence Interval for a Population Mean

A $c\%$ confidence interval for the mean μ in a normally distributed population is given by $\bar{x} - z_c\frac{\sigma}{\sqrt{n}} \leq \mu \leq \bar{x} + z_c\frac{\sigma}{\sqrt{n}}$, where $\bar{x}$ is the sample mean, n is the sample size, σ is the population standard deviation, and z_c depends upon the desired degree of confidence.

Note that it is assumed that the population is normally distributed and that you know the population standard deviation σ. In a more advanced statistics course, you can develop a confidence interval that does not depend upon a normally distributed population or knowing the population standard deviation.

Example 2 **For the given situation, find the specified confidence interval for the population mean.**

(A) In a random sample of 20 students at a large high school, the mean score on a standardized test is 610. Given that the standard deviation of all scores at the school is 120, find a 99% confidence interval for the mean score among all students at the school.

Identify the sample size n, the sample mean $\bar{x}$, the population standard deviation σ, and the value of z_c for a 99% confidence interval.

$n = 20$ $\bar{x} = 610$ $\sigma = 120$ $z_c = 2.576$

Substitute the values of n, $\bar{x}$, σ, and z_c into the formulas for the endpoints of the confidence interval. Simplify and round to the nearest whole number.

$\bar{x} - z_c\frac{\sigma}{\sqrt{n}} = 610 - 2.576 \cdot \frac{120}{\sqrt{20}} \approx 541$ $\bar{x} + z_c\frac{\sigma}{\sqrt{n}} = 610 + 2.576 \cdot \frac{120}{\sqrt{20}} \approx 679$

So, you can state with 99% confidence that the mean score among all students lies between 541 and 679.

(B) In a random sample of 30 students at a large high school, the mean score on a standardized test is 1514. Given that the standard deviation of all scores at the school is 141, find a 95% confidence interval for the mean score among all students at the school.

Identify the sample size n, the sample mean $\bar{x}$, the population standard deviation σ, and the value of z_c for a 95% confidence interval.

$n =$ 30 $\bar{x} =$ 1514 $\sigma =$ 141 $z_c =$ 1.96

Substitute the values of n, $\bar{x}$, σ, and z_c into the formulas for the endpoints of the confidence interval. Simplify and round to the nearest whole number.

$$\bar{x} - z_c \frac{\sigma}{\sqrt{n}} = 1514 - 1.96 \cdot \frac{141}{\sqrt{30}} \approx 1464$$

$$\bar{x} + z_c \frac{\sigma}{\sqrt{n}} = 1514 + 1.96 \cdot \frac{141}{\sqrt{30}} \approx 1564$$

So, you can state with 95% confidence that the mean score among all students at the school lies between 1464 and 1564.

Reflect

7. What must you assume about the test scores of all students to use the formula for the confidence interval?

Your Turn

8. In a random sample of 42 employees in a large company, the mean weekly number of minutes spent exercising is 86. Given that the standard deviation of all employees is 22.4, find a 99% confidence interval for the mean weekly number of minutes spent exercising among all employees in the company.

Explain 3 Choosing a Sample Size

In Part B of Example 2, you found the 95% confidence interval $1464 \le \bar{x} \le 1564$, which is a range of values centered at $\bar{x} = 1514$. You can write the confidence interval as 1514 ± 50, where 50 is called the *margin of error*. The **margin of error** is half the length of a confidence interval.

Margin of Error for a Population Proportion

The margin of error E for the proportion of successes in a population with sample proportion $\hat{p}$ and sample size n is given by $E = z_c \sqrt{\frac{\hat{p}(1-\hat{p})}{n}}$, where z_c depends on the degree of the confidence interval.

Margin of Error for a Population Mean

The margin of error E for the mean in a normally distributed population with standard deviation σ, sample mean $\bar{x}$, and sample size n is given by $E = z_c \frac{\sigma}{\sqrt{n}}$, where z_c depends on the degree of the confidence interval.

From the formulas you can see that the margin of error decreases as the sample size n increases. This suggests using a sample that is as large as possible. However, it is often more practical to determine a margin of error that is acceptable and then calculate the required sample size.

Example 3 **Find the appropriate sample size for the given situation.**

(A) A researcher wants to know the percent of teenagers in the United States who have social networking profiles. She is aiming for a 90% confidence interval and a margin of error of 4%. What sample size n should she use?

Step 1 Rewrite the margin-of-error formula for a population proportion by solving for n.

$E = z_c\sqrt{\frac{\hat{p}(1-\hat{p})}{n}}$ Write the formula.

$E^2 = z_c^2 \cdot \frac{\hat{p}(1-\hat{p})}{n}$ Square both sides.

$nE^2 = z_c^2 \cdot \hat{p}(1-\hat{p})$ Multiply both sides by n.

$n = z_c^2 \cdot \frac{\hat{p}(1-\hat{p})}{E^2}$ Divide both sides by E^2.

Step 2 Estimate the value of $\hat{p}$.

The researcher has not conducted the survey and is trying to find $\hat{p}$. So, she must estimate $\hat{p}$ as 0.5, which is the value of $\hat{p}$ that makes the expression $\hat{p}(1-\hat{p})$ as large as possible.

Step 3 Identify the values of E and z_c.

E is the margin of error written as a decimal and z_c is the z-score that corresponds to a 90% confidence interval. So, $E = 0.04$ and $z_c = 1.645$.

Step 4 Substitute the values of $\hat{p}$, E, and z_c in the rewritten margin-of-error formula from Step 1.

$$n = z_c^2 \cdot \frac{\hat{p}(1-\hat{p})}{E^2} = \frac{(1.645)^2 \cdot 0.5\,(1-0.5)}{(0.04)^2} \approx 423$$

So, the researcher should survey a random sample of 423 teenagers.

(B) Caleb is a restaurant manager and wants to know the mean number of seconds it takes to complete a customer's order. He is aiming for a 95% confidence interval and a margin of error of 6 seconds. Based on past experience, Caleb estimates the population standard deviation to be 21 seconds. What sample size n should he use?

Step 1 Rewrite the margin-of-error formula for a population mean by solving for n.

$E = z_c\frac{\sigma}{\sqrt{n}}$ Write the formula.

$E^2 = z_c^2 \cdot \frac{\sigma^2}{n}$ Square both sides.

$nE^2 = z_c^2 \cdot \sigma^2$ Multiply both sides by n.

$n = \frac{z_c^2 \cdot \sigma^2}{E^2}$ Divide both sides by E^2.

Step 2 Identify the values of E, σ, and z_c.

E is the margin of error, σ is the population standard deviation, and z_c is the z–score that corresponds to a 95% confidence interval. So, $E = 6$, $\sigma = 21$ and $z_c = 1.96$.

Step 3 Substitute the values of E, σ, and z_c in the margin of error for a population mean formula that was solved for n.

$$n = \frac{\left(1.96\right)^2\left(21\right)^2}{\left(6\right)^2} \approx 47$$

So, Caleb should survey a random sample of 47 orders.

Reflect

9. Discussion In Part A, do you expect the sample size to increase or decrease if the researcher decides she wants a smaller margin of error? Explain using the margin-of-error formula for a population proportion.

10. Discussion In Part B, do you expect the sample size to increase or decrease if Caleb decides he wants a 99% confidence interval instead of a 95% confidence interval? Explain using the margin-of-error formula for a population mean.

Your Turn

11. Zoe is an editor of a newspaper in a state capital and wants to know the percent of residents in her state who are in favor of banning the use of handheld cell phones while driving, a bill that is being considered in the state legislature. After researching similar polls conducted in other states, she estimates that $\hat{p} = 0.35$. She is aiming for a 95% confidence interval and a margin of error of 5%. What sample size n should Zoe use?

Elaborate

12. How can an interval that captures 95% of the sample proportions in a sampling distribution be used to find a 95% confidence interval for a population proportion?

13. Describe how increasing the sample size affects the confidence interval of a population mean.

14. Essential Question Check-in What is the relationship between a confidence interval and a margin of error for a population proportion or population mean?

Evaluate: Homework and Practice

- Online Homework
- Hints and Help
- Extra Practice

Identify the values of the sample proportion $\hat{p}$ that fall within 2 standard deviations of the given population proportion p for each situation.

1. Suppose that 44% of all employees at a large company attended a recent company function. Alannah plans to survey a random sample of 32 employees to estimate the population proportion. What are the values of $\hat{p}$ that she is likely to obtain?

2. Suppose the proportion p of a school's students who oppose a change to the school's dress code is 73%. Nicole surveys a random sample of 56 students to find the percent of students who oppose the change. What are the values of $\hat{p}$ that she is likely to obtain?

For the given situation, find the specified confidence interval for the population proportion.

3. Hunter surveys a random sample of 64 students at his community college and finds that 37.5% of the students saw a film at the local movie theater in the last 30 days. Find a 90% confidence interval for the proportion p of all students at the community college who saw a film at the movie theater in the last 30 days.

4. In a random sample of 300 U.S. households, 111 households have a pet dog. Find a 99% confidence interval for the proportion p of all U.S. households that have a pet dog.

5. A quality control team at a company that manufactures digital utility meters randomly selects 320 meters and finds 12 to be defective. Find a 95% confidence interval for the proportion p of all digital utility meters that the company manufactures and are defective.

6. In a random sample of 495 four-year-olds in a state, 54.7% can provide the first and last name of at least one parent or guardian. Find a 99% confidence interval for the proportion p of all four-year-olds in the state who can provide the first and last name of at least one parent or guardian.

For the given situation, find the specified confidence interval for the population mean.

7. An online website that tracks gas prices surveys a random sample of 73 gas stations in a state and finds that the mean price of 1 gallon of regular gasoline is \$3.576. If the website estimates from past surveys that the population standard deviation is \$0.117, find a 95% confidence interval for the mean price of regular gasoline in the state.

8. Caiden manages the security team at a large airport and surveys a random sample of 149 travelers. He finds that the mean amount of time that it takes passengers to clear security is 28.3 minutes. From past experience, Caiden estimates that the population standard deviation is 6.4 minutes. Find a 90% confidence interval for the mean amount of time that it takes passengers to clear security.

9. A quality control team at a company that manufactures smartphones measures the battery life of 24 randomly selected smartphones and finds that the mean amount of continuous video playback from a full charge is 12.70 hours. Given that the population standard deviation is 0.83 hour, find a 99% confidence interval for the mean amount of continuous video playback from a full charge.

10. Stephen surveys 53 randomly selected students at his large high school and finds that the mean amount of time spent on homework per night is 107.9 minutes. Given that the population standard deviation is 22.7 minutes, find a 90% confidence interval for the mean amount of time students at the school spend on homework per night.

Find the appropriate sample size for the given situation.

11. Executives at a health insurance company want to know the percent of residents in a state who have health insurance. Based on data from other states, they estimate that $\hat{p} = 0.8$. They are aiming for a 99% confidence interval and a margin of error of 1.5%. What sample size n should they use?

12. Tyler is a manager at a utility company and wants to know the mean amount of electricity that residential customers consume per month. He is aiming for a 90% confidence interval and a margin of error of 10 kilowatt-hours (kWh). From past experience, Tyler estimates that the population standard deviation is 91.1 kWh. What sample size n should he use?

13. Teneka is a restaurant owner and wants to know the mean amount of revenue per day. She is aiming for a 95% confidence interval and a margin of error of \$200. Given that the population standard deviation is \$870, what sample size should Teneka use?

14. **Biology** Miranda is a biologist who is measuring the lengths of randomly selected frogs of the same species from two locations.

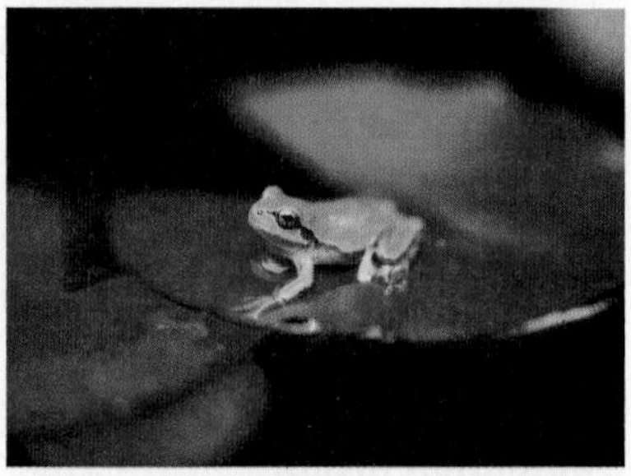

a. Miranda measures the lengths of 25 frogs from location A and finds that the mean length is 7.35 cm. Given that the population standard deviation is 0.71 cm, find a 95% confidence interval for the mean length of frogs from location A.

b. Miranda measures the lengths of 20 frogs from location B and finds that the mean length is 7.17 cm. Given that the population standard deviation is 0.69 cm, find a 95% confidence interval for the mean length of frogs from location B.

c. Is it clear that the mean length of frogs from one location is greater than the mean length of frogs from the other location? Explain your reasoning.

15. Which of the following sets of desired margin of error E, desired confidence level c, and given sample proportion $\hat{p}$ or population standard deviation σ require a sample size of at least 100? Select all that apply.

A. $E = 0.1$, $c = 95\%$, $\hat{p} = 0.5$

B. $E = 1000$, $c = 99\%$, $\sigma = 4000$

C. $E = 0.04$, $c = 90\%$, $\hat{p} = 0.9$

D. $E = 4$, $c = 95\%$, $\sigma = 18.6$

E. $E = 0.06$, $c = 99\%$, $\hat{p} = 0.3$

F. $E = 50$, $c = 90\%$, $\sigma = 309$

H.O.T. Focus on Higher Order Thinking

16. Multiple Representations The margin of error E for the proportion of successes in a population may be estimated by $\frac{1}{\sqrt{n}}$, where n is the sample size. Explain where this estimate comes from. Assume a 95% confidence interval.

17. Draw Conclusions In the Explore, you wrote an interval of the form $\mu_{\hat{p}} - 2\sigma_{\hat{p}} < \hat{p} < \mu_{\hat{p}} + 2\sigma_{\hat{p}}$ that captures 95% of the sample proportions. You know that $\mu_{\hat{p}} = p$, so you can rewrite the interval as $p - 2\sigma_{\hat{p}} < \hat{p} < p + 2\sigma_{\hat{p}}$. Solve this compound inequality for p. What does this result tell you?

18. Explain the Error A quality assurance team for an LED bulb manufacturer tested 400 randomly selected LED bulbs and found that 6 are defective. A member of the team performed the following calculations to obtain a 95% confidence interval for the proportion p of LED bulbs that are defective. Explain the error.

$n = 400 \qquad \hat{p} = \frac{6}{400} = 0.015 \qquad z_c = 1.96$

$$\hat{p} - z_c\sqrt{\frac{\hat{p}(1-\hat{p})}{n}} = 0.015 - 1.96\sqrt{\frac{0.015(1-0.015)}{400}} \approx 0.003$$

$$\hat{p} + z_c\sqrt{\frac{\hat{p}(1-\hat{p})}{n}} = 0.015 + 1.96\sqrt{\frac{0.015(1-0.015)}{400}} \approx 0.027$$

With 95% confidence, the proportion of LED bulbs that are defective lies between 0.3% and 2.7%.

Lesson Performance Task

Between 2010 and 2011, a research group conducted a survey of young working women and men, ages 18 to 34. Of the 610 women surveyed, 66% indicated that being successful in a high-paying career is either "one of the most important things" or "very important" in their lives. Of the 703 men surveyed, only 59% replied that they attach such importance to career.

a. Find a 95% confidence interval for each sample proportion.

b. Find the margin of error for each result at the 95% confidence level.

c. Is it possible that the population proportions could actually be equal? Explain.

24.2 Surveys, Experiments, and Observational Studies

Resource Locker

Essential Question: What kinds of statistical research are there, and which ones can establish cause-and-effect relationships between variables?

Explore Recognizing Different Forms of Statistical Research

Statistical research takes various forms depending on whether the purpose of the research is to measure a variable in a population, to see if there is evidence of an association between two variables, or to determine whether one variable actually influences another variable.

Suppose a graduate school researcher is considering three studies related to math and music. One study involves asking a random sample of high school students in a large school district whether they listen to music while doing math homework. A second study involves asking a random sample of students at a large university whether they are majoring in math and whether they also play a musical instrument or sing. A third study involves a group of adult participants where half will be randomly assigned either to listen to classical music for 15 minutes before taking a logical reasoning test or to listen to white noise for 15 minutes before taking the same test.

(A) Which study appears to look for an association between two variables without actively manipulating either one? What are those variables?

(B) Which study appears to be looking for evidence that one variable actually influences another variable? What are those variables, and which one is manipulated to see if it influences the other?

(C) Which study appears to be simply measuring a variable in a population? What is that variable?

Reflect

1. Discussion Describe the type of result or conclusion the researcher might obtain from each study.

Explain 1 Detecting Errors in Surveys

A **survey** measures characteristics of interest about a population using a sample selected from the population. As you saw in a previous lesson, a sample needs to be representative of the population in order for the measurements obtained from the sample to be accurate. Random sampling is generally the best way to ensure representation.

Even when random sampling is used, a survey's results can have errors. Some of the sources of errors are:

- *Biased questions:* The wording of questions in a survey can influence the way people respond to questions. Survey questions need to be worded in a neutral, unbiased way.
- *Interviewer effect:* If an interviewer asks the questions in a survey, the person being interviewed may give inaccurate responses to avoid being embarrassed.
- *Nonresponse:* Some people may be difficult to contact, or they may simply refuse to participate once contacted. If nonresponse rates are higher for certain subgroups of a population, then those subgroups will be underrepresented in the survey results.

Example 1 **Explain why the results of each survey are likely to be inaccurate, and then suggest a way to improve the accuracy of the survey.**

(A) The owner of a business, conducts interviews with a random sample of employees to have them rate how satisfied they are with their jobs.

Since the interviewer is the owner of the business, the employees may not be completely open about any job dissatisfaction they may have. The employees may feel that their job security is at stake. A better survey would involve a neutral interviewer or allow the employees to respond anonymously.

(B) In a random sample of town residents, a survey asks, "Are you in favor of a special tax levy to renovate the dilapidated town hall?"

The question is biased because the word "dilapidated" suggests that the town hall is in a state of disrepair, which makes it seem that a renovation is urgently needed.

A better survey would begin with a factual list of repairs that need to be made and then ask, "Are you in favor of a special tax levy to make these repairs?"

Reflect

2. Even if the survey question in Part B is revised to avoid being biased, do the people surveyed have enough information to give an informed and accurate response? Explain.

Your Turn

Explain why the results of the survey are likely to be inaccurate, and then suggest a way to improve the accuracy of the survey.

3. A teacher conducts one-on-one interviews with a random sample of her students to get feedback on her teaching methods.

Explain 2 Distinguishing Between Observational Studies and Experiments

In an **observational study**, researchers determine whether an existing condition, called a *factor*, in a population is related to a characteristic of interest. For instance, an observational study might be used to find the incidence of heart disease among those who smoke. In the study, being a smoker is the factor, and having heart disease is the characteristic of interest.

In an **experiment**, researchers create a condition by imposing a treatment on some of the subjects of the experiment. For instance, an experiment might be conducted by having some people with eczema take a vitamin E pill daily, and then observing whether their symptoms improve. In the experiment, taking the vitamin E pill is the treatment, and improvement of symptoms is the characteristic of interest.

Generally, an experiment is preferred over an observational study because an experiment allows researchers to manipulate one variable to see its effect on another. However, there may be practical or unethical reasons against performing an experiment. For example, it would be unethical to ask people to smoke in order to study the effects of smoking on their health. Instead, an observational study should be performed using people who already smoke.

Example 2 **Determine whether each research study is an observational study or an experiment. Identify the factor if it is an observational study or the treatment if is an experiment. Also identify the characteristic of interest.**

(A) Researchers measure the cholesterol of 50 subjects who report that they eat fish regularly and 50 subjects who report that they do not eat fish regularly.

This research study is an observational study. The factor is whether people eat fish regularly, and the characteristic of interest is cholesterol level.

(B) Researchers have 100 subjects with high cholesterol take fish oil pills daily for two months. They monitor the cholesterol of the subjects during that time.

This research study is an experiment. The treatment is taking fish oil pills daily.

The characteristic of interest is cholesterol level.

Reflect

4. **Discussion** Suppose the researchers in Part A find that considerably more people who eat fish regularly have normal cholesterol levels than those who do not eat fish regularly. Is it reasonable to conclude that eating fish regularly has an effect on cholesterol? Explain.

Your Turn

Determine whether the research study is an observational study or an experiment. Identify the factor if it is an observational study or the treatment if is an experiment. Also identify the characteristic of interest.

5. Researchers monitor the driving habits of 80 subjects in their twenties and 80 subjects in their fifties for one month by using a GPS device that tracks location and speed.

Explain 3 Identifying Control Groups and Treatment Groups in Experiments

Whether a study is observational or experimental, it should be comparative in order to establish a connection between the factor or treatment and the characteristic of interest. For instance, determining the rate of car accidents among people who talk on cell phones while driving is not instructive unless you compare it with the rate of car accidents among people who don't talk on cell phones while driving and find that it is significantly different.

While a comparative observational study can suggest a relationship between two variables, such as cell phone use while driving and car accidents, it cannot establish a cause-and-effect relationship because there can be *confounding variables* (also called *lurking variables*) that influence the results. For instance, perhaps people who talk on cell phones while driving are more likely to drive aggressively, so it is the aggressive driving (not the cell phone use) that leads to a higher rate of car accidents.

In an experiment, randomization can remove the problem of a confounding variable by distributing the variable among the groups being compared so that its influence on the groups is more or less equal. Therefore, the best way to establish a cause-and-effect relationship between two variables is through a **randomized comparative experiment** where subjects are randomly divided into two groups: the *treatment group*, which is given the treatment, and the *control group*, which is not.

Example 3 **Identify the treatment, characteristic of interest, control group, and treatment group for the given experiment. Assume all subjects of the research are selected randomly.**

(A) To see whether zinc has an effect on the duration of a cold, researchers have half of the subjects take tablets containing zinc at the onset of cold symptoms and the other half take tablets without any zinc. The durations of the colds are then recorded.

The treatment is having subjects take tablets that contain zinc at the onset of cold symptoms.
The characteristic of interest is the duration of the cold.
The control group consists of subjects who took tablets without zinc.
The treatment group consists of subjects who took tablets containing zinc.

(B) To see whether regular moderate exercise has an effect on blood pressure, researchers have half of the subjects set aside 30 minutes daily for walking and the other half not do any walking beyond their normal daily routines. The subjects also take and record their blood pressure at the same time each day.

The treatment is having subjects walk for 30 minutes daily.
The characteristic of interest is blood pressure.
The control group consists of subjects who do not do any walking beyond their normal daily routines.
The treatment group consists of subjects who walked for 30 minutes daily.

Your Turn

6. Identify the treatment, characteristic of interest, control group, and treatment group for the following experiment. Assume all subjects of the research are selected randomly.

To see whether reviewing for a test with a classmate improves scores, researchers ask half of the subjects to study with a classmate and the other half to study alone. The test scores are then recorded.

Explain 4 Evaluating a Media Report of Statistical Research

When you encounter media reports of statistical research in your daily life, you should judge any reported conclusions on the basis of how the research was conducted. Among the questions you should consider are the following:

- Is the research a survey, an observational study, or an experiment? In broad terms, a survey simply measures variables, an observational study attempts to find an association between variables, and an experiment attempts to establish a cause-and-effect relationship between variables.
- Was randomization used in conducting the research? As you know, random sampling is considered the best way to obtain a representative sample from a population and therefore get accurate results. Randomization also helps to dilute the effects of confounding variables.
- Does the report include the details of the research, such as sample size, statistics, and margins of error? The details help you judge how much confidence to have in the results of the research or how much importance to place on the results.

Example 4 **Evaluate the article by answering the following questions.**

- Is this a survey, an observational study, or an experiment? How do you know?
- Was randomization used in the research? If so, how?
- What details of the research does the article include? Is any important information missing?

(A)

Caring Doctors Shorten and Ease the Common Cold

Researchers have found that among patients with colds, those who gave their doctors perfect scores on a questionnaire measuring empathy have colds that did not last as long and were less severe. Empathy on the part of doctors included making patients feel at ease, listening to their concerns, and showing compassion.

A total of 350 subjects who were experiencing the onset of a cold were randomly assigned to one of three groups: no doctor-patient interaction, standard interaction, and enhanced interaction. Only subjects in the third group saw doctors who had been coached on being empathetic.

- Is this a survey, an observational study, or an experiment? How do you know?
  This study is an experiment because treatments were imposed on two groups of patients: those who had a standard interaction with a doctor and those who had an enhanced interaction with a doctor.
- Was randomization used in the research? If so, how?
  Randomization was used by randomly assigning subjects to a control group or one of two treatment groups.
- What details of the research does the article include? Is any important information missing?
  The report includes the number of subjects but no statistics, such as measures of cold duration or severity.

(B)

Fitness in Teen Years May Guard Against Heart Trouble Later

A study of almost 750,000 Swedish men suggests people who are aerobically fit as teenagers are less likely to have a heart attack later in life. Each 15 percent increase in the level of aerobic fitness as a teenager is associated with an 18 percent reduced risk of a heart attack 30 years later. Overall, teens and young adults who participate in regular cardiovascular training have a 35 percent reduced risk of a heart attack later in life.

The researchers analyzed medical data from men drafted into the nation's army, which requires a test of aerobic fitness at the time of induction. National health registers provided information on heart attacks the men had later in life.

- Is this a survey, an observational study, or an experiment? How do you know?
  This study is an observational study because the factor of aerobic fitness as a teenageris being related to the characteristic of interest, which is the risk of having a heart attacklater in life.
- Was randomization used in the research? If so, how?
  Randomization was not used in the research because all of the subjects were male draftees in the Swedish army. The subjects may not be representative of all adults because women were obviously excluded, and they may not be representative all adult males because only Swedish males were studied.
- What details of the research does the article include? Is any important information missing? The report includes the sample size and the following statistics: each 15 percent increase in the level of aerobic fitness as a teenager is associated with an 18 percent reduced risk of a heart attack 30 years later, and teens and young adults who participate in regular cardiovascular training have an overall 35 percent reduced risk of a heart attack later in life (presumably compared with teens and young adults who don't participate in regular cardiovascular training). What is missing is how the researchers defined "level of aerobic fitness" and "regular cardiovascular training" as well as how they calculated their reported statistics.

Reflect

7. **Discussion** What conclusion do you draw from the report in Part A? How much confidence do you have in that conclusion? Why?

Your Turn

8. Evaluate the article by answering the following questions.
   - Is this a survey, an observational study, or an experiment? How do you know?
   - Was randomization used in the research? If so, how?
   - What details of the research does the article include? Is any important information missing?

Study Finds One in Seven Would Fail Kitchen Inspection

Research suggests that at least one in seven home kitchens would flunk a health inspection that is given to restaurants. Only 61 percent of home kitchens would get an A or B if put through a restaurant inspection, compared with 98 percent of Los Angeles County restaurants. At least 14 percent of home kitchens would fail. The results are based on a questionnaire about food safety administered on the Internet and taken by about 13,000.

Elaborate

9. What are some sources of errors in a survey? Why should these errors be avoided?

10. Describe the difference between a factor in an observational study and a treatment in an experiment.

11. Explain what confounding variables are and describe how they are handled in a randomized experiment.

12. **Essential Question Check-in** How do the three kinds of statistical research discussed in this lesson study a characteristic of interest in a population?

Evaluate: Homework and Practice

Personal Math Trainer
- Online Homework
- Hints and Help
- Extra Practice

1. Members of a research team are considering three studies related to sleep and learning. The first study involves comparing the scores on a post-study test of learning from two groups of randomly chosen adults, with one group getting at least 7 hours of sleep per night for a week and the other group getting at most 6 hours of sleep per night for a week. A second study involves asking a random sample of students at a large university to report the average number of hours of sleep they get each night and their college grade point average. A third study involves asking a random sample of high school students in a large school district whether they feel they get enough sleep to stay alert throughout the school day.

a. Which study appears to look for an association between two variables without actively manipulating either one? What are those variables?

b. Which study appears to be looking for evidence that one variable actually influences another variable? What are those variables, and which one is manipulated to see if it influences the other?

c. Which study appears to be simply measuring a variable in a population? What is that variable?

Explain why the results of each survey are likely to be inaccurate and then suggest a way to improve the accuracy of the survey.

2. A store offers its customers a chance to win a cash prize if they call a toll-free number on a receipt and participate in a customer satisfaction survey.

3. A reporter for a local newspaper asks a random sample of people attending a holiday parade, "Since this holiday parade is so popular, do you support having the city provide the support for a larger parade next year?"

Determine whether each research study is an observational study or an experiment. Identify the factor if it is an observational study or the treatment if is an experiment. Also identify the characteristic of interest.

4. Researchers found that of patients who had been taking a bone-loss drug for more than five years, a high percentage of patients also had an uncommon type of fracture in the thigh bone.

5. Researchers found that when patients with chronic illnesses were randomly divided into two groups, the group that got regular coaching by phone from health professionals to help them manage their illnesses had lower monthly medical costs than the group that did not get the coaching.

6. A caretaker at a zoo is studying the effect of a new diet on the health of the zoo's elephants. She continues to feed half of the elephants their existing food, switches the other half to a new diet, and then monitors the health of the elephants.

7. A school district wants to know whether there is a relationship between students' standardized test scores and the amount of time they spend on extracurricular activities. The school board surveys students from each school in the system to gather data about the average number of hours per week spent on extracurricular activities and each student's most recent test scores.

8. Researchers want to know the effect of vitamin C as a dietary supplement on blood pressure. Half of the randomly assigned subjects take one 1000-milligram tablet of vitamin C daily for six months while the other half of the subjects take one placebo tablet daily for six months. The blood pressure of all subjects is taken weekly.

Identify the treatment, characteristic of interest, control group, and treatment group for the given experiment. Assume all subjects of the research are selected randomly.

9. A restaurant manager wants to know whether to keep using orange slices as a garnish or to change to tangerine slices. All of the subjects are blindfolded. Half of the subjects are asked to eat orange slices, and the other half are asked to eat tangerine slices. All subjects are asked whether they like the taste of the fruit.

10. A pharmaceutical company wants to know about the side effects of a new cholesterol medication. Out of 400 randomly selected volunteers who currently take the existing cholesterol medication, the researchers switch the old drug with the new drug for 200 of them, and continue to give the other 200 the old drug. They then monitor the two groups for side effects.

11. A park service wants to determine whether reintroducing a particular species of underwater plant to the lakes in the park system would be beneficial to a particular species of fish living in the lakes. The researchers reintroduce the plant in one lake. One year later, they study the health of the fish population in the lake where the plant was reintroduced, as well as in an ecologically similar lake without the plant.

12. A research team wants to know whether a new formula for a laundry detergent is more effective than the existing formula. The team members first wash a variety of fabrics with a variety of stains using the detergent with the new formula, and then they wash the same pairings of fabrics and stains using the detergent with the existing formula. They then compare the extent to which the stains have been eliminated.

Evaluate each article by answering the following questions.

- Is this a survey, an observational study, or an experiment? How do you know?
- Was randomization used in the research? If so, how?
- What details of the research does the article include? Is any important information missing?

13.

> ## Doctors Work When Sick
>
> Doctors know that they can get sick from their patients, but when they are sick themselves, do they stay away from their patients? Researchers asked 537 doctors-in-training to anonymously report whether they had worked while sick during the past year. The researchers found that 58% said they had worked once while sick and 31% said they had worked more than once while sick.

14.

> ## Antibiotic Use Tied to Asthma and Allergies
>
> Antibiotic use in infants is linked to asthma and allergies, according to a study involving 1401 children. Researchers asked mothers how many doses of antibiotics their children received before 6 months of age as well as whether their children had developed asthma or allergies by age 6. Children who received just one dose of antibiotics were 40% more likely to develop asthma or allergies. The risk jumped to 70% for children who received two doses.

15. Which of the following research topics are best addressed through an observational study? Select all that apply.

A. Does listening to loud music with headphones affect a person's hearing?

B. Does second-hand smoke affect the health of pets?

C. Does a particular medication make seasonal allergy symptoms less severe?

D. Does increasing the number of stoplights per mile on a road decrease the number of car accidents on the road?

E. Does drinking sports drinks before and while playing a game of baseball increase the number of runs scored?

F. Does a certain toothpaste prevent cavities in children better than another toothpaste?

H.O.T. Focus on Higher Order Thinking

16. Draw Conclusions Randomly assigning subjects to the control group or the treatment group for an experiment means that if a difference between the two groups is observed at the conclusion of the experiment, then the difference must be due either to chance or to the treatment. How do you think a researcher can conclude that the difference is due to the treatment?

17. Critique Reasoning Consider the following experiment: Mr. Jones wants to know what the condition of his deck would be if he did not continue to reapply wood sealant to it every spring to protect it. This spring, he uses the sealant on the entire deck except for several adjacent boards. He then observes how exposure to the weather affects those boards in relation to the rest of the deck.

Lindsay claims that the part of the deck to which the sealant is applied constitutes the treatment group because that is the part that is actually "treated." Is she correct? Explain.

18. Persevere in Problem Solving Give an example of a question that could be better answered by gathering data in an observational study than it could by gathering data in an experiment. Explain why an observational study would be more appropriate. Then describe an observational study that would answer the question.

Lesson Performance Task

Using an online search engine, look for a research-based article that interests you about teen health, teen fitness, or teen nutrition using the search terms "teen health articles," "teen fitness articles," or "teen nutrition articles." Print the article to give to your teacher, and include your analysis of the research on which the article is based. Your analysis should address the following points:

- On what type of research study is the article based? How do you know?
- Was randomization used in conducting the research? If so, how?
- What details about the research does the article include? Are there any details that appear to be missing?
- What is your overall evaluation of the research? How much importance do you place on the conclusions drawn from the research? Explain.

24.3 Determining the Significance of Experimental Results

Resource Locker

Essential Question: In an experiment, when is an observed difference between the control group and treatment group likely to be caused by the treatment?

Explore 1 Formulating the Null Hypothesis

You can think of every randomized comparative experiment as a test of a *null hypothesis*. The **null hypothesis** states that any difference between the control group and the treatment group is due to chance. In other words, the null hypothesis is the assumption that the treatment has no effect.

An unusual experimental result may be *statistically significant*. The determination of **statistical significance** is based on the probability of randomly getting a result that is the same as, or more extreme than, the result obtained from the experiment under the assumption that the null hypothesis is true. A low probability of getting the result, or a more extreme result, by chance is evidence in favor of rejecting the null hypothesis.

A statistically significant result does not prove that the treatment has an effect; the null hypothesis may still be true, and a rare event may simply have occurred. Nevertheless, standard practice in statistics is to reject the null hypothesis in favor of the *alternative hypothesis* that the result is, in fact, due to the treatment.

(A) Suppose 10 people with colds are treated with a new formula for an existing brand of cold medicine, and 10 other people with colds are treated with the original formula. The mean recovery times for the two groups are compared.

Is the null hypothesis that the mean recovery times for the two groups will be very different, or that they will be about the same?

(B) Suppose that the mean recovery time for both groups is 5 days. Does the result of the experiment appear to be statistically significant? Explain your reasoning.

(C) Suppose a potential growth agent is sprayed on the leaves of 12 emerging ferns twice a week for a month. Another 12 emerging ferns are not sprayed with the growth agent. The mean stalk lengths of the two groups of ferns are compared after a month.

State the null hypothesis.

(D) Suppose that the treated ferns had a mean stalk length that is twice the mean stalk length of the untreated ferns. Does the result of the experiment appear to be statistically significant? Explain your reasoning.

Reflect

1. **Discussion** In the U.S. legal system, a defendant is assumed innocent until guilt is proved beyond a reasonable doubt. How is what happens with a null hypothesis like what happens with a defendant?

2. Does the experimental result in Step B prove that the new formula is no more effective than the original formula? Explain.

3. Does the experimental result in Step D prove that the growth agent works? Explain.

Explore 2 Simulating a Resampling Distribution

Suppose a company that offers a college entrance exam prep course wants to demonstrate that its course raises test scores. The company recruits 20 students and randomly assigns half of them to a treatment group, where subjects take the course before taking the college entrance exam, and half to a control group, where subjects do not take the course before taking the exam. The table shows the exam scores of the 10 students in each group. How can you tell whether the course actually improved the scores of the students in the treatment group?

	College Entrance Exam Scores				
Treatment group	1440	1610	1430	1700	1690
	1570	1480	1620	1780	2010
Control group	1150	1500	1050	1600	1460
	1860	1350	1750	1680	1330

One thing you could do is compute the mean exam score for each group to see if the means are different. Obviously, the company expects the treatment group's mean to be greater than the control group's mean. But even if that is the case, how do you know that the difference in the means can be attributed to the treatment and not to chance? In other words, how do you know if the difference is statistically significant?

The null hypothesis for this experiment is that the college entrance exam prep course has no effect on a student's score. Under this assumption, it doesn't matter whether a student is in the treatment group or the control group. Since each group is a sample of the students, the means of the two samples should be about equal. In fact, any random division of the 20 students into two groups of 10 should result in two means whose difference is relatively small and a matter of chance. This technique of scrambling the data, called *resampling*, allows you to create a *resampling distribution* of the differences of means for every possible pairing of groups with 10 students in each. You can test the null hypothesis by using the resampling distribution to find the likelihood, given that the null hypothesis is true, of getting a difference of means at least as great as the actual experimental difference. The test is called a **permutation test**, also known as a *randomization test.*

Use the table of exam scores to construct a resampling distribution for the difference of means, assuming that the null hypothesis is true. Then determine the significance of the actual experimental result.

(A) State the null hypothesis in terms of the difference of the two group means.

(B) Calculate the mean score for the treatment group, $\bar{x}_T$, and the mean score for the control group, $\bar{x}_C$. Then find the difference of the means.

(C) Label the data in the table with the identifiers 1 through 20. Then follow these steps to complete each of the following tables.

- Use a graphing calculator's random integer generator to generate a list of 10 identifiers between 1 and 20 with no identifiers repeated.
- Record the scores that correspond to those identifiers as the scores for Group A. Record the remaining 10 scores as the scores for Group B.
- Find $\bar{x}_A$, $\bar{x}_B$, and $\bar{x}_A - \bar{x}_B$, and record them in the table.

	Resampling 1					Means	Difference of means
Group A	?	?	?	?	?	$\bar{x}_A =$?	$\bar{x}_A - \bar{x}_B =$?
	?	?	?	?	?		
Group B	?	?	?	?	?	$\bar{x}_B =$?	
	?	?	?	?	?		

	Resampling 2					Means	Difference of means
Group A	?	?	?	?	?	$\bar{x}_A =$?	$\bar{x}_A - \bar{x}_B =$?
	?	?	?	?	?		
Group B	?	?	?	?	?	$\bar{x}_B =$?	
	?	?	?	?	?		

	Resampling 3					Means	Difference of means
Group A	?	?	?	?	?	$\bar{x}_A =$?	$\bar{x}_A - \bar{x}_B =$?
	?	?	?	?	?		
Group B	?	?	?	?	?	$\bar{x}_B =$?	
	?	?	?	?	?		

(D) Report the differences of means that you found for simulations 1–3 to your teacher so that your teacher can create a frequency table and histogram of the class results. You should make your own copy of the frequency table and histogram using the intervals shown.

Interval	Frequency
$-320 \leq x < -240$	?
$-240 \leq x < -160$	?
$-160 \leq x < -80$	?
$-80 \leq x < 0$	?
$0 \leq x < 80$	?
$80 \leq x < 160$	?
$160 \leq x < 240$	?
$240 \leq x < 320$	?

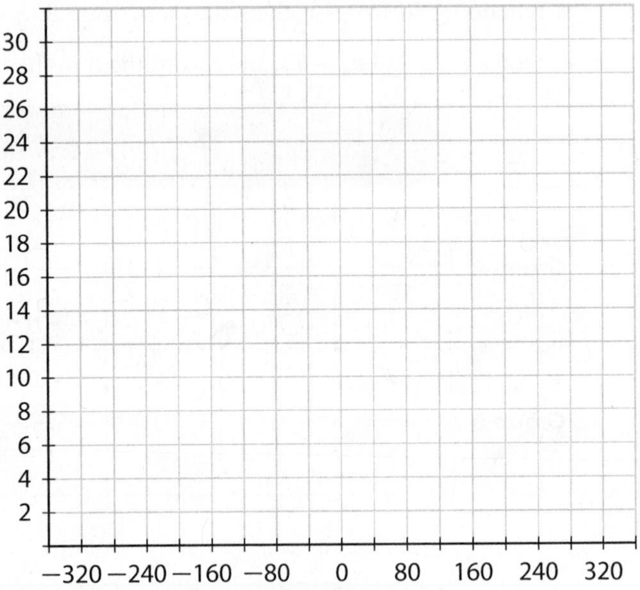

Reflect

4. Discussion Would you say that the resampling distribution provides sufficient evidence to reject the null hypothesis? Explain your reasoning.

Explain 1 Performing a Permutation Test

Once you use the resampling distribution to calculate the probability, called the *P–value*, of randomly getting a result that is the same as, or more extreme than, the result obtained from the experiment under the assumption that the null hypothesis is true, you can determine the significance of the result. Statisticians commonly use the following levels of significance:

- When $P > 0.10$, the result is *not significant*. The null hypothesis is not rejected.
- When $0.05 < P \leq 0.10$, the result is *marginally significant*. You can reject the null hypothesis at the 10% significance level.
- When $0.01 < P \leq 0.05$, the result is *significant*. You can reject the null hypothesis at the 5% significance level.
- When $P \leq 0.01$, the result is *highly significant*. You can reject the null hypothesis at the 1% significance level.

Example 1 **Determine the experimental result's significance and state a conclusion.**

(A) The histogram shows 90 resamples from Explore 2. Recall that the result obtained from the experiment was a difference of means of 160.

Step 1 Calculate the *P*-value.

Divide the sum of the frequencies for the intervals $160 \leq x < 240$ and $240 \leq x < 320$ by the sum of all frequencies (the total number of resamples). So, $P(x \geq 160) = \frac{2+1}{90} \approx 0.03.$

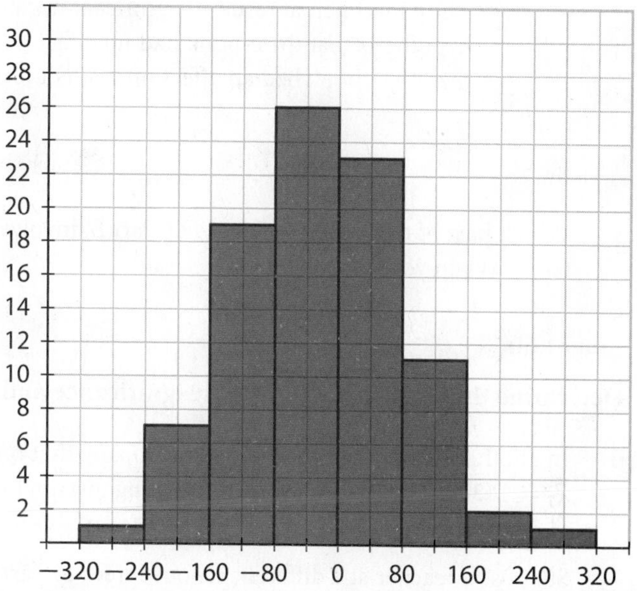

Step 2 Determine the significance.

Because the *P*-value is between 0.05 and 0.01, the experimental result is significant. Reject the null hypothesis that the exam prep course has no effect in favor of the alternative hypothesis that the course has a positive effect.

(B) A textbook company has created an electronic version of one of its books and wants to know what effect, if any, using the e-book has on student learning. A teacher who has two classes that already use the textbook agrees, with the permission of the school district, to participate in a research study. One of the classes uses the e-book for the next unit of instruction while the other class continues to use the print version of the book. After teaching the unit, the teacher gives the same test to both classes. The mean score for the class using the e-book is 82.3, while the mean score for the class using the print book is 78.2.

The resampling distribution for the difference of mean test scores, given that the null hypothesis is true, is normal with a mean of 0 and a standard error of 2. The distribution is shown.

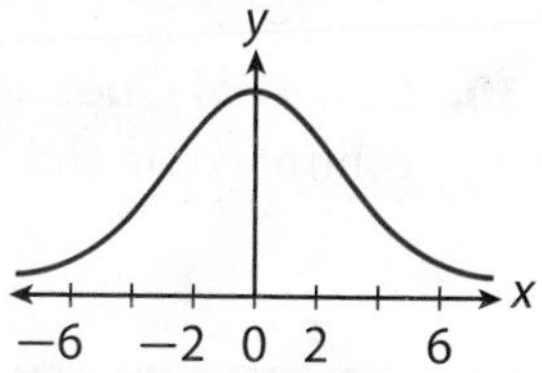

Step 1 State the null hypothesis in terms of the difference of the mean test scores. The difference of the mean test scores using the e-book and the print book is about 0.

Step 2 Identify the treatment group and its mean test score, $\bar{x}_T$, as well as the control group and its mean test score, $\bar{x}_C$. Then find $\bar{x}_T - \bar{x}_C$.

Treatment group: class using e-book

$\bar{x}_C =$ 82.3

Control group: class using print book

$\bar{x}_C =$ 78.2

$\bar{x}_T - \bar{x}_C =$ 4.1

Step 3 Use the resampling distribution to determine the significance of the experimental result.

The interval $-2\left(\boxed{2}\right) \leq x \leq 2\left(\boxed{2}\right)$, or $\boxed{-4} \leq x \leq \boxed{4}$, captures the middle 95% of the differences of the means in the resampling distribution.

The experimental result is significant because it falls outside the interval. Reject the null hypothesis that the e-book had no effect on student learning. Accept the alternative hypothesis that the e-book had an effect on student learning.

Reflect

5. Which part of this example, Part A or Part B, involves a *one-tailed* test and which part involves a *two-tailed* test? Explain your reasoning.

Your Turn

Determine the experimental result's significance and state a conclusion.

6. In another experiment for the same company that offers the college entrance exam prep course, $\overline{x}_T = 1632$, $\overline{x}_C = 1370$, and the resampling distribution is normal with a mean of 0 and a standard error of 83.

7. Suppose a teacher at a different school agrees to participate in the same research study using the e-book. For this school, the mean score for the class using the e-book is 81.7, while the mean score for the class using the print book is 77.9. The resampling distribution for this school is the same as the resampling distribution for the first school.

Elaborate

8. Describe how to obtain a resampling distribution given the data from an experiment.

9. Describe how to perform a permutation test using a resampling distribution.

10. Essential Question Check-In To what does the null hypothesis attribute any difference between the control group and the treatment group? To what does the alternative hypothesis attribute a difference?

Evaluate: Homework and Practice

Personal Math Trainer

- Online Homework
- Hints and Help
- Extra Practice

1. A research dietitian is investigating whether the consumption of fish improves the strength of bones in older adults. Two hundred older adults are recruited for an experiment in which half are asked to eat fish at least three times per week while the other half maintains their regular diet. The dietitian measures the bone density of the subjects at the beginning and end of the experiment and calculates the mean change in bone density for the two groups.

a. State the null hypothesis for this experiment.

b. If the dietitian finds that the difference of the mean changes in bone density for the two groups is not statistically significant, how does the dietitian interpret the results of the experiment?

2. An agricultural researcher investigates a new fertilizer by planting a field of corn using the new fertilizer and another field using standard fertilizer. At the end of the growing season, the researcher measures the corn yield from each plant in each field and then calculates the mean corn yields for both fields.

a. State the null hypothesis for this experiment.

b. If the researcher finds that the mean corn yield for the field with the new fertilizer is greater than the mean corn yield for the field with standard fertilizer and that the difference of the mean yields is statistically significant, how does the researcher interpret the results of the experiment?

In Exercises 3 and 4, follow these steps for creating a resampling distribution using a combination of a spreadsheet and a graphing calculator. (The steps assume 10 data values for the control group and 10 for the treatment group. You will need to make adjustments for different numbers of data values.)

Step 1 Enter the original data from the experiment in column A of a spreadsheet. List all the treatment group's data first, followed by all the control group's data. Then calculate the difference of the means by entering = **AVERAGE(A1:A10) − AVERAGE(A11:A20)**in cell A21.

Step 2 In cell B1, enter = **RAND()** and fill down to cell B20.

Step 3 Select the rows containing the data and choose **Sort...** from the **Data** drop-down menu. In the dialog box, indicate that you want the data sorted on **Column B.**

Step 4 Clicking OK in the dialog box puts the random numbers in numerical order and rearranges the data from the experiment at the same time. The first 10 data values become the new treatment group, and the last 10 become the new control group. Notice that the difference of the means in cell A21 is also recalculated.

Step 5 Enter the difference of the means in List 1 of a graphing calculator. Then return to the spreadsheet, highlight cell B1, and fill down to the last data value. Doing so creates a new list of random numbers in column B.

Step 6 Repeat Steps 3–5 as many times as desired. Then use the graphing calculator to obtain a histogram of the simulated resampling distribution and use trace to obtain the frequencies of the bars in the histogram in order to perform a permutation test.

3. A psychology researcher is testing whether it's possible to reduce test anxiety and improve test performance by having people write about their thoughts and feelings before taking a test. The researcher recruits 20 people, randomly assigning half to the control group, who sit quietly for 15 minutes before taking a test of general knowledge, and the other half to the treatment group, who write about their thoughts and feelings for 15 minutes before taking the same test. The table lists the scores on the test.

Control group	88	72	75	63	81	77	68	78	82	66
Treatment group	89	82	74	83	78	76	71	80	88	69

a. State the null hypothesis for the experiment.

b. Calculate the mean score for the treatment group, $\bar{x}_T$, and the mean score for the control group, $\bar{x}_C$. Then find the difference of the means.

c. Use a spreadsheet and a calculator to obtain at least 50 resamples of the data. Copy the results of the spreadsheet into a table, like the one shown.

Interval	Frequency
$-8 \le x < -4$	?
$-4 \le x < 0$	?
$0 \le x < 4$	?
$4 \le x < 8$	?

d. Calculate the P-value.

e. Determine the experimental result's significance and state a conclusion.

4. A medical researcher is testing a new gel coating for a pill and wants to know if it improves absorption into the bloodstream. The 12 subjects in the control group are asked to take the pill with the original coating, and the 12 subjects in the treatment group are asked to take the pill with the new coating. Blood samples are drawn from each subject 1 hour after ingesting a pill. The measured drug levels, in micrograms per milliliter, are listed in the table.

Control group	34	26	33	27	36	29	39	33	25	34	37	31
Treatment group	35	36	37	35	29	31	33	40	37	36	20	39

a. State the null hypothesis for the experiment.

b. Calculate the mean drug level for the treatment group, $\bar{x}_T$, and the mean drug level for the control group, $\bar{x}_C$. Then find the difference of the means.

c. Use a spreadsheet and a calculator to obtain at least 50 resamples of the data. Copy the results of the spreadsheet into a table, like the one shown.

Interval	Frequency
$-6 \le x < -4$	?
$-4 \le x < -2$	?
$-2 \le x < 0$	?
$0 \le x < 2$	?
$2 \le x < 4$	?
$4 \le x < 6$	?

d. Calculate the P-value.

e. Determine the experimental result's significance and state a conclusion.

5. A research gerontologist is interested in finding ways to help seniors who suffer from insomnia. She conducts an experiment in which 50 elderly volunteers are randomly assigned to two groups, one that receives informational brochures about insomnia and one that receives two in-person therapy sessions and two follow-up phone calls on how to overcome insomnia. Both groups are monitored for the amount of sleep they get each night. After 1 month, the mean change in the amount of sleep that each group gets is calculated and found to be 0.2 hour for the group that gets brochures and 1.4 hours for the group that gets therapy sessions and phone calls.

a. State the null hypothesis for the experiment.

b. Identify the treatment group and its mean amount of sleep, $\bar{x}_T$, as well as the control group and its mean amount of sleep, $\bar{x}_C$. Then find $\bar{x}_T - \bar{x}_C$.

c. The resampling distribution for the difference of the mean change in the amount of sleep, given that the null hypothesis is true, is normal with a mean of 0 and a standard error of 0.5. What interval captures 95% of the differences of the means in the resampling distribution?

d. Determine the experimental result's significance and state a conclusion.

6. A public health researcher is interested in knowing whether the calories that teenagers consume at fast food restaurants is affected by listing calorie counts on restaurant menu boards. He recruits 50 teenagers each from two localities, one where fast food restaurants are not required to post calorie counts and one where they are. The teenagers are asked to keep the receipt each time they eat at a fast food restaurant so that the researcher can determine the calorie count for the meal. The researcher finds that the mean calorie count for the teenagers living where restaurants do not post calorie counts is 554, while the mean calorie count for the teenagers living where restaurants do post calorie counts is 486.

a. State the null hypothesis for the experiment.

b. Identify the treatment group and its mean calorie count, $\bar{x}_T$, as well as the control group and its mean calorie count, $\bar{x}_C$. Then find $\bar{x}_T - \bar{x}_C$.

c. The resampling distribution for the difference of the mean calorie counts, given that the null hypothesis is true, is normal with a mean of 0 and a standard error of 40. What interval captures 95% of the differences of means in the resampling distribution?

d. Determine the experimental result's significance and state a conclusion.

7. A research botanist is investigating the health of plants that have been genetically engineered to be more disease resistant. The botanist measures the nitrogen levels in two groups of plants, ones that have been genetically engineered and ones that have not. Using the data from the experiment, the botanist creates the resampling distribution shown. The random variable X represents the difference of the mean nitrogen level for the genetically engineered plants and the mean nitrogen level for the standard plants. Use the resampling distribution to classify the significance of each value of X as highly significant, significant, marginally significant, or not significant.

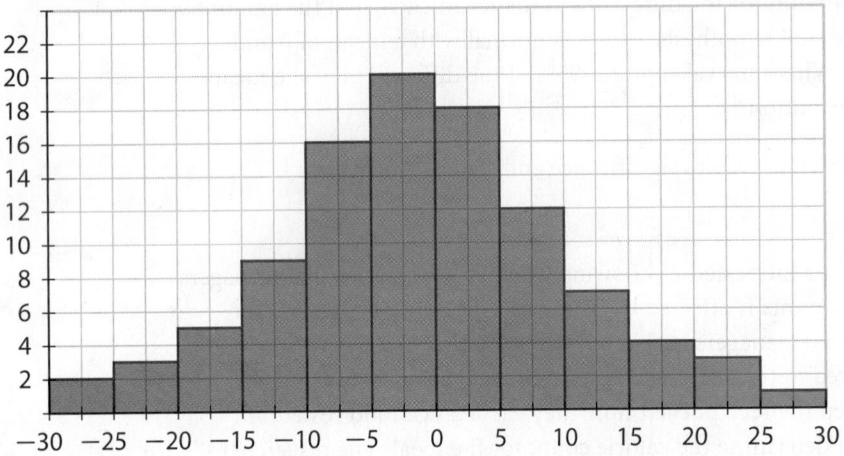

A. $X = 25$

B. $X = 15$

C. $X = -20$

D. $X = -10$

H.O.T. Focus on Higher Order Thinking

8. Draw Conclusions The reason that the statistical test you used in this lesson is called a *permutation* test is that the process of resampling assigns different permutations of the labels "treatment" and "control" to the data from an experiment. Although the number of permutations of n distinct objects is $n!$, the objects in this case are some number of "treatment" labels and some number of "control" labels, so the objects are not distinct. When a set of n objects contains n_1 copies of the first object, n_2 copies of the second object, ..., and n_L copies of the last object, then the formula for the number of permutations of the n objects becomes $\frac{n!}{n_1! \cdot n_2! \cdot \ldots \cdot n_L!}$.

a. Recall that in Explore 2, you had a control group with 10 students and a treatment group of 10 students. How many permutations of the "treatment" and "control" labels are possible? Did your class generate all possible resamples?

b. Suppose your class had generated all possible resamples. Explain why the resampling distribution would be perfectly symmetric and centered on 0.

9. Communicate Mathematical Ideas The table shows measurements obtained from an experiment involving 3 subjects in the control group and 3 subjects in the treatment group.

Control group	2	4	3
Treatment group	9	10	5

a. How many distinct resamples of the data are possible? Explain your reasoning.

b. Calculate the difference of the means for the given treatment and control groups. Is this difference significant at the 5% level using a one-tailed test? Explain why or why not.

10. Explain the Error A student was given the resampling distribution shown and asked to determine the P–value when the actual difference of means for the treatment and control groups from an experiment is 30. The student gave the answer $\frac{4}{77} \approx 0.052$. Is the student correct? Explain.

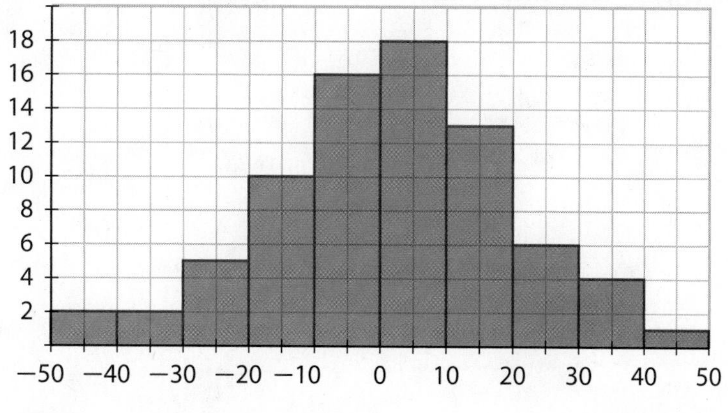

Lesson Performance Task

Researchers conducted an experiment where 12 teenage subjects were asked to use a driving simulator. At random intervals, a signal changed from green to red. Subjects were told to press a "brake" button as soon as they noticed that the signal changed to red. Each subject used the simulator under two conditions: while talking on a cell phone with a friend (the treatment) and while music was playing from a radio (the control). The table gives the data from the experiment.

Subject	Reaction Time (milliseconds)	
	Cell Phone (Treatment)	Radio (Control)
A	565	471
B	585	544
C	564	529
D	581	613
E	604	531
F	567	597
G	523	535
H	549	556
I	561	474
J	551	508
K	610	551
L	579	462

a. Calculate the mean reaction time for the treatment, $\overline{x}_T$, and the mean reaction time for the control, $\overline{x}_C$. Then find the difference of the means.

b. Because this experiment involved obtaining both the control data and the treatment data from the same subjects, resampling the data involves maintaining the pairing of the data but randomizing the order of the data within pairs. The table shows one resample where a coin was flipped for each of the 12 subjects. If the coin landed heads up, then the subject's reaction times were kept as they are. However, if the coin landed tails up, then the subject's reaction times were swapped. Using the data for the resample, find $\bar{x}_T$, $\bar{x}_C$, and $\bar{x}_T - \bar{x}_C$. How does the difference of the means for the resample compare with the difference of the means you obtained in part a?

Subject	Treatment Reaction Time (milliseconds)	Control Reaction Time (milliseconds)	Treatment Reaction Time for Resample	Control Reaction Time for Resample
A	565	471	565	471
B	585	544	544	585
C	564	529	564	529
D	581	613	581	613
E	604	531	531	604
F	567	597	567	597
G	523	535	535	523
H	549	556	549	556
I	561	474	474	561
J	551	508	551	508
K	610	551	551	610
L	579	462	462	579

c. State the null hypothesis for the experiment.

d. Under the assumption that the null hypothesis is true, researchers resampled the data 1000 times and obtained the resampling distribution shown in the table. Use the table to find the probability that a difference of the means from the resampling distribution is at least as great as the difference of the means that you found in part a.

Interval	Frequency
$-61 \leq x < -41$	5
$-41 \leq x < -21$	89
$-21 \leq x < -1$	390
$-1 \leq x < 19$	408
$19 \leq x < 39$	102
$39 \leq x < 59$	6

e. Using the *P*-value you obtained in part d, state the significance of the experimental result and the conclusion you can draw from the permutation test.

Making Inferences from Data

Essential Question: How can making inferences from data help to solve real-world problems?

Key Vocabulary
confidence interval *(intervalo de confianza)*
margin of error *(margen de error)*
survey *(estudio)*
observational study *(estudio de observación)*
experiment *(experimento)*
randomized comparative experiment *(experimento comparative aleatorizado)*
null hypothesis *(hipótesis nula)*
statistically significant *(estadísticamente significativa)*
resampling *(remuestro)*
permutation test *(prueba de permutación)*

KEY EXAMPLE *(Lesson 24.1)*

In a random sample of 100 clothing buyers at a particular clothing store, 64 bought a pair of jeans. Find a 90% confidence interval for the proportion p of clothing buyers at that particular store who will buy jeans.

$n = 100$
$\hat{p} = 0.64$
$z_c = 1.645$

Determine the sample size n, the proportion $\hat{p}$, and the value of z_c for a 90% confidence interval.

Substitute into the formulas for the endpoints of the confidence interval.

$$\hat{p} - z_c\sqrt{\frac{\hat{p}(1-\hat{p})}{n}} = 0.64 - 1.645\sqrt{\frac{0.64(1-0.64)}{100}} \approx 0.56$$

$$\hat{p} + z_c\sqrt{\frac{\hat{p}(1-\hat{p})}{n}} = 0.64 + 1.645\sqrt{\frac{0.64(1-0.64)}{100}} \approx 0.72$$

So, you can state with 90% confidence that the proportion of people that will buy jeans at that particular store lies between 0.56 and 0.72.

KEY EXAMPLE *(Lesson 24.2)*

Explain why the results of the survey are likely to be inaccurate, and then suggest a way to improve the accuracy of the survey.

Mr. Culberson, the owner of a sporting goods company, conducts one-on-one interviews with a random sample of employees to have them rate how satisfied they are with the quality of the goods they sell.

Because the person conducting the survey is the owner of the company, the employees may not be completely open about their feelings of the products. Some employees may not even buy the products. A better survey would involve a neutral interviewer, allow employees to respond anonymously, or to interview customers instead of employees.

In a random sample of town residents, a survey asks, "Are you in favor of a special tax levy to renovate the sad state of the city park?"

The question is biased because the words "sad state" suggest that the park is in such a state that it needs to be fixed, which makes it seem that the tax levy is necessary. The question should begin with a factual list of improvements, and then a question like, "Are you in favor of a tax levy to make improvements to the park?"

EXERCISES

In a random sample of 50 parfait buyers at Yo-Gurt Shop, 37 used vanilla frozen yogurt for their parfait. Find the proportion. *(Lesson 24.1)*

1. Find a 99% confidence interval for the population proportion p of parfait purchasers who will use vanilla frozen yogurt.

2. If the survey were expanded to 100 buyers, and 89 used vanilla frozen yogurt, find a 90% confidence interval for the population proportion p of parfait purchasers who will use vanilla frozen yogurt.

Explain why the results of the survey are likely to be inaccurate. *(Lesson 24.2)*

3. A survey of favorite sports for the school is taken after football practice.

MODULE PERFORMANCE TASK

Sports Nutrition

Twenty-four athletes training for the Olympics were randomly assigned to one of two groups for a sports nutrition study. The treatment group received a daily dosage of a particular nutritional supplement for 6 weeks. The control group received a placebo. Each athlete's power output was tested before and after the 6-week training period. Researchers reported the following gains for each athlete in watts per kilogram of body mass.

	Increase in Power (watts/kg of body mass)			
Treatment Group	0.52	0.21	0.38	0.36
	0.39	0.30	0.46	0.33
	0.41	0.53	0.27	0.40
Control Group	0.32	0.39	0.25	0.29
	0.28	0.41	0.18	0.28
	0.19	0.42	0.33	0.26

What is the difference in means between the treatment and control groups? Is this difference statistically significant?

Start by listing information you will need to solve the problem. Be sure to write down all your data and assumptions. Then use graphs, numbers, tables, words, or algebra to explain how you reached your conclusion.

Ready to Go On?

24.1–24.3 Making Inferences from Data

Personal Math Trainer

- Online Homework
- Hints and Help
- Extra Practice

State the null hypothesis.

1. Ten plants are given a new plant food once a week, in addition to regular watering. Ten other plants are only watered regularly. After one month, the mean heights of the two groups of plants are compared.

2. A sample group of patients suffering from frequent headaches are given a new medicine designed to significantly reduce the number of headaches per month. Another group of patients also suffering from frequent headaches are given a sugar pill. After 6 months, the mean numbers of headaches are compared for the two groups.

Find the proportion.

3. A local school took a random sample of 500 students, in which 378 carried backpacks. Find the proportion of students who carry backpacks with a 95% confidence interval.

ESSENTIAL QUESTION

4. How can making inferences from data help a test-prep writer?

MODULE 24
MIXED REVIEW

Assessment Readiness

1. A local band took a survey of 100 local music listeners about their favorite type of music. The results are as follows: 36 stated they preferred rock, 32 stated they preferred country, 25 stated they preferred hip-hop, and 7 stated they had no preference. Any probability uses a 95% confidence interval.

   Tell whether each statement is correct.

   A. The data have a normal distribution.

   B. probability of country: between 0.23 and 0.41

   C. probability of rock: between 0.27 and 0.45

2. Consider the situation where a company is testing a new pair of shoes. They give 20 runners a pair of their redesigned shoes and 20 runners a pair of the previous model of shoes. After one month, they will be testing the amount of wear on the shoes. Determine if each statement is True or False.

   A. The null hypothesis would be that both shoes wear the same amount.

   B. A potential problem with the test is not knowing how much each runner runs in a week. This cannot be avoided.

   C. The desired hypothesis for the shoe company would be that the older shoes worked better than the redesigned ones.

3. A local political group is taking surveys of potential voters in the next election. They are calling voters registered in the Democratic Party to see which candidate is most likely to win the election for mayor. Explain why the results of the survey are likely to be inaccurate, and then suggest a way to improve the accuracy of the survey.

4. What type of function is illustrated by the points $(-1, 16)$, $(0, 4)(1, 1)$, $\left(2, \frac{1}{4}\right)$ and $\left(3, \frac{1}{16}\right)$? Explain your answer.

Assessment Readiness

Personal Math Trainer
- Online Homework
- Hints and Help
- Extra Practice

1. Consider a survey to pick a new sport to add to the school. Is the suggested sampling method likely to result in an accurate result?

Answer Yes or No for A–C.

A. survey every 10 attendees at a football game

B. survey every teacher

C. survey every 20 students on the school roster

2. Consider a situation where a pizza company wants to improve its sauce. They give each of 15 testers two unlabeled samples of pizza; one with the new sauce and one with the old sauce.

Determine if each statement is True or False.

A. The null result would be both sauces tasting the same.

B. The desired result would be the customers preferring the new sauce.

C. The undesired result would be that the customers cannot tell between the two sauces.

3. Consider the survey where a company owner, Ms. Baker, takes a random sample of her customers' names and their opinion about the quality of her product in return for a free donut.

Determine if each statement is True or False.

A. The survey is biased because the customers may not be honest to the owner of the company since they have to give their names.

B. The survey would be more accurate if Ms. Baker would allow customers to survey anonymously.

C. All customers will be honest if they get a free donut for completing the survey.

4. Tell whether each equation has at least 2 real roots.

A. $f(x) = x^2 - 6$

B. $f(x) = x^2 + 2$

C. $f(x) = (x^2 - 2)(x + 2)(x - 4)$

5. Describe the difference between a normal distribution and a uniform distribution.

6. Suppose the average time a student spends traveling to school via walking, car, or bus is 22 minutes, with a standard deviation of 12 minutes. You choose a random sample of 100 students. What is the probability that your sample has a mean time up to 24.4 minutes? Explain.

7. Karissa solved the absolute value equation $5 = 2|x - 3| + 2$ as shown. Describe and correct Karissa's mistake(s).

$5 = 2\|x - 3\| + 2$	Subtract 2 from both sides.
$3 = 2\|x - 3\|$	Divide both sides by 2.
$1.5 = \|x - 3\|$	Separate equation into two equations.
$1.5 = x - 3$ and $-1.5 = x - 3$	Solve for x.
$x = -1.5$ and $x = -4.5$	

Performance Tasks

★ 8. Samples of the ages of members of two different athletic clubs in Smithville are shown.

Membership Information	
Power-Pump Gym	24, 28, 44, 50, 31, 20, 25, 54, 27, 19, 23, 37, 42, 25, 29, 40
Smithville Racket Club	14, 49, 30, 17, 28, 71, 64, 29, 12, 28, 60, 51, 23, 59, 66, 23

A. Determine the mean and standard deviation for each data set. Round to the nearest age.

B. What do the samples say about the age of a typical member at each club? Explain.

★★ **9.** A cable company wants to know if customers that pay for DVR service (to record shows) would cancel it if the ads in the shows could not be skipped when shows are viewed. A report from a survey shows that only 12% of customers that pay for DVR would cancel it.

A. Name at least three aspects of the survey that you would want to know more about to help determine if the report is valid.

B. The cable company ultimately wants more of its customers to pay for DVR service, since only 29% of customers currently subscribe to this service. How might this information affect the company's decision to disable fast-forwarding of ads? Write 3 statements about your reasoning.

★★★ **10.** The United States Association of Table Tennis (USATT) uses a rating system for members. The ratings are normally distributed with a mean of 1400 and a standard deviation of 490.

A. Ernesto says that about a third of all members have a rating between 900 and 1400. Is this correct? Explain.

B. An "expert" player is considered to have a rating of at least 1900. About what percent of members are *not* "experts"?

C. A USATT club in New York has 73 members. The club has an average member rating of 1870. Explain why the members of the club do not reflect the distribution of all USATT members.

MATH IN CAREERS

Pharmaceutical Scientist A pharmaceutical scientist is testing whether a certain medication for raising glucose levels is more effective at higher doses. In a random trial, the fasting glucose levels of 5 patients being treated at a normal dose (Group A) and 5 patients being tested at a high dose (Group B) were recorded. The glucose levels in mmol/L are shown in the table.

A	5.4	5.7	4.8	4.3	4.6
B	5.5	5.1	4.2	5.9	4.9

a. State the null hypothesis for the experiment.

b. Compare the results for the control group and the treatment group using box plots.

c. Do you think that the researcher has enough evidence to reject the null hypothesis?

Focus on Careers

The following Focus on Career pages can be used after you have completed each unit in the book. Each feature shows how mathematics is used in some career.

UNIT 1

Functions

Mathematics and Underwater Photography

Underwater photographers sometimes travel the world to photograph marine life. They are both photographers and commercial divers. As photographers they use math to calculate settings for their cameras including things such as shutter speed (the length of time a camera shutter is open) and aperture (a hole inside the lens that can be changed from small to large). As commercial divers they use math to calculate how long they can safely dive at different depths and how much air they will need in their tanks to complete their dives.

Like all divers, underwater photographers feel the pressure of the water on them increase as they dive deeper. The increasing water pressure causes a diver's body to absorb more nitrogen. If the diver returns to the surface too rapidly, the nitrogen in the diver's body fluids can form bubbles. The bubbles can cause "the bends," or decompression sickness. To prevent injury, the diver needs to return to the surface slowly. Using standard gear, a diver can go to a maximum depth of about 130 feet. The maximum recommended rate of ascent for divers is about 1 second per foot. The graph shows how the time needed to return to the surface is related to the depth of the dive.

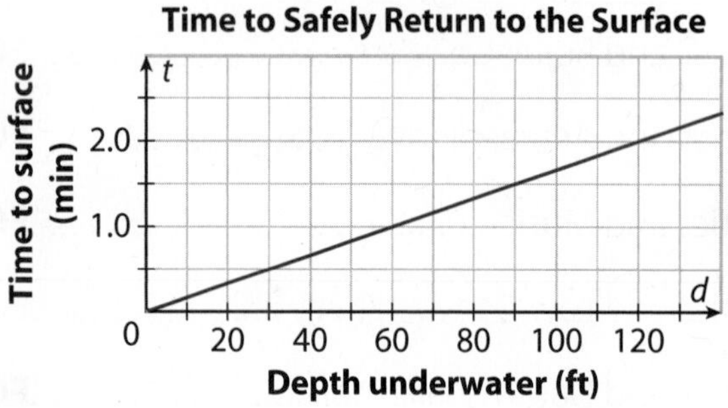

The rate of 1 second per foot is the same as $\frac{1}{60}$ minute per foot. The ascent time t (in minutes) at any depth d (in feet) is then modeled by $t(d) = \frac{1}{60}d$. Since the maximum depth is about 130 feet, the domain is restricted to the interval $0 \leq d \leq 130$.

Exercises

Suppose that a diver has just finished photographing a school of fish at a depth of 120 feet and it is time to return to the surface. To prevent the bends, the diver needs to ascend slowly. Sketch a graph of the following verbal descriptions, where depths below the surface are considered positive.

1. **a.** The diver ascends to the surface at a constant rate of 20 feet per minute.

   b. The diver ascends at a rate of 60 feet per minute with a decompression stop of 2 minutes at 60 feet and a second stop for 3 minutes at 15 feet.

One of the difficulties that an underwater photographer faces occurs because of the differences between the physical properties of water and air. Another issue is caused by the interaction of light rays between the camera housing and the water. The transition from the lens to the water causes the light to bend, thus magnifying the image and affecting the angle of view of the camera lens. The following graph shows the apparent angle of view of an underwater camera relative to that in air.

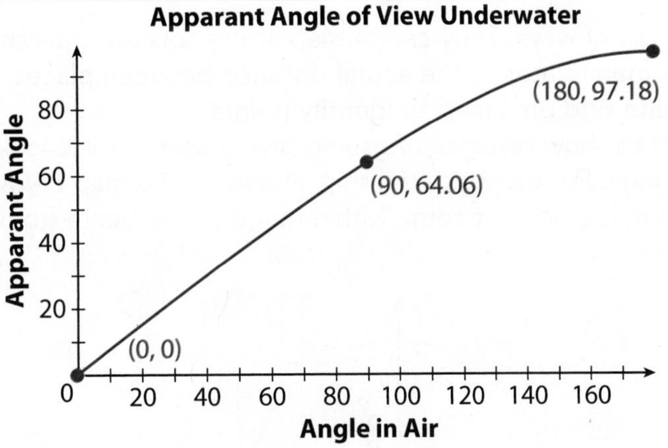

2. Give the domain and range of the function.

3. On what interval(s) is the function increasing? On what interval(s) is the function decreasing?

4. Find the function's average rate of change over each interval. Round your answers to the nearest hundredth.

   a. [0, 90]

   b. [90, 180]

   c. [0, 180]

UNIT 2

Quadratic Functions, Equations, and Relations

Mathematics and Cartography

Digital mapping, or digital cartography, is the process of compiling data collected over time to generate a virtual image of a specific region. The majority of the data is geographic in nature, but other types of information relevant to the map's application are also included. The chief purpose of this technology is to produce maps that accurately represent a particular area. Much of the data comes from satellite imagery, and for most applications, these maps must be updated regularly to provide the most accurate information.

Cartographers use math in lots of ways. They create map scales to show how the distance between places shown on a map relates to the actual distance between places. They can also superimpose a coordinate grid on a map to identify points.

Often maps can be used to show distance rings and give a user a quick look at what will be included within the rings. For example, the ship shown on the map below, where the coordinates are given in miles, has just come within range of the beam from the lighthouse.

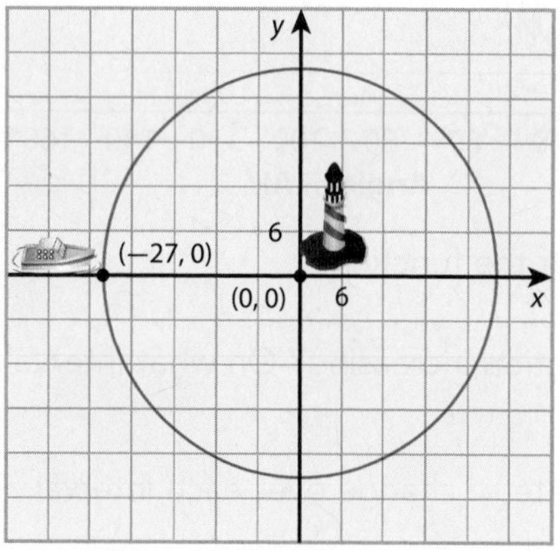

The circle represents the set of points that lie at the outer range of the lighthouse beam. The lighthouse is located at the origin, so the center of the circle is (0, 0). The distance between the ship and the lighthouse is 27 miles, so the radius is $r = 27$. Therefore the equation of the circle is $x^2 + y^2 = 27^2$ or $x^2 + y^2 = 729$.

The map can then be used to determine if other ships can see the beam. The inequality $x^2 + y^2 \leq 729$ represents the situation. To determine if a second ship with coordinates (24, 12) would be included in the ring, determine if the coordinates satisfy the inequality. Since $24^2 + 12^2 = 720$ and $720 \leq 729$, the second ship can see the beam from the lighthouse. Plotting the point on the map would give a visual confirmation that the second ship is indeed within the circle.

Exercises

One digital map created showed engine response time for a Massachusetts fire department. A coordinate grid was superimposed on a map of the town, with the fire station located at the origin. The map indicated a fire engine leaving the station could reach a fire that was within 1.6 miles of the station in less than 5 minutes.

1. Write an equation of the circle defining the region that a fire engine could reach within 5 minutes.

2. Suppose the station received an alarm from a building located at the map coordinates (0.9, 1.2). The fire chief said that the building was on the outer edge of the circle defining the 5-minute response time. Do you agree? Explain your reasoning.

3. Suppose a second fire station located at (1.6, 1.6) sometimes sent fire engines to help the fire department referred to in Exercises 1–2. Suppose this second fire station assisted with fires within a one-mile radius. Write an equation of the circle defining the region that the second station covered. Then determine whether the second station would assist with a fire at the building in Exercise 2.

A cellular phone network uses towers to transmit calls. The range of a tower can be defined by a circle. Suppose a cellular phone service company is installing towers in a town centered at the origin on a coordinate plane. Tower A will be located 19 miles due north of the town's center point and Tower B will be located 19 miles due south of the town's center point. Assume each tower has a range of 20 miles.

4. Find an equation of the circle that defines the range of Tower A.

5. Find an equation of the circle that defines the range of Tower B.

6. The table below gives the locations of several places within the town. Are there any places that are not within the range of at least one of the towers? Are there any places that are within the range of both of the towers?

Place	Location
School	(–3, 0)
Library	(7, 5)
Park	(12, –2)

UNIT 3

Polynomial Functions, Expressions, and Equations

Mathematics and Real Estate Sales

When people are looking to buy or sell a home, most turn to a real estate agent. These agents connect buyers and sellers for a percentage of the sale price or a commission. This means that real estate agents are going to be very interested in the home prices in the area where they work. While most of the day-to-day work of a real estate agent involves communicating with people, some agents use mathematics to examine the stability of the local housing market over time.

Since agents' earnings are based on property sales, some agents use home price data to create models to try and predict trends in the housing market. If agents can find a region where they think home costs are going to increase, they can focus their advertising in that area to try and find clients.

For example, home values in some cities, such as Pittsburgh and Houston, have changed very little over the period from 2003 to 2015, while home values in other cities have undergone drastic swings. After average home prices in Phoenix reached a high of approximately \$332,000 in the 1st quarter of 2006, they then fell by 57% to a low of approximately \$143,000 by the 3rd quarter of 2011, where the numbers have been adjusted to 2016 values to account for inflation.

The graph below shows the national average for home prices in the United States, in thousands of dollars and adjusted for inflation, for the 13-year period from 2003 through 2015. The national trend is similar to that of Phoenix, but the fluctuation in value is less extreme.

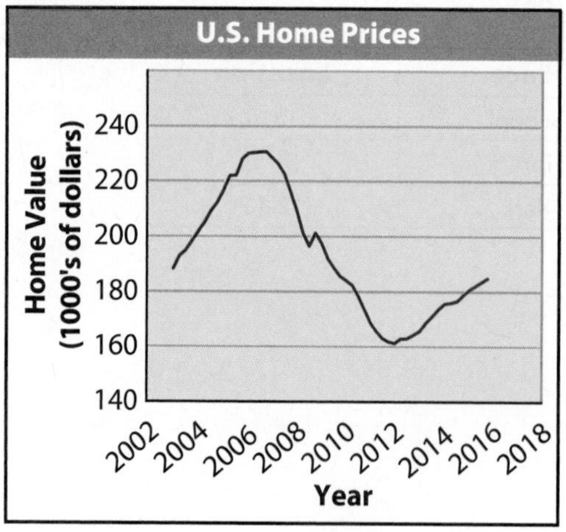

Exercises

The data in the following table give the 4th quarter values of U.S. home prices from 2003 through 2015, inclusive. The data are the same as those shown in the graph for the 4th quarter values.

Year	2003	2004	2005	2006	2007	2008	2009	2010	2011	2012	2013	2014	2015
Value ($1000's)	198.5	212.4	228.3	230.9	216.1	201.3	185.8	173.8	161.9	164.3	173.7	178.9	185.0

1. **a.** Examine the data in the table and on the graph. Notice that the values rise to a maximum, then fall to a minimum, then rise again. Would a linear function be appropriate to model this data? Would a quadratic function be appropriate?

b. What kind of function should be used to model this data, based on the observed behavior?

c. Use the cubic regression feature on a graphing calculator to find a function that can be used to model the data. Let x be the number of years since 2003 and y be the value of the home in thousands of dollars. Round all coefficients to the nearest hundredth.

d. On the graphing calculator, graph the function found in part (c) along with a scatter plot of the data points. How closely does the model match the data?

e. What does the function give as an estimate for the value of a home in the United States in 2010? Round to the nearest hundred.

f. What is the error in the estimated 2010 value to the nearest percent?

g. What does the function give for the value of a home in the United States in 2020? Round to the nearest hundred dollars. Do you think this value is realistic? Why or why not?

2. The following function can be used to model the inflation-adjusted value of home prices in San Francisco in the 4th quarter from 2003 through 2015, inclusive, where x is the number of years since 2003 and y is the value of the home in thousands of dollars.

$$y = 1.87x^3 - 29.17x^2 + 92.76x + 711.20$$

a. What is the domain of this function?

b. For what years does the model predict the value of a home to be $711,200? Round to the nearest year. Find the solutions algebraically, and then verify your answers with a graphing calculator.

UNIT 4

Rational Functions, Expressions, and Equations

Mathematics and Astronomy

Astronomy is the oldest of the natural sciences, which is remarkable because experiments cannot be performed directly. Modern astronomers can only observe the radiation that comes to Earth. They use sophisticated equipment to study multiple aspects of the universe and then use this knowledge to gain a better understanding of our solar system.

Astronomers who study galaxies are interested in how much the stars within them move. Physics tells us that the closer the orbit of a star is to the center of a galaxy, the faster it should move along its orbital path. These conclusions are based on observations that the planets closer to the sun move faster because of the stronger gravitational pull. Planets at the edge of the solar system travel much more slowly because the gravitational pull of the sun is weaker. Astronomers were quite surprised to discover, using powerful telescopes to measure the velocities, that the faint stars at the edges of galaxies were actually moving faster than those closer to the center! It seemed as though the stars were defying the laws of gravity, but astronomers now attribute this phenomenon to dark matter, a theoretical type of matter we cannot see.

Any two objects exert a gravitational force on each other. This gravitational force is given by the formula

$$F = G\,\frac{m_1 m_2}{d^2}$$

where m_1 and m_2 are the masses of the two objects, G is a universal constant called the gravitational constant, and d is the distance between the objects. The gravitational force is a function of the distance between the objects and decreases as the separation increases.

As an example, the graph shows the gravitational force between Earth and Voyager 2, a space probe launched by NASA in 1977 that is still in active use. It is now more than 17 billion kilometers from Earth and remains the only probe to have explored the outer planets of our solar system. Its journey will continue on into interstellar space. The force between the probe and Earth was approximately 9170 N at Earth's surface and decreased as the probe moved away from Earth. The relationship shown in the graph is an example of a rational function.

Gravitation Force between Voyager 2 and Earth

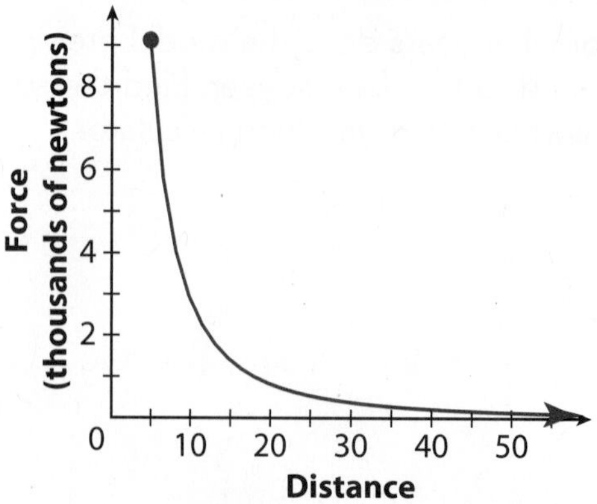

Exercises

Astronomers use a measurement called *apparent size* to describe how big an object in space looks from different locations. For example, the apparent size of the sun from the planet Mercury is about 2.58. This means that the sun appears about 2.58 times as wide on Mercury as it does on Earth. Use the table to answer the questions that follow.

Planet	Mean distance from sun (millions of miles)	Apparent size of sun
Mercury	36.0	2.58
Venus	67.2	1.38
Earth	93.0	1.00
Mars	142	0.655
Jupiter	484	0.192
Saturn	885	0.105
Uranus	1780	0.0522
Neptune	2790	0.0333

1. **a.** The size of the sun varies inversely with the distance from where it is observed because the product of distance and size is roughly constant. Write a rational equation that gives the sun's apparent size s as a function of the distance d in millions of miles from which it is observed.

   b. Ceres is an asteroid located between the orbits of Mars and Jupiter. The mean distance of Ceres from the sun is about 257 million miles. What is the apparent size of the sun from Ceres?

Astronomers use gravity to help explain the motion of objects in space. Earth is the source of gravity that affects you most directly. The gravitational force F, measured in newtons (N), that Earth exerts on a relatively small object of mass m (in kilograms) at a distance d (in meters) from the Earth's center is given by:

$$F = \frac{(4.0 \times 10^{14})m}{d^2}$$

In order to leave Earth, the space probe Voyager 2 had to overcome Earth's gravity.

2. Write an equation giving Earth's gravitational force on Voyager 2, which has a mass of 930 kilograms, as a function of the distance d from Earth's center.

3. The function you wrote in part (a) is graphed on the preceding page. What are the function's domain and range? (*Hint*: The radius of Earth is about 6.37×10^6 meters.) What value does Earth's gravitational force on Voyager 2 approach as the distance from Earth becomes greater and greater?

4. The average distance between the center of Earth and the center of the moon is about 3.84×10^8 meters. When Voyager 2 was this far from Earth's center, what was the gravitational force on the probe? How does this force compare with the force required to lift an algebra book (about 20 N)?

UNIT 5

Radical Functions, Expressions, and Equations

Mathematics and Roller Coasters

Hundreds of millions of people visit amusement parks in the United States annually, many seeking the thrills of the giant roller coasters. Roller coasters are designed by a licensed engineer who generally has a degree in mechanical, electrical, or structural engineering. The key to a popular ride is to keep it going as fast as possible at all the times, with twists and loops along the way. It is the job of the roller coaster designer to ensure that this happens, while preserving the safety of the ride.

One of the main duties of a roller coaster designer includes deciding how to place the track. Modern-day roller coasters can reach over 400 feet in height and can achieve speeds of up to 149 miles per hour. Besides downhill drops, they contain turns, loops, and corkscrews that induce feelings of weightlessness or other unnatural, disorienting sensations due to the acceleration caused by these curved motions.

Roller coaster designers often test rides many times to ensure that the ride is safe. In designing a ride, they need to make sure that the roller coaster is going fast enough to climb the hills. They must also take special care to ensure that the ride does not induce jerk, a sudden change in acceleration that can cause whiplash.

The maximum velocity that a roller coaster can achieve occurs at the bottom of a vertical drop and is determined by the height of the drop and by the acceleration due to gravity. Ignoring the effects of friction and air resistance, this velocity is given by the formula,

$$v = \sqrt{2gh}$$

where v is the theoretical maximum velocity in feet per second, h is the height of the drop in feet, and g is the acceleration due to gravity, a constant that equals 32 feet per second squared. This formula is an example of a radical function.

Exercises

Amusement park ride designers use physics to predict the velocity of a ride. If you ignore friction and air resistance, potential energy at the top is transformed into kinetic energy at the bottom, according to the equation

$$\text{kinetic energy} \quad \frac{1}{2}mv^2 = mgh \quad \text{potential energy}$$

where m is the mass, v is the velocity, g is the acceleration due to gravity, and h is the height of the drop.

1. Solve the equation for v. Does a roller coaster car drop faster when people are in it or when it is empty? Explain.

2. **a.** A roller coaster at an amusement park in Jackson, New Jersey involves a vertical drop of 418 feet. Using $g = 32$ ft/s², find the velocity of the car after it falls 418 feet, in both feet per second and miles per hour.

   b. By what factor would you have to change the height of the roller coaster in order to double the car's velocity at the bottom?

When designing a roller coaster, the designer can use the formula

$$v = \sqrt{2gh}$$

to find the maximum velocity of a roller coaster car, which occurs at the bottom of the first hill. For the exercises, ignore energy losses due to friction and air resistance.

3. **a.** In customary units, $g = 32$ ft/s². Use this fact to show that $v = \sqrt{2gh}$ can be simplified to $v = 8\sqrt{h}$.

   b. Find the maximum velocity of each of the roller coaster cars in the table, to the nearest foot per second, using the data for the greatest vertical drop distances.

Roller Coaster	Drop (feet)
Roller Coaster A	221
Roller Coaster B	256
Roller Coaster C	328
Roller Coaster D	400

   c. Use the results of part (b) to graph $v = 8\sqrt{h}$. Identify the points on the graph that represent the roller coasters shown in the table.

   d. Suppose you want to design a roller coaster whose maximum velocity is 125 miles per hour. Convert this velocity from miles per hour to feet per second. Use your graph or the equation to find the drop for the first hill.

UNIT 6

Exponential and Logarithmic Functions and Equations

Mathematics and Archaeology

Archaeologists study human history and activity through the recovery and analysis of artifacts and other physical remains. Did you know that it's also possible to determine if there was a human presence at a particular site even if no artifacts are found? Methods discovered in the late twentieth century that combine chemistry, geology, and topography have made this possible. Now, archaeological digs where no artifacts are found can still provide important information about the past.

While the presence of artifacts is fairly conclusive proof of a cultural presence, the lack of artifacts doesn't necessarily disprove a cultural presence. In fact, the multidisciplinary methods mentioned above can provide evidence of a cultural presence even without artifacts. By performing a chemical analysis on soil samples from a site where artifacts are found, the impact of the culture on the soil can be determined. Artifacts such as mollusk shells and animal bones break down and raise the concentration of calcium in the soil and affect the pH of the soil, making it more alkaline than normal. Even if digs in other locations do not yield cultural artifacts, if the soil pH in both sites is similar, a link can be established between the cultures of the peoples in the two sites.

A measure of the pH level of soil is really a measure of the concentration of hydrogen ions in the soil (pH stands for "potential of hydrogen"). The pH scale runs from 0 to 14, where 7 is neutral. Alkalinity increases as the numbers increase, and acidity increases as the numbers decrease.

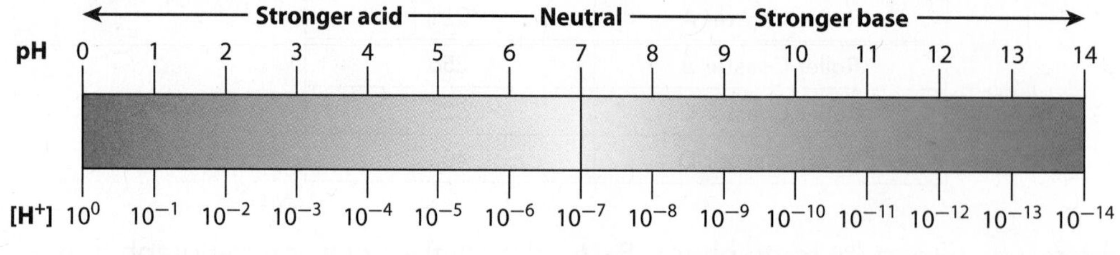

Since each whole-number increase in pH represents a ten-fold decrease in the concentration of hydrogen atoms, the pH scale is an example of a logarithmic scale. Specifically,

$$pH = -\log[H^+].$$

Furthermore, since pH is defined in terms of the common logarithm, then the hydrogen ion concentration can be found from the pH, using the inverse, exponential function,

$$[H^+] = 10^{-PH}.$$

Exercises

Archaeologists often make excavation grids like the one below on sites where they are searching for artifacts. An excavation grid consists of squares of earth separated by partitions called balks. Suppose a group is excavating a section of a large field. The group creates an excavation grid such that the area of each grid square and its surrounding balks is 25 square meters. Each person can excavate a grid square in 20 days.

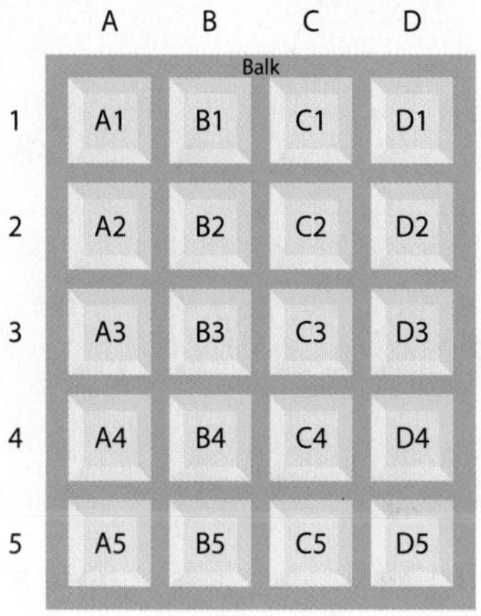

1. **a.** How many total square meters can a person excavate in 1 day? in 2 days? in 3 days?

b. Is the total number of square meters excavated by a person after n days an arithmetic or a geometric sequence? Write a recursive rule and an explicit rule for a sequence that models the situation.

c. If there are 10 people in the group, how many total square meters will the group have excavated in 10 days?

Archaeologists use the pH scale to rate the acidity of soils. The pH of a soil is given by the equation

$$\text{pH} = -\log[\text{H}^+],$$

where $[\text{H}^+]$ is the soil's hydrogen ion concentration in moles per liter. (An ion is an electrically charged atom, and a mole of ions contains about 6.02×10^{23} ions.) The greater a soil's pH, the more alkaline (or less acidic) the soil is.

2. **a.** At an excavation site, archaeologists found that the soil could be divided into three distinct layers. The hydrogen ion concentrations of the uppermost, middle, and bottommost layers of soil were 4.0×10^{-7}, 1.6×10^{-7} and 2.0×10^{-6}, respectively, all in units of moles per liter. Find the pH of each soil layer, rounded to the tenths place.

b. The presence of human artifacts increases a soil's alkalinity. Which of the soil layers in part (a) do you think contained the most artifacts? Explain.

3. At a separate excavation site, the pH of one soil layer was found to be 6.0, while that of another layer was found to be 6.6. Find the hydrogen ion concentration, $[\text{H}^+]$, in moles per liter, in each of the two layers. Express your answer in scientific notation using two significant digits.

4. Suppose the difference in pH of two soils, A and B, is 2. Compare the hydrogen ion concentrations in the soils.

UNIT 7

Trigonometric Functions

Mathematics and Music

While we may not all agree on a particular genre of music, we probably do agree that the quality of the recording plays a significant role in the enjoyment of our chosen music. While musicians know what they want their music to sound like, they cannot do it alone. While in the studio, musicians work closely with a recording engineer to create their sound. A recording engineer is a specialist in a field that merges several disciplines, including acoustics, psychoacoustics (the psychology of the perception of sound), electrical engineering, and music itself. Using a combination of digital recorders, listening devices, mixing boards, and specialized software, the recording engineer collaborates with the musician to shape the overall sound of the recording.

At its most basic, music is sound, a collection of waves moving through the air. When an object vibrates, it generates waves that move away from the object. These waves move in all directions, bouncing off anything they run into: the floor, the ceiling, and the walls. To avoid picking up a mixture of direct sound waves and their reflections, state-of-the-art recording studios hire acoustical engineers to design studios that minimize these reflections and any other noise that could show up on the recording. This is achieved through high ceilings, concrete walls and floors, and specially shaped foam insulation.

A representation of a sound wave can be displayed on an oscilloscope, an instrument used to study electrical signals. Pictured below are oscilloscope traces of a C-note played at three different volumes on a guitar. Each sound wave establishes a repetitive pattern, which can be modeled by sine functions.

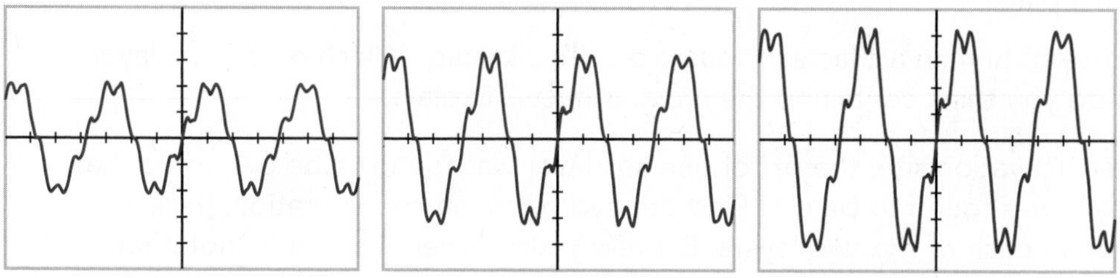

Guitar C-note at low volume | **Guitar C-note at normal volume** | **Guitar C-note at high volume**

While each wave follows the general trend of a sine curve, none of them appears to be a single sine wave. This is due to harmonics. When a guitar string is plucked, waves are produced with frequencies that are multiples of the fundamental frequency of the string. The output is the sum of the sounds from each of these frequencies. The magnitude of the harmonics of an open string can be controlled to some extent by the location along the string at which it is plucked.

Exercises

When music is recorded, it is the small pressure changes in the air that are recorded. If the atmospheric pressure is 15.000 pounds per square inch (psi), a loud noise might cause the pressure to vary between 14.999 psi and 15.001 psi. A pure musical tone will cause the air pressure to vary in a way that can be modeled with a sine function. The variation in pressure for a soft Concert A is given by

$$P = 0.0005 \sin 880\pi t$$

where P is the deviation from the average atmospheric pressure in psi and t is the time in seconds.

1. **a.** Graph the function.

b. What is the function's amplitude and period?

One way to tune a guitar is to use harmonics, the ringing tones you hear if you pluck a string while lightly touching the string at points one half, one third, or one fourth of the way along its length. To find the exact points to touch, you can use the 12th, 7th, and 5th frets as guides. The table shows the sound pressure equations for the harmonic tones of a guitar tuned in the key of A.

String (frequency)	Fundamental (open string)	1st harmonic (12th fret)	2nd harmonic (7th fret)	3rd harmonic (5th fret)
E($\frac{165}{2}$ Hz)	$P = \sin 165\pi t$	$P = \sin 330\pi t$	$P = \sin 495\pi t$	$P = \sin 660\pi t$
A (110 Hz)	$P = \sin 220\pi t$	$P = \sin 440\pi t$	$P = \sin 660\pi t$	$P = \sin 880\pi t$
D($\frac{440}{3}$ Hz)	$P = \sin \frac{880}{3}\pi t$	$P = \sin \frac{1760}{3}\pi t$	$P = \sin 880\pi t$	
G($\frac{1760}{3}$ Hz)	$P = \sin \frac{3520}{9}\pi t$	$P = \sin \frac{7040}{9}\pi t$		
B($\frac{495}{2}$ Hz)	$P = \sin 495\pi t$			
E (330 Hz)				

2. **a.** Look at the first two rows of the table. How do the equations of the 1st, 2nd, and 3rd harmonics compare with the fundamental equations?

b. Copy and complete the table.

c. Strings that vibrate according to the same equation sound the same. The first four strings can be tuned by comparing the 3rd harmonic of one string with the 2nd harmonic of the next. Explain how you might tune the last two strings based on the harmonics of one of the first four strings.

UNIT 8

Probability

Mathematics and Law

The role of a criminal lawyer in a jury trial is to convince the jury beyond a reasonable doubt of the defendant's innocence or guilt, depending, of course, on whether the lawyer represents the defense or prosecution. DNA (*deoxyribonucleic acid*) evidence—admissible in courtrooms since 1987—can go a long way towards that end. Though not infallible (for example, evidence can be mishandled or test results misread), DNA evidence is so powerful because of its ability to discriminate between individuals and hence convict or exonerate.

DNA testing can be used when samples of, say, a perpetrator's blood or hair are found at the scene of the crime. Scientists can analyze blood or hair samples by isolating the DNA contained within a cell nucleus. DNA is considered to be the chemical basis of heredity because it makes up the genes. Everyone in the world, except for identical twins, has a unique set of genes. The DNA found at a crime scene is compared with the DNA sample taken from the suspect to see if they match. The DNA samples are compared at several well-known sites on the DNA chain. The genetic sequence found at each site is called a *marker*. If all of the markers in two DNA samples "match up" (or coincide), then both samples probably came from the same person.

A single strand of DNA contains 3 billion markers. It is impossible to compare so many markers between two DNA samples using present technology. Typically, about a dozen distinguishing markers are compared. DNA testing is based on the idea that the markers occur independently of one another in a strand of DNA. In order to determine the probability that two different DNA samples come from the same person, the probabilities associated with each of the markers are multiplied.

Suppose, for example, that marker A occurs in 2% of the population and marker B occurs in 5% of the population. The probability of two DNA samples having both markers is 1 in 1000:

$$\text{Probability of having both markers} = \frac{2}{100} \times \frac{5}{100} = \frac{1}{1000}$$

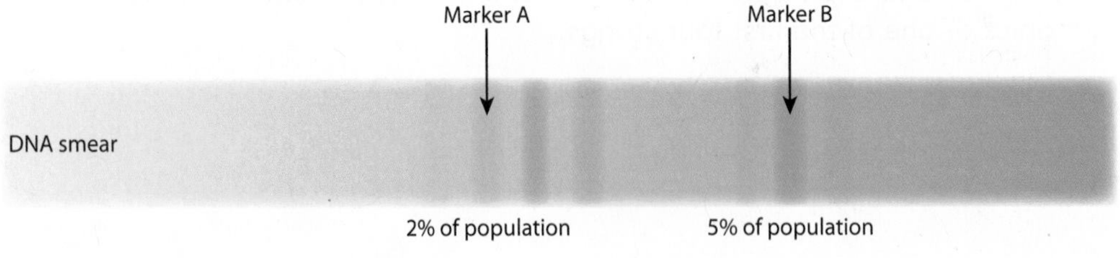

Exercises

Attorneys often rely on fingerprints to place a suspect at the scene of a crime. Fingerprint evidence is considered very strong because each person's fingerprints are assumed to be unique. This was established mathematically in 1892 by British scientist Sir Francis Galton, who wanted to estimate the probability that two fingerprints from two randomly chosen people match. He divided each of the two hypothetical fingerprints into 24 square sections. He then defined these three events:

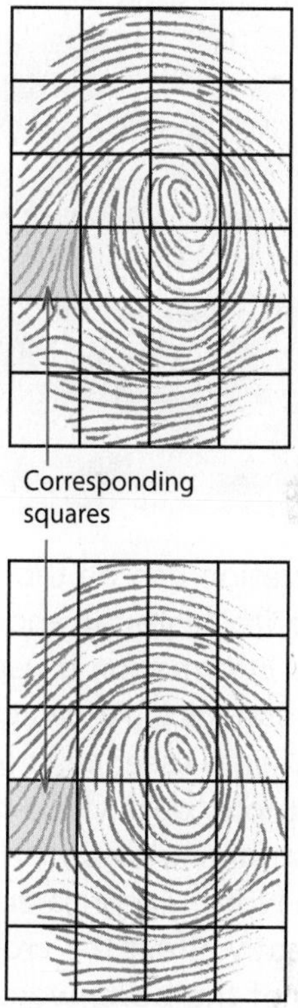

A: The same number of ridges pass through two corresponding squares.

B: The ridges adjacent to two corresponding squares have the same "general course."

C: Two corresponding squares match.

1. **a.** Galton claimed that $P(C) = P(C|A \text{ and } B) \cdot P(A \text{ and } B)$. He assumed *A* and *B* are independent events and estimated that $P(A) = \frac{1}{2^{1/3}}$, $P(B) = \frac{1}{2^{1/6}}$, and $P(C|(A \text{ and } B)) = \frac{1}{2}$. Find the probability that two corresponding squares match

b. Galton also assumed that matches between corresponding squares are independent events. Based on this assumption and your answer to part (a), what is the probability of a complete match between two fingerprints from two randomly chosen people?

In criminal court cases that require a unanimous decision, it is often difficult for a jury to reach a decision. Suppose the probability that any given jury member thinks the defendant is guilty is a constant, *p*. You will use two models to explore how this probability and the jury size affect the chances of a guilty verdict.

2. **a.** The *Friedman* model assumes that each jury member votes independently and that the defendant is declared guilty only if all members vote for conviction. Express the probabilities of conviction by a 6-member jury and by a 12-member jury as functions of *p*.

b. The *Walbert* model assumes that the majority will convince the minority. If the jury is initially split evenly, the *Walbert* model states that there is a 50% chance of eventual conviction. For example, according to this model, a 6-member jury will always vote for conviction if 4, 5, or 6 members initially think the defendant is guilty, and half the time if just 3 members believe the defendant is guilty. Express the probabilities of conviction by a 6-member jury and by a 12 member jury as functions of *p*.

c. Use your answers to parts (a) and (b) to find the probability of a conviction for each model and each jury size if $p = 0.9$.

UNIT 9

Statistics

Mathematics and Data Visualization

Data visualization involves creating accurate visual representations (i.e., graphics) of data in order to clearly communicate the information to readers or viewers. The data is encoded as visual objects—points, lines, or bars—that are contained in the graphics. Done properly, the graphical representation of a large batch of numerical (or even categorical) data will enhance the understanding of the information in a way that is not conveyed by a large table of numbers. A visual representation can also spotlight what a statistical measure like standard deviation means across an entire data set.

Data visualization can be thought of as a happy medium between art and science. It should be *both* aesthetic and functional, as a beautiful display that does not communicate its intended information is useless. For this reason, data visualization can also be viewed as descriptive statistics. Artists can make a significant contribution to these technical projects, because art is, in essence, a form of communication.

For example, data visualization has been used in the study of the European corn borer (species *Ostrinia nubilalis*), an insect that originated in Europe that can also be found throughout North America and northern Africa. This agricultural pest damages corn plants and can greatly affect the crop's yield. In the study, mathematical models of the larval and adult forms of the borer were created to determine how an insect disease would affect these two populations. The study also wanted to determine how the corn plants might be affected indirectly by the insect disease. These interactions were programmed into a computer, which produced billions of numbers; extracting useful information from these numbers was a tedious process.

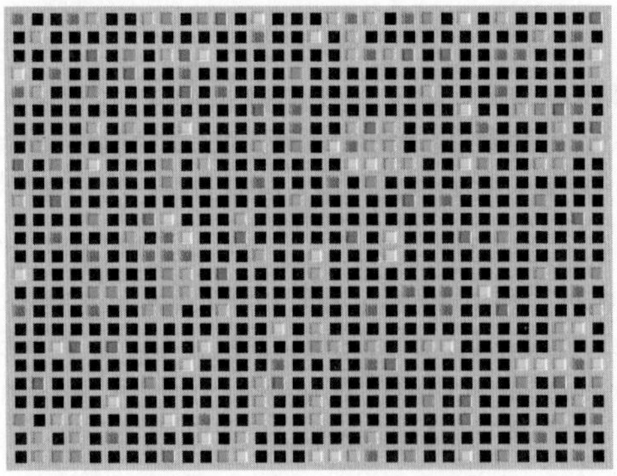

Using data visualization techniques, the information was also displayed graphically, as seen in the image above. The image shows a cornfield with 800 plants. The black squares show plants with no larvae, green squares show plants with healthy larvae, and red squares show plants with infected larvae. Other colors show plants with a mixture of healthy and infected larvae. In this image, color is used to present *categorical data*. Such a visual presentation can greatly enhance our understanding of the data.

Exercises

The matrix below gives typical cornfield data that a data visualization specialist might use to create a visual display. Each element of the matrix corresponds to a corn plant and has two values related to corn borer larvae. The numbers in the shaded column tell the total number of corn borer larvae on each plant. The numbers in the unshaded column tell how many of the larvae are infected. It is the healthy larvae that damage the crops.

	C1		C2		C3		C4		C5		C6		C7		C8		C9	
R1	3	1	7	4	0	0	4	1	8	3	5	3	9	6	8	7	11	5
R2	4	2	0	0	0	0	6	4	4	1	3	2	0	0	6	5	10	10
R3	0	0	0	0	0	0	3	2	3	0	3	3	5	2	1	0	9	7
R4	0	0	0	0	0	0	0	0	1	0	0	0	2	2	0	0	3	3
R5	0	0	0	0	3	0	0	0	0	0	0	0	7	3	9	5	5	1
R6	5	3	6	6	0	0	3	3	6	3	0	0	0	0	0	0	0	0
R7	0	0	0	0	0	0	0	0	0	0	2	0	0	0	0	0	1	0
R8	0	0	0	0	0	0	0	0	0	0	0	0	4	2	8	6	0	0
R9	0	0	0	0	0	0	0	0	0	0	0	0	0	0	3	0	0	0
R10	3	0	0	0	0	0	0	0	0	0	0	0	0	0	0	0	0	0

1. **a.** Select a sample of 10 plants that have larvae on them from the matrix above using each of the indicated methods: (i) cluster; (ii) systematic; (iii) random. For each method, calculate the percentage of infected larvae on each plant.

b. For each of your samples in part (*a*), calculate the mean percentage of infected larvae. Do these values agree with each other? If not, explain any discrepancies.

2. **a.** Using only the plants that actually have larvae on them, make a box plot of the data in the shaded columns of the matrix. Find the mean, median, standard deviation, and IQR of the data.

b. Using only the plants that actually have larvae on them, make a box plot of the data in the unshaded columns of the matrix. Find the mean, median, standard deviation, and IQR of the data.

c. How do corresponding values from parts (a) and (b) compare with one another?

3. **a.** Let X be a random variable that represents the number of healthy larvae on each plant. What are the possible values of X?

b. Make a table that shows all possible values and the probability for each value.

c. Make a histogram of the probability distribution.

d. What is the probability that the number of healthy larvae is not 0? How is this probability represented in the histogram?

UNIT 1 Selected Answers

MODULE 1

Lesson 1.1 Domain, Range, and End Behavior

Your Turn

6. Domain: $-\infty < x < +\infty$, $\{x \mid -\infty < x < +\infty\}$, $(-\infty, +\infty)$

   Range: $y \le 0$, $\{y \mid y \le 0\}$, $(-\infty, 0)$

   End behavior: As $x \to +\infty$, $f(x) \to -\infty$; As $x \to -\infty$, $f(x) \to -\infty$.

9. 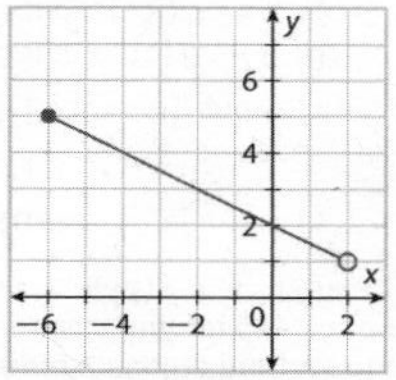

   The range is $1 < y \le 5$.

10. 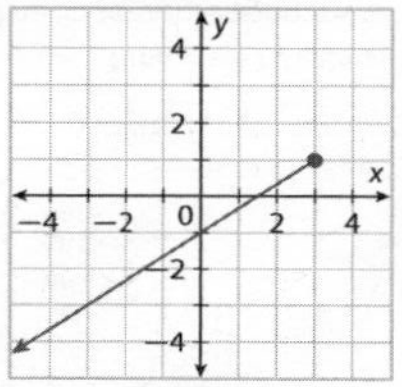

   The range is $(-\infty, 1]$.

12. The walkway's rate of motion is $\frac{5}{3}$ ft/s. The distance d (in feet) you travel at any time t (in seconds) is modeled by $d(t) = \frac{5}{3}t$.

   Domain: $\{t \mid 0 \le t \le 60\}$; range: $\{d \mid 0 \le d \le 100\}$.

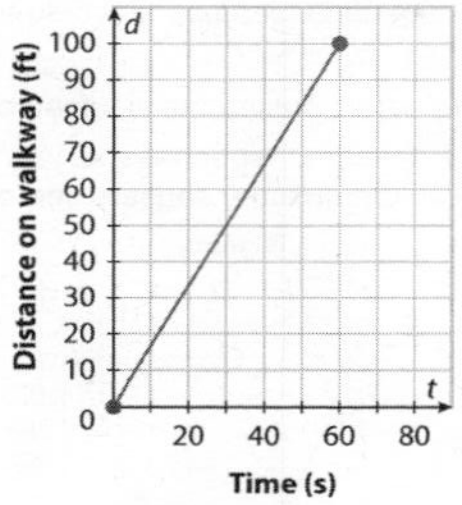

Evaluate

1. $x \ge 5$, $\{x \mid x \ge 5\}$, $[5, +\infty)$
3. $\{x \mid -25 \le x < 30\}$, $[-25, 30)$
5. Domain: $-\infty < x < +\infty$, $\{x \mid -\infty < x < +\infty\}$, $(-\infty, +\infty)$

   Range: $2 \le y < +\infty$, $\{y \mid 2 \le y < +\infty\}$, $[2, +\infty)$

   End behavior: As $x \to +\infty$, $f(x) \to +\infty$; As $x \to -\infty$, $f(x) \to +\infty$.
7. Domain: $-\infty < x < +\infty$, $\{x \mid -\infty < x < +\infty\}$, $(-\infty, +\infty)$

   Range: $-\infty < y < +\infty$, $\{y \mid -\infty < y < +\infty\}$, $(-\infty, +\infty)$

   End behavior: As $x \to +\infty$, $f(x) \to +\infty$; As $x \to -\infty$, $f(x) \to -\infty$.

9. 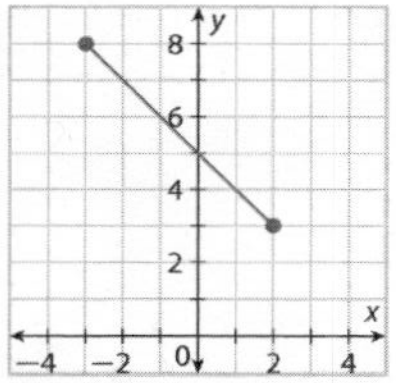

   The range is [3, 8].

11. $d(t) = 12t$. The domain is $\{t \mid 0 \le t \le 0.75\}$. The range is $\{d \mid 0 \le d \le 9\}$.

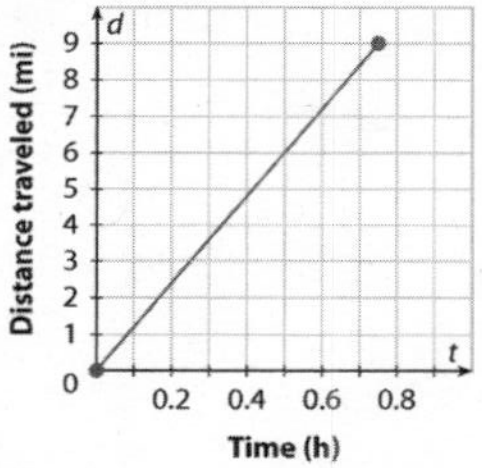

13. Cameron's function is correct, but the domain and range are incorrect. The domain should be $0 \le t \le 6$. The range should be $0 \le n \le 150$.

15. $y = -0.46x + 500$.

   Domain: $0 \le x \le 1091$, $\{x \mid 0 \le x \le 1091\}$, [0, 1091]

   Range: $0 \le y \le 500$, $\{y \mid 0 \le y \le 500\}$, [0, 500]

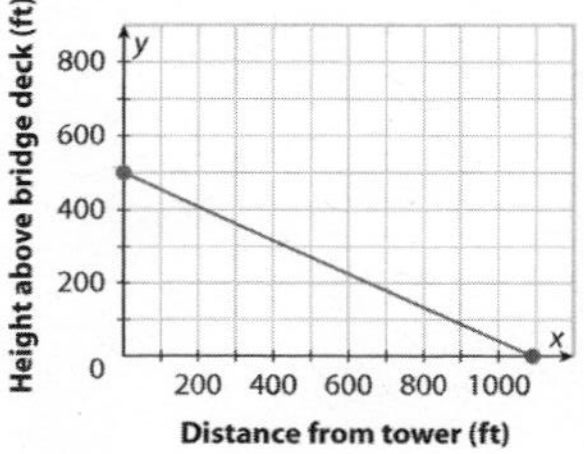

UNIT 1 Selected Answers

MODULE 1

Lesson 1.2 Characteristics of Function Graphs

Your Turn

4. **Strawberries on Shelves**

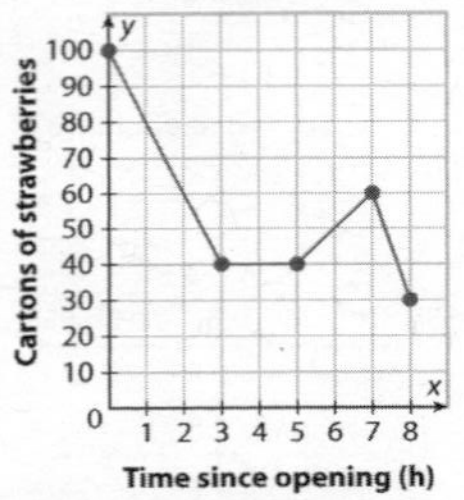

6. The linear regression model is $y = 2.4x + 11$ where x represents the day and y represents the number of hits. The model predicts that on day 15 there will be $y = 2.4(15) + 11 = 47$ hits.

Evaluate

1. $\{t \mid 3 \le t \le 13\}$
   $\{t \mid 0 \le t \le 3\}$ and $\{t \mid 13 \le t \le 18\}$
3. Domain: $\{t \mid 0 \le t \le 18\}$;
   Range: $\{V(t) \mid 0.75 \le V(t) \le 3\}$.
5. As n increases without bound, $P(n)$ approaches 0. This implies that as n increases without bound, the probability that every roll is a 5 approaches 0, that is, it becomes an impossible event.
7. a. 2; b. –2; c. –1; d. 4; e. –3; f. 0
9. $\{x \mid x < -3\}$ and $\{x \mid -1 < x < 2\}$.

11.

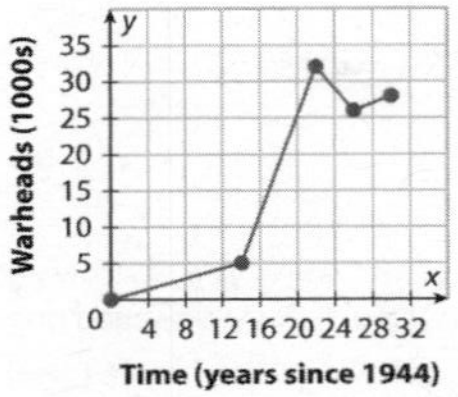

13.

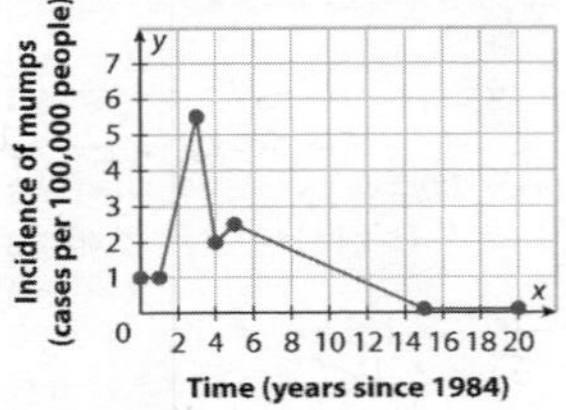

15. a.

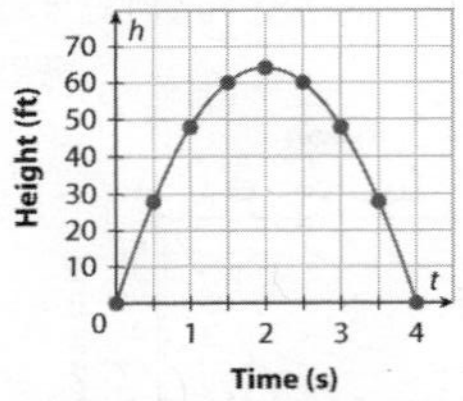

b. The ball reaches a maximum height of 64 feet in 2 seconds.

c. The height is increasing on the interval $\{t \mid 0 \le t \le 2\}$.

d. The height is decreasing on the interval $\{t \mid 2 \le t \le 4\}$.

17. The linear regression model is $h = 2.75\ell + 71.97$ where ℓ is the length of a woman's humerus (in centimeters) and h is her overall height (in centimeters).
The woman's height would be about 160 centimeters. Because 32 is in the domain of the regression model, the prediction is an interpolation.

19. The average rate of change on an interval uses only the endpoints of the interval in the calculation. If the endpoints happen to have the same y-coordinate, the average rate of change will be 0, but that doesn't mean the function remains constant throughout the interval. For example, the average rate of change for $f(x) = x^2$ on the interval $\{x \mid -1 \le x \le 1\}$ is $\frac{f(1) - f(-1)}{1-(-1)} = \frac{1-1}{1-(-1)} = \frac{0}{2} = 0$, but the function is decreasing from (–1, 1) to (0, 0) and then increasing from (0, 0) to (1, 1), so the function is clearly not constant on the interval.

UNIT 1 Selected Answers

MODULE 1

Lesson 1.3 Transformations of Function Graphs

Your Turn

12. The graph of $g(x) = f(-4(x-3)) + 1$ is a reflection of the graph of $f(x)$ across the y-axis, a horizontal compression by a factor of $\frac{1}{4}$, and a translation of 3 units to the right and 1 unit up.

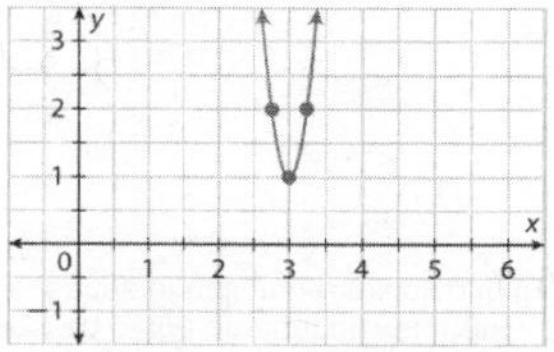

13. $g(x) = \frac{1}{25}f(x-3) + 3$. The domain of $g(x)$ is $\{x \mid -2 \le x \le 8\}$.

Evaluate

1.

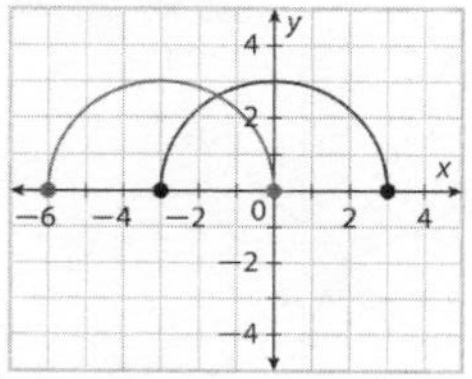

$g(x) = f(x+3)$

3.

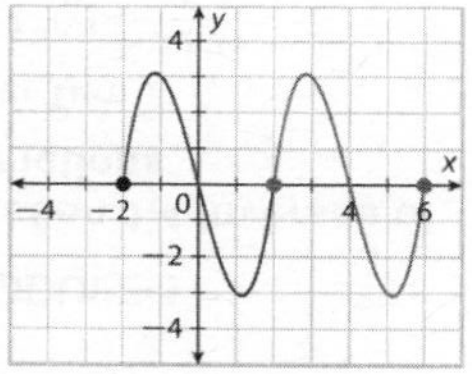

$g(x) = f(x-4)$

5.

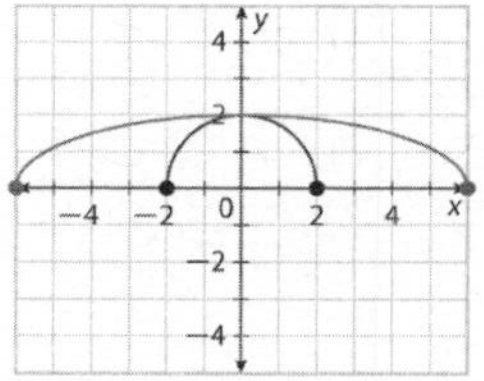

$g(x) = f\left(\frac{1}{3}x\right)$

7.

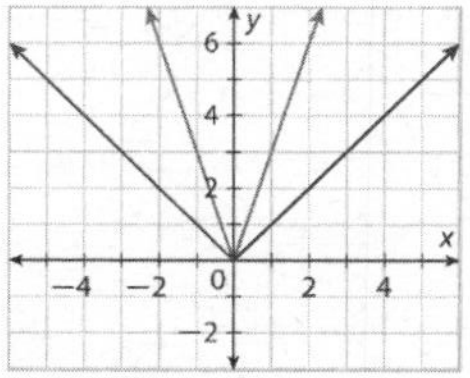

$g(x) = f(3x)$

9.

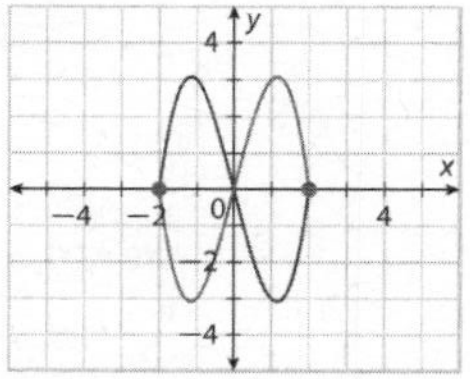

$g(x) = f(-x)$

11.

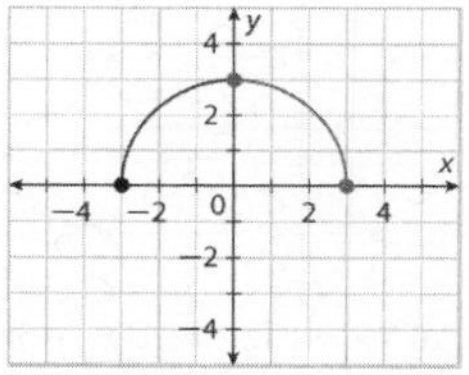

$g(x) = f(-x)$

13. a. Odd function; b. Even function; c. Neither

15. Reflection of the graph of $f(x)$ across the x-axis, a vertical compression by a factor of $\frac{1}{3}$, and a translation of 4 units to the left.

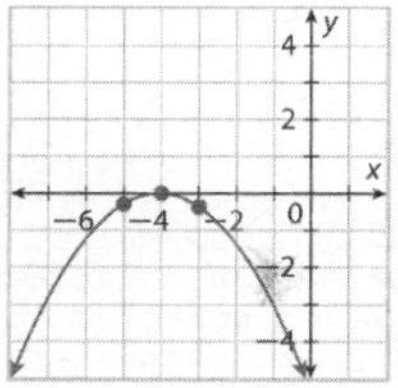

17. $g(x) = -\frac{1}{6}f(x-2) + 12$. The domain of $g(x)$ is $\{x \mid 2 \le x \le 8\}$.

19. The graph of $g(x)$ shows that the graph of $f(x)$ has been stretched horizontally by a factor of 2 and translated to the left 4 units. So, $g(x) = f\left(\frac{1}{2}(x-(-4))\right)$. This equation is equivalent to the given form of $g(x)$ because $x-(-4)$ can be rewritten as $x+4$, $\frac{1}{2}$, can be distributed to the terms of $x+4$, and $f(x)$ can be replaced by the action (squaring) that it performs on its input values. So, $g(x) = f\left(\frac{1}{2}(x-(-4))\right) = f\left(\frac{1}{2}(x+4)\right) = f\left(\frac{1}{2}x+2\right) = \left(\frac{1}{2}x+2\right)^2$.

UNIT 1 Selected Answers

MODULE 1

Lesson 1.4 Inverses of Functions

Your Turn

5. $f^{-1}(x) = \dfrac{-x+3}{2}$

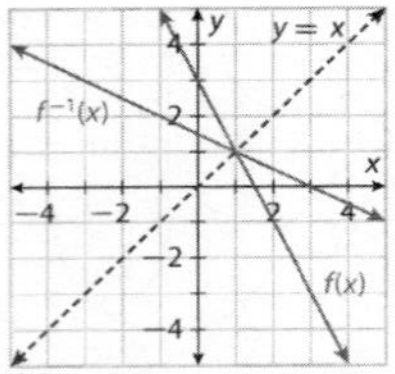

6. $\{w \mid 0 \le w \le 600\}$

$-\dfrac{1}{20}w + 30 = t$

The inverse function gives the time (in hours) the pool has been draining as a function of the amount of water (in thousands of gallons) remaining in the pool.

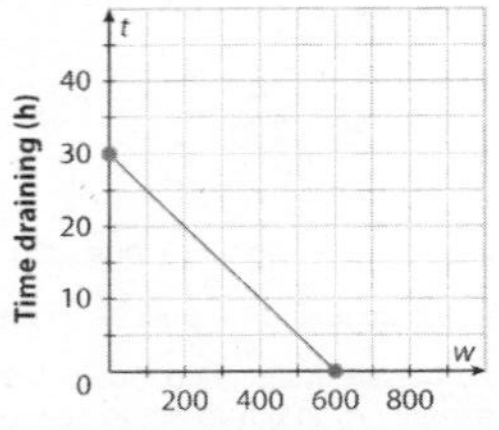

Evaluate

1. 16; 12; 18

The inverse is a function, because for each input there is only one output.

3. Inverse of function:

$\{(-3, -4), (-4, -2), (-2, 0), (0, 1), (3, 2)\}$

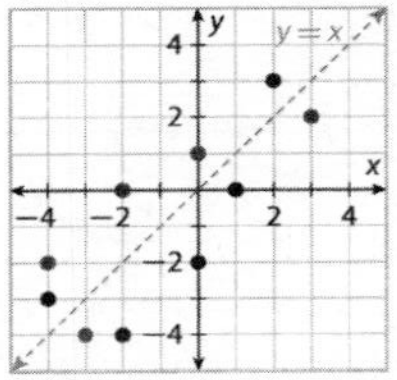

5. $f^{-1}(x) = \dfrac{x+8}{4}$

7. $f^{-1}(x) = 6x - 1$

9. $f^{-1}(x) = -\dfrac{1}{3}x + 1$

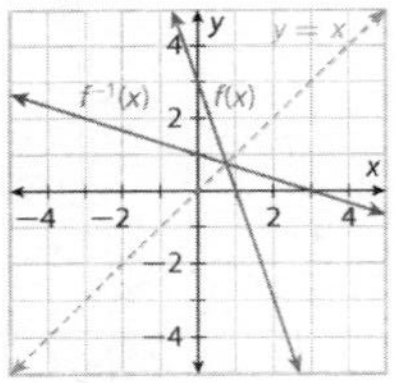

$f^{-1}(f(x)) = f^{-1}(-3x+3) = -\dfrac{1}{3}(-3x+3) + 1$

$= (x-1) + 1 = x$

$f(f^{-1}(x)) = f\left(-\dfrac{1}{3}x+1\right) = -3\left(-\dfrac{1}{3}x+1\right) + 3$

$= (x-3) + 3 = x$

11. The domain of the function $A = \dfrac{1}{2}(20)h$ is restricted.

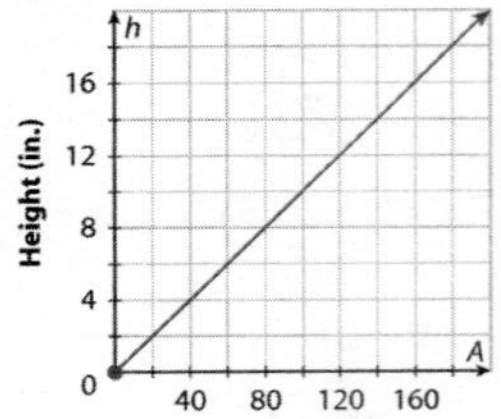

The inverse function is $h = \dfrac{A}{10}$.

The inverse function gives the height (in inches) of a triangle with a base of 20 inches as a function of the area (in square inches) of the triangle.

13. The function's inverse is not a function, because the function is many-to-one. If the domain is restricted to $\{x|x \le 0\}$, $\{x|x \ge 0\}$, or some subset of these sets, the function becomes one-to-one, and the inverse is a function.

15. A, B, F, G and H.

17. You have to restrict the domains of quadratic functions and absolute value functions, because these functions are many-to-one functions. For instance, the quadratic function $f(x) = x^2$ pairs both −2 and 2 with 4, and the absolute value function $f(x) = |x|$ pairs both −2 and 2 with 2. On the other hand, linear functions (excluding constant functions) and exponential functions are one-to-one functions, so their domains do not need to be restricted.

UNIT 1 Selected Answers

MODULE 2

Lesson 2.1 Graphing Absolute Value Functions

Your Turn

2. Vertex: $(h, k) = (-6, 4)$
   (4, 2)
   (−16, 2)

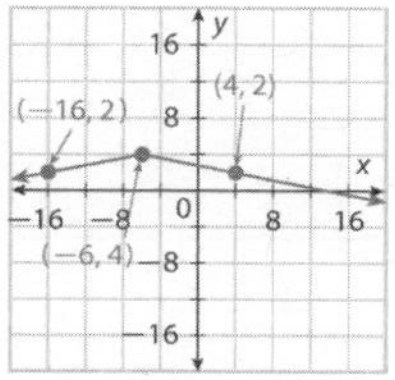

3. $g(x) = |2(x+5)| - 1$

4. The second student should stand 5.57 meters away from the first student.

Evaluate

1.

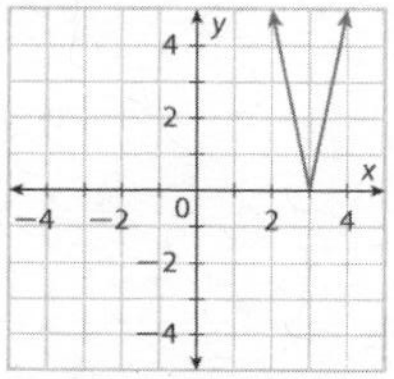

$g(x)$ is the graph of $f(x) = |x|$ vertically stretched by a factor of 5 and shifted 3 units to the right.

3.

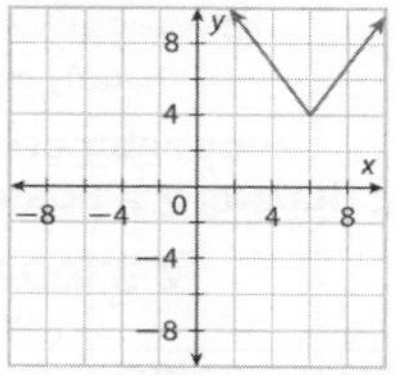

$g(x)$ is the graph of $f(x) = |x|$ horizontally compressed by a factor of $\frac{5}{7}$, shifted 6 units to the right and 4 units up.

5. $g(x)$ is the graph of $f(x) = |x|$ vertically stretched by a factor of $\frac{7}{4}$, shifted 2 units to the right, and 3 units down.

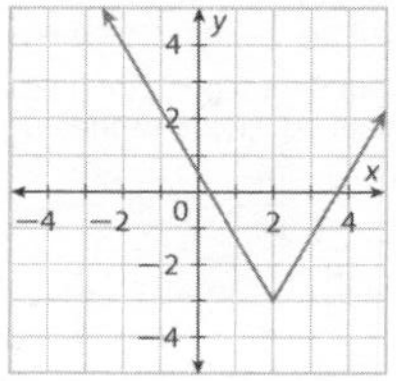

7.

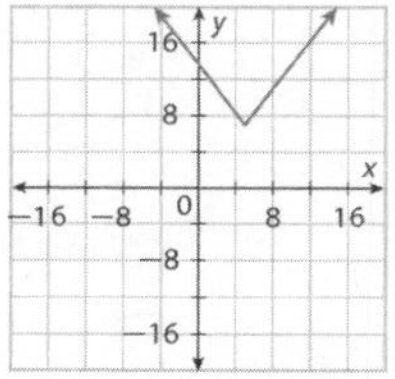

D: all real numbers; R: $y \geq 7$

9.

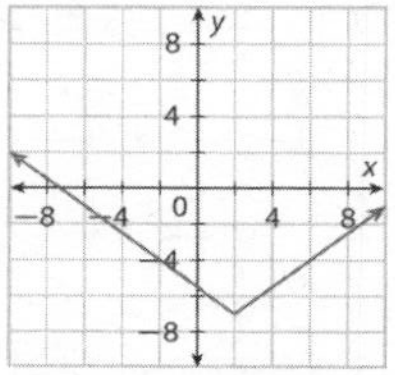

D: all real numbers; R: $y \geq -7$

11.

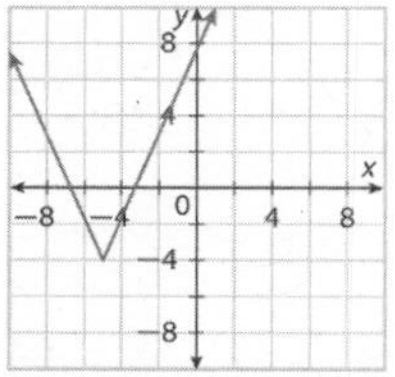

D: all real numbers; R: $y \geq -4$

13. $g(x) = -\frac{1}{4}|(x-4)| + 3$

15. a. An equation for the path of the ball is $y = \frac{5}{4}|x - 6|$.

    b. The point (10, 5) satisfies the equation, so the player does make the shot.

17. $y = -\frac{1706}{145}|x - 72.5| + 853$

19. The graph shown cannot be the graph of $y = |x+3| + 2$ because the +3 inside of the absolute value symbols means the parent graph should be shifted to the left 3 units. The graph shown is shifted to the right 3 units, so it represents $y = |x-3| + 2$.

UNIT 1 Selected Answers

MODULE 2

Lesson 2.2 Solving Absolute Value Equations

Your Turn

3. $x = 18$ or $x = -22$

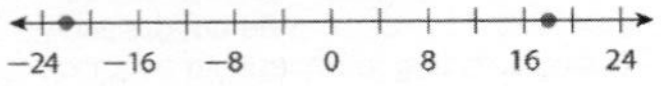

4. $x = \frac{8}{3}$ or $x = \frac{4}{3}$

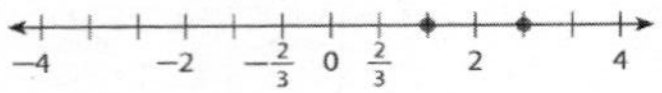

5. $\left|\frac{1}{2}x + 5\right| = -\frac{2}{3}$

No solution

6. $\left|\frac{4}{3}x - 2\right| = 0$

$x = \frac{3}{2}$

Evaluate

1.

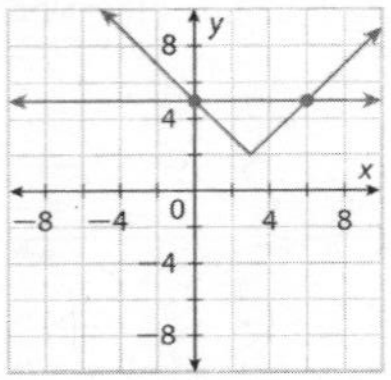

$x = 0$ or $x = 6$

3.

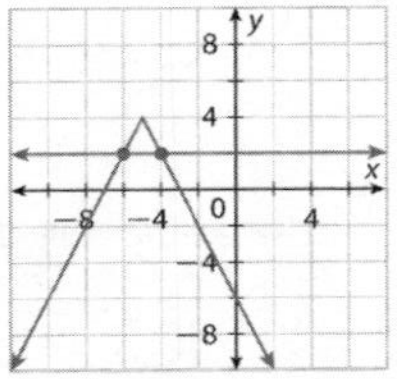

$x = -4$ or $x = -6$

5.

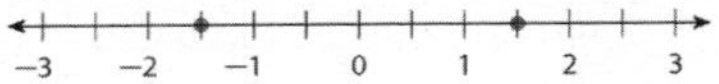

$x = \frac{3}{2}$ or $x = -\frac{3}{2}$

7.

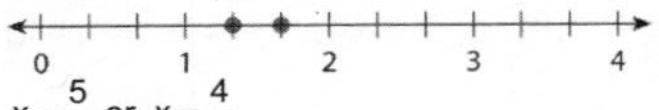

$x = \frac{5}{3}$ or $x = \frac{4}{3}$

9. No solution

11.

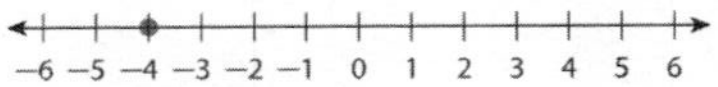

$|x + 4| = 0$

$x = -4$

13. No solution

15.

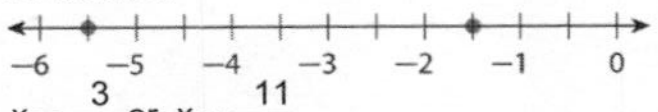

$x = -\frac{3}{2}$ or $x = -\frac{11}{2}$

17. The buoys should be placed at 150 ft and 330 ft from the left-hand shore.

19. The points are (–2, 0) and (8, 0).

21. No Solution. Terry does not have a spot on his roof that is 30 feet high.

23.

$3\|x - 2\| - 5\|x - 2\| = -7$			Subtraction Property of Equality
$(3 - 5)\|x - 2\| = -7$			Distributive Property
$\|x - 2\| = \frac{7}{2}$			Division Property of Equality
$x - 2 = \frac{7}{2}$	or	$x - 2 = -\frac{7}{2}$	Definition of absolute value
$x = \frac{11}{2}$	or	$x = -\frac{3}{2}$	Addition Property of Equality

25. Answers will vary. Sample answer: time, distance, height, length, speed.

UNIT 1 Selected Answers

MODULE 2

Lesson 2.3 Solving Absolute Value Inequalities

Your Turn

6. $x \geq -3$ and $x \leq 1$

9. The solution is $x \leq 4$ and $x \geq 10$.

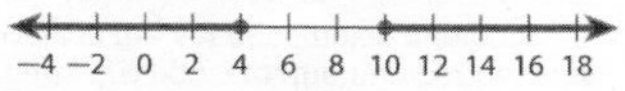

10. The solution is $-4 < x < 1$.

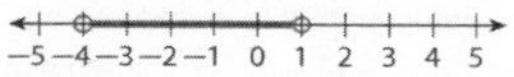

11. $|w - 13.8| \leq 0.1$

The range of acceptable weights of the cereal (in ounces) is $13.7 \leq w \leq 13.9$.

Evaluate

1. The integers from –5 to 5 that satisfy the inequality are –5, –4, –3, –2, –1, 3, 4, and 5.

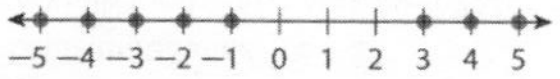

3.

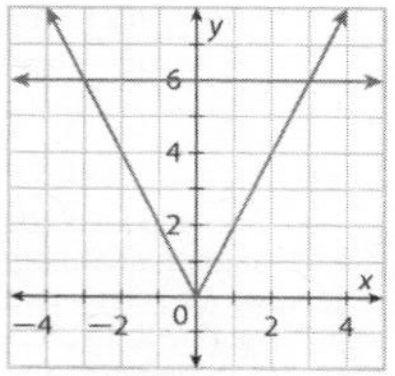

The solution is $-3 \leq x \leq 3$.

5.

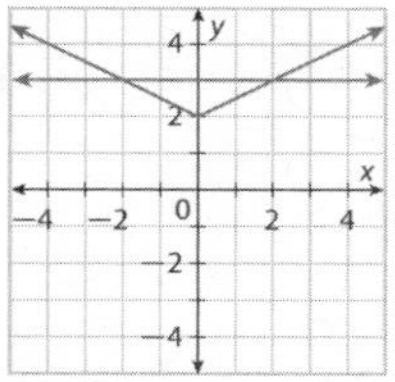

The solution is $-2 < x < 2$.

7. C. The solution is $x < -2$ or $x > 2$.

9. B. The solution is $-\frac{5}{2} < x < \frac{1}{2}$.

11.

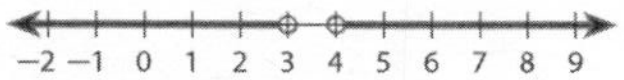

The solution is $x < 3$ or $x > 4$.

13. The solution is $x \leq -5$ or $x \geq -3$.

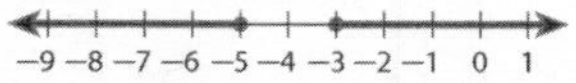

15. all real numbers

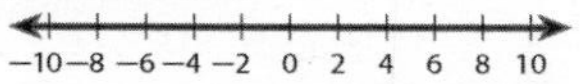

17. The range of house temperatures (in degrees Fahrenheit) is $66 \leq T \leq 70$.

19. The range of ages (in years) that a squirrel lives is $5 \leq a \leq 8$.

21. The range of typical speeds (in miles per hour) is $25 \leq s \leq 35$.

23. The student identified where the graph of $g(x)$ lies above the graph of $f(x)$, but the student should have identified where the graph of $f(x)$ lies above the graph of $g(x)$ because the inequality has the form $f(x) > g(x)$. So, the solution of the inequality is $x < -3$ or $x > 5$.

UNIT 2 Selected Answers

MODULE 3

Lesson 3.1 Solving Quadratic Equations by Taking Square Roots

Your Turn

3. $x = \pm 2\sqrt{6}$

4. $x = \pm -\frac{\sqrt{13}}{2}$

6. $50 - 16t^2 = 0$

The water balloon hits the ground in $\frac{5\sqrt{2}}{4} \approx 1.8$ seconds.

7. $\frac{8}{3}t^2 = 4$

The tool falls 4 feet in $\frac{\sqrt{6}}{2} \approx 1.2$ seconds.

9. $= -4$

10. $= -\frac{1}{3}$

11. $x = \pm 6i$

12. $x = \pm \frac{\sqrt{35}}{5}i$

Evaluate

1. a. $x = -3$ and $x = 3$.

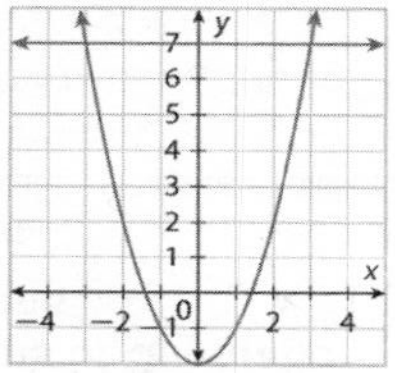

b. $x = -3$ or $x = 3$

c. $x = \pm 3$

3. $x = \pm\sqrt{6}$

5. $x = \pm\frac{\sqrt{2}}{2}$

7. $16t^2 = 20$

The acorn falls 20 feet in $\frac{\sqrt{5}}{2} \approx 1.1$ seconds.

9. So, the width of the rectangle is $\sqrt{15} \approx 3.9$ cm, and the length is $3\sqrt{15} \approx 11.6$ cm.

11. –9

13. $-\frac{1}{2}$

15. $x = \pm 4i$

The solutions are imaginary.

17. $x = \pm 9i$

19. $x = \pm\frac{2\sqrt{5}}{5}i$

21. The smaller square has a side length of $\sqrt{14} \approx 3.7$ cm, and the larger square has a side length of $2\sqrt{14} \approx 7.5$ cm.

23. a. Imaginary

b. Real

c. Real

d. Real

e. Imaginary

f. Real

25. The width of the screen is $16\sqrt{6} \approx 39.2$ inches, and the height of the screen is $9\sqrt{6} \approx 22.0$ inches.

UNIT 2 Selected Answers

MODULE 3

Lesson 3.2 Complex Numbers

Your Turn

4. The real part of 11 is 11, and the imaginary part is 0. Because the imaginary part is 0, the number belongs to these sets: real numbers and complex numbers.
5. The real part of $-1 + i$ is -1, and the imaginary part is 1. Because both the real and imaginary parts of $-1 + i$ are nonzero, the number belongs only to the set of complex numbers.
7. $8 - 16i$
8. $8 + 5i$
10. $-32 - 75i$
11. $73 + 173i$
13. Total impedance = $6 - 2i$

    Voltage for the first resistor = $72 + 24i$

    Voltage for the second resistor = $36 + 12i$

    Voltage for the inductor = $-18 + 54i$

    Voltage for the capacitor = $30 - 90i$

Evaluate

1. $7 - 3x$

   Replacing x with the imaginary unit i gives this result: $(3 + 2i) + (4 - 5i) = 7 - 3i$.
3. The real part is 5, and the imaginary part is 1. Because both the real and imaginary parts are nonzero, the number belongs only to the set of complex numbers.
5. The real part is 25, and the imaginary part is 0. Because the imaginary part is 0, the number belongs to these sets: real numbers and complex numbers.
7. $10 + 15i$
9. $-11 + 2i$
11. $-5 - 3i$
13. $1 + 2i$
15. $-9 + 19i$
17. $108 - 23i$
19. Total impedance = $1 - 3i$

    Voltage for the resistor = $12 + 36i$

    Voltage for the capacitor = $108 - 36i$
21. Total impedance = $6 - 8i$

    Voltage for the inductor = $-19.2 + 14.4i$

    Voltage for the capacitor = $96 - 72i$
23. A. B

    B. D

    C. A

    D. C
25. Show that the square of each number is $6i$.

$$\left(\sqrt{3}+i\sqrt{3}\right)\left(\sqrt{3}+i\sqrt{3}\right) = 3+3i+3i+3i^2$$
$$= 3 + 3i + 3i + 3(-1)$$
$$= 6i$$

$$\left(-\sqrt{3}-i\sqrt{3}\right)\left(-\sqrt{3}-i\sqrt{3}\right) = 3+3i+3i+3i^2$$
$$= 3 + 3i + 3i + 3(-1)$$
$$= 6i$$

UNIT 2 Selected Answers

MODULE 3

Lesson 3.3 Finding Complex Solutions of Quadratic Equations

Your Turn

5. There are two non-real solutions:

   $-4 + i$ and $-4 - i$.
6. There are two real solutions:

   $-5 + 4\sqrt{2}$ and $-5 - 4\sqrt{2}$.
7. Write the area A of the sail as a function of b. $A = \frac{1}{2}b(2b) = b^2$

   Substitute 10 for A. $10 = b^2$

   Subtract 10 from both sides. $0 = b^2 - 10$

   Find the discriminant. $0^2 - 4(1)(-10) = 0 + 40 = 40$

   Because the discriminant is positive, the equation has two real solutions, so the area of the sail can be 10 in^2.
8. The solutions are $\frac{4}{3}$ and $-\frac{1}{2}$.

   Check

$$6\left(\frac{4}{3}\right)^2 - 5\left(\frac{4}{3}\right) - 4 \stackrel{?}{=} 0$$
$$\frac{32}{3} - \frac{20}{3} - 4 \stackrel{?}{=} 0$$
$$0 = 0$$

9. The solution are $-3 + i\sqrt{3}$ and $-3 - i\sqrt{3}$.

$$\left(-3+i\sqrt{3}\right)^2 + 8\left(-3+i\sqrt{3}\right) + 12 \stackrel{?}{=} 2\left(-3+i\sqrt{3}\right)$$
$$6 - 6i\sqrt{3} - 24 + 8i\sqrt{3} + 12 \stackrel{?}{=} -6 + 2i\sqrt{3}$$
$$-6 + 2i\sqrt{3} = -6 + 2i\sqrt{3}$$

Evaluate

1. The graph of $g(x) = -6$ intersects the graph of $f(x)$ twice, so the equation $x^2 + 6x + 6 = 0$ has two real solutions. The graph of $g(x) = -9$ intersects the graph of $f(x)$ once, so the equation $x^2 + 6x + 9 = 0$ has one real solution. The graph of $g(x) = -12$. doesn't intersect the graph of $f(x)$, so the equation $x^2 + 6x + 12 = 0$ has no real solutions.
3. Two real solutions:

   $-2 + \sqrt{3}$ and $-2 - \sqrt{3}$.
5. Two non–real solutions:

   $\frac{5}{2} + \frac{i\sqrt{55}}{2}$ and $\frac{5}{2} - \frac{i\sqrt{55}}{2}$.
7. Two real solutions:

   $\frac{-13+\sqrt{309}}{14}$ and $\frac{-13-\sqrt{309}}{14}$.
9. The equation has two real solutions.
11. The equation has two non-real solutions.
13. $70w - w^2 = 1300$ the equation has two non-real solutions, so the gardener does not have enough fencing.
15. $x(5 - x) = 6.5$ the equation has two non-real solutions, so a student who is 6 feet 6 inches tall cannot walk through the arch without ducking.
17. The solutions are $4 + i\sqrt{11}$ and $4 - i\sqrt{11}$.

$$\left(4+i\sqrt{11}\right)^2 - 8\left(4+i\sqrt{11}\right) + 27 \stackrel{?}{=} 0$$
$$5 + 8i\sqrt{11} - 8\left(4+i\sqrt{11}\right) + 27 \stackrel{?}{=} 0$$
$$5 + 8i\sqrt{11} - 32 - 8i\sqrt{11} + 27 \stackrel{?}{=} 0$$
$$5 - 32 + 27 \stackrel{?}{=} 0$$
$$0 = 0$$

19. The two solutions are $\frac{1+\sqrt{13}}{2}$ and $\frac{1-\sqrt{13}}{2}$.

Check

$$\left(\frac{1+\sqrt{13}}{2}\right)^2-\left(\frac{1+\sqrt{13}}{2}\right)-3\stackrel{?}{=}0$$

$$\frac{14+2+\sqrt{13}}{4}-\left(\frac{1+\sqrt{13}}{2}\right)-3\stackrel{?}{=}0$$

$$\frac{14+2+\sqrt{13}}{4}-\left(\frac{2+2+\sqrt{13}}{4}\right)-3\stackrel{?}{=}0$$

$$\frac{12}{4}-3\stackrel{?}{=}0$$

$$0\stackrel{?}{=}0$$

21.

Equation	Two Real Solutions	One Real Solution	Two Non-Real Solutions
$x^2-3x+1=0$			
$x^2-2x+1=0$			
$x^2-x+1=0$			
$x^2+1=0$			
$x^2-x+1=0$			
$x^2+2x+1=0$			
$x^2+3x+1=0$			

23. The equation has two real solutions when $c<16$. The equation has one real solution when $c=16$. The equation has two non–real solutions when $c>16$.

UNIT 2 Selected Answers

MODULE 4

Lesson 4.1 Circles

Your Turn

3. $(x-1)^2+(y+4)^2=4$

4. $(x+2)^2+(y-5)^2=36$

5. $(x+2)^2+(y+3)^2=9$

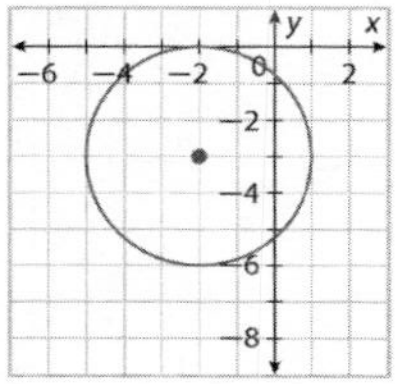

6. $(x-3)^2+(y-4)^2=\frac{16}{9}$

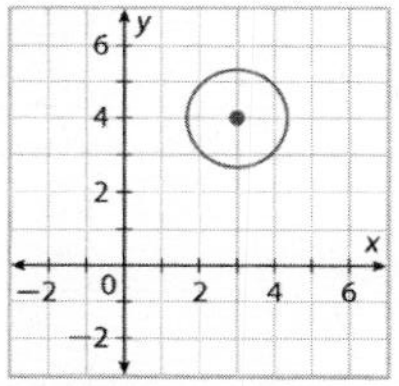

8. The inequality $x^2+(y+1)^2<16$ represents the situation.

Sasha delivers to the houses located at points *B*, *D*, and *E*.

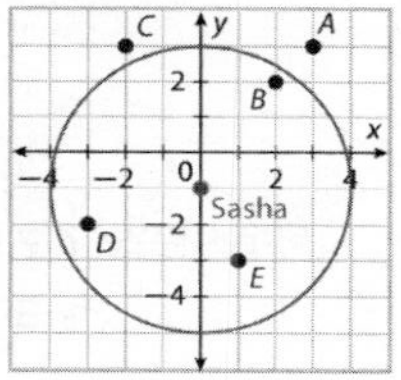

Evaluate

1. $(x-4)^2+(y+11)^2=256$

3. $(x+8)^2+(y-2)^2=65$

5. $(x-1)^2+(y-4)^2=4$

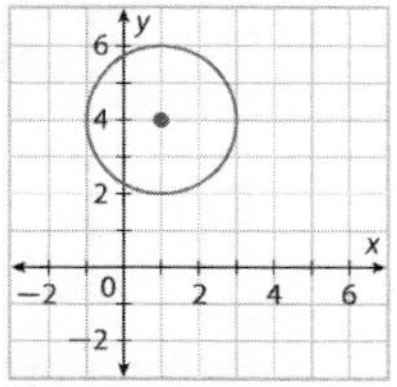

7. $(x+2)^2+(y+6)^2=1$

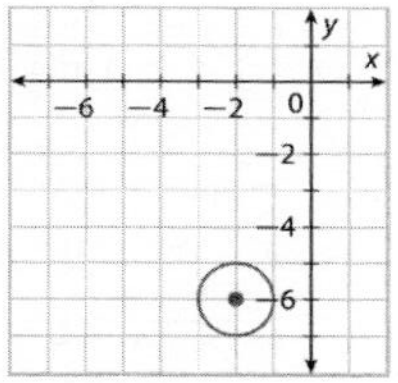

9. $(x-1)^2+(y-2)^2=16$

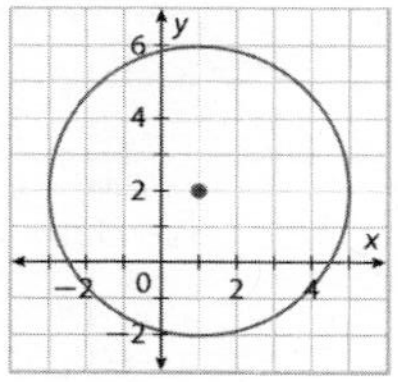

11. $(x-4)^2+(y-1)^2=\frac{1}{4}$

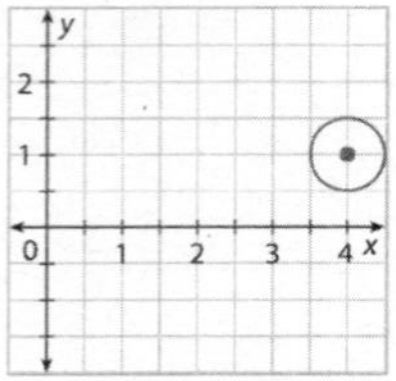

13. $(x-30)^2+(y-30)^2 \le 1225$

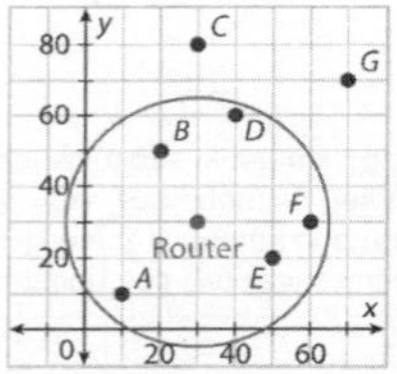

15. $(x-30)^2+(y-40)^2 \le 625$

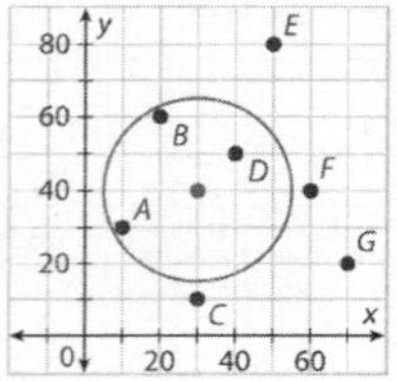

17. $(x-5)^2+y^2>100$

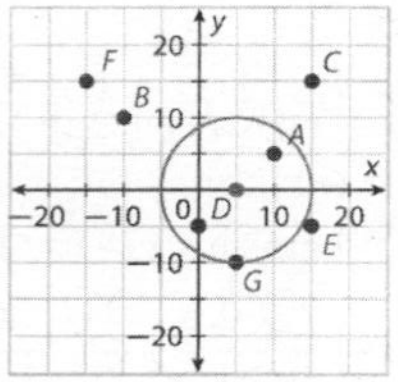

19. $(x+10)^2+(y+10)^2 \le 900$

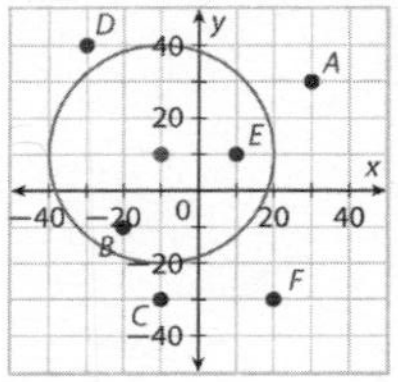

21. B, C, A, D

23. $x^2+y^2=4489$, Venus is approximately 67 million miles from the Sun.

25. Let the center of the sphere be *C* (*h*, *k*, *j*), the radius be *r*, and an arbitrary point on the sphere be *P*-prime (*x*, *y*, *z*). The plane $z=j$ includes the points *C* (*h*, *k*, *j*) and *P'* (*x*, *y*, *j*), which is the perpendicular projection of *P* (*x*, *y*, *z*) onto the plane. Because *C* and *P'* are both in the plane $z=j$, $CP'=\sqrt{(x-h)^2+(y-k)^2}$. Applying the Pythagorean Theorem to $\Delta CP'P$, which is a right triangle, gives the following:

$$(CP')^2+(P'P)^2=(CP)^2$$

$$\left(\sqrt{(x-h)^2+(y-k)^2}\right)^2+(z-j)^2=r^2$$

$$(x-h)^2+(y-k)^2+(z-j)^2=r^2$$

UNIT 2 Selected Answers

MODULE 4

Lesson 4.2 Parabolas

Your Turn

3.

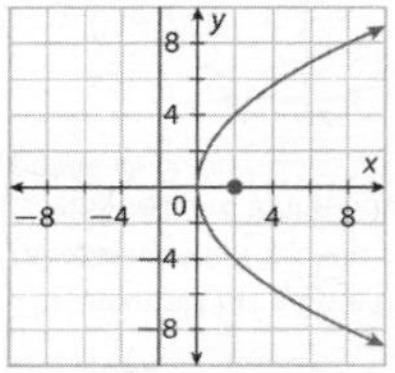

$y^2=8x$

4.

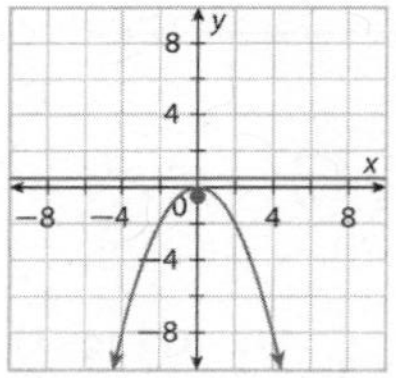

$x^2=-2y$

5.

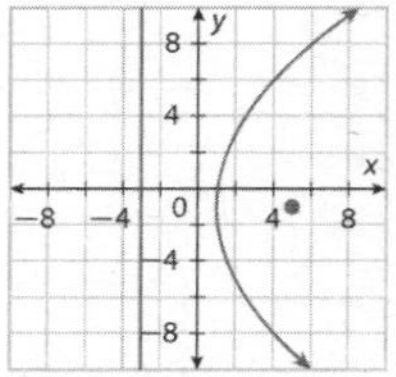

$(y+1)^2=16(x-1)$

6.

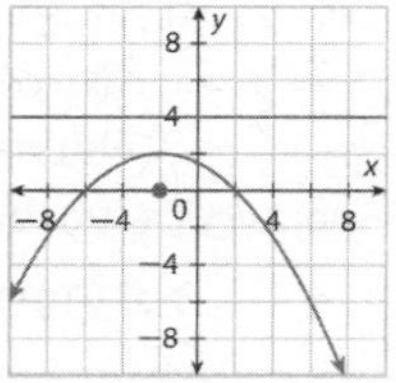

$(x+2)^2=-8(y-2)$

7.

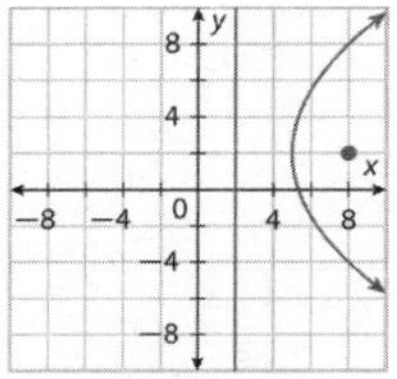

$(y-2)^2=12(x-5)$

8.

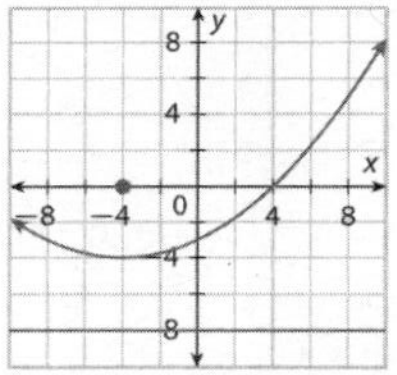

$(x+4)^2=16(y+4)$

9. The team wins the game.

Evaluate

1.

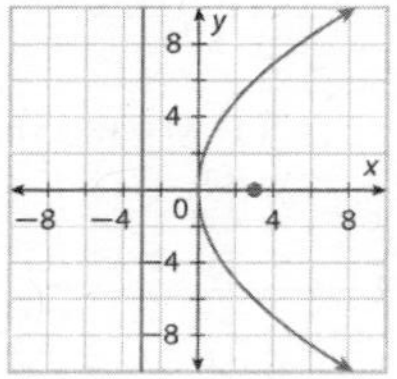

$y^2=12x$

3.

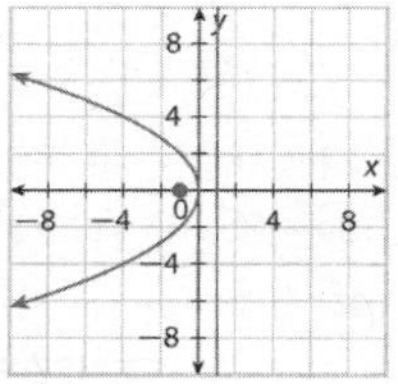

$y^2=-4x$

5. $(y-6)^2 = -5(x+3)$

7.
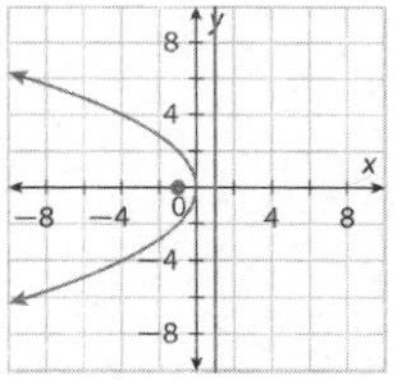

$(x-5)^2 = -8(y-5)$

9.
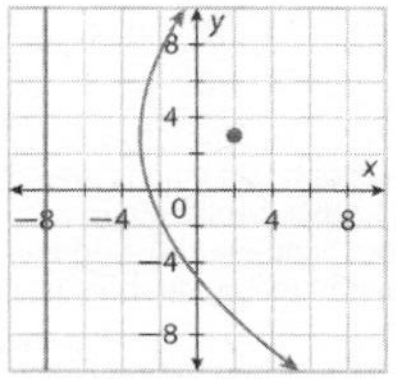

$(y-3)^2 = 20(x+3)$

11. The focus is 12.5 in. from the vertex of the cross section.

13. The ball travels 40 feet before it hits the ground.

15. B; C; A

17. $y^2 = -4px$

19. The parabola has the equation: $y^2 = 4px$. The axis of symmetry of this parabola is the x-axis. The line containing the latus rectum is perpendicular to the x-axis and goes through the focus so it has an equation of $x = p$. Setting $x = p$ in the equation above and solving for y we obtain the coordinates of the endpoints of the latus rectum. Their coordinates are $(p, 2p)$ and $(p, -2p)$. The length of this segment is $2p - (-2p) = 4p$ as expected for a vertical segment with those endpoints.

$y^2 = 4px$

$y^2 = 4p \cdot p$

$y^2 = 4p^2$

$y = \pm\sqrt{4p^2}$

$y = \pm 2p$

UNIT 2 Selected Answers

MODULE 4

Lesson 4.3 Solving Linear-Quadratic Systems

Your Turn

3.
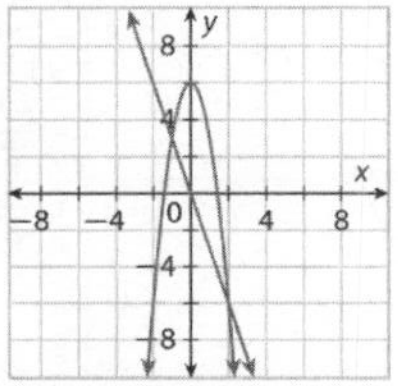

$(-1,3)$ and $(2,-6)$

4.
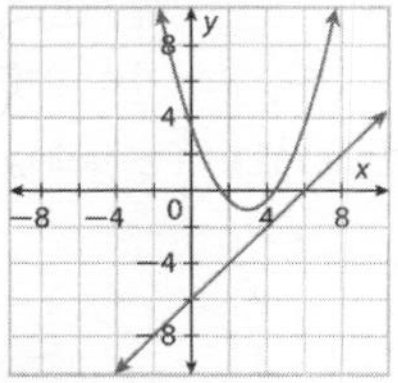

No solution

6. The solutions are $(0,6)$ and $\left(\frac{9}{2},-3\right)$.

7. The solutions are $(0,-7)$ and $(1,-6)$.

8. $(-1.17,-7.04)$ and $(1.65,-6.94)$

9. (4, 20)

Evaluate

1. 1

3.
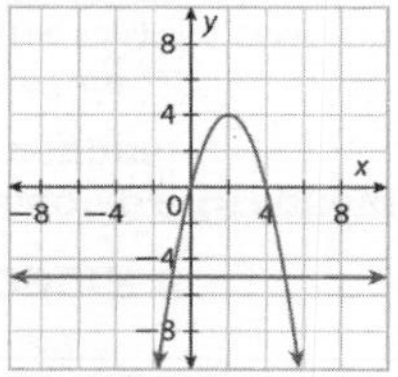

$(-1, -5)$ and $(5, -5)$

5.
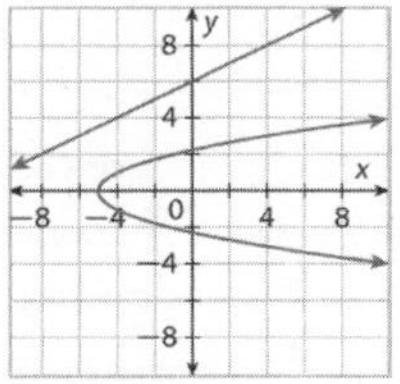

No solution

7.
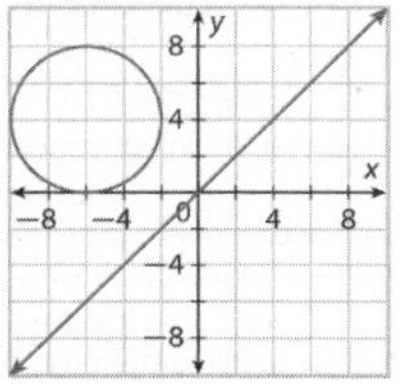

No solution

9. $(-3,2)$

11. $(1,-5)$ and $(5,-1)$

13. $(0,1)$ and $(1,2)$

15. It takes $\frac{1}{60}$ of an hour, or 1 minute, to catch up.

17. The quarter and the balloon will pass after 4 seconds.

19. B; D; A; C

21. The student did not give a linear equation. The first equation is a circle, and the second equation is a parabola.

23. Because the graphs are both parabolas that share a vertex, any line that goes through the vertex but is not horizontal or vertical will go through some other point on each parabola.

UNIT 2 Selected Answers

MODULE 4

Lesson 4.4 Solving Linear Systems in Three Variables

Your Turn

2. (1, 3, 1)
3. (2, –6, 3)
4. (1, 3, 1)
5. (2, –6, 3)
6. (1, 3, 1)
7. $t = 794$, $f = 2352$ and $r = 4496$

Evaluate

1. (0, 0, 3)
3. (0, 0, 3)
5. (–1, 4, –2)
7. (0.25, 0.75, 0)
9. (2,–3,1)
11. Angle *X* measures 160°, angle *Y* measures 15°, and angle *Z* measures 5°.
13. Stock A sold 4000 shares, stock B sold 1000 shares, and stock C sold 5000 shares.
15. The student did not add the last column of numbers representing the values to the right of the equals sign. The correct matrix set up should be as follows.

$$\begin{bmatrix} 5 & 7 & 9 & 0 \\ 1 & -1 & 1 & -3 \\ 8 & 1 & 0 & 12 \end{bmatrix}$$

UNIT 3 Selected Answers

MODULE 5

Lesson 5.1 Graphing Cubic Functions

Your Turn

4. The transformations of the graph of *f*(*x*) that produce the graph of *g*(*x*) are:
   - a vertical compression by a factor of $\frac{1}{2}$
   - a reflection across the *x*-axis
   - a translation of 3 units to the right

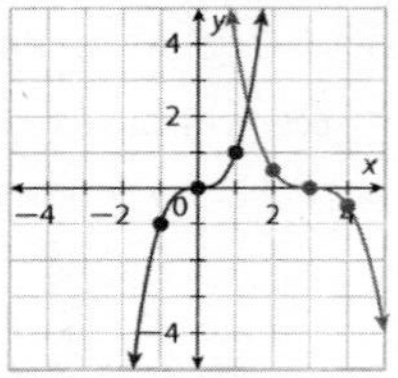

Points: $\left(2, \frac{1}{2}\right)$, (3,0), and $\left(4, -\frac{1}{2}\right)$

5. $g(x) = 3\,(x + 2)^3 - 2$
6. $g(x) = \left(\frac{1}{4}(x-1)\right)^3 - 1$
8. 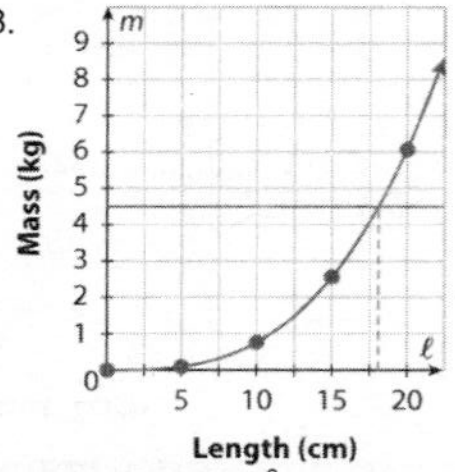

$m(\ell) = 0.00076\ell^3$

The inner edge length of the box is about 18 cm.

Evaluate

1. 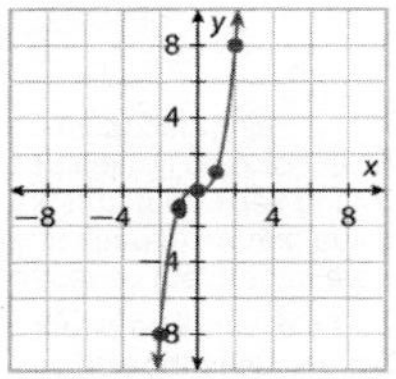

   a. The domain is ℝ, and the range is ℝ.

   b. As $x \to +\infty$, $f(x) \to +\infty$. As $x \to -\infty$, $f(x) \to -\infty$.

   c. The graph's only *x*-intercept is 0. The graph's only *y*-intercept is 0.

   d. The function has positive values on the interval $(0, +\infty)$ and negative values on the interval $(-\infty, 0)$.

   e. The function is increasing throughout its domain. The function never decreases.

   f. The function is odd because $f(-x) = (-x)^3 = -x^3 = -f(x)$.

   g. The graph is symmetric about the origin.

3. Vertical stretch of the graph of *f*(*x*) by a factor of 5 and a reflection across the *x*-axis.
5. Horizontal compression of the graph of *f*(*x*) by a factor of $\frac{1}{3}$.
7. Vertical compression of the graph of *f*(*x*) by a factor of $\frac{1}{4}$.
9. Horizontal stretch of the graph of *f*(*x*) by a factor of $\frac{3}{4}$ as well as a reflection across the *y*-axis.

11.

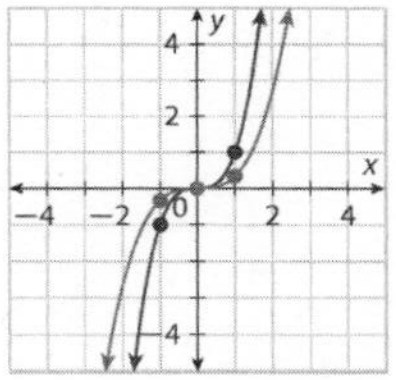

A vertical compression by a factor of $\frac{1}{3}$.

Reference points on the graph of $g(x)$ are $\left(-1, -\frac{1}{3}\right)$, (0,0) and $\left(1, \frac{1}{3}\right)$.

13.

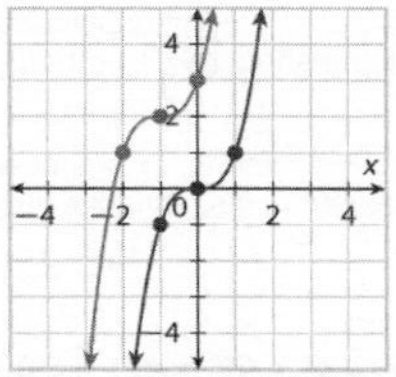

A translation of 1 unit to the left and 2 units up. Reference points on the graph of $g(x)$ are (−2, 1), (−1, 2), and (0, 3).

15. $g(x) = -3(x - 1)^3 + 4$

17. $g(x) = 0.5(x + 1)^3 + 2$

19. $V(r) = \frac{1}{2}\left(\frac{4}{3}\pi r^3\right) \approx 2.09r^3$.

The radius of the biodome is about 1.4 thousand (1400) ft.

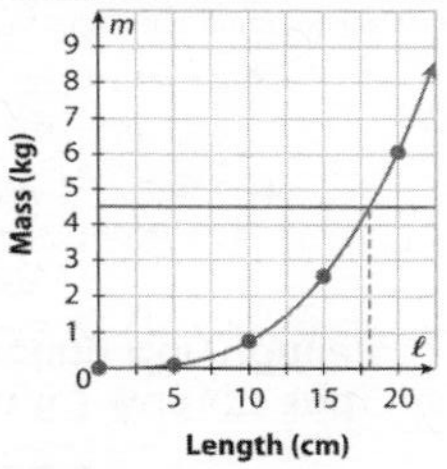

21. Horizontally stretching or compressing the graph of the parent cubic function by a factor of b results in the graph of the function $g(x) = \left(\frac{1}{b}x\right)^3$. You can rewrite $g(x)$ as follows:

$$g(x) = \left(\frac{1}{b}x\right)^3$$
$$= \left(\frac{1}{b}\right)^3 \cdot x^3$$
$$= \frac{1}{b^3} \cdot x^3$$

The function is now in the form $g(x) = ax^3$ where $a = \frac{1}{b^3}$. Notice that when $|b| > 1, |a| < 1$, which means that a horizontal stretch is equivalent to a vertical compression. Similarly, when $|b| < 1, |a| > 1$, which means that a horizontal compression is equivalent to a vertical stretch.

UNIT 3 Selected Answers

MODULE 5

Lesson 5.2 Graphing Polynomial Functions

Your Turn

5.

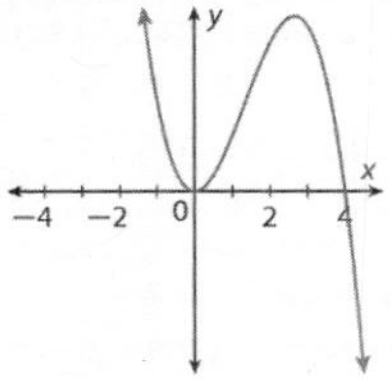

7. Maximum volume is about 402 cubic inches when square flaps with a side length of 2.7 inches are made in the corners.

Evaluate

1. Domain: $(-\infty, +\infty)$

   Range: $(-\infty, +\infty)$

   End behavior: As $x \to +\infty, f(x) \to +\infty$.

   As $x \to -\infty, f(x) \to -\infty$.

3. Domain: $(-\infty, +\infty)$

   Range: $[0, +\infty)$

   End behavior: As $x \to +\infty, f(x) \to +\infty$.

   As $x \to -\infty, f(x) \to +\infty$.

5. The graph has two turning points. The function has one local maximum value and one local minimum value.
7. The graph has two turning points. The function has one local maximum value and one local minimum value.
9.

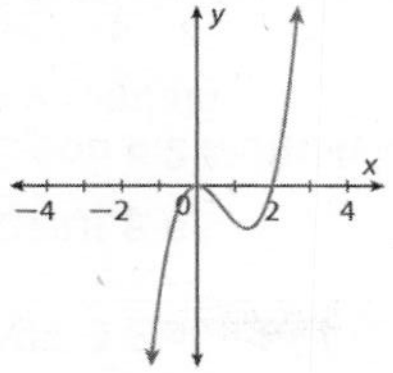

11.

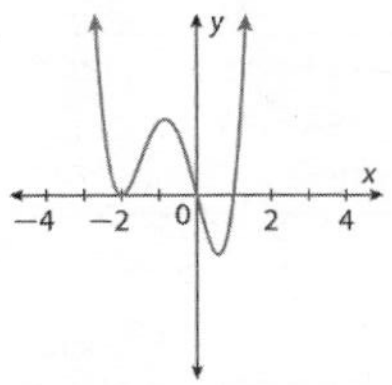

13. The volume function is $V(x) = x(17 - x)(36 - x)$. The box has a maximum volume of about 2032 cubic inches when the dimensions of the box are 7.3 inches, 9.7 inches, and 28.7 inches.
15. The specific function with $a = -1$ is $f(x) = -(x+2)^2(x-3)$.
17. The specific function with $a = -1$ is $f(x) = -(x+2)^2(x-3)^2$.
19.

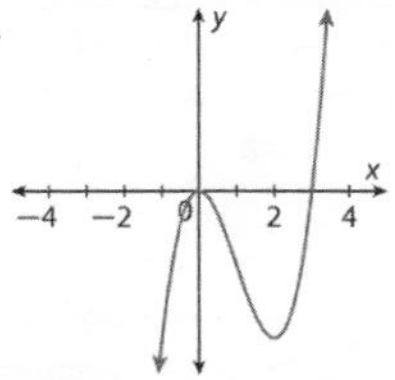

The student sketched the graph so that it crosses the x-axis at $x = 0$ and is tangent to the x-axis at $x = 3$. Instead, the graph should be tangent to the x-axis at $x = 0$ and cross the x-axis at $x = 3$.

21. $V(x) = \frac{1}{4\pi}(x-1)^2(18-x)$ the tube has a maximum volume of about 59.9 cubic inches when the length of the sides of the rectangle that form the ends of the tube is 12.3 inches.

UNIT 3 Selected Answers

MODULE 6

Lesson 6.1 Adding and Subtracting Polynomials

Your Turn

3. $-9x^7 + 17x^4 + 9x^3 + 16$
4. $3x^{11} + x^6 + 4x^4 - 9x + 17$
6. $23x^7 - 6x^2 - 30$
7. $-6x^5 + 7x^3 + 11x^2 + 13x$
8. 132,219 thousand automobiles were owned in the United States in 2005.

Evaluate

1. Standard Form: $x^9 - 23x^7 - 6x^3 + 2x^2 + 10$
   Degree: 9
   Leading Coefficient: 1
3. $-121x^{12} - 65x^2 + 15x$
5. $18x^2 + 9x$
7. $-10x^3$
9. $68x^4 + 17x^3 - 22x - 22$
11. $-17x^3 + 2x + 2$
13. $10x^2 - 14$
15. The width is 29,644 inches when the length is 21 inches.
17. ≈ 983 dollars
19. About 242,240 thousand students were enrolled in 2000.
21. a d e g
23. Janice will need to spend \$4030 on fencing.
25. The sum of two monomials, ax^m and bx^m, is another monomial, $(a+b)x^m$.

   $ax^m - bx^m = (a-b)x^m$

   The difference of two monomials, ax^m and bx^m, is another monomial, $(a-b)x^m$

   So, the sum or difference of two polynomials is a sum of monomials, which is another polynomial.

UNIT 3 Selected Answers

MODULE 6

Lesson 6.2 Multiplying Polynomials

Your Turn

3. $2x(5x^2) + 2x(-7x) + 2x(4) + 3(5x^2) + 3(-7x) + 3(4)$ Distribute the $2x$ and the 3.
   $10x^3 - 14x^2 + 8x + 15x^2 - 21x + 12$ Simplify.
   $10x^3 + x^2 - 13x + 12$ Combine like terms.
4. $x(-4x^2) + x(-8x) + x(3) - 6(-4x^2) - 6(-8x) - 6(3)$ Distribute the x and the -6.
   $-4x^3 - 8x^2 + 3x + 24x^2 + 48x - 18$ Simplify.
   $-4x^3 + 16x^2 + 51x - 18$ Combine like terms.
5. The total cost of making the toys can be modeled by the following polynomial, where x is the number of years since 2000.
   $T(x) = -0.0028x^4 - 0.048x^3 + 17.568x^2 - 51.84x + 575$
6. The left side of the identity is already fully simplified. Simplify the right-hand side.
   $a^5 - b^5 = a(a^4) + a(a^3b) + a(a^2b^2) + a(ab^3) + a(b^4) - b(a^4) - b(a^3b) - b(a^2b^2) - b(ab^3) - b(b^4)$
   $a^5 - b^5 = a^5 + a^4b + a^3b^2 + a^2b^3 + ab^4 - a^4b - a^3b^2 - a^2b^3 - ab^4 - b^5$
   $a^5 - b^5 = a^5 - b^5$
7. The right side of the identity is already fully simplified. Simplify the left-hand side.
   $a(a^2) + a(ab) + a(b^2) - b(a^2) - b(ab) - b(b^2) = a^3 - b^3$ Distribute a and b.
   $a^3 + a^2b + ab^2 - a^2b - ab^2 - b^3 = a^3 - b^3$ Simplify.
   $a^3 - b^3 = a^3 - b^3$ Combine like terms.
8. Substitute $x = 40$ and $y = 3$ into the identity and evaluate.
   $(40 + 3)(40 - 3) = 40^2 - 3^2$
   $43 \cdot 37 = 1600 - 9$
   $43 \cdot 37 = 1591$
9. $25 - 7 = 18$
   Substitute $x = 25$ and $y = 7$ into the identity and evaluate.
   $(25 - 7)^2 = 25^2 - 2 \cdot 25 \cdot 7 + 7^2$
   $18^2 = 625 - 350 + 49 = 625 - 301 = 324$

Evaluate

1. $x^3 + 6x^2 + 5x$
3.

	x^3		$+3x^2$		$+1$
×			$3x^2$	$+6x$	-2
	$-2x^3$		$-6x^2$		-2
$6x^4$	$+18x^3$			$+6x$	
$3x^5 + 9x^4$			$+3x^2$		
$3x^5 + 15x^4$	$+16x^3$		$-3x^2$	$+6x$	-2

   Multiply -2 and $(x^3 + 3x^2 + 1)$.
   Multiply $6x$ and $(x^3 + 3x^2 + 1)$.
   Multiply $3x^2$ and $(x^3 + 3x^2 + 1)$.
   Combine like terms.
5. $2x(3x^2) + 2x(-4xy) + 2x(2y^2) + 5y(3x^2) + 5y(-4xy) + 5y(2y^2)$ Distribute the $2x$ and the $5y$.
   $6x^3 - 8x^2y + 4xy^2 + 15x^2y - 20xy^2 + 10y^3$ Simplify.
   $6x^3 + 7x^2y - 16xy^2 + 10y^3$ Combine like terms.
7.

		$4x^2$	$+3x$	$+2$
	×	$3x^2$	$+2x$	-1
		$-4x^2$	$-3x$	-2
	$8x^3$	$+6x^2$	$+4x$	
$12x^4$	$+9x^3$	$+6x^2$		
$12x^4$	$+17x^3$	$+8x^2$	$+x$	-2

Multiply −1 and $(4x^2 + 3x + 2)$.
Multiply $2x$ and $(4x^2 + 3x + 2)$.
Multiply $3x^2$ and $(4x^2 + 3x + 2)$.
Combine like terms.

9. $R(x) = -0.02x^4 - 0.3x^3 + 4.4x^2 - 14.2x + 20$

11. $K + U = 1752$
Since the sum is a constant, this means that the energy of the object is constant and that as it gains kinetic energy by falling, it loses the same amount of potential energy.

13. The left side of the identity is already fully simplified. Simplify the right-hand side.

$$\begin{array}{r} a^4 - a^3b + a^2b^2 - ab^3 + b^4 \\ \times \qquad\qquad a + b \\ \hline a^4b - a^3b^2 + a^2b^3 - ab^4 + b^5 \\ a^5 - a^4b + a^3b^2 - a^2b^3 + ab^4 \qquad \\ \hline a^5 \qquad\qquad\qquad\qquad\qquad + b^5 \end{array}$$

15. $a^2(x^2) + a^2(y^2) + b^2(x^2) + b^2(y^2) = (ax)^2 - 2(ax)(by) + (by)^2 + (bx)^2 + 2(bx)(ay) + (ay)^2$
$a^2x^2 + a^2y^2 + b^2x^2 + b^2y^2 = a^2x^2 - 2axby + b^2y^2 + b^2x^2 + 2axby + a^2y^2$
$a^2x^2 + a^2y^2 + b^2x^2 + b^2y^2 = a^2x^2 + a^2y^2 + b^2x^2 + b^2y^2$

17. $32^2 = (30 + 2)^2$
$= 900 + 120 + 4$
$= 1024$

19. $47^2 = (50 - 3)^2$
$= 2500 - 300 + 9$
$= 2209$

21. $58 \cdot 68 = (63 + 5)(63 - 5)$
$= 63^2 - 5^2$
$= (60 + 3)^2 - 25$
$= 60^2 + 2 \cdot 60 \cdot 3 + 3^2 - 25$
$= 3600 + 360 + 9 - 25$
$= 3944$

23. a. 1 term
b. 2 terms
c. 2 terms
d. 4 terms

25. Since $ax^m \cdot bx^n = abx^{m+n}$ for real numbers a and b and whole numbers m and n, the product of two monomials is another monomial. Therefore, the product of two polynomials, which are sums of monomials, is again a sum of monomials, which is another polynomial.

UNIT 3 Selected Answers

MODULE 6

Lesson 6.3 The Binomial Theorem

Your Turn

8. The values in row 4 of Pascal's Triangle are 1, 4, 6, 4, and 1.
$(x - y)^4 = 1x^4(-y)^0 + 4x^3(-y)^1 + 6x^2(-y)^2 + 4x^1(-y)^3 + 1x^0(-y)^4$
$= x^4 - 4x^3y + 6x^2y^2 - 4xy^3 + y^4$

10. The probability that Ms. Banks will get exactly 2 of the next 3 students is $\frac{2}{9}$, or about 22.2%.

Evaluate

1. The path LLRRLLR leads to the fourth node in row 7. This node has a value of $15 + 20 = 35$ when Pascal's Triangle in Explore 1 is extended to row 7.

3. $(x + 6)^3 = 1x^3(6)^0 + 3x^2(6)^1 + 3x^1(6)^2 + 1x^0(6)^3$
$= x^3 + 18x^2 + 108x + 216$

5. $(x + 3)^6 = 1x^6(3)^0 + 6x^5(3)^1 + 15x^4(3)^2 + 20x^3(3)^3 + 15x^2(3)^4 + 6x^1(3)^5 + 1x^0(3)^6$
$= x^6 + 18x^5 + 135x^4 + 540x^3 + 1215x^2 + 1458x + 729$

7. $(3x + 4)^5 = 1(3x)^5(4)^0 + 5(3x)^4(4)^1 + 10(3x)^3(4)^2 + 10(3x)^2(4)^3 + 5(3x)^1(4)^4 + 1(3x)^0(4)^5$
$= 243x^5 + 1620x^4 + 4320x^3 + 5760x^2 + 3840x + 1024$

9. $(x + 2y)^5 = 1x^5(2y)^0 + 5x^4(2y)^1 + 10x^3(2y)^2 + 10x^2(2y)^3 + 5x^1(2y)^4 + 1x^0(2y)^5$
$= x^5 + 10x^4y + 40x^3y^2 + 80x^2y^3 + 80xy^4 + 32y^5$

11. $(5x + y)^4 = 1(5x)^4y^0 + 4(5x)^3y^1 + 6(5x)^2y^2 + 4(5x)^1y^3 + 1(5x)^0y^4$
$= 625x^4 + 500x^3y + 150x^2y^2 + 20xy^3 + y^4$

13. $(5x - 4y)^3 = 1(5x)^3(-4y)^0 + 3(5x)^2(-4y)^1 + 3(5x)^1(-4y)^2 + 1(5x)^0(-4y)^3$
$= 125x^3 - 300x^2y + 240xy^2 - 64y^3$

15. $-20x^3$

17. $1080x^3y^2$

19. $\frac{135}{512}$, or about 26.4%

21. about 0.000114, or about 0.0114%

23. B
D
A
C

25. If you think of a tree diagram like the one for Pascal's Triangle but with a and b substituted for L and R, you can see that a pathway from the top of the tree down to the node in, say, position 2 (counting from 0) of row 5, generates a string such as *aabab*, which is one way to produce the term with the variable part a^3b^2 in the expanded form of $(a + b)^5$. (In essence, the string *aabab* tells you to use the *a*-terms from the first, second, and fourth factors in the product $(a + b)(a + b)(a + b)(a + b)(a + b)$ and to use the *b*-terms from the third and fifth factors.) There are 9 other pathways that lead to position 2 of row 5: *bbaaa, abbaa, aabba, aaabb, baaab, abaab, baaba, ababa,* and *babaa*. So, there is a total of 10, or ${}_5C_2$, ways to produce the term with the variable part a^3b^2, which means that a^3b^2 has a coefficient of ${}_5C_2$. In general, the term in the expanded form of $(a + b)^n$ with the variable part $a^{n-r}b^r$ has the coefficient ${}_nC_r$, which is what the Binomial Theorem tells you.

UNIT 3 Selected Answers

MODULE 6

Lesson 6.4 Factoring Polynomials

Your Turn

4. $x(3x + 4)(x + 1)$
6. $40x^4 + 5x = 5x(2x + 1)(4x^2 - 2x + 1)$
7. $(x^2 + x + 1)(x + 2)$
8. The vault is 24 feet long, 12 feet wide, and 12 feet high.

Evaluate

1. $x(x + 4)(x - 3)$
3. $x^3 - 125 = (x - 5)(x^2 + 5x + 25)$
5. $8x^3 + 125 = (2x + 5)(4x^2 - 10x + 25)$
7. $216x^3 + 64 = 8(3x + 2)(9x^2 - 6x + 4)$
9. $10x^3 - 80 = 10(x - 2)(x^2 + 2x + 4)$
11. $x(x + 2)(x + 8)$
13. $(x^2 + 6)(x + 8)$
15. $(2x + 3)(4x^2 - 6x + 9)(x + 1)$
17. $(x^2 + 3)(x + 2)$
19. The lower floor is 32 feet long, 16 feet wide, and 10 feet high.
21. The tank is 8 feet long, 4 feet wide, and 4 feet high.
23. difference of two squares

    none

    none

    sum of two cubes

    none
25. There is no sum-of-two-squares factoring pattern because factoring any sum of two squares results in factors with imaginary constants.
27. (-4) — Rewrite as a difference

    $\sqrt{-4}$ $\sqrt{-4}$ — of two squares.

    $x - 2i$
29. $(x + 1)(x + i)(x - i)$

UNIT 3 Selected Answers

MODULE 6

Lesson 6.5 Dividing Polynomials

Your Turn

3. $5x - 10$

   $(3x^2 + 6x + 1)(5x - 10) + 63x - 2$

   $= 15x^3 - 30x^2 + 30x^2 - 60x + 5x - 10 + 63x - 2$

   $= 15x^3 + 8x - 12$

   $63x - 2$
4. $9x^2 + x - 133$

   $(x^2 + 16)(9x^2 + x - 133) - 16x + 2124$

   $= 9x^4 + x^3 - 133x^2 + 144x^2 + 16x - 2128 - 16x + 2124$

   $= 9x^4 + x^3 + 11x^2 - 4$

   $-16x + 2124$
6. $(x - 2)(2x^2 + 9x + 17) + 41$
7. $\left(x + \frac{1}{3}\right)(6x^3 - 27x^2 + 9x - 6) + 7$
8. Since the remainder is 0, $(x + 4)$ is a factor.

   $2(x + 1)(x^2 - x + 1)(x + 4)$
9. Since the remainder is 6, $x - 1$ is not a factor.

Evaluate

1. $p(-3) = -155$
3. $p(-3) = 0$
5. $(x^2 - 4)(18x - 3) + 73x - 13$
7. $(x^2 + 3x + 0.5)(x^2 - 3x + 8.5) - 18x - 6.75$
9. $(x - 8)(7x^2 + 52x + 16) + 28$
11. $(x + 1)(2.5x^2 + 3.5x - 9) - 1$
13. $x + 2$ is not a factor.
15. $x - 3$ is not a factor.
17. $x^2 - 3x$
19. $x^2 + 3x - 1$
21. $x^2 - 5x - 12$

    Check.

    $(3x + 4)\left(\frac{3x^2 - 15x - 36}{3}\right) - 2$

    $= (3x + 4)(x^2 - 5x - 12) - 2$

    $= 3x^3 + 4x^2 - 15x^2 - 20x - 36x - 48 - 2$

    $= 3x^3 - 11x^2 - 56x - 50$
23. Polynomials are similar to integers with respect to closure. They are closed under each operation except division.

UNIT 3 Selected Answers

MODULE 7

Lesson 7.1 Finding Rational Solutions of Polynomial Equations

Your Turn

7. The zeros are $x = 3$, $x = -1$, or $x = -5$.
8. The length is 4 inches. The width is 2 inches and the height is 7 inches.

Evaluate

1. $x = 4$, $x = -2$, or $x = -1$

   $f(x) = (x - 4)(x + 2)(x + 1)$
3. $x = 3$, $x = -\frac{1}{2}$, or $x = -2$

   $j(x) = (x - 3)(2x + 1)(x + 2)$
5. $x = 2$, $x = 4$, or $x = -1$

   $h(x) = (x - 2)(x - 4)(x + 1)$
7. $x = 1$ or $x = -1$

   $s(x) = (x - 1)(x + 1)(x - 1)$
9. $x = 1$, $x = -3$, or $x = -4$

   $k(x) = (x - 1)(x - 1)(x + 3)(x + 4)$
11. $x = -1$ or $x = 2$

    $h(x) = (x - 2)(x - 2)(x + 1)(x + 1)$
13. The width is 1 inch and the height is 15 inches.
15. The height is 6 inches, the length is 2 inches, and the width is 3 inches.
17. The zeros of $f(x)$ are $x = -3$, $x = 4$, and $x = 3$.

    $f(x) = x^3 - 4x^2 - 9x + 36$

    The zeros of $f(x)$ are all factors of the constant term in the polynomial function.
19. For any factor $(ax + b)$, a zero occurs at $-\frac{b}{a}$. Sabrina forgot to include the negative sign when converting from her factors to the zeros.
21. $p(x) = (x + 3)(x - 4)(x - 6)$; any constant multiple of $p(x)$ will also have degree 3 and the same zeros, so the equation can be any function of the form $p(x) = a(x + 3)(x - 4)(x - 6)$ where $a \neq 0$.

UNIT 3 Selected Answers

MODULE 7

Lesson 7.2 Finding Complex Solutions of Polynomial Equations

Your Turn

5. The roots are $\frac{3}{2}$, $\frac{-3+3i\sqrt{3}}{4}$, and $\frac{-3-3i\sqrt{3}}{4}$.
6. The roots are 0, 7, $3 + 2i$, and $3 - 2i$.
9. The polynomial function is $p(x) = x^4 - 12x^3 - 37x^2 + 224x - 1066$.
10. The radius of the rocket is 3 cm.

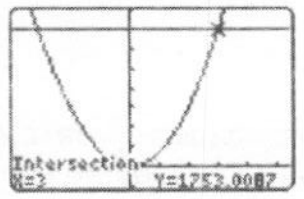

Evaluate

1. The zeros of $p(x)$ are 2, $\frac{2+i\sqrt{2}}{3}$, and $\frac{2-i\sqrt{2}}{3}$.
3. The roots are $\frac{3}{2}$, $-2i$, and $2i$.
5. $p(x) = x^4 - 2x^3 - 5x^2 + 10x$
7. $p(x) = x^6 + 2x^5 + 9x^4 + 16x^3 - x^2 - 18x - 9$
9. 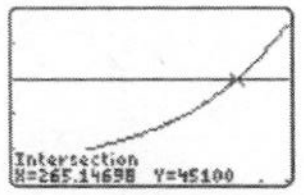

   The x-coordinate of the intersection gives the model's predicted height for a tree with the volume of the President tree. This predicted height is about 265 feet.
11. 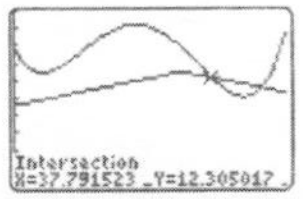

    The graphs intersect at x-values of about 38 and 47. This means that at those weeks of the year, the cash balance and stock balance in the account were the same.
13. The roots are -5 and 5, each with multiplicity 2, and $-5i$ and $5i$.
15. The least degree is 10. Since $3i$ is a root 3 times, then $-3i$ must also be a root 3 times. Since $2 - \sqrt{3}$ is a root 2 times, then $2 + \sqrt{3}$ must also be a root 2 times, and $3 + 3 + 2 + 2 = 10$.

UNIT 4 Selected Answers

MODULE 8

Lesson 8.1 Graphing Simple Rational Functions

Your Turn

4. The transformations of the graph of $f(x)$ that produce the graph of $g(x)$ are:
   - a vertical compression by a factor of $\frac{1}{2}$
   - a reflection across the x-axis
   - a translation of 1 units to the left and 3 units down

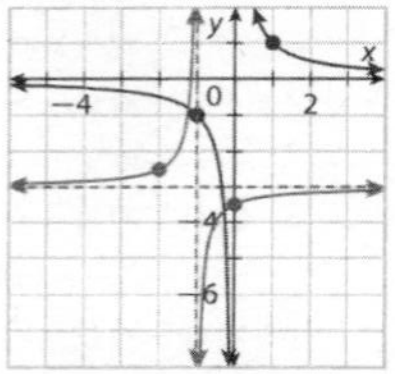

Vert. Asymp: $x = 0$ becomes $x = -1$

Horiz. Asymp: $y = 0$ becomes $y = -3$

$(-1, -1)$ becomes $\left(-2, -\frac{1}{2}\right)$

$(1, 1)$ becomes $\left(0, -\frac{7}{2}\right)$

Domain of $g(x)$:

Inequality: $x < -1$ or $x > -1$

Set notation: $\{x \mid x \neq -1\}$

Interval notation: $(-\infty, -1) \cup (-1, +\infty)$

Range of $g(x)$:

Inequality: $y < -3$ or $y > -3$

Set notation: $\{y \mid y \neq -3\}$

Interval notation: $(-\infty, -3) \cup (-3, +\infty)$

5. The transformations of the graph of $f(x)$ that produce the graph of $g(x)$ are:
   - a horizontal stretch by a factor of 2
   - a reflection across the y-axis
   - a translation of 2 units to the right and 1 unit up

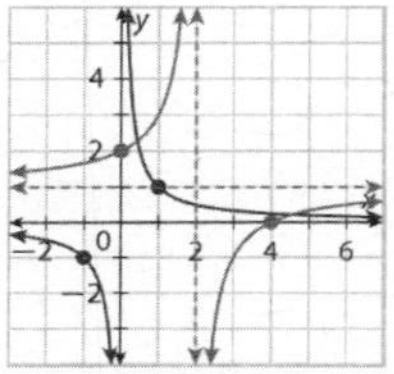

Vert. Asymp: $x = 0$ becomes $x = 2$

Horiz. Asymp: $y = 0$ becomes $y = 1$

$(-1, -1)$ becomes $(4, 0)$

$(1, 1)$ becomes $(0, 2)$

Domain of $g(x)$:

Inequality: $x < 2$ or $x > 2$

Set notation: $\{x \mid x \neq 2\}$

Interval notation: $(-\infty, 2) \cup (2, +\infty)$

Range of $g(x)$:

Inequality: $y < 1$ or $y > 1$

Set notation $\{y \mid y \neq 1\}$

Interval notation: $(-\infty, 1) \cup (1, +\infty)$

8. $g(x) = 3 + \frac{2}{x+2}$, or $g(x) = 2\left(\frac{1}{x+2}\right) + 3$.

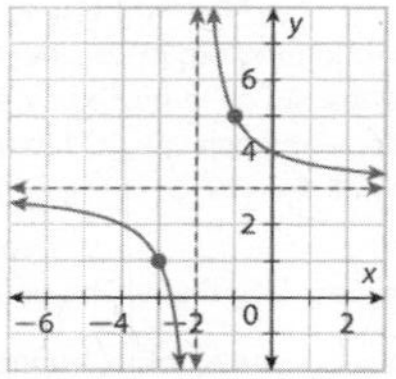

Domain of $g(x)$:

Inequality: $x < -2$ or $x > -2$

Set notation: $\{x \mid x \neq -2\}$

Interval notation: $(-\infty, -2) \cup (-2, +\infty)$

Range of $g(x)$:

Inequality: $y < 3$ or $y > 3$

Set notation: $\{y \mid y \neq 3\}$

Interval notation: $(-\infty, 3) \cup (3, +\infty)$

10. $g(x) = -4\left(\frac{1}{x-2}\right) + 1$.

11. $g(x) = \frac{1}{2(x-4)} - 3$.

12.

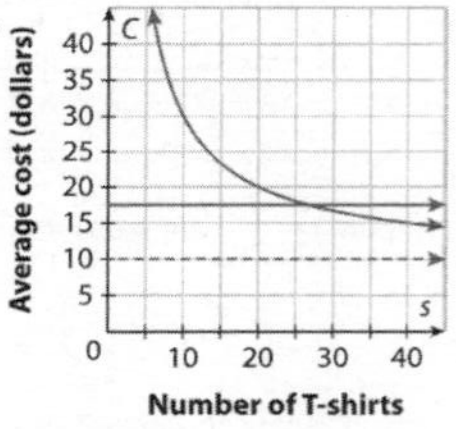

$C(s) = \frac{200}{s} + 10$

the minimum number of T-shirts that brings the average cost below $17.50 is 27.

Evaluate

1. The graph of $g(x)$ is a translation of the graph of $f(x)$ up 4 units.
3. The graph of $g(x)$ is a translation of the graph of $f(x)$ left 3 units.
5. The graph of $g(x)$ is a translation of the graph of $f(x)$ down 7 units.
7. The graph of $g(x)$ is a vertical compression of the graph of $f(x)$ by a factor of 0.1 as well as a reflection of the graph of $f(x)$ across the x-axis.
9. The transformations are:
   - a vertical stretch by a factor of 3
   - a translation of 1 unit to the left and 2 units down

Domain of $g(x)$:

Inequality: $x < -1$ or $x > -1$

Set notation: $\{x \mid x \neq -1\}$

Interval notation: $(-\infty, -1) \cup (-1, +\infty)$

Range of $g(x)$:

Inequality: $y < -2$ or $y > -2$

Set notation: $\{y \mid y \neq -2\}$

Interval notation: $(-\infty, -2) \cup (-2, +\infty)$

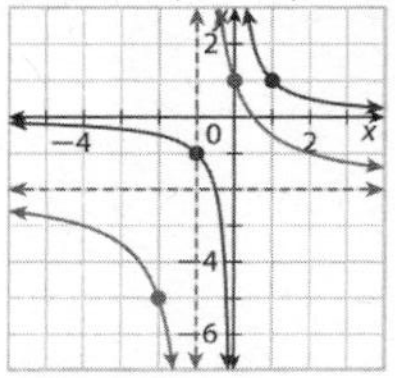

11. The transformations are:
    - a vertical compression by a factor of $\frac{1}{2}$
    - a reflection across the x-axis
    - a translation of 1 unit to the right and 2 units down

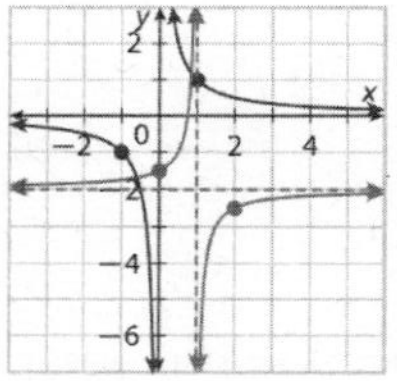

Domain of $g(x)$:

Inequality: $x < 1$ or $x > 1$

Set notation: $\{x \mid x \neq 1\}$

Interval notation: $(-\infty, 1) \cup (1, +\infty)$

Range of $g(x)$:

Inequality: $y < -2$ or $y > -2$

Set notation: $\{y \mid y \neq -2\}$

Interval notation: $(-\infty, -2) \cup (-2, +\infty)$

13. $g(x) = -2\left(\frac{1}{x-1}\right) + 3$

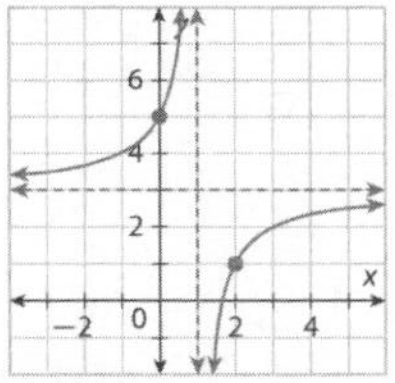

Domain of $g(x)$:

Inequality: $x < 1$ or $x > 1$

Set notation: $\{x \mid x \neq 1\}$

Interval notation: $(-\infty, 1) \cup (1, +\infty)$

Range of $g(x)$:

Inequality: $y < 3$ or $y > 3$

Set notation: $\{y \mid y \neq 3\}$

Interval notation: $(-\infty, 3) \cup (3, +\infty)$

15. $g(x) = 3\left(\frac{1}{x-2}\right) - 4$

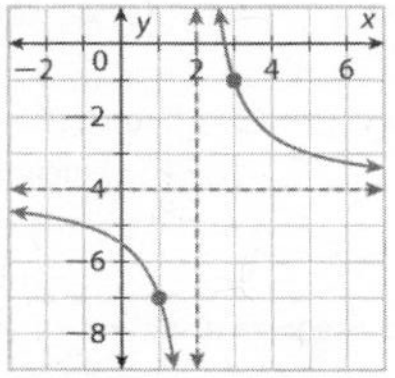

Domain of $g(x)$:

Inequality: $x < 2$ or $x > 2$

Set notation: $\{x \mid x \neq 2\}$

Interval notation: $(-\infty, 2) \cup (2, +\infty)$

Range of $g(x)$:

Inequality: $y < -4$ or $y > -4$

Set notation: $\{y \mid y \neq -4\}$

Interval notation: $(-\infty, -4) \cup (-4, +\infty)$

17. $g(x) = 3\left(\frac{1}{x-3}\right) + 4$

19. $g(x) = \frac{1}{2(x-3)} - 1$

21. $C(s) = \frac{100}{s} + 15$

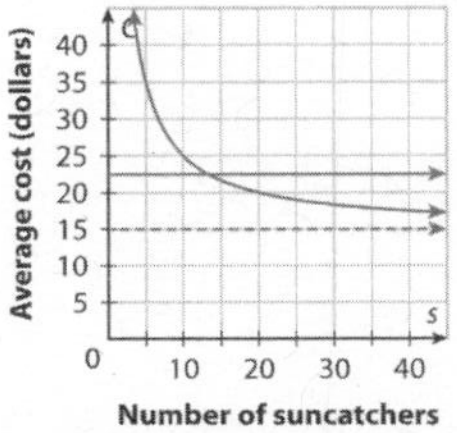

The minimum number of suncatchers that brings the average cost below $22.50 is 14.

23. B; E; G

25. The domain consists of all real numbers except for the value of x that makes the denominator equal to 0. Solving $px + q = 0$ for x gives $x = -\frac{q}{p}$. So, the domain is $\left\{x \mid x \neq -\frac{q}{p}\right\}$. When you divide the numerator by the denominator, the quotient of the leading coefficients determines the horizontal asymptote of the graph, and this y-value is the only real number that isn't in the range of the function. Dividing $mx + n$ by $px + q$ gives a quotient of $\frac{m}{p}$, so the range is $\left\{y \mid y \neq \frac{m}{p}\right\}$.

UNIT 4 Selected Answers

MODULE 8

Lesson 8.2 Graphing More Complicated Rational Functions

Your Turn

3.

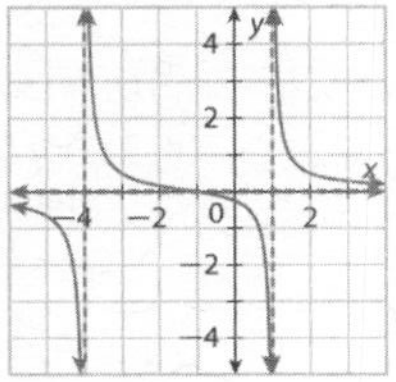

Domain:

Inequality: $x < -4$ or $-4 < x < 1$ or $x > 1$

Set notation: $\{x \mid x \neq -4$ and $x \neq 1\}$

Interval notation: $(-\infty, -4) \cup (-4, 1) \cup (1 + \infty)$

Range:

Inequality: $-\infty < y < +\infty$

Set notation: $\{y \mid -\infty < y < +\infty\}$

Interval notation: $(-\infty, +\infty)$

4. The amount of salt that the chemist should add is about 6.4 grams.

Evaluate

1. Domain:

Inequality: $x < -1$ or $x > -1$

Set notation: $\{x \mid x \neq -1\}$

Interval notation: $(-\infty, -1) \cup (-1, +\infty)$

vertical asymptote at $x = -1$

3. $f(x) = 3 + \frac{7}{x-2}$. As x increases or decreases without bound, $f(x)$ approaches 3.

Range:

Inequality: $y < 3$ or $y > 3$

Set notation: $\{y \mid y \neq 3\}$

Interval notation: $(-\infty, 3) \cup (3, +\infty)$

5. $f(x) = x - 4 + \frac{2}{x-1}$. As x increases without bound, $f(x)$ increases without bound, and as x decreases without bound, $f(x)$ decreases without bound.

Range (approximate):

Inequality: $y < -5.83$ or $y > -0.17$

Set notation: $\{y \mid y < -5.83$ or $y > -0.17\}$

Interval notation: $(-\infty, -5.83) \cup (-0.17, +\infty)$

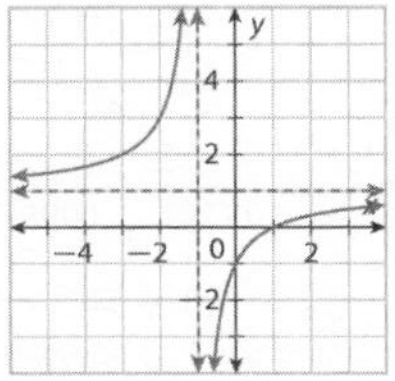

7. Domain:

Inequality: $x < -1$ or $x > -1$

Set notation: $\{x \mid x \neq -1\}$

Interval notation: $(-\infty, -1) \cup (-1, +\infty)$

Range:

Inequality: $y < 1$ or $y > 1$

Set notation: $\{y \mid y \neq 1\}$

Interval notation: $(-\infty, 1) \cup (1, +\infty)$

9.

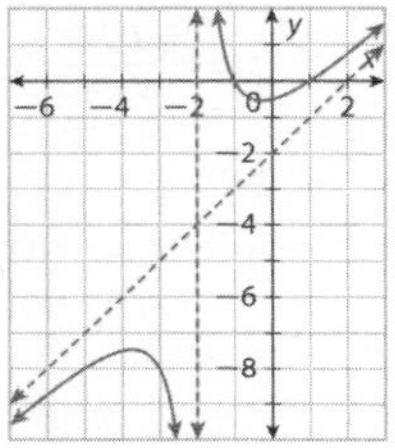

The line $y = x - 2$ is a slant asymptote.

Domain:

Inequality: $x < -2$ or $x > -2$

Set notation: $\{x \mid x \neq -2\}$

Interval notation: $(-\infty, 12) \cup (-2, +\infty)$

Range (approximate):
Inequality: $y < -0.54$ or $y > -7.46$
Set notation: $\{y \mid y < -0.54 \text{ or } y > -7.46\}$
Interval notation: $(-\infty, -0.54) \cup (-7.46, +\infty)$

11. 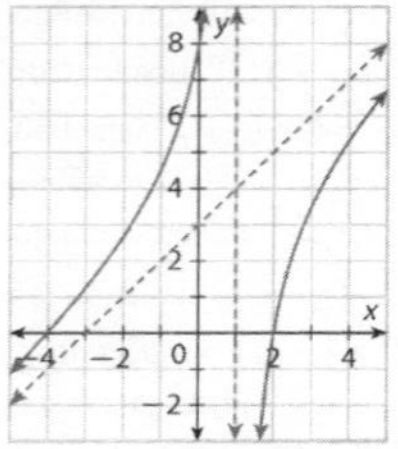

The line $y = x + 3$ is a slant asymptote.
Domain:
Inequality: $x < 1$ or $x > 1$
Set notation: $\{x \mid x \neq 1\}$
Interval notation: $(-\infty, 1) \cup (1, +\infty)$
Range:
Inequality: $-\infty < y < +\infty$
Set notation: $\{y \mid -\infty < y < +\infty\}$
Interval notation: $(-\infty, +\infty)$

13. $p(w) = \dfrac{16 + w}{23 + w}$
The domain of the rational function is $\{w \mid w \geq 0$ and w is a whole number$\}$.
The range is $\{p \mid 0.696 \leq p < 1\}$.
The number of consecutive wins needed to bring the team's winning percentage to 0.750 is 5.

15. $t(s) = \dfrac{13s - 9}{(s-3)(s+3)}$
The domain of the function is $\{s \mid s > 3\}$.
The range of the function is $\{t \mid t > 0\}$.
The kayaker's paddling speed was about 4.3 miles per hour.

17. A; D; E; G

19. The domain of $f(x)$ is $\left\{x \mid x \neq -\dfrac{1}{2}\right\}$, while the domain of $g(x)$ is $\left\{x \mid x \neq -\dfrac{1}{2} \text{ and } x \neq \dfrac{1}{2}\right\}$, so the student's claim is correct with respect to the domains. The range of $f(x)$ is $\{y \mid y \neq -1\}$, while the range of $g(x)$ is $\{y \mid y \neq -1$ and $y \neq 0\}$, so the student's claim is incorrect with respect to the ranges.

UNIT 4 Selected Answers

MODULE 9

Lesson 9.1 Adding and Subtracting Rational Expressions

Your Turn

2. $\dfrac{x+1}{(x-5)(x+1)}$
3. $\dfrac{1}{x}$
5. Taking the highest power of 2, the LCD is $2^3 \cdot 5(x-3) = 40(x-3)$.
6. The LCD is $3 \cdot 5(x+4)(x+5) = 15(x+4)(x+5)$.
7. $\dfrac{x^4 - x^2 + 1}{(1+x)(1-x)}, x \neq \pm 1$

   $\dfrac{x^4 - x^2 - 1}{(1+x)(1-x)}, x \neq \pm 1$
8. $\dfrac{x^2 - x + 2}{(2+x)(2-x)}, x \neq \pm 2$

   $\dfrac{(x-1)}{(2-x)}, x \neq \pm 2$
9. $\dfrac{55}{28}d$
10. $\cong 0.58d$

Evaluate

1. $x \neq 1, x \neq -4$
3. $\dfrac{x^2(x-7)}{x^3 + 8x^2}$ or $\dfrac{x^3 - 7x^2}{x^3 + 8x^2}$
5. $\dfrac{4}{(2-x)}$
7. $\dfrac{(2x+1)}{(x+1)}$
9. $6(x+8)(x-9)$
11. $10(x+2)(x+3)$
13. $21(x-9)(x+2)(x-2)$
15. $\dfrac{-x^2 + x + 1}{x(1+x)}, x \neq 0, -1$
17. $\dfrac{x^2 + x - 4}{x(x+2)}, x \neq 0, -2$
19. $x^2 + 2, x \neq \pm\sqrt{2}$
21. $\dfrac{-x^2 - 3x + 13}{(x+2)(x-2)}, x \neq \pm 2$
23. $\dfrac{2x^2 + 9}{(x+2)(x-2)}, x \neq \pm 2$
25. The cost can be represented by $= \dfrac{700 + 51q}{2q}$.
So the average cost per item to produce q items in each factory is $= \dfrac{700 + 51q}{4q}$.
27. $\dfrac{1600}{s} - \dfrac{1600}{s+12} = \dfrac{19{,}200}{s(s+12)}$ meters
29. a. C
b. D
c. B
d. A
31. Answers may vary. Sample answer: $\dfrac{a}{x(x-17)}$

UNIT 4 Selected Answers

MODULE 9

Lesson 9.2 Multiplying and Dividing Rational Expressions

Your Turn

2. $\frac{(x-3)}{2x(x-9)}$

   Excluded values: $x=-3$, $x=8$, $x=0$, and $x=9$.

3. $\frac{3x}{x+1}$

   Excluded values: $x=-1$ and $x=9$.

4. $\frac{(x+11)(x-1)}{8x}$

   Excluded values: $x=0$, $x=1$, and $x=-3$.

5. $\frac{4}{x^2}$

   Excluded values: $x=0$, $x=7$, and $x=8$.

7. The ratio as a function of time is $1+\frac{At}{2v_0}$.

Evaluate

1. Multiply $x-3$ by x^2-3x+4 to get the numerator of the product. Multiply 2 by x^2-2x to get the denominator of the product. Then, simplify by cancelling common factors in the numerator and the denominator.

3. $10x^2$

   Excluded value: $x=-5$.

5. $\frac{x}{x+4}$

   Excluded values: $x=-4$, $x=-1$, $x=0$, and $x=1$.

7. $\frac{9x}{4(x-2)}$

   Excluded values: $x=6$, $x=2$, $x=0$ and $x=-6$.

9. $\frac{(x-3)^2}{(x-6)^2}$

   Excluded values: $x=\pm6$, $x=\pm3$.

11. $\frac{1}{(x+5)^2}$

   Excluded values: $x=-5$, $x=-3$, and $x=5$.

13. $\frac{8}{x}$

   Excluded values: $x=0$, $x=-4$, and $x=6$.

15. $\frac{-2}{(x+1)(x-1)}$; the numerator and denominator are polynomials, so it is a rational expression.

17. $\frac{x-1}{x+1}$; the numerator and denominator are polynomials, so it is a rational expression.

19. The outer ring is 1.0625 times longer than the middle ring and about 1.13 times longer than the inner ring.

21. Maria did not multiply by the reciprocal.

$$\frac{x^2-4x-45}{3x-15}\div\frac{6x^2-150}{x^2-5x}=$$

$$\frac{x^2-4x-45}{3x-15}\bullet\frac{x^2-5x}{6x^2-150}$$

$$=\frac{(x-9)(x+5)}{3(x-5)}\bullet\frac{x(x-5)}{6(x+5)(x-5)}$$

$$=\frac{x(x-9)(x+5)(x-5)}{18x(x-5)(x+5)(x-5)}=\frac{x(x-9)}{18(x-5)}$$

23. a. Jordan's garden is $x+10$ feet wide.

   b. Karl's garden is 3 times wider than Jordan's garden.

   c. Jordan's garden:

   Length: $4+3=7$ feet

   Width: $4+10=14$ feet

   Karl's garden:

   Length: $4+6=10$ feet

   Width: $3(4+10)=42$ feet

UNIT 4 Selected Answers

MODULE 9

Lesson 9.3 Solving Rational Equations

Your Turn

2. The solutions are $x=9$ or $x=-5$.

4. $\frac{1}{7}(4)+\frac{1}{t}(4)=1$

   It would take Lara about 9 hours and 20 minutes to clean the tank by herself.

   The answer is reasonable because $9\frac{1}{3}$ is positive and $\frac{1}{7}(4)+\frac{1}{9\frac{1}{3}}(4)=1$.

Evaluate

1. The solution is $x=-3$.

3. The solution is $x=4$.

5. The solution $x=5$ is extraneous. There is no solution.

7. The solution is $x=2$ or $x=-6$.

9. $\frac{9+s}{12+s}=0.850$

11. The dimensions are 200 feet by 90 feet.

13. The speed of the current is about 4.5 km/h.

15. The average speed of the truck is 50 mph.

17. B; E

19. Possible answer: The graph of $y=\frac{(x-4)(x-3)}{x-4}=\frac{x^2-7x+12}{x-4}$ has the same graph as $y=x-3$ but has an open circle at $x=4$.

21. Substitute y for x in the expression, and substitute x for $f(x)$. Then solve for y.

   $f^{-1}(x)=\frac{2x-1}{x-1}, x\neq1$

UNIT 5 Selected Answers

MODULE 10

Lesson 10.1 Inverses of Simple Quadratic and Cubic Functions

Your Turn

3.

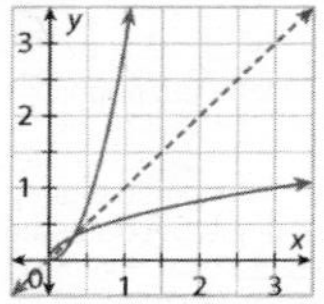

Restrict the domain. {x | x ≥ 0}

Find the inverse.

$\sqrt{\frac{x}{3}} = f^{-1}(x)$

Confirm the inverse relationship using composition.

$f^{-1}(f(x)) = f^{-1}(3x^2)$

$= \sqrt{\frac{3x^2}{3}}$

$= \sqrt{x^2}$

$= x$ for $x \geq 0$

Since $f^{-1}(f(x)) = x$ for $x \geq 0$, it has been confirmed that $f^{-1}(x) = \sqrt{\frac{x}{3}}$ for $x \geq 0$ is the inverse function of $f(x) = 3x^2$ for $x \geq 0$.

4. $r(A) = \sqrt{\frac{A}{\pi}}$

A circular object with an area of 40 cm^2 will have a radius of about 3.6 cm.

5.

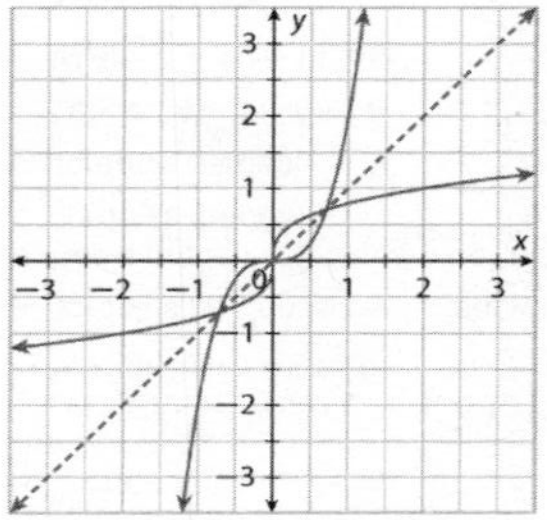

$f^{-1}(x) = \sqrt[3]{\frac{x}{2}}$ is the inverse function of $f(x) = 2x^3$

6. $\sqrt[3]{\frac{3}{44\pi}m} = r(m)$

Evaluate

1.

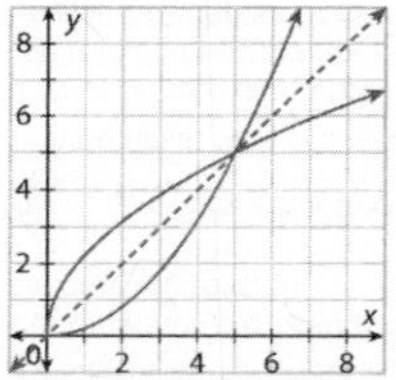

$f^{-1}(x) = \sqrt{5x}$ for $x \geq 0$ is the inverse function of $f(x) = 0.2x^2$ for $x \geq 0$.

3.

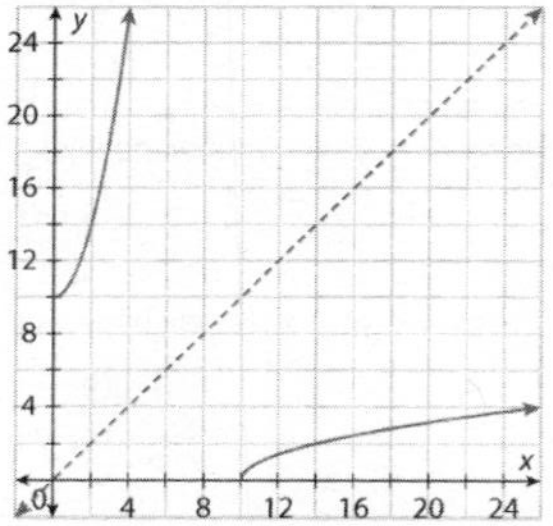

$f^{-1}(x) = \sqrt{x-10}$ for $x \geq 10$ is the inverse function of $f(x) = x^2 + 10$ for $x \geq 0$.

5. $f^{-1}(x) = \sqrt{x + \frac{3}{4}}$ for $x \geq -\frac{3}{4}$ is the inverse function of $f(x) = x^2 - \frac{3}{4}$ for $x \geq 0$.

7. $\sqrt{14.9d} = s(d)$

The speed of a tsunami over water with an average depth of 1500 feet is about 150 mi/h.

9.

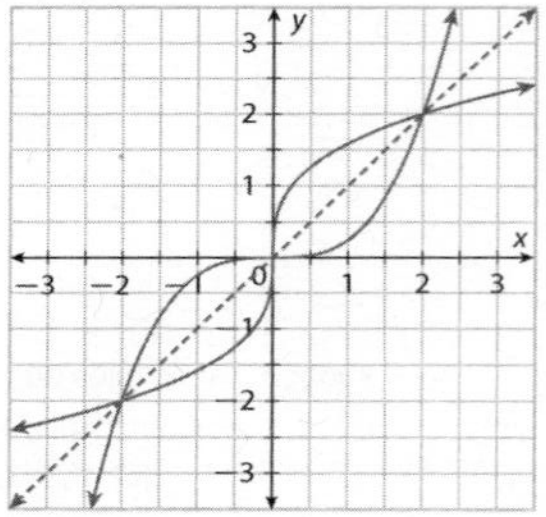

$f^{-1}(x) = \sqrt[3]{4x}$

11. $f^{-1}(x) = \sqrt[3]{x + \frac{5}{6}}$

13. $\sqrt[3]{\frac{m}{31}} = r(m)$

15. $\sqrt[3]{\frac{V}{2000}} - 1 = r(V)$

17. $C = 0.5\sqrt{a} + 6.2$

$c = 0.5\sqrt{a} + 0.2$

The total cost with installation would be $13.13.

UNIT 5 Selected Answers

MODULE 10

Lesson 10.2 Graphing Square Root Functions

Your Turn

4.

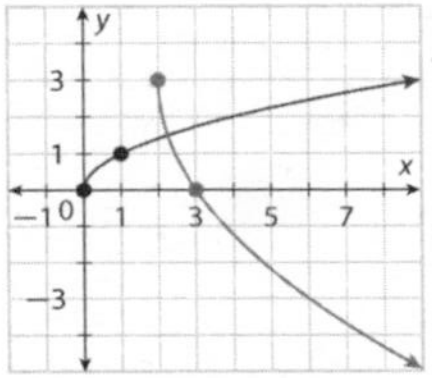

The domain is $\{x \mid x \geq 2\}$.

The range is $\{y \mid y \leq 3\}$.

5.

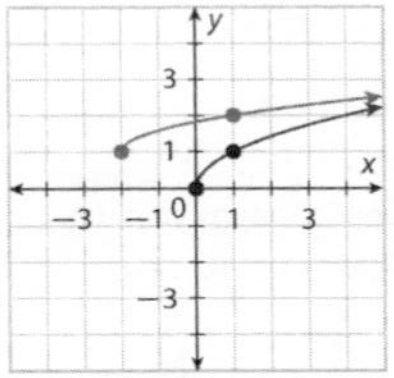

The domain is $\{x \mid x \geq -2\}$.

The range is $\{y \mid y \geq 1\}$.

6. $g(x)=\sqrt{2(x-1)}-1$

7. $g(x)=-3\sqrt{x+3)}+5$

8.

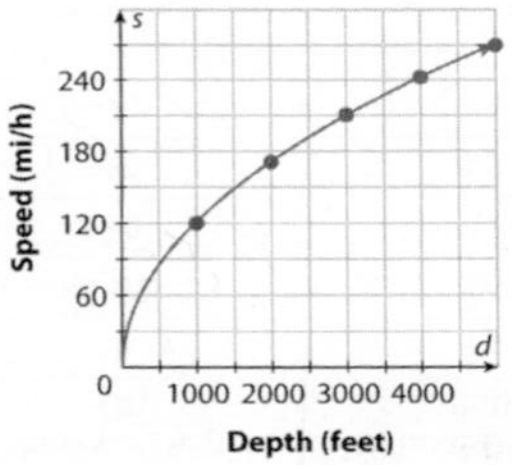

First interval:

$= 0.0505$

Last Interval:

$= 0.0288$

The average rate of change represents the increase in tsunami speed with each additional foot of depth.The speed increases less with each additional foot of depth.

Evaluate

1.

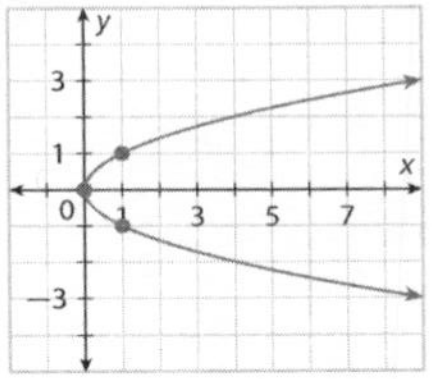

	$f(x)=\sqrt{x}$	$g(x)=-\sqrt{x}$
Domain	$\{x \mid x \geq 0\}$	$\{x \mid x \geq 0\}$
Range	$\{y \mid y \geq 0\}$	$\{y \mid y \geq 0\}$
End Behavior	$f(x) \to \infty$ as $x \to \infty$	$g(x) \to -\infty$ as $x \to \infty$

The functions are reflections of each other over the *x*-axis.

3. Stretch vertically by a factor of 5, reflect across *x*-axis, and translate down by 3 and left by 1.

5. Compress horizontally by a factor of $\frac{1}{7}$, reflect across *y*-axis, and translate right by 7.

7. Domain: $\{x \mid x \geq -4\}$

   Range: $\{y \mid y \geq 3\}$

9. Domain: $\{x \mid x \geq 3\}$

   Range: $\{y \mid y \leq -5\}$

11.

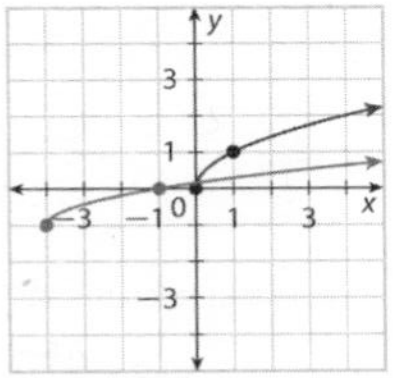

domain: $\{x \mid x \geq -4\}$

range: $\{y \mid y \geq -1\}$

13.

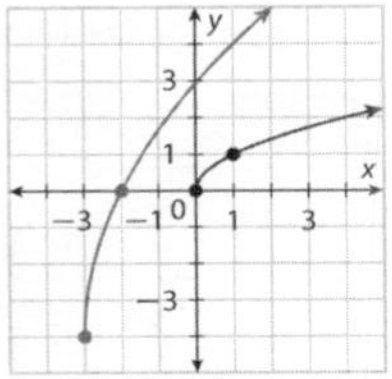

domain: $\left\{x \mid x < \frac{1}{2}\right\}$

range: $\{y \mid y \geq -2\}$

15. $g(x)=\sqrt{\frac{1}{2}(x+3)}$

17. $g(x)=-\frac{1}{2}\sqrt{x-\frac{1}{2}}+1$

19.

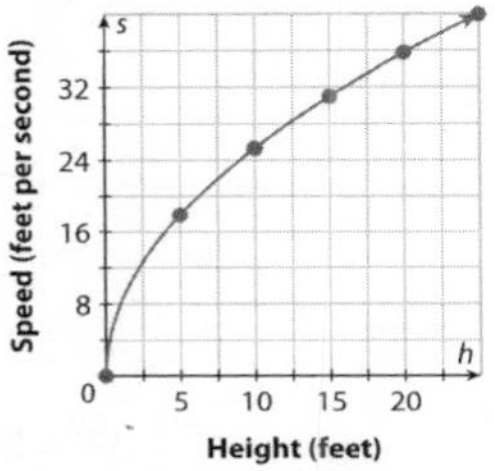

Points: (0, 0), (5, 17.9), (10, 25.3), (15, 31.0), (20, 35.8), (25, 40.0)

First Interval:

$= 3.58$

Last Interval:

$= 0.84$

The rate of change represents additional speed in feet per second for each additional foot of height. The rate of change decreases with increasing height. So, the additional speed decreases as the height increases.

21.

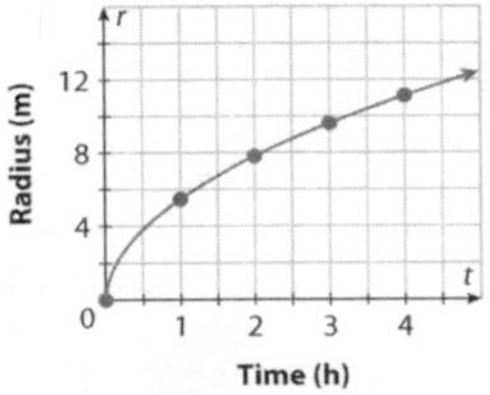

Points: (0, 0), (1, 5.64), (2, 7.98), (3, 9.77), (4, 11.28)

First Interval: $= 5.64$

Last Interval: $= 1.51$

The rate of change represents the increase in meters of the oil spill radius per hour. The rate of change decreases with increasing time. So, the increase in the radius of the oil spill decreases as the time increases.

23. The transformation is a horizontal compression by a factor of $\frac{1}{8}$, a reflection over the *y*-axis, a translation of 2 to the right, and a translation of 3 up.

25. a. The graph is translated left by *H* feet.

    b. The domain is given by $\{h : h \geq -0\}$.

    Although values of *h* between –*H* and 0 might seem reasonable because the expression under the square root symbol is still not negative, a negative value of *h* corresponds to being underwater, where the visibility over the horizon is not modeled by the function.

    c.

Observer Height (ft)	Buoy Distance (mi)
0	1.7
10	4.2
20	5.7
30	6.8
40	7.8

Observer Height (ft)	Sailboat Distance (mi)
0	5.4
10	6.6
20	7.7
30	8.6
40	9.4

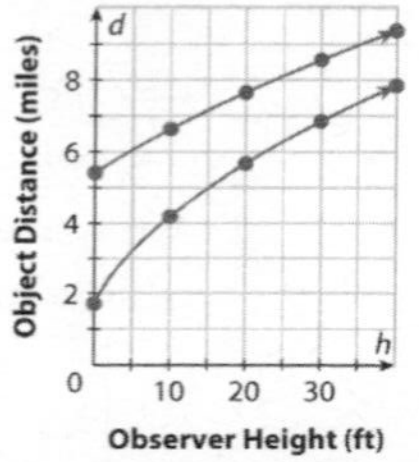

d. From 0 to 10 feet observing the 2-foot tall buoy.

UNIT 5 Selected Answers

MODULE 10

Lesson 10.3 Graphing Cube Root Functions

Your Turn

2.

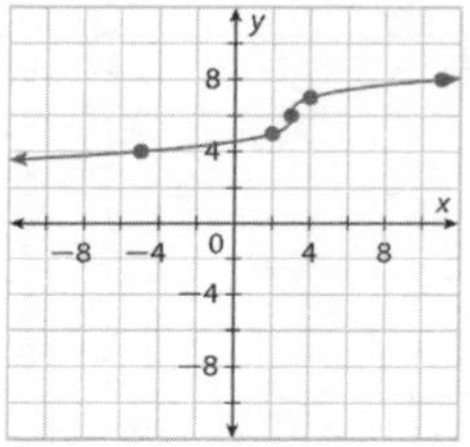

3. The function is $g(x)=2\sqrt[3]{(x+2)}-5$.

4. The function is $g(x)=\sqrt[3]{\frac{1}{2}(x+3)}+2$.

5.

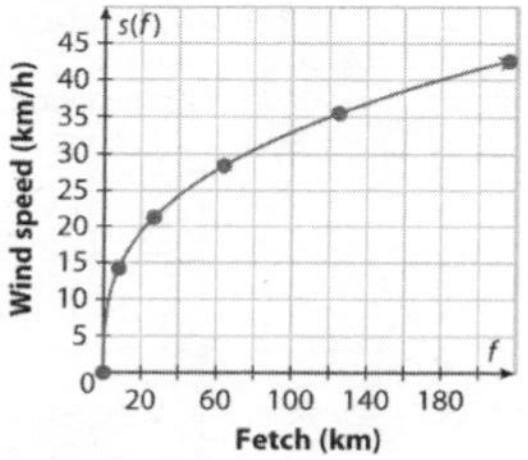

first interval: ≈ 0.19

second interval: ≈ 0.11

third interval: ≈ 0.08

The average rate of change is becoming less.

The speed of the wind is about 28.4 km/h.

Evaluate

1.

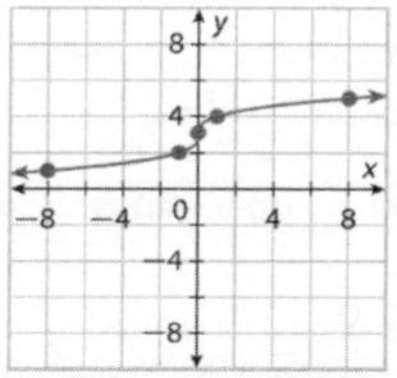

The domain is all real numbers.

The range is all real numbers.

3. The graph of $g(x)=\sqrt[3]{x}+6$ is the graph of $f(x)=\sqrt[3]{x}$ translated 6 units up.

5. The graph of $g(x)=\frac{1}{3}\sqrt[3]{-x}$ is the graph of $f(x)=\sqrt[3]{x}$ compressed vertically by a factor of $\frac{1}{3}$ and reflected across the y-axis.

7. The graph of $g(x)=-2\sqrt[3]{x}+3$ is the graph of $f(x)=\sqrt[3]{x}$ reflected across the x-axis, vertically stretched by a factor of 2, and then translated 3 units up.

9.

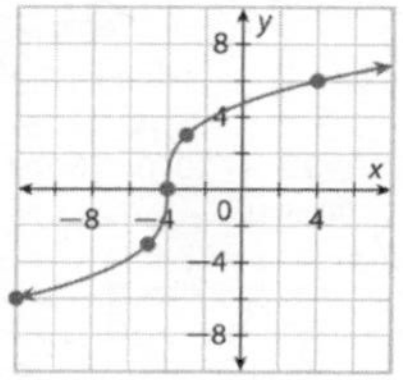

11. 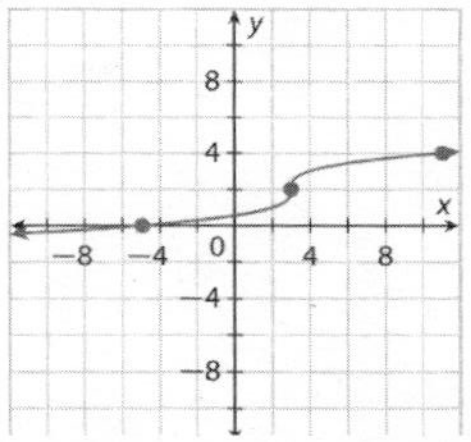

13. The function is $g(x) = -2\sqrt[3]{(x-2)} - 6$.

15. 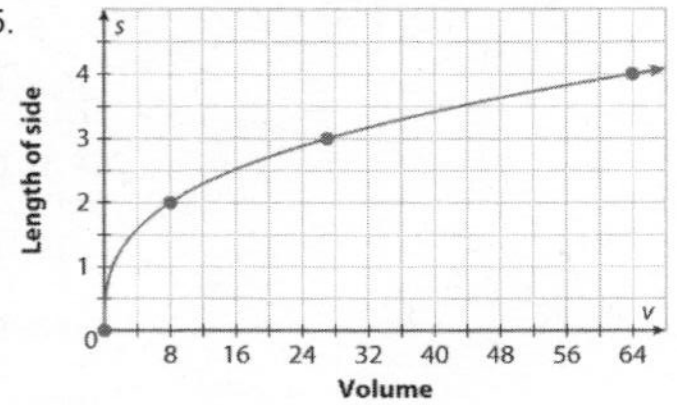

When $V = 48$, $s \approx 3.6$.

17. 1. Graph the parent function $f(x) = \sqrt[3]{x}$.
   2. Translate the graph of $f(x) = \sqrt[3]{x}$ 8 units to the left.
   3. Translate the resulting graph 11 units down.

19. $y = a\sqrt[3]{-h} + k$ or $y = -ah^{\frac{1}{3}} + k$

21. A
    G

23. Answers may vary. Sample answer: If you square a negative number you always get a positive number. Thus, you cannot take a square root of a negative number and this restricts the domain of the square root function to nonnegative numbers. However, if you cube a negative number, you get another negative number. Thus, you can take the cube root of a negative number, a positive number, and zero. Therefore, the domain of the cube root function is all real numbers.

UNIT 5 Selected Answers

MODULE 11

Lesson 11.1 Radical Expressions and Rational Exponents

Your Turn

5. a. $\frac{4}{9}$; b. $\left(\sqrt[c]{3y}\right)^b$ or $\sqrt[c]{(3y)^b}$; c. 0.125;
   d. $(st)^{\frac{v}{u}}$

8. a. Kleiber's law for lion: ≈ 3450 Calories
   Kleiber's law for human: ≈ 1750 Calories
   b. ≈ 1400 Cal.
   The rate for a human would be significantly lower than the actual prediction from Kleiber's law. Kleiber's law indicates that smaller organisms have a higher metabolic rate per kilogram of mass than do larger organisms.

Evaluate

1. 1024
3. 64
5. $-\frac{243}{32}$
7. $v\sqrt[3]{w^2}$ or $v\left(\sqrt[3]{w}\right)^2$
9. $y^{\frac{5}{7}}$
11. 243
13. $(bcd)^{\frac{2}{3}}$
15. 4
17. The fret should be placed about 45.25 cm from the bridge.
19. Yes; for this n and T, the Jean's mass is $M_J = 100(1000)^{-\frac{1}{2}}(-263 + 273)^{\frac{3}{2}}$
    $= \frac{100}{1000^{\frac{1}{2}}}(10)^{\frac{3}{2}} = 100$. The mass of the clump, 137, is greater than the Jean's mass, 100, so the clump will form a star.
21. C
23. For graph B, $m = n$, that is, $y = ax$. This is because the graph is that of a line, for which the exponent on x is 1 and the graph has a constant rate of change (slope). For graph A, $m > n$. This is because for a power greater than 1, the average rate of change of the graph increases as x increases, that is, the graph gets steeper. For graph C, $m < n$. This is because for a power less than 1, the average rate of change of the graph decreases as x increases, that is, the graph gets less steep.

UNIT 5 Selected Answers

MODULE 11

Lesson 11.2 Simplifying Radical Expressions

Your Turn

3. 1728
4. $\frac{36}{xy}$
5. $x^{\frac{5}{6}}$
6. 128
8. $6x^4y^5$
9. $\frac{2\sqrt[4]{x^2}}{x^4}$
11. The expression is $S = 5 \cdot 2^{\frac{1}{3}}V^{\frac{2}{3}}$, which gives $S = 6.30V^{\frac{2}{3}}$.

Evaluate

1. 4
3. 6561
5. $2x^{\frac{1}{2}}$
7. $5^{\frac{5}{6}}$
9. $3^{\frac{1}{4}}x^{\frac{1}{6}}$
11. $s^{\frac{1}{3}}t^{\frac{7}{6}}$.
13. 6
15. x^2y
17. a. $\frac{1}{6\pi^{\frac{1}{2}}} \cdot S^{\frac{3}{2}} \approx 0.094S^{\frac{3}{2}}$
    b. $V \approx 1050$ ft³
19. A; C; D; E
21. Aaron incorrectly applied the Quotient of Powers Property. He should have subtracted the exponents.
    625
23. For $0 < a < 1$; for $a < -1$ or $0 < a < 1$.

UNIT 5 Selected Answers

MODULE 11

Lesson 11.3 Solving Radical Equations

Your Turn

6. $x = 4$
8. $x = -75$
9. The elephant is about 47 years old.

Evaluate

1. The solution is $x = 34$.
3. The solution is $x = 1$.
5. The solution is $x = 32$.
7. The discriminant is negative. There are no real solutions.
9. $x = 31$
11. Because there are no real values of x for which $x^2 = -6$, the only solution $x = -15$.
13. $\frac{7}{3} = x$
15. Because there are no real values of x for which $8x^2 = -27$, the only solution is $x = 3$.
17. Because expected skid length under the conditions is 286 feet, and the actual skid distance was 250 feet, the car was not exceeding the speed limit when the skid began.
19. The buck is about 13 years old.
21. A. No solutions; B. One solution; C. One solution; D. One solution; E. One solution
23. When the student squared both sides, the coefficient 2 should also have been squared: $x = 11$
25. Possible answer: One way is to raise both sides to the reciprocal power. For example, to solve $(2x - 3)^{\frac{3}{5}} = 8$, raise both sides to the $\frac{5}{3}$ power to obtain $2x - 3 = 32$, which has the solution $x = 17.5$. You would need to be especially careful when the denominator of the power is even, indicating an even root.

UNIT 6 Selected Answers

MODULE 12

Lesson 12.1 Arithmetic Sequences

Your Turn

3. The explicit rule is $f(n) = -7 + 5n$ for $0 \le n \le 5$. The recursive rule is $f(0) = -7$ and $f(n) = f(n-1) + 5$ for $1 \le n \le 5$.
4. The explicit rule is $f(n) = 11 - 6(n-1)$ for $1 \le n \le 6$. The recursive rule is $f(1) = 11$ and $f(n) = f(n-1) - 6$ for $2 \le n \le 6$.
5. 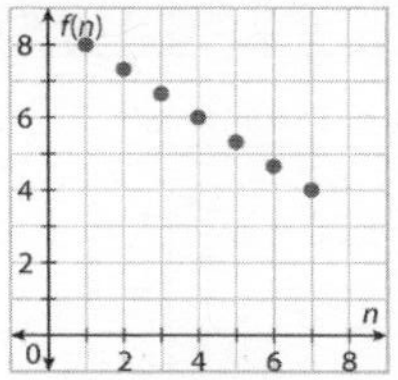

$8, 7\frac{1}{3}, 6\frac{2}{3}, 6, 5\frac{1}{3}, 4\frac{2}{3}, 4$

6. 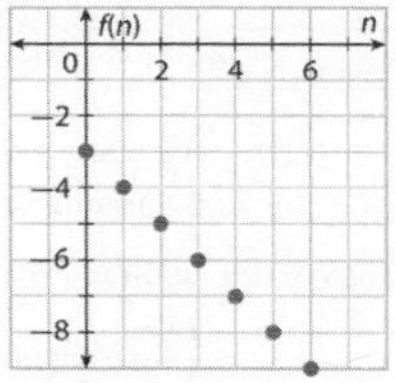

$-3, -4, -5, -6, \ldots$

7. Recursive rule: $f(1) = 395$ and $f(n) = f(n-1) + 45$ for $n \ge 2$.

   Explicit rule is $f(n) = 395 + 45(n-1)$ for $n \ge 1$.

   The summer camp runs for 8 weeks.

8. An explicit rule for the sequence is $f(n) = 38 + 12(n-1)$ for $n \ge 1$. A recursive rule is $f(1) = 38$ and $f(n) = f(n-1) + 12$ for $n \ge 2$.

   326 inches, or 27 feet 2 inches, long

Evaluate

1. The rule for $B(s)$ would remain unchanged while the rule for $T(s)$ would become $T(s) = 210 - 7.5s$.

   The domain of each function would change from {0, 1, 2, ..., 14} to {0, 1, 2, ..., 28}.

   The range of each function would likewise change from {0, 7.5, 15, ..., 105} to {0, 7.5, 15, ..., 210}.

3. Explicit rule is $f(n) = 8 - 3n$ for $0 \le n \le 4$. The recursive rule is $f(0) = 8$ and $f(n) = f(n-1) - 3$ for $1 \le n \le 4$.
5. $f(n) = 19 - 10(n-1)$ for $n \ge 1$
7. $f(0) = 14$ and $f(n) = f(n-1) + 8$ for $n \ge 1$.
9. 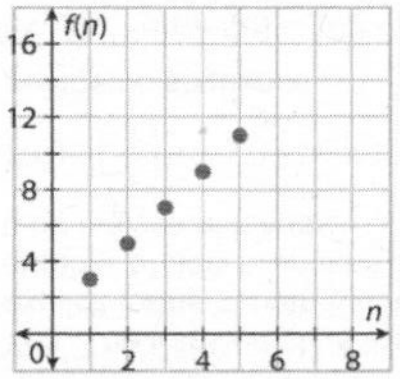

3, 5, 7, 9, 11

11. 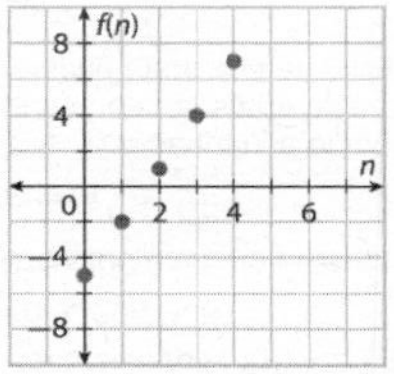

−5, −2, 1, 4, 7

13. Recursive rule: $f(1) = 4$ and $f(n) = f(n-1) + 4$ for $n \ge 2$.

    Explicit rule is $f(n) = 4 + 4(n-1)$ for $n \ge 1$.

    There are 68 panes in the 17th row.

15. An explicit rule for the sequence is $f(n) = 5 + 0.25(n-1)$ for $n \ge 1$.

    A recursive rule is $f(1) = 5$ and $f(n) = f(n-1) + 0.25$ for $n \ge 2$.

    A stack of 28 plastic cups will fit on the shelf without having a tight fit.

17. a. In each case, the sequence is 1, 3, 5, 7, 9, ... because the points on each graph have those numbers as their second coordinates.

    b. For sequence A, explicit rule is $f(n) = 1 + 2n$ for $n \ge 0$

       For sequence B, explicit rule is $f(n) = 1 + 2(n-1)$ for $n \ge 1$

    c. The explicit rule for sequence B is the result of replacing n in the rule for sequence A with $n - 1$. Doing so translates the graph of sequence A to the right 1 unit.

19. $f(0) = a$

    $f(1) = f(0) + d = a + d$

    $f(2) = f(1) + d = (a + d) + d = a + 2d$

    $f(3) = f(2) + d = (a + 2d) + d = a + 3d$

    $f(4) = f(3) + d = (a + 3d) + d = a + 4d$

    Generalizing these results gives $f(n) = a + dn$.

UNIT 6 Selected Answers

MODULE 12

Lesson 12.2 Geometric Sequences

Your Turn

4. Explicit Form: $f(n) = \frac{1}{27} \cdot (3)^n$

   Recursive Form: $f(n) = 3 \cdot f(n-1)$, $n \geq 1$

   and $f(0) = \frac{1}{27}$

5. Explicit Form: $f(n) = 0.001 \cdot (10)^{n-1}$

   Recursive Form: $f(n) = 10 \cdot f(n-1)$, $n \geq 2$ and $f(1) = 0.001$

6.

n	1	2	3	4	5	...
$f(n)$	**3**	**6**	**12**	**24**	**48**	...

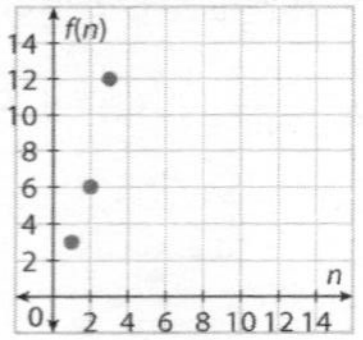

7.

n	1	2	3	4	5	...
$f(n)$	**2**	**6**	**18**	**54**	**162**	...

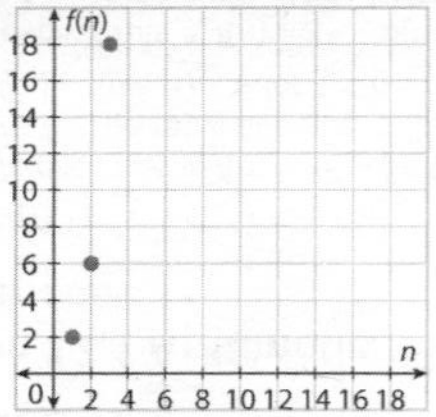

8. Explicit rule: $f(n) = 200 \cdot 2^n$, $n \geq 0$

   Recursive rule: $f(n) = 2 \cdot f(n-1)$, $n \geq 1$ and $f(0) = 200$

   819, 200 bacteria present after 4 hours

Evaluate

1. Yes. The sequence of lengths of the new branches per stage has a common ratio relating them and an initial value.

   The explicit form is: $f(n) = \left(\frac{1}{3}\right)^n$, $n \geq 0$.

3. Yes. The total length is the product of the explicit forms of both functions, the number of new branches per stage times their individual length:

   $f(n) = \left(\frac{1}{3}\right)^n 2^n = \left(\frac{2}{3}\right)^n$, $n \geq 0$. This is a geometric sequence.

5. Explicit Form: $f(n) = 100 \cdot (0.1)^n$

   Recursive Form: $f(n) = 0.1 \cdot f(n-1)$, $n \geq 1$ and $f(0) = 100$

7. Explicit Form: $f(n) = 10^{50} \cdot (10^{-3})^{n-1}$

   Recursive Form: $f(n) = 10^{-3} \cdot f(n-1)$, $n \geq 2$ and $f(1) = 10^{50}$

9.

n	0	1	2	3	4	...
$f(n)$	**0.5**	**1**	**2**	**4**	**8**	...

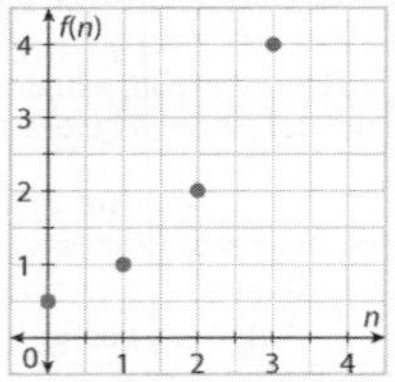

11.

n	1	2	3	4	5	...
$f(n)$	**1**	**0.666...**	**0.444...**	**0.296...**	**0.197...**	...

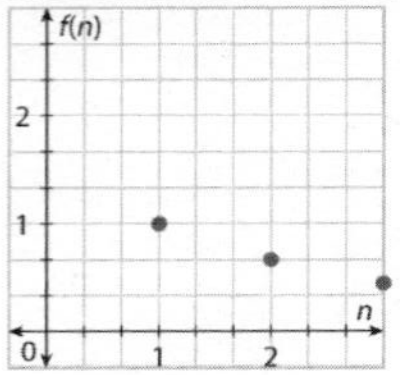

13. Explicit rule: $f(n) = 256\left(\frac{1}{4}\right)^{n-1}$, $n \geq 1$

    Recursive rule: $f(n) = \left(\frac{1}{4}\right) \cdot f(n-1)$, $n \geq 2$.

    and $f(1) = 256$

    The winner plays 5 games.

15. a. Explicit rule: $f(n) = \left(\frac{3}{4}\right)^{n-1}$, $n \geq 1$

    Recursive rule:

    $f(n) = \left(\frac{3}{4}\right) \cdot f(n-1)$, $n \geq 2$ and $f(1) = 1$

    b. Explicit rule: $f(n) = \left(\frac{8}{9}\right)^{n-1}$, $n \geq 1$

    Recursive rule:

    $f(n) = \left(\frac{8}{9}\right) \cdot f(n-1)$, $n \geq 2$ and $f(1) = 1$

    c. ≈ 0.702 square unit

17. A is incorrect because $f(4) = 6$, and if A were correct, then $f(4) = 16$.

    C is incorrect because $f(4) = 6$ and so $f(0) \neq 6$. If $n = 0$ is in the domain, then $f(0) = \frac{3}{8} = 0.375$.

    B, D, E, F, G, and H are all possible correct rules for different initial whole number values of either 0 or 1.

UNIT 6 Selected Answers

MODULE 12

Lesson 12.3 Geometric Series

Your Turn

6. –21

7. $\frac{85}{256}$

8. The present value of the delayed-payout plan, $837,484.63, is less than the lump-sum plan, so it makes sense to go with the lump-sum plan.

Evaluate

1. a.

Stage	Sum of the areas of the pieces that have been laid down	Difference of 1 and the area of the remaining piece
1	$\frac{3}{4}$	$1-\frac{1}{4}=\frac{3}{4}$
2	$\frac{3}{4}+\frac{3}{16}=\frac{15}{16}$	$1-\frac{1}{16}=\frac{15}{16}$
3	$\frac{3}{4}+\frac{3}{16}+\frac{3}{64}=\frac{63}{64}$	$1-\frac{1}{64}=\frac{63}{64}$
4	$\frac{3}{4}+\frac{3}{16}+\frac{3}{64}+\frac{3}{256}=\frac{255}{256}$	$1-\frac{1}{256}=\frac{255}{256}$

b. $\frac{3}{4}+\frac{3}{16}+\cdots+3\left(\frac{1}{4}\right)^n=1-\left(\frac{1}{4}\right)^n$

c. In the general formula $S(n)=a\left(\frac{1-r^n}{1-r}\right)$,

let $a=\frac{3}{4}$ and $r=\frac{1}{4}$.

$$S(n)=a\left(\frac{1-r^n}{1-r}\right)=\frac{3}{4}\left(\frac{1-\left(\frac{1}{4}\right)^n}{1-\frac{1}{4}}\right)$$

$$=\frac{3}{4}\left(\frac{1-\left(\frac{1}{4}\right)^n}{\frac{3}{4}}\right)=1-\left(\frac{1}{4}\right)^n$$

3. 255

5. $n=7$

$=-\frac{4372}{243}\approx-17.99$

7. $n=8$
585,936

9. 2 – 10 + 50 – 250 + 1250 – 6250
–5208

11. 1000 + 800 + 640 + 512 + 409.6 + 327.68 + 262.144
3951.424

13. A total of 15 matches were played.

15. a. a total of 3355 new cases
b. The number of cases will exceed 40,000 in the seventh week.

17. Since the delayed-payment option saves the business about $1000, it is the better deal.

19. The future value of the annuity is given by the finite geometric series $p+p(1+i)+p(1+i)^2+\ldots+p(1+i)^{n-1}$. Use the formula for the sum of a finite geometric series with $a=p$ and $r=1+i$.

$$FV=p\left(\frac{1-(1+i)^n}{1-(1+i)}\right)=p\left(\frac{1-(1+i)^n}{1-1-i}\right)$$

$$=p\left(\frac{1-(1+i)^n}{-i}\right)=p\left(\frac{(1+i)^n-1}{i}\right)$$

21. a. As $n\to+\infty$ $S(n)\to+\infty$, so a reasonable conclusion is that this series does not have a finite sum.
b. As $n\to+\infty$ $S(n)\to 2$, so a reasonable conclusion is that this series has a sum of 2.

UNIT 6 Selected Answers

MODULE 13

Lesson 13.1 Exponential Growth Functions

Your Turn

4. The domain of $g(x)$ is $\{x|-\infty < x < \infty\}$.

   The range of $g(x)$ is $\{y|y > -6\}$.

   $a = 4$ $h = -2$ $k = -6$

   The asymptote becomes $y = -6$.

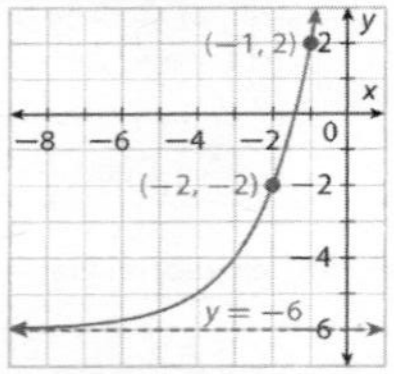

5. The domain of $q(x)$ is $\{x|-\infty < x < \infty\}$.

   The range of $q(x)$ is $\{y|y < 3\}$.

   $a = -\frac{3}{5}$ $h = -2$ $k = 3$

   The asymptote becomes $y = 3$.

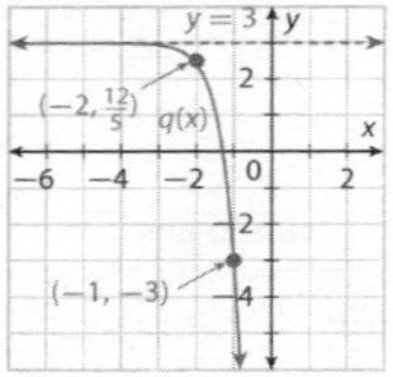

6. $g(x) = \frac{3}{2}(2^{x-3}) - \frac{5}{2}$

   Verify that $g(4) = \frac{1}{2}$.

   $g(4) = \frac{3}{2}(2^{4-3}) - \frac{5}{2} = \frac{1}{2}$

   The domain of $g(x)$ is $\{x|-\infty < x < +\infty\}$.

   The range of $g(x)$ is $\left\{y \mid y > -\frac{5}{2}\right\}$

8. $g(t) = 3.25\,(1.11)^t$.

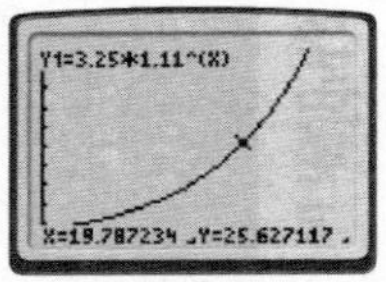

The card will be worth $26 approximately 20 years after John purchased it.

Evaluate

1.

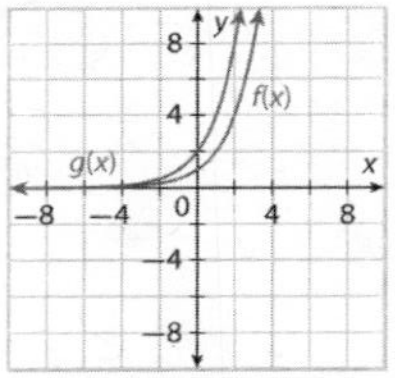

$g(x)$ is a vertical stretch (or horizontal compression) of $f(x)$. The domain of $f(x)$ is $\{x|-\infty < x < \infty\}$ and the range is $\{y|y > 0\}$. The domain of $g(x)$ is $\{x|-\infty < x < \infty\}$ and the range is $\{y|y > 0\}$. The y-intercept of $f(x)$ is 1 and the y-intercept of $g(x)$ is 2.

3.

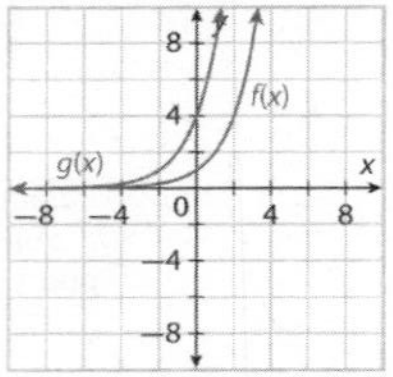

$g(x)$ is a shift to the left by 2 of $f(x)$. The domain of $f(x)$ is $\{x|-\infty < x < \infty\}$ and the range is $\{y|y > 0\}$. The domain of $g(x)$ is $\{x|-\infty < x < \infty\}$ and the range is $\{y|y > 0\}$. The y-intercept of $f(x)$ is 1 and the y-intercept of $g(x)$ is 4.

5.

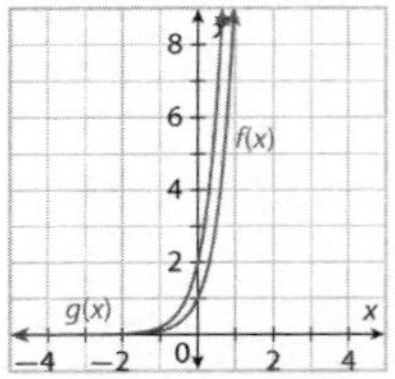

$g(x)$ is a vertical stretch (or horizontal compression) of $f(x)$. The domain of $f(x)$ is $\{x|-\infty < x < \infty\}$ and the range is $\{y|y > 0\}$. The domain of $g(x)$ is $\{x|-\infty < x < \infty\}$ and the range is $\{y|y > 0\}$. The y-intercept of $f(x)$ is 1 and the y-intercept of $g(x)$ is 2.

7.

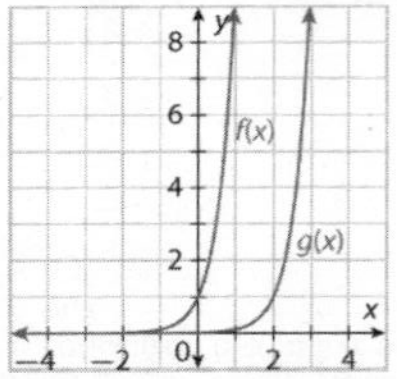

$g(x)$ is a shift to the right by 2 of $f(x)$. The domain of $f(x)$ is $\{x|-\infty < x < \infty\}$ and the range is $\{y|y > 0\}$. The domain of $g(x)$ is $\{x|-\infty < x < \infty\}$ and the range is $\{y|y > 0\}$. The y-intercept of $f(x)$ is 1 and the y-intercept of $g(x)$ is $\frac{1}{100}$.

9. The graph is shifted down by 4 and right by 3.

11.

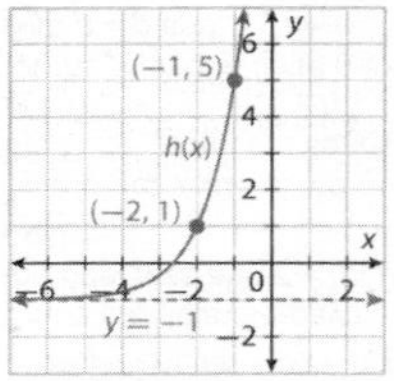

The domain is $\{x|-\infty < x < \infty\}$.

The range is $\{y|y > -1\}$.

(−2, 1) (−1, 5) $y = -1$

13.

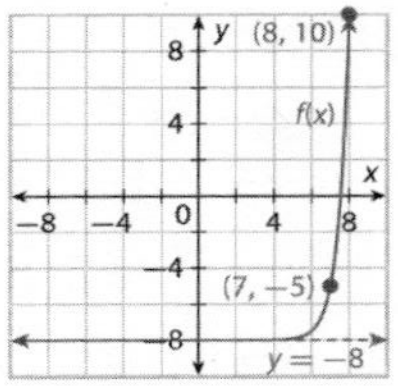

The domain is $\{x|-\infty < x < \infty\}$.

The range is $\{y|y > -8\}$.

(7, −8); (8, 10); $y = -8$.

15.

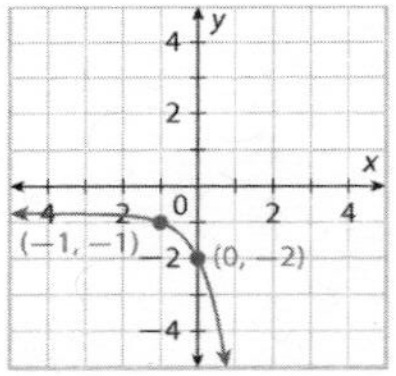

The domain is $\{x|-\infty < x < \infty\}$.

The range is $\left\{y \mid y < -\frac{3}{4}\right\}$.

(−1, −1) (0, −2) $y = -\frac{3}{4}$

17. $g(x) = 2.2(2^{x+1}) + 3$

    Verify that $g(0) = 7.4$

    $g(0) = 2.2(2^{0+1}) + 3 = 7.4$

    The domain of $g(x)$ is $\{x|-\infty < x < +\infty\}$.

    The range of $g(x)$ is $\{y|y > 3\}$.

19. $f(t) = 0.59(1.5)^t$

    approximately 5.74 days

21. $f(t) = 15{,}000(1.05)^t$

    approximately 10.47 years

23. For $g(x) = 2^x$, as $x \to +\infty$, $g(x) \to +\infty$ and as $\to -\infty$, $g(x) \to 0$.

    For $f(x) = x^2$, as $\to +\infty$, $f(x) \to +\infty$ and as $x \to -\infty$, $f(x) \to +\infty$.

    The two functions have the same end behavior as $x \to +\infty$, however as $x \to -\infty$, $f(x) = x^2$ is unbounded, whereas $g(x) = 2^x$ is bounded below by 0.

UNIT 6 Selected Answers

MODULE 13

Lesson 13.2 Exponential Decay Functions

Your Turn

3. Domain: $\{x \mid -\infty < x < \infty\}$

   Range: $\{y \mid y > -4\}$

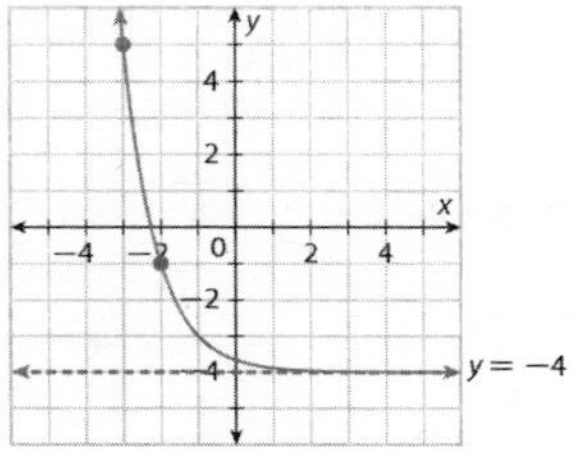

6. $g(x) = 2\left(\frac{1}{4}\right)^{x-1} - 4$

   Domain: $\{x \mid -\infty < x < \infty\}$

   Range: $\{y \mid y > -4\}$

9. about 5.79 years

Evaluate

1. Vertical translation up by 3.

   Domain: $\{x \mid -\infty < x < \infty\}$

   Range: $\{y \mid y > -3\}$

3. Reflection across the x-axis, translation right by 1 and up by 2.

   Domain: $\{x \mid -\infty < x < \infty\}$

   Range: $\{y \mid y < 2\}$

5. Domain: $\{x \mid -\infty < x < \infty\}$

   Range: $\{y \mid y < 2\}$

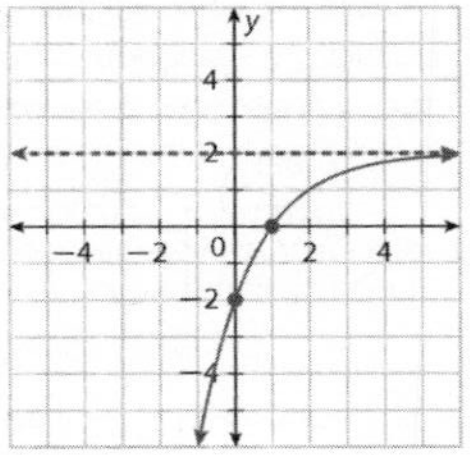

7. Domain: $\{x \mid -\infty < x < \infty\}$

   Range: $\{y \mid y > 2\}$

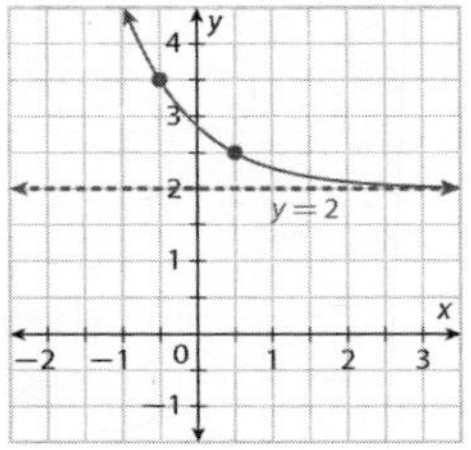

9. $g(x) = 4\left(\frac{1}{2}\right)^{x-4} - 1$

   Domain: $\{x \mid -\infty < x < \infty\}$

   Range: $\{y \mid y > -1\}$

11. $I(t) = 10(0.95)^t$ about 13.5 minutes

13. $a(t) = 0.75(0.75)^t$ about 7 seconds

15. The decay rate of the first quantity is 50% because the decay factor is $1 - r = \frac{1}{2}$, so the decay rate equals $\frac{1}{2}$, or 50%. The decay rate of the second quantity is 75% because the decay factor is $1 - r = \frac{1}{4}$, so the decay rate is $\frac{3}{4}$, or 75%. The decay rate of the second quantity is greater.

17. $R(t) = 500(0.725)^t$; Sample answer: I used the general exponential decay function $f(x) = ab^x$ and substituted 100 for $f(x)$, 500 for a, and 5 for x, resulting in $100 = 500(b^5)$.
    I then solved for b by dividing 100 by 500 to get 0.2 and then took the fifth root of 0.2, resulting in 0.724779, which I rounded to 0.725.

UNIT 6 Selected Answers

MODULE 13

Lesson 13.3 The Base e

Your Turn

2. Reference points:

   $(0, 1) \to (-2, -4)$

   $(1, e) \to (-1, -e - 3)$

   asymptote: $y = -3$

   Domain: $\{x \mid -\infty < x < \infty\}$

   Range: $\{y \mid y < -3\}$

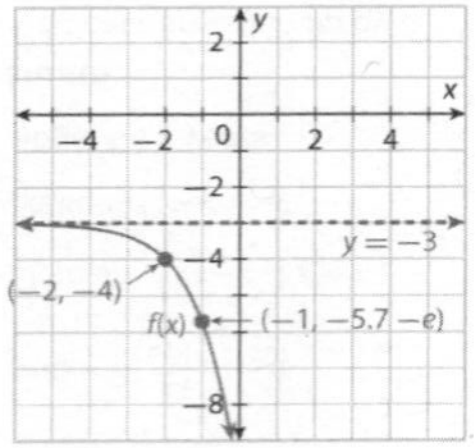

3. $g(x) = -e^{x+2} + 1$

   Domain: $\{x \mid -\infty < x < \infty\}$

   Range: $\{y \mid y < 1\}$

4. the fossil is about 15,800 years old.

   $r = 1 - e^{-0.00012} \approx 0.00012$

   So, the decay rate is 0.012%.

Evaluate

1. As $x \to \infty$, $f(x) \to e$.

3. The graph is translated $\frac{1}{2}$ unit to the right.

   There is no effect on the domain, range, or end behavior.

5. The graph is vertically compressed by a factor of $\frac{1}{4}$ and reflected across the x-axis. There is no effect on the domain, but the range changes to $\{y \mid -\infty < y < 0\}$.

   The end behavior as $x \to -\infty$ does not change, but the end behavior as $x \to \infty$ changes from $g(x) \to \infty$ to $g(x) \to -\infty$.

7. $(0, c - d)$

9.

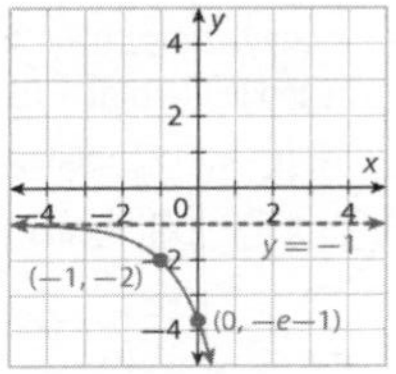

   $(-1, -2)$; $(0, -e - 1)$

   Domain: $\{x \mid -\infty < x < \infty\}$

   Range: $\{y \mid y < -1\}$

11.

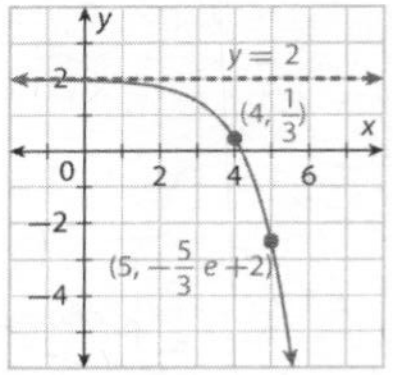

13. $g(x) = -6e^{x-4} + 2$

    Domain: $\{x \mid -\infty < x < \infty\}$

    Range: $\{y \mid y < 2\}$

15. The herd reached 25 million approximately 26 years after 1984, which would have been 2010.

    $r = e^{0.154} - 1 \approx 0.166$

    So, the growth rate is 16.6%.

17. a. approximately 2.3 minutes

    b. approximately 2.8 minutes

    c. approximately 17 minutes inside the coffee shop

    The coffee will never cool to 71°F on the patio.

UNIT 6 Selected Answers

MODULE 13

Lesson 13.4 Compound Interest

Your Turn

3. in approximately 12.9 years
4. in approximately 14.1 years
5. in approximately 6.4 years
6. Jaclyn should choose Account Y.

Evaluate

1. in approximately 16.8 years
3. 10.9 years longer
5. in approximately 77 years
7. in approximately 46.4 years
9. in approximately 12.8 years
11. The value of Lucy's investment equals the value of Juan's investment after approximately 31.2 years. The common value of the investments is approximately $5407.00.
13. Tanika should choose Account B.
15. A. C

    B. B

    C. E

    D. A

    E. D
17. The value of n in the function

    $V(t) = \left(1 + \frac{r}{n}\right)^{nt}$ is the number of times the

    interest is compounded per year, so the student should have used 4 instead of 3. the investment reaches a value of $16,500 after approximately 27.6 years.

UNIT 6 Selected Answers

MODULE 14

Lesson 14.1 Fitting Exponential Functions to Data

Your Turn

5. An approximate model is $f(x) = 2.15(0.92)^x$, where $f(x)$ is in million of tons.

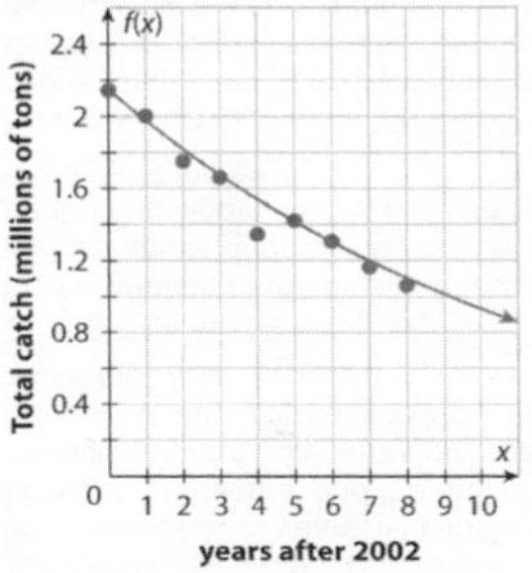

7. $f(x) = 2.119(0.9174)^x$

   The graphs are close together with almost the exact same amount of curvature. The regression model lies just a little lower than the model from YourTurn5, and thus is a better model

9. About 2018 or 2019; no, the model shows the fishery declining rapidly; possible elaboration: The model indicates that the reasons for the decline must be found and necessary changes made to ensure the productivity of the fishery. Some of these considerations are the total catch in the fisheries by other countries as well as by Iceland, whether and where overfishing is taking place, the health of the overall ocean environment in the areas, the health of the harvestable fish population as well as of species that it depends on, how quickly populations of different species can recover, and so on.

Evaluate

1. exponential growth.
3. A quadratic model is appropriate
5. Anja's model is $f(x) = 10(0.60)^x$.
7. Celia's model is $f(x) = 9.5(0.76)^x$.
9. a.

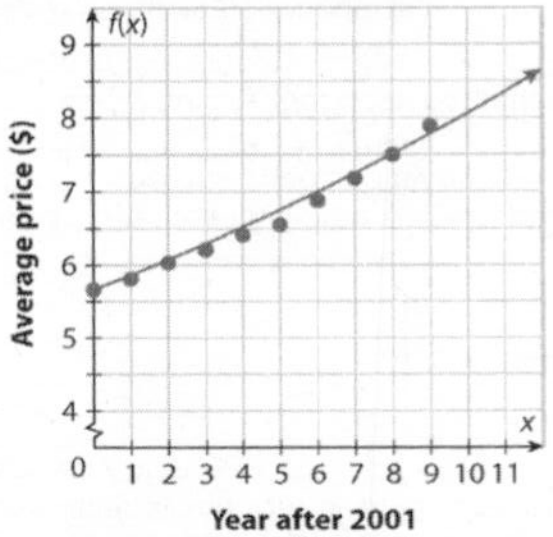

   An approximate model is $f(x) = 5.66(1.036)^x$. Overall, the model fits the trend fairly well, though it overestimates the price a little in the middle of the data, and passes below the last data point

   b. Regression model: $f(x) = 5.59(1.037)^x$

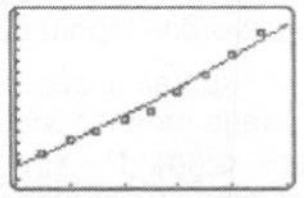

   The regression model is very close to the previous model. Its graph starts just a bit below the first model's graph, and it rises a tiny bit more steeply, but the models are very close together at the end of the period of the data.

   c. ≈ \$8.96; this is about \$.616 more per ticket than the actual. No, for the year, the revenue shortfall would be about $490(365)(0.66) \approx$ \$109,000, which is a large amount of money. \$0.61 accounts for about 7% of the individual ticket price which is a large amount.

11. a. $f(x) \approx 184.6(1.054)^x$, where x is in years
    b. $f(x) \approx 36.92(1.054)^x$.
    c. It will take about 2.7 years.
13. a
15. Notice that subtracting 3 from each y-value gives (0, 2), (1, 1), (2, 0.5), (3, 0.25), (4, 0.125), (5, 0.0625). This can be modeled by $f(x) = 2(0.5)^x$, so adding 3 to each function value will give the original data. So, you can use the model $f(x) = 2\,(0.5)^x + 3$.

UNIT 6 Selected Answers

MODULE 14

Lesson 14.2 Choosing Among Linear, Quadratic, and Exponential Models

Your Turn

4. Step 1: The life expectancy data are the data best modeled by a linear function, as its plot is the only one that does not show a distinct curve or change of direction. Although the average rate of change over the first and second halves of the data are somewhat different, the trend appears linear over the last several data points. The regression line will be a reasonably good fit, but not be really close. It will have a positive slope fairly close to the data's overall average rate of change of about 0.28.

   Step 2: A regression model is $y = 0.2901x + 49.62$ where x is the number of years after 1900 and y is the life expectancy in years. The initial value is about 49.6 years, and the rate of change is about 0.29 years per year, or about 2.9 years increase in life expectancy per decade.

   Step 3: The model is a good approximation of the overall trend, but it passes above, then below, then above the data points again, and is rising faster than the data at the end.

   Possible answer: I think the model may overestimate the life expectancy going forward, since it is rising faster than the data toward the end of the period. It does seem reasonable to predict that the increase can continue at about the rate shown by the data beginning in 1950, although with any significant health or medical advances, it could increase more.

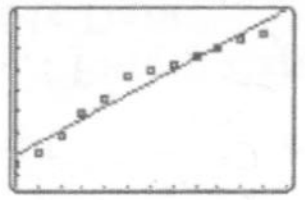

7. Step 1: The median age data appear to be the data best modeled by a quadratic function, as its scatter plot seems to show a single change of direction and a minimum point. The quadratic model for median age will have a positive leading coefficient since it opens upward. It appears that the vertex will not be too far from the minimum point on the plot, but the model's fit will not be very close, as the data appear to lie closer to the graph of an absolute value function.

   Step 2: A regression model is $y = 0.004048x^2 - 0.1093x + 29.90$ where x is the number of years after 1950 and y is the median age in years.

   Step 3: The model approximates the data trend pretty well, except that it misses the minimum data point by a considerable amount. It is also rising more quickly than the data at its right side.

   Possible answer: I think the model will not be accurate going forward because of the nature of the data set. The drop in median age around 1950 corresponds to the Baby Boom after World War II, when birth rates were very high.

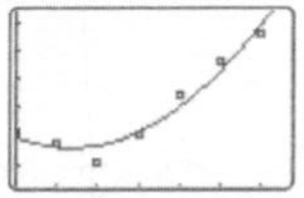

9. Step 1: The mean full-time wage appears to be the one best modeled by an exponential function, as it rises increasingly quickly, but does not reflect a change in direction.

   Step 2: A regression model is $y = 1.539(1.0567)^x$ where x is the number of years after 1940 and y is the mean full-time wage in thousands of dollars. The initial value for the model is 1.539, or about \$1540. The growth factor is 1.0567, and the growth rate is 0.0567, or about 5.67% per year. Because $1.056\,7^{10} \approx 1.74$, this is a growth rate of about 74% per decade.

   Step 3: The model is a fairly good fit, but it is rising more quickly at the end than the data indicate, as the last data value especially shows a decrease in the growth rate. Given that there was a recession in the decade after the year 2000, the model after 2000 would need a lower growth rate to be accurate.

Evaluate

1. A: IV

   B: I

   C: II

   D: III

3. a. Linear; the data show a clear linear pattern with no significant variation from it. The fit should be very close. The model will have a positive value for a since the graph is rising. Because the data are very far from the y-axis, the y-intercept of the model will not be meaningful in this context.

   b. The model is $y = 1.454x + 2.008$ where x is the frame size in cm and y is the inseam length in cm. The rate of change indicated by the model is 1.454 additional cm of inseam length per cm increase in frame size.

   c. The model is an extremely close fit for the individual values and for the overall trend.

   d. Possible answer: Yes; the model is a very close fit to the data. Also, this data point lies within the domain and range of the model data, so it should be safe to make the conclusion.

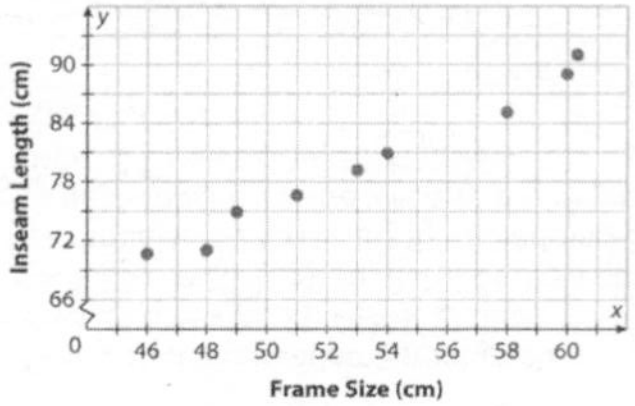

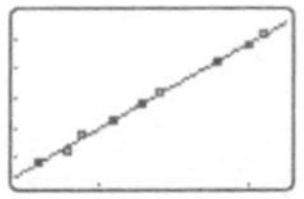

5.

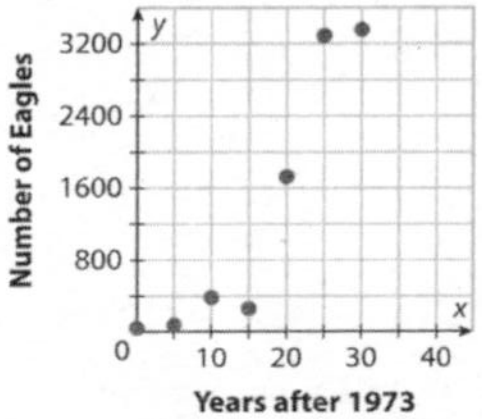

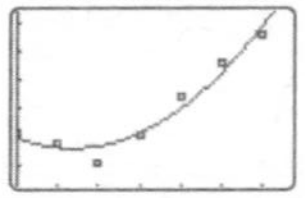

   a. Exponential; the data are clearly not linear, and appear to roughly approximate exponential growth, though it appears that a quadratic model could also be reasonable. Because the model shows growth, the growth factor will be greater than 1.

   b. The model is $y = 44.94(1.172)^x$ where x is the number of years since 1973 and y is the number of eagles counted. The parameter $a = 44.94$ is the model's estimate for the initial number in 1973. The growth factor is 1.172, which means that the annual growth rate is 17.2% annually.

   c. The model is very close to the first two data points, though it does not pass too close to the other points individually. Still, the model does look like a reasonable approximation of the data trend.

d. 2033: $y = 44.94(1.172)^{60} \approx 614{,}171$
Possible answer: very little confidence; there are many factors that affect eagle population, so the population would likely not continue to grow exponentially at the same rate.

7.

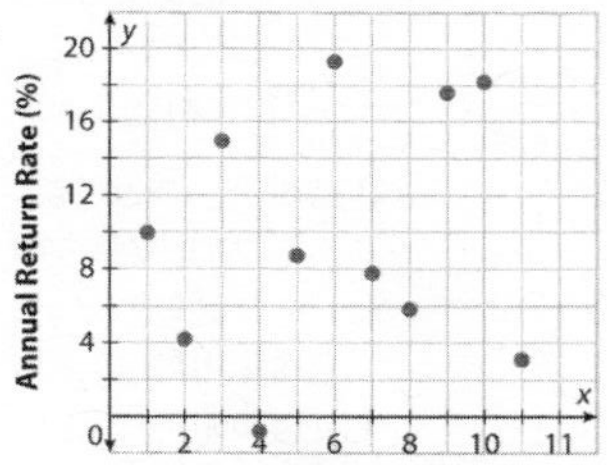

b. Possible answer: No model; there is no apparent pattern to the data.

c. Possible answer: The data give some prediction in the sense that they show that over the course of a decade, stocks have nearly always risen, and usually by at least several percent per year during the decade. So while the data give very little indication about any short period of time, they show that over a long enough time stocks generally rise several percent annually.

9. Possible answer: When you keep zooming out, you see that the model is actually parabolic in shape (opening downward), but to find a quadratic model, the calculator has had to make the neighborhood of the data such a tiny part of the curve of the parabola that it appears basically straight where it passes through the data. Additionally, the parameter a in front of the x squared term in the quadratic model is close to 0 and very small compared to b, and c.

11. The quadratic model is a slightly closer fit.

UNIT 6 Selected Answers

MODULE 15

Lesson 15.1 Defining and Evaluating a Logarithmic Function

Your Turn

8. $2^{-4} = \frac{1}{16}$

$\left(\frac{1}{3}\right)^y = x$

$\log_{10} 10{,}000 = 4$

$\log_{\frac{2}{5}} d = c$

9. $f(343) = 3$

$f\left(\frac{1}{49}\right) = -2$

$f\left(\sqrt{7}\right) = \frac{1}{2}$

11. $\log 0.25 \approx -0.602$

$10^{-0.602} \approx 0.25$

$\ln 0.25 \approx -1.386$

$e^{-1.386} \approx 0.25$

12. $\log 4 \approx 0.602$

$10^{0.602} \approx 4$

$\ln 4 \approx 1.386$

$e^{1.386} \approx 4$

13. The sound of the rock concert has an intensity level of about 125 dB.

14. After about 34 seconds

Evaluate

1. –2

–1

0

1

2

3

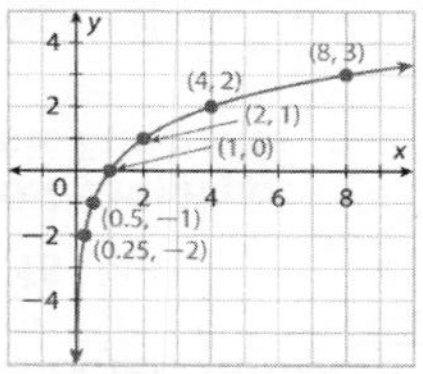

3. a. The domain of $f(x)$ is $\{x \mid -\infty < x < +\infty\}$, and the range is $\{y \mid y > 0\}$.

b. The exponential function is one-to-one, so no restriction on its domain is needed in order for its inverse to be a function.

c. $f^{-1}(x) = \log_3 x$

d. The domain of $f^{-1}(x)$ is $\{x \mid x > 0\}$, and the range is $\{y \mid -\infty < y < +\infty\}$.

5. $\log_5 125 = 3$

7. $\log_3 n = m$

9. $6^4 = 1296$

11. $8^y = x$

13. $f(243) = 5$

$f\left(\frac{1}{27}\right) = -3$

$f\left(\sqrt{27}\right) = \frac{3}{2}$

15. $f\left(\frac{1}{64}\right) = 3$

$f(256) = -4$

$f\sqrt[3]{16} = -\frac{2}{3}$

17. $\log 9 \approx 0.954$

$10^{0.954} \approx 9$

$\ln 9 \approx 2.197$

$e^{2.197} \approx 9$

19. $\log 0.31 \approx -0.509$

$10^{-0.509} \approx 0.31$

$\ln 0.31 \approx -1.171$

$e^{-1.171} \approx 0.31$

21. about 88 dB

23. The formula for finding the pH uses the common logarithm, not the natural logarithm. She should have found

$\log\frac{1}{[H^+]}$

$$pH = \log\frac{1}{[H^+]}$$
$$= \log\frac{1}{7.53\times10^{-9}}$$
$$\approx 8.1$$

So, the pH of the liquid is about 8.1.

25. a. Let $f(x) = \ln x$. Then $f^{-1}(x) = e^x$.

$$\ln e^2 = f(e^2)$$
$$= f(f^{-1}(2))$$
$$= 2$$

b. Let $f(x) = 10^x$. Then $f^{-1}(x) = \log x$.

$$10^{\log 7} = f(\log 7)$$
$$= f(f^{-1}(7))$$
$$= 7$$

c. $4^{\log_2 5} = (2^2)^{\log_2 5}$

$$= 2^{2\log_2 5}$$
$$= 2^{2\log_2 5 + \log_2 5}$$
$$= \left(2^{2\log_2 5}\right)\left(2^{2\log_2 5}\right)$$

Let $g(x) = 2^x$. Then $g^{-1}(x) = \log_2 x$.

$$2^{\log_2 5} = g(\log_2 5)$$
$$= g\left(g^{-1}(5)\right)$$
$$= 5$$

Substitute 5 for

$2^{\log_2 5}$ in $4^{\log_2 5} = \left(2^{\log_2 5}\right)\left(2^{\log_2 5}\right)$

$$4^{\log_2 5} = \left(2^{\log_2 5}\right)\left(2^{\log_2 5}\right)$$
$$= (5)(5)$$
$$= 25$$

UNIT 6 Selected Answers

MODULE 15

Lesson 15.2 Graphing Logarithmic Functions

Your Turn

2. Domain: $\{x \mid x > -1\}$

Range: $\{y \mid -\infty < y < +\infty\}$

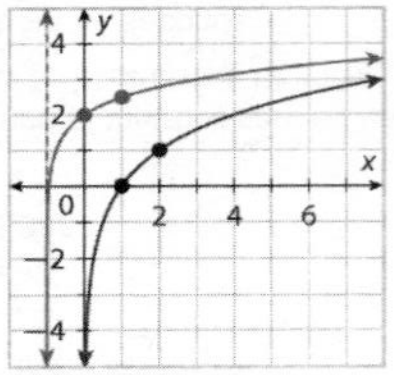

The transformations of the graph of $f(x) = \log_2 x$ that produce the graph of $g(x)$ are as follows:

- a vertical compression by a factor of $\frac{1}{2}$
- a translation of 1 unit to the left and 2 units up

Asymptote $x = -1$

Reference point (0, 2)

Reference point $\left(1, 2\frac{1}{2}\right)$

4. a. $B = 1000\,(1.02)^t$ where B is the account balance at time t (in years since the deposit was made).

b. The inverse of the exponential model is $t = 50 \ln \frac{B}{1000}$, which gives the time it takes for the account balance to reach a certain level.

c. A graphing calculator gives the logarithmic regression model $t = -349 + 50.5 \ln B$. Graphing this model and the inverse model from part b shows that the models are basically equivalent.

Evaluate

1.

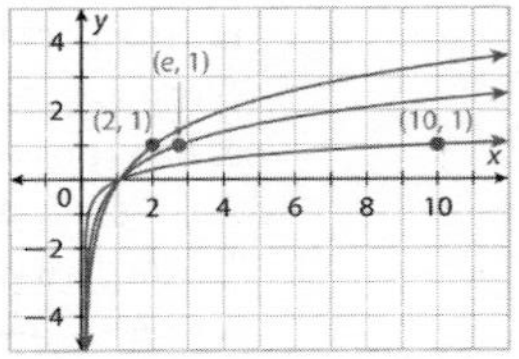

3. a. The graph of $g(x)$ is a vertical translation of the graph of $f(x)$ down 5 units. The attributes that change are the x-intercept and the intervals where the function is positive and where it is negative.

b. The graph of $g(x)$ is a vertical stretch of the graph of $f(x)$ by a factor of 4. No attributes change.

c. The graph of $g(x)$ is a horizontal translation of the graph of $f(x)$ left 6 units. The attributes that change are the domain, the end behavior, the vertical asymptote, the x-intercept, and the intervals where the function is positive and where it is negative.

d. The graph of $g(x)$ is a vertical compression of the graph of $f(x)$ by a factor of $\frac{3}{4}$ as well as a reflection across the x-axis. The attributes that change are the end behavior and whether the function increases or decreases throughout its domain.

e. The graph of $g(x)$ is a vertical translation of the graph of $f(x)$ up 7 units. The attributes that change are the x-intercept and the intervals where the function is positive and where it is negative.

f. The graph of $g(x)$ is a horizontal translation of the graph of $f(x)$ right 8 units. The attributes that change are the domain, the end behavior, the vertical asymptote, the x-intercept, and the intervals where the function is positive and where it is negative.

5. • a vertical stretch by a factor of 3

• a translation of 1 unit to the right and 1 unit down

Domain: $\{x \mid x > 1\}$

Range: $\{y \mid -\infty < y < +\infty\}$

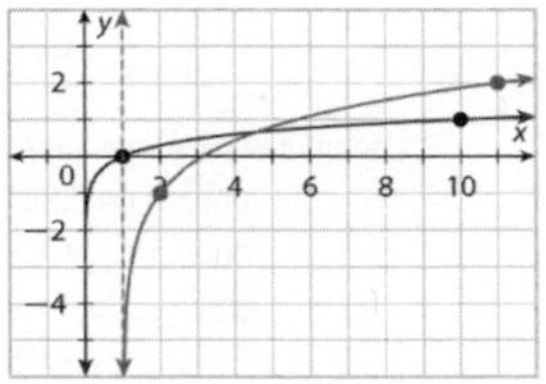

7. • a vertical compression by a factor of 4

• a reflection across the *x*-axis

• a translation of 4 units to the right and 3 units up

Domain: $\{x \mid x > 4\}$

Range: $\{y \mid -\infty < y < +\infty\}$

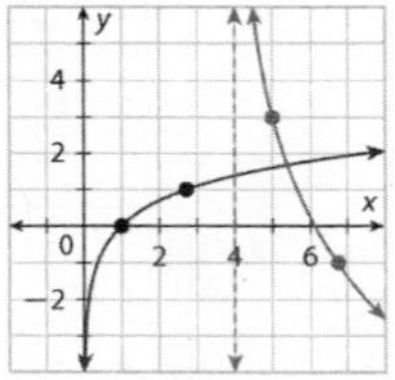

9. a. $p = 100(0.685)^t$ where *p* is the percent of fluorine-18 remaining at time *t* (in hours).

b. $t = -2.65 \ln \frac{p}{100}$, which gives the time it takes for the percent of fluorine-18 remaining to reach a certain level.

c. A graphing calculator gives the logarithmic regression model $t = 12.2 - 2.64 \ln p$. Graphing this model and the inverse model from part b shows that the models are basically equivalent

11. Using the function's rule:

$g(x) = \log(x - h)$

$1 = \log(7 - h)$

$10^1 = 7 - h$

$3 = -h$

$-3 = h$

Thinking in terms of the function's graph:

The graph of $g(x) = \log(x - h)$ is the graph of $f(x) = \log x$ translated *h* units horizontally. Since the graph of $f(x)$ passes through the point (10, 1), shifting the graph left 3 units causes it to pass through the point (7, 1). A shift of 3 units to the left means that $h = -3$.

13. Let $\log_{\frac{1}{b}} x = m$. In exponential form, the equation is $\left(\frac{1}{b}\right)^m = x$, so $\left(b^{-1}\right)^m = x$ and $b^{-m} = x$. In logarithmic form, the equation $b^{-m} = x$ is $\log_b x = -m$, or $-\log_b x = m$. By the transitive property of equality, $\log_{\frac{1}{b}} x = -\log_b x$.

UNIT 6 Selected Answers

MODULE 16
Lesson 16.1 Properties of Logarithms

Your Turn

4. $\log_4 64^3 = 9$
5. $\log_8 18 - \log_8 2 \approx 1.057$
6. 18.85 years

Evaluate

1. 4
3. 12
5. $x + 9$
7. 6
9. 9.2 is 3.98×10^{25} ergs
11. from 20 decibels to 60 decibels
13. $t = \dfrac{\log\left(\frac{50}{40}\right)}{\log(1 + 0.08)}$

about 2.90 years

15. about 14.3 minutes
17. a. C
b. A
c. E
d. D
e. B

19. Let $x = \log_c a$. Then $a = c^x$ by the definition of a logarithm.

$\log_b a = \log_b c^x$	Take the logarithm of both sides.
$\log_b a = x\log_b c$	Power Property of Logarithms
$\dfrac{\log_b a}{\log_b c} = x$	Divide both sides by $\log_b c$.
$\dfrac{\log_b a}{\log_b c} = \log_c a$	Substitution

21. Since the two terms have different bases, the Product Property of Logarithms cannot be used to simplify the expression.

$= 6$

23. Rewrite both expressions using the same base.

$\log_b a = \dfrac{\log a}{\log b}$ and $\log_{\frac{1}{b}} a = \dfrac{\log a}{\log\left(\frac{1}{b}\right)}$

$\dfrac{\log a}{\log\left(\frac{1}{b}\right)} = \dfrac{\log a}{\log b^{-1}} = \dfrac{\log a}{-\log b} = -\dfrac{\log a}{\log b}$

So $\log_{\frac{1}{b}} a$ is the opposite of $\log_b a$.

UNIT 6 Selected Answers

MODULE 16
Lesson 16.2 Solving Exponential Equations

Your Turn

4. $x = \ln 37.5 + 1 \approx 4.624$

5. $x = \dfrac{\log 12}{3\log 6} \approx 0.462$

6. about 98.2 quarters, or about 24.6 years

Evaluate

1.
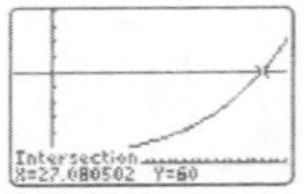

≈ 27.1

3.
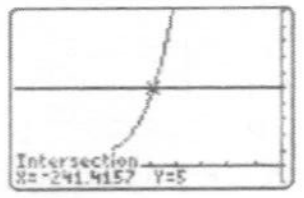

≈ -241.4

5.
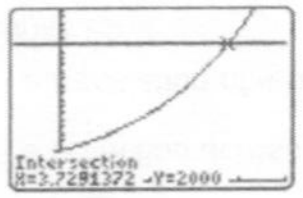

$x \approx 3.73$

Check:

$450e^{0.4(3.73)} \approx 2000$

$450e^{1.492} \approx 2000$

$2000.69 \approx 2000$

The answer is reasonable.

7. $x = \dfrac{\ln 6}{3} \approx 0.597$

9. $x = \dfrac{3\ln 250 + 1}{2} \approx 8.782$

11. $x = \dfrac{4\log 30}{\log 5} \approx 8.453$

13. about 27.4 years

15. from about 10.96 km to about 24.94 km above sea level.

17. about 36.5 years

19. after about 30 years, or around 2010

21. The student evaluated log *e* incorrectly. log *e* is not equal to 1. The student should have evaluated the logarithm correctly or used the natural log.

$e^{4x} - 6 = 10$	$e^{4x} - 6 = 10$
$e^{4x} = 16$	$e^{4x} = 16$
$\log e^{4x} = \log 16$	$\ln e^{4x} = \ln 16$
$4x\log e = \log 16$	$4x\ln e = \ln 16$
$x = \dfrac{\log 16}{4\log e} \approx 0.693$	$4x(1) = \ln 16$
	$x = \dfrac{\ln 16}{4} \approx 0.693$

23. The masses of the parent isotopes and daughter isotopes are equal when $t = h$. So, the masses of the isotopes will be equal after 1 half-life. This makes sense because after one half-life, the mass of the parent isotopes will be $\frac{1}{2}$ of the initial mass. Since the parent isotopes decay into the daughter isotopes, the other half is now made of daughter isotopes. So, the two masses are equal.

UNIT 7 Selected Answers

MODULE 17
Lesson 17.1 Angles of Rotation and Radian Measure

Your Turn

8. $-\dfrac{11\pi}{4}$

9. 195°

11. angular velocity.
≈ 4490 radians/second
distance the point travels in a second
$\approx 45{,}000$
The point travels about one fourth the speed of light.

12. Using degrees:

$\dfrac{103°}{360°} = \dfrac{x \text{ mi}}{24{,}860 \text{ mi}}$

$360x = 103(24{,}860)$

$x = \dfrac{103(24{,}860)}{360}$

$x \approx 7110$

The distance is about 7100 miles.

Using radians:
First convert to radians.

$\dfrac{\pi}{180°} \cdot 103° = \dfrac{103\pi}{180}$

Use the arc length formula.

$S = r\theta = \dfrac{24{,}860}{2\pi}\left(\dfrac{103\pi}{180}\right) \approx 7110$

The distance is about 7100 miles.

Evaluate

1. Possible answer:

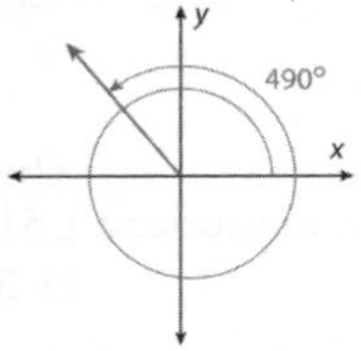

3. 444°, 804°, –276°, –636°

5. $\dfrac{5\pi}{3}, \dfrac{11\pi}{3}, -\dfrac{7\pi}{3}, -\dfrac{13\pi}{3}$

7. $\dfrac{7\pi}{18}$

9. $-\dfrac{21\pi}{4}$, or $-5\dfrac{1}{4}\pi$

11. 330°

13. –300°

15. The coordinates are 35.68° north latitude and 139.69° east longitude. The school is in Tokyo, Japan.

17. It would be about 1800 miles shorter to fly over the North Pole.

19. about 793 mi/h

21. 33 inches

23. A, B, D, E, F

25. about halfway between 1:05 and 1:06

27. $\frac{1}{2}r^2\theta$; A full circle has an area of πr^2. A full circle is 2π radians, so an angle of θ radians is $\dfrac{\theta}{2\pi}$ of the circle. Find the portion of the area of a full circle that this represents: $\dfrac{\theta}{2\pi} \cdot \pi r^2 = \dfrac{\theta}{2} \cdot r^2 = \dfrac{1}{2}r^2\theta$.

MODULE 17

Lesson 17.2 Defining and Evaluating the Basic Trigonometric Functions

Your Turn

5. $\frac{1}{2}$
6. –1
8. about 73.2 feet long

Evaluate

1. $\frac{4}{5}$; $\frac{4}{5}$; $-\frac{4}{5}$; $-\frac{4}{5}$
$\frac{3}{5}$; $-\frac{3}{5}$; $-\frac{3}{5}$; $\frac{3}{5}$
$\frac{4}{3}$; $-\frac{4}{3}$; $\frac{4}{3}$; $-\frac{4}{3}$
3. $-\frac{\sqrt{3}}{3}$
5. 1
7. –1
9. $\sqrt{3}$
11. –0.921
13. –0.993
15. –0.809
17. 0.530
19. $y \approx 2.14$
21. $y = 0.5 \sin(2\phi)$
23. ≈ 48 feet
25. ≈ 29.24 yards
27. Sven used his calculator in radian mode instead of degree mode. $\sin 10° \approx 0.1736$
29. Assume θ is in Quadrant I. Then $-\theta$ will be in Quadrant IV. $-\theta$ will have the same reference angle as θ, so their absolute values will be the same. Cosine is positive in both Quadrant I and Quadrant IV, so $\cos\theta$ and $\cos(-\theta)$ will have the same value. If θ is in Quadrant IV, then $-\theta$ is in Quadrant I, and the same reasoning holds. The same pairings work for Quadrants II and III. (If θ is in Quadrant II, then $-\theta$ is in Quadrant III, and vice versa. In both cases, the reference angles are the same angle, and the cosine of both θ and $-\theta$ is negative).

MODULE 17

Lesson 17.3 Using a Pythagorean Identity

Your Turn

7. $\cos\theta \approx -0.765$
8. $\tan\theta \approx -0.110$
11. $\sin\theta \approx 3.454$ $\cos\theta \approx -0.960$

Evaluate

1. $\cos\theta \approx 0.857$
3. $\cos\theta \approx 0.895$
5. $\cos\theta \approx -0.419$
7. $\sin\theta \approx 0.735$
9. $\cos\theta \approx -0.245$ and $\sin\theta \approx 0.972$
11. $\cos\theta \approx 0.130$ and $\sin\theta \approx 0.981$
13. $\cos\theta \approx 0.628$ and $\sin\theta \approx -0.777$
15. $\cos\theta \approx 0.148$ and $\sin\theta \approx 0.985$
17. A. Positive
B. Negative
C. Negative
D. Negative
E. Positive
19. $x^2 + y^2 = r^2 \Rightarrow (r\cos\theta)^2 + (r\sin\theta)^2 = r^2$
$r^2\cos^2\theta + r^2\sin^2\theta = r^2 \Rightarrow \cos^2\theta + \sin^2\theta = 1$
21. $\mu \approx 0.84$
23. $1 + \cos\theta$
25. The expression $\frac{\sqrt{1-\cos^2\theta}}{\sqrt{1-\sin^2\theta}}$ simplifies to $\tan\theta$. If you rewrite $\frac{\sqrt{1-\cos^2\theta}}{\sqrt{1-\sin^2\theta}}$ using the Pythagorean Identity, you get the result $\frac{\sqrt{\sin^2\theta}}{\sqrt{\cos^2\theta}}$. Taking the square root results in the expression $\frac{\sin\theta}{\cos\theta}$, which is equivalent to $\tan\theta$.

UNIT 7 Selected Answers

MODULE 18

Lesson 18.1 Stretching, Compressing, and Reflecting Sine and Cosine Graphs

Your Turn

9. vertically compressed by a factor of $\frac{1}{2}$ and horizontally compressed by a factor of $\frac{1}{4}$; $\frac{\pi}{2}$

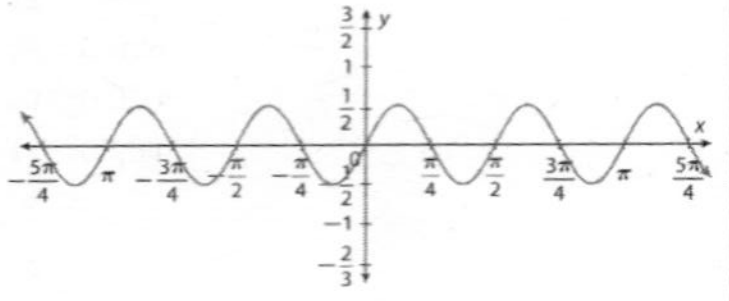

10. $y = 2\cos\frac{\pi}{2}x$

11. frequency $= \frac{1}{1.5} \approx 0.67$ Hz

The frequency represents the number of back-and-forth swings per second. The amplitude represents the pendulum's maximum horizontal displacement. The period represents the amount of time it takes the pendulum to complete a back-and-forth swing.

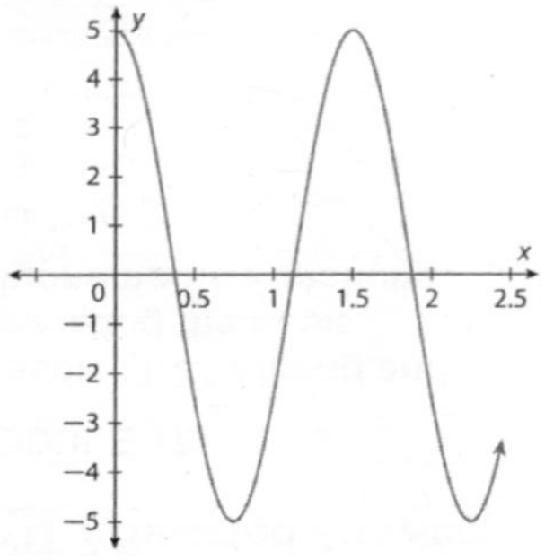

Evaluate

1.

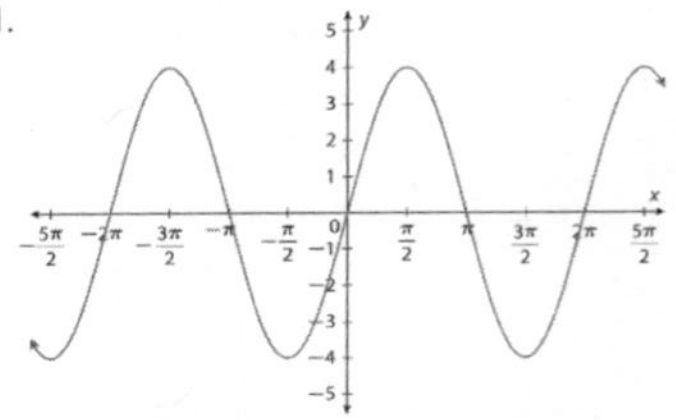

vertically stretched by a factor of 4 period: 2π

3.

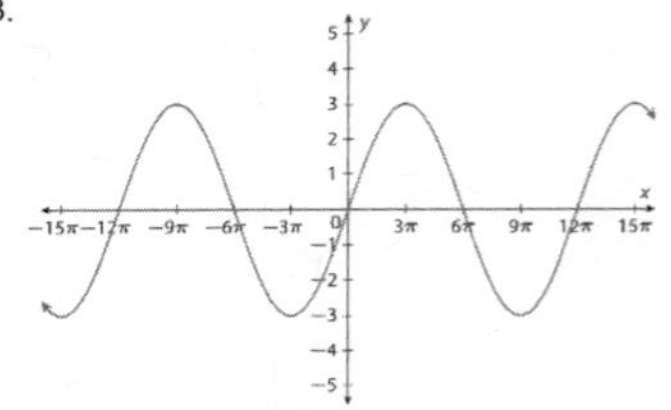

vertically stretched by a factor of 3; horizontally stretched by a factor of 6; reflected across the *x*-axis period: $2\pi \cdot 6 = 12\pi$

5.

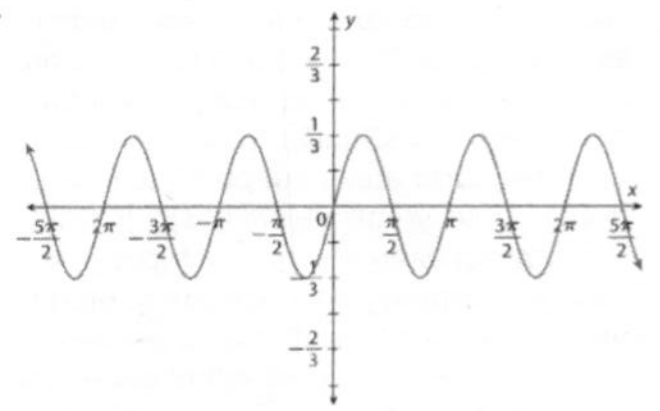

vertically compressed by a factor of $\frac{1}{3}$;

horizontally compressed by a factor of $\frac{1}{2}$

period: $2\pi \cdot \frac{1}{2} = \pi$

7. $y = 3\sin 2\pi x$

9. $y = -3\sin 2x$

11. $y = \frac{1}{2}\sin\frac{1}{2}x$

13. frequency $= \frac{1}{0.003} \approx 333$ Hz

The frequency represents the number of cycles of the sound wave every second. The amplitude represents the maximum change in air pressure. The period represents the amount of time it takes for the sound wave to repeat.

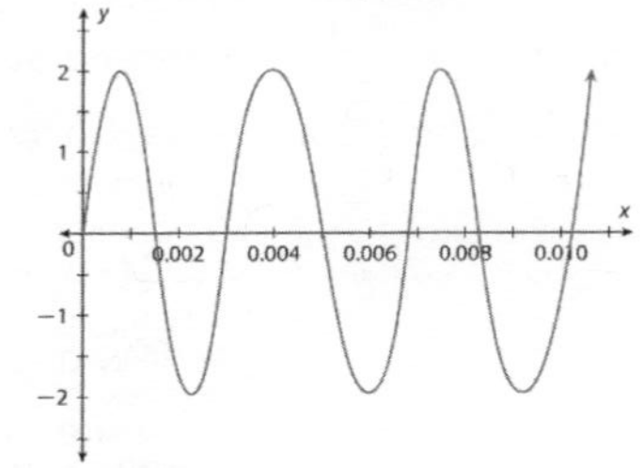

15. frequency $= \frac{1}{\pi} \approx 0.32$ Hz

The frequency represents the number of back-and-forth swings every second. The amplitude represents the the pendulum's maximum horizontal displacement. The period represents the amount of time for the pendulum to complete a back-and-forth swing.

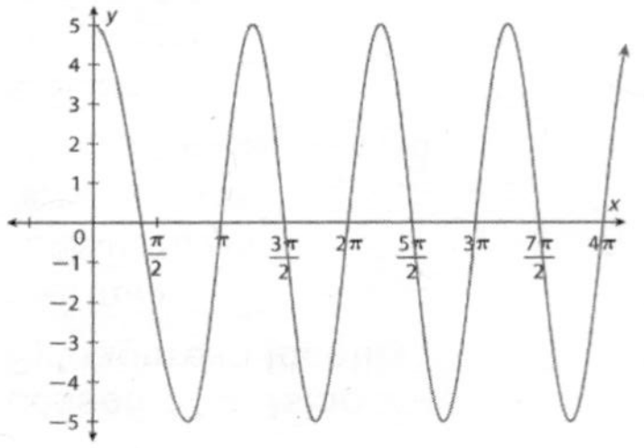

17. A. Domain: $\{x \mid x \in R\}$ Range: $\{y \mid -1 \le y \le 1\}$

B. Domain: $\{x \mid -\infty < x < +\infty\}$

Range: $\{y \mid -2 \le y \le 2\}$

C. Domain: $\{x \mid -\infty < x < +\infty\}$

Range: $\{y \mid -3 \le y \le 3\}$

D. Domain: $\{x \mid -\infty < x < +\infty\}$

Range: $\left\{y \mid -\frac{4}{5} \le y \le \frac{4}{5}\right\}$

E. Domain: $\{x \mid -\infty < x < +\infty\}$

Range: $\{y \mid -2 \le y \le 2\}$

A, B, C, D, and E all have the same domain. B and E have the same range.

19. The graphs of the cosecant and secant functions consist of U-shaped curves that alternate between (a) being above of the *x*-axis and opening up and (b) being below the *x*-axis and opening down. The cosecant function has asymptotes at multiples of π, while the secant function has asymptotes at odd multiples of $\frac{\pi}{2}$.

Neither function has *x*-intercepts. Both functions have a local maximum value of −1 and a local minimum value of 1.

21.

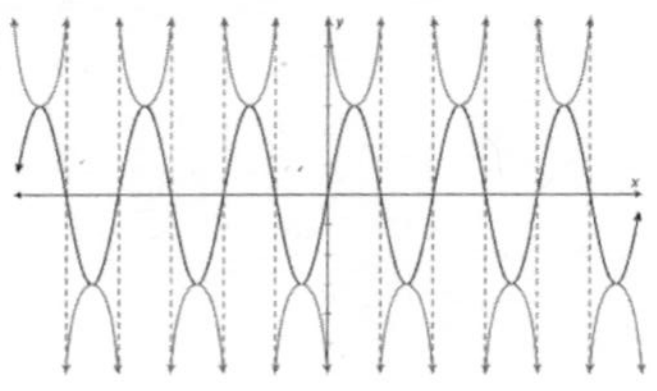

23.

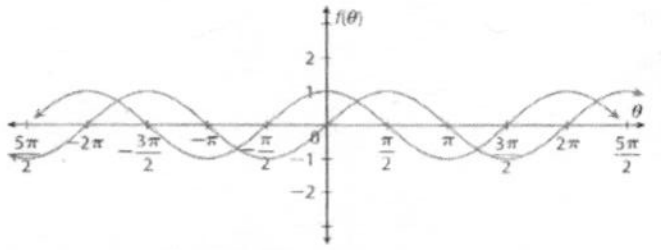

The sine and cosine functions are equal when $\theta = \frac{\pi}{4} + n\pi$, where n is an integer.

These angles correspond to the points where the line $y = x$ intersects the unit circle, which means that the x-and y-coordinates of those points are equal.

25. Domain:

$\left\{x \middle| 0 < x < \frac{\pi}{2}, \frac{\pi}{2} < x < \frac{3\pi}{2}, \frac{3\pi}{2} < x \le 2\pi\right\}$

Range: $\{y | -\infty < y \le -1, 1 \le y < +\infty\}$

Since the domain does not include $x = \frac{\pi}{2}$ or $x = \frac{3\pi}{2}$, while the range goes to either $+\infty$ or $-\infty$, there has to be vertical asymptotes at $x = \frac{\pi}{2}$ and $x = \frac{3\pi}{2}$.

UNIT 7 Selected Answers

MODULE 18

Lesson 18.2 Stretching, Compressing, and Reflecting Tangent Graphs

Your Turn

6.

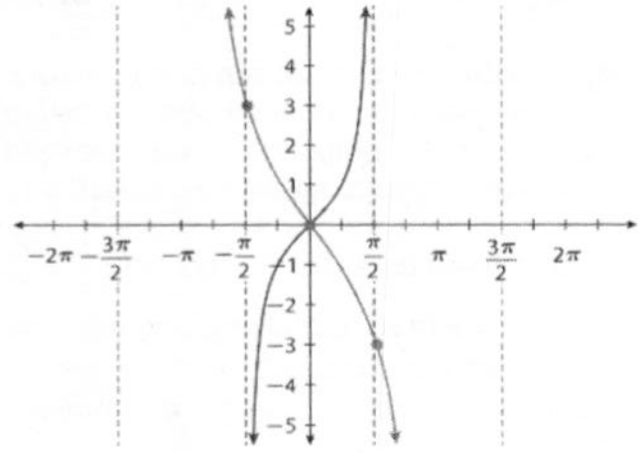

7. $f(x) = \frac{1}{2}\tan 2\pi x$

8. $f(x)$:
Period = 3
$g(x)$:
Period $= \frac{1}{3}$
The period of $g(x)$ is less than that of $f(x)$.

9. $h = 20\tan\theta$

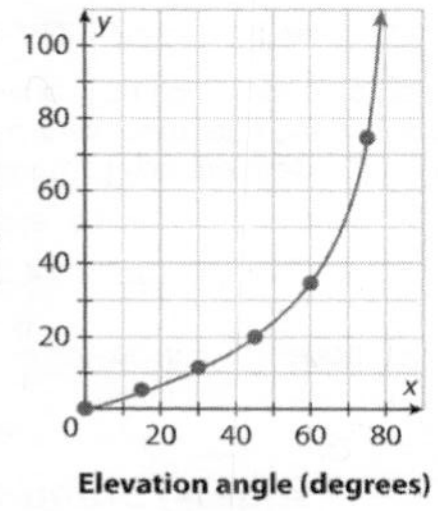

Evaluate

1. For $f(x) = \tan x$, asymptotes are at $x = \frac{\pi}{2} + n\pi$, for all integers n.
For $f(x) = \cot x$, asymptotes are at $x = n\pi$, for all integers n.

3.

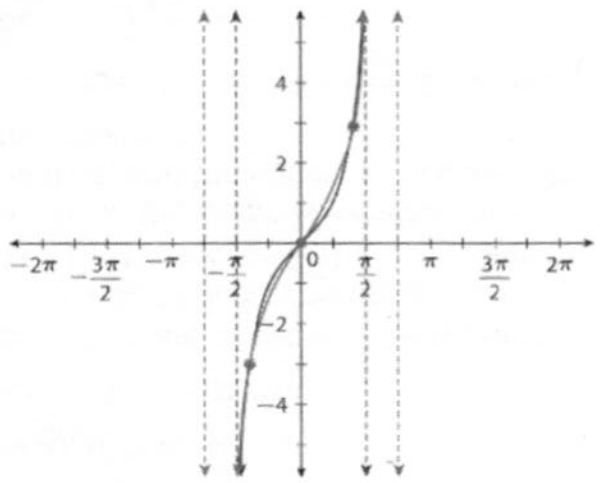

Asymptotes at $x = -\frac{3\pi}{4}$ and $x = \frac{3\pi}{4}$

Reference points at $\left[-\frac{3\pi}{8}, -3\right]$, $(0, 0)$, $\left[\frac{3\pi}{8}, 3\right]$

5.

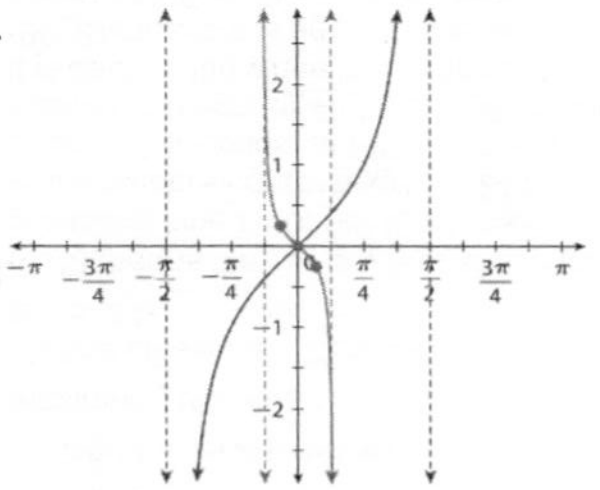

Asymptotes at $x = -\frac{\pi}{8}$ and $x = \frac{\pi}{8}$

Reference points at $\left[-\frac{\pi}{16}, \frac{1}{4}\right]$, $(0, 0)$, $\left[\frac{\pi}{16}, \frac{-1}{4}\right]$

7. $g(x) = -\frac{5}{2}\tan 2x$

9. $g(x) = 4\tan\frac{\pi}{4}x$

11. $g(x)$ has a greater period than $f(x)$.

13. $f(x)$ has a lesser period than $g(x)$.

15.

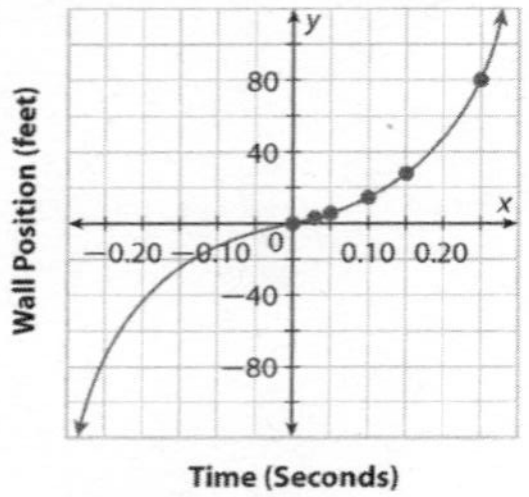

17. –0.1 mile and 0.1 mile

19. $t = -\frac{1}{8}$ second

21. Positioning the camera at –80° or 80° captures the longest stretch of the hallway. The shortest stretch occurs at the least steep portion of the graph, or when $\theta = 0°$.

23. The important reference points and asymptotes of the tangent function all occur at recognizable points in the sine and cosine graphs. The asymptotes will be at the cosine's x-intercepts, the tangent's x-intercepts will be at the sine's x-intercepts, and the halfway points occur where the sine and cosine functions intersect.

UNIT 7 Selected Answers

MODULE 18

Lesson 18.3 Translating Trigonometric Graphs

Your Turn

3. Period: $\frac{1}{b} = 2$, so $b = \frac{1}{2}$; period $= 2\pi \cdot \frac{1}{2} = \pi$

Midline: $y = k$, or $y = 1$

Amplitude: $a = 2$

The point (0, 1) on the graph of $y = \cos x$ is a local maximum, and lies 1 unit above the midline. The corresponding point for $f(x) = 2\cos 2\left(x - \frac{\pi}{2}\right) + 1$ will lie $a(1) = 2(1) = 2$ units above the midline, or at $y = 1 + 2 = 3$. There is also a translation $h = \frac{\pi}{2}$ units to the right. So, $\left(\frac{\pi}{2}, 3\right)$ is on the graph. The next local maximum is one cycle to the right, or at $\left(\frac{\pi}{2} + \pi, 3\right) = \left(\frac{3\pi}{2}, 3\right)$.

Minimum: $a = 2$ units below the midline, or $k - a = 1 - 2 = -1$; occurs one half cycle after the first maximum, or at $x = \frac{\pi}{2} + \frac{\pi}{2} = \pi$. So, $(\pi, -1)$ is on the graph.

The graph crosses its midline halfway between the first maximum and the minimum, and halfway between the minimum and the second maximum, or at $x = \frac{\frac{\pi}{2} + \pi}{2} = \frac{3\pi}{4}$ and $x = \frac{\pi + \frac{3\pi}{2}}{2} = \frac{5\pi}{4}$. So, $\left(\frac{3\pi}{4}, 1\right)$ and $\left(\frac{5\pi}{4}, 1\right)$ are on the graph.

6. $f(x) = 2\sin 2\left(x - \frac{\pi}{2}\right) - 1$

(Note that $f(x) = 2\sin 2\left(x + \frac{\pi}{2}\right) - 1$ also represents the graph.)

7. Period: 90; Midline; $h(t) = 24$

Amplitude: $|a| = 16$;

Maximum: 40

Minimum: 8

(0, 8) is a minimum

Second minimum: (90, 8)

Maximum: (45, 40)

Midline crossings: (22.5, 24) and (67.5, 24)

(0, 8) means the car is 8 feet above the ground at time $t = 0$; (22.5, 24) means it is at the wheel's center height of 24 feet after 22.5 seconds; at (45, 40) it is at its maximum height of 40 feet; at (67.5, 24) it is back at the wheel's center height; (90, 8) means it is again at the minimum height of 8 feet after a 90-second cycle.

Evaluate

1. Period: $2\pi \cdot 1 = 2\pi$;

Midline: $y = k$, or $y = 1$

Amplitude: $|a| = 3$

$h = -\pi$, $k = 1 \Rightarrow$ image of (0, 0) from $y = \sin x$ is $(-\pi, 1)$; other midline crossings are at cycle halfway point, $(-\pi + \pi, 1) = (0, 1)$ and cycle endpoint, $(-\pi + 2\pi, 1) = (\pi, 1)$. Plot $(-\pi, 1)$, $(0, 1)$, and $(\pi, 1)$. $a < 0$, so the graph is reflected in its midline, and the minimum occurs before the maximum.

Minimum: $k - |a| = 1 - 3 = -2$; occurs at $x = \frac{-\pi + 0}{2} = -\frac{\pi}{2}$.

Maximum: $k + |a| = 1 + 3 = 4$; occurs at $x = \frac{0 + \pi}{2} = \frac{\pi}{2}$. Plot $\left(-\frac{\pi}{2}, -2\right)$ and $\left(\frac{\pi}{2}, 4\right)$.

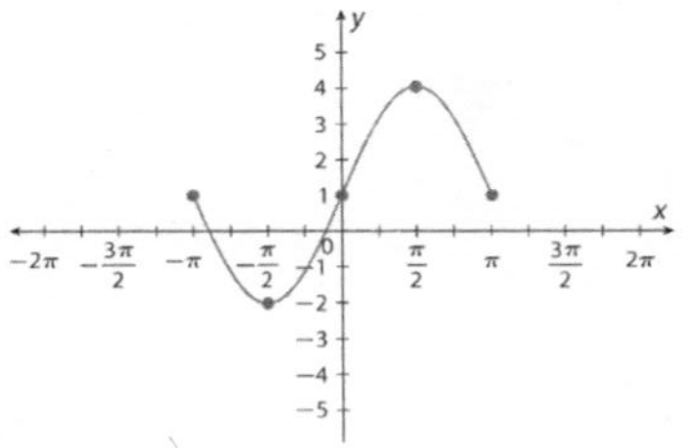

3.

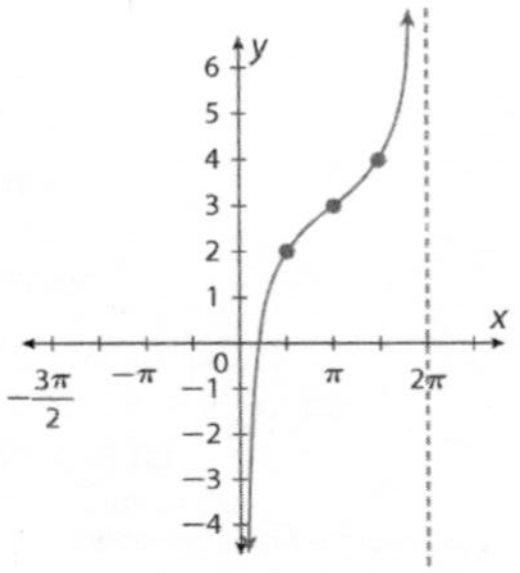

Period: $b = 2 \Rightarrow \pi \cdot b = 2\pi$; Midline: $y = k$, or $y = 3$; $h = \pi \Rightarrow$ midline crossing is translated π units to the right to $(\pi, 3)$; asymptotes are half a cycle to the left and right at $x = \pi - \pi = 0$ and $x = \pi + \pi = 2\pi$. Halfway points are halfway between the asymptotes and midline crossing, or at $x = \frac{\pi}{2}$ and $x = \frac{3\pi}{2}$. The points are $\left(\frac{\pi}{2}, 3\right)$ and $\left(\frac{3\pi}{2}, 3\right)$.

5. $f(x) = 2\sin(x - \pi) + 1$. (Note that $f(x) = 2\sin(x + \pi) + 1$ also represents the graph.)

7. $f(x) = 3\tan\frac{1}{2}x + 2$

9. Period: $\frac{1}{b} = \pi$, so $b = \frac{1}{\pi}$, and $2\pi \cdot b = 2$;

Midline: $k = 36$, so the midline is $h(t) = 36$.

Amplitude: $a = 10$; Maximum: $36 + 10 = 46$;

Minimum: $36 - 10 = 26$

$h(0) = 10 \sin\left(-\frac{\pi}{2}\right) + 36 = 26 \Rightarrow (0, 26)$ is on the graph.

This is a minimum. The next minimum is one cycle later at (2, 26). A maximum occurs halfway through the cycle at (1, 46). Midline crossings: halfway between first minimum and maximum at (0.5, 36) and halfway between maximum and second minimum at (1.5, 36).

(0, 26) means the toy is at its lowest point 26 inches above the floor t = 0; (0.5, 36) means it is at its midline (resting) height of 36 inches after 0.5 second; at (1, 46) it is at its maximum height of 46 inches, then back to the midline height at (1.5, 36), and finally back to the minimum height after 2 seconds.

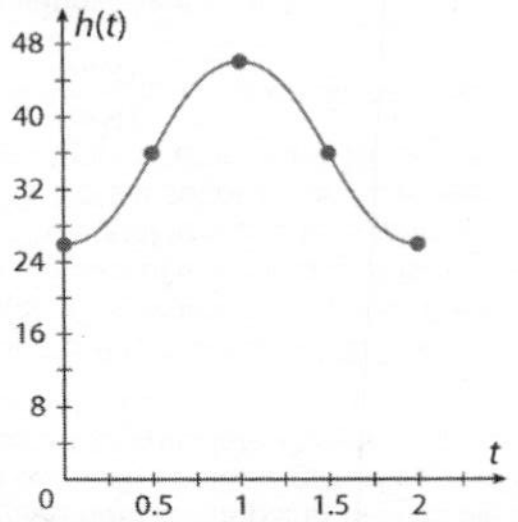

11. The key points are translated h units right for positive h, h units left for negative h, k units up for positive k, and k units down for negative k.

13. Yes, a sine curve with a negative coefficient a is the same as a curve with a positive coefficient a translated horizontally by half a cycle. For example, the graphs of $y = -\sin x$ and $y = \sin(x + \pi)$ are the same. Also, any cosine curve is the same as a sine curve translated by one fourth of a cycle, so a similar result holds for cosine graphs.

UNIT 7 Selected Answers

MODULE 18

Lesson 18.4 Fitting Sine Functions to Data

Your Turn

6. Rough-fit model:

$y = -8.3 \sin\frac{\pi}{6}(x - 4) + 19.7$.

Regression model:
$y = 8.13 \sin(0.52x + 1.05) + 19.79$
Both models fit the data equally well for all values of x.

7. From September 19 to March 23

Evaluate

1. a.

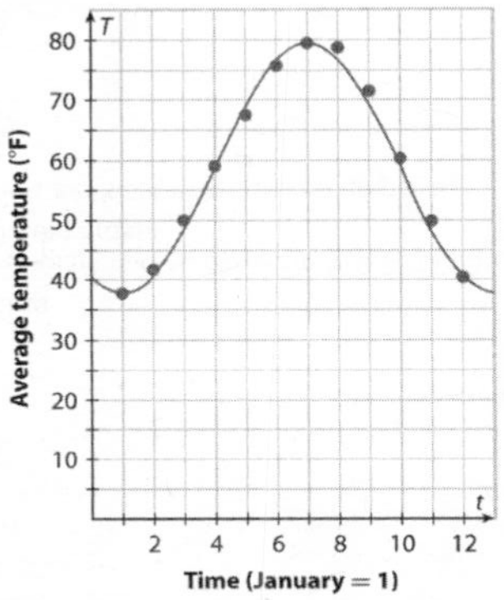

$y = 20.85 \sin\frac{\pi}{6}(x - 4) + 58.55$.

b. Regression model: $y = 21.02 \sin(0.51x - 2.01) + 58.61$

The models are very close together, and both fit the data well for all values of x.

3. a.

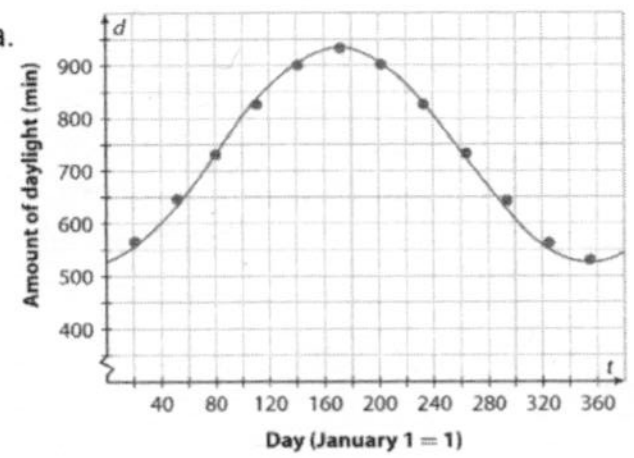

$y = 201.5 \sin\frac{2\pi}{365}(x - 80) + 731.5$.

b. Regression model: $y = 197.8 \sin(0.0168x - 1.32) + 728.7$

Both models fit the data very well for all values of x.

c. 94 days, which is a little over 3 months.

5. For cosine and sine functions that have the same amplitude, period, and vertical shift, translating the graph of the cosine function one fourth of a period to the right produces the graph of the sine function, or translating the graph of the sine function one fourth of a period to the left produces the graph of the cosine function. So, if you have a sine regression model, you can rewrite it as a cosine model if desired by a simple horizontal shift.

7. The regression model is in the form $y = a \sin(bx + c) + d$ instead of the form $y = a \sin\frac{1}{b}(x - h) + k$. Ryan needs to rewrite the model by factoring out the 0.0168 from the expression $0.0168t - 1.32$: $t = 78.6$, which corresponds to March 20.

UNIT 8 Selected Answers

MODULE 19

Lesson 19.1 Probability and Set Theory

Your Turn

3. $P(A)=\frac{1}{3}$
4. $P(A\cup B)=\frac{14}{30}$
5. $P(A\cap B)=\frac{1}{30}$
6. $P(A^c)=\frac{2}{3}$
8. $P(A)=\frac{3}{4}$
9. $P(A)=\frac{3}{5}$

Evaluate

1. Yes, because every element of *D* is also an element of *A*.
3. {2, 4, 6, 12}
5. {1, 2, 3, 4, 6, 8, 10, 12}
7. {5, 7, 9, 10, 11}
9. $P(A)=\frac{3}{5}$
11. $P(A\cup B)=\frac{4}{5}$
13. $P(A^c)=\frac{2}{5}$
15. $\frac{5}{6}$
17. $\frac{5}{6}$
19. $\frac{2}{3}$
21. a. $\frac{5}{36}$

    b. $\frac{31}{36}$
23. $\frac{12}{13}$; there are 4 aces in the 52-card deck, so $P(\text{ace})=\frac{4}{52}=\frac{1}{13}$. This means $P(\text{not ace})=1-\frac{1}{13}=\frac{12}{13}$.
25. $A\cap B\cap C=\varnothing$ because you can never draw a card that is both red and black. Therefore, $P(A\cap B\cap C)=0$.
27. No; choosing a black tile is not the complement of choosing a white tile since the bag also contains gray tiles. It is not possible to calculate $P(B)$ from the given information.
29. Assume *A* is a subset of *S*. Then $0\le n(A)\le n(S)$. For example, if *S* has 10 elements, the number of elements of *A* is greater than or equal to 0 and less than or equal to 10. No subset of *S* can have fewer than 0 elements or more than 10 elements. So $0\le\frac{n(A)}{n(S)}\le 1$. When all the outcomes are equally likely, $P(A)=\frac{n(A)}{n(S)}$. Therefore $0\le P(A)\le 1$.

UNIT 8 Selected Answers

MODULE 19

Lesson 19.2 Permutations and Probability

Your Turn

3. $\frac{1}{56}$
4. $\frac{5}{28}$
5. 34, 650
6. 210
7. $\frac{1}{15}$
8. $\frac{2}{5}$

Evaluate

1. The songs can be played in 479,001,600 different orders.
3. There are 3024 ways to arrange players.
5. $\frac{1}{165}$
7. $\frac{1}{56}$
9. 1680 ways
11. 15,120 row arrangements
13. $\frac{1}{20,160}$
15. $\frac{1}{35}$
17. $\frac{1}{21}$
19. $\frac{1}{720}$
21. $\frac{1}{5525}$
23. C. C, A, B
25. Yes, they have the same probability. The probability of drawing 4 aces from a deck of cards would be $P(A)=\frac{n(A)}{n(S)}=\frac{{}_4P_4}{{}_{52}P_4}$ because the 4 aces could be drawn in any order, and there are 52 cards in the deck. There are also 4 3s in the deck that could be drawn in any order, so the probability would be the same.
27. $n(A)$ should be 1 since the tiles must appear in the order B-E-A-D. The correct probability is $\frac{1}{360}$.

UNIT 8 Selected Answers

MODULE 19

Lesson 19.3 Combinations and Probability

Your Turn

4. The probability of getting exactly 3 heads is $\frac{1}{4}$.
5. The probability of getting all diamonds is $\frac{11}{230}$.
6. Because the questions are equally likely to be true or false, the probability that the test contains at most 2 true questions is $\frac{11}{32}$.
7. Because a senior is equally likely to be a boy or a girl, the probabilty that the council will contain at least 3 girls is $\frac{1}{2}$.

Evaluate

1. 15 ways
3. 27,405 groups
5. $\frac{10}{143}$
7. ≈ 11.8%
9. $\frac{193}{512}$
11. $\frac{93}{256}$
13. $\frac{1}{220}$
15. $\frac{4}{21}$
17. $\frac{1}{435}$
19. $\frac{14}{969}$
21. a. 84
    b. After you and your friends are chosen, 3 other contestants from the remaining 6 can be chosen in any combination, so event *A* consists of combinations of 3 contestants from the 6 who are left.
    $n(A) = {}_6C_3 = 20, P(A) = \frac{n(A)}{n(S)} = \frac{20}{84} = \frac{5}{21}$
23. In permutations, order matters. In combinations, order does not matter. In a permutation of *A, B,* and *C, ABC* is different from *CBA*, so they would be counted as two different permutations. In a combination, *ABC* is the same as *CBA*, and would not be counted again.
25. Using the formula for combinations and the fact that $0! = 1$,
    ${}_nC_n = \frac{n!}{n!(n-n)!} = \frac{n!}{n!0!} = \frac{n!}{n!} = 1$; this makes sense because there is only 1 combination of n objects taken *n* at a time.

UNIT 8 Selected Answers

MODULE 19

Lesson 19.4 Mutually Exclusive and Overlapping Events

Your Turn

4. The probability of a person having a headache or taking no medicine is $\frac{13}{25}$.

Evaluate

1. The probability that you choose a red marble or a green marble is $\frac{3}{4}$.
3. The probability that you choose a vowel or a letter in the word GEOMETRY is $\frac{5}{13}$.
5. $\frac{\text{Total Adults}}{\text{Total Drivers}} = \frac{97}{125}$
7. $\frac{\text{Total Teens}}{\text{Total Drivers}} = \frac{28}{125}$
9. $\frac{\text{Teens with 2+ accidents}}{\text{Total Drivers}} = \frac{9}{125}$
11. $\frac{\text{Towson and said no}}{\text{Total}} = \frac{1}{15}$
13. $\frac{\text{Yes}}{\text{Total}} = \frac{58}{75}$
15. $\frac{\text{Parkville or said Yes}}{\text{Total}} = \frac{61}{75}$
17. The probability that the sale was one of Becky's or Raul's successful sales is $\frac{5}{18}$.
19. The probability that the sale was one of Darrell's unsuccessful sales or one of Raul's unsuccessful sales is $\frac{7}{18}$.
21. The probability that the sale was a successful sale or one of Raul's attempted sales is $\frac{7}{12}$.
23. If 321 employees take only a train, and 445 total employees take a train, then 445 − 321 = 124 people take both a bus and a train to work.
    $n(A \cup B) = n(\text{bus}) + n(\text{train}) - n(\text{bus and train}) = 621 + 445 - 124 = 942$
    $n(S) = n(\text{total surveyed}) = 1108$
    $P(A \cup B) = \frac{n(A \cup B)}{n(S)} = \frac{942}{1108} = \frac{471}{554} \approx 85\%$
    The probability that a randomly chosen employee takes a bus or a train to work is 85%.
25. When finding $n(A \cup B)$, $n(A)$ should be added to $n(B)$, not multiplied.
    $P(A \cup B) = \frac{n(A) + n(B) - n(A \cap B)}{n(S)} = \frac{4 + 13 - 1}{52} = \frac{16}{52} = \frac{4}{13}$

UNIT 8 Selected Answers

MODULE 20

Lesson 20.1 Conditional Probability

Your Turn

5. $\frac{1}{3}$

6. $\frac{1}{4}$

Evaluate

1. ≈ 56%

3. ≈ 8%

5. ≈ 88%

7. Let L be the event of getting less than 6 hours of sleep, and let M be the event of getting more than 6 hours of sleep. Let Pa be the event of passing the exam, and let F be the event of failing the exam. Then

$$P(Pa|L) = \frac{P(L \cap Pa)}{P(L)} = \frac{0.100}{0.183} \approx 0.546 \approx 55\%,$$

and

$$P(F|M) = \frac{P(M \cap F)}{P(M)} = \frac{0.067}{0.817} \approx 0.082 \approx 8\%,$$

so the probability that a student who got less than 6 hours of sleep passed the exam is greater.

9. $\frac{1}{2}$

11. $\frac{1}{4}$

13. $\frac{1}{2}$

15. A. B
 B. D
 C. A
 D. C

17. 45%

19. Let $N1B$ be the event that a 1 is not rolled on the blue cube and $N1R$ be the event that a 1 is not rolled on the red cube.

$$P(N1B|N1R) = \frac{n(N1B \cap N1R)}{n(N1R)} = \frac{\frac{25}{36}}{\frac{5}{6}} = \frac{\frac{25}{36} \cdot 36}{\frac{5}{6} \cdot 36} = \frac{25}{30} = \frac{5}{6}$$

Given that not rolling a 1 on the red number cube has occurred, there are 30 possible outcomes (where the ordered pairs give the number on the red cube first): (2, 1), (2, 2), (2, 3), (2, 4), (2, 5), (2, 6), (3, 1), (3, 2), (3, 3), (3, 4), (3, 5), (3, 6), (4, 1), (4, 2), (4, 3), (4, 4), (4, 5), (4, 6), (5, 1), (5, 2), (5, 3), (5, 4), (5, 5), (5, 6), (6, 1), (6, 2), (6, 3), (6, 4), (6, 5), and (6, 6). Of these, all but 5 outcomes—(2, 1), (3, 1), (4, 1,) (5, 1), and (6, 1)—are successful because they involve a number that is not 1 on the blue cube. So, the probability of not rolling a 1 on the blue cube when a 1 is not rolled on the red cube is $\frac{25}{36} = \frac{5}{6}$.

21. Since $P(A|B) = \frac{n(A \cap B)}{n(B)}$, you can think of $P(A|B)$ as the ratio of the area of the overlap of the circles to the area of the entire circle labeled B. Since more of circle B lies inside the overlap than outside the overlap, $P(A|B) > \frac{1}{2}$. On the other hand, since $P(B|A) = \frac{n(A \cap B)}{n(A)}$, you can think of $P(B|A)$ as the ratio of the area of the overlap of the circles to the area of the entire circle labeled A. Since less of circle A lies inside the overlap than outside the overlap, $P(B|A) < \frac{1}{2}$. So, $P(A|B) > \frac{1}{2} > P(B|A)$.

23. The conditional probability $P(A|B) = \frac{n(A \cap B)}{n(B)}$ restricts the discussion to event B because that event is assumed to have occurred. The numbers used to calculate $P(A|B)$ both come from the highlighted row in the table: $n(A \cap B)$ is the number of outcomes in event B that are also in event A, while $n(B)$ is the number of all outcomes in event B. The rest of the table is irrelevant.

MODULE 20

Lesson 20.2 Independent Events

Your Turn

3. The events are not independent.
4. The events are not independent.
6. 6%
7. ≈ 11%
8. The events are not independent.
9. The events are independent.

Evaluate

1. a. $P(R) = \frac{3}{5}$ and $P(B) = \frac{2}{5}$

   b. $\frac{2}{5}$

   c. $\frac{8}{19}$

   d. Events R and B are independent when the first chip is returned to the bag because $P(B|R) = P(B)$ in that case.

3. The events are not independent.
5. ≈ 5.6%
7. 9%
9. ≈ 8.3%
11. ≈ 24.3%
13. $\frac{1}{8}$
15. The events are not independent.
17. The events are not independent.

19.

	Women	Men	Total
Prefers Writing with a Pen	40	60	100
Prefers Writing with a Pencil	20	30	50
Total	60	90	150

Examples showing independence of events will vary. Sample answer:
Let W be the event that a person is a woman. Let Pe be the event that a person prefers writing with a pen. $P(W) = \frac{60}{150} = \frac{2}{5}$, $P(Pe) = \frac{100}{150} = \frac{2}{3}$, and $P(W) \cdot P(Pe) = \frac{2}{5} \cdot \frac{2}{3} = \frac{4}{15}$.

Since $P(W \cap Pe) = \frac{40}{150} = \frac{4}{15}$ and $P(W \cap Pe) = P(W) \cdot P(Pe)$, the events are independent.

21. $P(A^c|B) = 1 - P(A|B)$ Definition of complementary events

    $= 1 - P(A)$ Definition of independent events

    $= P(A^c)$ Definition of complementary events

    So, events A^c and B are also independent.

MODULE 20

Lesson 20.3 Dependent Events

Your Turn

3. $\frac{4}{15}$
4. $\frac{2}{5}$
7. So, the probability that all three customers get a white car is $\frac{1}{5}$.
8. The probability that two customers get the silver cars and one gets a white car is $\frac{1}{5}$.

Evaluate

1. a. $P(C) = \frac{70}{110} = \frac{7}{11}$, $P(S) = \frac{60}{110} = \frac{6}{11}$, and $P(C \cap S) = \frac{50}{110} = \frac{5}{11}$.

   Since $P(S) \cdot P(C) = \frac{7}{11} \cdot \frac{6}{11} = \frac{42}{121}$ and $P(C \cap S) = \frac{5}{11} = \frac{55}{121}$, $P(C) \cdot P(S)$ $\neq P(C \cap S)$, so the events C and S are dependent.

   b. $P(C|S) = \frac{5}{6}$ and $P(S|C) = \frac{5}{7}$.

   Multiplying $P(C)$ and $P(S|C) = P(C \cap S)$.
   Multiplying $P(S)$ and $P(C|S) = P(C \cap S)$.

3. $\frac{3}{19}$
5. $\frac{2}{57}$
7. a. Of the 36 outcomes in the entire table, a sum of 7 appears 6 times, so $P(B) = \frac{6}{36} = \frac{1}{6}$. Of the 6 outcomes in the row labeled 2, a sum of 7 appears once, so $P(B|A) = \frac{1}{6}$. Since $P(B|A) = P(B)$, events A and B are independent.

   b. $\frac{1}{36}$

9. a. D

   b. A, C

   c. B

11. a. $\frac{34}{285}$

    b. $\frac{34}{57}$

13. $P(A \cap B \cap C) = P((A \cap B) \cap C)$ Group events A and B as one event.

    $= P(A \cap B) \cdot P(C|A \cap B)$ Apply the Multiplication Rule to $A \cap B$ and C.

    $= P(A) \cdot P(B|A) \cdot P(C|A \cap B)$ Apply the Multiplication Rule to A and B.

UNIT 8 Selected Answers

MODULE 21

Lesson 21.1 Using Probability to Make Fair Decisions

Your Turn

4. Possible answer: Choose an employee's name at random from a list of all employees. Each month, remove the previous winners from the list. Once every employee has won once, begin again with the list of all employees.
8. Possible answer: If the game is interrupted when the players are tied, they each have a probability of winning equal to $\frac{1}{2}$.

Evaluate

1. Possible answer: You could split the cost of a sixth pass to the climbing gym so that you each get a third visit for half of the price of an additional pass. Or you could toss a coin and the winner gets the fifth pass. Tossing a coin gives each of you a 50% (or equal) chance of winning the last pass.
3. Not fair; $P(\text{Meri wins}) = \frac{2}{6} = \frac{1}{3}$;

   $P(\text{Riley wins}) = \frac{3}{6} = \frac{1}{2}$
5. Fair; $P(\text{Meri wins}) = \frac{1}{2}$; $P(\text{Riley wins}) = \frac{1}{2}$
7. Fair; $P(\text{Meri wins}) = \frac{3}{6} = \frac{1}{2}$;

   $P(\text{Riley wins}) = \frac{3}{6} = \frac{1}{2}$
9. 0.30 0.12
   0.23 0.12
   0.18 0.05

   Find the total number of games won: 30 + 23 + 18 + 12 + 12 + 5 = 100. Assign numbers from 1–100 to the members so each has as many numbers assigned as the number of games won. Then use a random number generator to choose an integer from 1 to 100.
11. Possible answer: Write the names on slips of paper, place them in a box, and draw a slip at random. The probability that Paige wins is 1 out of 20, or 5%.
13. If the packages are attached randomly, then each seat has an equal chance of having a package containing a family pass.
15. $\frac{499}{500}$
17. ≈ 13.21%
19. Yes. Leon did 7 of the 53 completed puzzle problems. He was assigned 7 of the 53 possible winning numbers, and each number has the same chance of being chosen.
21. Sofia should get 16 or 17 of the toys. Perhaps they could agree that she gets only gets 16, but gets first choice. Then they take turns choosing until Alexa has 4. Then Sofia gets the rest.

UNIT 8 Selected Answers

MODULE 21

Lesson 21.2 Analyzing Decisions

Your Turn

7.

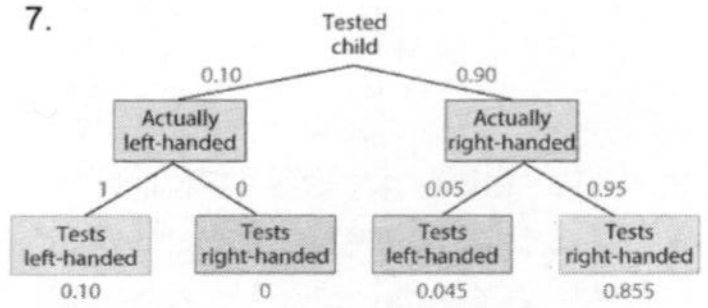

8. The probability that the test is correct in this case increases from 67.2% to 69.0%, or about 2 percentage points.
9. The probability that the test is correct in this case increases from 99.1% to 100%. or about 1 percentage point.

Evaluate

1. No; Of the 1,015 products that Helen completed, 50 were defective, which is about 4.9%. Of the 370 products that Kyle completed, 20 were defective, which is about 5.5%. Neither should be put on probation solely based on these data.
3.

	Bike	No bike	Total
On campus	9,000 (0.38) = 3,420	9,000 (0.62) = 5,580	10,000 (0.90) = 9,000
Off campus	1,000 (0.98) = 980	1,000 (0.02) = 20	10,000 (0.10) = 1,000
Total	4,400	5,600	10,000

Only 980 of the 4,400 bike-riding students live off campus, so only 22% of the coupons will go to the intended target of students living off campus. Therefore, this is not a good decision.

5.

	Test Positive	Test Negative	ssTotal
Allergy	196	4	200
No allergy	490	9,310	9,800
Total	686	9,314	10,000

No; Only 196 people out of the 686 who tested positive actually have the allergy. This is about 29% of those who test positive.

7. a. $\frac{1}{3}$; b. 0; c. $\frac{1}{3}$; d. $\frac{2}{3}$
9.

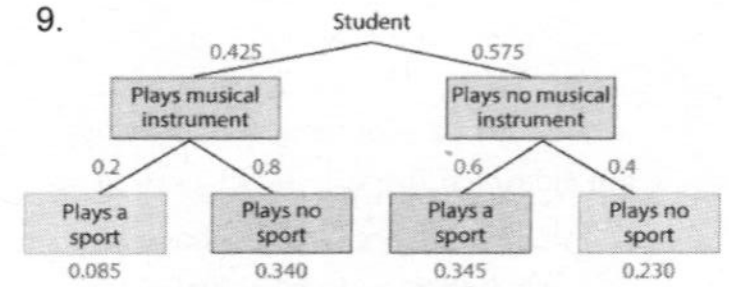

The probability that a student plays a musical instrument given that he or she plays no sport is about 60%. So, it is somewhat likely that a student who doesn't play a sport does play an instrument, but it would not be reasonable to assume that this is true.

11.

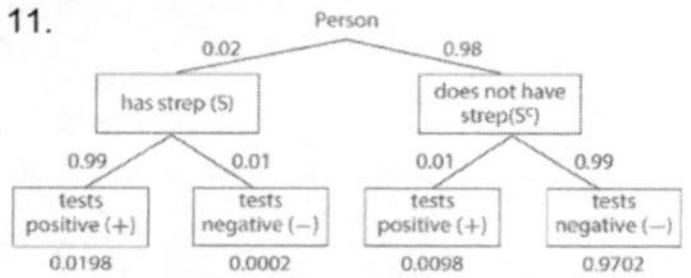

About 67% of those tested positively for strep throat actually have strep throat.

13. $P(B) \cdot P(A \mid B) = P(A) \cdot P(B \mid A)$;

Substitution, because $P(B \cap A) = P(A \cap B)$

$\frac{P(B) \cdot P(A \mid B)}{P(B)} = \frac{P(A) \cdot P(B \mid A)}{P(B)}$; Divide each side by $P(B)$.

$P(A \mid B) = \frac{P(A) \cdot P(B \mid A)}{P(B)}$; Bayes' Theorem

15.

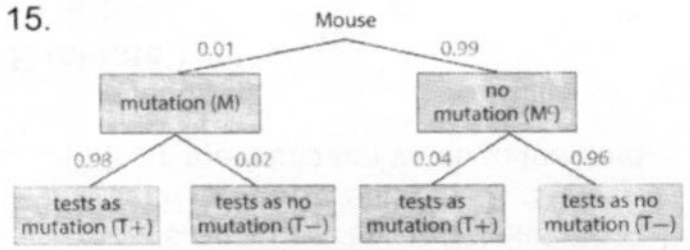

It is not a good decision, because there is only a 19.8% probability that a mouse that tests positive for the mutation actually has the mutation.

17. Based on the sample, Tomas is least likely to be late if he takes Route *C*.

19. Yes, because $P(B \mid C) = \frac{18}{40} = 0.45$, while

$P(C \mid B) = \frac{18}{72} = 0.25$. So, customers who bought cookies also bought bread almost half of the time, while customers who bought bread also bought cookies only a quarter of the time.

UNIT 9 Selected Answers

MODULE 22

Lesson 22.1 Data-Gathering Techniques

Your Turn

3. The population consists of adult residents of the city.
   a. Simple random sample. Likely to be biased; people who do not use cell phones (or did not give their cell phone numbers to the newspaper) are left out of the survey.
   b. Stratified sample. Not likely to result in a biased sample; a wide range of residents is surveyed.
5. Mean number of days skied: 12.125; mean number of lift rides taken per day: 11.625; predicted number of lift rides taken by a pass holder per season:

   $\approx$ 141 lift rides

Evaluate

1. a. Systematic sample
   b. Cluster sample
   c. Stratified sample
   d. Self-selected sample
   e. Convenience sample
3. This sampling method is likely not to be biased since the sample is random and all of the freshmen are available to be chosen.
5. Doctors from different specialties may have different opinions about the new rules. Using a simple random sample means that dermatologists, as a group, have less of a chance of having their opinions surveyed than any other group, and oncologists have a greater chance than any other group. Using a stratified sample guarantees that the opinions all of five specialties are surveyed.
7. The population consists of all computers at the assembly plant. This is a simple random sample.
9. a. Predicted number of cars 48
   b. Predicted number of cars 72
   c. Predicted number of cars 36
11. A. C
    B. F
    C. A
    D. D
    E. E
    F. B
13. a. The data are discrete because how many people live in household is a count. Another example of discrete data: number of televisions in a household.
    b. The data are nominal because the categories of male and female do not have an order. Another example of nominal data: subject's eye color.
    c. The data are continuous because time can be measured in hours, minutes, or even seconds. Another example of continuous data: subject's height.
    d. The data are ordinal because the categories have an order from youngest to oldest. Another example of ordinal data: the highest educational degree that a subject has attained (high school diploma, associate's degree, bachelor's degree, and so on).

UNIT 9 Selected Answers

MODULE 22

Lesson 22.2 Shape, Center, and Spread

Your Turn

7. a. The distribution has a central mound and symmetric tails, so it is a normal distribution.

   b. The interval for data that are within 2 standard deviations of the mean is $70.4 < x < 95.6$. The bars for x-values that satisfy $70.4 < x < 95.6$ have heights of 1, 1, 1, 1, 3, 6, 3, 1, 1, 1, and 1, so 20 data values out of 22, or about 91% of the data, are in the interval.

   c. The interval for data that are less than 2 standard deviations below the mean is $x < 70.4$. The only bar for x-values that satisfy $x < 70.4$ has a height of 1, so the probability that the test score is in the interval is $\frac{1}{22} \approx 0.05$.

8. a. The part of the box to the left of the median is slightly wider than the part to the right, and the "whisker" on the left is longer than the one on the right, so the distribution is skewed left.

   b. The probability is about 75%, or 0.75, because Q_1, the median, and Q_3 divide the data into four almost-equal parts and there are three parts that each represent about 25% of the data from the minimum value to the third quartile.

Evaluate

1. a.

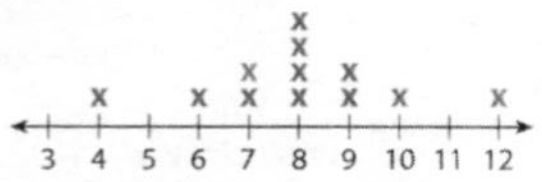

normal distribution

b.

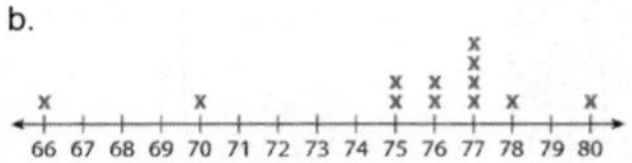

left-skewed distribution

c.

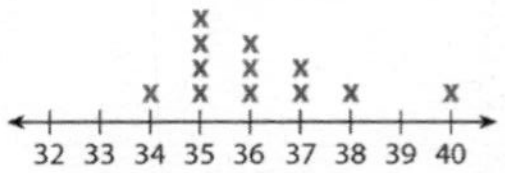

right-skewed distribution

3. a. $\bar{x} \approx 166$ Median = 165

   $s \approx 8.2$ IQR = 10

   b. normal distribution

   c. 13 data values out of 14, or about 93% of the data, are in the interval.

   d. $\frac{12}{14} \approx 0.86$ or 86%

5. a. $\bar{x} = 355$ Median = 375

   $s \approx 72.28$ IQR = 62.5

   The mean and median are significantly different, which indicates that the distribution is not symmetric.

   b. The part of the box to the left of the median is slightly wider than the part to the right, and the "whisker" on the left is longer than the one on the right, so the distribution is skewed left.

   c. The probability is about 50%, because Q_1, the median, and Q_3 divide the data into four almost-equal parts.

7. A. Normal

   B. Normal

   C. Skewed

   D. Skewed

   E. Normal

   F. Skewed

9. a. The box plot shows that the distribution is skewed right because the right "whisker" is longer than the left one.

   b. $\bar{x} = 2$ Median = 2

   $s \approx 1.3$ IQR = 2

   The mean and median are equal.

   c. The box plot does not change.

   The mean is less than the median.

   d. The part of the box to the right of the median is now wider than the part to the left, and the right "whisker" is now even longer than the left one.

   The mean is greater than the median.

   e. The general rule is that when a distribution is skewed right, the mean is greater than the median because the mean is increased by the data in the tail on the right. The investigation of the sibling data shows that this rule doesn't always apply.

UNIT 9 Selected Answers

MODULE 23

Lesson 23.1 Probability Distributions

Your Turn

5.

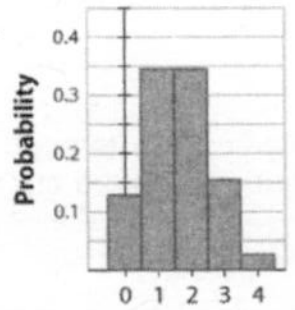

Number of heads	0	1	2	3	4
Theoretical probability	0.1296	0.3456	0.3456	0.1536	0.0256

The distribution is slightly skewed right.

$P(X \geq 2) = 0.5248$

$P(X < 4) = 0.9744$

6.

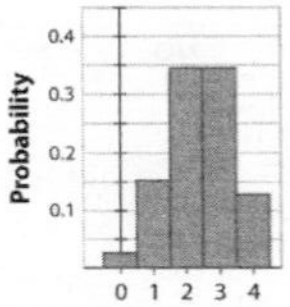

Number of heads	0	1	2	3	4
Theoretical probability	0.0256	0.1536	0.3456	0.3456	0.1296

The distribution is slightly skewed left.

$P(X \geq 2) = 0.5248$

$P(X < 4) = 0.8704$

Evaluate

1. a. 2, 3, 4, 5, and 6

b. 2; 3; 4; 5; 6; $\frac{1}{9}$; $\frac{2}{9}$; $\frac{3}{9}$; $\frac{2}{9}$; $\frac{1}{9}$

c.

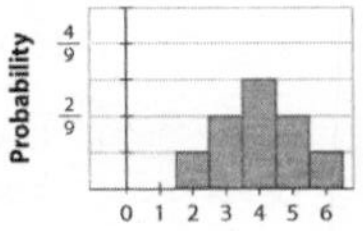

d. The probability is $\frac{8}{9}$. This is the sum of the areas of the bars for the outcomes 3, 4, 5, and 6.

3. a.

Number of heads	0	1	2	3	4	5	6	7
Theoretical probability	$\frac{1}{78,125}$	$\frac{28}{78,125}$	$\frac{336}{78,125}$	$\frac{2240}{78,125}$	$\frac{8960}{78,125}$	$\frac{21,504}{78,125}$	$\frac{28,672}{78,125}$	$\frac{16,384}{78,125}$

b.

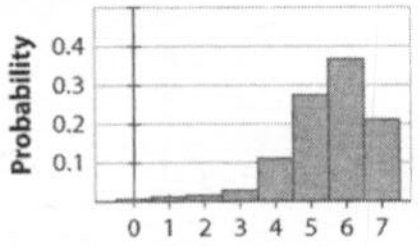

c. ≈ 0.577

d. ≈ 0.967

e. The probability of getting an odd number of heads is greater.

f. Answers may vary. Possible answer: The probability of getting 7 heads in 7 flips of a fair coin is $\left(\frac{1}{2}\right)^7 = \frac{1}{128} \approx 0.008$. The probability of getting 7 heads in 7 flips of the trick coin is $\frac{16,384}{78,125} \approx 0.210$. Since getting 7 heads on the trick coin is more than 26 times as likely to occur as getting 7 heads on the fair coin, I would question whether the coin is fair.

5. a. $\frac{1}{16}$; $\frac{2}{16}$; $\frac{3}{16}$; $\frac{4}{16}$; $\frac{3}{16}$; $\frac{2}{16}$; $\frac{1}{16}$

b.

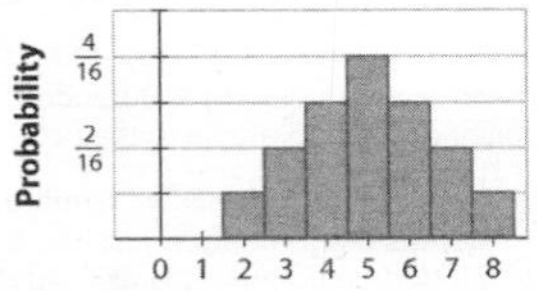

c. 0.375

d. $P(X > 5) = P(X < 5)$ because the histogram of the probability distribution is symmetric with respect to $x = 5$.

7. B; C; A, D; E, F

9. Rather than flip the coin just once, flip the coin twice. If you flip the coin twice and the results match, then completely disregard the results. If you flip the coin twice and the results are different, then use the first result and disregard the second result. To see why the process is fair, let p be the probability of getting heads and $1 - p$ be the probability of getting tails. For a biased coin, $p \neq 1 - p$. Assume that both probabilities are nonzero. Then the probability of getting two heads is p^2, the probability of getting two tails is $(1 - p)^2$, and these probabilities are not equal if p and $1 - p$ are not equal. However, the probability of getting heads followed by tails is p $(1 - p)$, the probability of getting tails followed by heads is $(1 - p)p$, and these probabilities are equal. So, by going with heads when heads appear first and going with tails when tails appear first, the two outcomes have equal probability, and the results are fair.

UNIT 9 Selected Answers

MODULE 23

Lesson 23.2 Normal Distributions

Your Turn

5. 99.7%
6. 0.15%
7. about 24.2%
8. about 18.41%

Evaluate

1. It is reasonable to use a normal curve for the distribution of heads when 6 coins are flipped because the distribution is symmetric and follows a bell-shaped curve.
3. 16%, or 0.16
5. 0.975
7. 0.815
9. 0.84
11. about 48%
13. 0.1587
15. 0.5
17. ≈ 0.477
19. ≈ 0.2023
21. About 11.11% of children are between 50 and 53 inches tall.
23. The student's answer is only correct if a is the mean. If a is not the mean, the area for the *x*–values less than a is p, and the area for *x*–values greater than a is 1 – *p*.

25.

			Values ≤ *x*	
z	Area ≤ *z*	*x*	Projected	Actual
–2	0.02	5.8	0.02 • 20 = 0.4 ≈ 0	1
–1	0.16	6.6	0.16 • 20 = 3.2 ≈ 3	4
0	0.5	7.4	0.5 • 20 = 10	9
1	0.84	8.2	0.84 • 20 = 16.8 ≈ 17	17
2	0.98	9	0.98 • 20 = 19.6 ≈ 20	20

The projected number of values that corresponds to each value of *z* is close to the actual number of data values. The data appear to be normally distributed.

UNIT 9 Selected Answers

MODULE 23

Lesson 23.3 Sampling Distributions

Your Turn

6. between 314.6 grams and 331.4 grams
7. about 0.93
8. between 34.5% and 45.5%
9. about 0.94

Evaluate

1. a. The best estimate of the population mean is the mean of the sample means: $\mu_{\bar{x}} = 24.1$.

   b. The best estimate of the population proportion is the mean of the sample proportions: $\mu_{\hat{p}} = 0.69$.

   c. The manager could have improved the accuracy of the estimates by using a sample size greater than 10.
3. between 417 and 433
5. about 0.38
7. between 53.6 kilograms and 106.4 kilograms
9. ≈ 0.00000000000000091
11. between 20.2% and 29.8%
13. about 0.81
15. between 14.5% and 41.5%
17. about 0.90
19. The student used the standard deviation of the population rather than the standard deviation of the sampling distribution.

   $\sigma_{\bar{x}} = \frac{\sigma}{\sqrt{n}} = \frac{25}{\sqrt{45}} \approx 3.73$

   $P(\bar{x} \le 401) =$ normalcdf (–1ᴇ99, 401, 400, 3.73) ≈ 0.606
21. Your random sample has produced a sample proportion that is 10 standard deviations below the mean. This result is so unlikely that you should reject your assumption.

MODULE 24

Lesson 24.1 Confidence Intervals and Margins of Error

Your Turn

6. With 95% confidence, the proportion of all voters in Isabelle's town who support raising property taxes in order to build a new library lies between 47% and 68%.
8. With 99% confidence, the mean weekly number of minutes spent exercising among all employees in the company lies between 77 minutes and 95 minutes.
11. Zoe should survey a random sample of 350 state residents.

Evaluate

1. The reasonably likely values of the sample proportion are between 26% and 62%.
3. With 90% confidence, the proportion of all students who saw a film at the movie theater in the last 30 days lies between 27.5% and 47.5%.
5. With 95% confidence, the proportion of digital utility meters that are defective lies between 1.7% and 5.8%.
7. With 95% confidence, the mean price of 1 gallon of regular gasoline in the state lies between $3.549 and $3.603.
9. With 99% confidence, the mean amount of continuous video playback from a full charge lies between 12.26 hours and 13.14 hours.
11. The executives should survey a random sample of 4719 state residents.
13. Teneka should survey a random sample of revenues from 73 days.
15. Answers: B, C, E, F
17. $\hat{p} - 2\sigma_{\hat{p}} < p < \hat{p} + 2\sigma_{\hat{p}}$

    The last inequality gives the confidence interval for the population proportion p.

MODULE 24

Lesson 24.2 Surveys, Experiments, and Observational Studies

Your Turn

3. Since the interviewer is the teacher, students may not be open about any dissatisfaction they may have with her teaching methods. The students may feel that how the teacher grades them will be influenced by their responses. A better survey would allow the students to respond anonymously.
5. This research study is an observational study. The factor is a person's age and the characteristic of interest is the person's driving habits.
6. The treatment is studying for the test with a classmate.

   The characteristic of interest is the student's test score.

   The control group consists of subjects who study for the test alone.

   The treatment group consists of subjects who study for the test with a classmate.
8. This study is a survey because a characteristic of interest (knowledge of food safety) was measured. Randomization was not used in the research because people volunteered to take the Internet questionnaire, which means that those who are interested in food safety are more likely to take the questionnaire. The report includes the sample size of 13,000 and the statistics that 61 percent of home kitchens would earn an A or B on a restaurant inspection and 14 percent would fail, but it is missing the margins of error for these statistics.

Evaluate

1. a. The study that looks for an association between two variables is the one that asks a random sample of students at a large university how much sleep they get and what their college grade point average is. The variables are average daily amount of sleep and academic performance (as indicated by college grade point average).

   b. The study that looks for evidence that one variable influences another is the one that randomly assigns adults to a group that gets at least 7 hours of sleep per night for a week or to a group that gets at most 6 hours per night of sleep for a week, with a test of learning given afterward. The variables are the daily amount of sleep and the ability to learn (as indicated by a score on a test). The amount of sleep is manipulated to see if it influences ability to learn.

   c. The study that simply measures a variable in a population is the one that involves asking high school students whether they feel they get enough sleep to stay alert throughout the school day. The variable is getting enough sleep to feel alert throughout the school day.
3. The reporter asks only people who are attending the parade and are more likely to support having a larger parade in the future, so there is nonresponse from people who do not attend the parade. Also, the phrase "since this holiday parade is so popular" biases the question. A better method is to ask a random sample of all residents a question that does not mention the popularity of this year's parade.
5. This study is an experiment. The treatment is the regular coaching by phone from health professionals that one group got. The characteristic of interest is the monthly medical costs.

7. This is an observational study. The factor is the average number of hours per week a student spent on extracurricular activities. The characteristic of interest is the student's most recent standardized test score.
9. The treatment is giving subjects the tangerine slices. The characteristic of interest is whether the subjects like the taste of the fruit. The control group consists of the subjects who are given the orange slices (the current garnish), and the treatment group consists of the subjects who are given the tangerine slices.
11. The treatment is reintroducing the underwater plant in one lake. The characteristic of interest is the health of the fish population. The control group consists of the fish in the lake without the plant. The treatment group consists of the fish in the lake with the plant.
13. This study is a survey because the only variable is doctors who work while sick. The report does not say whether random sampling was used but only doctors-in-training were surveyed. The report includes the sample size and sample proportions but does not include the margins of error.
15. A, B, D
17. Lindsay is incorrect because Mr. Jones is determining the effect of the board's exposure to the weather, which is the treatment. The part of the deck with the sealant is the control group because it is not exposed to the weather, and Mr. Jones has applied the sealant every spring.

UNIT 9 Selected Answers

MODULE 24

Lesson 24.3 Determining the Significance of Experimental Results

Your Turn

6. $\overline{x}_T - \overline{x}_C = 262$

   Since 3 standard errors above the mean is 3 (83) = 249, the experimental result falls in the part of the tail of the resampling distribution that is more than 3 standard errors above the mean. This means that the *P*-value for the experimental result is less than 0.15%, or 0.0015, according to the 68-95-99.7 rule for normal distributions, so the result is highly significant. Reject the null hypothesis that the exam prep course has no effect in favor of the alternative hypothesis that the course has a positive effect.

7. $\overline{x}_T - \overline{x}_C = 3.8$

   The experimental result is not significant because it falls inside the interval that captures the middle 95% of the differences of the means in the resampling distribution. The null hypothesis cannot be rejected. In this case, the conclusion is that the e-book had no effect on student learning.

Evaluate

1. a. The null hypothesis is that the mean change in bone density for the two groups will be about the same.
   b. The null hypothesis cannot be rejected, so the dietitian must conclude that the consumption of fish does not improve the strength of bones in older adults.
3. a. The null hypothesis is that the mean score on the test is the about the same for the two groups.
   b. $\overline{x}_T = 79$; $\overline{x}_C = 75$; $\overline{x}_T - \overline{x}_C = 4$
   c. 6, 18, 21, 5 Answers will vary. Possible answers (based on 50 resamples) are given in the table.
   d. Answers will vary. Possible answer:
      $P(x \geq 4) = \frac{5}{50} = 0.10$
   e. Answers may vary. Possible answer: Because the *P*-value equals 0.10, the result is marginally significant. The null hypothesis can be rejected. So, writing about thoughts and feelings for 15 minutes before taking a test improves test performance.
5. a. The null hypothesis is that the mean change in the amount of sleep that each group gets is about the same.
   b. Treatment group: those who receive therapy sessions and follow-up phone calls; $\overline{x}_T = 1.4$
      Control group: those who receive informational brochures; $\overline{x}_C = 0.2$
      $\overline{x}_T - \overline{x}_C = 1.2$
   c. $-1 \leq x \leq 1$
   d. The experimental result is significant because it falls outside the interval $-1 \leq x \leq 1$. Reject the null hypothesis that the therapy sessions and phone calls had no effect on the amount of sleep in favor of the alternative hypothesis that the therapy sessions and phone calls improved sleep.
7. a. Highly significant
   b. Marginally significant
   c. Significant
   d. Not significant
9. a. Use the permutations formula from the previous exercise to get $\frac{6!}{3! \cdot 3!} = 20$.
      Alternatively, think in terms of taking 6 data values and assigning 3 of them, without regard to order, to the control group (with the rest assigned to the treatment group). Then, ${}_6C_3 = 20$.

b. $\overline{x}_T - \overline{x}_C = 8 - 3 = 5$. Because the greatest data values are in the treatment group, this difference of means is greater than any other difference possible using resamples of the given data.

So, $P(x \geq 5) = \frac{1}{20} = 0.05$, and the difference is significant at the 5% level using a one-tailed test.

Glossary/Glosario

A

ENGLISH	SPANISH	EXAMPLES
absolute value of a complex number The absolute value of $a + bi$ is the distance from the origin to the point (a, b) in the complex plane and is denoted $\lvert a + bi \rvert = \sqrt{a^2 + b^2}$.	**valor absoluto de un número complejo** El valor absoluto de $a + bi$ es la distancia desde el origen hasta el punto (a, b) en el plano complejo y se expresa $\lvert a + bi \rvert = \sqrt{a^2 + b^2}$.	$\lvert 2 + 3i \rvert = \sqrt{2^2 + 3^2} = \sqrt{13}$
absolute value of a real number The absolute value of x is the distance from zero to x on a number line, denoted $\lvert x \rvert$. $\lvert x \rvert = \begin{cases} x & \text{if } x \geq 0 \\ -x & \text{if } x < 0 \end{cases}$	**valor absoluto de un número real** El valor absoluto de x es la distancia desde cero hasta x en una recta numérica y se expresa $\lvert x \rvert$. $\lvert x \rvert = \begin{cases} x & \text{si } x \geq 0 \\ -x & \text{si } x < 0 \end{cases}$	$\lvert 3 \rvert = 3$ $\lvert -3 \rvert = 3$
absolute-value function A function whose rule contains absolute-value expressions.	**función de valor absoluto** Función cuya regla contiene expresiones de valor absoluto.	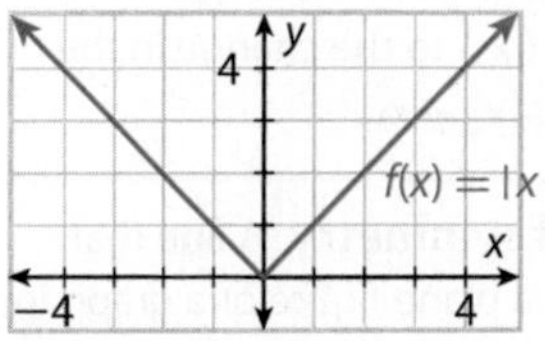
amplitude The amplitude of a periodic function is half the difference of the maximum and minimum values (always positive).	**amplitud** La amplitud de una función periódica es la mitad de la diferencia entre los valores máximo y mínimo (siempre positivos).	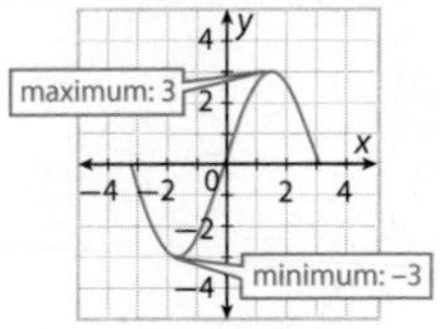 amplitude $= \frac{1}{2}\left[3 - (-3)\right] = 3$
angle of depression The angle formed by a horizontal line and a line of sight to a point below.	**ángulo de depresión** Ángulo formado por una recta horizontal y una línea visual a un punto inferior.	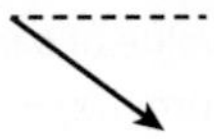
angle of elevation The angle formed by a horizontal line and a line of sight to a point above.	**ángulo de elevación** Ángulo formado por una recta horizontal y una línea visual a un punto superior.	
angle of rotation An angle formed by a rotating ray, called the terminal side, and a stationary reference ray, called the initial side.	**ángulo de rotación** Ángulo formado por un rayo en rotación, denominado lado terminal, y un rayo de referencia estático, denominado lado inicial.	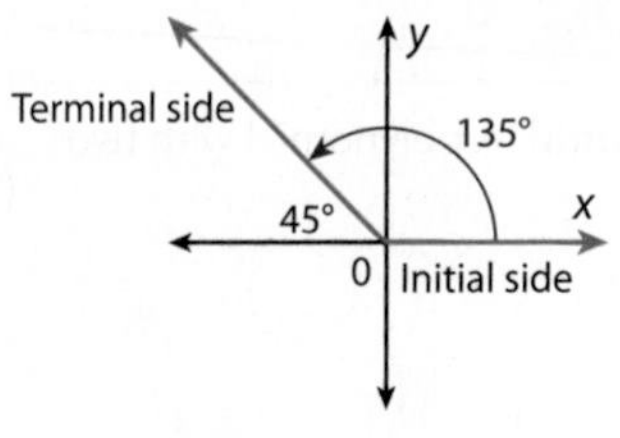

ENGLISH	SPANISH	EXAMPLES
arithmetic sequence A sequence whose successive terms differ by the same nonzero number d, called the *common difference.*	**sucesión aritmética** Sucesión cuyos términos sucesivos difieren en el mismo número distinto de cero d, denominado *diferencia común*.	4, 7, 10, 13, 16, ... $+3 + 3 + 3 + 3$ $d = 3$
arithmetic series The indicated sum of the terms of an arithmetic sequence.	**serie aritmética** Suma indicada de los términos de una sucesión aritmética.	$4 + 7 + 10 + 13 + 16 + ...$
asymptote A line that a graph approaches as the value of a variable becomes extremely large or small.	**asíntota** Línea recta a la cual se aproxima una gráfica a medida que el valor de una variable se hace sumamente grande o pequeño.	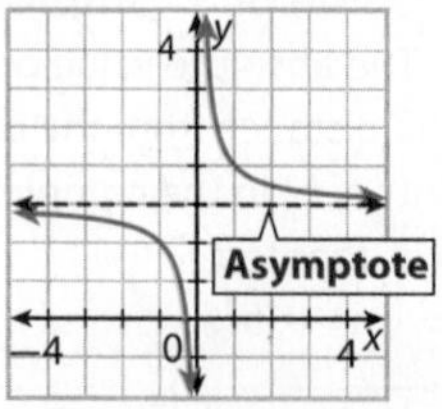
augmented matrix A matrix that consists of the coefficients and the constant terms in a system of linear equations.	**matriz aumentada** Matriz formada por los coeficientes y los términos constantes de un sistema de ecuaciones lineales.	System of equations: $3x + 2y = 5$, $2x - 3y = 1$ Augmented matrix: $\left[\begin{array}{cc\|c} 3 & 2 & 5 \\ 2 & -3 & 1 \end{array}\right]$
average rate of change The ratio of the change in the function values, $f(x_2) - f(x_1)$ to the change in the x-values, $x_2 - x_1$.	**tasa de cambio promedio** Razón entre el cambio en los valores de la función, $f(x_2) - f(x_1)$ y el cambio en los valores de x, $x_2 - x_1$.	
axis of symmetry A line that divides a plane figure or a graph into two congruent reflected halves.	**eje de simetría** Línea que divide una figura plana o una gráfica en dos mitades reflejadas congruentes.	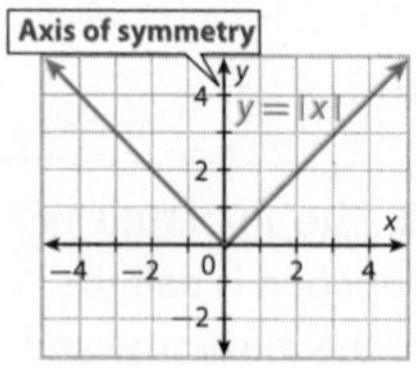

B

ENGLISH	SPANISH	EXAMPLES
base of an exponential function The value of b in a function of the form $f(x) = ab^x$, where a and b are real numbers with $a \neq 0, b > 0$, and $b \neq 1$.	**base de una función exponencial** Valor de b en una función del tipo $f(x) = ab^x$, donde a y b son números reales con $a \neq 0, b > 0$, y $b \neq 1$.	$f(x) = 5(2)^x$ ↑ base
biased sample A sample that does not fairly represent the population.	**muestra no representativa** Muestra que no representa adecuadamente una población.	
binomial A polynomial with two terms.	**binomio** Polinomio con dos términos.	$x + y$ $2a^2 + 3$ $4m^3n^2 + 6mn^4$

ENGLISH	SPANISH	EXAMPLES
binomial experiment A probability experiment consists of n identical and independent trials whose outcomes are either successes or failures, with a constant probability of success p and a constant probability of failure q, where $q = 1 - p$ or $p + q = 1$.	**experimento binomial** Experimento de probabilidades que comprende n pruebas idénticas e independientes cuyos resultados son éxitos o fracasos, con una probabilidad constante de éxito p y una probabilidad constante de fracaso q, donde $q = 1 - p$ o $p + q = 1$.	A multiple-choice quiz has 10 questions with 4 answer choices. The number of trials is 10. If each question is answered randomly, the probability of success for each trial is $\frac{1}{4} = 0.25$ and the probability of failure is $\frac{3}{4} = 0.75$.
binomial probability In a binomial experiment, the probability of r successes $(0 \leq r \leq n)$ is $P(r) = {}_nC_r \cdot p^r q^{n-r}$.	**probabilidad binomial** En un experimento binomial, la probabilidad de r éxitos $(0 \leq r \leq n)$ es $P(r) = {}_nC_r \cdot p^r q^{n-r}$.	In the binomial experiment above, the probability of randomly guessing 6 problems correctly is $P = {}_{10}C_6\,(0.25)^6\,(0.75)^4 \approx 0.016$.
Binomial Theorem For any positive integer n, $(x+y)^n = {}_nC_0\,x^n y^0 + {}_nC_1\,x^{n-1} y^1 + {}_nC_2\,x^{n-2} y^2 + \ldots + {}_nC_{n-1}\,x^1 y^{n-1} + {}_nC_n\,x^0 y^n$.	**Teorema de los binomios** Dado un entero positivo n, $(x+y)^n = {}_nC_0\,x^n y^0 + {}_nC_1\,x^{n-1} y^1 + {}_nC_2\,x^{n-2} y^2 + \ldots + {}_nC_{n-1}\,x^1 y^{n-1} + {}_nC_n\,x^0 y^n$.	$(x+2)^4 = {}_4C_0\,x^4 2^0 + {}_4C_1\,x^3 2^1 + {}_4C_2\,x^2 2^2 + {}_4C_3\,x^1 2^3 + {}_4C_4 x^0 2^4 = x^4 + 8x^3 + 24x^2 + 32x + 16$
branch of a hyperbola One of the two symmetrical parts of the hyperbola.	**rama de una hipérbola** Una de las dos partes simétricas de la hipérbola.	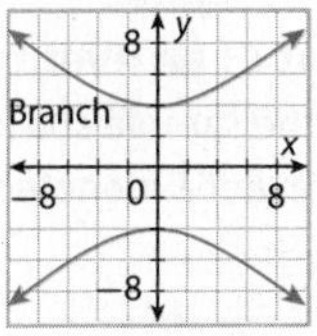

C

ENGLISH	SPANISH	EXAMPLES
categorical data Data that represent observations or attributes that can be sorted into groups or categories.	**datos categóricos** Datos que representan observaciones o atributos que pueden ser clasificados en grupos o categorías.	
census A survey of an entire population.	**censo** Estudio de una población entera.	
closure A set of numbers is said to be closed, or to have closure, under a given operation if the result of the operation on any two numbers in the set is also in the set.	**cerradura** Se dice que un conjunto de números es cerrado, o tiene cerradura, respecto de una operación determinada, si el resultado de la operación entre dos numerous cualesquiera del conjunto también está en el conjunto.	The natural numbers are closed under addition because the sum of two natural numbers is always a natural number.
coefficient matrix The matrix of the coefficients of the variables in a linear system of equations.	**matriz de coeficientes** Matriz de los coeficientes de las variables en un sistema lineal de ecuaciones.	System of equations: $2x + 3y = 11$, $5x - 4y = 16$; Coefficient matrix: $\begin{bmatrix} 2 & 3 \\ 5 & -4 \end{bmatrix}$

ENGLISH	SPANISH	EXAMPLES
combination A selection of a group of objects in which order is *not* important. The number of combinations of *r* objects chosen from a group of *n* objects is denoted ${}_nC_r$.	**combinación** Selección de un grupo de objetos en la cual el orden *no* es importante. El número de combinaciones de *r* objetos elegidos de un grupo de *n* objetos se expresa así: ${}_nC_r$.	For 4 objects *A*, *B*, *C*, and *D*, there are ${}_4C_2 = 6$ different combinations of 2 objects: *AB*, *AC*, *AD*, *BC*, *BD*, *CD*.
common difference In an arithmetic sequence, the nonzero constant difference of any term and the previous term.	**diferencia común** En una sucesión aritmética, diferencia constante distinta de cero entre cualquier término y el término anterior.	In the arithmetic sequence 3, 5, 7, 9, 11, ..., the common difference is 2.
common logarithm A logarithm whose base is 10, denoted $\log_{10}$ or just log.	**logaritmo común** Logaritmo de base 10, que se expresa $\log_{10}$ o simplemente log.	$\log 100 = \log_{10} 100 = 2$, since $10^2 = 100$.
common ratio In a geometric sequence, the constant ratio of any term and the previous term.	**razón común** En una sucesión geométrica, la razón constante *r* entre cualquier término y el término anterior.	In the geometric sequence 32, 16,18, 4, 2 ..., the common ratio is $\frac{1}{2}$.
complement of an event All outcomes in the sample space that are not in an event *E*, denoted $\overline{E}$.	**complemento de un suceso** Todos los resultados en el espacio muestral que no están en el suceso *E* y se expresan $\overline{E}$.	In the experiment of rolling a number cube, the complement of rolling a 3 is rolling a 1, 2, 4, 5, or 6.
completing the square A process used to form a perfect-square trinomial. To complete the square of $x^2 + bx$, add $\left(\frac{b}{2}\right)^2$.	**completar el cuadrado** Proceso utilizado para formar un trinomio cuadrado perfecto. Para completar el cuadrado de $x^2 + bx$, hay que sumar $\left(\frac{b}{2}\right)^2$.	$x^2 + 6x + \blacksquare$ Add $\left(\frac{6}{2}\right)^2 = 9$. $x^2 + 6x + 9$ $(x + 3)^2$ *is a perfect square.*
complex conjugate The complex conjugate of any complex number $a + bi$, denoted $\overline{a + bi}$, is $a - bi$.	**conjugado complejo** El conjugado complejo de cualquier número complejo $a + bi$, expresado como $\overline{a + bi}$, es $a - bi$.	$\overline{4 + 3i} = 4 - 3i$ $\overline{4 - 3i} = 4 + 3i$
complex fraction A fraction that contains one or more fractions in the numerator, the denominator, or both.	**fracción compleja** Fracción que contiene una o más fracciones en el numerador, en el denominador, o en ambos.	$\dfrac{\frac{1}{2}}{1 + \frac{2}{3}}$
complex number Any number that can be written as $a + bi$, where *a* and *b* are real numbers and $i = \sqrt{-1}$.	**número complejo** Todo número que se puede expresar como $a + bi$, donde *a* y *b* son números reales e $i = \sqrt{-1}$.	$4 + 2i$ $5 + 0i = 5$ $0 - 7i = -7i$
complex plane A set of coordinate axes in which the horizontal axis is the real axis and the vertical axis is the imaginary axis; used to graph complex numbers.	**plano complejo** Conjunto de ejes cartesianos en el cual el eje horizontal es el eje real y el eje vertical es el eje imaginario; se utiliza para representar gráficamente números complejos.	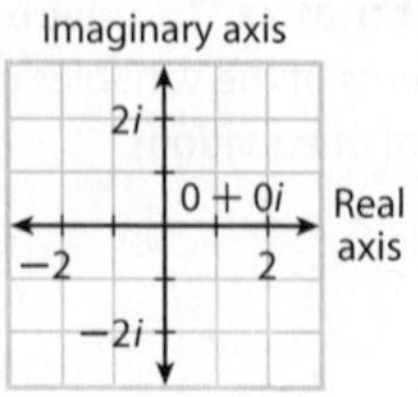

ENGLISH	SPANISH	EXAMPLES

composition of functions The composition of functions f and g, written as $(f \circ g)(x)$ and defined as $f(g(x))$ uses the output of $g(x)$ as the input for $f(x)$.

composición de funciones La composición de las funciones f y g, expresada como $(f \circ g)(x)$ y definida como $f(g(x))$ utiliza la salida de $g(x)$ como la entrada para $f(x)$.

If $f(x) = x^2$ and $g(x) = x + 1$, the composite function $(f \circ g)(x) = (x + 1)^2$.

---

compound event An event made up of two or more simple events.

suceso compuesto Suceso formado por dos o más sucesos simples.

In the experiment of tossing a coin and rolling a number cube, the event of the coin landing heads and the number cube landing on 3.

---

compound interest Interest earned or paid on both the principal and previously earned interest, found using the formula $A(t) = P\left(1 + \frac{r}{n}\right)^{nt}$ where A is the final amount, P is the principal, r is the interest rate given as a decimal, n is the number of times interest is compounded, and t is the time.

interés compuesto Interés ganado o pagado tanto sobre el capital inicial como sobre el interés previamente ganado. Se halla usando la fórmula $A(t) = P\left(1 + \frac{r}{n}\right)^{nt}$, donde A es la cantidad final, P es el capital inicial, r es la tasa de interés indicada en forma de número decimal, n es el número de veces que se reinvierte el interés y t es el tiempo.

---

compression A transformation that pushes the points of a graph horizontally toward the y-axis or vertically toward the x-axis.

compresión Transformación que desplaza los puntos de una gráfica horizontalmente hacia el eje y o verticalmente hacia el eje x.

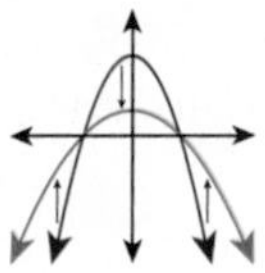

---

conditional probability The probability of event B, given that event A has already occurred or is certain to occur, denoted $P(B \mid A)$; used to find probability of dependent events.

probabilidad condicional Probabilidad del suceso B, dado que el suceso A ya ha ocurrido o es seguro que ocurrirá, expresada como $P(B \mid A)$; se utiliza para calcular la probabilidad de sucesos dependientes.

---

confidence interval An approximate range of values that is likely to include an unknown population parameter.

intervalo de confianza Un rango aproximado de valores que probablemente incluirá un parámetro de población desconocido.

---

conic section A plane figure formed by the intersection of a double right cone and a plane. Examples include circles, ellipses, hyperbolas, and parabolas.

sección cónica Figura plana formada por la intersección de un cono regular doble y un plano. Algunos ejemplos son círculos, elipses, hipérbolas y parábolas.

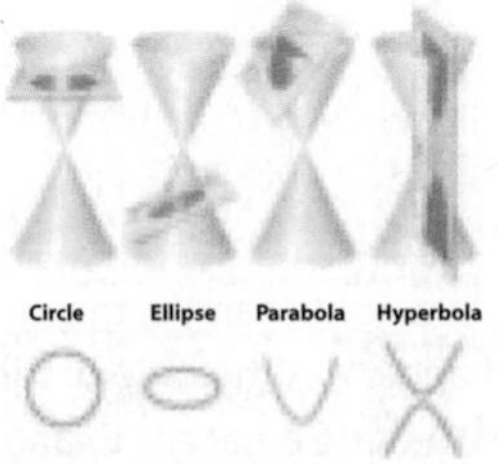

---

conjugate axis The axis of symmetry of a hyperbola that separates the two branches of the hyperbola.

eje conjugado Eje de simetría de una hipérbola que separa las dos ramas de la hipérbola.

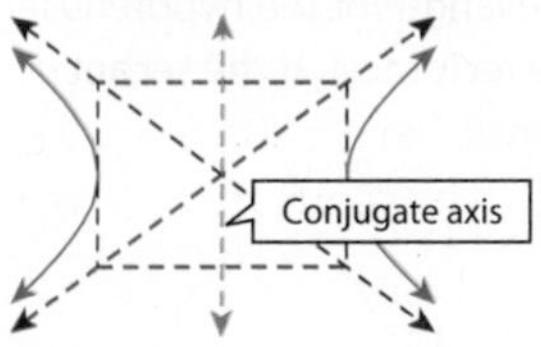

ENGLISH	SPANISH	EXAMPLES
constraint One of the inequalities that define the feasible region in a linear-programming problem.	**restricción** Una de las desigualdades que definen la región factible en un problema de programación lineal.	Constraints: $x > 0$ $y > 0$ $x + y \leq 8$ $3x + 5y \leq 30$ Feasible region 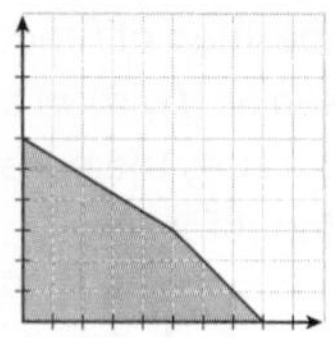
continuous function A function whose graph is an unbroken line or curve with no gaps or breaks.	**función continua** Función cuya gráfica es una línea recta o curva continua, sin espacios ni interrupciones.	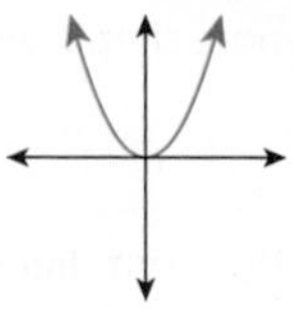
contradiction An equation that has no solutions.	**contradicción** Ecuación que no tiene soluciones.	$x + 1 = x$ $1 = 0x$
correlation A measure of the strength and direction of the relationship between two variables or data sets.	**correlación** Medida de la fuerza y dirección de la relación entre dos variables o conjuntos de datos.	Positive correlation 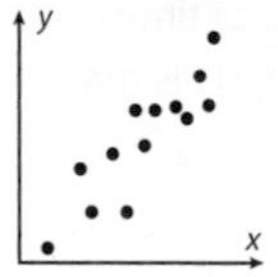 No correlation 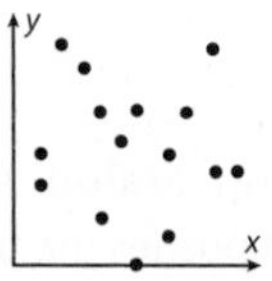 Negative correlation 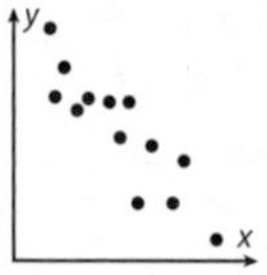
correlation coefficient A number r, where $-1 \leq r \leq 1$, that describes how closely the points in a scatter plot cluster around the least–squares line.	**coeficiente de correlación** Número r, donde $-1 \leq r \leq 1$, que describe a qué distancia de la recta de mínimos cuadrados se agrupan los puntos de un diagrama de dispersión.	An r–value close to 1 describes a strong positive correlation. An r–value close to 0 describes a weak correlation or no correlation. An r–value close to -1 describes a strong negative correlation.
cosecant In a right triangle, the cosecant of angle A is the ratio of the length of the hypotenuse to the length of the side opposite A. It is the reciprocal of the sine function.	**cosecante** En un triángulo rectángulo, la cosecante del ángulo A es la razón entre la longitud de la hipotenusa y la longitud del cateto opuesto a A. Es la inversa de la función seno.	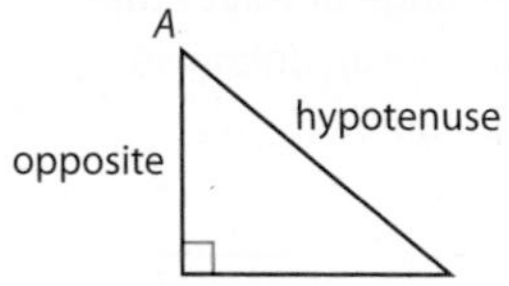 $\csc A = \frac{\text{hypotenuse}}{\text{opposite}} = \frac{1}{\sin A}$
cosine In a right triangle, the cosine of angle A is the ratio of the length of the side adjacent to angle A to the length of the hypotenuse. It is the reciprocal of the secant function.	**coseno** En un triángulo rectángulo, el coseno del ángulo A es la razón entre la longitud del cateto adyacente al ángulo A y la longitud de la hipotenusa. Es la inversa de la función secante.	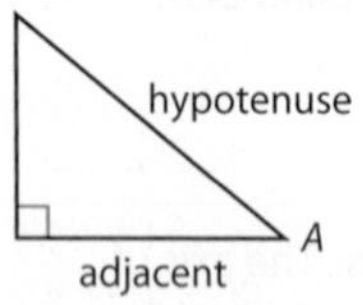 $\cos A = \frac{\text{adjacent}}{\text{hypotenuse}} = \frac{1}{\sec A}$

ENGLISH | SPANISH | EXAMPLES

cotangent In a right triangle, the cotangent of angle *A* is the ratio of the length of the side adjacent to *A* to the length of the side opposite *A*. It is the reciprocal of the tangent function.

cotangente En un triángulo rectángulo, la cotangente del ángulo *A* es la razón entre la longitud del cateto adyacente a *A* y la longitud del cateto opuesto a *A*. Es la inversa de la función tangente.

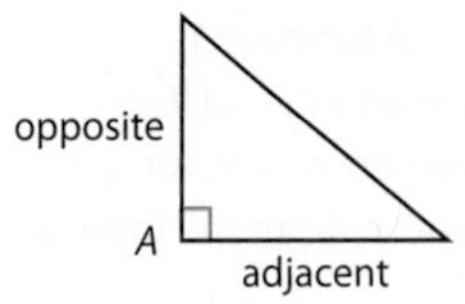

$\cot A = \frac{\text{adjacent}}{\text{opposite}} = \frac{1}{\tan A}$

---

coterminal angles Two angles in standard position with the same terminal side.

ángulos coterminales Dos ángulos en posición estándar con el mismo lado terminal.

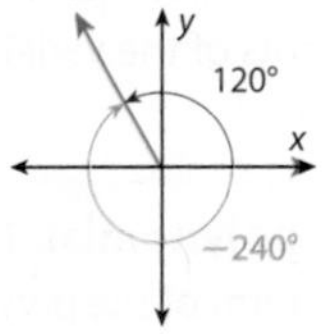

---

critical values Values that separate the number line into intervals that either contain solutions or do not contain solutions.

valores críticos Valores que separan la recta numérica en intervalos que contienen o no contienen soluciones.

---

cube-root function The function $f(x) = \sqrt[3]{x}$.

función de raíz cúbica La función $f(x) = \sqrt[3]{x}$.

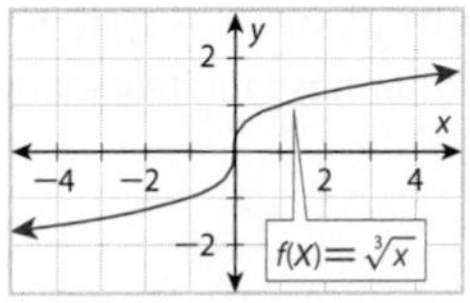

---

cubic function A polynomial function of degree 3.

función cúbica Función polinomial de grado 3.

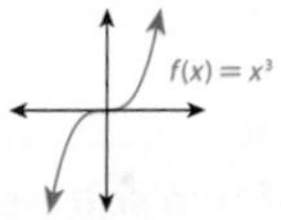

---

cumulative probability The probability that a random variable is less than or equal to a given value.

probabilidad acumulada La probabilidad de que una variable aleatoria sea menor o igual que un valor determinado.

---

cycle of a periodic function The shortest repeating part of a periodic graph or function.

ciclo de una función periódica La parte repetida más corta de una gráfica o función periódica.

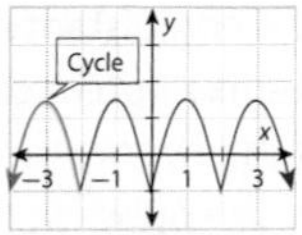

D

decay factor The base $1 - r$ in an exponential expression.

factor decremental Base $1 - r$ en una expresión exponencial.

$2(0.93)^t$

decay factor (representing $1 - 0.07$)

---

decay rate The constant percent decrease, in decimal form, in an exponential decay function.

tasa de disminución Disminución porcentual constante, en forma decimal, en una función de disminución exponencial.

In the function $f(t) = a(1 - 0.2)^t$, 0.2 is the decay rate.

Glossary/Glosario

ENGLISH	SPANISH	EXAMPLES
decreasing A function is decreasing on an interval if $f(x_1) > f(x_2)$ when $x_1 > x_2$ for any x-values x_1 and x_2 from the interval.	**decreciente** Una función es decreciente en un intervalo si $f(x_1) > f(x_2)$ cuando $x_1 > x_2$ dados los valores de x, x_1 y x_2, pertenecientes al intervalo.	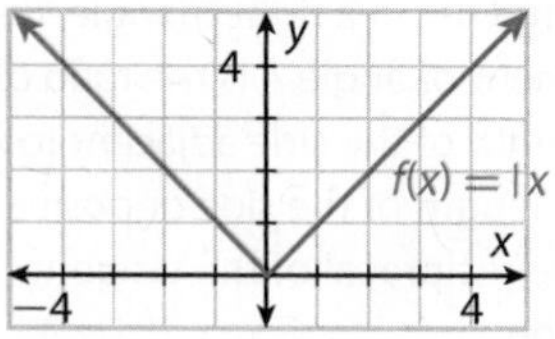 $f(x)$ is decreasing on the interval $x < 0$.
degree of a monomial The sum of the exponents of the variables in the monomial.	**grado de un monomio** Suma de los exponentes de las variables del monomio.	$4x^2y^5z^3$ Degree: $2 + 5 + 3 = 10$ 5 Degree: 0 $(5 = 5x^0)$
degree of a polynomial The degree of the term of the polynomial with the greatest degree.	**grado de un polinomio** Grado del término del polinomio con el grado máximo.	$3x^2y^2 + 4xy^5 - 12x^3y^2$ Degree 6 ↑ Degree 4 ↑ Degree 6 ↑ Degree 5
dependent events Events for which the occurrence or nonoccurrence of one event affects the probability of the other event.	**sucesos dependientes** Dos sucesos son dependientes si el hecho de que uno de ellos se cumpla o no afecta la probabilidad del otro.	From a bag containing 3 red marbles and 2 blue marbles, drawing a red marble, and then drawing a blue marble without replacing the first marble.
dependent system A system of equations that has infinitely many solutions.	**sistema dependiente** Sistema de ecuaciones que tiene infinitamente muchas soluciones.	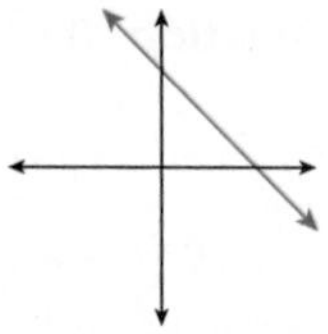 $\begin{cases} x + y = 3 \\ 2x + 2y = 6 \end{cases}$
difference of two squares A polynomial of the form $a^2 - b^2$, which may be written as the product $(a + b)(a - b)$.	**diferencia de dos cuadrados** Polinomio del tipo $a^2 - b^2$, que se puede expresar como el producto $(a + b)(a - b)$.	$x^2 - 4 = (x + 2)(x - 2)$
directrix A fixed line used to define a *parabola*. Every point on the parabola is equidistant from the directrix and a fixed point called the *focus*.	**directriz** Línea fija utilizada para definir una *parábola*. Cada punto de la parábola es equidistante de la directriz y de un punto fijo denominado *foco*.	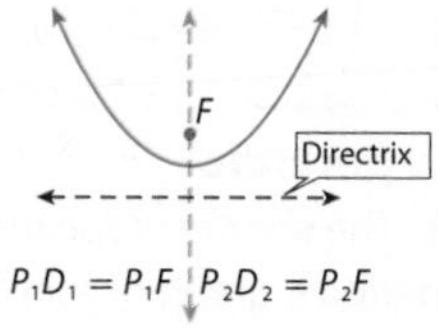
discontinuous function A function whose graph has one or more jumps, breaks, or holes.	**función discontinua** Función cuya gráfica tiene uno o más saltos, interrupciones u hoyos.	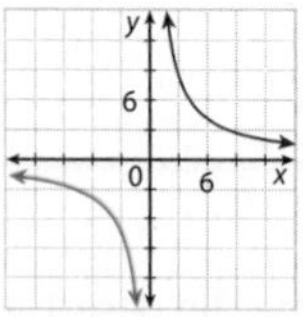
discriminant The discriminant of the quadratic equation $ax^2 + bx + c = 0$ is $b^2 - 4ac$.	**discriminante** El discriminante de la ecuación cuadrática $ax^2 + bx + c = 0$ es $b^2 - 4ac$.	The discriminant of $2x^2 - 5x - 3 = 0$ is $(-5)^2 - 4(2)(-3) = 25 + 24 = 49$.
distribution A set of numerical data that you can graph using a data display that involves a number line, such as a line plot, histogram, or box plot.	**distribución** Un conjunto de datos numéricos que se pueden representar gráficamente mediante una representación de datos que incluye una recta numérica, como un diagrama de puntos, un histograma o un diagrama de cajas.	

E

elementary row operations *See* row operations.

operaciones elementales de fila *Véase* operaciones de fila.

---

elimination A method used to solve systems of equations in which one variable is eliminated by adding or subtracting two equations of the system.

eliminación Método utilizado para resolver sistemas de ecuaciones por el cual se elimina una variable sumando o restando dos ecuaciones del sistema.

---

empty set A set with no elements.

conjunto vacío Conjunto sin elementos.

The solution set of $|x| < 0$ is the empty set, $\{\ \}$, or $\varnothing$.

---

end behavior The trends in the y-values of a function as the x-values approach positive and negative infinity.

comportamiento extremo Tendencia de los valores de y de una función a medida que los valores de x se aproximan al infinito positivo y negativo.

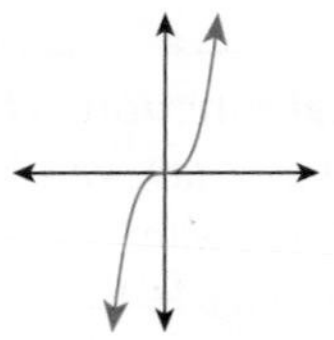

End behavior: $f(x) \to \infty$ as $x \to \infty$

$f(x) \to -\infty$ as $x \to -\infty$

---

even function A function in which $f(-x) = f(x)$ for all x in the domain of the function.

función par Función en la que para todos los valores de x dentro del dominio de la función.

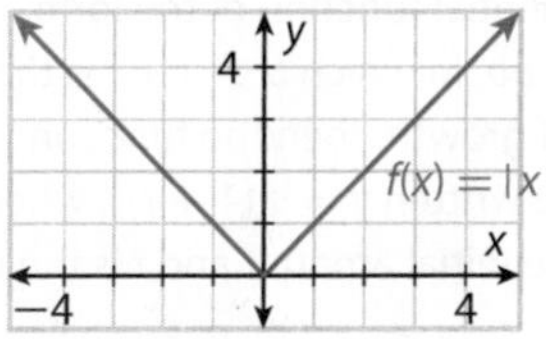

$f(x) = |x|$ is an even function.

---

event An outcome or set of outcomes in a probability experiment.

suceso Resultado o conjunto de resultados en un experimento de probabilidad.

In the experiment of rolling a number cube, the event "an odd number" consists of the outcomes 1, 3, and 5.

---

expected value The weighted average of the numerical outcomes of a probability experiment.

valor esperado Promedio ponderado de los resultados numéricos de un experimento de probabilidad.

The table shows the probability of getting a given score by guessing on a three-question quiz.

Score	0	1	2	3
Probability	0.42	0.42	0.14	0.02

The expected value is a score of $0(0.42) + 1(0.42) + 2(0.14) + 3(0.02) = 0.76$.

---

experiment An operation, process, or activity in which outcomes can be used to estimate probability.

experimento Una operación, proceso o actividad cuyo resultado se puede usar para estimar la probabilidad.

Tossing a coin 10 times and noting the number of heads.

---

experimental probability The ratio of the number of times an event occurs to the number of trials, or times, that an activity is performed.

probabilidad experimental Razón entre la cantidad de veces que ocurre un suceso y la cantidad de pruebas, o veces, que se realiza una actividad.

Kendra made 6 of 10 free throws. The experimental probability that she will make her next free throw is

$P(\text{free throw}) = \frac{\text{number made}}{\text{number attempted}} = \frac{6}{10}$.

ENGLISH	SPANISH	EXAMPLES

explicit formula A formula that defines the nth term a_n, or general term, of a sequence as a function of n.

fórmula explícita Fórmula que define el enésimo término a_n, o término general, de una sucesión como una función de n.

Sequence: 4, 7, 10, 13, 16, 19, …
Explicit formula: $a_n = 1 + 3n$

exponential decay An exponential function of the form $f(x) = ab^x$ in which $0 < b < 1$. If r is the rate of decay, then the function can be written $y = a(1 - r)^t$, where a is the initial amount and t is the time.

decremento exponencial Función exponencial del tipo $f(x) = ab^x$ en la cual $0 < b < 1$. Si r es la tasa decremental, entonces la función se puede expresar como $y = a(1 - r)^t$, donde a es la cantidad inicial y t es el tiempo.

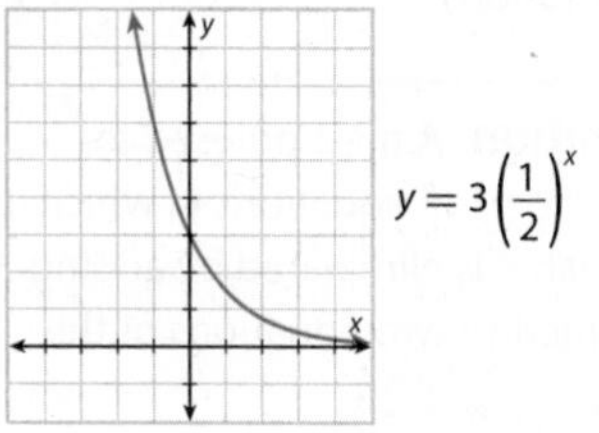

exponential equation An equation that contains one or more exponential expressions.

ecuación exponencial Ecuación que contiene una o más expresiones exponenciales.

$2^{x+1} = 8$

exponential function A function of the form $f(x) = ab^x$, where a and b are real numbers with $a \neq 0$, $b > 0$, and $b \neq 1$.

función exponencial Función del tipo $f(x) = ab^x$, donde a y b son números reales con $a \neq 0$, $b > 0$ y $b \neq 1$.

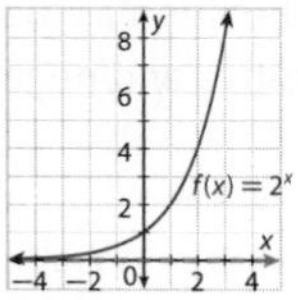

exponential growth An exponential function of the form $f(x) = ab^x$ in which $b > 1$. If r is the rate of growth, then the function can be written $y = a(1 + r)^t$, where a is the initial amount and t is the time.

crecimiento exponencial Función exponencial del tipo $f(x) = ab^x$ en la que $b > 1$. Si r es la tasa de crecimiento, entonces la función se puede expresar como $y = a(1 + r)^t$, donde a es la cantidad inicial y t es el tiempo.

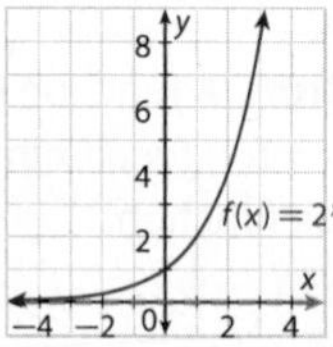

exponential regression A statistical method used to fit an exponential model to a given data set.

regresión exponencial Método estadístico utilizado para ajustar un modelo exponencial a un conjunto de datos determinado.

extraneous solution A solution of a derived equation that is not a solution of the original equation.

solución extraña Solución de una ecuación derivada que no es una solución de la ecuación original.

To solve $\sqrt{x} = -2$, square both sides; $x = 4$.
Check $\sqrt{4} = -2$ is false; so 4 is an extraneous solution.

F

Factor Theorem For any polynomial $P(x)$, $(x - a)$ is a factor of $P(x)$ if and only if $P(a) = 0$.

Teorema del factor Dado el polinomio $P(x)$, $(x - a)$ es un factor de $P(x)$ si y sólo si $P(a) = 0$.

$(x - 1)$ is a factor of $P(x) = x^2 - 1$ because $P(1) = 1^2 - 1 = 0$.

ENGLISH	SPANISH	EXAMPLES
factorial If n is a positive integer, then n factorial, written $n!$, is $n \cdot (n-1) \cdot (n-2) \cdot \ldots \cdot 2 \cdot 1$. The factorial of 0 is defined to be 1.	**factorial** Si n es un entero positivo, entonces el factorial de n, expresado como $n!$, es $n \cdot (n-1) \cdot (n-2) \cdot \ldots \cdot 2 \cdot 1$ Por definición, el factorial de 0 será 1.	$7! = 7 \cdot 6 \cdot 5 \cdot 4 \cdot 3 \cdot 2 \cdot 1 = 5040$ $0! = 1$
Fibonacci sequence The infinite sequence of numbers beginning with 1, 1 such that each term is the sum of the two previous terms.	**sucesión de Fibonacci** Sucesión infinita de números que comienza con 1, 1 de forma tal que cada término es la suma de los dos términos anteriores.	1, 1, 2, 3, 5, 8, 13, 21, …
finite geometric series A geometric series in which the sum of a finite number of terms of a geometric sequence is found.	**serie geométrica finita** Una serie geométrica en la que se halla la suma de un número finito de términos de una secuencia geométrica.	
finite sequence A sequence with a finite number of terms.	**sucesión finita** Sucesión con un número finito de términos.	1, 2, 3, 4, 5
finite set A set with a definite, or finite, number of elements.	**conjunto finito** Conjunto con un número de elementos definido o finito.	$\{2, 4, 6, 8, 10\}$
first differences The differences between y-values of a function for evenly spaced x-values.	**primeras diferencias** Diferencias entre los valores de y de una función para valores de x espaciados uniformemente.	see table below
focus (pl. foci) of a parabola A fixed point F used with a *directrix* to define a *parabola*.	**foco de una parábola** Punto fijo F utilizado con una *directriz* para definir una *parábola*.	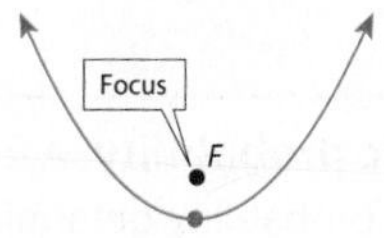
frequency of a data value The number of times the value appears in the data set.	**frecuencia de un valor de datos** Cantidad de veces que aparece el valor en un conjunto de datos.	In the data set 5, 6, 6, 6, 8, 9, the data value 6 has a frequency of 3.
frequency of a periodic function The number of cycles per unit of time. Also the reciprocal of the period.	**frecuencia de una función periódica** Cantidad de ciclos por unidad de tiempo. También es la inversa del periodo.	The function $y = \sin(2x)$ has a period of π and a frequency of $\frac{1}{\pi}$.
function rule An algebraic expression that defines a function.	**regla de función** Expresión algebraica que define una función.	$f(x) = 2x^2 + 3x - 7$ ↑ function rule

First differences example:

x	0	1	2	3
y	3	7	11	15
first differences		+4	+4	+4

Glossary/Glosario

ENGLISH	SPANISH	EXAMPLES
Fundamental Counting Principle For n items, if there are m_1 ways to choose a first item, m_2 ways to choose a second item after the first item has been chosen, and so on, then there are $m_1 \cdot m_2 \cdot \ldots \cdot m_n$ ways to choose n items.	**Principio fundamental de conteo** Dados n elementos, si existen m_1 formas de elegir un primer elemento, m_2 formas de elegir un segundo elemento después de haber elegido el primero, y así sucesivamente, entonces existen $m_1 \cdot m_2 \cdot \ldots \cdot m_n$ formas de elegir n elementos.	If there are 4 colors of shirts, 3 colors of pants, and 2 colors of shoes, then there are $4 \cdot 3 \cdot 2 = 24$ possible outfits.

G

ENGLISH	SPANISH	EXAMPLES
Gaussian Elimination An algorithm for solving systems of equations using matrices and row operations to eliminate variables in each equation in the system.	**Eliminación Gaussiana** Algoritmo para resolver sistemas de ecuaciones mediante matrices y operaciones de fila con el fin de eliminar variables en cada ecuación del sistema.	
general form of a conic section $Ax^2 + Bxy + Cy^2 + Dx + Ey + F = 0$, where A and B are not both 0.	**forma general de una sección cónica** $Ax^2 + Bxy + Cy^2 + Dx + Ey + F = 0$, donde A y B no son los dos 0.	A circle with a vertex at $(1, 2)$ and radius 3 has the general form $x^2 + y^2 - 2x - 4y - 4 = 0$.
geometric mean In a geometric sequence, a term that comes between two given nonconsecutive terms of the sequence. For positive numbers a and b, the geometric mean is $\sqrt{ab}$.	**media geométrica** En una sucesión geométrica, un término que se encuentra entre dos términos no consecutivos dados de la sucesión. Dados los números positivos a y b, la media geométrica es $\sqrt{ab}$.	The geometric mean of 4 and 9 is $\sqrt{4(9)} = \sqrt{36} = 6$.
geometric probability A form of theoretical probability determined by a ratio of geometric measures such as lengths, areas, or volumes.	**probabilidad geométrica** Una forma de la probabilidad teórica determinada por una razón de medidas geométricas, como longitud, área o volumen.	 The probability of the pointer landing the 80° angle is $\frac{2}{9}$.
geometric sequence A sequence in which the ratio of successive terms is a constant r, called the common ratio, where $r \neq 0$ and $r \neq 1$.	**sucesión geométrica** Sucesión en la que la razón de los términos sucesivos es una constante r, denominada razón común, donde $r \neq 0$ y $r \neq 1$.	1, 2, 4, 8, 16, ... $\cdot 2$ $\cdot 2$ $\cdot 2$ $\cdot 2$ $r = 2$
geometric series The indicated sum of the terms of a geometric sequence.	**serie geométrica** Suma indicada de los términos de una sucesión geométrica.	$1 + 2 + 4 + 8 + 16 + \ldots$

ENGLISH	SPANISH	EXAMPLES

greatest-integer function A function denoted by $f(x) = [x]$ or $f(x) = \lfloor x \rfloor$ in which the number x is rounded down to the greatest integer that is less than or equal to x.

función de entero mayor Función expresada como $f(x) = [x]$ o $f(x) = \lfloor x \rfloor$ en la cual el número x se redondea hacia abajo hasta el entero mayor que sea menor que o igual a x.

$\lfloor 4.98 \rfloor = 4$
$\lfloor -2.1 \rfloor = -3$

---

growth factor The base $1 + r$ in an exponential expression.

factor de crecimiento La base $1 + r$ en una expresión exponencial.

$12{,}000(1 + 0.14)^t$ ↑ growth factor

---

growth rate The constant percent increase, in decimal form, in an exponential growth function.

tasa de crecimiento Aumento porcentual constante, en forma decimal, en una función de crecimiento exponencial.

In the function $f(t) = a(1 + 0.3)^t$, 0.3 is the growth rate.

H

Heron's Formula A triangle with side lengths a, b, and c has area $A = \sqrt{s(s-a)(s-b)(s-c)}$, where s is one-half the perimeter, or $s = \frac{1}{2}(a + b + c)$.

fórmula de Herón Un triángulo con longitudes de lado a, b y c tiene un área $A = \sqrt{s(s-a)(s-b)(s-c)}$, donde s es la mitad del perímetro ó $s = \frac{1}{2}(a + b + c)$.

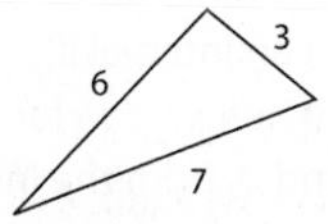

$s = \frac{1}{2}(3 + 6 + 7) = 8$
$A = \sqrt{8(8-3)(8-6)(8-7)}$
$= \sqrt{80} = 4\sqrt{5}$ square units

---

hole (in a graph) An omitted point on a graph. If a rational function has the same factor $x - b$ in both the numerator and the denominator, and the line $x = b$ is not a vertical asymptote, then there is a hole in the graph at the point where $x = b$.

hoyo (en una gráfica) Punto omitido en una gráfica. Si una función racional tiene el mismo factor $x - b$ tanto en el numerador como en el denominador, y la línea $x = b$ no es una asíntota vertical, entonces hay un hoyo en la gráfica en el punto donde $x = b$.

$f(x) = \frac{(x-2)(x+2)}{(x+2)}$ has a hole at $x = -2$.

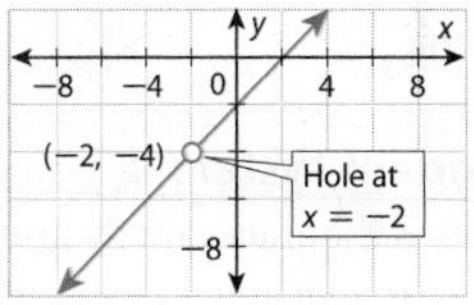

---

hypothesis testing A type of testing used to determine whether the difference in two groups is likely to be caused by chance.

comprobación de hipótesis Tipo de comprobación que sirve para determinar si el azar es la causa probable de la diferencia entre dos grupos.

I

imaginary axis The vertical axis in the complex plane, it graphically represents the purely imaginary part of complex numbers.

eje imaginario Eje vertical de un plano complejo. Representa gráficamente la parte puramente imaginaria de los números complejos.

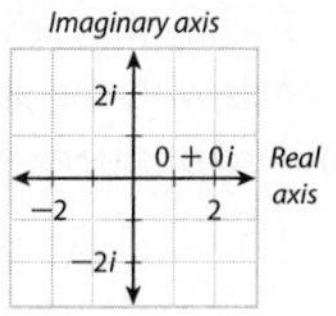

ENGLISH	SPANISH	EXAMPLES
imaginary number The square root of a negative number, written in the form *bi*, where *b* is a real number and *i* is the imaginary unit, $\sqrt{-1}$. Also called a *pure imaginary number*.	**número imaginario** Raíz cuadrada de un número negativo, expresado como *bi*, donde *b* es un número real e *i* es la unidad imaginaria, $\sqrt{-1}$. También se denomina *número imaginario puro*.	$\sqrt{-16} = \sqrt{16} \cdot \sqrt{-1} = 4i$
imaginary unit The unit in the imaginary number system, $\sqrt{-1}$.	**unidad imaginaria** Unidad del sistema de números imaginarios, $\sqrt{-1}$.	$\sqrt{-1} = i$
inconsistent system A system of equations or inequalities that has no solution.	**sistema inconsistente** Sistema de ecuaciones o desigualdades que no tiene solución.	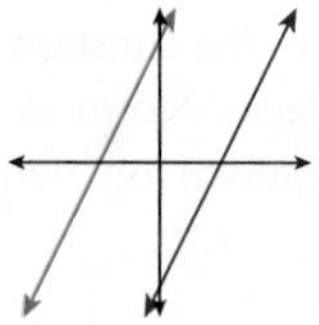 $\begin{cases} y = 2.5x + 5 \\ y = 2.5x - 5 \end{cases}$ is inconsistent.
Increasing A function is increasing on an interval if $f(x_1) < f(x_2)$ when $x_1 < x_2$ for any *x*-values x_1 and x_2 from the interval.	**creciente** Una función es creciente en un intervalo si $f(x_1) < f(x_2)$ cuando $x_1 < x_2$ dados los valores de x, x_1 y x_2, pertenecienlos al intervalo.	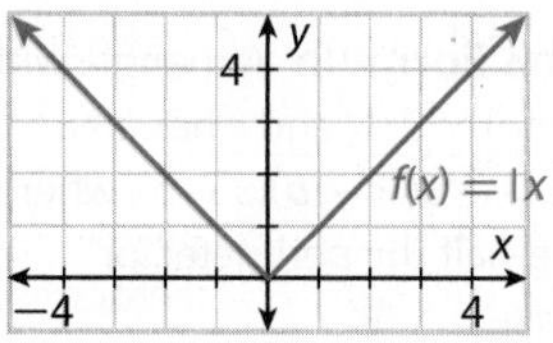 $f(x)$ is increasing on the interval $x > 0$.
independent events Events for which the occurrence or non-occurrence of one event does not affect the probability of the other event.	**sucesos independientes** Dos sucesos son independientes si el hecho de que se produzca o no uno de ellos no afecta la probabilidad del otro suceso.	From a bag containing 3 red marbles and 2 blue marbles, drawing a red marble, replacing it, and then drawing a blue marble.
independent system A system of equations that has exactly one solution.	**sistema independiente** Sistema de ecuaciones que tiene exactamente una solución.	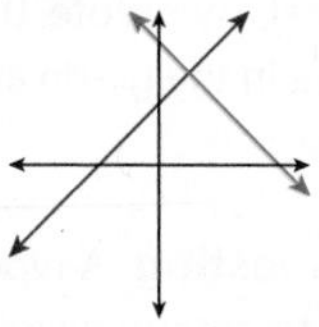 $\begin{cases} y = -x + 4 \\ y = x + 2 \end{cases}$ Solution: (1, 3)
independent variable The input of a function; a variable whose value determines the value of the output, or dependent variable.	**variable independiente** Entrada de una función; variable cuyo valor determina el valor de la salida, o variable dependiente.	$y = 2x + 1$ ↑ independent variable
initial side The ray that lies on the positive *x*-axis when an angle is drawn in standard position.	**lado inicial** El rayo que se encuentra en el eje positivo *x* cuando se traza un ángulo en la posición estándar.	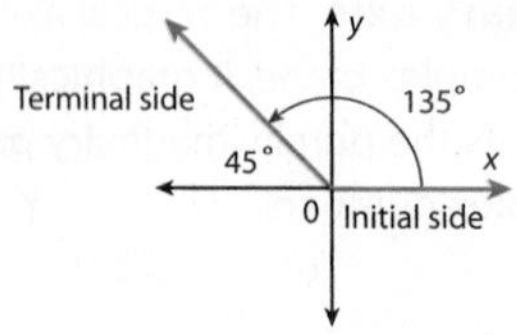

ENGLISH	SPANISH	EXAMPLES

interval notation A way of writing the set of all real numbers between two endpoints. The symbols [and] are used to include an endpoint in an interval, and the symbols (and) are used to exclude an endpoint from an interval.

notación de intervalo Forma de expresar el conjunto de todos los números reales entre dos extremos. Los símbolos [y] se utilizan para incluir un extremo en un intervalo y los símbolos (y) se utilizan para excluir un extremo de un intervalo.

Interval notation	Set-builder notation
(a, b)	$\{x \mid a < x < b\}$
$(a, b]$	$\{x \mid a < x \leq b\}$
$[a, b)$	$\{x \mid a \leq x < b\}$
$[a, b]$	$\{x \mid a \leq x \leq b\}$

inverse function The function that results from exchanging the input and output values of a one-to-one function. The inverse of $f(x)$ is denoted $f^{-1}(x)$.

función inversa Función que resulta de intercambiar los valores de entrada y salida de una función uno a uno. La función inversa de $f(x)$ se expresa $f^{-1}(x)$

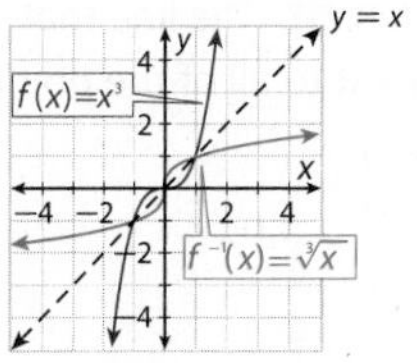

inverse relation The inverse of the relation consisting of all ordered pairs (x, y) is the set of all ordered pairs (y, x). The graph of an inverse relation is the reflection of the graph of the relation across the line $y = x$.

relación inversa La inversa de la relación que consta de todos los pares ordenados (x, y) es el conjunto de todos los pares ordenados (y, x). La gráfica de una relación inversa es el reflejo de la gráfica de la relación sobre la línea $y = x$.

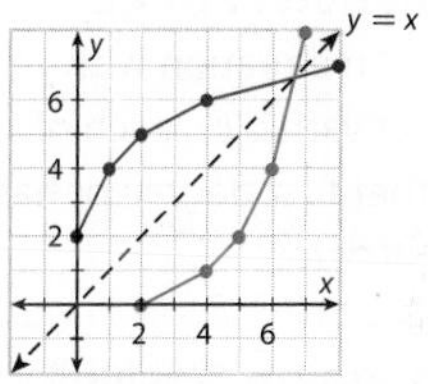

irreducible factor A factor of degree 2 or greater that cannot be factored further.

factor irreductible Factor de grado 2 o mayor que no se puede seguir factorizando.

$x^2 + 7x + 1$

J

joint relative frequency The ratio of the frequency in a particular category divided by the total number of data values.

frecuencia relativa conjunta La razón de la frecuencia en una determinada categoría dividida entre el número total de valores.

L

Law of Cosines For $\triangle ABC$ with side lengths a, b, and c,
$a^2 = b^2 + c^2 - 2bc \cos A$
$b^2 = a^2 + c^2 - 2ac \cos B$
$c^2 = a^2 + b^2 - 2ab \cos C$.

Ley de cosenos Dado $\triangle ABC$ con longitudes de lado a, b y c,
$a^2 = b^2 + c^2 - 2bc \cos A$
$b^2 = a^2 + c^2 - 2ac \cos B$
$c^2 = a^2 + b^2 - 2ab \cos C$

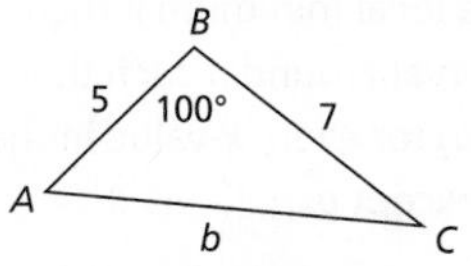

$b^2 = 7^2 + 5^2 - 2(7)(5)\cos 100°$
$b^2 \approx 86.2$
$b \approx 9.3$

Law of Sines For $\triangle ABC$ with side lengths a, b, and c,
$\frac{\sin A}{a} = \frac{\sin B}{b} = \frac{\sin C}{c}$.

Ley de senos Dado $\triangle ABC$ con longitudes de lado a, b y c,
$\frac{\text{sen}A}{a} = \frac{\text{sen}B}{b} = \frac{\text{sen}C}{c}$.

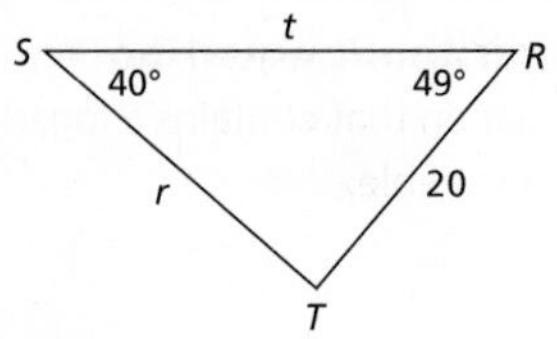

$\frac{\sin 49°}{r} = \frac{\sin 40°}{20}$
$r = \frac{20 \sin 49°}{\sin 40°} \approx 23.5$

Glossary/Glosario

Glossary/Glosario

ENGLISH	SPANISH	EXAMPLES
leading coefficient The coefficient of the first term of a polynomial in standard form.	**coeficiente principal** Coeficiente del primer termino de un polinomio en forma estandar	$3x^2 + 7x - 2$ ↑ Leading coefficient
limit For an infinite arithmetic series that converges, the number that the partial sums approach.	**límite** Para un serie que coverge, el número que se aproximan las sumas.	The series $\frac{1}{2} + \frac{1}{4} + \frac{1}{8} + \frac{1}{16} + \ldots$ has a limit of 1.
line of best fit The line that comes closest to all of the points in a data set.	**línea de mejor ajuste** Línea que más se acerca a todos los puntos de un conjunto de datos.	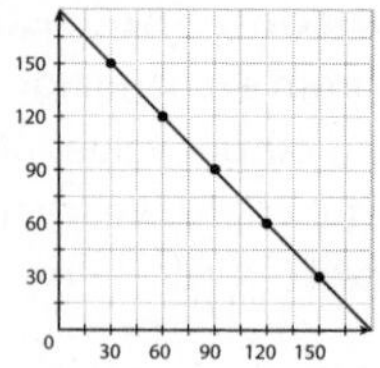
linear equation in three variables An equation with three distinct variables, each of which is either first degree or has a coefficient of zero.	**ecuación lineal en tres variables** Ecuación con tres variables diferentes, sean de primer grado o tengan un coeficiente de cero.	$5 = 3x + 2y + 6z$
linear regression A statistical method used to fit a linear model to a given data set.	**regresión lineal** Método estadístico utilizado para ajustar un modelo lineal a un conjunto de datos determinado.	
linear system A system of equations containing only linear equations.	**sistema lineal** Sistema de ecuaciones que contiene sólo ecuaciones lineales.	$\begin{cases} y = 2x + 1 \\ x + y = 8 \end{cases}$
local maximum For a function f, $f(a)$ is a local maximum if there is an interval around a such that $f(x) < f(a)$ for every x-value in the interval except a.	**máximo local** Dada una función f, $f(a)$ es el máximo local si hay un intervalo en a tal que $f(x) < f(a)$ para cada valor de x en el intervalo excepto a.	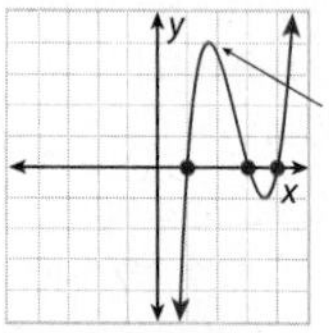
local minimum For a function f, $f(a)$ is a local minimum if there is an interval around a such that $f(x) > f(a)$ for every x-value in the interval except a.	**mínimo local** Dada una función f, $f(a)$ es el mínimo local si hay un intervalo en a tal que $f(x) > f(a)$ para cada valor de x en el intervalo excepto a.	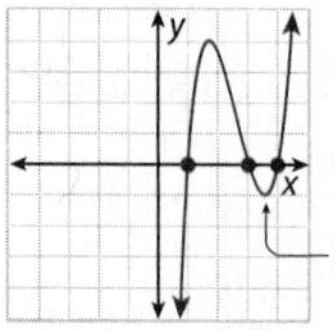
logarithm The exponent that a specified base must be raised to in order to get a certain value.	**logaritmo** Exponente al cual debe elevarse una base determinada a fin de obtener cierto valor.	$\log_2 8 = 3$, because 3 is the power that 2 is raised to in order to get 8; or $2^3 = 8$.
logarithmic equation An equation that contains a logarithm of a variable.	**ecuación logarítmica** Ecuación que contiene un logaritmo de una variable.	$\log x + 3 = 7$

ENGLISH	SPANISH	EXAMPLES
logarithmic function A function of the form $f(x) = \log_b x$, where $b \neq 1$ and $b > 0$, which is the inverse of the exponential function $f(x) = b^x$.	**función logarítmica** Función del tipo $f(x) = \log_b x$, donde $b \neq 1$ y $b > 0$, que es la inversa de la función exponencial $f(x) = b^x$.	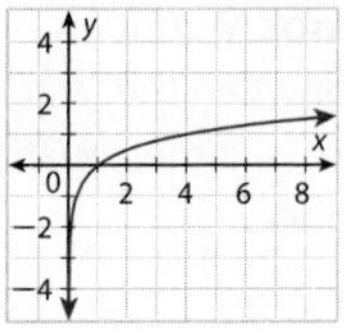 $f(x) = \log_4 x$
logarithmic regression A statistical method used to fit a logarithmic model to a given data set.	**regresión logarítmica** Método estadístico utilizado para ajustar un modelo logarítmico a un conjunto de datos determinado.	

M

ENGLISH	SPANISH	EXAMPLES
margin of error In a random sample, it defines an interval, centered on the sample percent, in which the population percent is most likely to lie.	**margen de error** En una muestra aleatoria, define un intervalo, centrado en el porcentaje de muestra, en el que es más probable que se encuentre el porcentaje de población.	
matrix A rectangular array of numbers.	**matriz** Arreglo rectangular de números.	$\begin{bmatrix} 1 & 0 & 3 \\ -2 & 2 & -5 \\ 7 & -6 & 3 \end{bmatrix}$
maximum value of a function The *y*-value of the highest point on the graph of the function.	**máximo de una función** Valor de *y* del punto más alto en la gráfica de la función.	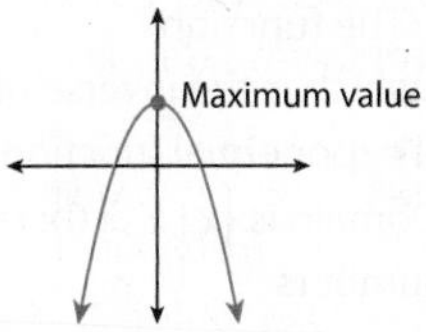
midline For the graph of a sine or cosine function, the horizontal line halfway between the maximum and minimum values of the curve; for the graph of a tangent function, the horizontal line through the point of each cycle that is midway between the asymptotes.	**línea media** En la gráfica de una función seno o coseno, la línea horizontal a medio camino entre los valores máximo y mínimo de la curva; en la gráfica de una función tangente, la línea horizontal que atraviesa el punto de cada ciclo que está a medio camino entre las asíntotas.	
minimum value of a function The *y*-value of the lowest point on the graph of the function.	**mínimo de una función** Valor de *y* del punto más bajo en la gráfica de la función.	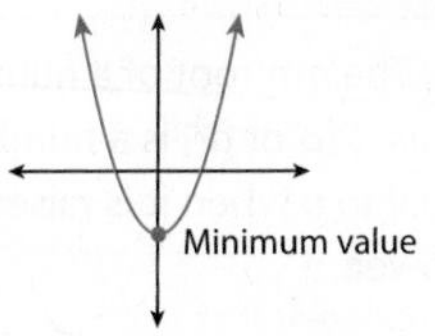
monomial A number or a product of numbers and variables with whole-number exponents, or a polynomial with one term.	**monomio** Número o producto de números y variables con exponentes de números cabales, o polinomio con un término.	$8x$, 9, $3x^2y^4$

ENGLISH	SPANISH	EXAMPLES
multiple root A root r is a multiple root when the factor $(x - r)$ appears in the equation more than once.	**raíz múltiple** Una raíz r es una raíz múltiple cuando el factor $(x - r)$ aparece en la ecuación más de una vez.	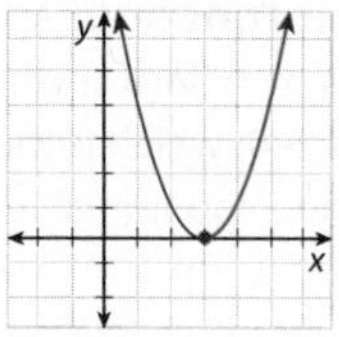 3 is a multiple root of $P(x) = (x - 3)^2$.
multiplicity If a polynomial $P(x)$ has a multiple root at r, the multiplicity of r is the number of times $(x - r)$ appears as a factor in $P(x)$.	**multiplicidad** Si un polinomio $P(x)$ tiene una raíz múltiple en r, la multiplicidad de r es la cantidad de veces que $(x - r)$ aparece como factor en $P(x)$.	For $P(x) = (x - 3)^2$, the root 3 has a multiplicity of 2.
mutually exclusive events Two events are mutually exclusive if they cannot both occur in the same trial of an experiment.	**sucesos mutuamente excluyentes** Dos sucesos son mutuamente excluyentes si ambos no pueden ocurrir en la misma prueba de un experimento.	In the experiment of rolling a number cube, rolling a 3 and rolling an even number are mutually exclusive events.

N

natural logarithm A logarithm with base e, written as ln.	**logaritmo natural** Logaritmo con base e, que se escribe ln.	$\ln 5 = \log_e 5 \approx 1.6$
natural logarithmic function The function $f(x) = \ln x$, which is the inverse of the natural exponential function $f(x) = e^x$. Domain is $\{x \mid x > 0\}$; range is all real numbers	**función logarítmica natural** Función $f(x) = \ln x$, que es la inversa de la función exponencial natural $f(x) = e^x$. El dominio es $\{x \mid x > 0\}$; el rango es todos los números reales.	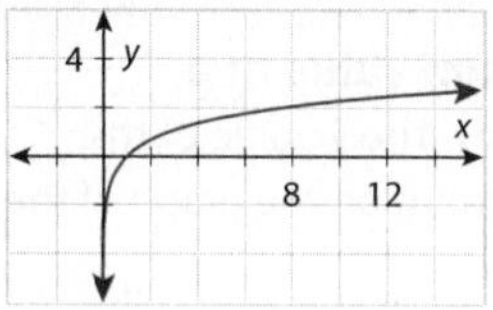
nonlinear system of equations A system in which at least one of the equations is not linear.	**sistema no lineal de ecuaciones** Sistema en el cual por lo menos una de las ecuaciones no es lineal.	$\begin{cases} y = 2x^2 \\ y = -3^2 + 5 \end{cases}$
normal distribution A distribution that is mounded in the middle with symmetric "tails" at each end, forming a bell shape.	**distribución normal** Una distribución que está elevada en el centro con "colas" simétricas en los extremos, lo que forma la figura de una campana.	
***n*th root** The nth root of a number a, written as $\sqrt[n]{a}$ or $a^{\frac{1}{n}}$, is a number that is equal to a when it is raised to the nth power.	**enésima raíz** La enésima raíz de un número a, que se escribe como $\sqrt[n]{a}$ or $a^{\frac{1}{n}}$, es un número igual a a cuando se eleva a la enésima potencia.	$\sqrt[5]{32} = 2$, because $2^5 = 32$.
null hypothesis The assumption made that any difference between the control group and the treatment group in an experiment is due to chance, and not to the treatment.	**hipótesis nula** La suposición de que cualquier diferencia entre el grupo de control y el grupo de tratamiento en un experimento se debe al azar, no al tratamiento.	

ENGLISH	SPANISH	EXAMPLES
numerical data Data that represent quantities or observations that can be measured.	**datos numéricos** Datos que representan cantidades u observaciones que pueden medirse.	

O

ENGLISH	SPANISH	EXAMPLES
observational study A study that observes individuals and measures variables without controlling the individuals or their environment in any way.	**estudio de observación** Estudio que permite observar a individuos y medir variables sin controlar a los individuos ni su ambiente.	
odd function A function in which $f(-x) = -f(x)$ for all x in the domain of the function.	**función impar** Función en la que $f(-x) = -f(x)$ para todos los valores de x dentro del dominio de la función	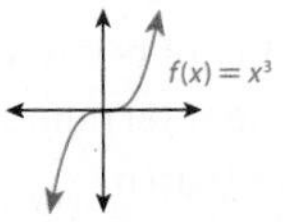 $f(x) = x^3$ is an odd function.
one-to-one function A function in which each y-value corresponds to only one x-value. The inverse of a one-to-one function is also a function.	**función uno a uno** Función en la que cada valor de y corresponde a sólo un valor de x. La inversa de una función uno a uno es también una función.	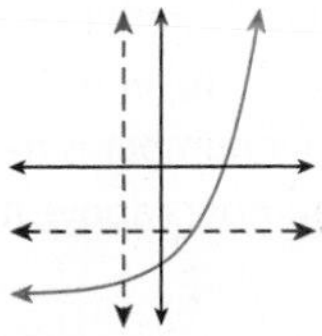
ordered triple A set of three numbers that can be used to locate a point (x, y, z) in a three-dimensional coordinate system.	**tripleta ordenada** Conjunto de tres números que se pueden utilizar para ubicar un punto (x, y, z) en un sistema de coordenadas tridimensional.	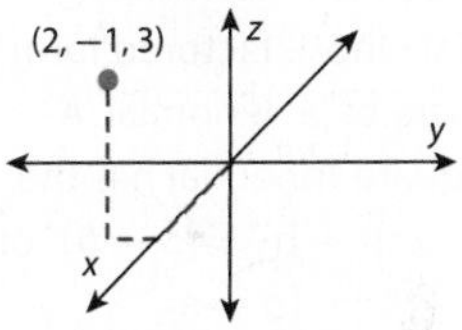
overlapping events Events in the sample space of a probability experiment that have one or more outcomes in common.	**eventos solapados** Eventos en el espacio muestral de un experimento de probabilidad que tienen uno o más resultados en común.	

P

ENGLISH	SPANISH	EXAMPLES
parabola The shape of the graph of a quadratic function. Also, the set of points equidistant from a point F, called the focus, and a line d, called the *directrix*.	**parábola** Forma de la gráfica de una función cuadrática. También, conjunto de puntos equidistantes de un punto F, denominado *foco*, y una línea d, denominada *directriz*.	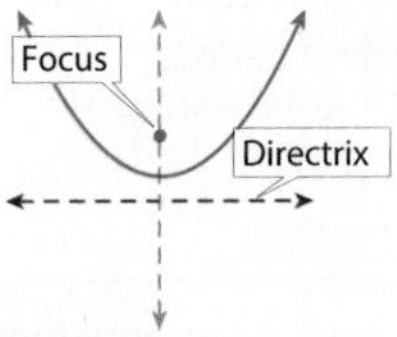
parameter One of the constants in a function or equation that may be changed. Also the third variable in a set of parametric equations.	**parámetro** Una de las constantes en una función o ecuación que se puede cambiar. También es la tercera variable en un conjunto de ecuaciones paramétricas.	$y = (x-h)^2 + k$ (h, k: parameters)
parent cube root function The function $f(x) = \sqrt[3]{x}$.	**función madre de la raíz cúbica** Función del tipo $f(x) = \sqrt[3]{x}$.	$f(x) = \sqrt[3]{x}$

Glossary/Glosario

ENGLISH	SPANISH	EXAMPLES
parent function The simplest function with the defining characteristics of the family. Functions in the same family are transformations of their parent function.	**función madre** La función más básica con las características de la familia. Las funciones de la misma familia son transformaciones de su función madre.	$f(x) = x^2$ is the parent function for $g(x) = x^2 + 4$ and $h(x) = 5(x + 2)^2 - 3$.
parent square root function The function $f(x) = \sqrt{x}$, where $x \geq 0$.	**función madre de la raíz cuadrada** Función del tipo $f(x) = \sqrt{x}$, donde $x \geq 0$.	$f(x) = \sqrt{x}$
partial sum Indicated by $S_n = \sum_{i=1}^{n} a_i$, the sum of a specified number of terms n of a sequence whose total number of terms is greater than n.	**suma parcial** Expresada por $S_n = \sum_{i=1}^{n} a_i$, la suma de un número específico n de términos de una sucesión cuyo número total de términos es mayor que n.	For the sequence $a_n = n^2$, the fourth partial sum of the infinite series $\sum_{k=1}^{00} k^2$ is $\sum_{k=1}^{4} k^2 = 1^2 + 2^2 + 3^2 + 4^2 = 30$.
Pascal's triangle A triangular arrangement of numbers in which every row starts and ends with 1 and each other number is the sum of the two numbers above it.	**triángulo de Pascal** Arreglo triangular de números en el cual cada fila comienza y termina con 1 y cada uno de los demás números es la suma de los dos números que están encima de él.	1 1 1 1 2 1 1 3 3 1 1 4 6 4 1
perfect-square trinomial A trinomial whose factored form is the square of a binomial. A perfect-square trinomial has the form $a^2 - 2ab + b^2 = (a - b)^2$ or $a^2 + 2ab + b^2 = (a + b)^2$.	**trinomio cuadrado perfecto** Trinomio cuya forma factorizada es el cuadrado de un binomio. Un trinomio cuadrado perfecto tiene la forma $a^2 - 2ab + b^2 = (a - b)^2$ o $a^2 + 2ab + b^2 = (a + b)^2$.	$x^2 + 6x + 9$ is a perfect square trinomial, because $x^2 + 6x + 9 = (x + 3)^2$.
period of a periodic function The length of a cycle measured in units of the independent variable (usually time in seconds). Also the reciprocal of the frequency.	**periodo de una función periódica** Longitud de un ciclo medido en unidades de la variable independiente (generalmente el tiempo en segundos). También es la inversa de la frecuencia.	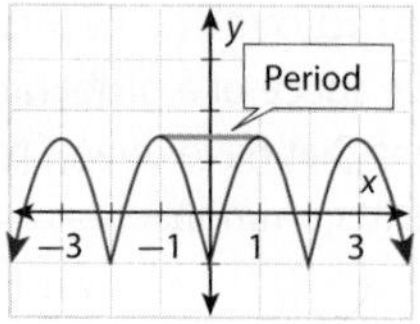
periodic function A function that repeats exactly in regular intervals, called *periods*.	**función periódica** Función que se repite exactamente a intervalos regulares denominados *periodos*.	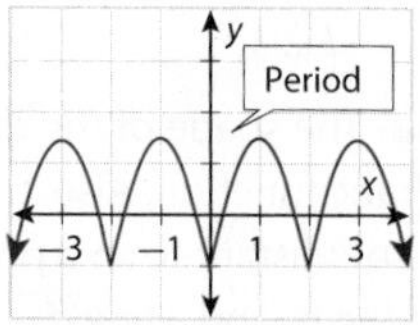
permutation An arrangement of a group of objects in which order is important. The number of permutations of r objects from a group of n objects is denoted $_nP_r$.	**permutación** Arreglo de un grupo de objetos en el cual el orden es importante. El número de permutaciones de r objetos de un grupo de n objetos se expresa $_nP_r$.	For 4 objects A, B, C, and D, there are $_4P_2 = 12$ different permutations of 2 objects: AB, AC, AD, BC, BD, CD, BA, CA, DA, CB, DB, and DC.

ENGLISH	SPANISH	EXAMPLES
permutation test A significance test performed on the results of an experiment by forming every possible regrouping of all the data values taken from the control and treatment groups into two new groups, finding the distribution of the differences of the means for all of the new group pairings, and then finding the likelihood, given that the null hypothesis is true, of getting a difference of means at least as great as the original experimental difference.	**prueba de permutación** Una prueba de significancia realizada sobre los resultados de un experimento al formar todos los reagrupamientos posibles de todos los valores de datos tomados de los grupos de control y de tratamiento en dos nuevos grupos, hallar la distribución de las diferencias de las medias para todos los emparejamientos nuevos, y luego hallar la probabilidad, suponiendo que la hipótesis nula es verdadera, de obtener una diferencia de medias al menos tan grande como la diferencia experimental original.	
phase shift A horizontal translation of a periodic function.	**cambio de fase** Traslación horizontal de una función periódica.	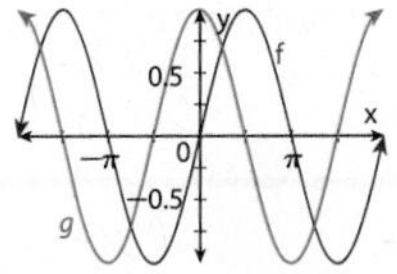 g is a phase shift of f $\frac{\pi}{2}$ units left.
piecewise function A function that is a combination of one or more functions.	**función a trozos** Función que es una combinación de una o más funciones.	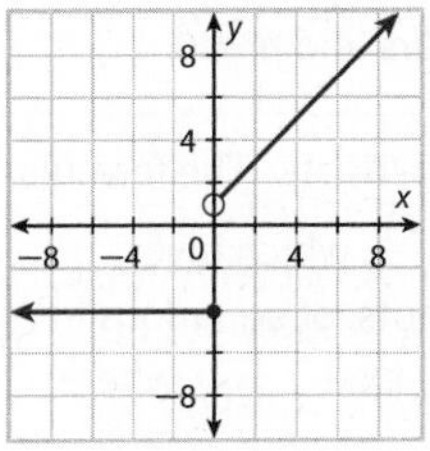 $f(x) = \begin{cases} -4 & \text{if } x \leq 0 \\ x+1 & \text{if } x > 0 \end{cases}$
polynomial A monomial or a sum or difference of monomials.	**polinomio** Monomio o suma o diferencia de monomios.	$2x^2 + 3x - 7$
polynomial function A function whose rule is a polynomial.	**función polinomial** Función cuya regla es un polinomio.	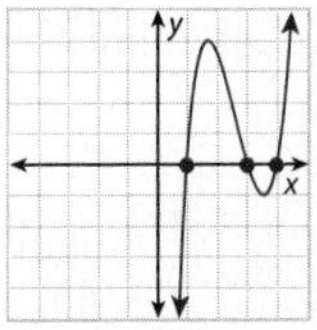 $f(x) = x^3 - 8x^2 + 19x - 12$
polynomial identity A mathematical relationship equating one polynomial quantity to another.	**identidad de polinomios** Relación matemática que iguala una cantidad polinomial con otra.	$(x^4 - y^4) = (x^2 + y^2)(x^2 - y^2)$
population The entire group of objects or individuals considered for a survey.	**población** Grupo completo de objetos o individuos que se desea estudiar.	In a survey about the study habits of high school students, the population is all high school students.
probability A number from 0 to 1 (or 0% to 100%) that is the measure of how likely an event is to occur.	**probabilidad** Número entre 0 y 1 (o entre 0% y 100%) que describe cuán probable es que ocurra un suceso.	A bag contains 3 red marbles and 4 blue marbles. The probability of choosing a red marble is $\frac{3}{7}$.

ENGLISH	SPANISH	EXAMPLES

probability distribution for an experiment The function that pairs each outcome with its probability.

distribución de probabilidad para un experimento Función que asigna a cada resultado su probabilidad.

A number cube is rolled 10 times. The results are shown in the table.

Outcome	1	2	3	4	5	6
Probability	$\frac{1}{10}$	$\frac{1}{5}$	$\frac{1}{5}$	0	$\frac{3}{10}$	$\frac{1}{5}$

---

probability sample A sample in which every member of the population being sampled has a nonzero probability of being selected.

muestra de probabilidad Muestra en la que cada miembro de la población que se estudia tiene una probabilidad distinta de cero de ser elegido.

---

pure imaginary number *See* imaginary number.

número imaginario puro Ver número imaginario.

$3i$

Q

quadratic equation An equation that can be written in the form $ax^2 + bx + c = 0$, where a, b, and c are real numbers and $a \neq 0$.

ecuación cuadrática Ecuación que se puede expresar como $ax^2 + bx + c = 0$, donde a, b y c son números reales y $a \neq 0$.

$x^2 + 3x - 4 = 0$

$x^2 - 9 = 0$

Quadratic Formula The formula $x = \frac{-b \pm \sqrt{b^2 - 4ac}}{2a}$, which gives solutions, or roots, of equations in the form $ax^2 + bx + c = 0$, where $a \neq 0$.

fórmula cuadrática La fórmula $x = \frac{-b \pm \sqrt{b^2 - 4ac}}{2a}$, que da soluciones, o raíces, para las ecuaciones del tipo $ax^2 + bx + c = 0$, donde $a \neq 0$.

The solutions of $2x^2 - 5x - 3 = 0$ are given by

$$x = \frac{-(-5) \pm \sqrt{(-5)^2 - 4(2)(-3)}}{2(2)}$$

$$= \frac{5 \pm \sqrt{25 + 24}}{4} = \frac{5 \pm 7}{4};$$

$x = 3$ or $x = -\frac{1}{2}$.

---

quadratic function A function that can be written in the form $f(x) = ax^2 + bx + c$, where a, b, and c are real numbers and $a \neq 0$, or in the form $f(x) = a(x - h)^2 + k$, where a, h, and k are real numbers and $a \neq 0$.

función cuadrática Función que se puede expresar como $f(x) = ax^2 + bx + c$, donde a, b y c son números reales y $a \neq 0$, o como $f(x) = a(x - h)^2 + k$, donde a, h y k son números reales y $a \neq 0$.

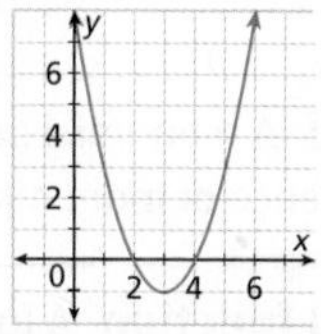

$f(x) = x^2 - 6x + 8$

---

quadratic model A quadratic function used to represent a set of data.

modelo cuadrático Función cuadrática que se utiliza para representar un conjunto de datos.

x	4	6	8	10
$f(x)$	27	52	89	130

A quadratic model for the data is $f(x) = x^2 + 3.3x - 2.6$.

---

quadratic regression A statistical method used to fit a quadratic model to a given data set.

regresión cuadrática Método estadístico utilizado para ajustar un modelo cuadrático a un conjunto de datos determinado.

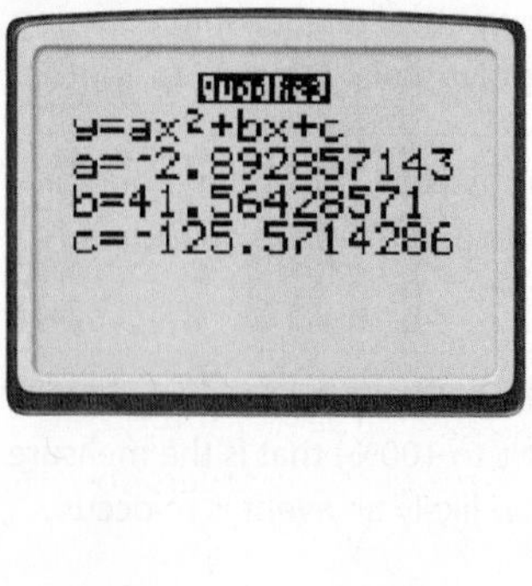

ENGLISH	SPANISH	EXAMPLES

R

ENGLISH	SPANISH	EXAMPLES
radian A unit of angle measure based on arc length. In a circle of radius *r*, if a central angle has a measure of 1 radian, then the length of the intercepted arc is *r* units. 2π radians $= 360°$ 1 radian $\approx 57°$	**radián** Unidad de medida de un ángulo basada en la longitud del arco. En un círculo de radio *r*, si un ángulo central mide 1 radián, entonces la longitud del arco abarcado es *r* unidades. 2π radianes $= 360°$ 1 radián $\approx 57°$	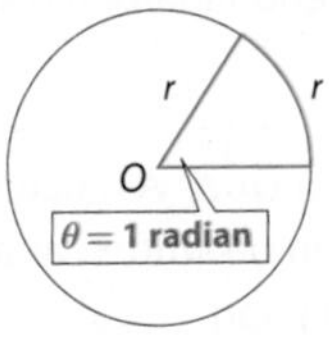
radical An indicated root of a quantity.	**radical** Raíz indicada de una cantidad.	$\sqrt{36} = 6$, $\sqrt[3]{27} = 3$
radical equation An equation that contains a variable within a radical.	**ecuación radical** Ecuación que contiene una variable dentro de un radical.	$\sqrt{x+3} + 4 = 7$
radical function A function whose rule contains a variable within a radical.	**función radical** Función cuya regla contiene una variable dentro de un radical.	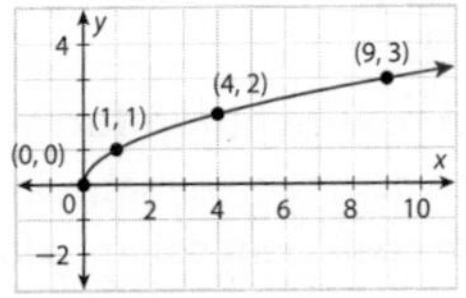 $f(x) = \sqrt{x}$
radicand The expression under a radical sign.	**radicando** Número o expresión debajo del signo de radical.	$\sqrt{x+3} - 2$ ↑ Radicand
random variable A variable whose value is determined by the outcome of a probability experiment.	**variable aleatoria** Una variable cuyo valor viene determinado por el resultado de un experimento de probabilidad.	
randomized comparative experiment An experiment in which the individuals are assigned to the control group or the treatment group at random, in order to minimize bias.	**experimento comparativo aleatorizado** Experimento en el que se elige al azar a los individuos para el grupo de control o para el grupo experimental, a fin de minimizar el sesgo.	
range of a function or relation The set of output values of a function or relation.	**rango de una función o relación** Conjunto de los valores desalida de una función o relación.	The range of $y = x^2$ is $\left\{y \mid y \geq 0\right\}$.
rational equation An equation that contains one or more rational expressions.	**ecuación racional** Ecuación que contiene una o más expresiones racionales.	$\frac{x+2}{x^2+3x-1} = 6$
rational exponent An exponent that can be expressed as $\frac{m}{n}$ such that if *m* and *n* are integers, then $b^{\frac{m}{n}} = \sqrt[n]{b^m} = \left(\sqrt[n]{b}\right)^m$.	**exponente racional** Exponente quese puede expresar como $\frac{m}{n}$ tal que, si *m* y *n* son números enteros, entonces $b^{\frac{m}{n}} = \sqrt[n]{b^m} = \left(\sqrt[n]{b}\right)^m$	$4^{\frac{2}{2}} = \sqrt{4^3} = \sqrt{64} = 8$ $4^{\frac{2}{2}} = \left(\sqrt{4}\right)^3 = 2^3 = 8$

Glossary/Glosario

ENGLISH	SPANISH	EXAMPLES
rational expression An algebraic expression whose numerator and denominator are polynomials and whose denominator has a degree ≥ 1.	**expresión racional** Expresión algebraica cuyo numerador y denominador son polinomios y cuyo denominador tiene un grado ≥ 1.	$\frac{x+2}{x^2+3x-1}$
rational function A function whose rule can be written as a rational expression.	**función racional** Función cuya regla se puede expresar como una expresión racional.	$f(x) = \frac{x+2}{x^2+3x-1}$
real axis The horizontal axis in the complex plane; it graphically represents the real part of complex numbers.	**eje real** Eje horizontal de un plano complejo. Representa gráficamente la parte real de los números complejos.	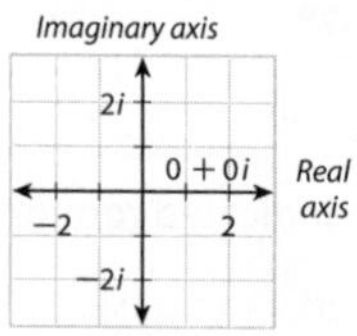
recursive rule A rule for a sequence in which one or more previous terms are used to generate the next term.	**Regla recurrente** Regla para una sucesión en la cual uno o más términos anteriores se utilizan para generar el término siguiente.	For the sequence 5, 7, 9, 11, ..., a recursive rule is $a_1 = 5$ and $a_n = a_{n-1} + 2$.
reduced row-echelon form A form of an augmented matrix in which the coefficient columns form an identity matrix.	**forma escalonada reducida por filas** Forma de matriz aumentada en la que las columnas de coeficientes forman una matriz de identidad.	$\left[\begin{array}{cc\|c} 1 & 0 & -1 \\ 0 & 1 & 3 \end{array}\right]$
reference angle For an angle in standard position, the reference angle is the positive acute angle formed by the terminal side of the angle and the x-axis.	**ángulo de referencia** Dado un ángulo en posición estándar, el ángulo de referencia es el ángulo agudo positivo formado por el lado terminal del ángulo y el eje x.	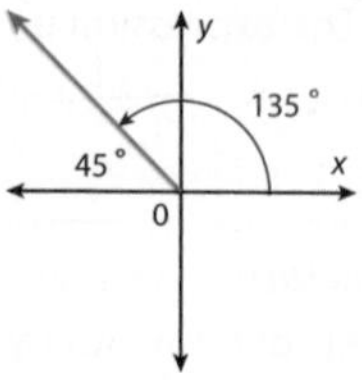
reflection A transformation that reflects, or "flips," a graph or figure across a line, called the line of reflection, such that each reflected point is the same distance from the line of reflection but is on the opposite side of the line.	**reflexión** Transformación que refleja, o invierte, una gráfica o figura sobre una línea, llamada la línea de reflexión, de manera tal que cada punto reflejado esté a la misma distancia de la línea de reflexión pero que se encuentre en el lado opuesto de la línea.	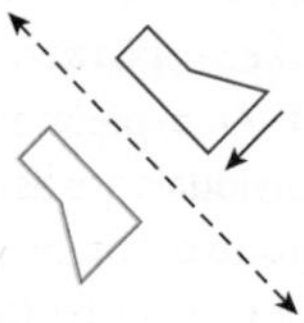
regression The statistical study of the relationship between variables.	**regresión** Estudio estadístico de la relación entre variables.	
Remainder Theorem If the polynomial function $P(x)$ is divided by $x - a$, then the remainder r is $P(a)$.	**Teorema del resto** Si la función polinomial $P(x)$ se divide entre $x - a$, entonces, el residuo r será $P(a)$.	
representative sample A sample that is a good estimator for its corresponding population parameter.	**muestra representativa** Una muestra que es un buen estimador para su parámetro de población correspondiente.	

ENGLISH	SPANISH	EXAMPLES

rotation A transformation that rotates or turns a figure about a point called the center of rotation.

rotación Transformación que hace rotar o girar una figura sobre un punto llamado centro de rotación.

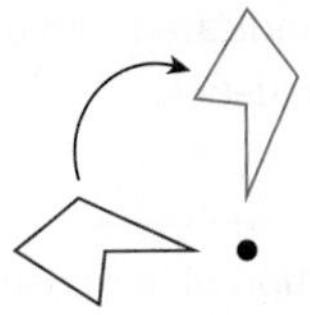

---

row operation An operation performed on a row of an augmented matrix that creates an equivalent matrix.

operación por filas Operación realizada en una fila de una matriz aumentada que crea una matriz equivalente.

$$\left[\begin{array}{cc|c} 2 & 0 & -2 \\ 0 & 1 & 3 \end{array}\right] = \left[\begin{array}{cc|c} \frac{1}{2}(2) & \frac{1}{2}(0) & \frac{1}{2}(-2) \\ 0 & 1 & 3 \end{array}\right] = \left[\begin{array}{cc|c} 1 & 0 & -1 \\ 0 & 1 & 3 \end{array}\right]$$

---

row-reduction method The process of performing elementary row operations on an augmented matrix to transform the matrix to reduced row echelon form.

método de reducción por filas Proceso por el cual se realizan operaciones elementales de filas en una matriz aumentada para transformar la matriz en una forma reducida de filas escalonadas.

$$\left[\begin{array}{cc|c} 2 & 0 & -2 \\ 0 & 1 & 3 \end{array}\right] = \left[\begin{array}{cc|c} \frac{1}{2}(2) & \frac{1}{2}(0) & \frac{1}{2}(-2) \\ 0 & 1 & 3 \end{array}\right] = \left[\begin{array}{cc|c} 1 & 0 & -1 \\ 0 & 1 & 3 \end{array}\right]$$

S

sample A part of the population.

muestra Una parte de la población.

In a survey about the study habits of high school students, a sample is a survey of 100 students.

---

sample space The set of all possible outcomes of a probability experiment.

espacio muestral Conjunto de todos los resultados posibles en un experimento de probabilidades.

In the experiment of rolling a number cube, the sample space is 1, 2, 3, 4, 5, 6.

---

sampling distribution A distribution that shows how a particular statistic varies across all samples of *n* individuals from the same population.

distribución de muestreo Una distribución que muestra de qué manera una determinada estadística varía a lo largo de todas las muestras de *n* individuos de la misma población.

---

second-degree equation in two variables An equation constructed by adding terms in two variables with powers no higher than 2.

ecuación de segundo grado en dos variables Ecuación compuesta por la suma de términos en dos variables con potencias no mayores a 2.

$ax^2 + by^2 + cx + dy + e = 0$

---

second differences Differences between first differences of a function.

segundas diferencias Diferencias entre las primerasdiferencias de una función.

x	0	1	2	3
y	1	4	9	16

first differences +3 +5 +7

second differences +2 +2

---

self-selected sample A sample in which members volunteer to participate.

muestra de voluntarios Muestra en la que los miembros se ofrecen voluntariamente para participar.

---

sequence A list of numbers that often form a pattern.

sucesión Lista de números que generalmente forman un patrón.

1, 2, 4, 8, 16, ...

ENGLISH	SPANISH	EXAMPLES
series The indicated sum of the terms of a sequence.	**serie** Suma indicada de los términos de una sucesión.	$1 + 2 + 4 + 8 + 16 + \ldots$
set A collection of items called elements.	**conjunto** Grupo de componentes denominados elementos.	$\{1, 2, 3\}$
set-builder notation A notation for a set that uses a rule to describe the properties of the elements of the set.	**notación de conjuntos** Notación para un conjunto que se vale de una regla para describir las propiedades de los elementos del conjunto.	$\{x \mid x > 3\}$ read, "The set of all *x* such that *x* is greater than 3."
simple event An event consisting of only one outcome.	**suceso simple** Suceso que contiene sólo un resultado.	In the experiment of rolling a number cube, the event consisting of the outcome 3 is a simple event.
simulation A model of an experiment, often one that would be too difficult or time-consuming to actually perform.	**simulación** Modelo de un experimento; generalmente se recurre a la simulación cuando realizar dicho experimento sería demasiado difícil o llevaría mucho tiempo.	A random number generator is used to simulate the roll of a number cube.
sine In a right triangle, the ratio of the length of the side opposite $\angle A$ to the length of the hypotenuse.	**seno** En un triángulo rectángulo, razón entre la longitud del cateto opuesto a $\angle A$ y la longitud de la hipotenusa.	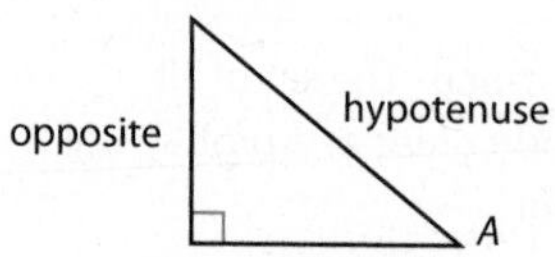 $\sin A = \frac{\text{opposite}}{\text{hypotenuse}}$.
skewed distribution A distribution that is mounded but not symmetric because one "tail" is much longer than the other.	**distribución sesgada** Una distribución que está elevada pero no es simétrica porque una de las "colas" es mucho más larga que la otra.	
square-root function A function whose rule contains a variable under a square-root sign.	**función de raíz cuadrada** Función cuya regla contiene una variable bajo un signo de raíz cuadrada.	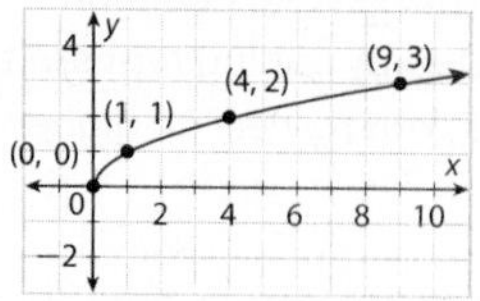 $f(x) = \sqrt{x}$
standard deviation A measure of dispersion of a data set. The standard deviation σ is the square root of the variance.	**desviación estándar** Medida de dispersión de un conjunto de datos. La desviación estándar σ es la raíz cuadrada de la varianza.	Data set: $\{6, 7, 7, 9, 11\}$ Mean: $\frac{6+7+7+9+11}{5} = 8$ Variance: $\frac{1}{5}(4 + 1 + 1 + 1 + 9) = 3.2$ Standard deviation: $\sigma = \sqrt{3.2} \approx 1.8$
standard error of the mean The standard deviation of the sampling distribution of the sample mean, denoted $\sigma_{\bar{x}}$.	**error estándar de la media** La desviación estándar de la distribución de muestreo de la media de la muestra, que se indica así: $\sigma_{\bar{x}}$.	

ENGLISH	SPANISH	EXAMPLES
standard error of the proportion The standard deviation of the sampling distribution of the sample proportion, denoted $\sigma_{\hat{p}}$.	**error estándar de la proporción** La desviación estándar de la distribución de muestreo de la proporción de la muestra, que se indica así: $\sigma_{\hat{p}}$.	
standard form of a polynomial A polynomial in one variable is written in standard form when the terms are in order from greatest degree to least degree.	**forma estándar de un polinomio** Un polinomio de una variable se expresa en forma estándar cuando los términos se ordenan de mayor a menor grado.	$3x^3 - 5x^2 + 6x - 7$
standard form of a quadratic equation $ax^2 + bx + c = 0$, where a, b, and c are real numbers and $a \neq 0$.	**forma estándar de una ecuación** cuadrática $ax^2 + bx + c = 0$, donde a, b y c son números reales y $a \neq 0$.	$2x^2 + 3x - 1 = 0$
standard normal distribution A normal distribution that has a mean of 0 and a standard deviation of 1.	**distribución normal estándar** Una distribución normal que tiene una media de 0 y una desviación estándar de 1.	
standard normal value A value that indicates how many standard deviations above or below the mean a particular value falls, given by the formula $z = \frac{x - \mu}{\sigma}$, where z is the standard normal value, x is the given value, μ is the mean, and σ is the standard deviation of a standard normal distribution.	**valor normal estándar** Valor que indica a cuántas desviaciones estándar por encima o por debajo de la media se encuentra un determinado valor, dado por la fórmula $z = \frac{x - \mu}{\sigma}$, donde z es el valor normal estándar, x es el valor dado, μ es la media y σ es la desviación estándar de una distribución normal estándar.	
standard position An angle in standard position has its vertex at the origin and its initial side on the positive x–axis.	**osición estándar** Ángulo cuyo vértice se encuentra en el origen y cuyo lado inicial se encuentra sobre el eje x.	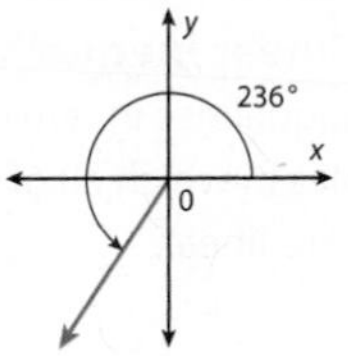
statistic A number that describes a sample.	**estadística** Número que describe una muestra.	
statistical significance A determination that the likelihood that an experimental result occurred by chance is so low that a conclusion in favor of rejecting the null hypothesis is justified.	**significación estadística** Una determinación de que la probabilidad de que un resultado experimental ocurriera por azar es tan reducida que está justificada una conclusión a favor de rechazar la hipótesis nula.	
step function A piecewise function that is constant over each interval in its domain.	**función escalón** Función a trozos que es constante en cada intervalo en su dominio.	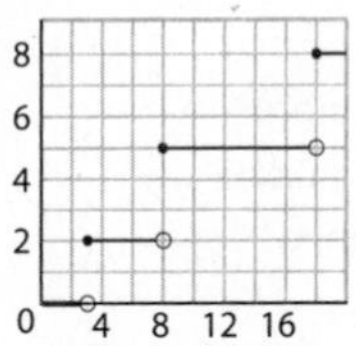

Glossary/Glosario

ENGLISH	SPANISH	EXAMPLES
stretch A transformation that pulls the points of a graph horizontally away from the *y*–axis or vertically away from the *x*–axis.	**estiramiento** Transformación que desplaza los puntos de una gráfica en forma horizontal alejándolos del eje y o en forma vertical alejándolos del eje *x*.	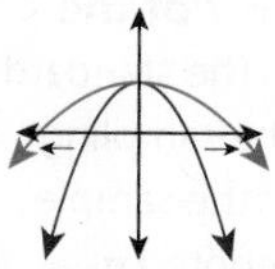
summation notation A method of notating the sum of a series using the Greek letter $\sum$ (capital *sigma*).	**notación de sumatoria** Método de notación de la suma de una serie que utiliza la letra griega $\sum$ (SIGMA mayúscula).	$\sum_{n=1}^{5} 3k = 3 + 6 + 9 + 12 + 15 = 45$
survey A data collection tool that uses questions to measure characteristics of interest about a population using a sample selected from the population.	**encuesta** Una herramienta para recopilar datos que usa preguntas para medir las características de interés sobre una población mediante una muestra seleccionada de entre la población.	
synthetic division A shorthand method of dividing by a linear binomial of the form $(x - a)$ by writing only the coefficients of the polynomials.	**división sintética** Método abreviado de división que consiste en dividir por un binomio lineal del tipo $(x - a)$ escribiendo sólo los coeficientes de los polinomios.	$(x^3 - 7x + 6) \div (x - 2)$ $\begin{array}{r\|rrrr} 2 & 1 & 0 & -7 & 6 \\ & & 2 & 4 & 6 \\ \hline & 1 & 2 & -3 & \boxed{0} \end{array}$ $(x^3 - 7x + 6) \div (x - 2) = x^2 + 2x - 3$
synthetic substitution The process of using synthetic division to evaluate a polynomial $p(x)$ when $x = c$.	**sustitución sintética** Proceso que consiste en usar la división sintética para evaluar un polinomio $p(x)$ cuando $x = c$.	
system of equations A set of two or more equations that have two or more variables.	**sistema de ecuaciones** Conjunto de dos o más ecuaciones que contienen dos o más variables.	$\begin{cases} 2x + 3y = -1 \\ x^2 = 4 \end{cases}$
system of linear inequalities A system of inequalities in two or more variables in which all of the inequalities are linear.	**sistema de desigualdades lineales** Sistema de desigualdades en dos o más variables en el que todas las desigualdades son lineales.	$\begin{cases} 2x + 3y \geq -1 \\ x - 3y < 4 \end{cases}$

T

term of a sequence An element or number in the sequence.	**término de una sucesión** Elemento o número de una sucesión.	5 is the third term in the sequence 1, 3, 5, 7, . . .
terminal side For an angle in standard position, the ray that is rotated relative to the positive *x*–axis.	**lado terminal** Dado un ángulo en una posición estándar, el rayo que rota en relación con el eje positivo *x*.	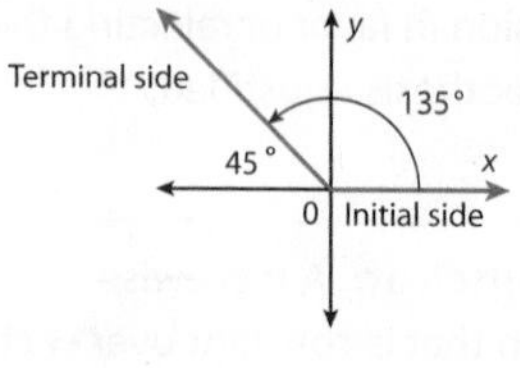

ENGLISH	SPANISH	EXAMPLES

theoretical probability The ratio of the number of equally likely outcomes in an event to the total number of possible outcomes.

probabilidad teórica Razón entre el número de resultados igualmente probables de un suceso y el número total de resultados posibles.

The theoretical probability of rolling an odd number on a number cube is $\frac{3}{6} = \frac{1}{2}$.

---

three-dimensional coordinate system A space that is divided into eight regions by an *x*–axis, a *y*–axis, and a *z*–axis. The locations, or coordinates, of points are given by ordered triples.

sistema de coordenadas tridimensional Espacio dividido en ocho regiones por un eje *x*, un eje *y* y un eje *z*. Las ubicaciones, o coordenadas, de los puntos son dadas por tripletas ordenadas.

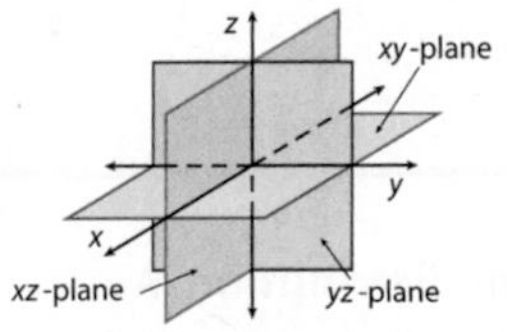

---

transformation A change in the position, size, or shape of a figure or graph.

transformación Cambio en la posición, tamaño o forma de una figura o gráfica.

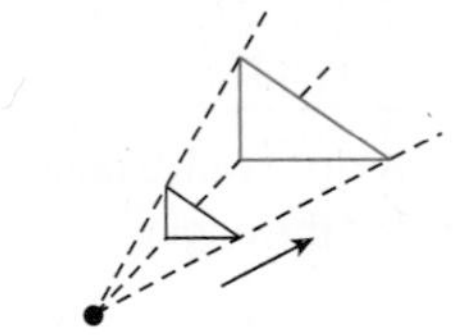

---

translation A transformation that shifts or slides every point of a figure or graph the same distance in the same direction.

traslación Transformación en la que todos los puntos de una figura se mueven la misma distancia en la misma dirección.

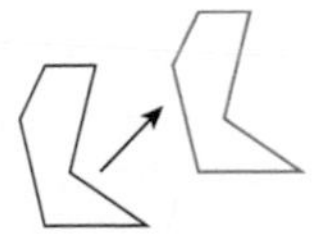

---

trial In probability, a single repetition or observation of an experiment.

prueba En probabilidad, una sola repetición u observación de un experimento.

In the experiment of rolling a number cube, each roll is one trial.

---

trigonometric function A function whose rule is given by a trigonometric ratio.

función trigonométrica Función cuya regla es dada por una razón trigonométrica.

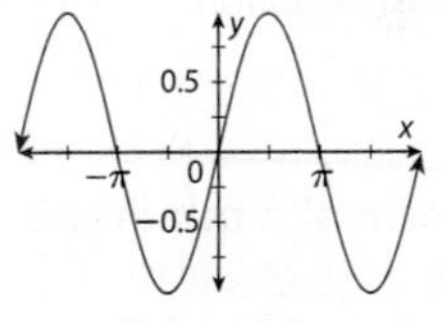

$f(x) = \sin x$

---

trigonometric ratio Ratio of the lengths of two sides of a right triangle.

razón trigonométrica Razón entre dos lados de un triángulo rectángulo.

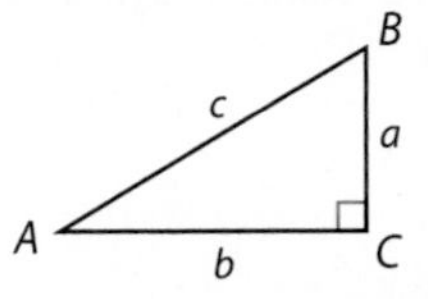

$\sin A = \frac{a}{c}$, $\cos A = \frac{b}{c}$, $\tan A = \frac{a}{b}$

---

trigonometry The study of the measurement of triangles and of trigonometric functions and their applications.

trigonometría Estudio de la medición de los triángulos y de las funciones trigonométricas y sus aplicaciones.

---

trinomial A polynomial with three terms.

trinomio Polinomio con tres términos.

$4x^2 + 3xy - 5y^2$

ENGLISH	SPANISH	EXAMPLES

turning point A point on the graph of a function that corresponds to a local maximum (or minimum) where the graph changes from increasing to decreasing (or vice versa).

punto de inflexión Punto de la gráfica de una función que corresponde a un máximo (o mínimo) local donde la gráfica pasa de ser creciente a decreciente (o viceversa).

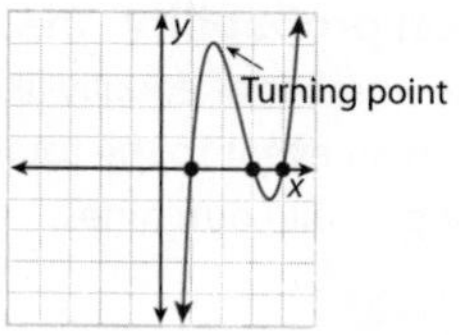

U

uniform distribution A distribution that is basically level, forming a shape that looks like a rectangle.

distribución uniforme Una distribución que es básicamente llana, formando una figura similar a un rectángulo.

unit circle A circle with a radius of 1, centered at the origin.

círculo unitario Círculo con un radio de 1, centrado en el origen.

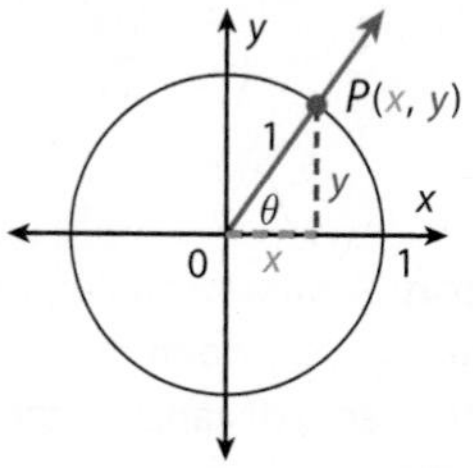

Unit circle

V

variance The average of squared differences from the mean. The square root of the variance is called the *standard deviation*.

varianza Promedio de las diferencias cuadráticas en relación con la media. La raíz cuadrada de la varianza se denomina *desviación estándar*.

Data set: is $\{6, 7, 7, 9, 11\}$

Mean: $\frac{6+7+7+9+11}{5} = 8$

Variance: $\frac{1}{5}(4+1+1+1+9) = 3.2$

vertex form of a quadratic function A quadratic function written in the form $f(x) = a(x-h)^2 + k$, where a, h, and k are constants and (h, k) is the vertex.

forma en vértice de una función cuadrática Una función cuadrática expresada en la forma $f(x) = a(x-h)^2 + k$, donde a, h y k son constantes y (h, k) es el vértice.

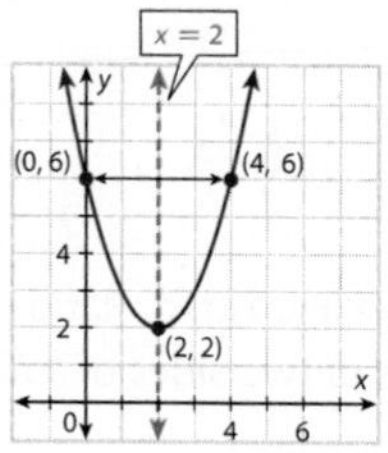

$f(x) = (x-2)^2 + 2$

vertex of an absolute-value graph The point where the axis of symmetry intersects the graph.

vértice de una gráfica de valor absoluto Punto donde en el eje de simetría interseca la gráfica.

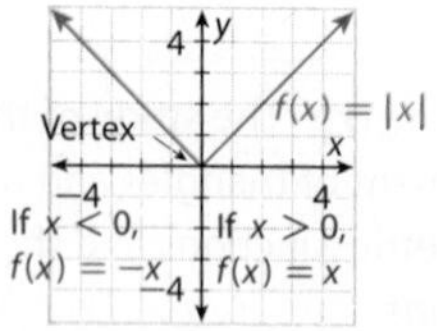

vertex of a parabola The highest or lowest point on the parabola.

vértice de una parábola Punto más alto o más bajo de una parábola.

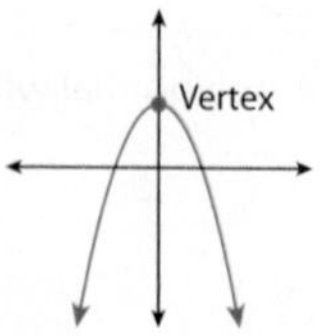

ENGLISH	SPANISH	EXAMPLES

Z

z-axis The third axis in a three-dimensional coordinate system.

eje z Tercer eje en un sistema de coordenadas tridimensional.

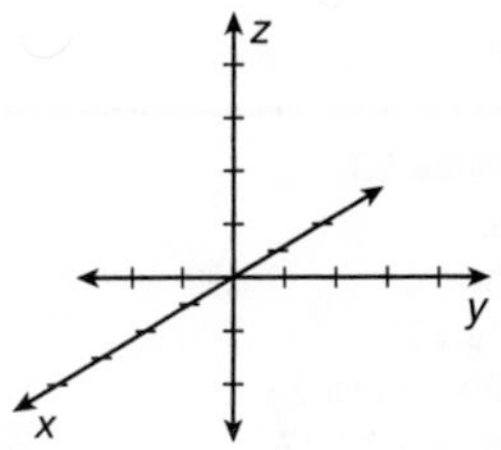

z-score A standardized data value from a normal distribution with mean μ and standard deviation σ found by using the formula $z = \frac{x - \mu}{\sigma}$ where x is the original data value.

puntaje z Un valor de datos estandarizado de una distribución normal con una media μ y una desviación estándar σ que se halla usando la fórmula $z = \frac{x - \mu}{\sigma}$, donde x es el valor de datos original.

zero of a function For the function f, any number x such that $f(x) = 0$.

cero de una función Dada la función f, todo número x tal que $f(x) = 0$.

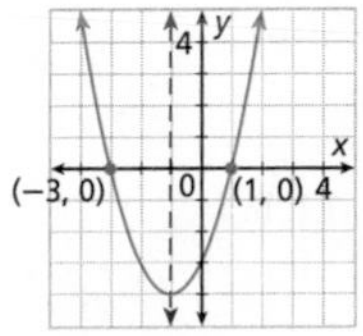

The zeros of $f(x) = x^2 + 2x - 3$ are −3 and 1.

Index

Index locator numbers are in Module. Lesson form. For example, 2.1 indicates Module 2, Lesson 1 as listed in the Table of Contents.

A

B

C

D

E

F

G

Index

N

O

P

Q

R

Table of Measures

LENGTH

1 inch = 2.54 centimeters

1 meter = 39.37 inches

1 mile = 5,280 feet

1 mile = 1760 yards

1 mile = 1.609 kilometers

1 kilometer = 0.62 mile

MASS/WEIGHT

1 pound = 16 ounces

1 pound = 0.454 kilograms

1 kilogram = 2.2 pounds

1 ton = 2000 pounds

CAPACITY

1 cup = 8 fluid ounces

1 pint = 2 cups

1 quart = 2 pints

1 gallon = 4 quarts

1 gallon = 3.785 liters

1 liter = 0.264 gallons

1 liter = 1000 cubic centimeters

Symbols

$\neq$	is not equal to
$\approx$	is approximately equal to
10^2	ten squared; ten to the second power
$2.\overline{6}$	repeating decimal 2.66666...
$\|-4\|$	the absolute value of negative 4
$\sqrt{}$	square root
π	pi: (about 3.14)
$\perp$	is perpendicular to
$\parallel$	is parallel to
$\overleftrightarrow{AB}$	line *AB*
$\overrightarrow{AB}$	ray *AB*
$\overline{AB}$	line segment *AB*
$m\angle A$	measure of $\angle A$

Formulas

Triangle	$A = \frac{1}{2}bh$		Pythagorean Theorem	$a^2 + b^2 = c^2$
Parallelogram	$A = bh$		Quadratic Formula	$x = \frac{-b \pm \sqrt{b^2 - 4ac}}{2a}$
Circle	$A = \pi r^2$		Arithmetic Sequence	$a_n = a_1 + (n - 1)d$
Circle	$C = \pi d$ or $C = 2\pi r$		Geometric Sequence	$a_n = a_1 r^{n-1}$
General Prisms	$V = Bh$		Geometric Series	$S_n = \frac{a_1 - a_1 r^n}{1 - r}$ where $r \neq 1$
Cylinder	$V = \pi r^2 h$		Radians	1 *radian* $= \frac{180}{\pi}$ *degrees*
Sphere	$V = \frac{4}{3}\pi r^3$		Degrees	1 *degree* $= \frac{\pi}{180}$ *radians*
Cone	$V = \frac{1}{3}\pi r^2 h$		Exponential Growth/Decay	$A = A_0 e^{k(t - t_0)} + B_0$
Pyramid	$V = \frac{1}{3}Bh$			